British Sculpture
1470 to 2000

British Sculpture
1470 to 2000

A Concise Catalogue of the Collection
at the Victoria and Albert Museum

DIANE BILBEY
with
MARJORIE TRUSTED

V&A Publications

The publication of this catalogue has been made possible by the generous support of the Crescent Trust, the Paul Mellon Centre for Studies in British Art, and the Henry Moore Foundation

First published by V&A Publications 2002

V&A Publications
160 Brompton Road
London SW3 1HW

Photography by Christine Smith and other members of the V&A Photo Studio.
Some additional photography by Philip Ward-Jackson and Mike Phipps of the
Conway Library, Courtauld Institute of Art, Mark Stocker and
Christie's Images Inc., New York.

ISBN 1 85177 395 9

A catalogue record for this book is
available from the British Library

Jacket front: *Self-portrait* by John Flaxman R.A., 1778 (cat. 102)

Jacket back: *Crouching youth* by Winifred Turner, about 1934 (cat. 763)

Frontispiece: *Mother and child* by Sir George James Frampton R.A., F.S.A., 1895 (cat. 394)

Typeset by M Rules
Designed by Sue Ryall
Printed in Italy by Grafiche Milani

V&A

V&A Publications
160 Brompton Road
London SW3 1HW
www.vam.ac.uk

Contents

For my mother, Sylvia Montague,
and in memory of my step-father, John Montague.

Foreword

In 1971, in his foreword to Margaret Whinney's *English Sculpture 1720–1830*, the late Sir John Pope-Hennessy remarked that 'the time for issuing a comprehensive catalogue [of the Museum's British sculpture collection] has not yet arrived'. Thirty years later, there can be no question that the time is ripe for the production of such a volume. In the intervening years, many acquisitions of the first importance have entered the Museum, so that the holdings in this area are now of a strength unparalleled elsewhere, and a great deal of new research has cast light on areas previously obscured by ignorance. It is also especially fitting that the publication of this catalogue follows closely the re-opening of the British Galleries covering the years 1500–1900: these galleries contain many of the most important sculptures to be found in the volume and demonstrate in the clearest manner possible the Museum's commitment to the study and display of British Art and Design.

Given the size of the collection and the need to make it accessible in convenient form, it was decided that the most appropriate approach would be to publish the material as a concise, rather than extended, catalogue. It is the intention that the reader should be able to find all the relevant facts in the entries – with references to more detailed studies where they exist for the more celebrated sculptures – and it is the hope that new avenues for research will be opened up by the provision of information on many of the unpublished or little-known pieces. Diane Bilbey deserves great credit for completing the massive task of compiling the catalogue while carrying out multifarious other duties, and for her determination in overcoming the difficulties inherent in such a project. She wrote nearly all the entries and organised the project with exemplary efficiency, while Marjorie Trusted gave valuable editorial and scholarly support.

It is a pleasure to thank three donors for their considerable contributions to the catalogue. The Paul Mellon Centre for Studies in British Art kindly provided two grants, one to allow for research and writing time for Diane Bilbey, the other a publication subvention; and the Henry Moore Foundation and the Trustees of the Crescent Trust also made extremely generous grants to subsidise production of the book. We are very grateful to all three bodies for their continuing support of sculpture studies.

Paul Williamson
Keeper of Sculpture, Metalwork, Ceramics & Glass

Acknowledgments

Completing a catalogue of this scale and scope would have been impossible without the help and encouragement of many individuals. Acknowledgments of this assistance have frequently been cited within the relevant catalogue entries, but I should also like to express my gratitude here. A great number of people have helped with the catalogue, both in a practical sense, as well as having given general support throughout the project. Initial work on the catalogue was made possible by a generous grant from the Paul Mellon Centre for Studies in British Art, enabling me to devote six months to the project. I should also like to express my thanks to Paul Williamson for providing me with the opportunity to undertake this work. Timothy Stevens actively encouraged and promoted the whole project, for which I am very grateful. I should especially like to thank Marjorie Trusted, without whose expertise and immense contribution this catalogue would not have been possible. I should like to express special thanks to the two other contributors to the catalogue, Alexandra Corney and Emma Hardy. Alexandra Corney, who not only researched and wrote the entries on objects by Jules Dalou, is also mentioned later in these acknowledgments to reflect my great appreciation for her assistance with the catalogue's photography programme. Emma Hardy wrote entries on three objects related to the Albert Memorial, and had also previously helped with the preparation for the catalogue at its early stages. I am also most grateful to Fiona Leslie for allowing us to publish her research on architectural models for the appendix. A number of individuals have been instrumental in the final format and presentation of the catalogue. I am particularly grateful to Philip Ward-Jackson, not only for his practical assistance in the photography of some of the objects, but also for his invaluable suggestions and amendments when reading through the text of the draft entries. I am similarly indebted to Malcolm Baker, Julius Bryant, the late Katharine Gibson, Martin Greenwood, John Kenworthy-Browne, Alexander Kader, John Sankey and Paul Williamson for their reading of the texts and for their helpful comments. Almost half the objects included had not previously been photographed. The huge task of coordinating the object moves and photography programme was carried out by Alexandra Corney, whose commitment and enthusiasm for the project I should particularly like to acknowledge. I am also immensely grateful to Christine Smith who undertook all the new photography with great skill and patience, particularly when further objects were added to the already lengthy list. I should also like to express gratitude to Mererid Roberts, who took over the photography programme in the latter stages, and to Ken Jackson, James Stevenson, and Mike Bergin of the V&A Photo Studio, and to Steve Woodhouse of the V&A Picture Library for their assistance in the photography programme. My thanks to Mark Stocker for allowing us to reproduce some of his photographs of objects by Joseph Edgar Boehm, to Mike Phipps for the photography of some further objects off-site, and to Christie's Images Inc., New York for their permission to illustrate the Inigo Jones caryatids (cat.nos. 6 and 7). Innumerable colleagues at the V&A have generously offered their support and encouragement during this project. All members of the Sculpture Department both past and present, including Rachel Akpabio, Wendy Fisher, Anna Hamilton, Norbert Jopek, Sally Korman, Shashi Sen, Eleanor Tollfree and Eleanor Townsend have over the months helped with varied aspects of the catalogue and have been generous in their encouragement and practical help. I should like to extend special thanks to Lucy Cullen for helping with the many queries asked of her, and for all her continued support, and to Peta Motture for her advice and encouragement. Similarly, I should would like to express sincere gratitude to Peter Ford, who has been happy to help on many occasions with technical support and advice concerning the database used for the project. Many additional members of V&A staff have assisted with the project and I should like to take this opportunity to thank colleagues in the Research Department, especially Malcolm Baker, who was constantly encouraging, as well as generously offering his expertise on relevant areas of the catalogue. I should also like to thank Jane Buller, Anthony Burton, Paul Greenhalgh, and the late Clive Wainwright. My thanks are extended to Charlotte Hubbard, Alexandra Kosinova, and Metaxia Ventikou, in the Sculpture Conservation Department at the Museum, and to the sculptor conservator Antonia Hockton, who conserved many of the plaster objects. Colleagues in Registry and the Archive of Art and Design have also been unending in their willingness to assist in this project, particularly Jo Hodden-Brown, Maureen Mulvanny and Michael Clark, as well as Guy Baxter, Serena Kelly, Elizabeth Lomas, Christopher Marsden and Lynn Young. I am also indebted to Lisa Murray and the staff of the Technical Services Department for their assistance in making objects accessible for photography. My gratitude is also extended to Mary Butler, Ariane Bankes, Geoff Barlow, Clare Davis, Miranda Harrison and Mary Wessel of the Publications Department for their assistance in the publication of this catalogue, with special thanks to Geoff Barlow for overseeing its production. Other V&A colleagues both past and present that I should like to thank include Martin Barnes, Terry Bloxham, James Cheshire, Rachel Church, Shaun Cole, Martin Durrant, Ann Eatwell, Richard Edgcumbe, Roy Edginton, Polly Elkin, Alun Graves, Mark Haworth-Booth, Robin Hildyard, Katherine Hugh, Elizabeth James, Andrew Kirk, Mirella Lord, Noreen Marshall, John Meriton, Wendy Monkhouse, Adrian Moore, Rebecca Naylor, Anthony North, Susan North, Fenella Page, Linda Parry, Clare Phillips, Lucy Pratt, Gordon Read, Alicia Robinson, Ananda Rutherford, Michael Snodin, Andrew Spira, Claire Sussums, Katie Swann, Eric Turner, Jonathan Voak, Helen Wilkinson, Dinah Winch, David Wright, James Yorke and Hilary Young. I should also like to thank Robyn Asleson, Charles Avery, Gordon Balderston, Joanna Barnes, David Bindman, Charles Bird, Susan Blake, Roger Bowdler, Jane Bowen, Charlotte Brunskill, Lucilla Burn, Hilary Chelminski, Alexandra Coldham, Paul Cox, Tina Craig, Roberta Cremoncini, François Delestre, Birgit Dohrendorf, Helen Dorey, Caroline Elam, Godfrey Evans, Peggy Fogelman, Lindsay Ford, Annette French, Moira Fulton, Christopher Gibbs, Cristiano Giometti, Andrew Glew, Anne Goodchild, Chris Green, Paul Hadfield, Jane Hamilton, Bridget Hanley, Robin Hamlyn, Rupert Harris, Annette Haudiquet, Andrew Heard, Alexandra B. Huff, Leslie Heitzman, Helen Hogg, Christine Hopper, Bryan Hyacinth, Donald Johnston, Alison Kelly, Tim Knox, David Lane, Michele Lefevre, Marika Leino, Léon Lock, Jerry Losty, Andrew Loukes, Alison Luchs, Ian Maine, Francis Marshall, Alison Moon, Andrew Moore, Edward Morris, Gerardine M. Mulcahy, Charles Napier, Victoria Nelson, Vanessa Nicolson, John Noble, Jane Nowosadko, Susan Palmer, Liz Paul, John Physick, Luisa Pontello, Martin Postle, Susan Rich, Helen Robinson, Megaklés Rogákos, Adeline van Roon, Rick Russell, Oliver H.D. Ryder, W.R. Serjeant, Peyton Skipwith, Helen Smailes, E.A. Smith, Yolanda Stațham, Hugh Stevenson, Simon Stock, Greg Sullivan, Daniela Tranquada, Ruth Trotter, Robert Upstone, Helen Valentine, Anne Verbrugge, Karen Wardley and Emma Williams. I am also grateful to the following lenders for allowing their objects to be included in this catalogue: the College Art Collections, University College, London; Mr Cheng Huan Q.C.; the London Diocesan Fund; the National Trust; and the Dean and Chapter of Westminster Abbey. I would like to express my sincere thanks to the three donors who have generously contributed towards the publication costs for this catalogue: The Crescent Trust , the Paul Mellon Centre for Studies in British Art, and the Henry Moore Foundation. Finally I would like to express my special thanks to family and friends, and especially to Vince Bridgman for his unending support and for designing the jacket for this book.

Diane Bilbey

Introduction

Post-medieval British sculpture is now seriously studied and appreciated, but this was not always the case. Very little had been written before the middle of the twentieth century; nevertheless the present catalogue is indebted to the pioneering work on virgin soil of a handful of scholars before then.[1] Perhaps because the study of this area of art history is a relatively recent phenomenon, this is the first catalogue of the unsurpassed collection of post-medieval British sculpture in the Victoria and Albert Museum, although a good proportion of the sculpture discussed here has been previously mentioned in disparate books and articles. Whilst certain groups of objects have been deliberately excluded,[2] with those exceptions, the catalogue is intended as a comprehensive record of the Museum's collection of British sculpture from the late fifteenth century onwards. The earliest objects included are three carved oak figures datable to about 1450–70 (cat.nos. 24a-c), the most recent being a bronze bust of Lord Carrington executed in 2000 by Marcelle Quinton (cat. no. 754). Although this is a concise catalogue, and the entries are not exhaustive, it is hoped that the bibliographical and other information to be found here will be of use to students in the field, and will provide the opportunity for further study of British sculpture both within and outside the context of the Museum's collection.

Fig 1. Anonymous photograph; between 1848 and 1872. Enfield railway station façade (cat.no. 24). Victoria and Albert Museum.

The Range of the Collection

The Victoria and Albert Museum houses the National Collection of post-classical sculpture, incorporating large and varied holdings of post-medieval British sculpture, unparalleled by any other collection, and which in its entirety could be said to provide a microcosmic history of the subject. A total of 773 pieces are included here, over a third of which have not hitherto been published. They range from architectural fragments and façades [fig. 1], sepulchral monuments and chimneypieces to portrait busts [fig. 2], statuettes, life-size figurative groups, small-scale models and reliefs. The materials covered include stone, marble, wood, terracotta, plaster, bronze, lead and iron. Current long-term loans of British sculpture to the Museum are also included by the kind permission of the lenders.

The work of over 200 individual sculptors, as well as 84 unattributed pieces, are represented, including virtually every major sculptor active in Britain during this period, such as Nicholas Stone, John Michael Rysbrack, Louis François Roubiliac, John Flaxman, and Alfred Gilbert. Alfred Stevens is the sculptor best-represented in the catalogue (148 of his works are in the collection),[3] though the volume of work by two other nineteenth-century sculptors, Sir Joseph Edgar Boehm and George Gammon Adams, is also substantial. It is therefore not surprising that the largest group of objects in the collection – just over 500 – date from the nineteenth century. Only 30 of the objects catalogued here were produced after 1900, this relatively small number being partly due to the fact that some British twentieth-century objects formerly in the collection were transferred to the Tate Gallery in 1983,[4] and partly because the Tate, rather than the V&A, concentrates on twentieth-century sculpture acquisitions.

The collection is particularly rich in sculptors' models, which broadly fall into three categories: those recording ideal works for which no finished work is known, such as the terracotta relief of two men fighting by John Flaxman (cat.no. 109); models produced by sculptors as competition entries, such as Nathaniel Smith's terracotta statuette of William Beckford, Alfred Stevens's memorial to the 1851 International Exhibition (neither of which was in the event executed), or Stevens's model for the monument to the Duke of Wellington erected in St Paul's Cathedral [fig. 3] (cat.nos. 208, 659, 576); and those (the majority) which served as studies for a finished work, such as Roubiliac's models for the memorials to the Duke and Duchess of Montagu (cat.nos. 165 to 167).

Fig 2. Anonymous photograph; after 1898 (inv.no. A.3:2-1995). Studio of Conrad Dressler showing the bust of his wife Nita Maria Schonfeld Resch (cat.no. 384). Victoria and Albert Museum, Sculpture Department archives.

The collecting of sculpture by the Museum in the nineteenth century had a particular educational slant. The Museum's educational role and its strong historical connections with the National Art Training School at South Kensington (later the Royal College of Art) are illustrated by the students' works in the collection, by practitioners who did not necessarily flourish subsequently as independent professional sculptors. For example, the model of an *Interior of a smithy* by A.W. Bowcher, a student of the National Art Training School and otherwise unknown, was purchased by the Museum from the sculptor in 1885, following its exhibition at the International Health Exhibition the previous year (cat.no. 337). The examples of Art Workmanship originally exhibited at the Society of Arts Art-Workmanship competitions also form an interesting period group within the present collection, even if they are rarely of the same quality as works by more renowned artists. They were often inspired by objects already in the Museum's collections, such as the carved *Putto on a dolphin* by George T. Sherborne, for which the prototype was a figure from an Italian renaissance chimneypiece (cat.no. 532). Similarly, no fewer than three versions of a *Virgin and child* relief – taken from an original terracotta panel in the style of Desiderio da Settignano (inv.no. 66–1866) – were exhibited by S. Beresford, T. Nichols, and H. C. Hatfield senior respectively at the Society of Arts Art-Workmanship competition of 1867, and were all acquired by the Museum a year later (cat.nos. 279, 520, 460). The teachers at the Royal College of Art, such as Felix Martin

Fig 3. Anonymous photograph; 1920. The Main Entrance to the Museum (Gallery 49) showing three plaster models by Alfred Stevens for the monument to the Duke of Wellington in St Paul's Cathedral (cat.nos. 576 to 578). Victoria and Albert Museum.

Miller, Alphonse Legros and Edouard Lanteri, some of whose works are also catalogued here, did however play an important role at the time as instructors, and were recognised as respected artists in their own right.

The Format of the Catalogue

Whilst new information on some of the objects in the collection has come to light in the course of the preparation of the catalogue, the information in the entries is based primarily on published sources, as well as on the observations of present and past curators of the Sculpture Department, as recorded in the departmental records kept since the 1950s. Official Museum files (known as Registered Papers) held by the Museum's Registry at the Archive of Art and Design at Blythe House, Hammersmith, have provided valuable and often previously unpublished information on the circumstances surrounding the acquisition of objects, as well as on the opinions of contemporary curators working in the Museum.[5]

The catalogue entries incorporate known information on provenance, bibliographical references and details of temporary loans to exhibitions when relevant. Short biographies of the sculptors have also been given, with bibliographical references. Physical descriptions are not included, since most objects are illustrated.[6] Whenever practicable, newly-taken measurements have been used, but where this has not been possible the recorded imperial measurements have been converted into metric; a small number of objects have not been measured for practical reasons. Indexes of provenance and subjects, and a concordance of inventory numbers are to be found at the end of the volume.

The catalogue has been arranged by century, and then alphabetically by sculptor. Within the section for each sculptor objects are generally ordered chronologically; works after an original model by a known sculptor are placed alphabetically under the relevant sculptor – for example William Wyon's version of John Bell's *Eagle slayer* is included under works by Bell as the original designer [fig. 4] (cat.no. 277). Exceptions to the chronological order occur when it is logical for works to be placed alongside similar objects by the same artist, such as the terracotta sketch models by Joseph Nollekens, which have all been grouped together, despite their differences in date. Unless they are directly related stylistically to a named sculptor, the unattributed objects are arranged chronologically at the end of each century.

Although the catalogue aims to be as inclusive as possible, the following categories have been excluded: ivories, alabasters, waxes, cameos, gems, mosaics, medals, models for medals, reproductive plasters, and architectural models; these last are listed as Appendix II. Some of these have already been published, while others, such as the waxes, plaster casts, and medals, form large coherent groups of several hundred items in themselves, and would not therefore necessarily form an appropriate part of the present publication.[7] Two sets of sculptors' tools are also excluded from this catalogue. One of these included items said to have originally belonged to the sculptor John Bacon the Elder [q.v.] (inv.nos. A.4 to 60–1998); the second set belonged to J.M. (Micky) Bickerdike (1894–1973), who had trained under Henri-Gaudier-Brzeska (1891–1915) (inv.nos. A.3:1 to 23–1992). It is anticipated that certain categories, such as the ivories and architectural models, will be the subject of future publications. The catalogue comprises objects which are held by the Sculpture Department only; it has not been possible to include the chimneypieces, often part of existing interiors, assigned to the Department of Furniture and Woodwork. Nor does the catalogue extend to the bronzes and ironwork by Alfred Stevens under the charge of the Department of Metalwork. Figurative sculpture on the façade of the Museum is excluded, as it has been fully discussed by John Physick (see Physick 1978; *idem* 1982). The sculpture held at Osterley Park, Ham House and Apsley House is also omitted but listed in Appendices III, IV and V respectively.[8]

British sculpture necessarily comprises work by artists active in this country who were not native to Britain, such as Claude David [fig. 5], Laurent Delvaux, Peter

Fig 4. Charles Thurston Thompson (1816–1868); about 1856 (inv.no. 33.966). Photograph of John Bell's *Eagle slayer* in front of the Brompton Boilers (cat.no. 276). Victoria and Albert Museum, Department of Prints, Drawings and Paintings.

Scheemakers, Michael Rysbrack, Louis François Roubiliac, Agostino Carlini, Raffaele Monti, Jules Dalou and Alphonse Legros. Although Francesco Fanelli is represented by the recently acquired miniature bronze portrait bust of *Charles I* (cat.no. 2), other small bronze figurative groups by this sculptor have been excluded, as these form a separate category to be covered by the relevant volume of the forthcoming *Catalogue of Italian Renaissance Bronzes*. Similarly, whilst the *Charles I* marble bust by Hubert Le Sueur has been catalogued (cat.no. 19; see also fig. 6), his small-scale bronzes have not.

The Formation of the Collection

British sculpture has been collected by the Museum since its inception, the earliest acquisition being a relief depicting a scene from Shakespeare's *Seven Ages* (cat.no. 474), given in 1853 by Henry Cole, the Museum's first Director. However, interest in different aspects of the collection has inevitably shifted over generations, with acquisition policies changing with an increased knowledge and understanding of British sculpture.[9] As noted above, in the first decades of the Museum's history, contemporary works (that is, nineteenth-century pieces) were purchased, partly because they were thought to serve as patterns for others to follow, and partly because the Museum patronised young British artists. Eighteenth- and early nineteenth-century British sculpture was not widely valued or studied until the 1950s, and it is thanks to curators such as Terence Hodgkinson [q.v.] that exceptionally important examples, such as Roubiliac's marble figure of *Handel* (cat.no. 156) were added to the collection in the 1960s. Hodgkinson was also instrumental in safeguarding church monuments which had been rendered homeless when certain churches became ruined or redundant; see for example the entries for the Finch monuments (cat.nos. 15, 16, 18). These were displayed in the newly-refurbished gallery of British sculpture on the ground floor of the Museum near the Main Entrance in 1969.[10]

Fig 5. Anonymous photograph; 1891. *Neptune* (previously known as *Time*) by Claude David in the grounds of the South Kensington Museum (cat.no. 96). Victoria and Albert Museum.

As well as purchases made by the Museum, many objects have been acquired as the result of gifts or bequests. The largest number of objects presented by any one individual are undoubtedly those given by Dr W.L. Hildburgh F.S.A. (1876–1955), who from the mid-1920s until his death contributed a total of 43 objects to the collection of British sculpture (as well as numerous gifts of continental sculpture, metalwork, and other items). In addition, the posthumous Hildburgh Bequest funded the acquisition of a further 12 British sculptures. Rupert Gunnis's bequest of sculpture in 1965 included amonst other items Samuel Joseph's busts of Lord and Lady Belhaven and Stenton (cat.nos. 475 and 476).[11]

In many instances sculptures have been given to the Museum directly by the artist, or by his heirs after his death. Examples include the collection of Alfred Gilbert's works presented to the Museum by the National Art Collections Fund in 1936, and the plasters from Sir Joseph Edgar Boehm's studio given by the executors of his estate in 1892 (see cat.nos. 176, 281 to 285, 288 to 336, 479, 737 to 740). A number of works by Sir George Frampton, including sketch models relating to the *Peter Pan* statue in Kensington Gardens, and the two *Mother and child* groups, were given by the sculptor's son Meredith in 1985 (cat.nos. 403 to 409, 394 and 395). The Museum's own funds for acquisitions are not infrequently supplemented by the generosity of funding bodies such as the National Art Collections Fund (now the Art Fund). A number of important purchases made by the Museum have only been made possible thanks to these donations, including the recently acquired marble bust of Daniel Finch by Rysbrack (cat.no. 177). The National Heritage Memorial Fund and National Art Collections Fund have also recently assisted in the Museum's purchase of the chimneypiece from the Great Drawing Room, Gower House, Whitehall, designed by Sir William Chambers (cat.no. 82), and the three carved oak figures from Naworth Castle (cat.nos. 24a-c).

Previous Publications

As mentioned above, a number of objects catalogued here have been cited in earlier specialist books and articles, and it may be useful to give a brief overview of twentieth-century publications on British sculpture. The following books have proved fundamental to the writing of the catalogue: Rupert Gunnis's *Dictionary of British Sculpture* (first published 1953; revised 1968);[12] Margaret Whinney's *Sculpture in Britain 1530–1830* (1964; revised by John Physick in 1988); John Physick's *Designs for English Monuments* (1969), and Margaret Whinney's selective handbook to the Museum's collection, *English Sculpture 1720–1830* (1971). The scholarship of Katharine Esdaile, including her monograph on Roubiliac (1928) – although this has to some extent been superceded by David Bindman and Malcolm Baker's study of Roubiliac's monuments (1995) – along with her numerous articles, deservedly established her as a pioneer in the study of British sculpture. M. I. Webb's writings on various British sculptors over a period of thirty years can be said to have culminated in her monograph *Michael Rysbrack Sculptor* (1954). Benedict Read's *Victorian Sculpture* (1982) and Susan Beattie's *The New Sculpture* (1983) are standard reference works for the field of nineteenth-century British sculpture.

The present publication is in the traditional format of a catalogue, but the hope is that this presentation of the collection will act as a body of information for the study of British sculpture in almost all its manifestations: monuments and models, religious and secular, masterpieces and half-forgotten study pieces, works destined for public, outdoor locations, and those intended for interiors, or private contemplation.

Fig 6. Anonymous photograph; c.1860s. The Chichester Cross, Sussex showing a bust of Charles I in the niche (see cat.no. 21). Victoria and Albert Museum, Sculpture Department archives.

Notes

1 Margaret Whinney drew attention to the pioneering work of Katherine Esdaile and Rupert Gunnis in particular in her 1971 publication on a selection of the Museum's British sculpture (Whinney 1971, p. 7).

2 For a listing of these groups, see below, p. xvi.

3 Apart from those pieces listed here, some plasters by Stevens in storage could not easily be accessed. The inventory numbers of these are as follows: 408–1889, 970–1903, A.27–1911 and A.74–1911. An iron cast by Stevens in the collection, inv.no. A.78–1911, as well as waxes by the artist, are also excluded from the catalogue.

4 These are listed as Appendix I.

5 A list of the most often cited names is given as Appendix VI.

6 A small percentage of objects, such as chimneypieces packed into cases, could not unfortunately be photographed.

7 Some wax objects by Alfred Gilbert are included, as they form part of a group of objects acquired from the studio of the sculptor. Similarly a group of plaster casts of hands of eminent personages, formerly in the studio of Sir Joseph Edgar Boehm at the time of his death, is also catalogued here, as is a mosaic head of Daniel by Alfred Stevens.

8 In 1996 Osterley Park and Ham House (previously administered by the V&A) were taken over by the National Trust; see Appendices III and IV. Apsley House is run by the V&A, but the collections form a separate cohesive group, relating above all to the 1st Duke of Wellington; see Appendix V.

9 For a full discussion of the formation of the collections in the Sculpture Department, see Williamson 1996, pp. 8–24. The Department of Architecture and Sculpture was formed in 1909 (the Department was re-named the Department of Sculpture in 1979). Acquisitions of sculpture prior to 1909 were made for the Museum; subsequently they were assigned specifically to the Department. Occasionally objects were transferred to Sculpture from other departments, notably the Circulation Department.

10 Room 50A. Although this display was modified in a redecoration programme of 1999, the central ideas of the 1969 configuration were retained, and the church monuments set into the North wall of the gallery remain.

11 For an account of Gunnis's collection see Knox 1998.

12 Gunnis's Dictionary is currently undergoing further revision under the editorship of Ingrid Roscoe (due for publication in about 2006).

THE 17TH CENTURY *and earlier*

Caius Gabriel Cibber

(b. Frensborg 1630 – d. London 1700)

Of Danish descent, Cibber was the son of the cabinetmaker to the King of Denmark. Around the age of seventeen he was sent to Rome, funded by the King of Denmark. He later travelled to the Netherlands, and arrived in England in about 1660 to work in the studio of John Stone (d. 1667), the son of Nicholas Stone the Elder [q.v.]. On Stone's death, Cibber established his own workshop. He was employed by the Duke of Devonshire at Chatsworth from 1687–90. His dramatic reclining figures depicting Melancholy Madness *and* Raving Madness *of about 1676, executed for the gates of Bethlem Hospital, Moorfields, were formerly on loan to the Museum: they are now at the Royal Bethlem Hospital, Beckenham, Kent. Cibber became prominent amongst the foreign sculptors working in England in the last quarter of the seventeenth century, and was appointed Sculptor to Charles II in 1667 (I am grateful to the late Katharine Gibson for this information). His son, the playwright Colley Cibber wrote a biography of the sculptor.*

Architect 1921; Gunnis 1968, pp. 101–3; Spink 1976; Allderidge 1977; Whinney 1988, pp. 110–15; Thieme-Becker, 6, p. 566; TDA, 7, pp. 297–9 [Physick].

1: Boy playing the bagpipes

about 1680–90
Portland stone
h. 108 cm.
A.3–1930

The somewhat confusing provenance of the present piece is recounted by Harold Faber in his 1926 monograph on Cibber, by Timbs in his *Curiosities of London*, and by Forster in the Stowe sale catalogue of 1848 (see Faber 1926, pp. 37–9; Timbs 1855, p. 618, Forster 1848, p. 272). Faber suggested that the group was 'probably made for the Duke [of Argyll] about the [sixteen] eighties when Cibber worked for several noblemen at their country seats', and that it had remained at Whitton Park for about one hundred years (Faber 1926, p. 38). However, a note by John Beckwith [q.v.] in the departmental records mentions that a Mr D.H. Simpson – then preparing a booklet on Whitton Park – stated that the first owner of Whitton Park was Archibald, 3rd Duke of Argyll, who succeeded in 1793: he did not buy land in Whitton before 1722, and so probably did not live there before the late 1720s. Beckwith concluded that it was unlikely that the group was at Whitton Park for 100 years as suggested by Faber. The group was then said to have been removed to London, first to Long Acre, then in front of 178 Tottenham Court Road, opposite the end of Howland Street, occupied by the studio of a sculptor named Mr Hinchliff, described as an assistant of Flaxman; it was later in the possession of Hinchcliff's son, with whom it remained until 1835 (or, according to Timbs, about 1825). At some point it was removed to Stowe House, Buckinghamshire. It was included in the Stowe sale of 1848, and was recorded by Forster as being sold as lot 134 on the thirty-sixth day of the sale, held on 3 October 1848 to a Mr J. Browne of University Street, London for £38 17s 0d. According to Forster's annotated catalogue of the Stowe sale, 'He [Mr Browne] was warmly opposed at the time by Mr. Redfern, on behalf of Mr Mark Philips, and the latter gentleman has since re-purchased the work of Mr Browne. It is now in the gardens at Snitterfield, Mr Philips' seat in Warwickshire' (Forster 1848, p. 272). Later in the possession of Sir George Trevelyan at Welcombe, Stratford-on-Avon, it was included in the sale of garden ornaments held by Sotheby's on 19 December 1929, lot 123, and bought in for £115; it was then acquired by the Museum by private treaty, via Alfred Spero and Kerin Ltd, 9 Clifford Street, New Bond Street, London, in 1930 for £150.

When the present piece came up at auction in December 1929 Margaret Longhurst [q.v.] noted, 'It is not very attractive but works by this sculptor very rarely come onto the market'. R.P. Bedford [q.v.] similarly commented, 'Although this work by Cibber is far from attractive I think that we should try to get it for our collections if it goes for a small price. We are unlikely ever to have a chance of getting a better work by the sculptor. It is possible that we may be able re-paint it so that it may be put in the Quadrangle'. The figure was considered to be of historical interest, and was described in the *Review of Principle Acquisitions during the Year 1930* as 'Historically, one of the most interesting pieces of English sculpture which the Department has acquired for a number of years' (*Review* 1930, p. 5).

The subject depicted in the present group has been associated with Daniel Defoe's Blind Piper, described by him in the *Journal of the Plague Year* (recounted in Faber 1926, pp. 38–9). This was originally noted by Timbs in his *Curiosities of London*, published in 1855: 'Among the many touching episodes of the Plague, is that of a blind Highland bagpiper, who having fallen asleep upon the steps of St. Andrew's Church, Holborn-hill, was conveyed away in the dead-cart; and but for the howling of his faithful dog, which waked him from his trance, he would have been buried as a corpse' (Timbs 1855, p. 618). Faber however noted, 'It is more than doubtful whether this group had originally any connexion at all with this remarkable occurance. It is more likely that the appearance of the group in Tottenham Court Road, while people still remembered Defoe's story, made somebody imagine a connexion and that thereafter Defoe's narrative was gradually changed to fit this theory. We find the story of the piper improved in 1820, evidently under the influence of Cibber's group, the dog for instance, of which Defoe has no mention, being made to play an important part' (Faber 1926, p. 39).

Margaret Whinney suggested the piece was related to genre sculpture produced in Holland by Pieter Xavery (b. about 1647; active 1667–74). Anthony Radcliffe has noted comparisons between the present piece and a figure by Cibber at Mapleduram House with bronze statuettes by Giambologna (1529–1608) (cf. *Giambologna* 1978, p. 9, see cat.nos. 135–139, pp. 164–66).

Bibliography

Timbs 1855, p. 618; *Architect* 1921, p. 163 and illus.; Faber 1926, pp. 37–9; *Review* 1930 pp. 5–6 plate V; Gunnis 1968, p. 102; Gibbon 1972, pp. 64–5; *Giambologna* 1978, p. 9; Whinney 1988, p. 114; Roscoe 1995, p. 39, fig. 3 on p. 39.

Francesco Fanelli

(b. Florence 1577; last documented London 1641)

Fanelli is best known for his small-scale bronze statuettes and groups, a number of versions of which are in the Museum's collection. Active in Florence and Genoa, Fanelli travelled to England in about 1631. In 1635 he received a pension from the King, and was later appointed Sculptor to the King.

Pope-Hennessy 1953; Radcliffe and Thornton 1978; DBI 1994 [Franchini Guelfi], p. 569; Schmidt 1998, n. 236 on p. 102; TDA, 10, pp. 786–7 [White].

2: Charles I (b.1600; r.1625–1649)

about 1635–40
Bronze
h. 16.4 cm.
A.3–1999

Recorded as being in the possession of Miss Daphne Ionides by 1952. Purchased by private treaty from Christie's, London, on behalf of the estate of Mrs M.E. Ionides for £240,000 in 1999. Acquired with the assistance of the National Art Collections Fund, and funds from the Murray Bequest, the Horn Bequest, the Hildburgh Bequest, the John Webb Trust, the Bryan Bequest, the Vallentin Bequest, the Barber Bequest and the J.R. Jones Bequest; and with the assistance of donations by The Crescent Trust, Mr Daniel Katz, The Sealed Knot Ltd, R.B.K. & C. Decorative & Fine Arts, G. Dockrell & Gift Aid, Mrs G. Wordsworth, R.J. Rankin, C.M. Diamond, and Mr B.R.E. Cox.

This is the only recorded bust of Charles I by Fanelli; its quality suggests it was originally executed for the King himself or a member of his court.

Bibliography

Pope-Hennessy 1953, p. 161, fig. 14; Radcliffe and Thornton 1978, p. 260; *DBI* 1994 [Franchini Guelfi], p. 569; TDA, 10, p. 787 [White]; Williamson 1999, p. 785, fig. VII; *NACF* 1999 [Motture], pp. 130–1, no. 4760; Murdoch 2001, p. 9 and fig.; Murdoch 2001 [Supplement] unpaginated, fig. 2.

Exhibited

British Antique Dealers Association, *The British Galleries at the V&A: New acquisitions and discoveries*, temporary display at the Duke of York's Headquarters, London, 21 to 27 March 2001.

3: Charles I (b.1600; r.1625–1649)

about 1700–50
Anonymous; style of Francesco Fanelli
Lead on a white marble base
h. (excl. base) 25 cm. h. (base) 12.5 cm.
A.213–1946

Included in the sale in the sale of Renaissance Furniture, Majolica and Objects of Art, the property of Mrs Arthur Bull, and removed from Tewin Water, Welwyn, Herts, formerly in the collection of the late Sir Otto Beit, Bt, K.C.M.G., held at Christie, Manson and Woods, Derby House, Stratford Place, Oxford Street, London, on 24 October 1946. Lot 75 was described as ' A lead bust of a man, possibly Charles I, wearing classical cloak and deep collar, on white marble socle'. Purchased from the sale by Frank Partridge, 144–146 New Bond Street, London, on behalf of the Museum for £33 12s 0d, under the terms of the John Webb Trust: a bronze statuette of *Amphitrite* was also purchased from the same sale (lot 50) by Partridge's on behalf of the Museum, inv.no. A.212–1946.

In a memorandum to the Director suggesting the purchase of the present piece from the Christie's sale, H.D. Molesworth [q.v.] wrote, 'In another category is the small lead bust No. 75, described as "possibly Charles I". I myself feel less doubtful of the subject and believe that the work is English or one of the foreign workers active in England either at the period of Charles I or at the Restoration: Le Sueur or Briot?'

The inventory numbers of bronzes by Fanelli not included in the present catalogue, but due for publication in the forthcoming *Catalogue of Italian Bronze Statuettes*, are listed below: A.103–1910, A.116 to 120–1910, A.124–1910, A.67–1951, A.37–1952, A.4 to 7–1953, A.5–1954, A.50–1956, A.58–1956, A.96–1956, A.19–1971, A.4–1975, A.20–1978, A.23–1979 and A.2–1981.

Busts of Charles I that show some areas of similarity either in style or treatment were also produced by François Dieussart (c. 1600–1661) and Hubert Le Sueur [q.v.].

Grinling Gibbons

(b. Rotterdam 1648 – d. London 1721)

Gibbons was the son of English parents, but was brought up in the Netherlands, and probably studied under Artus Quellinus I (1609–1668) in Amsterdam. He appears to have come to England in about 1667, and is first recorded in York, where he may have worked with the Etty family. By 1671 he was in London, where he attracted the attention of the diarist John Evelyn, who noted that he brought the young artist to the attention of King Charles II. Gibbons's workshop was and is most celebrated for the virtuoso wood reliefs and carvings produced for royal and aristocratic patrons, such as the work he carried out at Hampton Court, Windsor Castle, and Petworth House, Sussex. His workshop also produced statuary and church monuments in stone and marble, and statues cast in bronze; these may have been partly designed and executed by Gibbons's collaborator, Arnold Quellin [q.v.].

Gunnis 1968, pp. 167–70; Thieme-Becker, 13, pp. 593–4; TDA, 12, pp. 591–2 [Beard]; Gibbons 1998.

4: The stoning of St Stephen

1680–1710
Limewood and lancewood (with some later paint)
h. 184.3 cm. w. 134 cm.
446–1898

The present piece was recorded by Vertue as being in Gibbons's house in his Gallery of Pictures in Bow Street, Covent Garden, London, and he noted that it was later bought by James Brydges, 1st Duke of Chandos (*Vertue* 1938, p. 34). It may in fact have have been purchased by Brydges from the sale of Gibbons's effects in 1721. The relief was then at Canons, Edgeware until it was sold together with the contents of the house in 1747. Purchased from the sale by Mr Gore of Bush Hill Park near Enfield. By descent through the family, the relief was latterly with Mr Gore's grandson, William Mellish, M.P., in whose possession it is recorded in 1794. It later passed to Hector J. Gurdon Rebow (great-grandson of Mr Gore and uncle of Mellish) who on acquiring the relief removed it to Wivenhoe [Wyvenhoe] Park, near Colchester, Essex in 1839. The Museum purchased the relief from Mr Gurdon Rebow in 1898 (for details of the provenance and further bibliographical references, see Avray Tipping 1914, p. 51; Baker 1949, p. 166, n. 2; Green 1964, p. 36; Beard 1989, pp. 16, 186). In a letter published in the *Builder* of 1862, Mr Gurdon Rebow offered his understanding of the history of the relief, suggesting (with no evidence), that it was 'bought by Charles II of the artist, and presented by him to the Duchess of Chandos, and removed to Cannons, in Hertfordshire' (cited in Avray Tipping 1914, p. 51). However, a note on the records for the present piece suggests that the relief featured in a sale of the Executors of William Mellish, held by Christie's on 16 March 1839, lot 145. The sale catalogue recorded: 'This very important and unique work was purchased of the Artist by the great Duke of Chandos, and placed at his noble seat Canons, from whence, in 1747, at the destruction of that mansion, it was purchased and removed to Bush-Hill, the residence of the late Proprietor. It will be found that this celebrated work has been alluded to by Evelyn, Walpole, Chauncey, Lysons, and Clutterbuck'. If this is the case, it would suggest that Mr Gurdon Rebow may have purchased, rather than inherited the relief.

This relief was originally on loan to the Museum from Mr Gurdon Rebow immediately prior to its purchase, from 3 January 1898. The Museum authorities stipulated that 'as it is contrary to our regulations to receive objects on loan which are intended for immediate sale, except to the Department, we can only receive it upon the condition that during the period of the loan no negotiations for the sale of the carving shall be completed without first giving the Department the option of purchase at the most favourable price'. Mr Rebow subsequently offered the present piece to the Museum at the price of £3000; Caspar Purdon Clarke, then Director of the Museum, noted, 'Although this carving is probably Gibbons' masterpiece I am not sure that you would care to recommend its acquisition by the Museum except at a much more moderate price'. The response from Thomas Armstrong, then Director of Art – as anticipated by Purdon Clarke – was luke-warm; the relief 'is to me quite uninteresting & of no account artistically – The rendering of the architectural perspective is very ingenious and skillful and the piece is certainly a remarkable curiosity. If it were offered as a gift I do not think it would be refused but I should be sorry to see it bought even for one tenth of he price asked'. Purdon Clarke subsequently wrote to the owner stating, 'We are fully aware that the panel possesses great historical and antiquarian interest but for the purposes of our Museum we do not consider that it is worth more than £300 – for which we are prepared to purchase it'. The Museum purchased the relief from Mr Gordon Rebow later in 1898 for £300. Originally assigned to the Department of Furniture and Woodwork; transferred to the Department of Architecture and Sculpture on 19 April 1923.

When received on loan just prior to acquisition in 1898, the relief was observed to be 'badly damaged and many pieces of foliage and figures detached and missing'. There is a large crack in the foreground and further cracks occur along the bottom edge and at the top. Conservation carried out during 1992/3 revealed an inscription in pencil at the lower right hand edge of the backboard: Wm York & Sons Altered this Case June the 20th 1848.

Bibliography

Avray Tipping 1914, pp. 51–3, fig. 48; Esdaile 1927, p. 93; Brown 1934, p. 53; *Vertue* 1938, p. 34; Baker 1949, p. 166, n. 2; *Masterpieces* 1951, p. 80, no. 39, illus. on p. 81; Molesworth 1951, p. 14 and pl. XXI; Green 1964, pp. 36–7, fig. 18; Whinney 1988, pp. 116–7, fig. 74 on p. 442, n. 28; Beard 1989, pp. 16–17, 186, and fig. 5; *Gibbons* 1998, pp. 24,48–51, illus. on p. 35.

Exhibited

Grinling Gibbons and the Art of Carving, Victoria and Albert Museum, London, 22 October 1998 to 24 January 1999.

5: Putto with skull

about 1680–1700
Possibly circle of Grinling Gibbons or Arnold Quellin
Marble
h. 100.5 cm.
A.17–1982

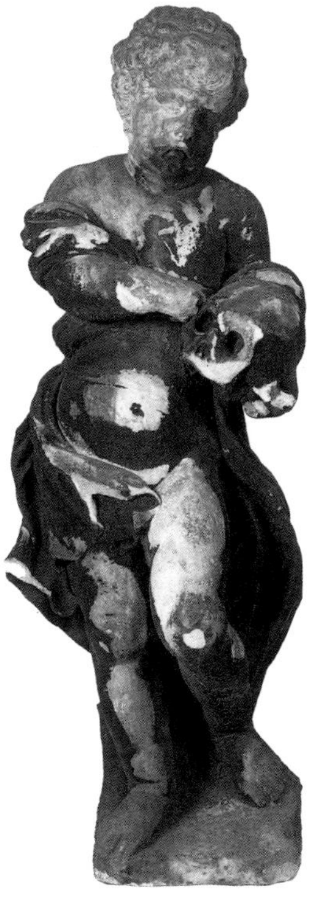

According to the vendor, previously at the Old Greycoat School, Westminster (founded in 1698) (Pevsner 1981 [London], pp. 665–6; Chancellor 1926, pp. 14–16). Purchased from the Heim Gallery, Jermyn Street, London in 1982 for £300.

The figure is badly eroded, possibly from weathering.

The attribution to the workshop of Grinling Gibbons or Arnold Quellin is suggested by comparisons with the carving on the Whitehall Palace altarpiece executed for James II in 1686; see entries for cat.nos. 12 and 13.

Inigo Jones

(b. London, bapt. 1573 – d. London 1652)

Though he began his career as a painter, Inigo Jones is best known for his work as an architect and designer, and between 1605–40 his work as a stage designer was much lauded by his contemporaries. The classical architectural motifs he studied on his travels to Italy directly inspired his architectural designs. In 1610 Jones was appointed Surveyor of Works to Henry, Prince of Wales, and in 1615, Surveyor General to James I, responsible for the design of buildings required by the King, including the Whitehall Banqueting House and Queen's House in Greenwich. Between 1625 and 1640 he was engaged on the repairs to St Paul's Cathedral.

Colvin 1995; pp. 554–61; Thieme-Becker, 19, pp.120–3; TDA, 17, pp. 633–9 [Tavernor/Peacock].

6: Caryatid figure

about 1636
After designs attributed to Inigo Jones
Stone
h. 129 cm.
A.7–1988

6 7

This caryatid figure, with its companion piece cat.no. 7, originally formed part of an overmantel for a chimneypiece at Wilton House, Wiltshire, and was possibly commissioned by Philip Herbert, 1st Earl of Montgomery and 4th Earl of Pembroke (1584–1650), who ascended to the Earldom in 1630 on the death of his elder brother, William Herbert, 3rd Earl of Pembroke (1580–1630). It is likely that the overmantel was in the South front of Wilton House before this part of the building was destroyed by fire around 1647 or 1648. Thence by descent through the family until sold at Christie's, London on 3 July 1961, lot 10, from 'A Selected Portion of the Collection of Ancient Marbles Formed by the 8th Earl of Pembroke (1674–1732)'. The caryatids were subsequently in the possession of Roland Starke, a private collector who now lives in Southern California, and who on a visit to the Museum in September 1998 told us that the caryatids had been bought for him by his godfather at the Christie's sale at Wilton in 1961 for Bolton House, Hampstead. In 1975 they were moved to the U.S.A. and were bought by the Museum together with cat.no. 7 at Christie's, New York sale on 23 April, 1988 lot 82 for £15,549.29.

Colvin records the involvement of Inigo Jones in designs for the interior for Wilton House in the 1630s, and in the rebuilding of the south front of Wilton House for Philip, 4th Earl of Pembroke, which was begun in 1636. However, it was Isaac de Caux or Caus (d. after 1655) who was commissioned to rebuild the south front; Colvin notes, 'De Caux's employment at Wilton is documented by a warrant dated 14 March 1635/6 in which the Earl authorizes him 'to take down . . . that side of Wilton House which is towards the Garden and such other parts as shall bee necessary & rebuild it anew with additions according to the Plott which is agreed" (see Colvin 1995, pp. 298, 561).

The similarity of the present caryatids with a drawing attributed to Inigo Jones dated 1636 in the collection of the Royal Institute of British Architects (due to come to the V&A in 2003) for an overmantel at Oatlands Palace near Weybridge, Surrey, suggests a date around 1636 for both (see *Inigo Jones* 1989, pp. 221–2, cat.nos. 69 and 70, illus. p. 223). The putti heads on the caryatids at Oatlands Palace have here been replaced with female ones. Roland Starke has suggested that the R.I.B.A. drawing is one of the few signed by Jones and unique in having a drawn-in scale. He has also advised that the drawing and stone figures were shown to match to the inch when the two were computed (personal communication, November 2001).

BIBLIOGRAPHY
Williamson 1991, p. 876.

EXHIBITED
Access All Areas: The RIBA's Architectural Collections at the V&A, Victoria and Albert Museum, London, 18 May 1998 to 24 September 2000.

7: Caryatid figure

about 1636
After designs attributed to Inigo Jones
Stone
h. 128.5 cm.
A.8–1988

Purchased by the Museum together with cat.no. 6 from Christie's, New York, 23 April, 1988, lot 82 for £15,549.29. For full provenance see entry for cat.no. 6.

BIBLIOGRAPHY
Williamson 1991, p. 876.

JOHN NOST I (THE ELDER)

(active 1686 – d. London 1710)

John Nost (or Jan van Oost) came to England from Mechelen, and is first recorded as working with John Vanderstaine, a stone carver, at Windsor Castle. He was then employed as a foreman by Arnold Quellin [q.v.], whose widow he married. Nost worked in marble and stone, but also designed and produced many garden statues in lead, notably those at Melbourne Hall, Derbyshire. He obtained many royal and aristocratic commissions, and executed work for Hampton Court in 1700 and 1701/2. He is now known to have died in 1710, rather than 1729 as previously thought (see Spencer-Longhurst and Naylor 1998, p. 39, note 26). For works by Nost the Younger see cat. nos. 148 and 149.

Gunnis 1968, p. 279–82; O'Connell 1987, pp. 802–6; Thieme-Becker, 25, pp. 522–3; TDA, 23, p. 253 [Murdoch]; Spencer-Longhurst and Naylor 1998, pp. 31–40.

8: William III (b.1650; r.1689–1702)

about 1695
Terracotta
h. 53 cm.
A.35–1939

Purchased from Montague Marcussen Ltd, Antiques & Works of Art, 98 Crawford Street, London, in 1939 for £25; the vendor believed the figure to be by a French modeller and to depict James II. On long-term loan to Historic Royal Palaces at Hampton Court from 1992 to 1999.

The left hand is placed on the hip, and the right (a restoration) raised and clutched, probably originally intended to hold a baton. On acquisition the model was gilded; the gilding was later removed to reveal the terracotta.

The present piece is thought to be the original model for the lifesize stone figure of William III on the Royal Exchange erected in 1695 (see entry for cat. no. 9). Katharine Esdaile, who later published the statuette (see Esdaile 1940 [William III]), was instrumental in suggesting the origin of the present piece. In a letter to H.D. Molesworth in July 1939 she wrote, ' I went to the B.M. after all, I looked at the Grace prints of the R. Exchange & the great Illustrated Pennant. There is no doubt that I am right. There is the crown at the back of the head, the tunic just above the [illegible], the attitude, the turn towards his Queen & all the rest. Poor as the prints are, they are decisive . . . even if the V&A has to go to the NACF we must get that statuette'.

In a memorandum to Margaret Longhurst [q.v.], H.D. Molesworth [q.v.] noted, 'I went to the Royal Exchange Assurance Co to look at the Carter drawings referred to by Mrs Esdaile. These are very slight pencil sketches some four inches high – consequently not very distinctive. The drawing of William III certainly looks very similar to the Marcussen terracotta, the major differences being that the position of the legs is reversed, and that the left hand held an orb, while the right with the sceptre was brought forward onto the other hand, as far as can be judged the comparison of the crown and cloak, and the emphasis of the garter and cloak cords is very similar as is the general feel and build up, on the whole it is however, not impossible that Mrs Esdaile is right'.

The Museum later acquired the model for the statue of Queen Mary; see entry for cat.no. 9.

BIBLIOGRAPHY
Esdaile 1940 [William III]; Esdaile 1947 [Sisters], p. 254 and plate C; Molesworth 1951, p. 14 and plate XIX: Staring 1965, p. 222 and n. 2, fig. 2; Whinney 1988, p. 445, n. 68; *Glorious Revolution* 1988, illus. on p. 19; *Going Dutch* 1989, illus.; TDA, 23, p. 253 [Murdoch]; Smith 1996, p. 12 n. 4, p. 25; Roscoe 1997, p. 175, fig. 62 on p. 176, Snodin and Styles 2001, fig. 17 on p. 13.

EXHIBITED

Drawings by English Sculptors 1680–1810, Ashmolean, Oxford; *Parliament and the Glorious Revolution 1688–1988,* Banqueting House, Whitehall, 1 July to 30 September 1988, cat.no. 13; *'Going Dutch'. Decorative Arts from the Age of William and Mary*. The Victoria and Albert Museum at the Bank of England, Bank of England Museum, London, 29 June to 4 October 1989.

9: Mary II (b.1662; r.1689–1694)

about 1695
Possibly by John Nost the Elder
Painted and gilt terracotta
h. 60 cm.
A.208–1946

Previously owned by the donor's mother, Lady Younghusband. The donor 'understood from her [mother] that it was one of the statues of Kings and Queens of England which stood in Gloucester Cathedral, until they were removed many years ago'. Given by Miss Eileen L. Younghusband, 24A Lansdowne Road, Holland Park, London, in 1946.

Though by family tradition thought to be from Gloucester Cathedral, the present piece is almost certainly the companion figure to the statuette of William III, which is also in the Museum's collections, and mentioned in Katharine Esdaile's article on the William III model in the *Burlington Magazine* of April 1940; she wrote, 'It would be too much to hope that the model for the companion statue of the Queen is still in existence, for the life of a terracotta is uncertain' (Esdaile 1940 [William III], p. 124).

As with the statuette of William III, Katharine Esdaile was 'exceedingly interested' in the present piece when it surfaced in 1946. In response to a letter written by John Pope-Hennessy she wrote, 'She Mary II (I don't think it is Queen Anne) was so much taller than William that the difference in size is not surprising, and one odd detail – the placing of the crown far back to allow for the Tour [Tower] of hair in front, corresponds with the way in which William's crown is pushed back to allow for the periwig'. Mrs Esdaile reported back on a visit to the Guildhall Library in which she found several related drawings: one engraving, signed 'Sutton Nicholls sculp', 'shows the Queen with a crown, sceptre in the V&A hanging ruffle on l. arm, and lines of jewels draped in loops on the chest (I studied all through a magnifying glass). This seems to me decisive – the Mary is our statuette. But what a relentless portrait of an elderly woman it is!'.

Although differences are apparent in drawings which relate to the figures for the Royal Exchange, and the terracottas, both are thought to be the models for the statues of William and Mary, executed by John Nost and placed on the Royal Exchange in 1695. A payment of £120 to Nost for the statues was recorded in the City's Cash Accounts for Michaelmas, 1696 (Roscoe 1997, p. 175). Both original statues, which stood in niches, vanished after the fire at the Royal Exchange in 1838. Ingrid Roscoe has noted the apparent differences between the present piece and its pendant, and an engraving showing the scheme of the Royal Exchange quadrangle, and suggests this might indicate 'that modifications were demanded by the supervisory committee, or conceivably, that the maquettes in fact relate to another commission . . . The model for Mary is slightly larger and looks less sophisticated because it is coated in polychrome paints, very likely original. The opulent colours, ranging from dark blues and red to flesh-tones and gilding, are consonant with other Exchange statues in State robes' (Roscoe 1997, p. 175).

Bibliography

Esdaile 1947 [Sisters], p. 254 and pl. B; *Glorious Revolution* 1988, illus. p.19; Whinney 1988, p. 445 and n. 68; *Going Dutch* 1989, illus.; TDA, 23, p. 253 [Murdoch]; Roscoe 1997, p. 175, fig. 63 on p. 176.

Exhibited

Parliament and the Glorious Revolution 1688–1988, Banqueting House, Whitehall, 1 July to 30 September 1988, cat.no. 14; *'Going Dutch', Decorative Arts from the Age of William and Mary.* The Victoria and Albert Museum at the Bank of England, Bank of England Museum, London, 28 June to 4 October 1989.

Arnold Quellin (Artus/Arnoldus Quellinus III)

(b. Antwerp 1653; d. London? after 9 December 1686)

Arnold Quellin was the son of the Netherlandish sculptor Artus Quellin II (1625–1700), and trained under his father in Antwerp. He went to London in about 1682, and there joined Grinling Gibbons's workshop. He specialised in marble sculpture, of which his monument to Thomas Thynne (c. 1682) in Westminster Abbey is a notable example; he may also have provided the models for the bronze statues of Charles II (1685) at Chelsea Hospital and James II (1686) in Trafalgar Square.

Beard 1989, passim, but especially pp. 51–64, 197; Thieme-Becker, 27, p. 508; TDA, 25, p. 813 [Kockelburgh].

10: Charles II (b.1630; r.1660–1685)

after 1685
Terracotta
h. 20.5 cm.
A.7–1945

According to Mr Winter, the Museum official who discovered the bust at Alfred Spero's premises, 134 New Bond Street, London, it was said to have belonged to the late brother of the vendor, almost certainly Maurice Spero, who had owned the bust for some time before it was passed to another dealer. It was later acquired by Alfred Spero, from whom the Museum purchased it in 1945 for £30.

The present bust was originally identified by Katharine Esdaile as a model for the upper portion of the full-length statue of Charles II (now lost), which was designed by Arnold Quellin for the Royal Exchange, and completed between 22 May 1685 and the end of that year, when Walpole recorded payment being made to Quellin. See the article 'A lost Stuart Statue' by Esdaile in the *Times*, 8 December 1928. A further terracotta full-length model for the

Royal Exchange figure of Charles II attributed to Artus Quellin is in Sir John Soane's Museum; see Gibson 1997, fig. 56 on p. 164. A note on the records for the present piece records 'Comparison with the Soane Museum statuette shows that this bust is an exact reproduction (a cast in my opinion) of the Soane figure with slight variation of the cloak at the base of the bust where it is finished off' (departmental records; H.D. Molesworth [q.v.]). For the Royal Exchange see also the entry for cat. no. 9.

Bibliography
Gibson 1997, p. 161, n. 142.

10

11

11: James II (?) (b.1633; r.1685–1688; d.1701)

about 1685
Probably by Arnold Quellin
Bronze
h. 32.3 cm.
A.20–1948

Purchased from Messrs Sotheby & Co, New Bond Street, London in 1948 for £16.

This statuette is a smaller variant of the bronze statue of James II situated outside the National Gallery in London, attributed to the studio of Grinling Gibbons, and probably executed by Arnold Quellin, originally erected in the Privy Gardens, Whitehall in 1685 (see Blackwood 1989 pp. 30–1).

The composition of the figure is comparable with two designs by John Nost the Elder [q.v.] for statues of William III (see Physick 1969, pp. 56–7, figs. 30 and 31).

Bibliography
Gibson 1997, p. 161, n. 142.

12: Putto holding the crown and coat of arms of Scotland

about 1686
Style of Arnold Quellin or Grinling Gibbons [q.v]
Marble
h. 95.9 cm. w. 69.1 cm.
A.3–1973

Purchased from Peter Hone Antiques, 110 Islington High Street, London, together with cat.no. 13 in 1973 for £600, using funds from the Hildburgh Bequest.

There is a fracture across the top right corner; the surface is weathered.

The attribution is based on comparisons of the shape and size of this relief and its companion cat.no. 13, with those now in the church of St Andrew at Burnham-on-Sea, Somerset, by Grinling Gibbons and Arnold Quellin (see Green 1964, figs. 61 and 63). In describing the reliefs at Burnham, Vivian-Neal noted, 'Some of the heads of the ten cherubs are of great beauty, but with one exception the six child-angels in the chancel have a struggling, almost tortured expression, common in many other works of the seventeenth century in which the vitality of the period was trammeled by convention' (Vivian-Neal 1935, p. 132).

The Burnham sculptures originally formed part of the altarpiece in the Roman Catholic chapel in Whitehall Palace (1686), which was dismantled following the fire in 1695, and re-erected as the High Altar of Westminster Abbey in 1706; around 1820 it was moved to Burnham and finally dismembered there. Some of the reliefs were kept at Westminster, and are now in the Dean's Yard (see *Wren Society* 1930, pp. 74–5, figs. on pp. 236–7, and pls. XIII to XIV; Vivian-Neal 1935, pp. 127–32; Green 1962; *idem*, 1964, pp. 60–1; Beard 1989, pp. 25–6; *Westminster Abbey* 1995, pp. 125–6). Vivian-Neal recorded, 'A Victorian architect removed certain of the marbles from Burnham Church; some of these were found by Prebendary G.L. Porcher in a lumber room at the old vicarage' (Vivian-Neal 1935, p. 131). There is no known visual record of the original arrangement of the altarpiece as it stood in Whitehall.

The stiff drapery on this relief and its pendant is similar to that found on monuments by Grinling Gibbons, including the Holder monument, St Paul's Cathedral, and the Robert Cotton monument, Conington, Cambridgeshire (see Green 1964, figs. 231 and 232). The poses of the putti also bear a resemblance to those holding crowns on the Fauconberg monument, Coxwold, Yorkshire (*ibid.*, figs. 235 and 236). The facial features are reminiscent of those found on a marble figure of *Autumn* – one of a pair with that of *Winter* – by Quellin of about 1680/90, formerly at Stowe, Buckinghamshire, and now in the Rijksmuseum, Amsterdam (inv.no. RBK 1970–29b); see *Europäische Barockplastik* 1971, fig. 129, cat.no. 249.

BIBLIOGRAPHY
Whinney 1988, p. 444, n. 45; Beard 1989, pp. 26 n. 28, 196.

13: Putto holding the crown and coat of arms of Ireland

about 1686
Style of Arnold Quellin or Grinling Gibbons [q.v.]
Marble
h. 95 cm. w. 68.9 cm.
A.4–1973

Purchased from Peter Hone Antiques, 110 Islington High Street, London, together with cat.no. 12 in 1973 for £600, using funds from the Hildburgh Bequest.

The surface of the relief is weathered.

Together with its companion cat.no. 12, this relief may derive from the Whitehall altarpiece. See entry for cat.no. 12.

BIBLIOGRAPHY
See entry for cat.no. 12.

William Stanton

(b. 1639 – d. 1705)

William Stanton was one of a family of sculptors; he was the father of Edward Stanton [q.v.]. William Stanton is mainly recognised for his funerary monuments, produced between about 1665 and 1705. Commenting on the Stanton family of sculptors, Katharine Esdaile noted, 'The Stantons were excellent examples of that traditional English training by which a sculptor began as an apprentice under an extablished master; worked his way up; became a member of the Masons' Company of which all three Stantons were in fact Master; and either carried on an existing business or started one of his own'.

Esdaile 1929 [Model], p. 197; Esdaile 1930, pp. 149–69; TDA, 29, p. 542 [Physick].

14: Lady Rebecca Atkins (d.1711)

about 1689
Terracotta
l. 36 cm.
A.1–1929

Purchased by Dr W.L. Hildburgh F.S.A. from the Pelham Galleries, 155 Fulham Road, Chelsea, London around 1929 for £9. Given to the Museum as a New Year gift by Dr Hildburgh in 1929.

This is a sketch model for the recumbent effigy from the marble monument to Sir Richard Atkins Bt. (d.1689) and Lady Rebecca Atkins (née Wright alias Bunkley) and their three children, in the North transept of St Paul's Church, Clapham (see *Historical Monuments* 1925, p. 93 and pl. 144). On acquisition this sketch was erroneously identified by Katharine Esdaile as the model for the female figure on the tomb of Richard (d. 1689) and Isabel (d. 1693) Shineburne or Sherburne of Stonyhurst, in the church at Mitton, Yorkshire, executed by William Stanton in 1699; it was published as such in an article by Mrs Esdaile in the *Burlington Magazine* in 1929 (see Esdaile 1929 [Model] and Whinney 1988 below; see also Esdaile 1927 frontispiece and Esdaile 1929 [Model], pl. B for illustrations of the Mitton monument). In her article, Katharine Esdaile noted the rarity of such seventeenth-century models, 'The monument of a private person… was of interest only to the family; and even if a model were made, the chances against its survival are overwhelming. If three eighteenth-century terra-cottas have, to my knowledge, fallen victims to the domestic duster within five years, the existence today of a seventeenth-century example seemed impossible to hope for' (Esdaile 1929 [Model], p. 196).

The differences between the finished Shirburn or Sherburne monument and the present piece were highlighted in the *Review of*

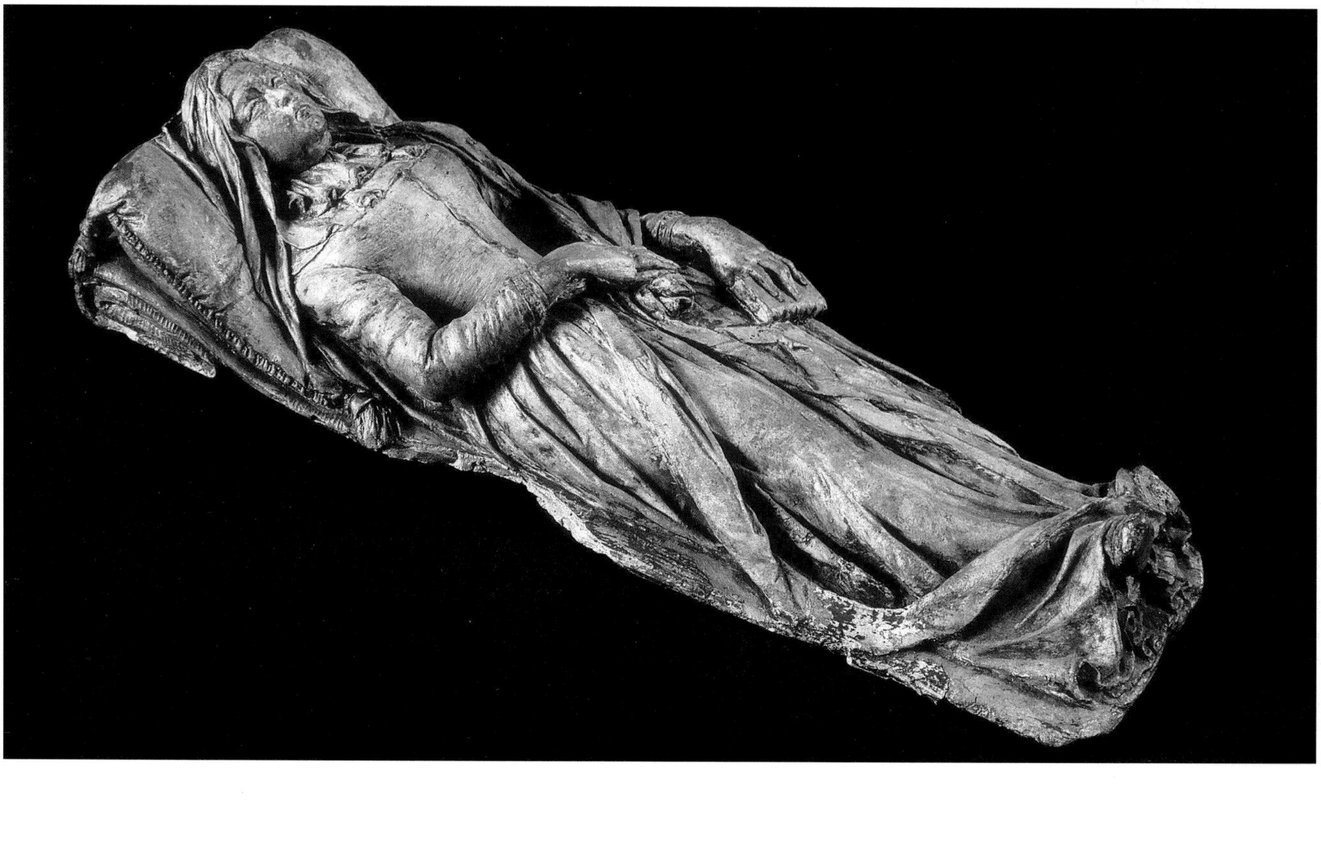

Principal Acquisitions during the Year 1929, 'The use of the recumbent position at so late a date in the 17th century, instead of the reclining pose, is an unusual archaism. It was fortunate that Stanton did not adhere in the finished work to the design of this charming little model, which, in the freshness and vivacity of the treatment of the draperies, recalls French work of the late 16th and early 17th centuries' (*Review* 1929, p. 4). The original identification of the present piece was later corrected by Katharine Esdaile to that of Lady Atkyns [sic] (Esdaile 1942, p. 185; I am grateful to Paul Williamson for this reference).

The will of Lady Rebecca Atkins is in the Prerogative Court of Canterbury (PROB 11/521, sig 119); a copy on microfilm is in the Family Records Centre, London (I am grateful to Dinah Winch for this information).

BIBLIOGRAPHY

Review 1929, pp. 3–4 and fig 5; Esdaile 1929 [Model], and pl. A; Esdaile 1942, p. 185; Molesworth 1951, p. 13 and pl. XVI; Whinney 1988, p. 446, n. 2 (there said to be the terracotta model for the female figure on the tomb of Richard and Isabel Shireburn; citing Esdaile 1929 [Model]).

EXHIBITED

Drawings by English Sculptors 1680–1810, Ashmolean Museum, 23 November to 10 December 1967.

NICHOLAS STONE THE ELDER

(b. near Exeter, 1586/7– d. London 1647)

Stone was the most important sculptor in England in the first half of the seventeenth century; his surviving tombs evince his training on the Continent, and his ability to absorb earlier sculptural traditions, particularly the antique. He served as an apprentice to the Netherlandish sculptor Hendrick de Keyser I (1565–1621) in Amsterdam, probably from 1607 to 1613, when he returned to England, having married de Keyser's daughter Maria. As well as executing memorials and garden sculpture for private clients, Stone received prestigious commissions from the English Court, being appointed Master Mason and Architect at Windsor Castle in 1626, and Master Mason to the Crown in 1632. He was also active as an architect, his most noteworthy commission being the Banqueting House in Whitehall (1619–21). With the outbreak of Civil War in 1642 Stone appears to have ceased working. His surviving notebook and account book (both at Sir John Soane's Museum) give exceptionally important information about the range of his sculpture, including many lost works.

Physick 1970 [Eastwell]; Whinney 1988, pp. 67–85; Colvin 1995, pp. 929–31; TDA, 29, pp. 713–4 [White]; White 1999, pp. 118–38.

15: Wall monument to Sir Heneage Finch (1580–1631)

1632
Marble
h. 243 cm.
A.184–1969

The inscription in Latin reads:

HENEAGIO FINCH/Equiti aurato, Servienti ad Legem Recordatori/per decennium Londinensi:/Ac Parlamentario, in secundis Sereniss: Caroli Regis/Ordinum Comitijs Proloquutori:/

MOILI FINCH et ELIZABETHÆ/(quæ viro superstes vicecometissae Maidston et/comitissae de Winchilsey dignitatibus aucta)

FILIO, OPTIMO, PATRONO, MARITO, AMICO VIRO/Ex Elizabetha coniuge secunda,/Antiquo Cradocorum genere orta, binis susceptis filiabus;/ac peracto iusti coniugij biennio. M. VII. D. XX./Spiritum in manus Salvatoris sui, cui constantissime in =/servivit, placidissime (dum hydrope corripitur) resolvit/V Die Dec: Ao. CHRISTI. M. D. C. XXXI./Vixit Annos L Men: XI Di: V

Franciscus frater natu non affectu minimus (vna cum Tho:/Twisden consobrino) ex testamenta hæres modicum hoc/ingentis Desiderij et Doloris/Monumentum P.

Habes (ô nunquam moriture) heu cito nimium/Quem ipse in vivis dictitasti tumulum:/Mori nempe negavit

Virtus inclyta, intemerata fides,/Assiduitas invicta, alma Iustitia./Inter Primos qui pie Literatus,/Nulli Bonitate Secundus extitisti./Abrepto in coelis A Dño quid invidemus./Cui parem in terris posteri vix videbunt.

Translation: To Heneage Finch,

the radiant knight who served London as a Recorder for decades, Member of Parliament, and under King Charles Speaker of the House of Commons.

To Moyle and Elizabeth Finch, the latter having survived her husband, and elevated with the titles of the Viscountess of Maidstone and Countess of Winchilsea

To the best son, husband, employer and friend, from Elizabeth his second wife, who came from the ancient family of Cradock, one of two daughters, having survived her husband by two years two months and seven days

He most serenely gave up his soul into the hands of his Saviour when he was taken away by the dropsy on the 5 September 1631.
He lived fifty years eleven months and five days.
Francis his brother, and heir (together with Thomas Twisden his brother-in-law) erected this small monument with enormous sorrow and grief.
Alas, you, (o Lord who will never die) have assigned too hastily this burial amongst those still living.
Renowned virtue never denies death nor does measured faith, unsurpassed zeal and gracious justice.

Among those who were best versed in religious text, you were second to none in virtue.
Taken into the heavens by the Lord, how envious are we who survive. They will hardly see your equal on earth in future times.
(We are grateful to Norbert Jopek and James Yorke for help with this translation).

The account book of Nicholas Stone records that the commission for the present piece was received in October 1632, 'Agreed with Mr Frances Finch Esquyer for 50£ agreed for the tombe of Ser Hanegs Finch Mr Recorder of London and receved 10£ in pres Rest due to me the tombe bing sett up and finished 40£' (Spiers 1919, p. 88). Originally in the south chancel aisle of the church of St Mary, Eastwell, Kent. Removed from the ruined church and given to the Museum by the Rector and Churchwardens of the Parish of Eastwell with Broughton Aluph in 1969, together with cat.nos. 16, 18, 48 and 498. For a full description of the monuments from Eastwell see Physick 1970 [Eastwell].

Sir Heneage Finch was Recorder of London, Sergeant-At-Arms, and Speaker of the House of Commons between 1626 and 1628. He was the fourth son of Sir Moyle Finch and Lady Elizabeth Finch (later Countess of Winchelsea); for their monument also in the Museum, see entry for cat.no. 16. Adam White suggests that the present piece is closely related to an earlier monument commemorating William Camden (d. 1623) in Westminster Abbey, supposed to have been erected by Sir Robert Cotton, 'Cotton's carefully conceived act of homage was stripped of its meaning by none other than Nicholas Stone, whose monument to Sir Heneage Finch imitates that of Camden in form but scarcely, if at all, in substance. That Britain's leading sculptor could work in this way clearly suggests the one reason why the new classicism was never widespread; quite simply, it was not widely understood or appreciated, particularly by artists' (White 1985, p. 31; see fig. 31 on p. 30 for the Camden monument). Another closely related monument executed by Stone the same year as the present piece, also for the sum of £50, was erected to the memory of Dr Hugh Barker in the ante-chapel of New College Chapel, Oxford (see Fyer 1912, p. 249, pl. XI (2) opp. p. 247).

Two cartouches with coat-of-arms displayed in the Museum above the monument, but not shown in the accompanying illustration, were originally displayed higher up on the wall of the chancel, and are described by Spiers as 'so characteristic of Stone's works blazoned in colours' (Spiers 1919, p. 88; see pl. XXXVIII opp. p. 86 for the monument in situ).

BIBLIOGRAPHY
Physick 1970 [Eastwell], p. 135, fig. 3 on p. 129, fig. 14 on p. 134; Kenworthy-Browne 1973, p. 574 and fig. 1; *Society of Antiquaries* 1977 no. 517; White 1985, p. 31 and fig. 12; *idem* 1999 p. 121, notes 143–5 on p. 132; Baker 2000 [Figured in Marble], p. 51, pl. 35 on p. 51.

16: Monument to Sir Moyle Finch (1551–1614) and his wife, Lady Elizabeth Finch, Countess of Winchilsea (1556–1634)

about 1615–30
Attributed to Nicholas Stone the Elder
Marble and alabaster
h. 172 cm.
A.186–1969

Inscribed with the names of the twelve children of Sir Moyle and Lady Elizabeth Finch around the bier anti-clockwise from the top right:

THEOPHILVS FINCH/HENEAGE FINCH/THOMAS FINCH IOHN FINCH/HENEAGE FINCH FRAVNCIS FINCH/WILLIAM FINCH/ROBERT FINCH/ELIZABETH FINCH ELIZABETH FINCH/KATHERINE FINCH ANN FINCH

Removed from the ruined church of St Mary, Eastwell, Kent. Given to the Museum by the Rector and Churchwardens of the Parish of Eastwell with Broughton Aluph in 1969, together with cat.nos. 15, 18, 48 and 498. For a full description of the monuments from Eastwell see Physick 1970 [Eastwell].

This monument was originally covered by an elaborate canopy supported by eight columns, which was removed in 1756 by Lord Nottingham to alleviate concerns that the effigies below – considered to be the most outstanding in Kent – might be endangered should the canopy collapse (see Physick 1970 [Eastwell],

Cat.no. 16 in situ in gallery 50A in 1970.

pp. 131–35). The monument was erected after the death of Sir Moyle Finch in 1614, and during the lifetime of his widow, who was made Viscountess Maidstone in 1623 and then Countess of Winchilsea in 1628. The names of their children are inscribed on the bier (see above and Physick 1970 [Eastwell], pp. 133–4). For the monument to their fourth son, Sir Heneage Finch, who died in 1631, see the entry for cat.no. 15. Marjorie Trusted has noted that the high quality of the carving of the present piece is particularly apparent in the portrait of Lady Elizabeth Finch, suggesting that it may have been taken from life. Comparison with the painted portrait of Lady Finch of 1600 by Marcus Gheeraerts the Younger corroborates this supposition; see *Dynasties* 1995, pp. 179–80, cat.no. 122. In his *Biographical Dictionary of London Tomb Sculptors*, Adam White rejects an earlier attribution of the monument (except the effigies) to the workshop of Nicholas Johnson (fl. about 1594 d. 1624). He also rejects the attribution of the effigies to either William Cure (Cuer) the Younger (fl. 1605 – d. 1632) or Nicholas Stone the Elder (see White 1999, p. 73; p. 45 and n. 51 on p. 47; p. 127, notes 328–30 on p. 137).

Bibliography

Esdaile 1935 pp. 230–4 and plate III; Physick 1970 [Eastwell], pp. 131–5 and figs 7, 9–12; *Dynasties* 1995, p. 180; Baker 1996 [Louvre], p. 75, fig. 1 on p. 87; Williamson 1996 [Trusted], p. 131; White 1999, pp. 45, n. 51 on p. 47; p. 73, notes 8–10 on p. 74; p. 127, notes 328–30 on p. 137; Llewellyn 2000, pp. 1, fig. 2a on p. 3, fig. 2b on p. 4, p. 164.

17: Monument to Sir Augustine Nicolls (1559–1616)

about 1616
Ascribed to Nicholas Stone the Elder
Alabaster and black marble
h. (overall) 325.5 cm.
A.9–1965

The monument contains four panels with inscriptions. The main inscription, found beneath the central figure depicting Sir Augustine Nicolls, reads:

TO THE MOST RELIGIOVS & RENOWNED MEMORYE OF SR AUGUSTINE NICOLLS KNIGHT LATE OF/FAXTON IN NORTHAMPTONSHEERE, WHO WAS SECOND SONNE OF THOMAS/NICOLLS ESQR OF THE SAME COVNTIE, HE WAS STVDENT OF THE LAWES IN/THE MIDDLE TEMPLE LONDON, BECAME READER THEREIN THE LAST YEARE OF/QUEENE ELIZABETH, OF WHOM HE RECEAVED HIS WRITT OF SERIEANT AT THE/LAWE YE MICHAELMAS TEARME IMMEDIATLY FOLLOWINGE AFTERWARD SERIEANT/TO PRINCE HENRY OF FAMOVS MEMORYE AND Y QVEENE HIS MOTHER; THEN ONE/OF HIS MATIES IVSTICES OF HIS COVRT OF COMMON PLEASE AND KEEPER OF THE/GREATE SELE TO THE MOST ILLVSTRIOVS AND MIGHTYE PRINCE CHARLES: WHO/HAVINGE LABOVRED IN THE HIGH AND PAINFVLL CALLINGE OF A MOST REVEREND &/IVST IVDGE FOR YR SPACE OF FOVRE YEARES FELL VNDER THE HEAVIE BVRTHEN/OF IT AT KENDALL SITTINGE THEN IVSTICE OF ASSISE AND COMMINGE TO/GIVE IVGGMENT VPPON OTHERS BY HIS COMFORTABLE & CHRISTIAN DEPARTVRE/RECEAVED (WEE ASSVREDED BELEEVE) HIS IVDGMENT WITH MERCYE IN YE YEARE/OF OVR LORD 1616 THE 3 DAY OF AVGVST THE 14TH YEARE OF YE RAINGE OF OR/SOVERAIGNE LORD KINGE IAMES: AND THE 57TH YEARE OF HIS AGE

Originally from the demolished church of St Denis, Faxton, Northamptonshire. Terence Hodgkinson [q.v.] noted in a memorandum to the Director, 'These have been in Mr Graham-Harrison's potting-shed for about fifteen years, following the demolition of the church at Faxton, to which they belonged'. Given to the Museum by the Rector and Churchwardens of Lamport with Faxton in 1965, together with cat.nos. 62, 126 and 260. For a full discussion of the Faxton monuments, see Hodgkinson 1971/2.

The allegorical figures represent: above, *Fortitude* and *Temperance*; and below, *Justice* and *Prudence*. Most of the head of the figure of Prudence is missing. The three smaller inscription panels are damaged.

Sir Augustine Nicolls was a Justice of Common Pleas; he was commemorated at Faxton, where he was Lord of the Manor, though he is buried at Kendal, Westmoreland, having died there while on circuit.

In his article on the monuments, Terence Hodgkinson described the present piece as 'The earliest and most eleborate of the Faxton monuments . . . The design of the memorial and especially of the allegorical figures is sophisticated for its date and strongly reminds one of the work of Nicholas Stone. In particular the nervous handling of the drapery in the two figures of the lower register is to be found elsewhere in the sculpture of Stone and, in his case, must have been learned in the workshop of his father-in-law, Hendrick de Keyser' (Hodgkinson 1971/2, pp. 337–9).

Bibliography
Hodgkinson 1971/2, pp. 337–9, pl. 6.

18: Wall monument to Frances, Lady Finch (d.1627)

about 1627
Attributed to Nicholas Stone the Elder
Marble
h. 212.5 cm.
A.185–1969

The inscription in Latin reads:

CONJVGI SVÆ/PLVSQVAM DESIDERATISSIMÆ/FRANCISCÆ/ EDMVNDI BELL DE BEVPREEHALL EQVITIS AURATI FILIÆ,/-CONJVGVM, MATRVM, FÆMINARUM OPTIMARVM, OPTIMÆ,/SECVLO HVIC NON INEPTÆ, CVJVS MORES TOLERAVIT,/VITA VERO RETVLIT ANTIQVI. POSTERIQVE RELIQVIT/SINGVLARIS EXEMPLI SVI FRVCTVM, DOLOREM BREVIS,/HENEAGIVS FINCH/EQVES AVRATVS, SERVIENS AD

LEGEM AC RECORDATOR/CIV. LOND. POST VNDECIM LIBEROS, vii. SCILICET FILIOS ET/iv. FILIAS PLACIDISSIMO QVATVORDECIM PLVS ANNORVM/CONJVGIO SVSCEPTOS, E QVIBVS FILIJ. iii. AC FILIA. i/QVIBVS ADSIS O DEVS/SVPERSVNT/HIC AD PARENTVM HVJVS SEPVLCHRVM/POSVI/SIBIQVE, QVOD ET IPSA DESIDERAVIT DESTINAT/OBIJT ILLA. xi. DIE APRIL./MDCXXVII/ILLE

Translation: To his most beloved wife Frances Daughter of Sir Edmund Bell of Beaupré Hall The best of wives, mothers and the best of womanhood, not unsuited to this century whose principles she sustained and brought with her in her own true life, those of ancient times. Moreover she left the fruits of her exceptional example for posterity.

Brief in mourning, Sir Heneage Finch serving as a lawyer and recorder to the City of London after having eleven children, seven sons and four daughters, and more than fourteen years marriage whence three sons and one daughter survive with God's protection. He erected this sepulchre of his family and to himself as she herself devised and ordained. She died on the eleventh of April 1627

He himself . . .

(We are grateful to Norbert Jopek and James Yorke for their help with this translation).

Removed from the ruined church of St Mary, Eastwell, Kent. Given to the Museum by the Rector and Churchwardens of the Parish of Eastwell with Broughton Aluph in 1969, together with cat.nos. 15, 16, 48 and 498. For a full description of the monuments from Eastwell, see Physick 1970 [Eastwell].

Lady Finch was the daughter of Sir Edmund Bell, and the first wife of Sir Heneage Finch.

The Latin inscription on this memorial tablet is incomplete, as it was originally intended that it should also commemorate Sir Heneage Finch, husband of Lady Finch, though this was not carried out: Sir Heneage later remarried and is commemorated separately in another monument by Nicholas Stone, which incorporates the arms of his two wives in cartouches displayed above his monument; see the entry for cat.no. 15.

Bibliography

Physick 1970 [Eastwell], pp.130–1 and fig 5; White 1999, p. 125, notes 273–4 on p. 136.

Hubert Le Sueur

(b. Paris about 1590 – d. Paris after 1658)

In 1614 Le Sueur, a noted bronze founder, was appointed Sculptor-in-Ordinary to Louis XIII of France. Le Sueur was active in England between 1625 and 1641: in 1625 he was appointed as Court Sculptor to Charles I following the marriage of Charles I to Henrietta Maria, the sister of Louis XIII, in 1625. He produced a number of equestrian groups, both large and small-scale; his life-size equestrian statue of Charles I in Trafalgar Square, London is one of his most noted works. A number of his bronze equestrian statuettes are in the Museum's collection, including the re-united group of Henry IV and Fallen Warrior *(inv.nos. A.46–1951 and A.1–1992). These are not catalogued here (see Introduction, p. xiv). Le Sueur executed a number of tombs in Westminster Abbey, as well as producing portrait busts.*

Avery 1978; idem 1988; TDA, 19, pp. 249–50 [Avery]; Evelyn 1995; idem 2000.

19: Charles I (b.1600; r.1625–1649)

signed and dated 1631
Marble
h. 87 cm.
A.35–1910

Signed and dated on the reverse: HVBERTVS/LE SVEVR/FACIEBAT/1631
Inscribed on the base at the front: CAROLVS REX/ÆTATIS SVÆ/AN: XXXI

According to Museum papers relating to its acquisition, the vendors believed this bust to have come from The Hague, and stated that it was formerly in the royal palace Huis ten Bosch (House in the Wood). Purchased from Messrs Durlacher Bros., 42 New Bond Street, London in 1910 for £540 (a reduction of 10% of the original asking price of £600).

Charles Avery has noted: 'The use of marble is unique among Hubert's portraits and the bust forms a prototype for a number of bronze variants which were cast in the following years. It is therefore likely that it was made for the King himself' (Avery 1978, p. 131). See also entry for cat. no. 22

Bibliography

Cust 1912; Webb 1928 (I), p. 15; *idem* (II), p. 81; Brown 1934, illus. on p. 48; *Illustrated London News* 1937; Avery 1978, p. 131, fig. 2 on p. 130; Avery 1988, pp. 181, 212, cat.no. 29, pl. 54a; Whinney 1988, p. 87, n. 88 on pp. 438–9; Howarth 1989, p. 88 and fig. 38; *Death, Passion and Politics* 1995, pp. 86–7; Evelyn 1995, p. 86, n. 7; TDA, 19, p. 249, [Avery], Snodin and Styles 2001, fig. 20 on p.15.

Exhibited

Kings and Queens of England, 1500–1900, Victoria and Albert Museum, London, 10 May 1937.

19

20: Unknown man

about 1630
Anonymous, style of Hubert Le Sueur
Bronze
h. 62 cm.
A.41–1951

In the possession of Frederick G. Powell & Co, Dealers in Antique and Decorative Furniture, 112 Brompton Road, London. Purchased for the Museum by Dr W.L. Hildburgh F.S.A. in 1951 for £12 10s 0d.

In a memorandum to the Director, H.D. Molesworth [q.v.] noted, 'I have long been interested in this life size 17th century bronze bust of a man. It is no great work of art but it is I think undoubtedly English & represents the lost tradition of the English baroque tomb makers. I should very much like to have it for the study collection. The price used to be £75 but since Mr Powell died the firm have been selling off stuff and I chanced on this at £12 10 [shillings] which seems to me a reasonable nominal figure'. The bust was purchased on behalf of the Museum by Dr Hildburgh, and the letter of thanks from the Director records his 'official and personal thanks for yet another gift in this field that you have made so very specially your own'.

The bust is no longer on the socle shown in the illustration.

The inventory numbers for works in the Museum by the French sculptor Hubert Le Sueur (not included in the present catalogue) are: A.155–1910, A.46–1951, A.47–1951, A.108–1956, A.1–1992, A.1–1994.

21: Charles I (b.1600; r.1625–1649)

about 1638
Anonymous; after Hubert Le Sueur
Painted plaster
h. 86 cm.
A.89–1929

Given by Mr Harold Lane, 40 Putney Hill, London in 1929.

Traditionally this bust was said to have been in a niche on the Old Chichester Cross, Chichester (see Introduction, fig. 6), and to have come into the possession of the donor in recognition of a donation made by him to Chichester Hospital. In a letter dated 7 May 1929, Mr Sydney E. Castle, who appears to have acted as intermediary in the gift of the bust to the Museum, wrote: 'the bust is stated as being the original stone given by Charles I himself to Chichester. In recent years the position of this was regarded as dangerous I understand and was replaced by a bronze or metal bust cast from the same mold, the original figure was then discarded and fell into the hands of Mr Lane as a result of a donation to something or the other!'.

The circumstances concerning the provenance of the bust were discussed by Katharine Esdaile in an article published in 1929 following its acquisition by the Museum. While suggesting Francesco Fanelli [q.v.] as the possible author, she commented on the confusion surrounding the origins of the bust: 'Now, as every visitor to Chichester is aware, as Pether's painting of 1794 in the Chichester Museum proves, and as Dalaway, Horsfield, and all subsequent historians of Chichester have mentioned, there has long been, and still is, a bronze bust of Charles I in the niche on the Cross originally occupied by the bust of its builder, Bishop Storey. That bust, along with the figures in the still empty niches, was destroyed by the Parliamentarians, and replaced at the Restoration by the bronze bust of the King, traditionally assigned to either Fanelli or Le Sueur, and the chalk bust, down to the minutest details, is a replica of the bronze' (Esdaile 1929 [Acquisitions], p. 387). Esdaile noted that the temporary removal of the bronze bust from the Cross between 1863 and 1867 was recorded in topographical publications, and that in 1863 it was removed to 'the Council-house, North Street'. She went on to record: 'Now the chalk bust which is an exact replica, but executed in a style suited to bronze, not stone, as the undercutting of the collar, the treatment of the hair and beard, and the incised, not modelled, lines which make the tippet proves, is also said to have been found 'lying about the Town Hall", ie. the Council House, and to have been received by its late owner from thence". Esdaile concluded that the present bust was an early copy of the bronze bust on the Chichester Cross (*ibid.*, p. 390).

Whilst asserting it to be a contemporary authentic work – probably executed by Francesco Fanelli around 1635–6 – in his 1931 article devoted to a discussion of the bust, Cyril Bunt rejected the traditional assumption that the bust formerly occupied a niche in Chichester Cross (Bunt 1931, p. 106). Charles Avery has more recently commented: 'Its exact correspondence with the bronze bust in Chichester suggests that it was cast from it at an indeterminable date, while the severe weathering proves that it has been exposed for a number of years: one wonders if it was indeed substituted for the bronze in the niche on the cross at some stage' (Avery 1988, p. 213). Comparing the present bust with the bronze version, now in the Council Chamber at Chichester, Avery has suggested, 'The time-consuming detailing of the chain of the Order of the Garter differentiates the bronze from the stucco cast in the Victoria and Albert Museum and proves that the [bronze] bust is the original' (*ibid.*, p. 213, cat.no. 32A; see also *idem* 1998, cat.nos. 32C and 32D for related versions).

Bibliography

Review 1929, pp. 2–3, fig. I on p. 3; Esdaile 1929 [Acquisitions], pp. 387, 390, and fig. 2 on p. 387; Bunt 1931; Avery 1988, p. 213, cat.no. 32B, fig. 57C on p. 187.

22: Charles I (b.1600; r.1625–1649)

about 1750–1850
Anonymous; after Hubert Le Sueur
Bronze
h. 77 cm.
A.12–1937

On loan to the Museum from Dr W.L. Hildburgh F.S.A. from 31 May 1934 (ex-loan 4803), and subsequently offered as a gift to the Museum by Dr Hildburgh in 1937 to celebrate the Coronation.

The present bust is a later variant of the bronze bust of Charles I by Hubert Le Sueur given to the Bodleian Library Oxford by Archbishop Laud in 1636, and installed in an oval niche in the Library in 1641 (see Avery 1988, p. 212, cat.no. 30B, pl. 55a on p. 183; Poole 1912, pl. VII opp. p. 41; Webb 1928 (II), pl. I (A)). A.12–1937 is also related to the marble bust of Charles I by Le Sueur of 1631 in the Museum's collections (cat.no. 19), as well as the one now described as a 'bronze cast of bust' in the National Portrait Gallery (*NPG* 1981, p. 106, no. 297; Cust 1912, pl. II, (B)). It is likely that both the present bust and the National Portrait Gallery version were cast from a copy of the Bodleian original, although differences are apparent in the two later versions: there are only three rows of studs around the neck in the National Portrait Gallery bust, whereas there are four in the present piece. Similarly the studs on the National Portrait Gallery version are embossed, whereas they are incised in the present piece.

JOHN TOMSON OR THOMPSON

(probably active 1670 – 1700)

Little is known about this sculptor, although it is likely that he was also responsible for the rectangular wooden relief depicting the Last Judgement, described as late seventeenth century, formerly on a gateway entering the south churchyard of the Church of St Stephen, Coleman Street, London, and later kept in the vestry: a plaster cast reproduction which replaced the original, together with the original itself, were destroyed by bombing during the Second World War. A further relief is in the wall of the bombed church of St Andrew's, Holborn Viaduct, and another over the gateway to St Giles in the Fields, dated 1687, was repositioned in a gateway of 1810. Comparisons may also be made with some reliefs by John Weston of Exeter (active 1696–1733), including that forming part of the monument of Jonathan and Elizabeth Ivie in St Petrock's Church, Exeter (1717); see Gunnis 1968, p. XXXI opp. p. 432; Easter 1995 (I am grateful to Dr Roger Bowdler for this information). John Tomson may be a variant spelling of a John Thompson (d.1700) who was recorded as a mason working at several City of London churches at this time. There are six entries for a mason called John Thompson in the parochial accounts of several London churches (including All Hallows, Lombard Street, St Christopher, Threadneedles Street, and St Mary Le Bow) between January 1670 and December 1694. The total cost for this work was £19,477. Gunnis recorded that a sculptor named John Thompson or Tomson worked at St Paul's from 1688 to 1700, becoming Master of the Masons' Company shortly before his death in 1700. A plain memorial tablet to a John Tomson, who died in 1700, is in the Parish Church of St Martin-in-the-Fields, Westminster.

Historical Monuments 1925, p. 112; Historical Monuments 1929, p. 75 and pl. 140; Wren Society 1933, pp. 46, 48, 50, 52, 54; Gunnis 1968 pp. 391–2.

23: The Last Judgement

signed; about 1680–1700
Boxwood
h. 13 cm. l. (excl. frame) 59 cm.
A.48–1932

Signed on the lid of the tomb depicted on the left: John Tomson./Fecit:

A ribbon, held by a cherub to the top left of the relief, under which are representations of the souls of the Blessed, is inscribed: Come ye Blessed

Purchased from Mr J.F. da C. Andrade, 8 Brook Street, London in 1932 for £7.

Some of the cherubs' trumpets and arms have been broken and replaced; the right arm of the angel Gabriel is missing.

The present piece was probably not intended as an independent relief but belonged to a series. Departmental records suggest that it was accompanied by a set of six small rectangular reliefs depicting scenes from the *Life of Christ*, and one larger relief of the *Nativity*. These were in the possession of the vendor of the present relief, and were later passed to Nyburg, presumably the dealer S.N. Nyburg of 16c Grafton Street, London. In 1947 what was described as an 'elaborate woodcarving in glass shade case' (possibly identical with the *Nativity* relief), was offered by Nyburg on approval for purchase by the Museum, but was declined (departmental records).

In the *Review of Principal Acquisitions during the Year 1932*, the unique quality of the present piece was noted: described as 'a curiously shaped boxwood relief . . . [it] makes an acquisition of considerable interest, as not only are English boxwood carvings of any quality rare, but, in addition, the present example is signed by an unknown artist, JOHN TOMSON. The style, which is highly individual, compares so closely with the relief of the Doom at present above a door in the vestry of the church of St Stephen, Coleman Street, that there can be little doubt that both are by the same hand, and it is very possible that research among the records will prove that this carver worked in more than one City church of the Wren period' (*Review* 1932, p. 5).

BIBLIOGRAPHY

Review 1932, p. 5.

Sir Christopher Wren

(b. East Knoyle 1632 – d. London 1723)

Sir Christopher Wren was the most prolific and successful architect in Britain of his generation. A self-taught architect – he had begun his career as a scientist – Wren is perhaps chiefly known as the architect responsible for the rebuilding of the City of London churches after the Great Fire of London of 1666, and St Paul's Cathedral.

Colvin 1995, pp. 1083–97; TDA, 33 [Downes], pp. 392–9.

24: Architectural façade from the front of a house, formerly Enfield railway station

before 1672
Possibly built by or for Edward Helder (d.1672), after a design by Sir Christopher Wren
Brick
h. (greatest) 506 cm.
324–1907

The house from which the façade was taken is thought to have been erected before 1672 for Edward Helder, a bricklayer to designs by Sir Christopher Wren (Whitaker 1891, pp. 174–6; Briggs 1934, p. 68). It was later purported to have formed part of the school-house in which the poet John Keats (1796–1821) was educated around 1803–10, and later the residence of Isaac Disraeli (1766–1848), father of Benjamin Disraeli (1804–1881). The building became Enfield Railway Station in 1848 (Tuff 1858, p. 188); the station was demolished in 1872. The façade was however saved, and originally purchased for the Structural Collection of the Science Museum (then part of the South Kensington Museum), from Messrs Patman and Fotheringham, 100 & 102 Theobald's Road, London, in February 1873 for £50. It was later transferred to the South Kensington Museum in April 1907, where it was registered as an example of decorative architecture and brickwork. Its acquisition in 1873 is recorded in a contemporary publication on Enfield by Edward Ford. He noted, 'the central part of the façade has been purchased . . . by the Directors of the South Kensington Museum where it has been erected as a screen for the structural division. It was taken down brick by brick, with the greatest of care, all being numbered and packed in boxes of sawdust for carriage. Nothing could exceed the beauty of the workmanship, the bricks having been ground down to a perfect face, and joined with bees-wax and rosin, no mortar or lime being used. In this manner the whole front has been first built in a solid block, the circular-headed niches, with their carved cherubs and festoons of fruit and foliage, being afterwards cut out with the chisel. The arches were built without *voussoirs*, the lines of the brickwork running straight across the work, with the joints so fine as scarcely to be perceptible to the nicest scrutiny' (Ford 1873, p. 206).

In May 1911 a boss from one of the capitals on the facade was accidentally broken off by a student from the London County Council Central School of Arts and Crafts, for whom a scaffolding had been erected to allow him to take detailed drawings from the facade (Museum records).

A number of historical connections relating to this façade have been suggested since its acquisition. A letter from a Mr J. Dykes Campbell, 29 Albert Hall Mansions, Kensington Gore, London to Sir Philip Cunliffe Owen [q.v.] of 2 March 1886, records:

'Sir

In the Terra Cotta Department of your Museum there is part of a beautiful old house-front removed some years since from Enfield – a happy specimen of old carved brickwork of the North Italian type – and, as such, well worthy of preservation. But this particular specimen has infinitely greater value and interest as having formed part of the house in which John Keats received the greater part of his education – and as to this fact the label is silent. I at least cannot make this silence a reproach to the Department, for I was myself ignorant of the associations of the brickwork until one day last week, when I received a letter from the venerable Mrs Charles Cowden Clarke, in which she asked if I had ever gone to see "the relic of Keats' old school-house at the S.K. Museum?" I had often seen the bricks, but my knowledge of what they were had been confined to what the label told me. There is no room for doubt that this old front formed part of the school-house in which Keats and Charles Cowden Clarke and Edward Holmes (the composer and biographer of Mozart) received their education – and it is also believed that Marryat and George Bidder were scholars there'. It was also suggested that the house was Disraeli's former residence, as noted by Edward Ford in his *History of Enfield* (Ford 1873, pp. 203–4).

A watercolour sketch showing the building when it belonged to the Great Eastern Railways, and served as Enfield Railway Station, signed 'Thomas Batterbury (Architect), sketched, September 23rd 1871.', is in the Sculpture Department archive. It is further annotated 'House, Enfield Middlesex (formerly belonging to the Earl of Essex)'. A photograph showing the façade in situ, when the building was still in use as a railway station, is also in the Sculpture Department archive (see Introduction, fig. 1).

There are a number of references to the façade in topographical publications relating to Enfield, which confirm the previous uses of the building from which this facade is taken, and also suggest the name of the architect. In 1891 Whitaker noted, 'A railway was built in 1849 to join the Eastern Counties line at Edmonton, the station being a disused school house. In 1872 this house was demolished and the present building erected. An illustration shows the house as it stood when first used as a station and another illustration shows the beautifully carved facade of the central upper story of the old station house, once a celebrated school kept by the father of Mr. Cowden Clarke. The sketch was made in 1910 from the carefully preserved relic in the Victoria and Albert Museum . . . The house was built by Edward Helder, a layer of bricks, who died in 1672, and was buried in the nave of the parish church . . . It was probably designed by Wren, and was almost certainly the birthplace of Isaac Disraeli in 1766. At Mr Clarke's school there were educated John Keats, the poet, Edward Holmes, the composer, Charles Cowden Clarke, the writer, and Edward Cowper, the engineer' (Whitaker 1891, pp. 174–6). In *Middlesex Old and New* the writer commented, 'The remaining old houses of Enfield are mainly brick buildings of the late 17th and 18th centuries. One of them, formerly used as the first railway station of the G.E.R., was a beautiful design, possibly by Wren, and was erected some time before 1672 for Edward Helder, a bricklayer. It was pulled down to make room for the present sordid station building, but the central pediment was fortunately preserved and subsequently erected in the Victoria and Albert Museum. There, that fragment of a bricklayer's house – and possibly relic of Wren's genius – is studied and measured annually by students of architecture' (Briggs 1934, p. 68).

BIBLIOGRAPHY

Tuff 1858, p. 188; Ford 1873, pp. 203–6 and fig.; Whitaker 1891, pp. 174–6, figs. on p. 175 and 177; Briggs 1934, p. 68; Corney 2001.

UNATTRIBUTED SCULPTURE (1470–1700)

24a: Knight or soldier in armour

about 1450-70
Oak
h. 109 cm.
A.11-2001

The present piece, together with cat.nos. 24b and 24c, was originally at Naworth Castle, Cumbria, the seat of the Dacre family. The three figures were first noted in 1772, in Francis Grose's *The Antiquities of England and Wales*, Vol. I, there described as being installed on the screen (probably designed by Vanbrugh) in the Great Hall, together with four heraldic figures of beasts. The beasts were also acquired by the Victoria and Albert Museum in 2000 (inv.nos. W.6 to W.9-2000). A number of re-workings of the interior of the Great Hall are recorded, although the three soldiers were again noted on the screen in 1810 (Britton and Brayley 1810, pp. 123-4), and once more in a watercolour of about 1830 showing the Great Hall (see Worsley 1987, fig. 14). They passed by descent to the Hon. Philip Howard, and were included in the Sotheby's, London sale of 7 July 1999, lot 50. Purchased from the sale by Daniel Katz Ltd, 59 Jermyn Street, London, they were the subject of an export stop, and were subsequently purchased by the Museum in 2001 for £220,000, with the assistance of contributions from the National Heritage Memorial Fund, and the Art Fund (formerly the National Art Collections Fund).

The figures may represent distinguished members of the Dacre family. They were probably originally displayed freestanding at Naworth, perhaps on a staircase, together with other sculptures which no longer survive. As noted above, they were positioned on the screen in the Great Hall by the late eighteenth century, and were later saved from a fire there in 1844 which destroyed the screen. Subsequently they were displayed in various positions around the house.

The three figures (cat.nos. 24a to 24c) were acquired by the Museum in December 2001, and were only added to the present catalogue at the time of going to press, hence their catalogue numbering.

BIBLIOGRAPHY

Grose I, 1772; Britton and Brayley 1810, pp. 123-4; Worsley 1987, fig. 14; *Katz* 2000 [Zock], cat.no. 7; *NACF* 2002.

24b

24c

24b: Youthful nobleman wearing a tunic and coronet

about 1450-70
Oak
h. 109 cm.
A.12-2001

Purchased together with cat.nos. 24a and 24c from Daniel Katz Ltd, 59 Jermyn Street, London in 2001. Originally at Naworth Castle, Cumbria, the seat of the Dacre family and probably made specifically for display in the Great Hall. For full provenance details see entry for cat.no. 24a.

BIBLIOGRAPHY
See entry for cat. no. 24a

24c: Standing man wearing a tunic and codpiece

about 1450–70
Oak
h. 109 cm.
A.13-2001

Purchased together with cat.nos. 24a and 24b from Daniel Katz Ltd, 59 Jermyn Street, London in 2001. Originally at Naworth Castle, Cumbria, the seat of the Dacre family and probably made specifically for display in the Great Hall. For full provenance details see entry for cat.no. 24a.

BIBLIOGRAPHY
See entry for cat. no. 24a

25: Chimneypiece with brickwork and tracery above

about 1470–1500
Stone with brickwork above
h. 507 cm.
455–1906

Originally part of the High Altar of the Priory Church, Prittlewell, Essex. See also entry for cat.no. 26. Uncovered during the demolition of a house called 'Reynoldes' in East Street, Prittlewell, near Southend, Essex during 1906. Purchased from Mr J.C. Flaxman, Southend-on-Sea, Essex in 1906 for £25. On loan to the Central Museum, Southend-on-Sea, Essex since 1973.

Prittlewell Priory was founded between 1086 and 1121 by Robert de Essex, Lord of the Manor of Rayleigh. A Guild or Fraternity of Jesus was established at Prittlewell in 1468, and the lands held by the Guild were called 'Reynoldes', probably after the original owner. The dissolution of the Priory took place in 1536, and it is possible that this fireplace and tracery, together with cat.no. 26, were removed during this period, and subsequently boarded up in 'Reynoldes' where they were discovered in 1906. According to Keating Clay's account of Prittlewell

Priory, it is likely that the fireplace came from the Priory refectory and the reredos from the Priory Church. These were evidently removed during the destruction of the monastery and placed in a private house.

A leaf and rose decoration is contained in both the spandrels of the fireplace. Above is a brickwork panel containing a Gothic arch, with three sections, the centre one is painted with the sacred monogram (I.H.S.) (Jesus Hominum Salvator – Jesus the Saviour of men) and those at the sides with fleur-de-lys.

A head of a window (inv.no. 453–1906) removed in 1906 from the same house is in the Department of Furniture and Woodwork.

BIBLIOGRAPHY
Keatinge Clay 1918, pp. 7, 16–18, also illus. (unpaginated); *English Chimneypieces* 1928, introductory page (unpaginated) and fig. 1.

26: Chimneypiece

about 1470–1500
Stone
h. 122 cm
454–1906

Purchased from Mr J.C. Flaxman, Southend-on-Sea, Essex in 1906 for £1. Uncovered during the demolition of a house called 'Reynoldes' in East Street, Prittlewell, near Southend, Essex during 1906.

See also cat.no. 25.

The chimney piece is of plain stonework with no ornament.

[Not illustrated].

27: God the Father

about 1480–1500
Oak and canvas
h. (incl. frame) 54.5 cm.
23–1881

Purchased from John Charles Robinson [q.v.] in 1881 for £4. This was one of a number of objects purchased from Robinson in 1881 for a total of £503 5s (inv.nos 18 to 48–1881). These objects had been collected by Robinson during his travels in Italy from October to November 1880. Despite being acquired in Italy this devotional relief is likely to be English, and may have been exported to the Continent at an early date. Large numbers of English alabaster reliefs were exported to Europe during the fifteenth century (see Cheetham 1984, pp. 45–8).

There are remains of gilding on the overlaid canvas.

BIBLIOGRAPHY
English Medieval Art 1930, p. 126, cat. no. 719.

EXHIBITED
English Medieval Art, Victoria and Albert Museum, London, 1930.

28: Chimneypiece from a house in Canterbury

about 1500
Stone
h. 180.5 cm.
256–1906

Said to have been taken from a house in Canterbury. Given by Mrs A. Turner, "Ye Denne", 28 Bath Road, Chiswick, London in 1906.

A note in the registered description for this object records that on acquisition the chimneypiece was in ten pieces, and that an eleventh was missing from the left side. The acquisition records also suggest that the chimneypiece was acquired with the bottom of a grate and two fire-dogs.

29 30

A.B. Skinner [q.v.] inspected the chimneypiece as well as an iron fireback then in the possession of Mrs Turner. He noted, 'In the garden there are two pieces of an old stone fireplace which, Mrs Turner says, were removed from the same house as the fireback at Canterbury . . . I examined this fireplace and found that she had got it wrongly set up. This is the reason why it looks so curious in the sketch . . . Although it is in a very wrecked condition I should like to have it . . . Although it is in a very dilapidated state through exposure, I beg to recommend that we accept it if she will give it to us'. The fireback referred to by Skinner, with the initials of Charles II, was also purchased by the Museum from Mrs Turner in 1906 for £5 (inv.no. 255–1906, under the charge of the Metalwork Department).

29: Spandrel from a fireplace

about 1500
Limestone
35.4 cm. x 27 cm.
A.124–1916

Given by Edward Ernest Leggatt, Esq, 'Chase Side', Enfield, Middlesex, together with cat.no. 30 in 1916. Discovered in the walls of the donor's house, 'Chase Side' in Enfield during renovations in 1916. Leggatt (an art dealer and donor to the British Museum and National Portrait Gallery), was responsible for saving the Tudor Palace at Enfield (former residence of Edward VI) which was to be demolished to make way for a cinema, by purchasing it around 1921.

Carved with the heraldic rose. See also entry for cat.no. 30.

BIBLIOGRAPHY
Review 1916, p. 8.

30: Spandrel from a fireplace

about 1500
Limestone
44.5 cm. x. 37.5 cm. d. 15 cm. (irreg.)
A.124:A-1916

Given by Edward Ernest Leggatt, Esq, 'Chase Side', Enfield, Middlesex in 1916. Discovered in the walls of the donor's house, 'Chase Side' in Enfield during renovations in 1916. See also entry for cat.no. 29.

Thought to be carved with the sunburst badge of Henry VII.

BIBLIOGRAPHY
Review 1916, p .8.

31: St John the Evangelist

about 1505
Terracotta
h. 48 cm.
A.76–1949

Purchased from Montague Marcussen, 98 Crawford Street, London in 1949 together with cat.no. 32 for £30.

This is a slightly reduced replica of the bronze figure of *St John the Evangelist* on the grate around the tomb of Henry VII and Elizabeth of York in Westminster Abbey (see Colvin, Ransome and Summerson 1975, p. 219 and Lindley 1995, p. 54; I am grateful to Paul Williamson for these references). Thermo-luminescence testing carried out in 1987 by Oxford University suggested that this figure and its pendant (see entry for cat.no. 32) were fired in the early to mid eighteenth century, and are not contemporary with the original bronze figures. The debate on the dating of these terracottas is noted in departmental records, the earlier date being suggested by the fact that the production of cast figures of saints, such as this and the *Unidentified Saint* (cat.no. 32) would have been unlikely after the Reformation. The taking of squeezes and casts in terracotta was known in London around the start of the 16th century. Six figures remain on the grate, and have been in place since the inventory of the early 18th century. The pendant figure, cat.no. 32, was considered to be so closely related to the grate figures that it was thought to have been a cast taken from one of the missing twelve statuettes. For these reasons, on stylistic grounds, and despite the thermo-luminescence tests, a date of around 1505, contemporary with the grate itself, has been given.

31

32

32: Unidentified saint

around 1505
Terracotta
h. 52 cm.
A.77–1949

Purchased from Montague Marcussen, 98 Crawford Street, London in 1949 together with cat.no. 31 for £30.

Along with the closely related *St John the Evangelist*, cat.no. 31, this figure may have been cast from one of the missing statuettes from the grate adorning the tomb of Henry VII and Elizabeth of York in Westminster Abbey.

33: Fragment of decoration, left profile of a girl

about 1518–22
Terracotta
h. 30.5 cm.
A.26–1938

Found during excavations in 1937 for a new building for Messrs Mosers on the site of Suffolk Place, Southwark, London, the palace of Charles Brandon, Duke of Suffolk (d. 1545), brother-in-law to Henry VIII. Mr Waddington of the Guildhall Museum informed Margaret Longhurst [q.v.] of the terracottas in the possession of Messrs Mosers. Subsequently given to the Museum by Messrs Mosers Ltd, Iron Steel & Hardware Merchants, 170 to 188 & 192 Borough High Street, Southwark, London in 1938, together with cat.nos. 34 to 43. The fragments are referred to in a history of the company, *Mosers of the Borough* (see *Mosers* 1938). Two further items of imported stoneware excavated from the site were also acquired by the Department of Ceramics and Glass.

This relief is cream-coloured terracotta.

On examining the objects offered to the Museum, Margaret Longhurst [q.v.] noted: 'Messrs. Mosers . . . wish to give the fragments to some museum where they would be appreciated and . . . I think that a group of them would be a distinctly interesting addition to our collection of architectural fragments . . . I imagine that they were used for wall decorations in the Tudor building . . . The palace was built between 1518 and 1522 by Charles Brandon for his wife Mary Tudor, sister of Henry VIII, and seems from van den Wyngaerde's drawing to have been most imposing. About 1537 it became Crown property and later was given by Queen Mary I to Nicholas Heath, Archbishop of York who sold it in 1557, after which it was in part, if not entirely, pulled down. We have nothing at all like these fragments in our collection and I feel that they would be of interest in connection with our terracotta bust of Henry VII [inv.no. A.49–1935] as I think the Italian designs must be due to the influence of Torrigiano'. Following the gift, the donor Mr Miller, Director and Secretary of Messrs Mosers Ltd wrote to the Museum commenting, 'we are disappointed that Torrigiano cannot be named as the sculptor!'. The Italian connection was noted in the *Review of Principal Acquisitions during the Year 1938*, 'The style of the decoration, in common with that of several Tudor buildings of the period, notably of course at Hampton Court, shows strong Italian influence, suggesting direct contact with, though probably not the actual hand of, one of the imported Italian workmen' (*Review* 1938, p. 4). Further terracotta examples, and a marble excavated from the same site are also in the Cuming Museum, London, inv.nos. 15011–15 (I am grateful to Bryan Hyacinth and Chris Green for this information). These and the present pieces were the subject of an unpublished study by Chris Green (Green 1986, esp. pp. 2, 5, 8).

An account of the circumstances surrounding the making of these casts is noted in a paper by G.L. Gomme, Clerk of the Council; see Gomme 1908.

According to the authors of an 1888 publication entitled *The Inns of Old Southwark*, Suffolk Place was said to have been on the site subsequently occupied by an inn, the Old Bull (Rendle and Norman 1888, p. 265 and n. 1). The history of Suffolk Place is also recorded in several topographical publications; see Stow 1908, pp. 59–60; Manning and Bray 1814, pp. 632–4; Kingsford 1920, pp. 35–7.

Anthony van den Wyngaerde's drawing of Suffolk Place is reproduced by Kingsford in his entry on Suffolk Place (see *ibid.*, pl. between pp. 36–7).

In his review of Maurice Howard's *The Early Tudor Country House* . . ., Phillip Lindley noted, 'The Suffolk Place terracottas are clearly connected with work at Layer Marney and elsewhere. The fact that the same motifs also appear in East Anglian tombs proves two things: first, that the same workmen supplied 'architectural' and 'tomb' decoration . . . and, secondly, that the relationship between East Anglian and metropolitan projects is a good deal more complicated than is generally supposed' (Lindley 1988, p. 65).

For a discussion of similar terracotta fragments from Laughton Place, see Howard 1991, pp. 133–52; see also Lindley 1991 and Morris 2000.

Bibliography

Review 1938, p. 4; *Mosers* 1938, p. 7, fig. A on p. 7; Green 1986, figs. 13 and 15; Gunn and Lindley 1988, p. 280, pl. XXIc; Lindley 1988, pp. 65–6; Morris 2000, esp. p. 180, n. 7; Snodin and Styles 2001, fig. 7 on p. 38.

34: Fragment of decoration, head of a crowned lion

about 1518–22
Terracotta
h. 32 cm.
A.27–1938

Excavated from the site of Suffolk Place, Southwark, London. Given to the Museum by Messrs Mosers Ltd, Iron Steel & Hardware Merchants, 170 to 188 & 192 Borough High Street, Southwark, London in 1938, together with cat.nos. 33, 35 to 43; see entry for cat.no. 33.

This relief is cream-coloured terracotta.

The present piece is discussed by Gunn and Lindley in connection with Charles Brandon's Suffolk house, Westhorpe: 'The formal repertoire employed in the Suffolk Place terracottas may have been extensive: in 1520, when Sir Nicholas Vaux wrote to enquire whether Suffolk would lend terracotta arms and beasts, Suffolk Place was probably still in process of construction, and these terracottas were undoubtedly originally intended to decorate the building. One of the Suffolk House fragments shows the same motif – Suffolk's badge, a head of a lion erased, crowned with a ducal coronet – as Westhorpe's surviving bridge panels; the London panel is of higher quality and probably formed part of a larger design as is suggested by its squared off edges' (Gunn and Lindley 1988, p. 280).

Bibliography

See references for cat.no. 33; *Mosers* 1938, fig. A. on p. 7; Green 1986, figs. 13 and 15; Gunn and Lindley 1988, p. 280, pl. XXIc.

35: Fragment of decoration, half length figure of Cupid

about 1518–22
Terracotta
h. 22 cm.
A.28–1938

Excavated from the site of Suffolk Place, Southwark, London. Given to the Museum by Messrs Mosers Ltd, Iron Steel & Hardware Merchants, 170 to 188 & 192 Borough High Street, Southwark, London in 1938, together with cat.nos. 33, 34, and 36 to 43; see entry for cat.no. 33.

This relief is pale pink-coloured terracotta.

Similar complete examples of cherubs related to the present piece, are to be found above the doorway to the south side of Sutton Place, Surrey (see Howard 1987, fig. 77 on p. 130). Howard suggests that they are similar to French examples, in particular to those found in the Hotel Lallement at Bourges, but that the most likely explanation for these similarities would 'have been the use of similar books of patterns and designs, as workshops of this period were dependent on much the same sources and presumably these were also what building patrons were looking at' (*ibid*., p. 130).

BIBLIOGRAPHY
See references for cat.no. 33.

36: Fragment of a pilaster, wth two winged griffins

about 1518–22
Terracotta
h. 35.5 cm.
A.29–1938

Excavated from the site of Suffolk Place, Southwark, London. Given to the Museum by Messrs Mosers Ltd, Iron Steel & Hardware Merchants, 170 to 188 & 192 Borough High Street, Southwark, London in 1938, together with cat.nos. 33 to 35, 37 to 43; see entry for cat.no. 33.

This relief is pink-coloured terracotta.

BIBLIOGRAPHY
See references for cat.no. 33; also *Mosers* 1938, fig. B on p. 8; Green 1986, fig. 14; Lindley 1988, fig. 1 on p. 66.

37: Fragment of a pilaster

about 1518–22
Terracotta
h. 35.5 cm.
A.30–1938

Excavated from the site of Suffolk Place, Southwark, London. Given to the Museum by Messrs Mosers Ltd, Iron Steel & Hardware Merchants, 170 to 188 & 192 Borough High Street, Southwark, London in 1938, together with cat.nos. 33 to 36, and 38 to 43; see entry for cat.no. 33.

This relief is pink-coloured terracotta. It is similar in style to cat.no. 36.

BIBLIOGRAPHY
See references for cat.no. 33.

38: Fragment of a frieze

about 1518–22
Terracotta
l. 36 cm.
A.31–1938

Excavated from the site of Suffolk Place, Southwark, London. Given to the Museum by Messrs Mosers Ltd, Iron Steel & Hardware Merchants, 170 to 188 & 192 Borough High Street, Southwark, London in 1938, together with cat.nos. 33 to 37, and 39 to 43; see entry for cat.no. 33.

This relief is cream-coloured terracotta.

BIBLIOGRAPHY
See references for cat.no. 33; see also *Mosers* 1938, fig. B on p. 8; Green 1986, fig. 14; Lindley 1988, fig. 1 on p. 66.

39: Fragment of a frieze

about 1518–22
Terracotta
l. 26 cm.
A.32–1938

38

39

Excavated from the site of Suffolk Place, Southwark, London. Given to the Museum by Messrs Mosers Ltd, Iron Steel & Hardware Merchants, 170 to 188 & 192 Borough High Street, Southwark, London in 1938, together with cat.nos. 33 to 38, and 40 to 43; see entry for cat.no. 33.

This fragment is similar to cat.no. 33, but has a moulded edge on either side. It is cream-coloured terracotta.

BIBLIOGRAPHY
See references for cat.no. 33; *Mosers* 1938, fig. B on p. 8; Green 1986, fig. 14; Lindley 1988, fig. 1 on p. 66.

40: Fragment of a frieze

about 1518–22
Terracotta
l. 15 cm.
A.33–1938

Excavated from the site of Suffolk Place, Southwark, London. Given to the Museum by Messrs Mosers Ltd, Iron Steel & Hardware Merchants, 170 to 188 & 192 Borough High Street, Southwark, London in 1938, together with cat.nos. 33 to 39, and 41 to 43; see entry for cat.no. 33.

This relief is similar to cat.nos. 38 and 39. It is cream-coloured terracotta.

BIBLIOGRAPHY
See references for cat.no. 33.

41: Fragment of a garland

about 1518–22
Terracotta
h. 25.5 cm.
A.34–1938

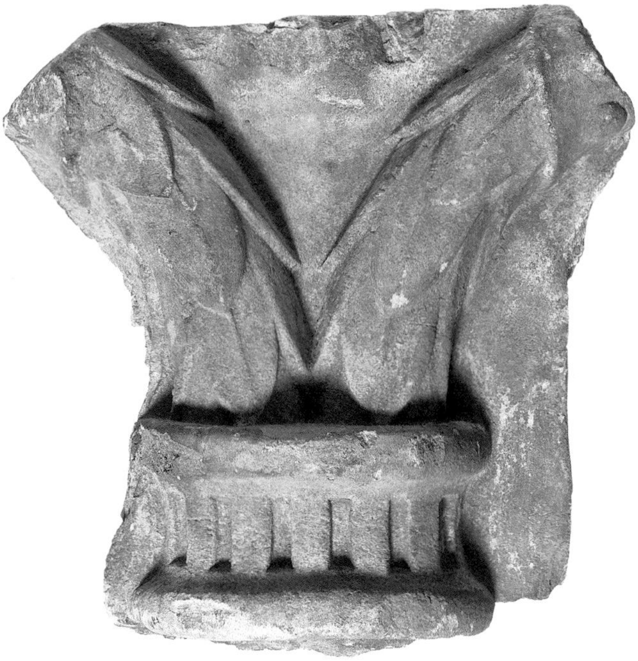

Excavated from the site of Suffolk Place, Southwark, London. Given to the Museum by Messrs Mosers Ltd, Iron Steel & Hardware Merchants, 170 to 188 & 192 Borough High Street, Southwark, London in 1938, together with cat.nos. 33 to 39, 42 and 43; see entry for cat.no. 33.

This relief is cream-coloured terracotta.

BIBLIOGRAPHY
See references for cat.no. 33; see also Green 1986, fig. 15.

42: Fragment of a garland

about 1518–22
Terracotta
h. 24.5 cm.
A.35–1938

Excavated from the site of Suffolk Place, Southwark, London. Given to the Museum by Messrs Mosers Ltd, Iron Steel & Hardware Merchants, 170 to 188 & 192 Borough High Street, Southwark, London in 1938, together with cat.nos. 33 to 41 and 43; see entry for cat.no. 33.

This relief is similar to cat.no. 41. It is pink-coloured terracotta.

BIBLIOGRAPHY
See references for cat.no. 33.

42

43: Fragment of a garland

about 1518–22
Terracotta
h. 26 cm.
A.36–1938

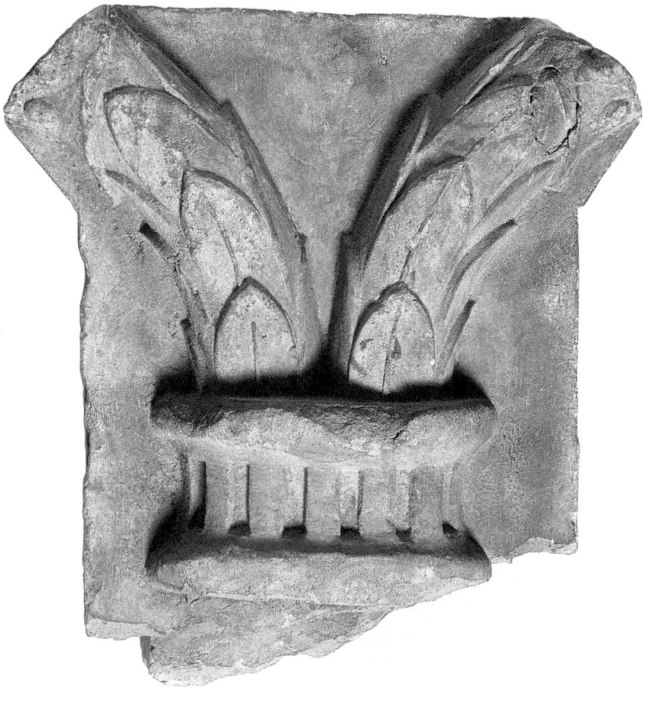

Excavated from the site of Suffolk Place, Southwark, London. Given to the Museum by Messrs Mosers Ltd, Iron Steel & Hardware Merchants, 170 to 188 & 192 Borough High Street, Southwark, London in 1938, together with cat.nos. 33 to 42; see entry for cat.no. 33.

This relief is similar to cat.nos. 41 and 42. It is cream-coloured terracotta.

BIBLIOGRAPHY
See references for cat.no. 33; see also Green 1986, fig. 15.

44: Wild boar running

about 1550
Terracotta
l. 29 cm. (irreg.)
A.122–1916

Probably originally belonging to the Royal Architectural Museum, and taken on by the Architectural Association, together with its premises in 1903. Given to the Museum by the Architectural Association in 1916 together with cat.no. 45.

A note on the departmental records records that several similar fragments were found at Westminster Abbey, and probably derive from the school of Pietro Torrigiani (1472–1528).

45: Floral decoration

about 1550–1600
Painted and gilt limestone
l. 46 cm.
A.121–1916

Probably originally belonging to the Royal Architectural Museum, and taken on by the Architectural Association, together with its premises in 1903. Given to the Museum by the Architectural Association in 1916 along with cat.no. 44. A total of 127 architectural fragments (inv.nos. A.13 to 123–1916), formerly belonging to the Royal Architectural Museum, were given by the Architectural Association to the Museum in 1916, as well as a further 3905 plaster casts (A.1916–1 to 3095), mainly English, although including some German, French and Italian pieces (see *Review* 1916, pp. 1–6). For a discussion of the relationship between the Royal Architectural Museum and the Architectural Association, see Wylde 1981.

A crimson coloured paint decoration is still visible on this fragment of a frieze.

46: Tudor coat of arms

about 1550–75
Stone with some traces of polychromy
h. 61.5 cm. w. 95 cm.
91–1890

Inscribed: HONI·SOIT·Q·MALE·Y·PENCE (Evil be to he who thinks evil).

Originally removed from a house formerly standing at Bideford, Devon. Purchased from Mr Richard Palmer, 34 Old Town, Bideford in 1890 for £25.

Rectangular relief carving with the Tudor royal arms. The initials E.R. may refer to Edward VI (r.1547–53) or Elizabeth I (r.1558–1603).

47: The Holy Trinity

dated 1553
Painted and gilt oak
h. 57 cm.
A.25–1917

Acquired from a dealer in Manchester by E. Peter Jones Esq. Given to the Museum by E. Peter Jones, Greenbank, Chester, though the National Art Collections Fund in 1917.

In a memo to the Director, R.P. Bedford [q.v.] commented on the present piece, 'From the proportions of the figure and the type of architectural setting I think it is almost certainly English work, with Flemish influence perhaps, and its date 1553 (the year Edward VI died and Mary came to the throne) makes it of peculiar interest from an historical point of view. The treatment of the subject is one common in the earlier alabaster groups, and it may well have been made under this influence. The conjunction of the Gothic group with the Renaissance framework is interesting – it was acquired in Manchester in which district the Gothic tradition remained longer than it did in the rest of England. I am not quite certain as to its original use; the two iron rings in the side suggest that it may have been a devotional mural tablet but the projecting base may rather point to its having been a small portable retable in a private chapel. Objects of this class are of extreme rarity as they were destroyed in great numbers during the iconoclastic outbursts of subsequent reigns, and the date and almost perfect preservation go to make this one of the most important acquisitions of recent years'. See also *Review* 1917, p. 2.

Prior to its acquisition, this relief was subject to a lengthy discussion when exhibited by its previous owner, Mr E. Peter Jones, at the Society of Antiquaries on 28 June 1917. The Chairman concluded that he 'could not agree as to the English origin of the panel, and thought it showed strong Flemish influence, especially in the grouping and the crown and beard of the chief figure; nor was the figure of Christ English in feeling' (*Society of Antiquaries* 1917, pp. 216–7).

BIBLIOGRAPHY
Society of Antiquaries 1917, pp. 214–7, and fig. on p. 215; *Review* 1917, pp. 2–3.

EXHIBITED
Exhibited by H. Clifford Smith on behalf of the owner, Mr E. Peter Jones at the Society of Antiquaries, Burlington House, on 28 June 1917.

48: Monument to Thomas Moyle (d. 1560) and his wife Katherine (d. after 1560)

about 1560
Caen stone
h. 115.8 cm.
A.187–1969

Inscribed above the shields from the north-west side: SYR THOMAS/KEMP AMYE/MOYLE; SYR THOMAS/MOYLE KATIERYN/IVRDAYN; SYR THOMAS/FFYNEHE KATHERYN/MOYLE; SYR THOMAS/MOYLE KATERYN/IVRDAYN; SYR THOMAS/MOYLE; SYR THOMAS/MOYLE KATERYN IVRDAYN; IOHN MOYLE/SIR ROBERT/DARCY; SYR/WALTER MOYLE/LVCOMBE

For details of the coats-of-arms and heraldry, see Physick 1970 [Eastwell], pp. 129–30.

Removed from the ruined church of St Mary, Eastwell, Kent. Given to the museum by the Rector and Churchwardens of the Parish of Eastwell with Broughton Aluph in 1969 together with cat. nos. 15, 16, 18 and 498.

Sir Thomas Moyle was the grandfather of Sir Moyle Finch; see entry for cat.no. 16, and great-grandfather of Sir Heneage Finch; see entry for cat.no. 15. The names on the tomb-chest are those of Sir Thomas's father and mother, grandfather, grandmother, wife, daughters and daughters' husbands. Physick records that the stone from which the monument was constructed must have formerly been used in a building, as there are some quatrefoil decorative details, arch-mouldings and part of a window-transom on the inside of the chest. For a full discussion of the Eastwell monuments see Physick 1970 [Eastwell].

BIBLIOGRAPHY
Physick 1970 [Eastwell], pp. 128–30 and figs. 2–4.

49: Chimneypiece

about 1580–1600
Limestone
h. 147.5 cm.
127–1907

Removed from a house called Market Garden, Baker Street, Enfield, Middlesex which is reputed to have formed part of the lodge of a mansion, now destroyed. Purchased together with a stone chimneypiece held by the

Furniture and Woodwork Department (inv.no. 128–1907) (illustrated in *English Chimneypieces* 1928, fig. 3), from Howard Rumney, Esq, 12 Craven Street, Charing Cross, London in 1907 for £100.

The upper part of the jambs and lower edge of the architrave have deep mouldings, with a rosette at the termination of the architrave on each side. In the centre of the frieze above there is a grotesque mask held within a cartouche, to the sides of which are birds, fruit, scrolls, vases with pea-pods and cherries, and monkeys in a symmetrical design.

50: Gateway, from Ascott House, near Stadhampton, Oxfordshire

about 1580–1600
Brick and stone with wrought iron gates and lunette
h. 4.27 m.
A.5–1925

The entablature bears the inscription: SI BONVS ES INTRES: SI. NEQVAM NEQVAQVAM
(If you are good, enter. If wicked, by no means)

The gate was originally the garden gate to Ascott Park, Ascott House, near Stadhampton, Oxfordshire, the ancestral home of the Dormer family: rebuilt around 1660, the house was destroyed by fire in 1662 (see Sherwood and Pevsner 1979, p. 776). Bought by Sir Paul Makins Bt. in 1924 with the intention of presenting it to the Museum, the gateway was at that time the entrance to a farmhouse. Given to the Museum by Sir Paul Makins, Brimpton Grange, Tiddington, Oxfordshire, in 1925. A stipulation of the gift was that the gateway should be removed by the Museum and replaced with plain walling and a wooden farm gate.

On examining the gateway and in his recommendation to the Director, H.P. Mitchell [q.v.] wrote, 'It is at present filled by a pair of wrought iron gates of simple design with a beautiful lunette of radiating scrollwork above. This ironwork is evidently of 18th century date, replacing the original doors. The lunette is in good condition; the gates have lost some of the smaller details, but are in substantially sound condition. Sir Paul Makins has bought the whole, including the short flanking walls, and since the land has been bought by the Local Authority for small holdings and the original house has disappeared he feels there is no sufficient reason for leaving this charming gate where it is. The stonework and the ironwork are both decaying under the action of the weather, and no proper care is bestowed on it . . . In my opinion, as a very pleasing and characteristic example of English building, in combination with excellent English ironwork of the 18th century, it would form an important acquisition for the Museum'.

Eric Maclagan [q.v.] supported Mitchell's recommendation, noting, 'We have no stonework of the period, and I feel sure it would be of the utmost use to students, who are very short of material on anything like a large scale for measuring'.

BIBLIOGRAPHY
Review 1925, p .5.

51: Floral scrolls in low relief

about 1590–1620
Plaster in a glazed wood frame
h. 7.6 cm. w. 23.8 cm.
311–1887

Formerly in the house owned by General Henry Ireton (1611–1651) at Highgate, London. Given by the architect Hugh Stannus Esq, F.R.I.B.A., 64 Larkhall Rise, Clapham, London in 1887.

This is a portion of a frieze.

BIBLIOGRAPHY
Bequests and Donations 1901, p. 244.

52: Chimneypiece, from 20 Colegate, Norwich

about 1600
Carved stone
Cornice h. 9 cm.; Architrave h. 42 cm.; Jambs h. 124.5 cm.
650–1902

Purchased from Messrs Jewson & Sons Ltd, St Clements, Norwich, in 1902 for £52 10s. According to information supplied by Mr Charles B. Jewson in March 1963, the mantelpiece originally came from 20 Colegate, St Clements, Norwich, then Head Office of Messrs Jewson & Sons Ltd.

Modern fills on the cornice, the outer side of the jambs and the architrave, were removed on acquisition.

An inspection report of the mantelpiece by T.G. Jackson on 2 April 1902, noted that, despite its condition, 'It is . . . a very good and interesting example of English Renaissance Art, and if it is to be turned out of its original home which I think would be a pity it would be a very useful acquisition for the Museum'. Following Mr Jackson's visit, Purdon Clarke noted on 3 April 1902, 'The interesting point in this object is that there are certain indications proving that it is of the same school as the fireplace purchased by us at Bromley and the old fireplace from Queen Elizabeth's robing-room at Westminster Palace, but it is better in style than either of these'. For the Bromley fireplace, see entry for cat.no. 56.

BIBLIOGRAPHY
English Chimneypieces 1928, fig. 4.

53: Scottish royal coat of arms

about 1603–88
Polychromed slate
h. 38.5 cm. w. 30.5 cm.
A.8–1945

Inscribed at the bottom: DIEV ET MON DROIT
Inscribed around the coat-of-arms: HON I SOIT QUI MAL Y PENCE
(God and my right/Evil be to he who thinks evil)

Given by Captain G. Owen Wheeler, 64 London Road, Worcester, in 1945.

The panel depicts the royal arms of Scotland.

I am grateful to Charles Bird, and to Timothy Duke at the College of Arms for their help in dating this piece.

54: Thomas, 3rd Baron Fairfax of Cameron (1612–1671)

before 1645 (?)
Elmwood
h. 38 cm
A.71–1927

Purchased from Mr R.W. Thomas, Antiques, 78 George Street, Portman Square, London in 1927 for £25, using funds from the Francis Reubell Bryan Bequest.

The nose is a replacement; the bust is worm-eaten.

In the *Review of Principal Acquisitions during the Year 1927* the bust, then unidentified, was considered 'particularly valuable as English wood busts are very unusual' (*Review* 1927, p. 5).

R.P. Bedford [q.v.] noted on its acquisition, 'This bust is carved in elm or chestnut and it appears to be of late 17th century date – it is impossible at present to say whom it represents. It is rather worm eaten, and a thick coat of varnish makes it difficult to see what parts have been restored; I think that possibly the nose may be modern. We have no English wood sculpture of the type in our collections nor do I know of a similar work'.

A similar bust in lead said to depict Fairfax, Commander-in-Chief of the Parliamentarian Army between 1645–50, has led to the suggestion that the present piece represents the same sitter. Weaver described the lead version as 'not only a fine achievement in sculptured likeness of a strong type, but is probably the oldest lead portrait bust in England'. He supported the theory that the bust was indeed a portrait of Fairfax by noting that the lead bust located in the Council Chamber of the York Philosophical Society is a replica of a bronze bust at Leeds Castle in Kent, a former home of the Fairfax family. He suggested that the Leeds bust was by the medallist and wax-modeller Abraham Simon (1617–1692), whose brother, the medallist Thomas Simon (1618–1665), also executed medals depicting Fairfax. However he noted, 'The attribution to Abraham Simon of the bust is nothing more than a guess, but it seems a reasonable one. Andrew Karne was in York somewhere between 1633 and 1638, but we do not know of his being there as late as 1645. He is a possible but unlikely author of the bust' (Weaver 1972, pp. 146–8, and fig. 238).

BIBLIOGRAPHY
Review 1927, p. 5, pl. 4.

55: Armorial relief with the arms of Brett

about 1650
Marble
h. 39.5 cm.
A.4–1945

Originally said to have come from Merchant Taylors' Hall in the City of London. On long-term loan from Mr H. Vincent Harley, 112 Campden Hill Road, London from 1927, and subsequently given to the Museum by him in 1945 in memory of his son H. Vincent Maldon Harley, killed by enemy action while on Government Service in 1944.

The Brett arms as described under Esher are as follows: 'Arms: Within an orle of crosses botony fitchée, or a lion ramp[ant] of the last. Crest: A lion passant gules' (*Burke's* 1980, p. 955).

56: Chimneypiece

about 1660
Stone
21–1894

Formerly in the Old Palace, Bromley-by-Bow, in East London. Built in 1606 (attributed to the architect John Thorpe (c.1565–1655?), it was the former residence of James I, but was demolished in 1893 by the London County Council School Board to make way for a new school (Hobhouse 1971 pp. 24–5). Purchased from Mr Joshua Binns, 186 Brompton Road, London in 1894 for £12. Further fragments from the interior of the Old Palace are held by the Furniture and Woodwork Department (inv.nos. 51&A-1894; 248 and A-1894; 430–1895; 1282 and B,N,O,X-1900; 859 to 861:A-1901).

The chimneypiece is in three parts. The lintel is carved in relief with a plain shield in the centre painted with the date 1660 (?), and surrounded by symmetrical vignette strapwork. The under portion of the lintel and the jambs are carved with deep flutings and rosettes.

57: Man in armour, possibly James II when Duke of York (b.1633; r.1685–8; d.1701)

about 1660
Boxwood
h. 38.5 cm.
A.17–1936

In the Henry Oppenheimer collection, and sold on the second day's sale of the collection held at Christie's, London on 16 July 1936, lot 206, described as 'a man in armour English 17th century . . . glass shade and stand. Said to be a portrait of James, Duke of York'. Purchased for £162 15s by the National Art Collections Fund and given to the Museum.

In a letter dated 13 June 1936 to Sir Robert Witt at the National Art Collections Fund prior to the Oppenheimer sale, Eric Maclagan [q.v.] wrote: 'The third object in which we are specially interested is the beautiful boxwood portrait statuette of a man in armour (lot 206); whether it really represents James Duke of York, I am not convinced. But it is first-class work. We doubt whether it is English; more likely German or Flemish'. In a memorandum to the Director on 2 July 1936, R.P. Bedford [q.v.] noted a visit by himself and Margaret Longhurst [q.v.] to view the sculpture included in the sale, noting, 'As the result there is one object which we feel we should be justified in buying out of Museum funds. This is the boxwood statuette of a man in armour. Although this work, as we had already pointed out, bears a certain similarity to two boxwood statuettes of emperors already in our collections, this similarity is confined chiefly to the treatment of the elaborate base; the figure itself is much more broadly conceived and seems obviously to be the work of another hand'. In relaying this information to Sir Robert Witt however, Eric Maclagan wrote that he thought the statuette could indeed be by the same hand as the statuettes of emperors already in the Museum's collections; he also noted, 'But the Oppenheimer figure with its contemporary costume is very much more interesting and I have always thought it finer; it is also in perfect state whereas one of ours has lost several fingers. They were tentatively ascribed by Berliner to a sculptor named Loth, but the Oppenheimer figure can be dated by the costume and would be too early for him; I do not think we ever found the suggestion a very convincing one'. In the *Review of Principle Acquisitions during the Year 1936*, a previous attribution to Grinling Gibbons was also noted (*Review* 1936, p. 5).

The two figures of emperors noted above as being already in the Museum's collections are those of *Alexander the Great* and *Julius Caesar* (inv.nos. 169 and 170–1864). They have more recently been published as related to three figures of *Lucretia*, *Cicero* and *Cleopatra* in the Burghley House collection, which are currently described as South Italian, last quarter of the 17th century (see *Treasure Houses* 1985, pp. 268–9, cat.no. 189). The present figure is unlikely to be Italian. Although here catalogued as British, it may have been produced by a Netherlandish artist, perhaps active in England.

The oceanic symbolism of sea-horses at the base implies the present piece commemorates a naval dignitary; it may therefore depict James, Duke of York on his appointment in 1660 as Lord High Admiral of the Fleet.

BIBLIOGRAPHY

Review 1936, pp. 5–6, p. 2 (a); *de Ruyter* 1957, p. 49, cat.no. 225.

EXHIBITED

Tentoonstelling ter herdenking van Michiel de Ruyter, Rijksmuseum Amsterdam and Nieuw Tehuis voor Bejaarden, Vlissingen, 23 March to 16 September 1957, cat.no. 225.

58: John Tillotson, Archbishop of Canterbury (1630–1694)

1660–80
Pearwood
h. 21.5 cm.
A.4–1925

Purchased from E. Hart Esq in 1925 for £10.

There is a crack to the left and right of the relief.

The Archbishop is shown wearing a doctor's gown and bands. Tillotson became Archbishop of Canterbury in 1666 (see *DNB* 1973, XIX, p. 875). This relief may commemorate this event, and is perhaps a reduced version of a life-size marble portrait. There is a medallion portrait of Tillotson on his monument of 1694 in St Lawrence Jewry, London, although it differs markedly from the present relief in style (see *Historical Monuments* 1929, p. 61 and plate 24 (1)). A later commemorative monument to Tillotson by Joseph Wilton [q.v.] was erected in Sowerby, West Yorkshire, Tillotson's birth-place, in 1796 (see Physick 1969, pp. 138–9; Whinney 1988, p. 269, illus. 195 on p. 268).

Two somewhat later oval pearwood medallions portraying Joseph Wilcocks (1673–1756), of similar size and technique to this portrait were auctioned at Sotheby's London on 9 December 1988, lots 302 and 303 (both unsold).

59: Charles II (b.1630; r.1660–1685)

about 1660–1700
Sycamore or limewood
h. 49.5 cm.
A.23–1933

Departmental records note that the present piece was formerly in the Peel Collection, possibly that amassed by Sir Robert Peel (for Peel's patronage of the arts, see Mordaunt Crook 1966). Given by Sir George Buckston Browne, F.R.C.S., F.S.A., 80 Wimpole Street, Cavendish Square, London in 1933.

The base shown in the accompanying illustration is no longer attached to the object.

When exhibited at the 1932 loan exhibition, the present piece was attributed to Grinling Gibbons [q.v.], but when published in the *Review of the Principal Acquisitions during the Year 1933* it was noted, 'After careful comparison with documented works of that artist, however, it seems unlikely that it is actually by his hand, though there is no doubt that it is a distinguished work of his period' (*Review* 1933, p. 7).

Listed under 'lesser works and attributions' in his monograph of Gibbons, Green commented, 'Although smashed, mended and varnished, this bust with its fine profile and cascading wig is seen at once to be a serious attempt at portraiture and, even now in its battered condition, a moving one. Attached to a blank cartouche, it may have been part of an overmantel, which had an answering bust of the Queen' (Green 1964, p. 137).

Bibliography

Loan Exhibition 1932, p. 44, cat.no. 342, and pl. XXVIII; *Review* 1933, p. 7, and pl. 4(d) opp. p. 7; Dobson and Wakeley 1957, p. 101 (I am grateful to Tina Craig for this reference); Green 1964, p. 137, and pl. 193.

Exhibited

Loan exhibition depicting the reign of Charles II, 22–23 Grosvenor Place, London, 28 January to March 1932, cat.no. 342; *Royal Exhibition*, Art and History Society, for the Queen's Silver Jubilee, Ealing Museum, London, 6 to 13 July 1977.

60: Unknown man

about 1670
Anonymous, possibly by a follower of John Bushnell
Terracotta
h. 73 cm.
A.7–1963

Purchased by John Hunt from an 'unimportant sale in the Midlands' and passed on by him to Ian Askew. Purchased together with cat.no. 61 for £350 from Ian Askew, Antiques and Decorations, 2 Queen's Elm Parade, Church Street, London in 1963, using funds from the Hildburgh Bequest.

The bust, together with its pendant, cat.no. 61, was covered with a thick grey paint which was removed on acquisition. The busts are each supported on an integral chimney-like support, which stands on a separate base.

Terence Hodgkinson [q.v.] noted on their proposed acquisition, 'These two life-size English terracotta portrait busts of unknown men are exceedingly rare in being dateable in the third quarter of the 17th century or, early in the last quarter'. It is likely that the busts were made as models for marble versions for a church monument; see entry for cat.no. 119. The age difference apparent in the sitters suggests that the busts may represent a father and son.

Rupert Gunnis tentatively attributed the busts to John Bushnell (about 1630–1702) (departmental records). Busts of a similar type by Bushnell may be seen on the monuments to David Walter (d. 1679) in Wolvercote, Oxfordshire, and that to Sir Thomas (d. 1676) and Lady Trevor (d. 1695) at Leamington Hastings, Warwickshire. A comparable terracotta bust of Charles II by Bushnell of about 1678 is in the Fitzwilliam Museum, Cambridge (inv.no. M1–1948; see *Fitzwilliam* 1958, p. 296, illus. on p. 297).

61: Unknown man

about 1670
Anonymous, possibly by a follower of John Bushnell
Terracotta
h. 74 cm.
A.8–1963

Purchased by John Hunt from an 'unimportant sale in the Midlands' and passed on by him to Ian Askew. Purchased together with cat.no. 60 for £350 from Ian Askew, Antiques and Decorations, 2 Queen's Elm Parade, Church Street, London in 1963, with funds from the Hildburgh Bequest.

See entry for cat.no. 60.

62: Monument to Sir Edward Nicolls (1619–1682)

about 1682
Alabaster with black marble tablet
h. (entire monument) 228.6 cm. h. (tablet) 56.2 cm.
A.10–1965

The Latin inscription reads: M[onumentum]. S[uum]./EDVARDI NICOLLS Baroneti,/Ab illustri Seimoror[u]m stirpe oriundi,/Corpus lapide vicino clauditur/Cujus Domus, dum vixit, universis,/pectus bonis & literatis, Arca agenis semper patuit/In quo prater caeteras, virtutes suas/Augustini patrui, religio probitasq[e]./Francisci patris in homines suos humanitas/Tanquam domesticae & hereditarie resplenduci/Uxores habuit duas/1. JUDITHAM ROLANDI S IOHN equitis filiam,/Quae 7 filias ipsi peperit./2. JANAM STEPHANI SOAMES equitis filiam 8/Ex qua suscepit filiolum unicaum EDVARDUM./Filiasq[e] duas SUSANNAM & JANAM,/Quos eiusdem Tutelae moriens reliquit/Vixit annos 63, menses i. Obijt Febrs. 28, 1682/Charis[sim]o Conjugi Uxor moerens/H[oc]: M[onumentum]: P[osuit].

Translation: This is the monument to Edward Nicolls, Baronet from the illustrious line of the Seymour, whose body is covered by a tombstone nearby. As long as he lived the doors of his house were open to good and civilised men, in which place remain his virtues and those of his uncle Augustine and the religion, honesty and humanity of his father Francis to all his people; and likewise his continual domestic and hereditary splendour.

He had two wives

1. Judith Roland, the daughter of the knight S John who gave him seven daughters.

2. Jane Stephen Soames, the eighth daughter of a knight. From her he received only one son Edward and two daughters Susanne and Jane who are left as his chief mourners.

He lived sixty-three years and two months and died on the 28 February 1682. His mourning wife erected this monument to her most beloved husband. (We are grateful to Norbert Jopek for help with this translation).

Originally from the demolished church of St Denis, Faxton, Northamptonshire. Given by the Rector and Churchwardens of Lamport with Faxton in 1965, together with cat.nos. 17, 126 and 260. For the Faxton monuments, see Hodgkinson 1971/2.

Sir Edward Nicholls was a great-nephew of Sir Augustine Nicolls; for his monument see entry for cat.no. 17.

BIBLIOGRAPHY

Hodgkinson 1971/2, p. 339, pl. 1 on p. 334 (for the monument when displayed in the Museum, in a filled (now open) entrance to gallery 50A); p. 339, pl. 3 on p. 336.

THE 18TH CENTURY

Robert Adam

(b Kirkcaldy 1728 – d. London 1792)

Robert Adam was one of the leading architects and designers of his generation, and a contemporary and rival of William Chambers [q.v.]. He embarked on the Grand Tour in October 1754, returning to London in January 1758. He established his architectural practice in London in 1763, in partnership with his younger brother James. He designed or altered a great number of seminally important public buildings and country houses, including Kedleston Hall, Derbyshire, Osterley Park, Middlesex, Kenwood House, London, and Luton Hoo, Bedfordshire.

Colvin 1995, pp. 51–62; TDA, 1, pp. 134–41 [Stillman].

63: Chimneypiece, from 15 Portman Square, London

about 1760
After a design by Robert Adam
Marble
h. (greatest) 171.5 cm.
A.14–1952

Originally from 15 Portman Square, London, which according to the donor once belonged to the Duke of Fife. In 1935 offered to Mr [John] Reginald Jones by the dealer Pratt, [possibly Calab Pratt, dealer in antique furniture, 185 to 188 Great Portland Street, 80 Bolsover Street, 108 Brompton Road, London] for £195, and presumably purchased by him then. On loan to the Museum from Mr Jones, Elm Lodge, Hendon, London from 28 September 1935, and subsequently bequeathed by him to the Museum in 1952, together with four Italo-Flemish plaquettes (inv.nos. A.15, A.15:A, B and C-1952). The present piece and the plaquettes reverted to being loans during the lifetime of Mr Jones's wife, Mrs E.M. Jones, who died in 1962.

In a letter to the Museum in September 1935, the donor Mr Jones wrote that the present piece was 'the best and most important of all the mantels in these 4 notable Adam houses . . . The centre panel is particularly good work on the purest marble. The method of construction is the same as on on other mantles I have seen and as can be seen in the book illustrations. A suggestion is made that such panels were brought from Italy – in a case like this possibly by Robert Adam himself, and a mantelpiece built to contain it'. However, Michael Snodin has recently suggested that the present piece could be after a design by the architect James Wyatt (1746–1813).

The central relief depicts Bacchus and Ariadne in a chariot drawn by panthers.

Thomas Ady or Adye

(active 1730 – 1753; d. before 1762)

A sculptor on whom little has been published, Adye is especially noted for the period between 1737 and 1744 when he was sculptor to the Society of Dilettanti, who commissioned him to carve an ornamental ballot-box depicting the Tomb of Bacchus, as well as other carvings in ivory. He also executed a number of funerary monuments of note, including one to Charles Sergison (d. 1732) at Cuckfield, West Sussex. Gunnis recorded that such monuments were often characterised by large portrait medallions accompanied by a cherub figure unveiling or holding the portrait.

Cust 1914, pp. 31–3; Gunnis 1968, p. 15; Redgrave 1970, p. 3; Whinney 1971, p. 71; idem 1988, p. 248, and fig. 179 on p. 247.

64: John Fane, 7th Earl of Westmorland (1682–1762)

signed and dated 1742
Marble
h. (incl. socle) 82.6 cm.
A.65–1949

Signed and dated on the right of the pedestal: Thos ADY 1742
Inscribed on the front of the base: Iohan^{s} Fane· Ea$^{L.}$ of Westmorel^{d}

The bust was almost certainly originally in the Temple of Friendship, Stowe House, Buckinghamshire (later in the Grenville Vestibule), and was included in the 1848 Stowe sale, as lot 764 on the sixth day, 21 August 1848. According to Forster's annotated catalogue of the Stowe sale, sold to "Russell" for £8 8s (Forster 1848, p. 49). Rupert Gunnis noted that Russell was a London dealer who sometimes acted as an agent for collectors (departmental records). The vendors of the present piece noted that was said to have come from the Earl of Jersey's collection; if this is correct the Earl must have acquired the bust from Russell or a subsequent owner. Purchased from Messrs Kerin, 15 Davies Street, London, in 1949, together with cat.no. 270, for £120 (£100 being the sum for the present piece).

John Fane, 7th Earl of Westmorland (the spelling 'Westmoreland' on the contemporary socle may be a mistake), was promoted to Major-General in 1742, the same year this bust was executed, and the emblems and his classical armour signify his military standing. A further version is at West Wycombe Park, Buckinghamshire in the collection of the late Sir John Dashwood, Bt., and the terracotta model for the base was recorded in the possession of Earl Fortescue, Ebrington Park, Gloucestershire (Gunnis 1968, p. 15). The West Wycombe bust is illustrated in an article of 1933 displayed over the portico to the doorway in the dining room, originally the saloon; see Oswald 1933, fig. 10 on p. 471; Whinney 1988, p. 248, n. 11 on p. 458.

For the bust of Viscount Cobham, also formerly at the Temple of Friendship, Stowe House, see entry for cat.no. 202.

Bibliography

Smith 1920, p. 48; *Vertue* 1934, p. 133; Esdaile 1949, p. 13; Molesworth 1951, p. 15 and pl. XXX; *Siècle de l'élegance* 1959, p. 33, cat.no. 28; Gunnis 1968, p. 15; Whinney 1971, p. 72, cat.no. 18, illus. on p. 73; Davies 1979, p. 148; Whinney 1988, p. 248.

Exhibited

Le Siècle de l'élegance La Demeure Anglaise au XVIII siècle, Musée des Arts Décoratifs, Paris, 26 February to mid-June 1959, cat.no. 28.

65: Paul Joddrell (1713–1751)

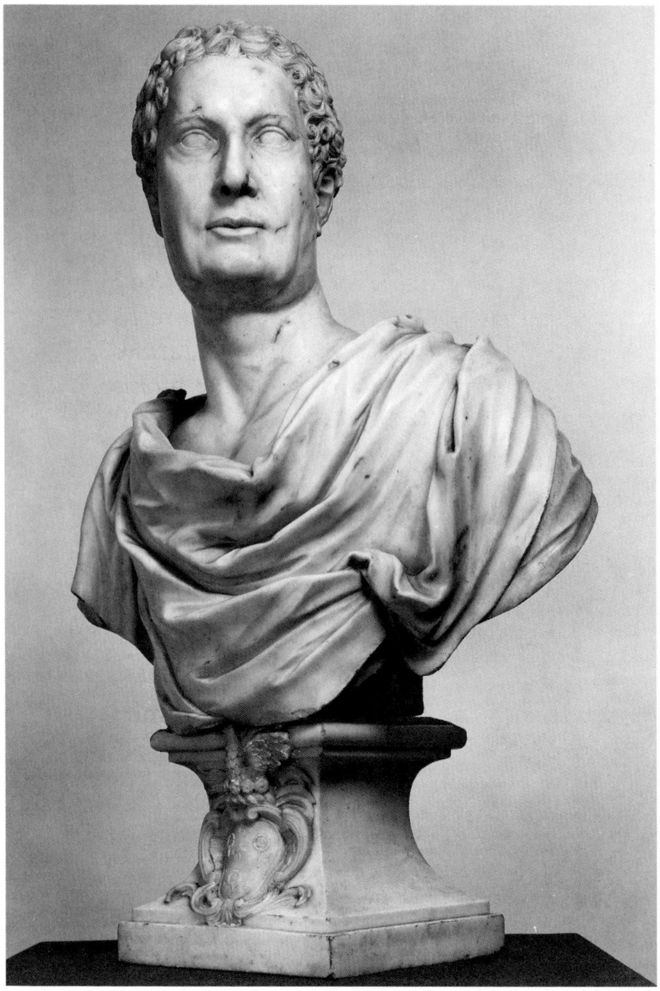

about 1740
Ascribed to Thomas Ady
Marble
h. (incl. socle) 85 cm.
A.1–1957

Acquired by Gerald Kerin, 15 Davies Street, London, from Commander Roger Coke, R.N. (retd), of Bayfield Hall, Holt, Norfolk. Bayfield Hall is recorded as the home of Henry Joddrell, the sitter's third son, and it is presumed the bust remained at Bayfield Hall until its sale to Gerald Kerin. Purchased by the Museum from Gerald Kerin in 1956 for £300, using funds from the Bequest of Francis Reubell Bryan.

The bust surmounts a socle with a cartouche containing the arms of Joddrell. Terence Hodgkinson [q.v.] suggested the sitter be identified with Paul Joddrell of Duffield, Derbyshire, Solicitor-General to Frederick, Prince of Wales (1707–1751), and noted, 'on grounds of style, there is little doubt that the bust dates from the second quarter of the eighteenth century, probably close to 1740' (departmental records).

In a memorandum to the Director, John Pope-Hennessy, Hodgkinson noted; 'Not enough is known of English sculpture of this date for us to propose an attribution with any confidence, though Dr Margaret Whinney's suggestion of Henry Scheemakers is worth considering. It is an exceedingly good bust, judging by what I have so far seen of English sculpture of this date and is, perhaps, rather more impressive than the marbles by Rysbrack, Peter Scheemakers and Thomas Ady, which we already possess'. Hodgkinson later attributed the bust to Ady, noting comparisons with the signed bust by Ady of the Earl of Westmorland; see entry for cat.no. 64 (departmental records).

Bibliography

Whinney 1971, p. 74, cat.no. 19, illus. on p. 75.

John Bacon the Elder R.A.

(b. London 1740 – d. London 1799)

Bacon was the head of a family of sculptors; his sons Thomas (1773–d. after 1800) and John Bacon the Younger [q.v.] worked in their father's studio. Bacon, a contemporary of Thomas Banks [q.v.] and Joseph Nollekens [q.v.], became one of the most prolific English neo-classical sculptors. He began his career apprenticed to Nicholas Crispe, in whose porcelain factory he trained. Bacon was awarded premiums at the Society of Arts between 1760 and 1778. He was a modeller in the Coade Manufactory [q.v.] and also produced models for ceramics for Wedgwood and Derby. In 1769 he enrolled at the Royal Academy, where he was awarded a Gold Medal for his Aeneas Escaping from Troy, *the first sculpture to be given such an award. A year later, Bacon was elected as an Associate of the Royal Academy. He returned to the Coade Manufactory in 1771, becoming its chief designer. Bacon also produced many funerary monuments; his monument of 1779 to Thomas Guy in Guy's Hospital, London, is regarded as his masterpiece. In 1784 he was awarded a commission to produce the monument to Admiral Rodney in Spanish Town, Jamaica, which marked the beginning of a number of such monuments for Jamaica. Bacon exhibited at the Royal Academy between 1769 and 1798.*

Cunningham 1830, pp. 200–46; Graves I, pp. 87–8; Cox-Johnson 1961; Gunnis 1968, pp. 24–8; Clifford 1985; Whinney 1988, pp. 303–13; Thieme-Becker, 2, p. 328; TDA, 3, pp. 25–6 [Bryant]; Coutu 1998.

66: Britannia, on the monument to Admiral Sir George Pocock (1706–1792)

about 1792–6
Plaster
h. 72 cm.
Cheng Huan Loan 1

Formerly in the possession of Sir Francis J.B. Watson, Esq, C.V.O., and lent by him to the Museum from February 1965. From October 1973 lent to the Museum by Mr Cheng Huan Q.C.

This is the model for the figure of Britannia on the monument to Admiral Sir George Pocock erected in the chapel of St John the Evangelist, Westminster Abbey in 1796. A related drawing is held in the Department of Prints, Drawings and Paintings (inv.no. E.1534–1931); see Physick 1969, pp. 158–60.

We are grateful to Mr Cheng Huan Q.C. for allowing us to include this in the catalogue.

Bibliography
Physick 1969, p. 159–60.

Exhibited
English Sculptor's Drawings, 1680–1860, Department of Prints, Drawings and Paintings, Victoria and Albert Museum, 3/4 November 1966 to 29 January 1967.

67: Unknown elderly man

about 1770–99
Attributed to John Bacon the Elder
Terracotta
h. 60.5 cm.
517–1868

Purchased from Mr Pratt in 1868 for £8.

The attribution of the present piece to Bacon was suggested on acquisition.

THOMAS BANKS R.A.

(b. London 1735 – d. London 1805)

Banks was ranked by Flaxman [q.v.] as the equal of Canova, and his interpretations of the antique were highly regarded by his contemporaries and later artists; he specialised in ideal subjects, but also carved some outstanding portrait busts, as well as some monuments. The son of the steward of the Duke of Beaufort, he was apprenticed for seven years to the mason and ornament-carver William Barlow in London. He worked in the evenings at the studio of Peter Scheemakers [q.v.], where he met Joseph Nollekens [q.v.], and where he also had the opportunity to study the antique from the models and copies Scheemakers had brought back from Rome. Banks enrolled in the life classes at the St Martin's Lane Academy after completing his apprenticeship, and by 1769 was probably working as an assistant to Richard Hayward. In 1772 he became the first sculptor to be awarded the Royal Academy's travelling stipend to Rome, where he was to spend seven years, partly thanks to the income of his wife, whom he had married in 1766. He returned to England in 1779, having acquired great skill in carving marble, which can be seen in his surviving reliefs and figures, notably Caractacus before Claudius *(Stowe House, Buckinghamshire), and the* Falling Titan *(Royal Academy, Diploma Work of 1785). He visited Naples in 1778, and then spent some months in Russia (1781–2), but thereafter was based in London, specialising in portraits and monuments, and supplementing his income by carving chimneypieces and architectural sculpture. He regularly exhibited works at the Royal Academy from 1770 to 1803 and was elected a member of the Royal Academy in 1785.*

Bell 1938; Gunnis 1968, pp. 37–40; Whinney 1988, pp. 322–36; Thieme-Becker, 2, p. 445; TDA, 3, pp. 183–5 [Bryant].

68: Achilles arming

about 1777
Terracotta
h. 47 cm.
A.22–1955

In the possession of Edward H. Corbould, and lent by him to the 1862 International Exhibition. On loan to the Museum from Mrs. M. Pott, 11 Scarsdale Villas, Kensington, London, from 11 February 1937 until 1955. Mrs Pott was the daughter of the former owner, E.H. Corbould. Given to the Museum by Mr Reginald H. Pott on behalf of his deceased wife in October 1955.

In a letter of October 1955 to the Museum Mr Pott noted, 'A burglar nearly smashed up the work "Achilles Arming"' (departmental records). On acquisition the model had been broken into many pieces; it was conserved shortly after its arrival.

A label beneath the base had a defaced inscription in a nineteenth-century hand, recording Banks as the sculptor of the present piece (departmental records; the label is no longer attached). Elvy O'Brien has suggested an attribution of the figure to Johan Tobias Sergell (1740–1814); see O'Brien 1982, pp. 316–7, no. 23. The present piece has been compared with the terracotta figure of a male nude by Banks in the Musée Girodet, at Montargis (see Bellenger 1996, p. 186, and fig. 3).

The subject matter is noted by Cunningham, who recorded, 'His [Banks's] favourite of all the heroes was Achilles. I have already mentioned two pieces in which he is introduced, and there are others even of superior merit – they are, however, both sketches – something rude, as all his sketches are, but full of that heroic feeling which made Flaxman his ardent admirer. The first I allude to is Achilles arming amidst his Myrmidons. He is represented placing on his head that helmet which was never soiled with dust' (Cunningham 1830, p. 109, quoted in part by Bell 1938, p. 193). A scene depicting *Thetis dipping Achilles into the River Styx* is incised on the helmet; see entry for cat.no. 71.

A version of the present piece in bronze – unsigned, but with the figure wearing a fig leaf – was recorded in a private collection in 1984 (noted by Malcolm Baker; departmental records). What appears to be a life-size version of Banks's *Achilles Arming* is included in an oil sketch of about 1846 by John Partridge (1790–1872), depicting *The Fine Arts Commissioners in 1846.* Bryant notes that 'Such a statue is not recorded and was presumably invented to represent the sculptor more prominently in Partridge's 'imaginary collection of the works of our principal deceased Artists . . .'" (Bryant 1983 [Banks], p. 742, fig. 16 on p. 743).

Bibliography

Cunningham 1830, pp. 109–10; *International Exhibition* 1862, p. 140; Bell 1938, p. 193, and pl. XLIII; Whinney 1971, p. 134, cat.no. 43, illus. on p. 135; *Neo-classicism* 1972, p. 190, cat. no. 295; *British Artists in Rome* 1974, cat.no. 55 and illus.; Sutton 1974, p. 402, and fig. 16; O'Brien 1982, pp. 316–7, no. 23, figs. 95 to 103 on pp. 496–504; Bryant 1983 [Banks], p. 742; Bryant 1985, p. 49; Bellenger 1996, p. 186.

Exhibited

International Exhibition of 1862, London, British Division, class XXXIX, A – Deceased artists, lent by E.H. Corbould, Esq.; *Age of Neo-classicism*, Royal Academy, 9 September to 19 November 1972, cat.no. 295; *British Artists in Rome 1700–1800*, The Iveagh Bequest, Kenwood, 8 June to 27 August 1974, cat.no. 55.

69: Thetis and her nymphs rising from the sea to console Achilles for the loss of Patroclus

1777–8; finished posthumously by assistants 1805–7
Marble
91.4 cm. x 118.7 cm.
A.15–1984

Commissioned by Frederick Augustus Hervey, Bishop of Derry, later 4th Earl of Bristol (1730–1803), but remained in the artist's possession, although it was not included in the Banks sale held by Mr Christie on 22 May 1805. However, Under 'Fancy objects', lot 76 was described as the 'Original Plaster Model executed at Rome, A Bas-Relief, the subject Thetis and Sea Nymphs rising from the Sea to Console Achilles for the loss of Briseis'; this plaster is now in Sir John Soane's Museum. Given by the artist's daughter Mrs Lavinia Forster to the National Gallery in 1845; its arrival was discussed in a lengthy article in the *Illustrated London News* (see below). A tablet commemorating the gift of Mrs Lavinia Forster to the National Gallery was acquired at the same time; see entry for cat.no. 70. Transferred from the National Gallery to the Tate Gallery at a date sometime between 1897 and 1902 (I am grateful to Charlotte Brunskill for this information) (Tate inv.no. 1763). Placed on indefinite loan from the Tate at the Victoria and Albert Museum in 1936 (ex-loan 45). Formally transferred from the Tate and accessioned by the V&A in 1984.

The relief – depicting a passage in Homer's *Iliad* – was begun by Banks in Rome, although in an article in the *Illustrated London News* noting its arrival at the National Gallery in 1846, the writer noted that that, 'Banks executed this beautiful composition of

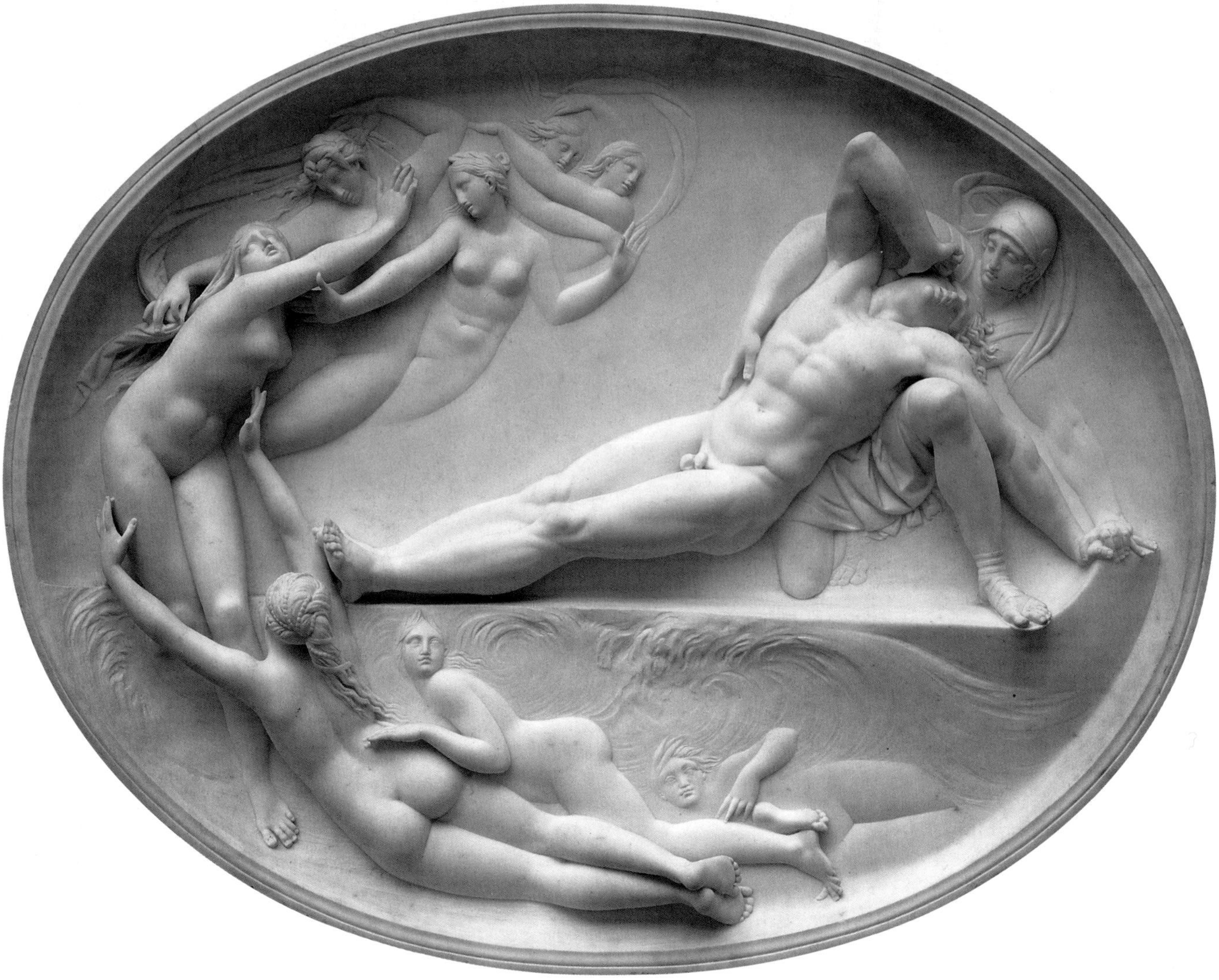

Thetis and her Nymphs Consoling Achilles during one of the sculptor's summer visits to Hafod, in Wales' (*Illustrated London News* 1846). The work was incomplete at Banks's death, and was completed probably by studio assistants; see *Director* 1807, cited by Bell 1938, p. 41. The plaster version in Sir John Soane's Museum may have been an early copy after the marble, rather than a model for it; another plaster is in a private collection in Scotland.

The offer of the gift of this piece to the National Gallery by Mrs Lavinia Forster was made through her son-in-law Ambrose Poynter, who wrote on 18 March 1845: 'My object in disposing of it will be to have it placed where it will remain in permanent safety, and on a situation where it will be before the eyes of the world to the honour of the eminent artist by whom it was executed'. In a letter dated 15 May 1845, Lavinia Forster wrote, 'This estimable work has been secured from the risk of injury and destruction, entirely by the exertions of the above mentioned Ambrose Poynter Esq. and it would be gratifying to me to combine his name with mine in offering it to you' (National Gallery MS NG5/60/1845; references supplied by Malcolm Baker). In a further letter, Mrs Forster recounted that the relief was commissioned by the Earl of Bristol and Bishop of Derry, but was not required by him, and returned with Banks to England in 1779 (*Art in Rome in the Eighteenth Century* 2000 [Baker], p. 228).

For further information and bibliographical references see *Art in Rome in the Eighteenth Century* 2000 [Baker], pp. 228–9, cat.no. 106. A comparable marble relief by Banks of *Alcyone discovering the body of her dead husband Ceyx* of 1775–9 taken from Ovid's *Metamorphoses*, is in the Leeds City Art Gallery (inv.no. 7.660/68); see Stainton 1974; *Leeds* 1996, p. 3.

I am grateful to Julius Bryant for his help with this entry.

BIBLIOGRAPHY

Director 1807; Cunningham 1830, pp. 100–1; *Illustrated London News* 1846; Graves I, p. 105, no. 538; Graves 1908, p. 22, no. 47; Bell 1938, pp. 35–6, 40–1; *Tate* 1947, p. 6; *Royal Academy* 1951, pp. 237–8, cat.no. 671; *Romantic Movement* 1959, pp. 273–4, cat.no. 466; Irwin 1966, p. 56, pl. 59; Gunnis 1968, p. 37; Keutner 1969, p. 333 and pl. 232; Whinney 1971, p. 128, cat.no. 40, illus. p. 129; Stainton 1974, pp. 327–8, fig. 51 on p. 329; *Fuseli* 1979, pp. 51–2, cat.no. 53, illus. on p. 52 (erroneously states the plaster relief painted to resemble bronze in the Sir John Soane's Museum

71

is terracotta) (reference supplied by Malcolm Baker); Bryant 1985, p. 61, fig. 10 on p. 62; Whinney 1988, p. 324 and fig. 235, n. 11 on p. 466 (erroneously states the plaster relief painted to resemble bronze in the Sir John Soane's Museum is terracotta); Ingamells 1997, p. 127; *Art in Rome in the Eighteenth Century* 2000 [Baker], pp. 228–9, cat.no. 106, Snodin and Styles 2001, fig. 32 on p. 200.

EXHIBITED

Royal Academy 1784, no. 538; British Institution, London, 1806, no. 47; There has been some confusion as to whether the present piece was exhibited at the International Exhibition of 1862. Bell noted that it was exhibited at the International Exhibition of 1862, lent by the National Gallery. In the exhibition catalogue for the *Romantic Movement* it was said to have been lent to the 'International Exhibition, National Gallery, 1862'. However, the *International Exhibition 1862 Official Catalogue of the Fine Art Department* records a plaster version was exhibited – under the British Division, class XXXIX, A – Deceased artists (see Bell 1938, p. 41; *International Exhibition* 1862, p. 140); *Winter Exhibition, 1951–52. The First Hundred Years of the Royal Academy 1769–1868*, Royal Academy, London, cat.no. 671; *The Romantic Movement. Fifth Exhibition to Celebrate the Tenth Anniversary of the Council of Europe*, Tate Gallery and Arts Council Gallery, London, 10 July to 27 September 1959, cat.no. 466; *New Hang*, Tate Gallery, 11 December 1989 to 11 June 1990; *Art in Rome in the Eighteenth Century*, Philadelphia Museum of Art, Philadelphia, and Museum of Fine Arts, Houston, 16 March to 17 September 2000, cat.no. 106.

70: Tablet for the relief Thetis and her nymphs rising from the sea to console Achilles for the loss of Patroclus

Marble
l. 61cm. h. 30cm.
A.15:A-1984

Inscribed: THETIS RISING FROM THE SEA /TO CONSOLE ACHILLES FOR THE/DEATH OF PATROCLUS./BY THOMAS BANKS, R.A./PRESENTED BY HIS DAUGHTER/Mrs LAVINIA FORSTER

This tablet commemorates the gift by the artist's daughter Mrs Lavinia Forster of the *Thetis* relief to the National Gallery in 1845. Transferred from the National Gallery to the Tate Gallery early in the twentieth-century, together with the relief. Placed on indefinite loan from the Tate at the Victoria and Albert Museum in 1936 (ex-loan 45a). Formally transferred from the Tate and accessioned by the V&A in 1984.

The tablet is no longer displayed alongside the relief; see entry for cat.no. 69.

[Not illustrated].

71: Thetis dipping Achilles into the river Styx

1790
Marble on wooden plinth
h. 85 cm.
A.101–1937

Commissioned by Colonel Thomas Johnes (1748–1816) of Hafod, Cardiganshire, and recorded in the Conservatory at Hafod in 1803 (see Bell 1938, p. 77). Chancellor noted that 'it occupied the place of honour' (Chancellor 1911, p. 153). The group, which survived the fire which destroyed much of Hafod on 13 March 1807, remained at Hafod and formed part of Johnes's estate, which was acquired by the 4th Duke of Newcastle in 1833 (*DNB* 1973, X, p. 890). It had been removed to Clumber House, home of the Duke of Newcastle by 1845, and was included in the Clumber House sale, held on 19 October 1937, lot 337, 'Mansion of Clumber Property of the Hon. the Earl of Lincoln inherited under the will of the late Henry Pelham Archibald Douglas Pelham-Clinton, 7th Earl of Newcastle', held by Messrs Christie, Manson and Woods, London, 19 – 22 October 1937. Included in the 3rd day's sale, held on 21 October, as lot 337, it was not ascribed to a particular artist, merely described as 'A statuary marble group of 'Thetis dipping Achilles in the River Styx and the octagonal pedestal for same'. Bell recorded that the whereabouts and authorship of the *Thetis* group had been forgotten, as is suggested by the Clumber House sale catalogue entry (Bell 1938, pp. 78–9). Purchased at the sale for £80 by Cecil Keitch and Kerin, 4 Bruton Place, London, who acted as agents for the Museum in bidding for the piece.

Charles Bell – a descendant of the sculptor – who originally offered to pay up to £50 to secure the figure for the Museum, in the event paid the full amount of £80 in order to present it to the Museum. The original octagonal wood pedestal was almost certainly acquired with the marble. Mrs Forster had written to Allan Cunningham in 1830 describing it as 'placed over a magnificent vase in the conservatory'; this suggests that the wood pedestal was made slightly later.

The heads of the two figures are those of Thomas Johnes's second wife Jane, and their daughter, Mariamne. In *Peacocks and Paradise,* the story of Hafod House, it was noted: 'Banks was, of course, invited to immortalize Jane in marble, for Johnes was one of his most generous patrons and had a warm affection for the man as a great admiration for the artist . . . The simplicity and goodness of his character, his frugal way of life and his complete absorption in perfecting his craft, strongly appealed to Johnes, and Banks spent many summers at Hafod' (Inglis-Jones 1950, pp. 98–9).

Bell incorrectly suggested the marks on the present piece were due to staining occurring from the result of the fire at Hafod in March 1807, and the one at Clumber in 1879, but these are in fact natural faults in the marble (Bell 1938, p. 79).

At the sale of the 'Extensive and valuable collection of original models in Terra Cotta, Moulds and Casts, of the late eminent Artist, Thos. Banks Esq., Dec' held by the Executors, at Mr Christie, London, 22 May 1805, under 'Fancy Subjects', lot 75 was described as: 'The much admired figure of Thetis dipping the Infant Achilles in the River Styx, Model in Plaister for the Marble in the possession of T. Johnes, Esq., M.P. at Hafod'.

A related terracotta model appeared on the Paris art market in 1988 (noted by Malcolm Baker, departmental records).

BIBLIOGRAPHY

Morning Post, 13 June 1789; *idem*, 28 August 1789; *idem*, 26 November 1789 (cited in Bell 1938, p. 75 and Inglis-Jones 1950, p. 99); Chancellor 1911, p. 153; *Clumber* 1908, illus. on p. 353 (displayed in the North-West corner of the Saloon in Clumber House); *Review* 1937, p. 8, and pl. 4(c); Graves I, p. 105, no. 658; Bell 1938, pp. 75–9, pl. XV and XVI; Inglis-Jones 1950, pp. 98–9, illus. opp. p. 99; *Royal Academy* 1968, p. 74, cat.no. 132; Whinney 1971, p. 130, cat.no. 41, illus. on p. 131; *idem* 1988, pp. 325–6, fig. 236 on p. 326; Williamson 1996 [Trusted], p. 162.

EXHIBITED

Royal Academy 1790, no. 658; *Royal Academy of Arts Bicentenary Exhibition 1768–1968*, Royal Academy, London, 14 December 1968 to 2 March 1969, cat.no. 132.

72: Dr Anthony Addington (1713–1790)

1790
Marble
h. (incl. socle) 76 cm.
A.2–1955

Purchased by David Piper of the National Portrait Gallery on behalf of Mr Piers Raymond at the sale of the possessions of the late Viscount Sidmouth, at Up-Ottery Manor House, Devon, held by J. Trevor & Sons, 22 July 1954, lot 413, where it was described as, 'A white marble bust of a gentleman'. Purchased by Dr W.L. Hildburgh F.S.A. from Mr Piers Raymond for £14 10s. Given by Dr Hildburgh to the Museum in 1955 as a New Year gift.

Dr Addington retired from practice as a doctor around 1780, purchasing the estate of Up-Ottery, Devon (*Royal College of Physicians* 1964, p. 18). Bell records an extract from the diary of Joseph Farrington: '1798, January 3rd. The Speaker shewed us his house – . . . a Bust of his father by Banks, from cast taken after death – but so like that Mr Pitt said 'it was the only bust he could ever talk to' (Bell 1938, p. 84; and cited by Whinney 1971, p. 132).

A contemporary press notice (date and newspaper unrecorded) noted, ' The fine bust of the late Dr ADDINGTON, made by BANKS, for the Speaker, is so much admired for fidelity and spirit, that the ingenious artist is making another for Lady CHATHAM' (Press Cuttings 1686–1835, II, p. 476, bound volumes in National Art Library – reference supplied by Marjorie Trusted). An oil painting of Anthony Addington by John Rowell (d. 1756) of about 1750 is in the Royal College of Physicians. Addington is described as 'Physician and confidant to Lord Chatham; and in 1788 called in by the Prince of Wales to advise on the mental condition of George III' (*Royal College of Physicians* 1977, p. 54, cat.no. 2, illus. on p. 55). A Coade stone bust of Addington by Banks of about 1790/1 – formerly thought to be marble – is also in the Royal College of Physicians, 'Presented in 1827 by the Earl of Chatham, whose father was a patient of Addington's' (*Royal College of Physicians* 1964, pp. 18–19, illus. on p. 19). This bust is possibly the one referred to in the press cutting cited above.

BIBLIOGRAPHY

Bell 1938, p. 84, pl. XIX (the property of Viscount Sidmouth); *Royal College of Physicians* 1964, p. 18; Whinney 1971, p. 132, cat.no. 42, illus. on p. 133.

EXHIBITED

A 'Bust of the late Dr Addington of Reading', was exhibited at the Royal Academy in 1791 (Graves I, p. 105, no. 636). Julius Bryant has noted (correspondence 2001), that a version in a private collection in the U.S.A. may have been the one exhibited at the Royal Academy.

73: Alderman John Boydell (1719–1804), Lord Mayor of London in 1790

about 1791
Painted plaster
h. 85 cm.
A.19–1931

Purchased from Miss Annie Bacon, 17 Gilston Road, London, together with cat.no. 261 in 1931 for £15. The bust belonged to Miss Bacon and her sister. Miss Bacon was apparently a descendant – possibly the great-granddaughter – of the sculptor John Bacon the Elder [q.v.]. Fifty-four drawings for monuments by John Bacon the Elder and John Bacon the Younger [q.v.] were also purchased from Miss Bacon at this time; the total price of £45 included the two busts. The drawings are held in the Department of Prints, Drawings and Paintings (inv.nos. E.1528 to E.1581–1931). A collection of sculptor's tools previously belonging to Bacon the Elder was given by the great-great-great granddaughter of the sculptor in 1998 (inv.no. A.4 to 60–1998).

Prior to the acquisition of the present piece and cat.no. 261, R. P. Bedford [q.v.] noted, 'Although these two plaster sketch models cannot be considered great works of art they have a certain interest for the history of English sculpture'.

The present piece is probably the model for the marble bust of Boydell originally in the Church of St Olave's Jewry, London. The church was demolished in 1888, and the bust was subsequently removed to the Church of St Margaret's, Lothbury. The original bust is signed 'Banks del. F. Smith sc.'. In his compilation of the *Annals of Thomas Banks,* Bell suggested, 'The strange signature may express Banks's recognition of the virtuosity of his workman, but it is more likely that the bust was executed by a carver, whose name seems to be unrecorded elsewhere, after Banks's death, from his model' (Bell 1938, p. 85). The original setting for the marble bust is described in George Godwin's *The Churches of London*. The inscription on Boydell's monument records that the remains of his niece, Mary Nichol, who died on 21 December 1820, were also placed in the same vault, and that at her request, the marble bust of her uncle was also placed there on her death (Godwin 1839, pp. 6, 9; I am grateful to Julius Bryant for this reference). The Boydell bust is noted by Gunnis in his entry for the sculptor Frederick William Smith (1797–1835), one of Chantrey's chief assistants (see Gunnis 1968, pp. 356–7). Citing a pamphlet produced in 1930 entitled *Some Historical Notes on the Church of St Margaret, Lothbury*, Bell recounted that Mrs Esdaile had apparently seen the terracotta from which the bust was made, ' "in a private collection belonging to two old ladies, and that the identity was absolute". Allowing for the fact that the cast, painted brown, is actually in plaster, it seems probable that this was the bust acquired by the Museum in 1931' (Bell 1938, p. 85).

Boydell was a print-seller and engraver, and patron of the arts (see TDA, 4, pp. 607–8 [West]. In her London diary of 1786, Sophie von la Roche recorded a visit to his shop on 28 September, describing Boydell as 'London's most famous print dealer' (La Roche 1933, pp. 237–9).

BIBLIOGRAPHY
Graves I, p. 105; *Review* 1931, p. 53; Bell 1938, p. 85; Whinney 1988, p. 334.

EXHIBITED
A bust of Boydell was exhibited by Banks at the Royal Academy in 1791, no. 662: an annotation on the record cards suggests that Katharine Esdaile thought this was the present piece.

74: Angel in Adoration

before 1792
Limewood
h. 42.8 cm.
A.8–1965

Executed by the sculptor for his daughter Lavinia Banks as a finial for her harp. Recorded by Lavinia Forster (neé Banks; see entry for cat. no. 69) in the possession of the sculptor Sir Francis Chantrey [q.v.], presumably following the posthumous sale of Banks's studio held by Mr Christie, 5 Newman Street, on 22 May 1805. Although I have been unable to find a definite match to any of the descriptions from the lots listed in the catalogue, lot 72 under 'Fancy Subjects' was described as 'Filial Piety, an elegant small kneeling female figure', although this may have been for a church memorial, whilst lot 61 was described as 'A model for a Term'. The sculptors Charles Francis Rossi and later Sir Francis Chantrey were entrusted with the safekeeping of the items not sold at the sale (Bell 1938, p. 196). The present piece appears to have been returned to Lavinia Forster, in whose possession it was recorded in March 1830 (see below). A letter from Ambrose Poynter to Phillip Hardwick R.A., dated 17 January 1863, later records the finial in his possession (see *Builder* 1863 II). By 1936 it was owned by Sir Hugh Poynter, Bt. Given to the Museum by Charles F. Bell, Esq., F.S.A., in 1965. Mr Bell – who in 1937 also gave to the Museum the Banks marble group *Thetis dipping Achilles in the Styx*; see entry for cat.no. 71 – was a descendant of the sculptor and his biographer (see Bell 1938).

There are faint traces of gilding. The hands have been broken and repaired.

The angel finial is shown in a portrait of Lavinia Banks with her harp by James Northcote (1746–1831) of 1792; see Bell 1938, pl. XXIV. Various recollections of the harp finial are recounted by Bell in his monograph on Banks (see Bell 1938, pp. 93–4). In a letter from Mrs Lavinia Forster to Allan Cunningham, dated 1 March 1830, she wrote: 'You will find among the models in Mr Chantrey's possession a little figure of an angel in the act of adoration, which he [Banks] designed for the top of my harp, and carved it in wood himself, that it might be, as it was, quite perfect. Nothing could exceed its beauty when just finished in the wood; but the sharpness of its execution was much impaired by the gilding. The harp was worn out and destroyed, but I have this precious remain in my possession, having had it displaced from the instrument of which it was so original and tasteful an ornament' *(Builder* 1863 [I], p. 4; cited and reprinted in Bell 1938, p. 93).

BIBLIOGRAPHY
Builder 1863 [I], p. 4; *Builder* 1863 [II]; Bell 1938, pp. 93–4, and pl. XXIV; *Bulletin* 1968, p. 163 and illus.

75: Dying warrior

about 1772–9
Perhaps by Thomas Banks
Terracotta
h. 15.5 cm.
A.11–1963

Incised on the integral base at the front beneath the shield: 

Formerly in the possession of Messrs Peel and Humphris Ltd. Bought by the Museum from Michael Ricketts Esq, 19 Emperor's Gate, London in 1963 for £85.

The present piece has not been identified with any specific sculpture project executed by Banks. The reclining figure and subject matter are however closely related to a plaster model by the sculptor, *The Dying Patriot*, in Sir John Soane's Museum. The oval shield on which the present subject lies is replaced in the Soane plaster by an altar, with the figure holding a shield, beneath which is an upturned crown (see Bell 1938, pl. XL). The style and size of the present piece may be compared with that of the terracotta *Achilles Arming*; see entry for cat.no. 68, which Tererence Hodgkinson [q.v.] suggested was a 'more developed conception of the same idea' (departmental records).

The subject matter of the dying hero was one used by Banks in a number of works, including the marble relief of the *Death of Germanicus* at Holkham Hall of 1774, Patroclus in the marble relief of *Thetis and her nymphs rising from the sea to console Achilles for the loss of Patroclus* of 1778; see entry for cat.no. 69, and in the design for a monument to Captain Cook and George Blagdon Westcott of 1804–5, in St Paul's Cathedral.

The present piece could have been one of those terracottas executed by Banks whilst in Rome (1772–9), which remained in his studio after his death. His daughter Lavinia Forster recorded, 'All the terracottas were models made by my father in Italy, and are valuable to me' (Bell 1938, p. 196). Julius Bryant has however recently suggested in correspondence that this piece may be by the Swedish sculptor Johan Tobias Sergel (1740–1814); cf Antonsson 1942, illus. on p. 163 and pl. 65. See also comparisons with Sergel's Othyryades: O'Brien 1982, pp. 297–302, cat. no. 17; for the terracotta version in the Louvre, see *Louvre* 1994, p. 98; and *Sergel* 1990, p. 227, no. 237 for the terracotta version in the Nationalmuseum, Stockholm. In her 1981 lecture on Sergel, Elvy Setterqvist made comparisons with the inscription on the present piece and the seal impression – a helmet motif – on Sergel's will beneath his signature (I am grateful to Julius Bryant for this information).

Francis Bird

(b. London 1667 – d. London 1730/1)

At the age of eleven, Bird was sent to the Netherlands to train in the studio of a sculptor called Cozins, who is otherwise unknown. He later travelled to Rome, returning to England around 1689 to work in the studios of Grinling Gibbons [q.v.] and Caius Gabriel Cibber [q.v.]. Bird returned to Rome some years later, where he worked in the studio of Pierre Legros (1629–1714). On his return to England in about 1700, Bird was engaged in work on the decoration of St Paul's Cathedral. He was also responsible for a number of the funerary monuments in Westminster Abbey: that to Dr Busby (d. 1695) was considered by Whinney to be the 'finest monument of the period in Westminster Abbey'.

Gunnis 1968, pp. 53–5; Rendel 1972; Whinney 1988, pp. 150–6; Thieme-Becker, 4. p. 49; TDA 4, p. 79 [Physick].

76: George I **(b. 1660; r.1714–1727)**

about 1725
Attributed to Francis Bird
Terracotta
h. 25.8 cm.
A.31–1984

Purchased from Cyril Humphris, 23 Old Bond Street, London in 1984 for £10,000.

There is a hole in the back of the head.

Shortly after its acquisition, this bust was noted by Anthony Radcliffe to be 'almost certainly by Francis Bird'. Analogies may be made with two monuments by Bird in particular: that to Sidney, 1st Earl of Godolphin (1645–1712) in Westminster Abbey, and William Russell, 1st Duke of Bedford (1613–1700) in St Michael's Church, Chenies, Buckinghamshire. In both instances the sitter wears a lace cravat, together with an identical Order of the Garter hanging from a chain of rosettes and ribbons.

Although it has been suggested that the size of the bust may indicate it was used as a model for a ceramic version (departmental records), this seems unlikely, as neither pottery nor porcelain figures were made in England until the 1740s. More probably the present piece was a model used to produce a wax from which a bronze version could have been executed (information kindly supplied by Robin Hildyard).

PETER BOSSI

(active Dublin 1785 – 1798; d. before 1815)

Bossi worked in Dublin from 1785 to 1798, where he is recorded in the trade directories as an 'inlayer in Marble and Stucco worker', from premises at 22, later 38, Fleet Street. Malcolm Baker has suggested that he may have been a member of the Italian family of stuccoists of the 17th and 18th centuries, who were active in Germany in the eighteenth century.

Thieme-Becker, 4, pp. 404–5; TDA, 4, p. 470 [Schianchi] (for Benigno Bossi); Saur 1996, 13, p. 221.

77: Chimneypiece from an unidentified house in Dublin

about 1790–1800
Style of Peter Bossi
Marble inlaid with coloured composition
h. 140.3 cm.
A.1–1909

Described by Eric Maclagan [q.v.] as coming from 'an old family mansion in Dublin'. Given by J.A. Dolmage Esq. on behalf of his son, the late Cecil Goodrich Dolmage, Esq., L.L.D., D.C.L., in 1907, together with a further two chimneypieces from the same house, cat.nos. 231 and 232. The chimneypiece was installed in the Director's Office at the Museum for Sir Roy Strong in the mid 1980s.

The inlaid details are red, brown, green and blue; the moulded cornice is inlaid with vertical stripes in dark green.

This chimneypiece, together with cat.nos. 231 and 232, was acquired as an example of the work of the Italian emigré workers of the late eighteenth century working in Ireland at that time. A chimneypiece with pilasters decorated with similar garlands of ivy leaves from a Georgian house in Ely Place, off St Stephens Green, Dublin, was with Partridge Fine Arts, in October 1989 (information supplied by Malcolm Baker). It was said to be in the style of Peter Bossi in *A Picture Book of English Chimneypieces* published in 1928 (see *English Chimneypieces* 1928, pl. 20).

BIBLIOGRAPHY
Georgian Society 1909, p. 22 and pl. XC (I); *English Chimneypieces* 1928, pl. 20.

Edward Burch R.A.

(b. London about 1730; d. London 1814)

Burch was a gem engraver and sculptor who trained at the Royal Academy schools during 1769. He exhibited at the Royal Academy between 1771 and 1808, having been elected an Academician in 1771. Forrer noted, 'Burch's name appears on a medal of Dr William Hunter, the anatomist, 1774; at that time the artist was in the employment of the Medallist and Gem-engraver, [James] Tassie [1735–1799], for whom he executed Portrait-medallions in wax'. Seidmann records that Burch 'enjoyed great success and attracted wide patronage for more than two decades', although his career declined from 1788 onwards. From 1794 to 1812 he acted as Librarian at the Royal Academy. Other examples of his gems may be found in the British Museum (see Dalton 1915, p. 161, cat.nos. 1132 and 1133). Gertrud Seidmann is currently preparing a monograph on Burch.

Forrer I, p. 311; Gunnis 1968, pp. 69–70; TDA, 5, p. 187 [Seidmann].

78: Anatomical figure

after 1761
Ascribed to Edward Burch, after an original wax by Michael Henry Spang or Spong
Bronze
h. 25.3 cm.
A.18–1945

Purchased from Messrs Alfred Spero, 134 New Bond Street, London in 1945 for £85, under the terms of the John Webb Trust.

On acquisition this figure was thought to be Italian, possibly Florentine, and to date from the middle of the 16th century. Comparisons were made between the present bronze – noted on departmental records as 'an unusually fine example' – and other versions, including one in Berlin dated by Bode to the second half of the 16th century (inv.no. 1973) (Bode 1904, p. 23, no. 399, pl. XXVI). The attribution of the present piece to Edward Burch was first suggested by Martin Kemp, at the time of the exhibition *Dr William Hunter at the Royal Academy of Arts* held at the University of Glasgow in 1975 (see Kemp 1975, p. 15; *idem* 1983, p. 383). In describing the present piece Kemp has suggested that it is 'indistinguishable in all respects' from the statuette shown in Mason Chamberlin's painting of Dr William Hunter (1769) in the Royal Academy of Arts, and is identical in size to the wax model in the Hunterian Museum, University of Glasgow. He continued, 'This unbroken series of associations suggests that the bronzes were designed to provide durable and portable mementos of the full-scale écorché which William Hunter used for his learned instructions to the Academicians and students' (*idem* 1975, p. 15, fig. 7 for the Chamberlin painting).

This écorché figure from which the various versions appear to derive was originally modelled in wax by the Anglo-Danish sculptor Michael Henry Spang (or Spong) (d. 1762) after a plaster cast of the flayed body of a criminal made for Dr William Hunter (1718–1783). Spang exhibited the wax at the Society of Artists in 1761 (Graves 1907, p. 242, no. 162), and Martin Kemp has proposed that 'Burch may have been responsible for its subsequent production in bronze. He exhibited two casts 'from a wax model' at the Royal Academy in 1775, which if not the écorché, do at least provide evidence of his involvement with casting' (Kemp 1983, p. 383). A bronze 'Cast of an Anatomy figure, after Spang,' was awarded a premium at the Society of Arts in 1767 (Baker 1996 [Production], pp. 150–1).

The various versions known in museum collections are listed by Kemp; see Kemp 1975, pp. 15–17, and p. 28, n. 9; Price Amerson 1975, pp. 349–52, nos. 41–9. In addition two further versions of the present piece are in the Science Museum (inv.nos. 1981–1911 and 1991–128/621, the latter formerly part of the Hunterian Society Collection).

Another version, described as late 18th century, was sold at Sotheby's, London, 8 December 1988, lot 282. A larger écorché figure by Ludovico Cigoli (1559–1613) is also in the Museum's collections (inv.no. A.25–1956). A bronze medal by Edward Burch of 1774, with a portrait of William Hunter on the obverse and a group attending a surgical demonstration on the reverse, is likewise in the Museum's collections (inv.no. 113–1888).

A touring exhibition entitled *The Quick and the Dead* held at the Royal College of Art, London, Mead Gallery, University of Warwick, and Leeds City Art Gallery, Leeds, included comparable pieces (see *Quick and the Dead* 1997).

BIBLIOGRAPHY
Kemp 1975, pp. 15, 28, fig. 9; Price Amerson 1975, II, p. p. 351–2, cat.no. 47 (there said to be identical with the version in the Staatliche Museum, Berlin); *L'Écorché* 1977, p. 43, cat.no. 5, illus. on p. 141; Kemp 1983, p. 383; *Artist's Model* 1991, pp. 95–6, illus. on p. 96, pl. XXI on p. 36, cat.no. 90; Bryant 1991, p. 410, fig. 2 on p. 410; *L'âme au corps* 1993, p. 532, cat.no. 1:17.

EXHIBITED
L'Écorché, Museé des Beaux-Arts, Rouen, 15 January to 28 February 1977, cat.no. 5; *The Artist's Model*, University Art Gallery, Nottingham and Iveagh Bequest, London, 30 April to 31 August 1991, cat.no. 90; *L'âme au corps – arts et sciences 1793–1993*, Grand Palais, Paris, 19 October 1993 to 28 February 1994, cat.no. 1:17.

AGOSTINO CARLINI R.A.

(about 1718 – 1790)

Carlini was a native of Genoa, but the circumstances of his early training are unknown. He worked in The Hague from 1748 to about 1753, is first recorded in London in 1760, and spent the rest of his working life in England. In Holland he had been employed as a decorative wood-carver; in England his work was largely in marble, and included funerary monuments, a bust of George III, and decorative heads for Somerset House.

Smith 1828, pp. 202–3; Trusted 1992; idem 1993; Baarsen 1998.

79: Joshua Ward (1685–1761)

about 1761–4
Marble
h. 213 cm.
A.2–1991

Presented to the Royal Society for the Encouragement of Arts, Manufactures and Commerce (the Royal Society of Arts) by Ralph Ward (the great-nephew of Joshua Ward, and one of his executors) in 1793. Purchased from the Royal Society of Arts with the assistance of funds from the Phillips Bequest in 1991 for £250,000.

The thumb and fingers of the right hand are modern resin replacements.

The subject was a renowned quack-doctor, who manufactured, advertised, and sold patent medicines, known as "Ward's Drop and Pill". The present figure may have been intended as part of a monument to Ward to be erected in Westminster Abbey, but this plan was never brought to fruition, perhaps because the project was incomplete at Ward's death. A drawing showing how the statue might have been intended to be seen within a niche is in the British Museum (inv.no.1920–4–20–4). For a full discussion of the present piece, see Trusted 1992.

BIBLIOGRAPHY
Smith 1828, pp. 202–3; Gunnis 1968, p. 81; Davies 1979, p. 146; Whinney 1988, p. 269 and fig. 196; Williamson 1991, p. 880; Trusted 1992, pp. 776, 778–81, fig. 15 on p. 779; *idem* 1993; Williamson 1996 [Trusted], pp. 160–1.

ANDREW CARPENTER (ANDRIES CARPENTIÈRE)

(b. about 1677 – d. London 1737)

Carpenter is first recorded in London in 1702, and was probably a native of the Netherlands or France. He worked in marble, but produced a great number of garden statues in lead, including work for Wrest Park, Bedfordshire, and Canons, Middlesex, and had worked with John Nost the Elder [q.v.] as his principal assistant. During the 1720s and 1730s he executed several important church monuments. George Vertue mentioned Carpenter's use of lead: 'for many years in the latter part of his life at this house in the road to High park [Hyde Park], imployd his time & study to Cast Leaden figures. of all kinds he being the most estteemd then run into much imployment – but soon that was run down in the prices, by under working. that he had much ado to hold up his head at last. he was a gros heavy man allwayes. but age and cares brought him to his end. about July 1737'.

Vertue 1934, p. 83; Gunnis 1968, pp. 82–3; TDA, 5, p. 827 [Murdoch].

80: Meleager

1720–30
Painted lead on stone base
h. (figure) 161 cm. h. (base) 33 cm.
A.5–1985

The original location of this figure is unknown. Latterly in the collection of Prince Littler, Chestham Park, Henfield, Sussex and sold by Christie, Manson and Woods Ltd at the sale of the Properties of Mrs Nora Prince-Littler and the late Prince Littler, C.B.E., Chestham Park, Henfield, held on 18 and 19 April 1977. Included in the sale as lot 499 under 'Garden Sculpture and Ornaments' – it was formerly situated within the Rotunda – it was described as 'A lead figure of Actaeon standing with horn and with left arm extended, a hound at his feet . . . 18th century octagonal stone plinth'. In an annotated copy of the catalogue held in the National Art Library it is noted that this figure was sold for £2,800. Purchased by T. Crowther & Sons Ltd, whose application to export the figure in 1984 was subject to an objection; the figure was subsequently purchased by the Museum in 1985 for £16,500, with assistance from the National Art Collections Fund and the Phillips Bequest.

The figure was conserved in 1990 to reveal the remains of the original ochre-coloured paint.

Although this figure is generally thought to represent Meleager, it could portray Actaeon; both mythical figures were renowned huntsmen and represented with hunting dogs. Its octagonal base, and comparisons with analogous figures, such as those at Carshalton Park, Surrey, suggest it may have originally surmounted a gate-pier.

The attribution to Carpenter was suggested by Anthony Radcliffe, who noted comparisons between the present figure and recorded lead works by the sculptor produced for the Duke of Kent in 1730 at Wrest Park, Bedfordshire. The four groups of figures, representing *Diana and Actaeon*; *Venus, Adonis and Cupid*; *The Rape of the Sabines* and *Aeneas and Anchises*, contain elements analogous with the present piece. The dog in the Wrest Park group of *Venus, Adonis and Cupid* is closely similar to the dog in the present piece, and the drapery is comparable with that found on the Wrest Park figures (see Weaver 1972, figs. 265, 266, 267 on p. 168, and fig. 269 on p. 169). A price list sent by Carpenter to the Earl of Carlisle in 1723 (retained in the archives of Castle Howard, noted by Gunnis; see Gunnis 1968, p. 83), detailed the lead statuary offered by Carpenter, and included six feet high figures of *Meleager* and of *Adonis* which were priced at £20 and £18 respectively (departmental records, noted by Anthony Radcliffe).

THOMAS CARTER THE YOUNGER

(d. London? 1795)

Carter was one of a family of mason-sculptors; he was the nephew and son-in-law of Thomas Carter the Elder (d. 1756/7), and the nephew of Benjamin Carter [q.v.]. His workshop, based in Piccadilly, London, produced a large number of chimneypieces for great houses, but he also executed church monuments, such as that to Chaloner Chute (see below).

Gunnis 1958, p. 334; idem 1968, pp. 85–6.

81: Chaloner Chute (about 1595–1659)

about 1775
Attributed to Thomas Carter the Younger
Terracotta
h. 6.4 cm.
A.8–1911

Given by Mr H. Avray Tipping, Mathern Palace, Chepstow, together with its leather case, in 1911. The case (probably nineteenth century) no longer survives.

Chaloner Chute was Speaker of the House of Commons.

The attribution of the present piece – now identified as a model for the marble monument to Chaloner Chute at the Vyne, Hampshire – has been subject to revision since its acquisition in 1911. The monument (and consequently this model) was originally ascribed to Roubiliac and the subject was thought to represent William Shakespeare. It was later ascribed to Thomas Banks, and was published as such by Bell in the description of the Vyne Monument in his monograph on the sculptor. Bell quoted Chaloner Chute (a descendant of the original subject) in his *History of the Vyne* of 1888, in which the Tomb Chamber was described as 'containing the fine marble monument, by Banks, of Chaloner Chute, recumbent in his Speaker's robes' (Bell 1938, pp. 46–7; Chute 1888, p. 23). The attribution of the Chute monument to Banks was given in the *Dictionary of National Biography* in the entry for Chute (*DNB* 1973, IV, p. 349). The monument has also been ascribed to John Bacon the Elder [q.v.] (see below).

On acquisition Eric Maclagan [q.v.] mentioned the attribution to Roubiliac, though he noted that a recumbent figure of Shakespeare was not cited by Sainte Croix in his 1882 monograph on the sculptor. The relationship with the present model and the monument to Chaloner Chute at the Vyne, Hampshire, was noted by Maclagan in May 1913; it had been identified by H. Clifford Smith, although it was then mistakenly thought to be by Thomas Banks [q.v.]. In a letter to the *Burlington Magazine* in January 1940, Katharine Esdaile [q.v.] suggested as the sculptor for the Vyne monument, and therefore of the present piece, John Bacon the Elder [q.v.], quoting a reference to the chapel at the Vyne in the *Topographer* of 1789 which recorded: 'To the side of this chapel, the late Mr. John Chute began to add a smaller one, for the purpose of erecting in it an altar-tomb of marble, to the memory of his ancestor, the Speaker. The present possessor has gone on with this design, which is not yet finished. However the altar-tomb is placed there, and on it, Recumbent, the figure of the Speaker in his robes, by Bacon from his picture by Vandyke, preserved here' (see Esdaile 1940 [Vyne]; citing *Topographer* 1789, pp. 59–60).

The attribution to Thomas Carter the Younger was made by Gunnis in 1952, following his examination of a bill for the Vyne monument presented by Thomas Carter to Thomas Chute, in which payments to Carter were recorded; he was paid in full in 1785 for the monument begun in 1775. The re-evaluation of the bill and subsequent re-attribution of the Vyne monument to Carter was published by Sir Charles L. Chute in *Country Life* in May 1954. Gunnis himself published an article in the *Architectural Review* in 1958, in which the discovery of the Thomas Carter bill and subsequent identification of the sculptor as Thomas Carter was made. In his article, Gunnis stated that the erroneous attribution of the monument to John Bacon the Elder made in the *Topographer* of 1789, recounting Sir Samuel Egerton Brydges's visit to the Vyne was puzzling; he wrote, 'It is difficult to understand how the mistake arose, considering that Sir Samuel visited the Vyne frequently . . . Carter certainly employed assistants, but I have found no mention of Bacon (of whom several lines were written shortly after his death) working for Carter. Moreover, when the Chute monument was ordered Bacon was too well known and too well established to work for another' (Gunnis 1958).

For an illustration of the monument itself see Chute 1954; Whinney 1988, fig. 184 on p. 253.

BIBLIOGRAPHY

Review 1911, p. 3; Bell 1938, p. 46; Esdaile 1940 [Vyne]; Chute 1954; Gunnis 1968, p. 86; *Grand Design* 1997, pp. 305–6, cat.no. 136, illus. on p. 305; Bowdler 2002.

EXHIBITED

Photographs of Monuments, Council for the Care of Churches, Church of All Hallows on the Wall, February 1964; *A Grand Design. The Art of the Victoria and Albert Museum*, travelling exhibition, Baltimore Museum of Art, Boston Museum of Fine Art, Toronto Royal Ontario Museum, Houston, The Museum of Fine Art, San Francisco, Fine Arts Museums and Victoria and Albert Museum, 12 October 1997 to 16 January 2000, cat.no. 136; *Precious*, Millennium Gallery, Sheffield, 5 April to 24 June 2001.

Sir William Chambers

(b. Göteborg 1723 – d. London 1796)

Chambers was one of the chief exponents of English Palladianism, and along with Robert Adam [q.v.], one of the most important British architects of the second half of the eighteenth century. His father was a Scottish merchant working in Sweden. After returning to England and being educated at Ripon, Yorkshire, Chambers later returned to Sweden at the age of sixteen, and began training as a merchant. Between 1740–69 he travelled to the Far East, and it was during these voyages that he began his studies in civil architecture. In 1749 Chambers began his professional education, attending J.F. Blondel's École des Arts in Paris. In 1750 he travelled to Italy, where he remained for five years. He moved to London in 1755, and in 1756, following his designs for the mausoleum for Frederick, Prince of Wales, at Kew, he was appointed tutor of architecture to George, Prince of Wales (later George III). In 1760 his standing and reputation was such that he was appointed joint architect – with Robert Adam – to the Office of Works. He was a founding member of the Royal Academy of Arts, and its first Treasurer.

Thieme-Becker, 6, pp. 345–7; Colvin 1995, pp. 236–42; Chambers 1996; TDA, 6, pp. 410–13 [Harris].

82: Chimneypiece from the Great Drawing Room, Gower House, Whitehall

about 1775
Designed by Sir William Chambers; probably carved by Joseph Wilton [q.v.]
Marble
h. 190 cm.
A.1–1998

Commissioned by Granville Leveson Gower, 2nd Earl Gower (1721–1803) for the Great Drawing Room at Gower House, Whitehall, London, designed by Chambers: Gower House was begun in 1765. Around 1807 Gower House was sold to Robert Smith, 1st Baron Carrington (1752–1838), and the present piece was removed by Charles Robert Wynn-Carrington, 1st Earl Carrington (1843–1928), when the house was demolished in 1886. It was taken to Daws Hill, High Wycombe, Buckinghamshire, around 1895 where it remained until its sale in 1995. Daws Hill was acquired by Wycombe Abbey School in 1929, who sold the chimneypiece at Sotheby's, London sale held on 15 November 1995, lot 60. Purchased from the sale by Christopher Gibbs Ltd for £76,727.50. Purchased by the Museum from Christopher Gibbs in 1998 for £125,000 with the assistance of the National Art Collections Fund and the National Heritage Memorial Fund.

Joseph Wilton – a friend of Chambers – is likely to have been the sculptor of the present piece. Gunnis records a number of instances when Chambers supplied the design from which Wilton worked, including a chimneypiece for the drawing room of the Duchess of Marlborough at Blenheim in 1772 (see Gunnis 1968, pp. 434–5; see also *Chambers* 1996 [Coutu] for a discussion of the working relationship between Chambers and Wilton).

A design for the wall on which the chimneypiece was installed is now in Sir John Soane's Museum, London (see *Chambers* 1996 [Snodin], fig. 206 on p. 143); photographs recording the chimneypiece in the Great Drawing Room at Gower House before its demolition are in the Department of Prints, Drawings and Paintings, inv.nos. 518–1886 and 520–1886.

Bibliography
Chambers 1996 [Snodin], fig. 207 on p. 144; Snodin 1998; for further bibliographical references see the comprehensive entry in the Sotheby's sale catalogue cited above; Williamson 1999, p. 787, fig. XV; Snodin and Styles 2001, fig. 26 on p. 197.

Sir Henry Cheere Bt.

(b. London 1703 – d. London 1781)

Cheere began his career as an apprentice mason and in about 1728 worked with Henry Scheemakers (d. 1748) on a monument to the Duke of Ancaster. Murdoch notes that he had set up in his own studio by 1726 near St Margaret's, Westminster: Gunnis recorded that he worked in a variety of materials 'marble, bronze, stone and lead'. He produced allegorical statues of Law, Physic *and* Poetry *for Queen's College, Oxford. Cheere also produced chimneypieces. Murdoch comments, 'He specialised in the production of decorative sculpture and provided chimneypieces for the Court Room, Goldsmiths' Hall, London (1735); Ditchley, Oxon (1738–41); Longford Castle, Wilts (1741–2); and Picton Castle, Dyfed [now Pembrokeshire] (1752)'. Gunnis noted, 'The rococo details of Cheere's monuments are often very similar to those of his chimneypieces, and they must have been admired in their day'.*

Webb 1958 [I and II]; Gunnis 1968, pp. 97–9; Baker 1986 (Cheere); Thieme-Becker, 6, p. 448; TDA, 6, p. 528 [Murdoch]; Craske 2000.

83: George Pitt M.P., of Stratfield Saye, Hampshire
(?1663–1735)

about 1738–41
Attributed to Sir Henry Cheere
Marble
h. 57.5 cm.
A.7–1981

Inscribed on the socle at the back: PRIOR

In the possession of W. Moreton Pitt who inherited Encombe House, Dorset, the home of George Pitt, together with its contents. At an unrecorded date sold to the dealer Mr Street of Brewer Street for £20. In the possession of Mr Webb, probably a Bond Street dealer, and purchased from him for £60 by the Duke of Buckingham. Included in the Stowe sale of 1848 (6th day's sale, held on 21 August 1848, lot no. 751), there described as 'A bust of Prior – an exquisite work of Roubiliac, on a square pedestal of different marbles'. Purchased by Sir Robert Peel for £136 10s. It is possible that Peel added the current pedestal, which does not appear to be original: it does not correspond with the description in the Stowe catalogue of a plinth of 'different marbles'. Peel may have changed the pedestal so that the bust would form a pair with his Roubiliac bust of Alexander Pope. Included in the Peel Heirlooms sale, held at Robinson and Fisher, 10 May 1900, lot 133, and purchased by Duveen for 550 guineas. The bust was published as being in a private collection by Katharine Esdaile in her 1928 monograph on Roubiliac. The bust was unlocated until 1981, when it was purchased in Edinburgh by Mr John Pinkerton. Purchased by the Museum from John Pinkerton in 1981 for £25,000 (departmental records).

Though listed in the 1848 Stowe catalogue as being the work of Roubiliac, doubts as to its authorship were raised at this early date. In H. Forster's catalogue of the sale, he described the bust as 'certainly one of the finest and most life-size marbles ever executed, though doubts have been expressed as to whether it is really the work of the great master whose name appears in the catalogue. When brought forward, the attention of everyone present was immediately directed to it: the biddings commenced with great spirit, and were carried on by several parties until after the price had exceeded 100 guineas . . . Sir Robert Peel will no doubt prize its possession very highly, the right honourable baronet's collection already containing a companion bust of Pope, which originally belonged to Mr. Bindley, of the Stamp Office, and subsequently to Mr. Watson Taylor ' (Forster 1848, p. 48, illus. opp. p. 174).

The 1848 Forster catalogue also illustrates the immense interest focused on the ownership of the bust. A single sheet inserted into one of the copies of the catalogue held in the National Art Library (Pressmark 23.S), has an anonymous lengthy printed ode entitled, 'Lines written on the Bust of Prior, by Roubilliac [sic], which was recently purchased by Sir R —— P ——, at Stowe. For one hundred and thirty guineas, after having refused to give fifty pounds for it, to a dealer' (I am grateful to Malcolm Baker for this reference). The ode begins:

'Five Years have passed since Francis Street,
With Bust of Prior chanced to meet,
Chef d'ouvre of Roubilliac,
Sans flaw, *sans* chip, *sans* stain, or crack;
On pedestal antique, it stood,
And all, *save one*, pronounced it good'.

The present bust was first published by Katharine Esdaile in her monograph on Roubiliac as a portrait of Matthew Prior (1664–1721), and it was there attributed to Roubiliac. Esdaile commented on its provenance, 'It once belonged to Nollekens [there is in fact no documentary or other evidence for Nollekens's ownership of the bust], was then at Stowe, whence it was bought by Sir Robert Peel for 130 guineas in 1848, and is now in a private collection'. Esdaile suggested a link between the bust with a 'little lead statuette from the Ionides Collection in the possession of Mr W.L. Phillips' (Esdaile 1928, p. 52). This statuette – in fact bronze – acquired by the Museum in 1931, has similarly been identified as George Pitt; see entry for cat.no. 84.

Shortly before its acquisition in 1981, the sitter was identified as George Pitt, M.P. by Malcolm Baker, who compared the present bust with another version on the monument to George Pitt in the parish church of St Michael, at Stinsford, Dorset. Baker suggested that payments made to Henry Cheere from the Pitt family account at Hoare's Bank in 1738, 1739 and 1741, related to the present bust and the Stinsford monument, amongst other items. He noted a description of the Stinsford bust in a contemporary topographical publication: J. Hutchins's 1774 edition of *History and Antiquities of the County of Dorset* (p. 463), stated that the Stinsford monument incorporated 'a neat bust of Mr Pitt in white marble executed to the life'. In later editions, including that for 1792, the description was expanded: 'At the west end of the north aisle is a very handsome cenotaph, or honorary monument, for the late Mr Pitt. It is made of various-coloured marble, adorned with a pediment, columns, and urns. Above is a neat bust of Mr. Pitt in white marble, executed from a model made after his death from recollection by his son John Pitt, esq.' (Hutchins 1863, p. 567). John Pitt (c. 1706–1787) was an amateur architect (Colvin 1995, pp. 757–8); he evidently collaborated with the sculptor on the commission. See also Baker 1999, pp. 529–30, and fig. 2 on pl. 529 for the Stinsford bust.

BIBLIOGRAPHY

Esdaile 1928, p. 52, pl. XI; *Rococo* 1984, p. 288, cat.no. S1; *Louvre* 1992, p. 72, fig. 21a, where it is compared with a bust of a man by John Nost the Younger (d. 1780) (inv.no. R.F. 4232); Baker 2000 [Figured in Marble], p. 103; Baker forthcoming [Pitt].

EXHIBITED

Rococo. Art and Design in Hogarth's England, Victoria and Albert Museum, London, 16 May to 30 September 1984, cat.no. S1; *Grosvenor House Antiques Fair*, Grosvenor House Hotel, London, 12 June to 21 June 1997.

84: George Pitt, M.P., of Stratfield Saye, Hampshire
(?1663–1735)

about 1738–41
Perhaps by Sir Henry Cheere or John Cheere [q.v.]
Lead
h. 54 cm.
A.30–1931

Property of Miss Ionides, sold at Sotheby's, London, 24 July 1931 lot 55, incorrectly described as 'A plaster figure of Pope, standing with book case behind, bronzed, 22 in.'. Purchased from the sale by 'Mooney' for £5 10s, presumably on behalf of Dr W.L. Hildburgh F.S.A. Given to the Museum by Dr Hildburgh in 1931.

The reference in Katharine Esdaile's 1928 monograph to 'the charming little lead statuette from the Ionides Collection in the possession of Mr W.L. Phillips', implies that prior to the sale at Sotheby's in 1931, the figure was with Messrs Phillips. Esdaile suggested that the statuette was closely related to the marble bust of Matthew Prior then in a private collection, and that the statuette was 'a lead cast from a lost terra-cotta by the younger sculptor' (see Esdaile 1928, pp. 52–3, and pl. XI). The marble bust referred to by Esdaile as being in a private collection was later acquired by the Museum in 1981; before its purchase the subject was identified as being that of George Pitt M.P., rather than Matthew Prior as had been previously assumed; see entry for cat.no. 83. Given the marble bust's attribution to Cheere, the lead statuette may be by the same sculptor, or perhaps more likely his brother John, who specialised in lead sculpture.

BIBLIOGRAPHY

Esdaile 1928, pp. 52–3, pl. XII opp. p. 55; *Review* 1931, p. 4, pl. 3(d).

85: Mourning figure

about 1739
By Sir Henry Cheere; from a design by Thomas Archer
Terracotta
h. 45.5cm
A.11–1934

Purchased by H.D. Molesworth [q.v.] on behalf of Dr W.L. Hildburgh F.S.A. from Charlesworth, J.F. da C. Andrade, Works of Art, 8 Avery Row, Brook Street, London on 16 May 1934 for £4, and immediately given by Dr Hildburgh to the Museum. H.D. Molesworth noted, 'When I found the object in Mr Andrade's shop he said that he thought it had come, through another dealer, from a mixed sale and had no other provenance' (Museum records).

On acquisition the figure was attributed to Joseph Nollekens [q.v.] on the basis of comments made by Katharine Esdaile [q.v.], who suggested it was possibly the model for the tomb of Lieut. General Bennet Noel, at Exton. However, Molesworth noted in 1934, 'This figure is undoubtedly very close but not, I feel, taken from this terracotta' (Museum records).

Annotations on the records for this object show that in June 1953 the model was re-evaluated and ascribed to Peter Scheemakers [q.v.]. It was thought to represent Eleanor Archer (d. 1703), first wife of the architect Thomas Archer (c. 1668–1743), and to have been a model for part of the Thomas Archer monument erected in Hale Church, Hampshire in 1739. Marcus Whiffen suggested the monument was probably designed by Archer himself (Whiffen 1950, p. 41). What was thought to be a related drawing by Scheemakers in Sir John Soane's Museum was later identified by Rupert Gunnis as a preparatory sketch by Scheemakers for another monument, that to Sir Christopher Powell (d. 1742) at Boughton Monchelsea, Kent (*Wren Society* 1940, pl. XLVI; Whiffen 1950, p. 41). However, the similarity in design of the Archer and Powell monuments, together with the mourning figures on other Scheemakers monuments, including that to Sir Hugo Chamberlen in Westminster Abbey (1731) and the Shelburne monument at High Wycombe (1754), seemed to support the attribution to Scheemakers.

Documentary evidence which came to light in 1988 however suggests the monument was executed by Henry Cheere: a payment of £100 was made to Cheere from Thomas Archer's bank account at Hoare's Bank on 19 January 1739 (information supplied by Ingrid Roscoe), although the evidence cited above suggests that Archer himself was responsible for the design of the monument. The figures on the monument are now considered to be allegorical, rather than representing Archer's two wives as previously thought. The pendant figure on the monument holding a skull is based on an engraving by Marcantonio Raimondi (about 1470/82–1527/34) (see Baker 1990, p. 27; fig. 1 on p. 15 for the monument).

A terracotta model of an *Allegorical figure* or *Tomb figure* of about 1740, originally attributed to Joseph Nollekens [q.v.], and possibly related to the present piece is in the Museum of Fine Arts, Boston, inv.no. 44.604. In 1984 Malcolm Baker had suggested an attribution to Peter Scheemakers of the Boston terracotta, making comparisons with the present piece (departmental records). I am grateful to Alexandra B. Huff for supplying information on the Boston figure.

BIBLIOGRAPHY

Review 1934, p. 5, pl. 4C; Williamson 1996, p. 19 and fig. 10 on p. 21; Baker 2000 [Figured in Marble], n. 9 on p. 176.

EXHIBITED

Exhibition of photographs of monumental sculpture, organised by the Council for the Care of Churches, Church of All Hallows on the Wall, 25 February to 20 March 1964.

86: William Augustus, Duke of Cumberland (1721–1765)

about 1746–7
Lead
h. (incl. socle) 66 cm.
A.12–1947

Inscribed on the socle at the front: REPUBLICA SERVATA/MDCCXLVI
Translation: In the service of the Republic/1746

Previously at Lowther Castle, near Penrith, Cumberland from an unrecorded date until its purchase by Cooper & Adams, 41 James Street, London, from the Castle sale in 1947. Noted in departmental records to have been erroneously catalogued as George III, the bust may possibly be identified as that included in the classical and other sculptures auctioned on the third day's sale held on 30 April 1947: lot 2379 was a 'bronzed compo bust George III, 26 in. high', sold together with a marble model of a hand; the height of 26 inches matches the height of the present piece with its socle. Purchased by the Museum from Cooper & Adams in 1947 for £50.

This bust commemorates the victory of the royal troops led by the Duke of Cumberland over the Highlanders at the Battle of Culloden on 16 April 1746. It has been suggested that the present bust represents a man older than twenty-five, the age of the Duke of Cumberland in 1746. However, comparisons with contemporary commemorative medals show Cumberland with similar features (see *Medallic Illustrations*, pls. CLXVII and CLXVIII).

In 1971 Whinney catalogued this bust as anonymous, 'Though it has some affinity to works by John Cheere, it would be rash to suggest that he was the sculptor' (Whinney 1971, p. 94). The present attribution came about in 1976 with correspondence between Anthony Radcliffe and General R.H. Whitworth concerning an identical bust at Belton House, Lincolnshire. General Whitworth wrote, 'The bust is exactly similar to a lead one belonging to Lord Brownlow at Belton and his is certainly by Sir Henry Cheere ... In the Cust family records is written "A leaden bust of William, Duke of Cumberland, the victor at Culloden executed by Cheere, is still at Belton House. Sir John Cust wrote from Marlborough Street to Lord Tyrconnel on November 7th 1747 and says he had paid Cheere the statuary £9 9 0, due by his uncle, for the Duke's bust ... This seems conclusive that it was executed by Cheere soon after Culloden. Mr Skipman at Belton House gave me this information from the family records' (letter 2 February 1976). Anthony Radcliffe noted that although the particular Cheere responsible for the bust is not specified, it is likely to have been produced by Henry Cheere, 'since John is not known as a portrait sculptor, and it was Henry who was to execute in 1770 the lead equestrian statue of the Duke for Cavendish Square. Furthermore, Henry Cheere executed in 1754 the monument to Viscount Tyrconnell in Belton Church. It is not impossible, however, that the bust was cast in the yard of John Cheere' (departmental records). However more recently Moira Fulton has pointed out that John Cheere did on occasion execute portrait busts, for example a gilt lead bust of the Duke of Argyll in 1743, on display at Blair Castle; Cheere charged 7 guineas for it, plus 2 guineas for gold bronzing it (Blair Castle Charter Room, Bundle 55). The similarity in price suggests that possibly John Cheere modelled the present piece (personal communication from Moira Fulton, February 2002). John Cheere also probably collaborated with his brother Henry to make the lead equestrian statue of the Duke of Cumberland in Cavendish Square (Webb 1958, p. 278). (We are grateful to Moira Fulton for her comments on this).

A reduced lead version of the bust was with the dealer Alfred Spero in October 1952 (noted by Terence Hodgkinson [q.v.] in departmental records). A small lead bust of the same subject attributed to Cheere (h. 21 cm), was exhibited at Trinity Fine Arts, 31 May to 20 June 1990, no. 19, and may be identical to that noted by Hodgkinson as being with Spero in 1952.

BIBLIOGRAPHY
Whinney 1971, p. 94, cat.no. 28, illus. on p. 95; Kerslake 1977 (I), p. 69.

EXHIBITED
George III. Bicentennial Exhibition, Yorktown Victory Center, Virginia, USA, April 1977 to 31 March 1978.

87: Dr William Henry Salmon of Holcombe, Somerset (d.1773)

about 1750
Probably after a model by Sir Henry Cheere; cast perhaps by John Cheere
Lead
h. (incl. socle) 70.8 cm.
A.19–1921

Purchased together with its pendant, cat.no. 88 from the Rev. J.D.C. Wickham, 8 Lansdown Place East, Bath in 1921 for £170. Rev. Wickham was a descendant of the sitter.

On arrival in the Museum this bust, like its pair, was covered with a later layer of white paint, which was removed.

On acquisition this bust and its pendant (cat. no. 88) were identified as Dr Salmon and his wife Mary respectively; further information on the identity of the sitters was supplied by A. Vivian Neal, who wrote in 1932, 'As you doubtless know they were portraits of Dr. William Henry Salmon who bought the manor of

Holcombe, Somerset in 1734, and his wife Mary (Tooker) of Norton Hall, Somerset. There was a curious tradition that a member of the Salmon family (I think circa 1790) decided to destroy his family portraits. The paintings he burnt, and he had arranged that these busts should be taken down to Weymouth and sunk in the channel, but died before his intention was carried out' (departmental records).

Prior to the acquisition of this bust and its pendant Eric Maclagan [q.v.] noted, 'They are admirable examples of this peculiarly English style of sculpture . . . This bust has been ascribed to Roubiliac, but, it appears, without any very good authority. They are in any case fine specimens of portrait sculpture of the first half of the 18th century'. The attribution of the busts to Roubiliac made by Katharine Esdaile in her monograph of 1928, and followed by Margaret Whinney in 1971, has recently been re-assessed. Malcolm Baker has suggested that the busts are probably by Sir Henry Cheere rather than Roubiliac, noting that the socles on the busts resemble one found on a bust by Cheere at Belton (departmental records) although Moira Fulton has pointed out that John Cheere's busts have similar socles (personal communication, February 2002). John Cheere, brother of Henry Cheere, was an experienced lead caster and may have executed this bust and its pendant, cat.no. 88.

Bibliography

Review 1925, pp. 10–11, fig. 9 on p. 10; Esdaile 1928, p. 93, n. 2; *Age of Rococo* 1958, p. 179, cat.no. 489; Whinney 1971, p. 88, no. 25, illus. on p. 89.

Exhibited

The Age of Rococo: Art and Culture of the Eighteenth Century, Residenzmuseum, Council of Europe, Munich, 15 June to 15 September 1958, cat.no. 489.

88: Mary Salmon (dates unknown)

about 1750
Probably after a model by Sir Henry Cheere; cast perhaps by John Cheere
Lead
h. (incl. socle) 73 cm.
A.20–1921

Purchased together with cat.no. 87 from the Rev. J.D.C. Wickham, 8 Lansdown Place East, Bath in 1921 for £170.

See entry for cat.no. 87.

Bibliography

Review 1925, pp. 10–11, fig. 10 on p. 11; Esdaile 1928, p. 93, n. 2; *Age of Rococo* 1958, p. 179, cat.no. 490; Whinney 1971, p. 90, no. 26, illus. on p. 91.

Exhibited

The Age of Rococo: Art and Culture of the Eighteenth Century, Residenzmuseum, Council of Europe, Munich, 15 June to 15 September 1958, cat.no. 490.

John Cheere

(b. London 1709 – d. London 1787)

John Cheere, the younger brother of the sculptor Sir Henry Cheere [q.v.], was apprenticed to a haberdasher for a period of seven years from 1725, but later joined his brother's studio. The younger Cheere is most noted for the production of lead figures, which he executed at this own studio at Hyde Park Corner from 1737. Cheere seems to have taken over the yard previously occupied by the Nost family. He also produced plaster figures and busts of eminent contemporaries, including those made for the Turner family of Kirkleatham.

Phillips 1964, pp. 76–7; Gunnis 1968, pp. 99–100; Cheere 1974; Kenworthy-Browne 1974; Clifford 1992; Baker 1995 [Roubiliac and Cheere]; TDA, 6, p. 528 [Murdoch].

89: Edmund Spenser (?1552–1599)

about 1749
Perhaps by John Cheere
Lead
h. 48.5 cm.
A.3–1955

Purchased by Belham (presumably on behalf of Dr W.L. Hildburgh F.S.A.) for £50 together with cat.no. 90 from the sale held at Sotheby's, London, on 29 May 1953, lot no. 3, there unattributed and incorrectly identified as Shakespeare and Milton. On loan to the Museum from Dr Hildburgh from 25 June 1953 (ex-loan no. 5242). Given by Dr Hildburgh in 1955.

A plaster version is in the Castle Museum, York, inscribed 'Cheere Ft 1749' and 'Spencer' (see *Cheere* 1974, cat.no. 52). See also entry for cat.no. 90.

This is one of a series of statuettes of historical figures or Worthies produced in lead by John Cheere. Ten such subjects, represented in the bronzed plasters formerly at Kirkleatham Hall, Yorkshire, and now owned by the Castle Museum, York (on permanent loan to York City Art Gallery), include Spenser, Homer, Rubens, Van Dyck, Pope, Newton, Inigo Jones, Locke, Milton and Shakespeare. Friedman noted: 'The bronzed plasters, with their strong literary associations, were intended for libraries, either perched on book-cases . . . or crowning presses, always placed high so as to enhance the illusion of real bronze' (Friedman 1973, p. 924). Though statuettes of Rubens, Van Dyck and Inigo Jones are inscribed 'Cheere ft 1749', they are in fact identical with models known to have been executed by John Michael Rysbrack [q.v.]; see entries for cat.nos. 197 and 198. The fact that these statuettes are inscribed 'Cheere' may only signify that he obtained models or moulds, from which he produced plaster versions, and it is therefore also possible that the remaining signed 'Cheere' plasters were also based on models by others. In his posthumous sale there was a collection of Rysbrack terracottas (an extract from the sale catalogue is in the Esdaile Papers, I, p. 194, at the Henry Moore Institute in Leeds. The sale catalogue itself is untraced. We are grateful to Moira Fulton for this reference). Friedman however proposed that the statuettes of Milton, Spenser and Pope are likely to be Cheere's original compositions; he suggested that the present piece, together with that of Pope, cat.no. 90 were 'almost certainly cast by Cheere' (Friedman 1973, p. 925). A related lead figure of John Locke by Cheere was included in the sale at Sotheby's, London, 9 November 1999, lot 65.

The influence of Peter Scheemakers's Shakespeare memorial in Westminster Abbey was such that the pose seen here 'became almost de rigueur for British poets. Pope too took on a similar pose in statuettes produced by the Cheere workshop, and also Spenser' (*Shakespeare* 1964, p. 24).

Bibliography

Shakespeare 1964, p. 24, and pl. 10(e) on p. 25; Friedman 1973, p. 925; *Cheere* 1974, cat.no. 53.

Exhibited

O Sweet Mr. Shakespeare I'll have his picture. The changing image of Shakespeare's person, 1600–1800, National Portrait Gallery, 18 April to 30 June 1964; *The Man at Hyde Park Corner: Sculpture by John Cheere 1709–1786*, Temple Newsam, Leeds, 15 May to 15 June 1974 and Marble Hill, Twickenham, 19 July to 8 September 1974, cat.no. 53.

90: Alexander Pope (1688–1744)

about 1749
Perhaps by John Cheere
Lead
h. 47 cm.
A.4–1955

Purchased by Belham (presumably on behalf of Dr W.L. Hildburgh F.S.A.) for £50, together with cat.no. 89, from the sale at Sotheby's, London on 29 May 1953, lot no. 3, where they were unattributed and incorrectly identified as Shakespeare and Milton. On loan to the Museum from Dr Hildburgh from 29 May 1953 (loan no. 5243). Given by Dr Hildburgh in 1955.

Together with cat.no. 89, this figure appears to be one of a series of historical portraits of Worthies produced by Cheere; see entry for cat.no. 89. Like the statuette of Spenser, Friedman suggests this lead version was 'almost certainly cast by John Cheere' (Friedman 1973, p. 925). A bronzed plaster version of the present piece inscribed 'Pope' and 'Cheere ft 1749' is owned by the Castle Museum, York, though currently at the York City Art Gallery (see *Cheere* 1974, cat.no. 63, pl. 10).

BIBLIOGRAPHY
Shakespeare 1964, p. 24, and pl. 10 (d); Friedman 1973, p. 925, n. 17; *Cheere* 1974, see cat.no. 63; Bassett and Fogelman 1997, illus. on p. 51.

EXHIBITED
O Sweet Mr. Shakespeare I'll have his picture. The changing image of Shakespeare's person, 1600–1800, National Portrait Gallery, London, 18 April to 30 June 1964.

91: Portrait of a man, perhaps William Hogarth (1697–1764)

about 1750
Perhaps by John Cheere
Lead
h. 75.5 cm.
A.62–1926

Previously lent to the Museum by Lieut. Col. G.B. Croft Lyons from 1913 to 1926 (ex-loan no. 728). Bequeathed to the Museum by Lieut. Col. Croft Lyons in 1926.

Eric Maclagan [q.v.] considered this 'an interesting English lead bust of Hogarth (style of Roubiliac)' when he saw it on exhibition at the Burlington Fine Arts Club during the winter of 1912 on loan from Lieut. Col. Croft Lyons.

On acquisition this bust was associated with the style of Roubiliac, and dated to the first half of the eighteenth century. Katharine Esdaile expressed doubts as to the identification of the sitter as Hogarth, whilst affirming her opinion 'that it is the work of Roubiliac' (Esdaile 1928, p. 51). The terracotta model for the bust of Hogarth in the National Portrait Gallery of about 1741 differs in certain details from the present bust, but may depict the same sitter (see *NPG* 1981, p. 280, no. 121). It was later suggested that the subject was copied from an oil sketch of John Gay (1685–1732) by Sir Godfrey Kneller (1646–1723). Terence Hodgkinson [q.v.] noted that the 'sketch and bust could represent the same man; but NPG doubt in fact the sketch represents Gay' (departmental records). The attribution and identity of the sitter in the sketch are still uncertain (*NPG* 1981, p. 704, no. 622).

In her annotated copy of Katharine Esdaile's monograph, Marjorie Webb suggested that the bust could be by John Cheere. More recently, Malcolm Baker has corroborated this attribution, considering the form of the bust and socle accord with the work of John Cheere. Cheere would certainly have known Hogarth, in his *Analysis of Beauty* Hogarth illustrated John Cheere's yard, and statues by him (we are grateful to Moira Fulton for comments on this).

BIBLIOGRAPHY
Burlington Fine Arts Club 1912, p. 32; *Review* 1926, p. 5, fig. 4 on p. 4; Esdaile 1928, pp. 50–1, n. 2; Brown 1934, p. 59; Edwards 1962, fig. 1 on p. 464 (where identified as Hogarth and by Roubiliac).

EXHIBITED
A Collection of Pictures Decorative Furniture and other Works of Art, Burlington Fine Arts Club, London, winter 1912.

William Collins

(b. 1721 – d. London 1793)

William Collins was apprenticed to Henry Cheere [q.v.], and was also a close neighbour and friend of John Cheere [q.v.] (advertisement in the London Evening Post *10–12 December 1751, British Library Burney 439b (we are grateful to Moira Fulton for this reference). Gunnis recorded that he 'was much employed as a modeller of bas-reliefs and tablets for chimneypieces. J.T. Smith [Nollekens and his Times, II, p. 243] describes these tablets as consisting of 'pastoral scenes which were understood by the most common observers, such, for instance, as a shepherd-boy eating his dinner under an old stump of a tree, with his dog begging before him; shepherds and shepherdesses seated upon a bank surrounded by their flocks; anglers, reapers, etc'. Collins was also commissioned to produce other decorative work, including medallions for Harewood House, Yorkshire. Collins was one of the original members of the Incorporated Society of Artists in Great Britain, founded in 1759, and showed works at the Society's exhibitions between 1760 and 1768.*

Gunnis 1968, p. 238; Thieme-Becker, 7, p. 238; TDA, 6, p. 528 [Murdoch].

92: Shepherd and shepherdess

about 1761
Attributed to William Collins
Marble on giallo marble backing, in a gilt wood frame
h. (excl. frame) 28.7 cm; l. (excl. frame) 52 cm
1152–1882

Bequeathed to the Museum by John Jones in 1882.

On acquisition this relief was considered to be the work of John Bacon the Elder [q.v.] and described as such in the *Catalogue of the Jones Collection*, published in 1924. In 1984 it was however suggested that it should be identified with one exhibited by Collins at the Society of Artists exhibition held at Spring Gardens in 1761 (no. 144), described as 'for a chimney-piece; a clown and country girl' (*Rococo* 1984, pp. 308–9, cat.no. S49; *Wedgwood* 1995, p. 131, no. F12).

A similar plaque is on a chimneypiece at Bretton Hall, near Wakefield, Yorkshire (unpublished), and others are in the Lady Lever Art Gallery (inv.nos. LL131, LL132 and LL133); see *Lady Lever* 1999, pp. 2–3. A closely related marble relief also acquired from the Jones collection, originally attributed to Joseph Nollekens [q.v.], has likewise recently been re-attributed to Sir

Henry Cheere or William Collins; see entry for cat.no. 93. Similarly carved reliefs depicting a ram and foliage – white marble on what appears to be a coloured marble backing – are on a chimneypiece carved by Cheere in the drawing-room of Picton Castle (see Girouard 1960, fig. 5 on p. 67). Cheere was commissioned to produce a number of chimneypieces for Picton Castle by Sir John Philipps, the 4th baronet of Picton, in connection with the redecoration of the castle. Girouard notes that letters were exchanged between Cheere and Sir John between August 1749 and July 1752 (*ibid.*, p. 69). Designs for chimneypieces by Sir Henry Cheere, including those at Picton Casle, Pembrokeshire and at Biddick Hall, Durham (formerly at Lambton Castle) are held in the Department of Prints, Drawings and Paintings (see Physick 1969, pp. 128–9, figs. 91 to 93). Several other designs for marble panels for chimneypieces are illustrated by Girouard (Girouard 1960, figs. 8, 9 and 10 on p. 69). Another related version was sold by Crowther's of Syon Lodge in 1987.

BIBLIOGRAPHY

Jones 1924, p. 101, no. 394, pl. 74; Powell 1984, fig. 6 on p. 102 and p. 103; *Rococo* 1984, pp. 307–8, cat.no. S49, illus p. 308; *Wedgwood* 1995 p. 131, cat.no. F12, illus. p. 131.

EXHIBITED

Rococo. Art and Design in Hogarth's England, Victoria and Albert Museum, London, 16 May to 30 September 1984, cat.no. S49; *The Genius of Wedgwood*, Victoria and Albert Museum, 1995, cat.no. F. 12.

93: Putti with a ram

about 1761
Attributed to William Collins
Marble in a gilt wood frame
h. (excl. frame) 28 cm. l. (excl. frame) 55 cm.
1176–1882

Bequeathed to the Museum by John Jones in 1882.

Though attributed to Joseph Nollekens [q.v.] on acquisition, and dated to the late eighteenth century, the present piece relates to another relief, depicting a *Shepherd and Shepherdess,* also acquired by the Museum through the Jones Bequest in 1882, and now similarly attributed to Sir Henry Cheere or William Collins; see entry for cat.no. 92. A closely comparable variant of the present piece (h. 30 cm. l. 54.5 cm.) described as *Putti Playing with Ram,* is in the Lady Lever Art Gallery, where it is attributed to Henry Cheere and said to have probably been intended as a decorative panel in a chimneypiece (see *Lady Lever* 1999, pp. 2–3, inv.no. LL132).

BIBLIOGRAPHY

Jones 1924, p. 100, no. 392, pl. 72.

Anne Seymour Damer

(b. Sundridge 1748 – d. London 1828)

Anne Seymour Damer (neé Conway) married the Hon. John Damer in 1767, but after his suicide in 1776 trained as a sculptor. Her cousin Horace Walpole bequeathed his estate Strawberry Hill to her in 1797; Whinney suggested that she 'might perhaps have been forgotten but for the devotion of Horace Walpole ... he doted on her delicacy and her talent, which he grossly-overpraised'. She was, perhaps due to this and her sex, considered by many an amateur. She exhibited at the Royal Academy from 1784 to 1818. Her self-portrait is in the British Museum. A painted portrait of Damer by Angelica Kauffman (1741–1807) of 1766 held at Chillington Hall, Staffs, depicts Damer in a traditional oval medallion, with sculptors' tools and a marble bust beneath.

Graves II, pp. 235–6; Noble 1908; Gunnis 1968, pp. 120–1; Thieme-Becker, 7, pp. 318–9; Petteys 1985, p. 178; Whinney 1988, pp. 319–20; TDA, 8, p. 481 [Eustace]; Yarrington 1997.

94: Mrs Freeman as Isis (or as a priestess of Isis)

signed; about 1789
Marble
h. 46 cm.
A.31–1931

Signed on the left side of the socle in Greek lettering: ΑΝΝΑΣ . /ΔΑΜ⩽Ρ/Η ΛΟΝΔΙΝΑΙΑ/ΣΠΟΙ⩽Ι
(Anna S. Damer. The Londoner made it).

Purchased by Messrs Spink from the collection of Thomas Hope (1769–1831), sold at Messrs Foster on Thursday 27 February 1930, lot 132. The annotated copy of the catalogue held in the National Art Library records it was sold for £4 10s to Spink, but also records the name of Balham. Presumably purchased from Messrs Spink by Dr W.L. Hildburgh F.S.A., and subsequently given to the Museum by him in 1931.

The relief on the socle is probably a sistrum, a musical instrument originally unique to Egypt and associated with the worship of Isis. The original owner of the bust Thomas Hope, owned and designed many pieces in the Egyptian style. The use of what is apparently Greek marble may have been considered appropriate for the subject.

Damer originally used the subject of *Isis* to accompany *Thamesis*, two masks carved as keystones for Henley Bridge opened in 1786. For the keystones see Tomalin 1975, p. 97. According to Noble, the mask representing Isis 'is said to be a portrait of Mrs Damer's intimate friend and neighbour, Miss Freeman of Fawley Court'. However it differs in some respects from the present bust. Although here cited as 'Miss' Freeman, the sitter is generally referred to as 'Mrs' Freeman; 'Mrs' may be a courtesy title, not necessarily indicating she was married. However, it is not certain whether the model used by Damer was Elizabeth Freeman, wife of Strickland Freeman, or one of his three sisters, who in the 1780s would have been in their twenties (I am grateful to Jane Bowen for this information). Damer also designed and executed the decorative woodwork for the Library of Fawley Court, near Henley, the home of the Freeman family (Noble 1908, pp. 80, 90–1).

This bust is similar in style to that of Damer's *Prince Henry Lubomirski as Bacchus* in the Ashmolean Museum, Oxford. Penny notes that the sistrum on the socle of the present piece is placed at an angle similar to that of the thrysus on the socle of the Prince Henry bust (*Ashmolean* 1992 [III], pp. 32–3).

BIBLIOGRAPHY
Graves II, p. 236; Noble 1908, p. 82; *Review* 1931, p. 53; *Royal Academy* 1951, p. 23, cat.no. 19; Gunnis 1968, p. 120; *Inspiration of Egypt* 1983, p. 23, cat.no. 32; *Orient* 1989, p. 426, cat.no. 1/79, illus. 510 on p. 429; *Ashmolean* 1992 [III], p. 33; Yarrington 1997, p. 38 and fig. 6.

EXHIBITED
Exhibited at the Royal Academy in 1789 (no. 613); *Royal Academy Winter Exhibition 1951–2. The First Hundred Years of the Royal Academy 1769–1868*, Royal Academy, London, cat.no. 19; *Europa und der Orient 800–1900*, Martin Gropius-Bau, Berlin, 28 May to 27 August 1989, cat.no. 1/79; *The Inspiration of Egypt*, Brighton and Manchester City Art Gallery, 7 May to 17 July 1983, cat.no. 32.

CLAUDE DAVID

(active London 1706 – 1722)

David came originally from Burgundy, but executed a number of works in marble in England from 1706 until 1722, including a design for a fountain in Cheapside. His signed monument to the Hon. Philip Carteret (d.1710) is in Westminster Abbey. He may be related to, or conceivably identical with the sculptor Claude David (b.1655) who was recorded in Spain, and who is said to have worked in ivory.

Gunnis 1968, p. 121; Estella Marcos 1984, pp. 110–111.

95: Vulcan, or possibly Prometheus chained to a rock

about 1710
Marble
l. 86.5 cm.
A.3–1981

Commissioned by Sir Andrew Fountaine (1676–1753) for Narford Hall, Norfolk, and included in the Narford inventory, dated 17 September 1738. Purchased by the Museum at the sale of the collection of Sir Andrew Fountaine, Narford Hall, Norfolk, held at Sotheby's, Parke, Bernet & Co, London on 11 December 1980, lot 221 (described as Prometheus). Purchased for £4460 using funds from the John Webb Trust.

The figure is closely related to David's statue of St Bartholomew in the Church of S. Maria di Carignano in Genoa (see Ceschi 1949, p. 50). Malcolm Baker has suggested that the present piece 'is one of the few free-standing sculptures of mythological figures to have been executed by a sculptor working in England in the first half of the 18th century' (Baker 1993, p. 15).

Though traditionally thought to represent *Prometheus* – it is noted as such in Blomefield's entry on Narford Hall in 1781 as, 'on the stair case. A piece of sculpture of Prometheus chained to, a rock, by Cavalier David' (Blomefield 1781, p. 64) – it has more recently been suggested that the figure represents Vulcan. Malcolm Baker has noted that this 'identification [is] seemingly confirmed by the presence of the anvil but leaving the spectator puzzling as to why the god is shown chained with his pincers unused beside him. An explanation is provided by an entry in the diary of Sir Matthew Decker who visited Narford in 1728 and saw the piece in its original setting. Placed on the landing halfway up the main stair, the figure was intended to be accompanied by a further figure of William III, and the sculptural ensemble was to be an allegorical representation of the avoidance of war as a result of William's arrival and The Glorious Revolution. Vulcan is accordingly represented as chained rather than fashioning the instruments of war' (Baker 1993, p. 15; see also Baker 2000 [Figured in Marble], pp. 30–1).

BIBLIOGRAPHY
Blomefield 1781, p. 64; Gunnis 1968, p. 121; Penny 1982; *Norfolk and the Grand Tour* 1985, p. 31; Parissien, Harris and Colvin 1987, p. 58; Whinney 1988, p. 449, n. 15; Baker 1993, pp. 14–15 (described as Vulcan), fig. 5 on p. 17 (described as Prometheus); Baker 2000 [Figured in Marble], pp. 30–1, fig. 16 on p. 29.

96: Neptune (previously known as Time)

about 1702
Attributed to Claude David
Marble
h. 177 cm.
A.3–1985

The possible provenance, identity and attribution of the figure were initially suggested by Katharine Esdaile; see below. The date and circumstances surrounding the arrival of this figure into the Museum is not recorded, but its existence on the premises is recorded by two official museum photographs which date from before 1872 (information supplied by Malcolm Baker). These early photographs show the figure when it was displayed outside in the Quadrangle, now the Pirelli Garden. Martin Durrant (Picture Library, Victoria and Albert Museum) has suggested that the photographs were probably taken between 1870–2. See also Introduction, fig. 5.

The figure is badly corroded from weathering. The facial features have been badly eroded; both the arms have been broken at the shoulder and some drapery over the right shoulder is now missing.

This figure was originally identified by Katharine Esdaile as *Time*, and attributed by her to Claude David, in the manuscript copy of the *Dictionary of Sculptors, English (or working in England, including modellers, artists who designed monuments, and others connected with the art of sculpture)*, compiled in the 1940s. Under her entry for Claude David, Esdaile noted: 'There is a marble baroque garden statue in the courtyard of the Victoria and Albert Museum representing Time, which came from the garden of Alford House, Kensington, whose head bears a singular resemblance to the head of Time on No. 3; can this be one of the missing statues from St James's. Its previous history is unknown' (Esdaile MS, David, p. 9; reference cited in Whinney 1988, p. 449, n. 15). [The No. 3 referred to is the signed monument by David to Philip Carateret (d. 1710) in Westminster Abbey (reference supplied by John Physick; see also Gunnis 1968, pl. VIII opp. p. 129 for the Carteret monument). John Physick has also noted that a source cited by Esdaile is incorrect: it is not Maitland's *London*, but Malcolm's *London Redivivum*. Published in 1807, the Park of St James is described by Malcolm: 'Part of it has been inclosed as a garden to the Palace, which contains nothing remarkable at present; but the Postman of 1702 informed the publick, "They set up some days ago, by order of her Majesty, in St James garden, two excellent figures of marble, made by Cavalier David, who was brought up by the famous Bernini, who was sent some time ago to the late King by Prince Vaudemont, to make the statues and figures, with which his Majesty intended to adorn the Royal Palaces. These are figures of a curious performance, and mightily commended by such who have any gust of things of this nature"' (Malcolm 1807, p. 242).

The gardens, redesigned by Henry Wise (d. 1738) only a few years after the park was opened, may have resulted in the present figure being moved to Wise's nurseries at Brompton Road. It is possible that the figure was later incorporated into the garden of Alford House, built in 1851 by Matthew Digby Wyatt (1805–1886) for Lady Marion Alford, sister-in-law of Edward Frederick Levenson Gower MP, the younger brother of George Levenson-Gower, 2nd Earl Granville (1815–1891), Vice-President of the 1851 Commission, who had close links with the formation of the Museum (information supplied by John Physick). Alford House, which formed part of the north-east corner of Wise's former property, was later renamed Ennismore Gardens. Alford House was demolished in 1955, but the existence of the figures in the photographs taken around 1872 suggests that prior to the building of Alford House the figure was removed, and travelled the relatively short distance to the South Kensington Museum site.

Interest in the figure was re-kindled around 1984–5 with John Physick's discovery of the Esdaile manuscript reference, suggesting the figure was formerly at Alford House, and it was formally registered in 1985.

Though traditionally considered to be a representation of *Time*, Malcolm Baker has recently suggested that the figure might depict the sea-god Neptune. This is corroborated in part by the shell-like form of the basin on which the figure stands.

Bibliography

Esdaile MS [David], p. 9; Whinney 1988, p. 449, n. 15; Baker 2000 [Figured in Marble], p. 29.

Laurent Delvaux

(b. Ghent 1696 – d. Nivelles 1778)

Delvaux trained in Antwerp under Pieter-Denis Plumier (1688–1721), with whom he was later to work in London alongside Peter Scheemakers [q.v.] on the monument to John Sheffield, 1st Duke of Buckingham in Westminster Abbey. Delvaux and Scheemakers went into partnership following Plumier's death, and executed monuments and some garden figures; Delvaux carved a marble figure of Hercules for Richard Tylney, Viscount Castlemaine in 1722 (now at Waddesdon Manor, Buckinghamshire). In 1728 both Delvaux and Scheemakers left London for Rome, where Delvaux was to remain until 1732, before returning to the Netherlands. While in Rome he executed a number of commissions for Italian and British patrons, including John Russell 4th Duke of Bedford, who commissioned a number of works inspired by antique sculpture (now at Woburn Abbey, Bedfordshire). He was appointed court sculptor in Brussels in 1733, and in 1734 settled in Nivelles where his workshop produced many religious works, including the monumental pulpit at St Bavo, Ghent. After 1750 Delvaux was employed by Charles of Lorraine (1712–1780), Governor of the Netherlands, to produce decorative work for his residences in Brussels, Tervuren and Mariemont.

Gunnis 1968, p. 126; Avery 1979; idem 1983; Whinney 1988, pp. 182–90; Thieme-Becker, 9, pp. 41–2; TDA, 8, pp. 698–9 [Bussers]; Jacobs 1999.

97: Vertumnus and Pomona

signed; about 1725
Marble
h. 129.5 cm.
A.1–1949

Signed faintly on the ribbon beneath the buckle: L. Delvo. f.

Formerly at Canons, near Edgware, Middlesex, the seat of James Brydges, Duke of Chandos (1673–1744). Margaret Whinney suggested that the present piece, together with the *Venus and Adonis* group executed by Peter Scheemakers [q.v.], was almost certainly commissioned by the Duke of Chandos specifically for Canons: Scheemakers and Delvaux were at this time working in partnership. However only just over twenty years later, in 1747, the drain of hereditary tax on an already spent fortune resulted in the demolition of Canons, and the sale of its contents (Forster 1848, p. 50). The two groups of *Vertumnus and Pomona* and *Venus and Adonis* were probably bought by Lord Cobham for Stowe House, Buckinghamshire at the Canons sale; they are first recorded at Stowe in 1773. In Steeley's *Stowe a Description* . . . of that year, the present piece, together with Scheemakers's *Venus and Adonis* is recorded in the Dining Room (Seeley 1773, p. 40). Seeley's *Description* . . . of 1797 notes that the two groups were removed from the Dining Room to the garden (*idem* 1797, p.13). Some two years later the groups were recorded by Smith, still located in the garden (Smith 1828, p. 45). The two groups were clearly viewed as a pair, displayed together whilst at Stowe House, and appearing as consecutive lots in both the 1848 and 1921 Stowe sale catalogues. The present group was offered as lot 782 on 21 August 1848, when it was described as being in the South Portico, noted in Forster's catalogue as sold to 'A. Robertson, Esq.' for £86 2s 0d (82 guineas). In the 1921 Stowe sale held by Messrs Jackson Stops, it was again in the South Portico, along with Scheemakers's *Venus and Adonis*. Whinney has noted that the inclusion of these groups in both Stowe sales may be because they were bought back by the family in the 1848 sale (Whinney 1971, p. 32). In the third and last Stowe sale catalogue of 1922 the present group is listed, though the *Venus and Adonis* is not. However, the accompanying illustration in the catalogue is of the *Venus and Adonis*, suggesting that the present piece had already been sold at the 1921 sale, and its inclusion in the catalogue an error (see Shaw 1922, pp. 50 and 69). The location of *Vertumnus and Pomona* is not recorded from 1921 until 1948, when it was acquired by Dr W. L. Hildburgh F.S.A. from Bert Crowther,

Isleworth, Middlesex, towards the end of 1948. It was given by Dr Hildburgh to the Museum as a customary New Year gift in 1949.

In 1957 Terence Hodgkinson [q.v.] noted on the records for the present piece that the *Venus and Adonis* was then in the possession of Mr A. Knight Loveday, of Beckwith & Son, Antique Dealers, Hertford, and published by Mr Knight Loveday in *Country Life* as, 'recently . . . discovered in the garden of a house in Hertfordshire' (Knight Loveday 1957). It is now in a private collection at St Paul's Walden Bury, Hertfordshire; see Jacobs 1999, p. 232.

A lead variant of the present group, supplied by John Cheere [q.v.] in 1756, is in the Royal Palace at Queluz, Portugal (see Correia Guedes 1971, illus. on p. 96; Jacobs 1999, p. 234, illus. on p. 233).

For a full discussion of the *Vertumnus and Pomona*; and related works by Delvaux, see Jacobs 1999, pp. 231–7. A terracotta model described as 'Vertumnus and Pomona, a Groop [sic] by ditto [Delvaux]' was included as lot 70 in the 1728 sale of the collection of works Delvaux and Scheemakers (*ibid*, pp. 190, 232, cat.no. SM100).

Bibliography

Seeley 1773, p. 40; Seeley 1797, p. 13; Willame 1914, pp. 8, 54, no. 20, pl. opp. p. 8 (then noted in the collection of 'Mme La baronne Kinloss, at Stowe); Shaw 1922, pp. 50, 69; Molesworth 1951, p. 14, and pl. XXIV; Gunnis 1968, p. 126; Whinney 1971, p. 32, cat.no. 3, illus. on p. 33; McCarthy 1973, p. 229 (comparing the present piece with the figurative work executed by James Lovell (active 1752–1778) at Stowe inspired by statues in the Orangerie at Versailles, engraved by Thomassin); Whitfield 1973, fig. 17 on p. 604; Avery 1979, pp. 160–2, fig. 9 on p. 160; Whinney 1988, p. 186, and fig. 126 on p. 186; Roscoe 1995, p. 42, and fig. 8 on p. 42; Jacobs 1999, pp. 116–7, 156–7 and fig. 50 on p. 156, 231–4, cat.no. S9 for further bibliography.

98: Kneeling Cupid

about 1730–2
Terracotta
h. 29.5 cm.
910–1855

Signed in monogram on the side of the pediment: L.D.

Purchased in 1855 for £1 0s 2d; vendor not recorded. A pendant figure to this was purchased at the same time; see cat.no. 99.

A putto with cornucopia of flowers, similarly signed in monogram, is illustrated by Willame in his monograph on Delvaux (Willame 1914, p. 83 cat.nos. 262–3, pl. between pp. 82–3; see also Jacobs 1999, p. 321, cat.no. 110, also p. 320, cat.no. S109). Similar putti signed 'L.D.', and an unsigned figure of the *Infant Hercules* attributed to Delvaux, were included in a sale at Christie's, London, 8 December 1992, lots 59 to 61 (lot 60 is most closely related; see Jacobs 1999, p. 246, cat.no. S28, illus. on p. 245). Jacobs has noted the similarity between such figures and the putti adorning funerary monuments executed by the Delvaux and Scheemakers partnership, particularly that to Dr Hugh Chamberlen of c. 1730–2 in Westminster Abbey, suggesting an approximate date for the terracottas; see entry for cat.no. 200. Malcolm Baker has however recently suggested that this present piece and its pendant might be later in date (Baker 2000 [Review], p. 782).

Bibliography

Devigne [n.d.], p. 149 and fig. IX on pl. 149; Jacobs 1999, p. 245 and illus. cat.no. S25; Baker 2000 [Review], p. 782.

99 98

99: Kneeling Cupid

about 1730–2
Terracotta
h. 29.5 cm.
911–1855

Signed in monogram on the side of the pediment: L.D.

Purchased in 1855 for £1 0s 2d; vendor not recorded. A pendant figure to this was purchased at the same time; see cat.no. 98.

See entry for cat.no. 98.

Bibliography

Devigne [n.d.], p. 149 and fig. IX on pl. 149; Jacobs 1999, p. 245 and illus. cat.no. S26; Baker 2000 [Review], p. 782.

100: Hercules, after the antique Farnese Hercules

about 1768
Terracotta
h. 52.5 cm.
A.56–1930

Included in the sale of the collections of Max and Maurice Rosenheim, sold by order of the Executors at Sotheby, Wilkinson & Hodge, 33–34 New Bond Street, London, 9 to 11 May 1923, lot 483.The annotated copy of the sale catalogue held in the National Art Library records it was sold for £5. Given to the Museum by Dr W.L. Hildburgh F.S.A. in 1930.

The neck is broken and repaired; part of the big toe of the left foot is missing.

The identification of the present piece as a model for the marble figure of Hercules – formerly in the Palace of the Duke of Lorraine in the Palais de Charles-Alexandre de Lorraine, Brussels, later the Musée de Peinture Moderne, and now the Musées Royaux des

Beaux-Arts – was noted on the records for the present piece by Terence Hodgkinson, who wrote, 'Although unsigned, this statuette may be ascribed unreservedly to Delvaux. It is certainly a preparatory model for the marble statue in Brussels'. The marble, executed during 1768–70, is signed and dated 1770; see Willame 1914 pl. between pp. 76–7. The arms of Charles, Duke of Lorraine, Governor of the States of Brabant 1750–1775, incised on the trunk on which the figure leans, confirms the connection of the present piece with the marble in Brussels.

The present piece is one of a number of models executed by Delvaux for this commission. The various models and their relationship with the finished marble are discussed by Alain Jacobs in his monograph on Delvaux; see Jacobs 1999, pp. 457–69, cat.nos. S267 to S274.

Bibliography

Jacobs 1999, pp. 458–9 (with further references), 464 cat.no. S270, illus. on p. 458.

101: Ceres

about 1720
Possibly by Laurent Delvaux
Oak
h. (figure) 183 cm. h. (base) 61.5 cm.
A.24–1941

Said to have been bought privately at an unknown date for a small sum by Sir Henry Solomon Wellcome (1853–1936) as Sarah Churchill, Duchess of Marlborough (1650–1744) (information supplied by Dr Johnson Saul of the Wellcome Museum to Dr W.L. Hildburgh in 1941). Included in the Wellcome sale (no. 5), held by Harrods for Allsop & Co, on 14 March 1938, lot 108, where it was bought by 'Johnson' for £5. Sold with the contents of 'The Museum', Finchingfield, Essex (the estate of Mr H.F. Ellis) on 10 June 1941, lot 424, where it was described as *Queen Anne* by Grinling Gibbons. Sold by Robinson and Foster, on 16 October 1941, on behalf of Mr Bowles, 96 Abbot Road, Poplar, London, described as Sarah, Duchess of Marlborough by Grinling Gibbons. The figure was purchased from this sale by Dr W.L. Hildburgh F.S.A. for £21, and subsequently given to the Museum. (I have been unable to verify the above sale details, which are recorded on the departmental records). A note on the records for this object suggests that on acquisition the figure was accompanied by a letter (now lost) from one of its previous owners, Mr Ellis, to Winston Churchill; dated 18 May 1938, it offered the figure presumably for purchase, as *Queen Anne*, formerly the property of the Duchess of Marlborough.

The figure stands on a base in the form of a fountain, which represents the head of a river-god. There are signs of gilding on the sun-motif brooch attached to the chest of the figure.

The suggestion (see above) that the figure may represent Sarah Churchill, Duchess of Marlborough is certainly plausible given her patronage of the arts (see Szpila 1997 for a discussion of her Blenheim commissions). The facial features resemble portraits of the Duchess (see *ibid.*, fig. 1 on p. 190). However, the features of the figure are also comparable to the portrait of Queen Anne after John Closterman's portrait, in the National Portrait Gallery, London; see *NPG* 1981, p. 14, no. 215. The figure may therefore simply represent ideal female beauty.

In requesting funding for the purchase of the present piece, Eric Maclagan [q.v.] wrote in October 1941, ' it is a life-sized statue in oak ... to be sold at Robinson and Fosters ... It is called in the catalogue "Sarah 1st Duchess of Marlborough" and ascribed to Grinling Gibbons; it is also said to have been formerly at Blenheim. It is as a matter of fact a goddess Ceres and I do not think it has anything to do with the Duchess. It certainly has nothing to do with Grinling Gibbons'. It was noted on the departmental records for this object, probably made shortly after acquisition, that 'The carving is certainly not by Grinling Gibbons but may be by one of his followers. The head, hands or details of the corn etc. are very carefully and well carved but the drapery is coarse. The figure is made up of several pieces, the back hollowed out and slabs of wood nailed over the opening. The base is obviously copied from a marble fountain'.

Paul Williamson and Malcolm Baker have recently suggested that Laurent Delvaux could be the sculptor of this piece. Similar radiating sun-motifs can be found on some Delvaux figures, including those of *Prudence* and *Christian Truth*; see Jacobs 1999, pl. 13 opp. p. 120; and fig. 43 on p. 131. A comparable feature is also used for the terracotta figure of *Religion* by François-Joseph Janssens (1744–1816), who worked in Delvaux's studio; see Jacobs 1999, fig. 28 opp. p. 89. In the sale catalogue of the collection of Delvaux and Scheemakers prior to their leaving for Italy, what is described as 'Two, Apollo and Ceres, by Plimier' were included as lot 49 in the first day's sale held on 16 April 1728 (cited in Jacobs 1999, p. 189). 'Plimier' was presumably Pieter-Denis or François Plumier (1688–1721).

Bibliography

The Times, 30 January 1958, illus. on p. 16.

Exhibited

Included in the Hildburgh Memorial Exhibition held in the Recent Acquisitions Court at the Victoria and Albert Museum, 30 January to March 1958.

John Flaxman R.A.

(b. York 1755 – d. London 1826)

Flaxman was one of the most celebrated English sculptors of his day, the only sculptor to whom Sir Joshua Reynolds devoted one of his Lectures, and was himself to become the first Professor of Sculpture at the Royal Academy in 1810. He was the son of a plaster-cast maker, and was a precocious artist, who first exhibited at the Royal Academy in 1771. He entered the Royal Academy Schools in 1770, and from 1775 onwards supplied designs for ceramics to Josiah Wedgwood, while trying to establish himself as a sculptor. From 1787 to 1794 Flaxman was in Rome, where he gained an international reputation. On his return to England he concentrated on funerary monuments and portrait busts, although his subject pieces, such as Satan overcome by St Michael, *executed for Petworth (1819–26) were greatly admired. He regularly exhibited at the Royal Academy from 1770 until 1827 (a posthumous work). A large collection of his plaster models was presented to University College London by his sister-in-law, Maria Denham in 1849.*

Chancellor 1911, pp. 236–59; Gunnis 1968, pp. 147–51; Flaxman 1979; Whinney 1988, pp. 337–59; Thieme-Becker, 12, pp. 79–83; TDA, 11, pp. 162–5 [Bindman].

102: Self-portrait

signed and dated 1778
Terracotta
diam. 18.8 cm.
294–1864

Inscribed anti-clockwise around the rim: + HANC SVI IPSIVS EFFIGIEM FECIT IOANNES FLAXMAN IVNIOR ARTIFEX STATVARIVM ET CŒLATOR ALVMNVS EX ACADEMIA REGALE • ANNO ÆTATIS XXIV A•D• MDCCLXXVIII
(John Flaxman the Younger, artist, sculptor and engraver made this image of himself; pupil of the Royal Academy at the age of 24 in the year 1778)

In the possession of Sir William Hamilton (1730–1803) in Naples by 14 July 1798, catalogued by Hamilton at this time, located in his library of the Palazzo Sessa, Naples (Fothergill 1969, p. 297 – citing BM Add. MSS 41200, ff. 121–6). Purchased by the Museum at Messrs Christie, Manson, 8 King Street, London, lot 988, from the collection of John Watkins Brett, deceased, of Hanover Square, London for £161 14s on the sixth day of the sale, 11 April 1864. The relief is illustrated in the catalogue in a beaded gilt wooden frame (opp. p. 74): the frame, which dates from some time after the relief, perhaps as late as the early 1860s, was removed at an unrecorded date after acquisition in 1864, and is currently in store. The relief is noted in departmental records as being purchased by Chaffens, probably on behalf of the Museum. Included in the same sale, lot 1115 on seventh day of sale, 12 April 1864, was the wax portrait of Flaxman's sister, executed in 1772, also purchased for the Museum (inv.no. 295–1864).

Constable incorrectly described the relief in his 1927 monograph on Flaxman as wax and dated 1779. The relief is related to two drawings, one in University College, London, the other in Earls High School, Halesowen, Worcestershire, as well as a further plaster relief in the British Museum, all of around the same date (see *Flaxman* 1979, pp. 38–9, cat.nos. 2, 3 and 4b). Further medallion portraits of Flaxman and his wife are in Sir John Soane's Museum.

Constable suggested, 'This is probably the self-portrait which Wedgwood contemplated reproducing in 1779, though he apparently did not do so' (Constable 1927, p. 23, n. 1).

Bibliography
Inventory 1864, p. 24; Graves III, p. 123, no. 91; Doin 1911, illus. p. 233 – though illustrating what appears to be the V&A version, the writer states the relief is in the British Museum; Constable 1927, pp. 23, n.1, 80–1, illus. pl. IX; Brown 1934, illus. p. 72 (engraving after the present piece); Deutsch 1943, p. 38, pl. A on p. 39; *Royal Academy* 1951, p. 167, cat.no. 426; Whinney 1971, p. 138, no. 44, illus. p. 139; Irwin 1979, p. 10; *Flaxman* 1979, p. 39, no. 4a; *Wedgwood* 1995, pp. 61–2, cat.no. C9; Williamson 1996 [Trusted], p. 164.

Exhibited
Royal Academy in 1779, described as 'Portrait in terracotta', no. 91; *The First Hundred Years of the Royal Academy 1769–1868*, Royal Academy, London, 1951–2, cat.no. 426; *John Flaxman, R.A.*, Royal Academy, London, 26 October to 9 December 1979, cat.no. 4a; *The Genius of Wedgwood*, Victoria and Albert Museum, 8 June to 17 September 1995, cat.no. C9.

103: Venus caging cupids

about 1788–94
Marble in a gilt wood frame
h. 66.5 cm. w. 33.5 cm.
1150–1882

Bequeathed by John Jones in 1882.

In the 1924 catalogue of the Jones Collection it was suggested that this relief is 'based on the Pompeian painting, "Cupids for sale", found at Stabiae and now in the Museo Nazionale, Naples' (*Jones* 1924, p. 100; citing Conforti 1901, pp. 38–9, pl. CXVII). Flaxman may have seen the painting during his time in Italy (1787–94).

Bibliography
Jones 1924, p. 100, cat.no. 393, pl. 73.

104: 'Come thou blessed' monument to Agnes Sarah Harriet Cromwell (d.1797)

about 1798
Plaster
h. 34.5 cm. w. 17.5 cm.
UCL Loan 3

On the death of Flaxman, this and other models by the artist passed to the artist's sister-in-law, and later adopted daughter, Maria Denman. Given by Miss Denman to University College, London in 1848 (UCL inv.no. 1102). On loan to the Victoria and Albert Museum from the College Art Collections, University College London, from August 1958.

This is a preliminary sketch model for the monument to Agnes Cromwell in Chichester Cathedral. The tablet beneath, left blank in the model, is filled with an inscription on the completed monument; the pediment is there inscribed with the title of the subject depicted, 'COME THOU BLESSED'. A further sketch by Flaxman for the figure on this monument, illustrating *Come Thou Blessed*, is also on loan to the Museum; see entry for cat.no. 105.

Another model, formerly on loan to the Museum and returned in 1992, is also in the collections of University College (inv.no. 1082); see Whinney and Gunnis 1967, pp. 15–16, cat.no. 10).

Flaxman had exhibited a marble bas-relief of this subject, 'Come, thou blessed' at the Royal Academy in 1800 (no. 1056), and it is possible that this sketch is a model for the exhibited piece, rather than specifically for the Agnes Cromwell memorial. For a discussion of the reliefs see Irwin 1979, pp. 127–8.

Agnes Cromwell, the daughter of Captain Henry Cromwell, R.N. and his wife Mary, died at the age of eighteen; the commission is recorded as being given on 23 June 1798 (see Croft-Murray 1939–40, p. 61).

Irwin comments, 'He [Flaxman] has fused the classicism of the stele and the draperies with his new-found Quattrocento elegance, using the basis for this composition the well established formula of an apotheosis. He has also brought to the design on the Cromwell monument his experience in working on the Homer illustrations . . . This small scale monument was to become one of Flaxman's most influential works, with many subsequent imitations by other sculptors' (Irwin 1979, pp. 127–8).

In a typed handlist produced on receipt of the Flaxman models from University College, following their loan to the Flaxman exhibition at the Hatton Gallery, Pope-Hennessy [q.v.] wrote: 'Amongst the earliest is an elegant panel in low relief representing the ascension of Miss Agnes Cromwell . . . In this it is easy to detect the influence of Thomas Banks, whose work Flaxman greatly admired and whose 'Thetis and her nymphs consoling Achilles' [cat.no. 69] is to be seen . . . at the Victoria and Albert Museum'.

Whinney and Gunnis record that Flaxman used this design on several other monuments (see Whinney and Gunnis 1967, p. 16).

We are grateful to the College Art Collections, University College London for allowing us to include this in the catalogue.

Bibliography

Ely 1900, p. 18, no. 17 – there described as 'The Reward of the Righteous'; Constable 1927, p. 87; *Flaxman* 1958, cat.no. 6; Whinney and Gunnis 1967, pp. 15, 55, cat.no. 97; *Flaxman* 1979, p. 103, cat.no. 116a and illus.

Exhibited

John Flaxman R.A. Sculptor, Hatton Gallery, King's College, University of Durham, Newcastle-upon-Tyne, 10 February to 21 March 1958, cat.no. 6; *John Flaxman R.A.*, Kunsthalle, Hamburg; Thorvaldsens Museum, Copenhagen; Royal Academy, London, 20 April to 9 December 1979, cat.no. 116a.

105: 'Come thou blessed' monument to Agnes Sarah Harriet Cromwell (d.1797)

about 1798
Plaster
h. 52.5 cm. w. 26 cm.
UCL Loan 4

See entry for cat.no. 104. On loan to the Museum from the College Art Collections, University College London from August 1958. UCL inv.no. 1101.

This was used as a sketch model for the relief illustrated on the memorial to Agnes Cromwell in Chichester Cathedral, though Flaxman had already executed it before receiving this commission. See entry for cat.no. 104.

We are grateful to the College Art Collections, University College London for allowing us to include this in the catalogue.

Bibliography

Ely 1900, p. 28, no. 104; Constable 1927, p. 87; *Flaxman* 1958, cat.no. 7, and illus.; *Romantic Movement* 1959, p. 282, cat.no. 482, and pl. 22 (b); Whinney and Gunnis 1967, pp. 55–6, cat.no. 98; *Neo-classicism* 1972, pp. 235–6, cat.no. 364, pl. 77; *Flaxman* 1979, p. 103, cat.no. 116b and illus.

Exhibited

John Flaxman R.A. Sculptor, Hatton Gallery, King's College, University of Durham, Newcastle-upon-Tyne, 10 February to 21 March 1958, cat.no. 7; *The Romantic Movement, Fifth Exhibition to celebrate the tenth anniversary of the Council of Europe*, Tate Gallery and Arts Council Gallery, London, 10 July to 27 September 1959, cat.no. 482; *The Age of Neo-classicism*, Royal Academy and Victoria and Albert Museum, London, 9 September to 19 November 1972, cat.no. 364.

106: Monument to the Hon. Barbara Lowther (d.1805)

about 1805
Plaster
h. 36 cm. w. 16.5 cm.
UCL Loan 13

See entry for cat.no. 104. On loan from the College Art Collections, University College London from August 1958. UCL inv.no. 1092.

This is a preliminary sketch model for a monument commemorating the Hon. Barbara Lowther, in the church of St Mary Magdalene, Richmond, Surrey. The monument to Barbara Lowther was commissioned by her sister, Katherine, Duchess of Bolton, and cost 220 guineas. The oval scratch in the pedestal marks the positioning of a medallion containing the portrait of the deceased. A later larger model for this monument is also on loan from University College; see entry for cat.no. 107. There are some differences between this sketch, the later model, and the finished monument. In the present piece, the portrait is not formalised, nor does it incorporate the lilies seeming to sprout from the base of the monument.

We are grateful to the College Art Collections, University College London for allowing us to include this in the catalogue.

BIBLIOGRAPHY
Ely 1900, p. 25, no. 85; Croft-Murray 1939–40, p. 86; *Flaxman* 1958, cat.no. 17; Whinney and Gunnis 1967, p. 59, cat.no. 107, pl 19 (a); *Neo-classicism* 1972, p. 237, cat.no. 367, pl. 76 (shows UCL loan 14).

EXHIBITED
John Flaxman R.A. Sculptor, Hatton Gallery, King's College, University of Durham, Newcastle-upon-Tyne, 10 February to 21 March 1958, cat.no. 17; *The Age of Neo-classicism*, Royal Academy and Victoria and Albert Museum, London, 9 September to 19 November 1972, cat.no. 367.

107: Monument to the Hon. Barbara Lowther (d.1805)

about 1805–6
Plaster
h. 116.2 cm. w. 66 cm.
UCL Loan 14

See entry for cat.no. 104. On loan from the College Art Collections, University College London, from August 1958. UCL inv.no. 1103.

This is a larger, more finished model for the monument to Barbara Lowther in the church of St Mary Magdalene, Richmond, Surrey; see entry for cat.no. 106.

We are grateful to the College Art Collections, University College London for allowing us to include this in the catalogue.

BIBLIOGRAPHY
Ely 1900, p. 32; Croft-Murray 1939/40; p. 86; *Flaxman* 1958, cat.no. 18 and illus.; *Romantic Movement* 1959, pp. 282–3; cat.no. 483; Whinney and Gunnis 1967, p. 59, cat.no. 107, pl. 16 (b); *Flaxman* 1979, p. 108, cat.no. 123, illus. 51; *Metropole London* 1992, p. 474, cat.no. 414 and illus.

EXHIBITED
John Flaxman R.A. Sculptor, Hatton Gallery, King's College, University of Durham, Newcastle-upon-Tyne, 10 February to 21 March 1958, cat.no. 18; *Romantic Movement*, Tate Gallery and Arts Council Gallery, London, 10 July to 27 September 1959, cat.no. 483; *John Flaxman R.A.*, Hamburg; Thorvaldsens Museum, Copenhagen; Royal Academy, London, 20 April to 9 December 1979, cat.no. 123; *Metropole London. Macht und Glanz einer Weltstadt*, Villa Hugel, Essen, 6 June to 8 November 1992, cat.no. 414.

108: Monument to Captain James Walker and Captain Richard Beckett (d.1809)

about 1811
Plaster
h. 71.5 cm. w. 45.5 cm.
UCL Loan 20

See entry for cat.no. 104. On loan from the College Art Collections, University College London, from August 1958. UCL inv.no. 1106.

This is a sketch model for the monument in the parish church of St Peter in Leeds, commemorating the death on active service in the Napoleonic War of two Leeds citizens who fell at the Battle of Talavera on 24 July 1809. The monument, which cost £700, was paid for by public subscription; see Irwin 1979, pp. 161–2, illus. 225 on p. 163.

We are grateful to the College Art Collections, University College London for allowing us to include this in the catalogue.

BIBLIOGRAPHY

Ely 1900, p. 15; Graves III, p. 124, no. 925; Constable 1927, p. 91; *Flaxman* 1958, cat.no. 23 and illus.; *Romantic Movement*, 1959, p. 283, cat.no. 484; Whinney and Gunnis 1967, p. 62, cat.no. 114, and pl. 20 (a).

EXHIBITED

Royal Academy in 1811, described as 'Victory leaning on a trophy; a monument to Captains Walker and Becket [sic] for the Town of Leeds', no. 925; *John Flaxman R.A. Sculptor*, Hatton Gallery, King's College, University of Durham, Newcastle-upon-Tyne, 10 February to 21 March 1958, cat.no. 23; *The Romantic Movement*, Tate Gallery and Arts Council Gallery, London, 10 July to 27 September 1959, cat.no. 484.

109: Two men fighting

signed; about 1807–17
Terracotta
h. 20 cm. w. 20.5 cm.
A.23–1934

Signed on the back: Flaxman Fec[t]

Given by Mr Richard B. Pilcher O.B.E., F.C.I.S. Institute of Chemistry of Great Britain and Ireland, 30 Russell Square, London, in accordance with the wishes of Mrs Thomas Bolas in 1934. Mrs Bolas (neé Eveline Dell), was a direct descendant of Isaac Dell, who served a seven year apprenticeship with Flaxman. Two indentures, one signed by Dell, the other by Flaxman, are held in the National Art Library (inv.no. 86.QQ. Box I, (ii)). Isaac Dell was indentured to Flaxman on 26 April 1788 by his mother Harriot Dell, who paid £31 10s to Flaxman. In return, Flaxman agreed to instruct Dell in the 'Moulding and Casting of Plaister Figures', though it was stipulated in an addendum that Dell's mother would fund her son in 'Washing, Mending and Apparel of all Sorts'. In the indenture, Flaxman describes himself as a 'Moulder and Caster of Plaister Figures'.

The relief has a crack through the centre, top to bottom. Damage is visible on the torso of the left-hand figure.

In the *Review of the Principal Acquisitions during the Year 1934* it was noted, 'The composition compares very closely with the artist's drawings for the *Theogony of Hesiod*, published in 1817, and may perhaps date from this period' (*Review* 1934, p. 5). Wark however suggests that Flaxman's work on this series may pre-date 1817: 'It is clear . . . that Flaxman had been working out the designs for at least a decade. A note in the *Athenaeum: A Magazine of Literary Information* for February 1807 (p. 172) mentions the fact that Flaxman was then employed on compositions from Hesiod' (Wark 1970, p. 38). For related drawings depicting *Gods and Titans* and *Giants and Titans*, studies for Hesiod's *Theogony*, see *Flaxman* 1979, p. 128, cat.no. 156; see also see *Flaxman* 1976, figs. 11 and 12 for *Prometheus chained* by Flaxman from the *Tragedies* of Aeschylus.

BIBLIOGRAPHY

Review 1934, p. 5; *Flaxman* 1958, cat. no. 3.

EXHIBITED

John Flaxman R.A. Sculptor, Hatton Gallery, King's College, University of Durham, Newcastle-upon-Tyne, 10 February to 21 March 1958, cat.no. 3.

110: St Michael overcoming Satan

about 1817
Plaster
h. (excl. spear) 78 cm.
312–1898

Given by Dr W. Stuart, 133 Gloucester Terrace, Paddington, London in 1898. Recorded in the original acquisition information as being acquired by Dr Stuart from the 'Denman sale at Christie's'. The sale catalogue of the remaining works by Flaxman from the collection of the late Miss Flaxman and Miss Denman, held at Messrs Christie, Manson and Woods, 8 King Street, London, on 26 April 1876, included as lot 74, 'St Michael Subduing Satan', under 'Plaster Models by J. Flaxman, R.A.', the annotated copy of the catalogue held in the National Art Library records that this was sold to 'Grindlay [?]' for £23 2s (22 guineas) (probably the art-dealer Mr W. Grindlay, Duke Street, St James's Square). A later sale of works by Flaxman, the property of the Denman family, was held at Messrs Christie, Manson and Woods, 8 King Street, London on 26 and 27 February 1883. Lot 368 included in the second day's sale was described as ' St Michael subduing Satan – cast', the annotated copy of the catalogue held in the National Art Library records it was sold to 'Rathbone' for £4 14s 6d. The present piece may be this one, or that sold in 1876.

Described in the original acquisition information as 'Flaxman's original design in clay (unbaked) for the Archangel Michael and Satan, the large plaster model of which is under the Dome of the University College Gower Street . . . Mr Armstrong has seen it and concurs in recommending its acceptance'.

A pedestal on which the figure originally stood was also offered by Dr Stuart, who requested it should be returned if not required. Though the group was accepted and registered in 1897, the pedestal was declined and returned.

This is a sketch-model for the marble group executed by Flaxman for the 3rd Earl of Egremont, which was completed, almost certainly by Thomas Denman, Flaxman's brother-in-law and pupil, in 1826, and installed (probably in the North Bay) at Petworth House, Sussex at some date after October 1827 (McEvansoneya 2001, p. 357). The group was commissioned in 1817 (*ibid.*, p. 352), and completed in 1824; a full-size plaster model, exhibited by Flaxman at the Royal Academy in 1822 (no. 985), is at University College, London (see Whinney and Gunnis 1967, p. 51. no. 88, pl. 24b; the model was on loan to the V&A between 1972 and 1994). Whinney noted, 'The St Michael overcoming Satan was one of . . . [Flaxman's] last works, and though the figure of the saint reveals Flaxman's profound admiration for Antiquity, the composition has certain links with sixteenth-century Italian sculpture, such as Benvenuto Cellini's 'Perseus', of which Flaxman made drawings when he was in Italy' (Whinney 1971, p. 144). Irwin comments that 'Contemporary and near-contemporary discussions of Flaxman's work frequently singled out the *St Michael* as one of the sculptor's outstanding achievements' (Irwin 1979, p. 180).

Reproductions of the *St Michael overcoming Satan* produced by William Wyon were commissioned by the Art Union and issued in 1844; this was the first bronze to be commissioned by the Art Union (see Aslin 1967, p. 15, fig 1. on p. 12; Avery and Marsh 1985, pp. 329–30). It was later reproduced by H.J. Hatfield; see entry for cat.no. 461.

A further small model is in Sir John Soane's Museum, London (inv.no. SC7).

BIBLIOGRAPHY
Bequests and Donations 1901, p. 247; Graves III, p. 124, no. 985; Whinney 1971, p. 144, no. 47, illus. p. 145, McEvansoneya 2001, p. 352, n. 9, fig. 40 on p. 353.

111: Crouching Cupid

about 1824
Plaster
h. (incl. integral plinth) 54 cm.
516–1868

Given by R.J. Lane Esq., A.R.A. in 1868.

This figure is probably related to the figure of Cupid executed by Flaxman for Samuel Rogers in 1824, together with a pendant figure of Psyche. Models for these are in Sir John Soane's Museum, inv.nos. S33 and S34 respectively (see Irwin 1979, p. 176, p. 230 n. 18; Bolton 1919, illus. p. 1). The Soane models of Cupid and Psyche are illustrated in an article on Flaxman in the *Gazette des Beaux-Arts* of April 1911 by Jeanne Doin, pp. 330–42. In connection with Flaxman's return to London in 1794, following his travels in Italy and France, Doin commented that these figures were illustrative of Flaxman's use of sources taken from the antique (*ibid.*, p. 330, illus. p. 331 and p. 332). The Psyche figure had been used earlier by Flaxman on the 1814–15 monument to Mary Tighe (1772–1810), author of a poem, *Psyche*. A model for this monument was exhibited at the Royal Academy in 1815 (no. 900) (see *Flaxman* 1979, p. 110, cat.no. 126).

BIBLIOGRAPHY
Bequests and Donations 1901, p. 186; Constable 1927, p. 96 – there described as a cast.

112: Seated youth with pan-pipes

about 1824
Terracotta
h. 24 cm.
534–1877

Purchased from A. Copeland Esq. in 1877 for £30.

Acquisition records note that the figure had been 'broken and mended'.

The attribution is based on the figure's similarity with the figure of a *Crouching Cupid* by Flaxman; see entry for cat.no. 111. Julius Bryant has however suggested in correspondence that this piece may be by Joseph Gott [q.v.].

BIBLIOGRAPHY
Constable 1927, p. 97 – there listed under 'undated authentic work' by Flaxman; *Flaxman* 1958, cat.no. 24.

EXHIBITED
John Flaxman R.A. Sculptor, Hatton Gallery, King's College, University of Durham, Newcastle-upon-Tyne, 10 February to 21 March 1958, cat.no. 24.

113: Frieze representing Greek comedy from the ancient drama on the theatre at Covent Garden

1809
Plaster
h. 39.1 cm. l. 185.4 cm.
A.8–1968

Formerly in the possession of the donor's great-grandfather, the sculptor Henry Westmacott [q.v.] and by descent to his son the sculptor James Sherwood Westmacott [q.v.]. By descent to Mr H. Barrs-Davies and given by him to the Museum in 1968, together with cat.nos. 114 to 116; see also cat. no. 702). In his report to John Pope-Hennessy [q.v.], Terence Hodgkinson [q.v.] wrote, 'The reliefs . . . constitute, so far as is at present known, the only surviving version of the complete Flaxman design for the friezes on the old Covent Garden Theatre. The stone reliefs on the theatre itself were mutilated when re-installed on the façade of the present Opera House and the plaster models at University College were almost entirely destroyed in the Second World War; the two surviving fragments are on loan from University College to this Museum . . . we cannot be absolutely sure, at this stage, that the Davies reliefs come from Flaxman's workshop, as it is just possible that they were cast after the University College models at some later date; (though not after about 1870). However, the fate of the University College reliefs gives the Davies versions considerable importance, at the least as a record of Flaxman's composition, and I recommend that they should be accepted'.

The present piece, together with cat.nos. 114 to 116, were on acquisition covered with black paint in imitation of bronze. According to the donor, this had been carried out around 1900, possibly after the death of James Sherwood Westmacott, who died in 1900. This paint was removed shortly after acquisition.

Of his non-funerary commissions, perhaps Flaxman's most influential work is that produced for the Covent Garden Theatre. He was commissioned in 1809 to produce two stone friezes for the façade of the Covent Garden Theatre (now the Royal Opera House), by the architect Robert Smirke (1780–1867) to represent the Ancient and Modern Drama (see Whinney 1965, for an account of the friezes). Whinney recorded that University College London owned models of both the Ancient and Modern Drama but that 'only two slabs of the Ancient Drama and none of the Modern Drama survived the Second World War. These appear to be later casts from the same mould as no. 45, for they are less fine in modelling and some of the detail has been lost' (Whinney 1971, p. 140, n. 1). The two surviving reliefs depicting the *Muse of Comedy confronting Aristophanes and Menander* and *Apollo driving his chariot of the sun*, were on loan to the Museum from University College, London from 1958 (V&A loan inv.nos. UCL 17 and 18); they were returned in 1992 (see Whinney and Gunnis 1967, pp. 60–1, cat.nos. 110 and 112, and pl. 21). The stone reliefs based on these plaster models were cut by John Charles Felix Rossi (1762–1839), who specialised in decorative architectural sculpture (see TDA, 27, p. 197 [Bryant]).

Whinney noted, 'The designs have considerable importance in the history of English sculpture, for they are probably the first example of the direct influence of the Elgin Marbles' (Whinney 1971, p. 140). Flaxman had seen the marbles from the Parthenon (now in the British Museum) in 1807, when he had been consulted with regard to their re-arrangement at the Park Lane residence of Lord Elgin (Smith 1916, p. 297, reference cited by Whinney 1971, p. 140; see also Irwin 1979, p. 174; see also *ibid.*, p. 172 and Constable 1927, p. 68). The present relief depicts the seated figures of the playwright Aristophanes and the poet Menander to the right, before them the Muses Thalia, Polyhymnia, Euterpe, Clio and Terpsichore. To the far left of the relief, Pegasus is surrounded by three nymphs.

The present display of the friezes differs considerably from that which was originally intended. A fire at the theatre in 1856, and the subsequent rebuilding by E.M. Barry in 1856–8, resulted in Flaxman's friezes being cut and re-arranged in the order in which they can be seen today (Irwin 1979, pp. 72–4).

A contemporary account of the new Theatre at Covent Garden (reference cited by Whinney 1971, p. 140, n.1) is given in the *Gentleman's Magazine* in 1809, in which the writer noted, 'The designs are classical, and the execution masterly . . . The designs of both Basso Relievos, and the models of the Ancient Drama, are by Mr Flaxman, and the execution in stone, is by Mr Rossi' (*Gentleman's Magazine*, 18 September 1809, LXXIX (ii), pp. 880–1). The writer also commented on the statue of Tragedy in the South wing, not that it was 'a fine figure, holding the Tragic mask and dagger. The sculptor is Mr. Rossi. Comedy holds the shepherd's crook with pedun, on her right shoulder, and the comic mask in her left hand. This is the workmanship of Mr Flaxman and occupies the Northern wing' (*ibid.*, p. 881)

Bibliography

Whinney 1971, p. 140, no. 45, illus. p. 141; Irwin 1979, p. 172.

114: Frieze representing Greek tragedy from the ancient drama on the theatre at Covent Garden

1809
Plaster
h. 39.1 cm. l. 180.8 cm.
A.9–1968

Given by Mr H. Barrs-Davies in 1968, together with cat. nos. 113, 115, 116 and 702; see entry for cat.no. 113.

This section of relief, the right section of the frieze depicting the Ancient Drama, depicts the playwright Aeschylus with Bacchus, leaning against a faun, and Athena and Melpome; taken from Aeschylus's *Eumenides*, Orestes is shown pursued by two Furies, fleeing towards Apollo in his chariot (Whinney 1971, p. 140). For further sections of relief, see entries for cat.nos. 113, 115, and 116.

Bibliography

Whinney 1971, p. 140, no. 45, illus. p. 141; Irwin 1979, fig. 239 on p. 173.

115: Frieze representing Shakespeare from the modern drama on the theatre at Covent Garden

1809
Plaster
h. 39.1 cm. l. 174 cm.
A.10–1968

Given by Mr H. Barrs-Davies in 1968, together with cat. no. 113, 114, 116 and 702; see entry for cat.no. 113.

This relief, the left section of the frieze for the Modern Drama, depicts the seated figure of Shakespeare to the right, in front of which are characters from the *Tempest* and *Macbeth*. For further sections of relief, see entries for cat.nos. 113, 114, and 116.

Bibliography

Whinney 1971, p. 142, no. 46, illus. p. 143; Irwin 1979, fig. 238 on p. 173.

116: Frieze representing Milton from the modern drama on the theatre at Covent Garden

1809
Plaster
h. 47.9 cm. l. 177.2 cm.
A.11–1968

Given by Mr H. Barrs-Davies in 1968, together with cat. nos. 113 to 115 and 702; see entry for cat.no. 113.

The relief, the right section of the frieze for the Modern Drama, depicts the seated figure of Milton to the left (as a pendant to that of Shakespeare in the adjoining relief), together with scenes from Milton's *Comus*. For further sections of the relief, see cat. nos. 113 to 115.

Bibliography

Whinney 1971, p. 142, no. 46, illus. p. 143.

113

114

115

116

Daniel Garrett

(d. 1753)

Garrett was an exponent of the Palladian style of architecture, having acted as clerk of works for many of Lord Burlington's (1694–1753) building schemes. In 1727 he was appointed Labourer in Trust at Richmond New Park Lodge in the Office of Works, and in 1729 given the same post at Windsor. By the time of his dismissal in 1737, he was already established as an architect in his own right, active mainly in the north of England. In 1747 Garrett published Designs and Estimates of farm-houses, etc. for the County of York, Northumberland, Cumberland, Westmoreland and Bishoprick of Durham. *Colvin describes Garrett as 'something of a pioneer in the use of rococo plasterwork . . . he designed several Gothick buildings in the manner of William Kent (?1685–1748)'.*

Colvin 1995, pp. 393–5.

117: Chimneypiece

about 1757
Designed by Daniel Garrett; carved by Benjamin Carter
(formerly ascribed to Joseph Wilton)
Marble
A.60–1951

Originally in Northumberland House, the Strand, London, which was demolished in 1874. Deposited with Messrs Bert Crowther, Syon Lodge, together with the overmantel, by the Duke of Northumberland; see entry for cat.no. 118. The chimneypiece was purchased by Dr W.L. Hildburgh F.S.A., and then given by him to the Museum in 1951.

This was one of a pair of chimneypieces made for the Gallery or Ballroom at Northumberland House. Its twin is now installed in the Billiard Room at Syon House, Middlesex. A similar chimneypiece – minus the overmantel – was given to the City of Birmingham Museum and Art Gallery in 1959. The destruction of Northumberland House was reported in the *Illustrated London News* in 1874–5. The house and site were purchased by the Metropolitan Board of Works from the Duke of Northumberland and his son Earl Percy, under a Special Act of Parliament, for £500,000. The article in the *Illustrated London News* reported its intended demolition was 'for the purpose of making a new street from Charing cross to the Victoria Thames Embankment. There was much discussion, at the time, upon the question of the necessity for destroying Northumberland House' (*Illustrated London News*, 25 July 1874, p. 89). The demolition is illustrated by three engravings in January 1875 (*ibid.*, 30 January 1875, p. 112). Illustrations of the gallery before the demolition of the house are also included in the *L.C.C. Survey of London*, XVIII (The Strand), 1937, pls 8 and 10 (departmental records).

The chimneypiece was originally ascribed to Peter Scheemakers [q.v.] by Terence Hodgkinson [q.v.] on the basis of a related drawing held in the Department of Prints, Drawings and Paintings (inv.no. E.912–1921) which was itself ascribed, incorrectly according to Hodgkinson, to Henry Keene (1726–1776). Hodgkinson noted that comparisons with signed drawings by Scheemakers suggested that the chimneypiece should in fact be attributed to him. The chimneypiece was later ascribed to Benjamin Carter, and recently it was suggested that it was designed by Joseph Wilton [q.v.], though carved by Benjamin Carter. This attribution

117 & 118

was based on the identification of Wilton in a painting by Francis Hayman of 1760, in which Wilton and his family were thought to be depicted, gathered around a design for the present piece shown on an easel (see Allen 1983, fig. 2 on p. 1983 – the painting was then in the collection of Sir Robert Kirkwood, and is now in the Department of Prints, Drawings and Paintings in the Victoria and Albert Museum, inv.no. P.7–1985). Benjamin Carter (d. 1766) specialised in carving marble chimneypieces, sometimes in partnership with his brother, Thomas; he also produced carved church monuments; his most celebrated work was however probably the lion he made in 1752 for Northumberland House in the Strand, London, and now at Syon Park, Isleworth, Middlesex (Gunnis 1958, p. 334; *idem* 1968, p. 84).

Jeremy Wood has recently re-attributed the chimneypiece: though agreeing with the attribution of Benjamin Carter as the carver, he proposed that the designer was Daniel Garrett, and that Simon Vierpyl (1725–1810), an English sculptor working in Rome, may have been responsible for making the models. Garrett had been commissioned by Algernon Seymour, 7th Duke of Somerset (1684–1750) in 1748 to assist with the re-design of Northumberland House, the main focus of which was the addition of a new wing to contain the Gallery (Wood 1999, pp. 401–2). Wood suggests, 'Although the carving of the chimney-pieces was carried out by Carter in London, Vierpyl's role would have been similar to that of the painters employed by Northumberland [Sir Hugh Percy Smithson, First Duke of Northumberland (1715–1786)] in Rome' (*ibid.*, p. 406). Wood also identified the figure depicted in Hayman's painting as Benjamin Carter, rather than Joseph Wilton, and suggests the painting dates from 1751/2. He notes that Wilton was in Italy during the time the Gallery at Northumberland House was conceived, and is not known to have been employed by the Duke of Northumberland until the early 1760s (*ibid.*, pp. 404–6, fig. 9 on pl. 404, and fig. 10 on p. 405). Carter, who specialised in chimneypieces, is known to have been paid £292 in 1757 for executing the pair (Allen 1983, p. 200, n. 46).

The caryatid figures at either side of the chimneypiece are based on the antique prototypes of the Farnese Captives (see Haskell and Penny 1981, pp. 169–72). Variants may also be found on a chimneypiece at Saltram in Devon (Whinney 1988, p. 461, n. 33).

The illustration shows the chimneypiece when displayed in gallery 63 in the Museum, prior to 1969.

Bibliography

Haskell and Penny 1981, p. 170, n. 17; Allen 1983; *Hayman* 1987, n. 5 on p. 106; Whinney 1988, p. 461, n. 33; Laing 1989, p. 248, fig. 11 on p. 249; Wood 1999, pp. 404–6, fig. 9 on pl. 404, and fig. 10 on p. 405.

118: Overmantel

about 1757
Designed by Daniel Garrett; probably executed by Benjamin Carter
Wood and plaster
A.60:A-1951

Originally in Northumberland House, The Strand, London, demolished in 1874. Deposited with Messrs Bert Crowther, Sion Lodge, together with the chimneypiece, by the Duke of Northumberland; see entry for cat.no. 117. The overmantel was given to the Museum by Bert Crowther Esq in 1951.

See entry for cat.no. 117.

The overmantel would originally have held a full-length portrait. A near-contemporary account of the Gallery at Northumberland House written in 1761, noted, 'The finishing above the chimneypieces consists of terms, sphinxes, festoons, etc., and within the spaces formed by these ornaments are placed whole length portraits of the Earl and Countess of Northumberland in their robes' (Dodsley 1761, p. 54).

The chimneypiece and overmantel, together with its companion, was illustrated in an engraving of the interior of the Gallery recorded by Sir Charles Barry in 1853, reproduced by Wood in his article (see Wood 1999, fig. 6 on p. 401). Describing the scheme of the overmantel, Wood notes, 'Below are pairs of sphinxes, while Barry's drawings show that the broken pediments above were embellished with trophies of weapons. These survive at the Victoria and Albert Museum, but have not been included in the most recent installation of the overmantel' (*ibid.*, p. 404, and n. 48).

Bibliography

Wood 1999, p. 404, fig. 10 on p. 405.

Giovanni Battista Guelfi

(b. Bergano 1690/1 – d. after 1734)

Guelfi was the most important Italian sculptor working in England in the first half of the eighteenth century, but much of his life remains obscure. He is first recorded in Rome in 1714, where he probably worked under Camillo Rusconi (1658–1728), almost certainly restoring antique marbles. By 1721 Guelfi was in England, restoring the Arundel marbles which were owned by Lord Leominster at Easton Neston in Northamptonshire. Guelfi also carved the monument to James Craggs (erected in 1727) in Westminster Abbey, and another similar one to Thomas Watson Wentworth (c. 1731) in York Minster, as well as some portrait busts for monuments. He also carved busts of Worthies for Queen Caroline's Hermitage at Richmond. He is last documented in 1732, and according to Vertue, left England around 1734, when he may have returned to Italy.

Esdaile 1948 [Guelfi]; Webb 1955; Gunnis 1968, p. 183; Whinney 1988, esp. pp. 159–61; TDA, 13, p. 782 [Eustace]; Giometti 1999.

119: Anne, Duchess of Richmond (d.1722)

about 1730–4
Terracotta
h. 68 cm.
A.19–1947

In the possession of the Dukes of Richmond at Goodwood House, Sussex, where it was discovered in the stables and purchased by Gerald Kerin. Purchased from Gerald Kerin, 15 Davies Street, Berkeley Square, London in 1947 for £50, using funds from the John Webb Trust.

When acquired, the bust was covered with peeling bronze paint which was removed.

On acquisition Terence Hodgkinson [q.v.] wrote, 'The bust was bought from Goodwood, which was acquired by the Duchess's husband (the natural son of Charles II and Louise de Kerouaille) in 1720. It may possibly be the model that Guelfi submitted before executing the monument'.

A year after its acquisition, Katharine Esdaile published an article discussing its recent discovery, 'I learnt that it came from the stables at Goodwood; its identity had clearly been forgotten, and it is certainly odd that Vertue, visiting Goodwood in 1739 and making notes, says nothing of it, for it cannot have been banished to the stables shortly after the Duchess's death' (Esdaile 1948 [Guelfi], p. 318).

This is a terracotta version of the marble bust on the monument to the Duchess of Richmond at Deene, Northamptonshire, erected in 1734 by her son. Margaret Webb points out that although the bust was executed by Guelfi, the monument itself is signed by another, 'It is clear, therefore, that Guelfi only carved the bust of the Duchess, and that the rest of the monument, which is very well cut, is by John Boson or Bossom' (Webb 1955, p. 143).

This is one of only two terracottas ascribed to Guelfi, the other being a model for the monument to James Craggs, in Sir John Soane's Museum, London (Giometti 1999, p. 29). Marble busts of Thomas Fermor and his wife Henrietta Louisa, Earl and Countess of Pomfret, in the Ashmolean Museum, Oxford have been attributed to Guelfi by Penny (*Ashmolean* 1992 [III], p. 96, cat.nos. 516 and 517), but Baker in his review of Penny in the *Burlington Magazine* has suggested that they may have been carved by a later sculptor (such as Wilton) at the time of the presentation of the Arundel marbles to Oxford (Baker 1994).

Whinney described the Duchess of Richmond bust as 'smoothly and roundly modelled, the forms being much generalized; the same characteristics appear in a group of monuments, all with busts, made under the will of Katherine, wife of the 6th Earl of Westmoreland, to her parents, Thomas and Katherine Stringer, at

Kirk Thorpe, West Yorkshire and to Thomas Stringer, a distant relative at Enfield, Middlesex . . . All Guelfi's portraits have the same long faces, large-featured, haughty and slightly horse-like – in fact, to an Italian, the typical English face' (Whinney 1988, p. 161). In a response to an enquiry by John Physick raised in the *Church Monuments Society Newsletter* concerning the Duchess of Richmond bust and the similar bust on the monument to Sir Thomas Stringer and Katherine Stringer (erected 1732) in Kirkthorpe, Yorkshire, Brian Breton confirmed, 'there is an identical pose and very similar hairstyle with loose curls on the left shoulder', though he also notes some subtle differences (*Church Monuments Society Newsletter*, Winter 1991, vol. 6, no. 2, p. 27 and *ibid.*, Summer 1991, vol. 7, no. 1, p. 10). For an illustration of the Stringer bust see Webb 1955, fig. 17.

BIBLIOGRAPHY

Esdaile 1948 [Guelfi], p. 318, figs. 16 and 17 on p. 319; Webb 1952, p. 217; *idem* 1955, p. 143; *British Portraits* 1956, pp. 70–1, cat.no. 191; *Italian Art* 1960, p. 74, cat.no. 173; Gunnis 1968, p. 183; Whinney 1971, p. 68, no. 17, illus. on p. 69; Whinney 1988, p. 161; *Ashmolean* 1992 [III], p. 96; TDA, 13, p. 782 [Eustace]; Giometti 1999, pp. 29–30, fig. 2 on p. 29.

EXHIBITED

British Portraits, Winter Exhibition 1956–57, Royal Academy, London, cat.no. 191; *Italian Art and Britain. Winter Exhibition 1960*, Royal Academy, London, cat.no. 173.

FRANCIS HARWOOD

(b. about 1727 – d. Florence 1783)

The dates of Harwood's birth and death, previously unrecorded, were established by Roberta Cremoncini in her 1992 Phd thesis (University of Siena). Like his contemporary Christopher Hewetson [q.v.], Harwood spent his working life in Italy. He travelled to Rome in 1752, and then went to Florence, where he resided from 1753 until his death. Although he was British, his exact place of birth is unknown. Little is known of Harwood's early career; he was however noted as being 'acquainted with Joseph Wilton [q.v.] who was then working in Florence'. Ingamells states, 'After Wilton returned to England in 1755 Harwood appears to have worked in a studio near SS. Annunziata with Giovanni Battista Piamontini'. Fleming and Honour have noted that the scope of Harwood's work was wide-ranging; as well as producing busts and copies after the antique, he also executed vases, chimneypieces and figures. I am grateful to Roberta Cremoncini for letting me see extracts from her Phd thesis on Harwood.

Gunnis 1968, p. 191; Fleming and Honour 1968; Cremoncini 1990/1; Ingamells 1997, pp. 472–3.

120: Seneca

signed and dated 1763
By Francis Harwood, after the antique
Marble
h. 67 cm.
A.26–1948

Signed and dated: F. Harwood Fecit 1763

Inscribed on the front: SENECA

Said to have come from Gordon Castle, Banffshire, Scotland. Given by Bert Crowther, Syon Lodge, Busch Corner, Isleworth, Middlesex in 1948, accompanying a set of pedestals purchased on the Museum's behalf by the Ministry of Works from Crowthers. Transferred from the Department of Architecture and Sculpture to the Circulation Department (part of Regional Services) in 1958, and on the closure of Regional Services in 1981, returned to the charge of the Sculpture Department. On long-term loan to Chiswick House (now administered by English Heritage) since 1958.

H.D. Molesworth [q.v.] noted in the departmental records relating to this object that a marble bust of Homer accompanied the acquisition of this bust, though Mr Crowther did not make a formal gift of it to the Museum until 1958; see entry for cat.no. 121.

On the reproduction of the image of Seneca, Haskell and Penny note, 'Busts of "ancient worthies" such as Seneca, Marcus Aurelius, Cicero and Homer which were frequently copied in marble and cast in plaster – especially in the eighteenth century as library ornaments, just as Cicero was known to have acquired busts for his library – were valued more because they represented great men (as did death masks which inspired similar veneration) than because they reproduced works of art. It is in any case often hard to discover the originals of these replicas because the antique portraits of such figures existed in many versions – for instance, about a dozen examples of the type of bust now called 'pseudo-Seneca' were known in the seventeenth century, and as many have been discovered since . . . The identification of Seneca . . . was first published in 1598, and thereafter the learned all over Europe looked with awe and devotion at the stoic philosopher, emaciated, even uncouth, disdainful of the corruption and luxury of Nero's court, and soon to commit suicide. They continued to do so until 1813, when an inscribed herm portrait of Seneca with quite different features was discovered (Staatliche Museum, Berlin) and even after that many scholars were reluctant to admit that their devotion had been misplaced' (Haskell and Penny 1981, p. 52; see p. 51, fig. 28 for a bust of Seneca similar to the present piece).

A closely related bust catalogued as *Pseudo-Seneca* and possibly by Joseph Wilton, is in the J. Paul Getty Museum, Malibu (inv.no. 87.SA.111); see *Getty* 1997, p. 56.

BIBLIOGRAPHY

Gunnis 1968, p. 191; Fleming and Honour 1968, p. 515, n. 12; Cremoncini 1990/1, p. 55, no. 12.

121: Homer

signed and dated 1764
By Francis Harwood, after the antique
Marble
h. (incl. socle) 71 cm.
A.8–1958

Signed and dated on the base beneath the left shoulder: F. Harwood Fecit 1764
Inscribed at the base: HOMERVS

Formerly at Gordon Castle, Banffshire, Scotland. Given by Bert Crowther, Syon Lodge, Busch Corner, Isleworth in 1958, though actually received into the Museum in 1948 together with its pendant bust of *Seneca*; see entry for cat.no. 120. Transferred from the Department of Architecture and Sculpture to the Circulation Department (part of Regional Services) in 1958, and on the closure of Regional Services in 1981, returned to the charge of the Sculpture Department. On long-term loan to Chiswick House from 1958; returned to the Museum in December 1990.

See entry for cat.no. 120.

BIBLIOGRAPHY

Gunnis 1968, p. 191; Fleming and Honour 1968, p. 515, n. 12; Cremoncini 1990/1, p. 56, no. 13.

122: Venus and Cupid

about 1763–5
Marble
l. 40 cm. w. 26.3 cm.
A.23–1948

Formerly at Gordon Castle, Banffshire, Scotland. Given by Bert Crowther, Syon Lodge, Busch Corner, Isleworth, Middlesex in 1948.

On acquisition H.D. Molesworth [q.v.] wrote: 'This small relief came from a fitting in Gordon Castle belonging to the same decoration as our bases – recently acquired. The whole, together with the busts, were executed by F. Harwood between 1763–65.' For the busts mentioned by Molesworth, see entries for cat.nos. 120 and 121.

Christopher Hewetson

(b. Kilkenny 1736/9 – d. Rome 1798)

The date of Hewetson's birth is unclear; Gunnis and Hodgkinson suggest 1739, de Breffny 1737, and more recently, a date of about 1736 has been proposed by Cullen. Brian de Breffny records that Hewetson initially worked in Dublin for the sculptor John Nost the Younger [q.v.], before travelling to Rome in 1765, where he remained for the rest of his life, and where he established himself as one of the prominent British sculptors working in Rome at that time. In the 1780s Hewetson was mainly involved in the execution of portrait busts: de Breffny records that his earliest work was the bust of Viscountess Sudley (1767–9). Perhaps his most prestigious commission was that for the monument to Dr Baldwin for Trinity College, Dublin. Commissioned from Hewetson in 1771, it was executed in Rome and on completion in 1781 shipped to Dublin and installed in the Examination Hall in 1784. Hewetson exhibited only twice at the Royal Academy, in 1786 a bust of Gavin Hamilton, and in 1790 a bust of an unidentified man.

Graves IV, p. 91; Strickland 1913, pp. 479–80; Hodgkinson 1952/4; Gunnis 1968, p. 199; de Breffny 1986; Thieme-Becker, 17, p. 13; TDA, 14, p. 500 [Cullen].

123: Pope Clement XIV (Lawrence Ganganelli)
(b. 1769; Pope from 1769; d.1774)

signed and dated 1773
Marble
h. (incl. socle) 75 cm.
A.22–1948

Signed on the side left truncation: Christ^{s}o Hewetson Fec^{t} Romæ 1773
Inscribed on the truncation at the back: CLEMENS XIV PONT MAX

Acquired by Thomas Mansel Talbot (1747–1813) probably from Gavin Hamilton (1723–1798). By descent with the Talbot collection. Purchased by Edward O'Sullivan, St Cuthberts, Theodore Road, Port Talbot, on 29 October, 1941 from the contents of the Margam Castle sale, Glamorganshire, Trustees of the late Miss Emily Charlotte Talbot, sold by Christie's, lot no. 461; incorrectly described as Pope Leo X and dated 1776, it was purchased for 8 guineas. Mr O'Sullivan wrote, 'I understand it formed part of a collection of ancient Marbles purchased by the late Mr Talbot, and I suppose it is of Italian origin'. Terence Hodgkinson noted that the bust was probably originally acquired by Miss Emily Charlotte Talbot's grandfather, Thomas Mansel Talbot (see following entry), 'together with a large collection of ancient marbles, many of which were bought through Gavin Hamilton. We know that the sculptor Hewetson was a friend of Hamilton's and exhibited a bust of him at the RA' (Museum records). The bust was purchased from Edward O'Sullivan by the V&A in 1948 for £35.

Terence Hodgkinson [q.v.] commented: 'By the standards of English sculpture of this period the bust is a very good one. There is also some interest in the fact that this Pope was very friendly to and much liked by the English in Rome & is said to have remarked that he wished the English would honour religion as much as they honoured him' (Museum records). Hodgkinson also points out that the date on the present piece was originally incorrectly read as 1776, when it was in fact 1773.

Four other marble versions of the bust are known: one, executed for Lord Hylton at Ammerdown, was acquired from the sale held at Christie's, London on 11 December 1990, lot 48, by the National Gallery of Scotland (inv.no. 2525; see *Art in Rome in the Eighteenth Century* 2000 [Baker], p. 255, cat.no. 130). A second, signed and dated 1772, is at Gorehambury, Hertfordshire. The third is at Beningborough Hall, York, dated 1771: previously published by Whinney and Hodgkinson respectively as whereabouts unknown (see Bibliography below). Hodgkinson's annotations to his 1952/4 article and departmental records later correct this and note the bust as still at Beningborough Hall (see *Treasure Houses* 1985, p. 270, cat.no. 190). A further marble version is at the Yale Center for British Art, New Haven. A plaster version, traditionally but probably erroneously ascribed to Canova is at Bassano del Grappa, Museo Civico (see Pavanello 1976, p.135, no. 378 and Bassi 1943, p. 16, and fig. 22). The versions mentioned above are cited by de Breffny 1986, p. 55, nos. 4a to b, c, e.

Ingamells records that whilst in Rome in 1773, Talbot commissioned Hewetson to produce this bust, together with a bust of himself; see entry for cat.no. 124.

Bibliography

Molesworth 1951, p. 16, pl. XXXIX; Hodgkinson 1952/4, p. 43, and n. 6, pl, XVII (B); Honour 1959, p. 226, n. 11 and fig. 5 on

p. 228; *Siècle de l'élegance* 1959, p. 41, cat.no. 64; Gunnis 1968, p. 199; *Irish Portraits* 1969, p. 85, cat.no. 162; Whinney 1971, p. 110, no. 33, illus. p. 111; *Treasure Houses* 1985, p. 270; de Breffny 1986, p. 55, no. 4d, illus. p. 63; *Three Graces* 1995, p. 11; Ingamells 1997, p. 924; *Art in Rome in the Eighteenth Century* 2000 [Baker], p. 255.

EXHIBITED

Le Siècle de l'élegance la Demeure Anglaise au XVIII siécle, Musée des Arts Décoratifs, Paris, 26 February to mid-June 1959, cat.no. 64; *Irish Portraits 1660–1860*, National Gallery of Ireland, Dublin 14 August to 14 October 1969; National Portrait Gallery, London 30 October 1969 to 4 January 1970; Ulster Museum, Belfast, 28 January to 9 March 1970, cat.no. 162.

124: Thomas Mansel Talbot of Margam Park and Penrice Castle (1747–1813)

signed; 1773
Marble
h. 61.5 cm.
A.41–1953

Signed on the truncation at the side: CHRŨS·HEWETSON·Fecit

Commissioned by the sitter in 1773 at a cost of £68. Possibly sold at the Margam Castle sale held by Christies on 29 October 1941, the Trustees of the late Miss Emily Charlotte Talbot, though the lot has not been identified. Lot 459 in the sale is described as 'A bust of a man – 24½" high'; though the size is similar, the bust is catalogued as standing on a white marble square pedestal. Purchased by Dr W. L. Hildburgh F.S.A. from Montague Marcussen of Crawford Street, London, for £25. Given by Dr Hildburgh to the Museum in 1953 on the occasion of his birthday.

On acquisition the bust was unidentified, though a date of 1790 was suggested. It was later proposed that the subject could be Augustus, Duke of Sussex (1773–1843); Hewetson is said to have executed a bust of the Duke of Sussex in 1794 (Esdaile 1947 [Hewetson], p. 135). However, this was rejected because of the inconclusive comparison with a known portrait of the Duke by Guy Head (1762–1800) in the National Portrait Gallery (see *NPG* 1981, p. 552, no. 648).

In correspondence, Mr Robert G. Stewart, Curator, National Portrait Gallery, Washington D.C., suggested that the subject was the American painter Henry Benbridge (1743–1812), who was in Italy from 1765–9, and shared a studio with Hewetson in Rome in 1765 (letter to Terence Hodgkinson [q.v.] 10 April 1970). Hodgkinson commented at the time, 'The bust does resemble portraits of Benbridge but suggests a handsomer subject. The identification, though possible, remains uncertain'. Nevertheless, the bust was illustrated in the exhibition catalogue accompanying the exhibition *Henry Benbridge 1743–1812,* held at the Smithsonian Institute, Washington, in 1971, p. 26.

The bust was identified as Thomas Mansel Talbot with the assistance of John Vivian Hughes, Local Studies Librarian, Central Library, Swansea, who wrote to Anthony Radcliffe in March 1977 stating, 'The photographs of the unidentified bust by Hewetson are quite exciting. I am sure this is Thomas Mansel Talbot, as you have suggested. It would appear to depict him in middle age. The resemblance to other Talbot family portraits is quite striking. The forehead and nose are distinctive and recognisable features in all generations of the Talbot family'.

Talbot had inherited the estates of Margam and Penrice, held in trust on the death of Rev. Thomas Talbot in 1758. Talbot travelled to Europe in 1770 on the Grand Tour, sending back the works of art he had amassed in June 1775 (Hughes 1975, p. 2). One of the sculptural items acquired from Hewetson by Talbot was the bust of Pope Clement XIV, signed and dated 1773, now also in the Museum's collections; see the entry for cat.no. 123. Ingamells records that Talbot travelled twice to Rome, once from 30 November 1771 to 30 June 1772, and later from May to August 1773; in 1773 Talbot commissioned two busts from Hewetson, and is recorded as paying £68 'in full for my Bust', and a further £140 for the bust of Pope Clement XIV; see entry for cat.no. 123 (Ingamells 1997, pp. 923–4). In July 1977 Anthony Radcliffe noted, 'Another bust by Hewetson of Thomas Mansel Talbot with classical draperies and short classicising hair in the possession of Mr C.P. M. Methuen-Campbell at Penrice Castle, Gower (formerly a residence of Thomas Mansel Talbot) shows the identical facial features and must be more or less contemporary with the present bust... Although the present bust is not identifiable in the catalogue of the Margam Castle sale, 1941, it may also have been there'.

BIBLIOGRAPHY

Hodgkinson 1952/4, p. 50, n. 4, pl. XVII, D; de Breffny 1986, p. 59, no. 299, illus. p. 72; Ingamells 1997, pp. 923–4.

125: Sir Thomas Gascoigne, 8th Bt. of Parlington
(1745–1810)

signed and dated 1778
By Christopher Hewetson, cast by Luigi Valadier (b. Rome 1726; d. Rome 1785)
Bronze
h. 51 cm. h. (incl. socle) 62 cm.
A.1–1986

Inscribed on hollow back: Sir Thomas Gascoigne Bart./Rome 1778/Lovis Valadier F

Given by John H.J. Lewis in 1986.

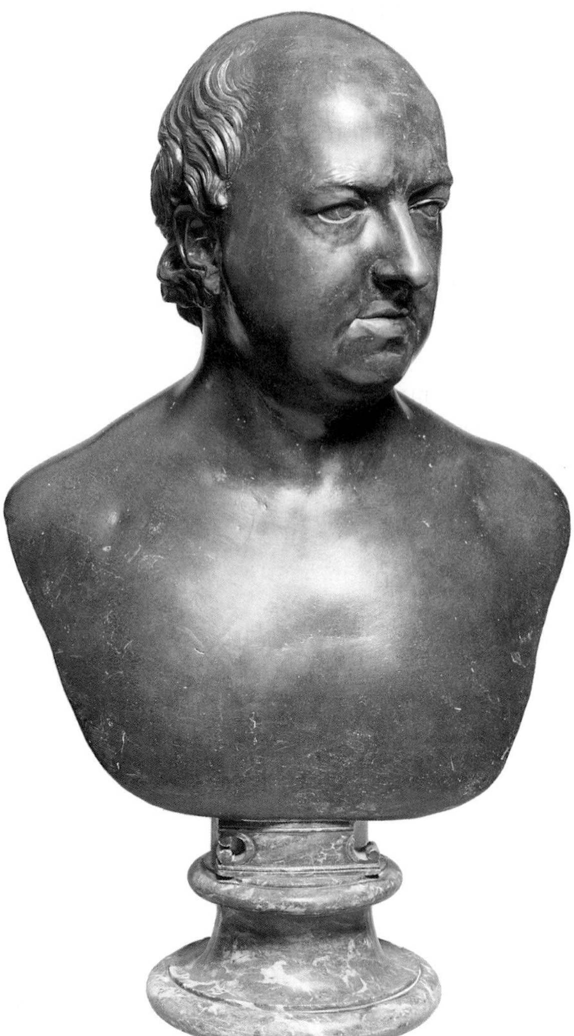

Gasgoigne travelled to the continent in 1764, initially visiting Turin. He first went to Rome in early 1765, returning there in March 1778 when he presumably sat for Hewetson (Ingamells 1997, p. 394).

The version originally commissioned by Gascoigne, including the same inscription as the present piece, was presented to Leeds City Art Galleries in 1968 as part of the Gascoigne Bequest (inv.no 71.123/68); (see Friedman 1976; p. 20, fig. 2; *Valadier* 1991, pp. 142–4, cat.no. 75; *Leeds* 1996, p. 3). The Leeds version is catalogued by de Breffny in his preliminary catalogue raisonné as attributed to Hewetson (see de Breffny 1986, p. 60, no. attr. 4, illus. p. 74). The V&A version, acquired in the same year as the article was published, is not cited.

Luigi Valadier was one of a family of goldsmiths of French origins, established in Rome in 1714 by his father, Andrea Valadier (1695–1759). On the death of his father, Luigi Valadier took over the family business; his skill as a hardstone-cutter, jeweller and gold- and silversmith, as well as a bronze caster helped establish him as one of the leading bronze-founders of the second half of the eighteenth century (see *Valadier* 1991; TDA, 31, p. 799 [Catello]; Wardropper 2000).

Bibliography
Penny 1991 [Rockingham], p. 19, p. 34 n. 97; Williamson 1991, p. 876.

John Hunt

(active Northampton 1710 – d. Northampton 1754)

Hunt was an active and productive sculptor, mainly of monuments, in Northamptonshire; he was a pupil of Grinling Gibbons, although he appears to have specialised in stone rather than wood.

Gunnis 1968, pp. 212–3.

126: Monument to John Nicolls Raynsford
(1723–1746)

signed; about 1746
Marble with some polychromy and gilding
h. 198.5 cm.
A.11–1965

Signed centrally at the bottom beneath the inscription tablet: John Hunt/Northampton/Fecit

The tablet is inscribed: Near this Place lie the Remains/of JOHN NICOLLS RAYNSFORD Esqr Descended by his Father & his Mother/From the Ancient Familys/of NICOLLS & ISHAM,/both of this Parish of Lamport;/Sole Proprietor of this Lordship/and Manor of Faxton

He Married ELIZABETH eldest Daughter /of the Rev^{d}: Sr John Dolben Bar^{t}/And Grand Daughter of William Lt Digby/of the KINGDOM of IRELAND; /By whom He left only one Female/INFANT, ELIZABETH,/ Happy in not being sensible/of the Loss of a Tender Parent,/Whose many Endearing Qualitys/have renderd His untimely Fate,/Greatly lamented by his most/Affectionate Wife & Mother,/By all His Relations, Friends, & Dependants,/But with the utmost Resignation/Submitted to That GOD,/Whose Name is ever to be Magnified/both by Life & by Death

He Died in the 24th Year of His Age,/September the 4th: 1746.

From the demolished church of St Denis, Faxton, Northamptonshire. Given to the Museum by the Rector and Churchwardens of Lamport with Faxton in 1965, together with cat.nos. 17, 62 and 260.

In his article on the Faxton monuments, Terence Hodgkinson [q.v.] commented on the present piece that, 'His [Hunt's] Faxton monument has charm; but the parts of the design cannot be said to form a convincing unity; the capitals of the pilasters, for instance, are awkwardly cut away to accommodate the slab bearing the inscription' (Hodgkinson 1971/2, p. 339).

John Nicolls Raynsford was the grandson of Sir Edward Nicolls, whose monument, also formerly in the church of St Denis, Faxton is also in the Museum; see entry for cat.no. 62.

BIBLIOGRAPHY
Hodgkinson 1971/2, p. 339, pl. 4 on p. 336.

P. H. Leader

(active 1790 – 1800)

P.H. Leader, described as a wax-modeller, resident at New Brentford, exhibited two wax models at the Royal Academy in 1797. This sculptor may also have been related to a G. Leader of 188, Oxford Street, also a wax modeller, who exhibited at the Royal Academy between 1792 and 1804. A wooden bust of Charles James Fox, signed and dated 1797 by G. Leader, was included in a sale at Sotheby's, 8 December 1988, lot 301. Pyke suggested that both G and P.H. Leader also worked as medallists.

Graves V, p. 11; Forrer VII, p. 540; Gunnis 1968, pp. 236–7; Pyke 1973, p. 77.

127: Unknown man, possibly George Washington (1732–1799)

signed; about 1790–1800
Boxwood
h. 18.2 cm.
A.24–1939

Signed on the truncation beneath the bust: P. Leader. Sculpt.

Purchased from Charlesworth, J. F. da C. Andrade, Works of Art, Brook Street, 8 Avery Row London in 1939 for £7 10s.

When at the Museum on approval for purchase, the relief was thought to depict Admiral Duncan (1731–1804): the word 'Duncan' was apparently written on the reverse of the mount, which was not original, and was subsequently replaced (departmental records). H.D. Molesworth [q.v.] noted, 'a comparison with such medals of the admiral as we have, though not dissimilar, would not seem to support the suggestion with absolute certainty. The subject is shown without uniform and I have not as yet been able to find any other portraits which could confirm the attribution'. Molesworth went on to note that the relief was 'particularly interesting in that it is signed "P. Leader" and is treated exactly in the manner of a wax portrait relief'. He also suggested that the portrait was not dissimilar to that found on a wax portrait relief thought to be Edmund Burke (1730–1797) by T.R. Poole (d. about 1821), formerly in the Mary Bate collection, inv.no. A.31–1970.

Wendy Fisher has suggested the sitter might be identified as George Washington (c.f. Reilly and Savage 1973, p. 332 (d); *Wedgwood* 1973, cat.no. 97 for the Wedgwood medallion).

A similar relief of George IV as a Hussar, also in boxwood, and signed 'LEADER' was brought into the Department in 1955 (departmental records).

BIBLIOGRAPHY
Gunnis 1968, pp. 236–7.

JOHN CHARLES LOCHÉE

(b. 1751 – active 1772; d. after 1791)

Lochée enrolled at the Royal Academy Schools in 1772 under the name Johannes Carolus Lochees. He is best known for his small-scale works in wax, and in the execution of portrait medallions and engraved gems. From 1774 Lochée was employed as a modeller for Josiah Wedgwood; he also worked for James Tassie. Lochée was also a portrait sculptor. He became Portrait Modeller to Prince William Henry around 1786, and received a number of royal commissions for portrait busts including those of Frederick Augustus, Duke of York, and George, Prince of Wales. Wax portraits of an unknown man, and Augustus Frederick, Duke of Sussex are also in the Sculpture Department (inv.nos. A.56–1930 and A.72–1970). Lochée exhibited at the Royal Academy between 1776 and 1790. In 1791 he was declared bankrupt, after which date he is no longer recorded.

Graves V, p. 79; Forrer III, p. 452; Gunnis 1968, p. 241; Hodgkinson 1969; Pyke 1973, pp. 80–1; Reilly and Savage 1973, p. 362; Thieme-Becker, 23, p. 305.

128: Richard Brinsley Sheridan (1751–1816)

about 1788–9
Marble
h. (excl. socle) 72 cm.
A.44–1950

Purchased from Gerald Kerin, 15 Davies Street, London in 1950 for £45.

On acquisition the sitter depicted was unidentified, and the bust thought to be probably by a German or North European sculptor working under French influence: the costume suggested a date of about 1730–50. The sitter was identified as Richard Brinsley Sheridan in March 1957 with the discovery of another version of the bust inscribed with the sitter's name in the Royal Collection at Windsor Castle (see *NPG* 1985, II, no. 1084). A drawing of the Windsor bust is to be found in the notebooks of Sir George Scharf (1820–1895) held at the National Portrait Gallery, where it was described as being "in corridor" on 4 November 1881. What is described as "a plaster cast from an original bust at Windsor" in the studio of the sculptor Francis at 56 Alban's Street, was also drawn by Scharf on 20 February 1862 (departmental records).

A further version, which differs slightly from the present piece, is illustrated in Walter Sichel's *Life of Richard Sheridan*, where it was recorded in the possession of Mr A.T.B. Sheridan (d. 1931) at Frampton Court, near Dorchester (subsequently demolished), and which Sichel tentatively attributed to Joseph Nollekens [q.v.] (Sichel 1909, p. 370; cited in Hodgkinson 1969, p. 156 and n. 20 on p. 160).

The bust was attributed to Lochée by Terence Hodgkinson in his

1960 article on the sculptor, in which he noted another version of the bust at the Museum of Art, Carnegie Institute, Pittsburgh (ibid., p. 156).

Lochée exhibited a bust of Sheridan at the Royal Academy in 1790, no. 547 (Graves V, p. 79), perhaps the present version or one of those cited above.

BIBLIOGRAPHY
Hodgkinson 1969, p. 156 and fig. 13, n. 18 on p. 160; *NPG* 1985, I, p. 452 (I am grateful to Malcolm Baker for these references).

JOSEPH NOLLEKENS R.A.

(b. London 1737 – d. London 1823)

Nollekens was most famous as a prolific sculptor of portrait busts, many of which are of high quality, while some, such as those of Charles James Fox and William Pitt the Younger, became the standard images of the sitters. Nollekens was the son of a painter, and was apprenticed to Peter Scheemakers [q.v.] in 1750. He went to Rome in 1762, and worked with Bartolomeo Cavaceppi (?1716–1799) restoring and copying antique marbles. He returned to England in 1770, and was elected an Associate of the Royal Academy in 1771, and a Royal Academician the following year. As well as busts, Nollekens executed several funerary monuments, and some ideal figures, such as those for the 2nd Marquess of Rockingham (1773–8) (see entry for cat.no. 131), and a Venus *and* Mercury *for the 1st Earl of Yarborough. Many drawings (some at the V&A), and some of his terracotta models survive (see entries below). The posthumous biography of Nollekens, by a former assistant, J. T. Smith, was written in some rancour, but provides a good, if not always accurate picture, of the sculptor's life and methods of working.*

Smith 1828; Gunnis 1968, pp. 276–9; Whinney 1988, pp. 287–302; Thieme-Becker, 25, p. 506; TDA, 23, pp. 189–90 [Kenworthy-Browne].

129: Monument to Sir John Tyrell (1726–1766) and Dame Mary his wife (1735–1766)

signed; about 1766–70
Marble
A.92–1970

Signed at the bottom left of the memorial: Nollekens F[t]

The memorial tablet is inscribed: Near this Place are interred,/Sir JOHN TYRELL, late of Heron, Bart./Who died 5 January, 1766 ; aged 40 Years:/And Dame MARY, his Wife ;/Who died 23 September, 1766; aged 31 Years./He was the only surviving Child, and Heir, of/Sir JOHN TYRELL; by Dame ELIZABETH, his Second Wife ;/to whose Memories, a Monument is erected in this Church./She was the only Child, and Heiress, of THOMAS CRISPE,/(late of Parbold, in the County Palatine of Lancaster ; and/of Elden, in the County of Suffolk,) Esquire ; deceased : by MARY, his Wife./This Monument is erected to their Memories,/by MARY TYRELL, and ELIZABETH TYRELL ;/their only Children, and Coheiresses.

Commissioned from the sculptor by Mary and Elizabeth Tyrell, the daughters of those commemorated. From the west wall of the South (Tyrell) chapel, Church of All Saints, East Horndon, Essex. Given by the Rector and Churchwardens of East Horndon with West Horndon in 1970.

The endangered plight of the church at East Horndon was reported in July 1970, and the serious levels of vandalism to the interior of the church prompted the Museum to acquire the present piece. The Diocesan authorities had approved the disposal of the church's contents to suitable recipients, and the removal of this monument, carried out as a matter of urgency, was endorsed by the Council for the Care of Churches.

BIBLIOGRAPHY
Gunnis 1968, p. 278.

130: Castor and Pollux

signed and dated 1767
Marble
h. 160.7 cm
A.59–1940

Signed and dated on the integral base to the side:
IOSEPH NOLLEKENS.FAC,ROMÆ, AN,D. MDCCLXVII

Commissioned by Lord Anson of Shugborough Hall, Staffordshire, and executed by Nollekens whilst in Rome. Included in the Shugborough Hall sale held by Mr George Robins on 1 August 1842 and the following thirteen days, the group was featured in the eighth day's sale, held on 9 August 1842, described as part of the large collection of antique and modern statuary at Shugborough Hall. Lot 90 located to 'The area of the Bust Gallery', it was described as 'A truly magnificent specimen of modern sculpture, the life size group of Castor and Pollux, in pure statuary marble, copied from the antique by Nollekens, it is 5 feet 4 [inches] high, and may be ranked as one of the finest efforts of this renowned English sculptor, also a stone pedestal, 2 feet 4 [inches] high'. The annotated copy of the sale catalogue held in the National Art Library records the group was sold for £320 3s 0d. Purchased by Mr H. Soden, the father of the donor Mrs H.B. Borradaile, around 1935. Bequeathed to the Museum by Mrs Borradaile in 1940, the group was given by Brigadier Gen. H. Borradaile, D.S.O. in accordance with the wishes of his late wife.

The plinth on which the present piece stands appears to be original. According to Greek mythology Castor and Pollux were the offspring of Leda, Queen of Sparta and the god Zeus. The group is a copy of the antique group acquired by Philip V of Spain, and now in the Prado, Madrid (see Haskell and Penny 1981, pp. 173–4, no. 19, illus. on p. 175; also Walker 1994 [Odescalchi], p. 1965–6, fig. 12 on p. 195). Haskell and Penny record, 'A copy of the group had been made by Coysevox for Louis XIV . . . and a cast probably made in connection with this copy, remained in the French Academy in Rome after the group's departure to Spain. This enabled other casts to be taken . . . and more copies to be made' (Haskell and Penny 1981, p. 174; see also Keller-Dorian 1920, pp. 69–70, no. 89, and pl. 138.). The existence of casts was noted by Montaiglon, who in 1758 noted a version in the French Academy of Painting and Sculpture at Rome, and it was probably this version which Nollekens used as his model for the present piece (de Montaiglon and Guiffrey 1901, p. 226; cited by Whinney 1988, p. 463, n. 4). In 1855 a cast of the group was recorded at the Museum at Wiesbaden (Bogler 1855, p. 1 and pl. 1). What was presumably Nollekens's terracotta model for the present piece was included in the third day's sale of Nollekens's effects held by Christie's on 5 July 1823, lot 50, under the heading Terracotta 'From the Modelling Room, First Floor' it was described as 'Castor and Pollux (Group at Madrid) by Nollekins [sic]'; the annotated sale catalogue held in the National Art Library records that this was purchased by 'Sarte' for £4. Its present location is unknown.

Bibliography

Gunnis 1968, p. 277 (noted as being at Shugborough Hall and erroneously thought to be dated 1768); Whinney 1971, p. 114, cat.no. 34, illus. on p. 115; Haskell and Penny 1981, p. 174, n. 18; Lord 1988, p. 915 n. 4; Whinney 1988, pp. 288, 463 n. 4; Bassett and Fogelman 1997, illus. on p. 39.

131: Diana

signed and dated 1778
Marble
h. (with scagliola pedestal) 124 cm.
A.5–1986

Signed and dated on the base: Nollekens Ft., 1778

Commissioned from Charles Watson-Wentworth, 2nd Marquess of Rockingham (1730–1782), together with three other statues of goddesses, between 1773 and 1778, and probably intended for a sculpture gallery at Wentworth Woodhouse, near Rotherham, Yorkshire, his ancestral home. Originally displayed in Lord Rockingham's house in London, but moved to Wentworth Woodhouse following his death in 1782. Sold at the disposal of the Wentworth Woodhouse collection held at Christie's, London, 15 July 1986, lot 85 and purchased by the Art Institute of Chicago. (The other three statues of goddesses were also included in this sale, lots 84, 86, 87 and were subsequently acquired by the J.Paul Getty Museum; see *Getty* 1998, p. 97, cat.no. 34, illus. on p. 97). The licence required by the Art Institute of Chicago to export the *Diana* was withheld by the Secretary of State for Trade and Industry and the Minister for the Arts following an objection being lodged to its export. The figure was subsequently purchased by the V&A from the Art Institute of Chicago in 1986 for £97,707.50.

The pedestal is probably original. The figure of Diana was the last of four statues commissioned by Lord Rockingham from Nollekens at a cost of £115. It is significant as a rare example of 'ideal' sculpture, in a period dominated by funerary sculpture and portrait busts. It has been suggested that the *Diana* could have formed part of a group of figures including *Venus*, *Minerva* and *Juno*, which were made as companion figures to an antique figure of *Paris* (now also in the J. Paul Getty Museum), forming a narrative of the *Judgement of Paris*, a unique concept in eighteenth-century English sculpture. However, the inventory of Lord Rockingham's London house indicates that the three other goddesses were displayed together in one room without the *Diana* (Penny 1991 [Rockingham], p. 23]), suggesting that the present figure was considered distinct from the others, which did indeed represent the *Judgement of Paris*. When all the statues (*Venus*, *Minerva*, *Juno*, *Paris* and the present *Diana*) were displayed in the Sculpture Room at Wentworth Woodhouse in 1834, they do not seem to have been shown as a narrative group (*ibid*., p. 27). The animated pose of the *Diana* differs from the other Nollekens sculptures in the group. Rather than being based directly on an antique source, it is related to a seventeenth-century French bronze figure of *Cupid* (see Baker 2000 [Figured in Marble], fig. 10 on p. 17). Four drawings showing the *Cupid* are included in Nollekens's sketchbook, following further preliminary designs for the *Diana* (departmental records).

A sketch by Nollekens showing Diana nude is in the Department of Prints, Drawings and Paintings, in the Victoria and Albert Museum (inv.no. E.643–1950) (information supplied by Malcolm Baker; see *ibid*., fig. 9 on p. 17).

BIBLIOGRAPHY

Graves V, p. 381, no. 217; Binney 1983, fig. 3 on p. 709 shown in situ in Wentworth Woodhouse; Whinney 1988, pp. 288–90; Penny 1991 [Rockingham], pp. 20, 30–1, and fig. 32; Williamson 1991, p. 879 and pl. XI; Williamson 1996 [Trusted], p. 163; Bassett and Fogelman 1997, p. 86; Baker 2000 [Figured in Marble], pp. 16–17, p. 36.

EXHIBITED

Royal Academy 1778, no. 217.

132: Sir George Savile Bt. (1726–1784)

signed and dated 1784
Marble
h. 75.9 cm.
A.16–1942

Signed on the back: Nollekens F[t].
Inscribed on the front of contemporary pedestal: Sir George Savile/1784·

Chichester Constable Collection. Bought from the Chichester Constable Collection by Cecil Leitch & Kerin, Ltd in 1932. Purchased that year by Dr W. L. Hildburgh F.S.A. from Leitch & Kerin. On loan to the Museum from Dr Hildburgh from 24 January 1933 (loan no. 4785). Given by Dr Hildburgh to the Museum on the occasion of his birthday in 1942.

Sir George Savile, 8th Baronet, was a well-known independent politician. In her London diary of 1786, Sophie von la Roche recorded a visit to the studio of Joseph Nollekens on 27 September 1786. She noted: 'This morning, directly after breakfast, we went to see the sculptor Nollekens, where I experienced the infinite pleasure of meeting this clever, modest man, whose talent is quite equal to that of the ancients ... I noticed with great pleasure that the artist was not only employed and supported by art lovers, but that friendship played its part; for Mr. Nollekens had over six bust portraits of the estimable Savile to complete for his friends, two of whom sent for him with great dispatch on the death of Savile, so as to have an immediate cast of his features. He showed us this mould, from which it is evident that the good man had passed beyond all feeling; for the warm, adhesive mass had torn some hairs away all round his forehead; the veins were still pulsing with the last beats of his charitable heart; pensiveness and spiritual suffering still left their mark on the tender, manly features' (La Roche 1933, pp. 233–4).

A further version with blank eyeballs, purchased from Leonard Partridge in 1947, is in the Fitzwilliam Museum, Cambridge (inv.no. M.19–1947; Whinney 1971, p. 116). Two other marble busts are known, one in a private collection, the other with Daniel Katz Ltd in 1992/3 (see *Katz* 1992, p. 45, illus. p. 46; entry by John Kenworthy-Browne). A bust was at Lord Yarborough's house, 19 Arlington Street, London and another at Holderness House, Hull (I am grateful to John Kenwnorthy-Browne for this information). A bust of Savile (perhaps this one or that now in Cambridge) was exhibited by Nollekens at the Royal Academy in 1785, though Whinney noted 'It is ... impossible to say whether either is the version exhibited at the Royal Academy in 1785' (Graves V, p. 381, no. 635; Whinney 1971, p. 116). Eric Maclagan [q.v.] considered this bust to be 'quite the finest Nollekens bust in the Museum' (departmental records).

BIBLIOGRAPHY

Smith 1920, II, p. 14; *Art Treasures* 1932, p. 146, cat.no. 1161; *British Art* 1934, p. 268, cat.no. 1198; *Masterpieces* 1951, p. 96, no. 47, illus. p. 97; Molesworth 1951, p. 16 and pl. XL; *Hildburgh* 1957, fig. 8 on p. 19; *Style, Truth and the Portrait* 1963, cat.no. 42 and illus. (unpaginated); Whinney 1971, p. 116, cat.no. 35, illus. on p. 117; *Ashmolean* 1992 [III], p. 142.

EXHIBITED

Art Treasures Exhibition 1932, British Antique Dealers' Association, held at Messrs Christie, Manson & Woods, 8 King Street, St James's, London, 12 October to 5 November 1932, cat.no. 1161 (exhibited by Cecil Leitch & Kerin, Ltd); *Exhibition of British Art 1934*, Royal Academy, London, January to March 1934, cat.no. 1198 (mistakenly refers to the Art Treasures Exhibition being held at the Grafton Galleries in 1932; the exhibition was held at Christie, Manson & Woods); *Style, Truth and the Portrait*, The Cleveland Museum of Art, Ohio, 1 to 10 November 1963, cat.no. 42.

133: The Hon. Charles James Fox (1749–1806)

signed; about 1802–3
Marble
h. (incl. socle) 72 cm.
A.1–1945

Signed on the back: J. NOLLEKENS. RA./SCULP.

Purchased by Dr W.L. Hildburgh F.S.A. at an unrecorded sale held at Christie's. On loan from Dr Hildburgh from 25 June 1937 (loan no. 5010). Given by Dr Hildburgh in 1945 as a New Year gift.

This is a version of Nollekens's second bust of Charles James Fox; the earlier bust depicts Fox in a flowing wig. For the earlier version, see *Katz* 1992, p. 42 (entry by John Kenworthy-Browne). Gunnis described the busts of Fox and of Pitt the Younger, as Nollekens's 'stock pieces'. Both versions of Fox's portrait bust were exhibited at the Royal Academy; the first in 1791 (no. 632), the second in 1802 (no. 1073). Whinney suggested, 'The sculptor's masterpiece in the Baroque manner, is, however, beyond question the earlier of his two busts of Charles James Fox (1791), though the existence of many replicas has perhaps tended to dull its interest. The flamboyance of Fox's character has been seized to perfection and the grossness of his physique has been emphasized rather than ignored ... The second bust, made in 1803 [sic, probably meant to be 1802], is also a splendid portrait, though the head, which has no wig is almost frontal, and so the ferocious energy of the sitter is less strongly revealed by the design' (Whinney 1988, pp. 300, 302).

A variant of the present piece is in the Lady Lever Art Gallery (*Lady Lever* 1999, p. 66, inv.no. LL726), another minus the drapery, incised and dated 1805, is in the National Portrait Gallery (*NPG* 1981, p. 207, no. 3887); a further example of 1803 is in the possession of George Howard Esq., at Castle Howard (see Irwin 1966, fig. 155). Dated examples of both busts may also be found at Holland House listed in the catalogue of 1904, 'In the breakfast Room is a bust of Mr Fox by Nollekens (1793), and another by the same (1807) is in the entrance Hall' (*Ilchester* 1904, p. 138). A wax cast of a bust of Fox by Peter Rouw (1770–1852), 'executed after his death in 1807', is also listed in the Ilchester catalogue (*ibid.*, p. 170, cat.no. 246). The 1791 bust executed by Nollekens for Lord Fitzwilliam was subsequently given by Fitzwilliam to Catherine II of Russia, and is now in the Hermitage (see Ettinger 1924, and illus. on p. 89; *Treasures* 2000, p. 132, cat.no. 213). A painting by Lemuel Francis Abbott (1760–1802) depicting Nollekens in front of the earlier version of his bust of Fox, is in the National Portrait Gallery (*NPG* 1981, p. 417, no. 30), an engraving of which is illustrated by Smith (see Smith 1920, I, illus. opp. p. 380). For the version at Carlton House, see *Carlton House* 1991, p. 52, cat.no. 2.

At the sale of Mr George Robins at Shugborough Hall, held on 1 August 1842 and following thirteen days, lot 14 on the eighth day was described as: ' A SPLENDID MARBLE BUST OF THE RIGHT HONOURABLE CHARLES JAMES FOX, with drapery, a noble specimen of sculpture, by NOLLEKENS, on small circular pedestal, together 28 inches high'. In the annotated facsimile copy of the catalogue held in the National Art Library, this lot is recorded as sold for £210.

John Kenworthy-Browne has suggested that the signature of the present bust is not typical, and was put on after Nollekens's lifetime, and that the bust may have been carved by one of his assistants, perhaps Alexander Goblet [q.v.], or Sebstian Gahagan (fl. 1800–35).

Busts by Nollekens of Fox and Pitt were often displayed as a pair; see entry for cat.no. 134.

Bibliography

Whinney 1971, p. 122, no. 38, illus. on pl. 123; Whinney 1988, p. 464, n. 20; TDA, 23, p. 190 and illus [Kenworthy-Browne].

Exhibited

George III. Bicentennial Exhibition, Yorktown Victory Center, Virginia, USA, April 1977 to 31 March 1978.

134: William Pitt the Younger (1759–1806)

signed; about 1806–23
Marble
h. 53.5 cm.
A.11–1925

Signed on the back truncation: J NOLLEKENS Fc^{t}

Given by Dr W.L. Hildburgh, F.S.A. in 1925.

On acquisition R.P. Bedford [q.v.] wrote, 'This is evidently one of the 74 marble busts of Pitt which were made by Nollekens [sic] masons after the death mask. There was a constant demand for busts of Pitt & Fox, they were known as "Nollekens' stock pieces". As is to be expected the work is dull but it is quite genuine'. Gunnis records that the busts of Pitt, taken from a mask produced immediately after his death, were sold by Nollekens for £120 each, and that Nollekens 'also made replicas of the mask itself, but in this case the original is in the possession of Earl Stanhope' (Gunnis 1968, p. 276). Nollekens also executed a full-size marble statue of Pitt, erected at Senate House, Cambridge in 1812.

In the relevant entry in the *Review of Principal Acquisitions during the Year 1929* in connection with the recent acquisition of busts of Charles and Henrietta Pelham – see entries for cat.nos. 135 and 136 – the writer (probably Bedford) notes, 'Of his bust of Pitt, which the sculptor made from a death mask, he carved no less than 74 examples in marble, and 600 were cast in plaster. These and Nollekens' other works were produced by pointing, a practice which was almost universal by that day, and his works have all the fault which that mechanical process gives' (*Review* 1929, p. 4); see also Smith 1920, I, pp. 370–1.

Busts by Nollekens of *Pitt* and *Fox* were often displayed as a pair; see entry for cat.no. 133.

Bibliography

Review 1925, p. 5; *Review* 1929, p. 4.

135: Charles Pelham, later 1st Earl of Yarborough (1781–1846)

signed and dated 1808
Marble
h. 72 cm.
A.119–1929

Signed and dated on the back: Nollekens Ft./ 1808.

From the collection of Lord Yarborough. Sold together with seventeen other portrait busts by Nollekens at Christie's, 11 July 1929, lot 146; purchased by Messrs Alfred Spero and Kerin Ltd, 9 Clifford Street, New Bond Street, London. Purchased by the Museum with its contemporary pedestal (A.119:A-1929) from Messrs Alfred Spero and Kerin Ltd in 1929 for £25.

Charles Anderson Pelham, later 1st Baron Yarborough, the father of the sitter, was one of Nollekens's chief patrons, for whom the sculptor produced over thirty works (see Lord 1988).

The present bust was purchased by Alfred Spero and Kerin at the same sale as that of cat.no. 136, later discovered to be its pendant. R.P. Bedford [q.v.] wrote, 'This is a typical male bust by Nollekens of the less official type and I think that it is very cheap. Both busts have charming wood pedestals of contemporary date'.

An earlier version, signed and dated 1806, is at Brocklesby Park, Lincolnshire, the Yarborough ancestral home (Lord 1988, p. 918). For Brocklesby Park see also Hussey 1934; for a discussion of the mausoleum at Brocklesby Park, see Lord 1992 [Brocklesby].

Bibliography

Smith 1920, II, p. 13; *Review* 1929, p. 4, pl. III; Gunnis 1968, p. 278; Lord 1988, p. 918, n. 25 (there incorrectly cited as inv.no. A.119–1950), and fig. 41.

Exhibited

Nollekens exhibited a bust of 'the Hon. Mr Pelham' at the Royal Academy in 1808 (Graves V, p. 382, no. 969), either the present bust or a variant.

136: Henrietta Pelham (m.1806; d.1813)

signed and dated 1810
Marble
h. (incl. socle) 66 cm.
A.120–1929

Signed and dated on the back: Nollekens Fc./ 1810.

From the collection of Lord Yarborough; sold at Christie's, 11 July 1929, lot 160; purchased by Messrs Alfred Spero and Kerin Ltd, 9 Clifford Street, New Bond Street, London for £37 16s. Purchased by the Museum with its contemporary pedestal (A.120:A-1929) from Alfred Spero & Kerin Ltd in 1929 for £37 16s.

See entry for cat.no. 135.

In his recommendation for acquiring the present bust, R.P. Bedford [q.v.] commented that though the other portrait busts by Nollekens in the sale at Christie's were 'mainly shop pieces, and are, as usual with works of this class, very dull, but Lot 160 – a portrait of Henrietta, wife of the first Earl of Yarborough, signed and dated 1810 – seems to be of a different character and to have all the marks of the artist's individual touch. It is carved in butter-coloured marble, highly polished, and is a most attractive object'.

An earlier version, signed and dated 1808, is at Brocklesby Park, Lincolnshire, the Yarborough ancestral home (Lord 1988, p. 918, fig. 42).

Bibliography

Smith 1920, II, p. 13; *Review* 1929, p. 4, pl. III; Graves V, p. 382, no. 874; Lord 1988, p. 918, n. 25 – there incorrectly cited as inv.no. A.120–1950).

Exhibited

A bust of the 'Hon. Mrs Pelham' was exhibited at the Royal Academy in 1810 (no. 874), which Lord suggested was the present piece (Lord 1988, p. 918, n. 25).

137: Lady Brownlow (1788–1814)

signed and dated 1814
Marble
h. (incl. socle) 66 cm.
A.60–1965

Signed and dated on the back: NOLLEKENS Ft. 1814.

Bequeathed by Rupert Gunnis Esq., Hungershall Lodge, Tunbridge Wells, Kent, in 1965. The Gunnis bequest included marble busts, a marble relief, waxes (inv.nos. A.60 to A.143–1965), also drawings of sculpture and monuments, now held in the Department of Prints, Drawings and Paintings. For a discussion of Gunnis as a collector, see Knox 1998.

The circular marble base is damaged.

Evidently the donor was uncertain about the identity of the sitter. In the first edition of *Dictionary of British Sculptors 1660–1851*, he identified the present bust as Mrs Tower (Gunnis 1953, p. 278), but in the 1968 edition it is called Lady Brownlow (Gunnis 1968, p. 278). Nollekens exhibited a bust of Lord Brownlow at the Royal Academy in 1810 (Graves V, p. 382, no. 766). Two busts of Lady Brownlow are listed by J.T. Smith in his list of busts executed by Nollekens (Smith 1920, II, p. 11).

The present bust is illustrated in situ in a photograph of the Drawing Room at Hungershall Lodge in 1965 (Knox 1998, p. 93, fig. 9). John Kenworthy-Browne has suggested this is a posthumous bust ordered by Lord Brownlow following his wife's death on 21 February 1814, aged 25. A further marble version with an inscriptional tablet is at Belton House, Lincolnshire, the Brownlow ancestral home (I am grateful to John Kenworthy-Browne for this information, and to Paul Hatfield for confirming its catalogue number BEL/SC/4).

BIBLIOGRAPHY
Gunnis 1968, p. 278; Knox 1998, p. 93, fig. 9.

138: Juno Pronuba

about 1765–70
Terracotta
h. 18.2 cm.
A.10–1944

Sold on the second day of Christie's sale of Nollekens's studio effects, held on 4 July 1823, lot 71, and purchased by the sculptor Peter Rouw for 13s, together with cat.no. 141 and one other model. Katharine Esdaile [q.v.] had suggested this might be a version of the *Juno Pronuba*, sold as lot 19 on the second day's sale held on 4 July 1823. Sold together with figures of *Religion* by Nollekens, and a '*Cupid with his Bow,* from the antique of Edmund Burke' lot 19 was purchased by Peter Rouw for 13s. Probably given by Rouw to Mrs C.H. Smith (née Fanny Riviere) (see below). Thence by descent to Miss Zoë Gordon Smith. Given by Miss Zoë Gordon Smith, The Close, 10 St Raphael Road, West Worthing in 1944, together with cat.nos. 139 to 142 and 146.

In a recent article Kenworthy-Browne rejects the suggestion that the six terracotta models presented to the Museum by Miss Gordon Smith had originally been given by Nollekens himself to the donor's grandmother, as proposed by Esdaile in her 1944 article and as also accepted by Whinney (Esdaile 1944, p. 220; Whinney 1971, p. 120), as she would have only been ten years old at the time of the gift. On examining this group of terracotta models, Eric Maclagan [q.v.] had noted on 17 December 1943, 'the grandmother whose name was perhaps Riviere, lived close to Nollekens and obtained the terracottas direct from him. Mrs Cater [a friend of the donor who helped instigate the gift to the Museum] thinks that she was connected in some way with Smith, the biographer of Nollekens'.

A letter from Mrs C.E. [Dora] Cater written on 2 January 1944 appears to confirm the statuettes were given by Peter Rouw to the Smith family; she writes, 'The Nollekens statuettes came to Miss Zoë Gordon Smith from her parents, Mr and Mrs P. Gordon-Smith, to whom they were left by his mother, Mrs Charles Harriett Smith, née Fanny Riviere. She was born in 1813, and married C.H. Smith as his second wife in 1833? -4. There appears to be no direct account of how the statuettes came into the C.H. Smiths' possession, whether by purchase or gift, but the few words about them in her "Letter to Gordon" will be useful, and, I think, some information about the C.H. Smiths themselves... When she was seventy-nine, in an effort to hand on the torch, she wrote a remarkable letter or memoir to her grandson which she called "Letter to Gordon"... "I was only ten when Nollekens died, but remember my elders talking of him and his queer ways – I afterwards became associated with those who knew him quite well – the Bonomis, Byrnes, and Rouws... ". Mrs C.H. Smith makes many personal references to Joseph Bonomi, and to Peter Rouw. I quote one to Peter Rouw to show her genuine acquaintance with Nollekens' friends. "Peter Rouw, the sculptor and modeller in wax, also lived near us – a fine, military-looking man. He gave us many fine examples of his own wax models – duplicates of some in South Kensington Museum"'.

Katharine Esdaile had been misinformed about the ownership of two of the terracottas included in her 1944 article, and in so doing mistakenly suggested this terracotta was on loan to the Museum from Mrs C.A. Cater, when in fact it was amongst those given by Miss Gordon-Smith. The figure described by Esdaile as the *Young*

Bacchus or perhaps *Young Apollo*, was not in fact in the possession of the Museum as stated by Esdaile, but was temporarily on loan from Mrs C.A. Cater (see Esdaile 1944, p. 223, no. 5, and pl. II (B).

Esdaile noted the 'subject was treated by Nollekens in the "bas-relief in terracotta of a marriage ceremony, modelled by Mr. Nollekens from the one [an antique original] over the dining-room door" at Towneley's [sic] house in Park Street' (*ibid.*, p. 223), and cites a passage from Smith's *Nollekens and his Times*, 'Over the chimney-piece in the drawing-room looking into Park-street, was a bas-relief in terracotta of a marriage ceremony, modelled by Mr. Nollekens from the one over the dining-room door. This performance was highly esteemed by Mr. Townley, who always spake of Mr. Nollekens as the first Sculptor of his day . . .The bride and bridegroom are seen with joined hands; behind and between them stands Juno Pronuba' (Smith 1920, I, p. 217, and n. 3).

Kenworthy-Browne comments that this figure of *Juno Pronuba* is 'unquestionably by Nollekens; his Rome period is indicated by rough surface treatment, and by the fact that this little model reproduces in miniature a statue of Ceres which was owned by Cavaceppi and published in Cavaceppi's *Raccolta* (1769), but with the addition of a wreath over the veil' (Kenworthy-Browne 1998, p. 73, and n. 17).

Bibliography

Esdaile 1944, p. 223, no, 7, pl. II (C) on p. 222, where it is incorrectly stated as being the property of Mrs C.A. Cater; Gunnis 1968, p. 277; Kenworthy-Browne 1998, pp. 73, 77, no. 3, and fig. 3 on p. 79.

139: Hero dying in the arms of Victory

about 1790
Terracotta
h. 22 cm.
A.7–1944

Sold on the second day of the Christie's sale of Nollekens's studio effects, held on 4 July 1823, lot 40, and purchased by the sculptor Peter Rouw for 15s. Given by Miss Zoë Gordon Smith, The Close, 10 St Raphael Road, West Worthing in 1944, together with cat.nos. 138, 140 to 142 and 146. See entry for cat.no. 138.

This model was identified by Katharine Esdaile as a *Young Man Sinking in Death*, the first sketch for the monument to Lord Robert Manners, in the event not executed, for the chapel at Belvoir Castle, exhibited at the Royal Academy in 1790 (no. 660). Esdaile commented, 'What seems to have been a sketch for the same subject, a group of two Figures, a Dying Hero and Victory, No. 15 in the third day's sale, is also on record. In the end, Lord Rockingham's head appeared as a medallion on Nelson's famous if overpowering Monument to the Three Captains in Westminster Abbey, the execution of which may, with the Duke's death, have put a stop to the idea of another at Belvoir' (Esdaile 1944, pp. 220, 3). However, Kenworthy-Browne suggests the present piece could alternatively be identified with the model exhibited at the Royal Academy in 1802 (Graves V, p. 382 no. 1067), described as 'A sketch of a monument for a naval officer expiring in the arms of Victory', or that exhibited at the British Institution in 1809, 'Model of a group of a naval officer expiring in the arms of Victory' (no. 338) (Kenworthy-Browne 1998, p. 77).

A related drawing by Nollekens showing the same subject with the hero held in a more upright position was acquired by the Department of Prints, Drawings and Paintings in 1950 (inv.no. E.618–1950). Kenworthy-Browne illustrates a related design for this monument, of about 1782–90, which is in the Ashmolean Museum, Oxford (*ibid.*, fig. 7 on p. 80), together with further related drawings.

In her London diary of 1786, Sophie von la Roche noted a visit to Nollekens's studio on 27 September where she saw two monuments to the Duke of Rutland. Though one was intended for Westminster Abbey, the composition of the other – apparently intended as a private commemoration for the Rutland estate – appears to relate to the present piece: ' . . . then the superb monument which the Duke of Rutland is having erected at Westminster Abbey to his beloved brother Manners. Lord Manners died at he age of twenty-four, a naval captain in the American war, from a cannon-ball from the enemy ships, which deprived him of both feet. This monument is very large and very noble. A kind of hill by the seashore, on which Time is supporting a rostral column, and pendent from it the bust of Lord Manners, and, at the duke's command, those of two other honest officers who served and died at his brother's side; a sea-horse bears a Triton to the shore, who mournfully points to the likenesses; the spirit of fame hovers over the monument, laurel wreaths in hand. The second monument is meant for the garden of his country estate – Lord Manners lies dying on the sea-shore, supported by the goddess of victory. The artist tactfully contrived to make the goddess in the image of the beautiful Duchess of Rutland, who gazes at him with a sister's tender sorrow, supporting him with one arm and offering him a palm of victory with her other hand' (La Roche 1933, pp. 233–4).

Katharine Esdaile discussed Nollekens's aptitude for terracotta modelling in an article in the *Burlington Magazine* of 1944: 'Nollekens's marbles tend to be frigid and sometimes meretricious; these sketches show him at work for his own pleasure; modelling either out of his head, or for orders, those in the last category being altogether more spontaneous than the finished marbles, which tend to be frigid and were usually carved by his workmen' (Esdaile 1944, p. 223). For a more recent discussion of the terracotta models by Nollekens, see Kenworthy-Browne 1998.

Bibliography

Graves V, p. 381, no. 660; Esdaile 1944, pp. 220–3, pl. I (C) on p. 221; Gunnis 1968, p. 277; Whinney 1971, p. 118, no. 36, illus. on

p. 119; Whinney 1988, p. 295; Kenworthy-Browne 1998, p. 77, no. 6, fig. 6 on p. 80.

EXHIBITED
Royal Academy 1790 no. 660.

140: Venus standing on a shell

about 1800?
Terracotta
h. 21 cm.
A.9–1944

Sold on the second day of the Christie's sale of Nollekens's studio effects, held on 4 July 1823, lot 40, together with cat.no. 142, purchased by the sculptor Peter Rouw for 18s. Given by Miss Zoë Gordon Smith, The Close, 10 St Raphael Road, West Worthing in 1944, together with cat.nos. 138, 139, 141, 142 and 146. See entry for cat. no. 138.

The forearm and hand are missing.

Katharine Esdaile had suggested that this model may be identified as the figure of *Modesty*, which was included in the Nollekens sale as lot 29, described as ' A female figure, Modesty' (Esdaile 1944, p. 223). However, lot 29 on any of the sale days does not appear to correspond with the present piece. Kenworthy-Browne has recently proposed that it is more likely to be a representation of *Venus standing on a shell* (Kenworthy Browne 1998, p. 78, no. 12).

BIBLIOGRAPHY
Esdaile 1944, p. 223, no. 4, and pl. II(A) on p. 222; Gunnis 1968, p. 277; Kenworthy-Browne 1998, p. 78, no. 12, fig. 16 on p. 82.

EXHIBITED
Nollekens exhibited 'Venus annointing her hair' at the Royal Academy in 1800 (no. 1031), possibly the present piece.

141: Woman with a book, possibly Religion, or Mrs Jane Coke of Holkham (1753–1800)

about 1800–2
Terracotta
h. 22 cm.
A.8–1944

Sold on the second day of the Christie's sale of Nollekens's studio effects, held on 4 July 1823, lot 19, and purchased by the sculptor Peter Rouw for 13s, together with cat.no. 138. Given by Miss Zoë Gordon Smith, The Close, 10 St Raphael Road, West Worthing in 1944, together with cat. nos. 138 to 140, 142 and 146. See entry for cat. no. 138.

In her 1944 article Katharine Esdaile suggested this model might relate to a number of monuments, 'The Victoria and Albert Museum has a larger and more finely finished example of the type, which was a favourite of the sculptor and is used, eg. on the Irwin Monument at Whitkirk, Leeds, the Kemys-Tynte at Goathurst, Somerset, and a Noel monument at Exton, Rutland. The exact marble has not yet been identified, but the Kemys-Tynte tomb is the nearest of those named to this first sketch' (Esdaile 1944, p. 220).

Traditionally unidentified and described as *Woman with a book*, Kenworthy-Browne suggests that this model may depict *Religion*, or Mrs Coke of Holkham, by comparing this model with drawings for the monument to Mrs Coke (d. 1800) at Tittleshall, Norfolk, held in Sir John Soane's Museum, the Department of Prints, Drawings and Paintings at the Victoria and Albert Museum (inv.no. E.636–1950) and the Ashmolean Museum, Oxford respectively; see Kenworthy-Browne 1998, figs. 10, 11 and 12 on p. 81. A further drawing related to this monument is in the Department of Prints, Drawings and Paintings (inv.no. E.4358–1920); see Physick 1969, fig. 114 on p. 150 and p. 151.

BIBLIOGRAPHY
Esdaile 1944, p. 220, no. 2, pl. I (B) on p. 221; Kenworthy-Browne 1998, p. 77, no. 8, fig. 9 on p. 81.

142: Maria, Mrs Henry Howard of Corby Castle, Cumberland and her child (d.1788)

about 1800–3
Terracotta
h. 14 cm.
A.5–1944

Identified by Kenworthy-Browne as being sold together with a figure of Venus standing on a shell cat.no. 140, on the second day of the Christie's sale of Nollekens's studio effects, held on 4 July 1823, lot 40; this sketch was amongst those purchased by the sculptor Peter Rouw (1770–1852), who paid 18s for this lot. In her article Katharine Esdaile had erroneously suggested they were sold as lot 41. Given by Miss Zoë Gordon Smith, The Close, 10 St Raphael Road, West Worthing in 1944, together with cat.nos. 138 to 141 and 146. See entry for cat. no. 138.

This terracotta was identified by Katharine Esdaile as a sketch for the marble monument to Mrs Howard, who died in childbirth in 1788, erected in Wetheral Church, Cumberland in 1803. Though Cunningham and subsequent writers, including Esdaile, have suggested the cost of the monument was £2000, Penny notes that it was in fact £1,500 (Cunningham 1830, p. 175; Penny 1975 [Church Monuments], p. 316, and n. 5). The finished monument differs from the model in a number of ways, as noted by Penny (*ibid.*, pp. 316–7). A design for the whole monument by Nollekens of about 1789 is in the Department of Prints, Drawings and Paintings in the Victoria and Albert Museum (inv.no. E.958–1965); see Physick 1969, p. 37, fig. 20 on p. 44. Another related drawing – inv.no. E.957–1965 – is also in the Department of Prints, Drawings and Paintings. J.T. Smith noted, 'It has been roundly asserted, that Nollekens took the composition of this monument from that erected to the Cardinal Richelieu. Be that as it may, the figure of the child alone is equal to any thing ancient or modern, and the praise bestowed on that, Nollekens is unequivocally entitled to. The figure of Religion, in this monument, was carved by Goblet' (Smith 1920, II, p. 15, n. 2).

A marble idealised portrait bust identified by Nicholas Penny as Maria, Mrs Henry Howard of Corby, is in the Ashmolean Museum, Oxford (see *Ashmolean* 1992 [III], p. 140, illus. on p. 141). Penny suggests, 'It was wholly characteristic of Nollekens to make a bust version as well as a full-length effigy' (*ibid.*, p. 140).

Bibliography

Graves V, p. 382, no. 1082; Esdaile 1944, p. 220, no. 1, and pl. 1 (A) on p. 221; Gunnis 1968, p. 277; Whinney 1971, p. 120, no. 37, illus. on p. 121; *Neo-classicism* 1972, p. 267, cat.no. 414; Penny 1975 [Church Monuments], pp. 317–8; Kenworthy-Browne 1998, p. 77, no. 7, fig. 8 on p. 80.

Exhibited

Nollekens exhibited at the Royal Academy in 1800 'A monumental group to the memory of a lady who died in child-bed, supported by Religion, etc.' (no. 1082), presumed to be the present piece; Exhibition of photographs of Monumental sculpture, Church of All Hallows on the Wall, London, February to March 1964; *Drawings by English Sculptors 1680–1810*, Ashmolean Museum, Oxford, 23 November to 10 December 1967; *The Age of Neo-classicism*, Royal Academy and Victoria and Albert Museum, 9 September to 19 November 1972, cat.no. 414; *The Art of Death*, Victoria and Albert Museum, 8 January to 22 March 1992.

143: The Three Graces

about 1802
Terracotta
h. 18.5 cm.
A.1–2000

Included in second day of the sale of Nollekens's effects, held at Christie's, 4 July 1823, lot 37, under the section headed 'Pensieri in Terra Cotta, by Mr. Nollekins [sic] From the Back Parlour, Ground Floor", described as 'A ditto [Group] The Three Graces'; it was purchased by Mrs Palmer for £2 12s 0d. Sold in the Mrs Russell sale held on 19 March 1847, lot 392, bought by Norton for £2 2s 8d. Included in the P. Norton sale held by Christie's on 19 January 1869, lot 1101, bought by 'B.B.' for £2 19s. Purchased by Peter and Linda Murray 'about 1962 at Petworth' (see Kenworthy-Browne 1998, p. 78; no further details known). Given to the Museum by Mrs Linda Murray F.S.A. in 2000.

The earlier provenance of the present piece is similar to that of another terracotta by Nollekens of *Laocoon and his sons*; see entry for cat.no. 145.

It is not known whether this group was intended as a model for a larger work; John Kenworthy-Browne has commented, 'Whether or not it had been intended for marble, this little group looks like the result of experiment and study' (Kenworthy-Browne 1998, p. 75). In comparing the present piece with Canova's *Three Graces*, a contemporary commentator suggested the Nollekens terracotta was the superior work, writing: 'There is a terra cotta by Nollekens, that far surpasses in design the Graces of the celebrated Venetian. The three sisters are most judiciously seated on an irregular mound, and their attitudes have all the simplicity and unaffected ease of which forms of immortal grace and beauty are susceptible. Unlike the draperied, simpering, mirror-taught, posture-studied "Ballerine", of Canova, these are really the "Decantes Gratiae", unconscious of their charms, and more modest and innocent for being represented in the *nuda veritas* of Nature' (Medwin 1839, p. 470; cited by Kenworthy-Browne 1998, p. 75). Canova's group of the *Three Graces* was jointly purchased by the Victoria and Albert Museum and the National Galleries of Scotland in 1994, inv.no. A.4–1994.

A drawing by Nollekens of a standing group of the *Three Graces* is in the Department of Prints, Drawings and Paintings (inv.no. E.625–1950).

I am grateful to John Kenworthy-Browne for his help with this entry.

BIBLIOGRAPHY

Graves V, p. 382, no. 1064; Medwin 1839, pp. 469–70 (cited by Kenworthy-Browne); Kenworthy-Browne 1998, pp. 73, 75, 78, no. 14, fig. 18 on p. 83; *V&A Magazine* 2000 [II], p. 2 and illus.

EXHIBITED

Royal Academy 1802, no. 1064. Recorded in the Christie's sale catalogue, 11 January 1869, as being 'Exhibited at Manchester', perhaps the Manchester Art Treasures Exhibition of 1857, although it is not listed in the published catalogue of the exhibition.

144: The Judgement of Paris

about 1803
Terracotta
h. 23 cm.
A.21–1955

Sold on the second day of the Christie's sale of Nollekens's studio effects, held on 4 July 1823, lot 36, purchased by Nevill for £2 10s. On loan from Mrs R.M. Pott, 11 Scarsdale Villas, Kensington, from 21 July 1939 (loan no 2). Given by Reginald H. Pott in 1955. In 1944 Mrs Pott also gave to the Museum a series of five models for hands, perhaps by Roubiliac, which had formerly been in the possession of her father, the Victorian painter and sculptor Edward Henry Corbould; see entries for cat.nos. 169 to 174. It is possible therefore that the present piece also formed part of his collection.

The remains of a label on the base is inscribed: Original Model of "The Judgement . . . by Nollikyns [sic]

Penny comments, 'The sinuous elegance and harmonious balance of the composition do not diminish the dramatic impact that derives from the nearly indecorous freedom of the goddesses' behavior [sic], such as is found in no earlier version of the subject in any medium and such as Nollekens would not perhaps have felt to be appropriate on a larger scale' (Penny 1991 [Rockingham], p. 29).

BIBLIOGRAPHY

Graves V, p. 382, no. 932; Gunnis 1968, p. 277, as lent by Mrs M. Pott; *Neo-classicism* 1972, p. 266, cat.no. 412; Penny 1991 [Rockingham], pp. 28–9, fig. 29 on p. 29, p. 34 n. 118; Kenworthy-Browne 1998, pp. 75, no. 17, 78 and fig 21 on p. 84.

EXHIBITED
In 1803 Nollekens exhibited at the Royal Academy a sketch of the *Judgment of Paris* (no. 932), thought to be the present piece; *The Age of Neo-classicism*, Royal Academy and Victoria and Albert Museum, 9 September to 19 November 1972, cat.no. 412.

145: Laocoon and his sons

about 1803–5
Terracotta
h. 26 cm.
A.12–1966

At the sale of Nolleken's effects held from 3 to 5 July by Mr Christie, lot 35 sold on second day of the sale, 4 July 1823, described as 'A Group of Laocoon, – treated differently from the antique', is noted on departmental records. In an annotated copy of the catalogue held in the National Art Library noted as purchased by 'Este' for 15s (identified as Rev. J.C. Este by Kenworthy-Browne, although he suggests that the model could probably be identified as that sold on the third day of the Nollekens sale, held on 5 July 1823, lot 63, described as 'A sitting female and Laocoon by Nollekins [sic]'); purchased by Mrs Palmer for £7. Kenworthy-Browne adds to the provenance by citing the model as being sold at the Mrs Russell sale on 19 March 1847, lot 397; purchased by Mr Peter Norton Esq, Soho Square, London for £1 13s. Sold at the sale of Peter Norton's collection held at Christie, Manson and Woods, 8 King Street, London on the seventh day of the sale, 19 January 1869, lot 1096, described as 'Laocoon, an original design, by Nollekins [sic] – glass shade and gilt stand'. In an annotated copy of the catalogue held in the National Art Library it is recorded that this was purchased by Benjamin for £1 12s. Another group by Nollekens was also sold to Benjamin: lot 1095, it too was in a glass shade and gilt stand, and was described as 'A group of Adam and Eve, with two children, a dog and a dove'. Purchased by the grandfather of the vendor around 1876. Purchased from Miss Dorothy Hartley, Froncysylltau Llangollen, North Wales, in 1966 for £250 under the Hildburgh Bequest.

According to the vendor, the family had assumed it to be the work of Giovanni Bologna. Miss Hartley wrote, 'Your dates 1770–1810 (as said) are correct by own known ownership, this is Sure. The name of the artist (Gio; Bologna) was family tradition, (and probably based on the European travels of my grandparent while young)'.

Whinney commented, 'The composition is freely adapted from the famous Hellenistic Group in the Vatican, Rome, but is entirely different in conception. In the antique model the three figures are set out in line as on a frieze, so that the group has only one viewpoint, and the sons are young adolescents. The present group is tied together in the form of a spiral and there is an additional note of sentiment in the idea of the young children meeting their doom' (Whinney 1971, p. 124; see also Haskell and Penny 1981, pp. 243–7).

The ascription to Nollekens is based on the similarity of the present piece to other terracotta sketch models known to be by him; see cat.nos. 138 to 144 and 146: this is supported by two related drawings by Nollekens in the Department of Prints, Drawings and Paintings (inv.nos. E.572 and 573–1950), and more convincingly a pencil study for a Laocoon group, which is in the Ashmolean Museum, Oxford.

BIBLIOGRAPHY
Graves VI, p. 382, no. 694; Gunnis 1968, p. 277; Whinney 1971, p. 124, illus p. 125; *Neo-classicism* 1972, pp. 265–6, cat.no. 411; Kenworthy-Browne 1998, pp. 75–6, 78 no. 18, fig. 22 on p. 84.

EXHIBITED
Nollekens exhibited 'A sketch of Laicoon [sic] and his two sons' at the Royal Academy in 1805 (no. 694), suggested by Whinney to be the present piece; *Drawings by English Sculptors 1680–1810*, Ashmolean Museum, Oxford, 23 November to 10 December 1967; *Age of Neo-classicism*, Royal Academy and Victoria and Albert Museum, London, 9 September to 19 November 1972, cat.no. 411; *Taste and the Antique*, Ashmolean Museum, Oxford, 25 March 1981 to 10 May 1981, cat.no. 54.

146: Venus and Adonis

about 1810
Terracotta
h. 22.5 cm.
A.6–1944

Given by Miss Zoë Gordon Smith, The Close, 10 St Raphael Road, West Worthing in 1944, together with cat.nos. 138 to 142. See entry for cat. no. 138.

The fingers are missing from *Adonis*.

In her article on the models acquired by the Museum from Miss Gordon Smith, Katharine Esdaile commented, 'The modelling of this group, artistically the finest of the seven, is exceptionally fine and careful' (Esdaile 1944, p. 223). She noted that although Nollekens did not exhibit the present piece at the Royal Academy, a figure of Adonis was exhibited there in 1782 (Graves V, p. 381, no. 535).

A related drawing dateable to about 1810 is in the Ashmolean Museum, Oxford (Kenworthy-Browne 1998, p. 78, and fig. 24 on p. 84).

BIBLIOGRAPHY

Esdaile 1944, p. 223, no. 6, and pl. II (D) on p. 222; Gunnis 1968, p. 277; Kenworthy-Browne 1998, pp. 76, 78, no. 19, fig. 23 on p. 84.

147: Dr Samuel Johnson (1709–1784)

after 1777
Anonymous after an original by Joseph Nollekens
Lead
h. 52.5 cm.
A.63–1926

Inscribed on the early nineteenth century pedestal: RAMBLER

On loan to the Museum, together with its mahogany pedestal (A.63:A-1926) from the donor from 16 August 1915 (loan nos. 810 bust, and 811 & 811A – pedestal in two parts) immediately prior to that on loan to the Burlington Fine Arts Club. Bequeathed by Lt. Col. G.B. Croft Lyons in 1926.

In 1915 when the bust was taken on loan, Eric Maclagan [q.v.] commented: 'This is a most interesting bust of Dr Johnson, apparently based on a (lost?) bust by Nollekens. The pedestal is really an early 19th century mahogany gin-cupboard, but serves the purpose very well'.

This bust is after a clay bust of Johnson executed by Nollekens in 1777. The bust rests on a plinth fashioned to resemble a bound volume of Johnson's Rambler writings: for a discussion of the Rambler essays, see Wiles [n.d.].

The production of this bust in lead, a relatively cheap material, implies that other versions might exist, but none is recorded. Four plaster versions are known: two at the Samuel Johnson Birthplace Museum, Lichfield, Staffordshire (inv.nos. 2000.282 and 2000.283; I am grateful to Annette French for confirming this information), and a further one at the Athenaeum, London. A terracotta version is also at the Athenaeum (I am grateful to John Kenworthy-Browne for this information).

Plaster cast versions of the head of the Johnson bust were offered for sale by the Museum's cast selling service: in the 1939 *Catalogue of Plaster Casts*, they were priced at 8s 6d (*Casts* 1939, p. 24, no. 244; *Supplement* [n.d.], no. 244).

The bust of Johnson is discussed by Smith in *Nollekens and his Times*, who noted: 'When the Doctor sat to Mr. Nollekens for his bust, he was very much displeased at the manner in which the head had been loaded with hair, which the Sculptor insisted upon, as it made him look more like an ancient poet. The sittings were not very favourable, which rather vexed the artist, who, upon opening the street-door, a vulgarity he was addicted to, peevishly whined – "Now, Doctor, you did say you would give my busto half an hour before dinner, and the dinner has been waiting this long time". To which the Doctor's reply was, "Bow-wow-wow!". The bust is a wonderfully fine one and very like, but certainly the sort of hair is objectionable; having been modelled from the flowing locks of a sturdy Irish beggar, originally a street pavior, who, after he sat an hour, refused to take a shilling, stating that he could have made more by begging!' (Smith 1920, I, pp. 46–7 and Smith 1920, II, n. 1 on p. 13).

BIBLIOGRAPHY

Review 1926, p. 5 and fig 5; *Country Life* 1928; *Johnson* 1984, pp. 123–5, cat.no. 91; Wiles [n.d.], p. 156, and fig. 1 opp. p. 156.

EXHIBITED

Festival of the City of London, Royal Exchange, 6 July to 4 August 1964; *Samuel Johnson 1709–84. A Bicentenary Exhibition*, Arts Council, 19 July to 14 September 1984, cat.no. 91.

John Nost III (the Younger)

(b. London 1713 – d. Dublin 1780)

Nost the Younger would appear to be the son of the sculptor John Nost II (d. 1729), who was the cousin of John Nost I (known as 'the Elder') [q.v.]. Nost the Younger trained under Henry Scheemakers (1670–1748) in London in 1726, travelling to Dublin in 1749 where he settled, and executed a number of portrait busts for the Dublin Society, and public monuments including a statue of George III for Dublin City Hall. Nost the Younger also appears sporadically to have lived and worked in London after 1749, where his bust of the actor David Garrick was apparently reproduced in many copies. He died in Mecklenburgh Street, Dublin in 1780, and was described by the London press as 'statuary to his majesty'. I am grateful to Greg Sullivan for his help with this biography.

Strickland 1913, II, pp. 478–87; Gunnis 1968, p. 282; O'Connell 1987; Davis 1991, p. 28; Louvre 1992 [Baker], pp. 71–4; Thieme-Becker, 25, p. 523; TDA, 23, pp. 253–4 [Murdoch]; Hill 1998, pp. 48–55; Spencer-Longhurst and Naylor 1998; Sullivan [forthcoming].

148: George III (b.1738; r.1760–1820)

signed and dated 1767
Marble
h. 66 cm.
A.3–1957

Signed and dated on the back: From the Life/ by/ Jan Nost Sculp/ 1767

Included in Sotheby's sale, 25 January 1957, lot 50, the property of the late Darcy Edmund Taylor Esq, sold by order of the Trustees. Purchased from the sale by Frank Partridge & Sons Ltd on behalf of the Museum for £140.

Gunnis noted a bust of George III of 1764 which was included in the sale of David Garrick Esq, deceased (Gunnis 1968, p. 282). The contents of the sale 'bought from the mansion of Mrs Garrick, deceased on the Adelphi Terrace, and from his [Garrick's] villa at Hampton', were sold by Mr Christie, in the Great Room, Pall Mall; lot 74 sold on 23 June 1823, was described as 'V. Nost, 1764. An early bust of his late Majesty, George III'. In the annotated copy of the catalogue held in the National Art Library, it is noted this was sold to 'Cord' for £21 10s 6d. What appears to be the same bust was later included in an anonymous sale held at Christie's on 13 March 1883, lot 107, sold to 'Innes' for £15 15s (noted by Terence Hodgkinson [q.v.], departmental records); it appears to have been the property of Major Paynter (I am grateful to Marika Leino for this information). The present bust has been compared to a bust of an unknown man by Nost the Younger in the Louvre, see *Louvre* 1992, p. 71.

Bibliography
Age of Rococo 1958, p. 176, cat.no. 482; *Louvre* 1992, p. 71; Snodin and Styles 2001, fig. 9 on p. 161.

Exhibited
The Age of Rococo: Art and Culture of the Eighteenth Century, Residenzmuseum, Council of Europe, Munich, 15 June to 15 September 1958, cat.no. 482; *George III. Bicentennial Exhibition*, Yorktown Victory Center, Virginia, USA, April 1977 to 31 March 1978.

149: Henry Frederick, Duke of Cumberland (1745–1790)

about 1770
Possibly by John Nost the Younger
Marble
h. 67 cm.
A.26–1941

Purchased by Dr W.L. Hildburgh F.S.A. from Rogers, Chapman and Thomas's Auction Rooms in Gloucester Road, London, for 'a few shillings' early in November 1941. Given by Dr Hildburgh to the Museum in 1941.

A portion of the base has been broken and repaired.

The present piece was originally thought to depict William Augustus, Duke of Cumberland (1721–1765) and in comparison with the signed busts of Richard Temple, Viscount Cobham – see entry for cat.no. 202, and that of Frederick, Prince of Wales, sold at Sotheby's, 9 May 1941, lot 66 and now in the Royal Collection – was tentatively attributed to Peter Scheemakers [q.v.]. In November 1941, Eric Maclagan [q.v.] wrote to Lady Constance Milnes Gaskell, asking if Queen Mary might help with the identification of the sitter. Lady Gaskell replied, 'Queen Mary is very much interested in the photograph of the bust, and thinks it is similar to one at Windsor of William Augustus, Duke of Cumberland'. A letter from O.F. Morshead, Librarian at Windsor Castle, followed, in which he suggested, 'If it is Royal at all, I think it ought to be one of 3 possibilities: a) William Augustus, Duke of Cumberland (b. 1721; died aged 44 in 1765); (b) George III (b. 1738); or (c) his younger brother Edward, Duke of York (b. 1739). I'm sorry; I cannot make it into the Duke of Cumberland. By the time he had attained the age of the bust he had become grossly fat about the chaps. I have compared it carefully with our bust of him, and for what my opinion may be worth they do not represent the same man. But I quite see that others might hold the contrary view. Neither, in my view, is it the Duke of York. In spite of certain superficial resemblances, the nose and mouth are different. He had a pretty little nose, slightly rounded; and a most distinctive mouth – like a parrot eating a cherry as Madame de Sévigné described someone else. My first reaction on seeing the 3/4 profile was "a slight look of George III in later life" – meaning that although this man is young, I can see him developing into what George III came to look like. I compared it with our marble bust of George III by Bacon dated 1775; and really in profile it is rather like. But Bacon's bust seen full-face shows George III with a very narrow tapering forehead, whereas this man has a broad one. So I cannot press George III either – although in my view it is nearer to him than the two others'. In response Margaret Longhurst [q.v.] wrote, 'I am sorry that you did not agree with my identification of the bust as William Augustus, Duke of Cumberland. I base this mainly on medals of 1745 which I take to be about the date of the bust as this would make Cumberland 24 – a very plausible age for the man represented, I should say. Yesterday Mr. Adams and I went through the Cumberland material at the Portrait Gallery and found an undated engraving showing the Duke on horseback with a battle in the background (Carlisle or Culloden). This engraving quite convinced us both that the bust represents the same person; the curious flattening at the root of the nose, the narrow bridge and rather flattened tip and also the curly pouting mouth, are just the same . . . I cannot yet definitely suggest any sculptor, though I think Scheemakers is not impossible'.

The suggestion that the bust might represent Henry Frederick, Duke of Cumberland was made by Mr John Woodward, who compared it with the facial features on the full-length portrait of the Duke of Cumberland of 1777 by (Thomas Gainsborough (1727–1888) in Buckingham Palace (see Waterhouse 1958, no. 176, pl. 183). An annotation by Terence Hodgkinson [q.v.] on the records for the present piece suggesting a comparison with a bust by Joseph Nollekens [q.v.] of Edward, Duke of York, in the Royal Collection, signed and dated 1766, may result in further re-evaluation. Hodgkinson noted – presumably at a later date and referring to the previous attribution to Scheemakers – 'Cannot see this as Scheemakers. Why not Rysbrack? It is v. like the Holland House & ivory busts. Holland House bust is signed Rysbrack & dated 1754'. Malcolm Baker has recently suggested the present piece could by by John Nost the Younger (personal communication).

John (Jean) Obrisset

(active about 1705 – 1727)

Obrisset probably came from a family of artists (Aubrisset) in Dieppe, and may have been a Huguenot who arrived in London in the late seventeenth century. Little is known of his life and work; he specialised in pressed horn and tortoiseshell portraits.

Forrer IV, pp. 296–7; Huguenots 1985, p. 208; Thieme-Becker, 25, p. 552; Schaverien 1998.

150: Queen Anne (b.1664; r.1702–1714)

signed and dated 1705

From a die moulded by John Obrisset; probably after a model by John Croker
Pressed tortoiseshell
h. 7.5 cm.
A.17–1924

Signed: OB.

Bequeathed by Miss Benett in 1924.

A medal executed by John Croker (1670–1741) to commemorate the union with Scotland and England is the likely source for this portrait medallion (see *Medallic Illustrations,* pl. CXXIV, no. 16). A tobacco box attributed to Obrisset, with a portrait of Queen Anne in pressed horn taken from the same source as the present piece is in the Worshipful Company of Horners; see Schaverien 1998, p. 33, fig. 5 on p. 34.

A closely related medallion similarly signed 'O.B.' and dated 1705, which forms the top to a tortoiseshell snuff box, is in the Metalwork Department (inv.no. 305–1875): it is thought to have been taken from a die cut by Obrisset from a medal by Christian Wermuth (1661–1739) (departmental records). For further depictions of Queen Anne connected with Obrisset's work in horn, see Phillips 1931, pp. 62–5, nos. 29 to 54: of the dated examples illustrated all are inscribed with the date 1705. Schaverein notes that 'only one surviving medal by him [Obrisset], cast in lead, is known: an obverse portrait of Queen Anne similar to that on a medal by John Croker, signed OB 1705 behind the bust; on the reverse is an allegorical design with the signature OB beneath the buckle of the garter' (Schaverein 1998, p. 33, n. 18 on p. 38). Forrer lists the Queen Anne 'boxes and medallions are found in both silver and tortoiseshell from O'Brisset's moulds, copied from a medal by C[hristian] Wermuth 'as amongst his 'best known productions' (Forrer IV, p. 297). The Wermuth medal is probably that commemorating the Union of England and Scotland at Leipzig of 1707 (see *Medallic Illustrations*, pl. CXXV, no. 2), which is similar to the Croker medal (see above).

Read noted, 'The boxes and medallions of Queen Anne are naturally more plentiful than any others, and are found both in silver and tortoiseshell, from Obrisset's moulds. They are generally of one type . . . copied from a medal by C. Wermuth, though as portraits they are by no means of equal merit, some of the busts having been subjected to tooling by inexpert hands. The two medallions in fig. 4 form the top and bottom of a silver box in the British Museum collection. The bust of Prince George of Denmark is equal, if not superior, in execution to that of the Queen, from which it is separated in date by three years, the bust of the Prince being signed 'I (star) OB (star) F, 1708' while the Queen's bears the signature 'OB 1705'.' (Read 1894, p. 5).

Bibliography

Review 1924, p. 6.

Jan Roettiers

(b. ?Antwerp 1631 – d. London 1703)

Jan Roettiers was a one of a Flemish family of medallists, engravers, and goldsmiths, active in France and England from the early 17th to the mid- 18th century. Previously employed at the Antwerp Mint, Jan Roettiers later worked at the Royal Mint in London, where he produced a large number of commemorative medals until around 1697.

Forrer IV, pp. 296–7; TDA, 26 [Attwood], pp. 532–3.

151: Charles II (b.1630; r.1660–1685)

around 1700
Anonymous; after Jan Roettiers
Marble
h. 19.5 cm.
A.30–1939

Given by Dr W.L. Hildburgh F.S.A. in 1939, together with its pendant, cat.no. 152.

With the exception of the wreath, the present piece appears to be based on the obverse portrait of Charles II on a Christ's Hospital medal of 1673, by the Flemish medallist Jan Roettiers. The wreath does however appear coupled with the short hair but slightly different drapery on the obverse of another portrait of Charles II by Roettier, commemorating the War with Holland, Battle of Lowestoft in 1665 (see *Medallic Illustrations*, pl. LVI, no. 9; *ibid.*, pl. XLVIII, no. 10).

Exhibited
Royal Exhibition, Ealing Museum Art and History Society, 6 to 13 July 1977 to commemorate the Silver Jubilee of Queen Elizabeth II.

152: James II (b.1633; r.1685–1688; d.1701)

around 1700
Anonymous; after Jan Roettiers
Marble
h. 19.8 cm.
A.31–1939

Given by Dr W.L. Hildburgh F.S.A. in 1939 together with its pendant, cat.no. 151.

The unusually short hair on the present piece may be compared with the portrait of James II on the obverse of the sixty-shilling piece of 1686, by the Flemish medallist Jan Roettiers (see Farquahar 1910, p. 235). The portrait may also be compared with that on the obverse of the 1686 coronation commemorative medal; the obverse is signed in monogram WR, possibly for W. Roukens (see *Medallic Illustrations*, pl. LXIII, no. 14).

Exhibited
Royal Exhibition, Ealing Museum Art and History Society, 6 to 13 July 1977 to commemorate the Silver Jubilee of Queen Elizabeth II.

Louis François Roubiliac

(b. Lyons 1702 – d. London 1762)

Roubiliac was one of the leading sculptors of his generation, and the his monuments and busts are amongst the most important sculpture produced in eighteenth-century Britain. The son of a merchant, he may have trained under Balthasar Permoser (1651–1732) in Dresden, and is recorded in Paris in August 1730 as a prize winner in the Prix de Rome competition for students at the Académie Royale de Peinture et Sculpture, but no works by him are known to survive from this date. In the same year he is recorded as being in London, where he was to reside for the rest of his life, apart from a brief visit to Rome in 1752. He is said to have worked initially with Thomas Carter (d.1756/7), and was certainly an assistant in Henry Cheere's workshop [q.v.]. He executed busts for John Conduitt and the Duke of Argyll in the mid 1730s, but his first major independent commission was the statue of Handel for Jonathan Tyers, completed in 1738 (see below); by 1740 he had set up his own studio in London. Roubiliac's portrait busts in terracotta and marble, such as his 1755 marble bust of Philip Stanhope, 4th Earl of Chesterfield (National Portrait Gallery, London; for a bronze version, see cat. no. 157) were of a liveliness and naturalistic expression not seen before in English sculpture; his funerary monuments, such as those to the Duke and Duchess of Montague (1752–3) at Warkton, Northamptonshire similarly transcended previous sculpture of this type. Roubiliac's radical departure from earlier styles remained controversial for some of his contemporaries and later commentators, although Canova remarked in 1815 that the figure of Eloquence on the monument to the Duke of Argyll in Westminster Abbey (for the model of which, see cat. no. 164) was one of the noblest statues he had seen in England. On the sculptor's death, his pupil Nicholas Read (c.1733–1787) took over the studio.

Esdaile 1928; Baker 1984 [Roubiliac]; Thieme-Becker, 29, pp. 107–8; Baker 1995 [Roubiliac and Cheere]; Bindman and Baker 1995; TDA, 27, pp. 242–5 [Murdoch].

153: Lord Chief Justice Robert Raymond (1672–1732)

about 1732
Marble
h. 60 cm.
A.1–1947

Inscribed on the back: ROBERTUS D.nus RAYMOND.Capital./ Justic. Anglice, obiit XVIIIo. Martii/ MDCCXXXII/ Aetat.LX.
(Robert Raymond, Lord Chief Justice of England, died 18 March 1732 at the age of 60).

Purchased by H.M. Calmann from the Filmer family of East Sutton, Kent at an unrecorded date). Purchased by Dr W.L. Hildburgh F.S.A. from H.M. Calmann for £25. Given by Dr Hildburgh in 1947 as a New Year gift.

The bust was knocked from its pedestal in 1975, resulting in a large chip under the right shoulder, which has been repaired.

The bust has been re-attributed on a number of occasions since its acquisition in 1947. When it was aquired Terence Hodgkinson [q.v.] noted, 'Baron Raymond of Abbot's Langley was Lord Chief Justice from March 1724–5 till his death in March 1732–3. He died of the stone at his house in Red Lion Square and & was buried in the chancel at Abbot's Langley Church. The monument was later moved to the south nave aisle. Mrs Esdaile states that the monument is signed by P Scheemakers . . . The bust is certainly in Scheemakers's manner & there seems no reason to doubt that it is by him'. The attribution of the bust to Henry Cheere [q.v.] was explored by Margaret Whinney, who recorded that the monument to Baron Raymond in Abbot's Langley Church,

Hertfordshire, is signed 'Westby Gill AR invenit H. Cheere fecit'. She writes, 'the attribution of the bust to Henry Cheere rests partly on the execution of the monument, but also on the rich treatment of the folded drapery which is quite unlike the handling of either Rysbrack or Scheemakers. The features, with plain eyeballs, seem a little tame compared with the drapery and with other known work by Cheere, and it may be that the bust was not made from life' (Whinney 1971, p. 64); for Westby Gill (1679–1746), see Colvin 1995, p. 410. For the monument see Whinney 1988, pp. 194–7, fig. 134 on p. 196. However Malcolm Baker has recently suggested that the finishing of the back is more characteristic of the work of Roubiliac, who was an assistant with Cheere in the early 1730s (departmental records). The sensitive treatment of the face and drapery supports this attribution, though more work needs to be done on the practices shared by Cheere and Roubiliac at this date.

Bibliography

Whinney 1971, p. 64, no. 16, illus. on p. 65; Davies 1979, p. 116 (there said to be by Sir Henry Cheere); Whinney 1988, p. 453, n. 8(i); Baker 2000 [Figured in Marble], pp. 80, 82.

154: Jonathan Tyers (1702–1767)

about 1738
Terracotta
h. 71 cm.
A.94–1927

Esdaile recorded that this bust and the marble version were in the possession of the great-grandson of Jonathan Tyers, the Rev. Jonathan Tyers Barrett, D.D., who resided at Brandon House, Suffolk, and then passed by descent to the Rev. Wellesley Foley, the great-nephew of Tyers's great-granddaughter. However, the vendor noted the name of the former owner of Brandon House was the Rev. William Weller Poley, not Wellesley Foley as noted by Esdaile (Esdaile 1928, p. 41). According to the vendor, in correspondence prior to the acquisition of the present piece in September 1927, the two busts had been sold at the Brandon House, Suffolk sale, by the nephew of the late Rev. Weller Poley, held in September 1919, and were purchased by his father, Mr R. Levine. They passed by descent to the vendor, G.J. Levine, 50 Prince of Wales Road, Norwich, and were purchased from him in 1927 for £50. (In a later letter of November 1971, G.J. Levine stated that his father had bought the two busts from the Marquess of Graham sale at Easton Park, Wickham Market, Suffolk, around 1924. However he may have been mistaken; I have been unable to trace the relevant sale catalogue to confirm or deny this statement.

There is an integral terracotta support at the back of the bust.

Jonathan Tyers was a collector and entrepreneur; he opened the Pleasure Gardens at Vauxhall in June 1732; these were predominantly for evening entertainment, where sculpture and paintings were displayed. Roubiliac was commissioned to produce a marble statue of Handel for the gardens; see entry for cat.no. 156. Whinney noted of the present bust, 'It is careful and competent in modelling, a convincing portrait of a shrewd business-man, and a good example of the sculptor's busts in informal dress, though it has not the superb quality of his later work in this manner' (Whinney 1971, p. 82).

The marble version for which this is a model was included in the sale of Jonathan Tyers's effects, sold by Mr Christie, King Street, London, on 28 April 1830, lot 79, described as 'A very fine Bust of the late Jonathan Tyers Esq, in marble'; the figure of *Handel* by Roubiliac was also included in this sale. In 1927, when the marble version was auctioned (Sotheby's, 24 June 1927, lot 77), Katharine Esdaile [q.v.] advised against its purchase. Margaret Longhurst [q.v.] recorded that on seeing the terracotta in 1927 Mrs Esdaile considered the 'marble was very much inferior, probably the work of a pupil'. This is borne out by Mrs Esdaile's comments on the bust in her monograph, 'The terra-cotta, now in the Victoria and Albert Museum, is assuredly from the hand of Roubiliac; the marble is curiously inferior in handling and less pleasing in effect; yet from the wart on the nose to the frill on the shirt its realism foreshadows the sculptor's later triumphs in the same field, that of undress portraits of contemporaries; we do not need the evidence of Hayman's portrait group of the Tyers family to convince us of the iconic value of the bust' (Esdaile 1928, p. 41). In January 1954 the marble bust was offered to the Museum for purchase by Mr Hand of 73 Wimpole Street, London, but was declined. In October 1956 it was exhibited at Sabin's Gallery in Cork Street, and was purchased by the Birmingham City Museum and Art Gallery (inv. no. P.18'56); see *Birmingham* 1987, p. 82; Whinney 1988, fig. 136 on p. 200; Ruch 1970, fig. 12 on p. 494. Whinney commented on the Tyers bust, 'the fact that Tyers had a plump, rounded face gives this bust, with its big fold round the shoulders, a largeness of form which is not entirely characteristic of the sculptor' (Whinney 1988, p. 200). The drapery pattern on the other hand is wholly typical and was used again on the busts of John Raymond and Henry Streatfield (Baker 1995 [Wren], p. 125).

Bibliography

Review 1927, p. 5, pl. 4; Esdaile 1928, p. 41; Whinney 1971, p. 82, no. 22, illus. on p. 83; Davies 1979, p. 139; Whinney 1988, p. 200;

Baker 1995 [Making of portrait busts], p. 827; *idem* 1995 [Wren], p. 125, fig. 83; *idem* 2000 [Figured in Marble], p. 82; Snodin and Styles 2001, fig. 26 on p. 228.

155: Alexander Pope (1688–1744)

from a model of about 1738
Marble
h. (incl. socle) 64 cm.
A.14–1947

Originally in the possession of Lady Neave, Dagenham Hall, Dagenham, Essex. Purchased from her by Bert Crowther Esq., Syon Lodge, Busche Corner, Isleworth, Middlesex and subsequently sold to Dr W.L. Hildburgh F.S.A.. Given by Dr Hildburgh to the Museum in 1947.

The somewhat confusing evidence about the many versions of this bust is considered in detail by Wimsatt, whose account adds extensively to the briefer discussions by Esdaile (see Esdaile 1928, pp. 47–9; Wimsatt 1965, pp. 248–57). All the many known versions in marble, terracotta and plaster ultimately derive from a terracotta model now in the Barber Institute, Birmingham, or a lost variant model. The four signed versions in marble differ in format and their dates range from 1738 to 1741. These are at Temple Newsam House, Leeds, dated 1738 (*Leeds* 1996, p. 2, inv. no. 6/42; Wimsatt 1965, pp. 235–7), the Earl Fitzwilliam Collection, Milton, Peterborough, dated 1740, (*ibid.* pp. 237–40) and at Shipley Art Gallery, Gateshead, dated 1741 (*ibid.* pp. 241–3). These all reproduce the head but truncate to different degrees the shoulders and drapery. However, the fourth signed version, dated 1741, formerly in the Rosebery collection and now in the Yale Center for British Art, New Haven, Conn. (*ibid.* pp. 244–7), along with the plaster acquired by the British Museum from Roubiliac's sale in 1762 (*British Museum* 1999, pp. 165-8, cat. no. 64), follow the Barber terracotta in its full format. The unsigned V&A marble likewise shows the bust complete. Although apparently attributed by Whinney to Roubiliac and his workshop (Whinney 1971, pp. 80, 82), the roughly carved back of this example differs in its facture from that characteristic of signed or documented busts by the sculptor. Though a later date cannot be excluded, the present version is probably one of those numerous eighteenth-century images that reproduced this celebrated sculptural portrait representing the most famous of contemporary writers (Baker forthcoming [Multiple Heads]). Other comparable replicas in other materials include a plaster in the National Portrait Gallery (*NPG* 1981, p. 455, no. 2483) and a bronze in Birmingham City Art Gallery, inv. No. P.18'59 (*Birmingham* 1987, p. 84, no. 251, illus on p. 85). A further marble version attributed to the workshop of Joseph Nollekens [q.v.] was included in Sotheby's sale in London, 13 December 2000, lot 99. For a related bronze portrait medallion of the same sitter by Roubiliac, see cat. no. 162. I am grateful to Malcolm Baker for his help with this entry.

Bibliography
Noad 1950, p. 30 illus.; Wimsatt 1965, p. 250, no. 57–61.3 and illus.; Whinney 1971, pp. 80, 82, cat.no. 21, illus. on p. 81.

Exhibited
Eighteenth Century Art in England and France, Montreal Museum of Fine Arts, 1950; *The Eighteenth Century*, Chiswick House, 7 June to 29 June 1969.

156: George Frederick Handel (1685–1759)

signed and dated 1738
Marble
h. (incl. base) 153.5 cm
A.3–1965

Signed on the seat on which the figure sits: L· F· ROUBILIAC/ IN.^{II} ET· SCUL·^{II}
On pedestal at the front is inscribed: HANDEL

Commissioned from Roubiliac in 1737 by Jonathan Tyers (1702–1767) for his Pleasure Gardens at Vauxhall; for a terracotta bust of Tyers, see entry for cat.no. 154. Erected in April 1738 in a Grand Niche, in the Grove (for a discussion of the figure and its display whilst at Vauxhall, see Hodgkinson 1965); the figure is last recorded in the Grove behind the Orchestra in 1813. Following the death of Jonathan Tyers in 1767, management of the Gardens was taken over by his two sons, Thomas and Jonathan. In 1809 the gardens came into the possession of George Rogers Barrett and the Revd. Jonathan Tyers Barrett, D.D., and in 1818 on the death of George Barrett, the responsibility for the gardens passed to Dr Jonathan Tyers Barrett, whose attempt to sell the gardens in 1818 was unsuccessful. Before the sale of Vauxhall Gardens, the *Handel* was removed to the Stockwell home of George Rogers Barrett, shortly before his death. Around 1818 the figure passed to Jonathan Tyers Barrett, and was placed in the front hall of his house in Duke Street, Westminster. The death of Tyers Barrett in 1830 resulted in the sale of the figure by Mr Christie, King Street, London on 28 April 1830, lot 80, when it was described as, 'The very celebrated original sitting figure of Handel, in marble; which was for so many years publicly admired in the Gardens of Vauxhall. This noble piece of sculpture, well calculated as an embellishment to any public Music Hall, is to be viewed at Messrs Newtons', Upholsterers, in Wardour Street'. The *Handel* was again sold in 1833 by Mr Squibb of Savile Row to 'the sculptor and marble contractor', Joseph Brown of University Street, London, for £215 5s. Purchased by the Sacred Harmonic Society from Joseph Brown in 1854 for 100 guineas; a pamphlet published by them in 1854 recorded its recent purchase (see Puttick 1854; cited by Hodgkinson 1965, n. 32 on p. 13). The purchase was also recorded in the *Art Journal* of 1855. The marble plinth on which the figure is now displayed was almost certainly made at this time. The statue was displayed in the Society's offices in Exeter Hall, Strand, London until 1880 when it moved premises. The figure was moved to the offices of Novello and Company at 1 Berners Street, London, and was later purchased by Henry Littleton, chairman of the company. It remained in his possession at his Sydenham home for about twenty years; it was then given by his son to Novello and Company, where it remained at 160 Wardour Street from about 1906 to 1964, until its purchase by the Museum in 1965. Purchased from Novello and Company Ltd in 1965 for £10,000 with assistance from the National Art Collections Fund.

Terence Hodgkinson recorded that the lyre was broken whilst the figure was in the possession of Tyers Barrett (Hodgkinson 1965, p. 10); the left foot has been replaced.

Handel is shown in the guise of Orpheus playing Apollo's lyre. The figure was unprecedented in public statuary in depicting full-length a living composer. It was also exceptional in the way its aesthetic qualities were celebrated from the start; one writer in 1738 applauded both the 'finish'd beauties of the sculptor's hand' and Tyers's patronage which would be remembered 'when times remote dwell on *Roubillac*'s name' (Baker 1998 [Tyers], p. 44). Bindman has argued that the representation of Handel as Orpheus calming the savage passions of the beasts signalled Tyers's wish to make Vauxhall more respectable by discouraging his visitors from indulging their animal appetites (Bindman 1997). Brian Allen has compared the present piece with the stance and drapery in Francis Hayman's painting of Captain Henry of 1745, noting Hayman's use of 'the sculptor's device of the precariously perched slipper' (Allen 1991, p. 231, fig. 18).

A terracotta model for the present piece is in the Fitzwilliam Museum, Cambridge; see Esdaile 1928, pl. VII; Hodgkinson 1965, fig. 11 on p. 10; *Rococo* 1984, p. 85, cat.no. F9; Jervis 1993, illus. on p. 81. Bronze reductions were produced by Elkington & Company during the second half of the nineteenth century. A medallic illustration of the figure, probably by William Hogarth, is found on a silver pass to Vauxhall Gardens of about 1760, a version of which was offered for sale by A.H. Baldwin, Commemorative Medals 1500 to the Present Day, 1998, lot 100.

BIBLIOGRAPHY

Art Journal 1855; Esdaile 1928, pp. 36–41, pl. VII; Whinney 1961, pp. 82–3, illus. on p. 82; Hodgkinson 1965; Draper 1970, p. 377, fig. 2 on p. 378; Whinney 1971, pp. 78 and 80, cat.no. 20, illus on p. 79; Pinkerton 1973, p. 277 and fig. 6; Mainstone 1976; Davies 1979, p. 58; Allen 1981, p. 231 and fig. 19; *Rococo* 1984, pp. 85–6, cat.no. F10; Whinney 1988, pp. 198–9, 400, fig. 135 on p. 199; Bindman 1992, p. 3 and illus.; Solkin 1992, pp. 111–4, fig. 34 on p. 113; Jervis 1993, p. 81; Bindman and Baker 1995, p. 49, and fig. 28; Williamson 1996 [Trusted], p. 158, illus. on p. 159; Bindman 1997; Baker 1998 [Tyers]; *idem* 2000 [Figured in Marble], p. 10, pl. 1 on p. 10, pp. 31–2 and n. 36, p. 72, pp. 81–2; Snodin and Styles 2001, fig. 58 on p. 275.

EXHIBITED

Rococo. Art and Design in Hogarth's England, Victoria and Albert Museum, London, 16 May to 30 September 1984, cat.no. F10.

157: Philip Dormer Stanhope, 4th Earl of Chesterfield (1694–1773)

about 1745
Bronze
h. 56 cm h. (excl. socle) 45 cm.
A.17–1959

Purchased from Alfred Spero, 4 Park Mansions Arcade, Knightsbridge, London in 1959 for £90.

Three versions of this bust in bronze, including the present piece, are known, cited by Baker 1996 [Production], p. 153, n. 35.

Two terracotta and three plaster versions of the bust were included in the sale of Roubiliac's effects in May 1762: the terracotta versions were sold on the second day's sale 13 May, lot 75 and on the third day's sale 14 May, lot 83. The plaster versions were sold on 13 May, lot 9, the third day's sale 14 May, lot 18 and fourth day's sale 15 May, lot 20. A plaster variant purchased by Dr Maty from the sale of Roubiliac's effects held in May 1762, was presented by him to the British Museum shortly after its purchase (see Esdaile 1928, p. 103, pl. XXIII (b) opp. p. 90; *British Museum* 1999, pp. 63–5, cat.no. 17, pl. 10). The British Museum plaster was suggested by Mrs Esdaile to have been taken from the marble version formerly in the possession of the family of Lord Carnarvon, sold at Christie's, London on 3 June 1918, lot 192, it was purchased by Colonel Sir E.A. Brotherton for £252 (Esdaile 1928, pp. 106–7).

The location of the bust was unknown until it was re-discovered in 1985 and offered for sale at Christie's, London, 3 April 1985, lot 70 (see Balderston 1985); it is now in the National Portrait Gallery (see *British Museum* 1999, fig. 23 on p. 63).

Another version in bronze was offered at Christie's, London, 16 April 1991, lot 45, owned by the descendants of the Rt. Hon. Nathaniel Clements M.P., but was unsold.

BIBLIOGRAPHY

Whinney 1971, pp. 86, 88, no. 24, illus. on p. 89; Murdoch 1983, p. 39; Baker 1996 [Production], p. 153, n. 36; *British Museum* 1999, p. 65 and n. 10.

158: Sir Mark Stuart Pleydell Bt. (d.1768)

signed and dated 1755
Marble
h. 55 cm.
National Trust Loan 1

Signed on the right side of the pedestal: ad vivum Sct./L.F. Roubiliac.
Inscribed on the truncation at the back: Sr Mark Stuart Pleydell Bt. 1755. æt. 63.

Commissioned by the sitter for his seat, Coleshill House, High Wycombe, Berkshire. Originally placed on the chimneypiece in the saloon of Coleshill House, the bust was saved from the fire which destroyed the house in 1952, although its survival was not recorded. Re-discovered in the Old Laundry of Coleshill in the early 1980s (Murdoch 1983, p. 39). By descent to Miss Katherine Pleydell-Bouverie. Bequeathed to the National Trust in 1956 as part of the fabric of Coleshill House. On loan to the Museum since September 1983 from the National Trust.

This bust, one of two similar busts of Pleydell displayed at Coleshill House, was originally placed as an integral feature on the chimneypiece in the saloon. The bust is illustrated in an article of 1919 in which it is shown there with two urns displayed either side (Avray Tipping 1919, II, fig. 2 on p. 139). The other bust of Pleydell located in the hall is also illustrated in situ by Avray Tipping (Avray Tipping 1919, I, fig. 12 on p. 115).

Information held in Sir Mark Pleydell's receipt book confirms that he sat for Roubiliac between 12 and 17 May 1755; the bust, for which Roubiliac charged £86, was delivered to Coleshill House on 13 February 1756 (Murdoch 1983, p. 39 and *Rococo* 1984, p. 300).

There are two references to the Pleydell bust in the sale catalogue of Roubiliac's effects held on 12 to 15 May 1762: both lots appear in the third day's sale, held on 14 May, lot 16 described as 'Sir Mark Pleydell' under the heading 'Busts and Heads in Plaister' [sic], also 'Sir Mark Pleydell' as lot 54 under 'Moulds in Plaister [sic] for the following Figures, Busts, etc'.

We are grateful to the National Trust for allowing us to include this in the catalogue.

BIBLIOGRAPHY

Avray Tipping 1919, II, fig. 2 on p. 139; Webb 1954, p. 176; Murdoch 1983, p. 39; *Rococo* 1984, pp. 300–1, cat.no. S33, illus. p. 301; Baker 1995 [Wren], p. 122, n. 47; Baker 1996 [Louvre], pp. 78–9, figs 5 and 6 on p. 89; Baker 1999, p. 529, fig. 1 on p. 528; Baker 2000 [Figured in Marble], p. 55, pls. 39–40 on p. 56.

EXHIBITED

Rococo. Art and Design in Hogarth's England, Victoria and Albert Museum, London, 16 May to 30 September 1984, cat.no. S33.

159: William Shakespeare (1564–1616)

signed and dated 1757
Terracotta
h. 42.2 cm.
32–1867

Signed on left of base on which the figure leans: F. Roubiliac/ 1757.

At the sale of the property of Edward Stevens (architect), held on 7 February 1776, lot 38 is described as 'A terracotta figure of Mr Roubiliac's Shakespeare'. Noted on departmental records as having been purchased by Mr. A. Myers from the Henry Farrer Esq, F.S.A. sale (held at Christie's between 12 and 18 June 1866). Sold on the second day's sale, 13 June 1866, as lot 218, described as 'Shakespeare, by Corbett: a copy of the statue by Roubillac [sic]'. The annotated catalogue held in the National Art Library records it was purchased by 'Myers' for £2. Lots 221 and 222 in the same sale, described as models for a tomb in Westminster Abbey, were also purchased by Myers for 10s each. The Shakespeare statuette was purchased by the Museum from Mr Myers in 1867 for £4 4s. A terracotta model by Rysbrack for the Locke monument was also purchased from Myers at this time; see entry for cat.no. 192.

Plaster filling has been used on the top of the figure's head, his right hand, and on the base.

This is the model for the marble statue of Shakespeare carried out by Roubiliac for the actor David Garrick (1717–1779) in 1758, and placed in Garrick's Temple of Shakespeare on the banks of the Thames at Twickenham: the marble figure was bequeathed by Garrick to the British Museum in 1779 (see *British Museum* 1999, pp. 192–204, cat.no 74). Roubiliac probably used as a model his own painted copy of the Chandos portrait of Shakespeare, now in the British Museum (*Huguenots* 1985, p. 144).

Several other versions are known. A larger version of the present piece, sold at the M. Édouard Chappey sale, Galerie Georges Petit, Paris (11 to 15 March 1907) as lot 391, is noted by Esdaile together with the present piece, and a further marble version in a private collection (see Esdaile 1928, pp. 124–6, pl. XXXIX (b), pl. XL (b) opp. p. 126). The larger terracotta version is now in the Folger Shakespeare Library, Washington D.C (see Bindman and Baker 1995, p. 77, fig. 42 on p. 78).

BIBLIOGRAPHY

Graves 1907, p. 219, no. 88; Esdaile 1928, pp. 124, 200, pl. XL (a) opp. p. 126; Brown 1934, illus. on p. 59; Gunnis 1968, p. 330; *Huguenots* 1985, p. 144, cat.no. 205, illus. on p. 145; Whinney 1988, p. 226; *British Museum* 1999, pp. 199, notes 21 and 22 on p. 204, fig. 54 on p. 199.

EXHIBITED

Society of Arts Exhibition 1760 no. 88, described as 'A model of Shakespear' [sic]; lent to the Royal Society of Arts for the Reception held on 3 March 1960 to celebrate the first English public art exhibition of 1760; *O Sweet Mr. Shakespeare I'll have his picture. The changing image of Shakespeare's person, 1600–1800*, National Portrait Gallery, 18 April to 30 June 1964; *Garrick*, British Library, 30 November 1979 to 11 May 1980; *The Quiet Conquest: The Huguenots 1685–1985*, Museum of London, 15 May to 31 October 1985, cat.no. 205; *Creative Quarters: The Art World in London 1700–2000, Museum of London*, 30 March to 15 July 2001.

160: George Frederick Handel (1685–1759)

about 1750–60
Terracotta
diam. 28.6 cm.
A.11–1961

Purchased from Messrs Peel and Humphris Ltd, 37 New Bond Street, London in 1961 for £250, using funds from the Hildburgh Bequest. On loan to the Theatre Museum, Covent Garden since April 1987.

Terence Hodgkinson [q.v.] noted on acquisition, 'A number of such circular medallions exists, with representations of Cromwell and Garrick among them. An ascription to Roubiliac, on the basis of similarity to his bust portraits is made more plausible by the fact that a bronze medallion of Garrick at the Garrick Club, similar in character to the terracotta under discussion, is signed and dated by Roubiliac in 1751'. For bronze portrait medallions of this style, see entries for cat.nos. 161 to 163.

At the time of acquisition of the present piece the Museum was also offered offered a similar relief depicting Isaac Newton, which was not acquired. The newly-acquired relief was published by J.V.G. Mallet in the *Burlington Magazine* for April 1962 (see Mallet 1962). Mallet discussed the relationship between the present terracotta portrait medallion of Handel and the bronze variant then in the possession of Sir Francis Watson, and now on loan to the Museum (see entry for cat.no. 161), suggesting that the terracotta version 'is of especial interest, since it is the only subject yet known in both bronze and terra-cotta ... A relationship clearly exists between the two versions, but it is hard to see exactly what sort of relationship it is. The differences in size and detail preclude all possibility that the bronze is a cast of the terra-cotta. Nor does the highly finished appearance of the Handel and other terra-cotta medallions point to their being rough bozzetti for the bronzes ... I am inclined to believe that the terra-cotta medallions formed a series parallel to, but quite independent of the bronzes' (*ibid.*, p. 157). For the full-size statue of Handel by Roubiliac, see entry for cat.no. 156.

Bibliography

Musical Times 1961, frontispiece, n. on p. 618; Mallet 1962, and fig. 23 on p. 155; Kerslake 1977 (I), p. 128; Kerslake 1977 (II), fig. 341; *Rococo* 1984, p. 87, cat.no. F12; Penny 1998, p. 291, cat. no. RBF672.

Exhibited

Rococo. Art and Design in Hogarth's England, Victoria and Albert Museum, London, 16 May to 30 September 1984, cat.no. F12.

161: George Frederick Handel (1685–1759)

about 1750–60
Cast after a model by Louis François Roubiliac
Bronze
h. 26.3 cm.
Cheng Huan Loan 3

Formerly in the collection of Sir Francis J.B. Watson, C.V.O. From 1974 lent by Mr Cheng Huan Q.C.

This is one of a series of bronze portrait medallions executed by Roubiliac; see also entries for cat.nos. 162 and 163. See also entry for cat.no. 160, a related terracotta relief of the same subject.

John Mallet noted, 'Though not based on any surviving bust in the round, its composition links it with the busts of Barrow and Ray at Trinity, Cambridge, and I feel convinced that it was modelled by Roubiliac. A sculptor who worked in bronze as seldom as Roubiliac is unlikely to have done his own casting ... [it] may have either been cast by a different and inferior founder to his Pope and Middleton, or else it may be a good contemporary aftercast from a plaque in bronze or some other material' (Mallet 1962, p. 155).

Comparing the bronze reliefs executed by Roubiliac of Middleton, Pope and Garrick, Malcolm Baker commented, 'Although differing from each other in technique and facture, all share features characteristic of Roubiliac's modelling style and probably belong to a group of "basso relievos" represented in the 1762 sale catalogue by an Inigo Jones, Cromwell, Pope and Handel (2nd Day, lots 92–93)' (Rococo 1984, p. 306).

Baker also noted, 'The same crisp casting and highly finished surfaces characteristic of the casting of the highest quality goldsmith's work are also to be seen on a group of other small bronzes attributable to Roubiliac ... portraits of Pope, Handel, Middelton, Newton and Garrick, which were closely connected with "Medals" of the same subjects recorded in Roubiliac's posthumous 1762 sale' (*idem*, 1996 [Production], p. 150).

We are grateful to Mr Cheng Huan Q.C. for allowing us to include this in the catalogue.

BIBLIOGRAPHY
Mallet 1962, fig. 30 on p. 156; *Rococo* 1984, p. 306 cat.no. S45; Penny 1998, p. 291, cat. no. RBF672.

EXHIBITED
Rococo. Art and Design in Hogarth's England, Victoria and Albert Museum, London, 16 May to 30 September 1984, cat.no. S45.

162: Alexander Pope (1688–1744)

about 1750–60
Cast after a model by Louis François Roubiliac
Bronze
h. 25 cm.
Cheng Huan Loan 4

Formerly in the collection of Sir Francis J.B. Watson C.V.O; purchased by him as a pair to that of Conyers Middleton, see entry for cat.no. 163. Since 1974 on loan to the Museum from Mr Cheng Huan Q.C.

This is one of a series of bronze portrait medallions executed by Roubiliac; see also entries for cat.nos. 161 and 163, and cat.no. 160.

Commenting on the present piece, together with that of Conyers Middleton, cat.no. 163, Mallet notes, 'The portrait busts on each of these medallions are cast separately from their oval bronze back-plates, which are cut through and welded on from behind' (Mallet 1962, p. 153). Another version of this medallion portrait is in the Yale Center for British Art (see Baker 1996 [Production], p. 150 and fig. 7 on p. 151).

For a marble bust of the same sitter by Roubiliac, see entry for cat.no. 155.

We are grateful to Mr Cheng Huan Q.C. for allowing us to include this in the catalogue.

BIBLIOGRAPHY
Mallet 1962, fig. 28 on p. 156; Wimsatt 1965, pp. 248–50, no. 57–61.1, illus. p. 251; Penny 1998, p. 291, cat. no. RBF672.

163: Dr Conyers Middleton (1683–1750)

about 1753
Cast after a model by Louis François Roubiliac
Bronze
h. 25.4 cm.
Cheng Huan Loan 5

Formerly in the collection of Sir Francis J.B. Watson C.V.O., purchased by him as a pair together with that of Alexander Pope; see entry for cat.no. 162. From 1974 on loan from Mr Cheng Huan Q.C.

This is one of a series of bronze portrait medallions executed by Roubiliac; see entries for cat.nos. 161 and 162. See also entry for cat.no. 160.

Katharine Esdaile recorded that Roubiliac was commissioned to execute a commemorative bust of Middleton by Middleton's widow in 1753 for Trinity College Library, Cambridge, where he had been the University Librarian, although this did not come to fruition. The monument to Middleton formerly in the church of St Michael's, Cambridge, which incorporated a medallion portrait by Roubiliac is now lost (Esdaile 1928, pp. 99 and 122). She suggested the following items listed in the sale catalogue of Roubiliac's effects were related to the lost monument to Middleton: Under 'Designs for Monuments, Basso Relievo's, &C' in the first day of the sale of Roubiliac's effects held on 12 May 1762, lot 67 included 'Three medals of Pope, Mr Garrick and Dr Middleton'; in the second day's sale, lot 27 under 'Sundries in Plaister [sic], 'a medal of Dr Middleton' is lot 51 under 'Moulds in Plaister [sic], 'Three medals of Sir Isaac Newton, Mr Middleton and Mr Pope' (Esdaile 1928, pp. 220, 222–3, p. 180).

An ivory portrait medallion of the same sitter by Giovanni Battista Pozzo (1670–1750) is also in the collection (inv.no. A.16–1941).

We are grateful to Mr Cheng Huan Q.C. for allowing us to include this in the catalogue.

BIBLIOGRAPHY
Mallet 1962 and fig. 29 on p. 156; Baker 1995 [Wren], p. 120, n. 42; Penny 1998, p. 291, cat. no. RBF672.

164: Model for the monument to John Campbell, 2nd Duke of Argyll and Greenwich (1680–1743)

signed and dated 1745
Terracotta against a modern slate backing
h. 89.5 cm
21–1888

Signed and dated to the left of the base: L.F. Roubiliac in.t et Fecit 1745

Possibly to be identified as the 'Design' included in the 1762 sale of Roubiliac's effects, as lot 70 on the 3rd day's sale, together with related items, including a mould and plaster of the relief (3rd day, lot 57; 4th day, lots 34 and 35, and plaster busts of Eloquence (4th day, lots 2 and 19) (Esdaile 1928, p. 62; *Rococo* 1984, p. 291; Bindman and Baker 1995, p. 294). Purchased by the Museum from Mr Benjamin Webb, 5 Cottage Place, Romilly Street, London, in 1888 for £5.

This is the sketch for the marble monument to the Duke of Argyll in the South transept of Westminster Abbey, commissioned from Roubiliac in 1745, and erected in 1749 (for the monument, see Bindman and Baker 1995, esp. pp. 286–94; see also Whinney 1971, pp. 84, 86; *Rococo* 1984, pp. 291–2, cat.no. S7; Esdaile 1928, pp. 61–5). For a full discussion of the monument and its relationship to the designs and contract, see Baker 1992.

A number of changes to the design of the present piece were made in the execution of the actual memorial; the front of the base is incised with a scale confirming its function as a working model. Malcolm Baker has noted, 'His [Roubiliac's] use of models, like other aspects of his workshop procedure, owes much to his French training' (Baker 1992, p. 789).

A number of designs for the monument exist; one in pen, ink and chalk, acquired by the Museum in 1878 is in the Department of Prints, Drawings and Paintings (inv.no. 8381); see Physick 1969, pp. 119–20, cat.no. 83, fig. 83 on p. 120. A further design is in the City Museum and Art Gallery, Plymouth; see *Rysbrack* 1982, p. 132, cat.no. 48; see also Baker 1998 [Materials and processes], pl. 16 on p. 522. Another design for the monument was exhibited at Hazlitt, Gooden and Fox, London, October-November 1990, p. 44 cat.no. 21 (reference supplied by Marjorie Trusted).

Bibliography

Brinckmann 1925, p. 110 and pl. 61; Esdaile 1928, pp. 62–3, 65 and n. 3, pl. XVI (b); *Masterpieces* 1951, p. 88, no. 43, illus. p. 89; Physick 1967, p. 33, figs. 11 on p. 35; Physick 1969, p. 119; Whinney 1971, pp. 84–6, cat.no. 23, illus on p. 85; Davies 1979, p. 3; *Rysbrack* 1982, fig. 42 on p. 132; *Rococo* 1984, pp. 291–2, cat.no. S7; Baker 1986 [Roubiliac], pp. 59–60, 63, fig. 3 on p. 73, fig. 15 on p. 81; Whinney 1988, p. 205; Galvin 1990, pp. 849–50, fig. 25 on p. 849; Baker 1992, esp. pp. 785, 788, 791–3, fig. 26 on p. 791; *Ashmolean* 1992 [II], p. 111; Bindman and Baker 1995, pp. 236 and fig. 200, 292–4, figs. 248–50 on pp. 290, 293; *Westminster Abbey* 1995, p. 138, cat.no. 30, illus. on p. 139; Williamson 1996 [Trusted], p. 157 and illus; *idem* 1998 [Materials and processes], pp. 520, pl. 18 on p. 524; *idem* 2000 [Figured in Marble], pp. 42–4, fig. 32 on p. 43.

Exhibited

Rococo. Art and Design in Hogarth's England, Victoria and Albert Museum, London, 16 May to 30 September 1984, cat.no. S7; *900 Years: The Restorations of Westminster Abbey*, St Margaret's Church, Westminster Abbey, 23 May to 30 September 1995, cat.no. 30.

165: John, 2nd Duke of Montagu (1690–1749)

about 1750
Terracotta
h. 34.8 cm.
A.6–1947

Possibly included in the sale of Roubiliac's effects (12 to 15 May 1762) in the third day's sale, 14 May as lot 67, described under the heading 'Designs for Monuments, Basso Relievos, etc.' as 'Five designs for the Duke of Montague's'. On the second day's sale, 13 May, under 'Moulds in Plaister for the following Figures, Busts, etc', lot 57 is described as 'Duke of Mountague's [sic] monument'. In the possession of Louis Meier, 23 Cecil Court, Charing Cross Road, London before 1947, and purchased from him by Dr W.L. Hildburgh F.S.A. for £25. Given by Dr Hildburgh to the Museum in 1947.

On acquisition this model was covered with terracotta-coloured paint which was subsequently removed.

This is a preliminary model for the monument to the Duke of Montagu in St Edmund's Church, Warkton, Northamptonshire; a second more finished model of plaster and wood for the same monument is on loan to the Museum from The Dean and Chapter of Westminster Abbey; see entry for cat.no. 166. Terence Hodgkinson [q.v.] noted, 'The early sketch differs from the Westminster model and the monument itself mainly in its architecture and accessories. In the late versions the upward spiral movement of the design is prolonged by the addition of a storey to the architectural background and by crowning the whole with a flaming urn. The profile portrait, which shows the Duke bewigged in the early sketch becomes classically wigless in the finished monument' (Hodgkinson 1947, p. 258). The vertical incision on the right may have been made in the wet clay as the reduction in width of the architectural component was under discussion in the studio, as Baker has suggested. The composition is exceptional among monuments of the period in the way it interlinks figures and architecture. For a discussion of the monument see Bindman and Baker 1995, esp. pp. 124–33, 227–31, 298–304, cat.no. 5; Murdoch 1980 and *idem* 1985, pp. 34–43.

Penny has compared the modelling of this terracotta with Roubiliac's model for the monument in Westminster Abbey to Handel in the Ashmolean Museum, Oxford (see *Ashmolean* 1992 [III], pp. 153–4, cat.no. 565).

BIBLIOGRAPHY

Esdaile 1928, p. 180; Hodgkinson 1947, p. 258, and fig (B) on p. 256; Physick 1969, p. 34, n. 2, fig. 16 on p. 39; Whinney 1971, p. 92, no. 27, illus. on p. 93; Davies 1979, p. 93; Murdoch 1980, p. 42, fig. 63 on p. 44; *Rococo* 1984, p. 294 and illus., cat.no. S14; Murdoch 1985; Baker 1986 [Roubiliac], pp. 62–3 , fig. 12 on p. 78, fig. 14 on p. 80; *Ashmolean* 1992 [III], p. 153; Bindman and Baker 1995, pp. 227–31, 302–3, and figs. 188–9 on p. 229, fig. 257 on p. 302, and pl. XVI; Bassett and Fogelman 1997, p. 62 illlus.

EXHIBITED

Drawings by English Sculptors 1680–1810, Ashmolean Museum, 23 November to 10 December 1967; *Rococo. Art and Design in Hogarth's England*, Victoria and Albert Museum, London, 16 May to 30 September 1984, cat.no. S14; *The Art of Death*, Victoria and Albert Museum, 8 January to 22 March 1992.

166: John, 2nd Duke of Montagu (1690–1749)

about 1750
Painted wood and plaster
h. 63.2 cm.
Westminster Abbey Loan 2

Discovered in the triforium of Westminster Abbey in 1870 by the great-grandson of Roubiliac; he noted its discovery and condition in articles in the *Builder* and the *Art Journal* of that year. The *Builder* recorded, 'The corresponding terra-cotta sketch of the Nightingale Monument is in the rood-loft of Westminster Abbey, – Death gone, and the head of Mr Nightingale gone, but the fainting form of the lady fine and effective . . .' *(Builder*, 2 July 1870, XXVIII, no. 1430, p. 520). The *Art Journal* commented: 'In the roodloft are to be found models in plaster of several of the sculpture in the Abbey, and the original sketch, by Roubiliac, in terracotta of the famous "Nightingale" monument. We believe that the Chapter have taken into consideration the propriety of the removal of these relics to a more accessible place. It is certainly much to be desired that this should be done' *(Art Journal*, 1 August 1870, p. 232). Katharine Esdaile, who recorded the 1870 discovery in her monograph on Roubiliac, followed up the account in September 1923 when she found in the triforium two other models for the monuments to the Duke and Duchess of Montagu in Warkton Church, Northants; see entries for cat.nos. 167 and 168 (Esdaile 1928, pp. 69–70). She commented, 'How they came there can only be conjectured . . . The sculptor must have shown his model for the Nightingale monument to the Dean and Chapter; comment on the niche-setting produced the sculptor's justification of his device in the shape of the final model for the duchess's monument. He sent for it from his studio; the servant brought the duke's as well; the success of the niche was apparent, and the design accepted; but Roubiliac's death in January, 1762, a few months after the Nightingale monument was in place, left the three models on the Chapter's hands' (*ibid*., p. 70). On loan from the Dean and Chapter of Westminster Abbey, from January 1970, together with cat.nos. 167 and 168.

This is one of two models in the Museum for the same monument; see also entry for cat.no. 165. The present piece is the model for the memorial to John, 2nd Duke of Montagu erected in 1754 in the chancel of St Edmund's Church, Warkton, Northants, opposite the monument to his wife, Mary 2nd Duchess of Montagu, also by Roubiliac; see entry for cat.no. 167. Bindman and Baker suggest 'its relationship to the terracotta and the finished monument leaves little doubt that it was produced by Roubiliac in connection with the Montagu commission. The way in which wood and plasters were made to simulate the effects of different coloured marbles makes it probable that both were made for approval by Martin Folkes and the Countess of Cardigan, before a final decision was made about the design and the choice of marbles' (Bindman and Baker 1995, p. 303).

This is likely to be a more advanced design for the monument than the rougher terracotta model, cat.no. 165.

We are grateful to the Dean and Chapter of Westminster Abbey for allowing us to include this in the catalogue.

Bibliography

Esdaile 1928, pl. XVII (B) opp. pp. 66, 70, 198; *British Art* 1934, p. 267, cat.no. 1193; Physick 1969, p. 34, n. 2; Kenworthy-Browne 1973, p. 575, and fig. 2 on p. 574; Davies 1979, p. 93; Murdoch 1980, p. 42, n. 30, fig. 63 on p. 44; *Rococo* 1984, p. 295 and illus. cat.no. S15.; Murdoch 1985, fig. 3 on p. 40; Baker 1986 [Roubiliac], fig. 13 on p. 79, p. 63; Bindman and Baker 1995, pp. 227–8, fig. 187 on p. 228, detail on p. 208, 303–4, fig. 258 on p. 303.

Exhibited

Commemorative Exhibition of British Art, Royal Academy of Arts, London, January to March 1934, cat.no. 1193; *Rococo. Art and Design in Hogarth's England*, Victoria and Albert Museum, London, 16 May to 30 September 1984, cat.no. S15; *The Art of Death*, Victoria and Albert Museum, 8 January to 22 March 1992.

167: Monument to Mary, 2nd Duchess of Montagu (d.1752)

about 1752–3
Painted wood and plaster
h. 63.2 cm.
Westminster Abbey Loan 3

Amongst the items offered in the sale of Roubiliac's effects were a number of items relating to the Duchess of Montagu commission. Under 'Designs for Monuments, Basso Relievo's, &C', on the first day of the sale, 12 May 1762, lot 73 is described as 'Dutchess [sic] of Mountagu's [sic] monument, in plaister [sic]. On the second day's sale, 13 May, under 'Moulds in Plaister [sic], for the following Figures, Busts, etc', lot 58 is described as 'Dutchess's [sic] ditto Mountague's [sic] Monument'. On the third day's sale, 14 May 1762, under 'Designs for Monuments, Basso Relievos, etc', lot 68 is described as 'Two designs for the Duchess of Mountague's [sic]'. Discovered in the triforium of Westminster Abbey in 1870 by the great-grandson of Roubiliac; see entry for cat.no. 166. On loan from the Dean and Chapter of Westminster Abbey from January 1970, together with cat.nos. 166 and 168.

This is a model for the monument to Mary, 2nd Duchess of Montagu in the chancel of St Edmund's Church, Warkton, Northants, erected in 1754 opposite that to her husband, John, 2nd Duke of Montagu. For models relating to the 2nd Duke of Montagu's monument, also by Roubiliac, see entries for cat.nos. 165 and 166. Unlike the finished monument to the 2nd Duke of Montagu in which a number of changes from the original model were encorporated, the finished monument to the Duchess of Montagu is close to the model; the exceptions are the faces of the *Fates*, which in the model are somewhat elderly, and were changed to younger ones in the finished monument (see Bindman and Baker 1995, pl. VI for the monument).

A contemporary account of the monument to the Duchess of Montagu is given in the *Spectator* of 25 December 1753. The writer concludes: 'In short the whole is a metamorphoses of stone into those different stuffs by the magic hands of a skilful sculptor, which I have not yet seen so perfectly attained to amongst antients [sic] or moderns' (cited by Esdaile 1928, appendix C, pp. 208–10 and Bindman and Baker 1995, appendix A, pp. 360–1).

For a discussion of the monument, see Bindman and Baker 1995, esp. pp. 124–33, 308–11, no. 8; Murdoch 1980; also Murdoch 1985, pp. 43–4.

We are grateful to the Dean and Chapter of Westminster Abbey for allowing us to include this in the catalogue.

Bibliography

Esdaile 1928, p. 70, pl. XVIII (b) opp. p. 198, p. 198; *British Art* 1934, p. 267, cat.no. 1194; Murdoch 1980, p. 42, n. 30; *Rococo* 1984, p. 295 and illus, cat.no. S16; Murdoch 1985, fig. 4 on p. 40;

Bindman and Baker 1995, pp. 309–11, fig. 196 on p. 234, and fig. 262 on p. 311.

EXHIBITED
Commemorative Exhibition of British Art, Royal Academy of Arts, London, January to March 1934, cat.no. 1194; *Rococo. Art and Design in Hogarth's England*, Victoria and Albert Museum, London, 16 May to 30 September 1984, cat.no. S16.

168: Joseph Gascoigne (d.1752) and Lady Elizabeth Nightingale (d.1731) (model for the Nightingale monument)

signed and dated 1758
Terracotta
h. 53 cm.
Westminster Abbey Loan 1

Signed and dated at the bottom to the left side: 1758/Roubiliac.in.

Possibly identifiable as the model sold on the third day of the Roubiliac sale, as lot 71 under 'Designs for Monuments, Basso Relievos, etc.' 'Mr Nightingale's', and that offered at the Mr Jackson sale, held at Christie's on 22 July 1807, lot 88 (no purchaser is recorded in Christie's archive, suggesting that the model was possibly purchased before the sale, or remained unsold – I am grateful to Donald Johnston for checking this reference). Discovered in the triforium of Westminster Abbey in 1870 by the great-grandson of Roubiliac; see entry for cat. no. 166. On loan from the Dean and Chapter of Wesminster Abbey from January 1970, together with cat. nos. 166 and 167.

A scale of 1 to 15 is etched on the right side of the model. Mrs Esdaile noted, 'None of Roubiliac's terra-cottas shows work more minute: it is as if such details as the rustication of the arch and the hinges of the doors had been somehow mechanically diminished from the marble instead of being wrought out centimetre by centimetre in clay. No other model moreover bears a scale of proportions marked on it' (Esdaile 1928, p. 157). Baker comments, 'The monument, however, was not completed until 1761 and, although retaining the same architectural structure as that in the model, shows a major change in the moment in the action that is depicted as well as corresponding changes in the poses of all the figures involved. Such modifications indicate that, though evidently more than a working sketch, the terracotta represents a fairly early stage in the development of the composition' (Baker 1986 [Roubiliac], p. 63).

There are a number of references to the Nightingales in the sale catalogue of Roubiliac's effects held in May 1762. On the first day of the sale, held on 12 May under the heading 'Mould in plaister, for the following Figures, Busts, Bass Relievo's, & C' lot 44 is described as 'Mrs Nightingale'. Busts in terracotta of 'Mr Nightingale and his lady' appeared in the second day of the sale, held on 13 May, lot 85; and on the third day, 14 May under 'Designs for monuments', lot 71 is described as 'Design for Mr Nightingale's'.

This model is discussed by Bindman and Baker with further bibliographical references, in conjunction with the finished monument; see Bindman and Baker 1995, esp. pp. 221–5, 268–9, 325–30. See also Bindman 1986.

We are grateful to the Dean and Chapter of Westminster Abbey for allowing us to include this in the catalogue.

BIBLIOGRAPHY
Esdaile 1928, pp. 69–70, 157, pl. XLVIII (b) opp. p. 172, p. 180, 199; Gunnis 1968, p. 330; *Rococo* 1984, p. 304, cat.no. S40; Baker 1986 [Roubiliac], p. 63, fig. 16 on p. 81; Bindman and Baker 1995, pp. 268–9, 328–9, fig. 237 on p. 269, figs. 273–4, on pp. 329–30.

EXHIBITED
Rococo. Art and Design in Hogarth's England, Victoria and Albert Museum, London, 16 May to 30 September 1984, cat.no. S40.

169: Female left hand

about 1750
Perhaps by Louis François Roubiliac
Terracotta
l. 32 cm.
A.17–1944

Possibly identifiable with one of four lots (lots 30 to 33), each consisting of twelve hands, which were included in the first day of the sale of Roubiliac's effects, 12 to 15 May 1762. In the possession of the Victorian painter and sculptor Edward Henry Corbould (1815–1905), father of the donor Mrs Reginald Pott, who gave the present piece together with a further five models for hands in 1944; see entries for cat.nos. 170 to 174. Mrs Pott also gave the model of Nollekens's *Judgement of Paris* in 1955; see entry for cat.no. 144.

This life-size hand would almost certainly have been used as a model, although no marble versions on monuments corresponding to it have been identified. It could alternatively have served as an example for students and assistants to copy. The Roubiliac sale from which these may have been purchased contained a number of anatomical models, including arms, legs, and knees (for the sale see Esdaile 1928, Appendix F, and Bindman and Baker 1995, pp. 262–7, Appendix B).

169

BIBLIOGRAPHY
Baker 1986 [Roubiliac], p. 64, n. 25.

170: Female right hand

about 1750
Perhaps by Louis François Roubiliac
Terracotta
l. 30.5 cm.
A.18–1944

In the possession of the Victorian painter and sculptor, Edward Henry Corbould (1815–1905), father of the donor Mrs Reginald Pott, who gave the present piece together with a further five models for hands in 1944; see entries for cat.nos. 169, 171 to 174.

See entry for cat.no. 169.

BIBLIOGRAPHY
Baker 1986 [Roubiliac], p. 64, n. 25.

171: Upright male right hand

about 1750
Perhaps by Louis François Roubiliac
Terracotta
h. 26.5 cm.
A.19–1944

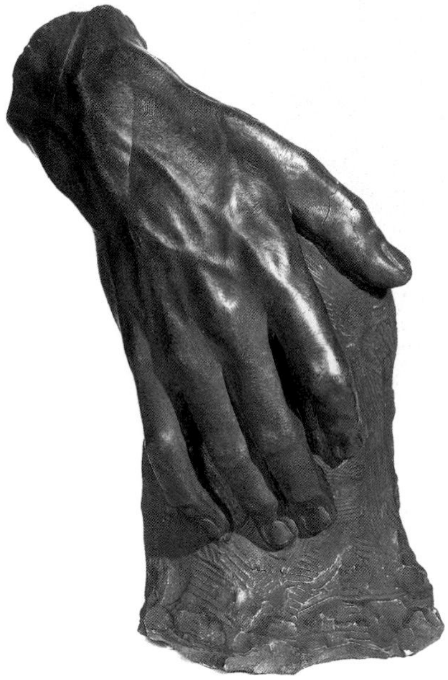

In the possession of the Victorian painter and sculptor, Edward Henry Corbould (1815–1905), father of the donor Mrs Reginald Pott, who gave the present piece together with a further five models for hands in 1944; see entries for cat.nos. 169 to 174

See entry for cat.no. 169.

An old torn label has '..oubiliac' and 'E.H. Corbould' written on it; also a further indecipherable inscription. There is also the fragment of a further label on which '. . ..odie' and '1762' is noted, possibly in connection with the Roubiliac sale of 1762.

BIBLIOGRAPHY
Baker 1986 [Roubiliac], p. 64, n. 25.

172: Female right hand holding a baton

about 1750
Perhaps by Louis François Roubiliac
Terracotta
h. 24 cm.
A.20–1944

In the possession of the Victorian painter and sculptor, Edward Henry Corbould (1815–1905), father of the donor Mrs Reginald Pott, who gave the present piece together with a further five models for hands in 1944; see entries for cat.nos. 169 to 171, 173 and 174.

See entry for cat.no. 169.

What remains of a label reads 'Roubiliac' together with a further indecipherable inscription.

BIBLIOGRAPHY
Baker 1986 [Roubiliac], p. 64, n. 25, and fig. 17 on p. 82.

173: Upright male left hand

about 1750
Perhaps by Louis François Roubiliac
Terracotta
h. 27.5 cm.
A.21–1944

In the possession of the Victorian painter and sculptor, Edward Henry Corbould (1815–1905), father of the donor Mrs Reginald Pott, who gave the present piece together with a further five models for hands in 1944; see entries for cat.nos. 169 to 172 and 174.

The thumb is missing.
See entry for cat.no. 169.

BIBLIOGRAPHY
Baker 1986 [Roubiliac], p. 64, n. 25.

174: Upright male left hand

about 1750
Perhaps by Louis François Roubiliac
Terracotta
h. 25.5 cm.
A.22–1944

In the possession of the Victorian painter and sculptor, Edward Henry Corbould (1815–1905), father of the donor Mrs Reginald Pott, who gave the present piece together with a further five models for hands in 1944; see entries for cat.nos. 169 to 173.

Three of the fingers merge into the block on which the hand is mounted.

See entry for cat.no. 169.
The decipherable inscription found on the remnants of a label reads: Terra Cotta by/ Roubiliac/Edward H.

BIBLIOGRAPHY
Baker 1986 [Roubiliac], p. 64, n. 25.

175: John Ray (1627–1705)

about 1850–1900
Anonymous; after Louis François Roubiliac
Plaster
h. 74 cm.
A.13–2000

Inscribed on the right of the base: L F Roubiliac Sc[t]
Inscribed on the base under the signature: JOA RAY

There is no information available on the provenance of the present piece, which until 2000 was recorded as an unregistered object in the Museum.

The casting lines on the bust suggest it was produced using piece moulds. See also entry for cat.no. 176 for a related version, in the studio of the sculptor Sir Joseph Edgar Boehm [q.v.] on his death.

176: John Ray (1627–1705)

about 1875–90
Anonymous; after Louis Francois Roubiliac
Plaster
h. 73cm.
1788–1892

Signed identically on both sides of the support: L.F. Roubiliac Sc[t]
Inscribed on the base: JOA.S RAY./1751/POSUIT/EDM. GARFORTH A.M.

Given by the Executors of the late Sir J. E. Boehm in 1892.

This bust of the naturalist John Ray appears to be taken from the marble original by Roubiliac, one of a series of portraits of distinguished members of Trinity College, Cambridge. The Garforth cited in the inscription was Edmund Garforth, the donor of the marble bust in the Wren Library. The terracotta model for this bust was purchased from the Roubiliac sale by Dr Matthew Maty and presented to the British Museum (Esdaile 1924 [Trinity College], pp. 13 and 15 and plate VI and VII, and Esdaile 1928, p. 100 and plate XXIX, *British Museum* 1999, pp. 170–3, cat.no. 66).

Malcolm Baker suggests the present piece 'appears to have been cast from the marble and is not an eighteenth-century multiple' (Baker 1995 [Wren], pp. 133–4).

See also entry for cat.no. 175.

Bibliography

Stocker 1988, p. 422, no. 355, p. 366 n. 29; Baker 1995 [Wren], pp. 133–4; *British Museum* 1999, p. 172, and n. 4 and 11 on p. 173.

John Michael Rysbrack

(b. Antwerp 1694 – d. London 1770)

Rysbrack was one of the most important sculptors active in England in the first half of the eighteenth century. The son of a landscape painter and etcher in Antwerp, he probably trained under Michel van der Voort I in that city from 1706 to 1712; in 1720 he moved to London, where he was to spend the rest of his life. His output was concentrated on portrait busts and funerary monuments, although he also executed garden and other outdoor pieces, such as the Saxon gods at Stowe, Buckinghamshire (see cat. nos. 181 and 182), work at Stourhead, Wiltshire, and the imposing bronze equestrian monument to William III in Bristol. Initially he collaborated with the architect James Gibbs (1682–1754), executing marble monuments for Westminster Abbey and elsewhere. He also worked with the architect William Kent (?1685–1748), again on monuments for Westminster Abbey. Towards the end of his career his work appears to have been in less demand, perhaps because of the rising popularity of Roubiliac [q.v.], although he was still producing major monuments, such as those to the Beaufort family at Badminton, Gloucestershire, and to Sir Nathaniel Curzon at Kedleston, Derbyshire.

Webb 1954; Gunnis 1968, pp. 333–8; Rysbrack 1982; Whinney 1988, pp. 162–81; TDA, 27, pp. 466–9 [Eustace].

177: Daniel Finch, 2nd Earl of Nottingham and 7th Earl of Winchilsea (1647–1730)

about 1723
Marble
h. 62 cm.
A.6–1999

Probably commissioned by William Finch, second son of the sitter, and displayed in his house in Savile Row, London. By 1774 the bust was displayed at the foot of the Great Staircase, Burley-on-the-Hill, Rutland. Thence by descent to G.S. Finch Esq., Ayston Hall, Rutland, Leicestershire, by whom it was sold in 1999. Included in the Sotheby's sale, London, 8 July 1998, lot 81, the bust was bought in and later purchased by the Museum for £350,000, with contributions from the National Art Collections Fund, the Parnassus Foundation through the American Friends of the V&A, the Hugh Phillips Bequest, the Henry Moore Foundation, and Sotheby's, whose donation was made in memory of Terence Hodgkinson [q.v.].

Monuments to other members of the Finch family are also in the Museum's collections; see entries for cat. nos. 16, 18 and 498. Daniel Finch was the eldest son of Sir Heneage Finch, 1st Earl of Nottingham; see entry for cat.no. 15.

The present bust, an early work by Rysbrack, helped establish and secure his reputation. Whinney has described the present bust as 'perhaps the most important of these early works by Rysbrack . . . a landmark in English sculpture (and indeed probably unique in the Europe of its day)' (Whinney 1988, pp. 166–7). As later studies have emphasised, the bust of Finch shows a severe antique convention being used in a precise and conscious manner, much as the French sculptor Edme Bouchardon (1698–1762) was to do for his British sitters. In discussing the importance of the present piece, Whinney noted that the portrait by Sir Godfrey Kneller of Daniel Finch now in the National Portrait Gallery, London, executed a few years previously, may have served as a model for the sculptor (for the Kneller portrait see *NPG* 1981, p. 619, no. 3910).

Bibliography

Vertue 1934, pp. 17, 56; Gunnis 1953, pp. 333, 336; Webb 1954, pp. 51, 222, fig. 6 on p. 28; *British Portraits* 1956, p. 183, cat.no. 596; Whinney 1988, pp. 166–8, fig. 106 on p. 166; Lord 1990, p. 867, fig. 54 on p. 867; Williamson 1999, p. 787, fig. XIII; *NACF* 1999 [Baker], p. 131, no. 4761; Baker 2000 [Portrait Bust], pp. 26–7, fig. 5 on p. 27; Baker 2000 [Grand Tour], p. 76, fig. 49a on p. 76; *V&A Magazine* 2000, [I], p. 2; Baker, Harrison and Laing 2000, p. 758 and fig. 31.

EXHIBITED
British Portraits, Winter Exhibition (1956–7), Royal Academy, London, cat.no. 596; *British Antique Dealers Association, The British Galleries at the V&A: New acquisitions and discoveries*, temporary display, at the Duke of York's Headquarters, London, 21 March to 27 March 2001.

178: James Gibbs (1682–1754)

signed and dated 1726
Marble
h. (excl. socle) 51 cm.
A.6–1988

Signed on the side of the black socle: Rysbrack/Sculp[r]
Signed and dated on the back: IAC: GIBBS Arch:/M[!] Rysbrack Sculp:/1726.
An engraved brass plaque (much-worn) on the front of the socle records the gift of the bust to St Martin-in-the-Fields:
THIS BUST BY RYSBRACK/OF/JAMES GIBBS/16 [82] 17 [54]/THE ARCHITECT OF THE CHURCH OF ST MARTIN IN THE FIELDS./WAS PRESENTED TO THE CHURCH/BY/WILLIAM BOORE, 1885
Inscribed on the front of the black socle: IAC GIBBS/Arch[t.]

Details concerning the provenance of the present bust have recently been revised (see below). It had previously been suggested the bust was commissioned by Edward Harley, 2nd Earl of Oxford, the primary patron of Gibbs and Rysbrack, both of whom lived close to one another on the Harley estate during the 1720s, and that it was subsequently acquired via the Horace Walpole sale by George Bubb Dodington, Lord Melcombe (see Baker 1990, pp. 17–18).

Gordon Balderston has recently discovered that, like Rysbrack's other bust of Gibbs, now in the Radcliffe Camera, Oxford (see below), the present bust belonged to the sitter himself, and, together with Rysbrack's bust of Alexander Pope, was displayed at his London residence at 5 Henrietta Street from the early 1730s (see Balderston 2001, pp. 9–15). Balderston records that on Gibbs's death these two busts – along with his house and its contents – were inherited by his friend the painter Cosmo Alexander (1724–1772), who in turn bequeathed them, with the rest of his collection, to his brother-in-law Sir George Chalmers (c.1729–1791). Chalmers sold the two busts at auction (Messrs Christie and Ansell, London, 28 March 1783, lots 88 and 89) see *ibid.*, p. 13. The bust of Gibbs was bought by Horace Walpole from the sale for seven guineas, and in 1784 it was recorded as being displayed on a coin cabinet in the Star Chamber at Strawberry Hill. It was subsequently included in the Horace Walpole sale, at Strawberry Hill, 17th day's sale, held on 13 May 1842, lot 99, there described in the Star Chamber as, 'A [n]oble marble bust of Gibbs, the architect, finely modelled and beautifully executed, on black marble pedestal, by Rysbrack'; the bust was sold to 'Forster' for seven guineas. The details of ownership of the bust are unknown following Forster's purchase in 1842, until 1885, when the bust was given by William Boore – thought to be 'an antique dealer and silver merchant of the Strand' (noted in a letter from the London Diocesan Advisory Committee for the Care of Churches; departmental records) – to the Church of St Martin-in-the-Fields, London. The question of the security of the bust at St Martin-in the-Fields was raised in 1986, by which time the bust was already no longer publicly displayed, and for this reason the church authorities decided to sell it by private treaty to a national institution. Purchased by the Museum from the Vicar and Churchwardens of the Parish of St Martin-in-the-Fields in 1988 for £465,000 with contributions from the National Heritage Memorial Fund, and the National Art Collections Fund (Eugene Cremetti Fund).

For a full discussion of the bust, see Balderston, *op. cit.* and Baker 2000 [Figured in Marble], pp. 98–9.

Marble on a contemporary black marble socle

The date of the pedestal is uncertain but it is based on a design by Gibbs (see Balderston 2001, p. 15).

The bust depicts the architect of St Martin-in-the Fields, James Gibbs; another portrait bust by Rysbrack of the same sitter, shown in a classicising manner without a wig, also dated 1726, is in the Radcliffe Camera, Oxford (see Baker 1990, fig. 5 on p. 19; *idem* 2000 [Figured in Marble], pp. 101–2, fig. 78 on p. 100, and Balderston 2001, fig. 5 on p. 6).

BIBLIOGRAPHY
Gunnis 1953, p. 335; Webb 1954, pp. 53–4, 216, fig. 10 on p. 39; *Painting and Sculpture in England* 1958, p. 26, cat.no. 49; *Eighteenth Century Portrait Busts* 1959, p. 26, cat.no. 28; *Gibbs* 1972, cat.no. 1; Kerslake 1977, I, p. 97 and II, pl. 262; Davies 1979, p. 51; *Rysbrack* 1982, pp. 74–5, cat.no. 10, illus. on p. 73; Friedman 1984, p. 15, n. 61 on p. 334, and frontispiece; Whinney 1988, p. 168, fig. 112 on p. 169; *V&A Album* 1988, p. 8 and front cover; *NACF* 1989, pp. 164–5, and illus. on p. 164; Baker 1990, pp. 16–18, fig. 4 on p. 17; Williamson 1991, p. 878; *idem* 1996 [Trusted], p. 155; Baker 2000 [Figured in Marble], pp. 95, 98–9, pl. 77 on p. 99; Balderston 2001; Snodin and Styles 2001, fig. 9 on p. 221.

EXHIBITED
Painting and Sculpture in England 1700–1750, Walker Art Gallery, Liverpool, 1958, cat.no. 49; *Eighteenth Century Portrait Busts*, the Iveagh Bequest, Kenwood, June to September 1959, cat.no. 28; *James Gibbs as a Church Designer*, Cathedral Church of All Saints, Derby, 1972, cat.no. 1; *Michael Rysbrack Sculptor 1694–1770*, Bristol City Art Gallery, 6 March to 1 May 1982, cat.no. 10.

179: William Shakespeare (1564–1616)

after 1726
After John Michael Rysbrack
Terracotta
h. 56 cm.
A.6–1924

Given by Mrs M.A. Miller, Anglesey House, Ryde, Isle of Wight in 1924 in memory of her father Augustus William Rixon, to whom the bust had previously belonged. A business card for E.W. Field, Dealer in Antiques and Works of Art, 28 Union Street, Ryde, Isle of Wight, was found amongst the papers relating to the objects offered as gifts to the Museum by Mrs Miller, and may indicate he acted as an agent for the donor.

There is some old damage to the right side of the face.

On acquisition this bust was thought to be 'a vigorous and characteristic work of Louis François Roubiliac' (*Review* 1924, p. 4). On inspection of the bust prior to its acquisition, Eric Maclagan [q.v.] wrote: 'It is not perhaps the most attractive kind of bust which Roubiliac did, but I think it quite likely that it is authentic, though I have not yet had time to look it up. It is considerably damaged, a good deal of the surface on one side of the face has been chipped off and repaired, but it is certainly a fine bold piece of modelling, and I think it would be quite worth accepting as a gift'. Katharine Esdaile published the bust in her monograph on Roubiliac, when discussing the Shakespeare busts, describing it as the 'curiously clumsy and probably very early terra-cotta… This work has nothing in common with any other Roubiliac Shakespeare, but bears a curious resemblance, in costume at least, to the bust round which Garrick throws his arm in Prior Park in Gainsborough's famous picture. But it shows no trace of the influence of the Chandos portrait, and artistically is much inferior to the rest' (Esdaile 1928, p. 128). In her copy of the Esdaile monograph (now in the Sculpture Department of the Victoria and Albert Museum), Marjorie Webb [q.v.] noted in the margin 'Rysbrack similar to his Shakespeare at Stowe Worthies'. The busts of Worthies at Stowe date from around 1726 to 1737 (Eustace 1998, pp. 33–4). The bust was later attributed to Rysbrack on stylistic grounds; a note on the departmental records suggests it was Geoffrey Webb (Marjorie Webb's husband) who identified the bust as being virtually identical with the stone bust of Shakespeare by Rysbrack amongst the series of busts of Worthies at Stowe (see Eustace 1998, fig. 6 on p. 33).

Discussing the Shakespeare busts produced in the eighteenth century, Webb commented, 'Earlier than any of these Rysbrack had cut a stone bust of Shakespeare to be one of the Worthies at Stowe. In the Victoria and Albert Museum is an unsigned terracotta which is almost certainly the model for this, for it is not only very similar but has that curious meanness of the body which I have already described as being peculiar to some of Rysbrack's early busts' (Webb 1954, p. 117).

Plaster casts of this bust were sold through the Museum's Cast Selling Service for of £1 15s each (*Casts* 1939, p. 20).

Bibliography

Shakespeare 1910, p. 24, cat.no. 173; *Review* 1924, p. 4, and fig. 3; Esdaile 1928, pp. 128, 186; Brown 1934, p. 59; Webb 1954, pp. 117, 224.

Exhibited

Shakespeare Memorial and Theatrical Exhibition, Whitehall Art Gallery, London, 12 October to 20 November 1910 (lent by the previous owner W. Rixon Esq.), cat.no. 173.

180: Canon Edward Finch (1664–1737)

signed and dated 1728
Terracotta
h. 61.6 cm.
A.27–1939

Signed on the back: Michael Rysbrack f. 1728

Purchased by Mr George H. Gabb Esq., 83 Crayford Road, Tufnell Park, London, from the auctioneers Foster's around 1934 for £36. According to Mr Gabb, the Museum were the underbidders at the sale, but H.D. Molesworth [q.v.] noted, 'I have not been able to trace any official papers on the matter, but Mr Bedford [q.v.] recalls some such attempt'. Offered by Mr Gabb to the Museum at the same price he claimed to have bought it for in 1934, and subsequently purchased in 1939 for £37 16s (36 guineas).

According to the vendor, the bust had been painted at least four times, and a layer of grey paint was removed on acquisition. The tip of the nose and parts of the cap and back of the robe have been restored.

The vendor suggested the bust 'undoubtedly' represented Jonathan Swift (1667–1745), and he continued to affirm this in a series of letters to Margaret Longhurst [q.v.], prior to its acquisition by the Museum. In one he wrote, 'I remember when I discussed the question of its identify with the late Chief of your Department he said that if they had it, he thought they would label it as – "Probably Jonathan Swift' – To which I added, "I don't think it would be long before the Probably' would be removed!' In a further letter to Margaret Longhurst, Mr Gabb wrote, 'No one has been able to suggest it can be anyone else as it is dated 1726 [it is in fact dated 1728], I may say I have identified some 12 important unknown portraits, four of which are now in the National Collection, which I think you will agree is an impressive record'.

Mr Gabb's proviso to selling the bust to the Museum was that the bust should be labelled as Jonathan Swift, and that he should be credited with its identification. Margaret Longhurst was adamant that such an identification could not be accepted by the Museum, as ' we are by no means convinced of it', though conceding the Museum would be prepared to label it 'possibly Jonathan Swift', but not 'probably Jonathan Swift'. Mr Gabb threatened to rescind the offer of the bust to the Museum, asking for it to be returned to Christie's, 'who I will instruct to sell it as: – "Probably Jonathan Swift – perhaps as, "Jonathan Swift", when it would probably fetch a much higher price than 36 guineas! I have now had such a long career as a Collector, that I have every reason to have confidence in my own judgment!'. Despite the somewhat acrimonious correspondence, the bust was purchased by the Museum from Mr Gabb.

Departmental records suggest the identity of the bust as Canon Finch was initially proposed by Edmund Esdaile (the son of the art historian Katharine Esdaile [q.v.]; I am grateful to John Physick for this information) in July 1956; he believed it to be a study for the bust of Canon Finch on Rysbrack's monument to two brothers, Dean Finch and Canon Edward Finch, in the south aisle choir of York Minster, though the bust on the monument is bareheaded (for the monument see Drake 1736, p. 513, and pl. opp. p. 513; Morrell 1944, pl. XXXVI and p. 40). This attribution was corroborated by John Mallett in October 1962. In *York Monuments*, Morrell made reference to a terracotta model of the Canon Finch bust at Burley-on-the Hill (Morrell 1944, p. 40). Canon Finch was also the brother of Daniel Finch, 2nd Earl of Nottingham and 7th Earl of Winchilsea (1647–1730); see entry for cat.no. 177. They were the grandsons of Sir Heneage Finch (1589–1631), whose monument is also in the Museum; see entry for cat.no. 15.

Bibliography

Webb 1954, pp. 182, 227, fig. 91 on p. 187; Whinney 1971, p. 36, cat.no. 4, illus. on p. 37; Davies 1979, p. 44; Whinney 1988, pp. 168, 187 (as 'Unknown clergyman'); Lord 1990, p. 867, n. 11.

181: Thuner

about 1728–30
Portland stone
h. 165.1 cm.
A.10–1985

The runic inscription reads: ᚦᚢᚼᚱ (THOR)

One of seven figures of Saxon gods commissioned by Richard Temple, 1st Viscount Cobham (1675–1749) from Rysbrack around 1728–30 for his gardens at Stowe House, Buckinghamshire. Originally located with the other six figures at Stowe, around an altar in an open grove known as the Saxon

Temple (*Vertue* 1934, p. 133). By 1744 they were removed to the Gothic Temple of Liberty, designed by James Gibbs (1682–1754), but by 1773 they moved again to a nearby grove (Kenworthy-Browne 1985, p. 226). The seven statues were dispersed in 1921 when they were included in the Stowe sale of that year, held by Messrs Jackson Stops, between 5 and 28 July 1921. Sold on the eighteenth day of the sale, described as 'Beautifully carved figure[s], executed in stone of "The Saxon deities" (by Rysbrack), denoting days of the week on a large stone pedestal', as lots 3793 to 3799. The purchasers at the sale were not recorded, and the significance of the figures was forgotten. The present piece and another of the Saxon gods, *Woden*, were rediscovered by Susan Moore in the gardens of Northcliffe School Hampshire in 1985 – presumably deposited there after the Stowe sale in 1921 – prompting their sale at auction that year. Included in the Phillips sale held on 18 June 1985, lot 169. Purchased by the Museum for £58,000 with assistance from the National Art Collections Fund.

The figure, which was covered in lichen, was cleaned in June 1991. The sceptre originally held in the figure's right hand has been broken.

Before its re-discovery and publication by Susan Moore, the present piece was unpublished in the Rysbrack literature. Moore noted that a photograph of *Thuner* taken in 1910 illustrated the Saxon gods 'on substantial pedestals that doubled their height' (Moore 1985, p. 251). This photograph – illustrated by John Kenworthy-Browne – shows both *Friga* and *Thuner* when they were at Stowe House; near to them are the foundations of the altar (Kenworthy-Browne 1985, fig. 22 on p. 227).

The seven statues depict Saxon gods and their associated days of the week; the present figure of Thuner, or Thor, the god of Thunder, is analogous to Thursday. The other statues were *Mona* (Monday) acquired by the Buckinghamshire County Museum, Aylesbury in 1991; *Tiw* (Tuesday) at Anglesey Abbey, near Cambridge (National Trust); *Woden* (Wednesday) in the collection of the late John Aspinall; *Friga* (Friday) formerly at Portmeirion, it was acquired by the Buckinghamshire County Museum, Aylesbury in 1994; *Seatern* (Saturday) is also in the collection of the late John Aspinall; *Sunna* (Sunday) was purchased by the V&A in 1997; see entry for cat.no. 182. For a full discussion of the Saxon deities, see Kenworthy-Browne 1985; Moore 1985. The figures executed by Rysbrack are directly inspired by Richard Verstegan's interpretation of the Saxon gods as noted and illustrated by him in his *Restitution of Decayed Intelligence in Antiquities Concerning the most noble, renowned English Nation* (first published in 1605), although Rysbrack's interpretation of Thor omits the twelve stars which surround the head of the figure as depicted by Verstegan. Under the title 'The Idoll Thor', Verstegan noted the characteristics of the god: 'The great reputed God, being of more estimation than many of the rest of like sort . . . was majestically placed in a very large, and spacious Hall, and there set, as if he had reposed himself upon a covered Bed. On his head he wore a Crowne of gold, and round in Compass above, and about the same, were set or fixed, twelve bright burnished golden starres. And in his right hand he held a kingly Scepter . . . That in the Aire he governed the winds, and the Cloudes; and being displeased did cause lightning, thunder, and tempests, with excessive Raine, Haile, and all ill weather. But being well pleased, by the adoration, sacrifice, and service of this suppliants, he then bestowed upon them most faire, and reasonable weather: and caused Corne aboundantly to growe: as also all sorts of fruites, & c. and kept away from them the Plague, and all other evill, and infectious diseases' (Verstegan 1634, pp. 74–5, illus. on p. 74). For further discussion of Richard Verstegan, see Parry 1995, pp. 49–69.

The significance of the political iconography of the Saxon gods at Stowe and Lord Cobham's allegiance, is discussed by George Clarke (Clarke 1973, pp. 568–71).

In a review of Alison Kelly's *Mrs Coade's Stone*, Nicholas Penny has suggested that moulds may have been inspired by the Saxon gods at Stowe, and that figures produced by Coade, as well as by Bridges of Knightsbridge, a rival firm, were taken from these moulds from the 1770s (Penny 1990; reference supplied by Marjorie Trusted).

A terracotta model of 'a Saxon God' was included in the Rysbrack sale held at Langford & Son, on 25 January 1766, lot 44.

Bibliography

Kenworthy-Browne 1985, esp. pp. 221, 223, fig. 6 on p. 222, fig. 22 on p. 227 (in a grove at Stowe House about 1905–10); Moore 1985, and fig. 1 on p. 250; Whinney 1988, p. 450, n. 21; Saumarez Smith 1989, pp. 10–12, fig. on p. 11 (I am grateful to Malcolm Baker for this reference); Davies 1991, p. 78, pl. 2:8; Williamson 1996 [Trusted], p. 156; Baker 2000 [Figured in Marble], p. 59.

182: Sunna

about 1728–30
Portland stone
h. 88.3 cm.
A.2–1997

One of seven figures of Saxon gods commissioned by Richard Temple, 1st Viscount Cobham (1675–1749) from Rysbrack around 1728–30 for his gardens at Stowe House, Buckinghamshire; see entry for cat.no. 181. Included in the Stowe House sale held by Messrs Jackson Stops of 1921 together with the other six figures, as lots 3793 to 3799. The whereabouts of the present piece only came to light in 1996: untraced for many years it was rediscovered by Tim Knox and Anthea Palmer of the National Trust, amongst shrubbery in a private collection in County Durham. It had previously been recorded in a photograph owned by Thomas Crowther & Son Ltd (see Davies 1991, p. 74, pl. 2:4). Included in the sale held by Christie's, London, on 1 July 1997, lot 8, the figure was purchased at the sale by a private collector, and was to have been exported to the United States. To allow it to remain in a national collection, the purchaser generously agreed to sell it to the Museum at the price he paid for it at auction. The figure was purchased by the Museum in 1997 for £135,862.50, with the assistance of the Heritage Lottery Fund, the Whiteley Trust, the Hildburgh Bequest, and an anonymous donor.

The figure was conserved in August 1997.

The present piece, representing Sunna, or Sunday, belongs to the series of seven Saxon gods representing the days of the week; a further figure from the series, that of Thuner, was acquired by the Museum in 1985; see entry for cat.no. 181. At the time of the discovery of the present piece in 1996, a mould was taken from it to enable casts to be made for display in the grounds of Stowe, now owned by the National Trust. Unlike the other figures, this is the only half-length figure in the series; it also lacks the runic inscription giving its name. The iconographical source was Richard Verstegan's *A Restititution of Decayed Intelligence in Antiquities,* (first published in 1605). Verstegan interpreted this particular deity as follows: 'First then, unto the day dedicated unto the especial adoration of the Idoll of the Sun, they gave the name of Sunday, as much to say, as the Sunsday, or the day of the Sun. This Idoll was placed in a Temple, and there adored, and sacrificed unto, for theat they beleeved that the sun in the firmament did with or in this Idoll correspond, and cooperate. It was made as here appeareth, like halfe a naked man, set upon a Pillar, his face as it were, brightened with gleames of fire, and holding with both his armes stretched out, a burning wheele upon his breast: the wheele being signific the course which he runneth round the world; and the fiery gleames, and brightnes, the light, and heat wherewith he warmeth, and comforteth the things, that live, and grow' (Verstegan 1634, pp. 68–9, illus. on p. 69).

Bibliography

Moore 1985, p. 252 (as whereabouts unknown); Davies 1991, p. 74, pl. 2:4 (as whereabouts unknown); *Royal Society of British Sculptors* 1997, p. 15 and illus; *V&A Magazine* 1998, p. 3; Williamson 1999, p. 786, fig. X; Knox 2001, p. 30, fig. 7 on p. 31 and n. 28 to 30.

183: Term (probably Socrates)

about 1729
Terracotta
h. 31.5 cm.
A.14–1955

Given by Lt. Col. H.W. Russell, "Innisfree", Avenue Road, Lymington, Hampshire in 1955. The model was originally sent to the Museum by the donor requesting an opinion; in the accompanying letter he wrote, 'The enclosed Terracotta figure which I obtained some years ago in Guildford the origin of which I cannot trace I would like to be identified if possible'. Although in his reply John Pope-Hennessy [q.v.] did not suggest an attribution to a specific sculptor, he wrote that it 'appears to date from the middle years of the 18th century and is probably English. It may perhaps have been the sketch model for part of a marble fireplace. At this period fireplaces were sometimes flanked with caryatids or terms of this kind, the mantelshelf being supported on the heads of the figures'. In his reply Col. Russell wrote that he would 'be pleased if you will dispose of the terracotta term in any way you like – I have no further interest in it', and the model was therefore subsequently accessioned by the Museum as a gift.

Confirming Pope-Hennessy's earlier supposition, the term was later identified as the model for the right-hand caryatid figure – possibly depicting the philosopher Socrates – on the marble chimneypiece in the Old East India House, Leadenhall and Lime Street, London, with an overmantel depicting *Britannia receiving the riches of the East*, commissioned from Rysbrack when it was rebuilt during 1726–9 by the architect Theodore Jacobsen (d. 1772) (see *Foreign and Commonwealth Office* 1996, fig. 20 for the chimneypiece). Jacobsen was also the architect for the Foundling Hospital; see entry for cat.no. 189. When the Old East India House was demolished in 1861, the chimneypiece was installed in the India Office Council Chamber of the Foreign and Commonwealth Office, Downing Street.

It is likely that the term on the left-hand side of the chimneypiece represents Plato, as a pendant to that of Socrates. Comparisons can be made between these and similar representations of these two philosophers on terms at Versailles (see Thomassin 1694, nos. 173 and 177 respectively).

The work carried out by Rysbrack on the marble relief which stood on the chimneypiece in the East India House is recorded by Vertue, who noted, ' in the East India house London being rebuilt. the great room for ye Council. or public Sales. – a chimney *bass-relievo*. first design'd by Mr. Rysbrac. & finely contriv'd, several figures well group'd and dispos'd. this design not pleasing the Directors, or advisors of the workes. another draught was made by their own directions and advice. by Mr-Pond a Gentleman who having some beginning in the principles of Painting under Mr. J. Vandrbank. went to Italy. (at the expence of his father a Wealthy Citizen) & at his return, in about two or three years <not so much as two> brought some few pictures. & c & was mightily commended by report, for his great industry & assiduous studys. abroad. but this design being on a half sheet of paper. – heightned – (as well as his paintings from the life) are a demonstrative contradiction. but to see Rysbrac's Model (with his design) so far far out done, is no agreable prospect to those, who ever thinks that travelling will qualify a painter, tho' it may as a Gentleman (but.) no other ways. probat.est <The Marble is intirely finisht very beautifull & masterly done admird by all Artists & lovers of Art. this will remain a sample of Mr. Rysbrack skill to posterity 1729.>' (*Vertue* 1934, p. 37; noted in Webb 1954, p. 131). Although this confirms Rysbrack as the author of the *Britannia* relief only, his recorded authorship of this relief, together with stylistic comparisons between the chimneypiece and other works by Rysbrack, strongly suggests that he was also responsible for the design of the chimneypiece. In her monograph on Rysbrack, Webb made no reference to the chimneypiece itself, only noting the relief as being by Rysbrack and finished about 1730 (*ibid.*, p. 228). A payment of £100 made to Rysbrack for the marble relief of *Britannia* is recorded on 22 April 1730 (Foster 1924, p. 35).

184: Sir Isaac Newton (1642–1727)

about 1730
Terracotta
h. 36 cm.
A.1–1938

Previously on loan to the Museum from Dr W.L. Hildburgh F.S.A. from 7 October 1935 (ex-loan 4899), and subsequently given by him to the Museum as a New Year gift in 1938.

The sale of Nollekens's effects held between 3 and 5 July 1823 included on the 2nd day of the sale, lot 59 – in the Groups and figures in terracotta from the Study – 'Rysbrack. A model of the Group of Figures of the Monument to Sir I. Newton, in Westminster Abbey'. The annotated catalogue held in the National Art Library records that it was sold to 'Neville' for £2 7s. What was described as 'A Terracotta Model, for the figure of Sir Isaac Newton, by Ryback [sic], for the tomb in Westminster Abbey; the books on which he leans are slightly different from those represented in the eventual sculpture – 14 fl in. high', featured as lot 86 in the sale of the collection formed by Edward Cheney Esq., Badger Hall, Shropshire, the property of Francis Capel-Cure Esq, held by Christie's, on 4 and 5 May 1905. The annotated catalogue held in the National Art Library records it was sold to Agnew for £19 19s (19 guineas).

In May 1958 the condition of the present piece was recorded as: 'Neck and left leg broken and repaired, left thumb restored in wax, and some make up on right foot and corner of base'. In January 1963 Ken Hempel of the Museum's Conservation Department recorded, 'The terracotta has been primed and finished to resemble terracotta again. At a later stage the object seems to have been painted again, white with possibly a black base. Thumb and first two fingers of left hand made up. Cloth held in right hand and right foot also restored. Base broken and made up with plaster. Break in left leg and neck. Drapery under right ankle restored. True colour obscured by dirt layer' (departmental records).

This is the terracotta sketch-model executed by Rysbrack from an original design by William Kent (about 1685/6–1748) for the monument to Sir Isaac Newton, commissioned by John Conduitt erected against the nave screen in Westminster Abbey in 1730. The *Gentleman's Magazine* of April 1731 recorded the monument being erected: 'On the Sarcophagus his own Figure is placed, in a cumbent Posture, his Elbow resting on the several incomparable Books written by him; two Boys stand before him with a Scroll, on which is drawn a remarkable *Diagram* relating to the *Solar System*; and over that a *converging Series*, an Invention which shews the utmost of human Understanding' (pp. 159–60, cited by Whinney

1971, p. 38). The design by William Kent, in pen, ink and wash, is in the Department of Prints, Drawings and Paintings, inv.no. E.424–1946; see Webb 1954, fig. 22 on p. 65; Physick 1967, fig. 3 on p. 28; Physick 1969, fig. 48 on p. 80; *Grand Design* 1999, fig. 115 on p. 306. The adapted design by Rysbrack from the Kent concept is in the British Museum (inv.no. 1859–7–9–100); see Webb 1954, fig. 23 on p. 65; Physick 1969, fig. 49 on p. 81. The authorship of the monument is noted by Vertue who recorded, 'April. 1731. Sett up in Westminster Abbey the Monument of Sr. Isaac Newton. a noble and Elegant work by Mr Michael Rysbrack. much to his Reputation. tho the design or drawing of it on paper was poor enough, yet for that only Mr Kent is honourd with his name on it (Pictor et Architect inventor.) which if it had been delivrd to any other Sculptor besides Rysbrack, he might have been glad to have his name omitted' (*Vertue* 1934, pp. 50–1; cited by Webb 1954, p. 84). For a discussion of the Newton commission see Webb 1954, pp. 82–5; Lord 1992 [Newton].

A related drawing in the Department of Prints, Drawings and Paintings (inv.no. 4910.19) shows a monument with the same composition, the main difference being the face of the figure, which appears more youthful than that represented in the present piece, and a coronet surmounting the cartouche on the pyramid may suggest an adaptation of the design from the Newton monument for 'some aristocratic dilettante, rather than an alternative sketch for this monument' (noted in departmental records). Francis Haskell also noted an early sketch by Alexander Pope among the Conduitt papers at King's College, Cambridge (Haskell 1975, p. 2, fig. 2 on p. 3; I am grateful to Malcolm Baker for this reference). A further drawing is in the Royal Institute of British Architects (information from Malcolm Baker), due to come to the V&A in 2003.

Nicholas Penny has compared the technique of the present piece with the modello in the Ashmolean Museum, Oxford for the monument to Handel by Roubiliac in Westminster Abbey (*Ashmolean* 1992 [III], p. 153, cat.no. 565).

The Rysbrack monument is illustrated on the reverse of a medal commemorating Sir Isaac Newton by Jean Dassier (1676–1763); see *Medallic Illustrations*, pl. CXLVII, no. 6.

BIBLIOGRAPHY

Review 1938, pp. 4–5, pl. 2(a); *Masterpieces* 1951, p. 87, no. 42, illus. on p. 86; Webb 1954, pp. 83, 222, fig. 21 on p. 65; *The Times*, 30 January 1958, illus. on p. 16; *Age of Rococo* 1958, p. 179, cat.no. 491; Physick 1967, p. 32, fig. 4 on p. 28; *idem* 1969, p. 81; Whinney 1971, p. 38, cat.no. 5, illus. on p. 39; Baker 1986 [Roubiliac], p. 64, fig. 18 on p. 83; Whinney 1988, n. 29 on p. 451; *Ashmolean* 1992 [III], p. 153; *Grand Design* 1999, p. 307, cat.no. 137, illus. on p. 306; *Precious* 2001, fig. 2 on p. 22.

EXHIBITED

Style in Sculpture, Victoria and Albert Museum, London, 1946; Included in the Hildburgh Memorial Exhibition held in the Recent Acquisitions Court at the Victoria and Albert Museum, 30 January to March 1958; *The Age of Rococo: Art and Culture of the Eighteenth Century*, Residenzmuseum, Council of Europe, Munich, 15 June to 15 September 1958, cat.no. 491; Exhibition of Drawings by English Sculptors 1680–1810, Ashmolean Museum, Oxford, 23 November to 10 December 1967; *A Grand Design. The Art of the Victoria and Albert Museum*, travelling exhibition, Baltimore Museum of Art, Boston Museum of Fine Art, Toronto Royal Ontario Museum, Houston, The Museum of Fine Art, San Francisco, Fine Arts Museums and Victoria and Albert Museum, cat.no. 137; *Precious*, Millennium Gallery, Sheffield, 5 April to 24 June 2001.

185: Putti supporting an architrave

about 1730
Possibly by John Michael Rysbrack
Marble
h. 133 cm.
A.4–1990

Possibly from the Great Saloon or Ball Room at Bedford House, London. In the possession of the dealers Poulter and Sons, Fulham Road, London, for a number of years, and by whom sold at Sotheby's, London on 7 December 1989, lot 169, where it was described as English with the suggestion that the details of the moulding were similar to those on the chimneypiece by Rysbrack at the Foundling Hospital. Reference was also made to the 'traditional belief' that the present piece derived from Carlton House where Peter Scheemakers [q.v.] executed several massive chimneypieces (Gunnis 1968, p. 342 and see below). Purchased for £14,966 on behalf of the Museum by Alex Wengraf Ltd, The Old Knoll, Blackheath, London; the relief was held until the following financial year, and accessioned in 1990. For further details of the possible provenance of the present relief see below.

The original purpose of the present relief is not known, though it may have formed part of a large chimneypiece or a doorframe. Malcolm Baker has suggested that although its size would have necessitated a chimneypiece of massive proportions, the vertical moulding on the related terracotta, cat.no. 187, 'would be consistent with the relief forming part of a chimneypiece or door frame' (departmental records). Stylistic comparisons may also be made with the winged putto on Rysbrack's monument to the Rev. Thomas Busby (d. 1725) erected in 1753 at Addington, Bucks; see Physick 1969, fig. 56 on p. 87. Similarities made with the putti found on the *Allegory of Charity* relief – see entry for cat.no. 189 – have also supported the suggested attribution to Rysbrack.

Malcolm Baker has suggested a source for the paired putti may be Michelangelo's putti on the Sistine Chapel ceiling in the Vatican (see *Michelangelo* 1992, figs. on pp. 363, 365, 371, 373, cat.nos. 90–3, 98–9 respectively). Timothy Stevens has proposed comparisons with an engraving by J. Miller published in 1763 showing a fragment of a Greek sarcophagus – one of the Arundel marbles – now in the Ashmolean Museum, Oxford (see Giometti 1999, fig. 11 on p. 34). See also entry for cat.no. 186 for stylistic comparisons with works by Bartolomeo Ammanati (1511–1592) and Jérôme Du Quesnoy the Younger (1602–1654).

Two closely comparable marble reliefs were included in the sale at Christie's, London, on 1 December 1911, lot 85, described as 'the property of a nobleman. Two portions of a chimneypiece . . . Italian 17th century'; bought by 'Harding' for £162 15s. This pair of reliefs 'of exactly similar design' were noted by Maclagan and Longhurst in their entry on the related terracotta reliefs, see entries for cat.nos. 186–7, and it had been thought that the present piece was one of the two. In an unpublished essay [1992] on the present piece, Chloë Archer has pointed out however that the difference in measurements would rule out this suggestion (departmental records). However, in the sale catalogue entry for a further pair of variant reliefs sold at Sotheby's on 10 July 1998, lot 79, it was mistakenly proposed that the reliefs sold in 1911 – which had been acquired by the 11th Duke of Norfolk as part of the Bedford House chimneypiece – could be identified with the present piece and another now in the USA. The suggestion that the present relief was 'traditionally' associated with Carlton House, London was rejected by Archer, who noted that it was merely based on the recollections of a mason working at Poulter and Son, Fulham Road, said to have seen the relief in the house; this however is patently absurd, since Carlton House was demolished in 1827 (the site cleared by 1861), and the mason arrived in London from Italy around 1918.

The present piece may have formed part of a chimneypiece executed by Rysbrack for John, 4th Duke of Bedford, between 1733 and 1736 for the Great Saloon or Ball Room at Bedford House; following the dismantling of the chimneypiece in 1800, the present relief may be identified with that sold at Christie's, Bedford House sale, held between 5–10 May 1800, lot 71, described as 'A Magnificent Statuary Marble Chimney Piece. The Cornice Supported by Four Bacchanalian Boys, in Alto Relievo': the buyer was Charles Howard, 11th Duke of Norfolk (see the entry for lot 79, Sotheby's, London, 10 July 1998). Two pairs were sold in 1891 and in 1911 respectively by the Duke of Norfolk (noted in sale catalogue as above). Those sold at the Arundel Castle sale, Sparks & Son, 14 and 15 April 1891, lots 298 and 299, were described as 'two figures of boys, in bold relief, supporting richly carved cornice, statuary marble, 4ft 3 in high; 3ft wide', and Archer suggests that the present relief may be one of those sold in the 1891 sale, probably originally acquired for Arundel Castle, rather than for the recently built Worksop Manor, Nottinghamshire.

As indicated above, several versions or variants relating to the present relief and cat.nos. 186 and 187 are known, recorded in auction house sales. In addition to those already noted, in the sale of the property of Mr Jackson, at Ebury House, near the Wooden Bridge, Chelsea, sold by Mr Christie, on 22 July 1807, lot 91 was described as 'Boys in Bass Relief, Rysbrack'. A pair of related reliefs in white marble was included in the sale at Sotheby's, London 4 December 1970, lot 79 (vendor D.W. Bull Ltd, purchased by Huxtable). The catalogue – which described them as 'Flemish' – suggested comparisons 'with the smaller pair of terracotta reliefs possibly maquettes for the present marbles, in the Victoria and Albert Museum'. A relief in marble related to cat.no. 186, which may have been executed by Peter Scheemakers [q.v.] for Carlton House, was sold at Christie's, London, 7 December 1989, lot 169. The architrave differs from the present piece. Another slightly smaller pair of marble variants (94 x 56.8 cm) with plain architraves were sold by Sotheby's, New York, 12 January 1993, lot 86, described as 'Italian White Marble Baroque Putti Supports'. Another pair of weathered marble versions was included in Sotheby's, London sale held on 3 December 1997, lot 226 – these were bought in but later sold privately to Peter Petrou, London. Another marble pair included in the Sotheby's, London sale on 10 July 1998, lot 79, was attributed to workshop of Rysbrack. A pair of closely related marble putti torchères, attributed to Rysbrack, second quarter of the eighteenth century, formerly the property of the Duke of Roxburghe, 2 Carlton House Terrace, London, was included in Sotheby's, London sale on 8 July 1998, lot 85.

Bibliography

Williamson 1991, p. 879, XII, and illus.

186: Putti supporting an architrave

about 1730
Perhaps by John Michael Rysbrack
Terracotta
h. 42 cm.
7717–1863

Purchased in London, together with cat. no. 187 for £6 6s (6 guineas) each; vendor not recorded.

Two possibly related lots were included in the Rysbrack sale held by Mr Langford and Son, at their House in the Great Piazza, Covent Garden on 24 and 25 January 1766 – lot 51 included in the first day's sale was described as 'Two boys, for a pediment', and lot 13 in the second day's sale under 'Models in Terra Cotta' was described as 'Two, boys on a side of a pediment'.

The present piece, together with its pendant, cat.no. 187 are models for marble originals, which were probably intended for use on the entablature of a doorway or chimneypiece; they may alternatively have formed part of the pediment of a monument. Both were originally ascribed to Alessandro Algardi (1598–1654) and published as such by J.C. Robinson in his 1862 catalogue of *Italian Sculpture of the Middle Ages and Period of the Revival of Art* at the then South Kensington Museum. The date of publication of the catalogue suggests that both were acquired before 1863, the year in which they were accessioned. Robinson suggested, 'These terracottas, originally part of the same decorative work, are executed altogether in the style of bronze sculpture. Their sharp and crisp execution resembles rather the work of the chasing chisel than the modelling tool. In an executive point of view, they are full of merit; recalling the clear and precise touch and graceful manipulation of the painter Guido, in the Sister art' (Robinson 1862, p. 183). The Algardi attribution was rejected by Maclagan and Longhurst in the 1932 *Catalogue of Italian Sculpture*, when the two terracottas were described as 'Italian 16/17th century . . . The ascription to Algardi in the Robinson catalogue is hardly put forward as more than a suggestion of Bolognese character in the reliefs' (Maclagan and Longhurst 1932, p. 156).

The traditional Italian attribution of the reliefs was later rejected, when it was first suggested they could be Flemish, first half of the eighteenth century, and later French, mid-seventeenth century. The reliefs were included by John Pope-Hennessy [q.v.] under 'rejected attributions' in his *Catalogue of Italian Sculpture in the Victoria and Albert Museum*; he proposed they could be 'English or Flemish eighteenth century' (Pope-Hennessy 1964, II, p. 699). Charles Avery has noted similarities with the putti on the balustrade by Bartolomeo Ammanati (1511–1592) in the Del Monte Chapel at S. Pietro in Montorio, Rome, suggesting a 'stylistic link with Francois Duquesnoy, [which] may point to Jerome Duquesnoy III (1602–1654), who borrowed from a Del Monte effigy for his Bishop Antoine Triest monument, St Bavo, Ghent' (departmental records). For the St Bavo monument, see Hadermann-Misguich 1970, fig. 14. Stylistic comparisons may also be made to the putti supporting the balustrade in the Ammanati tomb of the poet Jacopo Sannazaro (1457–1530) in Naples (see Kinney 1976, figs. 77–80 on pp. 299–300). In 1990 the Museum acquired a marble for which the present piece is a model; see entry for cat.no. 185. The probable attribution of the marble version to Rysbrack suggested that the closely comparable terracottas, although exhibiting some differences, notably in the archivtrave, were also likely to be by him.

Reproductions of the present piece, together with a cast showing putti heads by 'Flemingo' (François Duquesnoy (1594–1643)) were amongst those included in the *Preliminary list of Casts for the Use of Schools of Art, Art Classes, Technical Schools and public elementary schools*; see *Casts* 1901, fig. 26, 'Two casts. 7/6 each' Casts taken from the present piece and its pendant also appear in the 1939 *Catalogue of Plaster Casts* offered for sale by the Cast Department of the Victoria and Albert Museum, at a cost of £1 1s each; see *Casts* 1939, pp. 27–8, nos. 2687 and 2688.

Bibliography

Robinson 1862, p. 183; *Inventory* 1864, p. 171, no. 11940; Maclagan and Longhurst 1932, p. 156, pl. 105a; Pope-Hennessy 1964, II, p. 699.

187: Putti supporting an architrave

about 1730
Perhaps by John Michael Rysbrack
Terracotta
h. 42 cm.
7718–1863

Purchased in London, together with cat. no. 186 for £6 6s (6 guineas) each; vendor not recorded.

The present piece, together with its pendant cat.no. 186 are models for marble originals, probably used on the entablature of a doorway or chimneypiece; they may also have formed part of the pediment of a monument.

See entry for cat.no. 186.

Bibliography

Robinson 1862, p. 183; *Inventory* 1864, p. 171, no. 11941; Maclagan and Longhurst 1932, p. 157, pl. 105c; *Picture Book* 1932, pl. 15; Pope-Hennessy 1964, II, p. 699.

188: Thomas Wentworth, 3rd Earl Strafford
(1672–1739)

about 1740
Terracotta
h. 61.9 cm.
A.1–1954

In the possession of Sir Algernon Osborn Bt., Chicksands (date unknown; early twentieth century), and placed on loan by him at the Barking Museum, Barking, Essex. The model was subsequently lent by Sir Algernon to the Victoria and Albert Museum (loan no. 1) from 8 December 1936 until his death in 1948 (see below). Later purchased by Dr W.L. Hildburgh F.S.A. and on loan from him to the Museum from 17 June 1953 (ex-loan no 5240). Given to the Museum by Dr Hildburgh in December 1953, and registered as the first object acquired in 1954 by the Department of Architecture and Sculpture, later Sculpture Department. Hildburgh's enthusiasm in regularly offering as a gift the first object of the year to be accessioned by the Department of Architecture and Sculpture is commented upon by Leigh

Ashton [q.v.] in his letter of thanks to Dr Hildburgh for the gift of the present piece, 'I know you will not take it as greed but as a very sincere expression of our deep appreciation if I say that we hope and pray that many many A.1's may come in the future from the same source as they have over the last two decades'.

This is the sketch model for the full-size marble figure of Thomas Wentworth at Wentworth Castle.

The present piece was brought to the attention of the Museum in April 1936 by Mr H.B. Johnson of Barking Museum, where the model was on loan. H.D. Molesworth [q.v.] considered the statuette to be 'certainly English work, and I feel sure Rysbrack . . . The general treatment of the figure and the armour is extremely close to the statue of Henry, son of the 2nd Duke of Beaufort at Badminton, while the use of the pillar and the pose of the hands is almost exactly reproduced in the sketch for the Greenwich figure of George II; these are both by Rysbrack'. The sketch referred to is in the Museum's Department of Prints, Drawings and Paintings (inv.no. 8933–231). Later in 1936 Katharine Esdaile suggested an identification of the present piece as a sketch for the monument by Scheemakers to one of the Dukes of Ancaster at Edenham. In May 1951 Mrs Webb suggested that the terracotta was Rysbrack's model for the Earl of Strafford at Wentworth Woodhouse; this was confirmed later that year by photographic comparisons (see Whinney 1971, p. 40). The sculptor's tool marks are evident on the figure, especially on the face.

Bibliography

Webb 1954, p.162;
Whinney 1971, p. 40, cat.no. 6, illus. on p. 41; Davies 1979, p. 131; Whinney 1988, p. 450, n. 20.

189: Allegory of Charity

signed; about 1746
Terracotta painted grey
h. 67 cm. w. 105.4 cm.
A.58–1953

Signed on the bottom right: Mich: Rysbrack

Purchased by Sir Edward Littleton of Teddesley Hall, Staffordshire from Rysbrack in 1756. Said to have been sold at the Teddesley Hall sale, held on 20 March 1953 (I have been unable to verify this). Purchased by Montague Marcussen, 98 Crawford Street, London, and sold to the Museum in 1953 for £185. Teddesley Hall was demolished in 1954.

There is a vertical crack to the left of centre of the relief, and other cracks appear in the bottom right corner. The projecting horn of the cow – which has been broken off – is an old break, contemporary with the sale of the relief to Sir Edward Littleton by the sculptor, and is mentioned by Rysbrack in a letter to Sir Edward Littleton dated 7 April 1761: 'Sir, I am sorry for the accident which has happened to the Model, of the horn of the Cow, The horn is broke likewise of ye Marble Basso Relievo at the Foundling hospital, but it looks the more antique as Doctor Mead said of it. The accident may be repaired, by modelling the horn in Clay, and making a Mould upon it, and Cast it in Plaster of Paris, fix it on, and Paint it of the same colour as the Model is' (*Rysbrack* 1932, p. 26, letter XVIII; reprinted by Webb 1954, p. 205, letter XVIII; cited in Whinney 1971, p. 42).

This is the model for the marble relief which Rysbrack donated to the Foundling Hospital in 1746. The Foundling Hospital was established in London by Thomas Coram (1668–1751) in 1741. Rysbrack was one of a number of artists with close connections with the charity: he was elected Governor and Guardian of the Hospital in 1745 (see Brownlow 1865, pp. 60–1). On seeing the marble relief in October 1746 Vertue wrote, 'the Moddel of Clay of the same magnitude is admirably well done and therein shows his great Skill in the plastic Art wherein as the Materia is moleable, still permits the Artist to express his mind more Artfully & with greater freedom. than on the laborious or durable marble' (cited by Webb 1954, p. 135; Whinney 1971, p. 42). A terracotta figure of *Charity*, now in the Herron Museum of Art, Indianapolis, relates to the Charity figure depicted in the relief (Nicolson 1972, pp. 18, 88, and pl. 23; Webb 1954, fig. 62 on p. 124).

The Foundling Hospital was renamed the Thomas Coram Foundation for Children in 1954, and the marble relief is now displayed in the Court Room (see Webb 1954, pp. 131–2, 135; *Thomas Coram Foundation* 1965, p. 14, no. 78, described as Charity Children Engaged in Navigation and Husbandry; Nicolson 1972, p. 88, cat.no. 103, pls. 21, 48, 49).

Rysbrack also provided designs for a number of chimneypieces at Teddesley Hall, including one over which the present piece was to be displayed; see Physick 1969, pp. 101–3. Letters from the sculptor to Edward Littleton record the existence of these designs (see *Rysbrack* 1932, pp. 9, 11, 24, 26; also Webb 1954, pp. 195–6, 204–5, letters III, IV, XVI, and XVIII respectively). Mention of this chimneypiece is first made in a letter from Rysbrack to Littleton dated 12 February 1756, in which Rysbrack wrote, 'I really did not remember that I was to have given you a Design for a Chimney Piece, but if you please to send me the dimensions of the outside of the frame to the Model of Charity, and the Width of the light of the Chimney and the Height, I will send you a drawing for it, and you shall be heartily welcome'. Rysbrack wrote to Littleton again on 18 November 1756: 'According to Your Honour's desire I have made You a Drawing of a Chimney Piece Proportioned to Your Room and the Model of the Basso Relievo for the Foundling Hospital. I have tried a Great Many ways, but believe this will do, and I beg the favour that You shew it to all your Friends' (*Rysbrack* 1932, pp. 9 11; Webb 1954, pp. 195–6, letters III and IV respectively).

A design for the relief in pen, ink and wash, which differs slightly from the present piece – the cherub figure to the right of the relief is reversed – is in the Department of Prints, Drawings and Paintings (inv.no. E.415–1975).

The accompanying frame for the present piece was acquired by the Museum at the same time as the model, from the same source; see entry for cat.no. 190.

Bibliography

Rysbrack 1932, pp. 7, 9–11, 24, 26, letters I, III, IV, XVI and XVII; *Vertue* 1934, p. 132; Webb 1954, pp. 135, 194, 195, 196, 204–5, letters I, III, IV, XVI and XVIII; *Thomas Coram Foundation* 1965, p. 14; Wimsatt 1965, p. 99; Physick 1969, pp. 101–3; Whinney 1971, pp. 42, 44, cat.no. 7, illus on p. 43; Nicolson 1972, pp. 18, 88, pl. 22; Baker 1996 [Louvre], pp. 81–2; *idem* 2000 [Figured in Marble], pp. 56, 59.

189 and 190

190: Overmantle frame for the Allegory of Charity

about 1756
Anonymous, possibly after a design by John Michael Rysbrack
Wood
h. 183 cm. w. 177.2 cm.
A.59–1953

Commissioned by Sir Edward Littleton of Teddesley Hall, Staffordshire to frame the terracotta model of the Allegory of Charity, which was purchased from Rysbrack in 1756. Sold at the Teddesley Hall sale, held on 20 March 1953 (I have been unable to verify this). Purchased by Montague Marcussen, 98 Crawford Street, London and sold to the Museum with the terracotta relief; see entry for cat.no. 189; the frame was purchased in 1953 for £35.

See entry for cat.no. 189.

This frame may have been designed by Rysbrack at the request of Sir Edward Littleton, following his purchase in 1756 of the model for the *Allegory of Charity*, the marble original of which was executed and donated by Rysbrack to the Foundling Hospital. Littleton's request that Rysbrack should also supply a design for a chimney piece for Teddesley Hall, above which the terracotta relief was to be placed, is recorded in a series of letters from the sculptor to Littleton; see entry for cat.no. 189.

Though it has been suggested the frame is after a design by Rysbrack, a letter from the sculptor to Littleton dated 31 July 1756 in connection with the chimneypiece mentioned above suggests that Rysbrack was unaware of the dimensions of the frame in which Littleton had housed the relief (*Rysbrack* 1932, p. 9; Webb 1954, p. 195, letter III).

The present frame differs from that housing the Foundling Hospital relief, which was designed and donated by John Deval the Elder (1701–1774); for Deval, see *Thomas Coram Foundation* 1965, p. 14.

191: John Locke (1632–1704)

about 1750; after the original of 1733–4
After an original by John Michael Rysbrack
Plaster
h. (incl. base) 45 cm.
A.84–1921

Given by Percy Woods Esq., C.B., The Firs, London Road, Guildford, Surrey in 1921. In the year of his gift the donor noted in a letter to R.P. Bedford [q.v.], 'I have known the bust for nearly 79 years – it was one of several pieces of plaster of Paris – which belonged to my mother – and I believe that it came from her from a great aunt (by marriage) in Dorsetshire, altho it may have been (intermediately) in her grandmother's possession'. In a further letter of 23 September 1921, Mr Woods wrote, 'My mother had several groups of single busts – (in my childhood) – which I understood came to her from some Dorsetshire kinsfolk whose deaths did not take place so early as I imagined. I do not know how long the objects may have been in the possession of the Dorsetshire people before their deaths, but the latest date may even be 1834 that is to say the date of death of the old lady from whom they are supposed to have come to my mother'. On long-term loan to the Cecil Higgins Art Gallery, Bedford from February 1978; returned to the V&A April 2000.

On acquisition the sitter had not been identified, and the bust was described as an early contemporary cast from an original of the school of Roubiliac [q.v.]. A note on the departmental records relating to the present piece records that, 'Mrs Geoffrey Webb [M.I. Webb, the author of the monograph on Rysbrack] bought in a similar bronzed version of this bust, inscribed on the back J.P. PAPERA 16 Marylebone Street, Gordon Square'. Papera, described as a sculptor resident in London, exhibited three busts at the Royal Academy annually between 1829 and 1831 (Graves VI, p. 47). Mrs Webb also suggested the bust was a derivative of Rysbrack's *Alexander Pope* at the Athenaeum (departmental records).

Prior to its acquisition, R.P. Bedford [q.v.] noted on 15 September 1921, 'It is an early cast – I should think it dates from before 1800 – of an original work of the school of Roubilliac [sic] about the middle of the 18th century, and it will be a useful addition to our small collection of English portrait sculpture of the period'.

The present bust was identified by Terence Hodgkinson [q.v.], who noted on the departmental records in April 1947 that it was presumably after the marble bust of Locke executed by Rysbrack in 1733–4 for Queen Caroline's Grotto, Richmond, now in Kensington Palace. Malcolm Baker suggested the bust may be by John Cheere [q.v.] after Rysbrack.

BIBLIOGRAPHY
Wimsatt 1965, p. 106, n. 13.

192: John Locke (1632–1704)

signed and dated 1755
Terracotta
h. 58.4 cm.
33–1867

Signed and dated on the left of the base: Mich: Rysbrack: 1755

Possibly lot 56 in the second day's sale held on Rysbrack's retirement by Langford & Son, at their House in the Great Piazza, Covent Garden, London, 25 January 1766, under 'Models in Terra Cotta . . . A figure of Mr. Locke, for Oxford'. Included in the sale of Henry Farrer F.S.A. held at Christie, Manson & Woods, 8 King Street, London, 12 to 18 June 1866. Sold on the second day, 13 June 1866, lot 220, described as 'Statuette of Locke, holding a book', purchased by Mr A. Myers for 10s. Purchased by the Museum from Mr Myers in 1867 for £4 4s (4 guineas). Myers purchased the terracotta model of Shakespeare by Roubiliac from the same sale, which was also acquired by the Museum; see entry for cat.no. 159.

This is the sketch model for the marble statue of Locke executed by Rysbrack for the library of Christ Church, Oxford. Related drawings by Rysbrack are in the Art Institute of Chicago (see Harris 1971, p. 200, pl. 147 on p. 201, and pl. 148 on p. 202). A contemporary account in the *Public Advertiser*, 20 January 1757, records, 'A fine statue of that great and learned man, Mr. Locke, who was educated in Christ Church College, Oxon, is finished by Mr. Rysbrack, to be sent to that University' (Smith 1920, II, p. 51). Whinney commented, 'In general lines it is very close to the marble, but the relative size of the head is slightly greater, and the expression is more serious and less transient. This is one of the grandest works of Rysbrack's later years' (Whinney 1971, p. 48). Whinney suggested that the head is based on Sir Godfrey Kneller's portrait of 1697, now in the Hermitage Museum, St Petersburg, and that the pose is taken from Raphael's figure *Jonah*, painted in about

1510–11 for S. Maria della Place, Rome; 'It suggests that, had England required monumental religious sculpture, Rysbrack would have been well equipped to provide it' (*idem* 1988, p. 230).

BIBLIOGRAPHY

Hiscock 1946, p. 82; Webb 1954, pp. 169–70, 195, 220, fig. 84 on p. 166; Harris 1971, p. 200; Whinney 1971, p. 48, no. 10, illus. p. 49; Stewart 1978, fig. 19 on p. 214, n. 12 on p. 216, p. 219 and n. 22; Whinney 1988, pp. 229–30, fig. 164 on p. 230.

EXHIBITED

English Sculptors' Drawings 1680–1860, Department of Prints, Drawings and Paintings, Victoria and Albert Museum, 1967.

193: Flora

signed and dated 1759
Terracotta
h. 57.3 cm.
A.9–1961

Signed and dated to the right of the base: Mich: Rysbrack Fe[t]. 1759

Acquired by Sir Edward Littleton of Pillaton Hall, Staffordshire at an unrecorded date, probably around 1762. Pillaton Hall was demolished by Littleton in the mid-18th century, when he built a new ancestral seat at Teddesley, Staffordshire. The figure remained at Teddesley until around 1931, when it was included in the sale of items held at Spink & Sons, King Street, London, in July 1932 following the exhibition held there: Charleston and Wills record in their 1955 article that the records of Spink and Sons were destroyed in an air-raid, and the whereabouts of the piece was unrecorded until it was re-discovered and purchased by the Museum in 1961. The terracotta seems to have been sold at this time to Sir Robert Bland Bird, since it was to be purchased on behalf of the Museum by John O. Woodward, Esq., City Museum and Art Gallery, Birmingham, from the sale of the Executors of the late Sir Robert Bland Bird Bt, K.B.E., M.R.I. and the late Edith Lady Bird, O.B.E., The White House, Solihull, Warwickshire, held by Edwards, Son & Bigwood on the second day of the sale (20 to 22 June 1961) held on 21 June 1961, lot 456. Described as 'The costly and original, beautifully modelled terra-cotta figure – "The Flora", signed Mich. Rysbrack, Fect 1759'. Purchased using funds from the Hildburgh Bequest for £130.

On acquisition a later coating of wax and colour was removed.

This is a model for the marble statue commissioned by Henry Hoare the Younger (1705–1785) in 1759 as a pair to the figure of Hercules also executed by Rysbrack between 1747–52 for the Pantheon, a temple erected in the gardens at Stourhead, Wiltshire. The price paid for the marble is recorded in Henry Hoare's ledger: '1760 Dec 11 By Mr. Rysbrack for a Flora in part £200; 1761 Dec 14 By Mr. Rysbrack for the Flora in full £200' (cited in Webb 1954, p. 126). A further payment of £82 made in January 1762 is also recorded by Webb as probably being for the pedestal. She commented, 'Rysbrack took, as always, a great deal of trouble over the Flora, and the model at any rate pleased him and his clients, for his letters to Sir Edward Littleton contain several references to it, and Littleton bought the model' (Webb 1954, p. 126). One dated 21 January 1758 from Rysbrack to Sir Edward Littleton noted, 'But the little Figure of Flora, I Expect to work after sometime or other and therefore cannot part with it because it would be a Detriment to me' (*Rysbrack* 1932, p. 15, letter IX; Webb 1954, p. 199, letter IX). Another letter to Littleton dated 16 December 1758 records, 'I have Recd. the Picture of Shakespear from Mr. Wilson, but cannot begin the Model yet, I am so full of business, I have made a Model of Flora (which I am glad Every Body approve of) I have followed the Model of the Flora which I had by me, and likewise a Flora in Plaster, only altering some Places according to Mr. Hoare's Desire for whom I am going to do it in Marble; and hope when Your Honour comes to Town You will do me the Favour to Come and see it' (*Rysbrack* 1932, p. 20, letter XIII; Webb 1954, p. 202, letter XIII).

Rysbrack's *Flora* is based on the *Farnese Flora*, now in the Museo Nazionale in Naples (see Haskell and Penny 1981, pp. 80, 217–9, no. 41, and fig. 113 on p. 217). Katharine Esdaile noted, 'Thoroughly antique in spirit, the Flora, like the Hercules, is in fact original; no exact analogy can be found among the statues which have survived from antiquity, and none of them have the virginal charm of this little figure' (*Rysbrack* 1932, p. 43). In a discussion of the sculpture at Stourhead, Webb suggested, 'The Flora is not nearly such a good piece of work as the Hercules. By 1761 Rysbrack was sixty-seven, and his best works were behind him, though he did not finally retire till he was seventy-two' (Webb 1950, pp. 311–12).

Articles published in 1950 and 1956 discuss the present piece, whose location was at that time unknown (see Webb 1950, and Charleston and Wills 1956). The figure of Flora was reproduced in large numbers by the Bow porcelain factory, an example of which in the Department of Ceramics and Glass was ascribed to John Bacon on acquisition (inv.no. 533–1868) (see Charleston and Wills 1956).

A smaller more complete version in plaster, painted to resemble terracotta, is in Sir John Soane's Museum, said to have been cast from the present piece when in the possession of Sir Edward Littleton (see Charleston and Wills 1956, fig. V on pl. 127).

Bibliography

Rysbrack 1932, p. 15, letter IX, p. 31 letter XXIII, pp. 42–3, pl. VIII between pp. 32–3; Webb 1950, pp. 311–12, fig. 3 on p. 309; *idem* 1954, pp. 126, 199, 202, 215; Charleston and Wills 1956, pp. 125–7, and fig. I; Whinney 1971, p. 50, no. 11, illus. p. 51; Haskell and Penny 1981, fig. 43 on p. 90; *Rysbrack* 1982, pp. 164–6, illus. on p. 165; Kenworthy-Browne 1983, fig. 29 on p. 217; Lord 1983, p. 216, fig. 29 on p. 217; Lord 1990, n. 21 on p. 868.

Exhibited

The Art of Rysbrack in Terracotta, Spink and Sons Ltd, London, 1932; *Michael Rysbrack Sculptor 1694–1770*, Bristol City Art Gallery, 6 March to 1 May 1982, cat.no. 74.

194: George II (b.1683; r.1727–1760)

signed and dated 1760
By John Michael Rysbrack (workshop)
Marble
h. (incl. base) 89.5 cm.
A.10–1932

Signed and dated at the back: M.R/Sculp^{t}/1760

Purchased from Alfred Spero in 1932 for £105. In the sale of the property of the late W.J. Broderip Esq., held by Messrs Christie & Manson, 8 King Street, St James's, London, on 13 June 1859; lot 23 was described as, 'Bust of George II by Rysbrack from Shotover. Formerly the property of Baron Schutz'; it is not possible to confirm whether or not the bust is identical with the present piece (departmental records; noted by Terence Hodgkinson [q.v.]).

The present piece is a late, probably workshop version of an earlier bust of George II produced by Rysbrack in 1738, which may have been executed by Rysbrack shortly after the death of the King as a commemorative piece. Rysbrack produced two busts of George II in 1738, one in terracotta and another in marble, which are both in the Royal Collection at Windsor. Prior to entering the Royal Collections, the terracotta was exhibited at Messrs Spink & Sons Ltd in July 1932, and was included in *The Art of Rysbrack in Terracotta,* where it was paired with a terracotta bust of Queen Caroline (see *Rysbrack* 1932, pp. 41–2, pl. XI). In *English Ivories,* Margaret Longhurst illustrated the marble bust now at Windsor Castle, together with an ivory portrait bust by van der Hagen (active 1766–1779) – then the property of Miss D.K. Brown – which 'closely follows the marble'; a further oval ivory portrait relief, though a profile view, also probably by van der Hagen is also in the collections of the Victoria and Albert Museum (see Longhurst 1926, p. 61, pl. LXXIX on p. 169, inv.no. A.78–1923). The George II busts are discussed by Webb; see Webb 1954, pp. 155–6; the terracotta and marble busts at Windsor are illustrated on p. 150; see also Kerslake 1977, I, pp. 94–5.

Another version – signed M:RYSBRACK.F – was sold at Christie's, New York, 10 January 1990, lot 199A. A further version was auctioned at Christie's, London, 7 July 1998, lot 98 (unsold).

Bibliography

Review 1932, pp. 4–5, and pl. 4(b); Webb 1954, p. 156; Whinney 1971, p. 52, cat.no. 12, illus. on p. 53; Kerslake 1977, I, p. 94, Kerslake 1977, II, pl. 254; Whinney 1988, p. 450, n. 16; Snodin and Styles 2001, fig. 8 on p. 160.

195: Victory or Fame

signed and dated 1760
Terracotta
h. 58.1 cm.
A.1–1969

Signed on the base to the side: Mich^{l}: Rysbrack. fecit 1760.

Possibly included in the Rysbrack sale of 25 January 1766, under 'Models in terracotta', lot 9, which was described as a 'sketch of Fame for Admiral Vernon's monument'. Purchased by the Museum via private sale through Sotheby's, for £3000 (the model had been included in their 28 November 1968 sale, the property of Mrs Edna J. Harrie, lot 87); purchased with assistance from the Francis Reubell Bryan Bequest and the Hildburgh Bequest. In a letter from the vendor of the present piece to Howard Ricketts at

Sotheby's, Mrs Harrie recorded that the figure once belonged to the sculptor Peter Hollins [q.v.]: 'You will see I have found out a few interesting historical facts. You probably know from Dad, that our Uncle was a sculptor himself & that as a young man he took over the studio, equipment, various carvings & busts and the terracotta figure from the Birmingham sculptor named Peter Hollins' (reference noted by Malcolm Baker).

The present piece is the model for the figure on the marble monument by Rysbrack to Admiral Edward Vernon (1684–1757) erected in 1763 in the north transept of Westminster Abbey. A pen, ink and wash design for the monument – in which the figure is placed to the right of the bust unlike the final arrangement of the monument – is in the Department of Prints, Drawings and Paintings, inv.no. E.433–1946 (see Physick 1969, p. 109, no. 74, fig. 73 on p. 108). Katharine Eustace has noted that a further design, more closely related to the monument than the V&A design, is in the Yale Center for British Art, New Haven (inv.no. B1977.14.5719); see *Rysbrack* 1982, p. 184, n.1. In her monograph on Rysbrack, Webb suggested a connection between the Vernon monument and the monumental work executed by Roubiliac [q.v.]: 'In the Vernon monument Rysbrack has followed Roubiliac's lead and the static pose has given place to movement, for Fame is running to crown Vernon's Roman bust with a wreath of laurels. This and a few other works done in the 1750s and early 60s indicate that Rysbrack was to a certain extent influenced by the rococo fashion set by Roubiliac, though he was at the same time carrying out some of his most classical works' (Webb 1954, p. 91). Katharine Eustace has however suggested, 'it is more likely that the inspiration was both classical sculpture and the French tradition of Plumière and Delvaux. The pose closely parallels the "Discobolus" or "Borghese Gladiator"' (*Rybrack* 1982, p. 182).

Bibliography

Webb 1954, p. 226; Physick 1969, p. 109; Whinney 1971, p. 54, cat.no. 13, illus. on p. 55; *Rysbrack* 1982, pp. 182–4, cat.no. 88, illus. on p. 183; *Rococo* 1984, p. 307, cat.no. S48; Whinney 1988, p. 456, n. 12.

Exhibited

Rococo. Art and Design in Hogarth's England, Victoria and Albert Museum, London, 16 May to 30 September 1984, cat.no. S48; *Michael Rysbrack Sculptor 1694–1770*, City of Bristol Museum and Art Gallery, 6 March to 1 May 1982, cat.no. 88.

196: Inigo Jones (1573–1652)

about 1800–50
After John Michael Rysbrack
Painted cement
h. 75 cm.
488–1905

Formerly on the water-gate of the Thames near the Savoy, London. Given by J. Whitehead Esq., Mayes, East Grinstead, in 1905.

The surface is weathered.

According to the donor this bust was originally positioned on the water-gate of the Thames near the Savoy, London, and may well have had a commemorative purpose. In his letter offering it to the Museum, Mr Whitehead wrote, 'This bust came from the banks of the Thames, having formed an ornament to the Archway used for accep [sic] to the River boats. It stood somewhere [west? text unclear] of Waterloo Bridge, near the old Church. Mr Stevens of Carlisle St Soho is restoring it, and has been asked to send it to the Museum'.

Though historically attributed to Rysbrack and dated to around 1725–7, recent conservation analysis has revealed the bust to be made of painted cement, not terracotta as originally thought. For this reason, it is more likely to date from the nineteenth century, though based on the earlier representations of Inigo Jones by Rysbrack.

The subject is derived from a portrait of Inigo Jones by Van Dyck (1599–1641). Webb recorded, 'Burlington possessed Vandyck's drawing, and it is possible that Rysbrack also knew Vandyck's painted portrait of Inigo which Sir Robert Walpole bought and which went to Russia when his collection was sold . . . It is the head of the Vandyck drawing which Rysbrack has faithfully and admirable copied' (Webb 1954, p. 102). Webb suggested the bust of Inigo Jones executed for Lord Burlington around 1725, together with a bust of Palladio so pleased his client, that Rysbrack was commissioned to produce two statues of the same subjects for the entrance of his Villa at Chiswick (*ibid.*, fig. 38 on p. 89; see also Physick 1969, p. 78, fig. 46 for Kent's drawing of Rysbrack's statue at Chiswick). A further bust of Jones by Rysbrack dated 1727, and ordered for Stourhead, Wiltshire is also recorded by Webb, who commented, 'As Lord Burlington was the 'High Priest' of the Palladio-Inigo Jones cult, and as Rysbrack had a great deal of work in hand for the Burlingtonian circle by 1730, it seems very probable that it was Lord Burlington who set the fashion of employing Rysbrack for portraits of Inigo Jones, and that the sculptor made a pair of busts for the Earl before the statues were ordered' (Webb 1954, p. 101; see fig. 37 on p. 80 for the Chatsworth bust). Webb commented, 'In the Victoria and Albert Museum there is a terracotta bust of Inigo Jones [the present piece] which is probably an early Rysbrack as it has that slightly skimpy appearance already discussed; its surface has been damaged and not very happily repaired. In his letters to Littleton, Rysbrack describes his treatment of the surface of terracotta busts. The small cracks which occurred during the firing were stopped with plaster of Paris and then the bust was painted all over with a thin red paint made up, at least in one instance, of oil and turpentine coloured' (*ibid.*, p. 104). For the portrait busts and statues of Inigo Jones executed by Rysbrack, see *ibid.*, pp. 101–9, 218.

Webb suggested, 'The bust and statue of Inigo Jones were immediately popular and have been copied many times in various styles and materials by Rysbrack and other sculptors' (*ibid.*, p. 103). A similar bronze bust attributed to the studio of John Michael Rysbrack is in the Birmingham Museum and Art Gallery, inv.no. P.24'59 (see *Birmingham* 1987, p. 246, illus. p. 247). A bronze-coloured plaster cast variant of the same sitter, described as 'after Michael Rysbrack' is in the Royal Academy collection. A related terracotta statuette of Inigo Jones in the Royal Institute of British Architects was thought by Mrs Webb to be an early design of the statue at Burlington's Chiswick Villa; it is now thought to have been made after the Chiswick statue. (Webb 1954, p. 218). On a photograph of the R.I.B.A. statuette in the Sculpture Department archive annotated on the reverse by Margaret Whinney, Webb's suggestion is questioned, Whinney noting 'it seems more closely related to the Rubens/Van Dyck/Duquesnoy etc. figures of the 1740s'. An English seventeenth-century ivory portrait medallion of Jones taken from the same source is also in the Museum's collections, inv.no. (Circ.1–1947).

Plaster cast variants were available for sale by the Museum's Cast Selling Service at a cost of 8s 6d (*Casts* 1939, p. 24, no. 451).

Bibliography

Webb 1954, pp. 104, 218; *Treasure Houses* 1985, p. 223, cat. 144 (V&A version mentioned under related works).

197: Sir Peter Paul Rubens (1577–1640)

signed; probably about 1850
Cast by L. Genneau after a model by John Michael Rysbrack of 1743
Bronze
h. 60.5 cm.
A.24–1955

Signed on the side of the base of the column: Miche Rysbeack/1749
Faintly inscribed on the back of the base: L. Genneau
The name of the subject is inscribed on the back: D PETRVS PAVLVS RVBBENS EQVES

A bronze version of the Rubens statuette noted by Marjorie Webb in her monograph on Rysbrack, as being 'signed Mich Rysbeak [sic] 1749', was in the Hospital of St John and St Elizabeth, Grove End Road, London (Webb 1954, p. 224). In her annotated copy of her own monograph (now in the Sculpture Department at the V&A), Webb noted that this was 'Bought by V&A in 1956'. Later Whinney confirmed this by referring to the present piece and that of Sir Anthony Van Dyck, cat.no. 198, as being the pair of bronzes formerly in the Hospital of St John and St Elizabeth, London (Whinney 1971, p. 46). The pair of bronzes were included in Christie's, London, 24 November 1955, lot 15. Messrs Frank Partridge acted as agents for the Museum and were instructed to bid up to 100 guineas for this and cat.no. 198. The bronzes reached £200 – nearly twice the amount approved – but were purchased by Messrs Partridge who sold them to the Museum at a loss to themselves. Purchased together with cat.no. 198 from Frank Partridge & Sons Ltd, 144–6 New Bond Street, London, in 1955 for £120.

Though the present piece was acquired as an original work by Rysbrack the later discovery of the signature of L. Genneau, together with its quality, suggests it is a later French cast of the mid-nineteenth century.

The statuette of Rubens was one of a number of small-scale works executed by Rysbrack in the 1740s; others depict Van Dyck, and Fiammingo (Duquesnoy). For a full discussion see Webb 1954, pp. 109–12; Watson 1963; Whinney 1971, pp. 44, 46; *Rysbrack* 1982, pp. 142, 144; *Ashmolean* 1992 [III], pp. 156–7. The reproductive nature of the statuettes is recorded by Vertue, who noted in 1747: 'Mr. Van Aken had bought three Models most excellently done by M. Rysbracke Sculptor-& paid for them freely- one the portrait of Rubens at length. Vandyke. & Quesnoy fiamingo the Sculptor. of these three figures. molds were made & casts, at seaven guineas the three sold' (*Vertue* 1934, p. 135).

Bronzed plaster versions of the Rubens and Van Dyck statuettes formerly in the Kirkleatham Hospital collection, and inscribed 'Cheere ft 1749' and 'Cheere f 1749' are in the Castle Museum, York (see *Cheere* 1974, no. 67 and 68, pls. 22 and 23). Other similar statuettes which form part of this group – signed by Cheere – include depictions of Spenser, Pope, Homer, Locke, Newton, Milton and Inigo Jones. Also included is a further statuette of Shakespeare inscribed P. Scheemak(ers) F. 1740. It is likely that Cheere issued the plaster versions in some numbers (noted on departmental records).

For the terracotta version in the collection of the Earl of Harrowby, see also *Rysbrack* 1982, pp. 142, 144, illus. on p. 143, cat.no. 57; Whinney 1988, fig. 161 on p. 228. For the bronzed plaster versions at Stourhead, see Webb 1950, figs. 4 and 5 on p. 309; *idem* 1954, figs. 40 and 41 on p. 90. Ivory versions of the Palladio statuette together with those of Fiammingo and Inigo Jones adapted by Verkovis for the Horace Walpole's cabinet of 1743, are in the Victoria and Albert Museum, Department of Furniture and Woodwork (inv.no. W.52–1925); see Webb 1954, p. 112, fig. 42 on p. 90; Longhurst 1929, p. 85. A note made by Charles Avery on the records for the present piece records that a further pair of bronzes in the Beaverbrook Art Gallery, Fredericton, New Brunswick, Canada, dated 1743, are inscribed 'Société des Bronzes': The Société Des Bronzes de Paris flourished between 1870 and 1890 (Forrest 1988, p. 484). In 1956 a bronze version of the Rubens statuette was brought into the Sculpture Department for opinion, inscribed 'Miche Rysbrack 1743', and 'D. PETRVS PAVLVS RVBBENS EQVES'. The bronze was brought to the Department again in 1970, when it was compared with the present piece and its pendant, cat.no. 198; as a result, the two bronzes in the Museum were considered to be nineteenth-century: 'There is no evidence that bronze statuettes of such competence were produced in England in the middle of the 18th century and it is inherently improbable that any of the bronze versions of Rysbrack's models date before the middle of the 19th century' (departmental records). A related bronze version described as 'foundry or workshop of L. Genneau' inscribed 'Michel Rysbrack/1632' is in the Ashmolean Museum, Oxford (see *Ashmolean* 1992 [III], pp. 156–7, cat.no. 567).

Unsigned versions of the Fiammingo and Van Dyck terracotta-coloured plaster statuettes (though sold as terracottas) were auctioned as lot 99 at Sotheby's London, 4 December 1956; in the catalogue described as 'c. 1743', they were sold to 'Brunet' for £230 (listed in Watson 1963, p. 442, and fig 23, described as plaster painted in terracotta colour).

Bibliography

Webb 1954, p. 224; Watson 1963, pp. 442, 445; Whinney 1971, pp. 44, 46, cat.no. 8, illus on p. 45; *Ashmolean* 1992 [III], p. 156.

198: Sir Anthony Van Dyck (1599–1641)

about 1850
Anonymous, possibly cast by L. Genneau after a model by John Michael Rysbrack of about 1743
Bronze
h. 60 cm.
A.23–1955

The present statuette together with cat.no. 197 were identified by Margaret Whinney as those formerly in the Hospital of St John and St Elizabeth, Grove End Road, London. The pair of bronzes were included in Christie, London, 24 November 1955, lot 15. Messrs Frank Partridge acted as agents for the Museum, securing the two bronzes for £200 and later offering them to the Museum for the reduced price of £120. See entry for cat.no. 197.

On acquisition this statuette and its companion figure, cat.no. 197, were thought to be by Rysbrack and catalogued as such by Margaret Whinney, although she stated, 'the possibility that Nos. 8 [cat.no. 197] and 9 [cat.no. 198] are nineteenth-century copies of Rysbrack's models cannot be excluded' (Whinney 1971, p. 46). The pendant statuette of Rubens, cat. no. 197 is now known to have been cast by L. Genneau.

Bibliography

Webb 1954, p. 226; Watson 1963, p. 443; *Bristol* 1966, unpaginated; Whinney 1971, p. 46, no. 9, illus. p. 47; *Ashmolean* 1992 [III], p. 156.

T. Sanders

(active 1770 – 1790)

The precise identity of this sculptor is not known, though he may belong to a family of woodcarvers called Saunders who were active in the eighteenth century. A number of sculptors of this name are noted by Gunnis; one, a J.J. Sanders active 1812–46, was the son of 'J. Sanders, a mason'.

Review 1932, p. 6; Gunnis 1968, p. 339; Thieme-Becker, 29, p. 394.

199: Unknown man

signed; about 1770–90
Mahogany
h. 33.5 cm.
A.58–1932

Signed under the left shoulder: TS [monogram] Stamped underneath the base: T.W. SANDERS

Purchased from Messrs Charlesworth, 8 Avery Row, Brook Street, London in 1932 for £4 10s.

In recommending the present piece for purchase, Margaret Longhurst [q.v.] noted, 'This is an interesting and very unusual little bust in mahogany, dating apparently from between 1770 and 1790. The stamp with the name W. Sanders, on the front of the coat, underneath is similar to the stamps used on furniture from the late 18th century by firms such as Gillows. The initials T.S (or S.T?) carved on the back may be the name of the carver possibly a member of the same family'.

In the *Review of Principle Acquisitions during the Year 1932*, it was noted, 'The bust is signed under the shoulder with a monogram of the letters T S and stamped underneath T. (J?) Sanders. Though neither the monogram nor the stamped name can be traced to any recorded artist of the period, there was a family of woodcarvers, called Saunders of whom one member, Captain Richard Saunders, executed the Gog and Magog in the Guildhall in 1708, and it is possible that this bust may be the work of a descendant working in the second half of the century'.

Bibliography

Review 1932, p. 6 and pl. IV opp. p. 5.

Peter Scheemakers (Scheemaeckers)

(b. Antwerp 1691 – d . Antwerp 1781)

The sculptor trained under his father, Peter Scheemaeckers (1652–1714), a marble sculptor in Antwerp, before spending four years in Copenhagen. He arrived in England before 1721, and collaborated with Pieter-Denis Plumier (1688–1721) and Laurent Delvaux [q.v.] on the monument to John Sheffield, 1st Duke of Buckingham in Westminster Abbey (1722). Scheemakers continued in partnership with Delvaux, and together they produced further monuments, as well as garden statuary, some after the antique. The partners went to Rome in 1728, where Scheemakers remained for two years, after which he returned to England alone and set up another workshop in London. He was highly productive, and his busts, usually classical in style, chimneypieces, monuments and statues were in great demand. One of his most celebrated works was the marble figure of William Shakespeare for Westminster Abbey (1741). He also worked at Stowe, Buckinghamshire c.1737–40, alongside Rysbrack [q.v.], producing busts and figures. His brother Henry (1670–1748) and son Thomas [q.v.] were also sculptors. He exhibited at the Free Society of Artists from 1765 to 1767, and at the Society of Artists from 1777 to 1780.

Graves 1907, p. 227; Gunnis 1968, pp. 341–2; Thieme-Becker, 29, pp. 598–9; TDA, 28, pp. 63–4 [Roscoe]; Scheemakers 1996; Roscoe 1999, pp. 163–304.

200: Model for the tomb to Dr Hugh Chamberlen (1664–1728)

about 1728–30
Terracotta
h. 13.9 cm.
A.6–1927

Included in the sale of Scheemakers's effects by Mr Langford, at his House in the Great Piazza, Covent Garden, 'The Genuine, Large and Curious Collection of Models and Marbles, In groupes, Figures, Busts, &c. As likewise the Italian, Flemish and other Pictures of Mr. Peter Scheemaker, Statuary'. The present piece was included in the second day's sale held on 11 March 1756, lot 18 under the heading of Models, 'Dr Chamberlayne, and one of the side Figures of his Monument, by Mr. Scheemaker', the annotated catalogue records it was sold for £6 16s 6d. Sold at a mixed sale under other properties, held at Sotheby's on 3 December 1926, lot. 68, described as 'A fine 18th century model, in terra-cotta, for a tomb figure of a Chancellor of a University'. In the annotated copy of the catalogue held in the National Art Library, it is recorded that the model was sold to Belham for £8. Purchased by Dr W.L. Hildburgh F.S.A. and given by him to the Museum in 1927.

On acquisition the model was chipped and the arm restored.

This is the model for the monument to Dr Hugh Chamberlen in Westminster Abbey, the joint work of Peter Scheemakers and Laurent Delvaux [q.v.].

Whinney commented, 'A comparison of the finished work with the terracotta model in the Victoria and Albert Museum throws interesting light on the sculptor's outlook, for the head of the model is far more particularized. The brow is furrowed, and there is a deep depression on the bridge of the nose and sagging wrinkles under the eyes. In the marble all these have disappeared, and the head is ennobled and given an ideal beauty' (Whinney 1988, p. 185). For a full discussion of the monument, see Roscoe 1999, pp. 184–6, no. 6; see also *Vertue* 1934, p. 53.

Bibliography

Review 1927, p. 5, fig. 1 on p. 4; Esdaile 1927, p. 142; Whinney 1971, p. 58, no. 14, illus. on p. 59; Davies 1979, p. 22; Avery 1979, p. 159, and p. 170, n. 12; Whinney 1988, pp. 184–5, p. 452, n. 10; *Scheemakers* 1996, pp. 3, 10, fig. 5 on p. 3; Jacobs 1999, p. 242; Roscoe 1999, p. 185, fig. 40.

Exhibited

Peter Scheemakers 'The Famous Statuary 1691–1781', Centre for the Study of Sculpture, Henry Moore Institute, Leeds, 2 October 1996 to 5 January 1997, cat.no. 22.

201: Justice, from the tomb of Judge Francis Bernard (1664–1731)

about 1732
Terracotta, with remains of paint
h. 37 cm.
A.1–1989

Purchased from G.M.Heelas, 4 Loop Court Mews, Sandwich, Kent in 1989 for £4,000.

Originally painted with a dark brown patination to imitate bronze. Covered over with successive coats of grey and cream paint. These paint layers were removed shortly before the piece was acquired by the Museum.

The sword is broken off at the hilt and the front foot is missing.

This is the model for one of the figures on the monument by Peter Scheemakers to Judge Francis Bernard in Ballymoden Church, Bandon, County Cork. The monument is described in a study of Cork written by Charles Smith in 1893: 'In the other church is a fine monument to the memory of Francis Bernard, esq., one of the justices of the court of common pleas. On the right is a Minerva, reclining on her aegis; and on the left is Justice, leaning on her arm, her sword in her hand. Over an obelisk of a fine Egyptian marble is a coat of arms – viz., three escalop [sic] shells on a bend. On the table [plinth] is this inscription, in gilt letters of raised brass:

Francis Bernard, esq.,
Obiit Jun. XXIX., MDCCXXXI
Aetatis suae, LXVIII'
(Smith 1893, pp. 216–7)

For biographical information on Judge Bernard see Bennett 1862, pp. 182–5. Bennett mistakenly attributed the monument in Ballymoden church to Flaxman: 'a handsome white marble monument, by Flaxman, has been erected to his memory' (*ibid*, p. 185). The date of the present piece is suggested by Ingrid Roscoe's dating of the monument to about 1732 (see Roscoe 1999, pp. 188–9, no. 10 for the monument).

Bibliography

Williamson 1991, p. 876; Roscoe 1999, pp. 188–9 (incorrectly cited as inv. no. 1989–1).

Exhibited

Peter Scheemakers 'The Famous Statuary' 1691–1781, Centre for the Study of Sculpture, Henry Moore Institute, Leeds, 2 October 1996 to 5 January 1997, cat.no. 21.

202: Richard Temple, 1st Viscount Cobham
(1675–1749)

signed; about 1740
Marble
h. (with socle) 84.5 cm.
A.1–1942

Signed on the right side of the pedestal: P: Scheemakers Ft

Inscribed on the front of base beneath crest:
Rd Temple Viscount Cobham

One of a series of ten busts executed for Richard Temple, 1st Viscount Cobham for the Temple of Friendship at Stowe, Buckinghamshire, later moved to the Grenville Vestibule there. Sold on the sixth day of the Stowe sale, 21 August 1848, lot 770. In the published annotated catalogue of the sale by H.R. Forster it is recorded that the bust was sold for £18 18s to Mr Rainey, who may have acted as agent for the Temple family (Forster 1848, p. 49). Included in the sale of the Executors of the Rt Hon. Algernon William Stephen, 5th Earl Temple, removed from Newton Park, Bristol, held at Sotheby's, London, 9 May 1941, lot no. 65. In the annotated copy of the catalogue held in the National Art Library said to have been purchased by Dawson for £44. Acquired, probably through Dawson, by Dr W.L. Hildburgh F.S.A.; on loan from Dr Hildburgh from June 1941 (ex-loan 5066). Given by Dr Hildburgh as a New Year gift in 1942.

Forster recorded the aim of Lord Cobham 'was to collect the busts of all his political friends, and place them in a building to be erected for their reception, and honoured with the title of the Temple of Friendship. Unfortunately, the whole party, of which he formed so prominent a member, was broken up. The busts were, however, sculptured, and placed in the temple on its completion' (Forster 1848, pp. 49–50).

A closely related variant on an undecorated socle in the Lady Lever Art Gallery is attributed to Scheemakers, and described as a man in classical dress, possibly Grey, 3rd Lord Maynard (inv.no. LL735, see *Lady Lever* 1999, p. 71, illus. on p. 72).

For the bust of John Fane, 7th Earl of Westmorland, also formerly at the Temple of Friendship, Stowe House, see entry for cat.no. 64.

Bibliography

Forster 1848, p. 49; *Siècle de l'élegance* 1959, pp. 31–2, cat.no. 24; Whinney 1971, p. 60, no. 15, illus. on p. 61; Gibbon 1972, pp. 63–4; Clarke 1973, p. 544, fig. 11 on p. 548; Sutton 1973, p. 544, fig. 11 on p. 548; Davies 1979, p. 25; Whinney 1988, p. 187 and fig. 128; *Lady*

Lever 1999, p. 71, and n. 2; Roscoe 1999, p. 269; Baker 2000 [Portrait Bust], fig. 3 on p. 24.

EXHIBITED

Le Siècle de l'élegance la Demeure Anglaise au XVIII siècle, Musée des Arts Décoratifs, Paris, 1959, cat.no. 24 ; *Peter Scheemakers 'The Famous Statuary' 1691–1781*, The Centre for the Study of Sculpture, Henry Moore Institute, Leeds, 2 October 1996 to 5 January 1997, cat.no. 32.

203: Abundance, or perhaps Charity

about 1757–8
Terracotta
h. 41.9 cm.
A.2–1985

Christie's, London, 11 December 1984, lot no. 20, unidentified and described as 'terracotta statuette of a mourning woman'; sold for £432 to Cyril Humphris. Purchased from Cyril Humphris, 23 Old Bond Street, London in 1985 for £1,000.

This has been identified as a model for the allegorical figure on the left of the monument to the 2nd Lord Raymond (d. 1756) at the Church of St Lawrence, Abbot's Langley, Hertfordshire. The other pendant figure on the monument represents *Hope*. Though called *Abundance* (the sheaf held in the figure's hand being one of her attributes), Ingrid Roscoe suggests the figure may in fact be identified as *Charity*. Noting that Scheemakers delegated some modelling, Ingrid Roscoe compares the near-contemporary model of *Charity* for the monument to George Strode in the collection of the Centre for the Study of Sculpture, Leeds, with the present piece, 'The Strode Virtue has precisely detailed sleeves and hair and the underside of the base is smoothly finished. By contrast, the draperies of the Raymond figure are broadly rendered and the underside is coarse' (*Scheemakers* 1996, p. 10). For the Strode terracotta, see also *Leeds* 1996, p. 3 and Roscoe 1999, fig. 77; *ibid.*, pp. 231–2, no. 78, fig. 78 for the monument itself.

BIBLIOGRAPHY
Scheemakers 1996, p. 10, fig. 24 on p. 11; Roscoe 1999, p. 238 (incorrectly cited as inv. no. A.2–1986).

EXHIBITED
Peter Scheemakers 'The Famous Statuary' 1691–1781, Centre for the Study of Sculpture, Henry Moore Institute, Leeds, 2 October 1996 to 5 January 1997, cat.no. 50.

204: Sir Lionel Tollemache, 4th Baronet of Helmingham and 3rd Earl of Dysart (1648–1727)

dated Augt: 8th 1727
Attributed to Peter Scheemakers
Terracotta
h. 17.5 cm.
A.10–1981

The inscription on the underside of the model, made in the clay before firing, reads: Augt 8th 1727

Purchased from the Heim Gallery, 59 Jermyn Street, St James's, London in 1981 for £3,500.

The model had sustained a number of breaks which were repaired on acquisition. A conservation report written by Anne Brodrick in December 1981 recorded: 'When the object was first presented for inspection at the museum it was broken in two across the middle of the model. When finally acquired the model had been glued together'.

The present piece appears to be the model for the monument to Sir Lionel Tollemache, 3rd Earl of Dysart, who died on 23 February 1727, and whose monument is at St Mary's church, Helmingham, Suffolk. Pevsner recorded that the monument – though unsigned – is dated 1729 (Pevsner 1981 [Suffolk], pp. 58, 259). In his history of the Tollemaches, E.D.H. Tollemache recorded, 'A marble monument to his memory was placed in Helmingham Church, as he had ordered. Lord Dysart is dressed as a Roman warrior in toga and sandals, with his wife Grace weeping beside him' (Tollemache 1949, p. 98). The model bears close similarities with that of the figure of Lord Lexington (1661–1723) on the monument to the 2nd Baron and his wife, in St Wilfrid's Church, at Kelham, Nottinghamshire, and the present piece had until recently been thought to be connected with the Lord Lexington monument. The Lexington monument however, was erected in 1726: the inscribed date of 1727 on the present piece was therefore confusing, and seemed to imply its purpose was a record of the monument rather than a model for it (for the Lexington monument see Whinney 1988, pp. 246–7, fig. 178 on p. 246).

The pose of the figure also closely imitates that of John Sheffield, 1st Duke of Buckingham, on the marble monument to him in Westminster Abbey, designed by Pieter-Denis Plumier (1688–1721) and executed in about 1721 by Laurent Delvaux [q.v.] and Peter Scheemakers [q.v.]; see Whinney 1988, figs. 101 and 102 on pp. 158–9. Although the present piece was previously attributed to William Palmer (1673–1739) on the basis of the contract for the Lexington monument, recording the involvement of Palmer in the erection of the monument itself, he was probably the mason or 'setter-upper'; the figure on the monument is likely to have been designed and executed by Scheemakers (departmental records).

The conservation report carried out by Anne Brodrick in December 1981 (see also above) recorded, 'The chief features of the modelling are the scraped claw marks found on the mattress and the cloak. These are very similar to the modelling marks on Scheemaker's [sic] model of Dr Hugo Chamberlen'. For this model, see entry for cat.no. 200.

205: Unknown man (perhaps a member of the Shirley family)

about 1740
Ascribed to Peter Scheemakers
Marble
h. (excl. socle) 55.5 cm.
A.61–1965

Bequeathed by Rupert Gunnis in 1965.

The donor attributed this bust to Peter Scheemakers on stylistic grounds, although it is not listed in Roscoe 1999. The features found on the present bust are similar to those of members of the Shirley family, as seen in portrait busts by Scheemakers made of some family members before 1745, three of which were exhibited at the Royal Academy *British Portraits* Winter Exhibition, held in 1956–7, cat.nos. 40, 638 and 770; see also Roscoe 1999, pp. 269–70, no. 166. Terence Hodgkinson [q.v.] suggested that the sitter could be the Hon. Lawrence Shirley, a bust of whom is in the National Gallery of Victoria, Melbourne. However, it was subsequently felt that comparison of the profiles of these busts precludes the identity of the bust with Shirley, although a family resemblance is evident (departmental records). A further comparison of the subject with the first Duke of Ancaster on his monument at Edenham Lincolnshire by Henry Scheemakers and Henry Cheere [q.v.], has also been proposed (departmental records).

Bibliography
Knox 1998, p. 95, n. 13.

Thomas Scheemakers

(b. London 1740 – d. London 1808)

Thomas Scheemakers was the son of the sculptor Peter Scheemakers [q.v.], with whom he initially trained and worked until 1771. Gunnis recorded that he 'worked in collaboration with James Stuart (1713–1788), and the latter is responsible for the design of several of the more important monuments', several models of which were exhibited at the Free Society of Artists. His most impressive monument is considered to be that commemorating Mary Russell of 1787, in SS. Peter and Lawrence, in Powick, Worcester. He exhibited at the Royal Academy between 1780 and 1804, and at the Free Society of Artists between 1765 and 1783.

Graves 1907, pp. 227–8; Gunnis 1968, pp. 344–5; Thieme-Becker, 29, p. 599; TDA, 28, pp. 64–5 [Roscoe].

206: Arion

signed and dated 1773
Terracotta
h. 72.4 cm.
247–1869

Signed and dated on the back at the base: T. Scheemaker/F.t 1773.

Purchased from I. Aresti in 1869 for £50.

The thumb and fingers of the right hand are damaged.

It is likely that the present piece is a finished work, rather than a model for a larger piece. Arion was a mythical poet and skilled lyre player. Whilst on board a ship and being threatened by the crew, Arion jumped overboard. He was said to have been saved, by being carried ashore by a dolphin attracted by the sound of his lyre-playing (Hall 1980, p. 31).

Esdaile noted, 'there is an attractive model of Arion by his son [Thomas Scheemakers the son of Peter Scheemakers] in the Victoria and Albert Museum which but for the date (1773) might well be attributed to the father' (Esdaile 1922, p. 113).

A related Wedgwood jasper plaque of about 1850–75 depicting Apollo is in the City Art Gallery, Manchester (inv.no. 1918–337), there said to be by an artist working for Wedgwood in Rome, or a sketch produced by Peter Scheemakers [q.v.] in Rome and passed on to his son Thomas (information kindly supplied by Liz Paul). For variants described as *Apollo Musagetes,* and probably the model supplied by John Flaxman senior in 1775, see Reilly 1995, p. 22.

Bibliography

Graves 1907, p. 227, no. 199; Esdaile 1922, p. 113; Gunnis 1968, p. 344.

Exhibited

Scheemakers exhibited 'Arion – a model in terra cotta' at the Free Society of Artists in 1773 (no. 199), presumably the present piece.

Nathaniel Smith

(b. Eltham, London about 1741/3 – d. after 1800)

There is some disagreement as to Nathaniel Smith's date of birth; Gunnis gives a date of around 1741, whereas Rackham suggests about 1743. Rackham recorded that Smith studied at St Martin's Lane School, and was taken on in 1755 as a pupil of Louis François Roubiliac [q.v.] until his death; he was engaged in work on some of Roubiliac's monuments in Westminster Abbey. Smith's Society of Arts awards are cited in the catalogue entry below; he is listed by Graves as a sculptor and miniature painter in the Free Society of Artists, exhibiting between 1761 and 1773. In both 1772 and 1773 he exhibited a miniature portrait at the Royal Academy. He was a fellow student of Joseph Nollekens [q.v.], and around 1788 became his chief assistant; his son, John Thomas Smith, the author of Nollekens and his Times, *recorded that his father had 'lodged with Mr. Roubiliac. He had obtained in the course of four years six premiums for productions in art, all whilst under sixteen years of age'. On the death of Roubiliac, Smith worked in the studio of Joseph Wilton [q.v.], assisting with the monument to General Wolfe in Westminster Abbey. Gunnis recorded that in becoming the chief assistant to Nollekens around 1788, Smith 'therefore spent most of his life working for other sculptors'.*

Graves VII, p. 188; Graves 1907, p. 241; Chancellor 1911, p.160; Smith 1920, II, pp. 150–1; Esdaile 1928, pp. 215–6; Forrer VIII, p. 210; Rackham 1930, p. 125; Gunnis 1968, pp. 358–9; Thieme-Becker, 31, p. 175–6.

207: Bringing down the stag

signed and dated 1760
Terracotta in a black and gold wood frame
h. 31.5 cm. w. 50.7 cm.
414:1215–1885

Signed on a stone to the left foreground: Nathl Smith/inv^{t} et fec^{t}/1760

Gunnis recorded that Smith's 'Model of Animals', probably the present piece, which was awarded a Royal Society of Arts prize in 1760, was formerly in the possession of Lord Maynard (Gunnis 1968, p. 358). Acquired at an unknown date by Charles and Lady Schreiber. Given by Charles

Schreiber, M.P. and Lady Charlotte Elizabeth Schreiber in 1884. Transferred from the Ceramics Department to the Sculpture Department in 1988. This was part of a collection given to the Museum of mainly English porcelain, earthenware, enamels and glass, formed by Charles and Lady Schreiber from 1865.

The frame is slightly damaged.

In his catalogue of the Schreiber collection, Rackham commented, 'In 1760 a premium of nine guineas was awarded to him [Smith] for "a model of a Buck and Hounds", presumably the present plaque' (Rackham 1930, p. 125). The same prize is noted by J.T. Smith (son of the sculptor) and biographer of Joseph Nollekens [q.v.]; he noted, 'in 1760 for a model of a Buck and Hounds 9l 9s' (Smith 1920, II, p. 151). This refers to the award system presented by the Royal Society of Arts for the encouragement of young artists, discussed by Wood in the *Journal of the Royal Society of Arts*, where he noted, 'Hundreds of young artists received from the Society the first recognition of their powers, and were thus encouraged to persevere in careers which in many cases led to reputation and success – in some to fame and fortune' (Wood 1912, p. 735). Wood recorded that Smith received six premiums – in 1758, 1761 and 1762 – for figures modelled in clay; in 1758 he was awarded two premiums for drawings; his premium for a bas-relief in 1760 is the one mentioned by Rackham above, probably the present piece (Wood 1912, p. 752).

BIBLIOGRAPHY

Schreiber 1885, p. 137, no. 1215; Wood 1912, p. 752; *Review* 1928, p. 4; Rackham 1930, p. 125, no. 645, pl. 84; Forrer VIII, p. 210; Gunnis 1968, p. 358; Thieme-Becker, 31, p. 175.

208: Alderman William Beckford, Lord Mayor of London (1709–1770)

signed and dated 1770
Terracotta
h. 28 cm.
A.48–1928

Signed and dated on the side of the base on the tripod:/Nathl Smith/fec^{t}/July 31. 1770
Insribed on the scroll: The humble/Address

Possibly the model included in the sale of the collection of Richard Wyatt, Milton Place, Egham, Surrey, sold by Mr Daniel Smith. The sale took place on Friday 19 March 1813 and the following seven days, excluding Sunday. Lot 320 was described in the catalogue as, 'Ten models, Alderman Beckford in Terra Cotta, with a Bell Glass and 9 other pieces'; sold on the 6th day of the sale, 25 March 1813. Re-discovered on the London art market in 1928 by Mr Lans Clarke in the possession of the dealer J. Rochelle Thomas, The Georgian Galleries, 10–12 King Street, London, on sale for £12. Mr Clarke advised Eric Maclagan [q.v.] of the statuette, which was taken on by the Museum on approval. It was purchased by Dr W.L. Hildburgh, F.S.A. and given by him to the Museum as a Christmas gift in 1928.

This is the model submitted by Smith for the commemorative statue to Beckford, elected Lord Mayor of London in 1762–3 and 1769–70 respectively, to be erected in the Guildhall, London. The competition to produce the memorial was set up within a month of Beckford's death on 21 June 1770. Though other sculptors also submitted models, including Agostino Carlini [q.v.] and John Flaxman [q.v.], there were suggestions that the sculptor John Francis Moore (d. 1809) had in fact already been selected, and the commission was indeed awarded to him; his statue was erected in 1772. For the Flaxman competition entry see Esdaile 1924 [Beckford].

On acquisition, the model was noted as follows: 'If sculpture in England at the end of the 18th century – one can hardly speak of English sculpture, as most of the practitioners in this country at that time were foreigners – does not occupy a very high place in the history of Art, terracotta sketch models are sufficiently rare to make the acquisition of one a matter of some importance, especially when the model is a portrait of a famous London citizen' (*Review* 1928, p. 3).

A design for the Beckford statue in pen and ink, signed Mr Moore of Berners Street (presumably John Francis Moore), is in the Department of Prints, Drawings and Paintings (inv.no. 4910.12) (see Physick 1969, pp. 140–1, fig. 104 on p. 140).

BIBLIOGRAPHY

Smith 1920, II, p. 134; *Review* 1928, pp. 3–5, fig. 2 on p. 4; Physick 1969, p. 141, no. 105; Whinney 1971, p. 106, no. 32, illus. p. 107; Trusted 1993, p. 190, n. 7.

EXHIBITED

Drawings by English Sculptors 1680–1810, Ashmolean Museum, Oxford, 1967.

Sir John Soane

(b. Goring on Thames 1753 – d. London 1837)

Soane is regarded as the chief architect of his age. He attended the Royal Academy Schools from 1771, and his gold medal prize of 1774 for his design for a triumphal bridge included a three-year scholarship in Rome, and also gave him the opportunity to meet potential clients. Following his return he was in demand as an architect of country houses. In 1788 he was appointed Surveyor to the Bank of England, for which he undertook major rebuilding works. Sir John Soane's Museum, London, his former residence, is an outstanding monument to his collecting and taste: the collection includes plaster casts, models, paintings, and architectural drawings.

Colvin 1995, pp. 904–12; TDA, 28, pp. 904–10 [Watkin], Dean 1999.

209: Chimneypiece from Fairford Park, Gloucestershire

about 1789
Designed by Sir John Soane
Marble
h. 168 cm.
A.20–1955

Originally at Fairford Park, Gloucestershire, this chimneypiece was rescued by John Summerson, then Curator of Sir John Soane's Museum and Dorothy Stroud, Deputy Curator of the Museum, when the house was being demolished in 1955. In order to save the chimneypiece Mr Summerson purchased it from Oakley's, the demolition contractors at Fairford Park. He subsequently sold it to Dr W.L. Hildburgh F.S.A. at cost price plus expenses, a total of £35 8s (the price for the chimneypiece £30). Given by Dr Hildburgh to the Museum in 1955.

The mantel shelf was broken when being moved from Sir John Soane's Museum to the Victoria and Albert Museum.

The building of Fairford Park for Andrew Barker was begun in 1661. Alterations to the house were subsequently carried out by Sir John Soane for J.R. Barker in 1789, and designs for the present chimneypiece are in Sir John Soane's Museum (Colvin 1995, p. 909; Verey 1979, p. 248; Dean 1999; Soane inv.no. SM81/1/32, 36). Information given on acquisition by Dorothy Stroud, Deputy Curator at Sir John Soane's Museum 1946–1984, suggests that one of these designs is from 1789, giving an approximate date for the present piece. She also proposed that the relief on the frieze was based on a drawing after the antique made by Soane when in Rome. I am grateful to Helen Dorey and Susan Palmer for information on Dorothy Stroud, and for the reference to Ptolemy Dean's recent publication.

Bibliography

Verey 1979, p. 248; Dean 1999, p. 180.

[Not illustrated].

Michael Henry Spang

(b. Denmark; active 1756 – d. London 1762)

Little is known of Spang's origins; he was a native of Denmark, but was in England from about 1756 until his death. He made chimneypieces for the four principal rooms at Kedleston, Derbyshire in 1759, and received some London commissions, such as three statues for the front of Lord Spencer's house in St James's, London. He exhibited at the Society of Artists from 1760–2, but at his death left practically nothing; his widow was later granted a pension from the Royal Academy from 1769 until her death in 1785.

Gunnis 1968, p. 361; Thieme-Becker, 31, pp. 327–8.

210: William Hogarth (1697–1764)

signed; about 1765
Terracotta with bronze-coloured paint
h. 47.5 cm.
311–1885

Signed on the base of the urn: M·H· Spang in.F

Given by Herr K.A.V. Schmidt-Ciazynski, Cracow (formerly of Trafalgar Square, Fulham Road, London) in 1885.

The statuette may be a posthumous portrait of Hogarth, perhaps a model for a memorial not in the event executed.

On acquisition it was noted that the nose was damaged, though this was subsequently repaired. Parts of the fingers of the right hand are missing, as is part of the sketch book. As the bronze paint covers the broken hand and sketch book, it is unlikely to be original. The urn on which the figure of Hogarth leans is inset with a medallion portrait inscribed 'APELLES'.

A note on the record card for this object records the similarity between the present statuette and another statuette in the Museum's collection, previously identified as Matthew Prior and ascribed to Roubiliac (see entry for cat.no. 84). The writer suggested that the latter may have been executed by Spang, 'Alternatively, it may show that Spang was working in a manner very close to Roubiliac's when he executed the Hogarth statuette'. However cat.no. 84 is now thought to be by Cheere, and to be a portrait of George Pitt; it is almost certainly not connected with the present piece.

Bibliography
Bequests and Donations 1901, p. 234; Slomann 1932, p. 180, and fig. 3 on p. 181; Gunnis 1968, p. 361; Thieme-Becker, 31, p. 327.

Edward Stanton

(b. ?London 1681 – d. ?London 1734)

Stanton was one of a family of mason-sculptors, and specialised in tombs, more than 150 of which are recorded. He was Mason to the City of London from 1708, and Mason to Westminster Abbey from 1720; he became Master to the Masons' Company in 1719.

Esdaile 1930; Gunnis 1968, p. 366; Whinney 1988, pp. 139 and 142; Thieme-Becker, 31, p. 471; TDA, 29, pp. 542–3 [Physick].

211: Unidentified portrait of a lawyer?

about 1700–20
Attributed to Edward Stanton
Terracotta
h. 63 cm.
A.9–1936

Inscribed on the back with a crescent:

Originally on loan from Dr W.L. Hildburgh F.S.A. from 17 April 1935 (ex-loan 4866). Given to the Museum by Dr Hildburgh in 1936.

In the *Review of Principle Acquisitions during the Year 1936*, it is noted, 'English work of this period cannot vie with that produced in France during the 18th century, but this example is not without considerable merit. It is perhaps unlikely that the subject will be identified, but a small incised crescent on the back seems to be evidence of its being the work of Edward Stanton. Stanton's sculpture is known from signed monuments at Knebworth, Elmleigh Castle and elsewhere, which date from the first quarter of the 18th century. Around these signed examples of his work Mrs. Esdaile has grouped a number other monuments which make the identification of the sculptor of this bust almost a certainty. In addition, the Stantons of Woolverdington (Country Warwick), from whom Edward was descended, bore as their arms: Argent two chevrons and a bordure engrailed sable, with a crescent for difference in the case of Edward Stanton as younger son, and the crescent on the bust can only refer to him' (*Review* 1936, p. 7).

In *Westmonasterium or The History and Antiquities of St Peters Westminster*, a 'Mr Edward Stanton, Mason' is listed together with an illustration of his arms; a shield enclosing two stripes and a crescent (see Dart 1723, pl. VII).

The collar worn by the sitter may alternatively suggest he was a clergyman or an academic (I am grateful to Susan North for this suggestion).

Bibliography

Review 1936, p. 7 and plate 3(b).

212: Mourning child with skull

about 1700–20
Anonymous, possibly by Edward Stanton or Thomas Stayner
Marble
h. (excl. base) 46 cm.
A.62–1938

Purchased from Maurice Spero Esq., 23 Brook Street, London, in 1938, together with cat.no. 213 for £20.

This figure and its pendant figure acquired at the same time, cat.no. 213, would originally have adorned a funerary monument. In the *Review of Principle Acquisitions during the Year 1938*, it was noted, 'Such child figures, in keeping with the contemporary taste for allegorical representation, are occasionally to be seen in churches, standing or seated on the cornice or dado mouldings of some of the larger architectural monuments of the late 17th or early 18th century. The rounded rather exaggerated modelling of these figures is typical of the better English work of the period, and the acquisition of these examples makes a welcome addition towards a more representative exhibition of early 18th-century English sculpture. It has not yet been possible to attribute these figures definitely to any particular sculptor, though the name of Thomas Stayner (about 1668–1731) has tentatively been put forward by Mrs. Esdaile' (*Review* 1938, p. 5).

On acquisition H.D. Molesworth [q.v.] wrote, 'I have not yet been able to find any parallel sufficiently close, to permit of a School or workshop ascription for them, though they would certainly seem to be earlier and more purely English than the work of some of the later 18th century Continental artists as Rysbrack, Scheemakers, or Delvaux'. He suggested that the 'nearest comparison[s]' were two putti found on a tomb of Sir John and Lady Burgogne (1709), Sutton Church, Beds, ascribed to Edward Stanton.

BIBLIOGRAPHY
Review 1938, p. 5, pl. 2 (b).

213: Mourning child with hour glass

about 1700–20
Anonymous, possibly by Edward Stanton or Thomas Stayner
Marble
h. (figure) 43 cm.
A.63–1938

Purchased from Maurice Spero Esq., 23 Brook Street, London in 1938, together with cat.no. 212.

This figure, pendant to cat.no. 212, would have originally adorned a funerary monument. See entry for cat.no. 212.

BIBLIOGRAPHY
Review 1938, p. 5, pl. 2 (c).

Sir Robert Taylor

(b. 1714 – d. London 1788)

Taylor was the son of the master mason and monumental sculptor Robert Taylor. At the age of eighteen Robert Taylor junior was apprenticed to Henry Cheere [q.v.], and following his apprenticeship travelled to Rome to study. Following his father's death in 1742, he received financial assistance from friends of his father, the Godfrey family of Woodford, which allowed him to set up business as a sculptor. His most famous commissions were the sculpture in the pediment of the Mansion House of 1744, and the monument to Captain James Cornewall in Westminster Abbey of 1755. After about 1755 he concentrated more on his architectural practice.

Esdaile 1948 [Taylor]; Rococo 1984, pp. 285–6, pp. 186, 297–8, 208–9, cat.nos. L75, S21–24, S50, S51, S53–55; Colvin 1995, pp. 962–7.

214: Monument to Thomas Crosse (1694–1732) and Robert Crosse (1671–1741)

about 1745
Attributed to Sir Robert Taylor
Marble
h. approx. 488 cm.
A.183–1969

Inscribed: This MONUMENT was Erected/at the Expence of MARY MARTIN/the eldest Daughter of Thomas Crosse/of Westminster Esquire and Widow/and Relict of William Martin heretofore/of Netteswell Bury, Esquire/To the Memory of/Thomas Crosse her Nephew (the Son of/Robert Crosse of Westminster Esquire)/who died the 14th of August 1732 aged/38 Years: And of The said Robert/Crosse her Brother who died the 1st of/September 1741 aged 70 Years,/The said MARY MARTIN died the 8th/of October 1764 aged 97 Years./All three lie interred in the Vault belonging/to the Family of Crosse In the Parish/Church of St. Margaret Westminster.

From the south chancel of St Andrew's Church, Netteswell, Essex. Given to the Museum in 1969 by the Rector and Churchwardens of St Stephen's Tye Green with St Andrew's Netteswell, Essex.

The grey pyramid behind the standing figure is a modern copy, the original (which is shown in the accompanying illustration showing the monument in situ), having been destroyed.

The attribution to Sir Robert Taylor is based on similarities with known monuments by Taylor at Wooton-under-Edge and Westbury. Malcolm Baker has noted that drawings by Taylor of a monument with a medallion portrait, now in the Taylorian Institute, Oxford are closely comparable, and support an attribution to this artist (departmental records). The inscription records that the monument was erected by Mary Martin (1667–1764) – who is represented as the mourning figure – to commemorate her nephew Thomas Crosse and brother, Robert Crosse.

Bibliography

Baker 1996 [Louvre], pp. 75, 76, 80, 82, fig. 2 on p. 87, fig. 13 on p. 92; *idem* 2000 [Figured in Marble], pp. 51–2, 60, pl. 36 on p. 52, pl. 45 on p. 60.

Robert Town

(active 1756 – 1767)

Robert Town utilised the local seams of cannel, a fossilised material resembling jet, found in the coal seams near Wigan, Lancashire to produce a number of carvings, some of which are discussed by Tait, who noted that the earliest recorded instance of carved cannel dates from 1634.

Tait 1965.

215: Henry VIII (b.1491; r. 1509–1547)

about 1756–67; inscribed 1528
Attributed to Robert Town
Cannel coal with paste emerald fastening
h. 42.5 cm.
35–1870

Purchased from Mr P. Albert, London in 1870 for £20.

On acquisition this bust was described as carved jet, and thought to be either English or German. In 1869 Sir Matthew Digby Wyatt [q.v.], wrote to Henry Cole [q.v.] drawing his attention to this bust, together with an ivory diptych offered for sale at Mr Albert's Shop, 504 New Oxford Street, London, which he suggested the Museum might wish to consider for acquisition, 'The other was one of those very curious carvings in jet of which there are two in the British Museum . . . I do not think there can be a doubt as to its genuineness. Albert only wants £15 for it and I look upon it as one of those very rare historical monuments which should be secured for a National Museum even at five times that amount rather than be let slip. Albert bought it from a North Country dealer at a very low price . . . I fancy it may be the work of that most rare hand – Richard Atsyll. Every illustration of such a date as 1528 when England was in the throes of change from Gothic to Renaissance is most interesting: especially as illustrating British absorption of foreign influence'. Richard Atsyll was a cameo cutter in the service of Henry VIII, and Digby Wyatt no doubt surmised it to be by him because of the date 1528 incised on the back; the bust is however a historicising piece produced in the mid-eighteenth century. Robert Town's cannel carvings are fully discussed in an article by Hugh Tait, although the present bust is not cited. A portrait medallion of Henry VIII in cannel coal of about 1755 and also attributed to Town is in the Rijksmuseum (see Leeuwenberg 1973, p. 490, no. 855, inv.no. NM7283, and Tait 1965, p. 95 fig. 8). Similar busts are in the collection of Lord Astor of Hever (in 1965; dated 1755 by Tait), one was offered for sale at Montague Marcussen Ltd in 1961, illustrated in the *Connoisseur* March 1961, CXLVIII, no. 592, p. xxxvi, described as 'English early sixteenth century'; a further example is in the British Museum (dated to about 1770 by Tait), and another in the collection of Mr Meyer Oppenheim (in 1965; dated about 1760 by Tait). Tait concluded that these carvings were based on an engraving reproduced by Jacobus Houbraken (1698–1780) after Hans Holbein (1460/5–1534), printed in 1750.

Exhibited
Precious, Millennium Gallery, Sheffield, 5 April to 24 June 2001.

John de Vaere (De Vaare)

(b. Ghent 1754 – d. Tronchiennes (-lez-Gand) 1830)

De Vaere was trained in his youth in the Netherlands, but went to Paris in about 1774, and was employed by a goldsmith, executing models which were used for royal commissions. He then went to London, where he attended the Royal Academy Schools in 1786, and was also recorded as working for Wedgwood at this time. He went to Rome in 1787, and while there worked with Flaxman [q.v.]. He returned to England in 1790, and continued to work for Wedgwood until 1795, when he entered the employment of Mrs Coade [q.v.]. He established himself as an independent sculptor in about 1800, but returned to his native South Netherlands in 1810, and was appointed Professor of Sculpture at the Royal Academy in Ghent. He exhibited at the Royal Academy in London from 1797 to 1809.

Gunnis 1968, p. 128; Reilly & Savage 1973, p. 360; Thieme-Becker, 34, p. 33.

216: Louis-Engelbert, Duke of Arenberg (1750–1820)

signed and dated 1791
Marble
h. 54 cm.
A.9–1973

Signed and dated on the back: J. DE VAERE./ROME. 1791

A later inscription on the back reads: LOUIS ENGELBERT/DUC D'ARENBERG/NÉ 3 AOÛT 1750/✠ 7 MARS 1820

Purchased from Leopold Preston Esq., 4 Kensington Court, London in 1973 for £500, using funds from the Hildburgh Bequest. Mr Preston appears to have acted as agent for the owner of the bust, said to have been a descendant of the sitter; the bust was also said to have always belonged to the family.

The acquisition of the present piece is recorded in the *Catalogue général des peintures, cartes, plans, estampes achetés par le duc Louis Engelbert dans les voyages de 1789 et 1791 pour Bruxelles et Arenberg* held in the Arenberg Archives, Edingen, Biografie 100, 36/24: '10 juillet [Rome 1791]: payé à DEWAER sculpteur 200 louis pour la statue groupée de Crépuscule en marbre et le buste de Mgr. à faire". The bust is recorded in the inventories of the Arenberg residence in Brussels until the First World War; a copy of the bust was in the Arenberg residence in Brussels Marche-les-Dames in the Ardennes in 1913; this was taken to Germany (exact location uncertain) in 1918 (information kindly supplied by Anne Verbrugge).

The Duke of Arenberg, who lost his sight in a hunting accident in 1775, was an active figure in public life, and was once considered a possible candidate for the Netherlandish throne. He was involved in financing the first ascent of a gas-filled balloon in 1783.

Bibliography

Autour du néo-classicisme 1985, p. 36 and illus; the bust will appear in an article by Anne Verbrugge; see Derez, Nelissen, Tytgat, Verbrugge [forthcoming].

Joseph Wilton R.A.

(b. London 1722 – d. London 1803)

Wilton was the son of a London plasterer and manufacturer of papier-mâché ornaments, but received training as a sculptor on the Continent, first under Laurent Delvaux [q.v.] at Nivelles, and from 1744 under Jean-Baptiste Pigalle (1714–1785) in Paris. He went to Florence in 1751, and remained in Italy until his return to England in 1755. His marble portraits and monuments, as well as his copies after antique sculpture, reveal his study of the antique. In 1758 he became one of the directors, along with Giovanni Battista Cipriani (1727–1785), of the Richmond House Gallery, London, a collection of plaster and marble copies after the antique, owned by Charles Lennox, 3rd Duke of Richmond and Lennox. These were made available to students and artists for study and copying. Wilton won the competition for the monument to General James Wolfe in Westminster Abbey in 1760, and in 1761 he was appointed Statuary to His Majesty, George III. In 1768 he became a founder member of the Royal Academy, but on inheriting a large legacy from his father in the same year he neglected sculpture, and went bankrupt in 1793. In 1796 he was made Keeper of the Royal Academy, a post which he retained until his death.

Gunnis 1968, pp. 434–7; Whinney 1988, pp. 261–9; Thieme-Becker, 36, pp. 45–6; TDA 33, pp. 226–7 [Murdoch].

217: Dr Antonio Cocchi (1695–1758)

signed and dated 1755
Marble
h. 61.3 cm.
A.9–1966

Signed on the back: I. Wilton/Sct.
Inscribed on the medallion on the socle: ANT.ΚΟΚΧΙΟΣ ΞΑΨΝΕ ΓΗΡΑΣΚΩ ΔΙΔΑΣΚΟΜΕΝΟΣ (Antonio Cocchi/Age 60/1755/I go on learning, as I grow old).'

Commissioned from the sculptor by Francis, 10th Earl of Huntingdon (1739–1789), and recorded at his seat, Castle Donington, Leicestershire, by Horace Walpole in 1768: 'Donnington in Leicestershire Lord Huntingdon's disagreable park, but a noble view of the Trent from a Cliff on one side. miserable House, small and placed in a hole. two tawdry rooms like assemble [sic] rooms at Blackheath, added by the Countess Dowager. a few family pictures, but the best are in town. four Marble busts with greek mottoes of the present Earl, Dr Cocchi of Florence, Epicurus & Pythagoras. D° of Oliver Cromwell, with, "audent ea facta minores"' (Toynbee 1928, p. 64). The bust was later recorded in an inventory of 1788, when it was displayed in the Drawing Room as a pair to that of a bust of Huntingdon also by (Baker forthcoming [Wilton]). The bust of Huntingdon was until recently in the British Embassy in Paris (Government Art Collections). It was lent on long-term loan to the Museum from 2001 onwards, and is currently displayed in the British Galleries. The present bust was formerly in the collection of Sir Ian Walker-Okeover Bt., D.S.O. of Okeover Hall, Ashbourne, Derbyshire, and was included in the sale at Christie's, London, on 30 June 1966, lot 14. Purchased by the Museum from Cyril Humphris Ltd in 1966 for £950, using funds from the Bequest of M.L. Horn.

Dr Cocchi was an eminent scholarly physician in Florence, and from 1738 until his death the Keeper of the Grand-Ducal collections. He was acquainted with many Englishmen, including Horace Mann, the British envoy in Florence, as well as Lord Huntingdon and Joseph Wilton.

In his memorandum to the Director, Terence Hodgkinson [q.v.] commented, 'This is a magnificent bust, it may indeed come to be regarded as the finest English bust in the Museum'. On acquisition, the bust was subject to a full discussion by Terence Hodgkinson in the *V&A Bulletin*; see Hodgkinson 1967; see also Whinney 1971, p. 98. For a recent re-evaluation of the bust and the circumstances surrounding its execution; see Baker forthcoming [Wilton].

Malcolm Baker has suggested that the date inscribed on the present bust of 1755 records the date when Cocchi sat for Wilton, though the bust itself was probably not executed until early 1756, after Wilton's return to London (*ibid.*). The significance of the Huntingdon commissions – the bust of Dr Cocchi and that of the Earl of Huntingdon – and their display as pendants to each other, as recorded by the 1788 inventory, is also discussed by Malcolm Baker, who has suggested: 'This evidence about the commissioning and setting of the busts, together with that available about the Huntingdon family's relationship with Dr Cocchi, makes clear that these two portraits, though executed a few years apart, were employed to commemorate a friendship, and in a sense, to celebrate the patron's experience of the Grand Tour' (*ibid.*). I am grateful to Malcolm Baker for allowing me to read his article prior to publication

A bronze version of the present bust is incorporated into the monument to Dr Cocchi in Santa Croce, Florence (see Hodgkinson 1967, p. 80 and fig. 9; Villani 1991, fig. 78). A marble version of the bust by Francis Harwood, omitting the medallion at the front of the socle and dating from 1759, is recorded in a private collection in Florence (see *ibid.*, fig. 80). An engraving of the bust by Veremondo Rossi after Leonardo Frati is illustrated in *ibid.*, fig. 77.

Bibliography

Hodgkinson 1967; Whinney 1971, p. 98, cat.no. 29, illus. on p. 99; Kenworthy-Browne 1973, p. 575, and figs. 3; Russell 1975, pp. 117–8, fig. 8 on p. 118; *Norfolk and the Grand Tour* 1985, pp. 136–7, cat.no. 82, illus on p. 137; Villani 1991, pp. 69–70; *British Museum* 1999, p. 68, and n. 15; Coutu 2000, pp. 49, 51, n. 47 on p. 54; Baker 2000 [Grand Tour], pp. 76–7, fig. 50 on p. 77; *idem* forthcoming [Wilton].

Exhibited

Norfolk and the Grand Tour. Eighteenth-century travellers abroad and their souvenirs, Castle Museum, Norwich, 5 October to 24 November 1985, cat.no. 82.

218: Bust of Laocoon

signed and dated 1758
By Joseph Wilton, after an antique prototype
Marble
h. 61 cm.
A.84–1949

Signed and dated beneath the left shoulder: I. Wilton. f^{t} 1758.

Sales held in 1779, 1823 and 1830 respectively include references to a bust of Laocoon by Joseph Wilton, presumably the present piece: i) The late Earl Ferrers, 'Brought from his Lordships seat at Staunton, in the County of Leicester, and his House in Upper Seymour Street, Portman Square', held at Messrs Christie and Ansell, Great Room, next Cumberland House, Pall Mall, 2–3 June 1779. Included in the second day's sale held on 3 June 1779, lot 72, was described as, 'Mr Wilton – Bust of the LAOCOON, *fine sculpture*, from the antique'. ii) in 'The Whole and valuable collection of antique and modern sculpture of the late Joseph Nollekins [sic] Esq RA Decd', held at Mr Christie's, London 3–5 July 1823. Included in the third day's sale held on 5 July 1823, lot 100, was described as 'Head of the Laocoon by Wilton'. The annotated catalogue held in the National Art Library records the bust was bought by 'Paynter' for £36 15s [35 guineas]. An addendum to lot 100 notes that a bust of one of the sons of Laocoon, also probably by Wilton, was also included in the sale; no lot number being assigned, it was sold for £6 6s [6 guineas]. iii) 'The Property of J. Paine Esq, Architect (dec'd)' held at Mr Christie, 8 King Street, St James's Square, on 12 March 1830, included as the final item in the sale, lot 104, 'A fine bust of the Laocoon, from the antique, in statuary marble, by Wilton'; the copy of the catalogue held in the National Art Library suggests this was sold for £32 11s 6d. Purchased by Dr W.L. Hildburgh F.S.A from the dealer Arthur Einstein for £12 at an unknown date. Given by Dr Hildburgh to the Museum in 1949.

The present bust is a copy of the head of the central figure of Laocoon from the antique marble group of Laocoon and his sons now in the Musei Vaticani, Rome (see Haskell and Penny 1981, pp. 243–7).

Bibliography

Owsley and Rieder 1974, pl. 5 on p. 7.

219: Oliver Cromwell (1599–1658)

about 1760
Terracotta
h. (incl. base) 71 cm.
A.72–1965

Bequeathed by Rupert Gunnis, Hungershall Lodge, Tunbridge Wells, Kent in 1965.

The present piece was covered in white paint which was removed by the Museum's Conservation Department in July 1965.

This bust is related to the marble bust of Cromwell executed by Wilton in 1762, also in the Museum's collections; see entry for cat.no. 220. The present piece is noted in a letter from Terence Hodgkinson [q.v.] to Rupert Gunnis in July 1965, in which Hodgkinson suggested, 'I can see no reason to suppose that it is not the original model. It is virtually identical to our marble version, save that the eyes of the lions' masks are blank in the marble; in the terracotta, the irises are indicated'. Margaret Whinney later remarked, 'A comparison of the two, however, shows that the terracotta is far more sensitive in modelling, and that much has been lost in the marble . . . in the terracotta the passages around the eyes and the vein in the left temple show exceptional liveliness, and the ability which almost equals that of Roubiliac to create a portrait of a man long dead' (Whinney 1971, p. 102). However, it is now thought that the terracotta may well be cast after the marble, rather than having served as a model; its finished condition supports this idea.

A coloured plaster cast (h. 76.2 cm with base) which relates to the present bust and cat.no. 220 is in the Royal Academy collections (unpublished); it has the number 106 faintly inscribed on the front of the base (I am grateful to Helen Valentine for confirming this).

BIBLIOGRAPHY
Whinney 1971, p. 102, cat.no. 31 and illus. on p. 103; *idem* 1988, p. 460, n. 26.

220: Oliver Cromwell (1599–1658)

signed and dated 1762
Marble
h. 74.9 cm.
A.32–1930

Signed on the back behind the left shoulder: Opus./Josephi Wilton 1762

Sold on the second day of the sale of the Lansdowne Collection held on 6 March 1930, lot 34. The bust was bought by the dealers Spero and Kerin for 54 guineas. Prior to its acquisition by the Museum, R.P. Bedford [q.v.] noted, 'This price however did not represent what it cost the firm, and they are only able to offer it to us through Mr Alfred Spero (who has now left the firm and started on his own) for £70 because they have been able to sell the pedestal the bust was on for a good price'. The wood pedestal was described in the sale catalogue as 'carved with dolphins and foliage, and painted white' (I am grateful to Marika Leino for this information). The bust was purchased by the Museum from Alfred Spero, 4 Lower Street, London in 1930 for £70.

A number of versions of the Cromwell bust by Wilton are known, including a terracotta bust acquired by the Museum from Rupert Gunnis in 1965; see entry for cat.no. 219. Two busts were exhibited by Wilton at the Society of Artists in 1761 and 1766, nos. 168 and 221 respectively, described as a bust 'in marble, of Oliver Cromwell', and a bust of 'Oliver Cromwell, from the noted cast of his face, preserved in the Great Duke's Gallery at Florence' (Graves 1907, pp. 283–4). Margaret Whinney suggested the present bust was the one exhibited in 1766, from the cast formerly in the Great Duke's Gallery and thought to have been taken from the head of the funeral effigy, now in the Bargello, Florence (Whinney 1971, p. 100). Other versions include those in the Cromwell Museum, Huntingdon (see *Cromwell Museum* 1965, p. 3, cat.no. 13); another version, the 'property of the Marquis of Lansdowne and removed from Lansdowne House' was sold by Mr Christie on the second day's sale of the collection, 26 May 1810, lot 26, described as 'A very spirited bust of O. Cromwell by Wilton, and mahogany term'. This was possibly identical with the present piece; if so, it must have been either bought in at the 1810 sale, or bought by a member of the Lansdowne family either then or at a later date, before being auctioned once more in 1930. A marble bust of Cromwell is recorded in 1789 in the hall of Castle Donington, Leicestershire – opposite a bust of Peter the Great – the 'seat of Lord Rawdon, late of his uncle the Right Honourable the Earl of Huntingdon deceased': 'Here is a fine bust of Cromwell, in marble, done by Wilton; it secured the artist an honourable employment under his present Majesty' (Throsby 1789, pp. 173–4); a marble version in the Foreign Office – identical to the present piece except that it is undated and the base is of a different shape – signed I. WILTON, was bought by the Ministry of Works from Messrs Marcussen in 1947. A marble version recorded by Mrs Webb was formerly recorded at Anglesey Abbey, Lord Fairhaven collection, and later in the possession of Lord Fairhaven of South Walsham Hall, Norwich, Norfolk; it is unsigned (all the above noted by Terence Hodgkinson [q.v.] , departmental records).

BIBLIOGRAPHY
Graves 1907, p. 284, no. 221; *Review* 1930, p. 7, and pl. VI; *Illustrated London News* 1937; *Siècle de l'élegance* 1959, p. 43, cat.no. 73; Whinney 1971, p. 100, cat.no. 30, illus. on p. 101; *idem* 1988, pp. 262, 460, n. 26.

EXHIBITED
Society of Artists, 1766, no. 221; *Exhibition of Kings and Queens of England, 1500–1900*, Victoria and Albert Museum, London, May 1937; *Le Siècle de l'élegance la Demeure Anglaise au XVIII siècle*, Musée des Arts Décoratifs, Paris, 26 February to mid-June 1959, cat.no. 73.

221: Unknown man, possibly Dr Edward Archer (1717–1789)

signed and dated 1781
Marble
h. 78.4 cm.
A.160–1969

Signed on the back: J. Wilton.fecit./1781.

Previously in the collection of W.H. Du Cros, M.P. (date unknown; early twentieth century), the bust was subsequently inherited by Roy Du Cros and later given by him to Madame Y. T. Foo. In the possession of the Heim Gallery, London, from whom the bust was purchased by the Museum in 1969 for £2,600. However the sale was nullified as it was later discovered that the bust had previously been stolen from the London residence of Madame Foo, prior to its aquisition by the Heim Gallery. The bust was subsequently re-purchased by the Museum in 1972 for the original price from the legal owner, Madame Foo. The sum previously paid to the Heim Gallery was recovered by the Museum. The inventory number indicating its original purchase in 1969, ie. A.160–1969, was however, retained.

John Kerslake has suggested that the sitter may be identified as Dr Edward Archer, an eminent physician. The facial characteristics in the full-length portrait of Archer by Robert Edge Pine (d. 1788) of 1782 in the Royal College of Physicians bear some similarity to those of the present bust (see *Royal College of Physicians* 1964, pp. 30–1). The soft cap and dress also suggest the subject is professional, rather than aristocratic, political or military.

Unattributed Sculpture of the 18th Century

222: Sundial

about 1700
Stone
h. (of brick pedestal) 88.5 cm. (base of pedestal) 45 cm. x 46.4 cm.
h. (sundial) 32.5 cm.
A.42–1910

Said to have originally come from the village of Ryhope, near Sunderland. Purchased from Mr H.J. Reynolds, 104 Brompton Road, London in 1910 for £17 10s.

Three of the gnomons are missing and one loose.

The sundial has thirteen facets with metal gnomons and sits on a baluster shaped pedestal. For similar facet-headed sundials see Gatty 1900, p. 108 for English sundials, and pp. 149–65 for Scottish; see also MacGibbon and Ross 1892, pp. 357–514 on Scottish sundials; pp. 441–512 for faced-headed dials. On acquisition this type of sundial was said to be very common in Scotland, and only found in England in the northern counties. A suggestion was made (not in the event taken up) that this sundial be placed in the quadrangle of the Museum to be 'appreciated by those who have to design gardens in the old style'.

223: The arms of Trevor

about 1700–1710
Limewood
h. 44 cm.
321–1907

Purchased from Mr A.G. Smithers, 28 High Street, Tunbridge Wells, (Dealer in Antique and Decorative Art) in 1907 for £5 10s.

This carved painted and gilt heraldic coat of arms with crest, helmet and mantling bears the arms of Trevor.

John Meriton has identified the crest as follows: Arms: [Per bend sinister] ermine [& ermines] a lion rampart [or] with a label for difference. Crest on a gentleman's helm: On a chapeau a wyvern wings elevated [sable]. He suggests that the family may be identified with that of the Trevor (of Denbigh) and that the arms could belong to one of the Barons Trevor of Bronham – the label indicating their eldest son and heir status during the father's lifetime: Thomas Trevor (1658–1746), John Trevor (1695–1764), Robert Trevor, Viscount Hampden (1706–1783). Alternatively, Sir Thomas Trevor, Baron of the Exchequer (d. 21 December 1656 aet 84) or son and heir Sir Thomas Trevor, KB (d. 5 February 1676 aet 64).

224: William III (b.1650; r. 1689–1702)

about 1700
Boxwood
h. 37 cm.
A.39–1939

Purchased by Alexander Sandor, 89 High Street, Hemel Hempstead, Herts, formerly of 144 Brompton Road, London, for £17 17s [17 guineas] from the Christie's sale held on 14 December 1939, lot 76; described in the catalogue as, 'A Flemish Boxwood Figure of a Courtier, possibly William of Orange . . . *on ormolu wall bracket*'. A misunderstanding in the sale room resulted in the Museum missing the opportunity of purchasing the present piece; instead it went to the dealer Alexander Sandor, from whom it was subsequently bought by the Museum later that year for £27 10s.

The right arm of the putto has been broken off and the left arm has been repaired. The right hand of William III has been repaired below the wrist; there is a vertical crack at the rear of the base.

Margaret Longhurst [q.v.] enthusiastically endorsed the proposed purchase of this object; in her memorandum to the Director proposing its acquisition she wrote, 'This is I consider a very fine boxwood carving – & I do not agree with Mr Molesworth [q.v.] that it is not worth more than 20 guineas . . . Before the war it might easily have fetched £50–60. It represents William III probably between 1690 and 1700. The work has some English characteristics but is probably by one of the numerous Dutch artists then in England'. Acquired shortly after the acquisition of a terracotta statuette of *William III* by John Nost the Elder – see cat.no. 8 – it was considered to be an interesting pendant to it.

Terence Hodgkinson [q.v.] noted the similarities of the present piece to the central figure of John Digby, 3rd Earl of Bristol (d. 1698) on the marble monument to the Earl and his two wives Alice (d. 1658) and Rachel (d. 1708–9), by John Nost (active 1686 – d. 1729) in the South transept of the Abbey Church, Sherborne, Dorset (see *Historical Monuments* 1952, pl. 169 opp. p. 208, detail on pl. 170).

A related carved wood figure of *William of Orange* in classical armour, described as Dutch/English, late 17th century, was sold by Sotheby's, Bewley Court, Lacock, Wiltshire, on 17 May 1993, lot. 186.

The present piece may well be by a sculptor of Netherlandish origin; Malcolm Baker has recently suggested that it could be by John Nost the Elder [q.v.].

Bibliography

Stadhouder-Koning 1950, p. 125, cat.no. 572, and illus.; *Europäische Barockplastik* 1971, p. 335, cat.no. 293, and pl. 124.

Exhibited

De Stadhouder-Koning en zijn tijd 1650–1950, Rijksmuseum, Amsterdam, 18 March to 29 May 1950, cat.no. 572; *Europäische Barockplastik am Niederrhein. Grupello und seine Zeit*, Kunstmuseum, Dusseldorf, 4 April to 20 July 1971, cat.no. 293.

225: Cherub

about 1700
Pine
h. 26 cm.
A.54–1932

Purchased from F.H. Sikes, Esq., 4 Carlyle Studios, King's Road, Chelsea, London in 1932 for £3.

Worm-eaten. There is a rectangular dowel hole at the back.

The owner, Mr Sikes left the bust at the Museum for an opinion in September 1932. R.P. Bedford [q.v.] wrote to Mr Sikes, 'It is not anything very great and I doubt if it is worth more than £2 or £3, but it is a thing we should be quite glad to have here if it were for sale at about that price'. The owner considered it to be a 'hideous bust', and that he would accept £3 for it, exclaiming that 'I should be v. willing to see the last of the abomination'.

In his recommendation to the Director, Bedford wrote: 'This cherub head is not without charm, and it is certainly English work of the late 17th century'. This piece, carved in a broad style, almost certainly formed part of a large structure, probably a piece of church furniture. Pine was widely used for structural pieces, or broad forms, rather than fine details. Despite Bedford's certainty that it was English, the type of wood is commonly found in Alpine regions and this piece might indeed be from the Tyrol.

BIBLIOGRAPHY
Review 1932, p. 5

226: Chimneypiece from Devonshire or perhaps Berkeley House

about 1700
Marble
A.23–1924

Messrs Holland, Hannen and Cubitts Ltd, 258 Grays Inn Road, London in 1924 purchased Devonshire House from the Duke of Devonshire. Given by Messrs Holland, Hannen and Cubitts Ltd in 1924.

Information relating to its acquisition describes this as 'A very fine fireplace in the basement of dark red marble with Bolection moulding dating from the earlier House'. Devonshire House stood on the site of an earlier building, Berkeley House, erected in 1664/5 by Hugh May (1621–1684) for the 1st Lord Berkeley of Stratton. Berkeley House was demolished in 1733, and Devonshire House, built by William Kent (1685–1748) took its place. This chimneypiece may have come from the part of Devonshire House which was subsequently altered, or more probably, from the previous building on the site, Berkeley House. Devonshire House was itself demolished, and a new commercial building, also called Devonshire House, was built in its place during 1924–6 (Pevsner 1981 [London], pp. 65, 627).

BIBLIOGRAPHY
English Chimneypieces 1928, fig. 8.

227: Chimneypiece from Scarcroft Lodge, possibly originally from Chesterfield House, South Audley Street, Mayfair

about 1748–50
Anonymous; possibly from a design by Isaac Ware (d. 1766)
Marble
h. 152 cm h. (figures) 120 cm.
A.140–1956

Said to have come from Scarcroft Lodge, Wetherby Road, Scarcroft, near Leeds. Given by the General Electric Company Ltd in 1956.

A chimneypiece of different design but with slightly larger, but almost identical caryatid figures, originally from Chesterfield House, Mayfair, is in the Metropolitan Museum of Art, New York (Given by the Hearst Foundation in 1956; inv.no. 56.234.4). The New York caryatids are 147.5 cm in height, about 27.5 cm taller than those on the present piece. For a full discussion of the history of the New York chimneypiece, see Parker 1963, where it is dated to about 1748–50, and Murdoch 1983, p. 39, where Tessa Murdoch suggests Roubiliac [q.v.] as the sculptor. The similarity between the caryatid figures on the chimneypiece now in New York and the present piece suggests that the two chimneypieces may come from the same workshop, and could even may have been made for the same house. Parker records that Chesterfield House was sold in 1869, but prior to the sale 'a few of the contents of the house were transferred to Bretby the country seat of the Earls of Chesterfield in Derbyshire . . . Among the contents of the house that were consigned to Bretby was the [New York] caryatid chimneypiece' (Parker 1963, p. 210). It is possible that the present piece was also removed at the same time.

The architect of Chesterfield House was Isaac Ware (d. 1766). His remarks on chimneypieces in his architectural treatise (*A complete Body of Architecture;* published in 1796), accord with the style of the present piece (pp. 570–6). One of the engraved illustrations (Ware 1796, pl. 88 and p. 574) illustrates caryatid figures close to those seen here. For the design, see also Laing 1989, fig. 8 on p. 248. For Chesterfield House, see Avray Tipping 1922.

228: Inigo Jones (1573–1652)

about 1750
Limewood
diam. 19.8 cm.
467–1882

Purchased from Mr W.H. Cuddy, 17 King Street, Brighton in 1882 for £2. Originally assigned to the Department of Furniture and Woodwork, and on loan to the Department of Architecture and Sculpture, now Sculpture Department, from April 1923.

Originally thought to be seventeenth-century, it is likely that this relief in a medallic format of the architect Inigo Jones dates from the eighteenth century, as it relates to the historicising portraits of 'Worthies' produced during the eighteenth-century; see Mallet 1962. See also the entry for cat.no. 196 for a bust of Inigo Jones.

229: Unknown woman, based on the antique Zingara

signed; about 1750–60
Marble
h. (incl. base) 44.5 cm.
A.1–1944

Signed on the back: ROUBILIAC SC

In the collection of Lord Boston in 1928, and possibly formerly owned by his ancestor Sir William Irby. In the possession of Alfred Spero from whom it was acquired by Dr W.L. Hildburgh F.S.A. together with cat.no. 230, in 1944. Given by Dr Hildburgh to the Museum as New Year gift in 1944. On long-term loan to the Natural History Museum from 17 June 1998.

See also entry for the companion bust, cat.no. 230; these two busts were presumably intended to be displayed together. In her 1928 monograph on Roubiliac Esdaile commented, 'Two female heads of classical type on black marble stands, nymphs perhaps, are in the possession of Lord Boston, whose ancestor Sir William Irby, created Lord Boston in 1761, may well have commissioned them; a second pair lately in his possession, a young girl and a negro boy, I have not seen. One of the first pair, whose scarf is twisted round her hair and passes under the chin, has an eighteenth-century flavour in spite of her likeness to the classical type known to Roubiliac's contemporaries as the Zingara or gipsy' (Esdaile 1928, p. 131). Despite the signature there is nothing stylistically to suggest that this is the work of Roubiliac.

The antique statue of *Zingara* is now in the possession of the Louvre, and is displayed at Versailles. Haskell and Penny record that the figure was widely reproduced up to the mid-nineteenth century, although 'it was the head alone that was most commonly reproduced, in France (there is a colossal example with porto venere drapery in the reserve collection at Versailles) and especially in England, in marble by itself, and as the head on marble chimney-piece herms (Powderham Castle in Devon), in Derby biscuit porcelain, in cameos and gems, in earthenware by Ralph and Enoch Wood, in black basaltes by Wedgwood, and in sets of plaster casts made by Scheemakers, by Cheere and by Charles Harris' (see Haskell and Penny 1981, pp. 339–41, and fig. 180 on p. 340).

A marble version signed by Richard Cockle Lucas was on the London art market in 1991–2.

A pair of female marble busts with similar facial features was included in the sale at Sotheby's, London, 9 November 1999, lot 66.

BIBLIOGRAPHY
Esdaile 1928, p. 131; Haskell and Penny 1981, p. 341, n. 23.

230: Unknown female, probably after the antique

signed; about 1750–60
Marble
h. (incl. base) 36.5 cm. h. (socle) 8.5 cm.
A.2–1944

Signed on the back: ROUBILIAC./Sc.

In the collection of Lord Boston in 1928, and possibly formerly owned by his ancestor Sir William Irby. In the possession of Alfred Spero, from whom it was acquired by Dr W.L. Hildburgh F.S.A. together with cat.no. 229, in 1944. Given by Dr Hildburgh to the Museum as New Year gift in 1944.

See entry for cat.no. 229. Commenting on the present piece, Esdaile noted, 'her hair almost covered by a sphendone, has drapery of a most unclassic order, with a frill round the neck' (Esdaile 1928, p. 131). As with cat. no. 229, despite the signature there is nothing stylistically to suggest that this is the work of Roubiliac.

BIBLIOGRAPHY

Esdaile 1928, p. 131.

231: Chimneypiece from an unrecorded Dublin house

about 1775–1800
Marble
h. 130.8 cm.
A.2–1909

From an unrecorded house in Dublin. Given by J.A. Dolmage Esq., on behalf of his son the late Cecil Goodrich Dolmage Esq., L.L.D., D.C.L. in 1909, together with cat.nos. 77 and 232.

BIBLIOGRAPHY

English Chimneypieces 1928, pl. 19.

232: Chimneypiece from an unrecorded Dublin house

about 1775–1800
Marble
h. 138.8 cm.
A.3–1909

From an unrecorded house in Dublin. Given by J.A. Dolmage Esq., on behalf of his son the late Cecil Goodrich Dolmage Esq., L.L.D., D.C.L. in 1909, together with cat.nos. 77 and 232.

The frieze is decorated with a symmetrical scroll design. The console-shaped jambs have a heavy leaf which terminates in a small drop wreath. A pattern of small leaves is repeated on the cornice and inner moulding.

[Not illustrated].

233: Chimneypiece, from a house at Hinckley, Leicestershire

about 1790–1800
Black slate
h. 133.5 cm.
1110–1904

Originally from an old house at Hinckley in Leicestershire. Purchased from Mr Thomas S. Elgood, 90 New Walk, Leicester in 1904 for £10 10s, including 10s packing expenses.

The previous owner Mr Elgood initially wrote to the Museum in April 1904 enclosing a photogaph of the present piece, which he described as a 'unique carved Slate Chimney piece – taken out of an old house in this County', and in fourteen parts. A further letter from Mr Elgood of 22 August 1904, recorded: 'This was taken out of a House at Hinckley, Leicestershire, about the year 1880 – it is of local design & workmanship, & the Slate would be obtained from Charnwood Forest (probably *Groby* Quarry). There are many slate Gravestones in the County of similar character'.

In his recommendation for purchase, Purdon Clarke [q.v.] commented, 'The ornament is in the Adam style of the end of the 18th century but the carving in slate seems to be peculiar to Leicester where there are many tombstones of the same period well worth reproduction for fine ornament and good lettering'. The central panel depicts nymphs and putti dancing round an altar.

[Not illustrated].

THE 19TH CENTURY

George Gammon Adams

(b. Staines 1821 – d. Chiswick 1898)

Adams began his career as a medallist, training at the Royal Mint under the tutelage of William Wyon (1795–1851). In 1840 Adams commenced studies in sculpture at the Royal Academy Schools, and in 1846 travelled to Rome to train further under John Gibson [q.v.]. He exhibited regularly at the Royal Academy, mainly portrait busts and medals, between 1841 and 1885. Forrer recorded that 'G.G. Adams's success as a sculptor was equal to his success as a medallist'. The sculptor lent a plaster cast of his Ancient Briton *to the Museum at a date probably prior to 1865 (I am grateful to Christopher Marsden for this information), almost certainly the unidentified statue noted in the* List of Objects in the Art Division, South Kensington Museum . . ., (List *1871). An anonymous oil portrait of Adams aged 15, as well as another portrait of him by John Bagnold Burgess (1830–1897) are in the Department of Prints, Drawings and Paintings (inv.nos. P.43–1982, P.44–1982).*

Forrer I, pp. 22–5; Graves I, pp. 6–7; Gunnis 1968, pp.13–14; Thieme-Becker, 1, pp. 73–4.

234: Arthur Wellesley, 1st Duke of Wellington
(1769–1852)

about 1852
Marble
h. (incl. base) 67.5 cm.
A.113–1980

Given by Miss I.D. Adams, daughter of George Gammon Adams in 1980. In total 196 items were included in the Adams gift, which consisted of many models for medals, and medals (not included here), as well as the busts and figurative sculpture catalogued here. In most instances it is not possible to date conclusively the many items included in this gift. A photograph album, together with other related material was also received in the Sculpture Department at the time of acquisition of the models; this was transferred to the Archive of Art and Design in 1996 (AAD/1997/12; hereafter *AAD Adams*).

This bust depicts the Duke of Wellington and is inscribed WELLINGTON along the base. A version of this bust is illustrated in the G.G. Adams album of studio photographs (*AAD Adams*, pp. 19 and 44).

Adams exhibited two busts of the Duke of Wellington at the Royal Academy, one in 1854, the other in 1859 (Graves I, pp. 6–7, nos. 1513 and 1356). This bust is a variant of the busts produced by Adams in 1852 and located at Stratfield Saye, Hants and Corsham Court, Wilts. For a bronze variant of this bust see entry for cat.no. 235.

Adams was a favoured sculptor of the Duke of Wellington and was chosen to take the death mask of Wellington, considered by his son to be the best likeness produced of the Duke. A plaster cast of this is in the National Portrait Gallery (*NPG* 1981, p. 602, no. 2155a).

235: Arthur Wellesley, 1st Duke of Wellington
(1769–1852)

about 1852
Bronze
h. 35.5 cm.
A.125–1980

Given by Miss I.D. Adams, daughter of George Gammon Adams in 1980. See entry for cat.no. 234.

This is the only bronze item (other than medals), to be included in the Adams bequest. The bust stands on a black wood square stand. On the back what appears to be "G" and "P" are etched crudely on the back.

This bust bears a resemblance to representations of Wellington as shown in the Adams album. For a marble variant see the entry for cat.no. 234.

236: General Sir Charles James Napier G.C.B.
(1782–1853)

about 1853–5
Marble
h. (incl. socle) 72.5 cm.
A.115–1980

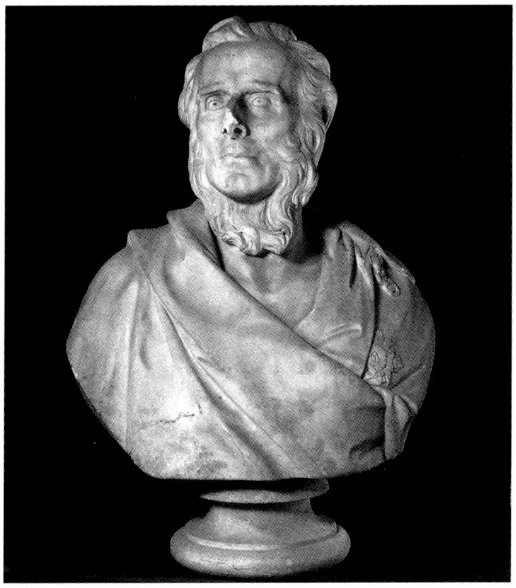

Given by Miss I.D. Adams, daughter of George Gammon Adams in 1980. See entry for cat.no. 234.

The nose is chipped.

This bust, depicting a bearded man possibly represents General Sir Charles James Napier. Photographs in the G.G. Adams album of studio photographs illustrate busts of Napier (*AAD Adams*, pp. 11 and 15); see also cat.no. 237.

Adams exhibited two busts of Sir Charles Napier at the Royal Academy, the first in 1854 (no. 1506), the other a year later in 1855 (no. 1444) (Graves I, pp. 6–7). A plaster cast of a closely related bust of Napier by Adams and dated 1853 was purchased by the National Portrait Gallery in 1899 (*NPG* 1981, p. 410, no. 1198).

237: General Sir Charles James Napier G.C.B.
(1782–1853)

about 1855
Plaster
h. 81 cm.
A.126–1980

Given by Miss I.D. Adams, daughter of George Gammon Adams in 1980. See entry for cat.no. 234.

The figure is cracked and chipped, the plaster peeling in patches.

This is probably a plaster model for the statue of General Napier erected in Trafalgar Square, although it varies from the finished work in some details. A discussion of public sculpture in the *Art Journal* in 1862 commented on Adams's statue of Napier, stating that those with 'the slightest attention to natural form and movement is all that is necessary for the condemnation of the statue of General Napier, in Trafalgar Square, as perhaps the worst piece of sculpture in England. The moral and relative worthlessness of the work exceeds tenfold its formal imperfection. To see in these days a mass so dull and soulless, and to remember that it is the work, less of a striving sculptor than of a company of gentlemen who constituted a committee of taste – to see and remember these things, we say, must lead to the conclusion that there is not even a modicum of taste or Art-intelligence shared by those committees who thus indecently expose their freshly dead friends to public animadversion' (*Art Journal*, 1 April 1862, p. 98; partly cited in Read 1982, p. 14, and fig. 9 on p. 10). The *Builder* was slightly more complimentary, though suggesting the statue was a useful lesson to others: 'The figure stands well, and the likeness is strongly marked. Simplicity and breadth characterise the treatment, and these are admirable qualities. We must, nevertheless, be permitted to say, rather with reference to works to follow than to this, that carried to extremes, especially in bronze, these qualities result in baldness and insipidity' (The *Builder*, 16 August 1856, XIV, no. 706, p. 446). See also the entry for cat.no. 236. For further information on the statue itself, see Blackwood 1989 pp. 256–7.

238: Major General Sir Henry Havelock K.C.B. (1795–1857)

about 1861
Plaster
h. 67 cm.
A.128–1980

Given by Miss I.D. Adams, daughter of George Gammon Adams in 1980. See entry for cat.no. 234.

I am grateful to Philip Ward-Jackson for identifying the subject. A bronze statue to Havelock by William Behnes [q.v.] in Trafalgar Square, was unveiled in 1861 (see Blackwood 1989, pp. 258–9 and *Art Journal*, 1 March 1864, p. 84 for a critique of the statue). A second cast was also erected in Mowbray Park, Sunderland, Tyne and Wear (Usherwood, Beach and Morris 2000, p. 183). It is likely that the present piece was executed by Adams in connection with the competition for the commission. A plaster bust of Havelock by Adams of 1858 is in the National Portrait Gallery (*NPG* 1981, p. 263, no. 1204).

239: Henry John Temple, 3rd Viscount Palmerston (1784–1865)

signed and dated 1866
Marble
h. 31cm. (excl. socle) h. 38.5 cm. (incl. socle)
A.120–1980

Signed and dated on the back: G.G.ADAMS.S./LONDON. 1866.

Given by Miss I.D. Adams, daughter of George Gammon Adams in 1980. See entry for cat.no. 234.

This bust portrays Palmerston in statesman's dress wearing a high collar, bow tie and sash with a sash and star of the Order of the Garter on his chest. On the back is a label attached to the bust, in the handwriting of the donor, Miss I.D. Adams, inscribed 'Small marble bust of Lord Palmerston, Prime Minister by George G. Adams sculptor'.

Palmerston first became Prime Minister in 1855 when the Crimean War was at its height, and then again during the period 1859–65. He was a dominant figure in English politics, and this bust may be a reduced verion of a larger bust commissioned from Adams to commemorate his death. Attached to the bust in an envelope was an extract from the *Times* of Wednesday 29 November 1865, reproducing a paragraph concerning a bust of Palmerston by Adams. This is annotated at the top: 'Mr Adams was permitted by the family to have a cast of the head and features [of Palmerston] after death'. The extract from the *Times* records: 'The Late Lord Palmerston – Yesterday Mr Adams, sculptor, had the honour to submit his bust of the late Premier for Her Majesty's inspection. The Queen was much pleased with the work, and thought it an excellent likeness. It really is, perhaps, as good a resemblance, in inanimate clay of the lamented statesman, as could be produced'. Beneath this paragraph is printed a copy of a letter from the Rt Hon. Lawrence Sullivan, Palmerston's brother-in-law, similarly commending the bust. As the cutting is dated 1865 the bust mentioned is likely to have been the model for the present work, which is signed and dated 1866. Adams exhibited a bust of Palmerston at the Royal Academy in 1867 (Graves I, p. 7, no. 1134). A plaster cast variant of the present bust was purchased in 1899 by the National Portrait Gallery (*NPG* 1981, p. 433, no. 1206).

240: Sir John Colborne, 1st Baron Seaton (1778–1863)

about 1866
Painted plaster
h. 78 cm.
A.127–1980

Given by Miss I.D. Adams, daughter of George Gammon Adams in 1980. See entry for cat.no. 234.

I am grateful to Philip Ward-Jackson for identifying the present piece as a model for the bronze statue of Field Marshal Lord Seaton, cast by Elkington at Devonport. An engraving of the statue was included in the *Illustrated London News*, 15 December 1866, p. 584. A plaster bust of Seaton by Adams dated 1863 is in the National Portrait Gallery, London (see *NPG* 1981, p. 509, no. 1205). A marble bust related to the plaster in the National Portrait Gallery was formerly in the United Services Club, London (Kilmurray 1979, p. 191).

241: Self-portrait

about 1850–98
Marble
h. 75 cm.
A.114–1980

Given by Miss I.D. Adams, daughter of George Gammon Adams in 1980. See entry for cat.no. 234.

The bust depicts Adams in casual attire, sporting a high collar and bow tie. A chest pocket holds what appear to be sculptor's tools, in the form of a knife and scraping instrument, though these are not clearly defined. For the possible plaster model for this bust see cat.no. 242.

242: Self-portrait

about 1850–98
Plaster
h. (incl. socle) 39.5 cm.
A.130–1980

Given by Miss I.D. Adams, daughter of George Gammon Adams in 1980. See entry for cat.no. 234.

The bust shows a man with beard and moustache wearing a bow tie and jacket with two buttons. A chest pocket holds tools which appear to be a knife and scraping tool, though these are not clearly defined. The back of the bust is hollowed out. This plaster bust may be a model for the marble self-portrait of Adams (see cat. no. 241). Another version of this bust is in the possession of Benedict Read (information supplied by Philip Ward-Jackson).

243: Unknown man

about 1850–98
Plaster
A.117–1980

Given by Miss I.D. Adams, daughter of George Gammon Adams in 1980. See entry for cat.no. 234.

This bust is in a fragmentary condition, to the extent that accurate measurements cannot be taken.

[Not illustrated].

244: Unknown man

about 1850–98
Plaster
h. (incl. socle) 78 cm.
A.124–1980

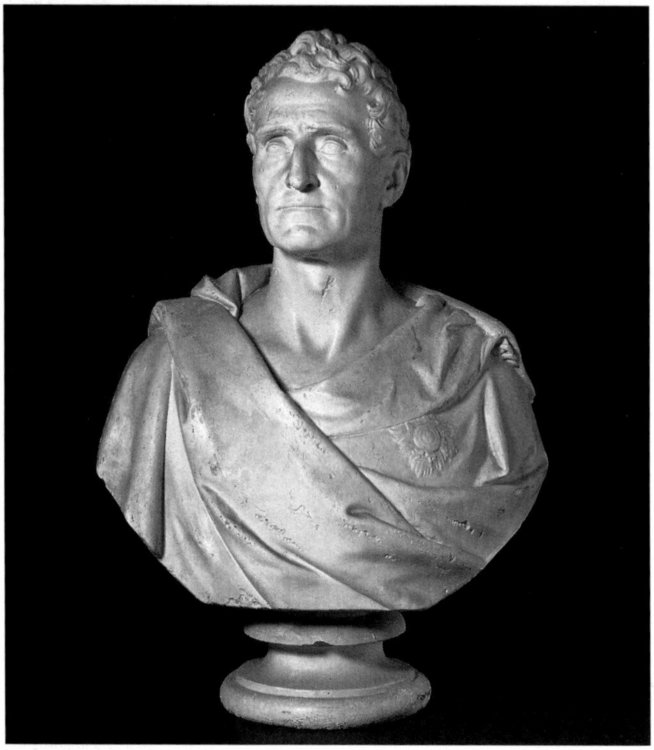

Given by Miss I.D. Adams, daughter of George Gammon Adams in 1980. See entry for cat.no. 234.

Bust of an unidentified man in classical dress.

245: Head of a young man

about 1850–98
Probably by George Gammon Adams
Painted plaster
h. (approx.) 27 cm.
A.12–2000

The present piece probably entered the Museum in 1980 with the gift of Miss I.D. Adams, daughter of George Gammon Adams in 1980; see entry for cat.no. 234. It was not however formally registered until 2000.

Fragmentary. Painted plaster, flaking. Two dowels emerge from the base of the head.

This may have been part of a model for a larger work.

246: Standing figure

about 1850–98
Plaster
A.118–1980

Given by Miss I.D. Adams, daughter of George Gammon Adams in 1980. See entry for cat.no. 234.

This figure is in a fragmentary condition, to the extent that accurate measurements cannot be taken.

[Not illustrated].

247: Seated female figure, Aegle

about 1850–98
Plaster
Oval base approx 47 cm. x 28 cm.
A.119–1980

Given by Miss I.D. Adams, daughter of George Gammon Adams in 1980. See entry for cat.no. 234.

In fragmentary condition.

This may be a model for a marble piece entitled *Aegle, Virgil*, which was exhibited at the Royal Academy in 1870 (Graves I, p. 7, no. 1166). The marble version is illustrated in the Adams album of studio photographs (*AAD Adams*, p. 18), and is annotated as being sold on the occasion of its exhibition at the Royal Academy. Aegle, the daughter of a Roman emperor, was pursued by the poet Virgil. In revenge for a trick she played on him, Virgil engulfed the city into darkness for several days. During this period of enforced darkness, the only way of lighting a torch was to place it in contact with the girl's body (Hall 1980, p. 323).

[Not illustrated].

248: Unknown woman

about 1850–98
Marble
h. 67 cm.
A.116–1980

Given by Miss I.D. Adams, daughter of George Gammon Adams in 1980. See entry for cat.no. 234.

The unidentified woman wears her hair in an ornate plaited bun, which is decorated with leaf-like ornament and what appears to be maize incorporated into the leaves.

249: Unknown woman, probably the sculptor's niece

about 1850–98
Painted plaster
h. (approx) 48 cm.
A.121–1980

Given by Miss I.D. Adams, daughter of George Gammon Adams in 1980. See entry for cat.no. 234.

A label on the back of the bust, probably attached by the donor, records the identity of the sitter as being the niece of the sculptor.

250: Unknown woman

about 1850–98
Plaster
h. 68.5 cm.
A.122–1980

Given by Miss I.D. Adams, daughter of George Gammon Adams in 1980. See entry for cat.no. 234.

The bust portrays a woman with hair loosely tied back with a rose; she has a plait-like decoration worn as a head-band. This bust is similar to one shown in the Adams album (*AAD Adams*, p. 41).

251: Unknown woman

about 1850–98
Marble
h. (incl. socle) 36.5 cm.
A.129–1980

Given by Miss I.D. Adams, daughter of George Gammon Adams in 1980. See entry for cat.no. 234.

The bust is of an unidentified woman with her plaited hair held in a bun. On the top of her head is a bow. The hair-style is similar to that of a bust of the Baroness Angela Georgina Burdett Coutts (1814–1906), as shown in the photographic album of Adams studio (*AAD Adams*, p. 38), though the woman depicted here appears slightly younger.

252: Unknown child

about 1850–98
Plaster
h. 53 cm.
A.123–1980

Given by Miss I.D. Adams, daughter of George Gammon Adams in 1980. See entry for cat.no. 234.

This bust depicts a child, probably a boy.

253: Owl

about 1850–98
Marble
h. 26.5 cm
A.131–1980

Given by Miss I.D. Adams, daughter of George Gammon Adams in 1980. See entry for cat.no. 234.

This statuette of an owl with beak open stands on a rocky base.

254: Spaniel in a kennel

about 1850–98
Plaster
h. 27 cm.
A.313–1980

Given by Miss I.D. Adams, daughter of George Gammon Adams in 1980. See entry for cat.no. 234.

This relief depicts a King Charles spaniel looking out from an arch-shaped wicker basket. The sentimental subject matter of this relief suggests it was perhaps a model for a funerary monument to a dog. The base of the relief has a space, possibly for an inscription. The back of the relief is hollowed out and there is a metal hook from the top from which it could be hung.

A white wax on slate model for a medal in the Museum's collections (inv.no. A.281–1980) possibly depicts a self-portrait of Adams with a spaniel.

Princess Louise Caroline Alberta, Duchess of Argyll and Marchioness of Lorne

(b. London 1848 – d. London 1939)

Princess Louise was Queen Victoria's sixth child; in 1871 she married the Marquis of Lorne, heir to the 8th Duke of Argyll, and became Duchess of Argyll and Marchioness of Lorne. According to Wake, Princess Louise's interest in sculpture was influenced by two female sculptors, Susan Durant and Mary Thornycroft (1814–1895). Susan Durant began teaching Princess Louise sculpture following her commissions to produce portraits of the royal children. In 1867 Mary Thornycroft was appointed to instruct the Princess in sculpture. In 1868 the Princess enrolled at the National Art Training School, attending the modelling classes together with the sculptor Henrietta Montalba [q.v.]. She exhibited at the Royal Academy in 1868, 1869 and 1874. In 1869 she exhibited 'Her Majesty the Queen' (no.1142), probably the same marble bust presented by the Queen to the Royal Academy in 1869, but withdrawn at the Princess's request in 1877, and substituted with another portrait of her mother in marble, signed and dated 1876. A terracotta portrait bust of Princess Louise, thought to be a self-portrait, is in the National Portrait Gallery (no. 4455). Louise later trained under the supervision of Sir Joseph Edgar Boehm [q.v.]. Spielmann recorded that Boehm was 'her chief instructor' and that 'applying herself under his advice . . . soon manifested singular skill in the art of sculpture, as a result of diligence applied to the cultivation of unusual natural ability.' Spielmann commented that her work as a sculptor, in particular the Kensington memorial (see entry for cat.no. 255 below), was worthy of merit, although 'it is commonly the lot of very prominent personages, that when they execute a really creditable work in the fine arts they rarely receive the full acknowledgement that is their due. The Princess, it should be understood, is a genuine artist and a hard worker'.

Spielmann 1901, pp. 160–1; Graves V, p. 95; NPG 1981, p. 354, no. 4455; Petteys 1985, p. 450; Wake 1988, esp. pp. 89–92; 302–5 (on Queen Victoria statue).

255: Queen Victoria (b.1819; r.1837–1901)

about 1888
Plaster
h. 102 cm.
A.30–1935

Given by the sculptor in 1935.

The figure was conserved in 2000. The surface appears to have been tinted a flesh-colour.

In a letter relating to its acquisition Princess Louise confirmed that this was the 'original first study' for the statue of her mother, erected in Kensington Gardens in 1893 by the Kensington Jubilee Memorial Committee to commemorate the fiftieth anniversary of the Queen's reign (Blackwood 1989, p. 65). The unveiling ceremony was held on Wednesday 28 June 1893 and was carried out by the Prince of Wales, though the Queen and Princess Louise were also in attendance; Princess Louise had symbolically 'handed to the Queen a silk cord, which her Majesty transferred to the Prince of Wales, and he, by pulling it, unveiled the statue' (*Illustrated London News*, 8 July 1893, CIII, no. 2829, p. 27; see also pp. 28 and 31). The statue is described as 'an excellent seated figure' by Gleichen, in his study *London's Open-Air Statuary*, London, p. 72. The statue was positioned in Kensington Gardens 'opposite the window of the room that she [Victoria] occupied in 1837, before her accession to the throne (*Illustrated London News*, 8 July 1893,

CIII, no. 2829, p. 27). The *Art Journal* commented that the sculpture 'has been placed in Kensington Gardens at a point visible from the rooms in Kensington Palace in which the Queen first saw the light, and first learnt that hers was the crown of Britain. The Princess has imagined her mother as she was in 1837, but has taken the liberty of giving the slender form of a girl of eighteen some of the attributes of later years more consonant with the support of her imperial responsibilities' (*Art Journal*, August 1893, p. 250).

The *Building News* recorded on 21 December 1888 that 'A sketch model of the statue has been shown to the committee for the memorial, and accepted'. The article went on to record, 'It represents the Queen as a young girl as at the time of her accession, and is founded on the well-known contemporary picture by Sir George Hayter' (*Building News*, 21 December 1888, LV, no. 1772, p. 834). For the Hayter portrait of Victoria see *NPG* 1981, p. 585, no. 1250.

In June 1893, the *Building News* commented that the statue was 'noteworthy as the first memorial executed by a woman erected in the metropolis' (*Building News*, 30 June 1893, LXIV, no. 2008, p. 893). The *Art Journal* similarly noted that 'This is the first statue, the work of a woman, that has been erected in London, and admirable in portraiture, and not wanting in some dignity and style, it reflects credit on the Princess as the most satisfactory of the many similar statues now in existence' (*Art Journal*, August 1893, p. 250). Comparing it with the newly erected Shaftesbury Memorial by Alfred Gilbert (see cat.no. 422), the *Magazine of Art* was less enthusiastic, commenting, 'Another addition, notable though less important as an artistic creation, has also been recently made to our public sculpture . . . It must be confessed that the artist seems rather to have aimed at the production of a figure typical of the dignity of the sovereign than at anything approaching portraiture. It is distinctly a work of beauty, and shows the Queen as she was at the time when she ascended the throne' (*Magazine of Art*, 1893, XVI, p. 394).

Spielmann commented that 'her [Princess Louise's] principal achievement is the large seated figure of Queen Victoria in Kensington Gardens. This statue would have done credit to some sculptors who enjoy considerable reputations, and who live by the practice of their profession' (Spielmann 1901, p. 161).

A reduced version in bronze of 1887, presented by the Earl of Halifax in 1922, is in the collections of the Leeds Museums and Galleries (see *Leeds* 1996, p. 14).

BIBLIOGRAPHY
Review 1935, p.1.

Henry Hugh Armstead

(b. London 1828 – d. London 1905)

Armstead was a sculptor, silversmith and illustrator. He was trained partly in the workshop of his father, John Armstead, a herald chaser, and subsequently at the Government School of Design, in the studio of Edward Hodges Baily [q.v.], and at the Royal Academy Schools. Early in his career Armstead concentrated mainly upon metalwork. However, he later turned to sculpture because he believed that his work in silver did not bring him sufficient critical recognition. The Art Union awarded him prizes in 1849 and 1851 for a relief of Boadicea *and a statuette of* Satan Dismayed, *and published them as small bronzes. He worked for the architect George Gilbert Scott [q.v.] on numerous occasions, most notably executing part of the podium frieze and four bronze statues for the Albert Memorial. He also produced church monuments, public statues and a few ideal works, such as* Ariel *(Christie's, South Kensington, 21 January 1998, lot 218), and* Remorse *(Tate Britain).*

Graphic 1875; Gosse 1883, pp. 171–5; Spielmann 1901, pp. 13–18; Obituary and letter in the Times, 6 December 1905; 9 December 1905, 11 December 1905; Haskell 1975; Houfe 1978 [Dictionary], p. 222; Read 1982 (various references); Beattie 1983, esp. pp. 33–4; Avery and Marsh 1985; Schroder 1988, pp. 276–9; TDA, 2, p. 474 [Ward-Jackson].

256: Sketch model for the poets and musicians frieze for the Albert Memorial

1864
Plaster
h. 53 cm. w. 173 cm.
178–1906

Given by the sculptor's widow, Mrs Sarah Armstead in 1906. Together with cat.no. 257 the present piece was originally displayed at Bethnal Green Museum, but was transferred to the Department of Architecture and Sculpture, later Sculpture Department, in 1965.

Both this relief and cat.no. 257 are the original plaster sketch-models for the central sections of the south and east sides respectively of the podium of the Albert Memorial; for the model of the memorial, see entry for cat.no. 531. Armstead made these one twelfth-scale models in order to test the content and arrangement of the frieze. Full-size plaster models were then made up, from which Armstead worked on the marble podium (Bayley 1981,

p. 69). There are few differences between the models and the finished podium friezes. These were designed in 1864 and executed in Campanella marble on the monument between 1866 and 1872. The north and west friezes, representing Architects and Sculptors respectively, are by John Birnie Philip (1824–1875).

The two sculptors seem to have been allowed considerable freedom in selecting the figures to be represented and deciding how they should be arranged. Armstead arranged the figures on both his friezes in groups according to geographical schools, whereas Philip arranged the Architects and Sculptors chronologically (*ibid.*, p. 69; Haskell 1975, p. 104). However, the sculptors worked under the guidance of George Gilbert Scott [q.v.], the architect of the memorial, and the Memorial Committee. Sir Charles Eastlake was appointed to advise on all artistic matters relating to the treatment of the frieze by the Queen in 1864 (Bayley 1981, p. 69).

The friezes were probably based upon Paul Delaroche's mural in the Amphithéâtre in the Hemicycle at the École des Beaux-Arts, Paris (1836–41), which depicts sixty-six artists from classical Greece up to the age of Louis XIV (*ibid.*, p. 67). Armstead's notebooks, now in the Royal Academy archive, show that he undertook a great deal of detailed research in order to produce, as far as possible, physiognomically accurate portraits.

For a discussion of Armstead's involvement see Haskell 1975, and also Bayley 1981, esp. pp. 67–86, and Brooks 2000 for a discussion of the memorial.

EH

257: Sketch model for the painters frieze for the Albert Memorial

1864
Plaster
h. 52 cm. w. 175 cm.
179–1906

Given by the sculptor's widow, Mrs Sarah Armstead, in 1906. Together with cat.no. 256 the present piece was originally displayed at Bethnal Green Museum, but was transferred to the Department of Architecture and Sculpture, later Sculpture Department, in 1965.

See entry for cat.no. 256.

EH

257

C. Atkins

(dates unknown; active 1869)

No infomation has been found on C. Atkins, presumably an amateur sculptor who exhibited at the South London Working Classes exhibition (see below).

258: Ivy

1869
Gilt metal in glazed wood frame
h. (relief) 34 cm. w. (relief) 13.5 cm.
h. (incl. frame) 43 cm. w. (incl. frame) 22.4 cm.
256–1869

Purchased from Mr C. Atkins, presumed to be the sculptor, in 1869 for £2 2s (2 guineas).

This plaque was purchased from the exhibitor from the South London Working Classes Exhibition of 1869. This exhibition is presumably the one which opened on 1 March 1869 at the Hall in Westminster Bridge Road, and described in the *Art Journal* as the South London Industrial Exhibition, the third annual exhibition of works 'by working men' (*Art Journal*, 1 April 1869, VIII, p. 116). The *Art Journal* commented that the exhibition was 'not satisfactory' and 'shows little or no improvement', but that 'we may not judge it, however, by ordinary rules. The productions shown are for the most part those of 'hard-handed men', whose labours all day long give them little leisure for study; who are in the strictest sense self-taught; and who at all events, look for no profit from their toil'. The *Art Journal* also noted the beneficial effects on both visitors to the exhibition as well as the exhibitors themselves, that 'minds and hearts are derived from exhibitions similar to those they saw around them; and those who competed in these displays would, in cultivating their tastes, find hidden refinement in things in which they never felt it existed before, and would be drawn into sympathy with the beautiful and the artistic' (*ibid.*, *loc.cit.*).

Exhibited
Westminster Hall South London Working Classes Exhibition of 1869.

John Bacon the Younger

(b. London 1777 – d. London 1859)

John Bacon the Younger was the son of the sculptor John Bacon [q.v.], in whose studio he initially trained. In 1789 Bacon attended the Royal Academy Schools, gaining silver and gold medals in 1793 and 1797 respectively. On the death of his father in 1799 he took over his father's prosperous studio. Cox-Johnson commented, 'The European Magazine *tells us that in 1803, 1813, and 1815 he had held exhibitions at his studio, open, free of charge, to the public. This unusual arrangement met with great success, and the public responded by applauding his work as heartily as they had approved of his father's'. Whinney noted 'like his father, he [Bacon the Younger] was a neo-classical artist by accident rather than desire, and the equestrian statue of William III, designed by the elder and carried out by the younger Bacon, is clear testimony of this; for it is still in the Baroque tradition, and might well be mistaken for a work of the 1730s'. Bacon exhibited at the Royal Academy between 1792 and 1824. In 1808, when he took on Charles Manning as his business partner, Bacon went into semi-retirement. One of the primary conditions in the indenture stipulated that all works produced would only bear the name of John Bacon. Cox-Johnson suggested, 'The contract with Manning explains why the younger Bacon was never elected to the Academy. To use the assistance of workmen was permissible; to employ a 'ghost' was unforgiveable. It also accounts for the vast body of work that bears the name of Bacon'. Whinney similarly comments, 'Bacon was unpopular with his fellow-artists, who never elected him even to an Associateship of the Royal Academy and who clearly felt with Flaxman [q.v.] that his works were flimsy, and that he had neglected the pure standards of sculpture'. See entry for cat.no. 260 for an example of the collaborative work of Bacon and Manning.*

Graves I, pp. 88–9; Cox-Johnson 1959; Gunnis 1968, pp. 28–32; Whinney 1988, pp. 313, 370; Thieme-Becker, 2, p. 328; TDA, 3, p. 26 [Bryant].

259: Monument to Anna Rhodes (1764–1796)

signed; about 1796
Marble
London Diocesan Fund Loan 1

Signed beneath the right hand standing figure in the upper half of the monument: J. Bacon, junr./Sculptor.

Inscribed: Erected by a Sister in Memory of her beloved ANNA CECILIA,/Daughter of CHRISTOPHER RHODES Esqr; of *Chatham* in the County of *Kent*. She departed/this Life, June 2d. 1796, aged 32. Her Remains were deposited in the 42d. Vault of this Chapel./Distinguished by her fine Understanding, and a most amiable Disposition of Heart,/She was the Delight of her Parents, and the Admiration of all who knew her./At the Age of 17, the Small-pox stripped off all the Bloom of youthful Beauty,/And being followed by a dreadful Nervous-disorder, withered those fair Prospects of earthly Happiness/Which were expected from her uncommon Affection, Sensibility and Tenderness./After enduring this afflictive Dispensation many Years,/When it was difficult to say which exceeded, her Sufferings or her Submission;/Her Friends' Concern for her Sorrows, or their Admiration of her Patience;/She was released by Death, and received into that World where there shall be no more Pain,/But GOD himself shall wipe away Tears from every Eye.

Alas! how vain are feeble Words to tell/What once she was, and why I lov'd so well:/None else but he who form'd the Heart can know/How great her Worth, or how extreme my Woe!/Blest Calv'ry, on thy crimson Top I see,/Suff'rings and Death, with Life and Love agree;/Justice severe and smiling Mercy join,/And thro' the Gloom we see the Glory shine.

From the now demolished church of St James's, Hampstead Road, London. On loan from the London Diocesan Fund, from 18 October 1967, together with cat.no. 361.

In June 1965, enquiries made by the Museum as to the fate of the dismantled memorials from the church of St James, Hampstead resulted in the loan to the Museum of the present piece and cat.no. 361. A preparatory drawing for the present piece, purchased from Miss Annie Bacon – a descendant of the sculptor – is held in the Department of Prints, Drawings and Paintings (inv.no. E.1556–1931); see Physick 1969, pp. 179–80, fig. 138 on p. 178. Physick noted that a further monument to Anna Rhodes, commissioned by the mother of the deceased from Bacon the Younger, erected in Whitfield's Tabernacle, Tottenham Court Road, London, was destroyed during the Second World War: a drawing for this monument is also in the Museum's Department of Prints, Drawings and Paintings (inv.no. E.1050–1966); see *ibid.*, p. 179

We are grateful to the London Diocesan Fund for allowing us to include this in the catalogue.

BIBLIOGRAPHY

Gunnis 1968, p. 29 (listed as in St James's Church, Hampstead); Physick 1969, p. 179; Busco 1994, p. 139, fig. 148 on p. 141 (not cited as being in the V&A).

Though this memorial is signed by John Bacon Junior, it is more likely to be by Charles Manning, with whom Bacon was in partnership from 1808. The indenture, signed on 24 June 1808 is discussed by Ann Cox-Johnson, who states: 'It has been known for a while that much of the later work credited to John Bacon was by Samuel Manning, but from these documents it seems that we must consider it possible, or even probable that any work executed between 1808 and 1812 may be partly or wholly by Charles Manning. Since the business was to be "carried on and conducted in the name of John Bacon only", we have no precise means of distributing the responsibility for any particular monument, though judging from the provision that Manning should devote his whole time to the business while Bacon was only to attend as much as the thought "fit and proper", it may well be that many works wrought during that period, which have hitherto been confidently attributed to Bacon, were, in fact by Manning' (Cox-Johnson 1959, p. 241; see also Graves V, p. 177 and Gunnis 1968, pp. 31–2, 251–3.).

BIBLIOGRAPHY

Hodgkinson 1971/2, p. 339, pl. 5 on p. 336.

260: Memorial plaque to Elizabeth Raynsford (1722–1810)

1810
By John Bacon the Younger and probably Charles Manning
Marble
h. 68.6 cm.
A.12–1965

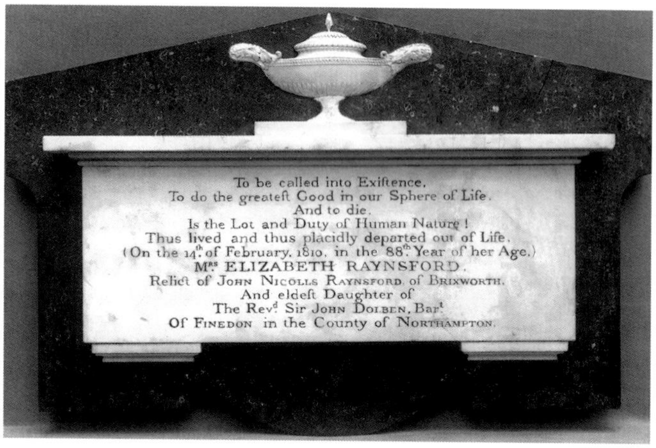

Signed and dated: J.BACON JUNr Ft LONDON 1810

Inscribed: To be called into Existence,/To do the greatest Good in our Sphere of Life,/And to die./Is the Lot and Duty of Human Nature !/Thus lived and thus placidly departed out of Life,/(On the 14th. of February. 1810, in the 88th. Year of her Age.)/MRS. ELIZABETH RAYNSFORD,/Relict of JOHN NICOLLS RAYNSFORD OF BRIXWORTH./And eldest Daughter of/The Revd. Sir JOHN DOLBEN, Bart./Of FINEDON in the County of NORTHAMPTON.

From the church of St. Denis, Faxton. Given by the Rector and Churchwardens of Lamport with Faxton, Northants, in 1965 together with cat.nos. 17, 62 and 126 in 1965.

See the entry for cat.no. 126 for an earlier monument by John Hunt to John Nicolls Raynsford, the husband of Elizabeth Raynsford.

261: Monument to Admiral Lord Rodney in St Paul's Cathedral (1719–1792)

signed; 1810
Plaster with metal armature
h. 49 cm.
A.20–1931

Signed at the front to the right of the base: I Bacon
Inscribed on the front: LD RODNEY

Purchased from Miss Annie Bacon, 17 Gilston Road, London in 1931 together with a bust of John Boydell; see entry for cat.no. 73; the price paid for the present piece was £15. Miss Bacon was a descendant of the sculptor John Bacon the Younger [q.v.].

The present piece was originally ascribed to John Bacon the Elder [q.v.] and thought to have been the model for the monument to Lord Rodney in Spanish Town, Jamaica, erected in 1784 to commemorate the victory of Lord Rodney over the French on 12th April 1782. Joan Coutu has recently re-attributed it to Bacon the Younger, and it is now thought to be the competition model he submitted in 1810 for the monument to Admiral Lord Rodney in St Paul's Cathedral. Joan Coutu has commented, 'The plaster model is similar, in its triangular composition and in its modern dress, to many of the monuments erected in St Paul's under the auspices of the Committee of Taste in the 1790s and early 1780s. The picturesque theatrical flair of the Victoria and Albert model is more in keeping with some of Bacon the Younger's grander designs – rather than Bacon the Elder's – such as the monument to General Sir George Moore (1810–1815) in St Paul's, which also has a very similar base to the Victoria and Albert model' (Coutu 1998, p. 55). The competition for the monument to Lord Rodney was in the event won by John Charles Felix Rossi (1762–1839).

For the previous attribution to Bacon the Elder and its probably erroneous connection with the Spanish Town monument, see Leslie and Taylor 1865, pp. 442–3; Cundall 1907, pp. 65–8; Cox-Johnson 1961, p. 30; Lewis 1967, pp. 365–73.

BIBLIOGRAPHY

Illustrated Souvenir 1924, p. 118, illus., cat.no. S.11; *Palace of Arts* 1924, p. 61, cat. S.11; *Review* 1931, p. 53; Esdaile 1946, p. 68; Cox-Johnson 1961, pp. 17, 29–31; Lewis 1967, p. 366; Whinney 1988, p. 308; Coutu 1998, pp. 52, fig. 8 on p. 54, p. 55.

EXHIBITED

British Empire Exhibition, Fine Art Section, Palace of Arts, Wembley, 1924, lent by Miss Bacon, cat.no. S.11.

Edward Hodges Baily R.A.

(b. Bristol 1788 – d. London 1867)

Baily began his career modelling portraits in wax. He was later introduced to John Flaxman [q.v.] in whose studio he remained for seven years, assisting Flaxman with many of his commissions. In 1808 Baily enrolled at the Royal Academy Schools, and was elected A.R.A. in 1817 and R.A. in 1820. From 1809 he was employed by Rundell and Bridge, the prestigious gold and silversmiths. Joseph Neeld was one of Baily's most important patrons, for whom the sculptor produced works for Grittleton House, Wiltshire. His public sculpture included reliefs on the Marble Arch, London and the figure of Nelson for the column in Trafalgar Square. Portrait sculpture was an important aspect of Baily's career. He exhibited at the Royal Academy between 1810 and 1862, and also at the British Institution between 1812 and 1840. A collection of papers relating to Baily and his works are held in the Department of Manuscripts, British Library (Manuscript no. 38678); I am grateful to Martin Greenwood for this information.

Art Journal, 1 June 1867, pp. 170–1; Graves I, pp. 93–5; Graves 1908, pp. 19–20; Kenworthy-Browne 1966; Gunnis 1968, pp. 32–6; Thieme-Becker, 2, pp. 374–5; Kader 1996; TDA, 3, pp. 78–9, [Eustace].

262: Eve at the fountain

about 1818
Plaster
h. 87 cm.
A.3–2000

There is no information on the provenance of the present piece, which until 2000 was an unregistered object in the Museum.

This is probably the plaster model for the marble group *Eve at the Fountain* executed by Baily in 1821 for the Philosophical Society of Bristol, and now in the Bristol City Art Gallery, which was exhibited at the Royal Academy in 1822 (*Bristol* 1966, inv.no. N.6929; Graves I, p. 93, no. 986). Gunnis suggested that it was in 1818 at the Royal Academy that Baily 'showed a model of his most celebrated work, "Eve at the Fountain", which at once gained him a European reputation; it is curious to reflect that he had made the original design as the handle of a cover for a soup-tureen for one of the City Companies. In 1821 "Eve" was executed in marble and purchased by the citizens of Bristol for their Literary Institute' (Gunnis 1968, p. 32). The model, referred to by Gunnis as being exhibited at the Royal Academy in 1818, is in fact probably either that exhibited in 1819 'Sketch for Eve, etc.' or 'Eve at the Fountain, etc.' exhibited in 1820 (Graves I, p. 93, nos. 1209 and 1008 respectively). Gunnis also noted that a replica, dated 1845, is in the Glyptotek, Copenhagen (Gunnis 1968, p. 35). A plaster *Eve at the Fountain* by Baily was exhibited at the 1853 Great Industrial Exhibition in Dublin, no. 1001 (see *Dublin* 1853, p. 174, no. 1001). A 'plaster statue' of *Eve at the Fountain* by Baily included in the 1862 International Exhibition, London, British Division, class XXXIX, B – Living artists, may be identical with the present piece (see *International Exhibition* 1862, p. 141).

263: Marius, among the ruins of Carthage

about 1833
Plaster
h. 163 cm.
8126–1862

Purchased from Mr R.J. Lane, A.R.A. in 1862 for £12, said to be a relative of the sculptor; I am grateful to Martin Greenwood for this information, which comes from the Baily papers held at the British Library; see biography above.

This is the original plaster model for the marble figure entitled 'Caius Marius sitting on the Ruins of Carthage, etc', exhibited at the Royal Academy in 1833 (Graves I, p. 94, no. 1182). For a summary of the history of Gaius [Caius] Marius and further references, see Hornblower and Spawforth 1996, p. 925.

Various references to Baily's *Marius* are to be found in the papers held at the British Library. An engraving of the figure is included in the *National Magazine* of 1857, and is discussed at length in the accompanying text: 'There are no statues in the world beside which this figure might not stand . . . Another reason why we have selected this particular performance of Mr. Baily's as our specimen of his art, is, because it remains uncommissioned in his studio; and we thus introduce our readers to a work with which they have not had such obvious opportunities of making acquaintance as have been afforded them in reference to so many another masterpiece from the same hand. There are few things finer than this in the English school; and it cannot, we imagine, be long ere it will find its way into marble' (*National Magazine* 1857); I am grateful to Martin Greenwood for this reference.

BIBLIOGRAPHY
International Exhibition 1862, p. 151, class XXXIX, British Division, B – Living artists, supplemental list; *Inventory* 1863, p. 171, no. 11944.

EXHIBITED
International Exhibition of 1862.

264: Maternal affection

signed and dated 1837
Marble
h. 94 cm.
A.33–1964

Signed on the base at the back: E.H. BAILY, RA./Sculpt/London/1837

Formerly in the Neeld Collection at Grittleton House, Wiltshire (see Kenworthy-Browne 1966). Purchased from Mallett at Bourdon House, 2 Davies Street, London, together with cat.no. 265 in 1964 for £250, under the bequest of Miss Ellen Barber. Mallett's acted as agents for Mrs J. Bourne (formerly Miss Neeld). Most of the Neeld Collection was later to be sold by Christie's on 22 September 1966. Joseph Neeld (1789–1856) was a Director of the silversmiths Rundell and Bridge, at which Baily was the chief modeller. Neeld's great-uncle was Philip Rundell; see entry for cat.no. 518.

The forefinger of the right hand and tips of three of the fingers on the left hand are missing.

This group was discussed and illustrated in an article in the *Art Union* of 1847, 'This is engraved from a very beautiful composition which was exhibited by Mr. Baily, in the plaster, in the year 1823. He received no commission for the first marble work that was executed from it in the following year, but brought it forward as a speculation. Not being, however, successful in effecting a sale, it was offered for disposal by lottery, with another smaller work; the prices of the two amounting to one thousand guineas. Not more than half of the numbers were taken, but the lottery was, nevertheless, determined, when the smaller work became the property of the Duke of Buccleugh; and the larger, as remaining allotted among the undrawn numbers, was still the property of the sculptor; he then announced a determination to sell the work for three hundred and fifty pounds, which being made known to Mr Neeld, he purchased it. The group was repeated in marble for the late Earl of Egremont, who will long be remembered as a liberal patron of art. In proportion, the figures are what is called small life size: the mother, if erect, would stand about five feet in height . . . The group is not of the high order of subject to which others by this artist belong, as for instance his 'Eve'; but it is, nevertheless, treated with utmost dignity of the art; thus the Mother is a figure, which, otherwise disposed, might be a Venus' (*Art Union*, 1 April 1847, p. 120, engraving facing page). However, there appears to be some discrepancy in this account; Baily exhibited 'Affection etc' at the Royal Academy in 1823, no. 1102; in 1825 he also exhibited 'Affection: a group' at the British Institution, no. 410, possibly the same piece. In 1837 he showed 'Group, Maternal Affection' at the Royal Academy, no. 1179, probably the present piece, which was later purchased by Joseph Neeld (Graves I, p. 94, nos. 1102 and 1179; Graves 1908, p. 20, no. 410). Another version of this group, signed and dated 1841 is known (Museum records; London art market 1966). The same or possibly a further version, signed and dated 1841 is in the Fitzwilliam Museum, Cambridge (inv.no. M.3–1974). The group was also reproduced in Parian ware (see Atterbury 1989, fig. 6 on p. 12; I am grateful to Alexander Kader for this reference).

BIBLIOGRAPHY

Kenworthy-Browne 1966, p. 712; TDA, 3, p. 79 [Eustace].

265: Prince Albert (1819–1861)

signed and dated 1841
Marble
h. 80 cm.
A.34–1964

Signed and dated on the back: E.H. BAILY, R.A./Sculpt London/1841

Commissioned from the artist by Queen Victoria and rejected; subsequently purchased by Joseph Neeld in 1848. Purchased from Mallett at Bourdon House, 2 Davies Street, London, together with cat.no. 264 in 1964 for a total of £250, under the bequest of Miss Ellen Barber. See entry for cat.no. 264.

The model for the present piece was made by Baily in Brussels while the Prince Consort was staying with the King of the Belgians. The bust was commissioned by Queen Victoria in 1840, though Kenworthy-Browne records that it was 'rejected because it made its subject look too old' (Kenworthy-Browne 1966, p. 712).

BIBLIOGRAPHY

Graves I, p. 94; Kenworthy-Browne 1966, p. 712.

EXHIBITED

In 1841 Baily exhibited 'Prince Albert (unfinished)' no. 1217 at the Royal Academy, presumably the present piece; *The Arts of the Victorians*, Japan, Kobe Hankyu store; Kyoto Museum of Art; Tokyo, Daimaru Museum; Fukouka, City Museum, 29 February 1992 to 5 June 1993, cat.no. 5.

266: Eve listening to the voice

signed and dated 1842
Marble
h. 96.5 cm.
468–1875

Signed and dated on the integral base at the back of the figure:

The Original EVE by/E.H. BAILY, R.A. Sculp. London 1842

Given by Wynn Ellis Esq. in 1875. Transferred on loan from the Department of Architecture and Sculpture to Bethnal Green Museum in 1928; returned to the Sculpture Department in 1987.

Departmental records note that in 1881 a toe was 'discovered by the Police [who at that date acted as security guards in the Museum] on the 26th October, 1881, to have been broken off. The piece was found, and the statue repaired', a crack through the right arm and on across the left knee was also recorded.

The figure depicts *Eve listening to the voice of Satan*, a subject probably inspired by Milton's *Paradise Lost*; the composition is related to the antique sculpture of a *Nymph with a shell* in the Louvre (see Haskell and Penny 1981, pp. 280–2). Another version, signed and dated 1849, which had been commissioned by Joseph Neeld for Grittleton House, Wiltshire, was sold by Christie's (the property of Mrs J. Bourne neé Miss Celia Kathleen Mary Neeld, formerly in the collection of the late Captain L.W. Neeld of Kelston Park and Grittleton) on 22 September 1966, lot 9. In 1996 this figure was with Daniel Katz (see *Katz* 1996, p. 118, cat.no. 56, illus. p. 119); it was later sold at Sotheby's, London on 6 June 1997, lot 62. A version of a closely related figure entitled *Eve at the Fountain* signed and dated 1822, is in the Bristol City Art Gallery (see *Bristol* 1966, [unpaginated]; TDA, 3, pp. 78–9, illus. on p. 78, [Eustace]). For a plaster model for that figure, see entry for cat.no. 262.

In a lecture delivered at the Royal Academy, the sculptor Henry Weekes commented, 'Baily, an earnest pupil of Flaxman, was a more finished modeler [sic] than his master, though with less feeling and sentiment, and less power in design. What he gained by the means I have alluded to, was knowledge, not genius, and it carried him a great way: the latter, even his great teacher could not impart to him, though he obtained under his tuition much that we may designate as purity of style and taste. You may think it strange in me if I say that, notwithstanding he produced one of the most beautiful examples of English ideal Sculpture as yet known to us – his Eve – he was wanting in genius!' (Weekes 1880, pp. 296–7).

In 1841 Baily exhibited 'Eve listening to the Voice, etc.' probably the plaster model for the present piece (Graves I, p. 94, no. 1219).

Bibliography
Bequests and Donations 1901, p. 152; Gunnis 1968, p. 35; *Katz* 1996, p. 118, cat.no. 56.

267: Unknown man, possibly David Kent
(dates unknown)

signed and dated 1850
Marble
h. (incl. base) 76 cm.
A.71–1965

Signed and dated on the back: E.H. Baily.R.A. Sculp. 1850

Bequeathed by Rupert Gunnis Esq., Hungershall Lodge, Tunbridge Wells, Kent. The bust is illustrated in situ at Hungershall Lodge prior to its acquisition by the Museum in 1965; see Knox 1998, fig. 3 on p. 88.

The identity of the sitter is not known. A photograph of another version of the present piece is identified in the Conway Library at the Courtauld Institute of Art as being David Kent (information supplied by Alexander Kader).

Bibliography
Knox 1998, fig. 3 on p. 88.

Exhibited
In 1850 Baily exhibited four male portrait busts at the Royal Academy; two were anonymous, one portrayed Lord Gough, and the other Sir John Herschel. The present piece does not appear to represent Lord Gough or Sir John Herschel, but could be one of those unidentified (nos. 1432 and 1437).

Percival Ball

(b. London 1845 – d. London 1900)

Percival Ball exhibited at the Royal Academy between 1865 and 1882. He showed mainly portrait busts, including one of Amelia Ann Edwards (no. 1554), presumably the version now in the National Portrait Gallery (no. 929). In 1868 he was commissioned to design two groups entitled Instruction, *for the external pediment of the Museum's Lecture Theatre, which were produced in terracotta around 1870 by Doulton and Co. Ball's close relationship between the Doulton potteries and the Lambeth School of Art is discussed by Beattie. Beattie recorded that in 1863 as he was about to enter the Royal Academy Schools (where he was awarded the Gold Medal for sculpture in 1865), Ball was appointed master of the modelling class at Lambeth. He travelled on the Continent, staying in Paris, Munich and Rome from 1870 to 1886. Beattie also noted that 'before he left for Australia in 1886, Ball was to establish a sound reputation among informed critics for work which reflects the influence of his master Henry Weekes's homely neo-classicism. He was by no means an innovator, but his introduction to Lambeth as a pupil-teacher was a significant step in Sparkes's plan to raise the status of the modelling class'. On his arrival in Melbourne and on the death of the Australian sculptor James Gilbert, Ball was given the task of completing the monument to Sir Redmond Barry and other works begun by Alfred Gilbert [q.v.]. In 1898 Ball was commissioned to produce a bronze relief panel depicting* Phryne before Praxiteles *for the exterior of the New South Wales National Gallery of Art in Sydney (1900). This relief, together with the marble and bronze statue of Sir William Wallace for the Botanical Gardens, Ballarat, Australia (1889), are generally considered to be the best examples of his work.*

Graves I, p. 101, no. 1554; Parkes 1921, p. 161; Moore 1934, p. 83; Scarlett 1980, pp. 34–6; NPG 1981, p. 181, no. 929; Physick 1982, p. 118, illus. 122; Beattie 1983, p. 18; NSW 1989, p. 7; Thieme-Becker, 2, p. 412; McCulloch 1994, p. 68.

268: Westminster boy

signed and dated 187 (3?)
From a model by Percival Ball; executed by Doulton & Watts
Terracotta
h. 146 cm.
A.23–2000

Signed and dated on base: P.BALL.SC.ROME 187 (3?)

The property of Baroness Burdett-Coutts, this figure was received into the Museum from 28 August 1873 by Messrs Doulton & Watts, Lambeth Pottery, who appear to have produced the figure and acted as intermediary for the loan (see biography above for relationship between Ball and Doulton & Watts). As a redundant loan the present piece was formally accessioned by the Sculpture Department in 2000.

There is a hole in the top of the head. The figure has recently been conserved.

A letter dated 23 August 1873 on the registered papers relating to the loan of this object to the Museum, records that this figure was intended by the lender Baroness Burdett Coutts to act as a fountain figure to be placed in Vincent Square, London. A John Hassard writes:

'Sir

Mr Percival Ball has lately executed, in Rome, a figure of a "Westminster Boy" for the Baroness Burdett-Coutts, – intended to ornament a fountain she intends to erect in Vincent Square, (the Westminster Boys play-ground). The figure has been most ably carried out in terracotta by Messrs Doulton & Co. The Dean of Westminster and Lady Augusta Stanley were in Rome – before the model left the studio, & expressed their high approval of it. As the fountain will not be erected before April next, the Baroness thinks that you may perhaps like to exhibit the Figure, in the South Kensington Museum, as a temporary loan'. The figure was in the event not installed in Vincent Square, but remained at the Museum as a loan, until officially registered in 2000.

A mortar board worn by the figure which is shown in a photograph accompanying the letter is now missing.

W.H. Barrett

(dates unknown; active 1868 – 1872)

A sculptor listed in Graves as W. Barrett, 2 Alma Terrace Kennington (the same address as noted in the Journal for the Society of Arts; *see below), exhibited* Innocence *at the Royal Academy in 1872 (no. 1486).*

Graves I, p. 129, no. 1486.

269: Head of a boy

1868
Marble
h. 25.5 cm. w. 22.5 cm.
253–1869

The monogram WXD is signed in pencil on the reverse.

Purchased from Mr W.H. Barrett, presumed to be the sculptor, in 1869 for £2.

This panel depicting a boy's head in high relief was entered by the sculptor, together with another carving by him under the pseudonym WXD, in the Society of Arts Art-Workmanship Competition of 1868. He also exhibited a pedestal for a bust, consisting of carved marble combined with mosaic (*Journal for the Society of Arts,* 5 March 1869, XVII, no. 850, p. 245, nos. 25, 30, 31). The judges' report recorded that the present piece was 'satisfactory'. Barrett was awarded a prize of £4 for this panel and for a medallion head of Michelangelo.

Exhibited
Society of Arts Art-Workmanship Competition of 1868.

William Behnes

(b. London 1794/5 – d. London 1864)

Behnes's exact date of birth is uncertain. In an obituary in the Art Journal *the writer suggested Behnes was born in about 1794, whereas Gunnis gives a date of 1795. Behnes was the son of a Hanoverian pianoforte maker living in London. The Behnes family, who had moved to Ireland, returned to London and, encouraged by his parents, Behnes commenced studies at the Royal Academy. He probably began work as an independent sculptor around 1819. The lengthy obituary on Behnes in the* Art Journal *recorded: 'The great majority of his busts, and all his large statues, were executed at Osnaburg Street, where he resided the greater part of his life'. In an earlier article in the* Art Journal *of 1862 discussing public sculpture, the writer commented: 'There is not in the history of sculpture any record of an artist who has been more uniformly successful as a bust-maker than Behnes . . . But his statues have nothing of the quality of his busts'. The* Art Journal *obituary further recorded, 'He held, till his death, the appointment of Sculptor in Ordinary to the Queen, but the distinction was so purely honorary that it did not produce a single commission'. Behnes exhibited consistently at the Royal Academy between 1815 and 1863, but died almost destitute, having been declared bankrupt in 1861. The* Art Journal *commented, 'The story of the latter part of his career is indeed melancholy, adding another to the not too rare instances of men of genius falling victims to their own self-indulgence'. Correspondence and papers relating to this sculptor are held at Manchester University, John Rylands Library.*

Art Journal, 1 April 1862, p. 98; Art Journal, 1 March 1864, pp. 83–4; Graves I, pp. 166–8; Gunnis 1968, pp. 45–8; Thieme-Becker, 3, p. 204; TDA, 3, pp. 509–10 [Greenwood].

270: Unknown woman

signed and dated 1827
Marble
h. 69 cm.
A.66–1949

Signed on the back: W. BEHNES/SCULPR. LONDON. 1827.

Purchased from Messrs Kerin, 15 Davies Street, London together with cat.no. 64 in 1949. The purchase price for the two busts was £120, the individual price for this bust being £20.

The identity of the subject of this bust is unknown. Behnes exhibited two busts of female sitters at the Royal Academy in 1827: the Countess of Jersey, and Lady Southampton (Graves I, p. 167, nos. 1103 and 1113).

271: John Singleton Copley, 1st Baron Lyndhurst (1772–1863) created Baron Lyndhurst in 1827

signed and dated 1841
Plaster
h. 84 cm.
A.27–2000

Signed on truncation at the back: W. BEHNES SCUP^r^ Publis^d^/as the Act Directs/1841

On loan from the sculptor, William Behnes from a date prior to 1870, and probably one of the four 'Plaster busts, &c' described as lent by 'the late W. Behnes, Esq' to the Museum prior to 1870 (*List* 1870, p. ii). As a redundant loan the present piece was formally accessioned by the Sculpture Department in 2000.

This is a plaster model of the bust of Lord Lyndhurst produced for Trinity College, Cambridge in 1844 (Gunnis 1968, p. 47; Kilmurray 1979, p. 137). The obituary for Behnes in the *Art Journal* recorded his bust of Lord Lyndhurst as being of 'very high character' (*Art Journal*, 1 March 1864, p. 83). Behnes exhibited a bust of Lord

Lyndhurst together with that of the Duchess of Somerset at the display 'Sculpture of the United Kingdom', held at the South Kensington, later Victoria and Albert Museum in July 1857; see also entries for cat.nos. 272, 274, 276, 392 and 500.

The inscription implies the bust may have been intended to be executed in bronze, although I have been unable to find any surviving versions.

272: Duchess of Somerset (perhaps Lady Emily Somerset) (dates unknown)

signed and dated 1866
Plaster
h. 77 cm.
A.26–2000

Signed and dated on the truncation: W BEHNES Sculpt LONDON 1866

On loan from the sculptor, William Behnes from a date prior to 1870, this is probably one of the four 'Plaster busts, &c' described as lent by 'the late W. Behnes, Esq' to the Museum prior to 1870 (*List* 1870, p. ii). As a redundant loan the present piece was formally accessioned by the Sculpture Department in 2000.

The identification of the sitter as the Duchess of Somerset is noted in departmental records.

According to Gunnis, Behnes produced a statue of Lady Emily Somerset in 1844 (Gunnis 1968, p. 46). Gunnis cites the *Builder* of 1844, a review of an exhibition held at Westminster Hall. No. 147 is noted as 'A Portrait statue of Lady Emily, daughter of the Duke of Beaufort, by Behnes' (*Builder*, 27 July 1844, LXXVII, pp. 367–8). The exhibition was described by the *Art Journal* as 'highly creditable; it contains many respectable and many fine works'. Behnes exhibited busts of the Duke of Somerset at the Royal Academy in 1846 and 1856 (Graves I, pp. 168–9, nos. 1502 and 1317).

At the exhibition of 'Sculpture of the United Kingdom' held at the South Kensington, later Victoria and Albert Museum in July 1857, Behnes exhibited busts of 'Lord Lyndhurst and the Duchess of Somerset, the latter is a sweet production' (*Building News*, 17 July 1857, p. 740); see also entries for cat.nos. 271, 274, 276, 392 and 500.

273: Benjamin Disraeli, 1st Earl of Beaconsfield (1804–1881)

about 1850
Possibly by William Behnes
Plaster
h. 78 cm.
A.10–2000

There is no information available on the provenance of the present piece, which until 2000 was recorded as an unregistered object in the Museum. It may have been one of the four 'Plaster busts, &c' described as lent by 'the late W. Behnes, Esq' to the Museum prior to 1870 (*List* 1870, p. ii).

Several busts of Disraeli, including one in marble by William Behnes, are housed at Hughenden Manor, High Wycombe, Bucks, though none relates to the present piece (I am grateful to Victoria Nelson for this information).

274: Lord William George Frederic Cavendish Bentinck (1802–1848)

about 1850–7
Possibly by William Behnes
Painted plaster
h. (greatest) 91 cm.
A.11–2000

There is no information available on the provenance of the present piece, which until 2000 was recorded as an unregistered object in the Museum. It may have been one of the four 'Plaster busts, &c' described as lent by 'the late W. Behnes, Esq' to the Museum prior to 1870 (*List* 1870, p. ii).

Fragmentary; the bottom half of this model is missing.

A statue of Bentinck by Thomas Campbell [q.v.] was erected in Cavendish Square, London in 1851 (see Blackwood 1989, p. 182). I am grateful to Philip Ward-Jackson for his identification of the sitter of the present piece.

Behnes exhibited a statuette of Lord George Bentinck at the Royal Academy in 1853 (Graves I, p. 168, no. 1339). Described in the *Art Journal* review of the exhibition as, 'Statuette of Lord George Bentinck, W. BEHNES. The figure stands in a relieved pose on one foot; it is easy and graceful' (*Art Journal*, 1 June 1853, p. 152). It is not known if this was the present piece or a marble version. Although this may have been intended as a model for a statue of Lord Bentinck, none is recorded by Gunnis. Behnes exhibited a statuette of Lord George Bentinck at the exhibition 'Sculpture of the United Kingdom', held a the South Kensington, later Victoria and Albert Museum in July 1857; see also entries for cat.nos. 271, 272, 276, 392 and 500.

275: Sir Robert Peel (1788–1850)

about 1852–5
Plaster
h. 99 cm.
A.28–2000

On loan from the sculptor, William Behnes from a date prior to 1870, this is probably one of the four 'Plaster busts, &c' described in 1870 as lent by 'the late W. Behnes, Esq' (*List* 1870, p. ii). As a redundant loan the present piece was formally accessioned by the Sculpture Department in 2000.

Though identified on the original Museum records as Lord George Bentinck, Philip Ward-Jackson has suggested Sir Robert Peel as the identity of the sitter.

Gunnis recorded that Behnes executed three statues of Peel: in Leeds (1852), Bradford (1855) and another formerly at Cheapside, now part of the Police College, Hendon, London (Gunnis 1968, p. 46). Comparison with an engraving in the *Illustrated London News* of the Leeds version, and a photograph of the Cheapside version, bears some resemblance to the present piece, though differences are apparent in the position of the scroll and drapery over the left shoulder (see *Illustrated London News*, 28 August 1852, p. 157). I am grateful to Philip Ward-Jackson for this reference; see also Blackwood 1989, p. 184).

JOHN BELL

(b. Hopton 1811 – d. London 1895)

Bell began his career as a monumental mason carving gravestones; in 1829 he started attending the Royal Academy Schools. Gunnis recorded the diverse scope of his work; a number of objects, including fish-knives and a doorstop, were exhibited by Bell at the British Manufacture and Decorative Art exhibition of 1848. Bell also collaborated with Copeland, Coalbrookdale [q.v.] and Felix Summerly (alias Henry Cole [q.v.]) Art-Manufactures. A wax model by Bell of Two Kissing Cupids *(a design for a paperweight) was produced by Minton, and an example was given to the Museum by Henry Cole, who was a friend of the artist, in 1854 (inv.no. 205–1854). A further example of Bell's diversity is recorded by Gunnis, 'In 1845 he had designed for Colbrookdale [sic] Company a fearsome object called "the deerhound hall table," which consisted of four life-sized deer-hounds, cast in iron and seated on their haunches, supporting a table decorated with "emblems of the chase and with leaves and fruit of the vine"'. Among his best-known works are the* Eagle Slayer *(cat.no. 276), and the marble corner group* America *for the Albert Memorial in Hyde Park. Further examples of his monumental work are the Guards Crimean War Memorial, the Wellington Memorial at Guildhall, and Guards Memorial in Waterloo Place. Bell gave an address on 19 April 1858 entitled* British Sculpture in connection with the Department of Science and Art, *in which he lamented the lack of encouragement and opportunity for young British sculptors. Bell exhibited at the Royal Academy between 1832 and 1879, and at the British Institution between 1837 and 1845. Despite widespread contemporary critical acclaim for Bell's work, most significantly for the* Eagle Slayer, *Gunnis was to comment, 'his later groups exhibited at the Royal Academy were remarkable for nothing but bad taste and sickly sentimentality . . . They were much admired at that time and are typical of the work which has brought the sculpture of the late Victorian era so deservedly into disrepute'. Bell is known to have given three plaster models to the Museum: in 1879 he gave a model of an obelisk for the memorial to the 1851 International Exhibition to the Structural Division (present location unknown, probably no longer in existence); in 1884 a model of Oliver Cromwell (inv.no. 1121–1884) was acquired – irreparable damage meant however that it was de-accessioned in 1935; and a statue of the 'late Prince Consort, represented as a Christian Knight in armour' was given by Bell to the Museum in 1894 (inv.no. 336–1894); it too was de-accessioned, in 1958.*

Graves I, pp. 174–5; Graves 1908, p. 40; Gunnis 1968, pp. 48–9; Bonython 1982 [Cole], p. 27; Atterbury 1989, pp. 22, 59, 103, fig. 274, p. 260; Thieme-Becker, 3, pp. 226–7; TDA, 3, p. 629 [Stocker]; Barnes 1999.

276: The Eagle slayer

about 1851
By John Bell; cast by the Coalbrookdale Company [q.v.]
Cast iron
h. 247 cm.
A.28–1959

A photograph taken by Charles Thurston Thompson (1816–1868) shows the *Eagle Slayer* in front of the 'Brompton Boilers', the early ironwork structures in which the collections of the South Kensington Museum were first housed [see Introduction, fig. 4] (Department of Prints, Drawings and Paintings, inv.no. 33.966; see Haworth-Booth and McCauley 1998, no. 8, illus. p. 22; I am grateful to Martin Barnes for this reference). Reference is made to Bell's *Eagle Slayer,* which 'every one knows', was included in the collection of 'Sculpture of the United Kingdom', established by the Sculptors' Institute and displayed at the then South Kensington Museum during 1857 (*Building News,* 17 July 1857, p. 740; I am grateful to Anthony North for this reference; see also cat.nos. 271, 272, 274, 392 and 500). The location of the figure at the South Kensington Museum, later the Victoria and Albert Museum, was recorded by Bell in 1890 in connection with the plaster version then at Kensington Town Hall (see below); he noted that it stood in the 'entrance court of the South Kensington Museum' (Barnes 1999, p. 25, citing J. Bell, *Catalogue of Statuary in Kensington Town Hall,* London, 1890). In his recent monograph on Bell, Richard Barnes has confirmed previous suppositions that the *Eagle Slayer* was presented by the Coalbrookdale Company to the South Kensington Museum (Barnes 1999, p. 83).

The figure is first mentioned in Museum records in 1913, when the Works Department, H.M. Office of Works at Imperial College of Science, requested the statue be moved. H.A Coward wrote, 'we are re-erecting "Cash Cottage" on a site close to Block A. The statue "Eagle Slayer" is right in the centre of the new position'. At a date prior to 1913, the *Eagle Slayer* was displayed in the quadrangle of the Museum, now the Pirelli Garden.

Eric Maclagan [q.v.] wrote in 1913, 'Mr Skinner [q.v.] and I could never trace the history of the Eagle Slayer. It does not seem to be a V&A Museum object. Science Museum has several figures in cast iron, and it may possibly belong to them'. In 1926 a Mr Hitchcock, presumably of the Museum's Central Inventory, noted, 'I can find no record of Registration, either as gift, purchase or loan. In view of John Bell's association with the Museum in the 'fifties, it is exceedingly likely that the object falls into a classification at one time rather numerous, that of objects "contributed" without specified conditions, or allowed to remain after an Exhibition'. The figure was displayed in front of the Modelling School at the V&A prior to its transfer to the Bethnal Green Museum from the Department of Architecture and Sculpture on 19 October 1926. Although its status was once again discussed, it was decided not to accession the figure. The installation of the figure at Bethnal Green in 1927 was recorded in the local press: the *Star* on 11 April 1927, and the

Sphere on 30 April 1927 (I am grateful to Noreen Marshall for these references). After further investigations in 1959, it was formally accessioned as a Museum object, officially placed under the charge of the Bethnal Green Museum, and re-sited there on a new plinth in the front garden.

The figure is now without its bow, although the photograph by Thurston Thompson mentioned above shows the bow in place. A press cutting showing the installation at Bethnal Green from the *Sphere,* 30 April 1927, shows the bow had been removed by this time.

Bell exhibited 'The eagle shooter' at the Royal Academy in 1837, no. 1176, which Read suggests was probably a plaster version. It was later exhibited as *The Archer* or *Eagle Slayer* at Westminster Hall in 1844. Read notes that the *Eagle Slayer* 'was eventually transferred to marble, bronze, and iron, though in what medium it was presented at its next appearance in 1844 is not clear' (Read 1982, pp. 27, 83). In its review of the Westminster Hall exhibition, the *Builder* commented, 'The story intended to be conveyed is, that an eagle having just slain a lamb, soars high aloft; scared from his prey by the shepherd (represented in the statue), who has just launches a successful shaft at the wide-winged robber. – A very fine work, seeming to live' (*Builder*, 27 July 1844, no. LXXVII, p. 367, no. 106). This figure was purchased by the Art Union and published in several editions, initially in 1845; see entry for cat.no. 277. A marble version of the *Eagle Slayer* exhibited at the 1862 International Exhibition, formerly in the Wentworth Woodhouse collection, Rotherham, Yorkshire, was sold by the Trustees of the Fitzwilliam Settlement, at Christie's, 15 July 1986, lot 95; see Read 1982, p. 27. Purchased by the 5th Earl Fitzwilliam, and probably the version subsequently included in the sale held at Sotheby's, New York, on 26 May 1994, lot 71.

In 1959 Michael Rix of the University of Birmingham and Charles Gibbs-Smith, Keeper of Public Services at the Victoria and Albert Museum, thought it highly likely that the present version was the one exhibited at the 1851 International Exhibition, and included under the list of objects exhibited by the Coalbrookdale Company in the official catalogue as no. 641, class 22 (General Hardware), Vol. II, Section III, p. 659, illus. pl. 112 in Vol. II, illustrated beneath an ornamental cast-iron dome also manufactured by the Coalbrookdale Company.

Two versions of Bell's *Eagle Slayer* – in cast iron and bronze respectively – were exhibited at the 1851 International Exhibition. The version in cast iron was included in class XXX, division A, Sculpture and works of Plastic Art. Sculpture on a large scale. The bronze was included in class XXX, division A. Sculpture as a Fine Art, section A. 2. In the *Jury Reports* for the exhibition, it was noted: 'The Eagle-Slayer, cast in bronze, and also in iron. This figure represents a powerful man in very strong action, at the moment after shooting an arrow into the air. The violence of the exertion has brought the muscles into full play. The artist has admirably succeeded in expressing the momentary and transient character of the action, and the form is modelled with a knowledge and truth of detail which are seldom found in the English school. His work has, therefore, obtained the Prize Medal' (*Jury Reports* 1851, p. 1551; see also ibid., p. 1533, pl. 109, for the bronze). The Coalbrookdale Company, which was responsible for producing both the cast iron and bronze versions, were awarded a prize in class XXX, Fine Art Casting, Castings in Iron, for 'A very successful cast of Bell's Eagle-Slayer'. It was further noted in the *Jury Reports* that, 'The cast of Bell's figure of the Eagle-Slayer shows great perfection, both in the casting and subsequent tooling' (*Jury Reports* 1851, pp. 1586–7).

Cat.no. 276 displayed outside Bethnal Green Museum in 1937.

In his appraisal of the fine arts exhibited at the 1851 International Exhibition, the sculptor Henry Weekes [q.v.] commented, 'The first specimen exhibited by this artist [Bell] is, the "Eagle Slayer", which will bear comparison for correctness of form with any of the foreign productions. If Mr Bell values the lasting of his reputation he will execute this statue in marble; may be he has already done so. His name will then have a good chance of a place among the classics of English Sculpture' (Weekes 1852, p. 91).

Departmental records list a further version at Kensington Town Hall (information supplied by Michael Rix to Terence Hodgkinson [q.v.]). In 1961 Hodgkinson visited Kensington Town Hall to discover that this piece, a plaster, had been irreparably damaged during the Second World War. A full-size bronze version is in a private collection (I am grateful to James Cheshire for this information).

BIBLIOGRAPHY

Gunnis 1968, p. 49; Bonython 1982 [Cole], p. 27; Read 1982, illus. p. 28 pl. 19, p. 29; TDA, 3, p. 629 [Stocker]; Barnes 1999, pp. 6, 25, 83, 90. fig. 82 on p. 182.

277: The Eagle slayer

signed and dated 1846
After John Bell; by Edward William Wyon
Bronze
h. 63 cm.
A.75–1970

Inscribed on the side behind the Eagle Slayer's right foot:
EXECUTED BY/E.W. WYON/AFTER THE ORIGINAL OF/J. BELL/FOR THE ART UNION OF LONDON/1846

Bequeathed by the Hon. Dame Ada Macnaghten, widow of the Hon. Sir Frederick Macnaghten, a former chairman of British American Tobacco (d. 1955).

This is a mechanically reduced version of the full-size statue produced by John Bell, a cast iron version of which is in the Museum's collections; see entry for cat.no. 276. Another version, executed in bronze by H.J. Hatfield in 1889, was sold at Christie's, London, on 4 November 1982, lot 54, and a marble version, auctioned by the Trustees of the Fitzwilliam Settlement, Cambridge, was sold at Christie's, London on 15 July 1986, lot 95.

The subject of the *Eagle Slayer* was chosen by the Art Union for reproduction in 1845: the first version produced by John Bell had been exhibited at the Royal Academy in 1837. Avery and Marsh comment that after it was shown at the Art Union exhibition of 1844, it was deemed a suitable subject for reproduction (Avery and Marsh 1985, p. 332). Wyon was later commissioned to produce 'A Tazza modelled from a Greek Design for the Art Union of London', which was shown at the International Exhibition of 1851 (Gunnis 1968, p. 449). Wyon's reduced version of *St Michael overcoming Satan* by John Flaxman [q.v.], had been the first bronze to be commissioned by the Art Union in 1842, and was distributed in 1844 (see Avery and Marsh 1985, p. 328, fig. 1, and pp. 329–30).

Edward William Wyon (1811–1885) was a member of the prominent family of medallists active from the mid-eighteenth century; he chose to work almost exclusively as a sculptor (see Graves VIII, pp. 389–91; Forrer VI, p. 586; Forrer VIII, pp. 295–6; Gunnis 1968, pp. 449–50; Blackwood 1989, pp. 90–1; TDA, 33, p. 455 [Stocker]).

278: Eve

signed; about 1853
By John Bell, manufactured by Messrs Elkington & Company
Bronze
h. 74.5 cm.
4332–1854

Signed on the back of the tree trunk: IOHN BELL

Purchased from Messrs Elkington & Company in 1854 for £22 10s or £25 (discrepancies between the registered description for the object and the printed inventories). This is one of the early acquisitions by the Museum, and was originally in the collections at the Museum of Ornamental Art in Marlborough House, later to become the South Kensington Museum. Displayed at the Bethnal Green Museum at an unrecorded date. Transferred from the Circulation Department to the Department of Architecture and Sculpture, later Sculpture Department, in 1966.

Richard Barnes has recently suggested that the present piece is a reduction of the half life-size marble figure executed by Bell for Lord Truro (Barnes 1999, p. 44).

BIBLIOGRAPHY

Robinson 1861, p. 19, no. 540; *Inventory* 1863, p. 13, no. 540; Barnes 1999, pp. 6, 44, 136, and illus. no. 36 on p. 136.

EXHIBITED

The *Inventory of the Objects forming the Art Collections of the Museum* of 1863 records that the present piece was exhibited at the Paris Exhibition of 1855 (*Inventory* 1863, p. 13, no. 540).

S. BERESFORD

(dates unknown; active 1867)

No information has been found on S. Beresford other than his address '189 Oxford Street, Stepney E'. He was presumably an amateur sculptor who exhibited at the Society of Arts Art-Workmanship Competition of 1867.

Journal for the Society of Arts, 14 February 1868, XIV, no. 795, p. 241, no. 17.

279: Virgin and child

1867
By S. Beresford; after Desiderio da Settignano
Bronze
h. 40.5 cm. w. 33.5 cm.
856–1868

Purchased from S. Beresford, presumed to be the sculptor, in 1868 for £15.

This chased bronze panel is a copy of the relief in the Museum's collection, which is in the style of Desiderio da Settignano (1429/32 – about 1464) inv.no. 66–1866 (Pope-Hennessy 1964, I, pp. 142–3, no. 117, fig. 136). It was a prize object in the Society of Arts Art-Workmanship competition of 1867. Three examples of this composition entered in the competition of 1867 were subsequently acquired by the Museum; see cat.nos. 460 and 520. This piece was awarded a prize of £15.

EXHIBITED

Society of Arts Art-Workmanship Competition of 1867.

SIR JOSEPH EDGAR BOEHM BT. R.A.

(b. Vienna 1834 – d. London 1890)

Boehm was born in Vienna and trained initially under his father, Joseph Daniel Boehm (1794–1865), who was Court Medallist and Director of the Imperial Mint at Vienna. After a period in London where he attended Leigh's art academy, he returned to Vienna and attended the Akademie der Bildenden Künst. Boehm later travelled to Italy and between 1859 and 1862 worked in Paris. He returned to London in 1862, where he was to settle for the remainder of his life, and in the same year made his début at the Royal Academy. He exhibited consecutively each year, from 1862 until his death, with the exception of 1869. Boehm enjoyed a substantial amount of royal patronage and was a favourite of Queen Victoria, becoming Sculptor-in-Ordinary in 1880. He also acted as tutor to Princess Louise [q.v.], who became a sculptor in her own right. His final Academy work was exhibited posthumously in 1891. Though chiefly known as a sculptor of portrait busts, Boehm's work as an animalier sculptor is also significant, as is his work in terracotta. Boehm is also remembered for what was considered at the time to be a prodigous failure, the equestrian statue of the Duke of Wellington at Hyde Park Corner; see cat.nos. 309 and 316.

Graves I, pp. 218–20; Stocker 1988; Thieme-Becker, 4, pp. 194–5; TDA, 4, pp. 220–1 [Stocker].

280: Herdsman with bull

signed and dated 1868
Bronze
l. 61.5 cm.
1323–1901

Signed on the ground: BOEHM/1868
The group stands on an oval base, which is stamped on the edge: H YOUNG & CO/FOUNDERS/PIMLICO.

Purchased from Messrs Manson, Christie and Woods sale on Friday 29 November 1901, lot 50, for £19 19s [19 guineas]. Transferred from the Circulation Department to the Department of Architecture and Sculpture, later Sculpture Department, in 1956.

Museum papers record that this group was considered to be 'useful in Circulation [Department] and in our modern collection as a specimen of good modern casting ... we have a small collection of modern bronzes by Barye, Fremiet, Meunier but nothing by Sir Edgar'.

Boehm exhibited a plaster group entitled *Short horned Bull and Herdsman*, dated 1869 at the London International Exhibition of 1871 (Division I, Class II, no. 2509), which was advertised as being available in plaster for 500 guineas and in bronze for 1000 guineas. A marble group entitled *Young bull and herdsman* was exhibited at the Royal Academy in 1887 (no. 1798). In its review of the 1887 Royal Academy exhibition, the *Art Journal* commented that 'some works there were of considerable merit, but nothing remarkably striking arrests attention with the exception perhaps of no. 1798 '*Young Bull with Herdsman*', J.E. Boehm, R.A., the plaster model of which, shown some years ago, has now been admirably reproduced in a magnificent block of Sicilian marble' (*Art Journal*, September 1887, L, p. 318). Presumably this was the same marble group which was exhibited at the 1888 Centennial International Exhibition in Melbourne (no. 135), and purchased by the Victoria Art Gallery, now National Gallery of Victoria, Melbourne, for £1000. Donated to the Royal Agricultural Society of Victoria in 1941, this group is now described as 'in a rather dilapidated condition at the Royal Melbourne show grounds' (*National Gallery of Victoria* 1987, p. 27). Boehm also exhibited a bronze group *Shorthorn bull and English peasant* at the Vienna International Exhibition in 1873 (Group XXV, no. 187).

In 1871 Boehm entered the *Herdsman with Bull* group as part of a design for the competition for the Smithfield Fountain arranged by the Markets Committee of the Corporation of the City of London, in collaboration with the architect Thomas Jeckyll (1827–1881) (see *Builder* 1871, p. 161; I am grateful to Philip Ward-Jackson for this information and reference).

This bronze was acquired as a reduced copy of a plaster study for the same subject already in the possession of the Museum. Purchased in 1891 for £10 from the Executors of the late Sir J. E. Boehm (inv.no. 314–1891), this life-size plaster was de-accessioned in 1946. At the time of acquisition, this plaster group was considered by the officials recommending its purchase as 'good as anything he [Boehm] did outside his special arts of bust making' (Stocker 1988, pp. 301, 380 n. 61, p. 385 n. 20 – inv. no. for the written-off plaster study incorrectly cited as 314–1901). See Stocker 1988, pp. 17, 299–305 for a discussion of the Herdsmen and Bull groups.

BIBLIOGRAPHY

Stocker 1988, p. 399, no. 60 (incorrectly cited as plaster model when in fact bronze), illus. no. 323.

281: Equestrian statue of the hunter of early days

about 1868
Plaster
h. 140 cm.
1806–1892

The remains of an inscription '[H]UNTER' is visible on the front of the pedestal for the figure.

Given by the Executors of the late Sir J. E. Boehm in 1892. This was one of the plasters which remained in the studio of Boehm at the time of his death in 1890. A number of casts taken by Boehm of hands were also included in this gift, though registered as reproductions rather than original objects; see entry for cat.no. 288.

The figure has recently been conserved. The spear is missing from the figure's right hand.

This is a design for the bronze equestrian statue of *The Hunter of Early Days,* now in a private collection (see Stocker 1988, figs. 335 and 336). Boehm exhibited *The Hunter of Early Days* at the Royal Academy in 1868 (Graves I, p. 219, no. 991).

BIBLIOGRAPHY

Stocker 1988, p. 399, no. 50.

282: Louis-Gustave Ricard (1823–1873)

signed and dated 1870
Terracotta
h. 47 cm.
1787–1892

Signed at the bottom on the front to the left: J·E· BOEHM·fecit
Inscribed on the front at the base: G: + RICARD + ÆTATIS SVÆ XLVII NOVEMB. MDCCCLXX [G. Ricard at the age of 47 November 1870]
The back of the bust is hollowed out; the following inscription is visible: G. Ricard (PainTer)/[illegible]/LONDRES NOV 1870

Given by the Executors of the late Sir J. E. Boehm in 1892; see entry for cat.no. 281.

Boehm exibited a terracotta bust of 'Monsieur Ricard' at the Royal Academy in 1871 (Graves I, p. 219, no. 1182), which the *Athenaeum* described in its review as a 'spirited terra-cotta bust, in the cinque-cento style . . . not elaborate, but skilful and vigorous' (*Athenaeum*, 10 June, 1871, no. 2276, p. 727) The *Art Journal* review of the exhibition similary enthusiastically commented that Boehm's terracottas 'continue unrivalled for character, animation, and piquant sharpness in touch' (*Art Journal*, July 1871, p. 180). For Ricard, see TDA, 26, pp. 315–6 [Davenport].

BIBLIOGRAPHY
Stocker 1988, pp. 70–1, 402, no. 92, illus. 59.

283: Sir John Everett Millais (1829–1896)

signed and dated 1871
Terracotta
h. 62 cm.
1774–1892

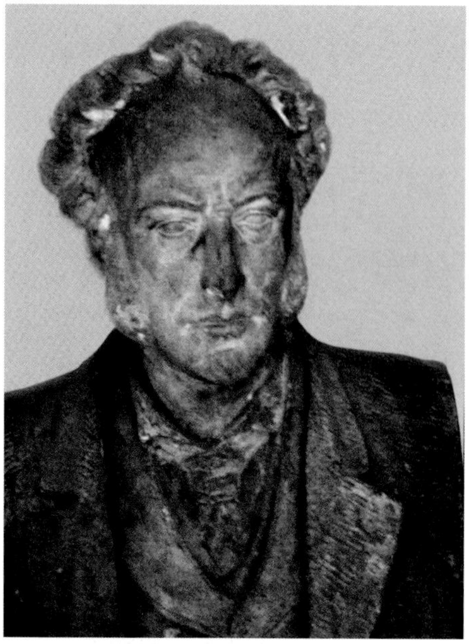

Signed and dated on the left shoulder: I·E·BOEHM·fecit MDCCCLXXI·

Given by the Executors of the late Sir J. E. Boehm in 1892; see entry for cat.no. 281.

Three busts of Millais were acquired in 1892 from the Boehm bequest, and one of these was presented by the authorities at South Kensington to the Wolverhampton Art Gallery in that same year (see *Bequests and Donations* 1901, p. 17, and *Wolverhampton* 1913, p. 123, no. 561).

In 1863 Boehm exhibited 'J.E. Millais, Esq ARA' (presumably a bust) at the Royal Academy (Graves 1905, I, p. 218, no. 1102). In 1883 he showed a bronze bust of Millais at the Royal Academy, which was described as a diploma work (Graves I, p. 220, no. 1581). This is now in the permanent collections of the Royal Academy.

See cat.no. 284.

BIBLIOGRAPHY
Stocker 1988, p. 403, no. 103; Stocker records that an identical example exists in the Walker Art Gallery, Liverpool, and that a terracotta bust was exhibited at the London International Exhibition of 1872 (no. 2534), presumably either the V&A or Walker Art Gallery bust.

284: Sir John Everett Millais (1829–1896)

signed and dated 1882
Plaster
h. 62 cm.
1773–1892

Signed at the back beneath the right arm: BOEHM. Fecit 1882
Inscribed on the back: J.E.MILLAIS./PicTor.

Given by the Executors of the late Sir J. E. Boehm in 1892; see entry for cat.no. 281.

A terracotta bust of Millais was also acquired by the Museum in 1892 from the estate of the sculptor; see cat.no. 283.

BIBLIOGRAPHY
Kilmurray 1981, p. 143; Stocker 1988, p. 413, no. 236.

285: Lioness on a pedestal

signed and dated 1871
Plaster
h. (incl. base) 180 cm.
1797–1892

Signed and dated on the base: BOEHM fecit/1871

Given by the Executors of the late Sir J. E. Boehm in 1892; see entry for cat.no. 281.

This appears to be a plaster model for the bronze lioness executed by Boehm, exhibited at the London International Exhibition in 1872 (no. 2536), and now located at Holkham Hall, Norfolk. A companion plaster model of a lion (inv.no. 1796–1892), the bronze of which is also at Holkham, was de-accessioned in 1939 (Stocker 1988, p. 403, no. 105). In 1910 Professor Edward Lanteri wrote to the Museum authorities asking if the present piece – then displayed in the entrance to the Southern Gallery of the Science Museum – could be lent to the Royal College of Art, writing: 'I should like to have it in the Modelling School for a few weeks'.

Bibliography
Stocker 1988, p. 403, no. 106.

286: Sir Henry Cole, K.C.B. (1808–1882)

signed and dated 1875
Terracotta
h. 71.5 cm.
525–1883

Purchased from the sculptor in 1883 for £52 10s [50 guineas].

Sir Henry Cole [q.v.], founder of the South Kensington Museum, was Secretary of the Science and Art Department, appointed Joint Secretary and Inspector of the Department of Science and Art in 1853, and sole Secretary and Director of the South Kensington Museum from 1858. He resigned his post on 22 May 1873. For further information on Cole see Bonython 1982 [Cole], Physick 1982, *Grand Design* 1997, and Bonython and Burton 2001.

The bust stands on a contemporary gilt pedestal base on which the name of the sitter is inscribed. It is currently displayed in a niche in the entrance to the Henry Cole Wing, opened in 1983, and named in memory of the founder of the Museum.

A draft letter to Boehm held on Museum papers records the fact that the Museum authorites were 'pleased to have an example of his art in connection with the founder of the Museum'. Cole noted eight sittings for Boehm in his diary for 1875, presumably for a version of this bust (Stocker 1988, p. 366, no. 17).

Several versions of this portrait exist (Stocker 1988, p. 407 no. 158). In 1876 Boehm exhibited a marble bust of Cole at the Royal Academy (Graves I, p. 219 no.1453), which is now in the Royal Albert Hall. A cast of one of the busts was made by the London-based Spence's Metal Company, who presented it to the former National Gallery of Victoria, now Victoria Art Gallery, Melbourne in 1876 (see *National Gallery of Victoria* 1908, p. 48, no. 120). The National Portrait Gallery, London purchased a plaster cast of the Cole bust in 1891, which was noted together with other purchases, in the *Magazine of Art*, 1891, p. xlvi, (see *NPG* 1981, p. 122, no. 865).

Bibliography
Stocker 1988, p. 407, no. 158; Thieme-Becker, 4, p. 195.

287: Thomas Carlyle (1795–1881)

signed; about 1875–81
Terracotta
h. 51 cm.
A.84–1930

Signed on the top face of the base beneath the chair: J·E·BOEHM

Given by Miss Fanny Crosbie (niece of John Forster) in 1895, to be placed with other objects known collectively as the Forster Bequest, bequeathed to the Museum in 1876. Formally registered in 1930.

This reduced copy of the seated figure of Carlyle was apparently made by Boehm at the request of the sitter. On 1 May 1874, Carlyle had noted: 'On May-day I am to give my first sitting for a statuette by Boehm' (*Carlyle* 1954, p. 55). Stocker comments that there was a large production run for reduced versions of the life-size model, and that Boehm charged 20 guineas for the more common versions in terracotta (Stocker 1988, p. 226). Terracotta versions are known to exist in Carlyle's House (24 Cheyne Row, London), and in the Royal Collection at Windsor Castle. Amongst those items given by the Executors of the Boehm Estate in 1892 (see cat.no. 281) was an object described as 'Thomas Carlyle', which was presented to Edinburgh (see *Bequests and Donations* 1901, p. 17). This is presumably the plaster version formerly in the Royal Scottish Museum, Edinburgh, which was destroyed in about 1945 (Stocker 1988, p. 406, no. 146A).

Following the death of the essayist and historian Thomas Carlyle in February 1881, the Memorial Committee obtained permission from Lord Rosebery for a replica of his statue of Carlyle to be erected as a public monument. The monument, erected on Chelsea Embankment, was unveiled on 26 October 1882 (Blackwood 1989, pp. 126–7). In November 1882, the *Builder* commented: 'Shortly after the death of Carlyle, some of his friends commissioned Mr Boehm to execute in bronze a replica of the statue he had modelled from the life some six years before. The statue had pleased Carlyle at the time' (*Builder* 1882). On its unveiling, the *Illustrated London News* commented that Boehm had produced 'a fine work of art, and also that much rarer acquisition, a vivid likeness of the man sought to be represented' (*Illustrated London News* 1882, p. 466). A replica of the Chelsea Embankment statue was erected in Carlyle's birth-place, Ecclefechan, Dumfries and Galloway, in 1929.

Portraits of Carlyle by Boehm were exhibited at the Royal Academy in 1875, 1881 and 1882 respectively. Commenting in 1878 on the version the magazine described as having been exhibited at the Royal Academy in 1875, the *Art Journal* remarked that it had considered it to be 'the "great portrait" of the year . . . The 'philosopher' is seated rather ungracefully – that is, sideways – in his chair, wearing a loose morning gown; but the position and the man, while his features, though showing strong marks of advanced age, are wonderfully animated and intellectually expressive – quite characteristic of the individual' (*Art Journal*, July 1878, XVII, p. 148). The marble version, commissioned by Lord Rosebery in 1881 and exhibited a year later at the Royal Academy (Graves I, p. 220, no. 1672), is now in the Scottish National Portrait Gallery (inv.no. PG1218) (*SNPG* 1990, p. 58, illus. p. 61). For a review of the 1882 Royal Academy exhibition see *Athenaeum*, 3 June 1882, no. 2849, p. 706.

In an article devoted to 'Some Portraits on Carlyle', the *Magazine of Art* commented on the 'difficulties which beset all modern work of this kind. It is hard to make coats and trousers look statuesque if, indeed, it is not impossible' (*Magazine of Art*, September 1884, II, pp. 76–83). An article entitled 'Thomas Carlyle. Statuette at Potsdam', by J.A.S. Barrett in the *Scotsman*, 15 August 1933, discussed a version in terracotta dated 1874, formerly in the Museum für Angewandte Kunst, Vienna, and a bronze in the Stadtschloss, Potsdam. For a discussion of the relationship between Carlyle and Boehm, and for the various versions of the Carlyle statue, see Stocker 1985; *idem* 1988, pp. 212–242, 406, nos. 148A to E.

Bibliography

Stocker 1988, p. 406, no. 148E.

288: Crossed hands of Thomas Carlyle (1795–1881)

about 1874–5
Plaster
l. 33 cm.
1892–97

Given by the Executors of the late Sir J.E. Boehm in 1892. This series of casts of hands (cat.nos. 289, 293, 315, 321 to 336, 479 and 737 to 740), were acquired by the Museum in 1892 from the Executors of the late Sir Joseph Edgar Boehm. Unlike the other objects acquired from the estate (see cat.no. 281) these were not registered as original objects, but instead assigned reproduction inventory numbers, and published as such in the *List of Reproductions in Electrotype and Plaster acquired by the South Kensington Museum in the Year 1892* (see *List* 1892, pp. 12–23 for the entire list of casts acquired). Comments made on 13 April 1893 by A.B. Skinner [q.v.] noted on the registered papers relating to the Boehm gift, indicate that these objects were regarded differently from the 'original' objects by Boehm: 'Original objects given by the executors of the late Sir Edgar Boehm registered, Nos. 1770 to 1806–1892'. Originally 107 objects (inv.nos. 1892–83 to 188), this series of casts was additional to the main gift of other sculpture by him acquired in 1892. Mainly corporeal fragments of hands of eminent personages – though a further 67 were taken from unidentified subjects – some were intended as models for finished works, although these do not always seem to have been executed. The sixty-seven casts of hands taken from unidentified subjects were included in a Board of Survey held in the Museum in 1956, and were written-off as they were seen to be redundant and/or damaged and of no further use (inv.nos.1892–85, 91, 93 to 95, 98 to 102, 106, 108 to 110, 112, 115 to 117, 120 to 124, 126, 130 to 133, 135 to 141, 143, 143A to 155, 157 to 159, 162 to 167, 169 to 178). Also included in the objects registered as reproductions were a number of unidentified figures, which not attributed to Boehm, may have also been used as source material in the Boehm studio (inv.nos 1892–178 to 188; inv.no. 1892–178; a draped female figure drawing aside a curtain, was written off in 1956). Although the majority of the hands are said to be by Boehm and are described as 'moulded from nature' in the *List of Reproductions. . .. 1892,* some pieces (cat.no. 737 to 740) are here described as anonymous, since they were executed before 1862 when Boehm settled in London. A cast of Boehm's right hand is recorded as having been modelled by Edouard Lanteri; see entry for cat.no. 479. A further cast included in the gift but not included in the present catalogue was described as French, late eighteenth-century, and was said to be of the left hand and wrist of the Comte de Lorge, a famous prisoner in the Bastille, taken after his death by the great-grandmother of Mr J.T. Tussaud; inv.no. 1892–129.

A plaster version incised 1875, described by Stocker as cast by Brucciani and Co. after Boehm, is in the National Portrait Gallery (see *NPG* 1981, p. 94, no. 1623); a further plaster cast of Carlyle's hands of 1874 is in Carlyle's House, Chelsea, London together with a bronze cast of the NPG hands (see Stocker 1988, p. 406, 148F, and fig. 254). The dates given to these hands suggests an approximate date for the present piece.

The hands appear to relate to the hands on the statue to Carlyle executed by Boehm and erected on Chelsea Embankment in 1882. A reduced-size terracotta version of the statue is in the Museum's collections; see entry for cat.no. 287. For a discussion of the relationship between Boehm and Carlyle, see Stocker 1988 pp. 212–42, 443.

BIBLIOGRAPHY
List 1892, p. 13.

289: Right hand of Mrs Carlyle (1801–1866)

about 1862–6
Plaster
l. 25.2 cm.
1892–87

Given by the Executors of the late Sir J.E. Boehm in 1892; see entries for cat.nos. 281 and 288.

'Mrs Carlyle' is presumably Jane, the wife of Thomas Carlyle (1795–1881); see entries for cat.no. 287 and 288. The purpose of this model is unknown.

BIBLIOGRAPHY
List 1892, p. 12.

290: Sir D. Younge

about 1875–90
Plaster
h. 70 cm.
1779–1892

Given by the Executors of the late Sir J. E. Boehm in 1892; see entries for cat.nos. 281 and 288.

This is a plaster model for a bust. Although cited by Stocker, no additional information on the sitter has been found.

BIBLIOGRAPHY
Stocker 1988, p. 421, no. 338.

290

291: Standing man

about 1875–90
Plaster
h. 89 cm.
1795–1892

Given by the Executors of the late Sir J. E. Boehm in 1892; see entries for cat.nos. 281 and 288.

The figure has a break in his right arm at the elbow. The model is pitted and spotted with brown dots. It stands on a rectangular base.

Though originally described as a plaster cast on acquisition, this is more likely to be a plaster model for an unidentified work by Boehm. The casting is very rough and pencil lines and numbers are visible on the figure, suggesting it was possibly a working model for a larger figure. The stance of the figure suggests it represents a groom holding a horse (now lost).

Bibliography
Stocker 1988, p. 421, no. 340.

292: Equestrian statue of Albert Edward, Prince of Wales (later Edward VII) (b.1841; r.1901–1910)

about 1876
Plaster
h. (figure) 154 cm.; h. (base) 84 cm.
1804–1892

Given by the Executors of the late Sir J. E. Boehm in 1892; see entries for cat.nos. 281 and 288.

The equestrian group, though not the base, has recently been conserved.

This is the plaster model for the equestrian statue of the Prince of Wales, which was originally erected on the Esplanade, in Bombay, but following vandalism was moved to a location near the Bhau Daji Lad Museum (formerly Victoria and Albert Museum, Bombay) (Stocker 1988, p.102). The present piece includes the model for the pedestal to which two reliefs representing scenes in the Princes of Wales's visit to India are attached.

The statue, commemorating the visit of 1875–7 of the Prince of Wales to India, was unveiled on 26 June 1879. It had been commissioned by Sir Albert Sassoon at a cost of £10,000, and, as noted by the *Magazine of Art*, was presented 'to his fellow-townsmen of the loyal city of Bombay'. The article continued: 'No better illustration of European sculpture could have been sent to represent contemporary art in our Eastern dependency' (*Magazine of Art*, November 1878–9, I, p. xxvii). The *Magazine of Art* also records that the statue was followed to India by the four panels which were used to decorate the pedestal. However, Boehm had not been the first choice for the commission; Matthew Noble [q.v.] had originally been employed by Sassoon, but his death on 23 June 1876 had meant that the commission was passed to Boehm. The *Art Journal* commented, 'It is understood that the equestrian statue of the Prince of Wales, which Sir Albert Sassoon had commissioned the late Mr M. Noble to execute, as a gift to the city of Bombay, will now be the work of Mr Boehm' (*Art Journal*, XV (new series), November 1876, p. 350). Stocker notes that from the late 1870s Boehm's interest turned to equestrian subjects, and that this was his first such commission (Stocker 1988, p. 19).

What was described as a 'sketch of a colossal equestrian statue of H.R.H. the Prince of Wales, given by Sir Albert Sassoon to the city of Bombay in commemoration of H.R.H.'s visit to India, 1875–1877', was exhibited by Boehm at the Royal Academy in 1878 (Graves I, p. 220, no. 1479). In its review of the Royal Academy exhibition of 1878, the *Art Journal* commented '. . . and the Prince of Wales Mr Boehm shows us mounted on horseback, in such gallant guise as only the late John Foley could have equalled' (*Art Journal*, October 1878, p. 199). The model was again exhibited with the plaster model of the pedestal, in front of the Indian Court of the Paris Exhibition in 1878.

The statue was generally well-received in the contemporary press. The *Illustrated London News* commented, 'The design of the statue is quite familiar to us in Europe, since the plaster cast was conspicuous in front of the Indian Court at the Paris Exhibition last year' (*Illustrated London News*, 2 August 1879, no. 2094, LXXV, pp. 117–8).

BIBLIOGRAPHY

Stocker 1988, pp. 101–2, 408, no. 173.

Base of cat.no. 292

293: Left hand of Albert Edward, Prince of Wales (later Edward VII) (b.1841; r.1901–1910)

about 1862–76
Plaster
l. 21.8 cm.
1892–113

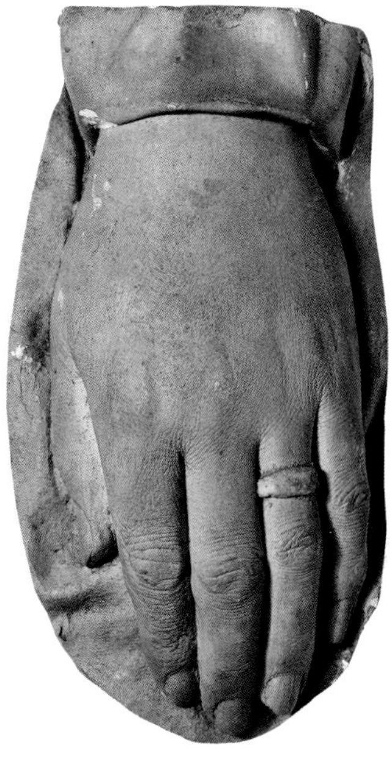

Given by the Executors of the late Sir J.E. Boehm in 1892; see entries for cat.nos. 281 and 288.

Boehm executed a number of works associated with the Prince of Wales, perhaps most notably the equestrian monument for Bombay (see various references in Stocker 1988). See the entry for cat.no. 292 for a plaster model for the monument.

BIBLIOGRAPHY

List 1892, p. 15.

294: Lord John Russell, 1st Earl (1792–1878)

signed and dated 1879
Plaster
h. 63.5 cm.
1783–1892

Signed and dated on the left shoulder: BOEHM·fecit·1879
Inscribed on the truncation at the back: LORD JOHN RUSSELL

Given by the Executors of the late Sir J. E. Boehm in 1892; see entry for cat.no. 281.

Lord John Russell was Prime Minister from 1846 to 1852. This portrait is the plaster model for Boehm's marble bust, executed 1879–80 for Westminster Abbey. Boehm was additionally commissioned to produce a funerary monument to Russell for Westminster Abbey. In 1880 he also exhibited 'Lord John Russell; model for statue for Houses of Parliament' at the Royal Academy (Graves I,

p. 220, no. 1590). See Stocker 1988, pp. 93, 133 and 146 for the Westminster Abbey monument to Russell.

BIBLIOGRAPHY
Stocker 1988, p. 410, no. 196.

295: Sir Frederick Burton, R.H.A. (1816–1900)

signed and dated 1880
Plaster
h. 70 cm.
1784–1892

Signed and dated on the left shoulder: BOEHM·1880·
Inscribed on the back truncation: FRED BURTON PAINTER

Given by the Executors of the late Sir J. E. Boehm in 1892; see entry for cat.no. 281.

Sir Frederick William Burton was a painter, and Director of the National Gallery of Ireland 1874–94. Boehm exhibited a terracotta bust of him at the Royal Academy in 1880 (Graves I, p. 220, no. 1636).

BIBLIOGRAPHY
Stocker 1988, p. 411, no. 217.

296: Professor Thomas Henry Huxley, LL.D., F.R.S. (1825–1895)

signed and dated 1881
Plaster
h. 64.6 cm.
1772–1892

Signed on the truncation: BOEHM·Fecit·
Inscribed on the back: PROFESSOR HUXLEY/1881·

Given by the Executors of the late Sir J. E. Boehm in 1892; see entry for cat.no. 281.

Huxley was Professor of Comparative Anatomy at the Royal College of Surgeons from 1863 to 1869; he was also a Trustee of the Hunterian Museum, Glasgow. A terracotta version was exhibited by Boehm at the Royal Academy in 1882, (Graves I, p. 220, no. 1600). This plaster model was transferred to the Royal College of Science in 1899; on permanent loan to Imperial College, it is now displayed in the entrance to the Huxley Building, 180 Queen's Gate, London (part of the Imperial College site).

BIBLIOGRAPHY
Stocker 1988, p. 412, no. 223.

297: William Ewart Gladstone (1809–1898)

signed and dated 1881
Plaster
h. 56 cm.
1785–1892

Inscribed on the back: W.E. GLADSTONE Sat MAY·10th 1881·
Signed beneath: J·E·BOEHM fecit
Also inscribed on the back near the base: III

Given by the Executors of the late Sir J. E. Boehm in 1892; see entry for cat.no. 281.

Gladstone was Prime Minister of Great Britain between 1868 and 1874. Boehm exhibited a marble bust of Gladstone at the Royal Academy in 1881 (Graves I, p. 220, no. 1497).

See also cat.no. 298 for a similar bust. Stocker notes that the Gladstone bust had 'a soft palpability', and that Boehm had 'hollowed out the eyes more deeply, the effect being to make them look more penetrating' (Stocker 1988, p. 68).

Bibliography
Stocker 1988, p. 411, no. 211.

298: William Ewart Gladstone (1809–1898)

signed and dated 1881
Plaster
h. 56 cm.
1786–1892

Signed on the back: J.E. Boehm fecit
Inscribed on the back: W.E. GLADSTONE/[Sat?] MAY 10TH 1881

Given by the Executors of the late Sir J. E. Boehm in 1892; see entry for cat.no. 281.

See entry for cat. no. 297.

Bibliography
Stocker 1988, p. 411, no. 211.

299: B. Bertrand (dates unknown)

signed; about 1882
Plaster on wood base
h. (excl. base) 50 cm.
1789–1892

Signed on the left shoulder: BOEHM· fecit
The square wood base is inscribed: B. BERTRAND

Given by the Executors of the late Sir J. E. Boehm in 1892; see entry for cat.no. 281.

Boehm exhibited a terracotta of Bertrand at the Royal Academy in 1882 (Graves I, p. 220, no. 1618), described as 'Monsieur B. Bertrand, fencing-master of the late Prince Imperial Louis Napoleon'. Stocker comments, 'No other Boehm bust conveys the dramatic immediacy or the sense of colour of Bertrand's startled, upward glance'. This may be a plaster model taken from the terracotta in preparation for a marble version.

BIBLIOGRAPHY
Stocker 1988, pp. 66–7, 412 no. 230, illus. 53.

300: Sir John (later 1st Baron) Lawrence (1811–1879)

about 1882
Plaster
h. 82 cm
1790–1892

Given by the Executors of the late Sir J. E. Boehm in 1892; see entry for cat.no. 281.

On acquisition this bust was mistakenly identified as a model for an unidentified portrait of the explorer David Livingstone. It was catalogued as such by Stocker, who suggested a date of about 1874. The bust has recently been identified by Philip Ward-Jackson as a model for the upper portion of the statue for Lord Lawrence, erected at Waterloo Place in March 1882. For further information on the statue itself see Blackwood 1989, pp. 198–9.

BIBLIOGRAPHY
Stocker 1988, p. 405, no.144.

301: Professor Henry John Stephen Smith (1826–1883)

signed and dated 1883
Plaster
h. 74.5 cm.
1775–1892

Signed and dated on the back beneath the inscription: BOEHM·fecit/1883
Inscribed on the back: PROFESSOR/HENRY SMITH

Given by the Executors of the late Sir J. E. Boehm in 1892; see entry for cat.no. 281.

Smith was Professor of Geometry at Oxford University from 1861 until his death. A marble bust by Boehm of 1883 is at the University Museum, Oxford. Smith is depicted wearing academic robes over his suit. This plaster model relates to cat.no. 304. Four plaster busts of Smith were included in the Boehm bequest of 1892; two depicting Smith in academic robes, the others in plain dress. A closely related terracotta bust of Smith was presented to the National Portrait Gallery by the sculptor in 1888; see *NPG* 1981, p. 523 no. 787.

BIBLIOGRAPHY
Stocker 1988, p. 414, no. 250A – also lists other versions.

302: Professor Henry John Stephen Smith (1826–1883)

signed and dated 1883
Plaster
h. 66 cm.
1776–1892

Signed and dated on the back beneath the inscription: BOEHM fecit/1883
Inscribed on the back: PROFESSOR/HENRY SMITH

Given by the Executors of the late Sir J. E. Boehm in 1892; see entry for cat.no. 281.

This plaster model of a bust shows Smith in plain dress and is a variant of cat.no. 303.

BIBLIOGRAPHY
Stocker 1988, p. 414, no. 250B.

303: Professor Henry John Stephen Smith (1826–1883)

about 1883
Plaster
h. 60 cm.
1777–1892

Given by the Executors of the late Sir J. E. Boehm in 1892; see entry for cat.no. 281.

This plaster model of a bust shows Smith in plain dress, and is a variant of cat. no. 302.

BIBLIOGRAPHY
Stocker 1988, p. 414, no. 250B.

304: Professor Henry John Stephen Smith (1826–1883)

about 1883
Plaster
h. 67.5 cm.
1778–1892

Given by the Executors of the late Sir J. E. Boehm in 1892; see entry for cat.no. 281.

This is a plaster model for a bust depicts Smith in academic robes and is a variant of cat.no. 301.

BIBLIOGRAPHY
Stocker 1988, p. 414, no. 250A.

305: Garnet Joseph, General the Rt. Hon. Viscount Wolseley, K.P., G.C.B. (1833–1913)

signed; about 1883–4
Plaster
h. 70 cm.
1770–1892

Signed on the truncation at the back beneath his right shoulder: BOEHM
Inscribed on the front of the integral socle: WOLSELEY

Given by the Executors of the late Sir J. E. Boehm in 1892; see entry for cat.no. 281.

This is a model for a bust of Garnet Joseph, 1st Viscount Wolseley, depicted in full military attire. A closely related, slightly larger version of this bust was acquired in the the same bequest; see cat.no.

306. A related bronze bust dated 1883 was presented to the National Portrait Gallery in 1919 by the sitter's widow, Dowager Lady Wolseley (see *NPG* 1981 p. 623, no. 1840). Boehm exhibited a bronze bust of Lord Wolseley at the Royal Academy in 1884 (Graves I, p. 220 no. 1722).

BIBLIOGRAPHY
Stocker 1988, p. 415, no. 257.

306: Garnet Joseph, General the Rt. Hon. Viscount Wolseley, K.P., G.C.B. (1883–1913)

about 1883–4
Plaster
h. 72.5 cm.
1771–1892

Inscribed on the front of the integral socle: WOLSELEY

Given by the Executors of the late Sir J. E. Boehm in 1892; see entry for cat.no. 281.

See entry for cat.no. 305.

BIBLIOGRAPHY
Stocker 1988, p. 415, no. 257.

307: Herbert Spencer (1820–1903)

signed and dated 1884
Plaster
h. 72 cm.
1791–1892

Signed and dated to the right on the truncation: J·E· BOEHM·84

Given by the Executors of the late Sir J. E. Boehm in 1892; see entry for cat.no. 281.

A terracotta model for a bust of the philosopher Herbert Spencer was also included in the Boehm bequest, see cat. no. 308. The original wax model for this bust is also in the Museum's collections (inv.no. 1793–1892). A marble bust of Spencer by Boehm was bequeathed by the sitter to the National Portrait Gallery in 1904 (*Art Journal,* March 1904, p. 104 and *NPG* 1981, p. 533 no. 1359).

BIBLIOGRAPHY
Stocker 1988, p. 415, no. 259; Stocker erroneously stated that there are two plaster versions of the Spencer bust, when in fact there is one plaster (the present version) and one terracotta, cat. no. 308.

308: Herbert Spencer (1820–1903)

signed; about 1884
Terracotta
h. 68.5 cm.
1792–1892

Signed on the back: J·E·BOEHM Fecit

Given by the Executors of the late Sir J. E. Boehm in 1892; see entry for cat.no. 281.

See entry for cat. no. 307. Boehm exhibited a terracotta bust of Herbert Spencer at the Royal Academy in 1884 (Graves I p. 220, no. 1784).

BIBLIOGRAPHY
Stocker 1988, p. 415, no. 259 (erroneously listed as plaster).

309: Equestrian statue for the Wellington Monument

about 1885
Plaster
h. 137 cm. l. 105 cm. d. (base) 35 cm.
1798–1892

Given by the Executors of the late Sir J. E. Boehm in 1892; see entry for cat.no. 281.

The monument to Arthur Wellesley, 1st Duke of Wellington (1769–1852) at Hyde Park Corner was unveiled on 21 December 1888 by the Prince of Wales; Boehm was in attendance. The *Illustrated London News* commented that there were no addresses, 'but when the statue was unveiled, the Prince and the company saluted, and the crowd outside raised a responsive cheer'. The monument had been commissioned as part of the re-design of Hyde Park Corner, which had been begun in 1883. This involved the removal of the previous statue of Wellington by Matthew Cotes Wyatt [q.v.], which was re-erected in Aldershot, Hampshire in August 1885 (*Illustrated London News*, 29 December 1888, XCIII, no. 2593, pp. 769–70 and Blackwood 1989, pp. 248–9).

This is one of two plaster models of the equestrian statue to Wellington; see also cat.no. 310. See also cat. no. 316 for a model of the horse, Copenhagen; and cat.nos. 311 to 314 for the plaster models of the four over life-size figures of guards representing the forces of England, Scotland, Ireland, and Wales.

Boehm had finished the design for the Wellington Monument by January 1886 (*Magazine of Art*, January 1886, p. xiii). In 1887 an article was published in the *Art Journal* which was to be a precursor of the general critical reaction to the new Wellington statue: '. . . the model has been placed, viewed, and judged, and was to be expected; the character of the work is imitative and realistic – the reverse, in fact, of monumental. There is not much connection between the rider and the horse; but there is excellent drawing in both, and as a piece of portraiture the statue may be considered a fair success. What was wanted, however, was not imitative, but Monumental Art; and the new 'Wellington', good and skilful as in certain ways it is, will be a standing subject of regret that the work was not thrown open to competition, as, being a national affair, it might and should have been' (*Art Journal*, January 1887, p. 32).

The *Builder* similarly suggested that improvements in design and execution of the monument could have been made: 'The new Wellington Statue by Mr Boehm is a successful and satisfactory portrait monument rather than a work of genius . . . it is an unobtrusive and simply-treated portrait statue; a good and recognisable likeness, according to the many extant portraits of the Duke; but it does not strike us as anything more than that. It is hardly even dignified, as far as the principal figure is concerned; it certainly is not impressive. It is possible to be too much afraid of 'effect' in a portrait statue, and to go to the other extreme of a rather prim simplicity . . . On the whole, there is a certain disappointment in the feeling that, though the monumental statue of our great captain is admirably free from any kind of bad taste, there might have been something more made of it; some touch of the heroic which we cannot discern here' (*Builder*, 29 December 1888, LV, no. 2395,

p. 464). There was however, some praise for the figures of guards which surmounted each corner of the monument, and for the horse.

See Stocker 1988, pp. 149–67 for the Wellington Monument commission.

BIBLIOGRAPHY
Stocker 1988, p. 416, no. 274A, illus. 156.

310: Equestrian statue for the Wellington Monument

about 1885
Plaster
h. (incl. base) 137.5 cm.
1799–1892

Given by the Executors of the late Sir J. E. Boehm in 1892; see entry for cat.no. 281.

This group has recently been conserved. This model is a slightly smaller version of cat.no. 309.

BIBLIOGRAPHY
Stocker 1988, p. 416, no. 274A.

311: Grenadier guard

about 1884–8
Plaster
h. 264.5 cm.
1800–1892

Given by the Executors of the late Sir J. E. Boehm in 1892; see entry for cat.no. 281.

In 1912, the present piece, and the three other plaster models for Guards for the Wellington Monument (cat.nos. 312 to 314) were displayed at the Science Museum, where some damage was sustained to the present piece on two separate occasions. On 29 May 1912, a Police report [the police at this time acted as warders] recorded: 'I beg to report that at 5.55 pm, 28th as Henry Sage, age 12 . . . was walking along the passage into Southern Gallery he caught hold of the side arm of the plaster cast of a Grenadier when it fell down and was broken. Sage when spoken to by P.C. 683 Sheppard, said, "I just caught hold of it when it fell down and broke". Another Police report of 6 June 1912 recorded that P.C. 232B Sandall 'found that the gun of one of the plaster cast soldiers standing in entrance to Southern Gallery Science Museum had broken off. P.C. was unable to ascertain by whom the damage was done, but during that morning a large aeroplane was carried in and it may have been accidentally done then. Foreman Garrard in charge of aeroplane stated that his men did not touch it'.

This is the plaster model for the bronze statue of a Grenadier Guard (British Guardsman, 1st Regiment from the early part of the nineteenth century) on the monument to the Duke of Wellington at Hyde Park Corner; see also cat.nos. 309 and 310. Over life-size plaster models for the other three guards on the monument were also included in this bequest; see cat.nos. 312 to 314. Boehm exhibited this plaster model together with that for cat.no. 314 at the Royal Academy in 1889 (Graves I, p. 220, no. 2018), where it was described as 'The British Guardsman of 1818, for Wellington monument'. For a discussion of the guards see Stocker 1988, pp. 158–66.

There was much critical appraisal of the Wellington Monument in the contemporary press. The *Magazine of Art* commented in its feature on *Sculpture of the Year* that 'on the same plane stand Sir Edgar's "British Guardsman of 1818," and "Enniskilling" Dragoon of 1815. As statues they are no doubt beyond suspicion; but we look for more than fidelity and archaeological accuracy in a work of art.' (*Magazine of Art*, XII, pp. 373–4).

The *Builder* was however more complimentary about the guards represented on Boehm's completed monument: 'we also very much admire the supporting figures of soldiers at the angles of the pedestal, representing a Grenadier, a Highlander, a Lancer and a Dragoon. There is a great deal of character about these figures, in which the sculptor has quite steered clear of the common-place dressed-up soldier figure that we frequently see in sculpture; these are fine hardy types of man who look as those who have seen hard service and know more of war than its mere parade' (*Builder*, December 1888, LV, no. 2395, p. 464).

The *Illustrated London News* commented: 'At the four corners stand, rather above life-size, four warriors: at the north-east, the British Grenadier of the early part of this century; at the north-west, the representative of the Scotch, in a soldier of the Highlander, wearing the kilt; at the south-east corner, an Irish Dragoon; and at the south-west, a Welsh Fusilier. All these are cast in bronze. Cast by Messrs Moore & Co, Thames Ditton' (*Illustrated London News*, 29 December 1888, XCIII, no. 2593, p. 770; an engraving of the monument is shown on p. 769). A reduced bronze version (h. 45 cm.) by Elkington & Co was included in the sale at Christies, South Kensington, London, 18 November 1992, lot 105.

BIBLIOGRAPHY
Stocker 1988, p. 416, no. 274B.

EXHIBITED
Royal Academy 1889, no. 2018; Tercentenary Exhibition of the Grenadier Guards, St James's Palace, 29 May to 23 June 1956.

[Not illustrated].

312: Welsh fusilier guard

about 1884–8
Plaster
h. 298.8 cm.
1801–1892

Given by the Executors of the late Sir J. E. Boehm in 1892; see entry for cat.no. 281.

This model has suffered from some damage. The sword scabbard, a lance blade and a toe have become detached.

This is the plaster model for Boehm's Welsh Fusilier for the Wellington Monument. See entry for cat.no. 311.

BIBLIOGRAPHY
Stocker 1988, p. 416, no. 274E.

[Not illustrated].

313: Royal highlander guard

about 1884–8
Plaster
h. 251.5 cm.
1802–1892

Given by the Executors of the late Sir J. E. Boehm in 1892; see entry for cat.no. 281.

This is the plaster model for the figure of the Royal Highlander from the 42nd Regiment for the Wellington Monument. See entry for cat.no. 311.

BIBLIOGRAPHY
Stocker 1988, p. 416, no. 274D.

314: Irish dragoon (Enniskillen) guard

about 1884–8
Plaster
h. 257 cm.
1803–1892

Given by the Executors of the late Sir J. E. Boehm in 1892; see entry for cat.no. 281.

This is the plaster model for the Enniskillen guard for the Wellington Monument. This plaster model was exhibited at the Royal Academy in 1889 (Graves I, p. 220, no. 2041), along with that of the Grenadier Guard cat.no. 311.

The two models were discussed in the *Art Journal* review of the Royal Academy exhibition: 'These are considered by many to be the most successful part of the undertaking; that of the 'Inniskillen Dragoon' is singularly personal and vigorous' (*Art Journal*, August 1889, p. 247). The Enniskillen guard is illustrated in the article 'The late Sir Joseph Edgar Boehm, Bart., R.A., Sculptor' by M. H. Spielmann in the *Magazine of Art* of 1891, pp. 132–5, fig. on p. 133.

BIBLIOGRAPHY
Stocker 1988, p. 416, no. 274C.

[Not illustrated].

315: Right hand of Arthur Wellesley, 1st Duke of Wellington (1769–1852)

about 1884–8
Plaster
l. 19 cm.
1892–119

Given by the Executors of the late Sir J.E. Boehm in 1892; see entry for cat.no. 288.

This is a model for the hand of the Duke of Wellington on the Wellington Monument at Hyde Park Corner. See also cat.nos. 292, 309 to 314, and 316. In the *List of Reproductions . . . 1892*, the present piece is described as 'cast from an original model in clay'.

BIBLIOGRAPHY
List 1892, p. 16.

316: Horse, probably for the Wellington Monument

about 1885
Plaster
h. 99 cm.
1805–1892

Given by the Executors of the late Sir J. E. Boehm in 1892; see entry for cat.no. 281.

This model has recently been conserved.

This is probably a model for Wellington's famous horse, Copenhagen for the Wellington Monument (see also cat.nos. 309 and 310). As shown by this model and that of the Duke of Wellington groups, cat.nos. 309 and 310, Boehm had originally 'portrayed "Copenhagen", the Duke's charger, in a restless, pawing posture, which gave it some resemblance to Stevens's monument' (Stocker 1988, p. 153). Although the *Builder* was critical of the artistic worth of the monument itself – see cat.no. 309 – the writer commented, 'These remarks do not apply to the horse, which is a great success, a very fine and spirited animal indeed' (*Builder*, 29 December 1888, no. 2395, LV, p. 464).

A bronze cast from around 1890–1, taken from the present piece, was sold by Boehm to Ferdinand de Rothschild, and remains at Waddesdon Manor, Buckinghamshire (see Stocker 1988, p. 154, illus. 158) .

Bibliography
Stocker 1988, p. 416, no. 274A.

317: Anthony Ashley-Cooper, 7th Earl of Shaftesbury (1801–1885)

about 1885
Plaster
h. 97 cm.
1794–1892

Given by the Executors of the late Sir J. E. Boehm in 1892; see entry for cat.no. 281.

This is the plaster model for the monument to the Earl of Shaftesbury in Westminster Abbey (1885–8). Stocker notes that this model differs slightly from the finished memorial; in the model the sitter looks downward. This model shows the original design for the figure of the Earl of Shaftesbury; Boehm in fact used the bust of Shaftesbury he had produced in 1875 for the memorial. A plaster cast of the 1875 Shaftesbury bust is held in the National Portrait Gallery (*NPG* 1981, p. 512, no. 862). For a further bronze bust of the sitter by Boehm, see also *Gilbert* 1986, pp. 142–3, cat.no. 51.

Bibliography
Stocker 1988, pp. 207–8, 417, no. 282, illus. 242.

318: Abbé Franz Liszt (1811–1886)

signed and dated 1886
Plaster
h. (excl. base) 46 cm.
1780–1892

Inscribed on the back: Abbé Liszt/May/1886/Boehm

Given by the Executors of the late Sir J. E. Boehm in 1892; see entry for cat.no. 281.

This is one of three similar models for busts of the composer Franz Liszt acquired at the same time from the Boehm bequest in 1892; see cat.nos. 319 and 320. A terracotta version of a bust of Liszt was lent by the Executors of Sir Edgar Boehm to the Victorian Exhibition, The New Gallery, London, 1891–2; see the catalogue for the exhibition, p. 204, no. 1078. As with the busts of Professor Smith (see cat.nos. 301 to 304), four portraits of Liszt were apparently originally received as part of the Boehm bequest, one of which was presented by the authorities of the South Kensington Museum to the Wolverhampton Art Gallery in 1892. In 1865 Liszt was received into orders of the Catholic Church and became known as Abbé. In 1886, at the age of 74, he travelled to London for celebrations held in his honour.

Bibliography
Stocker 1988, pp. 66, 417, no. 287; illus. 51.

319: Abbé Franz Liszt (1811–1886)

about 1886
Plaster
h. 48.5 cm.
1781–1892

Given by the Executors of the late Sir J. E. Boehm in 1892; see entry for cat.no. 281.

See entry for cat. no. 318.

Bibliography
Stocker 1988, pp. 66, 417, no. 287.

320: Abbé Franz Liszt (1811–1886)

about 1886
Plaster
h. (excl. base) 46 cm.
1782–1892

Given by the Executors of the late Sir J. E. Boehm in 1892; see entry for cat.no. 281.

See entry for cat.no. 318.

Bibliography
Stocker 1988, pp. 66, 417, no. 287.

321: Right hand of Abbé Franz Liszt (1811–1886)

about 1886
Plaster
l. 20.2 cm.
1892–104

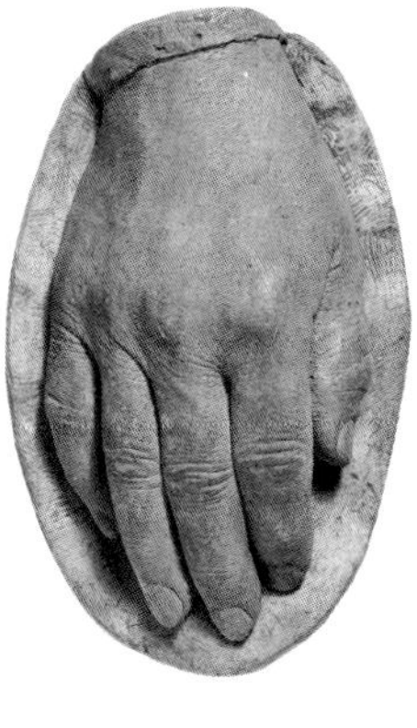

Given by the Executors of the late Sir J.E. Boehm in 1892; see entry for cat.no. 288.

Three plaster busts of Liszt by Boehm were also included in the Boehm gift to the Museum; see entries for cat.nos. 318 to 320. The date given to these busts suggests a date for the present piece.

BIBLIOGRAPHY
List 1892, p. 14.

322: Left hand and portion of arm of Lady Richard Grosvenor (dates unknown)

after 1862
Plaster
l. 33.5 cm
1892–83

Given by the Executors of the late Sir J.E. Boehm in 1892; see entry for cat.no. 288.

Lady Elizabeth Mary Levenson-Gower was married to Richard Grosvenor, 2nd Marquis of Westminster (1795–1869). The purpose of this model is uncertain.

BIBLIOGRAPHY
List 1892, p. 12

323: Left hand of Mrs (?Mary) Thornycroft (1814–1895)

after 1862
Plaster
l. 22.8 cm.
1892–88

Given by the Executors of the late Sir J.E. Boehm in 1892; see entry for cat.no. 288.

This subject is probably the hand of Mary Thornycroft, neé Francis, daughter of the sculptor John Francis (1814–1895). She and her husband, the sculptor Thomas Thornycroft [q.v.], were contemporaries of Boehm; see entry for cat.no. 686. The purpose of this model is unknown.

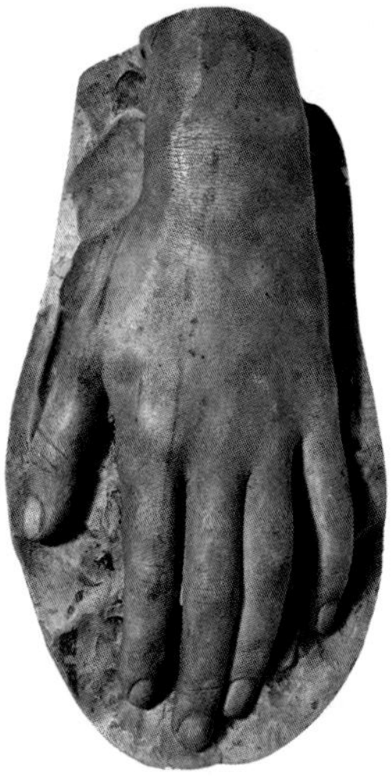

323

BIBLIOGRAPHY
List 1892, p. 12.

324: Left hand of H.R.H. Princess Louise, Duchess of Argyll and Marchioness of Lorne (1848–1939)

after 1862
Plaster
l. 19.2 cm.
1892–92

Scratched into the base: The [hand?] Prin[cess]

Given by the Executors of the late Sir J.E. Boehm in 1892; see entry for cat.no. 288.

Princess Louise was Queen Victoria's sixth child. She married the Marquis of Lorne, heir to the 8th Duke of Argyll, in 1871, and became the Duchess of Argyll and Marchioness of Lorne. Princess Louise was a sculptor in her own right, completing part of her training in Boehm's studio; see entry for cat.no. 255. The purpose of this model is unknown.

BIBLIOGRAPHY
List 1892, p. 13.

325: Right hand of Lord Savile, possibly John Savile, 1st Baron Savile of Rufford (1818–1896)

after 1862
Plaster
l. 22.5 cm.
1892–107

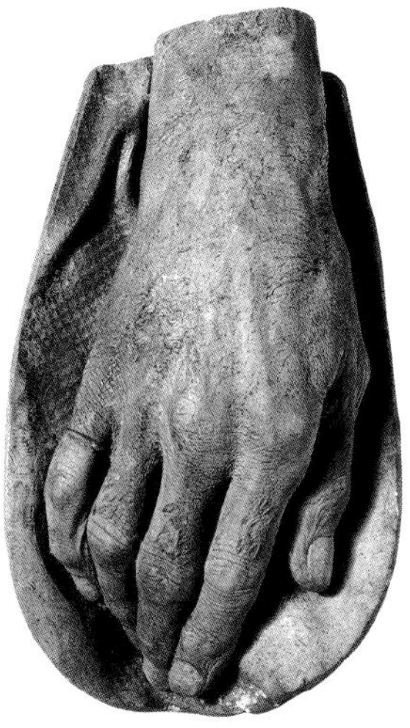

'Savil' is scratched into the base.

Given by the Executors of the late Sir J.E. Boehm in 1892; see entry for cat.no. 288.

Stocker does not list any works carried out by Boehm in connection with Lord Savile. The purpose and exact identity of this model are therefore uncertain.

BIBLIOGRAPHY
List 1892, p. 15.

326: Left hand of Miss Boehm (dates unknown)

after 1862
Plaster
l. 23.8 cm.
1892–111

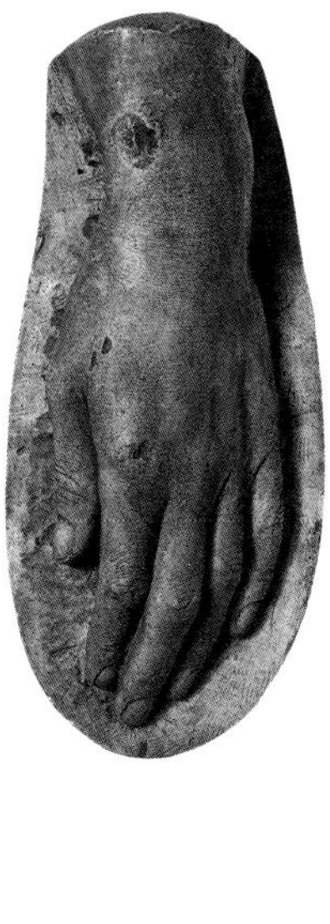

Given by the Executors of the late Sir J.E. Boehm in 1892; see entry for cat.no. 288.

The sitter was presumably a relative of the sculptor. The purpose of this model is unknown.

BIBLIOGRAPHY
List 1892, p. 15.

327: Right hand of Mr (? George) Leigh (dates unknown)

after 1862
Plaster
l. 21.4 cm.
1892–114

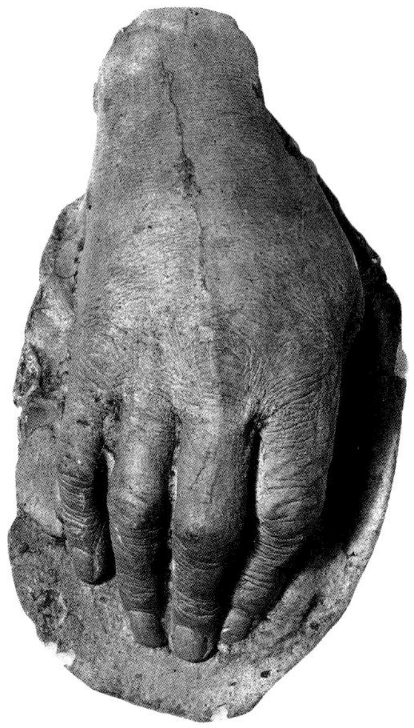

Scratched into the bottom: Mr G[eo?] Leigh

Given by the Executors of the late Sir J.E. Boehm in 1892; see entry for cat.no. 288.

Stocker records a number of known works executed by Boehm for a family named Leigh, including a statue of Mr Leigh and busts of Mr Leigh's two brothers (Stocker 1988, pp. 421–2, nos. 350A-E, 351, 352–3). The purpose of this model is unknown.

BIBLIOGRAPHY
List 1892, p. 15.

328: Right hand of Carl von Angeli (dates unknown)

after 1862
Plaster
l. 20.5 cm.
1892–134

Given by the Executors of the late Sir J.E. Boehm in 1892; see entry for cat.no. 288.

The sitter was the Court Painter to Queen Victoria (see Stocker 1988, pp. 79–114). A paintbrush would probably have been held between the thumb and forefinger. The purpose of this model is unknown.

BIBLIOGRAPHY
List 1892, p. 18.

329: Right hand and fore-arm of Lady Cardigan
(dates unknown)

after 1862
Plaster
l. 52.3 cm.
1892–156

Given by the Executors of the late Sir J.E. Boehm in 1892; see entry for cat.no. 288.

Boehm was commissioned in 1868 by Lady Cardigan (possibly the same Lady Cardigan whose hand and arm were cast), to execute a monument to her husband John Thomas Brudenell, 7th Earl of Cardigan (1797–1868). Stocker records that this was significant for Boehm, as it was his first commission for a recumbent monument. The monument, which is in St Peter's Church, Deene, Northamptonshire, was executed between 1869–70 (see Stocker 1988, pp. 171–6, p. 399, no. 59 for the monument).

BIBLIOGRAPHY
List 1892, p. 20.

330: Right hand of Lord Ashburton, possibly William Bingham Baring, 2nd Baron Ashburton
(1799–1864)

about 1862–4
Plaster
l. 21 cm.
1892–90

Scratched into the base on the bottom: ASHBURTON

Given by the Executors of the late Sir J.E. Boehm in 1892; see entry for cat.no. 288.

A marble bust of Louisa, Lady Ashburton is cited by Stocker, exhibited at the Grosvenor Gallery in 1880 (Stocker 1988, p. 411, no. 218). The purpose of the present model is unknown.

BIBLIOGRAPHY
List 1892, p. 13.

331: Left hand of Lord Palmerston, probably Henry John Temple, 3rd Viscount Palmerston
(1784–1865)

about 1862–5
Plaster
l. 24.8 cm.
1892–118

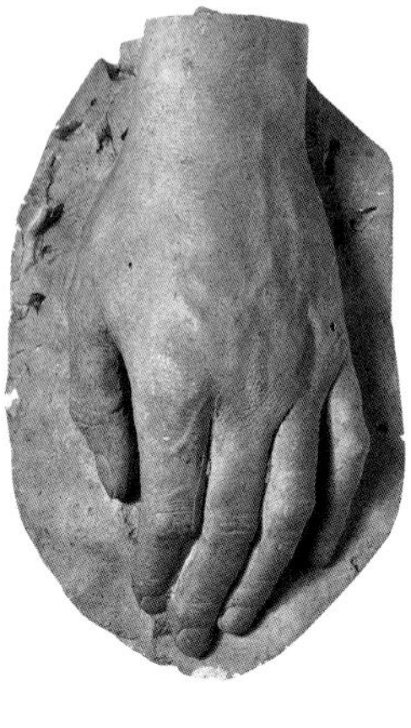

Given by the Executors of the late Sir J.E. Boehm in 1892; see entry for cat.no. 288.

Stocker does not record any works by Boehm connected with Palmerston.

Bibliography
List 1892, p. 16.

332: Hands of Sir Stratford Canning, 1st Viscount de Redcliffe (1788–1880)

about 1862–80
Plaster
l. 25.5 cm.
1892–105

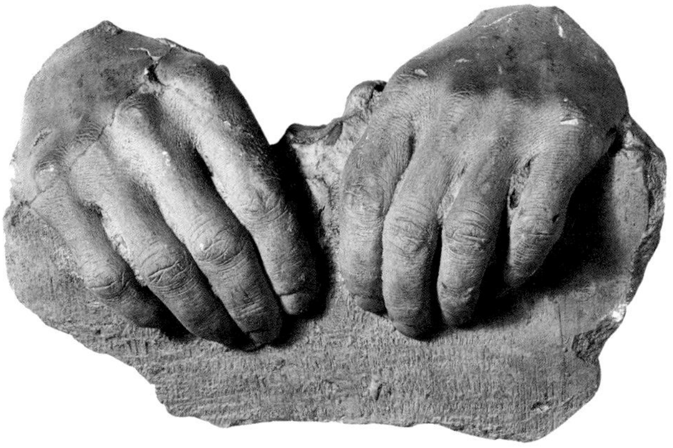

Given by the Executors of the late Sir J.E. Boehm in 1892; see entry for cat.no. 288.

The hands grasp a representation of a piece of wood.

Stocker records that a marble bust of the Viscount de Redcliffe executed by Boehm in 1864, exhibited at the Royal Academy in 1865, led to the commisssion for the monument to de Redcliffe in Westminster Abbey, unveiled in 1884 (see Stocker 1988, p. 207, p. 397, no. 27; Graves I, p. 218, no. 953).

Bibliography
List 1892, p. 14.

333: Left hand of General Giuseppe Garibaldi (1807–1882)

about 1862–82
Plaster
l. 22.5 cm
1892–84

Given by the Executors of the late Sir J.E. Boehm in 1892; see entry for cat.no. 288.

Stocker does not record Boehm having produced any works connected with Garibaldi, and the purpose of this model is unknown. For a bust of Garibaldi executed by Matthew Noble, see entry for cat.no. 522.

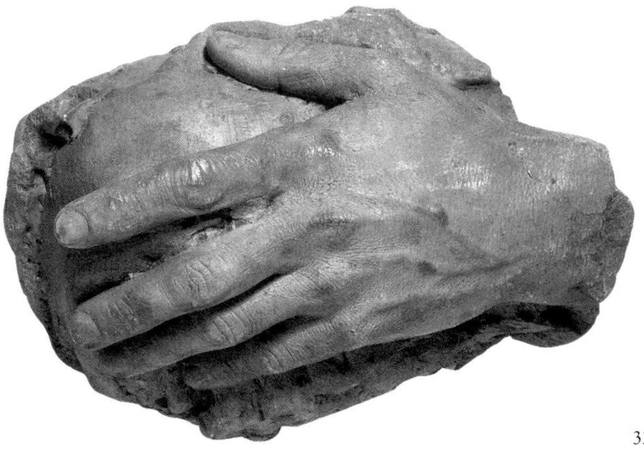

333

Bibliography
List 1892, p. 12.

334: Crossed hands of H.R.H. Princess Beatrice (Princess Henry of Battenberg) (1857–1944)

signed and dated 1877
Plaster
l. 22.5 cm.
1892–86

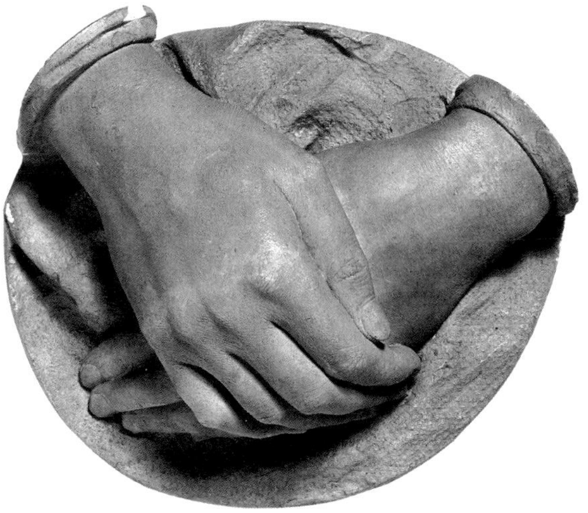

Signed on the side: J.E.B.
Inscribed around the rim at the front: HANDS of H·R·H·PRINCESS BEATRICE 1877·

Given by the Executors of the late Sir J.E. Boehm in 1892; see entry for cat.no. 288.

This subject is presumably Princes Beatrice Mary Victoria Feodor, fifth daughter of Queen Victoria. Stocker records a bronze statuette of Prince Leopold and Princess Beatrice, executed by Boehm in 1872, and in the Royal Collection at Windsor (see Stocker 1988, p. 403, no. 114). The purpose of the present model is unknown.

Bibliography
List 1892, p. 12.

335: Right hand of Benjamin Disraeli, 1st Earl of Beaconsfield (1805–1881)

about 1881–3
Plaster
l. 22 cm.
1892–103

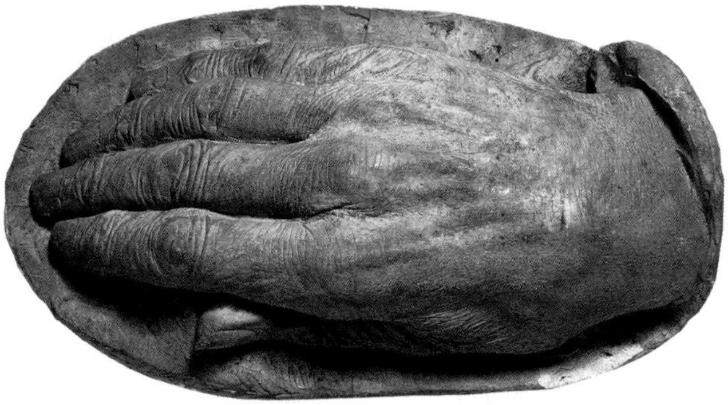

Given by the Executors of the late Sir J.E. Boehm in 1892; see entry for cat.no. 288.

Boehm also executed the monument to Disraeli in Westminster Abbey, executed between 1881–3, unveiled in 1883 (see Stocker 1988, pp. 208–9, p. 412, no. 227).

BIBLIOGRAPHY
List 1892, p. 14.

336: Folded hands of Archibald Campbell Tait, Archbishop of Canterbury (1811–1882)

about 1882
Plaster
l. 28.5 cm.
1892–96

Given by the Executors of the late Sir J.E. Boehm in 1892; see entry for cat.no. 288.

According to the entry in the *List of Reproductions* . . . this cast was 'moulded from nature after death'. Boehm was commissioned to produce a monument to Archbishop Tait for Canterbury Cathedral, which he executed between 1883–5 (see Stocker 1988, pp. 185–6, p. 414, no. 244).

BIBLIOGRAPHY
List 1892, p. 13.

A. (Alfred?) W. Bowcher

(dates unknown; active about 1884 – 1889)

Bowcher trained at the National Art Training Schools, South Kensington, and the piece catalogued below was probably produced whilst he was still a student. An Alfred W. Bowcher, Oakley Cottage Studio, Chelsea is listed as a sculptor who exhibited at the Royal Academy between 1886 and 1889. A series of photographs illustrating clay models for terracotta frieze decorations carried out by A.W. Bowcher for St James's Square, London in 1885 is held in the Sculpture Department.

Graves I, p. 255.

337: Interior of a smithy

signed; about 1884
Terracotta in glazed wood frame
Relief approx. 50 cm. square
17–1885

Signed beneath the anvil: A BOWCHER

Purchased from the sculptor, 72 Stroud Green Park, London in 1884 for £15, when it was shown at the International Health Exhibition for that year (see below). This was one of a total of 33 objects which were selected for consideration for purchase from the objects exhibited by the then South Kensington Museum.

'No 13' is inscribed in pencil on the top left of the relief. The number 13 is also pencilled in the top right hand corner on the integral frame.

This terracotta relief depicts a traditional image of a blacksmith's workshop.

EXHIBITED

This relief was entered into the *Students' Exhibition at the International Health Exhibition of 1884,* cat.no. 927. In 1858 an exhibition of works of art manufacture designed and executed by the students of the Schools of Art had been held under the auspices of the Science and Art Department of the South Kensington Museum. The Science and Art Department of the Committee of Council on Education considered a similar display would provide 'a stimulus . . . to the Artizan [sic], the Designer, and the Manufacturer, and useful information imparted to the public' (Museum records). The exhibition was planned for May 1884 'in immediate connection with and as part of the Health Education International Exhibition'. All items exhibited in the exhibition had to be either the work of former or present students of the Schools of Art, or be executed from designs by such students. The exhibition covered such topics as food, dress, the dwelling, the school, and the workshop.

Sir Thomas Brock

(b. Worcester 1847 – d. London 1922)

Brock initially trained with John Henry Foley [q.v.], and in 1867 attended the Royal Academy Schools, where in 1869 he won a Gold Medal for sculpture. He completed works left unfinished by Foley on his death in 1874, including the seated figure of the Prince Consort for the Albert Memorial. Brock executed a number of portrait busts as well as public monuments, including twelve statues of Queen Victoria, one of which is is his most well-known work, the Queen Victoria Memorial, Buckingham Palace, unveiled in 1911; see the entries below. He was knighted in 1911.

Spielmann 1901, pp. 25–33; Beattie 1983, sep. pp. 228–30; TDA, 4, p. 835 [Stocker]; Sankey 2002.

338: Queen Victoria, from a model for the Victoria Memorial, Buckingham Palace

about 1902
After a model by Sir Thomas Brock; cast by John Webb Singer
Bronze
h. 42 cm.
A.7–1977

Given by Mr and Mrs Roland Morris, 6 Highfields, Lakenheath, Brandon, Suffolk, in 1977, together with cat.nos. 339 and 340. Cast by John Webb Singer & Co. of Frome, Somerset. Mr Roland Morris's father was William Thomas Morris (1874–1944), Chairman and Managing Director of the Morris Singer Company.

The square column is surmounted by a figure of *Victory,* with *Constancy* and *Courage* at the base. The figure of Queen Victoria enthroned at the base of the column is surrounded by groups symbolising *Justice, Truth,* and *Motherhood,* the latter to symbolise the Queen's love for her people. Fruits, flowers and naval and military trophies adorn the corners of the plinth on which the figure rests.

This cast was probably taken from the first clay model commissioned by Brock from the Queen Victoria Memorial Committee in March 1901. The original model, which no longer survives, but which is illustrated in the *Magazine of Art* of 1902, appears to correspond with the central portion of the present piece *(Magazine of Art,* 1902, p. 140). In an article in the *Times* of 15 May 1911, p. 10, 'The Queen Victoria Memorial. Statement by Mr Brock. The Design and its Execution', Brock reported a visit of Edward VII to his studio to see the model, at which time certain alterations were suggested and incorporated into the final memorial. The differences between the present piece, later models and the executed memorial are most notable in the groups depicting *Truth* and *Motherhood* respectively. Inspected by Edward VII in June 1901, and on view at the Foreign Office on 26 July 1901, it was later placed on public exhibition at St James's Palace from 1 November to 7 December 1901. A second model by Brock was completed and approved by the King in June 1902, and it is this version to which the casts of the figures of *Queen Victoria* and *Truth* relate; see entries for cat.nos. 339 and 340. The lower portion of the memorial was opened to the public on 24 May 1909, though the monument itself was not officially unveiled until 16 May 1911. The two groups representing *The Army and Navy*, and *Science and Art* were not installed until April 1924, two years after Brock's death. In 1921 the Victoria Memorial was described by Kineton Parkes as 'Sir Thomas Brock's biggest undertaking, and the most considerable work of a monumental kind in recent London sculpture' (Parkes 1921, p. 65).

The plaster model for the memorial executed by Brock, and exhibited by him at the Royal Academy in 1904, was temporarily deposited at the Victoria and Albert Museum from 10 July 1905, until its return to Brock's studio on 28 March 1912. Lord Esher had suggested to the sculptor that this would be desirable until the memorial was completed, as a precaution against fire destroying the model which was then situated in Brock's studio. Brock's request to the Museum authorities specified that he did not wish the model to be exhibited, merely stored at the Museum. On 18 March 1912 Brock wrote to the Museum authorities that the three boxes containing the model should be returned to his studio, and that he would 'communicate with the Memorial Committee and ascertain what should be done with the model' (Museum records; I am grateful to John Sankey for alerting me to this information).

For further information on the memorial, see *Builder* 1901; *The Times* 27 July 1901, p. 14; *Magazine of Art* 1902; Cundall 1904; *The Times,* 15 May 1911, p. 8 (Queen Victoria Memorial. Tomorrow's Ceremonial. Official Programme); p. 10 statement by Brock); Parkes 1921, pp. 65–7; Darby 1978; *British Sculpture in the Twentieth Century* 1981, pp. 40–2; Read 1982, pp. 371–9.

In 1832 John Webb Singer established himself as a silversmith in Frome, Somerset, and by 1848 had set up the Frome Art Metal Works. The company of J.W. Singer of Frome was founded by Singer in 1852, who continued to work with the assistance of his two sons until his death in 1904. The foundry Spital and Clark of Birmingham and London was incorporated into the Singer business in 1914, which was in turn absorbed by William Thomas Morris (1874–1944) into the Morris foundry. To accommodate the merger of the two, the business was moved from Frome to premises in Dorset Road, London in 1927. The foundry later moved to Basingstoke, Hampshire from where it still trades. In January 1973 the Morris Singer Foundry Ltd and Susse Fondeur SA were amalgamated. An exhibition entitled *Bronze, Silver & Gold* commemorating this event took place at the Alwin Gallery, London between 21 August and 14 September 1973 (Sculpture Department records) (*British Sculpture in the Twentieth Century* 1981, p. 249; Beattie 1983, p. 241).

Bibliography

Beattie 1983, p. 241 (incorrectly suggesting the present piece and cat.nos. 339 and 340 were on loan to the V&A); *Kunst der Historismus* 1996, p. 475, cat.no. 12.21.

Exhibited

"Objects" The V&A Collects 1974–78, Victoria and Albert Museum, London, May 31 to Aug 13 1978; *British Sculpture in the Twentieth Century.* Part 1: Image and Form 1901–50 Whitechapel Art Gallery, London, 11 September to 1 November 1981, cat. no. 2; *Der Traum von Glück. Die Kunst des Historismus in Europa*, Künstlerhaus, Vienna, 13 September 1996 to 6 January 1997, cat. no. 12.21.

339: Queen Victoria, from a model for the Victoria Memorial

about 1902
By Sir Thomas Brock; cast by John Webb Singer
Bronze
h. 55 cm.
A.8–1977

The plinth is inscribed VICTORIA at the front.

Given by Mr and Mrs Roland Morris in 1977 together with cat.nos. 338 and 340. Cast by John Webb Singer & Co. of Frome, Somerset. Mr Roland Morris's father was William Thomas Morris (1874–1944), Chairman and Managing Director of the Morris Singer Company.

See entry for cat.no. 338.

Seated statue of Queen Victoria, holding in her right hand a sceptre and in her left hand the Orb, surmounted by a group of St. George and the Dragon.

This bronze, together with the bronze cast of *Truth* cat.no. 340, were probably taken from Brock's second more elaborate model, produced at a scale of 1/10 full size.

Bibliography
Darby [Victoria Monument] 1978, illus. p. 1647; *idem* 1983, p. 107.

Exhibited
British Sculpture in the Twentieth Century, Part I: Image and Form 1901–50, Whitechapel Art Gallery, London, 11 September to 1 November 1981, cat. no. 3.

340: Truth, from a model for the Victoria Memorial

about 1902
By Sir Thomas Brock; cast by John Webb Singer
Bronze
h. 51.5 cm.
A.9–1977

Given by Mr and Mrs Roland Morris in 1977 together with cat.nos. 338 and 339. Cast by John Webb Singer & Co. of Frome, Somerset. Mr Roland Morris's father was William Thomas Morris (1874–1944), Chairman and Managing Director of the Morris Singer Company.

See entry for cat.no. 338.

Standing winged figure of *Truth* holding a mirror in her right hand and trampling with her left foot on a snake. She is flanked by a nude boy carrying a palm branch and a seated girl reading. A full size plaster model of *Truth* was exhibited at the Rome International Exhibtion in 1911 with a model of *Justice* (I am grateful to John Sankey for this information).

As with cat.no. 339, this cast was probably taken from Brock's second, more elaborate model for the Victoria Memorial, which was completed and approved by the Edward VII in 1902.

ALFRED BROWN

(active 1845 – 1856)

Brown was first recorded in 1845, when he won the Royal Academy Gold Medal for his work The Hours Leading out the Horses of the Sun. *At the 1851 International Exhibition he exhibited a statue of* David before Saul. *As well as being a sculptor, Brown also worked in silver, designing a trophy for the Ascot races in 1845, and a large centrepiece for the Earl of Stamford in 1856, amongst other works. Grant commented, 'His art was chiefly poetical and mythological, but he excelled in horses, whilst statues of General Sir C. Napier and one of David displayed another side of his accomplishment'. Brown exhibited at the Royal Academy between 1845 and 1855; he also showed one work at the British Institution on 1853, a statuette of the* Duke of Wellington *in plaster, no. 575.*

Graves I, pp. 304–5; Grant 1953, p. 44; Gunnis 1968, p. 64; Thieme-Becker, 5, pp. 77–8.

341: General Sir Charles James Napier G.C.B.
(1782–1853)

about 1852
Bronzed plaster with leather and wire for bridle and stirrups, on a wood plinth
h. (figure) 99 cm. h. (plinth) 16 cm.
A.21–1936

Originally received on loan on 23 October 1875 from James Brown Esq, formerly of 25 South Street, Thurloe Square, London. Formally accessioned in 1936. The donor was presumably a relative of the sculptor. On 14 June 1876 James Brown was also recorded as lending to the Museum the plaster bas-relief *The Hours Leading out the Horses of the Sun*, and plaster statues of *The Dying Standard Bearer (*exhibited at the Royal Academy in 1853), *Satan falling from Heaven,* and *David* (exhibited at the Royal Academy in 1850) (see *List* 1876, p. 33). These appear to have been held in store at Bethnal Green Museum. In 1932 it was noted on Museum records that three of these plasters had deteriorated and broken beyond repair. The location of the *Satan* statue is not recorded.

In a fragmentary condition.

There has been some confusion as to the identity of the sitter of the present piece. Though originally noted in the *List of Art Objects in the South Kensington Museum . . . Lent during the Year 1875* as General Sir C.J. Napier, G.C.B., in Museum papers from 1932 it is noted as being Gen. Sir C.G. Napier, and in departmental records in 1936 as Sir E.J. Napier. I am grateful to Charles Napier and Philip Ward-Jackson for their efforts in identifying the sitter.

In 1852 Brown exhibited at the Royal Academy a 'Sketch for statue of General Sir Charles James Napier G.C.B., as Governor of Scinde and Belochistan' (Graves I, p. 305, no. 1323); this may have been the present piece. The location of the statue for which this was a model, if one survives, is unknown.

BIBLIOGRAPHY

List 1875, p. 203; Thieme-Becker, 5, p. 78.

Albert Bruce-Joy

(b. Dublin 1842 – d. Hindhead 1924)

Bruce-Joy trained at the South Kensington Schools, where he was a pupil of John Henry Foley [q.v.], at the Royal Academy Schools, and in Rome, where he remained for three years. On the death of Foley in 1874, Bruce-Joy took over his outstanding commissions. He also completed a statue of Robert James Graves for the Royal College of Physicians in 1877, for which Foley had previously executed three other figures of physicians. Bruce-Joy exhibited regularly at the Royal Academy between 1866 and 1923, and at the Royal Hibernian Academy of Arts between 1870 and 1914. Spielmann commented on the volume of his work, 'The list of his works is so long that – the expression is used in no uncomplimentary sense – it is surprising that they are so good'. He was prolific in the production of portrait busts and statues, and was also a medallist. He travelled extensively in North America, producing the Ayer Colossal Lion for Lowell, Boston amongst other works. Parkes commented, 'Albert Bruce-Joy is not only the oldest Irish sculptor, but he is the doyen of the sculptors of the British Isles . . . During a life so long as that of Bruce-Joy, an artist has ample opportunity of making some change in his outlook or style, but Bruce-Joy has been singularly consistent, and those banes of the artist, Committees, have felt safe with him, for they could count on a standard work'.

Hooe 1880, p. 15; Spielmann 1901, p. 24; Graves IV, pp. 289–92; Forrer III, p. 91; Parkes 1921, pp. 151–3; Royal Academy I, pp. 219–20; Thieme-Becker, 19, p. 211; Read 1982, pp. 75–6; Thomas 1982 (I am grateful to Martin Greenwood for this reference); Royal Hibernian Academy I, pp. 92–3.

342: Sunshine

about 1865–6
Marble
h. 65 cm.
A.11–1984

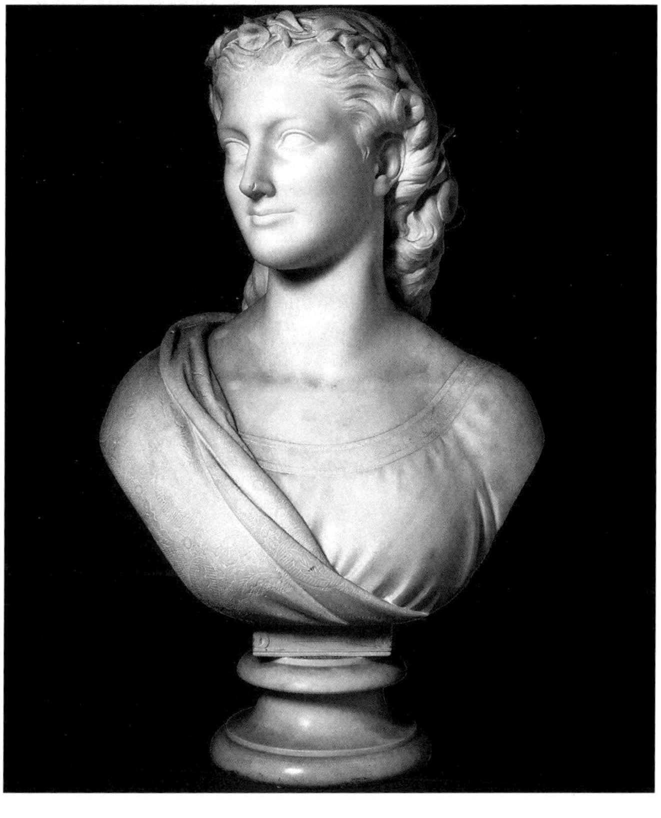

Bequeathed by Mrs Kate Blanche Thompson in 1984, together with cat.nos. 343 and 344. Previously owned by Mrs K.B.M. Bentall (the donor's daughter), who on her death in 1981 bequeathed this and the two other Bruce-Joy busts to her mother. Bruce-Joy lived at Haslemere in Surrey at periods between 1895 and 1905, as did the donor Mrs Thompson.

The cartouche beneath the bust is blank.

Bibliography
Graves IV, p. 289, no. 974; *Royal Hibernian Academy* I, p. 92, no. 386.

Exhibited
Bruce-Joy exhibited *Sunshine* at Royal Academy in 1866, no. 974, presumed to be the present piece. Thomas records the sculptor's 'first work to be exhibited at the Royal Academy, the figure of a young girl entitled *Sunshine* achieved rapturous acclaim: critics spoke of the radiant sweetness which lights up the finely cut features' (Thomas 1982, pp. 1688–9); Bruce-Joy exhibited *Sunshine* at the Royal Hibernian Academy of Arts 1870, no. 386, presumably the present piece. A 'life-size plaster bust' of Sunshine of 1865 was exhibited at the 1871 International Exhibition (see *London Exhibition* 1871 *[revised]*, p. 124, no. 2577).

343: Beatrice

signed; about 1866–7
Marble
h. 66.5 cm.
A.7–1990

Signed on the back: A.B.JOY Sc.
Inscribed on the cartouche: BEATRICE

Bequeathed by Mrs Kate Blanche Thompson in 1984, together with cat.nos. 342 and 344, though not written on until 1990; see entry for cat.no. 342. In the possession of the sculptor in 1868.

The star on the veil is chipped.

With her veil surmounted by a star, the present bust is thought to depict Dante's *Beata Beatrix*, 'a vision of the dead Beatrice as a woman wrapt in contemplation of heavenly bliss' (Hall 1980, pp. 42–3).

BIBLIOGRAPHY
Leeds 1869, p. 205, no. 636p; Graves IV, p. 289, no. 1156; *Royal Hibernian Academy* I, p. 92, no. 612.

EXHIBITED
Royal Academy 1867 no. 1156; National Exhibition of Works of Art at Leeds, 1868, section E, gallery J, no. 636p, lent by the sculptor. In 1870 Bruce-Joy exhibited *Beatrice* at the Royal Hibernian Academy of Arts, no. 612, presumably the present piece. At the 1871 International Exhibition, a marble bust of Beatrice by Bruce Joy was lent by the artist; the catalogue for the exhibition records it was priced at 80 guineas (*London Exhibition* 1871 *[revised]*, p. 124, no. 2575).

344: Young Apollo

about 1871
Marble
h. (incl. socle) 49 cm.
A.10–1984

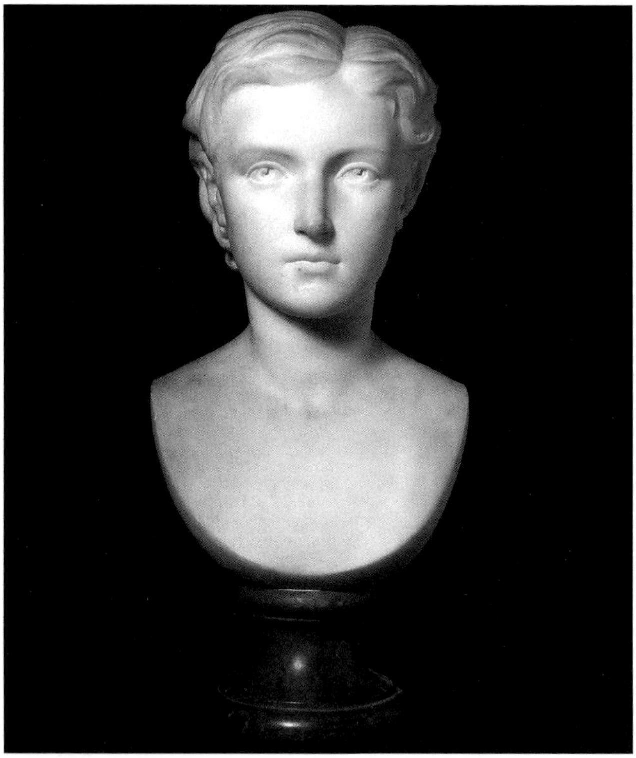

Bequeathed by Mrs Kate Blanche Thompson in 1984, together with cat.nos. 342 and 343; see entry for cat.no. 342.

BIBLIOGRAPHY
Graves IV, p. 289, no. 1281; Parkes 1921, p. 152.

EXHIBITED
Royal Academy 1871, no. 1281 there described as 'The young Apollo. "He listerned and he wept, etc." – Keats'.

Henry Behnes Burlowe

(b. 1796 or 1802 – d. Rome 1837)

There is confusion over the date of birth for Burlowe; Gunnis records a date of 1802, whereas the entry by Brockwell in Thieme-Becker suggests he was born in Dublin in about 1796. Burlowe was the younger brother of the sculptor William Behnes [q.v.]; Henry exhibited under the name of Burlowe to avoid confusion between the two. He exhibited busts at the Royal Academy in 1831 and 1833, and in 1834 travelled to Rome, where he was in demand as a portrait sculptor, until his death from cholera in 1837.

Graves I, p. 350; Redgrave 1970, p. 63; DNB 1973, II, p. 131; Thieme-Becker, 3, p. 204.

345: Samuel Carter Hall (1800–1889)

signed and dated 1834
Marble
h. 84 cm.
A.5–2000

Signed on the back: HB. BURLOWE/SCULPTOR/AND PHRENOLOGIST/ *LONDON*/1834

Inscribed across the back of the shoulders: SAMUEL CARTER HALL

Previously recorded at Bethnal Green Museum, the present object was unregistered until it was written on by the Museum in 2000. It was certainly at Bethnal Green Museum at a date prior to 1953, when it was noted by Gunnis (Gunnis 1953, p. 70).

Samuel Carter Hall was a writer and Editor of the *Art Journal*.

A bust of Carter Hall by Burlowe was exhibited at the Royal Academy in 1833 (see Graves I, p. 350, no. 1121).

Bibliography

Gunnis 1953, p. 70; Gunnis 1968, p. 70; Kilmurray 1981, p. 86.

Randolph Caldecott

(b. Chester 1846 – d. St. Augustine, Florida 1886)

Beginning his professional career as a bank clerk, Caldecott's lifelong passion for art was such that at around the age of 27 he left banking to 'shake off the trammels and routine of the desk, and devote himself entirely to art' (Brasenose Club *1888, p. 7). Though Caldecott is chiefly known as an illustrator, it is evident from the contemporary biography by Blackburn that his interests and work were varied, and not confined to book illustration. A number of his sketchbooks are held in the Department of Prints, Drawings and Paintings (Circ.431–1932, E.3678 to 3683–1932). A connection between Caldecott and the South Kensington Museum existed prior to the acquisition of cat.no.346 in 1902. Blackburn noted 'On the 16th April [1872] he [Caldecott] went to the Slade School to attend the Life Class under E.J. Poynter, R.A., until the 29th June. As this was the turning point in Caldecott's career, it should be recorded that at this time, and ever afterwards, Mr Armstrong, the present Art Director at the South Kensington Museum, was his best friend and counsellor. In a private letter to the writer of this memoir, dated 2nd November, 1876, Caldecott says:- "Pen can never put down how much I owe, in many ways, to T.A."'* (Blackburn *1886, p. 30). Caldecott exhibited at the Royal Academy and Grosvenor Gallery, and was a member of the Manchester Academy of Fine Arts, and Institute of Painters in Watercolours.*

For contemporary accounts of Caldecott see Phillips 1886; Blackburn 1886; Brasenose Club 1888, pp. 5–11. See also Caldecott 1977, pp. 3–17; Thieme-Becker, 5, pp. 380–1; TDA, 5, pp. 421–42 [Treuherz].

346: Cat

signed and dated 1874
Terracotta
h. 23.5 cm.
232–1902

Signed: R. Caldecott 1874 scratched into the ground behind the life-size figure of a cat, which sits on an integral terracotta base.

Purchased from the sale of the collection of Alexander A. Ionides Esq., held at Christie, Manson and Woods, 8 King Street, London on 14 March 1902, lot 273, for £7 7s (7 guineas).

As well as Thomas Armstrong [q.v.], the sculptor Aimé-Jules Dalou [q.v.] had a profound effect on Caldecott's artistic output. 'He [Caldecott] went with a letter of introduction to Dalou, the French sculptor, then living in Chelsea. Of this interview he writes, "M. Dalou very kind in hints, showing me clay & c". A friendship followed, cemented in the first instance by a bargain that Caldecott should come and work at the Studio and teach the sculptor to talk English, whilst Dalou helped him in his modelling! Caldecott profited by the arrangement, and often spoke in after years of the value of Dalou's practical teaching. Many visits were paid to the sculptor's studio in the year 1873.' (Blackburn 1886, pp. 63–4). Engen suggests the present piece is the most important of Caldecott's three-dimensional works to emerge from his contact with Dalou (*Caldecott* 1977, p. 14).

Blackburn recorded that 'On the 19th of November and following days Caldecott was "working at Dalou's on a cat crouching for a spring". He had a skeleton of a cat, a dead cat, and a live cat to work from. This model in clay was finished on the 8th December 1874.' (Blackburn 1886, p. 114).

Bibliography
Blackburn 1886, p. 114; *Aesthetic Movement* 1973, p. 57, no. 65, illus p. 56; *Caldecott* 1977, pp. 14, 29 and illus p. 29 – there said to be similar to the cat that killed the rat, in 'The House that Jack Built'; Watson 1986, pp. 148, illus. p. 149.

Exhibited
The Aesthetic Movement 1869–1890, Camden Arts Centre, London, 15 August to 7 October 1973, cat.no. 65; *Randolph Caldecott 1846–1886, A Christmas Exhibition of the work of the Victorian book illustrator*, Manchester City Art Gallery, 13 December 1977 to 28 January 1978, cat.no. 64.

347: Horse fair

signed; about 1874–6
Terracotta
h. 13 cm. w. 33 cm.
A.95–1927

Signed to the right: RC
Inscribed on the front to the right: AT LE FOLGUET/BRITTANY

Bequeathed by James Richardson Holliday Esq. in 1927. Holliday was Director of the Fitzwilliam Museum, Cambridge. He also bequeathed his large collection of mainly English watercolours and pre-Raphaelite drawings to various museums and institutions. A number of drawings by Caldecott, described as 'many good examples', were bequeathed by Holliday to the Fitzwilliam Museum in 1927 (*Fitzwilliam* 1928, pp. 2, 8).

The colour of this relief is a vivid orange, as opposed to the neutral-coloured pastiglia reliefs by Caldecott of around the same date, cat.nos. 348 and 349. Blackburn commented that Caldecott's favoured material was French clay (Blackburn 1886, p. 112). He also noted that during 1874 and 1878 Caldecott travelled to Brittany to make drawings for what was to be a publication entitled *Old Christmas*. Blackburn suggested that 'Caldecott's studies with M. Dalou, the sculptor, in 1874, and the great proficiency he had already obtained in modelling in clay enabled him to make several successful groups from his Brittany subjects' (*ibid.*, p. 111).

Blackburn also noted that 1874 was a very productive year for Caldecott, and that during October he began work on the wax bas-relief of a '"Brittany horse fair", afterwards cast in metal' (*ibid.*, p. 112, illus. p. 137). This is the metal version exhibited at the Royal Academy in 1876 (no. 1499) (Graves I, p. 375), and Blackburn (apparently the owner of the relief), commented that it attracted a good deal of critical praise, and was mentioned in the *Times* of that year, and in the *Saturday Review*, June 10th 1876: 'Of low relief – taking the Elgin frieze as the standard – one of the purest examples we have seen for many a day is Mr Caldecott's bas-relief, 'A Horse Fair in Brittany'. Here a simple and almost rude incident in nature has been brought within the laws and symmetry of art' (Blackburn 1886, p. 136). This metal verion is also discussed in Watson 1986, p. 148, illus. fig 3 on p. 149.

A terracotta frieze of the *Horse Fair, Le Folquet* [sic], *Brittany* was exhibited at the Brasenose Club in 1888 by a Mr William Clough (*Brasenose Club* 1888, no. 47, p. 31). Two other versions, described as electro-bronze, and bas-relief, bronzed, were exhibited by a Mr Thomas Hughes and Mrs Caldecott respectively (*ibid.*, cat.nos. 26 and 44, pp. 30–1). A plaster cast version from a bronzed bas-relief was exhibited at the Royal Institute of Painters in Water Colours exhibition of 1889, lent by Mrs Caldecott (*Royal Institute of Painters in Water Colours* 1889, p. 21, cat.no. 722).

BIBLIOGRAPHY

Review 1927, p. 90.

348: Girl feeding calves

signed; about 1874–8
Pastiglia (modelling paste) in a glazed wood frame
h. 16.5 cm. w. 22 cm.
448–1905

Signed in the upper left hand corner: RC

Purchased from Mrs M.H. Caldecott, the widow of the sculptor, in 1905 for £20. Formerly on loan to the Museum from Mrs Caldecott, together with cat.no. 349, between July 1899 and its purchase in 1905. In a letter to the Museum, Mrs Caldecott asked for £20 for each relief, in compensation for her losing the right to reproduce them. The reproductive value of Caldecott's works is illustrated by Mrs Caldecott exhibiting six different subjects described as 'plaster casts from bas-reliefs (bronzed)', at the Royal Insititute of Painters in Water Colours, in June 1889. A plaster cast version of the *Girl Feeding Calves* was also exhibited (*Royal Insititute of Painters in Water Colours* 1889, p. 21, no. 725).

Museum papers relating to the acquisition of this relief, and that of a *Hunting scene*, cat.no. 349, record that they were 'strongly recommended for purchase as being very characteristic of his [Caldecott's] work'.

This may be one of the subjects undertaken by Caldecott as a result of his study trips to Brittany during 1874 and 1878; see also cat.no. 347.

Bibliography
Brasenose Club 1888, p. 30, cat. 36, p. 31, cat.no. 42; *Caldecott* 1977, p. 29, cat. no. 66.

Exhibited
Two versions, (one of which was possibly the present piece), were lent by Mrs Caldecott to the Brasenose Club exhibition of 1888. See entry for cat.no. 350 for the Brasenose Club. One was described as a 'bas-relief, waxed – *Feeding Calves,* (cat.no. 36), the other a 'bas-relief, bronzed – *Girl feeding Calves* (cat.no. 42); *Randolph Caldecott 1846–1886, A Christmas Exhibition of the work of the Victorian book illustrator*, Manchester City Art Gallery, 13 December 1977 to 28 January 1978, cat.no. 66.

349: Hunting scene

signed; about 1874–8
Pastiglia (modelling paste) in a glazed wood frame
h. 18.5 cm. w. 28 cm.
449–1905

Signed in the upper left hand corner: RC

Purchased from Mrs M.H. Caldecott, the widow of the sculptor, in 1905 for £20. Formerly on loan to the Museum from Mrs Caldecott, together with cat.no. 348, between July 1899 and its purchase in 1905.

See entry for cat.no. 348. On the reverse of the frame is a label inscribed, 'On loan from Mrs Caldecott 18 . . .'; (the year has not been inserted). This is probably the label for the Brasenose Club exhibition of 1888.

Bibliography
Brasenose Club 1888, p. 31, no. 45; *Caldecott* 1977, p. 29, cat.no. 67.

Exhibited
A version of this relief described as 'bas-relief, bronzed – Huntsmen and Hounds', was lent by Mrs Caldecott to the Brasenose Club exhibition of 1888, cat.no. 45; *Randolph Caldecott 1846–1886. A Christmas Exhibition of the work of the Victorian book illustrator*, Manchester City Art Gallery, 13 December 1977 to 28 January 1978, cat.no. 67.

350: Hunting scene (Three jovial huntsmen)

signed and dated 1877
Plaster
h. 68 cm. w. 117 cm.
275–1903

Signed in the upper right hand corner: RC

Purchased from the sale at Christie, Manson and Woods, held on 6 April 1903, lot 80, for £9 9s. Catalogued as 'from the artist's sale'.

Described in the Christie's catalogue as 'the original plaster model in relief, by Randolph Caldecott; designed for bronze, but never executed' (Catalogue of porcelain, objects of art decorative furniture & tapestry from numerous sources, Messrs Christie, Manson and Woods, Monday 6 April 1903, p. 12). Museum papers relating to the acquisition of this relief suggest that Caldecott was highly regarded as a sculptor; the Director, A.B. Skinner [q.v.] commented, 'It is a very interesting specimen of Caldecott's work and I should like to have it to add to our specimens of the work of this very clever artist already in the Museum'. On acquisition it was described as having 'been roughly painted. The colour could be washed off and a more delicate coat given'.

Watson notes that Caldecott's interest in hunting was one which continued throughout his life, influencing his artistic work (Watson 1986, pp. 148–9). Though described on acquisition as a *Hunting Scene*, it is likely that the correct title for this relief is *Three Jovial Hunstmen*. A number of works by Caldecott depicting *Three Jovial Huntsmen* showing the same composition were included at the exhibition of his work in 1977 (see *Caldecott* 1977, pp. 22–3, nos. 23–8).

Bibliography
Brasenose Club 1888, p. 31, no. 51; *Royal Institute of Painters in Water Colours* 1889, p. 21, no. 741.

Exhibited
What is described as a bronzed bas-relief of *Three Jovial Hunstmen* (possibly this object), was exhibited three years after the death of Caldecott at the Loan Collection of the Works of Randolph Caldecott, held at the Brasenose Club, Manchester, March 1888, no. 51, lent by Mrs Caldecott. Mrs Caldecott also

lent what is described as a plaster cast (bronzed) of *Three Jovial Huntsmen* to the exhibition at the Royal Institute of Painters in Watercolours: The English Humourists in Art, Piccadilly, June 1889, no. 741. Described as 'Original model for a Frieze, made at Florence by R. CALDECOTT, unpublished. Hunting Party'. Though this was described as 'bronzed', Museum records confirm that the present piece is the version of the relief which was exhibited.

Thomas Campbell

(b. Edinburgh 1790 – d. London 1858)

Campbell was initially apprenticed to John Marshall, a marble-cutter, and later James Dalzell, to whom the business passed on the death of Marshall. With the assistance of his patron Gilbert Innes, Deputy Governor of the Bank of Scotland, Campbell later trained at the Royal Academy Schools. During this period he also worked in the studio of the sculptor Edward Hodges Baily [q.v.]. In 1818, again with the help of Innes, Campbell travelled to Rome, where he remained for a number of years. Though he returned to England in 1830, establishing a studio in London, he retained his studio in Rome. Another of his important patrons was the 6th Duke of Devonshire, for whom he executed in 1828 a statue of Princess Pauline Borghese, the sister of Napoleon. Campbell exhibited at the Royal Academy between 1827 and 1857. Correspondence relating to this sculptor is held at the National Library of Scotland, Department of Manuscripts.

Graves I, pp. 386–7; Gunnis 1968, pp. 76–7; Redgrave 1970, p. 69; Smailes 1987; Virtue and Vision [Smailes] 1991, pp. 64–71; Thieme-Becker, 5, pp. 458–9; British Museum 1999, p. 212.

351: Ganymede

about 1821–41
Plaster
h. 150 cm.
1859–4

Purchased for £2 – vendor not recorded. Though accessioned in 1859, the present piece was recorded in the Museum during April of the previous year (see below).

Though badly chipped, a letter 'O', presumably the remnants of a signature, is apparent on the base.

The present piece was apparently wrongly identified on its arrival in the Museum. In the *Inventory of Plaster Casts of Objects of Art . . .*, it was described as 'Ganymede and the Eagle. A restoration by Benvenuto Cellini of an antique torso. The original is in the Museum of the Uffizi, Florence' *(Inventory* 1869, p. 22). Though the present group is clearly inspired by the Cellini *Ganymede* (now in the Museo Nazionale del Bargello, Florence) it is not a plaster cast of it as stated in the *Inventory of Plaster Casts.* The vendor may have been unaware of the authorship of the present piece. It seems to be related to a lost ideal work by Campbell, although it is unclear whether it is a plaster cast after Campbell's *Ganymede* or a model for it. A reference made by M.W. Brockwell to a model of *Ganymede* by Campbell being in the South Kensington Museum presumably refers to the present piece (Thieme-Becker, 5, p. 459). However in the obituary of Campbell in the *Art Journal* for 1 April 1858, mention is made of 'a "Ganymede" with the eagle, the plaster cast of which is now in the gallery of the South Kensington Museum' (Donaldson 1858, p. 107).

Gunnis recorded that in 1821 Campbell executed a *Ganymede* for Lord Kinnaird, at Rossie Priory, Perthshire (Gunnis 1968, p. 72). I have been unable to confirm whether this is so; if it was executed it is now apparently lost (I am grateful to Helen Smailes for her comments on this). Campbell certainly exhibited a

Ganymede in 1841 (see below); the date of the present piece is uncertain, but could be any time between 1821 and 1841.

Bibliography
Donaldson 1858, p. 107; *Inventory* 1869, p. 22; Thieme-Becker, 5, p. 459.

Exhibited
In 1841 Campbell exhibited ' A model – Ganymede' at the Royal Academy (Graves I, p. 387, no. 1239).

352: Psyche

signed; about 1830 (?)
Plaster
h. 147 cm.
A.4–2000

Signed on the base: THO[S] CAMPBELL/ROME . . .

There is no information available on the provenance of the present piece, which until 2000 was recorded as an unregistered object in the Museum. We are grateful to Philip Ward-Jackson for identifying it.

A weathered marble version of closely comparable height (146 cm.) was included in the sale held at Sotheby's, London, 7 July 1988, lot 292, described as Psyche, signed and dated 'THOS. CAMPBELL, FECIT, ROMAE, MDCCCXXII', on a composition stone base inscribed 'ROSHER CHELSEA' (I am grateful to Philip Ward-Jackson and Mike Phipps for this reference). In 1830 Campbell exhibited at the Royal Academy a 'Marble statue of Psyche', possibly the version later sold in 1988 (Graves I, p. 386, no. 1174). Redgrave recorded that, 'Having at this time large commissions to execute in England, he returned in 1830, but retained his studio in Rome, and exhibited at the Academy a marble statue of "Psyche" with other works' (Redgrave 1970, p. 69). Amongst the works by Campbell Gunnis noted a *Psyche* of 1830 'For R.N. Hamilton' (Gunnis 1968, p. 77). In Campbell's obituary in the *Art Journal* of April 1858 – in which the Ganymede figure (see cat.no. 351) was also mentioned – the author noted: 'His works of fancy were few, but they are admirable for their chaste simplicity. Among these . . . a "Psyche" opening the vase, for R. Christopher Nisbett Hamilton, Esq.,' (Donaldson 1858, p. 107).

As with cat.no. 351 the present piece is probably a model for the original marble, although it could be a plaster cast after it.

Holme Cardwell

(b. Manchester 1820; active 1837 – 1856; d. about 1864)

Cardwell attended the Royal Academy Schools in 1834, and in 1841 travelled to Paris where he studied under David d'Angers (1788–1856). Cardwell later settled in Rome. He exhibited at the Royal Academy between 1837 and 1856, at the British Institution in 1840, and twice at the Suffolk Street Galleries.

Graves I, p. 393; Gunnis 1968, p. 78; Thieme-Becker, 6, pp. 590–1.

353: Cupid and Pan

signed and dated 1862
Marble
h. 130 cm.
1076–1871

Signed and dated on the side of the base behind forearm of Pan:
HOLME CARDWELL/OF/MANCHESTER/Sculpt^{r}. ROME 1862.

Given by John Malcolm Esq., Poltalloch in 1871.

This group is based on the theme of Love the Conqueror, in which Cupid is shown overcoming Pan, who is crouched on one knee, by holding one of his horns, 'Since Pan stood for carnal lust, the theme was seen as the combat of divine and earthly love, Cupid in this case having the more virtuous role. But Pan also personified universal nature, so it equally illustrated the all-embracing power of love' (Hall 1980, p. 88).

BIBLIOGRAPHY
International Exhibition 1862, class XXXIX, British Division, B – Living artists, p. 143, lent by John Malcolm Esq.; *Bequests and Donations* 1901, p. 194.

EXHIBITED
Lent by the previous owner John Malcolm to the International Exhibition of 1862, London.

354: Christ

1865
By Holme Cardwell, after the original by Bertel Thorvaldsen
Marble
h. (excl. plinth) 62 cm.
416–1906

Given by Sir Edwin Durning-Lawrence, Bart., King's Ride, Ascot, Berkshire in 1906. On loan to the Bethnal Green Museum from the Department of Architecture and Sculpture (now the Sculpture Department), from 1928; returned to the Sculpture Department in 1982.

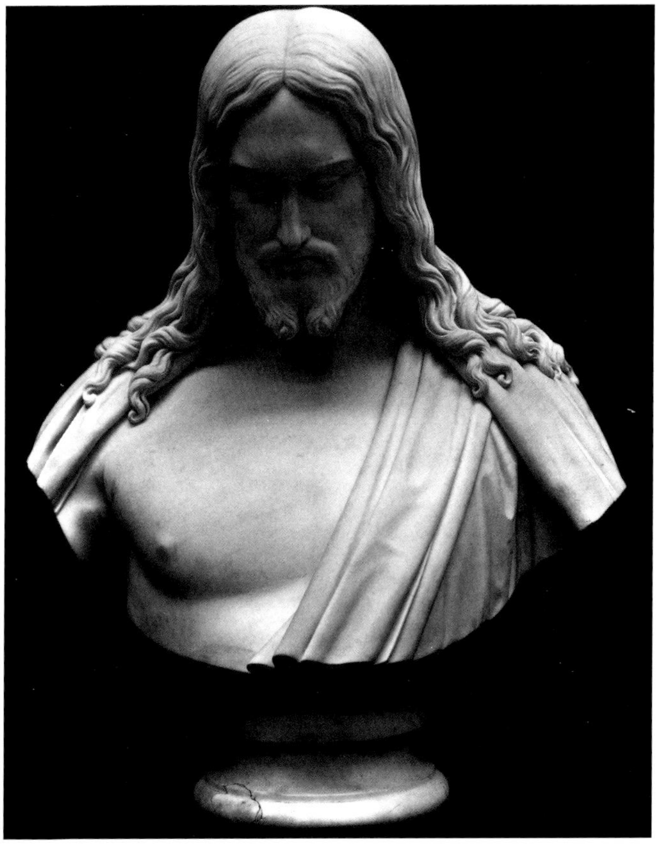

The pedestal for the bust is said to have formed part of a column from the Forum of Trajan in Rome. According to the donor, this bust was executed by Cardwell when in Rome in 1865. It is a reduced copy of the original full-length figure of Christ produced by Bertel Thorvaldsen (1768/70–1844) during 1821 for the Church of Our Lady, Copenhagen, now Copenhagan Cathedral. Accompanying figures of the Twelve Apostles were produced by Thorvaldsen between 1821–42, which together with the Christ were displayed in the interior of the Church. 'The figure of Christ, which is regarded as one of the best-known and most affecting religious images of the 19th century, was widely copied and imitated' (TDA, 30, p. 765 [Jørnaes]).

Sir Francis Legatt Chantrey R.A.

(b. Norton, nr Sheffield 1781 – d. London 1841)

Chantrey was probably the most successful British portrait-sculptor of his day. The son of a carpenter and tenant farmer, he was originally apprenticed to Robert Ramsay of Sheffield, a dealer in prints and plaster models, and decorative carver and picture restorer. In 1802 however he cancelled his apprenticeship and moved to London, resolving to be a portraitist in crayon and miniature. He was working for a German wood-carver by 1803, and seems to have started sculpting more seriously at around this date. In 1805 he received his first known sculpture commission, a monument to the Reverend Wilkinson in Sheffield Cathedral. He began specialising in sculpture, and his marriage in 1809 to his cousin, Mary Ann Wale, who brought a large dowry with her, enabled him to set up a studio in Pimlico. He travelled to Paris in 1814 and 1815, and to Italy in 1815; he took Canova to see his new statue of George III when the Italian sculptor visited England in 1815. Although he never formally enrolled at the Royal Academy schools, he studied there in the evenings when he was first resident in London, and exhibited there from 1804 to 1842 (two posthumous exhibits). His finest portraits and monuments exhibit a liveliness of execution and finish, indicating his powers of observation and his skilled technique in handling marble. On his death he left a fortune initially to his wife of about £150,000, which on her death was bequeathed to the Royal Academy, and is known as the Chantrey Bequest, to be used for the 'Encouragement of British Fine Art in Painting and Sculpture'. Additionally Chantrey's many plaster models and casts after the antique were given by his wife to the Ashmolean Museum, Oxford, where some of them remain, though the majority were unfortunately destroyed in 1939.

Whinney 1971, pp. 147–8; Chantrey 1981; Whinney 1988, pp. 422–3; Penny 1991 [Chantrey/Westmacott]; Ashmolean 1992 [III], pp. 213–50; Thieme-Becker, 6, pp. 366–7; Yarrington 1994; TDA, 6, pp. 455–8 [Bindman]; Yarrington 2000.

355: Unknown man, possibly Samuel Shore of Norton (d.1836)

signed and dated 1817
Marble
h. (incl. socle) 62 cm.
A.66–1965

Signed and dated on the back: CHANTREY/Sculptor 1817

Bequeathed by Rupert Gunnis Esq, Hungershall Lodge, Tunbridge Wells, Kent in 1965.

Chantrey exhibited seven busts of male sitters at the Royal Academy in 1817, including one of 'S. Shore, Esq' (Graves II, p. 41, no. 1059). Chantrey's ledgers record that on 30 November 1816 an order was raised by a Samuel Shore Esq. of Norton, Derbyshire, commissioning Chantrey to execute a bust of himself in marble, for which he was charged £84. However, 'A letter from Ward dated 11 July 1814 records that Chantrey was to come to Sheffield that summer and "model a bust of Mr Shore", well before an order was formally recorded in the Ledger' (Yarrington 1994 [Potts], p. 30, no. 13a). The present piece is not cited in the entry on Shore; however Malcolm Baker suggests that the amount charged by Chantrey of £84 was appropriate for a bust of this type.

Bibliography
Knox 1998, p. 95 n. 24.

356: Sir Archibald Macdonald Bt. (1747–1826)

signed and dated 1818
Marble
h. (incl. socle) 61 cm.
A.64–1965

Signed and dated on the back: CHANTREY/SC: 1818.
Inscribed on the truncation at the back: [SI]R ARCH^{D} MACDONALD.

Montague Marcussen Ltd, 98 Crawford Street, London. Purchased by Rupert Gunnis. Bequeathed by Rupert Gunnis Esq., Hungershall Lodge, Tunbridge Wells, Kent in 1965.

The sitter was appointed Solicitor General in 1784, and Attorney General in 1780. He was knighted in 1780 and served as a judge from 1793 to 1813. The bust had been called Dr Archibald Macdonald by Montague Marcussen, the previous owners; it was Rupert Gunnis who identified the sitter as Sir Archibald Macdonald. In his ledger, Chantrey records that he received an order from Sir Archibald to produce his bust in 1817, for which he was paid £105. A related drawing by Chantrey of this sitter is in the National Portrait Gallery, inv.no. 316A-166.

BIBLIOGRAPHY
Graves II, p. 41, no. 1043; Kilmurray 1979, p. 139; Yarrington 1994, p. 78, no. 60b, figs 44, 45; Knox 1998, p. 95 n. 24.

EXHIBITED
Chantrey exhibited a bust of 'Sir Arc. Macdonald' at the Royal Academy in 1820 no. 1043, presumably the present piece.

357: Henry Cowper (1758–1840)

signed and dated 1818
Marble
h. 69 cm.
A.65–1965

Signed and dated on the back: CHANTREY. SC./1828.

Bequeathed by Rupert Gunnis Esq., Hungershall Lodge, Tunbridge Wells, Kent in 1965.

Henry Cowper was Deputy Clerk of the Houses of Parliament, and Clerk Assistant of the House of Lords. A plaster model for this bust was included in the gift presented by Lady Chantrey to Oxford University in 1843, and is now held in the Ashmolean Museum, Oxford (*Ashmolean* 1992 [III], p. 230, no. 695; see *ibid.* 1992, pp.xxvii-xxiii, and pp. 213–4 for the Chantrey gift). Two preliminary sketches for the bust are in the National Portrait Gallery (*NPG* 1981, p. 135, no. 316 (a).

BIBLIOGRAPHY
Kilmurray 1979, p. 53; *Ashmolean* 1992 [III], p. 230; Yarrington 1994, p. 190, no. 165b; Knox 1998, p. 95 n. 24.

358: John Raphael Smith (1752–1812)

signed and dated 1825
Marble
h. 66 cm.
A.15–1920

Signed and dated on the back: CHANTREY, SC./1825.

Commissioned by Sir Simon Clarke Bt.; an entry in Chantrey's ledger on 16 December 1827 records the cost of the bust, £105, but it was still in Chantrey's studio on 14 February 1835 (Yarrington 1994 [Potts], p. 200). Given by Mrs O. Stuart Andreae and her sister Miss South, Kenna House, Kensington Palace Gardens, London in 1920.

Smith, a friend of Chantrey, was a painter and engraver. His self-portrait in pastel is in the National Portrait Gallery (see *NPG* 1981, p. 524, no. 981). Commenting on the present piece, Whinney suggested, 'The portrait is among the sculptor's most striking works. It shows his ability, for which he was so much praised, in rendering the softness of flesh, and also reveals his gift of conveying character. Smith was deaf, and the peculiarity of listening is conveyed with unmistakable precision, by the turn of the head, the straining of the eyes, and the slightly open mouth' (Whinney 1971, p. 148).

Chantrey exhibited the plaster model for the present bust at the Royal Academy in 1811 (Graves II, p. 40, no. 936); a second plaster is in the Ashmolean Museum, Oxford; see *Ashmolean* 1992 [III], p. 244, cat.no. 759.

Bibliography

Review 1920, p. 4; Gunnis 1968, p. 94, there mistakenly noted as J.T. Smith; Whinney 1971, p. 148, cat.no. 48, illus. on p. 149; *Chantrey* 1981, p. 18, cat.no. 10; Whinney 1988, p. 422 and pl. 314 on p. 419; *Ashmolean* 1992 [III], p. 244; Yarrington [Potts] 1994, p. 200; no. 176b, and fig. 117; TDA, 6, p. 456, fig. 2 on p. 457 [Yarrington].

Exhibited

British Portraits Exhibition, Bucharest, Romania and Budapest, Hungary, 1972–3; *Sir Francis Chantrey 1781–1841. Sculptor of the great*, National Portrait Gallery, London and Mappin Art Gallery, Sheffield, 16 January to 17 May 1981, cat.no.10.

359: Reginald Heber, Bishop of Calcutta (1783–1826)

about 1827
Clay
h. 24.5 cm.
A.29–1933

Said by the donor to have belonged to Henry Williams Chisholm, who may have been a London art dealer, 'probably given to him by Chantrey himself'. Given by Mrs E.B. (Hugh) Chisholm, 3 Ellerdale Road, Hampstead, London in 1933.

Prior to its acquisition, H.D. Molesworth [q.v.] commented: 'The finished monument shows certain considerable differences from this model; the position of the arms has been reversed in the finished monument, the left hand holds a book instead of a scroll, there are also differences in the drapery, so that it was probably not from this sketch, which bears the number 3, that the final statue was done . . . It is a fresh and pleasing work and would be a welcome addition to our series of sketches for monuments'.

Heber was made second Bishop of Calcutta in 1823. This is an unfired clay model for the marble monument to Heber executed by Chantrey for the Church of St John at Calcutta, later moved to St Paul's Cathedral, Calcutta (see Wilson 1896, p. 1, no. 1). Chantrey recorded the commission in his ledger on 19 March 1827; although the monument was not erected until 1835, it was moved to the newly constructed St Paul's Cathedral around 1847. A fee of £2000 was paid to Chantrey for the monument. This was one of four monuments to Heber commissioned from Chantrey. The first for St George's Cathedral, Madras, was completed in 1831. Chantrey received an order from Miss Alanson of Hodnet for a memorial to be placed in the Church of St Luke, Hodnet, Shropshire, completed in 1829. A reduced version of the Calcutta statue, commissioned for St Paul's Cathedral, London, was completed in 1835 (see Yarrington 1994, pp. 221–3, nos. 198a and 198b, 199a).

A plaster fragment of a head of Reginald Heber – the complete figure was damaged in the Second World War – which relates to the present piece, is in the Ashmolean Museum, Oxford (see *Ashmolean* 1992 [III], p. 218, no. 642). A further fragment of the head and shoulders from a similarly damaged figure relates to the monument to Heber in St George's Cathedral, Madras (*ibid.*, p. 219, no. 643). A plaster bust of Heber is also in the Ashmolean Museum, Oxford (*ibid.*, p. 234, no. 714).

Whinney commented that this 'rough sketch shows his [Chantrey's] method of concentrating on broad forms' (Whinney 1971, p. 152). Penny compares the present piece 'in colour of clay and summary handling', with the model for a statue of Mrs Dorothy Jordan with her children in the Ashmolean Museum, Oxford (see *Ashmolean* 1992 [III], p. 16, cat.no. 456).

BIBLIOGRAPHY

Review 1933, p. 7, pl. 4a; Whinney 1971, p. 152, cat.no. 50, illus. p. 153; *Neo-classicism* 1972, p. 218, cat.no. 336; Penny 1977, pp. 76–9, fig. 56 on p. 77; Kilmurray 1979, p. 105; Yarrington 1994, p. 223, no. 199a, and fig. 137.

EXHIBITED

The Age of Neo-classicism, Royal Academy and Victoria and Albert Museum, 9 September to 19 November 1972, cat.no. 336.

360: William Stuart, Archbishop of Armagh (1755–1822)

signed and dated 1828
Marble
h. 64 cm.
A.137–1956

Signed and dated on the back: CHANTREY. SC./1828.

With Robert Tunstill, presumably of Old Manor House, Bradford-on-Avon, from whom a bust of George IV by Samuel Joseph was also purchased by the Museum in 1956; see entry for cat.no. 477. Presumably sold to John Teed, and subsequently purchased from John Teed, 17 Silver Street, Bradford-on-Avon, in 1956 for £75. According to the vendor this bust was 'sold as Melbourne at the Culham House sale in 1938'.

On acquisition this bust was mistakenly identified as the Revd. George Crabbe (1754–1832) on the basis comparisons with representations of the same sitter as seen in drawings in the National Portrait Gallery. Margaret Whinney correctly identified the bust as William Stuart; she compared it to the plaster bust in the Ashmolean Museum, Oxford; on its original pedestal, it is inscribed with the name of the Archbishop of Armagh (see *Ashmolean* 1992 [III], p. 245, no. 766). Whinney commented, 'The bust is a good example of Chantrey's variant of the classicizing formula. The drapery, though indeterminate in character, is arranged in straight falling folds, and so gives a hint of a contemporary cloak; but the bare throat remains true to classical convention' (Whinney 1971, p. 150).

This bust was commissioned from Chantrey by the son of the Archbishop of Armagh in 1824, at a cost of £157 10s (155 guineas) (Yarrington 1994, p. 219). Whinney suggested, 'The date 1828 on the back of the present bust remains unexplained. It could be a second version, or possibly suggest delay in delivery' (Whinney 1971, p. 150). Chantrey also records in his ledger that on 24 February 1824 he was commissioned to produce a monument to Stuart for the Cathedral in Armagh (see Yarrington 1994, p. 191, no. 166a, and fig. 102).

BIBLIOGRAPHY

Whinney 1971, p. 150, cat.no. 49, illus. p. 151; Kilmurray 1979, p. 202; *Ashmolean* 1992 [III], p. 245; Yarrington 1994, p. 219, no. 196b, and fig. 123.

Coade and Sealy

(founded Lambeth 1769)

The Coade manufactory, established by Eleanor Coade (1733–1821) at Lambeth in 1769, specialised in the production of a wide variety of decorative, figurative, monumental, and architectural details in artificial stone, which could be cast from moulds. The sculptor John Bacon the Elder [q.v.] was closely associated with the business, and from 1771 acted as its chief designer. John Sealy (1749–1813), a cousin of Eleanor Coade, was made a partner in the firm in 1799, and the company name and stamp was changed accordingly to COADE & SEALY. On the death of Eleanor Coade in 1821, the company was bought by William Croggon (fl. 1814–35) who had worked at the manufactory, but the business foundered in 1833, and Croggon died bankrupt in 1835. His son Thomas John Croggon refounded the firm in 1835, though by this time had moved away from Lambeth, and once the moulds had been sold in 1843, no further Coade stone was produced. (I am grateful to Alison Kelly for her advice and information).

Ruch 1968; Kelly 1973; idem 1980, Kelly 1990; TDA, 7, p. 480 [Kelly].

361: Monument to Sir William Hillman (1740–1793)

signed and dated 1800
Coade stone
London Diocesan Fund Loan 2

Signed and dated at the bottom of the pedestal: COADE & SEALY/LAMBETH/1800.

Inscribed on the face of the pedestal: Near this place rests the Body of/Sir WILLIAM HILLMAN Knt./Of His Majesty's Board/of Green Cloth./Late of New Cavendish Street,/Portland Place./His Heart was benevolent,/His Charities Liberal,/And his Virtues without ostentation./He died the 7th February 1793,/Aged 53 Years./This Monument is erected/pursuant to the Will of/His only Sister ELIZTH. WALTER,/relict of Capt, JAMES WALTER/of Andover, Hants./Son of JOHN WALTER Esqr: MP/Late of Bushbridge House/in the County of Surrey.

Originally in the demolished church of St James's, Hampstead Road, London. On loan from the London Diocesan Fund from 18 October 1967, together with cat.no. 259.

The reproductive nature of Coade stone is illustrated by the number of known derivations of the present memorial. In a letter of 1972, prior to the publication of her comprehensive study of Coade stone, Alison Kelly noted, 'It does not appear in the Coade catalogue of 1784, but what sounds like it is described in Coade's Gallery, 1799, the descriptive handbook of the firm's showroom. Item 40 (p. 23) is: – "A Monument – a female figure standing, her right hand encircling an urn, finely expressive of sadness, on the die of the pedestal which supports the urn, and on which she leans, is the following inscription:

Viro optimo,/Poetae,/Si quis alius./Culto, pio, casto."

Copies (or slight variations) of it occur at Langley Marish, Slough (where the left hand hangs down, holding a book) Paddington, which is a mirror image, with the urn on the right, and Battersea Parish Church . . . I think that the Battersea one must be the first in this design, as there is a long article in the *Gentleman's Magazine*, 1792, vol. II, p. 588 describing its qualities, as if it were unique. There followed an animated correspondence in the magazine (p. 805 and 903) on its suitability, the main criticism being that a "vestal is out of place on the tomb of a married woman" . . . The urn is a variant of a catalogue number – in fact there seem to be three models which are hardly distinguishable from one another. A close relation of the urn, with the paterae in the swags instead of joining them, appears at Stow in the Wold, where the local stonemason, short of imagination, repeated it twice – in marble, in the round, and in bas-relief at the top of a plaque.'

For the Langley Marish version, see Betjeman and Piper 1948, figs. 130 on p. 88; the Paddington Parish Church version (laterally inverted), is illustrated in Kelly 1990, p. 248 illus.

We are grateful to the London Diocesan Fund for allowing us to include this in the catalogue.

Bibliography

Gunnis 1968, p. 108 (cited as being in St James's Church, Hampstead Road); Kelly 1990, p. 248 illus.

Coalbrookdale Company

The Coalbrookdale Company was established in 1709 by Abraham Darby I, who moved to Coalbrookdale from Bristol the year before. The company produced a range of cast-iron industrial products, including railway lines and bridges, diversifying in the early nineteenth century to include the more decorative domestic items including gates, benches, ornamental vases and umbrella stands, garden furniture and fountains, and stoves, later expanding production further to include more decorative objects such as statuettes, plaques and medallions. The company ceased production in 1959.

Ironbridge 1972, pp. 5–6.

362: Subjects from Milton's *Paradise Lost*

about 1856
Produced by the Coalbrookdale Company; designed by T. and W.J. Wills
Electro-bronze
h. 152.5 cm.
7229–1860

Purchased from the Coalbrookdale Company in 1860 for £50.

This vase was produced by electrolysis, and is an example of the decorative work produced by the Coalbrookdale Company; it was purchased by the Museum as a modern example of such work. The frieze around the vase depicts two scenes from Milton's *Paradise Lost*: *The Expulsion of Satan* and *The Expulsion of Adam and Eve;* a snake is coiled around the stem of the vase. An example of this vase is illustrated in a trade catalogue, *Coalbrookdale. Designs for Iron Gates, railings, balconies, stoves, fenders, tables, hatsstands, garden chairs, vases, fountains etc.*[n.d.], as registered design no. 18 'The Milton Vase'; plate 120. Philip Ward-Jackson has recently identified the sculptors of this vase as T. and W.J. Wills. The Milton vase was featured in the *Illustrated London News*, 31 January 1857: 'This interesting work of sculpture attracted much admiration at the last exhibition of the Royal Academy . . . The Vase is a joint production of two rising young artists T. and W.J. Wills, of Harrison-street, Gray's-inn-road. We are glad to see artistic skill applied to works of this class: the present design, if carried out in terra-cotta, would form a grand object for a garden or lawn.' (*Illustrated London News* 1857; I am grateful to Philip Ward-Jackson for this reference). For the 1856 exhibition at the Royal Academy, see Graves VIII, p. 302, no. 1247, under W.J. Willis.

W.J. and T. Wills (active 1857–1884) were brothers who worked in London; Graves noted two of their London addresses as 5 Douro Cottages, St John's Wood, and 12 Euston Road. They exhibited work at the Royal Academy between 1857 and 1884, including two models for drinking fountains in 1860, executed for the Metropolitan Free Drinking Fountain Association. T.Wills also exhibited *Perseus and Andromeda* at the British Institution in 1856, and again at the British Institution the Wills Brothers showed a 'Vase in Egyptian ware, subject Actaeon' in 1860. The brothers also executed public statuary, including a commemorative figure of Richard Cobden for Camden Town, the model for which was shown at the Royal Academy in 1866. I am grateful to Philip Ward-Jackson for providing me with material from his forthcoming publication on public sculpture in the City of London for this biographical summary (*Illustrated London News* 1857; Thieme-Becker 36, p. 36; Graves VIII, p. 302; *idem* 1908, p. 593; Ward-Jackson 2002).

Giovanni Battista Comolli

(b. Valenza 1775 – d. Milan 1830)

Comolli initially trained under Giuseppe Franchi (1731–1801) and later studied at the Accademia di Brera, Milan and then in Rome, possibly under Antonio Canova (1757–1822). From 1802 to 1814 he was Professor of Sculpture at the Imperial Academy of Arts (Ateno) in Turin. Francesco Melzi-d'Eril (1753–1816) was Comolli's chief patron. Comolli lost his position as Professor of Sculpture under Ferdinand I of Austria, and moved to Milan. He was active in England around 1820.

Gunnis 1968, p. 112 (incorrectly spelt Comelli); Thieme-Becker, 7, pp. 279–80; TDA, 7, p. 662 [Balderston].

363: William Frederick, 2nd Duke of Gloucester
(1776–1834)

about 1820
Attributed to Giovanni Battista Comolli
Marble
h. 67 cm.
A.69–1965

Bequeathed by Rupert Gunnis Esq., Hungershall Lodge, Tunbridge Wells, Kent in 1965.

On acquisition the subject of the present piece was unidentified, and the bust ascribed to John Francis (1780–1861). The donor had however previously suggested Earl Grey as the possible sitter, presumably Charles Grey, the 2nd Earl Grey (1764–1845), though the features of the bust do not seem to resemble him. A 'Bust in marble of Earl Grey' was exhibited by John Francis at the Royal Academy in 1832 (Graves 1905, III, p. 159, no. 1148).

Another version, also unsigned, is identified by an inscription on its accompanying pedestal as H.R.H. William Frederick, Duke of Gloucester; it was in the collection of Captain Fortescue, Boconnoc, Cornwall when the present piece was acquired. It differs slightly from the present bust, as it is without the decorative border on the tunic, and it has a tassel attached to the tunic at the bottom, which is missing from the Museum's version. The Boconnoc version was one of a number of busts mainly attributed to Comolli and placed on identical pedestals, which had passed to Captain Fortescue by descent. These include the Rt. Hon. George Grenville, the Rt. Hon. Thomas Grenville, Richard Grenville, Marquess of Buckingham, Lord Grenville, and William Wyndham, Lord Grenville. The Boconnoc bust of Thomas Grenville is apparently identical with the version in the Grenville Library at the British Museum, which is known to be by Comolli (departmental records; see also *British Museum* 1999, pp. 109–11).

Busts by Comolli of 'the late Duke of Gloucester', of William Wyndham, Lord Grenville (both bought by the Marquis of Chandos) and the Rt. Hon. Thomas Grenville (bought by the Earl of Ellesmere), were included in the Stowe sale of 1848 (see Forster 1848, p. 49, lots 762, 760 and 761 respectively). It is not possible to determine whether the bust of the Duke of Gloucester included in the Stowe sale was identical with that later at Boconnoc or the present piece; it could also conceivably be a third version. A bust of the Duke of Gloucester supposedly by Comolli was recorded outside the Old Plough Restaurant, Eaton Socon on the Great North Road (departmental records 1965).

Gordon Balderston has recently suggested that the bust might represent Richard Temple Nugent Grenville, 2nd Marquess of Buckingham (1776–1839) (personal communication).

Bibliography

TDA, 7, p. 662 [Balderston], (ascribed to Comolli); Knox 1998, p. 90, n. 25 on p. 95 (described as *Earl Grey* by John Francis).

Aimé-Jules Dalou

(b. Paris 1838 – d. Paris 1902)

Dalou was the son of a glove-maker, and initially trained in drawing at the Petit École in Paris in order to be of assistance in his father's business. Whilst studying he was noticed by Jean-Baptiste Carpeaux (1827–1875), who encouraged him to become a sculptor. In 1854 he entered the École des Beaux-Arts, where he trained for four years. During the early part of his career he worked on small scale sculpture, his first critical acclaim coming in 1870 when he won a medal for La Brodeuse, *which was exhibited in the Salon of that year. Dalou was known for his left-wing political sympathies, and was involved both actively and ideologically in the establishment of the Paris Commune in March 1871. After its overthrow he was forced into exile in London, where he lived from mid-1871 until his return to Paris after the amnesty of 1879. All of the sculpture by Dalou in the V&A, except* Workman with a Shovel, *cat.no. 379, and* Peasant, *cat.no. 380, dates from this period. His style at this time is characterised by small-scale works of an intimate domestic nature, and portraits for private commissions. He exhibited frequently at the Royal Academy, and as his reputation grew he was given a teaching appointment at the National Art Training School at South Kensington (later the Royal College of Art), where he had a profound effect on the development of British sculpture. After his return to Paris, Dalou executed a number of public monuments, whilst continuing to exhibit at the Salon.*

Dreyfous 1903; Caillaux 1935; Peasant in French 19th Century Art 1980, pp. 115–7; TDA, 8, pp. 472–3 [Hunisak].

364: Woman sewing

about 1870
Terracotta
h. 31.5 cm.
A.37–1934

Bequeathed by Miss S. Mary Forbes in 1934 (with cat.nos. 368, 370 and 373). Transferred to the Bethnal Green Museum in 1970, and returned to the V&A in 1983.

This is possibly a sketch for the figure *La Brodeuse*. Two plaster versions of this composition were made, one of which was shown in the Paris Salon of 1870. Its success was such that a marble version was commissioned by the French government, but work was not begun on it until 1880, after Dalou's return to Paris from exile in London. During the fulfilment of the commission Dalou became frustrated with the composition and destroyed both the marble version and the plaster model.

One of the plaster versions of *La Brodeuse* had been brought to England by Dalou, where it was used as the model for two bronze editions by Eugène Legrain (d. 1915), one of which was exhibited at the Royal Academy in 1873. This plaster is now in the Petit Palais, Paris.

A lost-wax bronze edition of *La Brodeuse* was produced by A.-A. Hébrard, Paris, examples of which are in the Musée Despiau-Wlérick, Mont-de-Marsan, France and the Staatliche Kunsthalle, Karlsruhe, Germany. The plaster version formerly owned by A.-A. Hébrard was sold at Sotheby's, London on 25 April 1968, lot.no. 298.

Exhibited
Design of the Times: 100 Years of the Royal College of Art, Royal College of Art, London, 7 February to 20 March 1996.

AC

365: Standing girl

signed; about 1872
Terracotta
h. 61 cm.
A.4–1952

Signed on the base: DALOU

Given by Dr. W. L. Hildburgh F.S.A.in 1952; for full provenance see entry for cat. no. 371.

The original of this composition was exhibited at the Royal Academy in 1872, and entitled *Jour des Rameaux à Boulogne* (Palm Sunday at Boulogne). This was the first piece Dalou executed after his arrival in England from Paris in 1871, and was bought by George Howard, later Earl of Carlisle. It is significant as the first of Dalou's series of peasant compositions.

Another terracotta version of this composition was exhibited at the Bruton Gallery, Bruton, Somerset in 1979 (cat. no. 33) and again in 1981–2 (cat. no. E27).

Bibliography
Radcliffe 1964, pp. 244–5; Hunisak 1977, p. 94, pl. 50; *French Sculpture* 1979, p. 54, cat. no. 33; *French Sculpture* 1981, cat. no. E27; Read 1982, p. 302.

AC

366: Peasant woman nursing a baby

signed and dated 1873
Terracotta
h. 136.5 cm.
A.8–1993

Signed and dated on the base: DALOU/1873

This group was made for Sir Lionel Coutts Lindsay for 300 guineas in 1873, and was exhibited at the Royal Academy in the same year. Subsequently it was in the collections of Lord and Lady Wantage of Lockinge, Oxfordshire, and then A. Thomas Loyd (also of Lockinge, Oxon.). Loyd presented it to the Tate Gallery in 1924 (inv. no. 4002). Transferred to the V&A in 1969 on long-term loan, this piece was at the Bethnal Green Museum between 1973 and 1983, and was formally accessioned by the V&A in 1993.

According to Dreyfous, this composition was based on a group entitled *Juno Suckling the Infant Hercules,* which Dalou later destroyed (Dreyfous 1903, pp. 59–60).

Two slightly reduced versions of this composition exist, one in the Hermitage, St. Petersburg, and the other also at the V&A, cat. no. 367. The slight reduction in size of these two versions suggests they were cast from a mould taken from the present piece, but they may also have been slightly re-worked by the artist.

There are also a number of small-scale versions of this group. A terracotta (h. 45 cm.) in the collection of Mr and Mrs Michael Travers (formerly in the collection of P. M. Turner), is signed and dated 1872. It is possible that this is the original sketch model, as it is the earliest dated version of the group. Other terracottas are in the Fitzwilliam Museum, Cambridge (inv. no. M3–1927), dated 1873 (h. 49 cm.), and two in private collections. Alley refers to a quarter life-size terracotta in the Ionides collection, which may be one of these. A plaster version is in the Petit Palais, Paris (h. 52 cm.). The latter was the model for editions by Susse Frères in bronze, and Sèvres in biscuit porcelain (no. 1045).

A marble version of the same group, probably a workshop piece (h. 94.5 cm.), was sold by Matthiesen's, London in 1955 to an English private collection (*Tate* 1959, p. 50). From there it passed to a French private collection in 1986 (*Leighton* 1996 pp. 38–9).

An engraving of this composition (a mirror image) was made by Achille-Isodore Gilbert, and published in an article about the London art world in the journal *L'Art* in 1876. A drawing was then made from this engraving by Vincent Van Gogh (see Heugten 1997, pp. 76–78). I am grateful to Martin Bailey for the information concerning the Van Gogh drawing.

BIBLIOGRAPHY

Art Journal 1873; *Athenaeum* 1873; Dreyfous 1903, pp. 59–60; Caillaux 1935, pp. 81–2, 127; *Tate* 1959, pp. 49–50; Avery 1972, p. 238; Hunisak 1977, p. 97; *Peasant in French 19th Century Art* 1980, pp. 116–7; Read 1982, p. 302, pl. 364; *Rhode Island* 1991, pp. 137–42; *Leighton* 1996, pp. 38–39.

AC

367: Peasant woman nursing a baby

signed; about 1873
Terracotta
h. 126 cm.
A.27–1912

Signed on the left of the base: DALOU

Made for James Staats Forbes. Given by his daughter Miss S. Mary Forbes in 1912. Transferred to the Bethnal Green Museum in 1970, and returned to the V&A in 1983.

For a full discussion of this object and bibliography, see cat. no. 366. The present piece is a slightly reduced version, cast from cat.no. 366.

BIBLIOGRAPHY

Caillaux 1935, pp. 81–2, 127; *Tate* 1959, pp. 49–50; Radcliffe 1964, pp. 244–5; Hunisak 1977, pp. 97, fig. 36B-E; *Peasant in French 19th Century Art* 1980, pp. 116–7; *Leighton* 1996, pp. 38–39, cat. no. 10; *European Sculpture* 2000 [Lindsay], p. 99 and fig. 2.

EXHIBITED

The Peasant in French 19th Century Art, Douglas Hyde Gallery, Trinity College, Dublin, 1980, cat. no. 15; *Albert, Prince Consort*, Royal College of Art, London, 1983–4.

AC

368: Hush-a-bye baby

about 1874
Terracotta
h. 53 cm.
A.39–1934

Inscribed on the base:
"Hush a bye baby on the tree top
When the bough bends the cradle will rock"

Bequeathed by Miss S. Mary Forbes in 1934 with cat.nos. 364, 370, and 373. Transferred to the Bethnal Green Museum in 1970, and returned to the V&A in 1983.

This terracotta was shown at the Royal Academy in 1874. It is a study for the marble group entitled *The Rocking Chair* made for the Duke of Westminster. Signed and dated 1875, the marble was shown at the Royal Academy in 1876 under the title *La Berceuse*, and remains in the collection of the Dukes of Westminster.

A plaster version, slightly smaller than the marble and therefore probably cast from it, was sold at Sotheby's, London, 24 April 1968, lot no. 141.

BIBLIOGRAPHY

Graves II, p. 233, no. 1530; Caillaux 1935, p. 128; Hunisak 1977, pp. 70–74, pl. 31A-F; Read 1982, p. 302; Burton and Haskins 1983, p. 112.

EXHIBITED

Royal Academy 1874, no. 1530.

AC

369: Eugénie Maria Wynne (b. about 1827)

signed and dated 1875
Terracotta
h. 56.5 cm.
A.2–1984

Signed and dated under the left shoulder: DALOU/1875

Purchased by Mr David Lane from the North London Auction House in about 1983 for around £160. Displayed in his lighting and decor shop Home Lights in Berwick Street, Soho, London, where it was purchased by the Display Manager of Maple & Co for around £220. Purchased by the Museum from Maple & Co, London in 1984 for £535.

John Steegman in his *A Survey of Portraits in Welsh Houses* (National Museum of Wales, Cardiff, 1957–62) lists a bust of Mrs Eugenie Maria Wynne (née Crowe) by Dalou at Garthewin, Llanfair Talhaearn, Denbighshire, probably the present bust.

The sitter was the daughter of the journalist Eyre Evans Crowe (1799–1868) and his first wife Margaret, whom he had married in 1823. The sitter's eldest brother, Eyre Crowe (1824–1910) was an artist who trained under Paul Delaroche (1797–1856). A portrait of Mrs Wynne when younger by Eyre Crowe is currently on loan to the National Library of Wales. In 1867 he was appointed one of the 13 Art Referees at the South Kensington Museum, following the departure of J. C. Robinson [q.v.]. Another of Mrs Wynne's brothers, Sir Joseph Archer Crowe, was the art historian who published prolifically in collaboration with Giovanni Battista Cavalcaselle.

Eugénie Marie was married to Robert Wynne, whose portrait was also at Garthewin. On the death of their grandson, R.O.F. Wynne, who inherited the estate from an uncle, the house was sold and the portraits within it (with the exception of the present bust) were lent to the National Library of Wales.

This bust was exhibited at the Society of French Artists, London in 1875, soon after its execution. Although it was published by Dreyfous in 1903 and Caillaux in 1935 (in both publications mistakenly called Mrs Gwene), its location was unknown until its appearance in London in the 1980s.

A painted plaster cast of this bust was recently acquired by the National Museum of Wales (previously sold at Sotheby's, London, 5 July 2000, lot 174). According to the entry in the Sotheby's catalogue, the production of the piece-moulds and cast was initiated by Dalou's pupil Edouard Lanteri [q.v.]. Lanteri passed the cast on to his pupil Albert Toft [q.v.], who in turn gave it to the sculptor Patrick Synge-Hutchinson. It was offered for sale at Sotheby's by the subsequent owner.

I am indebted to Timothy Stevens for his assistance in compiling this entry.

BIBLIOGRAPHY

Dreyfous 1903, pp. 67–8; Lami 1916, II, p. 7; Caillaux 1935, p. 130.

EXHIBITED

Close Encounters of the Art Kind, Victoria and Albert Museum, London, 1 November 2001 to 13 January 2002.

AC

370: Woman reading

about 1875
Terracotta
h. 23.5 cm.
A.38–1934

Bequeathed by Miss S. Mary Forbes in 1934 with cat.nos. 364, 368 and 373. Transferred to the Bethnal Green Museum in 1970, and returned to the V&A in 1983.

This is a sketch model for a larger version, of which several appear to have been made. A terracotta (h. 79.5 cm.) is now in the City Art Gallery, Manchester (inv. no. 1921.24); formerly in the collection of Constantine Alexander Ionides, it was donated by his daughter Helen Ionides in 1921.

A bronze edition of this composition was produced by Susse

Frères, Paris, during Dalou's lifetime. Versions were sold at Sotheby's London on 26 November 1998, lot 50, and 2 November 2001, lot 244. Another is in the collection of the Mead Art Museum, Amherst College, Massachusetts (see *Romantics to Rodin* 1980, pp. 187–8, cat.no. 68, illus. on p. 188).

A biscuit porcelain version was produced by the Sèvres factory (no. 1234).

BIBLIOGRAPHY
Avery 1972, p. 238 and fig. 8; Hunisak 1977, 32c.

AC

371: Head of a girl

dated 1876
Terracotta
h. 38 cm.
A.2–1952

Dated on the back: 1876

This object and cat. no. 365 were bought for the Museum by Dr W. L. Hildburgh F.S.A. for £50 from Mr G. C. Wilson of St. Osyth, Essex, through his agent F. T. Dent. According to the vendor they had been bought 'before the war' with a number of other Dalou effects from 'someone who had them from the studio.' Transferred to the Bethnal Green Museum in 1970, and returned to the V&A in 1983.

This is possibly a portrait of the artist's daughter, Georgette (1867–1915). Of numerous bronze versions, one is in the Musée d'Orsay (RF3951), and another is in the William Morris Gallery, Walthamstow, London; both are signed and dated 1876. A terracotta version is in a private collection.

BIBLIOGRAPHY
Tomory 1963, cat. no. 13, and illus.; Hunisak 1977, p. 133, pl. 90.

EXHIBITED
Sculpture in France 1880–1920, Auckland City Art Gallery (also Wellington and Christchurch), New Zealand, 1963, cat. no. 13.

AC

372: Alphonse Legros (1837–1911)

about 1876
Painted plaster
h. 51 cm.
A.7–1993

According to the donor, this bust was once owned by Edouard Lanteri [q.v.]. It was then in the possession of Mr and Mrs Guy Knowles, and was presented to the National Gallery by Mrs Knowles in 1922, and transferred to the Tate Gallery in the same year. It was transferred to the V&A in 1969. Between 1973 and 1983 it was at the Bethnal Green Museum, but was not formally accessioned by the V&A until 1993.

Alphonse Legros [q.v.] was a French-born artist who was brought to England in 1863 by James McNeill Whistler (1834–1903), and who succeeded Edward John Poynter (1836–1919) as Slade Professor of Fine Art at the University of London. Legros and Dalou had both trained under Lecoq de Boisbaudran at the Petite École in Paris, and it was on Legros's recommendation that Dalou was given a teaching post at the National Art Training School (later the Royal College of Art). After two years' teaching Dalou was succeeded by his pupil and the subsequent owner of the present bust, Eduoard Lanteri. It is likely that the bust dates from the time of Dalou's exile in England.

The present work is all that remains of a half-length figure of Legros, holding a palette in one hand and a brush in the other. Dalou had become dissatisfied with the figure and smashed it. According to Alley the dismembered head was retrieved by Lanteri.

Plaster versions are in the Musée de Dijon and the Strang Collection at the Slade School of Fine Art, London. The Strang Collection also formerly held a bronze version, the location of which is currently unknown. Another bronze is in the Fitzwilliam Museum, Cambridge, inv. no. M.16–1950 (like the present version, formerly in the collection of Guy Knowles). Alley states that the Dijon and Fitzwilliam pieces are believed to have been owned by Lanteri. Bronze versions are also in the Cleveland Museum of Art (Gift of John F. Kraushaar, inv. no. 1925.648), the National Museum of Wales, Cardiff (formerly in the collection of Arnold Haskell, purchased from the Bruton Gallery, Somerset in 1975, inv. no. NMW A 303) and the National Gallery of Art, Washington (inv. no. 1956.14.2).

BIBLIOGRAPHY

Dreyfous 1903, p. 66, illus. on p. 49; Caillaux 1935, p.128; *Tate* 1959, pp. 48–9; *Nineteenth Century French Sculpture* 1971, cat. no. 36, p.108, ill. p. 111; Hunisak 1977, fig. 86; *French Sculpture* 1979, cat. no. 28, p. 48; *European Sculpture* 2000 [Lindsay], p. 110.

EXHIBITED

Design of the Times: 100 Years of the Royal College of Art, Royal College of Art, London, 7 February to 20 March 1996.

AC

373: Charity

about 1877
Terracotta
h. 77 cm.
A.36–1934

Bequeathed by Miss S. Mary Forbes in 1934 with cat.nos. 364, 368 and 370. Transferred to the Bethnal Green Museum in 1970, and returned to the V&A in 1983.

This is one of many variations and versions of this composition, all of which were carried out around 1877/8. It is possible that it was based on a group of the *Madonna and Child with St. John the Baptist*, which was later destroyed by the artist.

A marble version was executed for a fountain at the back of the Royal Exchange in the City of London, and although it was finished by 1877 the fountain was not assembled until 1879. Once in place, the group deteriorated rapidly. This was due to adverse weather conditions, but may have been accelerated by dripping coming from a bronze canopy ironically erected for the purpose of protecting it. In 1897 the marble was replaced by a bronze version, and the canopy was removed in 1954. The present location of the removed marble version is unknown. It is not however the marble version now in the V&A (cat. no. 374). If, as may be supposed, the bronze now in situ behind the Royal Exchange was cast from its marble predecessor, a comparison of that with the V&A marble would reveal similarities. However, the proportions and details of the two groups differ markedly. Additionally, the *Magazine of Art* refers to both marbles at the same time when describing one at Maclean's Gallery in 1897 (likely to be the V&A version) saying, 'There is a fine little marble group of Dalou's "Charity" – unfortunately rather too deeply pointed – which is the more interesting and valuable, as the larger work at the Royal Exchange is rapidly perishing from climate and weather'.

A terracotta sketch model (h. 38 cm.), apparently modelled from life, is in the Musée d'Orsay (inv. no. RF 2314), from which a bronze edition was cast. An identical plaster is in the Petit Palais. There is another terracotta version at the V&A; see cat. no. 375.

The bronze edition was made by A.-A. Hébrard, one of which is in the David Daniels Collection, New York, and was exhibited at the J. B. Speed Art Museum. Louisville, Kentucky in 1971 (see *Nineteenth Century French Sculpture* 1971, p. 108, cat.no. 37, illus. on p. 112). Another bronze is at the Los Angeles County Museum of Art, inv. no. 23.3.2 (see *Los Angeles* 1987, p. 128).

I am grateful to Philip Ward-Jackson for his assistance in compiling this entry.

BIBLIOGRAPHY
Caillaux 1935, pp. 38, 129; *Masterpieces* 1951, p. 100, no. 49, illus. on p. 101; *Tate* 1959, pp. 47–8; *Nineteenth Century French Sculpture* 1971, p. 108, cat. no. 37, illus. on p. 112; Avery 1972, p. 238; *Musée d'Orsay* 1986, p. 110.

AC

374: Charity

about 1877
Marble
h. 91 cm.
A.6–1993

Signed on the back of the base: Dalou

Probably with Thomas McLean's Gallery, London, in 1897. In the possession of Lt.-Col. Henry Louis Florence by 1909. Bequeathed by the latter to the National Gallery in 1916, and transferred to the Tate in the same year (inv. no. 3052). Transferred to the V&A in 1969, it was at the Bethnal Green Museum between 1973 and 1983 and was formally accessioned in 1993.

For a full discussion of the *Charity* group see cat. no. 373.

BIBLIOGRAPHY
Magazine of Art 1897; Caillaux 1935, p. 129; *Tate* 1959, pp. 47–8; Avery 1972, p. 238; Read 1982, p. 302, pl. 365; Beattie 1983, pp. 14–15; *Musée d'Orsay* 1986, p. 110.

AC

375: Charity

about 1878
Terracotta
h. 71 cm.
A.27–1948

Inscribed on the base: Dalou

Formerly in the collection of Sir Edmund Davies. Given by Mr J. E. Bullard, in memory of Mr H. H. Bullard in 1948. Transferred to the Bethnal Green Museum in 1970, and returned to the V&A in 1983.

See cat.no. 373 for a full discussion of the Charity groups. Here the composition is virtually reversed, and an additional child is looking over Charity's shoulder. This is possibly an earlier version of the final composition for the Royal Exchange drinking fountain group. A smaller version of the present composition, also in terracotta, is in Birmingham Museum and Art Gallery, inv. no. P.I'57.

BIBLIOGRAPHY
Tate 1959, pp. 47–8; Avery 1972, p. 238; *Musée d'Orsay* 1986, p. 110.

AC

376: Angel with a dead child

about 1878
Bronze
h. 31 cm.
A.29–1917

Signed Dalou below the Angel's right foot, and stamped A.-A. Hébrard below a fold in the drapery near the left foot.

Bequeathed by Mr H. L. Florence, presumably Lt. Col. Henry Louis Florence, in 1917; see entry for cat.no. 374. Transferred to the Bethnal Green Museum in 1969, and returned to the V&A in 1983.

The present composition is an early variant of the terracotta *Monument to the Grandchildren of Queen Victoria* in the Private Royal Chapel at Windsor Castle. The finished composition comprises a seated angel holding three sleeping babies with two older children at his feet, one standing, the other seated. Queen Victoria's daughter Princess Louise [q.v.] obtained the commission (dated 1878) for Dalou. The work was probably executed and installed at Windsor without being publicly shown.

For a detailed discussion of the development of this composition see the exhibition catalogue *French Sculpture* at the Bruton Gallery, Bruton, Somerset, 7 April – 26 May 1979, p. 52, cat. no. 31, where two bronze editions were exhibited, one of each version of the composition.

There is a terracotta version of the present composition in the Petit Palais, Paris (inv. no. 14, see Hunisak 1977, pl. 46B), which is likely to have been used as the model for the present bronze.

This edition was cast by A.-A. Hébrard. Another bronze version, belonging to the Museum of Art, Rhode Island School of Design was shown at the exhibition *Nineteenth Century French Sculpture: Monuments for the Middle Class*, at the J. B. Speed Art Museum, Louisville, Kentucky in 1971, cat.no. 38, illus. on p. 113. Another is at the Minneapolis Institute of Arts.

Bibliography

Caillaux 1935, p. 130; Tomory 1963, cat. no. 12; *Nineteenth Century French Sculpture* 1971, p. 109, cat. no. 38, illus. on p. 113.

Exhibited

Sculpture in France 1880–1920, Auckland City Art Gallery, New Zealand (also Wellington and Christchurch),1963, cat. no. 12.

AC

377: Bacchanal

signed and dated 1879
Painted plaster
diam. 175 cm.
434–1896

Signed and dated on the edge beneath the reclining female figure: J. DALOU/1879

Lent to the Museum by Sir Joseph Edgar Boehm [q.v.] in 1887; given by Boehm's daughter in his name in 1896. Transferred to the Bethnal Green Museum in 1969, and returned to the V&A in 1983.

This is the first of several versions of Dalou's *Bacchanal*; it was exhibited at the Royal Academy in 1879.

The relief first entered the Museum in 1887 when it was accepted on loan from the sculptor Sir J. E. Boehm, who no longer had room to house it in his studio. After his death the relief was given to the Museum by his daughter, who asked for it to be registered as the late Sir Edgar Boehm's gift, and its date of accession to be recorded retrospectively as the year when it entered the museum. This however does not appear to have taken place, and the relief's accession number dates from the year when Boehm's daughter confirmed the gift (1896).

Another plaster version was exhibited at the Salon of the Société Nationale des Beaux-Arts in 1891, and was subsequently acquired by the Ville de Paris in 1893. It was accessioned by the Musée des Beaux-Arts, Calais in 1975.

The composition was later re-worked in marble (on a slightly larger scale, 180 cm. in diameter); this version now adorns the *Fontaine du Fleuriste* at Auteuil, under the title *Scène Bacchique*.

There are several reduced versions of this piece in existence: a unique bronze is now in the Musée d'Orsay, Paris (inv. no. RF1692), cast by A.-A. Hébrard in 1899. There is a small plaster version in the Petit Palais, Paris (inv. no. 282), and another was shown at the exhibition *Dalou Inédit* at the Galerie Delestre, Paris in 1978, and is now in a private collection. A biscuit porcelain version was produced by the Sèvres factory (no. 1360).

BIBLIOGRAPHY

Dreyfous 1903, pp. 144–5; Lami 1916, II, p. 8; Caillaux 1935, pp. 92–93, pl. XIII and p. 140; Radcliffe 1964 p. 244; Avery 1972, p. 238; Hunisak 1977, pp. 123 and 217, fig. 76; *Dalou* 1978, cat. no. 15; Hunisak 1978, p. 133; Burton and Haskins 1983, p. 113; *Musée d'Orsay* 1986, pp. 106–7; Thieme-Becker, 8, p. 307.

AC

378: Miss Helen Ionides (1871–1967)

signed; 1879
Terracotta
h. 46.5 cm.
A.10–1956

Signed under the left shoulder: DALOU

Given by the sitter in 1956. Transferred to the Bethnal Green Museum in 1970, and returned to the V&A in 1983.

This bust was made as a gift for the sitter's father, the collector Constantine Alexander Ionides (1833–1900). According to a letter from the donor of 11 August 1956 (now in the National Art Library), 'In 1877 my father bought "La Liseuse", the first work Dalou sold in England. He was so grateful, he enquired of my mother, whether there was anything he could model as a gift, that would give special pleasure to my father. My mother suggested a bust of me! I was born in 1871.'

The Museum has an oil painting by George Fredrick Watts O.M. R.A. (1817–1904), dated 1881, depicting the same sitter aged 10 years, and entitled "Lallie" (inv. no. CAI 1144). Also in the Prints, Drawings and Paintings Collection of the V&A is an album of photographs (inv. no. PH.2–1980) of the Ionides Collection, showing the present bust as it was displayed in the Ionides's house. Helen Euphrosyne Ionides received an M.B.E. in recognition of her work for the Red Cross during the Second World War; she never married (I am grateful to Helen Robinson of the Bruton Gallery for her assistance with these references).

According to the letter cited above, Dalou was commissioned to do two bronze casts of the bust by John Macallan Swann (1847–1910), the animalier sculptor, such was his admiration of the bust; these two versions were cast by Dalou's foundry, Cantoni of London in about 1879; see also entry for cat.no. 381. A bronze, possibly one of these two, was shown at Agnew's, London between 29 October and 11 December 1981 in an exhibition entitled *Sculpture and Works of Art* (cat. no. 28). It had previously been in the collection of R. Shaw-Kennedy, and was acquired by Agnew's from the Marquesa de Guadalmina on 6 August 1981. It was sold to the Bruton Gallery, Bruton, Somerset on 9 November 1981 for £3,750. Another bronze version was acquired by Agnew's in June 1992 from the Fine Art Society (*Gibson to Gilbert: British Sculpture 1840–1914*, cat. no. 10), and was sold to Mr and Mrs A. R. W. Smithers in November 1994. The donor's letter also states that a bronze version was 'sold at Christie's this year [1956] and bought by Agnew's.' This however must be an error, since Agnew's only dealt in sculpture from the late 1970s to the mid-1990s.

BIBLIOGRAPHY

Avery 1972, p. 238; Hunisak 1977, p. 133, pl. 89A-B; *Agnew* 1981, p. 36, cat. no. 28; *Gibson to Gilbert* 1992, pp. 14 and 52, cat.no. 10; *European Sculpture* 2000 [Lindsay], fig. 3 on p. 104.

AC

379: Workman with a shovel

signed; about 1894
Bronze
h. 19.2 cm.
A.31–1971

Inscribed at the front of the base: Susse Frs Ed^{n} Paris, on the back of the base to the left: cire perdue, and to the right: DALOU

A brass stamp set into the back of the piece is inscribed *SUSSE FRERES PARIS LOITEURS,* and in the middle of the stamp is a trademark of blacksmiths' tools.

Given by Dr Neville Goodman in 1971. Transferred to the Bethnal Green Museum in 1974, and returned to the V&A in 1983.

According to departmental records, this figure was cast from a maquette dating from 1894–9, now in the Petit Palais, Paris. Like cat. no. 380, it was initially intended for Dalou's projected *Monument to the Workers,* which was never brought to completion. This particular study was rejected in favour of a variant. A further version in bronze was included in the Sotheby's, London sale, 2 November 2001, lot 241.

A biscuit porcelain version was produced by Sèvres, no. 1353.

AC

380: Peasant

signed; about 1897–9
Bronze
h. 59 cm.
A.9–1993

Signed on the back of the rock: DALOU.
Stamped on the back of the base: Susse Ed^{n} Paris

This object was presented to the Tate Gallery by Mme. Susse in memory of her husband André in 1963 (inv. no. T614). Transferred on long term loan to the V&A in 1979: it was formally accessioned in 1993.

This figure is a reduced version of a figure which was part of Dalou's projected *Monument to the Workers*, on which he worked from 1889 onwards, but which was never brought to completion. A life-size version in bronze is in the Musée d'Orsay, Paris (inv. no. RF2999) and one in plaster is in the Petit Palais, Paris. Another small bronze is in the Los Angeles County Museum of Art, inv. no. M86.219.1 (see *Los Angeles* 1987, p. 128) and another was exhibited at the Bruton Gallery, Bruton, Somerset in 1979. *Worker with a Shovel* (cat. no. 379) was also a model for the same project. A biscuit porcelain version was produced by Sèvres, no.1282. A bronze version was sold at Sotheby's, London 11 July 2001, lot 245.

Bibliography

Tate 1963–4, p. 48; Elsen 1974, p. 8, pl. 7 (wrongly attributed to Constantin Meunier); *French Sculpture* 1979, cat. no. 32, p. 54.

Exhibited

Design of the Times: 100 Years of the Royal College of Art, Royal College of Art, London, 7 February to 20 March 1996.

AC

381: Rosalind Frances Howard, Countess of Carlisle, the Hon. Mrs George Howard (1845–1921)

1908, after the original of 1872; signed J. Dalou, 1872
After Aimé-Jules Dalou; cast by Enrico Cantoni
Bronze
h. 53 cm.
A.1–1985

Signed on the base: Dalou/1872

Purchased from Signor Enrico Cantoni, 100 Church Street, Chelsea, London in 1908 for £25. Cantoni was commissioned by the Museum to produce this bronze, which was cast from the original plaster by Dalou then in his Chelsea studio. Apart from the bronze at Castle Howard (see below), this was the only bronze cast made. The figure was initially accessioned as a reproduction (inv.no.1908–14), but was re-classified and written on as an original work in 1985. A tinted plaster cast of the same piece was also purchased in 1908 for £3 (inv.no. 1908–14A), though this was subsequently de-accessioned in 1952. On acquisition the bronze was assigned to the Art Museum and the plaster to the Department of Circulation. The bronze was transferred to the Bethnal Green Museum in 1968, and returned to the V&A in 1983.

The original bronze, now at Castle Howard, was commissioned from Dalou in 1872 soon after his arrival in England by George Howard MP, later 9th Earl of Carlisle (see Dreyfous 1903, pp. 52–3). Permission for the bronze and plaster casts to be taken from the plaster model used to produce the bronze was given in a letter of 1907 (Museum records), with the stipulation that the name of the lady represented was not mentioned on the label. This proviso was revoked in 1970. Rosalind Frances Howard was a promoter of women's political rights and temperance reform (*DNB* 1961, p. 222). This bronze was included in the sale held at Sotheby's, London on 20 May, 1994, lot 119.

Enrico Cantoni (active 1882–1912) cast the present version after Dalou's original model in 1908. A 'Moulder for sculptors. Also bronzing and colouring' is the description on Cantoni's letter-head; his address is given as 100 Church Street, Fulham Road. He was commissioned to produce other, mainly plaster cast reproductions for the Museum between 1882 and 1912, copies of which were often also supplied to other museums such as those in Edinburgh and Dublin. David McGill [q.v.] exhibited a bronze bust of 'Enrico Cantone, Esq' at the Royal Academy in 1894, no. 1810 (Graves V, p. 139). For Cantoni, see also the entry for cat.no. 378.

BIBLIOGRAPHY

Register, p. 243; *List* 1908, p. 15; Caillaux 1935, p. 127; Radcliffe 1964, pp. 244–5, n. 3; Hunisak 1977, p. 137, figs. 92A and 92B (there said to be by Dalou and to date from about 1873; reference supplied by Alexandra Corney); *Treasure Houses* 1985 [Radcliffe], p. 635, cat.no. 566; *Fake* 1990, p. 51, cat.no. 28b.

EXHIBITED

Fake? The Art of Deception, British Museum, London, 7 March to 3 September 1990, cat.no. 28b.

G. H. Deere

(dates unknown; active 1869 – 1870)

No information has been found on G. H. Deere other than two of his addresses: 23 Weston Street Pentonville in 1869, and 11 Hermes Street, Pentonville in 1870. In 1870 Deere exhibited a head of a satyr 'blocked by W. Theuerkauff, and chased by G. Deere'. A prize of £4 was awarded to Theuerkauff and £3 to Deere.

Journal for the Society of Arts, 10 February 1871, XIX, no. 951, p. 230 no. 57.

382: Mask from the group of Laocoon and Sons

signed; 1869
Copper repoussé
h. 22.7 cm. w. 22.2 cm.
101–1870

Signed in the bottom right hand corner: G.H. DEERE

Purchased from G. Deere, presumed to be the sculptor, in 1870 for £7.

This mask was a prize object in the Metalwork section of the Society of Arts Competition for 1870; Deere was awarded a prize of £2 (*Journal for the Society of Arts*, 5 March 1869, XVII, no. 850, p. 245, no. 11). See also cat.no. 691.

Exhibited
Society of Arts Art-Workmanship Competition of 1870.

Christopher Dresser

(b. Glasgow 1834 – d. Mulhouse, Alsace 1904)

Between 1847 and 1854 Dresser trained at the Government School of Design, London, where he came into contact with the reforming ideas of Henry Cole, Owen Jones and Richard Redgrave. Dresser had a special interest in botany, a subject on which he both lectured and published, in particular on the relationship of science and art. His designs were applied to a range of materials, including furniture, textiles, wallpaper and silver. Two of his notebooks are held in the Department of Prints, Drawings and Paintings (inv.nos. E.1498–1987, E.1499–1987).

Studio 1899; TDA, 9, p. 295 [Allwood]; Halén 1990.

383: Chimneypiece from Bushloe House, Wigston Magna, Leicestershire

about 1880
Possibly by Christopher Dresser
Slate with gilded decoration
Circ.661:A-1962

Said to have originally come from Bushloe House, Wigston Magna, Leicestershire. Given by the City of Leicester Museum and Art Gallery to the Museum in 1962. Initially held in the Circulation Department, it was transferred to the Department of Architecture and Sculpture, later Sculpture Department, in 1973.

On its transfer from Circulation Department to the Department of Architecture and Sculpture, the present piece was described as being of 'black slate with incised gilded decoration designed by Dresser, and is in 13 pieces, with 32 tiles (some broken). It was presented through Leicester Museum, and came with a fireplace . . . The items are fully documented as from Bushloe House, Wigston Magna, and are dated from c. 1880.'

[Not illustrated].

Conrad Gustav d'Huc Dressler

(b. Streatham, London 1856 – d. France 1940)

Dressler initially studied at the Royal College of Art under Edouard Lanteri [q.v.], and later with Sir Joseph Edgar Boehm [q.v.] in Paris. An exhibition was held in 1889 in which Dressler showed thirty busts of leading men. Spielmann records that Dressler established his own foundry in Chelsea, and experimented with electrotyping, one of the techniques he used for the panels executed for the church of St Francis Xavier, in Liverpool. Dressler was a co-founder of the Della Robbia pottery in Birkenhead in 1894; Miller commented that Dressler 'embarked upon a long and trying voyage before he could hope to sail into port, when he took up the work of a practical potter'. Around 1897 Dressler left Birkenhead to set up on his own, founding the Medmenham Pottery at Great Marlow, and producing the faience frieze for Lever Bros. Factory at Port Sunlight. Dressler, listed as a sculptor by Graves, exhibited at the Royal Academy between 1883 and 1907.

Miller 1900; Spielmann 1901, pp. 85–8; Royal Academy II, p. 188; Della Robbia Pottery 1980, section 6; Beattie 1983, pp. 241–2; Thieme-Becker, 9, p. 556; Walker 1994; Trusted 1996 [Dressler].

384: Nita Maria Schonfeld Resch (1864–1928)

signed and dated 1898
Painted terracotta on painted wood socle
h. (incl. socle) 64 cm. h. (excl. socle) 45 cm.
A.3–1995

Signed and dated on the back: Conrad Dressler/Dec 1898.

Purchased along with a photograph and autograph letter (see below) from Ted Few, 97 Drakefield Road, London in 1995 for £3,500.

The socle is original.

Nita Maria Schonfeld Resch was the wife of the sculptor. Another bust of her by Dressler of 1893 is in the Walker Art Gallery, Liverpool (inv.no. WAG 8622; see Trusted 1996 [Dressler], n. 10). A closely related coloured plaster relief of the same subject in a similar pose is also in the Walker Art Gallery (inv.no. 10740; see, *ibid.* n. 11). A photograph of about 1900 showing the bust in the sculptor's studio was acquired at the same time as the present piece (inv.no. A.3:2–1995); see Introduction, fig. 2. An autograph letter from Dressler also acquired at the same time is in the National Art Library (MSL 1995/7).

Bibliography

Miller 1900, p. 174 illus; Trusted 1996 [Dressler] and fig. 1; Williamson 1999, p. 788, fig. XVI.

Alfred Drury R.A.

(b. London 1856 – d. Wimbledon, London 1944)

Drury initially trained at the Oxford School of Art, and during the late 1870s, encouraged by Sir Thomas Brock [q.v.] at the National Art Training School (later Royal College of Art), studied under F.W. Moody (d. 1893), and more significantly Jules Dalou [q.v.]. The influence of Dalou was such that when the political situation in France improved, Drury accompanied Dalou on his return to France where he worked as his assistant from 1881 to 1885. In 1885 Drury first exhibited at the Royal Academy and was also employed in the studio of Sir Joseph Edgar Boehm [q.v.]. In 1905 Drury was commissioned to produce six architectural sculptures of the Prince Consort, Queen Victoria, St Michael and St George, and Imagination and Knowledge, for the main entrance of the Victoria and Albert Museum, together with nine soffit reliefs. He exhibited at the Royal Academy between 1885 and 1942, and was commissioned to produce the figure of Sir Joshua Reynolds (1723–1792) for the forecourt of Burlington House. In 1900 Drury was made an Associate of the Royal Academy, and was elected a Royal Academician in 1913.

Baldry 1900; Baldry 1906; Parkes 1921, pp. 78–81; Royal Academy II, pp. 193–4; Physick 1978; idem 1982, pp. 228–8; Thieme-Becker, 9, p. 591; TDA, 9, pp. 305–6.

385: The Genius of Painting

signed and dated 1886
Terracotta
h. (excl. base) 39.5 cm.
A.4–1991

Signed and dated on the base: A. DRURY/1886

Included in Christie's, Nineteenth century sale, London, 29 September 1988, lot 272. Purchased from Richard Coats, 32 Grantham Road, London in 1991 for £1500.

There is a crack beneath the figure of Cupid.

This statuette is an allegory of Painting. In her left hand the figure holds a panel showing the head of Peter Paul Rubens (1577–1640), while her right hand is poised, possibly to hold a pen or brush, no longer extant. The portrait of Rubens is taken from a self-portrait of the artist in the Royal Collection at Windsor (see Vlieghe 1987, pp. 153–7, no. 135, and figs. 171 and 176; also *Carlton House* 1991, pp. 83–4, cat.no. 35). The painting was shown at the Royal Academy in the *Winter Exhibitions of Old Masters* held in 1870 and 1876 (nos. 126 and 152 respectively), and it is possible that Drury may have seen the painting whilst it was exhibited, or known it through a reproduction. The present piece is one of Drury's earliest known works, executed on his return from Paris in 1885. He exhibited a similar terracotta statuette entitled the *Genius of Sculpture* at the Royal Academy in 1888 (Graves II, p. 378, no. 2056).

Exhibited
Design of the Times: 100 Years of the Royal College of Art, Royal College of Art, London, 7 February to 20 March 1996.

386: The Age of Innocence

signed and dated 1897
Plaster
h. 67.7 cm.
A.31–2000

Signed on the back of the integral base : A. DRURY/97

According to the donor, the bust was given to her mother in the late 1930s by the sculptor, who lived opposite the family in Wimbledon when the donor was a child. Given by Mrs Joy Way, 'Wasp Well', Outwood, Redhill, Surrey, in 2000.

The signature and date is incised into the surface of the plaster after casting had taken place, suggesting that it was produced in 1897, rather than being an aftercast.

The model for this bust was Gracie Doncaster, the daughter of one of Drury's friends (*Reverie* 1992, p. 35). The bust is considered by Benedict Read to be one of the 'major icons' of the late nineteenth-century English movement known as the 'New Sculpture' (*ibid.*, p. 21).

The present version is likely to have been the sculptor's plaster model, probably used in the production of subsequent closely related versions: it is known to have been reproduced in marble and bronze (see below). This plaster is likely to have been cast from an original clay or terracotta bust now lost, and is significantly larger than most of the other known versions in bronze. However the version sold at Christie's on 3 July 1985 (see below) was comparable in size with the present piece, and similarly signed and dated 1897. Bronze versions have appeared in various auctions in the 1980s and 1990s, though some may have reappeared: – Christie's, 3 July 1985, lot 154; Christie's, 15 May 1986, lot 34; Sotheby's, 14 December 1983, lot 228; Sotheby's, 18 March 1987, lot 180; Sotheby's, 29 November 1991, lot 207; Sotheby's, 20 May 1994, lot 116; Christie's, 31 October 1996, lot 399; Sotheby's, 14 May 1999, lot 220 and Phillips, 23 September 1997, lot 132. Bronze versions are also in the Laing Art Gallery, Newcastle upon Tyne, the Manchester City Art Gallery (inv.no. 1911.23), and the Harris Museum and Art Gallery, Preston (inv.no. S40); see *Reverie* 1992, p. 35.

Later reworked examples in marble are in the Cartwright Hall Art Gallery, Bradford (inv.no. 1906–200; h. 67 cm, signed and dated 1901), and in the Blackburn Museum and Art Gallery (signed and dated 1908; see Read 1982, fig. 389 on p. 328); a further version was formerly in the Luxembourg Museum, Paris (Beattie 1983, p. 242). A bronze was exhibited at the Royal Academy in 1897, and it has been suggested that this was the version sold by Phillips on 23 September 1997 (signed and dated 1896; see above). The date of this bronze, a year earlier than the date on the present piece, would suggest that Drury had to make another model. What appears to be a marble or plaster version is illustrated by Spielmann (see Spielmann 1901, p. 114 and p. 115 illus.). A marble version was exhibited by Drury at the International Fine Arts Exhibition, Rome in 1911 (*International Fine Arts Exhibition* 1911, p. 70, no. 1105).

Thomas Earle

(b. Hull 1810 – d. London 1876)

Thomas Earle, the son of the sculptor John Earle (1779–1863) initially trained in the workshop of Sir Francis Chantrey [q.v.], later attending the Royal Academy Schools in 1832. He exhibited regularly at the Royal Academy between 1834 and 1873, and at the British Institution between 1843 and 1865.

Graves III, pp. 4–5; Graves 1908, p. 173; Gunnis 1968, pp. 137–8; Thieme-Becker, 10, p. 282.

387: Hyacinthus

signed and dated 1854
Plaster
h. 150 cm.
383–1876

Signed at the back of the support: T. EARLE/S^{c}./1854

Inscribed on integral pedestal at the front: [HY]ACINTHUS

Given by Mrs Earle – presumed to be the sculptor's widow – in 1876, together with cat.no. 388. These two pieces may have been lent to the Museum by the sculptor prior to their acquisition. What were described as two 'plaster casts' (probably the present pieces) are recorded as being lent to the Museum prior to 1870 by a 'T. Earle, Esq.' (*List* 1870, p. iv).

Hyacinthus was a beautiful youth loved by Apollo, and died after being accidentally struck on the head by a discus, the hyacinth flower springing up where his blood had been spilt (Hall 1980, p. 158).

What was described as a 'Model. "Hyacinthus" a Youth, playing Quoits, life size', is listed as number 51 in a leaftlet entitled *Works Designed and Modelled by Mr. Thomas Earle, Vincent-Street, Ovington Square*; two copies are held in the Archive for the Town Docks Museum, Hull (information supplied by Gerardine Mulcahy).

EXHIBITED
Earle exhibited *Hyacinthus* at the Royal Academy in 1855 (no. 1415). It has been suggested that this exhibit was the present piece, as no evidence of Earle executing the figure in marble is recorded (information supplied by Gerardine Mulcahy). He also exhibited a plaster statue of *Hyacinthus* (again, perhaps the present piece) at the International Exhibition of 1862, London, British Division, class XXXIX, B – Living artists, probably the present piece (*International Exhibition* 1862, p. 144).

388: Miranda

about 1865
Plaster
h. 181 cm.
382–1876

Inscribed on the front of the integral pedestal: MIRANDA

Given by Mrs Earle – presumed to be the sculptor's widow – in 1876, together with cat.no. 387. These two pieces may have been lent to the Museum by the sculptor prior to their acquisition. What were described as two 'plaster casts' are recorded as being lent to the Museum prior to 1870 by a 'T. Earle, Esq.' (*List* 1870, p. iv).

The left hand is missing. A shell seems to have been used to imprint into the plaster base (noted by Philip Ward-Jackson).

This is a plaster model for the marble statue of Miranda from Shakespeare's *The Tempest*, 'What is 't, a spirit?' exhibited at the Royal Academy in 1866 (no. 900) (Graves III, p. 5). In its review of the Royal Academy exhibition in 1866, the *Art Journal* commented acidly '. . . How comes it to pass, then, that the Council of the Royal Academy do not find themselves in a position to reject examples of sculpture of such debased quality? Again, what excuse can be offered for Mr Earle's "Miranda" (900), which, as a work of Art is absolutely poverty-stricken? The cast of the drapery is commonplace, and no poetry comes to take the figure out of the sphere of everyday life'.

A figure of *Miranda* (material unknown) was lent by Earle's widow to the Exhibition of the Works of Local Arts', Hull in 1881. What was described as a 'Model. Statuette of "Miranda", from the Tempest', is listed as number 52 in a leaftlet entitled *Works Designed and Modelled by Mr. Thomas Earle, Vincent-Street, Ovington Square*; two copies are held in the Archive for the Town Docks Museum, Hull (information kindly supplied by Gerardine Mulcahy).

EXHIBITED
In 1865 Earle also exhibited at the British Institution what was described as 'Miranda. I might call him a thing divine; for nothing natural, I ever saw so noble – Tempest, act i, sc. 3' by Shakespeare' (no. 639), offered in marble at £100, and cast, 5 guineas. Earle exhibited 'Miranda. Model of a statue. 1866. 400 guineas, in marble' at the *London International Exhibition* of 1871, possibly the present piece (see *London Exhibition* 1871 *[revised]*, p. 121, no. 2527).

Morton Edwards

(b. London 1834 – d. San Francisco 1917)

In 1879 Edwards published A Guide to Modelling in Clay and Wax, *in which he described himself as Professor of Modelling, Secretary to the Society of Sculptors 1862; editor of the* Fine Art Magazine *and* Sculptors' Journal 1863; *Secretary of Literary and Artistic Society 1872 and Secretary of the Glyptic Society in 1876. In the preface he noted that he studied under William Behnes [q.v.] from 1852 to 1854, and in Rome under John Gibson [q.v.] in 1859. Edwards exhibited at the Royal Academy between 1864 and 1870. As well as showing* The Bather *(see entry for cat.no. 389 below) at the 1871 International Exhibition, Edwards exhibited two busts. According to Susan Rich, a descendant of Edwards, he spent 27 years in the United States, and in 1910 was planning to return to London from San Francisco, in order to raise funds to finance his book* The History of Sculpture from the earliest period to the present time. *He is listed in the City Directory as being resident in San Franciso from 1889 to 1910. I am most grateful to Yolanda Statham for Edwards's dates.*

Exhibition 1871, p. 121; Graves III, p. 28; Hughes 1989, p. 166; Thieme-Becker, 10, pp. 351–2.

389: Bather

1867
Tinted marble
h. 68.5 cm.
372–1872

Purchased from the sculptor in 1872 for £52 10s.

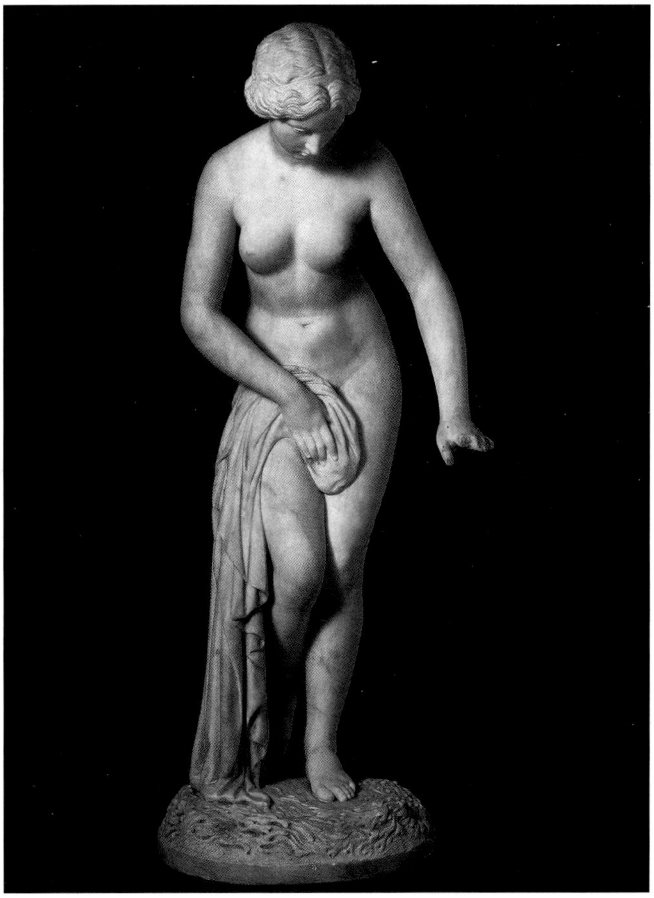

Four fingers on the left hand are missing.

In his *Guide to Modelling in Clay and Wax* of 1879 Edwards commented on the interest in tinted statuary, noting that John Gibson revived the process of colouring marble, and that 'There seems to have been latterly a much more favourable opinion respecting its employment, for there are many who think very highly of the results obtained by colouring or tinting marble statues both among sculptors and artists . . . The public generally say, Give us a picture – sculpture is too cold; and they are in a measure right. What should we say of anyone who esteemed a black and white crayon drawing of a picture more than the picture itself in all its glory of colour?' (Edwards 1879, pp. 8–9).

Bibliography

London Exhibition 1871, p. 121, no. 2531; Graves III, p. 28 no. 1174.

Exhibited

A 'chromoglyph', presumably this tinted marble sculpture of *The Bather*, was exhibited by Edwards at the Royal Academy in 1868 (no. 1174); at the International Exhibition of 1871 Edwards exhibited probably the same piece, described as a 'tinted marble statuette', class II, no. 2531.

EMILY ADDIS FAWCETT

(active London 1883 – 1908)

Little is known about Emily Addis Fawcett, whose addresses listed by Graves were 70 Westbourne Terrace, London and later, 42 Linden Gardens, London. She exhibited at the Royal Academy between 1883 and 1896, where she showed works in terracotta, marble and bronze. She also exhibited at the Society of Women Artists in 1895, 1896 and 1908, and at the Walker Art Gallery, Liverpool, and the Salon des Artistes Français, Paris.

Graves III, p. 94; Petteys 1985, p. 241; Society of Women Artists 1996, II, p. 39.

390: Profile head of a bearded man

signed and dated 1888
Probably by Emily Addis Fawcett
Marble
h. 52.4 cm. w. 41.8 cm.
A.18–2000

Signed in the bottom left hand corner: E A Fawcett. 1888

There is no information available on the provenance of the present piece, which until 2000 was an unregistered object in the Museum.

JOHANN JACOB FLATTERS

(b. Krefeld 1786 – d. Paris 1845)

A German by birth, Flatters spent most of his life in France; he settled in London in 1842; the bust catalogued below was executed a year after his arrival. Flatters was trained at the École des Beaux-Arts, Paris under Jean-Antoine Houdon (1741–1828) and Jacques-Louis David (c. 1748–1825). Between 1810 and 1839 he exhibited at the Salon in Paris, and was created a Chevalier de la Légion d'Honneur. Flatters produced a number of portrait busts of notable personages, including that of Louis XVIII and Goethe. In 1842 he came to London, exhibiting at the Royal Academy in the same year, when his address was listed as 2 Ranelagh Grove, London. Flatters also worked as a book-illustrator.

Graves III, p. 123; Schmidt 1957; Thieme-Becker, 12, p. 76.

391: Queen Victoria (b.1819; r.1837–1901)

signed and dated 1843
Marble
h. 67.3 cm.
A.36–1952

Signed on the sitter's left shoulder: Flatters/.1843

Purchased at an unrecorded sale early in 1952 by Dr W.L. Hildburgh F.S.A., and given by him to the Museum that year.

The bust was acquired primarily because of its value as a historical document. In his recommendation to the Director, H.D. Molesworth [q.v.] commented:

'Though I know you do not like this bust may I ask for your support in taking it as a gift from Hildburgh since I did definitely encourage him to buy it as a document (though not at the price he paid) when it was reported the afternoon before the sale, it would be a matter of no little embarrassment to hand it back to him . . . although not very beautiful it does seem fairly typical of the day and as such may perhaps qualify as borderline'.

In this relatively unadorned portrait of the young Queen, Flatters replaces the formality of a crown with a headdress made of roses; she wears a simple tunic. The royal status of the sitter is however affirmed by a coat-of-arms at the front of the socle.

For a comparative portrait of Prince Albert by Edward Hodges Baily, executed in 1841; see entry for cat.no. 265. The busts were exhibited together in the Victorian galleries of the Museum during the 1980s and 1990s.

Bibliography

Schmidt 1957, p. 66, figs. 6 and 7 on p. 69; *Romantic Movement* 1959, p. 433, cat.no. 980.

Exhibited

The Romantic Movement. Fifth Exhibition to celebrate the tenth anniversary of the Council of Europe, Tate Gallery and Arts Council Gallery, London, 10 July to 27 September 1959; *The Arts of the Victorians*, Japan: Hankyu Store, Kobe; Museum of Art, Kyoto; City Museum, Fukuoka, 29 September to 5 June 1993.

JOHN HENRY FOLEY R.A.

(b. Dublin 1818 – d. London 1874)

John Henry Foley, brother of the sculptor Edward Arlington Foley (1814–1874), began his education at the Royal Dublin Society's Schools in 1831, attending the Royal Academy Schools between 1835 and 1838. Gunnis commented that following the critical acclaim of his Youth at the Stream, *exhibited at Westminster Hall in 1844, 'Commissions for busts and statues . . . began to flow in and Foley soon found himself in the front rank of British contemporary sculptors'. Possibly Foley's most prestigious commission was that connected with the Albert Memorial, which included the colossal central bronze figure of Prince Albert, as well as one of the four marble groups depicting the continents, that of* Asia; *for the Albert Memorial model; see entry for cat.no. 531. Another acclaimed work was the bronze statue of* Oliver Goldsmith *for Trinity College, Dublin, a plaster version of which, possibly by Sir George Hodson or Hudson, is in the Museum's collection, cat.no. 466. He exhibited at the Royal Academy between 1839 and 1861. A marble figure of Foley by James Gamble is amongst those decorating the facade of the Museum. Thomas Brock [q.v.], a pupil of Foley, completed some works left unfinished at Foley's death, including the figure of Prince Albert for the Albert Memorial. Read comments on the role played by Foley, '. . . and in his production of memorial statues of his contemporaries in which the real men were given in addition a certain heroic aura, he was among the most effective commemorators of the age in which he lived'.*

Graves III, pp. 131–2; Gunnis 1968, pp. 153–4; Read 1974; Physick 1978; Thieme-Becker, 12, p. 150; TDA, 11, pp. 237–9 [Stocker]; Murphy 1999; Sankey 1999; see also various references in Brooks 2000 for his involvement in the Albert Memorial.

392: John Sheepshanks (1787–1863)

signed and dated 1866
Marble
1–1881

Signed and dated on the back: J.H. FOLEY R.A. Sc./LONDON 1866.

Given by Miss A. Sheepshanks, the sister of the sitter, in 1867, but not formally registered until 1881.

Sheepshanks was an art collector and generous public benefactor; in 1856 he gave his large collection of paintings to the Museum, for which a new gallery, known as the Sheepshanks gallery, designed by Captain Francis Fowke, was erected in 1857; see entries for cat.nos. 709 and 710; see also Physick 1982, pp. 33–9; *Art Journal*, 1 August 1857, pp. 239–40. In 1857 Foley exhibited at the Royal Academy 'The late Richard Sheepshanks, A.M.; posthumous bust in marble' no. 1343 (Graves III, p. 132, no. 1343); this was a bust of John Sheepshanks's younger brother Richard, the astronomer (1794–1855). This may be the same bust which was exhibited at an exhibition of 'Sculpture of the United Kingdom' held at the South Kensington, later Victoria and Albert Museum in July 1857; see enties for cat.nos. 271, 272, 274, 276 and 500; see also *Building News*, 17 July 1857, p. 740.

BIBLIOGRAPHY
Bequests and Donations 1901, p. 237; *Irish Art* 1971, p. 84, cat.no. 149.

EXHIBITED
Irish Art in the 19th century. An exhibition of Irish Victorian Art at Crawford Municipal School of Art, Dublin, 31 October to 29 December 1971, cat.no. 149.

Edward Onslow Ford

(b. London 1852 – d. London 1901)

Ford initially studied painting in Antwerp and Munich, sharing a studio whilst in Munich with Edwin Roscoe Mullins (1848–1907), and returning to England in 1875 to pursue a career as a portrait sculptor. He joined the Art Workers' Guild in 1884. Beattie commented, 'In close contact with Gilbert after 1884 and highly responsive to new ideas, [Ford] began series of ideal nudes and busts which, hailed then as daringly "realist", are imbued with delicate, melancholy symbolism . . . His best work, however, whether on a large or small scale, has a daintiness and intensity that reflects his love for Flemish Renaissance paintings and places it among outstanding achivements of New Sculpure Movement'. Ford exhibited at the Royal Academy between 1875 and his death.

Parkes 1921, pp. 125–6; Beattie 1983, pp. 242–3; TDA, 11, pp. 302–4 [Brook].

393: Fate

about 1900
Bronze
h. 53 cm.
501–1905

Purchased from the Fine Art Society Ltd, London in 1905 for £31 10s (30 guineas).

An exhibition of statuettes and busts by the late Edward Onslow Ford was held at the Fine Art Society, New Bond Street, London in 1905. The sculptor Thomas Brock [q.v.] who acted for the Museum as an advisor, recommended, 'that the bronze statuette 'Fate' (sketch) be purchased for the Museum . . . Although unfinished the work has considerable charm and would, I think, be a valuable addition to the Collections of small bronzes now being formed in the Museum'. The feet and hands on this statuette are unfinished. The subject depicts Fate, the scissors in her right hand ready to cut the thread of life which would have been held in her left. A comparable version is held in the Lady Lever Art Gallery (inv.no. LL121); see *Lady Lever* 1999, pp. 32–3.

Bibliography
Lady Lever 1999, p. 32.

SIR GEORGE JAMES FRAMPTON R.A., F.S.A.

(b. London 1860 – d. London 1928)

Frampton was a sculptor and medallist. He studied at the London School of Art under W.S. Frith (1850–1924), attended the Royal Academy Schools in 1882, and later travelled to Paris, returning to London in 1889. Like Lanteri [q.v.], Frampton was involved in the external decoration of the Museum, executing the sprandrel reliefs of Truth and Beauty *above the Main Entrance at the same date as the death mask of Sir Henry Irving, cat.no. 402. His diversity was noted by Spielmann: 'Highly accomplished and firmly based on the true principles of his art, he is at home in every branch of it – portraiture, decoration, ideal work, metal work, goldsmithery, jewellery, enamel, and furniture; indeed, he covers the whole field'. Frampton exhibited frequently at the Royal Academy between 1884 and 1928, and was awarded a knighthood in 1908. Archival material is held in the Archive of Art and Design (AAD 13–1988), and at the Henry Moore Institute, Leeds. A copy of the Henry Moore Institute archive relating to Frampton is also held at the Courtauld Institute of Art.*

Studio 1896 (for a contemporary interview with Frampton); Spielmann 1901, pp. 88–95; Forrer I, p. 136; Graves III, pp. 155–6; Physick 1978; Royal Academy III, pp. 106–7; Physick 1982 pp. 227–31; Stevens 1989 [Frampton]; Thieme-Becker, 12, pp. 281–3; TDA, 11, pp. 499–500 [Skipwith]; Cullen 1996.

394: Mother and child

signed and dated 1895
Silvered bronze
h. 102 cm.
A.8–1985

Signed and dated on the left side: G^EO FRAMPTON/1895

Given by Meredith Frampton, son of the sculptor in 1984, together with cat.no. 395, though not formally accessioned until 1985; see also entries for cat.nos. 396, 400, 401, and 403 to 411.

The group depicts Frampton's wife Christabel (1863–1951), whom he married in 1893, and son Meredith (1894–1984) (the donor), and was acquired at the same time as the plaster model; see entry for cat.no. 395.

Spielmann recorded, 'The next year [1895] there appeared the charming "Mother and Child", an experiment in polychromatic figure-work. The figures are in bronze against a bright copper plaque, with a disc of white behind the head. Here was something new, very effective, and highly pleasing in taste, if not convincing to the orthodox and the purists . . . in reality a family group of Frampton's own' (Spielmann 1901, pp. 90, 93). The plaque and disc mentioned by Spielmann are now missing. In 1896 Frampton exhibited, 'Mother and son (silvered bronze) £300' at the Royal Glasgow Institute (*Royal Glasgow Institute* II, p. 69, no. 838), presumably the version illustrated by Beattie (see Beattie 1983, fig. 154 on p. 160).

Frampton's wife Christabel was the subject of another work by her husband entitled *Christabel*; this bust, illustrated by Spielmann, is now untraced (Spielmann 1896, p. 208 illus.).

BIBLIOGRAPHY

Studio 1896, p. 205 fig; *Exposizione Venice* 1897, pp. 56, 145; *International Fine Arts Exhibition* 1911, p. 71, no. 1120; Forrer I, p. 136; Graves III, p. 155 (no. 1644); Beattie 1983, fig. 154 on p. 160; Stevens 1989 [Frampton], p. 76; Glaves-Smith 1992, p. 20; Williamson 1996 [Kader], p. 180, fig. 181.

EXHIBITED

Royal Academy 1895 no. 1644; *Seconda Exposizione Universelle*, Venice 1897, no. 10; Paris Exposition Universalle, 1900; International Fine Arts Exhibition, Rome, 1911, no. 1120 (I am grateful to Robert Upstone for this reference).

395: Mother and child

about 1895
Plaster
h. 94 cm.
A.9–1985

Given by Meredith Frampton, son of the sculptor in 1984, together with cat.no. 394, though not formally accessioned until 1985; see also entries for cat.nos. 396, 400, 401 and 403 to 411.

The hem on the child's robe was chipped and is now repaired.

This is the model for the bronze group depicting Frampton's wife Christabel and son Meredith (the donor), acquired at the same time as the original bronze; see entry for cat.no. 394.

396: Victory

about 1893–1910
Plaster
h. 13 cm.
A.21–1991

Given by the late Meredith Frampton, son of the sculptor in 1985, together with cat.nos. 400, 401, and 403 to 411; see also entries for cat.nos. 394 and 395. The present piece together with cat.nos. 400, 401, and 403 to 411 were not formally accessioned at the time of their arrival. The gift to the Museum was subsequently authorised by Meredith Frampton's niece Jill Dickins in 1991, in accordance with the wishes of the late Meredith Frampton. Five plaster models for medals, and one cast of a gem which also formed part of the gift, are not included in the present catalogue (inv.nos. A.16 to A.20–1991, and A.22–1991).

Chipped; some of the metal armature is emerging through the surface of the plaster in several places.

It is not known whether this model was used for a finished work.

397: Agriculture

before 1896
Marble
h. 41.3 cm. w. 58.5 cm.
A.5–1964

Incised on the front: AGRICVLTVRE

Given by the Commonwealth Institute, formerly the Imperial Institute, in 1964, together with cat.nos. 398 and 399.

This relief, together with cat.nos. 398 and 399 originally formed part of a large hooded fireplace in black marble inset with two bronze plaques, and the three marble reliefs catalogued here, which was produced by Frampton for the Imperial Institute (later the Commonwealth Institute), London, from whom they were given to the Museum in 1964. There is no further record of the bronze plaques – presumably removed at the same time as the present panels – though they did not form part of the gift to the Museum from the Commonwealth Institute in 1964.

In an interview given by Frampton to the *Studio* in 1896, he commented, 'I have certainly done a good deal of interior work, both in churches and public buildings . . . I have also done some fireplaces and other work at the Imperial Institute' (*Studio* 1896, p. 206).

Bibliography

Studio 1896, p. 206.

398: Literature, Art and Science

before 1896
Marble
h. 41 cm. w. 59 cm.
A.6–1964

Given by the Commonwealth Institute, formerly the Imperial Institute, in 1964, together with cat.nos. 397 and 399.

Top left edge broken off, also bottom corners damaged.

This relief together with cat.nos. 397 and 399 formed part of a fireplace produced by Frampton for the Imperial Institute, later Commonwealth Institute. See entry for cat.no. 397.

399: Commerce

before 1896
Marble
h. 41 cm. w. 56 cm.
A.7–1964

Given by the Commonwealth Institute, formerly the Imperial Institute, in 1964, together with cat.nos. 397 and 398.

Bottom right corner broken.

This relief together with cat.nos. 397 and 398 formed part of a fireplace produced by Frampton for the Imperial Institute, later Commonwealth Institute. See entry for cat.no. 397.

400: Mask, probably for Lamia

about 1899–1900
Gilded plaster
h. 17 cm.
A.14–1991

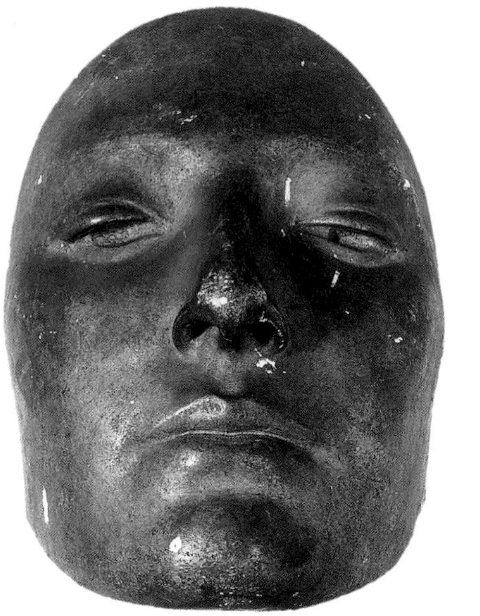

Pencilled on the reverse of this model is the inscription: '??LAMIA'.

Given by the late Meredith Frampton, the son of the sculptor in 1985, together with cat.nos. 396, 401, and 403 to 411, though not formally accessioned until 1991; see entry for cat.no. 396.

The gold surface colouring is lost in some areas. A metal bar is fixed horizontally across the back, and a metal loop is soldered around it for suspension.

This seems to be the original model for the face on Frampton's bronze and ivory bust *Lamia* of 1899–1900, which was exhibited at the Royal Academy in 1900, and is in the collections of the Royal Academy (see Spielmann 1901, pp. 93, 95, illus. p. 94; *Royal Society of British Sculptors* 1939, p. 34 illus; Beattie 1983, pp. 160–2, 243, fig. 155). A polychromed plaster version of *Lamia* of about 1900, signed 'Geo Frampton' is in the Birmingham City Museums and Art Gallery (see *Birmingham* 1987, p. 40, no. 112 (inv.no. P.29'73); *Pre-Raphaelite* 1991 [Greenwood], p. 100 cat.no. 10).

401: Design for badge commemorating the foundation of the Art Workers' Guild

signed; about 1902
Plaster
h. 11.8 cm. w. 9.3 cm.
A.15–1991

Inscribed on the nimbus: THE ART WORKERS GVILD/FOVNDED 1884
At the bottom, on a scroll, is inscribed part of the motto for the Art Workers' Guild: ART VNITY
At the top eminating from three bush motives behind the central figure representing Art: SCVLPTVURE ARCHITECTVRE
Around the plain surface of the model appear instructions incised in presumably Frampton's own hand. To the right of the model: From top of tree to bott[om]/of ball/Model to be reduced to/this size
Also to the left: This is not/to be . . .

Signed in the bottom right hand corner: Geo Frampton

Given by the late Meredith Frampton, son of the sculptor in 1985, together with cat.nos. 396, 400, and 403 to 411, though not formally accessioned until 1991; see entry for cat.no. 396.

Chipped in areas especially on top of the central bush motive.

The Art Workers' Guild, originally founded in 1884, was established as a forum for discussion between designers and artists of different disciplines (see TDA, 2, p. 575 [Galicki]).

Frampton was a member of the Art Workers' Guild from 1887 onwards, and became Master in 1902. In a contemporary account in the *Art Journal* detailing Frampton's career, entitled 'George Frampton, A.R.A., Art Worker', he is described as 'A master in many methods, Mr Frampton is truly an art worker, and he esteems it an honour to belong to the Art Workers' Guild and the Arts and Crafts Society' (*Art Journal*, November 1897, p. 321). For a discussion of Frampton's medals, see Jezzard 1994, especially pp. 54–8.

In an article in the *Medal* discussing plasters acquired by the Museum from the studio of Frampton, Lucy Cullen suggests, 'Although they seem to have formed some part of Frampton's working process, they cannot accurately be called models, but rather records of models. One (the Art Worker's Guild badge) reproduces traces of incised instructions in the sculptor's hand . . . It may be that these casts were made for Frampton's own use or reference from models in plaster or a more delicate medium such as wax. Some seem to have been produced as part of the production process, but others may have been intended to give an idea of what the finished article would look like. The sizes of some of them, significantly larger than the dimensions of the finished objects, suggest they were taken from working models' (Cullen 1996, p. 49).

Frampton exhibited a version of the badge commemorating the foundation of the Art Workers' Guild at the Royal Academy in 1908, included in a case of six other badges and medals (*Royal Academy* III, p. 106, no. 1953; cited by Forrer VII, p. 317).

Bibliography

Cullen 1996, p. 49, fig. 8 on p. 53, and notes 12, 15, 16 on p. 53.

402: Sir Henry Irving (1838–1905)

1905
Gilded plaster in a glazed wood case
h. (incl. case) 42 cm. (excl. case) 21.6 cm.
A.20–1932

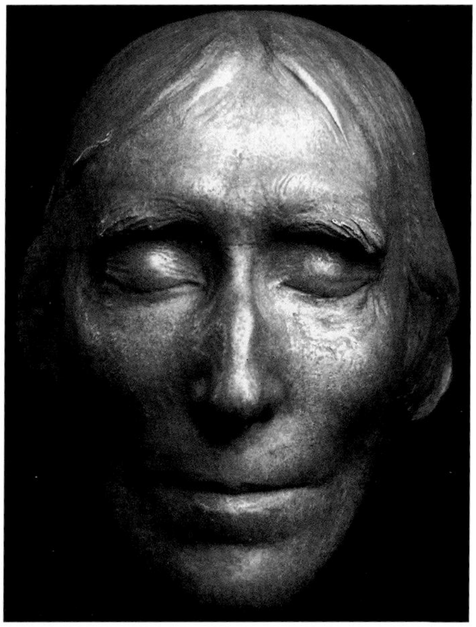

According to Museum records, a death mask of Irving was commissioned by the actor-manager Sir George Alexander (1858–1918) who was employed by Irving, accompanying him to America in 1884–5 (*DNB* 1982, p. 9). The mask was subsequently given to Mrs Aria, a great personal friend of Irving, by Lady Alexander, in the late 1920s. Bequeathed to the Museum by Mrs E. Aria, 8 Wimpole Street, London, in 1932. This is apparently the only original mask in existence; other surviving versions are cast after it (Museum records). Although outside the normal scope of the Museum's collections, the mask was accepted and originally displayed with other objects from the Theatrical Collection (now the Theatre Museum).

Two further plaster death masks of the actor Sir Henry Irving by Frampton are in the Museum of London; one is bronze-coloured, the other is surrounded with a wreath of leaves, and set on a slate board (inv.nos. 70.98/113 and A23950 respectively). A bronze statue of Irving by Thomas Brock [q.v.] is outside the National Portrait Gallery, London (Blackwood 1989, pp. 138–9). A bronze figure of Irving cast from a model by Edward Onslow Ford [q.v.] was included in a sale at Christie's, London, 14 February 1991, lot 72. A terracotta bust of Irving also by Onslow Ford was on the London art market in November 2001 (William Agnew & Co Ltd).

Bibliography

Review 1932, p. 50; Bassett and Fogelman 1997, p. 27 & illus.

403: Head of Peter Pan

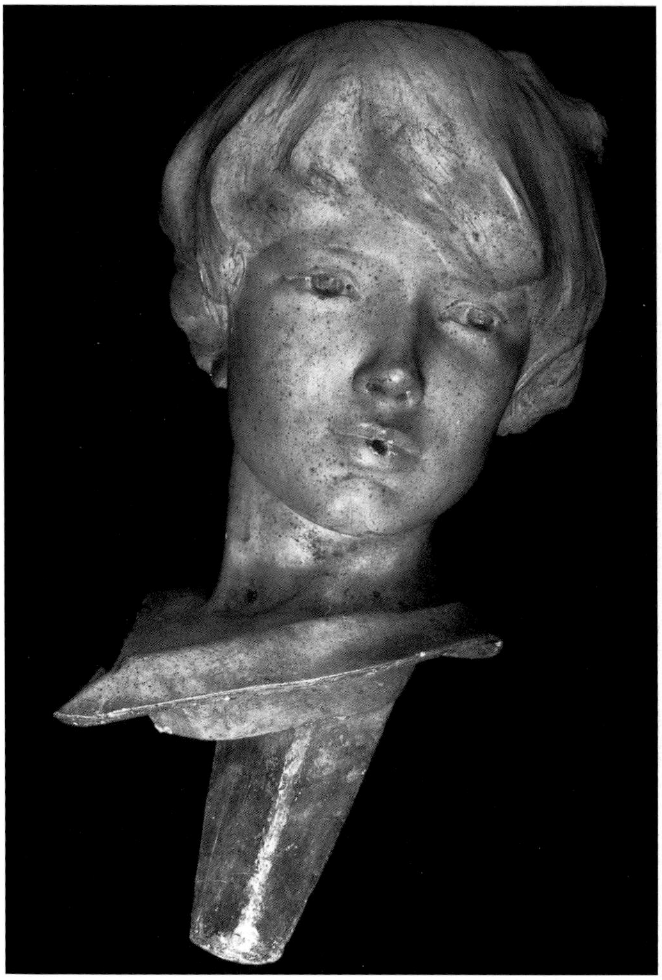

about 1910
Plaster
h. 41 cm.
A.5–1991

Given by the late Meredith Frampton, son of the sculptor, in 1985, together with cat.nos. 396, 400, 401, and 404 to 411, though not formally accessioned until 1991; see entry for cat.no. 396.

Minor chips on the surface of the plaster; some damage to back of the collar. An integral dowel extends from the neck. There is a small hole between the lips where the pipes would be fitted.

This and the following entries, cat.nos. 404 to 409 are the original plaster models for some of the component parts of the bronze figure of Peter Pan in Kensington Gardens (see Gleichen 1928, pp. 68–9; Blackwood 1989, pp. 136–7; Darke 1991, p. 61). This figure was commissioned anonymously by Sir James M. Barrie, the author of *Peter Pan,* and secretly erected on 29th and 30th April 1912, so that its appearance the next day would seem magical, and perpetuate the *Peter Pan* enigma, 'It is placed at the point where Peter Pan lands for his nightly visit to the Gardens' (Gleichen 1928, p. 69).

A further version of the *Peter Pan* group in bronze, unveiled on 16 June 1928, is in Sefton Park, Liverpool; see Cavanagh 1997, pp. 193–4. Bronze reductions of the Peter Pan figure were included in sales held by Sotheby's, London, on 5 July 2000, lot 163, and on 14 December 2001, lot 180.

At the Royal Academy in 1911 Frampton exhibited "Peter Pan". To be erected in bronze in Kensington Gardens' (*Royal Academy* III, p. 106, no. 1960).

BIBLIOGRAPHY
Cavanagh 1997, pp. 193–4.

404: Right arm of Peter Pan

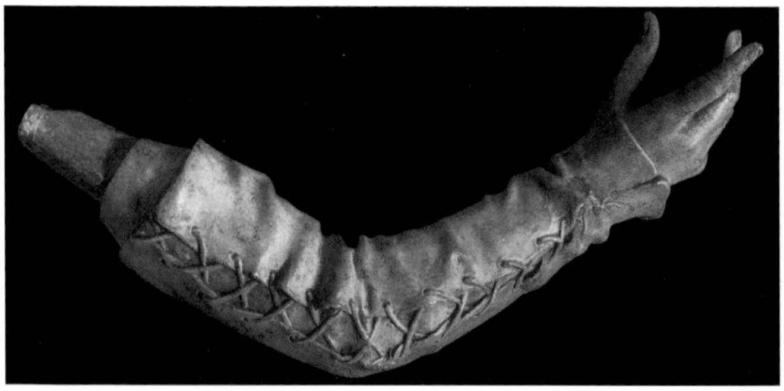

about 1910
Plaster
l. 64 cm.
A.6–1991

Given by the late Meredith Frampton, son of the sculptor, in 1985, together with cat.nos. 396, 400, 401, 403, 405 to 411, though not formally accessioned until 1991; see entry for cat.no. 396.

A crack is visable along the thumb. Some scratches are apparent. The fore-finger is chipped; there are minor chips elsewhere.

This is the model for right arm of the figure of Peter Pan in Kensington Gardens. See entry for cat.no. 403.

BIBLIOGRAPHY
Cavanagh 1997, pp. 193–4.

405: Left arm of Peter Pan

about 1910
Plaster
l. 64 cm.
A.7–1991

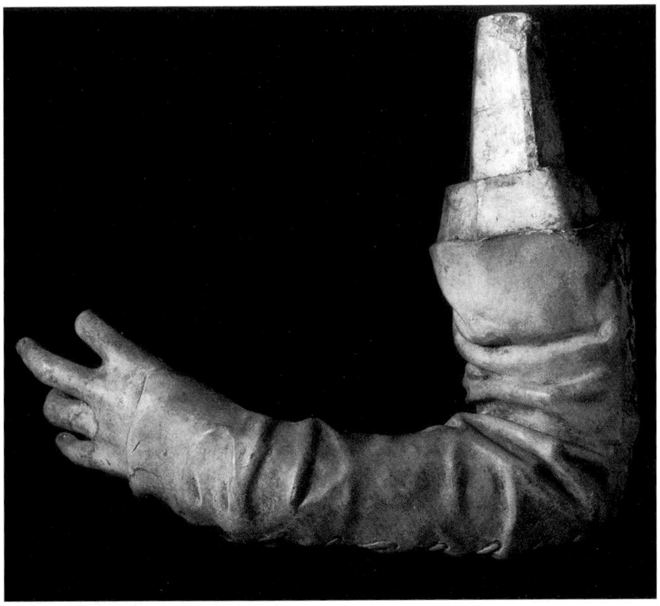

Given by the late Meredith Frampton, son of the sculptor, in 1985, together with cat.nos. 396, 400, 401, 403, 404, 406 to 411, though not formally accessioned until 1991; see entry for cat.no. 396.

There is some damage to the thumb where the pipes would have been attached; there is a surface break near the little finger.

This is the model for the the left arm of *Peter Pan* in Kensington Gardens. See entry for cat.no. 403.

BIBLIOGRAPHY
Cavanagh 1997, pp. 193–4.

406: Pipes of Peter Pan

about 1910
Plaster
l. 46 cm.
A.8–1991

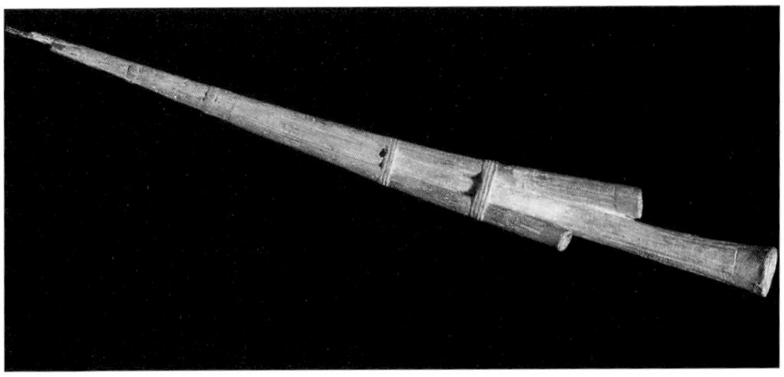

Given by the late Meredith Frampton, son of the sculptor, in 1985, together with cat.nos. 396, 400, 401, 403 to 405, and 407 to 411, though not formally accessioned until 1991; see entry for cat.no. 396.

Some plaster is missing from the end of the pipes, which would have been inserted into the mouth of *Peter Pan*; see entry for cat.no. 403.

BIBLIOGRAPHY
Cavanagh 1997, pp. 193–4.

407: Head of fairy

about 1910
Plaster
h. 12 cm.
A.9–1991

Given by the late Meredith Frampton, son of the sculptor, in 1985, together with cat.nos. 396, 400, 401, 403 to 406, and 408 to 411, though not formally accessioned until 1991; see entry for cat.no. 396.

Minor discoloration and chips are apparent; there is a crack above her right eye. A length of metal piping has been drilled into the base of the neck.

This is a model for one of the heads of the figures of fairies on the base of the bronze statue of Peter Pan in Kensington Gardens; see entry for cat.no. 403. For further heads of fairies, see also entries cat.nos. 408 and 409.

BIBLIOGRAPHY
Cavanagh 1997, pp. 193–4.

408: Head of fairy

about 1910
Plaster
h. 13.5 cm.
A.10–1991

Given by the late Meredith Frampton, son of the sculptor, in 1985, together with cat.nos. 396, 400, 401, 403 to 407, and 409 to 411, though not formally accessioned until 1991; see entry for cat.no. 396.

Minor discolouration and chips are visable; there is a red mark above the left eye. A small length of metal piping is drilled into the base of the neck. This is a further model for one of the heads of the figures of fairies on the *Peter Pan* statue in Kensington Gardens, see entry for cat.no. 403, also cat.nos. 407 and 409.

BIBLIOGRAPHY
Cavanagh 1997, pp. 193–4.

409: Head of fairy

about 1910
Plaster
h. 12.5 cm.
A.11–1991

Given by the late Meredith Frampton, son of the sculptor in 1985, together with cat.nos. 396, 400, 401, 403 to 408, 410 and 411, though not formally accessioned until 1991; see entry for cat.no. 396.

This is a further model for one of the heads of the figures of fairies on the *Peter Pan* statue in Kensington Gardens, see entry for cat.no. 403, also cat.nos. 407 and 408.

BIBLIOGRAPHY
Cavanagh 1997, pp. 193–4.

409

410: Female head, perhaps the New Testament

about 1910
Plaster
h. 9 cm.
A.12–1991

Given by the late Meredith Frampton, son of the sculptor, in 1985, together with cat.nos. 396, 400, 401, 403 to 409, and 411, though not formally accessioned until 1991; see entry for cat.no. 396.

Some wear or loss of surface pigmentation on the left side of the head, nose and chin.

The left side of the head is flat, with a hole for fixing. This is probably the pair of cat.no. 411; the two heads were intended for fixing, one on each side, to a central element. The originals to which these models for ideal heads relate is not known. It has been suggested that the blindfolded head, cat.no. 411 could represent the Old Testament, which would imply that this model personifies the New Testament.

411: Female head (blindfolded), perhaps the Old Testament

about 1910
Plaster
h.10.5 cm.
A.13–1991

Given by the late Meredith Frampton, son of the sculptor in 1985, together with cat.nos. 396, 400, 401, and 403 to 410, though not formally accessioned until 1991; see entry for cat.no. 396.

Some wear or loss of surface pigmentation, right surface of the head coated with varnish. Small chip at the end of the nose. The right side of the face is flattened and a hole drilled in for fixing.

The face of the female is blindfolded, and could personify the Old Testament. As with cat.no. 410 its probable pendant, the hair is held by a broad headband and swept back into a bun.

Charles Francis Fuller

(b. 1830 – d. Florence 1875)

Fuller joined the army in 1847, but left in 1853 and travelled to Florence, where he studied under the American sculptor Hiram Powers (1805–1873). Fuller was to exhibit a terracotta bust of Powers at the Royal Academy in 1873 (no. 1414). His obituary in the Art Journal *of 1875 records that during his time under the tutelage of Powers, Fuller 'made such progress that in a comparatively short space of time, his own studio was much frequented by the English who took interest in his works . . . Mr Fuller's works must not be classed with the best examples of modern sculpture, either British or foreign, but they evidence, generally, refined taste and poetic design'. Fuller exhibited regularly at the Royal Academy between 1859 and 1875. He appears to have lived in Florence from 1859 to about 1869, then at Rome for a period around 1871–5. His address whilst at Florence was Via della Nunziatina, almost certainly where the piece catalogued below was modelled.*

Art Journal, June 1875, p. 178; Graves III, pp.180–1; Redgrave 1970, pp. 162–3; Thieme-Becker, 12, p. 581.

412: Centurion

signed and dated 1869
Terracotta
h. 56.5 cm.
A.91–1923

Signed on the back of the bearskin cape: C.F. Fuller/1869

Purchased by Princess Louise and her husband the Marquis of Lorne whilst in Florence on their wedding tour in the 1870s. Given by H.R.H. Princess Louise, Duchess of Argyll in 1923; see also cat.no. 255. In a letter relating to its acquisition, Princess Louise commented: 'It was modelled by Mr Fuller, an English Sculptor settled out there [Florence], and is entitled "A Centurion". It is very cleverly executed, and he took a great deal of trouble with it, and it went through all sorts of processes to give it an ancient look'.

There is a hole in the top of the head and another through the back.
On acquisition Eric Maclagan [q.v.] commented that it was 'realistically modelled with some skill in the style of the later Italian Renaissance'.

BIBLIOGRAPHY
Art Journal, June 1875, p. 178; Graves III, p. 181, no. 1409; *Review* 1923, p. I.

EXHIBITED
In 1873 Fuller exhibited *A Roman centurion* at the Royal Academy (no. 1409), possibly the present piece prior to its purchase by Princess Louise and her husband.

GEORGE GARRARD

(b. London 1760 – d. London 1826)

Garrard initially trained as a painter under Sawley Gilpin (1733–1807) whose daughter he later married. He enrolled at the Royal Academy Schools in 1778, specialising in animal and sporting subjects until about 1795, when Gunnis commented, 'he deserted painting for sculpture'. Deuchar records that Garrard was encouraged by Samuel Whitbread M.P. to diversify, and that by 1800 he 'was attempting to gain additional recognition as a sculptor of both animal and human form'. In 1798 he was successful in campaigning to get a Bill passed by Parliament to safeguard the copyright interests of sculptors.

Garrard 1961; Gunnis 1968, pp. 163–4; TDA, 12, p. 164 [Deuchar].

413: Chimneypiece and grate from 4 Carlton Gardens

about 1800
Anonymous, possibly from a design by George Garrard
Marble
h. 135 cm.
A.56–1932

From 4 Carlton Gardens, London. Purchased by Mr T. Crowther & Sons from the contents of the house when it was demolished in 1932; see also the entry for cat.no. 726. Purchased for £100 together with cat.no. 726 from Mr T. Crowther & Sons, 282 North End Road, Fulham, London in 1932, by Mr G. Flint Clarkson, A.R.I.B.A. through the National Art Collections Fund, in memory of Mrs Jane Clarkson. Presented to the Museum in 1932.

Although 4 Carlton Gardens (now the official residence of the Foreign Secretary) was built around 1830, the style of this chimneypiece and that of cat.no. 726 suggest an earlier date. Two closely related chimneypieces with caryatid figures possibly by George Garrard are in the Carnarvon Room and in Queen Mary's Empire Room, Buckingham Palace. The Carnarvon Room chimneypiece is described by Clifford Smith as 'an admirable example of the early Regency style, and may perhaps be by the hand of the sculptor George Garrard, who is known to have worked for Holland at Carlton House. In the centre of the frieze is an oval panel carved with a female figure in a chariot drawn by serpents and accompanied by cherubs, with double cornucopias on either side; it is supported by detached columns in the form of terminal female figure with veiled heads' (Clifford Smith 1931, p. 208). The attribution of the Buckingham Palace chimneypieces to Garrard was proposed by Professor A.E. Richardson (*ibid.*, p. 209, n. 1); Clifford Smith suggested they dated from about 1800. In 1796 Garrard exhibited at the Royal Academy a 'Tablet for a chimneypiece' (Graves III, p. 207, no. 884). The fireplaces contained in this chimneypiece and that of cat.no. 726 are virtually identical.

BIBLIOGRAPHY
Review 1932, p. 7, pl. 5 facing p. 8.

JOHN GIBSON R.A.

(b. Conway 1790 – d. Rome 1866)

The Gibson family left Conway, Gwynedd, Wales intending to emigrate to America, but as Gibson recorded, on their arrival at the Liverpool docks, 'When my mother saw the great ships in the docks, she formed the most determined resolution never to put her foot in any one of those'; they settled where they found themselves, in Liverpool. At the age of fourteen Gibson was apprenticed to a firm of cabinet-makers in Liverpool, Gunnis recorded that his meeting with F.A. Legé (1779–1837) who worked for the Liverpool statuary firm of Messrs Francis, changed the course of his career. Gibson's evident talent as a sculptor was such that Mr Francis bought Gibson out of his apprenticeship and he was instead soon employed in their workshop. Gibson stated he would 'rather serve the remaining years in prison than continue at this disgusting wood-carving'. In 1817 he travelled to Italy, where he encountered Antonio Canova (1757–1822) and Bertel Thorvaldsen (1768/70–1844), in whose studios he worked. Greenwood records, 'By the 1830s Gibson was the leader of a colony of British sculptors working in Rome that included Richard James Wyatt, Lawrence Macdonald and Joseph Gott'. Perhaps his best-known work is the polychromed marble figure, the Tinted Venus, *exhibited at the London 1862 International Exhibition, and now in the Walker Art Gallery, Liverpool. Eastlake noted that the only pupil Gibson taught in his studio was the American sculptor Harriet Hosmer (1830–1908). Gibson exhibited at the Royal Academy between 1816 and 1864.*

Eastlake 1870; Graves III, p. 230; Matthews 1911; Gunnis 1968, pp. 171–3; Thieme-Becker, 13, pp. 600–2; TDA, 12, pp. 597–9 [Greenwood].

414: John Walter Watson Taylor (dates unknown)

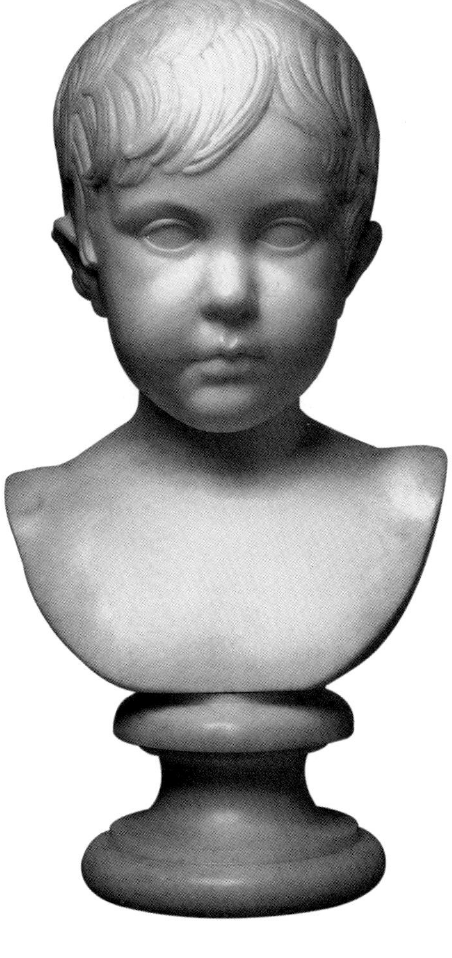

signed and dated 1816
Marble
h. 39 cm.
A.211–1969

Inscribed on the back: I GIBSON F^{T} 1816/IOHN WALTER/WATSON TAYLOR

Commissioned by Mr G. Watson Taylor in 1816. Sold as part of the Watson Taylor Collection, Erlestoke Park, Devizes, Wilts, by Mr George Robins, on 25 July 1832, lot 182. Purchased from L. Lipman Esq., 30 Robin Hood Road, Brentwood, Essex in 1969 for £350.

Gibson recorded that he was introduced by Mr Christie to Mr Watson Taylor, initially executing a bust of him and later his wife, his first commission after leaving Liverpool: 'Then I had commissions from them for all the children in turn, ending with the baby – a little thing with no shape at all'; Gibson noted a date of 1817 for the introduction, which must be incorrect given the date of the present bust (Eastlake 1870, p. 41). Matthews cites a similar account (Matthews 1911, pp. 34–5). A letter held in the Roscoe Papers (1730) in Liverpool Library records the relationship of Gibson and his new patron, Taylor, '. . . I have been introduced to Mr Christie and Mr G.W. Taylor who has employed me since my arrival in London. He is kind, liberal and rich, and as I think determined to be of use to the arts in all its departments. He has expressed himself particularly delighted with what I have done for him – 3 busts of his children in Marle [sic]' (information kindly supplied by Timothy Stevens). This bust and those of four other Watson Taylor children formed part of the Watson Taylor Collection, Erlestoke Park, Devizes, Wilts, sold by Mr George

Robins, on the fifteenth day of the sale, 25 July 1832. Described as: 'Busts in statuary marble of the Sons and Daughters of George Watson Taylor, Esq., M.P.'; the four busts (not three as cited above) are recorded as being executed by Gibson in 1816. Stevens comments that the present bust is 'animated by his [Gibson's] extraordinary manual dexterity and appreciation of the innocence of childhood', and notes that the busts of Watson Taylor's family 'were modelled while Gibson was staying with him in the Isle of Wight but carved in Rome' (Stevens 1989 [Liverpool], p. 46).

Bibliography

Matthews 1911, p. 246; Brumbaugh 1973, p. 122 and p. 123 fig. 2, there suggested to have been exhibited at the Royal Academy in 1816; Stevens 1989 [Liverpool], p. 46 and fig. 8 on p. 47.

Exhibited

In 1817 Gibson exhibited busts of Master S.W. Taylor (no. 1032) and Master J.W.W. Taylor (no. 1034), presumably the present piece, at the Royal Academy. A bust of Mrs Watson Taylor was also shown at the Royal Academy in 1819 (no. 1205).

415: Helen of Troy

signed; about 1825–30
Marble
h. (incl. socle) 61.5 cm.
A.25–1950

Signed on the truncation at the back: I GIBSON FECIT ROMÆ

Given by Mrs Borradaile in 1950.

This may be Gibson's earliest idealised bust, probably executed a few years after his arrival in Rome in 1817. According to myth, Helen was the daughter of Zeus who in the guise of a swan had seduced Helen's mother Leda. Helen hatched from an egg, indicated in this bust by the eggshell seen on her head. Variants exist in Derby Art Museum and in the New South Wales Gallery, Australia. A version formerly in the collection of Sir John Hanmer, Bettersfield Park, Shropshire, was at Thomas Agnew & Sons Ltd, London in 1981 (*Agnew* 1981, p. 20, cat.no. 12 and illus.).

416: Venus and Cupid

signed; about 1839
Marble
h. 118.7 cm.
A.22–1963

Signed on the bottom right: I GIBSON FECIT/ROMÆ

Purchased from Mr Leigh Underhill, 100 Islington High Street, London in 1963 for £150 using funds from the Hildburgh Bequest.

Two versions of a *Venus and Cupid* relief are listed by Lady Eastlake in her work on Gibson of 1870: one in the ownership of the Marquis of Albercorn and another owned by Howard Galton Esq. of Hadzor (Eastlake 1870, p. 253; see also Matthews 1911, p. 244). The present piece may be one of these. Its provenance before 1963 is unknown. Two versions are in the Royal Academy: one in marble, and another in plaster painted to imitate terracotta. Gibson exhibited a relief of Venus and Cupid at the Royal Academy in 1839, no. 1298, possibly the plaster now in the Royal Academy (Graves III, p. 230, no. 1298).

A version entitled 'Aphrodite. Eros' is illustrated in an engraving drawn by P. Guglielmi and engraved by Thomas Langer (Langer, Ufer and Siedentopf 1861, pl. LVIII).

Bibliography

Cooper 1971, pp. 88, fig. 7 on p. 90 (there erroneously said to be exhibited at the Royal Academy in 1833).

417: Grazia

signed and dated 1843
Marble
h. 61 cm.
1149–1882

Signed on the back truncation: I.GIBSON.FT. ROMÆ
Inscribed at the front: GRAZIA/PVELLA CAPVENSIS/1843 (Grazia, the girl from Capua)

Bequeathed by John Jones in 1882.

The accompanying pedestal shown here was also acquired through the Jones Bequest (inv.no. 1165–1882).

An article in the *Cornhill Magazine* entitled 'Recollections of Gibson the sculptor', recorded, 'His most beautiful model, Grazia, was the frequent subject of his conversation. Her sordid avarice, her fierce chastity, her furious temper, were studies to him; and the contract which her moral nature presented to her beauty, was graphically described . . . An English lady who had often heard of Grazia's marvellous beauty, asked permission to see her as she was sitting for her bust to Gibson. The lady looked at her and said she was handsome, but that her expression was bad. "She looks as if she had a vile temper". Grazia did not understand the words, but she read from the expression that it was something unfavourable. She started up. "Signor Giovanni, that woman has insulted me, I know. What did she say? Tell her *I* am a Roman, and that *she* is a miserable foreigner. Tell me what she said, or I will go and never return." "She said you were very beautiful, Grazia". "What else?" "What else *could* she say?" Grazia believed in him implicitly and was satisfied. He said she was quite capable of personally maltreating the lady if he had said the truth' (*Cornhill Magazine* 1868, p. 545). An account of Grazia is also to be found in Matthews 1911, pp. 205–12.

Marble versions exist in the City Art Gallery, Manchester and in the Royal Collection. A marble version of the Grazia bust by John Gibson's youngest brother, Benjamin Gibson (1811–1851), was included in the sale at Christie's, London, 27 September 1990, lot 130. A plaster bust is in the Royal Academy. Gibson recorded, 'I finished the model of the bust, and executed it for Lord Kilmorey. Afterwards I executed a repetition for Queen Victoria, and on the front of the bust is inscribed GRAZIA./FILIA CAPUENSIS.' (Eastlake 1870, p. 210). Gibson also recorded, 'I had often meditated a bust of Grazia, but delayed on account of her insolent and capricious ways. One day Lord Kilmorey encouraged me to begin, saying that he wished her bust in marble' (Eastlake 1870, p. 207).

Bibliography

Jones 1924, p. 101, no. 397; Gunnis 1968, p. 173; Sutton 1972, p. 158, fig. 6 on p. 159.

418: Pandora

signed; 1856
Marble
h. (figure) 173 cm. h. (pedestal) 46.5 cm.
A.3–1922

Signed at the back on the base: IOANNES GIBSON ME FECIT ROMÆ

Bought from the sculptor by John Penn in about 1860. The figure is shown in a photograph of around 1900 showing the drawing room at The Cedars, Belmont Hill, Lee (photograph in the possession of Lady Penn). It was included in the sale at The Cedars, by order of the Executors of the late Mrs Ellen Penn, which was held between 1–5 July 1912, by Farebrother, Ellis & Co, London, lot 634, described as 'A repetition (uncoloured) of the statue in marble exhibited at the International Exhibition, 1862' (information supplied by Lady Penn). It seems to have remained unsold, and was later given to the Museum by Mrs Constance Penn, 34 Wilton Crescent, London, SW1 in 1922 in accordance with the wishes of her husband, the late Mr William Penn. In a letter of 1922 relating to the offer of the piece to the Museum Mrs Penn noted, 'The statue is a very old friend, as it was bought direct from the studio in Rome at least 60 or 70 years ago by Mr Penn's father'. In another letter written by Mrs Penn she noted that her father-in-law, John Penn paid £900 for the figure; she continued, 'I only mention the price to show it was considered a good piece of work' (Museum records). However, Stevens records two letters from John Penn to Gibson relating to the present piece, suggesting that a price of £700 was paid for the figure (*Lady Lever* [Stevens] 1999, p. 38). On the death of her father-in-law, the figure passed to the donor and her husband. Mrs Penn recorded that they had attempted to sell it at the Christie, Manson and Wood sale of 21 December 1921, lot 70, but the high reserve placed on the figure was not reached; she stated, 'I am not altogether sorry as I would rather send it to the Museum' (Museum records).

Gibson recorded,'The figure is motionless, but her mind is in full activity, labouring under the harassing feelings of intense curiosity, fear, and perplexity. Her thoughts have dwelled too long on what she bears. The box is still unopened, but Pandora is already lost' (Eastlake 1870, p. 216).

The original painted plaster version commissioned by the Duke of Wellington, but purchased by Lady Marian Alford from the sculptor, formerly in the possession of Lord Brownlow, was auctioned at Christie, Manson and Woods on 3 May 1923, lot 55, but did not sell. Eastlake listed three versions of this subject, and records them as belonging to Lady Marian Alford, – Penn, Esq (presumably the present piece), and Mr Laurence, Mossley Hill, Liverpool (Eastlake 1870, p. 251). Gunnis incorrectly cites the Alford version as being in the V&A (Gunnis 1968, p.173); the Alford version is in fact the one in the Lady Lever Art Gallery, Port Sunlight (see *Lady Lever* 1999, pp. 35–9). Stevens suggests that the third version, commissioned by George Hall Laurence is the version 'with Peter Hone Art, Brighton in 1974, later sold Sotheby's, Belgravia, 13 November 1974 (lot 23) (£1,150)' (*ibid.*, p. 39). The *Pandora* is discussed in Gibson's biography (see Eastlake 1870, pp. 214–7–; also Matthews 1911, pp. 186–92).

Bibliography
Avers 1966, p. 167 and fig. 240, p. 292; Fletcher 1974, p. 3, fig. 2 on p. 2; Williamson 1996 [Trusted], p. 173; *Lady Lever* [Stevens] 1999, pp. 38–9.

419: Edith Margaret Mozley (1847–1909)

signed; 1864
Marble
h. 58 cm.
A.15–1968

Signed on the left side: OPVS IOANNIS GIBSON/ROMÆ
Inscribed on the front: EDITH MARGARET MOZLEY

Given by Contessa Bona Gigliucci, Piazza Savonarola, Florence, in 1968. The donor was the sitter's daughter. In a letter to John Pope-Hennessy [q.v.], Marion Rawson, the donor's cousin, wrote: 'In due course I or my cousin could send you details about her mother the Contessa Edith, who was born in Liverpool – which perhaps accounts for the contact with Gibson, although the bust was done in Rome before her marriage, and must have been one of Gibson's last works'. According to a further letter from Marion Rawson, Edith Mozley was 'the daughter of a rich and cultivated Liverpool banker there is nothing of importance to say, though she was much loved in social and artistic circles in Florence till her death early this century. The interest lies in her marriage to the younger son of Count Gigliucci of Fermo in the Marche, whose wife was the famous English soprano Clara Novello, daughter of Vincent Novello, founder of the London firm of music publishers'. Edith Mozley, who was sixteen years old when the bust was executed, may have been introduced to Gibson by Liverpool friends.

A letter from Gibson in Rome to Edith Mozley in Liverpool dated 9 July 1864 concerning her portrait bust was acquired from the same source in 1971; it is in the National Art Library (inv.no. L. 3520/71). Gibson wrote, 'I have the pleasure to say that I have finished your bust in marble and in two or three days will be delivered to Messrs Maclean to be sent by them to England . . . Before your bust was packed up I had a photo taken from the marble and it is beautiful . . . I am glad your Greek net is liked – you should display it now and then – "her fair locks were woven up in gold" another little thing I wish you to adopt it is to get a comb made like the one sculptured at the back of the bust – please look at it. You see I want your ornaments to be in good taste – you are very pretty – the old Greek poet, Charnus said, – "Beauty when unadorned, adored the most"- there is great truth in this, still a little ornament is elegant – Mrs Mozley perhaps will disapprove of this advice of mine fearing I shall make you vain, but I believe there is no danger of vanity – you have talent good [sic] with modesty . . . When they unpack the bust it must not be touched with the fingers, towels round it – place it for the moment within 6 feet from the window, covering the lower part so that the light streeks [sic] down upon the bust, but I dare say you are all up to this'.

A closely similar but slightly smaller plaster bust (h. 55.3 cm), painted to imitate terracotta, similarly inscribed on the front, EDITH MARGARET MOZLEY, and additionally numbered 30, is in the Royal Academy.

SIR ALFRED GILBERT R.A.

(b. London 1854 – d. London 1934)

Gilbert initially trained at Hetherley's School of Art in London between 1872 and 1873. He later enrolled at the Royal Academy Schools in 1873, and between 1872 and 1875 was assistant to Sir Joseph Edgar Boehm [q.v.]. A year later he went to Paris to study under Pierre-Jules Cavalier at the École des Beaux-Arts, and then in 1878 travelled to Rome, returning to England in 1884. In 1890 he produced the memorial to Randolph Caldecott [q.v.] in St Paul's Cathedral. In 1900 Gilbert was appointed Professor of Sculpture at the Royal Academy, but was declared bankrupt a year later. The latter part of his career was spent in self-imposed exile, largely in Bruges. He returned to London in 1926, finally completing the Clarence Memorial, originally begun in 1892, in 1928. Gilbert was also an accomplished jeweller and silversmith. The Tate Gallery Archive holds material relating to this sculptor, as does the archive of the Centre for the Study of Sculpture, Leeds.

Spielmann 1901, pp. 75–85; British Sculpture 1850–1914 1968, p. 24; Victorian 1978, pp. 158–67; Dorment 1985; Gilbert 1986, esp. pp. 13–18; Thieme-Becker, 14, pp. 23–4; TDA, 12, pp. 610–3 [Stocker].

420: Perseus arming

signed; about 1882
Bronze
h. 37 cm.
77–1904

Signed on the circular base: A. Gilbert.

In the collection of Alfred Higgins at the time of his death. Purchased at the sale of a collection of plaquettes, statuettes, etc., the property of the late Alfred Higgins, Esq., C.B., held at Christie, Manson and Woods on 29 January 1904, lot no. 37; there described as *Hermes*. Purchased for £65 2s (£68 7s 1d with commission) by Mr F.E. Whelan of Messrs Rollin and Feuardent on behalf of the Museum. See also entries for cat.nos. 421 and 425.

The sculptor Thomas Brock [q.v.], who was a member of the Museum's Council for Advice on Art, recommended the purchase of this piece, together with cat.nos. 421 and 425. He commented, 'I find that they are reductions of his original statuettes of these subjects, which are considerably large, nevertheless I consider the purchase of one or more of these would be desirable for the Museum, as they are admirable examples of his work and would prove instructive to students'. Brock's order of preference placed the present piece as most desirable for purchase, followed by cat.nos. 425 and 421 respectively.

Controversy about the authenticity of this bronze is discussed by Penny (*Ashmolean* 1992 [III], pp. 71–2), who concluded that the present piece 'turns out not to be an aftercast as one might suppose or even a poorly finished cast but to be identical in quality to the authorized version in Brocklebank's collection' . The Revd. J.W.R. Brocklebank bequeathed his collection of thirty-five bronze statuettes to the Ashmolean Museum in 1926; included were twelve examples of Alfred Gilbert's works (*ibid.*, pp. xxxv-xxxviii). However Eric Maclagan [q.v.] recorded a visit to the Museum by Mr Herbert Wheller, a friend of Gilbert's, who commented that the present piece and other Gilbert bronzes were 'merely commercial copies' and that the figure contained 'what is practically a forged signature'. Maclagan went on to state, 'I understand from Mr Watts that Gilbert himself called one Saturday afternoon four or five years ago and made a similar complaint, particularly repudiating the Perseus'.

Further versions are in the Leeds City Art Gallery (see *Leeds* 1996, p. 13; *Victorian* 1978, pp. 174–5, no. 91a), and the Ashmolean Museum, Oxford (*Ashmolean* 1992 [III], pp. 71–4, nos. 497, 498 and 499). For a miniature version offered for sale by Robert Bowman Ltd, London, see *Bowman* 2000, pp. 46–7. A version was also included in the Sotheby's, London sale, 2 November 2001, lot 247.

In an interview given for the *Easter Art Annual*, Gilbert records that he conceived the idea for this figure whilst in Florence: 'When I returned to Rome, and at once set to work to make a statuette called "Perseus Arming "... After seeing the wonderful and heroic statue of Cellini, amazed as I was by that great work, it still left me somewhat cold, insomuch that it failed to touch my human sympathies. As at that time my whole thoughts were of my artistic equipment for the future, I conceived the idea that Perseus before becoming a hero was a mere mortal, and that he had to look to his equipment. That is a presage of my life and work at that time. And I think the wing still ill-fits me, the sword is blunt, and the armour dull as my own brain ... But now comes the astonishing thing about the figure. I sent it to the Salon; it was accepted, and obtained for me honourable mention. This gave me great encouragement to continue the task I had set myself – that was, to go on writing my own history by symbol' (Hatton 1903, p. 10).

Bibliography

McAllister 1929, p. 57; *Ashmolean* 1992 [III], p. 71–2.

421: Offering to Hymen

about 1884–6
Bronze
h. 30.5 cm.
79–1904

In the collection of Alfred Higgins at the time of his death. Purchased at the sale of a collection of plaquettes, statuettes, etc., the property of the late Alfred Higgins, Esq., C.B., held at Christie, Manson and Woods on 29 January 1904, lot no. 39, described as a 'nude statuette of a girl, holding in her hand the figure of Victory'. Purchased for £24 5s 1d by Mr F.E. Whelan of Messrs Rollin and Feuardent on behalf of the Museum. See also entries for cat.nos. 420 and 425.

In other versions of this piece the female figure holds a silver goblet or sprig of hawthorn; in this case the figure holds a sprig of hawthorn together with a statuette depicting *Anteros*, which she presents to the god of marriage, Hymen (see *Victorian* 1978, pp. 178–9 and 181, cat.nos. 95 a and b and cat.no. 98). The other versions include one with plaster details in the Winchester Museum; these are cited in the above reference; see also *Ashmolean* 1992 [III], p. 77. no. 501. A version was at Thomas Agnew & Sons Ltd, London in 1981 (*Agnew* 1981, p. 39, cat.no. 30 and illus.).

Bibliography

Gilbert 1936, p, 16; Bury 1954, p. 70; *Victorian* 1978, p. 179; *Ashmolean* 1992 [III], p. 77.

422: Eros

about 1886
Plaster
A.6–1985

Given by Mr Gerald Keith, 18 Southampton Road, Holborn, London in 1937, it was registered as a reproduction until 1985, when it was given an inventory number for that year (see below). Mr Keith was the former Director of A.B. Burton, Founders, Thames Ditton and Gilbert's former solicitor and major legatee. The founders A.B. Burton cast the Liverpool replica of *Eros* for Sefton Park, as well as Gilbert's Alexandra Memorial; they also cast Frampton's statue of *Peter Pan* for Kensington Gardens; see entry for cat.no. 403.

In several sections; torso and head, right arm, left arm, right leg, left leg, right wing, left wing (both with detachable feathers), head-dress in two parts.

The original aluminium figure of *Eros* on an elaborate bronze pedestal, a memorial to Anthony Ashley-Cooper, 7th Earl of Shaftesbury (1801–1885), was unveiled in Piccadilly Circus, London on 29 June 1893 (see *Victorian* 1978, pp. 185–8; *Gilbert* 1986, pp. 135–43 and *Eros* 1987). The commission to produce the memorial had initially been given to Joseph Edgar Boehm [q.v.], but due to Boehm's other commitments, the commission was passed to his former pupil Gilbert. In his interview in the *Easter Art Annual* Gilbert commented: 'As to the figure surmounting the whole, if I must confess to a meaning or a raison d'être for its being there, I confess to have been actuated in its design by a desire to symbolise the work of Lord Shaftesbury; the blindfolded Love sending forth indiscriminantly, yet with purpose, his missile of kindness, always with the swiftness the bird has from its wings, never ceasing to breathe or reflect critically, but ever soaring onwards, regardless of its own peril and dangers' (Hatton 1903, p. 16). For comment on the unveiling, see the *Magazine of Art*, XVI, 1893, p. 394.

Museum correspondence records that a Mr Toft, probably the sculptor Albert Toft [q.v.], had in 1937 drawn this model to the attention of R.P. Bedford [q.v.], then Keeper of the Department of Architecture and Sculpture. In November 1937 Bedford noted on visiting the model kept at the Thames Ditton foundry that, 'It is in more or less perfect condition, but it is not the original full-scale model by Gilbert as I was led to believe. Instead, it is a cast made for Gilbert from the mould of the fountain which was made for a replica put up a few years ago in Sefton Park, Liverpool. It is thus only a cast, but it is a very decorative figure and I think we should do well to accept it. The Tate Gallery has a bronze made from Gilbert's original smaller sketch-model but the full-scale model is, I believe, lost'. With Bedford's opinion that this was merely a cast, it was originally recorded as such and assigned the reproduction inv.no. of A.1937–1. In 1984 Anthony Racliffe recorded on examination of the model that it appeared not to have been entirely original, concluding that the original parts comprised the torso, head, both arms, the right leg and parts of the wings. He suggested that the other sections were possibly made at the time of the casting of the Sefton Park version in 1931–2. Following this reassessment, the object was regarded as an original work rather than a reproduction, and it was allocated its present inventory number.

The bronze at the Tate Gallery was cast by the Royal Academy in 1926 from the original model (see *Victorian* 1978, pp. 188–9, cat.no. 103). The wood and plaster model for the Shaftesbury memorial is in the Museum and Art Gallery, Perth (see *Gilbert* 1986, pp. 140–1, cat.no. 47). For the aluminium version, unveiled on 23 July 1932 at Sefton Park, Liverpool, see Cavanagh 1997, pp. 195–6. Versions in bronze and aluminium were sold at Sotheby's, London on 29 September 1999, lot 388, and on 22 May 1996, lot 159 (I am grateful to Alexander Kader for this information).

In connection with the Royal Academy exhibition, *Sir Alfred Gilbert R.A.* held in London in 1986, the present piece was lent to Charles Henshaw & Sons, Edinburgh. In Dorment 1986 Timothy Bidwell discusses the restoration of the figure in Piccadilly Circus; the figure was sent to Charles Henshaw & Sons Ltd in July 1984, and the left leg and both arms of the present piece were lent to the foundry. Casts were taken from these to aid with the necessary repairs. Ten aluminium casts were also made from the present model under the auspices of the Fine Art Society; one was sold at Sotheby's in 1993 for £199,500 (see *Eros* 1987, pp. 11–15 for restoration and *Gilbert* [Bidwell] 1986, pp. 39–42).

Bibliography

Gilbert 1986 [Bidwell], pp. 40–2; *Eros* 1987, pp. 12, 15.

[Not illustrated].

423: Water nymphs

about 1890
Bronzed plaster
h. 13 cm.
A.98–1936

In the studio of the sculptor at the time of his death. Given by Mr Sigismund Goetze and the National Art Collections Fund in 1936, together with cat.nos. 426 to 429, and 433 to 439.

Though described on acquisition and by Machell Cox as a salt-cellar, this could be a preliminary idea for the cistern of the Shaftesbury Memorial; see entry for cat.no. 422. Machell Cox recorded that a 'more finished model of a section of this object, is in the possession of Mr Sigismund Goetz [sic.], shows the moulded base replaced by a plateau of swirling water, and the plain lip developed into a vertical band of ornament. The design as thus extended gains greatly in consistency and effect' (*Gilbert* 1936, pp. 25–6). The object noted as in the collection of Sigismund Goetze may be the model of a cistern given to the Royal Academy in 1936 (see *Gilbert* 1986, p. 140, cat.no. 46). What appears to be the present piece is shown in a photograph taken in 1935 of the interior of Alfred Gilbert's studio in Kensington Palace (see Dorment 1985, fig. 198 on p. 328).

Bibliography

Gilbert 1936, pp. 25–6, cat.no. 40; Bury 1954, p. 70, no. 40, pl. XVIII.

Exhibited

Models and Designs by the late Sir Alfred Gilbert R.A., Victoria and Albert Museum, Autumn 1936, cat.no. 40.

424: Victory

about 1891
Bronze
h. 33 cm. h. (incl. base) 43 cm.
1050–1905

In the collection of the actor-manager Sir Henry Irving (1838–1905) at the time of his death. Dorment records that the figure of Victory was 'a favourite present which Gilbert gave to friends: John Singer Sargent,

Seymour Lucas, Henry Irving, and Mark Senior were all presented with casts, very often completed with elaborate bronze bases below the spheres' (*Gilbert* 1986, p. 129). Purchased from the sale of the collection of Theatrical Relics, Costumes, Bronzes, Silver, Furniture and Decorative Objects. The Property of Sir Henry Irving (deceased), held at Christie, Manson & Woods on 14 and 15 December 1905. This figure sold on 14 December, lot 81 for £131 5s. Purchased by Messrs Ernest Brown and Phillips, Leicester Galleries, Leicester Square, London on behalf of the Museum. Prior to this sale, a silver figure of *Victory* was offered to the Museum by Messrs Brown and Phillips in November 1905, together with a bronze, *Needless Alarms* by Leighton [q.v.]. The silver statuette, priced at £52 10s (50 guineas), was considered too expensive, and when the present piece became available, it was returned. A similar statuette in silver, possibly the one offered to the Museum in 1905, was exhibited at the Royal Academy in 1891, no. 2069. The Leighton figure was however purchased; see entry for cat.no. 490.

The figure was originally designed to surmount the orb held by the figure of Queen Victoria in the Queen Victoria Jubilee Memorial in the Great Hall at Winchester Castle, executed by Gilbert in 1887 (see *Gilbert* 1986, p. 127).

The statuette was recommended for purchase by the sculptor Thomas Brock [q.v.], who was a member of the Museum's Council for Advice on Art. He wrote, 'I have inspected the small bronze statuette 'Victory' by Alfred Gilbert R.A. lot 81 to be sold at Christie's tomorrow, and I consider it a very beautiful work and one which should, if possible, be acquired for the Museum. This figure has evidently been cast under Mr Gilbert's supervision, therefore has additional value'. A.B. Skinner [q.v.], the Director of the Museum, added to Brock's comments, 'We are gradually forming a collection of bronze statuettes by artists of recent times, and among the most beautiful and valuable are those of Mr Gilbert. It is not often that the work executed either by him or under his immediate supervision comes into the market – commercial replicas are to be had, but these we would rather not possess . . . It is in every sense a beautiful figure and the bronze has a fine quality about it, so very different in tone to the examples found in the trade'.

Another version exists in the Ashmolean Museum, Oxford, said to be identical to the present piece (*Ashmolean* 1992 [III], p. 78, no. 502, illus. p. 79); a further example is in the Leeds City Art Gallery (*Leeds* 1996, p. 13, inv.no. SW210/25; see *Reverie* 1992, p. 46, cat.no. 20). A sketch model for the Victoria Jubilee Memorial now in the Royal Academy collection was exhibited by Gilbert at the Royal Academy in 1888, no. 1940. The Royal Academy also owns a bronze figure of Victory.

Bibliography
Gilbert 1936, p. 24.

425: Comedy and Tragedy: 'Sic vita' [Such is life]

about 1891–2
Bronze
h. (incl. pedestal) 40 cm.
78–1904

In the collection of Alfred Higgins at the time of his death. Purchased at the sale of a collection of plaquettes, statuettes, etc. the property of the late Alfred Higgins, Esq., C.B., held at Christie, Manson and Woods on 29 January 1904, lot 38. Purchased for £62 2s (£68 7s 1d including commission). See also entries for cat.nos. 420 and 421.

As with the figure of Perseus, in his interview given in the *Easter Art Annual*, Gilbert related this statuette to his personal life, as being 'the climax to my cycle of stories . . . It represents a boy carrying a comic mask. He is stung by a bee – the symbol of Love. He turns, and his face becomes tragic. The symbol is in reality fact. I was stung by that bee, typified by my love for my art, a consciousness of its incompleteness, my love was not sufficient . . . I was living a kind of double life at that time, enjoying the society of Irving and Toole and other famous and pleasant members of the Garrick Club going to the theatre at night, and with Tragedy in my private life, living my Comedy publicly, if not enjoying it'. A one-act play at the Lyceum called "Comedy and Tragedy" inspired Gilbert, and he 'conceived the notion of harking back to the old Greek stage upon which masks were always worn, and I conceived a kind of stage property boy rushing away in great glee with his comedy mask, and on his way being stung by a bee. This was the only way in which I could present the hidden pain and passion of the boy' (Hatton 1903, pp. 11–12).

A version of the present piece, also dated about 1891–2, in the

Castle Museum and Art Gallery, City of Nottingham Museums was exhibited in *Reverie, Myth, Sensuality. Sculpture in Britain 1880–1910*, cat.no. 21 (*Reverie* 1992, p. 47). Another version of 1892 is in the Leeds City Art Gallery (see *Leeds* 1996, p. 14); versions in the Ashmolean Museum, Oxford and the Tate Gallery date from 1891–2; others are cited by Dorment (see *Gilbert* 1986, pp. 116–8). Versions were also included in sales at Sotheby's, London on 16 April 1986, lot 253; 26 November 1986, lot 57; 23 June 1987, lot 83; 30 April 1993, lot 182; 9 December 1993, lot 157; and 20 May 1994, lot 110 (I am grateful to Alexander Kader for this information).

BIBLIOGRAPHY
Gilbert 1936, p. 17; McAllister 1929, p. 88; *Ashmolean* 1992 [III], p. 83.

426: Comedy and Tragedy 'Sic vita'

about 1891–2
Plaster
h. 68 cm.
A.90–1936

In the studio of the sculptor at the time of his death. Given by Mr Sigismund Goetze and the National Art Collections Fund in 1936, together with cat.nos. 423, 427 to 429, and 433 to 439.

This is a model for the bronze statuette produced by Gilbert; see entry for cat.no. 425 for a bronze version.

Although the present piece was previously thought to have been exhibited at the Royal Academy in 1892, Alison Luchs has recently suggested that a bronze version may have been shown (*European Sculpture* 2000 [Luchs], p. 269). For the bronze version in the National Gallery of Art, Washington, see *European Sculpture* 2000 [Luchs], pp. 266–71.

BIBLIOGRAPHY
Graves III, p. 233, no. 2004; *Gilbert* 1936, p. 17, no. 8, and pl. V; McAllister 1929, p. 88; *Review* 1936, p. 8, n. 1; Bury 1954, p. 70; *European Sculpture* 2000 [Luchs], pp. 268–9, p. 270, n. 12 and 20, fig. 2 on p. 268.

EXHIBITED
Models and Designs by the late Sir Alfred Gilbert R.A., Victoria and Albert Museum, Autumn 1936, cat.no.8.

427: Prince Albert Victor, Duke of Clarence and Avondale (1864–1892)

1892
Plaster, plasticine and wax
h. 30 cm.
A.89–1936

In the studio of the sculptor at the time of his death. Given by Mr Sigismund Goetze and the National Art Collections Fund in 1936, together with cat.nos. 423, 426, 428, 429, and 433 to 439.

This is Gilbert's working model for the tomb of the Duke of Clarence in the Albert Memorial Chapel, St George's, Windsor. The tomb, commissioned in 1892 shortly after the death of the Duke, was not finally completed until 1928. The finished monument differs considerably from this sketch-model. A further plaster model now in the possession of H.M. the Queen was completed by Gilbert in 1894, and exhibited at the Royal Academy in that year (no. 1849); see *Gilbert* 1986, pp. 159–60, cat.no. 67. Original information on the acquisition of the present piece records, 'The model, which is in plaster upon a wooden base with elaborations in plasticine, is of interest as embodying Gilbert's first conception of the central feature of his most important monument'. According to Dorment this is the model which was designed by Gilbert between 23rd and 25th January 1892, whilst at Sandringham (*ibid.*, p. 159).

Dorment notes that the bust of a *Bishop Saint* was to have been incorporated into the scheme (*Gilbert* 1986, pp. 165–6, cat.no. 74); see entry for cat.no. 431.

Bibliography

Gilbert 1936, p. 17, cat.no. 9 (a), pl. VI; *Review* 1936, p. 7; Bury 1954, pp. 70, 87, pl. XIII; Handley-Read 1968, p. 86 and fig. 2; *Victorian* 1978, p. 192; *Gilbert* 1986, p. 159, n. 3 on p. 160 and fig. 58 on p. 159.

Exhibited

Models and Designs by the late Sir Alfred Gilbert R.A., Victoria and Albert Museum, Autumn 1936, cat.no. 9 (a).

428: Kneeling figure on the back of a mermaid

about 1892
Plasticine and wax
h. 23.5 cm.
A.91–1936

In the studio of the artist at the time of his death. Given by Mr Sigismund Goetze and the National Art Collections Fund in 1936, together with cat.nos. 423, 426, 427, 429, and 433 to 439.

Machell Cox suggested, 'It is possible that the group is to be connected with two figures forming part of the decoration of the St Michael on the tomb of the Duke of Clarence' (*Gilbert* 1936, p. 25, cat.no.39). Though the present model is described as a kneeling figure on the back of a mermaid, the group of figures noted by Machell Cox is described by Dorment as 'a naked female soul . . . dragged down by a pursuing winged demon with horrible claws' (*Gilbert* 1986, p. 164). What appears to be the present piece – together with cat.no. 429 – is shown in a photograph taken in 1935 of the interior of Alfred Gilbert's studio in Kensington Palace (see Dorment 1985, fig. 197 on p. 328).

For the Duke of Clarence tomb, see the entry for cat.no. 427; see also entry for cat.no. 431.

Bibliography

Gilbert 1936, p. 25, no. 39 and pl. XVII; Bury 1954, p. 70.

Exhibited

Models and Designs by the late Sir Alfred Gilbert R.A., Victoria and Albert Museum, Autumn 1936, cat.no. 39.

429: St George and the dragon

about 1895
Plasticine and wax on a wood base
h. 20 cm.
A.88–1936

In the studio of the sculptor at the time of his death. Given by Mr Sigismund Goetze and the National Art Collections fund, together with cat.nos. 423, 426 to 428, and 433 to 439.

The model has suffered some damage.

Machell Cox suggested that this was possibly a preliminary model for the group surmounting the silver rose-water ewer and dish presented to King George V when Duke of York, as a wedding gift by the officers of the Brigade of Guards (see *Gilbert* 1986, pp. 146–7, cat.no. 56 and illus. p. 75). The ewer, begun in 1894, was eventually completed in 1901; it was exhibited, presumably in an unfinished state, at the Royal Academy in 1897, no. 2090.

Bury noted, 'The monumental quality of this note [sic.] is eloquent of the power of Gilbert's impulse as a modeller. So vital is it that we can almost feel the intensity of the sculptor's mind and see his hands moulding the form out of the cold, dead clay' (Bury 1954, p. 86). Bury similarly commented on the equestrian figure of St George as 'wholly in keeping with the general decorative scheme. The motif of St George was irresistible to Gilbert and he returned to it again and again' (Bury 1954, p. 86).

What appears to be the present piece – together with cat.no. 428 – is shown in a photograph taken in 1935 of the interior of Alfred Gilbert's studio in Kensington Palace (see Dorment 1985, fig. 197 on p. 328).

BIBLIOGRAPHY

Review 1936, p. 8, fig 1 on p. 9; *Gilbert* 1936, p. 24, cat.no. 34 (b), pl XIV; Bury 1954, pp. 70, 86, pl XVIII; *Gilbert* 1986, p. 147 and n. 1.

EXHIBITED

Models and Designs by the late Sir Alfred Gilbert R.A., Victoria and Albert Museum, Autumn 1936, cat.no. 34 (b).

430: Post Equitem sedet atra cura (Behind the rider sits dark care)

1899
Bronze
diam. 41.5 cm.
A.7–1972

Previously owned by Robert Dunthorne (Rembrandt Gallery, Vigo Street, London), who had purchased the roundel from the sculptor in May 1899. David Peel, Mount Street, London; Handley-Read Collection (probably purchased from David Peel in 1966 for £300). Purchased from Thomas Stainton, Madeley Penn Road, Beaconsfield, Buckinghamshire in 1972 for £605.

A label attached to the reverse is inscribed in ink: July 1966/from David Peel/Mount St Lond/£300.

The earliest version of this roundel with integral bronze frame, exhibited at the Royal Academy in 1887, no. 1819, is in the Birmingham Museum and Art Gallery; see *Reverie* 1992, p. 44, no. 18; *Victorian* 1978, pp. 176–7, no. 93; *Gilbert* 1986, pp. 176–7, no. 88. Another version is in the Royal Scottish Academy, Edinburgh. Spielmann commented that, 'The fine design and superb execution of "Post equitem sedet atra cura" made such a sensation in the Academy at the time of its exhibition that it is hardly likely to be forgotten' (Spielmann 1901, p.170).

Dorment comments, 'The startling polychromed effect of the Victoria and Albert Museum version was achieved by casting the medallion in an alloy of lead, copper and gold, the latter replacing the usual zinc and tin so that after the application of certain pickling solutions (verdigris, sulphate of copper, nitre, common salt, sulphur, water, vinegar) a rich reddish patination was obtained' (*Gilbert* 1986, p. 177).

A related marble roundel was on the London art market (Daniel Katz Ltd) in 2001; see *Katz* 2001, cat.no. 20.

BIBLIOGRAPHY

Peel 1967, cat.no. 22; *From Vittoria to Dalou* 1967, cat.no. 22 (states exhibited at Royal Academy in 1887); *British Sculpture 1850–1914*, 1968, p. 25, no. 65, pl. F (incorrectly states exhibited at Royal Academy in 1887); Handley-Read 1968, p. 25 and illus.; *Handley-Read* 1972, p. 108, cat.no. F.22 and illus. (there said to have been possibly exhibited at the Royal Academy 1887, and at the Fine Art Society 1902); *Victorian* 1978, pp. 176–7; Dorment 1985, p. 53, and fig. 24 on p. 52; *Gilbert* 1986, p. 177, cat.no. 89.

EXHIBITED

From Vittoria to Dalou. An Exhibition of European Works of Art, David Peel, April to May 1967, London, cat.no. 22; *Fine Art Society. British Sculpture 1850–1914*, 30 September to 30 October 1968, cat.no. 65; *Victorian and Edwardian Decorative Art: The Handley-Read Collection,* Royal Academy, London, 1972, cat.no. F.22; *Alfred Gilbert: Sculptor and Goldsmith*, 21 March to 29 June 1986, Royal Academy, cat.no. 89; *Knights, Chivalry, Romance, Legend*, Laing Art Gallery, Newcastle upon Tyne, 13 September 1995 to 18 February 1996.

431: Bishop saint

1899
Bronze and ivory
h. (overall) 29.5 cm. h. (bust) 19 cm. h. (base) 12 cm.
A.4–1995

Originally sold by the sculptor to Robert Dunthorne in 1899. Sold by Dunthorne to William Vivian; by descent to Lady Jean Makins, Cheriton, and Lady Harvey of Tasburgh. Given by Lady Harvey of Tasburgh in accordance with the wishes of Lady Jean Makins M.B.E.

This bust was produced by Gilbert as part of the Duke of Clarence tomb for the Albert Memorial Chapel in Windsor, but was not in the event incorporated; see also entries for cat.nos. 427 and 428. The bust was constructed out of the torso of the *St George* figure used for the tomb, with additions being made of the cope, ivory head and mitre. Commenting on the Vivian collection in 1905, Maskell described this bust as that of a bishop, and stated that together with a figure of St Elizabeth, it was a copy of a figure on the Clarence memorial, 'The bishop was to have been full length, but Gilbert changed his mind' (Maskell 1905, p. 411). The bust may however be an early study for the figure of St Boniface (see *Gilbert* 1986, p. 157; Gilbert 1987, pp. 9, 22–3, n. 12).

Bibliography

Hatton 1903, p. 32, illus. on p. 27 as Edward the Confessor; Maskell 1905, p. 411; *Victorian* 1978, p. 202, cat.no. 111, illus. on p. 201; Dorment 1985, p. 201, fig. 126 on p. 200; *Gilbert* 1986, pp. 165–6, cat.no. 74, and illus. on pp. 63 and 165; Williamson 1999, p. 788, fig. XVII.

Exhibited

The Victorian High Renaissance, Manchester City Art Gallery, Minneapolis Institute of Arts, Brooklyn Museum, 1 September 1978 to 8 April 1979, cat.no. 111; *Alfred Gilbert: Sculptor and Goldsmith*, Royal Academy of Arts, London, 21 March to 29 June 1986, cat.no. 74.

432: Charity

about 1899
By Sir Alfred Gilbert; cast by Alessandro Parlanti
Bronze
h. 38.1 cm.
A.8–1972

Originally owned by the family of the artist Alfred Drury [q.v.], in the possession of Anthony Radcliffe, and latterly in the Handley-Read collection. Purchased from Thomas Stainton, Madeley Penn Road, Beaconsfield, Buckinghamshire in 1972 for £412.50.

This figure illustrates Gilbert's practice of colouring bronze, a technique in which he became interested during the 1890s; see also entry for cat.no. 430. The figure of Charity is taken from one of the figures on the memorial candlestick to the Rt. Hon Lord Arthur Russell (1825–1892), commissioned from Gilbert in 1892, completed in 1900: it is in the Bedford family chapel at St Michael Chenies, Buckinghamshire (see *Victorian* 1978, pp. 189–90, Dorment 1985, pp. 193–7 and *Gilbert* 1986, pp. 177–80).

Versions were included in sales held at Sotheby's, London, 11 July 2001, lot 251 and on 2 November 2001, lot 251.

Bibliography

Handley-Read 1972, p. 109, cat.no. F.29; *Victorian* 1978, pp. 190–1, cat.no. 104; *Gilbert* 1986, p. 179, cat.no. 90, and p. 83 illus.; *Colour of Sculpture* 1996, p. 199, cat.no. 69.

Exhibited

Victorian and Edwardian Decorative Arts: The Handley-Read Collection, Royal Academy, London, 4 March to 30 April 1972, cat.no. F.29; *The Victorian High Renaissance*, Manchester City Art Gallery, Minneapolis Institute of Arts, Brooklyn Museum, 1 September 1978 to 8 April 1979, cat.no. 104; *Alfred Gilbert*, Royal Academy, 21 March to 29 June 1986, cat.no. 90; *The Colour of Sculpture 1840–1910*, Van Gogh Museum Amsterdam, and Henry Moore Institute, Leeds, 26 July to 6 April 1997, cat.no. 69.

433: Nymph and two cupids

about 1903 (?)
Plasticine and wax on an armature of split cane
h. 22 cm.
A.92–1936

In the studio of the artist at the time of his death. Given by Mr Sigismund Goetze and the National Art Collections Fund in 1936, together with cat.nos. 423, 426 to 429, and 434 to 439.

Machell Cox suggested that this may be a model for a group of figures designed to decorate the cover of a cup.

Bibliography

Gilbert 1936, p. 25, no. 36, and pl. XVI; Bury 1954, p. 70.

Exhibited

Models and Designs by the late Sir Alfred Gilbert R.A., Victoria and Albert Museum, Autumn 1936, cat.no. 36.

434: Decorative spoon depicting Europa and the bull

about 1903 (?)
Wax and other materials applied to a wood caddy spoon
h. 23.5 cm.
A.93–1936

This set of five decorative spoons were amongst items left in the artist's studio in Kensington Palace at the time of his death in 1934. Purchased by Sigismund Goetze and the National Art Collections Fund from the Executors of Gilbert's estate, this set of spoons was presented to the Museum in 1936, together with other items from Gilbert's studio (cat.nos. 423, 426 to 429, 433, and 434 to 439). Other sketches and models were similarly purchased by Goetze and the N.A.C.F., and presented to a number of other British museums and galleries. These include three decorative spoons (only one of which survives), in the collections of Birmingham Museum and Art Gallery (*Birmingham* 1987, p. 46, no. 134), as well as various maquettes for sculpture and metalwork in the Leeds Museums and Galleries *(Leeds* 1996, p. 18). Sir William Reid Dick [q.v.], Albert Toft [q.v.], Sir William Goscombe John and Sir William Reynolds-Stephens were amongst the Committee of Sculptors involved in the selection of material from Gilbert's studio for dispersal to various museums. Reynolds-Stephens and Toft were friends and pupils of Gilbert.

Some of the foil has flaked away at the bottom ridge of the bowl.

A short stemmed spoon of laquered and painted wood forms the bowl and stem. The top is modelled in wax formed around a base of wire and split cane, and depicts at the head of the stem, Europa astride the neck of a bull. The spoon is covered with foil, which is embossed with a decorative pattern.

Dorment suggests these spoons are of Japanese origin and may have been purchased by Gilbert at Liberty's. He felt it unlikely they were made as models for spoons to be fashioned in silver, but that Gilbert produced them for no other purpose than for his own amusement, he suggested they were made in about 1930. However they may date from an earlier period. Gilbert's early interest in intricate working is mentioned in an interview in the *Easter Art Annual* of 1903, in response to the question as to when he began to take an interest in art, Gilbert responded: 'I suppose my earliest inclination must have been in that direction. To get off fagging at Aldenham I used to go down to an adjacent chalk-pit and amuse myself. I collected walking sticks, and carved heads upon them, and by judicious presents of the same obtained immunity from some of my lessons' (Hatton 1903, p. 20). Spielmann similarly recorded, 'Even the lead-foil from his [Gilbert's] tobacco packet will become twisted by his inspired fingers into some interesting form – and so it is that his work suggests all through the mind ever busy to keep pace with infinitely dexterous hands' (Spielmann 1901, p. 84).

The Hatton article on Gilbert of 1903 includes an illustration showing sketch models for various objects, including spoons (Hatton 1903, fig. on p. 18).

Bibliography
Gilbert 1936, p. 27, cat.no. 48, pl. XX; *Review* 1936, pp. 7–8; Bury 1954, p. 70; *Gilbert* 1986, pp. 151–2, cat.no. 63 (for a discussion of the models acquired from Gilbert's studio).

Exhibited
Models and Designs by the Late Alfred Gilbert R.A., Victoria and Albert Museum, London, Autumn 1936, cat.no. 48 (see *Gilbert* 1936 above); *Alfred Gilbert: Sculptor and Goldsmith,* Royal Academy of Arts, London, 21 March to 29 June 1986, cat.no. 63 (see *Gilbert* 1986 above).

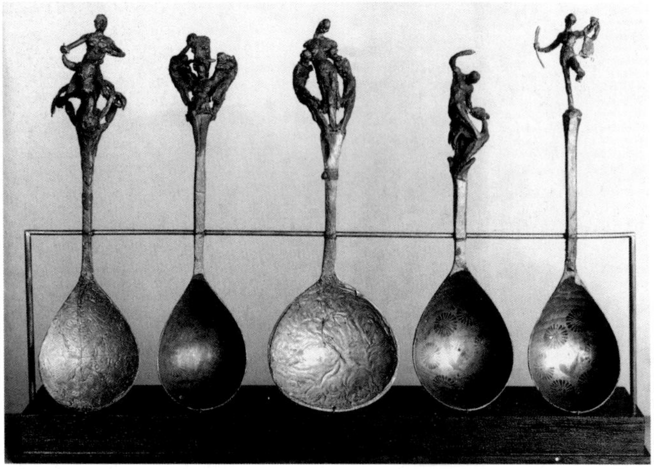

434 435 436 437 438

435: Decorative spoon depicting a winged man with a dragon

about 1903 (?)
Wax and other materials applied to a wood caddy spoon
h. 22.5 cm.
A.94–1936

In the studio of the sculptor at the time of his death. Purchased by Sigismund Goetze and the National Art Collections Fund from the Executors of Sir Alfred Gilbert's estate. See entry for cat.no. 434.

A short-stemmed spoon of laquered and painted wood forms the bowl and stem. The head and neck of a dragon curving over a winged armless figure of a man is modelled in wax upon foundations of wire and split cane. The bowl is outlined with an orange/gold lacquer with a design of six painted geometric sunburst motifs, in a rough circle around the inner bowl; a v-shaped design is painted in the centre of the bowl. Two other spoons have a similar decoration; see cat.nos. 437 and 438.

Bibliography
Gilbert 1936, p. 27, cat. 49, pl.XX; see also entry for cat.no. 434.

Exhibited
See entry for cat.no. 434.

436: Decorative spoon depicting a naked woman standing between two scrolled arabesques

about 1903 (?)
Wax and other materials applied to a wood caddy spoon
h. 23.5 cm.
A.95–1936

In the studio of the sculptor at the time of his death. Purchased by Sigismund Goetze and the National Art Collections Fund from the Executors of Sir Alfred Gilbert's estate. See entry for cat.no. 434.

The foil on the bowl appears to have puckered.

A short-stemmed spoon of laquered and painted wood forms the bowl and stem. The top is modelled in wax upon foundations of wire and split cane, and depicts a naked woman standing between two scrolled arabesques. In style, the bowl of this spoon covered in foil relates closely to cat.no. 434.

Bibliography
Gilbert 1936, p. 27, cat. 50, pl.XX; see also entry for cat.no. 434.

Exhibited
See entry for cat.no. 434.

437: Decorative spoon depicting a man in combat with a dragon

about 1903 (?)
Wax and other materials applied to a wood caddy spoon
h. 22.5 cm.
A.96–1936

In the studio of the sculptor at the time of his death. Purchased by Sigismund Goetze and the National Art Collections Fund from the Executors of Sir Alfred Gilbert's estate. See entry for cat.no. 434.

A short-stemmed spoon of laquered and painted wood forms the bowl and stem. A naked man striking at a dragon coiling up the stem behind him is modelled in wax upon foundations of wire and split cane. Like cat.nos. 435, 437 and 438, the bowl is outlined with an orange/gold lacquer with a design of six painted geometric sunburst motifs in a rough circle around the inner bowl; a v-shaped design is painted in the centre of the bowl.

Bibliography
Gilbert 1936, p. 27, cat. 51, pl. XX; see also entry for cat.no. 434.

Exhibited
See entry for cat.no. 434.

438: Decorative spoon depicting Apollo dancing

about 1903 (?)
Wax and other materials applied to a wood caddy spoon
h. 24.5 cm.
A.97–1936

In the studio of the sculptor at the time of his death. Purchased by Sigismund Goetze and the National Art Collections Fund from the Executors of Sir Alfred Gilbert's estate. See entry for cat.no. 434.

A short-stemmed spoon of laquered and painted wood forms the bowl and stem. A figure of Apollo dancing, holding a lyre in his left hand, is modelled in wax upon foundations of wire and split cane. The bowl is outlined with an orange/gold lacquer with a design of six painted geometric sunburst motifs, in a rough circle around the inner bowl; a v-shaped design is painted in the centre of the bowl. Two other spoons have a similar decoration; see cat.nos. 435 and 437.

BIBLIOGRAPHY
Gilbert 1936, p. 27, cat. 52, pl. XX; see also entry for cat.nos. 434.

EXHIBITED
See entry for cat.no. 434.

439: Tombstone, memorial to James Roger Cross (about 1917–1932)

about 1932
Plaster
h. 153.5 cm.
A.99–1936

Contained in the cross-shaped inset relief: JAMES·ROGER·CROSS/ sept·22nd·1932/aged/15/years.

In the studio of the sculptor at the time of his death. Given by Mr Sigismund Goetze and the National Art Collections Fund in 1936, together with cat.nos. 423, 426 to 429, and 433 to 438.

The central relief which contains the inscription is in coloured plaster, as are the rosettes, three of which are missing. The two remaining show traces of gilding.

According to Machell Cox, this is the working model for a memorial to be carried out in marble and bronze. It is not known whether the memorial was erected.

Alderman James Conrad Cross (1879–1952) was Lord Mayor of Liverpool in 1931 and 1932 (information kindly supplied by Edward Morris). Cross unveiled the aluminium replica of the Eros figure on 23 July 1932, given to the City of Liverpool by Mr George Audley (Bury 1954, p. 84; see Cavanagh 1997, pp. 195–6; see also cat.no. 422). If the subject to be commemorated

was a relative of the mayor (perhaps his son), he may have commissioned a memorial from Gilbert after the unveiling.

BIBLIOGRAPHY
Gilbert 1936, p. 20, cat.no. 15.

EXHIBITED
Models and Designs by the late Sir Alfred Gilbert R.A., Victoria and Albert Museum, Autumn 1936, cat.no. 15.

Count Victor (Prince Viktor) Gleichen (Hohenlohe-Langenburg)

(b. Langenburg 1833 – d. London 1891)

Viktor Ferdinand Franz Eugen Gustav Adolf Constantin Frederick, Prinz von Hohenlohe-Langenburg generally known as Count Victor Gleichen, was the son of a half-sister of Queen Victoria. In 1867 he was made Governor General and Constable of Windsor Castle. He became a sculptor on losing his wealth after a bank crash, studying under William Theed the younger [q.v.], and was given a studio in St James's Palace by the Queen; he exhibited at the Royal Academy between 1868 and 1892. His daughter, Her Serene Highness Fedora, the Countess Gleichen was also a sculptor and pupil of her father; she produced a memorial to him in Sunningdale Church, Berkshire.

Hooe 1880, p. 13; Graves III, pp. 247–8; Thieme-Becker, 17, p. 316.

440: Queen Victoria (b.1819; r.1837–1901)

signed and dated 1888
Marble
h. (incl. socle) 84 cm
A.16–1963

Signed in monogram on the back: G./1888.

The bust is set into a marble block which is inscribed: VICTORIA REGINA/PRESENTED BY/SIR GEO. MARTIN HOLLOWAY/1889

Given by Messrs Gerald Kerin Ltd, 9 Mount Street, London in 1963.

The Queen wears the Garter sash over her left shoulder, together with the Garter star, the badge of the Royal Order of Victoria and Albert, the badge of the Imperial Order of the Star of India, and the Royal Red Cross. A bust of Disraeli in Windsor Castle, documented as being by Gleichen, has an identical monogram to that found on the present bust.

A further marble bust by Gleichen depicting a younger Queen Victoria, dated 1875, is in the Walker Art Gallery, Liverpool (inv.no. 4171), as are portraits by Gleichen of Edward VII, Prince of Wales, Alexandra, Princess of Wales and the Duke and Duchess of Edinburgh. In 1876 Gleichen exhibited a marble bust of Queen Victoria at the Royal Academy (no. 1509), almost certainly the Liverpool version (Graves III, p. 248; no. 1509).

(Lewis) Alexander Goblet

(b. 1764 – d. after 1823)

Goblet enrolled at the Royal Academy Schools in 1792, and in 1794 became an assistant to Joseph Nollekens [q.v.]. Whinney recorded that Goblet was 'for many years principal carver in Nollekens workshop', and this bust of his master depicts Nollekens two years before his death. Nollekens bequeathed to Goblet his sculptor's tools and some unworked marble. Goblet exhibited at the Royal Academy between 1799 and 1822.

Gunnis, p. 175; Whinney 1971, p. 155; Thieme-Becker, 14, p. 283.

441: Joseph Nollekens (1737–1823)

about 1821
Marble
h. 45 cm.
A.70–1965

Inscribed on the front: JOSEPH NOLLEKENS. Esqr. R.A./Aged 84.

Christies, 5 July 1823 sale, of 'the whole of the highly valuable collection of Antique and Modern Sculpture of the late Joseph Nollekins [sic] Esq RA. Dec' (3rd day of sale, which began on 3rd July), lot 112 'A Bust of Mr Nollekins [sic] in marble, by Goblet'; Dowager Marchioness of Lansdowne deceased sale, held on 3 May 1834, Messrs Christie, Manson and Christie, at King Street, St James's Square, London, lot 115, described as 'A marble bust of Nollekins, by Goblet' (no purchaser is recorded in the Christie's archive; a line has been drawn through the catalogue entry for this bust, suggesting that it was withdrawn or possibly sold privately; I am grateful to Donald Johnston for checking this reference). Bequeathed by Rupert Gunnis, Hungershall Lodge, Tunbridge Wells in 1965.

Although the bust is unsigned, Whinney recorded, 'the identification is supported by a plaster version, recently on loan to the Ashmolean Museum, Oxford, which is signed and dated L.A. GOBLET, fec[it] 1821' (Whinney 1971, p. 156).

Bibliography

Graves III, p. 252, no. 1041; Gunnis 1968, p. 175; *Royal Academy* 1968, pp. 96–7, no. 202; Whinney 1971, p. 156, illus. p. 157; Kilmurray 1979, p. 158.

Exhibited

Goblet exhibited two busts of Nollekens at the Royal Academy in 1816 and 1822 (nos. 945 and 1041); the present piece is presumably the one exhibited in 1822, no. 1041; *Royal Academy Bicentenary Exhibition 1768–1968,* 14 December 1968 to 2 March 1969, no. 202.

Joseph Gott

(b. Leeds 1786 – d. Rome 1860)

Between 1798 and 1802 Gott served his apprenticeship under John Flaxman [q.v.], and in 1805 enrolled at the Royal Academy Schools; in 1819 he won a gold medal at the Royal Academy for a group of Jacob wrestling with an angel. *In 1822 Gott moved to Rome, where he was to remain for the rest of his life, though he returned regularly to England to meet his patrons and gain commissions. Gott produced a number of works containing groups of animals and children. Friedman comments that 'Gott was never attracted by the austere neo-Greek style practised by Gibson and Richard James Wyatt: his sculpture is unheroic, pastoral, romantic'. He exhibited at the British Institution in 1821 and 1822, and at the Royal Academy between 1820 and 1848.*

Graves III, pp. 279–80; Graves 1908, p. 222; Gunnis 1968, pp. 176–8; Thieme-Becker, 14, pp. 419–20; TDA, 13, p. 213 [Friedman].

442: Possibly a whippet or toy terrier

signed; about 1823–60
Marble
h. 38 cm.
1183–1882

Signed at the back of integral base: J. GOTT. F^{T}

Bequeathed by John Jones in 1882. On loan to 1 Carlton Gardens, Foreign and Commonwealth Office between 1991 and 1995.

The date of this piece is uncertain, but it is likely to have been produced during Gott's time in Rome. I am grateful to Daniela Tranquada and Luisa Pontello of the Kennel Club for their help in identifying the breed of dog.

Bibliography
Jones 1924, p. 101, no. 396; *Gott* 1972, p. 52, no. G.112 and pl. 53.

Exhibited
Joseph Gott 1786–1860 Sculptor, Leeds Temple Newsam House, 23August to 14 October 1972; Walker Art Gallery, Liverpool, 3 November to 3 December 1972, cat.no. G.112.

443: Little Red Riding Hood

signed; 1827
Terracotta
h. 27 cm.
A.30–1975

Signed on the base: J.GOTT F^{T}

Purchased from Mrs Marion Dutta, 164 The Grampians, London in 1975 for £300, under the Murray bequest.

The original stone socle is lost, although it was recorded in a photograph of 1975, when the object was apparently with the London dealer Alberto Colzi, shortly before its arrival in the Museum (Museum records).

This figure, executed by Gott in Rome for Lord Gower, may be identified as the figure listed as untraced in the catalogue of the exhibition devoted to Joseph Gott, held in Leeds in 1972 (see *Gott* 1972, p. 53, no. G115). Friedman quotes a letter written by Gott to William Gott [his patron, no relation] from Rome on 26 May 1832,

'I am thinking of sending 2 small statues to Leeds for the Exhibition to be ready whenever it may occur again . . . the other Red Ridinghood they were begun before I was in England last time & have been in progress since that time your father saw a terra Cotta Model of the Red riding hood at Lord F.L. Gower's & was much pleased with it'; the letter is quoted fully in *Gott* 1972, p. 63, no. 24.

EXHIBITED
"*Objects*", Victoria and Albert Museum, 31 May to 13 August 1978.

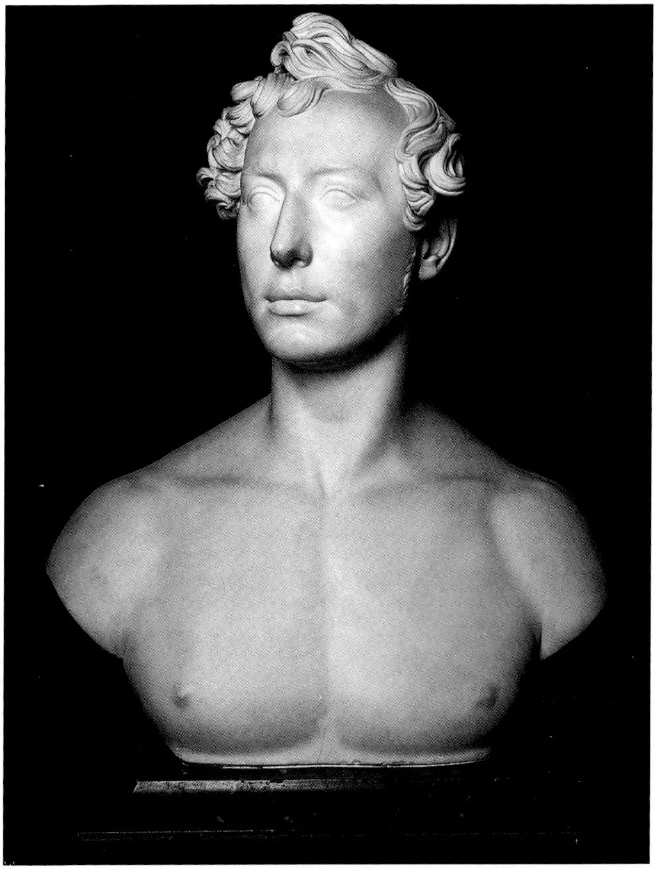

444: Unknown man

signed; about 1830–40
Marble
h. 60.5 cm.
A.16–1982

Signed on the truncation at the back: J.GOTT. F^{T}

Purchased from the Heim Gallery, 59 Jermyn Street, London in 1982 for £2000.

BIBLIOGRAPHY
Gott 1972, p. 47, no. G.75, and pl. 7.

EXHIBITED
Joseph Gott 1786–1860 Sculptor, Leeds Temple Newsam House, 23 August to 14 October 1972; Walker Art Gallery, Liverpool, 3 November to 3 December 1972, cat.no. G.75.

JOHN HANCOCK

(b. Fulham, London 1825 – d. 1869)

James records that Hancock attended the Royal Academy Schools in 1842, and around the same time made contact with the Pre-Raphaelite brotherhood through meeting Dante Gabriel Rossetti (1828–1882); he also later shared a studio with the Pre-Raphaelite sculptor Thomas Woolner [q.v.]. In 1862 Hancock completed the marble figure La Penserosa *for the Corporation of London at Mansion House. Hancock exhibited at the Royal Academy from 1843 to 1864. In 1864–5 he produced reliefs symbolising* Agriculture, Navigation, Science and Engineering, Cottage Industries, Commerce and The Arts, *for the Bishopgate Offices of the National Provincial Bank, now the National Westminster Bank. James suggests that these 'remain the largest monument to Hancock's work. They may also represent his swan-song. After 1864 he ceased to exhibit at the Royal Academy and the details of his life are unknown'. Hancock appears to have taught for the Science and Art Department of the then South Kensington Museum; a note on the* Précis of the Minutes of the Science and Art Department, *16 February 1852 to 1 July 1863 records on 5 January 1856 under the name of John Hancock 'change in share of fees in modelling class of Female School' (I am grateful to the late Clive Wainwright and Anthony Burton for alerting me to this source).*

Graves III, pp. 372–3. no. 1303; Gunnis 1968, pp. 186–7; Read 1982, pp. 222, 24, 25; Pre-Raphaelite 1991 [James], pp. 71–6; ibid. [Greenwood], pp. 104–8; Thieme-Becker, 15, p. 578.

445: Beatrice

signed; about 1851
Plaster
h. 183 cm.
Anonymous loan

Signed on the integral base towards the back: IOHN.HANC [OCK]... LONDON.
Inscribed at front of integral plinth: GUARDAMI BEN BEN SON BEN SON/BEATRICE [Look at me well; I am, I am indeed Beatrice]
Taken from Dante's *Purgatorio*

This object was taken on loan from G. Hancock Esq. (presumably a relative of the sculptor) at a date unrecorded, prior to 1870, perhaps in 1869, after the death of the sculptor. On loan to Queen's Park Museum, Manchester from May 1884; returned April 1903.

Hancock executed other versions of *Beatrice*, following the exhibition of the present piece at the Royal Academy in 1850 (no. 1303), and at the International Exhibition of 1851. In Mrs Jameson's *A Hand-Book to the Courts of Modern Sculpture* of 1854, she recorded: 'The original model [of *Beatrice*] was in the Great Exhibition of 1851, and has since been executed in marble for Miss Burdett Coutts' (p. 24); Gunnis also cites a marble version (Gunnis 1968, p. 186). In his appraisal of the 1851 International Exhibition, the sculptor Henry Weekes [q.v.] commented, 'Will he [the visitor to the exhibition] not stop before the beautiful spiritualized figure of "Beatrice", by Hancock, and become for a moment as absorbed in expression as is the plaster itself?' (Weekes 1852, p. 65; also cited by Gunnis 1968, p. 186, and *Pre-Raphaelite* 1991 [Greenwood], p. 106). The Jury Reports for the 1851 Exhibition similary recorded: 'To this list [of prizewinners] the name of HANCOCK deserves, in my opinion, to be added, for his statue in plaster of the Beatrice of Dante, in her beatified state. The figure is distinguished by a pure and noble expression of the head although many defects may be remarked in the drapery' (*Jury Reports* 1851, pp. 1552–3; I am grateful to James Cheshire for this reference). In 1854 Hancock exhibited 'Dante's Beatrice; a statuette in bronze. "Guardami ben, ben son, etc"' at the Royal Academy (no. 1416), and in 1862 'Beatrice; bust in marble, etc', (no. 1054) (Graves III, p. 373). Gunnis recorded that a version was also exhibited at the Paris International Exhibition of 1855 (Gunnis 1968, pp. 186–7; see *Paris Exhibition* 1855, class XXIX, p. 86, no. 1135). In an article in the *Builder* of 26 July 1856, entitled 'Notes on Sculpture with Reference to the Royal Academy Exhibition', Walter Smith remarked: 'Concerning this [*Maidenhood*] and another of Mr. Hancock's works, both of which were in the Paris Exhibition, a celebrated French critic wrote, that "the "Maidenhood" and the "Beatrice" of Mr. Hancock, *possess* what Gibson's works *require*, viz. life' (*Builder*, 26 July 1856, XIV, no. 703, p. 406).

Bibliography

International Exhibition 1851, p. 849, and fig. 151 opp. p. 849; Weekes 1852, p. 65; Graves III, p. 373, no. 1303; Gunnis 1968, pp. 186–7; *Pre-Raphaelite* 1991 [James and Greenwood], pp. 73, 104, 106, cat.no. 16; Ward-Jackson 1992, p. 134, fig. 86 on p. 134.

Exhibited

Royal Academy exhibition of 1850 (no. 1303), as 'Beatrice. "Last All-Saints' holiday even now gone by, etc."'; International Exhibition of 1851, catalogued under Miscellaneous objects, Main Avenue; *Pre-Raphaelite Sculpture: Nature and Imagination in British Sculpture 1848–1914*, Matthiesen Gallery, London, 31 October to 12 December 1991, and Birmingham City Museum and Art Gallery, 15 January to 15 March 1992, cat.no. 16.

Jonathan Harmer

(b. Heathfield 1762 – d. Heathfield 1849)

Jonathan Harmer was the son of Jonathan Harmer Senior (d. 1800), who bequeathed to his two sons Jonathan Jr and John 'all such Portland and other stone, together with my working Tools and utensils belonging to the Trade of a Stone Mason and Bricklayer, and Land Surveying Books'. In 1796 Jonathan Harmer Jr left for America, settling in New York, where he worked as a mason and painter, returning to Heathfield in May 1800. Harmer's younger brother John had previously settled in New York but also later returned to Heathfield. Lucas recorded that on his return: 'He [Jonathan Harmer Jr] seems to have taken up the family business, but soon turned his attention to the manufacture of terra-cotta bas-reliefs, used principally in his work as a monumental mason'. Lucas recorded the process employed by Harmer in the production of reliefs used as ornaments for gravestones and memorials in local churches. The terracotta 'having been first pressed in the mould, was afterwards made sharp by a tool, and then baked in the wood oven of the house intended for baking bread. The material is extremely hard, sometimes twisted and cracked by the heat, and varies in colour from cream and buff to a brilliant red'. Gunnis recorded: 'The best examples of his [Harmer's] work in situ are in the interior and churchyard of Cade Street Chapel, [Heathfield] Sussex.' Jonathan Harmer's son Sylvan Harmer (d. 1884) was the original writer of the manuscript history of the parish of Heathfield, written between 1821–31, on which Perceval Lucas based his Heathfield Memorials *cited above and in the following entries. According to Manwaring Baines, Harmer produced the terracotta ornaments by re-using his own clay moulds, for inclusion in funerary monuments he had made.*

Lucas 1910, pp. 104–8; Remnant 1962; Gunnis 1968, p. 188; Manwaring Baines 1980, pp. 166–7.

446: Basket of fruit and flowers

signed; about 1800–49
Terracotta
h. 16 cm. l. 26 cm.
A.7–1919

Stamped on either side of the basket relief at the bottom: HARMER FECIT

William Cleverly Alexander J.P. of Heathfield Park, Heathfield purchased pottery and notebooks remaining in Portland Square, Heathfield (the family home of the Harmer family) sometime after September 1897. According to Lucas, 'The stock consisted of a great number of the vases and paterae, two of the angel . . ., but with crown and rays [see cat.no. 448], also the crown by itself, and one new pattern – a small coat-of-arms, those of the second Duke of Newcastle, Clinton, with Pelham in pretence'. These were inherited by Miss W.T. Lister, Heathfield Park, Heathfield, Sussex from her father, and she subsequently (in 1919) gave the present piece, together with cat.nos. 447 to 459, to the Museum, from this stock. Miss Lister also gave three examples of Harmer's pottery to the Department of Ceramics and Glass (inv.nos. C.366 to C.368–1919). A complete set of the pottery reliefs produced by Harmer was given in 1908 by Mr Alexander to the Archaeological Museum of Sussex, now Sussex Archaeological Society, located at Barbican/Anne of Cleves House, Lewes.

This relief is framed with other Harmer reliefs; see cat.nos. 447, 450 to 453. On acquisition this series of reliefs were described as illustrating 'An interesting industry, now no longer in existence' (*Review* 1919, p. 4). The edge of the relief is grooved for fixing to a memorial with plaster or cement; the reliefs were commonly inserted as ornamental decoration into the top section of a memorial, and were produced by Harmer in his native village of Heathfield. Examples of this relief were noted by Alexander as being found on monuments at Framfield, Heathfield (on a monument dated 1818), Hurstmonceaux (on monuments dated 1800 and 1813, and on two other undated memorials), Mayfield, Warbleton (see Remnant 1964, pl. III, B, memorial to John Fox), and Wartling. A further version is to be found at Glynde on a headstone of 1811 dedicated to Marianne New (see *idem*. 1962, pl. IV). A variant of the present piece was used twice on a memorial together with an example of the cherub relief; see cat.no. 448. This is to be found on a tablet dedicated to Mary Luck (d. 1819), in Wadhurst, Sussex. Alexander recorded that a tombstone with Harmer's basket of flowers cast in iron, probably produced at the Ashburnham Furnace, East Sussex, was found in Wartling Church Yard (Lucas 1910, p. 108). For an illustration of this relief see *ibid.*, plate facing p. 112. A further example is held in the Brighton Museum (see Manwaring Baines 1980, p. 167 illus.).

Bibliography
Review 1919, p. 4.

447: Charity

signed; about 1800–49
Terracotta
h. 16.5 cm. l. 22.5 cm.
A.8–1919

Stamped at the top left side of the oval relief: HARMER FECIT

Given by Miss W. T. Lister in 1919. See entry for cat.no. 446.

The edge of the relief is grooved. This relief is framed with other Harmer reliefs; see cat.nos. 446, 450 to 453. The Charity relief is recorded by Alexander as being used in memorials found at Heathfield, Hurstmonceaux, Mayfield and Warbleton (Lucas 1910, p. 108).

Bibliography
Review 1919, p. 4.

447

448: Cherub head

about 1800–49
Terracotta
h. 53.5 cm. w. 41.5 cm.
A.9–1919

Given by Miss W.T. Lister in 1919. See entry for cat.no. 446.

The cherub head is set in a background of rays which radiate from a crown. An example of this relief is illustrated by Lucas (see Lucas 1910, plate facing p. 136). A version was used on the memorial to Mary Luck (d. 1819) found in Wadhurst, Sussex (see Remnant 1964, pl. 1). Two basket and flower reliefs were added, placed on either side of the cherub relief; see cat.no. 446. Examples of this relief used in memorials may also be found at Hurstmonceaux (described by Alexander as an Angel, on a memorial dated 1831), and Mayfield (again described by Alexander as an Angel); see Lucas 1910, p. 108 and Remnant 1962, pl. IV (memorial to Judith Curtis, 1810). A variant, omitting the rays and crown decoration, is to be found on a memorial to Mary Hall of 1818 at Heathfield (see Remnant 1962, pl. VI, A). A further example is held by the Sussex

Archaeological Society at Barbican/Anne of Cleves House, Lewes (*ibid.*, pl. II).

BIBLIOGRAPHY
Review 1919, p. 4.

449: Urn with rams' heads

signed; about 1800–49
Terracotta
h. 44 cm. w. 23.5 cm.
A.10–1919

Stamped on the top of the body of the urn: HARMER FECIT

Given by Miss W.T. Lister in 1919. See entry for cat.no. 446.

An example of this relief is illustrated by Lucas (Lucas 1910, pl. facing p. 124). Versions are to be found at Hailsham (recorded by Alexander as being seen in 1895), Hurstmonceux (on monuments dated 1812, the cast dated 1808 and 1817), and Mayfield (signed and dated Harmer fecit 1808) (*ibid.*, p. 108). Remnant recorded a further use of the urn on the altar tomb to Thomas Hicks at Salehurst (illus. Remnant 1962, pl. VI, B).

BIBLIOGRAPHY
Review 1919, p. 4.

450: Patera

about 1800–49
Terracotta
diam. 9 cm.
A.11–1919

Given by Miss W.T. Lister in 1919. See entry for cat.no. 446.

This relief is framed with other Harmer reliefs see cat.nos. 446, 447, and 451 to 453. An example of this patera is illustrated by Lucas, together with four other patera; see cat.nos. 451 to 459 (Lucas 1910, plate facing p. 164). The Sussex Archaeological Society, Barbican/Anne of Cleves House, Lewes holds 22 examples of ornamental paterae together with 10 of the original clay moulds; some of which are illustrated by Remnant (Remnant 1962, pl. III).

BIBLIOGRAPHY
Review 1919, p. 4.

451: Patera

about 1800–49
Terracotta
diam. 9 cm.
A.12–1919

Given by Miss W.T. Lister in 1919. See entry for cat.no. 446.

This relief is framed with other Harmer reliefs; see cat.nos. 446, 447, 450, 452 and 453. An example of this patera is illustrated by Lucas, together with four other patera, cat.nos. 450, 452 to 459; see Lucas 1910, plate facing p. 164.

BIBLIOGRAPHY
Review 1919, p. 4.

452: Patera

about 1800–49
Terracotta
diam. 6 cm.
A.13–1919

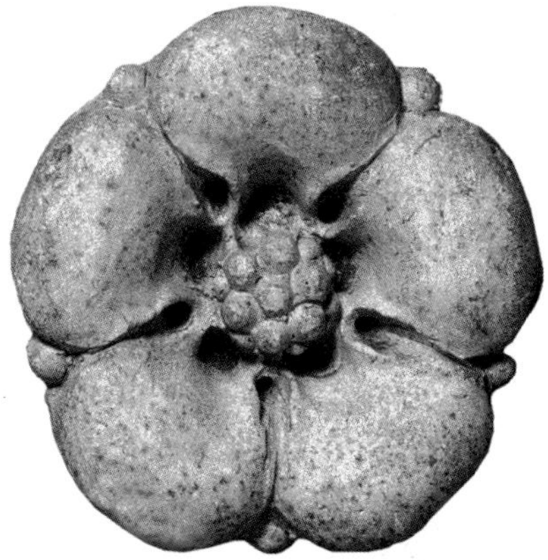

Given by Miss W.T. Lister in 1919. See entry for cat.no. 446.

This relief of which there are two examples in the collection – see also cat.no. 453 – is framed with other Harmer reliefs; see cat.nos. 446, 447, 450, 451, and 453. An example of this patera is illustrated by Lucas, together with four other patera; see cat.nos. 450 and 451, and 453 to 459; see Lucas 1910, plate facing p. 164.

BIBLIOGRAPHY
Review 1919, p. 4.

453: Patera

about 1800–49
Terracotta
diam. 6 cm.
A.13:A-1919

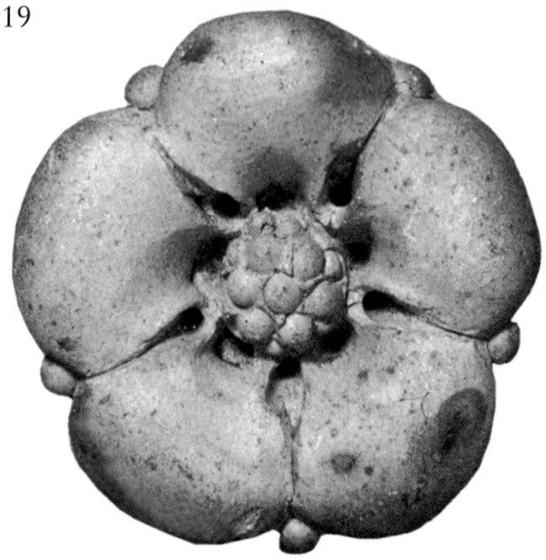

Given by Miss W.T. Lister in 1919. See entry for cat.no. 446.

This relief, of which there are two examples in the collection – see also cat.no. 452 – is framed with other Harmer reliefs; see cat.nos. 446, 447, and 450 to 452. An example of this patera, is illustrated by Lucas, together with four other patera cat.nos. 450 to 452, and 454 to 459; see Lucas 1910, plate facing p. 164.

BIBLIOGRAPHY
Review 1919, p. 4.

454: Patera

about 1800–49
Terracotta
h. 2.5 cm. diam. 6 cm.
A.14–1919

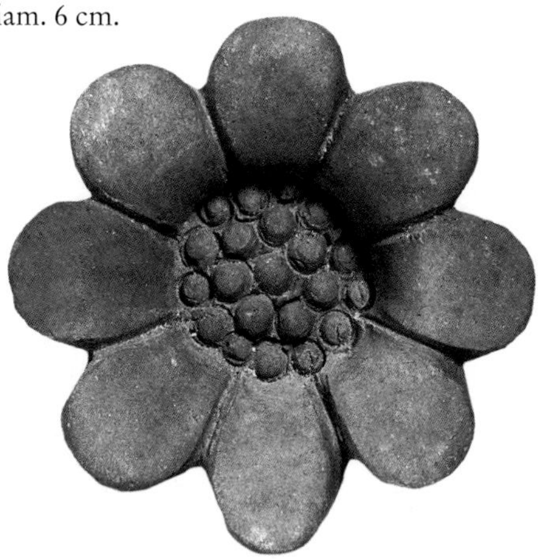

Given by Miss W.T. Lister in 1919. See entry for cat.no. 446.

This relief, of which there are two examples in the collection – see also cat.no. 455 – is framed with other Harmer reliefs; see cat.nos. 455 to 459. A variant of this patera is illustrated by Lucas, together with four other patera, cat.nos. 450 to 453, 455 to 459; see Lucas 1910, plate facing p. 164.

BIBLIOGRAPHY
Review 1919, p. 4.

455: Patera

about 1800–49
Terracotta
h. 2.5 cm. diam. 6 cm.
A.14:A-1919

Given by Miss W.T. Lister in 1919. See entry for cat.no. 446.

This relief, of which there are two examples in the collection – see also cat.no. 454 – is framed with other Harmer reliefs see cat.nos. 454, 456 to 459. A variant of this patera and that of another similar paterae – see cat.no. 456 – is illustrated by Lucas, together with four other patera cat.nos. 450 to 454, 456 to 459 and 459; see Lucas 1910, plate facing p. 164.

BIBLIOGRAPHY
Review 1919, p. 4.

456: Patera

about 1800–49
Terracotta
h. 2.5 cm. diam. 6.2 cm.
A.15–1919

Given by Miss W.T. Lister in 1919. See entry for cat.no. 446.

This relief, which is similar to cat.nos. 454 and 455, is framed with other Harmer reliefs; see cat.nos. 454, 455, 457 to 459. A variant of this patera, and that of cat.nos. 454 and 455, is illustrated by Lucas, together with four other paterae, cat.nos. 450 to 455, and 457 to 459; see Lucas 1910, plate facing p. 164.

Bibliography
Review 1919, p. 4.

457: Patera

about 1800–49
Terracotta
diam. 4.5 cm.
A.16–1919

Given by Miss W.T. Lister in 1919. See entry for cat.no. 446.

This relief, of which there are three examples in the collection – see also cat.no. 458 and 459 – is framed with other Harmer reliefs; see cat.nos. 454 to 456, 458 and 459. An example of this patera is illustrated by Lucas, together with four other patera, cat.nos. 450 to 456, 458 and 459; Lucas 1910, plate facing p. 164. The stone mould for this patera is held in the Department of Ceramics and Glass (inv.no. C.368–1919).

Bibliography
Review 1919, p. 4.

457

458: Patera

about 1800–49
Terracotta
diam. 4.8 cm.
A.16:A-1919

Given by Miss W.T. Lister in 1919. See entry for cat.no. 446.

This relief, of which there are three examples in the collection – see also cat.no. 457 and 459 – is framed with other Harmer relief; see cat.nos. 454 to 457, and 459. An example of this patera is illustrated by Lucas, together with four other patera cat.nos. 450 to 457, and 459; Lucas 1910, plate facing p. 164.

Bibliography
Review 1919, p. 4.

459: Patera

about 1800–49
Terracotta
diam. 4.5 cm.
A.16:B-1919

Given by Miss W.T. Lister in 1919. See entry for cat.no. 446.

This relief, of which there are three examples in the collection – see also cat.nos. 457 and 458 – is framed with other Harmer reliefs; see cat.nos. 454 to 458. An example of this patera is illustrated by Lucas, together with four other patera, cat.nos. 450 to 458; Lucas 1910, plate facing p. 164.

Bibliography

Review 1919, p. 4.

H.C. Hatfield senior

(dates unknown; active 1867)

No information has been found on H.C. Hatfield Senior, presumably an amateur sculptor who exhibited at the Society of Arts Art-Workmanship Competition of 1867. He may have been a member of the Hatfield's firm of bronze workers active from the 1840s, founded by J.A. Hatfield [q.v.]; see entry for cat.no. 462.

460: Virgin and child

signed; 1867
By H.C. Hatfield senior; after Desiderio da Settignano
Bronze
h. 40.5 cm.
858–1868

Signed in the bottom right hand corner: H.C. HATFIELD.SEN. R.

Purchased from H.C. Hatfield, presumed to be the sculptor, in 1868 for £16 6s (16 guineas).

This version of a relief in the style of Desiderio da Settignano (1429/32 – c. 1464) was awarded a prize of £10 in the Art-Workmanship Competition of 1867; see entries for cat.nos. 279 and 520 for two further examples. In a report on the 1867 competition written by the Art Referees Richard Redgrave and Matthew Digby Wyatt this relief was highlighted: 'Of the works sent in accordance with the prescribed designs, the most uniform excellence is shown in the various processes of metal working. Mr Dufour's repoussé work is excellent, as is Mr Hatfield's (senior) chasing of the Virgin and Child. In the last-mentioned we recognised an element not often to be met with in these competitions – the handicraft was kept in due subordination, and not suffered to divert the spectator's attention from the general scope and artistic purpose of the model. Too often in such objects the chasing of an angel's wing is made more telling than the angel's head; or the flowers trodden on by an amorino's foot may have had infinitely more pains bestowed upon them than has been given to the definition of the foot itself. So the major is often, through the art-workman's egotism, made to hide its head before the minor; but of this solecism Mr Hatfield, sen., has steered clear with the most commendable taste' (*Journal of the Society of Arts*, 14 February 1868, XIV, no. 795, p. 240).

Exhibited
Society of Arts Arts-Workmanship Competition of 1867.

H.J. Hatfield

(active London 1843 – 1874)

H.J. Hatfield was almost certainly a member of the Hatfield's firm of bronze workers, which was active from the 1840s. He is recorded as having produced a number of bronzes for the Art Union; see entry for cat.no. 462.

461: Hercules slaying a centaur

about 1850
By H.J. Hatfield after a model by Giambologna
Bronze
h. 41 cm.
A.100–1956

Purchased by Dr W.L. Hildburgh F.S.A. from an unrecorded sale just prior to its loan to the Museum commencing on 25 October 1952 (ex-loan 5218), when it was described as *Hercules and Nessus* in the style of Francesco Susini (d. 1646), and thought to date from the early seventeenth-century. Given to the Museum by Dr Hildburgh in 1956. Transferred from the Department of Architecture and Sculpture to the Circulation Department in 1969; returned to the Department of Architecture and Sculpture, later Sculpture Department, in 1977.

On acquisition, the present piece was thought to represent *Hercules and Nessus* after the marble group by Giambologna (1529–1608); see *Giambologna* 1978, fig. on p. 130, cat.no. 82. The reattribution of the present piece to H.J. Hatfield was made at some date after 1974; a further bronze group of *Hercules and Antaeus* was also re-attributed following the discovery of the Hatfield foundry stamp concealed beneath the foot of the Hercules figure; see entry for cat.no. 462. H.J. Hatfield, presumably a relative of J.A. Hatfield [q.v.] and H.C. Hatfield senior [q.v.], is noted in an article by Avery and Marsh as producing two bronzes for the Art Union: *St Michael overcoming Satan* after John Flaxman [q.v.] was issued in 1843; it was the first bronze to be commissioned by the Art Union and though originally produced by Edward William Wyon (1811–1885), it was later reproduced by H.J. Hatfield; see also entry for cat.no. 110. The other figure after John Henry Foley [q.v.] of *Caractacus* was cast by H.J. Hatfield in 1874 (see Avery and Marsh 1985, pp. 328 fig. 1, 329–30 and pp. 333–4, p. 333 fig. 13). However, unlike the present piece, the Hatfield bronzes cited above were stamped with the impression stating that they were cast for the Art Union.

Exhibited
The present piece was included in a travelling exhibition of twenty-two bronzes organised by the Circulation Department which ended in January 1974, entitled *Italian Renaissance Bronzes*; it was then thought to be Florentine; early seventeenth century.

John Ayres Hatfield

(active 1840 – 1849)

John Ayres Hatfield established a firm of art metal workers based in London in the 1840s, and supplied the Art Union with bronze statuettes. Hatfields are still in business under the name of H.J. Hatfield & Sons, Restorers, 42 St Michael's Street, London (information kindly supplied by Anthony North and Eric Turner). It is probable that H.C. Hatfield Senior [q.v.] and H.J. Hatfield [q.v.] were also members of the Hatfield family of bronze-workers.

Avery and Marsh 1985, pp. 329–39, 337 n. 13.

462: Hercules and Antaeus

about 1840–49
Bronze
h. 47 cm.
A.110–1956

Bequeathed by Dr W.L. Hildburgh F.S.A. in 1956. Previously on loan from Dr Hildburgh from May 1953 (ex-loan no. 5237).

On acquisition this bronze was considered to be possibly German 18th century. The Hatfield foundry stamp is concealed under the right foot of the Hercules figure. The stamp was discovered in about 1982 when the figure was removed from its base to repair the ankle which had become cracked; see also cat.no. 461. This group, with certain modifications, is based on a bronze held in the Royal Collection at Windsor. It may have been made for the Art Union of London, for whom J.A. Hatfield is known to have produced a bronze version of *Hebe* by Alfred Gatley (1816–1863) in 1845 (see Avery and Marsh 1985, pp. 329–30, and p. 329, fig. 3). A bronze by H.J. Hatfield, presumably a relative of J.A. Hatfield, is also in the Museum's collections; see entry for cat.no. 461.

Samuel James Bouverie Haydon

(b. Heavitree, Exeter 1815 – d. 1891)

According to Gunnis, Haydon originally trained as a lawyer, setting himself up in practice in Exeter, but later travelled to London to train under the sculptor Edward Hodges Baily [q.v.]. Gunnis quotes G. Pycroft's Art in Devonshire, *1883, who noted that Haydon's sculpture was 'so good that it is more the pity they are so few. It was not from want of genius, power or personal merit that he failed to make for himself a far greater name'. Wills recorded that in 1870 Haydon had intended applying for the Curatorship of the Antique School in the Royal Academy, though he did not actually do so. Haydon exhibited at the Royal Academy between 1840 and 1876.*

Graves IV, pp. 36–7; Wills 1962; Gunnis 1968, p. 193; Thieme-Becker, 16, p. 172.

463: Unknown man

1843
Bronze on contemporary marble base
h. (incl. base) 25 cm.
A.2–1918

Inscribed on the truncation: HAYDON

Given by Mr Charles Ricketts in 1918. The bust was apparently purchased by a West End dealer for £4 14s 6d from the sale of the collection of S. Willson, Esq., Jun., Down Lodge Epsom, held at Messrs Christie, Manson and Woods on 15 May 1917, lot 67. An annotated catalogue held in the National Art Library gives the name of 'Amor' as the purchaser; purchased by Charles Ricketts from this dealer in 1918.

The donor purchased this bust to present to the Museum, believing it to be by Alfred Stevens [q.v.]. However, by 1920, the date of publication of the *Review of Principle Acquisitions during the Year 1918*, the attribution had changed: 'This fine portrait bust strongly suggests the style of Alfred Stevens, and has been tentatively ascribed to him; the inscription, however, which is impressed with a punch or punches, suggests that it may rather be the work of Samuel J.B. Haydon, a sculptor who at any rate occasionally worked on a small scale . . . The person represented has not been identified, but can hardly be either Benjamin Haydon (1776–1846), or George Haydon (1822–1891), who was steward of Bridewell and Bethlem Hospitals and a friend of Cruikshank and other artists of the period' (*Review* 1918, p. 1).

The acquisition of a wax portrait in 1937 signed by Haydon and dated 1843 of the same unidentified subject (inv.no. A.44–1937) confirmed the attribution of the present piece to Samuel Haydon. Pyke noted that this wax is the only one known by the sculptor (Pyke 1973, p. 65, pl. 127).

Bibliography
Review 1918, p. 1, fig. 1 on p. 2; Wills 1962, p. 787, fig. 2 on p. 786.

464: Unknown child; possibly the son or daughter of the Rev. F. Fanshawe

signed and dated 1861
Marble
h. 41 cm.
A.7–1970

Signed and dated on the truncation: S.HAYDON-1861.

Given by the Heim Gallery Ltd, 59 Jermyn Street, London in 1970.

This memorial bust of a child wearing a shroud stands on a base in the form of a book, almost certainly a bible, surrounded by a wreath of immortelles and a rosebud.

BIBLIOGRAPHY
Graves IV, p. 37, no. 1041.

EXHIBITED
In 1861 Haydon exhibited at the Royal Academy 'Child of the Rev. F. Fanshawe; Posthumous marble bust' no. 1041, perhaps the present piece.

ROBERT HENDERSON

(active 1820 – 1834)

The works exhibited by Henderson at the Royal Academy between 1820 and 1832 were mainly animal groups, including the equestrian group catalogued below. He also exhibited at the British Institution between 1825 and 1828.

Graves IV, p. 68; Gunnis 1968, p. 196; Thieme-Becker, 16, p. 378.

465: Equestrian statuette of George III
(b.1738; r.1760–1820)

signed and dated 1821
Bronze
h. 37 cm.
A.4–1937

Signed on the edge of the base: ROBERT HENDERSON 1821. On an integral pedestal, stamped at the back: GEORGIUS/TIRTIUS

Purchased from Alfred Spero, London in 1937 for £25.

This equestrian statuette was one of three portraits of George III acquired by the Museum in 1937; for the others see entries for cat.nos. 692 and 704. The *Review of the Principal Acquisitions during the Year 1928* stated, 'It is an admirable little work and the modelling of the horse in particular bears witness to the truth of C.R. Leslie's remark when he says that he always knew "Little Bob Henderson to be a good judge of a Horse", in a letter to Constable' (*Review* 1938, p. 9). This refers to Leslie's letter to the painter John Constable of 6 September 1834. According to departmental records, he must be the Henderson who allowed John Constable to have a room in which to paint after a fire at his home in 1812. In 1825 Henderson exhibited an equestrian figure of George IV (Graves IV, p. 68, no. 1014)

BIBLIOGRAPHY
Graves IV, p. 68, no. 1140; *Review* 1928, p. 9; Gunnis 1968, p. 196.

EXHIBITED
Royal Academy 1821, no. 1140.

Sir George Frederick Hodson or Hudson

(b. 1806 – d. 1888)

There is a discrepancy in the spelling of the surname of this artist; he is listed in Strickland and Thieme-Becker as Hodson, though in Museum records and the Museum's Review of Principal Acquisitions during the Year 1930, *as Hudson. He was an Irish artist, who exhibited landscapes and figures at the Royal Hibernian Academy from 1827.*

Strickland 1913, I, pp. 488–9; Thieme-Becker, 17, p. 179.

466: Oliver Goldsmith (1728–1774)

after 1860
Possibly by Sir George Frederick Hodson or Hudson after John Henry Foley [q.v.]
Plaster, painted with bronze-coloured pigment
h. (incl. base) 101.5 cm.
A.83–1930

Signed on the base: G.F.H.
Inscribed on one side on the edge of the base: J.H. FOLEY.R.A.SC./ LONDON:1860

Given by G.F. Hudson to Mr John Forster. Given by Miss Fanny Crosbie to be placed with the Forster Bequest, received in 1876. See also entry for cat.no. 287.

Damage has occured to the right leg and toe; the left foot and right hand are detached from the figure. Chipped elsewhere, including on the book.

The figure stands on an integral rectangular base.

The suggestion that this sculpture might be by Sir George Frederick Hodson was made by R.P. Bedford [q.v.] in the correspondence relating to its acquisition. Bedford wrote, 'it is signed G.F.H. and must be a copy of Foley's statue by G.F. Hudson, but I have so far been unable to find out anything about the copyist (perhaps Sir George Frederick Hodson, Hon. R.H.D., mentioned in Strickland, A dictionary of Irish artists, but not as a sculptor)'.

This is a reduced copy of the statue depicting the novelist and playwright Oliver Goldsmith by John Henry Foley, erected in 1864 for Trinity College, Dublin. The *Art Journal* commented on the inauguration of the statue that 'the public had been enabled to pronounce their verdict upon it as a work of Art, and there had been an unanimous expression of opinion that it is "one of which Ireland may justly feel proud, not only as a worthy memorial of historic greatness, but as an evidence and trophy of living genius". There seems, indeed, to be but one opinion everywhere – that the work is one of the most perfect and admirable productions of Art the world has of late years seen.' (*Art Journal*, 1 February 1864, p. 57). The plaster model for the statue was given to the Royal Dublin Society, and was used for the reproduction of bronze statuettes by Elkington and Company (reference kindly supplied by Alexander Kader). One of the Elkington casts is in the Royal Collection, Windsor (see Read 1974, p. 266, fig. 5). Another was included in the Christie's, London sale of 27 September, 1990, lot 101. A bronze version was acquired by the Yale Center for British Art, New Haven in 1997, inv.no. B1997.24.2; see *Yale* 1998, p. 4 (I am grateful to Jane Nowosadko for information on this). A plaster version formerly in the vestibule of the Birmingham Museum and Art Gallery was damaged during the Second World War, and had to be destroyed (see *Birmingham* 1987, introduction).

Bibliography

Review 1930, p. 87

W. Holliday

(dates unknown; active 1863)

No information has been found on W. Holliday, presumably an amateur sculptor who exhibited at the Society of Arts Art-Workmanship Competition of 1863. Graham comments that the 'makers remain obscure figures', and that often only their addresses are known.

Graham 1993, p. 414.

467: Psyche

1863
Chased by W. Holliday; cast by Domenico Brucciani and C. Delpech after an original by John Gibson [q.v.]
Copper
h. 21.5 cm.
135–1864

On the reverse of the bust at the back D. BRUCCIANI/C.DELPECH/BED . . ./ LONDON
An indecipherable monogram is also scratched on the reverse.

Purchased from the Society of Arts Exhibition of 1864 for £6.

This bust appears to be taken from the central figure of *Psyche* in John Gibson's [q.v.] marble group *Psyche and the Zephyrs*, executed in 1822 for Sir George Beaumont and now untraced (see Matthews 1911, fig. opp. p. 54 and p. 241). The present bust, entered as an example of chasing in metal, was a prize object in the Society of Arts Exhibition of 1863. The Society of Arts Art-Workmanship Competitions held between 1863–71 were established 'for the encouragement of art-workmanship applicable to manufactures' (*Journal of the Society of Arts*, 27 March 1863, cited in Graham 1993, p. 411). Graham comments that, 'between 1864 and 1870 the Museum purchased sixty-one of the winning entries from a series of competitive exhibitions organised by the Society of Arts, and intended to encourage higher standards of craftsmanship and design amongst workmen employed in the applied arts industries' (*ibid.*, p. 411). The report of the Committee stated, 'The designs will be by artists of great reputation, to be translated into the various modes of workmanships, and photographs and castings of such designs will be sold by the Society, at the Society's House, at cost price, to persons desiring to be competitors' (*Journal of the Society of Arts*, 27 March 1863, XI, no. 540, p.321). The objects entered into the competitions were therefore mainly reproductions of known works, such as this present piece. Under the category of 'Chasing in metal', the Psyche bust is described: 'a) The Human figure – One prize of £10 for the best and a second prize of £5 for the next best, work executed after a reduced copy of Gibson's Psyche. A rough casting in bronze, upon which the chasing must be executed, will be supplied by the Society, price, 12s. A plaster cast may be obtained from D. Brucciani, 39 Russell-street, Covent-garden, W.C. Price, 3s 6d' (*idem* 2 April 1863, XI, no. 541, p. 341). Some of the most important plaster casts acquired by the Museum were commissioned through the Anglo-Italian firm established by Domenico Brucciani (b. Lucca 1815–d. London 1880). His most illustrious achievement was the cast of the Portal of the Cathedral at Santiago de Compostela (inv.no.1866–50); see Baker 1982. The importance of the Brucciani cast-selling business in the supply of casts to art schools, and the strong connections with the British Museum and this Museum were such that when the company ran into financial difficulties in 1921, it was taken over by the Board of Education as a public service, and organised as an educational branch of the V&A, named the Department for the Sale of Casts. The sale of casts continued at the Museum until 1951. For Brucciani see also the *Builder*, 1 May 1880, p. 556 (obituary) and Jenkins 1990, pp. 108–10. For a full discussion of the Art-Workmanship Competitions, see Graham 1993.

Bibliography
Inventory 1864, p. 11.

Exhibited
Society of Arts Art-Workmanship Competition of 1863.

Peter Hollins

(b. Birmingham 1800 – d. Birmingham 1886)

Hollins initially trained in Birmingham under his father, the architect William Hollins (1763–1843), but went to London in about 1822 to work in the studio of Sir Francis Chantrey [q.v.]. Parry-Jones recorded that during the 1830s (Gunnis stated in 1828), Hollins set himself up in a studio which he shared with the Birmingham painter Harry Room. In 1835–6 Hollins travelled to Italy, but in 1843 on the death of his father returned to the family business in Birmingham. Stocker comments that Hollins's success was marred 'because of his provincial status'.

Graves IV, pp. 133–4; Gunnis 1968, pp. 205–6; Parry-Jones 1981; Thieme-Becker, 17, p. 382; TDA, 14, p. 686 [Stocker].

468: Unknown man

signed and dated 1847
Marble on an integral base
h. 74 cm.
A.14–1982

Signed and dated on the back: PETER HOLLINS/SCULPTOR/1847.

Purchased from the Heim Gallery, 59 Jermyn Street, London in 1982 for £750.

The identity of the sitter is not known; Gunnis does not record this bust. During the period in which this bust was produced Hollins was working on the Warneford Hospital, Oxford project (see Parry-Jones 1981).

W.M. Holmes

(dates unknown; active 1866)

Holmes was a carver by trade, based in Soho, and unusually for an entrant in the Art-Workmanship Competitions made this piece to his own design.

Graham 1993, p. 414.

469: Festoon of fruit, flowers and foliage

1866
Caen stone
h. 8 cm. w. 10 cm.
24–1867

Purchased from Mr W.M. Holmes, presumed to be the sculptor, in 1867 for £5.

This panel was an entry for the Society of Arts Competition for Art-Workmen in 1866. The sculptor appears to have been influenced by the naturalistic carvers of the late seventeenth and early eighteenth century such as Grinling Gibbons [q.v.].

Bibliography
Graham 1993, p. 414, illus. p. 413 fig. 47.

Exhibited
Society of Arts Art-Workmanship Competition of 1866.

Henry Richard Hope-Pinker

(b. 1849 – d. 1927)

Pinker studied at the Royal Academy Schools and in Rome. Whilst at the Royal Academy Schools he produced a bust of Dr Benson, first headmaster of Wellington College, which was exhibited at the Royal Academy in 1875 (no. 1247). Spielmann recorded that this work led to other commissions. Pinker (after 1893 Hope-Pinker, though Graves cites him as Hope-Pincker) exhibited at the Royal Academy between 1875 and 1904. He produced a number of outdoor statues, including a bronze figure of W.E. Forster, unveiled on 1 August 1890 in Victoria Embankment Gardens. Spielmann commented: 'It is a feature of Mr Pinker's work that it has life, and that it is distinguished besides by a quality which, for want of a better word, I may term "roughness;" whereby the artist avoids that close resemblance to actual clothing which, whether in marble or bronze, is so distressing a quality in many statues. For dignity and simplicity the "Henry Fawcett", in the market-place of Salisbury, is probably Mr Pinker's most remarkable open air monument'.

Spielmann 1901, pp. 63–6; Blackwood 1989, pp. 202–3; Thieme-Becker, 27, p. 61.

470: Robert Henry Soden Smith, M.A. (1822–1890)

signed and dated 1884
Terracotta
diam. 14.5 cm.
518–1908

The reverse is incised: R.H.SODEN-SMITH.M.A. by his friend H.R.Pinker.Sc.1884
On the obverse around the margin is inscribed: R.H.SODEN-SMITH:M.A.:NATIONAL.ART.LIBRARY.1868–1890:HR.H-P.Sculp.

Given by the sculptor in 1908.

The acquisition details record that Hope-Pinker produced this commemorative portrait medallion a number of years prior to its acquisition by the Museum in 1908, but that he had recently completed some minor details on it. An obituary by C. Drury E. Fortnum in the *Academy* records the death of Soden Smith: 'one whose solid but unobtrusive life-work has been too little known and less recognized – the organiser, though not absolutely the founder, of the Art Library at the South Kensington Museum, now one of the most important in its class . . . The library was yet in embryo when Mr Smith was made its provisional keeper in 1857 . . . As Sir J.C. Robinson was practically the organiser of the Art Museum, so Mr Soden Smith was really the organiser of the Art Library'; Smith was given a permanent post in 1868, which he held until his death in 1890 (*The Academy*, 5 July 1890, no. 948, p. 16); reference kindly supplied by Anthony Burton; see also Burton 1999, fig. 8.2 on p. 118 for a contemporary portrait of Soden Smith.

Thomas Hopper

(b. Rochester 1776/7 – d. London 1856)

Hopper was an architect who worked in a range of architectural styles. He exhibited at the Royal Academy between 1807 and 1848. In 1807 he showed two designs for the 'Conservatory building for H.R.H. the Prince of Wales at Carlton House' (nos. 1011 and 1053); see entry below.

Graves IV, pp. 152–3; Thieme-Becker, 17, p. 489; Colvin 1995, pp. 512–16; TDA, 14, p. 753 [Burton].

471: Candelabrum

dated 1810
Probably designed by Thomas Hopper; manufactured by Coade and Sealy [q.v.]
Coade stone
h. 205.9 cm.
A.92–1980

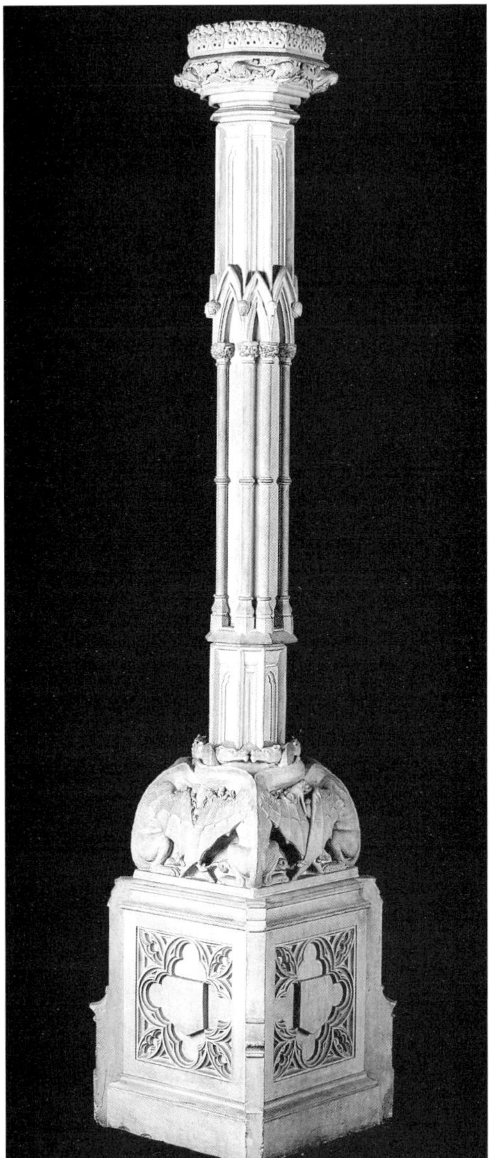

Inscribed on the base: COADE & SEALY LAMBETH.1810

Originally one of a set of ten ordered by George, Prince of Wales, later George IV from Coade & Sealy for the Gothic Conservatory at Carlton House, London and delivered on 9 February 1811; the total cost for the set was £500, and included brass lamps and black marble plinths. Following the demolition of Carlton House in 1827, the candelabra were installed in the Coffee Room at Windsor Castle that same year: they were later removed from Windsor Castle and the Royal Collection. As well as the candelabra or torchères for the Carlton House Conservatory, five figures for the niches – two kings, two bishops and one pilgrim, together with an octagonal fountain – were also supplied by Coade & Sealy (see de Bellaigue and Kirkham 1972, p. 28; Kelly 1990, pp. 219–21; *Carlton House* 1991, pp. 224–5, no. 200, illus. on back cover). The present piece was purchased by the Museum from Christopher Gibbs Ltd, 118 New Bond Street, London, in 1980 for £1500.

Versions of the candelabra include: one sold at Christie's, London, 13 April 1989, lot 19, purchased by the National Museum of Wales, Cardiff (see Hardy 1989; *NACF* 1990, p. 206; *National Museum of Wales* 1990, p. 755, pl. XIV; Bourne and Brett 1991, p. 183, no. 602 and illus.); another sold by Christie's, London, 4 July 1991, lot 49, signed 'T. Dubbin' and dated 1809, formerly at Chicksands Priory, and illustrated in situ in the hall of Chicksands in a photograph of 1893 (see Houfe 1978 [Chicksands], p. 228; reference supplied by John Hardy). A further pair was sold at Sotheby's, London, 4 July 1997, lot 12. Another version was on the London art market in 2001/2 (Hilary Chelminski; see *Apollo*, CLIV, October 2001, p. 8), and included in the exhibition *Coade Comfort* at Hilary Chelminski, Chelsea, London, 10 September to 10 November 2001. The previous owner had acquired it from a Bonham's sale sometime in the 1990s. A further version is in a private collection (I am grateful to Hilary Chelminski for this information).

Although Hopper is known to have designed the Conservatory in which the candelabra were placed, no documentary evidence exists on the authorship of the candelabra (Information kindly supplied by Micheal Snodin).

Bibliography

de Bellaigue and Kirkham 1972, pp. 20, 28 and pl. 13B; *Metropole London* 1992, p. 385, cat.no. 279, pls. I & II.

Exhibited

'Gothick' 1720–1840, Royal Pavilion, Brighton, 6 May to 17 August 1975, lent by Christopher Gibbs; *Metropole London. Macht und Glanz einer Weltstadt 1800–1840*, Villa Hügel, Essen, 4 June to 8 November 1992, cat.no. 279; *Pugin: A Gothic Passion*, Victoria and Albert Museum, London, 15 June to 11 September 1994.

George Jackson & Sons Ltd

(founded 1780)

The firm, named after its founder George Jackson (1756–1840) was established in 1780 in premises at 49 Rathbone Place, London. Jackson's specialised in the casting of decorative plasterwork for interiors, and were closely associated with the architect Robert Adam [q.v.], whose designs were executed in plasterwork. In an attempt to find a cheaper way of producing ornamental detail required for his interior designs, Adam had purchased from John Liardet his patented recipe for the composition, which he then passed to Jackson, who carved the moulds in boxwood, and used the plaster formula to press out the ornamental detail. The firm later moved to Rainville Road, Hammersmith, by which time the collection of moulds numbered around 20,000. The company was taken over around 1988 by Clark & Fenn Ltd.

Leighton 1977; Evans 1982.

472: Female allegorical figure with putto and ram

about 1820
Cast by George Jackson & Sons Ltd, possibly designed by Henry Stothard
Plaster or composition
h. 85 cm. w. 74 cm.
A.5–1990

The relief was one of those at the Rathbone Works, Rainville Road, Hammersmith, London works of George Jackson & Sons, selected for the Museum when the firm moved premises in 1989. A further 850 objects were also acquired by the Department of Furniture and Woodwork [inv.nos. W.20 to W.836–1989 – moulds for plasterwork; W.837 to W.850–1989 – composition boards; W.851 to W.867–1989 miscellaneous ornaments; W.868–1989 – plaster roundel after Thorvaldsen's *Night*; W.869–1989 – plaster roundel depicting an Egyptian mask]. Given by George Jackson & Sons Ltd, c/o J.C. England Esq., Director, Clark & Fenn Ltd, Mitcham House, Croydon, in 1990. Pattern boards with 'positives' were acquired from Jackson's by the Weald and Downland Open Air Museum, Chichester at around the same time.

On acquisition it was suggested that this relief was designed by a follower of John Flaxman [q.v.], possibly Henry Stothard (1795–1847), and that it was cast from an early 19th-century mould. The relief would probably have been used as part of an interior decorative scheme.

Robert Jackson

(active 1840 – 1878)

Gunnis recorded that Jackson was chief assistant to the sculptor John Thomas [q.v.], and was involved in the sculpture for the Houses of Parliament. He also produced fountains in St James's Park and Regent's Park. He exhibited at the Royal Academy between 1851 and 1878.

Graves IV, pp. 229–30; Gunnis 1968, p. 217.

473: The Hon. Alexander Francis Henry Campbell (b.1855)

signed; about 1872
Marble
h. 147.3 cm.
A.191–1969

Signed on the left of the base: R- JACKSON- Sc/29. MAIDA VALE

Included in the second day of the sale of the furniture and effects of Viscount Emlyn, Stackpole Court, held by Strutt & Parker, Lofts & Warner, London, on 20 November 1962, lot 557, there described as a 'White sculptured marble statue – A. Campbell wearing the kilt'. Purchased by the Museum from David Kenrick Antiques for £350 in 1969, under the bequest of Dr W.L. Hildburgh F.S.A.

On acquisition the identity of the subject was not known, and the piece was entitled *Boy in Highland Dress*. A marble bust of Alexander Campbell by Robert Jackson dated 1868 in a private collection depicts the same sitter as the present piece (information kindly supplied by the Rt. Hon. the Earl of Cawdor in 1984). In 1867 Jackson exhibited at the Royal Academy 'The Hon. A. Campbell, youngest son of the Earl of Cawdor' no. 1062, possibly a plaster version of the present piece. In 1872, a G.R. Jackson, Sculptor of 29 Maida Vale, exhibited at the Royal Academy 'The Hon. A. Campbell, son of the Earl of Cawdor; marble statue' (Graves IV, p. 225, no. 1512). This is almost certainly the present piece.

Bibliography

Graves IV, p. 229, no. 1062.

(Pierre)-Emile Jeannest

(b. 1813 – d. 1857)

The contemporary reputation of Emile Jeannest is illustrated in his lengthy and eulogistic obituary in the Art Journal*: 'The higher class of Art-manufacture in England has sustained a severe loss in the death of M. Jeannest . . . Son of M. Louis Jeannest, a manufacturer of bronzes, in which department of art he was employed early in life. He was for a period a pupil of the celebrated Paul Delaroche, and came to England about 1845 or 1846. He was resident in London for about 2 years, but does not appear to have been very successful. It was at this period that he was first employed by Mr. Herbert Minton, of Stoke-on-Trent; but the work executed appears to have been so ultra-French in its design, that after its manufacture it was not successful. Subsequently Mr. Minton induced M. Jeannest to settle for a period in the Staffordshire Potteries, and devote his attention to the production of works in parian – a material just then coming into public favour. During this period he appears to have been usefully and successfully employed in the Potteries School of Design, and laid the foundation for the education of the class of young modellers, which has proved so valuable to the staple trade of that district. About seven or eight years ago, the late Mr Henry Elkington, of Birmingham, engaged M. Jeannest to take the direction of the Fine-Art department which he founded in connection with the manufacturing firm of which he was so distinguished a member'.*

Art Journal, 1 July 1857, pp. 227–8; Atterbury and Batkin 1990, p. 276.

474: Child from Shakespeare's *Seven Ages*

about 1850–3
By (Pierre)-Emile Jeannest after a design by Daniel Maclise R.A.
Plaster
h. 17.8 cm
247–1853

Given by Henry Cole C.B. [q.v.] in 1853. At some stage held at the Bethnal Green Museum; transferred to the Department of Architecture and Sculpture, later Sculpture Department in 1977.

This semi-circular model in low relief is one of the earliest acquisitions in the Sculpture Department's collections, and was originally given to the Museum of Ornamental Art by the founder of the South Kensington, later Victoria and Albert Museum. In the *Inventory of Objects forming the Collections of the Museum of Ornamental Art*, the present piece is described as an 'Original finished model' (Robinson 1856, p. 8, no. 600). The model was one of two objects presented by Cole in 1853; the other was a closely-related semi-circular wax model of the *Old Man from Shakespeare's 'Seven Ages'*, executed by J. Rivers, again after a design by Daniel Maclise (inv.no. 248–1853).

The subject, *The Seven Ages of Man* comes from Jacques's speech in Shakespeare's 'As You Like It' (Act II, scene vii).

Daniel Maclise (1806–1870), of Irish origin, was active in England. He was particularly interested in Shakespearean themes, and in 1848 exhibited at the Royal Academy 'Shakspear's [sic] seven ages – a design to form the border and centre of a plateau, to be executed in porcelain' (Graves V, p. 155, no. 990). O'Driscoll records this in the memoirs of Maclise, commenting that four pictures were exhibited at the Royal Academy, 'These drawings were originally intended for embellishment of a porcelain card-tray; they are boldly and beautifully drawn, and vividly realise the descriptions of the great author. The drawings were made in accordance with the earnest request of some eminent persons interested in the development of art manufacture in England: for some unexplained reason this purpose was not carried out, and the drawings eventually came into the possession of the 'Art Union', who purchased them for £160; they were engraved by Goodall, and distributed amongst the subscribers' (O'Driscoll 1871, pp. 96–7).

Bibliography

Robinson 1856, p. 8, no. 600; *idem* 1860, p. 13, no. 575; *Inventory* 1863, p. 7, no. 201; *Bequests and Donations* 1901, p. 137.

Samuel Joseph

(b. London 1791 – d. London 1850)

Joseph studied under the sculptor Peter Rouw (1770–1852) and later attended the Royal Academy Schools. Friedman comments that 'Joseph had failed in 1817 to secure a RA travelling scholarship to Rome and instead found himself aligned to a clique of sculptors, led by Chantrey, who regarded an Italian education as unnecessary and preferred to stay at home pursuing the idea of a sculpture of naturalism. In the 1820s Joseph emerged as its most brilliant exponent'. Joseph went to Edinburgh in 1821, becoming one of the founding members of the Royal Scottish Academy in 1826, at which he exhibited from 1827 until 1844. A number of portrait busts by Joseph are in the National Gallery of Scotland, the Scottish National Portrait Gallery, as well as in the National Portrait Gallery, London. Joseph also exhibited at the Royal Academy between 1811 and 1846. Friedman records that 'unable to secure a major public commission', Joseph returned to London in 1829. Gunnis suggested that despite his return to London, Joseph 'never received, either in his lifetime or posthumously, the credit he deserved'. His monument to William Wilberforce, erected in Westminster Abbey in 1838, is described by Gunnis as 'the sculptor's masterpiece . . . though much criticized at the time, [it] is now generally agreed to be a magnificent work'.

Graves IV, pp. 286–8; Gunnis 1968, pp. 222–3; Whinney 1971, p. 159; Thieme-Becker, 19, p. 176; Royal Scottish Academy 1991, II, pp. 385–6; Virtue and Vision 1991 [Friedman], pp. 59–62.

475: Robert Montomery Hamilton, 8th Lord Belhaven and Stenton (1793–1868)

signed and dated 1826
Marble
h. (incl. socle) 67 cm.
A.67–1965

Signed and dated at the back: S.JOSEPH Sculpt./EDIN^R. 1826.

Bequeathed by Rupert Gunnis Esq., Hungershall Lodge, Tunbridge Wells, Kent in 1965.

The nose has been repaired.

The sitter was Lord High Commissioner to the General Assembly of the Church of Scotland and Lord Lieutenant of Lanarkshire; he became Baron Hamilton in 1831. He married Hamilton, daughter of Walter Frederick Campbell of Shawfield and Islay on 26 December 1815 (Burke's 1980, p. 232); see also entry for cat.no. 476 for the companion bust of his wife. This bust, together with its pendant is illustrated in the Blue Hall at Gunnis's home, Hungershall Lodge, just prior to their acquisition in 1965.

Bibliography
Knox 1998, fig. 4 on p. 88, p. 90, p. 95 n. 24.

476: Hamilton, Lady Belhaven and Stenton (d.1873)

signed and dated 1827
Marble
h. (incl. socle) 70 cm.
A.68–1965

Signed and dated on the back: S. JOSEPH Sculpt./EDIN^R. 1827.

Bequeathed by Rupert Gunnis Esq., Hungershall Lodge, Tunbridge Wells, Kent, in 1965.

This bust of Lady Belhaven is the companion bust to that of her husband, Lord Belhaven; see entry for cat.no. 475. Unlike the bust of Lord Belhaven, the present bust is on an integral marble socle.

Bibliography

Knox 1998, fig. 4 on p. 88, p. 90, p. 95 n. 24.

477: George IV (b.1762; r.1820–1830)

signed and dated 1831
Marble
h. (incl. socle) 87.5 cm
A.12–1956

Signed and dated on the truncation at the back: S.JOSEPH.SCULP.T./1831.

Purchased from Robert Tunstill, Old Manor House, Bradford-on-Avon, in 1956 for £60.

Whinney commented, 'The bust, which is posthumous, gives an idealized representation of the subject, similar to the famous portrait by Sir Thomas Lawrence' (Whinney 1971, p. 160). Friedman describes the bust as 'swaggering, Berniniesque' (*Virtue and Vision* [Friedman], 1991, p. 59).

Bibliography

Graves IV, p. 288, nos. 1265 and 1052; *Romantic Movement* 1959, p. 433, cat.no. 981; Gunnis 1968, p. 222; Whinney 1971, p. 160, no. 52, illus. p. 161; *Royal Scottish Academy* 1991, II, p. 386, no. 312, Snodin and Styles 2001, fig. 10 on p. 161.

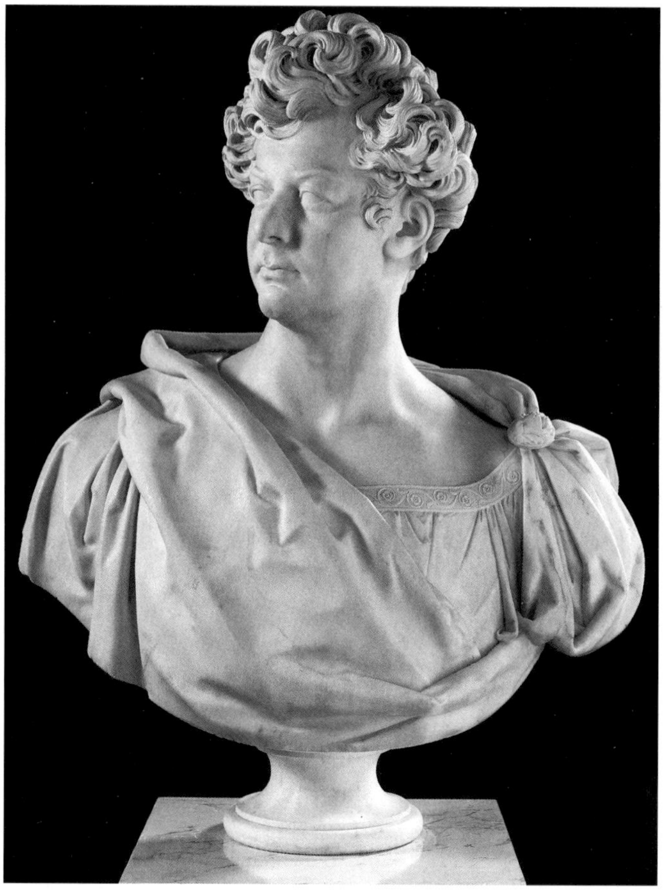

Exhibited

In 1830 Joseph exhibited at the Royal Academy a ' Bust in marble, of his Most Gracious Majesty George the Fourth, executed by command of His Majesty' (no. 1265). Together with ten other busts, Joseph exhibited possibly the same marble bust of 'His late Majesty George IV; executed by command of His Majesty' at the Exhibition of the Society of British Artists, Suffolk Street, London in 1831, (no. 876) (cited by Gunnis 1968, p. 222). Joseph also exhibited a bust of George IV at the Royal Academy in 1835, (no. 1052), and at the Royal Scottish Academy in 1833 a bust entitled 'His Most Gracious Majesty George IV – marble bust' (no. 312). In a letter to Pope-Hennessy in 1956, the previous owner Mr Tunstill recorded that the bust had been on loan to the Brighton Pavilion 'for their exhibition a couple of years ago'. This was presumably one of the Regency Exhibitions held in Brighton from the mid 1940s to mid 1950s, though I have been unable to confirm this. *The Romantic Movement*, Fifth exhibition to celebrate the tenth anniversary of the Council of Europe, Tate Gallery and Arts Council Gallery, London, 10 July to 27 September 1959, cat.no. 981; *Virtue and Vision*, Royal Scottish Academy, Edinburgh, 18 July to 15 September 1991.

Sir Edwin Henry Landseer R.A.

(b. London 1802 – d. London 1873)

Landseer is chiefly known as a painter, and was indeed one of the most popular British painters of his day. He studied initially under Benjamin Robert Haydon (1786–1846), later attending the Royal Academy Schools. He was a prolific exhibitor at the Royal Academy between 1815 and 1873, appointed an Associate of the Royal Academy in 1826, and Royal Academician in 1831. He was knighted in 1850. The Tate Gallery Archive holds material relating to this artist. Correspondence and papers for Landseer are also held in the National Art Library.

Graves IV, pp. 369–73; Thieme-Becker, 22, p. 304; TDA, 18, pp. 722–3 [Upstone].

478: Head of a lion

about 1858–66
Painted plaster
h. (approx.) 149 cm.
317–1880

Given by Mrs Mackenzie and Miss Landseer, sisters of the sculptor, in 1880.

This model has sustained much damaged, though the integral features of the head remain intact.

On acquisition, this colossal head of a lion was described as an experimental design for the figures of lions at the base of Nelson's column in Trafalgar Square. Landseer was commissioned in 1858 to design the four bronze lions to sit at the four corners of the column. The lions, which were cast by Carlo Marochetti [q.v.] in 1866, and unveiled in January 1867, represent Landseer's first use of bronze (TDA, 18, p. 723 [Upstone]). A study for a lion on canvas of about 1862 in the Tate Gallery relates to Landseer's Trafalgar Square commission (inv.no. N01350). I am grateful to Robin Hamlyn for confirming this; see *Landseer* 1981 [Hamlyn], pp. 204–6 for a full discussion of the Trafalgar Square lions.

Blackwood recorded that the main section of the memorial to Vice-Admiral Horatio Nelson (1758–1805) was completed by 1843; the figure of Nelson was executed by Edward Hodges Baily [q.v.]. Blackwood noted, 'The famous lions took a full sixty-two years to assume guard. The first sculptor commissioned, John Lough, failed to provide any. Thomas Milnes' lions were so lacking in spirit that they were rejected. Finally, on the strength of his skill as a painter of animals, Sir Edwin Landseer was brought in' (Blackwood 1989, p. 254). Gleichen commented that the lions were 'couchant and somewhat conventional . . . Only two lions were modelled, the other two being replicas: heads and tails being turned different ways'. He stated that the lions cost £18,000, although Blackwood recorded the cost as £20,000 (Gleichen 1928, p. 8; Blackwood 1989, p. 252).

Bibliography

Bequests and Donations 1901, pp. 186, 193.

Edouard Lanteri

(b. Auxerre 1848 – d. London 1917)

Lanteri, a sculptor and medallist, was a native of Burgundy, and initially trained under Aimé Millet (1819–1891) and M. Lecoque de Boisbaudran, and later at the École des Beaux-Arts under Eugène Guillaume (1822–1905) and Pierre-Jules Cavalier. On the suggestion of Jules Dalou [q.v.], another emigré artist, Lanteri settled in England from 1872, and was naturalised in 1901. At the age of 23 he became chief assistant to Sir Joseph Edgar Boehm [q.v.], a position he held until Boehm's death in 1890. In 1874 Lanteri was appointed Master of Modelling at the National Art Training School (now Royal College of Art), and in 1900 became the first Professor of Modelling. During 1905/6 he supervised students working on the figures of Fame, Sculpture and Architecture for the Exhibition Road façade of the Museum. Lanteri wrote a three volume guide to modelling, published in 1902, 1904 and 1911. He exhibited at the Royal Academy between 1885 and 1917, but was perhaps chiefly renowned as a teacher. Spielmann recorded: 'As a teacher he has no superior, and many a successful sculptor of to-day owes much to his untiring energy, encouragement, and interest, such as he takes in all who have the good fortune to come under his care'.

Spielmann 1901, pp. 125–8; Lanteri 1902; Staley 1903; Lanteri 1904; idem 1911; Forrer 1907, pp. 302–3; McAllister 1912; Forrer VII, p. 7; Parkes 1921, pp. 92–3; Physick 1978; and 1982 pp. 228–9, 231–2; Royal Academy IV, pp. 220–1; Thieme-Becker, 22, p. 361; TDA, 18, p. 751 [Attwood].

479: Right hand of Sir Joseph Edgar Boehm
(1834–1890)

about 1882
Moulded by Edouard Lanteri
Plaster
l. (excl. wooden compasses) 19 cm.
1892–125

Given by the Executors of the late Sir J.E. Boehm in 1892; see entry for cat.no. 288.

This cast of Boehm's hand seems to have been used as a model for the right hand on the monument to Sir Francis Drake, executed by Boehm. Stocker records two versions of the monument, one erected in Fitzford, Tavistock, and a replica erected at The Hoe, Plymouth (executed 1882–3 and 1882–4 respectively). Stocker also notes a related statuette in Woburn Abbey, and records that Boehm additionally produced a medal depicting Drake (see Stocker 1988, pp. 413, nos. 238A-E and 239, 132–3, figs. 130–5).

Bibliography
List 1892, p. 17.

480: Beatrice

signed; about 1885–1904
Marble in oak frame
h. 46 cm. w. 30.5 cm.
A.158–1920

Signed in the bottom left corner of the portrait: ED.LANTERI
Incised in a band beneath the portrait: BEATRICE

The oak frame is inscribed: MARBLE RELIEF BY/EDWARD LANTERI/B.1848, D.1917/GIVEN BY MRS LUDWIG MOND.

Purchased from the widow of the sculptor by Mrs Ludwig Mond. Given by Mrs Ludwig Mond and Mr Robert Mond, 20 Avenue Road, Regents Park, London in 1920.

This relief, an imaginary portrait of Dante's Beatrice, was accepted 'contrary to our practice to accept sculpture by modern artists working in England'. However, it was acquired as a piece of modern sculpture of 'peculiar interest to the Museum, with which the artist was so closely connected' (*Review* 1920, p. 4); see also entry for cat.no. 481. Plaster cast reproductions of the present piece were offered for sale by the Museum's cast selling service. In the *Catalogue of Plaster Casts* for January 1939, casts were available at a cost of £12 6d (*Casts* 1939, p. 27).

BIBLIOGRAPHY
Lanteri 1920, p. 7, no. 12; *Review* 1920, p. 4.

EXHIBITED
Exhibited at the commemorative exhibition of Lanteri's work held at *The Leicester Galleries*, London, January 1920, cat.no. 12.

481: Pax

signed and dated 1896
Plaster
h. 178 cm.
2015–1900

Signed and dated: Ed Lanteri 1896

Purchased from the sculptor in 1896 for £100.

During 1894 Thomas Armstrong [q.v.] wrote a memorandum suggesting the benefits to schools of art of providing themselves with casts of full-length figures. The memo, which was widely circulated, stated: 'It is very desirable to have casts of better quality from life size full length statues than any that are to be obtained at present from the well known and much used antique figures in the Vatican Museum. Although I hope that in time the opposition to the making of new moulds of them may be withdrawn, I think it well in the meantime to look out elsewhere for suitable figures which may be available . . . Monsieur Lantéri proposes to model from the living model a standing female figure 5ft high. On casts of this figure drapery could be arranged for study. Both arms of this piece will be free of the torso, from a little above the elbow, so that the arrangement of drapery on the figure may be made as easy as possible. One of the arms will have a joint, so that the lower part of it may be removed and replaced by another with a somewhat different movement. The cost of each cast of this figure, if a sufficient number of copies be ordered, will be eight guineas. This figure in my opinion will be very useful: and a copy of it will be ordered for the N.A.T.S. [National Art Training School]'.

A copy of the cast produced by Lanteri was purchased for the Edinburgh Royal Institute of Art in 1894, although in a memo dated 8 January 1895 Armstrong recorded that only about half the required number of twenty had been ordered by art schools, in order to keep the cost of each copy to £8 (perhaps an error for 8 guineas). He therefore suggested 'that the Department should pay for the original figure cast from the clay model in plaster', at a cost of £100. He qualified his statement by continuing that it 'may seem a great deal but it is not much for the work of a man of Mon. Lanteri's ability and he calculates on spending three or four months of his spare time in modelling the figure which he will finish in the extremities'. It was agreed that the figure would belong to the Department, and that casts of it (to be taken by Cantoni), would be authorised at a reduced price of £7 each; see also entry for cat.no. 381. All casts would however be signed and passed by Lanteri personally.

The present piece is Lanteri's original model of the standing female figure, purchased on 21 May 1896 for the National Art Training School at Armstrong's suggestion; it was registered in 1900. A mould was made of the original Lanteri model in Armstrong's studio at the Royal College of Art (formerly the National Art Training School).

BIBLIOGRAPHY
Staley 1903, p. 243; Thieme-Becker, 22, p. 361.

EXHIBITED
Staley recorded that the plaster cast of the *Pax* figure 'which was exhibited at the Royal Acadmy in 1900, is the version now in the Victoria and Albert Museum. It is a splendidly conceived and well-worked out representation quite natural and very graceful'. This appears to be erroneous; in 1897 Lanteri exhibited 'Pax; statue' no. 1964, but this was almost certainly a reduced bronze version and not the present piece (Graves IV, p. 385, no. 1964).

482: Term with putti

signed; about 1900
Bronze with marble base
h. (incl. base) 39.5 cm.
A.21–1971

Signed on the side of the base: Ed. Lanteri

Purchased by Dr Neville M. Goodman, C.B. for £20 from the London dealer Alfred Spero on 23 October 1943. Given by Dr Goodman in 1971, together with fifteen other bronzes, inv.nos. A.17 to 32–1971.

There are some areas worn to a paler colour and polished. Small chips are visible on the top and bottom rims of the marble base.

The term, a bearded old man's head on a column adorned with garlands, is surrounded by four dancing putti. The bronze is dowelled into a marble socle. On the base of the socle is a label, which reads:

75. Therme with putti. Edouard Lanteri (1848–1917) Spero. 1943. £20 £150 [the second figure in red ink].

The relatively unfinished forms indicate that this piece was cast from a clay sketch, probably for a garden ornament, which does not appear to have been executed. Describing a terracotta version of this piece, Spielmann suggested the composition shows the 'lighter side' of Lanteri's work: "Richness, joyousness, fine sensuousness, and movement are in this work, which ought not to be allowed to remain in this state, but should be carried out".

A 'garden ornament', perhaps a related object, was lent by Lady Harris to the exhibition of the sculpture by the late Professor E. Lanteri held at the Leicester Galleries, London in January 1920 (see *Lanteri* 1920, cat.no. 1). A plaster of the same subject was also exhibited (cat.no. 16).

Bibliography

Spielmann 1901, pp. 125, 7 terracotta model illus. p.125; Cooper 1975, p. 76 and fig. 72 (erroneously described as terracotta).

Exhibited

Design of the Times: 100 Years of the Royal College of Art, Royal College of Art, London, 7 February to 20 March 1996.

483: Alfred Stevens (1817–1875)

signed and dated 1911
Plaster
h. (incl. moulded base) 76 cm.
A.6–1912

Signed and dated on the back: Ed. Lanteri/1911

Given by the sculptor in 1912.

This is a cast used for the production of the bronze bust of Stevens by Lanteri acquired by the Tate Gallery in 1911 (inv.no.N02853), presented by the Alfred Stevens Memorial Committee. The artist himself supplied the plaster from the founders. According to the Tate's *Catalogue: British School 1936–7*, Lanteri used photographs and advice from those who personally knew Alfred Stevens to produce this likeness (*Tate* 1947, p.150). McAllister described Lanteri as 'one of the keenest and most understanding admirers of the work of Alfred Stevens' (McAllister 1912, p. 31).

Bibliography

Review 1912, p. 4.

John Lawlor

(b. Dublin 1820 – d. London 1901)

Lawlor initially studied at the Royal Dublin Society Schools; in 1845 he travelled to England and attended the Royal Academy Schools. He exhibited at the Royal Academy between 1848 and 1879, and at the British Institution between 1848 and 1865. At the 1851 International Exhibition, Lawlor exhibited A Bather, *which won him a prize medal. Gunnis recorded his 'best-known work is the group representing "Mechanics" which he executed in 1864 for the Albert Memorial'. He also records that Lawlor travelled to America in 1886, returning to London in 1901.*

Graves IV, pp. 395–6; Graves 1908, p. 337; Gunnis 1968, pp. 235–6; Thieme-Becker, 22, p. 481; Murphy 1999, pp. 71–2.

484: John Jones (1799–1882)

signed and dated 1882
Marble
h. (incl. socle) 69.5 cm. h. (socle) 13.3 cm.
A.79–1970

Signed and dated on the truncation at the back: J. LAWLOR Sc 1882.
The pedestal is inscribed: JOHN JONES ESQ/1800~1882/Sculptor. J. Lawlor

Held on the premises of the military tailors Rogers, John Jones Ltd, 33 Bruton Street, London (exact dates unknown; though possibly in their possession from 1882). Passed into the possession of Mrs Margaret Charters Kirk, an employee at the firm. Purchased together with its marble pedestal, inv.no. A.79:A-1970, from Mrs Margaret Charters Kirk, 11 Azalea Walk, Pinner, London in 1970 for £50.

John Jones bequeathed a large collection of mainly French eighteenth-century furniture to the Museum in 1882. He has been a sleeping partner in the firm of military tailors, Rogers, John Jones Ltd since 1850 (see Provenance above). As Jones died on 7 January 1882 this bust is almost certainly a posthumous commemorative portrait. A plaster version was formerly owned by the Museum (inv.no. 12–1900). The firm of John Jones Ltd asked if they could acquire this plaster version, and it was subsequently de-accessioned in 1971, and sold to the present firm of Rogers, John Jones Ltd, 16 Clifford Street, London for £5.

Bibliography

Sutton 1972, fig. 2 on p. 157, p. 158.

Richard Arthur Ledward

(b. Burslem 1857/8 – d. London 1890)

Richard Arthur Ledward trained in the South Kensington Schools, where he also later taught. He exhibited at the Royal Academy between 1882 and 1890. His second son, Gilbert Ledward [q.v.] also became a sculptor; see entry for cat.no. 750.

Graves V, p. 15; Thieme-Becker, 22, p. 540.

485: Sir (Francis) Philip Cunliffe-Owen K.C.B., K.C.M.G., C.I.E. (1828–1894)

signed and dated 1884
Terracotta
h. (incl. base) 72.5 cm.
495–1893

Inscribed and signed on the back truncation: SIR PHILIP CUNLIFFE OWEN. C.B. C.I.E. R.A LEDWARD Sc/1884

Given by Sir Philip Cunliffe-Owen in 1893, the year of his retirement from the Museum.

Sir Philip Cunliffe-Owen was Director of the South Kensington Museum (later Victoria and Albert Museum) from 1874 to 1893 (Bonython 1982 [Cole], p. 45). R.A. Ledward had also produced another bust commemorating a former member of the Museum's staff, Richard Redgrave (1804–1888). His son Gilbert Ledward produced a bust of Redgrave in 1915–16 based on his father's earlier bust of 1881; see entry for cat.no. 750.

Bibliography
Art Journal, The Glasgow exhibition special number, 1888, p. 26, illus. p. 27; Graves V, p. 15.

Exhibited
A terracotta bust of Sir Philip Cunliffe-Owen was exhibited by Ledward at the Royal Academy in 1884 (no. 1770). At the Glasgow International Exhibition of 1888 Ledward exhibited a bust of 'Sir P. Cunliffe Owen', described in the special number of the *Art Journal* as 'an excellent likeness '.

Alphonse Legros

(b. Dijon 1837 – d. Watford 1911)

Spielmann recorded the diversity of Legros: 'Mr Legros' name is great in art – in painting, sculpture, etching, and teaching'. Legros was initially apprenticed to a sign-painter, but in 1863 travelled to England and was appointed as teacher of an engraving class at the South Kensington Museum. In 1876 he became Professor at the Slade School, University College, London, where he remained until 1894; in 1881 he became a naturalised British citizen. Bénédite recorded, 'It was inevitable that some day or other he must attempt sculpture . . . His entire work, whether painted, drawn, engraved, or sculptured, represents enormous achievement, in which exceptionally fine results abound'. Legros was also a medallist and President of the Society of Medallists. An obituary notice in the Burlington Magazine *further records the high esteem in which Legros was held, 'It is sufficient at present to state that in our opinion the residence of M. Legros in London was one of the landmarks in the history of the Fine Arts in England during the latter part of the nineteenth century'. The Tate Gallery holds archival material relating to this sculptor.*

Spielmann 1901, pp. 166–8; Bénédite 1903, esp. pp. 21–2; Forrer III, pp. 375–8; Burlington Magazine, January 1912, XX, no. 106, p. 191; Thieme-Becker, 22, pp. 574–5; TDA, 19, pp. 89–90 [Wilcox].

486: Head of a satyr

about 1885–95
Plaster
h. 82 cm
A.125–1916

Given by Victor Ames Esq, The Manor House, Marylebone Road, London in 1916.

On acquisition this was considered to be 'a boldly modelled and characteristic example of the artist's work' (*Review* 1916, p. 9), and was thought to be a mascaron designed for street decoration. The relief is however more probably related to the satyr masks on one of the two fountains, the South fountain and the Terrace fountain, produced by Legros for the Duke of Portland at Welbeck Abbey.

Spielmann commented, 'Heads and masks by the Professor are fine in style, such as we see in the fountain for the Duke of Portland, which, I believe, is not yet completed . . . And so Mr. Legros' heads, when he pushes them to the limit of exaggerated expression, become almost grotesques – yet decorative and full of spirit and individuality; until to those who understand them they become "objets aimables"' (Spielmann 1901, p. 167).

Bibliography

Review 1916, p. 9; *Art and Design* 1987 [Radcliffe], p. 151, illus. on p. 150.

487: Female torso

signed and dated 1890
Plaster
h. 52.5 cm.
378–1891

Signed at the base of the left leg to the side: A. Legros/1890

Given by the sculptor in 1891.

The casting lines have been left visible on the plaster. This figure was given to the Museum whilst Legros was Slade Professor of Fine Art at University College, London. According to the original acquisition information, the cast was held in the Masters' Room in the National Art Training School and 'could be obtained through Monsieur Lanteri on one of the days which he is taking the Modelling Class'.

In his article on Legros, Bénédite described the present piece as 'that delightful little torso which is as much admired at the South Kensington Museum as at the Luxembourg' (Bénédite 1903, p. 22). Kineton Parkes commented in *Sculpture of To-day*, 'In the South Kensington Museum is a cast of a small female torso, very beautiful and suave in its simple lines' (Parkes 1921, pp. 91–2). Gronau recorded that the present piece was cast after the marble original (Gronau 1909, p. 55). Whilst presumably commenting on the marble, Spielmann is similarly complimentary, 'But in sculpture Mr Legros' great merits do not hide the defects. In the exquisite "Torso of a Woman" the artist is seen at his best; complete in its beauty it is, however, not the beauty of a complete thing, being, after all, a fragment' (Spielmann 1901, p. 167).

A slightly reduced bronze variant (h. 46 cm.) of this torso is in the Fitzwilliam Museum, Cambridge, and was exhibited at the Fine Art Society in 1902 and 1968 (see *British Sculpture 1850–1914,* 1968, p. 27, no. 97, and pl. J). A marble version of the same height as the bronze was exhibited at the Royal Academy in 1972; see *Victorian and Edwardian Decorative Art. The Handley Read Collection,* cat.no. F35: it is now in the Birmingham City Art Gallery, inv.no. P.41'73; see *Birmingham* 1987, p. 188, illus. on p. 189.

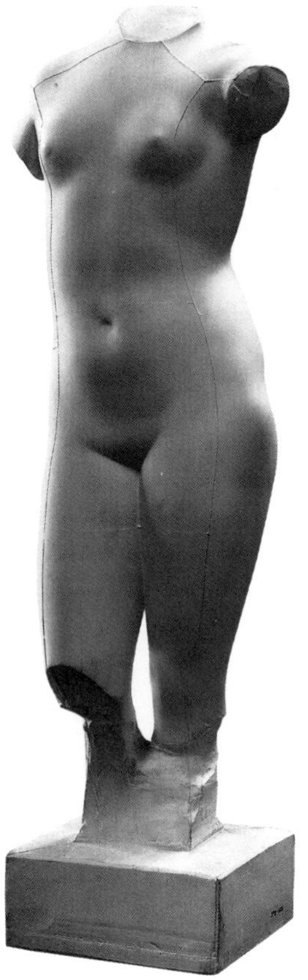

BIBLIOGRAPHY

Bequests and Donations 1901, p. 188; Bénédite 1903, p. 22; Gronau 1909, p. 55; Parkes 1921, pp. 91–2; *Pioneers* 1973, p. 109, cat.no. 28; Bassett and Fogelman 1997, illus. on p. 44.

EXHIBITED

Pioneers of Modern Sculpture, 20 July to 23 September 1973, Arts Council, Hayward Gallery, London, cat.no. 28.

FREDERIC LORD LEIGHTON R.A.

(b. Scarborough 1830 – d. London 1896)

Leighton's name is more commonly associated with painting, although his influential contribution to the movement in British sculpture known as the New Sculpture has recently been re-affirmed by the exhibition held in 1996, Leighton and his sculptural legacy. *Jones records that 'Leighton's interest in sculpture was a natural extension of his increasingly sculptural treatment of the painted canvas'. Following the critical acclaim for his* Athlete struggling with a python *– see entry below – Barrington recorded that 'Many were the voices heard exclaiming that Leighton ought to give himself entirely to sculpture. His masterly power in understanding form, and givng expression to it in Art, was readily understood and appreciated when he worked in the round, whereas it had been but scantily appreciated in his painting; the fact being, that the public is unaccustomed to find that power developed in modern pictures, whereas in sculpture it is the principal and obvious aim in any statue'. Leighton produced two frescoes:* The Industrial Arts as Applied to War *(1878–80), and* The Industrial Arts as Applied to Peace *(1884–6) for the interior of the Museum; these were recently conserved and re-displayed in 1996, the centenary of his death. He exhibited at the Royal Academy between 1855 and his death, and was elected President of the Royal Academy in 1878. The Tate Gallery Archive holds material relating to this artist.*

Barrington 1906, esp. p. 200; Graves V, pp. 29–33; Thieme-Becker, 22, pp. 593–4; TDA, 19, pp. 103–4 [Jones]; Leighton 1996; Read 1996.

488: Athlete struggling with a python

about 1874
Plaster
h. 25 cm.
A.38–1954

Given by the sculptor to G.F. Watts. Purchased by H.D. Molesworth [q.v.], on behalf of Dr W.L. Hildburgh F.S.A. from Cavendish, Hood & Co. Ltd, Antiques and Interior Decoration, 2 Baker Street, London, on 9 April 1954 for £1 5s, and given subsequently given to the Museum by Dr Hildburgh.

The casting lines are visible on the surface.

In the justification for its acceptance Molesworth wrote, 'This is a fairly historical little object since it represents the first sketch for the statue of Python by Leighton. The clay model was given by Leighton to Watts. Watts sent it to be cast and after making the mould the caster apparently destroyed the clay. Another of these casts is in Leighton house but the present example is inscribed in what has been identified as Watt's handwriting 'Sketch . . . given to me/by Fredk. Leighton/afterwards P R. Acady March 1878'. Quite apart from any merits on its own much interest lies in the great admiration which the thing aroused in its own day and which is recorded in contemporary letters'. In her *Life* of Leighton, Barrington commented on Leighton's group *Cymon and Iphigenia*, 'Leighton gave this group to Watts, who expressed to me an unbounded admiration for it. "Nothing more beautiful has ever been done! Pheidias never did anything better. I believe it was better even than Pheidias!" were the words Watts used when deploring the fact that he had lent it to a sculptor to be cast – something had gone wrong in the process of casting, and it had been destroyed. When giving me the modelled sketch for the "Python", Watts said, "I am giving you the most beautiful thing I have in my place"' (Barrington 1906, p. 198, n. 2). Molesworth may have misinterpreted Barrington in his statement suggesting that the sketch for the Python was destroyed by the caster: the destroyed model was more probably that produced for Leighton's *Cymon and Iphigenia*.

Tate Britain has the full-size bronze version of this composition, signed and dated 1877, and exhibited at the Royal Academy in that year (Tate inv.no.N01754). A replica of this was produced in marble in 1890 for the Glyptothek, Copenhagen, and was exhibited at the Royal Academy in 1891 (no. 2099). A letter in the manuscript collection of the National Art Library from F.W. Pomeroy to A.L. Baldry of 4 August 1898 outlined Pomeroy's career, and noted that Pomeroy [q.v.] carved the marble now in Copenhagen (NAL pressmark MSL/1972/4950/122). The Royal Academy has the original plaster model for the full-size bronze at Leighton House; it was presented to the Royal Academy by the sculptor in 1886. Three further versions in bronze, and one in waxed plaster are also in the Royal Academy collection. A plaster sketch given by Alphonse Legros in 1897 (inv.no. N01761), is in Tate Britain. A further version in bronze is in the Ashmolean Museum Oxford (see *Ashmolean* 1992 [III], p. 113, no. 532).

In Edmund Gosse's article in the *Art Journal* of 1894 entitled 'The New Sculpture', which discussed the emergence of a different type of sculpture, Gosse drew particular attention to the Leighton bronze: 'The Athlete and the Python', even with shortcomings which it may now not be difficult to point out, gave the start-word to the New Sculpture in England' (Gosse 1894, p. 140; reference cited by Beattie 1983).

BIBLIOGRAPHY

Ashmolean 1992 [III], p. 113; *Leighton* 1996, p. 47, no. 17.

489: The Sluggard

about 1890–1900
By Frederic, Lord Leighton, published by Arthur L. Collie
Bronze
h. 52.5 cm.
820–1901

Signed on the front of the base: FRED LEIGHTON
Inscribed at the front of the base: THE SLUGGARD
Inscribed at the back: PUBLISHED BY ARTHUR COLLIE/39B OLD BOND STREET LONDON/MAY 1ST 1890.

Purchased from the Fine Art Society Ltd, 148 New Bond Street, London in 1901 for £15 15s (15 guineas). Transferred from the Circulation Department to the Department of Architecture and Sculpture, later Sculpture Department, in 1956.

Original acquisition information records that this bronze was cast from the clay sketch-model for the bronze statue which was exhibited at the Royal Academy in 1886. Radcliffe comments that the original bronze statue 'was intended as a pendant to Leighton's only other life-sized sculpture, An Athlete Struggling with a Python, finished and exhibited in 1877, also now at Leighton House'. He continues that the date which appears on many of the bronze versions produced, including the present piece, 'refers to the date of first publication, and not, as has sometimes been supposed to the actual date of casting' (*Treasure Houses* 1985, p. 630).

The *Sluggard* or *Athlete awakening from sleeping*, was produced in large numbers, originally published by Arthur L. Collie in 1890, cast in the Singer Foundry in Frome. The copyright passed from Collie to J.W. Singer & Sons Ltd sometime in the early decades of the twentieth century; it appears in the Singer's trade literature around 1914 (cited by *Ashmolean* 1992 [III], p. 114; originally cited by Beattie 1983, p. 260, n. 59); a copy of the Singer brochure is in the registered papers under Roland Morris, in the Archive of Art and Design.

The Royal Academy has a bronze statuette cast from a plaster version given to the Royal Academy by the sculptor's sisters, Mrs Orr and Mrs Matthews in 1896. The original model for the life-size bronze statue of 1885 was presented to the Tate Gallery, and is now on loan to Leighton House. Another version produced by Collie was auctioned at Christie's, London, 29 October 1992, lot 19; another cast by Singer, though also retaining Collie's name, was sold at Sotheby's, London, 6 June 1997, lot 90. Published versions include those in the Leeds City Art Gallery (*Leeds* 1996, p. 14, and *Treasure Houses* 1985, p. 630, no. 562), in the Ashmolean Museum, Oxford (*Ashmolean* 1992 [III], p. 114, cat.no. 533); and in a private collection (*Leighton* 1996, p. 50, cat.no. 20; see also Read 1996, pp. 68–9). A version dated 1885 is in the Tate Gallery (inv.no. N01752).

BIBLIOGRAPHY

Ashmolean 1992 [III], p. 114.

490: Needless alarms

1897
After a model by Frederic, Lord Leighton; published by
Arthur Leslie Collie
Bronze
h. 50 cm. h. (base) 17 cm.
1054–1905

Inscribed on the base at the back: Pubd By Arthur L. Collie/39B Old Bond Street/London November 11 1897

Purchased from Messrs Ernest E. Brown & Phillips, The Leicester Galleries, 20 Green Street, Leicester Square, London in 1905 for £15 15s (15 guineas); see also entry for cat. no. 424.

Original acquisition information states that this bronze is a replica of the original statuette exhibited at the Royal Academy in 1886 (no.1922).

The figure depicts a girl frightened by a frog or toad. The sculptor Thomas Brock [q.v.], who acted as an advisor for the Museum on acquisitions, reported, 'I have examined the statuette "Needless Alarms" the bronze by the Late Lord Leighton P.R.A. and I consider it a good reproduction of the original made by Leighton for Millais. The price is reasonable and therefore I recomend its purchase at 15 guineas'.

Penny compares the composition of the figure with that of *Folly* by Edward Onslow Ford [q.v.] (*Ashmolean* 1992 [III], p. 67). A black wax study for *Needless Alarms* was presented to the Tate Gallery in 1913 (inv.no. N02945); a bronze version was also presented to the Tate Gallery in 1940 (inv. no. N05120). Versions were sold at Christie's, London on 16 June 1994, lot 357, and at Sotheby's, London, 5 July 2000, lot 169. Two further versions, one plaster and one bronze are discussed in *Leighton* 1996, p. 51, cat.nos. 21 and 22, p. 52, fig. 22. A full-size coloured plaster version and a bronze statuette are in the Royal Academy collections (I am grateful to Helen Valentine for this information).

BIBLIOGRAPHY

Parkes 1921, p. 131; *Ashmolean* 1992 [III], p. 67.

John Graham Lough

(b. Shotley 1798 – d. London 1876)

Lough began his career as a stonemason, initially working as an ornamental sculptor, executing work for the Library and Philosophical Society in Newcastle-upon-Tyne. In 1826 he entered the Royal Academy Schools; his success was such that he secured a commission from the Duchess of Buckingham for a bust in his first year. Between 1834 and 1837 he worked in Rome, and on his return settled in London. One of his chief patrons was Sir Matthew White Ridley, for whom he produced a series of compositions around a Shakespearean theme. Boase recorded, 'the early forties clearly marked a critical period in Lough's career. He had been forgotten in Rome, a risk that these Roman journeys were well known to entail. Busts and these single standing Shakespearean figures with an occasional minor monument were all the work that seems to have come his way'; however his fortune changed with the exhibition of two models for The Mourners *and* The Battle of the Standard, *at an exhibition of sculpture proposed for the new Houses of Parliament. He exhibited at the Royal Academy between 1826 and 1863, and at the British Institution between 1833 and 1863.*

Graves V, pp. 94–5; Graves 1908, pp. 353–4; Boase 1960; Lough and Merson 1987; Thieme-Becker, 23, p. 414; TDA, 19, p. 720 [Greenwood].

491: Duncan's horses devouring one another, from *Macbeth*

about 1834
Bronze
h. 34 cm.
92–1889

Signed on the base: J.C. Lough

Given by Miss Bishop, 42 Harewood Square, London in 1889. Miss Bishop was the niece of Mrs Lough, the sculptor's wife. Documentation relating to the acquisition of this group records that 'it was the wish of her [the donor's] aunt [Mrs Lough] that the bronze group of mad horses designed and executed by her late husband Mr John Graham Lough should be presented to the South Kensington Museum'. Transferred from Bethnal Green Museum to the Circulation Department in 1963, and later transferred to the Sculpture Department.

The bronze was treated for verdigris in 1921.

This is an example of Lough's use of Shakespearean themes; see also entries for cat.nos. 492 to 494. The subject is taken from *Macbeth*, Act II, scene iv:

'And Duncan's horses, – a thing most strange and certain, -
Beauteous and swift, the minions of their race,
Turn'd wild in nature, broke their stalls, flung out,
Contending 'gainst obedience, as they would make
War with mankind'

On acquisition this group was originally described as 'Mad horses'. Thomas Armstrong [q.v.] examined this group in connection with its possible acquisition and reported, 'The subject is not a pleasant one, a group of horses fighting, but the metal is good and artistically it is, I dare say, as good as most modelled work done at the time it was produced . . . Miss Bishop told me that her uncle, Mr Lough, not being satisfied with the . . . [illegible] bronze used by French foundries had the metal made on purpose. Lough was a man of some note in his time and this is as small a specimen of his work as we could hope to get, besides being of good material . . . '

Lough and Merson record that this group was the earliest work by the artist inspired by a Shakespearean theme, 'The subject was ideally suited to Lough's taste, since he was able to combine his genuine love and knowledge of horses with a highly dramatic subject' (Lough and Merson 1987, p. 57). A large marble version, and a plaster one of similar proportions to the present piece are known in private collections. A further plaster version is in the Los Angeles County Museum of Art, inv.no. M.81–263 (*Los Angeles* 1987, p. 143). Boase recorded that 'Several casts may have been taken' and that 'Joseph Buonaparte gave Lough a gold vase that had belonged to Napoleon as a token of his admiration for the work' (Boase 1960, p. 280).

Boase suggested that the *Duncan's Horses* exhibited at the Royal Academy in 1832, (no. 1159), was 'probably a model for a bronze', and therefore not the present piece; see also the *Athenaeum*, 30 June 1832, no. 244, p. 419.

Exhibited

In 1833 Lough exhibited 'A Group of Horses', no. 548, and a year later in 1834, 'A Group of Horses, in bronze', no. 568, at the British Institution, possibly the present piece.

Bibliography

Graves V, p. 94, no. 1159; *idem* 1908, p. 353; Boase 1960, pp. 279–80; Lough and Merson 1987, pp. 57, 84, illus. on dust-jacket.

492: Puck, from *A Midsummer Night's Dream*

signed; about 1847–60
Marble
h. 122 cm.
323–1867

Signed on the integral base: J.C.LOUGH

Bequeathed by William Minshull Bigg, together with cat.nos. 493 and 494, in 1867. Transferred on loan from the Department of Architecture and Sculpture to Bethnal Green Museum in 1928; returned to the Department of Architecture and Sculpture, later the Sculpture Department in 1951.

The subject is taken from Shakespeare's *A Midsummer Night's Dream*, Act II, scene i. Lough specialised in Shakespearean themes; see also entries for cat.nos. 491, 493 and 494. Lough and Merson discuss Lough's Shakespearean works, noting that he began work on his series in 1841; the ten works were commissioned from Sir Matthew White Ridley, a local landowner, for his London home, 10 Carlton House Terrace (Lough and Merson 1987, pp. 57–9).

In the *Descriptive Catalogue of the Lough and Noble Models of Statue, Bas-reliefs and Busts in Elswick Hall, Newcastle upon Tyne*, produced around 1910, a version of the present piece is listed, presumably plaster: 'no. 92 "PUCK, or Robin Goodfellow. One of Shakespeare's most amusing creations . . ."' The marble statue is in the possession of Lord Ridley' (Robinson n.d., p. 31, no. 92). For a discussion of the fate of the Lough objects formerly at Elswick Hall, see Lough and Merson 1987, pp. 73–80.

Two marble figures entitled *Puck*, both of 1849 and similar in height to the present piece, h. 122 and 124.5 cm respectively, were formerly in the collection of W.H. Lever (*Lady Lever* 1999, p. 81). A marble figure of Puck by Lough (h. 125 cm.) was sold at Sotheby's, London, 2 November 2001, lot 115.

Bibliography

Bequests and Donations 1901, p. 18; Boase 1960, p. 283 n. 30; Gunnis 1968, p. 244; Lough and Merson 1987, pp. 36, 59, 84, fig. 17.

Exhibited

The *Literary Gazette* records that in early July 1847 Lough opened his studio 'for the exhibition of several Shaksperian [sic] conceptions . . . Puck . . . He is truly the merriest and most mischievous of sprites. His head is young in form, but old in frolic, and cunning, and archness. That fellow cannot move without a trick; and how he stands, the mushroom Colossus, not of Rhodes, but of a hundred ways to fun and knavery. He is the quintessence of shrewdness and elfish whimsicality. It is a happy performance, and the true representative of all we fancy in our fairy love' (*Literary Gazette*, 10 July 1847, no. 1590, p. 507).

Lough and Merson record that this figure was 'Exhibited at the British Institution in 1850, but completed by 1847' (Lough and Merson 1987, p. 84). Lough also exhibited a plaster version of the present piece at the 1851 International Exhibition in London, and in the same year at the Guildhall, an exhibition of Lough's Shakespearean works was displayed, in which a version of 'mischievous Puck' was included, together with that of 'Titania, the fairy queen'; see entry for cat.no. 493 (*Builder*, 22 November 1851, IX, no. 459, p. 743).

493: Titania, from *A Midsummer Night's Dream*

signed and dated 1863
Marble
h. 75 cm.
324–1867

Signed and dated on the integral base: J.C. LOUGH./1863.

Bequeathed by William Minshull Bigg, together with cat.nos. 492 and 494, in 1867. Transferred on loan from the Department of Architecture and Sculpture to Bethnal Green Museum in 1928; returned to the Department of Architecture and Sculpture, later the Sculpture Department, in 1951.

The subject is taken from Shakespeare's *Midsummer Night's Dream*, Act IV, scene i. As with cat.no. 492, Lough appears to have produced a number of versions of this figure. Though this particular piece is signed and dated 1863, an exhibition of 'Mr Lough's sculptures' held at his studio during July 1847, confirms that a figure of *Titania* was completed by this time: 'Close by is a Titania, *of whom* (for they are so life-like we cannot say *of which*) we may simply observe that she is moulded in the most pure and graceful shape of female loveliness; and the accessories and effects of the drowsy potion admirably done' (*Literary Gazette*, 10 July 1847, no. 1590, p. 507). A version was exhibited at the International Exhibition of 1851, 'Among the productions of our native artists we must make special mention of . . . the "Titania" by Lough' (*The Illustrated Exhibiter*, no. 2, 14 June 1851, p. 22). The *Builder* commented on the display of Shakespearean works by Lough held at the British Institution in 1850, which included 'Titania, the fairy queen, . . . on the last occasion, the arrangement was particularly successful, and did honour to the sculptor to whom England may point with great satisfaction, we mean Mr. Lough . . . on pedestals on either side were ranged Mr. Lough's fine embodiments of some of his wonderful creations' (*Builder*, 22 November 1851, IX, no. 459, p. 743). A *Titania* of 1866 was formerly in the collection of William Hesketh Lever (*Lady Lever* 1999, p. 81). The model for this figure (which no longer survives) was amongst those bequeathed by the sculptor to the city of Newcastle-upon-Tyne, displayed at Elswick Hall, Newcastle-upon-Tyne from 1877 onwards (Robinson [n.d.], p. 75, no. 273). For a discussion of the fate of the Lough objects formerly at Elswick Hall, see Lough and Merson 1987, pp. 73–80.

Bibliography

Boase 1960, p. 283 and n. 30; Gunnis 1968, p. 244; Lough and Merson 1987, pp. 59, 84.

494: Jaques, from *As You Like It*

signed and dated 1865
Marble
h. 68.5 cm.
325–1867

Signed and dated on the base below the right foot of Jaques: J. C. LOUGH./1865.

Bequeathed by William Minshull Bigg, Esq., together with cat.nos. 492 and 493, in 1867. Transferred on loan from the Department of Architecture and Sculpture to Bethnal Green Museum in 1928; returned to the Department of Architecture and Sculpture, later the Sculpture Department, in 1987.

The subject is taken from Shakespeare's *As You Like It*, Act II, scene i. In the *Descriptive Catalogue of the Lough and Noble Models of Statues, Bas-Reliefs and Busts in Elswick Hall, Newcastle upon Tyne*, another version, presumably plaster is cited, (no. 31); see also entries for cat.nos. 492 and 493. For a discussion of the fate of the Lough objects formerly at Elswick Hall, see Lough and Merson 1987, pp. 73–80.

BIBLIOGRAPHY

Boase 1960, p. 283 and n. 30; Gunnis 1968, p. 244; Lough and Merson 1987, p. 84.

Richard Cockle Lucas

(b. Harnham Mill, Salisbury 1800 – d. Chilworth, near Romsey 1883)

Lucas is mainly known as a sculptor in wax and ivory, but he also worked in glass, marble and bronze, as well as being a painter; in his unpublished autobiography The Life of An Artist; Being the Autobiography of R.C. Lucas, Sculptor of Chilworth Tower, Hants *(held at Southampton, Collections of Southampton City Cultural Services), Lucas wrote, 'During my now long life I have had many fyttes [sic] of different pursuits'. Lucas began his career as an apprentice to his uncle, a cutler, where his skills as a carver were noticed. In his autobiography Lucas noted, 'I soon became proficient in the art of making scissors . . . I made twelve pairs of scissors so small that they were enclosed in a peach stone; this I elaborately carved . . . made hinges to it, wrote on its polished insides the Lord's Prayer so that it could be magnified and read, and sold it to a lady for a golden guinea'. He joined the Royal Academy Schools in 1828, training under Richard Westmacott (1775–1856). In 1865 he was granted a Civil List Pension of £150 aided by the support of his patron Lord Palmerston (a letter from Lord Palmerston to Earl Granville dated 10 July 1865, concerning a Civil List pension for Lucas in return for his gift of ivory carvings to the Museum, is in the National Art Library). Lucas recorded this in his* Essay on Art, *'then I wrought in ivory some of these specimens are wonderful, and I gave many of them to the South Kensington Museum (when Lord Palmerston gave me a pension), where they are now exhibited, and it is a comfort to me to live and yet be exhibited as an old master'. Lucas's gift in 1865 consisted of 22 ivories, 12 waxes, and the marble group catalogued below (inv.nos. 173 to 209–1865). Lucas exhibited frequently at the Royal Academy between 1829 and 1859.*

Lucas 1861, part 1, p. 12 (I am grateful to Karen Wardley and Lindsay Ford for their help with this reference); idem 1870; Graves V, pp. 105–7; Gunnis 1968, pp. 244–5; Pyke 1973, pp. 82–6; Thieme-Becker, 23, p. 433; British Museum 1999, pp. 118–9.

495: Sleep (formerly known as Mother and child)

about 1835
Marble
h. 40 cm.
209–1865

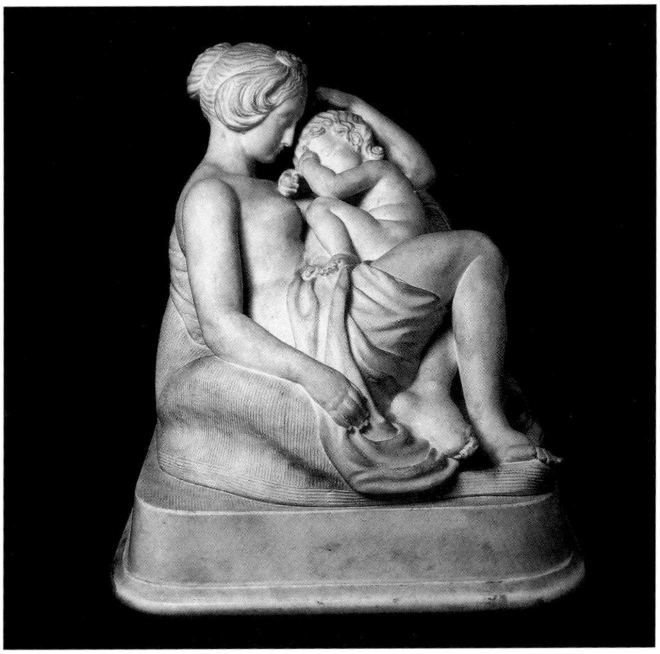

Given by the sculptor in 1865. Originally in the Bethnal Green Museum and transferred to the Circulation Department in 1963. Transferred to the Department of Architecture and Sculpture, later Sculpture Department, in 1966.

Though originally described as *Mother and Child* on departmental records, a photograph illustrating this group annotated, 'Sleep; marble in South Kensington Museum' is included in an album of 33 photographs taken and compiled by Lucas, and annotated as being in the South Kensington Museum, acquired by the Department of Prints, Drawings and Paintings in 1998 (inv.no. E.646:29–1998).

Bibliography
Graves V, p. 106, no. 901.

Exhibited
In 1865 Lucas exhibited a group entitled *Sleep* at the Royal Academy (no. 901), presumably the present piece.

496: Catherine, Lady Stepney, as Cleopatra (d.1845)

about 1836
Marble
h. 67.3 cm.
A.8–1964

Given by Miss A. Toomer, Wayside, Bickwell Valley, Sidmouth, in accordance with the wishes of the late Miss Dorothy Manners in 1964. Miss Manners was a descendant of Lady Stepney.

Correspondence relating to this bust, held in the Museum's registered papers, was also received at the time of acquisition. A letter from the artist David Wilkie (1785–1841) to Lady Stepney of 27 April 1836 records the installation of the bust at the Royal Academy, 'The bust of your Ladyship is placed on the right hand as you enter near the centre between the door and the window, Sir Francis Chantrey having taken as much care as he could of it. If the bust is adapted for that light, it is in other respects an excellent situation and on a level with the eye'.

A letter of 14 December 1909 from Stephen Manners (Lady Stepney's grandson) sent to Albert Durer Lucas (Cockle Lucas's son) refers to correspondence in the *Times* on his father's work, asking for information he might have, 'of these or of the replica of the marble bust which, as a boy, I remember stood in the entrance to the Coliseum in Regents Park', as well as the wax portrait of Lady Stepney also produced by Lucas, now also in the Victoria and Albert Museum (see below). A response from Albert Durer Lucas to Stephen Manners, dated 15 December 1909 does not refer to the Coliseum bust, but Lucas recalls, 'I well remember going with my father to Lady Stepney's house in Henrietta Street; and of her kindness, I have often thought. The bust and the little statue too, I remember, but have no memorandums of them'.

BIBLIOGRAPHY

Graves V, p. 106 (no. 1145); Gunnis 1968, p. 245; *Royal Academy* 1968, p. 105, no. 232; *Cleopatra* 2001, p. 350, cat.no. 372.

EXHIBITED

Lucas exhibited a bust of Lady Stepney at the Royal Academy in 1836 (no. 1145), presumably the present piece. He also exhibited a small full-length wax portrait (no. 1128), mentioned in the extracts from the correspondence cited above; this wax (inv.no. A.9–1964) was also bequeathed to the Museum at the same time as the present piece; *Royal Academy Bicentenary Exhibition 1768–1968*, 14 December 1968 to 2 March 1969, cat.no. 232; *Cleopatra of Egypt: From History to Myth*, British Museum, 10 April to 26 August 2001, cat.no. 372.

497: Thomas Willis Fleming (dates unknown)

signed and dated 1853
Marble
h. 48.5 cm.
A.7–1982

Inscribed on the rim at the top: THOS WILLIS FLEMING ESQ and signed: R.C. LUCAS SCF:
Inscribed on the rim below the portrait: GIVEN BY HIM TO CAROLINE HIS WIFE ON HER BIRTHDAY. 1853

Bequeathed by Miss Winifred Ellen Baylis in 1982.

No information has been found on the sitter.

LAWRENCE MACDONALD

(b. Gask 1799 – d. Rome 1878)

Gunnis recorded that Macdonald began his career apprenticed to a local mason, Thomas Gibson. In 1822 he entered the Trustees' Academy in Edinburgh, and later that year travelled to Rome. Gunnis recorded he became 'one of the founders of the British Academy of Arts in that city', where he was to remain almost permanently, until his death, and that 'He was one of the most popular portrait-sculptors of his day'. The writer of an article in the Art Journal *of 1854 noted that Macdonald's studio represented 'the peerage done into marble, a plaster galaxy of rank and fashion, row after row, in room after room, of noble and illustrious personages appear, until they become quite common as to quantity. All who ever figured in the "Court Journal" are here, looking as classical as drapery and hair-dressing can make them, otherwise indifferently so, certainly; yet, a potent family likeness pervades them all, it is perfectly astonishing: one really quite realises here the fact that they are all born of one common parent –* Macdonald *I mean, not* Adam*'. Greenwood records that 'Macdonald obtained the patronage of Prince Albert, for whose sculpture gallery at Osborne House he executed such ideal works such as* Hyacinthus*'. He exhibited at the Royal Academy between 1828 and 1857, and at the Royal Scottish Academy between 1832 and 1880, as well as at the 1851 International Exhibition. He was the father of the sculptor Alexander Macdonald (b. 1847).*

Art Journal, 1 October 1854, pp. 350–55; esp. p. 351 (cited by Gunnis, but incorrectly cited as Art Journal 1851); Graves V, pp. 134–5; Royal Scottish Academy 1991, III, pp. 115–6; Virtue and Vision 1991 [Smailes], pp. 64–71; TDA, 19, p. 878 [Greenwood].

498: Monument to Emily Georgiana, Lady Winchilsea (1809–1848)

signed and dated 1850
Marble
h. 180.3 cm.
A.188–1969

Signed and dated on the top of the couch: L. MACDONALD FECIT. ROMÆ./1850

Inscribed, in centred lettering on the front of the plinth: SACRED/TO THE MEMORY/OF/EMILY GEORGIANA/THE BELOVED WIFE/OF/GEORGE WILLIAM/EARL OF WINCHILSEA AND NOTTINGHAM/WHO/DIED JULY THE 10TH 1848/AGED 39 AND WAS/BURIED IN THE CHANCEL OF EWERBY CHURCH/LINCOLNSHIRE

Inscribed on the left side of the plinth: I/When the knell rung for the dying/Soundeth for me/And my corse coldly is lying/Neath the green tree

II/When the turf strangers are heaping/Covers my breast/Comes not to gaze on me weeping/I am at rest

Inscribed on the right side of plinth:

III/All my life coldly and sadly/The days have gone by/I who dreamed wildly and madly/Am happy to die

IV/Long since my heart has been breaking/Its pain is past/A time has been set to its aching/Peace comes at last/E.G.W. &. N.

Inscribed on the scroll held in her right hand: I AM HAPPY INDEED HAPPY IN THE WORD/GOD IS WAITING FOR ME

From the ruined church of St Mary, Eastwell, Kent, the south porch. Physick recorded, 'It was not damaged by the fall of the nave roof in 1951, but was exposed to the weather on its north side (front) until 1968' (Physick 1970, p. 136). Given by the Rector and Church wardens of the Parish of Eastwell with Broughton Aluph together with cat.nos. 15, 16, 18, and 48 in 1969 (see Physick 1970 [Eastwell] for a full account of the Eastwell monuments).

Lady Winchilsea, daughter of the Governor General of Canada, the Rt. Hon. Sir Charles Bagot, G.C.B., (1781–1843) was the second wife of George Finch-Hatton, the tenth Earl of Winchilsea and Nottingham.

Described by Gunnis as 'His most successful statue . . . which shows the lady reclining, like Madame Recamier, on a day-bed. The work is graceful and charming and, though not carved until 1850, has all the distinction and elegance of the Regency' (Gunnis 1968, p. 248).

BIBLIOGRAPHY
Gunnis 1968, p. 248; Physick 1970 [Eastwell], pp. 135–6, no. 5. fig. 16; *Virtue and Vision* 1991 [Smailes], p. 68; TDA, 19, p. 878 [Greenwood].

499: Eleanor Watt (d.1904)

signed and dated 1861; begun 1859
Marble
h. (incl. socle) 67 cm.
252–1904

Signed on the truncation at the back: L. MACDONALD.FECIT. ROMÆ. 1861.

Bequeathed by the sitter in 1904. Transferred on loan to the Bethnal Green Museum from the Department of Architecture and Sculpture in 1928; returned to the Sculpture Department in 1987.

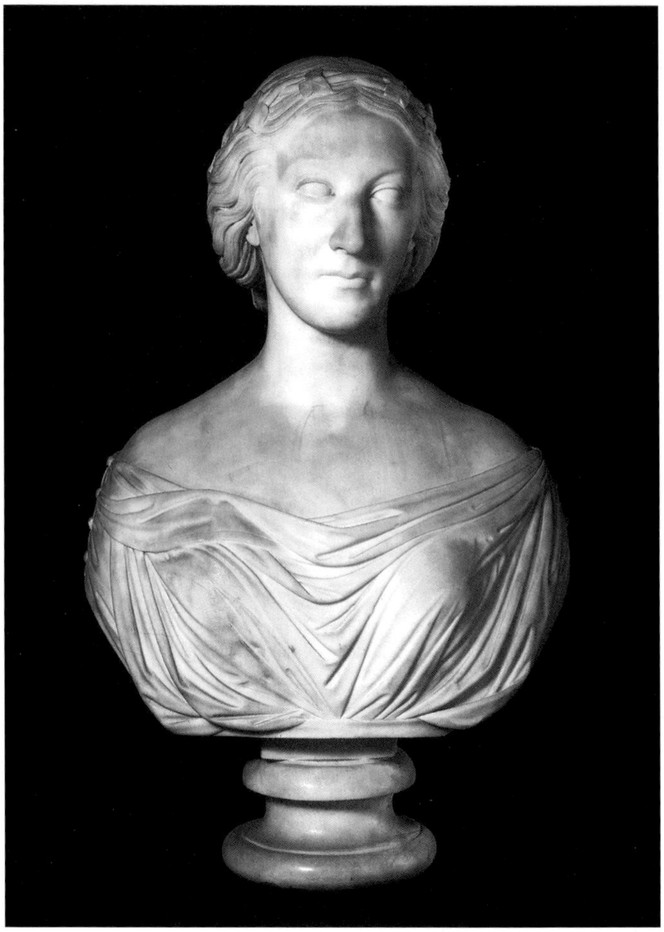

Although the present piece is dated 1861, the sitter recorded in her will that it was 'done by Macdonald at Rome in the year 1859'. Mrs Watt's bequest to the Museum also included a number of Japanese bronzes, together with items of lacquer work, enamel and porcelain. Documentation relating to its acquisition records that the bust was 'characteristic of the period . . . we would also like to have the bust, as a nucleus is being formed of portraits, busts, &c of benefactors to the Museum. Somewhere, in the new building, a place could be found for exhibiting them together'.

BIBLIOGRAPHY
Gunnis 1968, p. 249.

Patrick Macdowell R.A.

(b. Belfast 1799 – d. London 1870)

After initially being apprenticed to a London coachbuilder, MacDowell trained under the sculptor Peter Francis Chenu (b. 1760 – d. after 1822). Gunnis recorded that in 1830, on the recommendation of John Constable, MacDowell attended the Royal Academy Schools, 'but, once there, he made such rapid progress that only two years later he had a well-merited and secure reputation as a sculptor'. He exhibited at the Royal Academy between 1822 and 1870, and at the Royal Hibernian Academy of Arts between 1843 and 1863. Turpin observes that his most important work is the memorial to Frederick Richard Chichester, Earl of Belfast (d. 1853) in Belfast Castle, which 'combines observation and sentiment within a neo-classical format'. He is however perhaps best known for his group depicting Europe *for the Albert Memorial in Kensington Gardens; for the Albert Memorial model, see entry for cat.no. 531.*

Graves V, pp. 136–8; Strickland 1913, II, pp. 59–63; Gunnis 1968, pp. 249–50; Royal Hibernian Academy II, p. 221; Thieme-Becker, 23, p. 510; TDA, 19, p. 879 [Turpin].

500: Eve

signed and dated 1850
Marble on granite pedestal
h. 121.5 cm.
29–1886

Signed on the side of the base beneath the tree trunk: P. MAC DOWELL R.A. SCULP. *LONDON*/1850

Bequeathed by Mrs Dorothy De la Fosse in 1885. Transferred on loan to the Bethnal Green Museum from the Department of Architecture and Sculpture, later Sculpture Department in 1928; returned to the Sculpture Department at a date not recorded.

The first finger of the right hand has been broken and repaired.

Thomas Armstrong [q.v.] wrote in 1886, 'The artistic value of this marble replica is not as great as that of the cast we already possess but I think we should accept it if no conditions are imposed'. The cast referred to by Armstrong is in fact the plaster model for this statue on loan from the Royal Collection (loan no. 76), originally lent by King Edward VII, it was returned in 1999.

A letter from the sculptor dated 31 October 1850 from his address at 75 Margaret Street, Cavendish Square, where he resided from 1838 onwards, was included in the acquisition documentation, presumably given by the donor's executor, her husband Colonel H. De la Fosse C.B. Although the recipient of the letter is not named, the fact that it was owned by the De la Fosse family suggests the donor and her husband were the original owners of the figure:

'My dear Sir

When would you like the statue sent to your house? She is both ready and willing to change her abode, as at present she is little more than "an unprotected female"'.

However, Gunnis recorded that a version of *Eve* was sold on 7 July 1877 by an anonymous owner at Christie's for £189; it was described in the catalogue as 'life-size statue from the Manley Hall Collection', lot 37 (Gunnis 1968, p. 249). The purchaser is noted as 'Barry' in an annotated copy of the sale catalogue held in the National Art Library.

MacDowell exhibited the model for this figure entitled 'Eve, His words replete with guile, etc. Paradise Lost' at the Royal Academy in 1849, no. 1119, presumably the plaster now in the Royal Collection. In its review of the Royal Academy exhibition, the *Art Journal* commented, 'The subject is the temptation of Eve, who stands with the right arm raised, the hand resting on the head. She is supported against a tree, round which the serpent is twined. We have never seen such a piece of sculpture containing so little allusive accessory, in which the subject was so clearly defined. We see at once that it is Eve, – she listens to the voice of the Tempter, whose

'. . . words replete with guile
Into her heart too easy entrance won'.

She is lost in thought on the import of what she has heard; – the pose is easy and natural, and in the proportions of the figure we behold the recognition of living graces in preference to everlasting conventionality' (*Art Journal*, 1 June 1849, p. 176).

The *Athenaeum* also wrote at length on this figure (*Athenaeum*, 26 May 1849, no. 1126, pp. 549–50). The plaster model was also exhibited at the 1851 International Exhibition and at Dublin in 1853 (no. 1168); for the 1851 Exhibition see *Jury Reports* 1851, p. 1551. In its review of the 1851 British Institution exhibition, the *Art Journal* recorded: 'A "Marble Statue of Eve", by P. MACDOWELL, R.A., is the admirable statue which was exhibited at the Royal Academy the season before last. It is smaller than the plaster, but here, nevertheless, the purity and elegance of the conception are fully developed by the minute finish, of which marble is susceptible. The subject is, properly, the Temptation of Eve; the serpent has attached itself to the tree, by which she stands and – "Pausing awhile to herself she mused". The play of line on the right side of the figure is marked by a flowing grace, which is beyond description' (*Art Journal*, 1 March 1851, p. 75). What appears to be a plaster version was exhibited at the South Kensington Museum, in July 1857, and its merits were discussed in an article in the *Building News*, when Eve was described as 'a figure of surpassing excellence, conceived in the purest style of which plastic art is susceptible. For our own part we unhesitatingly pronounce it infinitely superior to any single statue ever produced by Canova, for it is devoid of the mannerism and voluptuousness of expression that characterises most of the works of that great artist. Although the figure is entirely nude, it does not offend the eye by anything approaching to

500

meretriciousness, and there is a charming innocence of expression in the countenance. If fault is to be found at all, it is with the outline of the statue on its right side, from the uplifted arm downwards, which is open to improvement. The right knee and leg also want anatomical development, and the ancle [sic] is evidently too thick. These defects, however, we are convinced were not in the original clay model of the artist, but, we presume, are attributable to the process of moulding or casting in the production of the figure in plaster' (*Building News*, 17 July 1857, p. 740; reference kindly supplied by Anthony Burton; see also enties for cat.nos. 271, 272, 274, 276, and 392).

BIBLIOGRAPHY

Athenaeum 1849 (marble version); *Bequests and Donations* 1901, p. 30; Graves V, p. 137, no. 937; Strickland 1913, II, p. 63; Gunnis 1968, p. 250; Read 1982, p. 13; Thieme-Becker, 23, p. 510; Murphy 1999, p. 71, fig. 4, and n. 71 and 73.

EXHIBITED

A marble version, presumably the present piece, was exhibited at the Royal Academy in 1865, no. 937. In its review of the exhibition, the *Art Journal* considered the figure warranted 'a fair meed of praise . . . after the manner of modern romance, graceful and refined' (*Art Journal*, 1 June 1865, p. 172; see also the *Athenaeum*, 27 May 1865, no. 1961, p. 723).

501: Sir Joshua Jebb K.C.B. (1793–1863)

about 1865
Marble
h. (incl. socle) 81 cm.
550–1883

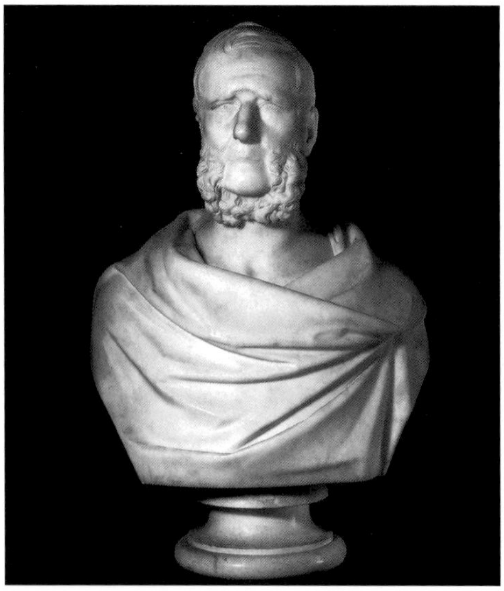

The present bust may have been lent to the Museum prior to its acquisition. What was described as a 'Marble bust' is recorded as on loan to the Museum before 1870 by a 'Lady A. Jebb' (*List* 1870, p. vi). Given by Lady Amelia Jebb, widow of the sitter, in 1883. Transferred from the Bethnal Green Museum to the Sculpture Department in 1987.

Sir Joshua Jebb was Surveyor General of Prisons, responsible in part for the construction of Pentonville, described as the 'Model prison', and for designing the prison in Portland, the Isle of Wight

(*DNB* 1973, X, pp. 698–9). This bust is a posthumous portrait, probably commissioned by the sitter's widow.

BIBLIOGRAPHY

Bequests and Donations 1901, p. 180; Graves V, p. 137, no. 935; Strickland 1913, II, p. 62; Gunnis 1968, p. 250; Kilmurray 1979, p. 120.

EXHIBITED

In 1865 MacDowell exhibited a posthumous marble bust of Sir Joshua Jebb, presumably the present piece (no. 935).

502: Richard Perrott (dates unknown)

signed and dated 1870
Marble
h. (incl. socle) 67 cm.
718–1902

Signed and dated on the back: P. MACDOWALL, R.A/SCULP/1870.
Inscribed on the front of the socle: RICHARD PERROTT, ESQ.

Given by F.D. Perrott, Esq., 6 Middle Temple Lane, The Temple, London son of the sitter, together with cat.no. 503. Transferred on loan from the Department of Architecture and Sculpture, now Sculpture Department in 1928 to Bethnal Green Museum; returned to the Sculpture Department in 1987.

This portrait bust was commissioned from the sculptor together with its pendant, a bust of his wife cat.no. 503. They are possibly amongst the last commissions undertaken by MacDowell, who died in the same year they were executed. It is not known whether they were produced for a special purpose; the donor described his father and mother as 'private persons'. Nothing further is known of the sitters.

In his letter offering the busts to the Museum, the donor recorded the fact that MacDowell, even at the age of 71, was still actively involved in his work, 'I remember as a child that I heard Macdowall [sic] say – the bust of my father was one of his best, and I know it was asked for Exhibition purposes'.

BIBLIOGRAPHY

Gunnis 1968, p. 250.

503: Mrs Richard Perrott (dates unknown)

signed and dated 1870
Marble
h. (incl. socle) 68 cm.
719–1902

Signed and dated on the back: P. MACDOWALL, R.A./SCULP/1870.
Inscribed on the front of socle: MRS RICHARD PERROTT.

Given by F.D. Perrott, Esq., 6 Middle Temple Lane, The Temple, London, son of the sitter, together with cat.no. 502. Transferred on loan from the Department of Architecture and Sculpture, now Sculpture Department in 1928 to Bethnal Green Museum; returned to the Sculpture Department in 1987.

See entry for cat.no. 502.

BIBLIOGRAPHY

Gunnis 1968, p. 250.

Baron Carlo Marochetti R.A.

(b. Turin 1805 – d. Passy, Paris 1867)

Marochetti initially studied in Paris, where he was resident, intermittently returning to Italy between 1822 and 1827. Following the 1848 Revolution, Marochetti settled in England; he produced a number of public monuments and became a favourite of royalty, producing the effigies of Queen Victoria and Prince Albert for Frogmore, Windsor. He exhibited at the Royal Academy between 1851 and 1867. He was elected as a Royal Academician in 1866. Plaster busts of Sir Anthony Panizzi and William Makepeace Thackeray, on loan to the Museum from 1868, were returned to a descendant of the sculptor in 2001.

Graves V, pp. 187–8; Thieme-Becker, 24, p. 126; TDA, 20, pp. 454–5 [Ward-Jackson]; Ward-Jackson 2000.

504: George Washington (1732–1799)

about 1851–3
Plaster
h. 63.5 cm.
1152–1868

Given by the Baroness Marochetti, the sculptor's widow, in 1868, together with cat.no. 505.

George Washington was the first President of the United States, elected in 1789; he retired as President in 1797. Calderini recorded that Marochetti produced a colossal equestrian monument to Washington for the 1855 New York Exhibition (the exhibition actually took place in 1853); it was destroyed by fire (Calderini 1928, pp. 31, 59 and note 1). An engraving and appraisal of the equestrian statue of Washington by Marochetti was reproduced in the *Illustrated London News*, 6 August 1853, XXIII, no. 636, p. 72; reference kindly supplied by Philip Ward-Jackson.

A related small-scale bronze, a reduction of the New York equestrian figure of Washington by Marochetti, was illustrated by Calderini and was said to be located in the Castello Marochetti at Vaux (Calderini 1928, pl. XXIX): it was later in the Château de Cheverny in the possession of the Comtesse de Vibraye, a distant relative of Marochetti (information kindly supplied by Philip Ward-Jackson). The present bust does not seem to be related to the equestrian monument.

Bibliography

Bequests and Donations 1901, p. 195.

505: Gioacchino (Antonio) Rossini (1792–1868)

about 1864
Plaster
h. 161.3 cm.
1153–1868

Given by the Baroness Marochetti, the sculptor's widow, in 1868, together with cat.no. 504.

The original bronze monument to the composer Rossini, for which this is the model, is located in the Liceo Musicale Rossini, Pesaro; it was donated by Gustave Delahante and José di Salamanca, and inaugurated on 21 August 1864. Philip Ward-Jackson has suggested that the portrait may have been taken from a photographic *carte de visite*.

506: Sir John Charles Robinson (1824–1913)

about 1864–5
Bronze
h. 38.5 cm.
A.202–1929

Given by the family of Sir John Charles Robinson in 1929.

Original acquisition information records that R.P. Bedford [q.v.] considered 'it would be interesting to have a portrait of a man who has done so much towards forming our collections'. In the introduction to the *Catalogue of Italian Sculpture* in the Museum, published in 1932, it is noted that the bust was originally shown 'in close proximity to the Italian sculpture which he collected' (Maclagan and Longhurst 1932, p. viii). It is now displayed in the offices of the Sculpture Department.

In 1853 Robinson was appointed the first Keeper of the Museum of Ornamental Art at Marlborough House, a predecessor of the South Kensington, later Victoria and Albert Museum, where he was instrumental in the formation of the collections, particularly sculpture and metalwork. Following disagreements highlighted by the Board's refusal to give Robinson the title of Director, he resigned as Keeper but was retained as Art Referee; he retired from the Museum in 1868 (see Maclagan and Longhurst 1932, pp. vii-viii; Bonython 1982 [Cole], pp. 44–5; TDA, 26, pp. 472–3 [Davies]; *Grand Design* 1997, pp. 151–4, 157–9).

Robinson was a friend of Marochetti from the late 1850s (recorded in Robinson papers in the Ashmolean Museum, Oxford). A bronzed plaster version was given by a descendant of Robinson to the Ashmolean Museum in 1998 (inv.no. WA 1998.183). Robinson and Marochetti were also founding members of the Collector's or Fine Arts Club (Eatwell 1994, p. 25).

Bibliography

Maclagan and Longhurst 1932, p. viii, p. xiii plate; Baker 1984 [Robinson], p. 341, fig. 2; Davies 1992, II, fig. 10; Eatwell 1994, fig. 1 on p. 26; Trusted 1996 [Spanish], p. 4, fig. 2; Williamson 1996, p. 11, p. 9, fig. 1.

Robert Wallace Martin

(b. London 1843 – d. Southall, London 1923)

Robert Wallace Martin (known as Wallace Martin) was principally a potter, active from the 1860s. He studied alongside George Tinworth [q.v.], who was to become his life-long friend, at the Lambeth School of Art and the Royal Academy schools. During 1871 Martin worked briefly for the Watcombe Terra-Cotta Co. Ltd [q.v.], based in Torquay. In 1877 he established a pottery works at Southall, in partnership with his three younger brothers, under the name of R.W. Martin & Bros, which became chiefly known for its original use of stoneware, branded 'Martin-ware'. Robert Wallace Martin acted as the sculptor and modeller; he was left the sole survivor of the brothers on the death of Edwin Bruce Martin in 1915. He exhibited at the Royal Academy between 1863 and 1888. Beard commented, 'Necessity made him a potter; his genius made him a great potter. But he was first and always a sculptor'. Records relating to the Martin Brothers business are held at the Ealing Local History Library.

Beard 1936; Haslam 1978; Bergesen 1991, pp. 172–9; Thieme-Becker, 24, p. 162; TDA, 20, p. 485 [Mawer].

507: Queen Victoria **(b.1819; r.1837–1901)**

signed and dated 1899
Terracotta
h. 59.2 cm. w. 46.8 cm.
A.4–1943

Signed on the truncation at the bottom: R·Wallace Martin·Sc·1899·

Originally commissioned by the Museum but rejected, the relief remained in the possession of the firm until it was purchased by Mr Maurice J. Isaacs from the sale of Martinware held at Sotheby's 25 October 1924, lot 54. Originally offered to the Museum for sale by Mr Isaacs in September 1938 at the price of £5 5s (5 guineas), described in correspondence as 'a quarter the amount arranged by your Council and the late Mr Martin'. Isaacs went on to record, 'I was informed by his brother Edwin [Edwin Bruce Martin (1860–1915)], that it was cancelled, through a complaint, which caused offence, & that this plaque was the only one of a celebrated personage . . . executed by the Martin Bros'. The offer to purchase the relief from Mr Isaacs was declined; the relief was later given to the Museum by Mr Isaacs, 8 Blomfield Street, Upper Westbourne Terrace, London in 1943.

Four holes have been drilled into the two sides and bottom of the relief.

Robert Wallace Martin was commissioned by the Museum to produce this relief, which was to commemorate the laying of the foundation stone of the Museum by Queen Victoria on 17 May 1899, the last public state ceremony she attended (see Physick 1982, pp. 213–4).

In a letter from Mr Isaacs at the time of its gift to the Museum, he wrote of the circumstances of the sale, 'I have a faint recollection of hearing, this was the stock of the Mr Martin, who died some time previous to this Sale. The Mr Martin whose acquaintance (through sitting next to him at the Sale) I made, did not have any interest, only attended to see what these items fetched, & advised me to buy the Plaque, telling me after the Sale, it was ordered for the V.&.A. Museum, & through the Purchaser criticising it, they refused delivery, which was to have been erected on the Wall just inside the Main Entrance'.

Beard recorded that 'Wallace was always the sculptor and portraitist of the family' and that his 'revived interest in portraiture had one interesting result', that of the portrait medallion of Queen Victoria, based on a well-known contemporary photograph of Victoria taken in 1897 by Bassano. Beard recorded that this relief was 'completed and fired in 1899 . . . Thereafter it was submitted to the authorities at the Museum for approval. Only one fault was found with it – it was not coloured. Wallace always hated criticism by those whom he considered unfit to pass artistic judgment, and in a fit of anger he put the plaque under his arm and marched out of the building. Later he gave orders for its destruction. Fortunately for future generations he did not insist upon this act of vandalism being carried out, and the plaque remained in the possession of the firm until the dispersal of the Martin Collection at Sotheby's in October, 1924. It is now in private possession, and it is to be hoped that it may one day find its way back, if not to the position which it was originally intended that it should occupy, at least to the great institution for which it was designed' (Beard 1936, p. 29).

Bibliography

Beard 1936, p. 29.

508: Ecce homo

dated 1914
Terracotta in a glazed wood frame
h. 9.5 cm.
A.7–1974

Inscribed into the dry clay on the underside of the truncation: Southall·1914 (I am grateful to Charlotte Hubbard for confirming this). A label on the back of the frame has the typed information: 'ECCE HOMO. Modelled by Wallace Martin, the Art Pottery, Southall.'

Given by Miss N.V. Wade, 14 Warfield Crescent, Waterlooville, Portsmouth in 1974, together with 17 examples of pottery from the Martin Brothers studio and photographic material, which are under the charge of the Department of Ceramics and Glass.

This present piece is one of a small number of figurative works produced by Wallace Martin. It is perhaps influenced by the sculptor Alexander Munro (1825–1871), for whom he had worked in the 1860s, or Jean-Charles Cazin (1841–1901), the sculptor and potter who taught Martin during his period at the Lambeth School of Art (Bergesen 1991, p. 178).

Felix Martin Miller

(b. 1820; active 1842 – 1880)

In Sculptors of the Day, *published in 1880, Miller is recorded as being at the Art School, South Kensington Museum: he was Master in the Modelling Class from about 1860 to 1880. He exhibited at the Royal Academy between 1842 and 1880, and at the British Institution between 1847 and 1866. Mentioned in the obituary of the sculptor John Henry Foley [q.v.] in the* Art Journal *of 1874, Miller was described as 'one of the few sculptors whose genius is manifest and who has produced works, chiefly bas-reliefs, that are unsurpassed by any productions of their class in modern Art: Foley thought so well of Miller that he commissioned more than one of his works in marble: indeed, the great artist was the principal patron of his struggling brother-artist'. The writer continued, 'if we are the means of directing the attention of Art-patrons to an artist who in his special department is unsurpassed, but whose evil fortune it has been to obtain much praise with little recompense'.*

Art Journal, October 1874, p. 306; Hooe 1880, p. 17; Graves V, pp. 249–51; Gunnis 1968, pp. 259–60; Physick 1982, pp. 141–2; Beattie 1983, pp. 12, 14, 16; Thieme-Becker, 24, p. 562.

509: Ariel

signed; about 1850–5
Marble, partly gilt
h. (incl. frame) 112 cm h. (relief) 99 cm.
2638–1856

Signed at the bottom left hand corner: F.M.MILLER.SC.
Inscribed at the bottom: ARIEL

Purchased from the Paris International Exhibition of 1855 for £50.

The subject is taken from Shakespeare's *The Tempest*.

EXHIBITED
Paris International Exhibition of 1855.
The subject was one used by Miller in a number of compositions exhibited at the Royal Academy between 1850 and 1870 (see Graves V, pp. 250–1). In 1852 Miller exhibited 'Ariel bas-relief in marble etc' (Graves V, p. 250, no. 1362), possibly the present piece. In 1867 the gem-engraver James Ronca (b. 1826–d. after 1908) exhibited 'Ariel; from a medallion by F.M. Miller', (*idem* VI, p. 356, no. 1108). In the same year he exhibited a further work inspired by Miller; see entry for cat.no. 510.

510: David Livingstone (1813–1873)

signed and dated 1857
Plaster
h. 72.5 cm.
349–1872

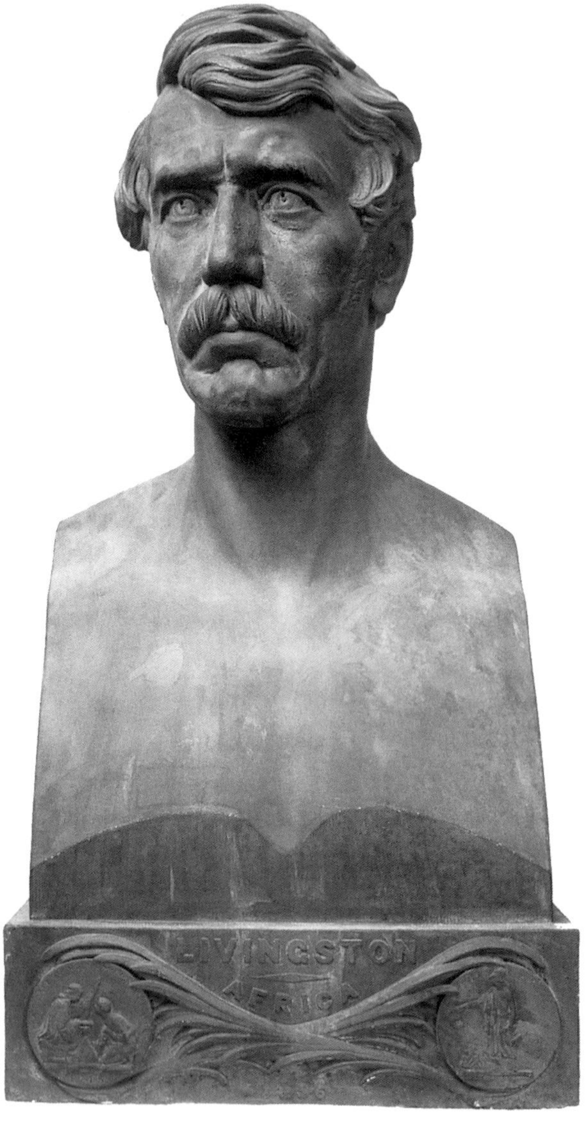

Signed and dated on the back: F·M·Miller/1857
Inscribed on the front: LIVINGSTONE/AFRICA/1856

Given by the sculptor in 1872 together with cat.no. 511.

This plaster bust of the explorer David Livingstone was said to have been 'modelled from life shortly after his return from Africa in 1856'. The two medallions on the base depict allegorical scenes. The left hand medallion is inscribed: PRÆDICATE EVANGELIUM· OMN[I] CREATURAE (preach the gospel to all creatures) and in the exergue L.M.S.; and the right hand medallion: TERRAS RECLUSAS (distant lands) and in the exergue R.C.S. or R.G.S.

Versions of the bust, dated 1867, omitting the base containing the medallions, were produced by Minton (see Atterbury 1989, p. 123, fig. 443; shape 443).

In 1857 Miller exhibited a bust of Livingstone at the Royal Academy (Graves V, p. 250, no. 1329). He showed a further 'cabinet bust of Dr Livingstone' a year later in 1858 (no. 1287). The gem-engraver James Ronca (b. 1826; d. after 1908) exhibited at the Royal Academy in 1867 'The late Dr Livingstone; from a bust by F.M. Miller' (Graves IV, p. 356, no. 1106). In the same year he showed another work inspired by Miller; see entry for cat.no. 509.

BIBLIOGRAPHY
Bequests and Donations 1901, p. 202.

511: Samuel Taylor Coleridge (1772–1834)

signed; about 1862
Plaster
h. 81 cm.
348–1872

Inscribed on the back truncation of the bust:
S.T. COLERIDGE/F.M.MILLER.Sc

Given by the sculptor in 1872 together with cat.no. 510.

A posthumous bust of the poet and philosophical writer, Samuel Taylor Coleridge was exhibited by Miller at the Royal Academy in 1862 (Graves V, p. 250, no. 1052).

BIBLIOGRAPHY
Bequests and Donations 1901, p. 202.

512: Engineer's blacksmith

signed; 1866
Tinted plaster
h. 103 cm.
304–1876

Signed on the base at the back: F.M. MILLER/SC

Given by the sculptor in 1876.

At the time of acquisition of this relief Miller was a teacher of modelling at the National Art Training School, South Kensington (later Royal College of Art).

BIBLIOGRAPHY
Bequests and Donations 1901, p. 202.

513: Hero signalling to Leander

signed; 1873
Plaster, painted and partly gilt
h. (excl. frame) 109 cm. w. (excl. frame) 51.1 cm.
114–1877

Signed in the centre at the bottom of the relief, beneath the shell detail: F.M. MILLER

Given by the sculptor in 1877.

This plaster relief is painted to imitate terracotta. On acquisition it was said to date from 1873. It depicts the legend of Hero and Leander, in which Leander, swimming across the waters at night to meet his lover Hero, is drowned (see Hall 1980, p. 154).

EXHIBITED
In 1843 Miller had exhibited at the Royal Academy 'Hero and Leander; sketch for an alto-relievo "On her lover's bosom breathed her last"', (Graves V, p. 249, no. 1471), perhaps an early variant of the present piece. In 1874 Miller exhibited 'Hero signalling to Leander; at the base the curtain of night is upraised showing the episode, etc.' (*ibid.*, p. 251, no. 1442), possibly the present piece.

HENRIETTA SKERRETT MONTALBA

(b. London 1856 – d. Venice 1893)

An obituary in the Art Journal *recording the death of Henrietta Skerret Montalba noted that she was 'the youngest of the brilliant quartette [sic] of artist-sisters so well known to the British and Continental public. Miss Henrietta Montalba followed Art in many forms; but unlike her sisters was most assiduous and successful in sculpture'. Henrietta's painter sisters were Clara, Hilda and Ellen, all of whom exhibited at the Royal Academy; the Montalba family moved from Kensington to Italy during the latter part of the nineteenth century. Beattie recorded that Montalba studied at the National Art Training School some time between 1868 and 1877, and that 'Only one sculpture student from South Kensington, Henrietta Montalba, emerged with credit during that period'; during 1868 she studied alongside Princess Louise [q.v.] in the modelling classes. Following her time at South Kensington, Montalba studied at the Scuola delle Belle Arti in Venice, and whilst he was resident in London, she worked under the French sculptor Jules Dalou [q.v.]. The bulk of her work were portrait busts executed mainly in terracotta. She exhibited at the Royal Academy between 1875 and 1893, and at the Glasgow International Exhibition of 1888.*

Art Journal, December 1893, p. 363; Hepworth-Dixon 1894; Graves V, pp. 273–4; DNB 1973, XIII, pp. 724–5; Beattie 1983, p. 18; Petteys 1985, p. 503; Thieme-Becker, 25, p. 79.

514: Venetian boy catching a crab

signed; about 1893
Bronze
h. 75 cm.
A.20–2000

Signed in the rocks beneath the left leg of the figure: Henrietta.S.Montalba

On loan to the Bethnal Green Museum from Miss Clara Montalba, 11 Campden House Mews, Campden Hill, London, from 16 October 1905. Clara Montalba (1842–1929) was the sculptor's sister, and a painter in her own right. She appears to have been the last surviving member of the Montalba family: attempts to locate any heirs in 1968 and 1976 were unsuccessful. Transferred from Bethnal Green Museum to the Department of Architecture and Sculpture, later Sculpture Department, in 1978. As a redundant loan the present piece was formally accessioned by the Sculpture Department in 2000.

The crab appears to have been cast from life. According to the obituary of the sculptor in the *Art Journal*, the figure depicts a Venetian fisher-boy (Hepworth-Dixon 1894, p. 216).

BIBLIOGRAPHY
Chicago Exhibition 1893, p. 271, cat.no. 30; Hepworth-Dixon 1894, pp. 215–6, illus. on p. 217; Graves V, p. 274, no. 1674; *DNB* 1973, XIII, p. 724.

EXHIBITED
Royal Academy 1893, no. 1674; Chicago Exhibition 1893, World's Columbian Exposition, Department K, Group CXXXIX, Fine Arts, Painting, Sculpture, Architecture, and Decoration, cat.no. 30; exhibited by Montalba when resident at Palazzo Trevisan, 809 Campo St. Agnese, Venice.

Raffaelle Monti

(b. Iseo 1818 – d. London 1881)

The son of a sculptor, Monti was trained in Milan, but came to London in 1846, and eventually settled there from 1848 until his death. His speciality was the carving in marble of illusionistic veiled figures, and he undertook a number of commissions for English patrons, as well as executing decorative sculpture for the grounds of the reconstructed Crystal Palace at Sydenham. He also became involved with the production of electrotypes for Elkington's, and executed the largest known electrotype monument in 1861, an equestrian statue of Charles Stuart, 3rd Marquess of Londonderry (Durham, market-place). Towards the end of his life he carried out work for Copelands Statuary Porcelain, and designed silver for the firm of C.F.Hancock.

Radcliffe 1965; Thieme-Becker, 25, p. 95; TDA, 22, pp. 27–8 [Ward-Jackson].

515: The sleep of sorrow and the dream of joy (an allegory of the Italian risorgimento)

signed and dated 1861
Marble
h. 175.3 cm.
A.3–1964

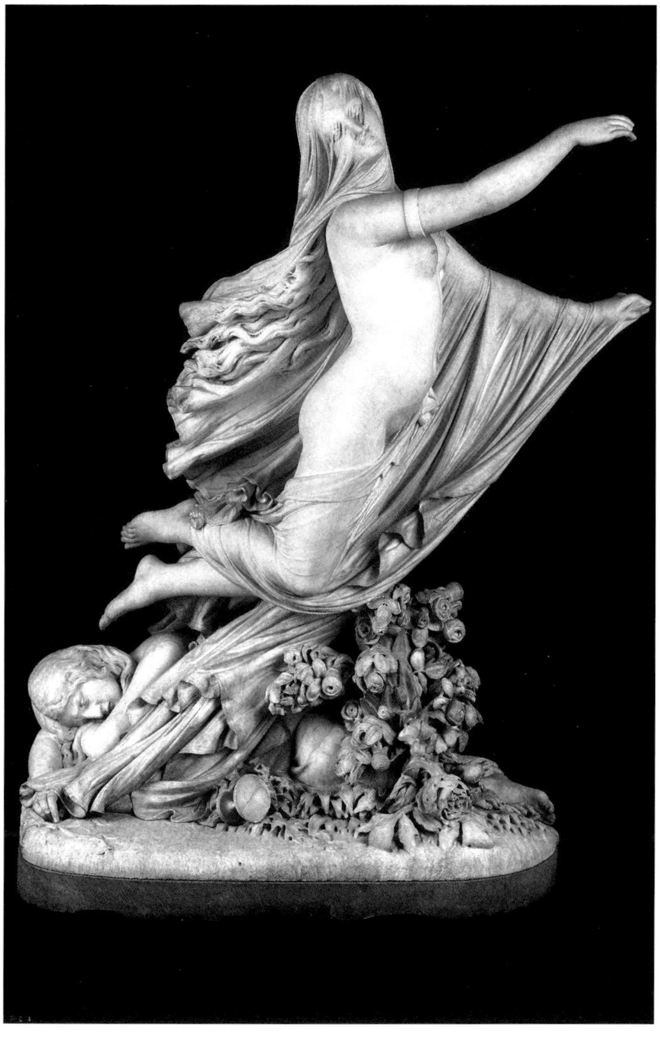

Signed on the base at the back: MONTI/1861

Shown at the International Exhibition, London of 1862. Possibly purchased from the exhibition by Mr Nottage, Chairman of the London Stereoscopic Company (see below). At a later date in the possession of the Croft family, Fanhams Hall, near Ware, Hertfordshire. In the collection of Anne, Lady Brocket of Fanhams Hall, and on her death sold by order of the Fanhams Estate Co. Ltd and Major R.A. Page Croft. Bought by Dr Hoda from the Sotheby's sale of Fanhams Hall contents on the final day's sale, 5 October 1950 (sale began on 2 October), included in the contents of the Winter Garden as lot 1000, for £5. In a letter written by Mrs Hoda in 1962, she noted that the figure was originally bought for £1200: 'I simply repeat what I was told by the late Lord Croft whom I met during the sale.' Purchased by the Museum from Mrs Sara S. Hoda, 1 Broomhill Walk, Woodford Green, Essex, in 1964 for £300.

The subject of this sculpture was a topical comment on the contemporary political situation in Italy, following the formation of the Kingdom of Italy, proclaimed on 17 March 1861. A biography of Monti in the *Illustrated London News* accompanying a discussion of the present group when exhibited at the 1862 International Exhibition, recorded, 'Returning to Milan [from England], he joined the Popular party and, as one of the chiefs of the National Guard of Milan, was sent in the following year on a mission to the camp of Charles Albert. On the defeat of that Monarch he fled to this country, and has since enjoyed great and deserved popularity' (*Illustrated London News*, 27 September 1862, XLI, no. 1166, p. 346, illus. on p. 345). J.B. Waring's contemporary publication *Masterpieces of Industrial Art & Sculpture of the International Exhibition, 1862,* published in 1863, commented on the symbolism of the sculpture in relation to recent political events (see Waring 1863, pl. 231 and opp. page). The images in this publication, including that of the present group, were taken by the London Photographic and Stereoscopic Company. The image of Monti's group was later acquired by the Museum, and is now in the Department of Prints, Drawings and Paintings (inv.no. E.1306–1992, no. 61). Also included in the Fanhams Hall sale (see provenance above) was another sculpture from the 1862 International Exhibition, *La Leggitrice* (*The Reading Girl*) by Pietro Magni (1817–1877), which was sold as lot 1001 for £5 to Lady Pearson; it was recently sold in the Sotheby's, London sale held on 5 July 2000, lot 148. Unlike that of the Monti group, the provenance of the Magni figure is recorded. Purchased after the 1862 exhibition from the Italian Ministero della Pubblica Instruzione by Mr Nottage, Chairman of the London Stereoscopic

Company, it then passed from his collection to the Croft family, where it was sold at the Fanhams Hall sale in 1950. It is likely that the Monti, which was in the same collection as the Magni by 1950, shared the same provenance (departmental records).

The present work had remained untraced since its exhibition in 1862 until 1962, when the then owner Mrs Hoda contacted the Museum on hearing of the 1862 centenary exhibition to be held at the Museum that year. She lent the group, which had been kept outside in her garden, to the commemorative exhibition, and subsequently offered it to the Museum for purchase.

Parian ware versions dated 1871 and 1875 respectively were produced for the Ceramic and Crystal Palace Art Union (Atterbury 1989, fig. 507 on p. 148). For a full discussion of the group see Radcliffe 1965.

Bibliography

International Exhibition 1862, p. 258, no. 2376; Waring 1863, pl. 231 and opp. page; *Art Journal* 1866; Molesworth 1951, pl. LV; Radcliffe 1965; Evers 1966, pp. 157, 167–8; Cogo 1996, p. 300, fig. 112 on p. 299; Williamson 1996 [Kader], p. 174, illus. on p. 175; TDA, 22, p. 28 and illus. [Ward-Jackson]; Boström 2000, p. 155, fig. 5 on p. 154.

Exhibited

International Exhibition of 1862, London, class XXXIX, Italian Division, no. 2376; *The International Exhibition of 1862*, Victoria and Albert Museum, 20 July to 30 September 1962.

Samuel Moutrie

(dates unknown; active 1869)

Little is known about the sculptor of the present piece other than his address: 219 Stanhope Street, Hampstead Road, London. Moutrie was presumably an amateur sculptor who exhibited at the Society of Arts Art-Workmanship Competition of 1869.

516: Female head

1869
Marble on gilt wood mount
h. 18 cm.
104–1870

Purchased from Samuel Moutrie, presumed to be the sculptor, in 1870 for £6.

A label on the reverse of the object is inscribed 'Samuel Moutrie' in ink.

Clare Graham identified the sculptor as Samuel Moutrie, and the bracket as a prize-winning entry from the Society of Arts Art-Workmanship Competition of 1869.

Bibliography

Graham 1993, p. 414 and fig. 48.

Exhibited

Society of Arts Art-Workmanship Competition of 1869.

Alexander Munro

(b. Inverness 1825 – d. Cannes 1871)

In 1844, with the assistance of Harriet Egerton, the Duchess of Sutherland, Munro was sent to London, where under John Thomas [q.v.] he assisted on the carving for the new Houses of Parliament. In order to improve his modelling skills Munro worked in the studio of Edward Hodges Baily [q.v.], before re-applying to the Royal Academy Schools (he had been unsuccessful in his first attempt in 1846, but gained entry in 1847). Whilst at the Royal Academy Schools he met Dante Gabriel Rossetti (1828–1882), John Everett Millais (1829–1896), and others who were members of the Pre-Raphaelite Brotherhood, which had a profound influence on his work. He exhibited regularly at the Royal Academy from 1849 to 1870, at the Royal Glasgow Institute in 1865, and at the Royal Scottish Academy between 1839 and 1858.

Graves V, pp. 326–8; Pre-Raphaelite 1991 [Macdonald], pp. 46–8, 57–65, 111–130; Royal Scottish Academy 1991, III, p. 329; Royal Glasgow Institute III, p. 272; Thieme-Becker, 25, p. 275; TDA, 22, p. 314 [Stocker].

517: Fountain nymph

about 1863
Plaster
h. (approx.) 171 cm.
A.15–2000

There is no information available on the provenance of the present piece, which until 2000 was recorded as an unregistered object in the Museum. A letter from the sculptor's wife, Mary Munro (see below) suggests that the model was in the Museum by 1869.

This plaster is related to the figure of a *Fountain Nymph* incorporated into the monument to Herbert Ingram at Boston, Lincolnshire. Katharine Macdonald has noted that the bronze figure, produced by Elkington, was installed on the monument in September 1863, the statue of Ingram having been unveiled earlier in 1862 (*Pre-Raphaelite* 1991 [Macdonald], p. 125).

Three further versions of the *Fountain Nymph* are recorded: a fragmentary plaster model, similar to the present piece and the model for the Elkington figure (*ibid., loc.cit.*), a further marble version, executed by Munro as a drinking fountain installed in Berkeley Square, London, and a reduced marble reproduction of the Berkeley Square version, erected in Park Town Gardens, Oxford around 1971 (*ibid., loc.cit.*).

The present piece is referred to in a letter written by the sculptor's wife, Mary Munro, to her sister in 1869: 'Alick [sic] thinks you did quite right to sell the fragment. He would like Mr Boulton to know that he himself thinks it the best thing in the room . . . He is wondering if Mr Boulton would prefer the entire figure for 30 gns. It is at the Kensington Museum' (*ibid., loc.cit.*).

We are grateful to Philip Ward-Jackson for his identification of the present piece.

Bibliography
Pre-Raphaelite 1991 [Macdonald], p. 125

William Grinsell Nicholl

(b. 1796 – d. 1871)

Nicholl is chiefly known for his architectural work, including the frieze and pediment for the Fitzwilliam Museum, Cambridge and the pediment for St George's Hall, Liverpool. He exhibited at the Royal Academy between 1822 and 1861.

Graves V, p. 364; Gunnis 1968, pp. 271–2; Thieme-Becker 25, p. 441.

518: Philip Rundell (1743–1827)

about 1827
Marble
h. 53.5 cm.
A.1–1995

Signed on the side: W.G. NICHOLL SCULPTOR
Inscribed at the front: PHILIP RUNDELL

Originally commissioned by Joseph Neeld of Grittleton, the sitter's nephew; given by Neeld to the Draper's Hall, London in 1827. Purchased from Sotheby's Nineteenth and Twentieth Century sculpture sale, 12 May 1995, lot 173, for £2823.

Philip Rundell was a prominent figure in the silver trade in the nineteenth century; on his death he was said to be 'the wealthiest tradesman in the Kingdom' (see Tanner 1991, pp. 91–102). Purchased jointly by the Departments of Sculpture and Metalwork, the bust is displayed in the Museum's newly refurbished Silver Galleries; it is probably a posthumous portrait of Rundell.

The sale of Joseph Neeld's collection by Christie's at Grittleton, Wiltshire took place on 22 September 1966; lot nos. 7 and 8 were two busts of Rundell by Edward Hodges Baily [q.v.], signed and dated 1838 and 1840 respectively (lot 8 is illustrated by S. Tanner in the article devoted to an obituary of Philip Rundell, see *ibid.*, fig. 1, p. 92). The other bust, lot 7, was re-sold at Christie's Nineteenth Century sale, London on 30 May 1996, lot 228, and was there erroneously identified as possibly David Gilbert; it was purchased by the National Portrait Gallery.

T. Nichols

(dates unknown; active 1864 – 1867)

No information has been found on T. Nichols other than his address, 4 Evrilda Street, Hemingford Road, London. He was presumably an amateur sculptor, and exhibited at the Society of Arts Art-Workmanship Competitions of 1864 and 1867.

519: Clytie

signed; 1864
By T. Nichols, after the Roman original
Bronze
h. 34 cm.
39–1865

Signed on the back of the base: T, N

Purchased from Mr T. Nichols, presumed to be the sculptor, in 1865 for £15.

This bust was a prize object in the Society of Arts Exhibition of 1864; it is a bronze version of the marble bust of *Clytie* in the

British Museum; inv.no. GR 1805.7–3.79 (see *Fake* 1990, cat.no. 3, pp. 32–3, illus. on p. 32). Versions of this piece, which came originally from Charles Townley's collection, were reproduced in marble, plaster and Parian ware (Haskell and Penny 1981, p. 68). The present bust was on long-term loan to the Cecil Higgins Art Gallery, Bedford from February 1978 to March 1981. A report on the objects to be reproduced in the 1864 competitions commented: 'A noble subject has been given for a model to the class of chasing in bronze, the section of the figure, by a machine reduced cast from the well-known antique bust generally styled 'Clytie', but also recognised by the name of 'Isis '. . . I do not know where it was discovered, but the original is now in the British Museum – where I beg competitiors to study it – numbered 79, and was originally part of the famous Towneley [sic] collection' (*Journal of the Society of Arts*, 15 April 1864, XII, no. 595, pp. 355–6). Nichols also exhibited a bronze plaque of the *Virgin and Child* after Desiderio da Settignano at the Society of Arts Art-Workmanship Competition in 1867 see cat.no. 520 below.

EXHIBITED
Society of Arts Art-Workmanship Competition of 1864.

520: Virgin and child

signed and dated 1867
By T. Nichols; after Desiderio da Settignano
Bronze
h. 40.5 cm. w. 33.5 cm.
857–1868

Signed at the bottom: T. Nichols, and dated 1867 on the rim to the right.

Purchased from Mr T. Nichols, presumed to be the sculptor, in 1868 for £15.

This panel is after a work in the Museum's collection in the style of Desiderio da Settignano (1429/32–c.1464). Nichols also exhibited a bronze bust of *Clytie* at the Society of Arts Art-Workmanship Competition in 1864; see cat.no. 519. Two other versions of this group were acquired at the same time; see cat.nos. 279 and 460.

EXHIBITED
Society of Arts Art-Workmanship Competition of 1867.

Matthew Noble

(b. Hackness 1817 – d. London 1876)

Noble trained in London under John Francis (1780–1861). His 1856 monument to the Duke of Wellington in Manchester made his reputation as a sculptor; Stocker records that Noble received a number of other commissions in Manchester, including the city's Albert Memorial, completed between 1862 and 1865. He exhibited prolifically at the Royal Academy between 1845 and 1876. Noble's models were presented by his widow to the city of Newcastle-upon-Tyne, and were displayed for a time at Elswick Hall, together with models by John Graham Lough [q.v.]; Stocker records that only six of these survive. Noble also worked in ivory, and an ivory portrait bust of Albert, Prince Consort is also in the Museum (inv.no. A.221–1969).

Graves V, pp. 376–8; Gunnis 1968, pp. 274–5; Thieme-Becker, 25, pp. 494–5; TDA, 23, pp. 171–2 [Stocker].

521: Oliver Cromwell (1599–1658)

signed and dated 1860
Marble
h. (incl. socle) 81 cm.
448–1884

Signed and dated on the back: M.NOBLE Sc/LONDON/1860

Inscribed on the back truncation: CROMWELL

Given by Charles Seeley, Esq., M.P. in 1884 with a pedestal, together with cat.no. 522. Originally displayed at Bethnal Green Museum; returned to the Sculpture Department in 1983.

Noble produced two further busts of Cromwell, recorded by Gunnis: one of 1860 at the Reform Club, London, another of 1874 in the Manchester City Hall. The Reform Club version is similar to the present bust. Noble also produced a bronze statue of Cromwell in 1875 for Wythenshawe Park, Manchester.

In 1861 Noble exhibited at the Royal Academy 'Oliver Cromwell. To be presented to the Peel Park Museum, Salford, by T.B. Potter, Esq.' (Graves V, p. 377, no. 1040). In 1873 he also exhibited 'Oliver Cromwell; marble statuette' (*ibid.*, p. 378, no. 1581).

Bibliography
Gunnis 1968, p. 275 (erroneously dated 1862).

522: General Giuseppe Garibaldi (1807–1882)

signed and dated 1867
Marble
h. (incl. socle) 81 cm.
449–1884

Signed and dated on the back: M. NOBLE Sc/LONDON/1867
Inscribed on the back truncation: GARIBALDI

Given by Charles Seeley, Esq., M.P. in 1884 with a pedestal, together with cat.no. 521. Originally displayed at Bethnal Green Museum; returned to the Sculpture Department in 1983.

Garibaldi visited England in April 1864.

Bibliography
Gunnis 1968, p. 275.

Exhibited
Noble exhibited 'General Garibaldi, marble bust' at the Royal Academy in 1867 (no. 1138), and in the same year he also exhibited a marble bust of Charles Seeley, Esq., M.P. (no. 1135), the donor of the present bust and cat.no. 521 (Graves V, p. 378).

Patric Park

(b. Glasgow 1811 – d. Warrington 1855)

Gunnis notes that Park was initially apprenticed to a stonemason, Mr Connell, who was employed at Hamilton Palace, and it was here that he gained experience in decorative stone carving. Grant recorded that on his arrival in Rome in 1831, Park was introduced by the Duke of Hamilton to Bertel Thorvaldsen (1770–1843), with whom he was to study for a period of two years. Park was particulary prolific in the production of portrait busts; Gunnis commented that this was 'a type of work at which he was at his best'. He exhibited at the Royal Academy between 1836 and 1855, and at the Royal Scottish Academy between 1839 and 1855; he was made an Associate of the Royal Scottish Academy in 1849, and an Academician in 1851.

Graves VI, pp. 53–4; McKay 1917, pp. 299–301; Grant 1953, p. 184; Gunnis 1968, pp. 290–1; Thieme-Becker, 26, pp. 238–9; Royal Scottish Academy 1991, III, pp. 413–5.

523: Napoleon III (1808–1873)

signed and dated 1855
Marble
h. 80 cm.
2637–1856

Signed on the back: PATRIC PARK/RSA/JANY 1ST/MANCHESTER/1855

Purchased from the Paris International Exhibition in 1855 for £150. Originally displayed at Bethnal Green Museum; transferred to the Department of Architecture and Sculpture, later Sculpture Department in 1976.

Charles Louis Napoleon Bonaparte was President of the Second French Republic between 1850 and 1852, and from 1852 to 1870 Emperor of the French. A plater version of the present bust, probably the model for it, was formerly in the Kelvingrove Art Gallery, Glasgow, presented by the sculptor's son in 1906 (inv. no. S.94); it was probably destroyed during bombing in the Second World War (I am grateful to Hugh Stevenson for this information).

Bibliography
Graves VI, p. 54, no. 1467; Gunnis 1968, p. 291; Thieme-Becker, 26, p. 238.

Exhibited
Paris International Exhibition of 1855. Park exhibited 'Napoleon III', possibly the present piece or the model for it, at the Royal Academy in 1855 no. 1467. In 1855 Park exhibited at the Royal Scottish Academy, 'Bust of Napoleon III. The Model executed at St Cloud 1854 for a Marble. Lent by the Duke of Hamilton' (McKay 1917, p. 300, no. 747).

FREDERICK WILLIAM POMEROY R.A.

(b. London 1856 – d. Cliftonville 1924)

Spielmann recorded that Pomeroy was initially 'apprenticed to a firm of architectural carvers, and under them acquired considerable skill in the manual side of the sculptor's art, occupying his evenings with drawing at the Lambeth schools'. He later attended the South London Technical Art School, where Jules Dalou [q.v.] was master of the modelling class. A letter dated 4 August 1898 in the manuscripts collection of the National Art Library from Pomeroy to A.L. Baldry is the source for Baldry's biographical article on Pomeroy for the Studio, *published in November 1898. In it Pomeroy apologises for the delay in his response: 'The fact is, that to put into writing anything pertaining to our Art, is more difficult to me than making a statue, and this is really the cause of my procrastination'. He continued, 'It was not until "Dalou" came to instruct in the New Modelling Schools founded and endowed by the City Guilds at Kennington [The South London Technical Art School] in 1899, than any decided progress was noticeable. But the enthusiasm & knowledge he brought to bear on the Students, resulted in the founding of a really good modelling class'. Pomeroy recorded that the progress made under the tutelage of Dalou enabled him and his fellow students, including George Frampton, to enter the Royal Academy Schools. Whilst at the Schools, Pomeroy was the recipient of a number of awards. In 1882 he won the silver medal for the best model from the antique, in 1882 the silver medal for the best model from life, in 1884 £50 for the best set of models produced during that year, and in 1885 the Gold Medal and travelling scholarship. This scholarship enabled the sculptor to study in Paris in the studio of Marius-Jean-Antonin Mercié (1845–1916) in 1886, and he later toured Italy at the suggestion of Frederic, Lord Leighton [q.v.]. Pomeroy also noted that he became acquainted with J.D. Sedding in 1887, and 'executed many things for him, notably the bronze work at Church, Sloane Square; & also Welbeck Abbey Chapel, & Douglas Castle'. He also recorded the sculpture for the new Science Gallery and Museum in Liverpool as his current commission in 1898. He joined the Art Workers' Guild in 1887, and was made Master of the Guild in 1908. He exhibited at the Royal Academy between 1885 and 1904; he was made Associate of the Royal Academy in 1907 and Royal Academician in 1917.*

Pomeroy 1898; Baldry 1898; Spielmann 1901, pp.114–8; Graves VI, pp. 175–6; Thieme-Becker, 27, p. 234; TDA, 25, p. 187 [Pearson].

524: Perseus

signed and dated 1898
Bronze
h. 49.8 cm.
A.9–1972

Signed and dated on the side of the base: F.W.POMEROY/SC 1898·

The name Perseus is inscribed on the base at the front in Greek lettering: ΠΕΡΣΕΥΣ

Originally in the Handley-Read collection. Purchased from Thomas Stainton, Madeley Penn Road, Beaconsfield, Buckinghamshire for £231 in 1972.

The figure depicts Perseus as he averts his eyes from the stare of the gorgon, Medusa. Spielmann commented, 'In 1898 came a very important statue of "Perseus", which, although the pose is different, deliberately changes the masterpiece of Benvenuto Cellini in general attitude and accessory, very wisely, however, omitting the corpse of Medusa at his feet. Canova, it is true, also produced a "Perseus" that was an echo of Benvenuto's, but he departed somewhat more obviously from the original' (Spielmann 1901, p. 117, illus. p. 19). Spielmann is probably commenting on the life-size plaster version exhibited by Pomeroy at the Royal Academy in

1898, described as 'Perseus; as a symbol of the subduing and resisting of Evil: statue' (Graves VI, p. 175, no. 1964). Beattie however commented, 'The work of F.W. Pomeroy and Onslow Ford in the late 1890s shows a marked reluctance to break new ground and an increasing reliance on received ideas. Pomeroy's monumental bronze Perseus of 1898 is little more than a restatement of the technical and expressive objectives of Mercié's *David*, a work he must have first encountered at least seventeen years earlier' (Beattie 1983, p. 177). The bronze by Mercié is now in the Musée d'Orsay in Paris. Beattie also records that at the exhibition held at the Fine Art Society in 1902 versions of Pomeroy's *Perseus* statuette were offered for thirty guineas (Beattie 1983, p. 199).

Penny notes that examples of the smaller bronze are quite common and that 'The Victoria and Albert's version is a lost-wax cast with a lively surface; others such as the Ashmolean's have the dead uniformity of the electrodeposit' (*Ashmolean* 1992 [III], p. 149).

The life-size bronze version is in the National Museum of Wales, Cardiff. Another version, larger than the present piece, was formerly in the collection of William Hesketh Lever (*Lady Lever* 1999, p. 81). Versions were at Sotheby's, London, 5 October 2000, lot 193, and with Robert Bowman Ltd, London in 2000; see *Bowman* 2000, pp. 80–1.

BIBLIOGRAPHY

British Sculpture 1850–1914, 1968, p. 30; *Handley-Read* 1972, p. 111, cat.no. F45, illus.; *Ashmolean* 1992 [III], p. 149.

EXHIBITED

British Sculpture 1850–1914, Fine Art Society, London, 30 September to 30 October 1968, cat.no. 12; *Victorian and Edwardian Decorative Art: The Handley-Read Collection*, Royal Academy, London, 1972, cat.no. F45.

Augustus Welby Northmore Pugin

(b. London 1812 – d. Ramsgate 1852)

Pugin was the leading exponent of the Gothic revival in nineteenth-century architecture, and is most celebrated for his interiors for the Houses of Parliament; he was also a designer of furniture, textiles, and stained glass.

Thieme-Becker, 27, pp. 453–4; Pugin 1994; TDA, 25, pp. 711–6 [Wedgwood].

525: Chimneypiece from the Bishop's House, Bath Street, Birmingham

about 1840–1
Designed by Augustus W.N. Pugin
Stone
h. 100.3 cm.
Circ.351–1961

Originally in the Bishop's House, Bath Street, Birmingham. Following its demolition, given by His Grace the Archbishop of Birmingham to the Museum in 1961. Initially acquired by the Circulation Department (Regional Services), it was later transferred to the Sculpture Department in 1981 following the closure of the Circulation Department. Two chairs also designed by Pugin were also given to the Museum at the same time as the present gift; inv.nos. Circ.352 and Circ. 353–1961 – also initially acquired by the Circulation Department – these are now in the Furniture and Woodwork Department.

The overmantle is inset with three heraldic shields.

On hearing of the planned demolition of the Bishop's House in Bath Street, Birmingham due to a planned road-widening scheme, Peter Floud, Keeper of the Circulation Department, contacted the Rev. Kevin J. Good and the Most Rev. Francis Joseph Grimshaw D.D. asking about the fate of the decorative fittings and furniture designed by Pugin, which were in the house. As a result, some of these were presented to the Museum. The Bishop's House, built by George Myers (1804–1875) during 1840–1, was located opposite the Cathedral (TDA, 25, p. 713 [Wedgwood]).

[Not illustrated].

George Rennie

(b. Phantassie 1802 – d. London 1860)

Rennie's father was George Rennie (1749–1828) the agriculturalist, and his uncle the engineer John Rennie (1794–1874), of whom he executed a bust, exhibited at the Royal Academy in 1831, no. 1202. He studied in Rome, probably in the studio of Bertel Thorvaldsen (1768–1844), returning to England in 1828. Gunnis recorded that his best-known sculpture is The Archer, *produced in 1828, and now at the Athenaeum Club, London. Rennie mooted the idea of the formation of the Parliamentary Committee which led to the establishment of the Government School of Design at Somerset House, a forerunner of the Victoria and Albert Museum; he was also involved in attempts to ensure public access to monuments and works of art held in public buildings and Museums. Rennie was elected as Liberal M.P. for Ipswich in 1841, and in 1847 he became Governor of the Falkland Islands.*

Gunnis 1968, p. 318; DNB 1973, XVI, pp. 903–4.

526: Cupid kindling the torch of Hymen

signed; about 1831
Marble
h. 143.8 cm.
A.22–1936

Signed on the left of base: GEORGE RENNIE.- FECIT.

Included in the sale of the collection of the sculptor held by Messrs Christie & Manson, King Street, London, on 9 June 1843, lot 43 was described as 'Hymen and Cupid – Cupid kindling the torch of Hymen, a very beautiful classical group'. Originally on loan from W.H. Rennie Esq., 19 Victoria Street, Westminster, London from February 1868. From 1918 various attempts to contact the lender or its rightful successive owner failed; communication with a Brig. Gen. George A.P. Rennie during 1934 and 1936 suggested that no descendant could be found, and that the Museum should consider the group its own. The object was consequently registered by the Museum in 1936.

The style of the present piece reflects the influence of Bertel Thorvaldsen (1768–1844) on Rennie's work. The sculptor's collection of his own original models, bronzes, and marbles, as well as original models by Thorvaldsen and Richard James Wyatt (1795–1850), 'collected during a residence on the Continent' were sold at Messrs Christie & Manson, King Street, London on 9 June 1843. As well as Rennie's *Cupid and Hymen*, the presence of Thorvaldsen's works in this collection testifies to the connection between Rennie and the Danish sculptor during Rennie's time in Rome. A 'Very fine bust of Thorwaldsen – the joint work of that sculptor and Mr Rennie' was amongst the items included in the sale of Rennie's collection in 1843, lot 42.

Bibliography
International Exhibition 1862, p. 142; Graves VI, p. 266, no. 1196; Gunnis 1968, p. 318; *DNB* 1973, p. 903.

Exhibited
International Exhibition 1862, London, British Division, class XXXIX, A- Deceased artists, lent by Mrs G. Rennie; Royal Academy 1831, no. 1196.

John Augustus Richter

(b. Dresden 1730 – d. after 1809)

According to Gunnis, Richter came to England from Dresden before 1770, and set himself up as a senior partner in Richter and Bartoli, a firm of Scagliolists (manufacturers of scagliola) located in Newport Street, Long Acre, London. In October 1773 Sir William Chambers noted that the firm were the 'best makers of scagliola'. In 1769 Richter was responsible for the scagliola inlay of a white marble chimneypiece, executed for Horace Walpole for the Round Tower at Strawberry Hill. In 1774 he was again employed by Walpole, completing the mosaic decoration for the shrine of Capoccio also at Strawberry Hill. Roget records that Richter, '"Artist, Engraver, and Scagliolist", came over from Saxony with the Marquis of Exeter, was introduced by him to King George the Third, and executed several public works in imitation of marble, some columns at Greenwich Hospital among the rest'. In 1782 and 1783 Richter exhibited five examples of scagliola work at the Free Society of Artists: two pedestals, two chimney-pieces and a table; in 1782 he also jointly entered with Hodgson (described as a sculptor), three 'drawings' in scagliola. According to information found in departmental records supplied by Mr Clifford Smith, in 1795 Richter was paid £300 for work carried out for George, Prince of Wales at Carlton House.

Roget 1891, p. 384; Graves 1907, pp. 213, 121; Walpole 1927, pp. 15, 129, 133, 154, 159; Gunnis 1968, p. 321; Thieme-Becker, 28, p. 296.

527: Scene from Ossian

signed and dated 1809
Scagliola
h. 32.8 cm. w. 37 cm.
A.25–1932

Inscribed on the reverse in ink:

Ossian/"On the harp arose the white hands of/Oina-morul. She waked her own/sad tale, from every trembling string./I stood in silence; for bright in/her locks was the Daughter of/many Isles./Inlaid by/JOHN AUGUSTUS RICHTER,/Scagliolist, London 1809, Aet: 79.

Given by Mrs B. Theodore, 45–47 East Street, Baker Street, London in 1932.

On acquisition this panel of inlaid coloured plaster was considered an interesting example for technical purposes, no other example being in the collection at the time. Scagliola, a technique originating in Italy, is plaster coloured in imitatation of marble or stone.

The relief depicts the legend of Ossian, supposedly a 3rd century Irish warrior and bard, whose poems were said to have been collected and translated by James Macpherson (1736–1796), who was in fact the author of the poems.

John Augustus Richter was the father of the painter Henry J. Richter (1772–1857), who exhibited two watercolours from the poems of Ossian at the Royal Academy in 1792 (Graves VI, p. 294, nos. 419 and 420). Henry J. Richter is described by Roget as a 'successful painter of subject pieces' and active member of the Society of the Old Water-Colour Society (see Roget 1891, pp. 383–8). Henry J. Richter may have designed this panel, later produced in scagliola by his father. In 1795 John Augustus and Henry Richter published an illustrated edition of Milton's *Paradise Lost*, the plates of which were mostly produced by Henry (*ibid.*, pp. 384–5).

Bibliography

Review 1932, p. 50; Neumann 1959, p. 148, n. 343, p. 149 fig. 130; Thieme-Becker, 28, p. 296.

Exhibited

Knights, Chivalry, Romance, Legend, Laing Art Gallery, Newcastle-upon-Tyne, 13 September 1995 to 18 February 1996.

John Singer Sargent

(b. Florence 1856 – d. London 1925)

Sargent, an American by birth, is known chiefly as a painter, but began sculpting in the 1890s, initially working on moulded reliefs for the mural decoration on the Boston Public Library, which Spielmann described: 'The originality of this relief is as undeniable as its beauty, with its gorgeousness of colour and the ordered disorder (as it appears to the recollection) of its strange and magnificent design'. Sargent exhibited a lunette and portion of ceiling, part of the decoration for the Boston Public Library, at the Royal Academy in 1894 (no. 423). He exhibited at the Royal Academy between 1882 and 1904. The Tate Gallery Archive holds material relating to this artist.

Spielmann 1901, p. 166; Charteris 1927; Graves VII, pp. 25–6; Pre-Raphaelite 1991 [Barnes], p. 136; Thieme-Becker, 29, p. 466; TDA, 27, pp. 839–42 [Ormond].

528: How they met themselves

after 1900
Bronze
h. 25 cm.
A.10–1972

This bronze may be identified with that described in a manuscript notebook listing the contents of Sargent's studio on his death (Collection R.L. Ormond, ms notebook p. 8; cited by *Pre-Raphaelite* 1991 [Barnes], p. 136): 'Bronze. Four figures, after Rossetti. The lovers meeting their own souls, by J.S. Sargent. 10 inches high'. In the studio of the artist on his death; Handley-Read Collection. Purchased from Thomas Stainton, Madeley Penn Road, Beaconsfield, Buckinghamshire in 1972 for £220.

The composition of this piece is based on a drawing by Dante Gabriel Rossetti (1828–1882) now in the Fitzwilliam Museum Cambridge, and shows two lovers meeting with their doubles in a wood at midnight – perceived to be an omen of death. According to Charteris, a small engraving of Rossetti's *The Meeting of Arthur and Guinevere* was displayed in Sargent's studio.

Another version was included in the Sotheby's, London sale held on 13 December 2000, lot 177.

Bibliography

Charteris 1927, p. 88; *Handley-Read* 1972, p. 112 cat.no. F.50 & illus; Read 1982, p. 273; *Singer Sargent* 1989, cat. no. 90; *Pre-Raphaelite* 1991 [Barnes], p. 136, cat. no. 47.

Exhibited

Victorian and Edwardian Decorative Art: the Handley-Read Collection, Royal Academy, London, 4 March to 30 April 1972; *John Singer Sargent*, Tokyo, Yamaguchi, Kumamoto, Otsu, 26 January to 11 June 1989; *Pre-Raphaelite Sculpture*, Matthiesen Gallery, London, 31 October to 12 December 1991, and Birmingham City Museum and Art Gallery, 15 January to 15 March 1992.

SCHULTZE

(active around 1859)

It has not been possible to identify this sculptor.

529: My own little girl

signed and dated 1859
Plaster
h. 46 cm.
A.24–2000

Signed on the back: Schultze/1859

A plaster bust was on loan to the Museum from R. Schultz Esq. at an unrecorded date prior to 1870 (*List* 1870, p. ix). What is presumably the same bust (and identical with the present piece) is later recorded on departmental records as being lent by the architect Robert Weir Schultz Weir (1860–1951), who is likely to have been a relative of the sculptor. As a redundant loan the present piece was formally accessioned by the Sculpture Department in 2000.

Philip Ward-Jackson has suggested that the present work is possibly derived from similar busts executed by Jean-Antoine Houdon (1741–1828); that of *Louise Brongniart* is comparable (see Réau 1964, pl. XLIV- XLV). The sculptor may have been Fritz Schulze [sic] (1838–1914) (see Thieme-Becker, 30, p. 335). However many artists are listed under Schultze/Schulze. A bust of Mademoiselle de Schultze was exhibited by H. Kachler (probably Heinrich Daniel Kaehler) at the Royal Academy in 1837 (Graves IV, p. 299; I am grateful to Marjorie Trusted for this information).

Sir George Gilbert Scott

(b. Gawcott 1811 – d. London 1878)

Sir George Gilbert Scott was one of the best known architects of the Victorian Gothic Revival. He began his career in partnership with William Bonythbon Moffat (1812–1887) between 1835 and 1845, initially specialising in workhouses. However, Scott increasingly turned to ecclesiastical architecture, both designing new churches and restoring medieval churches and cathedrals. St Giles, Camberwell (consecrated in 1844) was particularly admired for its archaeologically correct gothic detailing. Scott's work as a restorer of old buildings has often been criticised, and the establishment of the Society for the Protection of Ancient Buildings was prompted by his imminent restoration of Tewkesbury Abbey. By this time he had restored over three hundred churches and cathedrals, including the cathedrals of Ely, Hereford, Lichfield, and Salisbury, and Westminster Abbey. Scott's best-known secular structures include the Foreign and India Offices (1863–8) and the Home and Colonial Offices (1870–4) in Whitehall, London, which are decorated in an Italian Renaissance style, as well as the Gothic Midland Hotel (1866–76) at St. Pancras Station, London, and the Albert Memorial (1863–76) in Kensington Gardens, London. Scott saw sculpture as an integral part of his architecture. He also took a great interest in encouraging craftsmen, frequently employing firms such as Clayton and Bell and Skidmore in the decoration of his churches. Towards the end of his life he worked in a partnership with his son, John Oldrid Scott (1841–1913), who took over the practice on his father's death in 1878.

Read 1982, pp. 265–72; TDA, 28, pp. 277–80 [Howell].

EH

530: Model for the proposed restoration of the monument to Queen Philippa of Hainault (d.1369)

about 1850–1
Designed by Sir George Gilbert Scott: the statuettes made by John Birnie Philip, the marble background and alabaster niches by Samuel Cundy; the painting and gilding executed by Thomas Willement
Painted and gilt alabaster and marble
h. 110 cm
A.15–1973

One of nine previously unregistered models found in the Museum which were accessioned by the Department of Architecture and Sculpture, later Sculpture Department in 1973 (inv.nos. A.10 to A.15–1973). This model may have arrived in the Museum sometime after the Architectural Exhibition of 1852, at which it was exhibited. The model is mentioned by Scott in his *Recollections* . . . of 1879, as having been deposited in the South Kensington Museum, though it remained the property of the Architectural Museum. An editor's note contemporary with the 1879 edition [the author's son, G. Gilbert Scott F.S.A. was the editor] observed however, 'It is now in the architectural museum in Westminster' (Scott 1995, p. 165). This would suggest that although the model may have once been at South Kensington, by 1879 (the date of the editorial note), it had been returned to the Architectural Museum. The Royal Architectural Museum – founded in 1852 with Sir George Gilbert Scott as its head – merged with the Architectural Association in 1903 (see Wylde 1981). In 1916, with the demise of the Architectural Association, 127 architectural fragments (inv.nos. A.13 to A.123–1916) formerly belonging to the Royal Architectural Museum, together with 3905 plaster casts (A.1916–1 to 3095), were transferred to the Victoria and Albert Museum. It may have been at this time that the model was returned – unrecorded – to the Museum.

In his role as Surveyor of the Fabric of Westminster Abbey, a post to which he was appointed in 1849, Scott was charged with the task of surveying the Abbey's sepulchral monuments. The present piece is the design he submitted for the proposed restoration to the tomb-end of the sepulchral monument of Queen Philippa of Hainault. Scott had presumed that some of the missing pieces from the tomb were acquired by the architect Lewis Nockalls Cottingham (1787–1847). This was confirmed by Samuel Cundy's discovery of fragments in Cottingham's office, which he had bought some years earlier from the Abbey mason. Scott's investigation of the tomb itself, together with the discovery of the fragments resulted in the design for the proposed model (Lethaby 1906, pp. 251–2; Scott 1995, pp. 164–5; also recounted in *Victorian Church Art* 1971, p. 56).

The model was exhibited by Samuel Cundy (1816–1867) at the 1851 International Exhibition, where it received an Honourable Mention and was awarded a prize medal in class XXX, Sculpture and Works of Plastic Art, Architectural Models (*Jury Reports* 1851, pp. 1543, 1561). Cundy, a member of the Cundy family of architects/builders of the eighteenth and nineteenth century, was the son of the designer James Cundy (1793–1826). His work was mainly concerned with repairs to churches; he worked as foreman for Scott on a number of other projects, including work at the Church of St Stephen and the Abbey in St Albans. (*Builder* 1867; Gunnis 1968, p. 118; Thieme-Becker, 8, p. 195). The statuettes on the model were made by John Birnie Philip (1824–1875). Thomas Willement (1786–1871), who was responsible for the painting and gilding, worked as a designer and painter of heraldic stained glass (Thieme-Becker, 36, p. 14)

Contemporary comment on the proposed restoration was mixed. The Architectural Exhibition at the Portland Galleries attracted the critical comment of the *Builder*, which noted, 'We have here, too, Mr Cundy's restoration of part of Queen Philippa's monument in Westminster Abbey . . . which on several grounds entitles him to praise. We must, nevertheless, express our earnest hope that the original monument will be maintained. We may mention that Mr Cottingham has recently placed in the hands of the dean and chapter several large fragments, including two entire canopies, of the alabaster work which formed part of the original tomb. It appears these were purchased by the late Mr Gayfere, the abbey mason, by his father, nearly thirty years ago, and ever since have been most carefully preserved. Among the fragments are many of the deficient pieces of the canopy of the effigy. Some of the foliated parts are more like chased silver than carved stone' (*Builder* 1852). In an obituary for Samuel Cundy in the *Builder on* 29 June 1867, it was noted, 'His restoration – in – stone, with mosaic and gilding – of the Westminster Abbey tomb of Philippa, Queen of Edward III, will be in the memory of all who remember the Hyde-park Exhibition of 1851. It was done with taste and the true antiquarian feeling of an heraldic mason' (*Builder* 1867). A divergent view was later expressed by Noppen, who suggested the present piece 'is not a work of art, and the sculptor of the "weepers" cannot be congratulated, but it is sufficient to show the design of one end of the tomb' (Noppen 1931, p. 117).

Bibliography

Builder 1852; *Builder* 1867; Lethaby 1906, p. 252; Noppen 1931, p. 117, pl. C between pp. 114–7; *Victorian Church Art* 1971, p. 56, cat.no. F1; Morand 1991, fig. 20 on p. 69; Morganstern 1992, pp. 176–7, fig. 2 on p. 183; Scott 1995, pp. 164–5; *Westminster Abbey* 1995, p. 157, cat.no. 46, pl. 124 on p. 157.

Exhibited

International Exhibition of 1851, Main Avenue (West) no. 60; Architectural Exhibition of 1852, held at Portland Galleries, Regent Street, London, third room, no. 1; *Victorian Church Art*, Victoria and Albert Museum, London, November 1971 to January 1972, cat.no. F1; *900 Years: The Restoration of Westminster Abbey*, St Margaret's Church, Westminster, 23 May to 30 September 1995, cat.no. 46.

531: Sketch model of the National Prince Consort Memorial (Albert Memorial)

about 1863
Designed by George Gilbert Scott; made by Farmer and Brindley; sculptural groups modelled by Henry Hugh Arrmstead; paper mosaics made by Antonio Salviati
Plaster on a metal armature
Central architectural portion: h. 201 cm (approx.); Group, Europe: h. 15.5 cm.; Group, Asia: h. 17.8 cm.; Group, Africa: h. 15 cm.; Group, America: h. 17.8 cm.
A.13–1973

Signed 'Armstead Sculpt.' on the left side of Prince Albert's throne.

The four paper mosaics representing the arts of Poetry, Painting, Sculpture and Architecture are inscribed 'POESIS', 'PICTURA', 'SCULPTURA' and 'ARCHITECTURA'.

The model was initially displayed at Buckingham Palace, so that it could be referred to during discussions about the design of the memorial, and was later shown at the 1867 Paris Exhibition. On its return from the exhibition it was deposited at the South Kensington Museum. It was officially loaned to the Museum in 1871, through the sculptor Matthew Noble [q.v.], and finally presented to the Museum by George Gilbert Scott in 1873, although it was not formally registered in the Museum's records at that time. Twelve samples of the granite and stone used in the monument's final construction, including Correnie granite, Castlewellan granite, Isle of Mull pink granite and Sicilian marble, were acquired with the model. The model remained in store for many years unrecorded. During the 1960s John Physick, then Assistant Keeper of Public Services, was alerted to the possibility that the model might still be in the Museum, when he found a wood-engraved illustration in a nineteenth-century weekly journal, showing the Albert

Memorial Model displayed in the Museum's North Court. Some years later the model was discovered in one of the stores. It was then accessioned, restored and exhibited in the Marble Halls exhibition held at the Victoria & Albert Museum in 1973 (see *Marble Halls* 1973, pp. 213–4, cat.no. 150).

A month after the unexpected death of Prince Albert (1819–1861), on 14 December 1861, a meeting was held at the Mansion House to consider how best to commemorate him. As a result of this meeting several architects (George Gilbert Scott, James Pennethorne, T. L. Donaldson, P. C. Hardwick, Matthew Digby Wyatt and Charles Barry) were invited to submit designs for a memorial, to be erected in Kensington Gardens near the site of the 1851 International Exhibition. The commission was eventually awarded to Scott. In November 1863 more detailed discussions about the design took place, and shortly afterwards working drawings and this plaster model – executed by Farmer and Brindley – were produced (for Farmer and Brindley, see Hardy 1993). The sculpture was sketched in by John Richard Clayton for the first elevation drawings, and the three-dimensional models were made by Henry Hugh Armstead [q.v.] (Read 1982, p. 99). For a full discussion of the sculpture on the memorial, see Brooks 2000 [Read], pp. 160–205.

Work started on the site of the actual memorial in Kensington Gardens in May 1864, and it was completed in 1876. The complex sculptural programme includes four free-standing groups representing *Europe, Asia, Africa* and *America* by Patrick MacDowell [q.v.] John Henry Foley [q.v.], William Theed [q.v.] and John Bell [q.v.] respectively. The smaller groups at the base of the columns represent *Agriculture, Commerce, Manufactures,* and *Engineering*. These were executed by William Calder Marshall (1813–1894), Thomas Thornycroft [q.v.], Henry Weekes [q.v.] and John Lawlor [q.v.]. The reliefs below the statues, by Armstead and Birnie Philip, contain portraits of sculptors, musicians, poets, architects and painters (see cat. nos. 256 and 257).There are figures of the Sciences on the corner pillars: *Astronomy, Chemistry, Rhetoric* and *Medicine* by Armstead, and *Geometry, Geology, Physiology* and *Philosophy* by Birnie Philip. Higher up are figures of Virtues by James Redfern, and, at the summit, angels by Birnie Philip. William Brindley supplied the ornamental carvings of foliage and gargoyles. The model also shows the elaborate polychromatic scheme of decoration which was executed in metal and mosaic by Skidmore and Salviati. Antonio Salviati (1816–1890) founded his glass manufactory in Venice in 1859. The firm played a crucial role in the revival of the Venetian glass industry, initially concentrating on mosaics, but soon producing blown glass too, mainly in historicising styles (see Salviati 1862; *idem* 1866; Liefkes 1994; TDA, 32, pp. 204–5 [d'Alconzo]; Bova 1998). As executed the Memorial differs in a number of details from the present model; for instance the figure of Albert is in a slightly different pose, and holds the catalogue of the 1851 exhibition, rather than a scroll as here.

Only four years after its unveiling, the impact of the Albert Memorial on the development of English sculpture was discussed in an article entitled 'English Sculpture' in 1880 (see *Cornhill Magazine* 1880). For a guide to the memorial published in 1873, see *National Memorial* 1873.

Scott considered the small-scale sculpted groups made by Armstead for the model to be at least as successful as the sculpture of the actual memorial. He later wrote in his memoirs, 'Without derogating from the merits of the sculpture as eventually carried out, it is but just to say that I doubt whether either the central figure or a single group, as executed, is superior to the miniature models furnished by Mr Armstead. They remain to speak for themselves; while the two sides of the podium and the four bronzes, which he designed, give a fair idea of what his models would have proved if carried out to the real size. I mention this in justice both to him and to myself, as his small models were the carrying out of my original intention, and have in idea been the foundation of the result' (Scott 1995, p. 266).

Bibliography

Physick 1969, p. 191; *Marble Halls* 1973, pp. 213–4, cat.no. 150; Bayley 1981, p. 52; Brooks 2000 [Read], p. 172, fig. 134 on p. 173.

Exhibited

Universal Exhibition, Paris, 1867, group I, class V, no. 77 (174); South Kensington Museum, Museum of Construction. no.41a. Y; *'Marble Halls'. Drawings and Models for Victorian Secular Buildings*, Victoria and Albert Museum, London, August to October 1973, cat.no. 150.

EH

George T. Sherborne

(dates unknown; active 1864)

No information has been found on George T. Sherborne, presumably an amateur sculptor who exhibited at the Society of Arts Art-Workmanship Competition in 1864.

532: Putto on a dolphin

signed; 1864
By George T. Sherborne; after the workshop of Desiderio da Settignano
Marble
h. 60.3 cm.
153–1865

Signed on the top in monogram:

Purchased from Mr George T. Sherborne, presumed to be the sculptor, in 1865 for £15. Transferred from the Bethnal Green Museum to the Sculpture Department in 1988.

This bracket supported by a cupid on a dolphin's back was a prize object in the Society of Arts Competition of 1864. It is a copy of the chimneypiece in grey sandstone acquired by the Museum in 1859, inv.no. 5896–1859 (Pope-Hennessy 1964, I, pp. 135–8, no. 113; III, figs. 131–4; the present piece relates to the cherub bracket on the left of the chimneypiece) which is now attributed to the workshop of Desiderio da Settignano (1429/32 – c. 1464). On acquisition considered to be either by Donatello or Desiderio da Settignano, it was thought to be an excellent example for reproduction: 'It is difficult to conceive a finer example of execution, or one better fitted for application to modern uses, than the beautiful group of a boy and dolphin, which is offered as the theme for the first prize in Class 1 carving in marble, stone or wood. Such a work may be employed as a bracket, as a console, or cantilever; it might be placed over a fireplace, under a balcony, or in any other similar situation. The subject is one of those spirited themes so often adopted with perfect success by the great Italian sculptors, who gave their attention to the production of decorative works' (*Journal of the Society of Arts*, 1 April 1864, XII, no. 593, p. 321).

Exhibited
Society of Arts Art-Workmanship Competition of 1864.

Sarah Siddons

(1755 – 1831)

Sarah Siddons is chiefly known as a tragic actress; however she took up sculpture around October 1789, certain that she could produce better portraits of herself than many of the artists who had previously attempted to represent her. Siddons was the subject of nearly 400 portraits executed by many of the leading artists of the period, including Sir Joshua Reynolds (1723–1792). The Dictionary of National Biography *records 'in the following season (1789–90) she retired from Drury Lane, partly on account of ill-health, partly because of the difficulty of getting money from Sheridan [Richard Brinsley Sheridan (1751–1816)] . . . In this period also she practised modelling, to which she had always a disposition . . . She herself executed busts of herself and of her brother John'. Siddons was a friend of the sculptor Anne Seymour Damer [q.v.], who produced a bust of Siddons as the Tragic Muse. Noble records Siddons 'owed much to Mrs. Damer, in whose studio she, with other fair dames arrayed in mob-caps and aprons, wielded the mallet and chisel, kneading wax and clay with their white hands. Mrs. Siddons mentions that whenever she was with Mrs. Damer they indulged in their passion for Sculpture'. According to Robyn Asleson, Siddons's personal letters often refer to her current sculptural work. Siddons exhibited a bust of* Adam *from Milton's* Paradise Lost *at the Royal Academy in 1802 (no. 1058). For a detailed biography of Siddons, see Asleson 1999, pp. xii to xv. (I am grateful to Robyn Asleson for much of this information and advice generally on Siddons).*

Graves VII, p. 212; Noble 1908, pp. 164–5; Smith 1920, I, p. 370; DNB 1973, XVIII, pp. 195–202; NPG 1981, p. 519, no. 642; Hartnoll 1985, p. 768; Blackwood 1989, p. 130, illus. p. 131; Asleson 1999.

533: Self-portrait

1820s?
By Sarah Siddons; cast by Robert Shout
Plaster
h. (incl. socle) 65 cm.
Dyce 3329

Bequeathed by William Dyce. Received with objects collectively known as the Dyce Bequest in 1869.

Stamped on the back of the integral base: R SHOUT/HOLBORN

Robert Shout (about 1763–1843) was one of a family of masons and civil engineers from the North of England. He and his brother Benjamin moved to London, setting up premises in High Holborn. There they produced plaster casts and funerary monuments (see Colvin 1995, p. 867). A book containing designs for monuments and fireplaces by Robert Shout is held in the Department of Prints, Drawings, and Paintings at the Victoria and Albert Museum (inv.no. E.3000 to E.3169–1980); I am grateful to Greg Sullivan for these references. See also Clifford 1992, pp. 46–7; 63–4, fig. 8 on p. 47 (I am grateful to Moira Fulton for this reference).

A plaster bust of the same subject is in the Theatre Museum (inv.no. S.86–1978), the gift of the British Theatre Museum Association in 1978. On the self-portraits executed by Siddons, Robyn Asleson suggests, 'In these works she deliberately accommodated her features to the idealized conventions of Greek sculpture' (see Asleson 1999, p. 67, fig. 22). The Theatre Museum bust differs only slightly from the present one, in that it does not have the band at the front. Information supplied by the British Theatre Museum Association states that the bust was a self-portrait. In his biography of Damer, Noble commented that Mrs

Siddons 'was often a guest at Strawberry Hill, spending many hours in the studio, where, under the tuition of Mrs Damer, she practiced modelling. She is said to have first learnt the art at Birmingham, where, so the story runs: "Going one day into a shop and seeing a bust of herself which the shopman, not knowing whom he was addressing, told her was a likeness of the greatest actress in the world, Mrs Siddons bought the bust, thinking she could make a better replica of her own features. She set to work, and from that time made modelling one of her favourite pursuits"' (Noble 1908, pp. 164–5). Smith, quoting from Dallaway's *Anecdotes of the Arts*, 1800, recorded: 'The first tragedian of the English stage, Mrs. Siddons, has executed the busts of herself and her brother, Mr John Kemble, with astonishing truth and effect' (Smith 1920, I, p. 370). Robyn Asleson also attributes the Theatre Museum bust to Siddons, and in so doing suggests the same attribution for the present piece. There is also documentary evidence to uphold the Siddons attribution; a letter by Mary Siddons (granddaughter of Sarah Siddons) of 1861 claimed the bust was a self portrait. In unpublished research Robyn Asleson cites a letter from Sarah Siddons in 1808 to her son George (father of Mary Siddons), which is held in the Bodleian Library, Oxford (MS Film 1686, letter 10) in which she states; 'I send you a little Bust of myself, and by myself. I hope you'll like it' (I am grateful to Andrew Kirk for this information).

John Charles Felix Rossi (1762–1839) also exhibited a bust of Mrs Siddons at the Royal Academy in 1792 (no. 744).

Benjamin Evans Spence

(b. Liverpool 1822 – d. Rome 1866)

Benjamin Spence was the son of the sculptor William Spence (1793–1849). Timothy Stevens has ascertained that Spence's middle name is Evans and not Edwards as had been previously thought (entry on Spence in the forthcoming revised edition of the Dictionary of National Biography*). Spence attended the Liverpool Academy Schools in 1838. In 1846 he travelled to Rome, initially to work in the studio of John Gibson [q.v.], and later that of Richard James Wyatt (1795–1850). Gunnis recorded that on the death of Wyatt, 'Spence completed his unfinished works and also took over the studio, indeed he spent nearly all his working life in Italy, only going to England about once a year to visit the Royal Academy Exhibition'. Stevens notes that Spence set up his independent studio in 1848 in the Via degli Incurabili in Rome. He exhibited at the Royal Academy between 1849 and 1866.*

Graves VII, p. 215; Gunnis 1968, pp. 362–3; Stevens 1971.

534: Oberon and Titania, from *A Midsummer Night's Dream*

signed and dated 1866
Marble
h. 106 cm.
A.214–1969

Signed and dated on the side of the base: B.E. SPENCE/F^{T} ROMÆ. 1866.

In the possession of Mrs Ruby Gibbs by 1968 (information supplied by Timothy Stevens). Purchased from Mrs A. Gibbs (probably identical with Mrs Ruby Gibbs), Lingarden, Wilderton Road, Branksome Park, Poole in 1969 for £200 under the bequest of Dr W. L. Hildburgh F.S.A.

This group was produced in the year of the sculptor's death. The subject is taken from Shakespeare's *A Midsummer Nights Dream* (Act II, scene ii):

Oberon:
'What thou seest, when thou dost wake
(squeezes the flower on Titania's eyelids)
Do it for thy true love take'

At least one other version of this group seems to have been executed by the sculptor. On 4 June 1870 a sale of the 'remaining works of that highly-distinguished sculptor, Benjamin E. Spence' (the contents of Spence's studio in Rome) was held at Christie, Manson and Woods. Included amongst the items described as life-size statues was 'Oberon and Titania – a fine large group' (lot 166). In the annotated copy of the sale catalogue now in the National Art Library this group appears to have been sold for £200 to 'Vokins', a London dealer (information supplied by Timothy Stevens). Further items were categorised as second and third-size statues; the present piece, which is under life-size, may not therefore be the version sold in 1870.

Alfred Stevens

(b. Blandford Forum 1817 – d. London 1875)

Alfred Stevens is the best represented British sculptor in the collection; the bulk of the Stevens material was largely acquired during the late nineteenth and early twentieth century, and the collection reflects the interest in Stevens as a designer and sculptor; a further indicator of his esteem are the retrospective exhibitions of his work held in 1911, 1912 and 1975 respectively. Stevens was the son of a joiner and decorator. On leaving school he began working in his father's workshop, but his early promise as a painter was noticed by Samuel Best, the Rector of Blandford St Mary, in Dorset. Best sought to encourage Stevens in his artistic career, initially attempting to secure an apprenticeship for him with Sir Edwin Landseer [q.v.]. This idea did not come to fruition as a fee of £500 was required. In 1833 Best organised a collection to send Stevens to Italy to study; he sailed to Naples in 1833 and travelled extensively, remaining in Italy for the next nine years. The influence of the Italian Renaissance is evident in much of Stevens's work, and is perhaps best reflected in the Wellington Monument; see entry for cat.no. 576. During 1841–2 he was in Rome, and acted as an assistant to Bertel Thorvaldsen (1768/70–1844). Stevens returned to England in 1843, and between 1845–7 was an assistant at the Government School of Design in Somerset House. His diversity is illustrated by his time spent designing stoves for Messrs Henry E. Hoole and Co. Ltd at Sheffield between 1850–7 (see entries for cat.nos. 535 to 571), as well as his work for the Sheffield cutlers Wostenholm & Son Ltd; see entries for cat.nos. 650 to 653. Most of Stevens's major projects are illustrated in the collection, including models relating to the proposed redecoration of St Paul's Cathedral, cat.nos 608 to 619, the Wellington Monument, cat nos. 576 to 607, Dorchester House, cat.nos. 620 to 644, and the memorial to the 1851 exhibition, cat.no. 659. Two of his most illustrious projects, the Wellington Monument and the Dorchester House dining-room fireplace, were not completed during his lifetime, but were finished by his pupils Hugh Stannus and James Gamble respectively; see entries for cat.nos. 576 and 627. The plasters catalogued here were all part of the process of producing a finished work. Cast from Stevens's original models, they were then used as models for bronzes. Two important collections of Stevens material was acquired by the Museum during 1911, both originating from the collections of previous pupils of Stevens: Reuben Townroe and James Gamble, described by Towndrow as 'Stevens' most active assistant upon the final stages of the Wellington Monument' (Towndrow 1939, p. 98). A collection of 43 designs and drawings by Stevens were acquired at the same time, also purchased from Mrs Gamble and held in the Department of Prints, Drawings and Paintings (inv.nos. E.2075 to 2117–1911). The Tate Gallery Archive holds material on this sculptor.

Armstrong 1881; Southern 1925; Towndrow 1939; idem 1951; Ollett 1963; Stevens 1975; Thieme-Becker, 32, pp. 26–7; TDA, 29, pp. 645–7 [Stocker].

Work for Messrs Henry E. Hoole & Co. Ltd

535: Right-hand spandrel of an iron stove-front

about 1850
Plaster
h. 55 cm.
960–1903

Purchased from Hugh Stannus, 64 Larkhall Rise, Clapham, London, together with cat.nos. 537, 538, 541, 544, 547 to 549, 558, 559, 568, 569, 589, 590, 601, 644, 666, 667, 678 to 680 in 1903 for £35. This model was included in the large purchase of material by Stevens in the possession of Stannus, a former pupil of Stevens who wrote a monograph on the sculptor in 1891.

This is a model for the right-hand spandrel of an iron stove-front designed by Stevens for Messrs Henry E. Hoole & Co Ltd. See Hoole [n.d.] p.7 and fig. 2 on p. 8 for the stove-front.

Between 1850 and 1857 Stevens was involved in the design and modelling of grates and fenders for Messrs Hoole and Co at their Green Lane Works in Sheffield (see Hoole [n.d.] p. 4; *Stevens* 1975, pp. 8–11). Armstrong recorded that Messrs Hoole and Robson 'were manufacturers of stoves, fenders, and other iron work of a similar class, and they had either the good fortune or the sound judgment to retain his [Stevens's] services at a fixed yearly salary, with the consequence that soon after the opening of the 1851 Exhibition they found themselves famous as makers of some fire-paces of such exquisite design that they stood pre-eminent above all other works of their kind' (Armstrong 1881, p. 11).

536: Section of a fender

about 1850
Plaster
l. 27 cm.
A.48–1911

Purchased from Mrs Ada Gamble, 12 Stanlake Villas, Shepherd's Bush, London, together with cat.nos. 539, 540, 542, 543, 545, 546, 550 to 557, 560, 562 to 567, 570 to 575, 579, 596, 600, 607, 622, 632 to 637, 643, 647, 650, 652, 663, 668 to 677, and 681 in 1911 for £175. Mrs Gamble was the widow of James Gamble, a pupil of Stevens, who had a large collection of designs and drawings by his former master.

This portion of a fender relates to the cast-iron openwork fender designed by Stevens whilst he was employed at Messrs Henry E. Hoole & Co Ltd. A version of the fender is in the Metalwork Department (inv.no. 977–1903). For the fender see Stannus 1891, pl. XVII, p. 10, n. 88, and p. 11, n. 100.

537: Torus moulding

about 1850–1
Plaster
h. 14 cm. w. 7.5 cm.
966–1903

Purchased from Hugh Stannus, 64 Larkhall Rise, Clapham, London, together with cat.nos. 535, 538, 541, 544, 547 to 549, 558, 559, 568, 569, 589, 590, 601, 644, 666, 667, and 678 to 680 in 1903 for £35.

This is a sketch for moulding with raised inter-laced strapwork. A cast iron example of this is held in the Graves Art Gallery, Sheffield. Stevens designed what was called the 'Console Stove' consisting of a grate and chimneypiece, for Messrs Henry E. Hoole & Co Ltd during 1850–1, exhibited at the International Exhibition of 1851; for Hoole & Co Ltd. See Hoole [n.d.], p. 4 for the fireplace, and p. 5 for details. See also entries for cat.nos. 538 to 541 for further models from the same stove.

538: Model for angle-pieces on stove

about 1850–1
Plaster
h. 22.5 cm.
974–1903

Purchased from Hugh Stannus, 64 Larkhall Rise, Clapham, London, together with cat.nos. 535, 537, 541, 544, 547 to 549, 558, 559, 568, 569, 589, 590, 601, 644, 666, 667 and 678 to 680 in 1903 for £35.

This is a sketch for the bronze angle-pieces on the hot-air stove, designed by Stevens for Messrs Henry E. Hoole & Co Ltd during 1850; see entry for cat.no. 537. See also entries for cat.nos. 539 to 541.

539: Part of the side of a fireplace

about 1850–1
Plaster
l. 22 cm.
A.42–1911

Purchased from Mrs Ada Gamble, 12 Stanlake Villas, Shepherd's Bush, London, together with cat.nos. 536, 540, 542, 543, 545, 546, 550 to 557, 560, 562 to 567, 570 to 575, 579, 596 to 600, 607, 622, 632 to 637, 643, 647, 650, 652, 663, 668 to 677, and 681 in 1911 for £175.

This is probably a model for a spandrel panel on the Console Stove designed by Stevens for Messrs Henry E. Hoole & Co Ltd. See Hoole [n.d.], fig. on p. 4 for the fireplace, and fig. 1 on p. 5 for the spandrels. For further models relating to the 'Console Stove', see entries for cat.nos. 537, 538, 540 and 541.

540: Female figure

about 1850–1
Plaster
h. 9 cm.
A.43–1911

Purchased from Mrs Ada Gamble, 12 Stanlake Villas, Shepherd's Bush, London, together with cat.nos. 536, 539, 542, 543, 545, 546, 550 to 557, 560, 562 to 567, 570 to 575, 579, 596 to 600, 607, 622, 632 to 637, 643, 647, 650, 652, 663, 668 to 677, and 681 in 1911 for £175.

This is a model for a figure similar to that found on the frieze portion of the Console Stove designed by Stevens for Messrs Henry E. Hoole & Co Ltd for the International Exhibition of 1851; see entry for cat.no. 539. See Hoole [n.d.], p. 4, illus, and p. 5, fig. 5. See also entries for cat.nos. 537 to 539 and 541.

541: Design of openwork fender

about 1850–1
Plaster
l. 30.5 cm.
978:A-1903

Puchased from Hugh Stannus, 64 Larkhall Rise, Clapham, London, together with cat.nos. 535, 537, 538, 544, 547 to 549, 558, 559, 568, 569, 589, 590, 601, 644, 666, 667, and 678 to 680 in 1903 for £35.

This is a model for the design of an openwork fender front in cast iron, which was designed by Stevens whilst he was in Sheffield in 1850, employed by Messrs Henry E. Hoole & Co Ltd. A specimen of this design in cast iron (inv.no. 978–1903) is in the Department of Metalwork. This is possibly related to the Console Stove, see entries for cat.nos. 537 to 540.

542: Corner from the top of a stove

about 1850–1
Plaster
l. 21 cm.
A.38–1911

Purchased from Mrs Ada Gamble, 12 Stanlake Villas, Shepherd's Bush, London, together with cat.nos. 536, 539, 540, 543, 545, 546, 550 to 557, 560, 562 to 567, 570 to 575, 579, 596 to 600, 607, 622, 632 to 637, 643, 647, 650, 652, 663, 668 to 677, and 681 in 1911 for £175.

This is a model for part of a hot-air stove, designed and modelled by Stevens for Messrs Henry E. Hoole & Co Ltd. A version of the stove, in bronze with printed earthenware panels, is in the Metalwork Department (inv.no. 4030–1853). For the stove see Stannus 1891, pl. XVI, and p. 11, n. 98, and Armstrong 1881, p. 3. See entries for cat.nos. 543 to 545 for further related models.

543: Segment from the top of a stove

about 1850–1
Plaster
h. 23 cm.
A.39–1911

Purchased from Mrs Ada Gamble, 12 Stanlake Villas, Shepherd's Bush, London, together with cat.nos. 536, 539, 540, 542, 545, 546, 550 to 557, 560, 562 to 567, 570 to 575, 579, 596 to 600, 607, 622, 632 to 637, 643, 647, 650, 652, 663, 668 to 677, and 681 in 1911 for £175.

This is probably taken from the hot-air stove, designed by Stevens for Messrs Henry E. Hoole & Co Ltd. See Hoole [n.d.], fig. 1 on p. 11 for the top of the stove; see entry for cat.no. 542.

544: Angle-pieces on a hot-air stove

about 1850–1
Plaster
h. 23 cm.
973–1903

Purchased from Hugh Stannus, 64 Larkhall Rise, Clapham, London, together with cat.nos. 535, 537, 538, 541, 547 to 549, 558, 559, 568, 569, 589, 590, 601, 644, 666, 667, and 678 to 680 in 1903 for £35.

This is a model for the bronze angle-pieces on a hot-air stove designed by Stevens for Messrs Henry E. Hoole & Co Ltd, and exhibited at the International Exhibition of 1851; see Hoole [n.d.], fig. 3 on p. 11 for anglepiece. See entry for cat.no. 542.

545: Corner-piece of a stove

about 1850–1
Plaster
l. 39 cm.
A.37–1911

Purchased from Mrs Ada Gamble, 12 Stanlake Villas, Shepherd's Bush, London, together with cat.nos. 536, 539, 540, 542, 543, 546, 550 to 557, 560, 562 to 567, 570 to 575, 579, 596 to 600, 607, 622, 632 to 637, 643, 647, 650, 652, 663, 668 to 677 and 681 in 1911 for £175.

This is a sketch for the corner-piece of a stove designed by Stevens and executed by Messrs Henry E. Hoole & Co Ltd, and exhibited at the International Exhibition of 1851. See Hoole [n.d.], fig. 2 on p. 11 for detail; see entry for cat.no. 542.

546: Female figure with scrolls

about 1850–1
Plaster
h. 19.2 cm.
A.40–1911

Purchased from Mrs Ada Gamble, 12 Stanlake Villas, Shepherd's Bush, London, together with cat.nos. 536, 539, 540, 542, 543, 545, 550 to 557, 560, 562 to 567, 570 to 575, 579, 596 to 600, 607, 622, 632 to 637, 643, 647, 650, 652, 663, 668 to 677, and 681 in 1911 for £175.

This is part of a fireplace designed by Stevens for Messrs Henry E. Hoole & Co Ltd, and exhibited at the International Exhibition of 1851. A version of the fireplace is in the Metalwork Department (inv.no. 4028–1853). For the fireplace see Hoole [n.d.], figs. 1 and 2 on p. 22, and Armstrong 1881, p. 25 for detail.

547: Caryatid figure

about 1851
Plaster
h. 38 cm.
958–1903

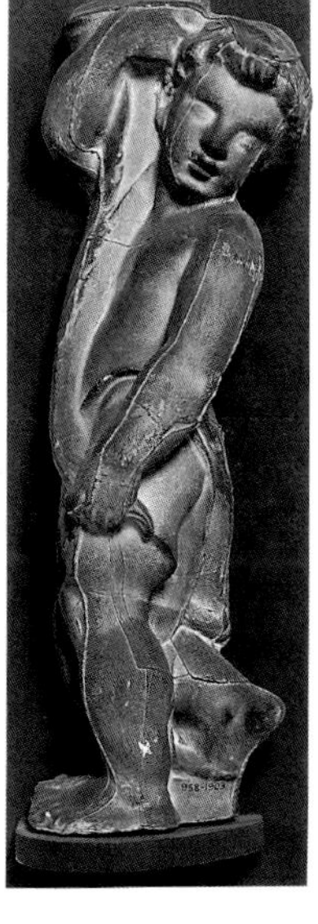

Purchased from Hugh Stannus, 64 Larkhall Rise, Clapham, London, together with cat.nos. 535, 537, 538, 541, 544, 548, 549, 558, 559, 568, 569, 589, 590, 601, 644, 666, 667, and 678 to 680 in 1903 for £35.

This is a model for part of a bronze, lacquered brass and steel fireplace known at the 'Boy' stove designed by Stevens for Messrs Hoole & Co Ltd in 1851, and exhibited at the International Exhibition of that year. A version of this fireplace is in the Metalwork collection (inv.no. 4029–1853; see *Stevens* 1975, illus. on back cover). For a pendant figure see cat.no. 548. For the fireplace and figure, see Hoole [n.d.], fig. 3 on p. 22.

548: Caryatid figure

about 1851
Plaster
h. 38.5 cm.
958:A-1903

Purchased from Hugh Stannus, 64 Larkhall Rise, Clapham, London, together with cat.nos. 535, 537, 538, 541, 544, 547, 549, 558, 559, 568, 569, 589, 590, 601, 644, 666, 667, and 678 to 680 in 1903 for £35.

This is a model for part of a bronze, lacquered brass and steel fireplace known at the 'Boy' stove designed by Stevens for Messrs Hoole & Co Ltd in 1851; see entry for cat.no. 547.

549: Female mask

about 1850–7
Plaster
h. 19.5cm.
967–1903

Purchased from Hugh Stannus, 64 Larkhall Rise, Clapham, London, together with cat.nos. 535, 537, 538, 541, 544, 547, 548, 558, 559, 568, 569, 589, 590, 601, 644, 666, 667, and 678 to 680 in 1903 for £35.

This is a sketch for a female mask; the purpose of the original model is unknown, but it may be part of a fireplace designed for Messrs Henry E. Hoole and Co Ltd. It is similar to the mask ornament on the frieze of a chimneypiece designed by Stevens during his stay in Sheffield (see Hoole [n.d.], p. 7 illus, p. 8 fig. 1).

550: Seated male figure

about 1850–7
Plaster
h. 45 cm
A.25–1911

Purchased from Mrs Ada Gamble, 12 Stanlake Villas, Shepherd's Bush, London, together with cat.nos. 536, 539, 540, 542, 543, 545, 546, 551 to 557, 560, 562 to 567, 570 to 575, 579, 596 to 600, 607, 622, 632 to 637, 643, 647, 650, 652, 663, 668 to 677, and 681 in 1911 for £175. Transferred to the Tate Gallery in 1952 (Tate inv.no. 6117); returned to the V&A in 1975.

This is a sketch model for a section of a firedog; see also cat.no. 551 for a pendant figure and cat.no. 552 a model for another part of the firedogs. A bronze variant is in the Walker Art Gallery, Liverpool. Together with its pendant, the figures were used as models for firedogs for a grate and fender designed by Stevens for Messrs Henry E. Hoole & Co, Sheffield. For illustrations of this firedog see Hoole [n.d.], p. 18; also Armstrong 1881, p. 34 illus.

Bibliography

Royal Academy 1890, p. 51, no. 97; *Review* 1911, pp. 6–7; *Stevens* 1911, p. 11, no. 78; *Tate* 1953, p. 230, no. 6117.

Exhibited

James Gamble Esq. exhibited a 'Figure designed as an Andiron' at the Winter exhibition of *Drawings and Models by Alfred Stevens*, no. 97, possibly the present piece or its pendant; At the *Loan Collection of Works by Alfred Stevens* at the National Gallery, British Art, London (now Tate Gallery), 15 November 1911 to 15 January 1912, Mrs Gamble lent 'Pair of Boy figures for bases of ornament of a grate' (no. 78), possibly the same figures.

551: Seated male figure

about 1850–7
Plaster
h. (incl. board) 41.5 cm
A.26–1911

Purchased from Mrs Ada Gamble, 12 Stanlake Villas, Shepherd's Bush, London, together with cat.nos. 536, 539, 540, 542, 543, 545, 546, 550, 552 to 557, 560, 562 to 567, 570 to 575, 579, 596 to 600, 607, 622, 632 to 637, 643, 647, 650, 652, 663, 668 to 677, and 681 in 1911 for £175. Transferred to the Tate Gallery in 1952 (Tate inv.no. 6118); returned to the V&A in 1975.

This is a sketch model for a section of a firedog designed by Stevens for Messrs Henry E. Hoole & Co Ltd; see also entry for cat.no. 550

its pendant figure, and cat.no. 552 for a model for another part of the firedog. For illustrations of this firedog see Hoole [n.d.], p. 18, and Armstrong 1881, p. 35 illus.

Bibliography
Royal Academy 1890, p. 51, no. 97; *Review* 1911, pp. 6–7; *Stevens* 1911, p. 11, no. 78; *Tate* 1953, p. 230, no. 6118.

Exhibited
James Gamble exhibited a 'Figure designed as an Andiron' at the Winter exhibition of *Drawings and Models by Alfred Stevens*, no. 97, possibly the present piece or its pendant; At the *Loan Collection of Works by Alfred Stevens* at the National Gallery, British Art, London (now Tate Gallery) 15 November 1911 to 15 January 1912, Mrs Gamble lent 'Pair of Boy figures for bases of ornament of a grate' (no. 78), possibly the same figures.

552: Leaves and mask

about 1850–7
Plaster
h. (max.) 13.5 cm.
A.46–1911

Purchased from Mrs Ada Gamble, 12 Stanlake Villas, Shepherd's Bush, London, together with cat.nos. 536, 539, 540, 542, 543, 545, 546, 550, 551, 553 to 557, 560, 562 to 567, 570 to 575, 579, 596 to 600, 607, 622, 632 to 637, 643, 647, 650, 652, 663, 668 to 677, and 681 in 1911 for £175. Transferred to the Tate Gallery in 1952; returned to the V&A in 1975.

This is a model for a boss from the base of a firedog designed for Messrs Henry E. Hoole & Co Ltd. It is a slightly larger study for the leaves supporting the pedestals of the andiron figures; see entries for cat.nos. 550 and 551.

Bibliography
Review 1911, pp. 6–7.

553: Half-bearded mask

about 1850–7
Plaster
l. 29.8 cm. w. 7.5 cm.
A.41–1911

Purchased from Mrs Ada Gamble, 12 Stanlake Villas, Shepherd's Bush, London, together with cat.nos. 536, 539, 540, 542, 543, 545, 546, 550, 552, 554 to 557, 560, 562 to 567, 570 to 575, 579, 596 to 600, 607, 622, 632 to 637, 643, 647, 650, 652, 663, 668 to 677, and 681 in 1911 for £175. Transferred to the Tate Gallery in 1952; and returned to the V&A in 1975.

This is a cast from a sketch by Stevens for a section of a fireplace designed by Stevens, probably for Messrs Henry E. Hoole & Co Ltd.

Bibliography
Review 1911, pp. 6–7.

554: Foliage and lions' heads

about 1850–7
Plaster
h. 30.5 cm.
A.44–1911

Purchased from Mrs Ada Gamble, 12 Stanlake Villas, Shepherd's Bush, London, together with cat.nos. 536, 539, 540, 542, 543, 545, 546, 550 to 553, 555 to 557, 560, 562 to 567, 570 to 575, 579, 596 to 600, 607, 622, 632 to 637, 643, 647, 650, 652, 663, 668 to 677, and 681 in 1911 for £175. Transferred to the Tate Gallery in 1952; and returned to the V&A in 1975.

This is a model for a fireplace back, probably designed by Stevens for Messrs Henry E. Hoole & Co Ltd.

Bibliography
Review 1911, pp. 6–7.

Exhibited
Alfred Stevens 1817–1875, Victoria and Albert Museum, 15 May to 14 September 1975.

555: Acanthus decoration

about 1850–7
Plaster
l.19 cm.
A.66–1911

Purchased from Mrs Ada Gamble, 12 Stanlake Villas, Shepherd's Bush, London, together with cat.nos. 536, 539, 540, 542, 543, 545, 546, 550 to 554, 556, 557, 560, 562 to 567, 570 to 575, 579, 596 to 600, 607, 622, 632 to 637, 643, 647, 650, 652, 663, 668 to 677, and 681 in 1911 for £175. Transferred to the Tate Gallery in 1952; returned to the V&A in 1975.

This is a model for a section of a fender from an unidentified fireplace; the moulding is decorated with acanthus leaves. It was perhaps part of the decoration for a fender designed by Stevens during his stay at Messrs Hoole & Co Ltd, Sheffield.

Bibliography
Review 1911, pp. 6–7.

556: Female profile

about 1850–7
Plaster
h. 14 cm
A.71–1911

Purchased from Mrs Ada Gamble, 12 Stanlake Villas, Shepherd's Bush, London, together with cat.nos. 536, 539, 540, 542, 543, 545, 546, 550 to 555, 557, 560, 562 to 567, 570 to 575, 579, 596 to 600, 607, 622, 632 to 637, 643, 647, 650, 652, 663, 668 to 677, and 681 in 1911 for £175. Transferred to the Tate Gallery in 1952; returned to the V&A in 1975.

This is a model showing an ornamental detail of a female left-facing profile used as a bracket supporting a moulding or entablature. It is possibly part of the decoration for a stove designed by Stevens during his stay at Messrs Hoole & Co Ltd. A closely related though more complete variant of this model is in the National Gallery of Scotland, Edinburgh.

557: Ornament detail with female profile

about 1850 –7
Plaster
h. 21 cm.
A.72–1911

Purchased from Mrs Ada Gamble, 12 Stanlake Villas, Shepherd's Bush, London, together with cat.nos. 536, 539, 540, 542, 543, 545, 546, 550 to 556, 560, 562 to 567, 570 to 575, 579, 596 to 600, 607, 622, 632 to 637, 643, 647, 650, 652, 663, 668 to 677, and 681 in 1911 for £175. Transferred to the Tate Gallery in 1952; returned to the V&A in 1975.

This is a model showing a detail of ornament with female profile. It is a detail for a bronze finger-plate designed by Stevens for Messrs Henry E. Hoole & Co Ltd for folding doors (see Hoole [n.d.], p. 24 illus). An oak door with an example is held in the Sheffield Graves Art Gallery.

Bibliography
Review 1911, pp. 6–7.

558: Rape of Proserpine

about 1855
Plaster
h. (in centre) 27.5 cm.
957–1903

Purchased from Hugh Stannus, 64 Larkhall Rise, Clapham, London, together with cat.nos. 535, 537, 538, 541, 544, 547 to 549, 559, 568, 569, 589, 590, 601, 644, 666, 667, and 678 to 680 in 1903 for £35.

This panel is concave. It is almost certainly a model for the *Rape of Proserpine* fireback for the 'Dog grate' designed by Stevens for Messrs Henry E. Hoole & Co Ltd of Sheffield in 1855. See also entries for cat.nos. 559 to 561. Armstrong recorded that 'In his designs for fire-grates Stevens so happily combined bronzes, brass, and steel that he gave those articles a place among the finest of modern decorative works . . . The whole of the work which he did for his Sheffield employers displays to perfection that union of grave with power, of beauty of line with depth and coherence of expression which should be the highest aim of the designer' (Armstrong 1881, p. 12). A copy of the grate, which was exhibited at the 1862 International Exhibition, was acquired by the South Kensington Museum in 1863 (inv.no. 8532–1863 illustrated in *ibid.*, pp. 20, 21 fig.1 (detail of Proserpine fireback); *Stevens* 1926, fig. 15; *Stevens* 1975, p. 27 fig. 22). Towndrow commented that the '"Dog grate" for the International Exhibition of 1862 was such a work, of exquisite modelling and original spirit, and must have been a magnificent background to the living flames of a fire' (Towndrow 1939, p. 102). An original wax model for this was lent by Messrs Henry E. Hoole & Co to the *Loan Collection of Works by Alfred Stevens,* held at the National Gallery, British Art (now Tate Gallery), between 15 November 1911 and 15 January 1912, no. 77, and at the *Loan Collection of Works by Alfred Stevens* held at the Mappin Art Gallery, Sheffield between April and June 1912, no. 178. A stove designed by Stevens with a group in relief of the *Rape of Proserpine* is under the charge of the Metalwork Department (inv.no. 8532–1863).

BIBLIOGRAPHY
Royal Academy 1890, p. 46, no. 35.

EXHIBITED
A 'Rape of Proserpina bas-relief for the decoration of the back of a fireplace. Plaster' was lent by Hugh Stannus to the commemorative exhibition of Stevens's work held at the Royal Academy in 1890, *Drawings and Models by Alfred Stevens*, no. 35, possibly the present piece.

[Not illustrated].

559: Finial of a firedog

about 1855
Plaster
h. 60 cm.
959–1903

Purchased from Hugh Stannus, 64 Larkhall Rise, Clapham, London, together with cat.nos. 535, 537, 538, 541, 544, 547 to 549, 558, 568, 569, 589, 590, 601, 644, 666, 667, and 678 to 680 in 1903 for £35.

This is a model for two female demi-figures for the finial for the 'Dog grate' irons on the *Rape of Proserpine* fire-back designed by Stevens for Messrs Henry E. Hoole & Co Ltd; see entry for cat.nos. 558, 560 and 561.

560: Two dolphins

about 1855
Plaster
h. 14.5 cm.
A.45–1911

Purchased from Mrs Ada Gamble, 12 Stanlake Villas, Shepherd's Bush, London, together with cat.nos. 536, 539, 540, 542, 543, 545, 546, 550 to 557, 562 to 567, 570 to 575, 579, 596 to 600, 607, 622, 632 to 637, 643, 647, 650, 652, 663, 668 to 677, and 681 in 1911 for £175. Transferred to the Tate Gallery in 1952; returned to the V&A in 1975.

This is a model for the finial of a fire-dog designed by Stevens for Messrs Henry E. Hoole & Co Ltd; see also entries for cat.nos. 558–559 and 561. In the catalogue of Stevens's work whilst at Messrs Hoole & Co between 1850–57, the firedogs, which were cast in bronze or 'armour bright', are described as accompanying the *Rape of Proserpine* fireback, 'Amongst those who are familiar with Stevens' work, this is one of the best known compositions. It is handled in a very bold and masterly manner' (Hoole [n.d.], p. 20 and illus, p. 21 fig. 2 (the finial itself), see also fig. 4; see Armstrong 1881, p. 20 illus). A wax model of a firedog in the form of a dolphin was lent by Messrs Henry E. Hoole & Co Ltd to the *Loan Exhibition of Stevens work* held at the Mappin Art Gallery, Sheffield from April to June 1912, cat.no. 186.

BIBLIOGRAPHY
Review 1911, pp. 6–7.

561: Mask satyr

about 1855
Plaster
h. 6 cm.
A.91–1911

Purchased from Mrs Townroe, 48 Gertrude Street, London, together with cat.nos. 593, 608 to 610, 612, 614, 651, 653, and 664 in 1911 for £25. Transferred to the Tate Gallery in 1952; returned to the V&A in 1975. Mrs Townroe was the widow of Reuben Townroe, a pupil of Stevens, who was also involved in a number of projects connected with the decoration of the Museum. According to Towndrow, whilst Stevens was at Sheffield working for Messrs Hoole & Co Ltd as Chief Designer between 1850 and 1857, he 'invited Reuben a promising art student, to learn the craft under his own instruction at the Green Lane Works. The boy was with Stevens most of the Sheffield period, and gained a faculty in modelling and an unusual insight into the decorative use of metals' (Towndrow 1939, p. 99). A collection of 274 studies and sketches by Stevens was also acquired by the Museum from Mrs Townroe in 1911, and are held in the Department of Prints, Drawings and Paintings (inv.nos. E.2467 to 3003–1911). They include studies for details of many of Stevens's best-known works also represented by sketch-models, including those for St Paul's Cathedral, the Wellington monument and the memorial to the 1851 exhibition. Drawings and copies from tracings and drawings by Stevens from Reuben Townroe were also acquired at this time.

This is cast from a sketch of a mask of a satyr, the beard terminating in foliage, possibly a model for as an ornament for a stove or fender produced whilst Stevens was employed as Chief Designer at Messrs Henry E. Hoole & Co in Sheffield during 1850–7. It is similar to a detail on the *Rape of Proserpine* grate made by Hoole & Co in 1855; see entry for cat.no. 558; as well as entries for cat.nos. 559 and 560.

BIBLIOGRAPHY
Review 1911, pp. 6–7.

562: Table upright foliage terminating in animal heads

about 1857
Plaster
h. 78.5 cm.
A.34–1911

Purchased from Mrs Ada Gamble, 12 Stanlake Villas, Shepherd's Bush, London, together with cat.nos. 536, 539, 540, 542, 543, 545, 546, 550 to 557, 560, 563 to 567, 570 to 575, 579, 596 to 600, 607, 622, 632 to 637, 643, 647, 650, 652, 663, 668–677, 681 in 1911 for £175. Transferred to the Tate Gallery in 1952; returned to the V&A in 1975.

This is a model for the upright side of a cast-iron table designed by Stevens, and produced by Messrs Henry E. Hoole & Co Ltd. Several of these tables were used in the former Refreshment Room (now the Gamble and Morris rooms) in the South Kensington Museum; see Hoole [n.d.], p. 15; Armstrong 1881, p. 40 illus; Physick 1982, pp. 138–9, n. 88. For further models for the same table see entries for cat.nos. 563 and 564.

BIBLIOGRAPHY
Review 1911, pp. 6–7.

[Not illustrated].

563: Cross-bar of a table

about 1857
Plaster
l. 83 cm.
A.35–1911

Purchased from Mrs Ada Gamble, 12 Stanlake Villas, Shepherd's Bush, London, together with cat.nos. 536, 539, 540, 542, 543, 545, 546, 550 to 557, 560, 562, 564 to 567, 570 to 575, 579, 596 to 600, 607, 622, 632 to 637, 643, 647, 650, 652, 663, 668 to 677, and 681 in 1911 for £175.

This model for part of a cast-iron table designed by Stevens for Messrs Henry E. Hoole & Co Ltd. For further models for the same table see entries for cat.nos. 562 and 564.

564: Table top corner

about 1857
Plaster
17.5 cm. sq.
A.36–1911

Purchased from Mrs Ada Gamble, 12 Stanlake Villas, Shepherd's Bush, London, together with cat.nos. 536, 539, 540, 542, 543, 545, 546, 550 to 557, 560, 562, 563, 565 to 567, 570 to 575, 579, 596 to 600, 607, 622, 632 to 637, 643, 647, 650, 652, 663, 668 to 677, and 681 in 1911 for £175. Transferred to the Tate Gallery in 1952; returned to the V&A in 1975.

This is a model for the top of a cast iron table designed by Stevens for Messrs Henry E. Hoole & Co Ltd. For further models for the same table see entries for cat.nos. 562 and 563.

Bibliography
Review 1911, pp. 6–7.

Exhibited
Alfred Stevens 1817–1875, Victoria and Albert Museum, 15 May to 14 September 1975.

565: Section of a fender

about 1850–7?
Plaster
l. 34.5 cm.
A.47–1911

Purchased from Mrs Ada Gamble, 12 Stanlake Villas, Shepherd's Bush, London, together with cat.nos. 536, 539, 540, 542, 543, 545, 546, 550 to 557, 560, 562 to 564, 566, 567, 570 to 575, 579, 596 to 600, 607, 622, 632 to 637, 643, 647, 650, 652, 663, 668 to 677, and 681 in 1911 for £175.

This portion of a fender may have been designed by Stevens whilst he was employed at Messrs Henry E. Hoole & Co Ltd.

566: Section of a fender ?

about 1850–7?
Plaster
l. 23 cm.
A.63–1911

Purchased from Mrs Ada Gamble, 12 Stanlake Villas, Shepherd's Bush, London, together with cat.nos. 536, 539, 540, 542, 543, 545, 546, 550 to 557, 560, 562 to 565, 567, 570 to 575, 579, 596 to 600, 607, 622, 632 to 637, 643, 647, 650, 652, 663, 668 to 677, and 681 in 1911 for £175.

This may be a model for a section of a fender, but has so far been unidenfied. It may have been designed by Stevens whilst he was employed at Messrs Henry E. Hoole & Co Ltd.

567: Part of the side of a fireplace ?

about 1850–7?
Plaster
l. 21 cm.
A.69–1911

Purchased from Mrs Ada Gamble, 12 Stanlake Villas, Shepherd's Bush, London, together with cat.nos. 536, 539, 540, 542, 543, 545, 546, 550 to 557, 560, 562 to 566, 570 to 575, 579, 596 to 600, 607, 622, 632 to 637, 643, 647, 650, 652, 663, 668 to 677, and 681 in 1911 for £175.

This may be a model for part of a fireplace; it has so far been unidentified. It may have been designed by Stevens whilst he was employed at Messrs Henry E. Hoole & Co Ltd.

568: Mould for a cast-iron fender front

about 1850–7?
Plaster
l. 35.4 cm.
969–1903

Purchased from Hugh Stannus, 64 Larkhall Rise, Clapham, London, together with cat.nos. 535, 537, 538, 541, 544, 547, 549, 558, 559, 569, 589, 590, 601, 644, 666, 667, and 678 to 680 in 1903 for £35.

This is a model for a portion of a cast-iron fender front so far unidentified. A plaster cast version of it is in the Museum's collections, inv.no. 1907–8. The illustration is of the present piece above the plaster cast version, which shows its reverse image. It may have been designed by Stevens whilst he was employed by Messrs Henry E. Hoole & Co Ltd.

569: Winged monster

about 1850–7?
Plaster
l. 21 cm.
965–1903

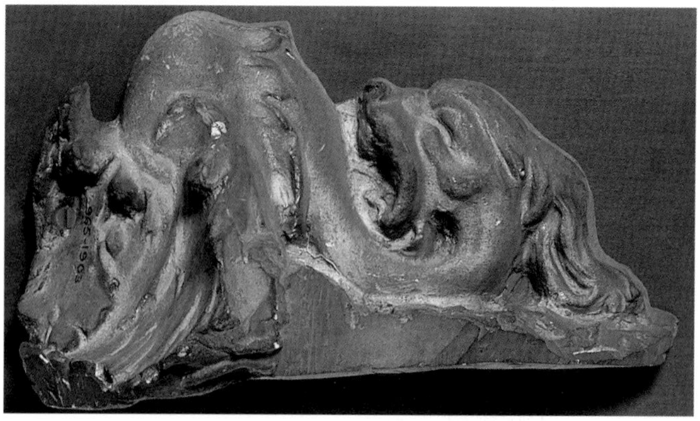

'HS' for Hugh Stannus is inscribed on the reverse.

Purchased from Hugh Stannus, 64 Larkhall Rise, Clapham, London, together with cat.nos. 535, 537, 538, 541, 544, 547 to 549, 558 to 559, 568, 589, 590, 601, 644, 666, 667, 678 to 680 in 1903 for £35.

The is model may relate to work designed by Stevens for Messrs Henry E. Hoole & Co Ltd; see also entry for cat.no. 570.

570: Dragon

about 1850–7?
Plaster
h. 29 cm.
A.58–1911

Purchased from Mrs Ada Gamble, 12 Stanlake Villas, Shepherd's Bush, London, together with cat.nos. 536, 539, 540, 542, 543, 545, 546, 550 to 557, 560, 562 to 567, 571 to 575, 579, 596 to 600, 607, 622, 632 to 637, 643, 647, 650, 652, 663, 668 to 677, and 681 in 1911 for £175.

This corner ornament may have been a model for a figure grate designed by Stevens for Messrs Hoole & Co Ltd; see also entry for cat.no. 569.

571: Hinge

about 1850–7?
Plaster
h. 19.5 cm.
A.67–1911

Purchased from Mrs Ada Gamble, 12 Stanlake Villas, Shepherd's Bush, London, together with cat.nos. 536, 539, 540, 542, 543, 545, 546, 550 to 557, 560, 562 to 567, 570, 572 to 575, 579, 596 to 600, 607, 622, 632 to 637, 643, 647, 650, 652, 663, 668 to 677, and 681 in 1911 for £175.

This may have been a model for a fender end designed by Stevens for Messrs Hoole & Co Ltd.

Work for Coalbrookdale Iron Company

572: Frieze section

about 1856
Plaster
l. 39 cm. w. 17 cm.
A.54–1911

Purchased from Mrs Ada Gamble, 12 Stanlake Villas, Shepherd's Bush, London, together with cat.nos. 536, 539, 540, 542, 543, 545, 546, 550 to 557, 560, 563 to 567, 570 to 571, 573 to 575, 579, 596 to 600, 607, 622, 632 to 637, 643, 647, 650, 652, 663, 668 to 677, and 681 in 1911 for £175. Transferred to the Tate Gallery in 1952; returned to the V&A in 1975.

This section of a festooned frieze is cast from a sketch by Stevens for the top section of moulding from a fireplace produced by the Coalbrookdale Iron Company. A related drawing is held in the Department of Prints, Drawings and Paintings (inv.no. 2692–1911). A further lithograph is in the Royal Institute of British Architects (due to come to the V&A in 2003); see *Stevens* 1975, fig. 27. For other models relating to designs for this fireplace, see entries for cat.nos. 573 to 575.

Bibliography
Review 1911, pp. 6–7.

Exhibited
Alfred Stevens 1817–1875, Victoria and Albert Museum, 15 May to 14 September 1975.

573: Mask and scroll-work

about 1856
Plaster cast
h. 19.5 cm.
A.65–1911

Purchased from Mrs Ada Gamble, 12 Stanlake Villas, Shepherd's Bush, London, together with cat.nos. 536, 539, 540, 542, 543, 545, 546, 550 to 557, 560, 562 to 567, 570 to 572, 574 to 575, 579, 596 to 600, 607, 622, 632 to 637, 643, 647, 650, 652, 663, 668 to 677, and 681 in 1911 for £175. Transferred to the Tate Gallery in 1952; returned to the V&A in 1975.

This is possibly a sketch for the double pilasters forming a fender for part of a fireplace on one of the same Coalbrookdale mantlepieces as discussed in the entries for cat.nos. 572, 574 and 575.

Bibliography
Review 1911, pp. 6–7.

Exhibited
Alfred Stevens 1817–1875, Victoria and Albert Museum, 15 May to 14 September 1975.

574: Double pilaster

about 1856
Plaster
h. 69 cm. w. 26 cm.
A.68–1911

Purchased from Mrs Ada Gamble, 12 Stanlake Villas, Shepherd's Bush, London, together with cat.nos. 536, 539, 540, 542, 543, 545, 546, 550 to 557, 560, 562 to 567, 570 to 573, 575, 579, 596 to 600, 607, 622, 632 to 637, 643, 647, 650, 652, 663, 668 to 677, and 681 in 1911 for £175. Transferred to the Tate Gallery in 1952; returned to the V&A in 1975.

This is a double pilaster for a mantlepiece designed by Stevens for the Coalbrookdale Company in 1859. For futher models relating to this piece see entries for cat.nos. 572, 573 and 575.

Bibliography
Review 1911, pp. 6–7.

Exhibited
Alfred Stevens 1817–1875, Victoria and Albert Museum, 15 May to 14 September 1975.

575: Ornament detail: profile of a ram

about 1856
Plaster
h. (irreg.) 20 cm.
A.73–1911

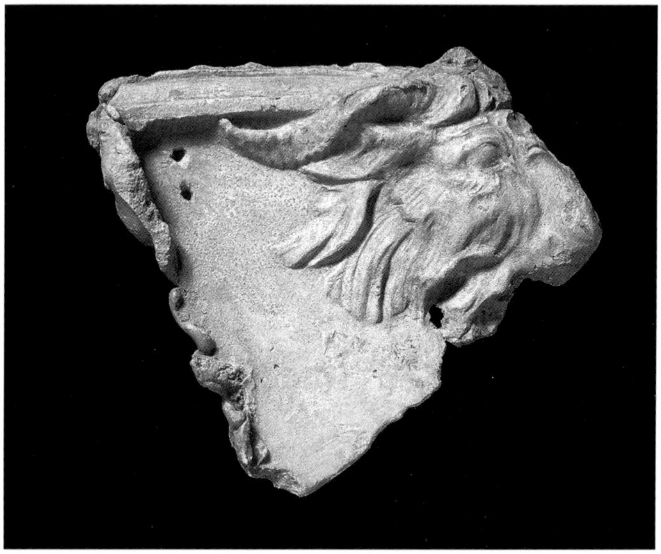

Purchased from Mrs Ada Gamble, 12 Stanlake Villas, Shepherd's Bush, London, together with cat.nos. 536, 539, 540, 542, 543, 545, 546, 550 to 557, 560, 562 to 567, 570 to 574, 579, 596 to 600, 607, 622, 632 to 637, 643, 647, 650, 652, 663, 668 to 677, and 681 in 1911 for £175. Transferred to the Tate Gallery in 1952; returned to the V&A in 1975.

This is a cast from a sketch by Stevens showing the detail of an ornament of a profile of a ram. A curved moulding is supported on the ram's horns. It was the model for the corner of a fire-back for a grate designed by Stevens for the 'Festoon' chimneypiece for Coalbrookdale in 1856. See cat.nos. 572 to 574. See *Stevens* 1975, fig. 26.

Bibliography
Review 1911, pp. 6–7.

Exhibited
Alfred Stevens 1817–1875, Victoria and Albert Museum, 15 May to 14 September 1975.

Wellington Monument, St Paul's Cathedral, London

576: Model for the Wellington Monument in St Paul's Cathedral

1857
Plaster and wax
h. 310 cm.
44–1878

Given by H.M. Office of Works in 1878.

Evidence of pointing is apparent on the surmounting equestrian group. I am grateful to Charlotte Hubbard for drawing this to my attention; see Hubbard 2001.

This is the competitive sketch model produced by Stevens for the Wellington Monument in St Paul's Cathedral, London, and was amongst those exhibited at Westminster Hall in 1857. In 1856 the Government had announced that a competition was to be held for a monument to the Arthur Wellesley, 1st Duke of Wellington (1769–1852). This model is the only one to survive out of a total of eighty-three submissions. Although Stevens came equal fifth in the competition, the winner being the Scottish sculptor William Calder Marshall (1813–1894), he was eventually given the commission, as his design was felt to be more in keeping with the interior of St Paul's Cathedral. The monument, the main part of which was completed after Stevens's death by his pupil Hugh Stannus (1840–1908), the equestrian figure completed by John Tweed [q.v.] was unveiled in 1912; it differs in some respects from this original design. For the full-size models for this monument, see entries for cat.nos. 577, 578 and 581. For a design for the monument in pen and ink in the Department of Prints, Drawings and Paintings (inv.no. 1119–1884), see Physick 1969, pp. 186–8. See also introduction, fig. 3.

Bibliography

Armstrong 1881, p. 16 illus and p. 22; *Royal Academy* 1890, p. 53, no. 125; Stannus 1891, p. 20, pl. XXXVIII; MacColl 1903, fig. 11 p. 96, p. 87; Brown 1934, p. 70 illus.; Towndrow 1939, p. 159 illus; Physick 1969, p. 186, fig. 145 on p. 188; Physick 1970 [Wellington], pls. 34–9; see pp. 51–82 for the preparation of the model; Read 1982, pp. 29, pl. 20, 84; *Ashmolean* [III] 1992, p. 161; Bassett and Fogelman 1997, p. 57 illus.; Hubbard 2001.

Exhibited

Drawings and Models by Alfred Stevens, Royal Academy Winter exhibition 1890, no. 125.

577: Sarcophagus with effigy of Arthur Wellesley, 1st Duke of Wellington

designed 1857; 1867–8
Plaster
l. 320 cm.
321–1878

Purchased from Alfred Pegler Esq., Maybush Lodge, Old Shirley, Southampton, together with the other portions of the full-size model for the Wellington Monument, cat.nos. 578 and 581 in 1878 for £150. The portions had been kept at Young & Co. Eccleston Iron Works, Pimlico.

This sarcophagus and effigy, together with the groups of *Valour and Cowardice* and *Truth and Falsehood* (cat.nos. 581 and 578), are the full-scale models for the Wellington monument; see entry for cat.no. 576, the original competition model; this was followed by a full-size model completed in 1866. The actual monument was not completed until 1912, thirty-seven years after Stevens's death. The vendor Alfred Pegler was a long-standing friend of Stevens. Pegler was keen for the Museum to accept this collection of models in its entirety; he stated that for 'educational purposes, I feel assured that when the present commission for the Wellington Monument is completed, it will be seen how necessary it will be to carry out the design of Mr Stevens in its integrity'. When the models were being considered for acquisition in 1875 Edward J. Poynter [q.v.] considered that the monument's 'interest is greatly enhanced by the fact that, as Mr Stevens died before the completion of the work in St Paul's, the groups of figures on the monuments must be carried out by other hands so that the original models by Mr Stevens himself will be all that remains of his own work'. There was some discussion as to the ownership of the present models offered for sale by Alfred Pegler. H.M. Office of Works wrote in 1876 that it was the property of the Government. See also Introduction, fig. 3.

BIBLIOGRAPHY

Stevens 1926, fig. 4; Brown 1934, p. 70 illus; Physick 1970 [Wellington], pls. 52–5 on pp. 72–3; *Stevens* 1975, p. 37 fig. 43; Read 1982, p. 29 and fig. 20.

EXHIBITED

Alfred Stevens 1817–1875, Victoria and Albert Museum, 15 May to 14 September 1975, cat. no. 43.

578: Truth and Falsehood

designed in 1857; about 1866
Plaster
h. 228 cm.
321:A-1878

Purchased from Alfred Pegler Esq., Maybush Lodge, Old Shirley, Southampton, together with cat.nos. 577 and 581 in 1878 for £150; see entry for cat.no. 577.

This is a full-size model for the bronze group of *Truth and Falsehood* on the Wellington monument. The group depicts Truth pulling out the tongue of Falsehood. See entries for cat.nos. 577 and 581 for other portions of the model. See also introduction, fig. 3.

BIBLIOGRAPHY

Stannus 1891, pp. 19–20, pl. XXXVI; *Stevens* 1926, fig. 5; Brown 1934, p. 78 illus; Physick 1970 [Wellington], pp. 59 and 60 on pp. 78–9; Kenworthy-Browne 1973, p. 575, and fig. 5; *Ashmolean* 1992 [III], p. 161; Williamson 1996 [Trusted], p. 176.

EXHIBITED

Alfred Stevens 1817–1875, Victoria and Albert Museum, 15 May to 14 September 1975, cat. no. 43.

579: Truth and Falsehood

about 1857
Plaster
h. 19 cm.
A.22–1911

Purchased from Mrs Ada Gamble, 12 Stanlake Villas, Shepherd's Bush, London, together with cat.nos. 536, 539, 540, 542, 543, 545, 546, 550 to 557, 560, 562 to 567, 570 to 575, 596 to 600, 607, 622, 632 to 637, 643, 647, 650, 652, 663, 668 to 677, and 681 in 1911 for £175. Transferred to the Tate Gallery in 1952 (Tate inv.no. 6102); returned to the V&A in 1975.

The head and left arm of this seated female figure are missing.

This is an early design for the group *Truth and Falsehood* on the Wellington monument. Another figure is partly indicated on the rough base at the feet of the female figure represented. See also cat.nos. 577 and 578.

BIBLIOGRAPHY
Review 1911, pp. 6–7; *Tate* 1953, p. 230, no. 6102.

580: Truth and Falsehood

about 1876–96
Cast after a model by Alfred Stevens
Bronze
h. 60 cm.
265–1896

Purchased from Messrs John Webb Singer & Sons, Frome, Somerset, together with cat.no. 584 in 1896 for £25 each. On loan to the Mappin Art Gallery, Sheffield from 1969; returned to the V&A in 2001.

This is a cast of the reduced version of the figure of *Truth and Falsehood* from the Wellington monument. See entry for cat.no. 584 for its pendant. Another version is in the Tate Gallery (inv.no. N02270).

BIBLIOGRAPHY
Ashmolean 1992 [III], p. 161.

581: Valour and Cowardice

designed 1857; 1866
Plaster
h. 236 cm.
321:B-1878

Purchased from Alfred Pegler Esq., Maybush Lodge, Old Shirley, Southampton, together with cat.nos. 577 and 578 in 1878 for £150; see entry for cat.no. 577.

This is a full-size model for the bronze figure of *Valour and Cowardice* on the Wellington Monument. See entries for cat.nos. 577 and 578 for the other portions of this model. For further models relating to the *Valour and Cowardice* group, see entries for cat.nos. 582 to 584.

Bibliography
Physick 1970 [Wellington], pp. 176–7 (illus. p. 177); *Stevens* 1975, fig. 44 on p. 38; *Ashmolean* 1992 [III], p. 161; Williamson 1996 [Trusted], p. 176, illus. p. 177.

Exhibited
Alfred Stevens 1817–1875, Victoria and Albert Museum, 15 May to 14 September 1975, cat. no. 43.

582: Valour and Cowardice

about 1863
Plaster, coloured bronze
h. 67 cm.
A.6–1975

Probably one of four sets of casts included in the sale of Stevens's studio effects held on 19 and 20 July 1877 by Messrs Robinson and Fisher. Given to the Tate Gallery by Sir Herbert Cook in memory of the former owner, Sir James Knowles K.C.V.O. through the National Art Collection Fund in 1908. Transferred from the Tate in 1975 (Tate inv.no. 2269).

This cast is taken from a study by Stevens for one of the bronze figures on the Wellington monument. The pendant to this group, *Truth and Falsehood*, was retained by the Tate Gallery (Tate inv.no. 2270). A sketch model of the same subject was lent by John R. Clayton at the exhibition of *Drawings and Models by Alfred Stevens*, at the Royal Academy Winter exhibition, 1890, no. 29. For further models relating to the *Valour and Cowardice* group, see entries for cat.nos. 581, 583 and 584.

Bibliography
British Art 1934, pp. 269–70, cat.no. 1203; Towndrow 1950, p. 84, no. 164; *Tate* 1953, p. 227, no. 2269.

Exhibited
Commemorative Exhibition of British Art, Royal Academy of Arts, London, January to March 1934, cat.no. 1203.

583: Valour and Cowardice

about 1857
Clay
h. 27.5 cm.
A.7–1912

Purchased from W. Onslow Ford Esq., 62 Acacia Road, St John's Wood, London in 1912 for £25. Transferred to the Tate in 1952 (Tate inv.no. 6101); returned to the V&A in 1975.

This is the original clay model produced by Stevens for the group depicting *Valour and Cowardice* on the Wellington monument. A nude armless female figure is seated above a roughly modelled male figure cowering beneath a shield. On acquisition Eric Maclagan [q.v.] commented: 'It is certainly the best of all the small Stevens plastic sketches I have ever seen; and shows his relation to the Italian cinque-cento in a most interesting way'. For further models relating to the Valour and Cowardice group, see entries for cat.nos. 581, 582 and 584.

Bibliography
Stevens 1926, fig. 6; Physick 1970 [Wellington], pl. 48 on p. 68.

584: Valour and Cowardice

about 1876
After a cast by Alfred Stevens by J.W Singer
Bronze
h. 66.2 cm.
264–1896

Purchased from Messrs John Webb Singer & Sons, Frome, Somerset, together with cat.no. 580 in 1896 for £25 each. On loan to the Mappin Art Gallery, Sheffield from 1969; returned to the V&A in 2001.

The present cast is taken from a plaster formerly in the possession of John R. Clayton, which was itself cast from the original sketch-model for the Wellington monument. Stevens exhibited a bronze group of *Valour and Cowardice* (possibly the present piece) for the Wellington monument at the Royal Academy in 1876 (no. 1427), together with a recumbent figure in bronze of the Duke of Wellington (no. 1522) (Graves VII, p. 255). The full-size plaster model for the *Valour and Cowardice* and the *Truth and Falsehood* groups are also in the Victoria and Albert Museum; see entries for cat.nos. 577, 578 and 581. Further versions of the *Valour and Cowardice* and *Truth and Falsehood* groups are in the Fitzwilliam Museum, Cambridge, the Walker Art Gallery, Liverpool, the Ashmolean Museum, Oxford (see *Ashmolean* 1992 [III], pp. 161–2), the National Gallery of Ireland, Dublin, the National Gallery of Scotland, Edinburgh, the Fogg Art Museum, Cambridge (inv.nos. 1943.11.22 and 23; I am grateful to Francesca Bewer for this information), the South African National Gallery, Cape Town, the National Gallery of Victoria, Melbourne. Bronze versions of *Truth and Falsehood* and *Valour and Cowardice*, the property of J.W. Singer & Sons Ltd, were included in the sale held at Sotheby's, London, 20 May 1994, lot 121. For further models relating to the *Valour and Cowardice* group, see entries for cat.nos. 581 to 583.

Bibliography

Ashmolean 1992 [III], p. 161.

585: Winged cherub head

about 1860
Plaster
h. 28 cm.
A.7–1975

Transferred from the Tate Gallery in 1975 (part of Tate inv.no. 2269). Given to the Tate Gallery by Sir Herbert Cook in memory of the former owner, Sir James Knowles through the National Art Collections Fund in 1908. The cast was probably sold at the disposal of Stevens's effects in 1877.

This is a model for a detail of the bronze frieze with cherub heads on the entablature of the Wellington monument; see entry for cat.no. 586. For the preparatory drawings for the frieze, see Physick 1970 [Wellington], pp. 61–2; pls. 41–2.

586: Winged cherub head

about 1860
Plaster
h. 29 cm.
A.7:A-1975

Transferred from the Tate Gallery in 1975 (part of Tate inv.no. 2269). Given to the Tate Gallery by Sir Herbert Cook in memory of the former owner, Sir James Knowles through the National Art Collections Fund in 1908, probably sold at the disposal of Stevens's effects in 1877.

This is a pendant to cat.no. 585, and is a detail of the entablature on the Wellington monument.

587: Cherub head

about 1860–70
Plaster
h. 65.5 cm.
406–1889

Purchased from John Webb Singer & Sons in 1889 for £8.

This is part of a model for the Wellington monument. See Stannus 1891, p. 19, pl. XXXIV.

588: Cherub head

about 1860–70
Painted plaster
h. 24.5 cm.
A.3–1913

Given by Messrs. Omar Ramsden and Alwyn C.E. Carr, St Dunstan's Studio, Seymour Place, Fulham Road, London, in 1913. Ramsden and Carr were silversmiths, active until 1918. They studied in Sheffield and at the Royal College of Art.

This is a model for a cherub head for the projecting portion of the architrave of the Wellington monument.

589: Cherub head

about 1860–70
Plaster
h. 50 cm.
955–1903

'HS' for Hugh Stannus is scratched into the surface.

Purchased from Hugh Stannus, 64 Larkhall Rise, Clapham, London, together with cat.nos. 535, 537, 538, 541, 544, 547 to 549, 558–559, 568, 569, 590, 601, 644, 666, 667, and 678 to 680 in 1903 for £35.

This is an original model for the bronze cherubs in the soffit of the Wellington monument.

590: Two cherub heads

about 1860–70
Painted plaster on wood fitting
l. 79.5 cm.
956–1903

Purchased from Hugh Stannus, 64 Larkhall Rise, Clapham, London, together with cat.nos. 535, 537, 538, 541, 544, 547 to 549, 558, 559, 568, 569, 589, 601, 644, 666, 667, and 678 to 680 in 1903 for £35.

This is the original model for part of the bronze frieze of cherubs on the architrave of the Wellington monument, see Stannus 1891, p. 19, pl. XXXIV.

EXHIBITED
Alfred Stevens 1817–1875, Victoria and Albert Museum, 15 May to 14 September 1975.

591: Three cherub heads

about 1860–70
Plaster in oak frame
l. (relief) 95 cm. l. (incl. wood frame) 123 cm.
A.53–1927

Given by Sannyer Atkin Esq. on behalf of his brother H.W. Atkin Esq., 49 Elm Park Gardens, London, together with cat.no. 592 in 1927.

In his letter offering the two reliefs to the Museum, Sannyer Atkin wrote, 'I think they are casts from which the bronzes were actually struck'.

The present piece and its pendant, cat.no. 592, relate to the frieze on the Wellington monument. Examples of these cherubs' heads already being in the Department of Architecture and Sculpture at the time, R.P. Bedford [q.v.] suggested that they could be assigned to the Circulation Department – where objects were circulated to provincial museums and schools of art, and who were, 'anxious to get some examples of Alfred Steven's work'. In the event, the reliefs were assigned to Architecture and Sculpture. Bedford noted the fact that they were, 'supposed to be two of the casts which were actually used in casting the bronze relief. They are therefore very fresh, and as they are different from the Stevens cherub heads we already have I think they should be in the main collections rather than in circulation. They are mounted in dreadful varnished oak frames of about 1890'.

BIBLIOGRAPHY
Review 1927, pp. 89–90.

592: Three cherubs heads

about 1860–70
Plaster in oak frame
l. (relief) 95.5 cm. l. (incl. wood frame) 123 cm.
A.54–1927

Given by Sannyer Atkin Esq. on behalf of his brother H.W. Atkin Esq., 49 Elm Park Gardens, London, together with cat.no. 591 in 1927.

This relates to the frieze on the Wellington monument; see entry for cat.no. 591.

BIBLIOGRAPHY
Review 1927, pp. 89–90.

593: Four cherub heads

about 1860–70
Plaster
l. 35 cm.
A.88–1911

Purchased from Mrs Townroe, 48 Gertrude Street, London, together with cat.nos. 561, 608 to 610, 612, 614, 651, 653, and 664 in 1911 for £25; see entry for cat.no. 561.

This portion of frieze may be related to similar cherub head friezes on the Wellington monument.

594: Two figures supporting a shield

about 1860–70
Plaster
h. 43 cm.
407–1889

Purchased from John Webb Singer & Sons in 1889 for £6. On loan to the Walker Art Gallery, Liverpool between March 1951 and April 1971.

This is the model for the heraldic achievement as originally conceived for the Wellington monument. It was altered in the finished monument (Physick 1970 [Wellington], p. 75).

Bibliography
Physick 1970 [Wellington], fig. 56 on p. 75.

Exhibited
Alfred Stevens 1817–1875, Victoria and Albert Museum, 15 May to 14 September 1975.

595: Rosette

about 1860–70
Plaster
h. 41 cm. w. 122.3 cm.
353–1899

Purchased from James Gamble Esq., 24 Rich Terrace, South Kensington, London in 1899, together with cat.no. 665 for £12 10s each.

Small portions are missing. This panel is the model from which the bronze work was cast for the ceiling at the extremeties of the Wellington monument immediately above the columns. On acquisition, this and cat.no. 665 were considered 'characteristic bits of Alfred Stevens work and though imperfect and wanting cleaning . . . the original models have a distinct value over and above their artistic merits which are high' (Museum records).

596: Heraldic lion

about 1860–70
Plaster
h. 29.5 cm.
A.32–1911

Purchased from Mrs Ada Gamble, 12 Stanlake Villas, Shepherd's Bush, London, together with cat.nos. 536, 539, 540, 542, 543, 545, 546, 550 to 557, 560, 562 to 567, 570 to 575, 579, 597 to 600, 607, 622, 632 to 637, 643, 647, 650, 652, 663, 668 to 677, and 681 in 1911 for £175.

This is a model for a concave shield on the Wellington monument.

597: Rosette and foliage

about 1860–70
Plaster
l. 121 cm. w. 38.5 cm.
A.28–1911

Purchased from Mrs Ada Gamble, 12 Stanlake Villas, Shepherd's Bush, London, together with cat.nos. 536, 539, 540, 542, 543, 545, 546, 550 to 557, 560, 562 to 567, 570 to 575, 579, 596, 598 to 600, 607, 622, 632 to 637, 643, 647, 650, 652, 663, 668 to 677, and 681 in 1911 for £175. Transferred to the Tate Gallery in 1952; returned to V&A in 1975.

This is a model for a ceiling panel for the Wellington monument; see entry for cat.no. 607.

Bibliography
Review 1911, pp. 6–7.

598: Corinthian capital

about 1860–70
Plaster
h. (max.) 39 cm.
A.30–1911

599

598

Purchased from Mrs Ada Gamble, 12 Stanlake Villas, Shepherd's Bush, London, together with cat.nos. 536, 539, 540, 542, 543, 545, 546, 550 to 557, 560, 562 to 567, 570 to 575, 579, 596, 597, 599, 600, 607, 622, 632 to 637, 643, 647, 650, 652, 663, 668 to 677, and 681 in 1911 for £175. Transferred to the Tate Gallery in 1952; returned to V&A in 1975.

This is a model for a corinthian capital in two pieces for the Wellington monument.

Bibliography
Review 1911, pp. 6–7.

599: Corinthian capital

about 1860–70
Plaster
h. 25 cm.
A.30:A-1911

Purchased from Mrs Ada Gamble, 12 Stanlake Villas, Shepherd's Bush, London, together with cat.nos. 536, 539, 540, 542, 543, 545, 546, 550 to 557, 560, 562 to 567, 570 to 575, 579, 596 to 598, 600, 607, 622, 632 to 637, 643, 647, 650, 652, 663, 668 to 677, and 681 in 1911 for £175.

This is a model for a corinthian capital for the Wellington monument. For illustration see previous entry.

Bibliography
Review 1911, pp. 6–7.

600: Corner piece

about 1860–70
Plaster
h. (max.) 16 cm.
A.64–1911

Purchased from Mrs Ada Gamble, 12 Stanlake Villas, Shepherd's Bush, London, together with cat.nos. 536, 539, 540, 542, 543, 545, 546, 550 to 557, 560, 562 to 567, 570 to 575, 579, 596 to 599, 607, 622, 632 to 637, 643, 647, 650, 652, 663, 668 to 677, and 681 in 1911 for £175. Transferred to the Tate Gallery in 1952; returned to the V&A in 1975.

This is a model for the moulding on the base below the sarcophagus on the Wellington monument.

Bibliography
Review 1911, pp. 6–7.

601: Moulding

about 1860–70
Plaster
l. 15.5 cm.
962–1903

Purchased from Hugh Stannus, 64 Larkhall Rise, Clapham, London, together with cat.nos. 535, 537, 538, 541, 544, 547 to 549, 558, 559, 568, 569, 589, 590, 644, 666, 667, and 678 to 680 in 1903 for £35.

This is a model for part of the moulding on the cornice of the podium on the Wellington monument.

602: Young woman

about 1866
Plaster
h. 42 cm.
1357–1900

Purchased from J.N. Forsyth Esq., The Studios, 325 Finchley Road, Hampstead, London in 1900 for £8 10s. Transferred to the Tate Gallery in 1952 (Tate inv.no. 6100); returned to the V&A in 1975.

This is a model possibly used for one of the Virtues on the Wellington monument; see also entries for cat.nos. 603 and 604 for further versions of the bust in bronze and plaster. On acquisition the bust was painted. The original acquisition information from the vendor records, 'It was modelled absolutely entirely by Stevens from his model, & was given to her some few years before his death, it has been in the possession of her husband since. There is no possible doubt of its genuiness [sic]'. James Gamble was happy to testify to its authenticity and stated, 'Mr Stevens never painted it. I have the original unpainted. Buy it'.

A plaster bust of a woman, possibly a study for *Valour*, was lent by Mrs Gamble to the *Loan Collection of Works by Alfred Stevens* held at the National Gallery, British Art (later Tate Gallery), between 15 November 1911 and 15 January 1912, no. 10.

602

603

According to Towndrow, Stevens preferred to use friends or members of his household as models, and he had a 'handsome woman as a housekeeper when he was living at North End, Fulham Road, who probably was his model, and may have been the unnamed subject of the Wellington Monument' (Towndrow 1939, pp. 138–9).

BIBLIOGRAPHY
Towndrow 1939, p. 138 and pl. 26.

603: Young woman

about 1866
Plaster
h. 41 cm.
A.26–1975

Purchased by the Tate Gallery (Royal Academy Gift Fund) in 1950. Transferred from the Tate in 1975 (Tate inv.no. 5937).

This cast is based on the plaster model of a young woman modelled by Stevens for the *Virtues* on the Wellington monument. A bronze aftercast of the present piece was taken at the Tate in 1950; see entry for cat.no. 604; see also cat.no. 602 for a further plaster version.

BIBLIOGRAPHY
Tate 1953, p. 229, no. 5937.

604: Young woman

1950; original about 1866
Bronze
h. 41 cm.
A.24–1975

Commissioned by the Trustees of the Tate in 1950.Transferred from the Tate Gallery in 1975 (Tate inv.no. 5954).

This bust was commissioned in 1950 by the Trustees of the Tate Gallery, cast after the plaster model held by the Tate for *Valour* and *Truth*, the figures of *Virtues* on the Wellington monument. For two plaster versions see entries for cat.nos. 602 and 603.

BIBLIOGRAPHY
Tate 1953, p. 229, no. 5954; *British Sculpture 1850–1914* 1968, p. 31, no. 142.

EXHIBITED
A bust described as a replica of the model for the *Virtues* on the Wellington Monument was lent by the Trustees of the Tate Gallery to the exhibition *British Sculpture 1850–1914*, held at the Fine Art Society, London, 30 September to 30 October 1968, no. 142, presumably the present piece.

605: Arthur Wellesley, 1st Duke of Wellington
(1769–1852)

about 1866–70
Plaster
h. 32 cm.
A.16–1975

Purchased by Hugh Stannus at the sale of Stevens's studio effects held by Robinson and Fisher on 19 and 20 July 1877. Given to the Tate Gallery by the Wellington Memorial Completion Committee in 1913. Transferred from the Tate Gallery in 1975 (Tate inv.no. 2944).

This head was part of the original plaster model for the figure of Wellington on the equestrian statue on the Wellington monument. According to MacColl, Stannus removed the head for safe-keeping, 'It has been preserved, since his [Stevens's] death, in the crypt of St Paul's; the casual visitor did not see it there, because it was covered up; and even when it was uncovered, the bad light, its closeness to the wall, and the absence of the Duke's head, which Mr Stannus had sawn off made it difficult to form an exact idea of the design and of its condition' (MacColl 1903, p. 87). See also the entry for cat.no. 606, a bronze aftercast taken in 1950.

BIBLIOGRAPHY
MacColl 1903, p. 87, fig. 7 on p. 92; Towndrow 1939, pp. xxii, xvi; Towndrow 1950, p. 85, no. 167 and pl. 26; *Tate* 1953, p. 228, no. 2944; Physick 1970 [Wellington], p. 85, no. 167.

606: Arthur Wellesley, 1st Duke of Wellington
(1769–1852)

1950; original about 1866
Bronze
h. 31 cm.
A.25–1975

Commissioned by the Trustees of the Tate in 1950. Transferred from the Tate Gallery in 1953 (Tate inv.no. 5959).

This head of the Duke of Wellington was cast in 1950 after the plaster model for the equestrian statue on the Wellington monument, cat.no. 605.

BIBLIOGRAPHY
Tate 1953, p. 229, no. 5959.

607: Rosettes and foliage

about 1860–70
Plaster
l. 122 cm. w. 22.5 cm.
A.29–1911

Purchased from Mrs Ada Gamble, 12 Stanlake Villas, Shepherd's Bush, London, together with cat. nos. 536, 539, 540, 542, 543, 545, 546, 550 to 557, 560, 562 to 567, 570 to 575, 579, 596 to 600, 622, 632 to 637, 643, 647, 650, 652, 663, 668 to 677, and 681 in 1911 for £175. Transferred to the Tate Gallery in 1952; returned to V&A in 1975.

This is a model for a narrow ceiling panel possibly for the Wellington monument; see entry for cat.no. 597.

BIBLIOGRAPHY
Review 1911, pp. 6–7.

[Not illustrated].

REDECORATION OF ST PAUL'S CATHEDRAL, LONDON

608: St Mark

about 1862
Plaster
h. 20 cm.
A.82–1911

Purchased from Mrs Townroe, 48 Gertrude Street, London, together with cat.nos. 561, 593, 609, 610, 612, 614, 651, 653, and 664 in 1911 for £25; see entry for cat.no. 561. Transferred to the Tate Gallery in 1952 (Tate inv.no. 6107), and returned to the V&A in 1975.

The figure is set on an integral base.

Between 1862 and 1865 Stevens was engaged in producing designs for the proposed redecoration of St Paul's Cathedral, London, a project which failed to come to fruition.

On acquisition this group of five models for the proposed decoration of St Paul's Cathedral, London, cat.nos. 608–610, 612 and 614 was considered to be the most important element in the collection purchased from Mrs Townroe in 1911, 'Although these are only roughly blocked out they convey an astonishing affect of impressive dignity which can hardly be matched except in the finest work of the Italian Renaissance' (*Review* 1911, p. 7). Eric Maclagan [q.v.] considered they were of 'considerable importance . . . The five sketches in the round – Jael, Judith, David, St Mark & St John, are all first ideas for the great scheme of decoration for the dome and central portions of St Paul's, a scheme for which there are numerous drawings. Sir Charles Holroyd has duplicates of the two first named, and sets great store by them'; see cat.nos. 613, 611 and 615. A.P. Oppé [q.v.] commented, 'they are not casts from finished works such as could be made at any time, but plaster models showing a stage in carrying out the design' (Museum records).

This is a model for the recumbent figure of *St Mark* proposed by Stevens to be carried out in marble for the decoration of the dome in St Paul's Cathedral. See cat.no. 609 for its pendant.

BIBLIOGRAPHY
Review 1911, pp. 6–7; *Tate* 1953, p. 230.

EXHIBITED
Alfred Stevens 1817–1875, Victoria and Albert Museum, 15 May to 14 September 1975.

609: St John

about 1862
Plaster
h. 20.7 cm.
A.83–1911

Purchased from Mrs Townroe, 48 Gertrude Street, London, together with cat.nos. 561, 593, 608, 610, 612, 614, 651, 653, and 664 in 1911 for £25; see entry for cat.no. 561. Transferred to the Tate Gallery in 1952 (Tate inv.no. 6106); returned to the V&A in 1975.

The figure is set on an integral base. This is a model for the recumbent figure of *St John* proposed by Stevens for the decoration of the dome in St Paul's Cathedral; see entry for cat.no. 608. A bronze version is in the National Gallery, Melbourne (Towndrow 1939, fig. 33).

BIBLIOGRAPHY
Review 1911, pp. 6–7; *Tate* 1953, p. 230.

EXHIBITED
Alfred Stevens 1817–1875, Victoria and Albert Museum, 15 May to 14 September 1975.

610: Judith

about 1862
Plaster
h. 24 cm.
A.84–1911

Purchased from Mrs Townroe, 48 Gertrude Street, London, together with cat.nos. 561, 593, 608, 609, 612, 614, 651, 653, and 664 in 1911 for £25; see entry for cat.no. 561. Transferred to the Tate Gallery in 1952 (Tate inv.no. 6105); returned to the V&A in 1975.

This is a model for a figure of Judith proposed by Stevens for the decoration of the dome of St Paul's Cathedral; see entry for cat.no. 608. A bronze version, formerly in the collection of Sir Charles Holroyd, was later acquired by the Museum in 1975; see cat.no. 611.

610

BIBLIOGRAPHY
Review 1911, pp. 6–7; *Tate* 1953, p. 230, no. 6105.

611: Judith

about 1862
Bronze in plaster niche
h. (niche) 42.5 cm. h. (figure) 22 cm
A.10–1975

Given by Sir Charles Holroyd to the Tate in 1912. Sir Charles Holroyd was the first Keeper of the National Gallery, British Art (now Tate Gallery), and later Director of the National Gallery, London. Transferred from the Tate Gallery in 1975 (Tate inv.no. 2887).

This figure was cast by Sir Charles Holroyd after Stevens's plaster model for the planned re-decoration of the dome in St Paul's Cathedral. For a plaster version see entry for cat.no. 610.

Versions of *Judith* and *Jael* in bronze were included in the sale held at Sotheby's, London, 16 April 1986, lot 261, and 2 November 2001, lot 250.

BIBLIOGRAPHY
Stevens 1911, p. 8, no. 46; *Stevens* 1912, p. 39, no. 209; Towndrow 1950, p. 115, no. 342; *Tate* 1953, p. 227, no. 2887.

EXHIBITED
Loan Collection of Works by Alfred Stevens, National Gallery, British Art, London (now Tate Gallery), 15 November 1911 to 15 January 1912, no. 46 lent by the original owner Sir Charles Holroyd, together with cat.nos. 613 and 615; *Loan Collection of Works by Alfred Stevens*, Mappin Art Gallery, Sheffield, April to June 1912, no. 209 lent by Sir Charles Holroyd, together with cat.nos. 613 and 615; *Alfred Stevens 1817–1875*, Victoria and Albert Museum, 15 May to 14 September 1975.

612: Jael

about 1862
Plaster
h. 23 cm.
A.85–1911

Purchased from Mrs Townroe, 48 Gertrude Street, London, together with cat.nos. 561, 593, 608 to610, 614, 651, 653, and 664 in 1911 for £25; see entry for cat.no. 561. Transferred to the Tate Gallery in 1952 (Tate inv.no. 6104); returned to the V&A in 1975.

This is a model for the figure of Jael for Steven's proposed decoration of the dome of St Paul's Cathedral; see entry for cat.no. 608. A bronze version, formerly in the collection of Sir Charles Holroyd was later acquired by the Museum in 1975; see cat.no. 613.

BIBLIOGRAPHY
Review 1911, pp. 6–7; *Tate* 1953, p. 230, no. 6104.

613: Jael

about 1862
Bronze in plaster niche
h. (niche) 42.5 cm. h. (figure) 22 cm.
A.12–1975

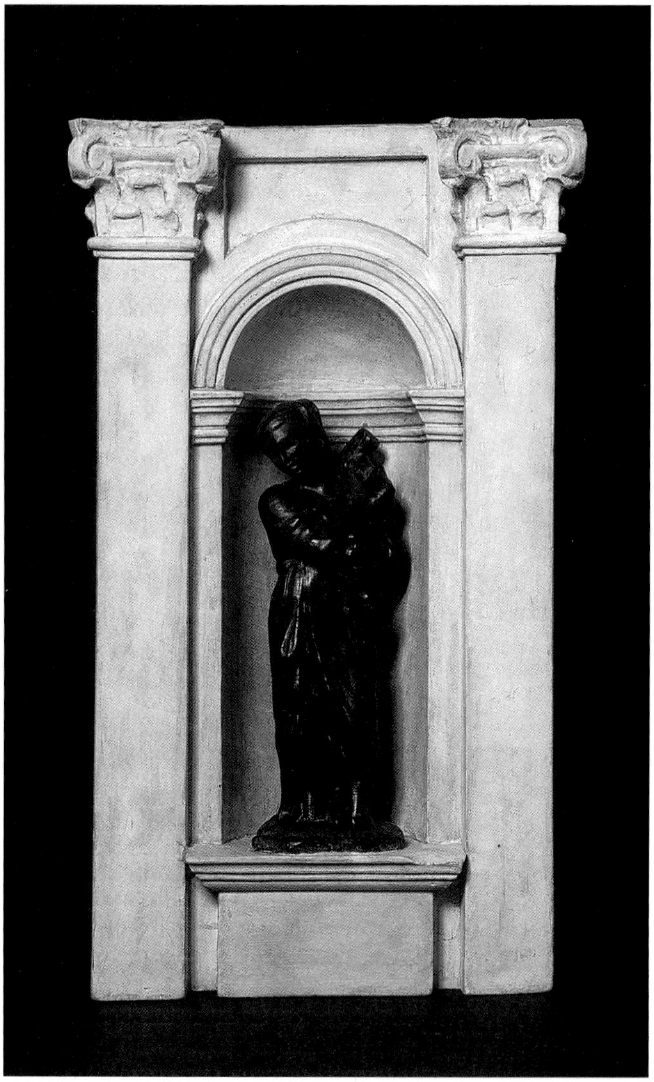

Transferred from the Tate Gallery in 1975 (Tate inv.no. 2889). Given by Sir Charles Holroyd to the Tate in 1912.

This figure is a cast after a model produced by Stevens for the planned re-decoration of the dome in St Paul's Cathedral. For a plaster version, see entry for cat.no. 612.

Versions of *Jael* and *Judith* in bronze were included in the sale at Sotheby's, London, 16 April 1986, lot 261.

Bibliography
Stevens 1911, p. 8, no. 48; *Stevens* 1912, p. 39, no. 211; Towndrow 1950, p. 115, no. 344; *Tate* 1953, p. 227, no. 2889.

Exhibited
Loan Collection of Works by Alfred Stevens, National Gallery, British Art, London (now Tate Gallery), 15 November 1911 to 15 January 1912, no. 48; *Alfred Stevens 1817–1875*, Victoria and Albert Museum, 15 May to 14 September 1975.

614: David

about 1862
Painted plaster
h. 25.5 cm
A.86–1911

Purchased from Mrs Townroe, 48 Gertrude Street, London, together with cat.nos. 561, 593, 608 to 610, 612, 651, 653, and 664 in 1911 for £25; see

entry for cat.no. 561. Transferred to the Tate Gallery in 1952; returned to the V&A in 1975.

This is a model for the figure of David proposed by Stevens for the dome of St Paul's Cathedral; see entry for cat.no. 608. A bronze version formerly in the collection of Sir Charles Holroyd was later acquired by the Museum in 1975; see cat.no. 615.

Bibliography
Review 1911, pp. 6–7; *Tate* 1953, p. 230, no. 6103.

Exhibited
Alfred Stevens 1817–1875, Victoria and Albert Museum, 15 May to 14 September 1975.

615: David

about 1862
Bronze
h. 22.5 cm.
A.11–1975

Transferred from the Tate Gallery in 1975 (Tate inv.no. 2888). Given by Sir Charles Holroyd to the Tate in 1912.

This figure is a cast after a model produced by Stevens for the planned re-decoration of the dome in St Paul's Cathedral. For a plaster version, see entry for cat.no. 614.

BIBLIOGRAPHY
Stevens 1911, p. 8, no. 47; *Stevens* 1912, p. 39, no. 210; Towndrow 1950, p. 115, no. 343; *Tate* 1953, p. 227, no. 2888.

EXHIBITED
Loan Collection of Works by Alfred Stevens, National Gallery, British Art, London (now Tate Gallery), 15 November 1911 to 15 January 1912, no. 47.

616: Isaiah

1862
Painted and gilt canvas on plaster
h. 53 cm
1955–1897

Given by F.C. Penrose Esq., Surveyor to the Fabrick of St Paul's, The Chapter House, St Paul's Churchyard, in 1897, together with cat.nos. 617 and 618. In July 1897 Penrose wrote that he was leaving his position imminently and was anxious to find a suitable home for these models.

This is a model for a mosaic spandrel proposed by Stevens between the dome arches of St Paul's Cathedral. The mosaic was executed by Salviati [q.v.] and was unveiled in 1864 (see Stannus 1891, p. 25, pl. LI). A number of studies for this mosaic are held in the Tate Gallery. Armstrong commented that although the space was similar to the Sistine Chapel and that comparisons with Michelangelo were apparent, 'It is obvious . . . that far from being a servile imitation of the great Florentine, his Isaiah is a bold attempt to rival him on his own ground' (Armstrong 1881, p. 25). See also entries for cat.nos. 617 and 618.

617: Jeremiah

1862
Painted and gilt canvas on plaster
h. 53 cm.
1956–1897

Given by F.C. Penrose Esq. in 1897; see entry for cat.no. 616.

This is a model for a spandrel proposed by Stevens for the mosaic decoration between the dome arches of St Paul's Cathedral, London (Stannus 1891, p. 25, pl. LII). See entries for cat.nos. 616 and 618. This model was never executed in mosaic.

618: Daniel

about 1862
Painted and gilt canvas on plaster
h. 52.5 cm.
1957–1897

Given by F.C. Penrose Esq. in 1897; see entry for cat.no. 616.

This is a model for a spandrel proposed by Stevens for the mosaic decoration between the dome arches of St Paul's Cathedral, London (see Stannus 1891, p. 25, pl. LIII). The design was partly executed in mosaic but never completed; see entry for cat.no. 619; also cat.nos. 616 and 617. Armstrong considered the design for Daniel as being the 'most vigorous and original of the three' (Armstong 1881, p. 25).

619: Head of the prophet Daniel

about 1864
Mosaic
h. 107 cm. w. 67 cm.
108–1873

Given by Jesse Rust Esq. in 1873.

This is an experimental panel for a mosaic designed by Stevens for one of the spandrels between the dome arches of St Paul's Cathedral, London. Beattie commented on the St Paul's Cathedral dome project, which was to include mosaic and sculpture, noting that it was 'potentially the most important decorative scheme he [Stevens] ever devised' (*Stevens* 1975, p.14). Armstrong commented, 'The Isaiah was executed by Salviati [q.v.] in glass mosaic, and its appearance when put up was so unsatisfactory to the artist that he had a portion of his Daniel carried out experimentally by an English firm. This fragment . . . was so much more to his mind, especially in the matter of colour, that any further work of the kind been sought from him he would have employed the same hands' (Armstrong 1881, p. 26). The English firm mentioned by Armstrong was probably Messrs Jesse Rust & Co: the mosaic was presented to the Museum by Jesse Rust.

BIBLIOGRAPHY
Armstrong 1881, p. 23 illus, p. 26; *Bequests and Donations* 1901, p. 230; *Stevens* 1975, p. 45 illus. 59.

EXHIBITED
Alfred Stevens 1817–1875, Victoria and Albert Museum, 15 May to 14 September 1975, cat.no. 59.

DORCHESTER HOUSE, PARK LANE, LONDON

620: Caryatid

about 1860–9
Plaster
h. 188 cm.
129–1879

Cat.nos. 620 and 621 Caryatids shown on model of chimneypiece in 1907.

Purchased from James Gamble, 24 Rich Terrace, London, together with cat.no. 621 the pendant figure, in 1879 for £75 (£37 10s each). Transferred to the Tate Gallery in 1952 (Tate inv.no. 6108); returned to the V&A in 1975.

Around 1858 Stevens was commissioned by Robert Holford to redesign the dining-room of Dorchester House, Park Lane; he also designed the mantelpiece for the saloon. This is a model for the right-hand caryatid figure for the mantelpiece for the Dorchester House dining-room; see entry for cat.no. 621 for the model for its pendant. According to Stannus, Stevens spent 1860 preparing the designs for the decoration of Dorchester House, and executed the fittings from 1863–5 (Stannus 1891, p. 26). The chimneypiece was finally installed in about 1869, though the caryatid figures were finished at a later date by Stevens's former pupil and the previous owner of the present piece, James Gamble. Armstrong commented on the caryatid figures on the finished mantlepiece: 'The two caryatid figures are works as fine and strong as anything produced during the last three centuries; but they make no attempt to appear superior to their work; they are entirely part of the architectural combination to which they are attached' (Armstrong 1881, p. 28). Dorchester House was demolished in 1929, and the chimneypiece was presented to the Tate Gallery in 1931 by the Dorchester House Syndicate Ltd; it was transferred to the V&A in 1976; see also entry for cat.no. 627. A plaster version of the chimneypiece was transferred from the Tate in 1975, having been originally presented to the Tate in 1911 by the Alfred Stevens Memorial Committee; see entry for cat.no. 628. For a reduced plaster version of this caryatid, see entry for cat.no. 625; for reduced versions of the left-hand figure, see entries for cat.nos. 622 to 624.

Bibliography
Armstong 1881, p. 6 illus; *Stevens* 1926, fig. 13; *Masterpieces* 1951, p. 103, no. 50, illus. pp. 102; *Tate* 1953, p. 230, no. 6108.

Exhibited
Alfred Stevens 1817–1875, Victoria and Albert Museum, 15 May to 14 September 1975.

621: Caryatid

about 1860–9
Plaster
h. 188 cm.
130–1879

Purchased from James Gamble, 24 Rich Terrace, London, for £37 10s in 1879, together with cat.no. 620, in 1879 for £75 (£37 10s each). Transferred to the Tate Gallery in 1952 (Tate inv.no. 6109); and returned to the V&A in 1975.

This is a model for the left-hand caryatid figure designed by Stevens for the mantelpiece for the Dorchester House dining-room; see entry for cat.no. 620. For reduced plaster versions of this caryatid figure, see entries for cat.nos. 622 to 624.

Bibliography
Armstrong 1881, p. 7 illus; *Stevens* 1926, fig. 12; *Tate* 1953, p. 230, no. 6109; Bassett and Fogelman 1997, p. 17.

Exhibited
Alfred Stevens 1817–1875, Victoria and Albert Museum, 15 May to 14 September 1975.

622: Caryatid

about 1873
Plaster
h. 19.5 cm.
A.23–1911

Purchased from Mrs Ada Gamble, 12 Stanlake Villas, Shepherd's Bush, London, together with cat.nos. 536, 539, 540, 542, 543, 545, 546, 550 to 557, 560, 562 to 567, 570 to 575, 579, 596 to 600, 607, 632 to 637, 643, 647, 650, 652, 663, 668 to 677, and 681 in 1911 for £175. Transferred to the Tate Gallery in 1952 (Tate inv.no. 6110); returned to the V&A in 1975.

The left hand is missing.

This is a model for the left-hand caryatid figure for the mantlepiece for the dining-room at Dorchester House, Park Lane, London; for the full-size model, see entry for cat.no. 621.

Bibliography
Review 1911, pp. 6–7.

623: Caryatid

about 1873
Plaster
h. 23 cm.
A.25–1934

Purchased from Miss Margaret Bagshawe, 63 Wostenholm Road, Sheffield, together with cat.nos. 624 and 625 in 1935 for £25. Originally on loan to the Museum in 1916 by Professor Randolph Schwabe, to whose care they had been entrusted by the owner, Private William Wyatt Bagshawe, an artist serving in Her Majesty's Forces. On the death of Private Bagshawe in 1916, no living relatives could be traced, and Professor Schwabe gave the present piece, together with cat.nos. 624 and 625, to the Museum in 1934. Subsequently Miss Margaret Bagshawe, Private Bagshawe's sister and heir came forward, and the figures were purchased from her a year later in 1935: the original inventory numbers relating to the previous year were retained. According to Towndrow, Bagshawe's father was 'one of Stevens's Sheffield circle' (Towndrow 1939, p. xvii). Transferred to the Tate Gallery in 1952 (Tate inv.no. 6111); returned to the V&A in 1975.

This is a further model for the left-hand caryatid figure on the Dorchester House mantelpiece. For the full-size model, see entry for cat.no. 621.

BIBLIOGRAPHY
Stevens 1911, p.15, no. 137; *Review* 1934, p. 5; *Tate* 1953, p. 230, no. 6111.

EXHIBITED
Two models of caryatids were lent by Mr W.W. Bagshawe to the *Loan Collection of Works by Alfred Stevens*, National Gallery, British Art (later Tate Gallery), 15 November 1911 to 15 January 1912, cat.nos. 130 and 137. It is probable that the present piece was exhibited as no. 137; see also entry for cat.no. 625.

624: Caryatid

about 1873
Plaster
h. 18.3 cm.
A.26–1934

Purchased from Miss Margaret Bagshawe, 63 Wostenholm Road, Sheffield, together with cat.nos. 623 and 625 in 1934 for £25; see entry for cat.no. 623. Transferred to the Tate Gallery in 1952 (Tate inv.no. 6112); returned to the V&A in 1975.

This is a further study for the left-hand caryatid figure on the Dorchester House mantelpiece; see entry for cat.no. 623. See also entry for the full-size model cat.no. 621.

BIBLIOGRAPHY
Review 1934, p. 5; *Tate* 1953, p. 230, no. 6112.

625: Caryatid

about 1873
Plaster
h. 25 cm.
A.27–1934

Purchased from Miss Margaret Bagshawe, 63 Wostenholm Road, Sheffield, together with cat.nos. 623 and 624 in 1934 for £25. Transferred to the Tate Gallery in 1952 (Tate inv.no. 6110); returned to the V&A in 1975. See entry for cat.no. 623.

This is a study for the right-hand caryatid figure on the Dorchester House mantelpiece. For the full-size plaster model see entry for cat.no. 620.

BIBLIOGRAPHY
Stevens 1911, p. 15, no. 130; *Review* 1934, p. 5; *Tate* 1953, p. 230, no. 6113.

EXHIBITED
Two models of caryatids were lent by Mr W.W. Bagshawe to the *Loan Collection of Works by Alfred Stevens*, National Gallery, British Art (later Tate Gallery), 15 November 1911 to 15 January 1912, cat.nos. 130 and 137. It is probable that the present piece was exhibited as no. 130; see also entry for cat.no. 623.

626: Overmantel

about 1863
Plaster
h. 76.2 cm.
A.15–1975

Originally belonging to Messrs Vincent Robinson; bought by them from the Stevens sale held by Robinson and Fisher on 19 and 20 July 1877. Purchased by the National Art Collections Fund in 1912 for £30. Transferred from the Tate Gallery in 1975 (Tate inv.no. 2893).

This is a study for the marble overmantel designed by Stevens for Dorchester House. The original is now held in the Walker Art

Gallery, Liverpool (illustrated Stannus 1891, p. 26). A paper design for the top panel of the overmantel is in the Tate Gallery (inv.no. N03786).

BIBLIOGRAPHY
Stevens 1911, p. 8, no. 45; *Tate* 1953, p. 227, no. 2893; Towndrow 1950, p. 122, no. 390.

EXHIBITED
Loan Collection of Works by Alfred Stevens, National Gallery, British Art (now Tate Gallery), 15 November 1911 to 15 January 1912, no. 45, lent by Messrs Vincent Robinson.

[Not illustrated].

627: Chimneypiece

Partly installed about 1869; completed by James Gamble about 1873
Carrara, grey bardiglio, and red marbles
h. 4.45 m
A.2–1976

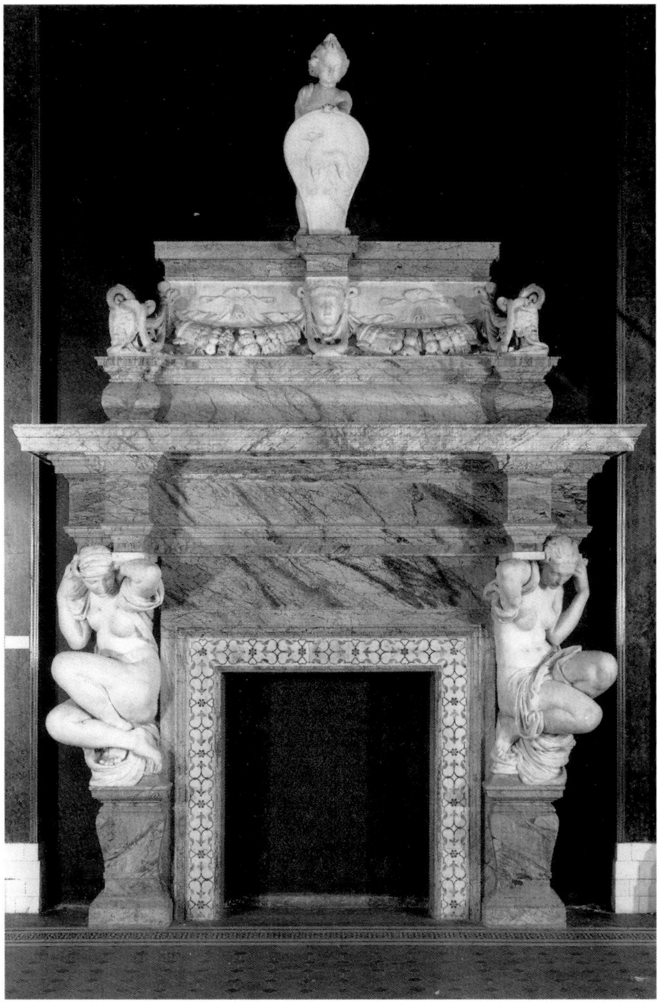

Originally from the dining-room at Dorchester House, Park Lane, London. Presented to the Tate Gallery in 1931 by the Dorchester House Syndicate Ltd. Transferred from the Tate in 1975 and formally registered at the V&A in 1976 (Tate inv.no. 4575).

This is the mantlepiece commissioned from Stevens by Robert Holford for the dining-room at Dorchester House, Park Lane. Although the mantelpiece was installed in about 1869, the caryatid figures were finished by James Gamble in 1873 (Stannus 1891, p. 31); see entry for cat.no. 620. Stannus commented: 'The Ornaments, and the Putto with the armorial shield of the Super-mantle, are modelled in a large manner; and the whole work is probably the finest Mantle-piece out of Italy' (Stannus 1891, p. 32). A plaster cast of the mantelpiece was transferred from the Tate Gallery in 1975; see entry for cat.no. 628; for the two full-size models for the caryatids see cat.nos. 620 and 621.

BIBLIOGRAPHY
Stannus 1891, pp. 31–2; pl. LVI and LVII; Gronau 1909, p. 51; Towndrow 1950, pp. 119–20, no. 376, pl. 25; *Tate* 1953, p. 229, no. 4575; Laing 1989, p. 251, fig. 14 on p. 251, n. 54 on p. 254; TDA, vol, p. 646, fig. 2 on p. 647 [Stocker].

EXHIBITED
Alfred Stevens 1817–1875, Victoria and Albert Museum, 15 May to 14 September 1975.

628: Mantelpiece

about 1911
Plaster and wood
h. 157 cm.
A.29–1975

Presented to the Tate Gallery by the Alfred Stevens Memorial Committee in 1911 (Tate inv.no.2785). Transferred from the Tate in 1975.

The marble mantelpiece from the dining room at Dorchester House for which this is probably a model, was also transferred to this Museum from the Tate Gallery in 1975; see entry for cat.no. 627. Plaster models for the caryatid figures are also in the collection; see entries for cat.nos. 620 and 621.

[Not illustrated].

629: Mirror frame

about 1863
Plaster in glazed wood frame
h. 91.5 cm. w. 77 cm.
594–1890

Purchased from John R. Clayton Esq. in 1890 for £10. This may be the 'small-scale plaster cast of frame of mirror in Dorchester House' purchased by Clayton for 7s at the sale of Stevens's studio effects by Messrs Robinson and Fisher, on 19 July 1877 (lot 32). The sale is noted as an appendix to Towndrow 1950; an annotated copy of the catalogue for the first day's sale is also held in the National Art Library (see Towndrow 1950, p. 129).

According to Museum records, this mirror frame was cast in a waste-mould taken from the original model executed by Stevens as part of the decoration of the dining-room at Dorchester House. Stannus recorded that the fittings for Dorchester House were designed and executed between 1863 and 1865, and that 'The MIRRORS of which there are eight, are treated with marginal frames of grotesques. The plaster model made for these is in South Kensington Museum, and some idea may be formed from the Title-page in Mr W. Armstrong's "study"' (Stannus 1891, p. 25; for title page referred to, see Armstong 1881). The completed mirror frames were carved in wood.

Bibliography
Royal Academy 1890, p. 45, no. 12; Stannus 1891, p. 25.

Exhibited
A mirror frame described as 'Plaster, afterwards executed in wood at Dorchester House', was lent by John R. Clayton Esq. to the Royal Academy Winter exhibition of *Drawings and Models by Alfred Stevens*, Winter 1890, no. 12, and is probably the present piece; *Alfred Stevens 1817–1875*, Victoria and Albert Museum, 15 May to 14 September 1975.

630: Head of a mirror frame

about 1863
Plaster
l. 46 cm.
312–1895

Purchased from Reuben Townroe, 48 Gertrude Street, Chelsea, London, in 1895 for £3 10s.

This is a model for the head of a mirror frame executed by Stevens for Dorchester House.

631: Door-knocker

about 1863
Plaster
h. 29 cm.
311–1895

Purchased from Reuben Townroe, 48 Gertrude Street, Chelsea, London, in 1895 for £1.

This is a model for a door-knocker executed by Stevens for Dorchester House.

632: Back view of half-length female nude

about 1863
Plaster
diam. 32 cm.
A.16–1911

Purchased from Mrs Ada Gamble, 12 Stanlake Villas, Shepherd's Bush, London together with cat.nos. 536, 539, 540, 542, 543, 545, 546, 550 to 557, 560, 562 to 567, 570 to 575, 579, 596 to 600, 607, 622, 633 to 637, 643, 647,

650, 652, 663, 668 to 677, and 681 in 1911 for £175. Transferred to the Tate Gallery in 1952 (Tate inv.no. 6116 for all six roundels, cat.nos. 632 to 637); returned to the V&A in 1975.

This is one of six roundels cast in plaster from sketches by Stevens for carved walnut doors in Dorchester House, Park Lane. For further roundels see cat.nos. 633 to 642. The walnut doors into which the panels are set are now in the Walker Art Gallery, Liverpool.

On acquisition this group of sketch models was considered especially important as a record of the original working models produced by a sculptor: 'The majority of these are plaster casts from clay models, (which would themselves usually be destroyed on completion), and represent the first plastic conception of the artist' (*Review* 1911, p. 6). They were considered 'an important series of plaster models of details . . . The work of this great artist, who was so intimately connected with this Museum, is of great interest to all students of design . . . The plaster casts represent a stage in Stevens's method of production: they include figure studies, designs for metalwork and ceilings, details of fireplaces, stoves, fenders, etc.' Eric Maclagan [q.v.] commented, 'I have no doubt whatever that they will be of great use to students and of great interest to the public'.

BIBLIOGRAPHY
Review 1911, pp. 6–7; *Stevens* 1926, fig. 11; *Tate* 1953, p. 230, no. 6116; *British Sculpture 1850–1914* 1968, p. 31, no. 141.

EXHIBITED
Six roundels for door panels at Dorchester House were lent by the Trustees of the Tate Gallery to the exhibition *British Sculpture 1850–1914*, held at the Fine Art Society 30 September to 30 October 1968, cat.no. 141, presumably the present piece, together with cat.nos. 633 to 637; *Alfred Stevens 1817–1875*, Victoria and Albert Museum, 15 May to 14 September 1975, cat.no. 51.

633: Figure with a sash

about 1863
Plaster
diam. 33.5 cm
A.17–1911

Purchased from Mrs Ada Gamble, 12 Stanlake Villas, Shepherd's Bush, London, together with cat.nos. 536, 539, 540, 542, 543, 545, 546, 550 to 557, 560, 562 to 567, 570 to 575, 579, 596 to 600, 607, 622, 632, 634 to 637, 643, 647, 650, 652, 663, 668 to 677, and 681 in 1911 for £175. Transferred to the Tate Gallery in 1952 (Tate inv.no. 6116); returned to the V&A in 1975.

This is one of six roundels cast in plaster for a door in Dorchester House, Park Lane; see entry for cat.no. 632.

BIBLIOGRAPHY
Review 1911, pp. 6–7, fig 5; *Stevens* 1926, fig 11; Tate 1953, p. 230, no. 6116; *British Sculpture 1850–1914* 1968, p. 31, no. 141.

EXHIBITED
See entry for cat.no. 632.

634: Figure playing a harp

about 1863
Plaster
diam. 34 cm.
A.18–1911

Purchased from Mrs Ada Gamble, 12 Stanlake Villas, Shepherd's Bush, London, together with cat.nos. 536, 539, 540, 542, 543, 545, 546, 550 to 557, 560, 562 to 567, 570 to 575, 579, 596 to 600, 607, 622, 632 to 633, 635 to 637, 643, 647, 650, 652, 663, 668 to 677, and 681 in 1911 for £175. Transferred to the Tate Gallery in 1952 (Tate inv.no. 6116); returned to the V&A in 1975.

This is one of six roundels in plaster for a door in Dorchester House, Park Lane; see entry for cat.no. 632.

BIBLIOGRAPHY
Review 1911, pp. 6–7, fig. 5; *Stevens* 1926, fig. 11.

EXHIBITED
See entry for cat.no. 632.

635: Figure with a shell

about 1863
Plaster
diam. 33.5 cm.
A.19–1911

Purchased from Mrs Ada Gamble, 12 Stanlake Villas, Shepherd's Bush, London, together with cat.nos. 536, 539, 540, 542, 543, 545, 546, 550 to 557, 560, 562 to 567, 570 to 575, 579, 596 to 600, 607, 622, 632 to 634, 636 to 637, 643, 647, 650, 652, 663, 668 to 677, and 681 in 1911 for £175. Transferred to the Tate Gallery in 1952 (Tate inv.no. 6116); returned to the V&A in 1975.

This is one of six roundels in plaster for a door in Dorchester House, Park Lane; see entry for cat.no. 632.

Bibliography
Review 1911, pp. 6–7; *Stevens* 1926, fig 11; *Tate* 1953, p. 230, no. 6116; *British Sculpture 1850–1914* 1968, p. 31, no. 141.

Exhibited
See entry for cat.no. 632.

636: Reclining figure

about 1863
Plaster
diam. 25.5 cm.
A.20–1911

636

Purchased from Mrs Ada Gamble, 12 Stanlake Villas, Shepherd's Bush, London, together with cat.nos. 536, 539, 540, 542, 543, 545, 546, 550 to 557, 560, 562 to 567, 570 to 575, 579, 596 to 600, 607, 622, 632 to 635, 637, 643, 647, 650, 652, 663, 668 to 677, and 681 in 1911 for £175. Transferred to the Tate Gallery in 1952 (Tate inv.no. 6116); returned to the V&A in 1975.

This is one of six roundels cast in plaster for a door in Dorchester House, Park Lane; see entry for cat.no. 632.

Bibliography
Review 1911, pp. 6–7; *Tate* 1953, p. 230, no. 6116; *British Sculpture 1850–1914* 1968, p. 31, no. 141.

Exhibited
See entry for cat.no. 632.

637: Mother and child

about 1863
Plaster
diam. 25.5 cm.
A.21–1911

Purchased from Mrs Ada Gamble, 12 Stanlake Villas, Shepherd's Bush, London, together with cat.nos. 536, 539, 540, 542, 543, 545, 546, 550 to 557, 560, 562 to 567, 570 to 575, 579, 596 to 600, 607, 622, 632 to 636, 643, 647, 650, 652, 663, 668 to 677, and 681 in 1911 for £175. Transferred to the Tate Gallery in 1952 (Tate inv.no. 6116); returned to the V&A in 1975.

This is one of six roundels in plaster for a door in Dorchester House, Park Lane; see entry for cat.no. 632.

BIBLIOGRAPHY
Review 1911, pp. 6–7; *Tate* 1953, p. 230, no. 6116; *British Sculpture 1850–1914* 1968, p. 31, no. 141.

EXHIBITED
See entry for cat.no. 632.

638: Woman with double pipes

about 1863
Plaster
diam. 29 cm.
A.18–1975

Given to the Tate Gallery in 1928 by the executors of Sir George Holford through the National Art Collections Fund. Transferred from the Tate in 1975 (Tate inv.no. 4386a).

This roundel and cat.nos. 632 to 637 and 639 to 642 are studies for panels for the walnut doors in the dining-room at Dorchester House, Park Lane, London, now in the Walker Art Gallery, Liverpool.

BIBLIOGRAPHY
Towndrow 1950, p. 119, no. 371; *Tate* 1953, p. 229, no. 4386; *Stevens* 1975, p. 41, no. 51.

EXHIBITED
Alfred Stevens 1817–75, Victoria and Albert Museum, 15 May to 14 September 1975, no. 51.

639: Kneeling woman holding a vessel aloft

about 1863
Plaster
diam. 27 cm.
A.19–1975

639

Given to the Tate Gallery in 1928 by the executors of Sir George Holford through the National Art Collections Fund. Transferred from the Tate in 1975 (Tate inv.no. 4386b).

This roundel is a further study for panels for the walnut doors in the dining-room at Dorchester House, Park Lane, London, now in the Walker Art Gallery, Liverpool. See also entries for cat.nos. 632 to 638 and 640 to 642.

BIBLIOGRAPHY
Towndrow 1950, p. 119, no. 372; *Tate* 1953, p. 229, no. 4386.

640: Woman leaning on a capital

about 1863
Plaster
diam. 24 cm.
A.20–1975

Given to the Tate Gallery in 1928 by the executors of Sir George Holford through the National Art Collections Fund. Transferred from the Tate in 1975 (Tate inv.no. 4386c).

This roundel is a further study for panels for the walnut doors in the dining-room at Dorchester House, Park Lane, London, now in the Walker Art Gallery, Liverpool; see also entries for cat.nos. 632 to 639 and 641 to 642.

BIBLIOGRAPHY
Towndrow 1950, p. 119, no. 373; *Tate* 1953, p. 229, no. 4386.

641: Woman on a dolphin

about 1863
Plaster
diam. 24 cm.
A.21–1975

Given to the Tate Gallery in 1928 by the executors of Sir George Holford through the National Art Collections Fund. Transferred from the Tate in 1975 (Tate inv.no. 4386d).

This roundel is a further study for panels for the walnut doors in the dining-room at Dorchester House, Park Lane, London, now in the Walker Art Gallery, Liverpool; see also entries for cat.nos. 632 to 640 and 642.

BIBLIOGRAPHY
Towndrow 1950, p. 119, no. 374; *Tate* 1953, p. 229, no. 4386.

642: Seated woman

about 1863
Plaster
diam. 28 cm.
A.22–1975

642

Given to the Tate Gallery in 1928 by the executors of Sir George Holford through the National Art Collections Fund. Transferred from the Tate in 1975 (Tate inv.no. 4386e).

This roundel is a further study for panels for the wooden doors in the dining-room at Dorchester House, Park Lane, London, now in the Walker Art Gallery, Liverpool; see entries for cat.nos. 632 to 641.

BIBLIOGRAPHY
Towndrow 1950, p. 119, no. 375; *Tate* 1953, p. 229, no. 4386.

643: Panel of a pilaster

about 1863
Plaster
h. 45 cm.
A.33–1911

Purchased from Mrs Ada Gamble, 12 Stanlake Villas, Shepherd's Bush, London together with cat.nos. 536, 539, 540, 542, 543, 545, 546, 550 to 557, 560, 562 to 567, 570 to 575, 579, 596 to 600, 607, 622, 632 to 637, 647, 650, 652, 663, 668 to 677, and 681 in 1911 for £175.

This pilaster forms part of a sideboard executed by Stevens for Dorchester House, Park Lane, London. See Armstrong 1881, p. 30 and Stannus 1891, pl. LV, p. 26 n. 235, for the sideboard.

644: Pilaster

about 1863
Plaster
l. 44 cm.
961–1903

'HS' for Hugh Stannus is scratched into the surface.

Purchased from Hugh Stannus, 64 Larkhall Rise, Clapham, London together with cat.nos. 535, 537, 538, 541, 544, 547 to 549, 558, 559, 568, 569, 589, 590, 601, 666, 667, and 678 to 680 in 1903 for £35.

This may relate to the work Stevens executed for Dorchester House, Park Lane,

Haverstock Hill, London

645: Nude figure with arms raised

about 1866
Plaster
h. (max.) 54.5 cm.
A.18–1912

Given by Charles Ricketts, Lansdowne House, Lansdowne Road, Holland Park, London in 1912 together with cat.no. 648. Transferred to the Tate Gallery in 1952 (Tate inv.no. 6123); returned to the V&A in 1975.

645

This is a cast for a fountain figure designed by Stevens for his own garden at 9 Eton Villas, Haverstock Hill, London, where he remained from September 1862 until his death in 1875. See also cat.no. 646 for a version in bronze cast from the present piece. On acquisition Eric Maclagan [q.v.] commented: 'These [see also cat.no. 648] are two figure-studies by Alfred Stevens – I believe they are plaster casts from the original (?) plasters belonging to Sir Charles Holroyd'. The donor also had versions in bronze.

Bibliography
Tate 1953, p. 230, no. 6123.

646: Nude figure with arms raised

1866–7
Bronze
h. 52 cm.
A.14–1975

Given to the Tate Gallery by Sir Charles Holroyd in 1912. Lent by the Tate Gallery to Leighton House; returned to the V&A in 1989. Transferred from the Tate in 1975 (Tate inv.no. 2891).

This figure was designed by Stevens as a figure for the fountain in his garden at 9 Eton Villas, Haverstock Hill, London. It was cast from the plaster also in the collection; see entry for cat.no. 645.

BIBLIOGRAPHY
Stevens 1911, p. 7, no. 34; *Stevens* 1912, p. 39, no. 212; Towndrow 1950, p. 123, no. 395; *Tate* 1953, p. 227, no. 2891.

EXHIBITED
Loan Collection of Works by Alfred Stevens, National Gallery, British Art, (now Tate Gallery) 15 November 1911 to 15 January 1912, no. 34, lent by Sir Charles Holroyd the original owner; *Loan Collection of Works by Alfred Stevens*, Mappin Art Gallery, Sheffield, April to June 1912, no. 212, lent by Sir Charles Holroyd the original owner.

MISCELLANEOUS WORKS ABOUT 1842 ONWARDS

647: Cannon

about 1842–65
Plaster
l. 42 cm. max.
A.51–1911

Purchased from Mrs Ada Gamble, 12 Stanlake Villas, Shepherd's Bush, London, together with cat.nos. 536, 539, 540, 542, 543, 545, 546, 550 to 557, 560, 562 to 567, 570 to 575, 579, 596 to 600, 607, 622, 632 to 637, 643, 650, 652, 663, 668 to 677, and 681 in 1911 for £175. Transferred to the Tate Gallery in 1952 (Tate inv.no. 6120); returned to the V&A in 1975.

On the breech is a group representing a lion and winged dragon struggling; above the trunnions (which are now missing) is a figure of Mars in armour, seated amidst foliage. This cast is from the same design as inv.no. A.79–1911 (not included in this catalogue), a wax cannon on turned wood base designed by Stevens for the son of his friend Alfred Pegler, but certain small differences between the plaster and the wax suggest the plaster was not in fact cast from the wax, or that the plaster version was possibly re-worked subsequently. The wax cannon, together with the present piece, was acquired from the Gamble collection of works by Stevens, described on acquisition as one of the 'most important of all . . . the elaborate toy-cannon on which he employed himself at intervals almost all through his life' (*Review* 1911, p. 7). Stannus recorded that during 1865 'a small toy cannon was cast this year. It had been designed, many years before for his Friend, in their boyhood; and at length he finished the model, and had it cast in brass intending it as a present to his Friend's son. The Breech was increased in bulk by the figure of the Dragon coiled round it, which was added in gesso or wax in the model, the mouth of the monster serving as the touch-hole. A figure of Mars on his shield, in basso-rilievo [sic], decorated the part between the breech and the trunnions, the Trunnions bore heads of British Bull-dogs; and the shaft was fluted. The whole was about 1'6" long. The work is described as being beautiful and suggestive. It is not to be found, and is either concealed or lost' (Stannus 1891, pp. 26–7). The 'Friend' was Alfred Pegler, and the version made for Pegler's son was cast in brass by Messrs Henry E. Hoole & Co Ltd around 1865 (Towndrow 1939, p. 141).

BIBLIOGRAPHY
Review 1911, pp. 6–7; *Tate* 1953, p. 230, no. 6120.

648: Three struggling figures

about 1844
Plaster
h. 27 cm.
A.19–1912

Given by Charles Ricketts Esq., Lansdowne House, Lansdowne Road, London, in 1912 together with cat.no. 645. Transferred to Tate Gallery in 1952; returned to V&A in 1975.

Stevens made numerous studies from around 1844 depicting three struggling figures. These groups have not as yet been identified, though all of the following titles have been suggested: the *Rape of Deianeira*, the *Massacre of the Innocents*, and the *Judgement of Solomon* (departmental records). See also entry for cat.no. 649 for a version in bronze.

BIBLIOGRAPHY
Stevens 1926, fig. 8.

EXHIBITED
Alfred Stevens 1817–1875, Victoria and Albert Museum, 15 May to 14 September 1975.

649: Three struggling figures

cast about 1912 after a model of about 1844
Bronze
h. 267cm.
A.13–1975

Given to the Tate Gallery by Sir Charles Holroyd in 1912 (Tate inv.no. 2890). Transferred from the Tate to the V&A in 1975.

This group was cast in bronze, possibly by the original donor Sir Charles Holroyd, from the original plaster presented to the Museum by Charles Ricketts in 1912; see entry for cat.no. 648.

Towndrow noted that the original purpose intended for the group is not known, but suggests it may have been a study for a painting of the *Massacre of the Innocents*.

BIBLIOGRAPHY
Stevens 1911, p. 8, no. 50; *Stevens* 1912, no. 39, no. 213; Towndrow 1950, p. 60, no. 31; *Tate* 1953, p. 230, no. 2890; *Stevens* 1975, p. 48, no. 66 illus.

EXHIBITED
Loan Collection of the Works by Alfred Stevens, National Gallery, British Art, (now Tate Gallery) 15 November 1911 to 15 January 1912, no. 50 lent by the original donor, Sir Charles Holroyd; *Loan Exhibition of the Works of Alfred Stevens*, Mappin Art Gallery Sheffield, April to June 1912, no. 213 lent by the original donor, Sir Charles Holroyd; *Alfred Stevens 1817–1875*, Victoria and Albert Museum, 15 May to 14 September 1975, no. 66; *Design of the Times: 100 Years of the Royal College of Art*, Royal College of Art, London, 7 February to 20 March 1996.

GEORGE WOSTENHOLM & SON LTD

650: Dagger sheath base

about 1850
Plaster
h. (of whole) 17.5 cm. h. (of knife sheath) 12 cm.
A.49–1911

Purchased from Mrs Ada Gamble, 12 Stanlake Villas, Shepherd's Bush, London, together with cat.nos. 536, 539, 540, 542, 543, 545, 546, 550 to 557, 560, 562 to 567, 570 to 575, 579, 596 to 600, 607, 622, 632 to 637, 643, 647, 652, 663, 668 to 677, and 681 in 1911 for £175. Transferred to the Tate Gallery in 1952; returned to the V&A in 1975.

This is the base of a dagger-sheath for a hunting knife which is embedded in a plaster panel, taken from the same sketch by Stevens as cat.no. 651; see also cat.nos. 652 and 653 for further models for dagger sheaths. Stevens was commissioned by the cutlers George Wostenholm & Son Ltd of Sheffield to produce a set of daggers and sheaths specifically for their stand at the 1851 International Exhibition. According to Stannus they were 'much admired' (Stannus 1891, p. 12). This sheath is illustrated with the other knives and sheaths in a watercolour held in the Walker Art Gallery, Liverpool, and by Stannus in an engraving (see Towndrow 1951, fig. p. 14; Stannus 1891, plate XXI; *Stevens* 1975, p. 25, fig. 20). The three original hunting knives, together with their sheaths of etched steel, with handles of nickel silver, ebony and ivory, were on loan to the Museum from 1953 until 1994, when they were returned to their owners, George Ibberson (Sheffield), the company incorporating George Wostenholm & Son Ltd. Although these daggers have been described as for Wostenholm's South American trade, the Director George Darby wrote in 1952 that this was not the case, and that they were designed by Stevens purely as show pieces for the 1851 exhibition. He commented, 'They are not the type of knife for which there could be any regular sale'. According to Towndrow, 'they were designed with not only the required richness of decoration, but with precise balance and shape, and were yet another demonstration of the universality of Steven's invention and technique' (Towndrow 1951, p. 16).

BIBLIOGRAPHY
Review 1911, pp. 6–7.

651: Dagger sheath

about 1850
Plaster
h. 15.5 cm.
A.90–1911

Purchased from Mrs Townroe, 48 Gertrude Street, London, together with cat.nos. 561, 593, 608 to 610, 612, 614, 653, and 664 in 1911 for £25; see entry for cat.no. 561. Transferred to the Tate Gallery in 1952; returned to the V&A in 1975.

This is a sketch-model for the base of a dagger-sheath designed by Stevens for the cutlers George Wostenholm & Son Ltd, and exhibited at the 1851 International Exhibition. It was cast from the same model as cat.no. 650.

BIBLIOGRAPHY
Review 1911, pp. 6–7.

652: Dagger sheath

about 1850
Plaster
h. 23.3 cm.
A.50–1911

Purchased from Mrs Ada Gamble, 12 Stanlake Villas, Shepherd's Bush, London, together with cat.nos. 536, 539, 540, 542, 543, 545, 546, 550, 557, 560, 562 to 567, 570 to 575, 579, 596 to 600, 607, 622, 632 to 637, 643, 647, 650, 663, 668 to 677, and 681 in 1911 for £175. Transferred to the Tate Gallery in 1952; returned to the V&A in 1975.

Some metal corrosion has been caused by the metal core, which has also produced a crack at the back and top of the sheath.

This is a cast for the sheath of a hunting-knife, designed for George Wostenholm & Son Ltd of Sheffield. It is modelled on one side only. At the top are a snake and a bird (see Armstrong 1881, p. 12 illus).

BIBLIOGRAPHY
Review 1911, pp. 6–7.

653: Dagger sheath

about 1850
Plaster cast
h. 10.2 cm.
A.89–1911

Purchased from Mrs Townroe, 48 Gertrude Street, London, together with cat.nos. 561, 593, 608 to 610, 612, 614, 651, and 664 in 1911 for £25; see entry for cat.no. 561. Transferred to the Tate Gallery in 1952; returned to the V&A in 1975.

This is a cast from a sketch for the central section of a dagger-sheath produced by Stevens for the Sheffield cutlers George Wostenholm & Son Ltd for the 1851 International Exhibition.

Bibliography
Review 1911, pp. 6–7.

Lions for the British Museum

654: Lion

about 1852
Bronze
h. 35 cm.
A.21–1945

Bought by Lewis F. Day from the sale of Alfred Stevens's effects, Robinson and Fisher, 19 and 20 July 1877. On the second day's sale, lot 122 was described in the catalogue as 'A bronze casting of lion executed for the rails of the British Museum' (cited in the appendix of Towndrow 1950, p. 133 from an annotated copy, which records the lot was purchased by Lewis F. Day for £4 5s). Bequeathed by the widow of Lewis F. Day to Miss Florence H. Steele. Given by Miss Florence Steele, Geranium Cottage, Reigate, in memory of Lewis F. Day Esq. in 1945.

This bronze is taken from a model made by Stevens in about 1852 for the lion sejant on the dwarf posts outside the British Museum, by the entrance lodges. Towndrow recorded: 'The masterpiece of the year was the modelling of the Lion Sejant for the dwarf-posts of the forecourt of the British Museum . . . The model was the fine cat of a friend, and Stevens always spoke of the finished work as his 'cat'' (Towndrow 1939, pp. 113–4, and fig. 18). According to Stannus, 'Mr Smirke [Sydney Smirke, the architect] desired something like the well-known lion on the newel of the Bargello cortile at Florence, but the problem was more difficult by reason of the smallness of the space on which the Museum lion was to sit'. Stevens's skill was such that he managed to render the lion 'large and dignified . . . The number of imitations of this lion by other artists is their sincerest tribute; and technically it is equally a triumph for Stevens in the small number (20) of pieces which are necessary in the mould for casting it' (Stannus 1891, p. 14, illus. of two plaster models pl. XXIV). Armstrong commented, 'They display, perhaps, the nearest approach to the Gothic spirit of which Stevens was capable' (Armstrong 1881, p. 15). The lions are no longer in position, having been removed in 1896 to railings outside the Charles Holden part of the Law Society building in Chancery Lane (Bradley and Pevsner 1997, p. 308; I am grateful to Philip Ward-Jackson for this reference). Others were placed on the railings around the Wellington monument, St Paul's Cathedral, London after Stevens's death, between 1892 and 1912, when the tomb was removed from the Consistory Chapel in St Paul's (I am grateful to Philip Ward-Jackson for this information; see also *ibid.*, p. 171, and Towndrow 1939, p. 114). Two further plaster versions of the British Museum lion figure were acquired in 1975, transferred from the Tate Gallery; see entries for cat.nos. 655 and 656. A further bronze version of the lion was lent by Mr H.J. Potter in 1912, to the *Loan Collection of Works by Alfred Stevens*, held at the Mappin Art Gallery, Sheffield, April to June 1912, no. 216. A further pair of plaster lions were lent by Mrs Gamble and Mr Holden to the Loan Collection of Works by Alfred Stevens held at the National Gallery, British Art (later Tate Gallery), 15 November 1911 to 15 January 1912, no. 44. A plaster cast version of Stevens's lion (inv.no. 1891–133b) was transferred to the Department for the Sale of Casts in 1938, from which further castings were produced and offered for sale. Reduced and enlarged versions were also available for sale (see *Casts* 1939, p. 36; *Supplement* [n.d.] illus. 241, 444). Stevens was also commissioned to re-design the Reading Room at the British Museum; the architectural model for this is also in the Museum's collections (inv.no. 349–1890).

Bibliography
Towndrow 1939, fig, 18.

Exhibited
Alfred Stevens 1817–1875, Victoria and Albert Museum, 15 May to 14 September 1975.

655: Lion

about 1852
Bronzed plaster
h. 35 cm.
A.8–1975

Given to the Tate Gallery by Enrico Cantoni in 1912. For Cantoni, see also the entry for cat.no. 381. Transferred from the Tate in 1975 (Tate inv.no. 2869).

This was originally designed as a model for lions to crown the dwarf-posts on the railings of the forecourt screen of the British Museum; see entry for cat.no. 654. Another plaster figure of a lion was acquired at the same time from the Tate transfer; see entry for cat.no. 656.

Bibliography
Towndrow 1950, p. 72, no. 95; *Tate* 1953, p. 227, no. 2869; *British Sculpture 1850–1914* 1968, p. 31, no. 139.

Exhibited
A model for the bronze lions for the British Museum forecourt was lent by the Trustees of the Tate Gallery to the exhibition *British Sculpture 1750–1914*, held at the Fine Art Society between 30 September and 30 October 1968, cat.no. 139 – presumably the present piece or cat.no. 656.

656: Lion

about 1852
Bronzed plaster
h. 35 cm.
A.9–1975

Given to the Tate Gallery by Enrico Cantoni in 1912. For Cantoni see also entry for cat.no. 381. Transferred from the Tate in 1975 (Tate inv.no. 2869).

See entry for cat.no. 655. This is a further plaster version of the lion produced by Stevens for the British Museum railings; see also entry for cat.no. 654.

Bibliography
Towndrow 1950, p. 72, no. 95; *Tate* 1953, p. 227, no. 2869.

Exhibited
See entry for cat.no. 655.

Miscellaneous Works about 1852–1870

657: Leonard Collmann (dates unknown)

about 1852
Plaster
h. 44.5 cm.
758–1899

Purchased from Reuben Townroe Esq. together with cat.no. 658 in 1899 for £5. Transferred to the Tate Gallery in 1952 (Tate inv.no. 6115); returned to the V&A in 1975.

This is a plaster cast of a bust of the son of Leonard William Collmann, of and brother of Herbert Collmann; see also cat.no. 658. A bronze variant of about 1860 is in the Tate Gallery (NO2932).

In the *Victoria and Albert Museum. A Picture Book of Children in Sculpture*, it was noted: 'The bust of Master Collmann by Alfred Stevens has a note of wistfulness about it which seems lacking in the great Italians by whom Stevens was a belated disciple' (*Picture Book* 1927, page opp. pl. 1).

A bust of 'Leonard Collmann when a child' was lent by Mrs Hugh Stannus to the *Loan Collection of Works by Alfred Stevens* held at the Mappin Art Gallery, Sheffield during April to June 1912, no. 218. Mrs Stannus also lent a plaster bust of 'Herbert Collman when a child'; see entry for cat.no. 658.

Bibliography

Stevens 1926, fig. 14; *Picture Book* 1927, pl. 20, and page opp. p. 1; *Tate* 1953, p. 230, no. 6115.

658: Herbert Collmann (dates unknown)

about 1854
Plaster
h. 46 cm diam.
757–1899

Purchased from Reuben Townroe Esq. together with cat.no. 657 in 1899 for £5. Transferred to the Tate Gallery in 1952 (Tate inv.no. 6114); returned to the V&A in 1975.

This is a portrait bust of the son of Leonard William Collmann, and brother of Leonard Collmann; see also cat.no. 657; it is on an integral moulded pedestal. Stevens produced painted portraits of Mr L.W. Collmann and his wife Mary Ann around 1854, and it is possible that this plaster bust of their son was also produced at about this time (the portrait of Mary Ann Collmann is in the Tate Gallery; the companion portrait of Leonard William Collmann is in the Fogg Art Museum, USA – both are illustrated by Beattie; see *Stevens* 1975, p. 31, figs. 32 and 33). Collmann, an architect and decorator, was a friend of Stevens, and often acted as an intermediary in the commissioning of works from the sculptor; he liaised between the Government and Stevens on the commission for the Wellington Monument for St Paul's Cathedral, London. Stannus recorded,' Thus the artistic part was preserved to Stevens, and the financial and business works was undertaken by Collmann' (Stannus 1891, p. 29). A bronze variant of about 1860 is in the Tate Gallery (NO2931).

A bust of 'Herbert Collmann when a child' was lent by Mrs Hugh Stannus to the *Loan Collection of Works by Alfred Stevens* held at the Mappin Art Gallery, Sheffield during April to June 1912, no. 217. Mrs Stannus also lent a plaster bust of Leonard Collmann when a child; see entry for cat.no. 657. Mrs Stannus probably lent the same piece, entitled a 'Head of Herbert Collmann when a child', to the *Loan Collection of Works by Alfred Stevens* held at the National Gallery, British Art (now Tate Gallery), between 15 November 1911 and 15 January 1912, no. 28. It is likely that these pieces were those sold on the first day of the sale of Stevens's studio, held on 19 and 20 July 1877 by Robinson & Fisher; lot 82, described as 'Two busts of Boys', was sold to Stannus for £2 12s 6d (see Towndrow 1950, p. 130).

Bibliography

Tate 1953, p. 230, no. 6114.

659: Competition model for the 1851 International Exhibition Memorial

about 1857
Wood and plaster
h. 211cm
318–1880

Inscribed on the front of the plinth: TO COMMEMORATE/THE EXHIBITION/ON THIS GROUND/IN THE YEAR 1851/OF THE WORKS OF/ART AND INDUSTRY/OF ALL NATIONS

Purchased from Mr James Gamble in 1880; purchase price not recorded. In an annotated copy (copy held in the National Art Library; also cited in the appendix of Towndrow 1950, p. 129) of the Robinson and Fisher sale catalogue of Stevens's studio, held on 19 July 1877, lot 34, described as 'A plaster cast of the original competitive design for memorial of Exhibition 1851' was sold to 'Gamble', presumably James Gamble, for £2 10s.

A public competition to design a suitable memorial to the 1851 International Exhibition to be erected in Hyde Park was announced in July 1857, with entries to be received by 2 February 1858. According to Stannus, Stevens worked on his submission during 1857, and the present piece is his design proposal; the memorial was however never carried out. Towndrow commented: 'It is a nobly serene work, unlike the Wellington Memorial in its purely classical spirit, and, in the model, so finely suggested, even to the modelling of all but the smaller details, that it rests to-day only waiting that intelligence which will see it carried to a satisfactory and splendid completion in the large' (Towndrow 1939, p. 136). Armstrong similarly commented in 1881 that 'The model was left by the artist in a state of practical completion, and but little is required to make it ready for the founder'; he concluded that if the model remained and the monument was not erected, that 'it will afford one more proof, where, however, no proof is needed, that when England has the good fortune to possess a great sculptor she is too perverse to profit by the event' (Armstrong 1881, p. 47).

A plaster plinth with two recumbent winged figures – part of a model for the International Exhibition – was purchased by the Museum in 1889 for £6 (inv.no. 408–1889); its present location is unknown.

Bibliography

Armstrong 1881, pp. 14–15, 47 fig. 37; *Royal Academy* 1890, p. 51, no. 95; Stannus 1891, pp. 21–2 and plate XXXIX; *Stevens* 1926, fig. 2; Towndrow 1939, pp. 136–7, figs 23, 24a & b, 25; *Stevens* 1975, p. 42 illus. 53.

Exhibited

Royal Academy Winter exhibition 1890. *Drawings and Models by Alfred Stevens,* cat.no. 95; *Alfred Stevens 1817–1875*, Victoria and Albert Museum, 15 May to 14 September 1975; *Albert, Prince Consort*, Royal College of Art, 11 October to 22 January 1984.

660: Warriors defending a bridge

about 1861
Painted plaster
diam. 45.7 cm.
44–1897

Purchased from Reuben Townroe Esq., c/o W.G. Townsend Esq., 16 Coleherne Mansions, Bolton Gardens, London, in 1897 for £5. Transferred to Circulation Department in 1954. Transferred to the Department of Architecture and Sculpture, later Sculpture Department, in 1979.

This plaster plaque is a design for the decoration of a plate, probably designed for Messrs Minton & Co, with whom Stevens collaborated during 1861. Acquisition information records that the plaque was painted by Stevens himself; it is painted in blue with warriors in classical costume defending a bridge. The rim is coloured in blue and brown with scrolling stems and cornucopiae. For two further examples of plates designed by Stevens see Stannus 1891, p. 24 pls. XLVIII and XLIX; Armstrong 1881, pp. 4–5 illus.

BIBLIOGRAPHY
Stevens 1926, fig. 16.

EXHIBITED
Alfred Stevens 1817–1875, Victoria and Albert Museum, 15 May to 14 September 1975.

661: Medusa

about 1865
Plaster
h. 37 cm.
A.17–1975

Given to the Tate Gallery by Sir George Holford in 1922. Transferred from the Tate in 1975 (Tate inv.no. 3691).

This is a model for the mask of Medusa forming part of the decoration of a frieze designed by Stevens for Weston Birt House, the country residence of the original donor of this piece, Sir George Holford; see also entry for cat.no. 662.

BIBLIOGRAPHY
Towndrow 1950, p. 123, no. 393.

662: Door-knocker

about 1865
Bronze
h. 33 cm.
A.23–1975

Previously owned by Mr John R. Clayton (dates unknown). Purchased from the Lewis Publications 'A' Fund by the Tate Gallery in 1930. Transferred from the Tate in 1975 (Tate inv.no. 4559).

This knocker was probably designed for Weston Birt House, Sir George Holford's country home. See also entry for cat.no. 661.

BIBLIOGRAPHY
Stevens 1912, p. 40, no. 214 and illus.; Towndrow 1950, p. 122, no. 392; *Tate* 1953, p. 229, no. 4559.

EXHIBITED
Loan Collection of Works by Alfred Stevens, Mappin Art Gallery, Sheffield, April to June 1912, no. 214.

663: Reclining figure

about 1855–70
Plaster
l. 29 cm.
A.24–1911

Purchased from Mrs Ada Gamble, 12 Stanlake Villas, Shepherd's Bush, London, together with cat.nos. 536, 539, 540, 542, 543, 545, 546, 550 to 557, 560, 562 to 567, 570 to 575, 579, 596, 600, 607, 622, 632 to 637, 643, 647, 650, 652, 668 to 677, and 681 in 1911 for £175. Transferred to the Tate Gallery in 1952 (Tate inv.no. 6126); returned to the V&A in 1975.

The left hand is missing.

This is a sketch model for a reclining female figure, so far unidentified.

BIBLIOGRAPHY
Review 1911, pp. 6–7; *Tate* 1953, p. 231, no. 6126.

664: Winged head

about 1855–70
Plaster
h. 8.5 cm.
A.92–1911

Purchased from Mrs Townroe, 48 Gertrude Street, London, together with cat.nos. 561, 593, 608 to 610, 612, 614, 651, 653, and 664 in 1911 for £25; see entry for cat.no. 561. Transferred to the Tate Gallery in 1952; returned to the V&A in 1975.

This sketch model for a winged head, is so far unidentified. It was apparently intended to be set between four medallions (departmental records).

BIBLIOGRAPHY
Review 1911, pp. 6–7.

665: Ceiling portion

about 1855–70
Plaster
h. 126 cm.
354–1899

Purchased from James Gamble Esq., 24 Rich Terrace, South Kensington, London in 1899, together with cat.no. 595 for £12 10s each.

This is a model for a portion of a ceiling decoration so far unidentified.

[Not illustrated].

666: Mouldings of a cornice

about 1855–70
Plaster
l. 21 cm.
964–1903

Purchased from Hugh Stannus, 64 Larkhall Rise, Clapham, London, together with cat.nos. 535, 537, 538, 541, 544, 547 to 549, 558, 559, 568, 569, 589, 590, 601, 644, 667, and 678 to 680 in 1903 for £35.

This is a model for the mouldings of a cornice so far unidentified.

667: Moulding of a cornice

about 1855–70
Plaster
l. 25 cm.
971–1903

Purchased from Hugh Stannus, 64 Larkhall Rise, Clapham, London, together with cat.nos. 535, 537, 538, 541, 544, 547 to 549, 558, 559, 568, 569, 589, 590, 601, 644, 666, and 678 to 680 in 1903 for £35.

This is a model for portion of a moulding of a cornice so far unidentified.

668: Rosette

about 1855–70
Plaster
h. 26 cm.
A.52–1911

Purchased from Mrs Ada Gamble, 12 Stanlake Villas, Shepherd's Bush, London, together with cat.nos. 536, 539, 540, 542, 543, 545, 546, 550 to 557, 560, 562 to 567, 570 to 575, 579, 596 to 600, 607, 622, 632 to 637, 643, 647, 650, 652, 663, 669 to 677, and 681 in 1911 for £175.

This is possibly a model for a ceiling so far unidentified.

669: Corner of a ceiling panel

about 1855–70
Plaster
h. 28.4 cm.
A.53–1911

Purchased from Mrs Ada Gamble, 12 Stanlake Villas, Shepherd's Bush, London, together with cat.nos. 536, 539, 540, 542, 543, 545, 546, 550 to 557, 560, 562 to 567, 570 to 575, 579, 596 to 600, 607, 622, 632 to 637, 643, 647, 650, 652, 663, 668, 670 to 677, and 681 in 1911 for £175.

This model for the corner of a ceiling panel is so far unidentified.

670: Section of a cornice

about 1855–70
Plaster
l. 40 cm.
A.31–1911

Purchased from Mrs Ada Gamble, 12 Stanlake Villas, Shepherd's Bush, London, together with cat.nos. 536, 539, 540, 542, 543, 545, 546, 550 to 557, 560, 562 to 567, 570 to 575, 579, 596 to 600, 607, 622, 632 to 637, 643, 647, 650, 652, 663, 668, 669, 671 to 677, and 681 in 1911 for £175.

This is a model of a section of cornice so far unidentied.

671: Section of a moulded cornice

about 1855–70
Plaster
l. 21.7 cm.
A.55–1911

Purchased from Mrs Ada Gamble, 12 Stanlake Villas, Shepherd's Bush, London, together with cat.nos. 536, 539, 540, 542, 543, 545, 546, 550 to 557, 560, 562 to 567, 570 to 575, 579, 596 to 600, 607, 622, 632 to 637, 643, 647, 650, 652, 663, 668 to 670, 672 to 677, and 681 in 1911 for £175.

This moulded cornice is so far unidentified.

672: Section of a moulded cornice

about 1855–70
Plaster
h. 15.5 cm.
A.57–1911

Purchased from Mrs Ada Gamble, 12 Stanlake Villas, Shepherd's Bush, London, together with cat.nos. 536, 539, 540, 542, 543, 545, 546, 550 to 557, 560, 562 to 567, 570 to 575, 579, 596 to 600, 607, 622, 632 to 637, 643, 647, 650, 652, 663, 668 to 671, 673 to 677, and 681 in 1911 for £175.

This section of moulded cornice is so far unidentified.

673: Corner of a moulded cornice

about 1855–70
Plaster
h. 15 cm.
A.59–1911

Purchased from Mrs Ada Gamble, 12 Stanlake Villas, Shepherd's Bush, London, together with cat.nos. 536, 539, 540, 542, 543, 545, 546, 550 to 557, 560, 562 to 567, 570 to 575, 579, 596 to 600, 607, 622, 632 to 637, 643, 647, 650, 652, 663, 668 to 672, 674 to 677, and 681 in 1911 for £175.

This section of moulded cornice is so far unidentified.

674: Section of a moulding

about 1855–70
Plaster
h. 12 cm.
A.56–1911

Purchased from Mrs Ada Gamble, 12 Stanlake Villas, Shepherd's Bush, London, together with cat.nos. 536, 539, 540, 542, 543, 545, 546, 550 to 557, 560, 562 to 567, 570 to 575, 579, 596 to 600, 607, 622, 632 to 637, 643, 647, 650, 652, 663, 668 to 673, 675 to 677, and 681 in 1911 for £175.

This section of moulding is so far unidentified.

675: Section of a moulding

about 1855–70
Plaster
l. 27 cm.
A.60–1911

Purchased from Mrs Ada Gamble, 12 Stanlake Villas, Shepherd's Bush, London, together with cat.nos. 536, 539, 540, 542, 543, 545, 546, 550 to 557, 560, 562 to 567, 570 to 575, 579, 596 to 600, 607, 622, 632 to 637, 643, 647, 650, 652, 663, 668 to 674, 676 to 677, and 681 in 1911 for £175.

This section of moulding is so far unidentified.

676: Section of a moulding

about 1855–70
Plaster
l. 24 cm.
A.70–1911

Purchased from Mrs Ada Gamble, 12 Stanlake Villas, Shepherd's Bush, London, together with cat.nos. 536, 539, 540, 542, 543, 545, 546, 550 to 557, 560, 562 to 567, 570 to 575, 579, 596 to 600, 607, 622, 632 to 637, 643, 647, 650, 652, 663, 668 to 675, 677, and 681 in 1911 for £175.

This section of moulding is so far unidentified.

677: Section of a band ornament

about 1855–70
Plaster
l. 39 cm.
A.61–1911

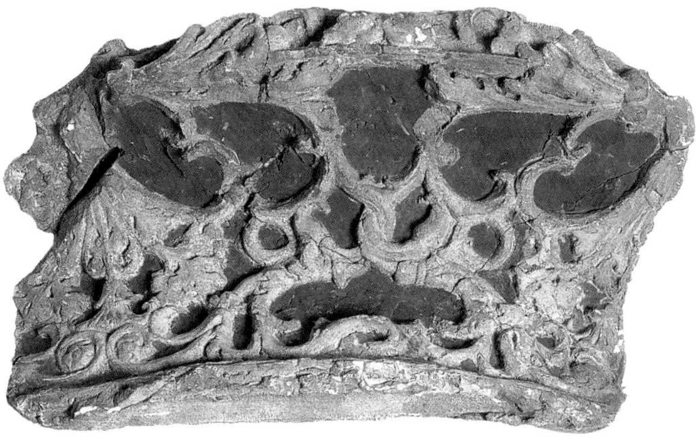

Purchased from Mrs Ada Gamble, 12 Stanlake Villas, Shepherd's Bush, London, together with cat.nos. 536, 539, 540, 542, 543, 545, 546, 550 to 557, 560, 562 to 567, 570 to 575, 579, 596 to 600, 607, 622, 632 to 637, 643, 647, 650, 652, 663, 668 to 676, and 681 in 1911 for £175.

This section of ornamental band is so far unidentified.

678: Frame moulding

about 1855–70
Plaster
l. 30 cm.
963–1903

'HS' for Hugh Stannus is scratched into the surface.

Purchased from Hugh Stannus, 64 Larkhall Rise, Clapham, London, together with cat.nos. 535, 537, 538, 541, 544, 547, 549, 558, 559, 568 to 569, 589 to 590, 601, 644, 666 to 667, and 679, 680 in 1903 for £35.

This is a model for a portion of frame moulding so far unidentified.

679: Angle of a torus-moulding

about 1855–70
Plaster
l. 21.9 cm.
968–1903

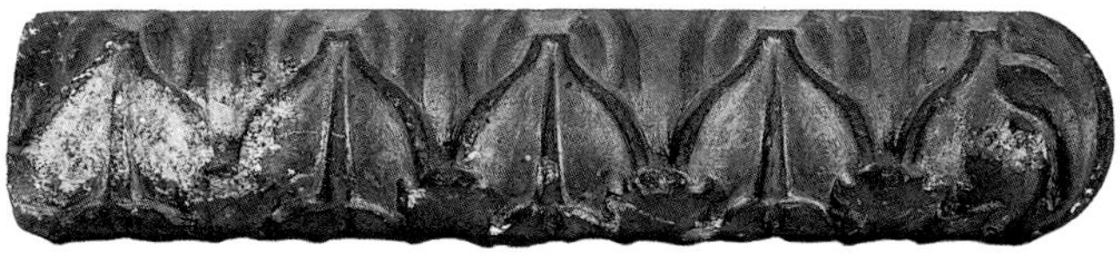

Purchased from Hugh Stannus, 64 Larkhall Rise, Clapham, London, together with cat.nos. 535, 537, 538, 541, 544, 547 to 549, 558, 559, 568, 569, 589, 590, 601, 644, 666, 667, 678, and 680 in 1903 for £35.

This is a model for a torus moulding so far unidentified.

680: Angle of a frame-moulding

about 1855–70
Plaster
h. 21 cm.
972–1903

Purchased from Hugh Stannus, 64 Larkhall Rise, Clapham, London together with cat.nos. 535, 537, 538, 541, 544, 547 to 549, 558, 559, 568, 569, 589, 590, 601, 644, 666, 667, and 678, 679 in 1903 for £35.

This is a model for the angle of a frame moulding so far unidentified.

681: Ornament side-piece

about 1855–70
Plaster
l. 35.5 cm.
A.62–1911

Purchased from Mrs Ada Gamble, 12 Stanlake Villas, Shepherd's Bush, London, together with cat.nos. 536, 539, 540, 542, 543, 545 to 546, 550 to 557, 560, 562 to 567, 570 to 575, 579, 596 to 600, 607, 622, 632 to 637, 643, 647, 650, 652, 663, and 668 to 677 in 1911 for £175.

This is a model for a portion of moulding so far unidentified.

682: Mask

about 1855–70
Plaster
h. 25.5 cm.
A.28–1914

Given by Sannyer Atkin Esq., 49 Elm Park Gardens, London in 1914. Previously in the possession of Mr Atkin's father, who had acquired a number of casts of Alfred Stevens's works.

This is a sketch model for a portion of a moulding for a piece of furniture, so far unidentified.

Bibliography
Review 1914, p. 4.

Thomas Stothard R.A.

(b. London 1755 – d. London 1834)

Stothard was one of the most accomplished artists of his generation, a painter and illustrator as well as a designer, and a contemporary and friend of the sculptor John Flaxman [q.v.]. Stothard studied at the Royal Academy Schools in 1777, and began work as a book-illustrator in 1779. He was elected a member of the Royal Academy in 1794, and in 1812 was appointed its librarian. Stothard exhibited at the Royal Academy between 1778 and 1834.

Bray 1851; Graves VII, pp. 283–5; Forrer V, pp. 696–7; Thieme-Becker, 32, pp. 139–40; TDA, 29, pp. 731–2 [Stocker].

683: Wellington shield

around 1822
Designed by Thomas Stothard
Painted plaster
diam. (approx) 99 cm.
A.23–1936

On loan, with a view to purchase, from Robert Green Esq., 78 Leman Street, Whitechapel, East London, from 13 August 1868. A drawing, described as the original design for the Wellington Shield by Thomas Stothard R.A., along with an engraved portrait of Stothard by William Henry Worthington (b. 1790) after George Henry Harlow (1787–1819), were also lent to the Museum at the same time. Attempts to return the loans were made in June 1903, (although a later report suggests a letter to the vendor was not sent, possibly because it was noted that the lender's former address no longer existed), and it was subsequently decided by the Museum authorities that the objects should be officially registered. The portrait of Stothard engraved by Worthington was later registered by the Department of Prints, Drawings and Paintings (E. 1220–1921), as was Stothard's original full-scale design for the Wellington Shield (E.1221–1921). What were described as '4 portions of fittings for Shield' were also deposited on loan. The present piece was not formally registered until July 1936.

When deposited on loan in 1868 the damage sustained by the present piece was noted: 'The centre figure broken in several places, and the shield much chipped'.

The purpose of this plaster is not certain, although its acquisition from the same source as the above-mentioned objects relating to Stothard suggests it is a model; the original documentation relating to its loan describes it as such. The fact that it is painted with bronze-coloured paint may suggest its use as a specimen piece, produced to illustrate the form the shield was to take. Alternatively it may be a cast of a model – perhaps the clay model – the format of which was subsequently changed: the scenes depicted on the present piece, though arranged in the same order as the finished shield, appear to have been assembled out of sequence (I am grateful to Ann Eatwell, Michael Snodin and Hilary Young for their comments on this).

The original shield in silver gilt, commissioned in 1814 for presentation to Arthur Wellesley, 1st Duke of Wellington, was executed by the firm of silversmiths Green, Ward & Green, who appointed Stothard to produce the design, which was cast by Benjamin Smith; it is now displayed at Apsley House, The Wellington Museum (I am grateful to Jonathan Voak for this information). The various scenes depicted reflect landmarks in Wellington's career.

In her *Life of Thomas Stothard, R.A.* of 1851, Mrs Bray recounts Stothard's involvement with the models for the Wellington Shield: 'But the wonder of Stothard's talents concerning the Wellington Shield, was not confined to the manner in which he executed the designs. It was of course necessary, before the chasing of the silver was commenced, that an exact model of the drawings to be so chased, should be executed as a guide to the persons who were to be employed in so nice a work. A Mr. Tollemach was chosen, but he died suddenly, soon after he was appointed to the task, and some difficulty arose as to who should succeed him; when, to the extreme surprise of all, Stothard offered to make the models himself from his own designs; and, with a rapidity scarcely less extraordinary than his former exertions, and wholly unpracticed as he was in this branch of art, he produced one of the most masterly models ever executed of its kind. The peculiar and *original* means he adopted in the execution of this work, and the beautiful and extraordinary effects produced by those means, are worthy of record. Stothard in the production of the various masses in the model, employed a *camel's hair pencil;* and with this he laid on the clay in as pulpy a state as possible. Such a process completely answered. It enabled him to give those graceful and flowing lines, whether of the human form, or of the drapery of his subject, with a taste and a delicacy that equalled even the drawings he had made. If painters were surprised by the great conceptions of his genius in the designs for the shield, sculptors were absolutely astonished at the models he had made from them. These were finished and placed before the persons who were chosen to execute the chasing in the silver: the latter were resident at Camberwell, near London; and here commenced the vexations and disappointing part of this great work, to Stothard. He complained that there was no Benvenuto Cellini to catch the spirit of his model, or to preserve it in the chasing of the shield' (Bray 1851, pp. 153–4).

The fact that the present piece appears to have the remains of bronzing tallies with Stothard's personal preference for the actual shield to have been made in bronze rather than silver. Mrs Bray recorded: 'I often heard Stothard talk a great deal about it; and I know he agreed in the opinion that a *bronze* shield, though less costly, would have been a richer and more classical material for his designs, and one more likely to go down to posterity; since, in times of tumult and civil strife (and who can say such would never occur again in England?) if they fall into the hands of the rude soldiery, or of the multitude, trophies of this nature are less likely to escape pillage when executed in silver than in bronze' (*ibid.*, p. 155).

Two models or casts in wax of two sections of the Wellington Shield by Stothard, purchased in 1857, are also in the Museum's collections (inv.nos. 4364 and 4365–1857); the scenes represent the *Entry into Toulouse* (1814) and the *Passage of the Douro and Liberation of Oporto* (1809) respectively.

William Theed III

(b. Trentham 1804 – d. London 1891)

Theed initially trained under his father William Theed II (1764–1817). He attended the Royal Academy Schools and trained for five years under the supervision of Edward Hodges Baily [q.v.]. He travelled to Rome in 1826, studying under Bertel Thorvaldesn (1768/70–1844), John Gibson [q.v.], and Richard James Wyatt (1795–1850). Theed, like Baron Carlo Marochetti [q.v.], was a favoured sculptor of Queen Victoria. He exhibited at the Royal Academy between 1824 and 1885.

Gunnis 1968, pp. 386–7; Thieme-Becker, 32, p. 586; TDA, 30, p. 703 [Stocker].

684: Prince Albert (1819–1861)

signed and dated 1864
By William Theed, cast by Elkington & Co
Bronze
h. 38 cm.
A.1–1996

Signed and dated: W. THEED.SC.LONDON 1864
Stamped to the side: ELKINGTON.&. Co.FOUNDERS.
Inscribed on the back: GIVEN TO HENRY COLE/BY QUEEN VICTORIA ON/THE FORTY FIFTH/ANNIVERSARY OF THE/PRINCE CONSORT'S/ BIRTHDAY/XXVI AUGUST/MDCCCLXIV.

Previously in the possession of Mrs Shirley Bury, formerly Keeper of the Department of Metalwork (1982–5). Purchased from Sotheby's Colonnade sale, London, 15 March 1996, lot 85 for £1,646.75.

The present bust is cast after the posthumous marble bust of the Prince Consort by Theed at Osborne House, Isle of Wight, one of two busts of Prince Albert which were commissioned by Queen Victoria, and completed by Theed in 1862. In the same year Theed exhibited one of the busts at the Royal Academy (no. 992); a Parian version of the present bust, together with a companion bust of Queen Victoria was produced by W.T. Copeland for the Art Union in 1865 (see Atterbury 1989, p. 136, and p. 182 fig. 596).

Bibliography
Bonython 1982 [Cole], p. 54; *idem*. 1982 [Album], p. 27 fig. 7.

Exhibited
Inventing New Britain: The Victorian Vision, Victoria and Albert Museum, London, 5 April to 29 July 2001.

John Thomas

(b. Chalford 1813 – d. London 1862)

Gunnis recorded that Thomas began his career as a stone-mason, but that at the end of his apprenticeship he travelled to Birmingham, where his work was noticed by Sir Charles Barry, who commissioned him to provide all the carved stone and woodwork for Birmingham Grammar School, which Barry was then designing. This was the start of a long and industrious career, in which Thomas gained commissions for both decorative works on public buildings, as well as for freestanding sculpture. Barry later employed Thomas to supervise the stone carving at the Houses of Parliament. In 1848 he was commissioned by Prince Albert to produce two reliefs of War *and* Peace *for Buckingham Palace. Gunnis recorded that 'In 1849 he supplied a chimney-piece for Mr. Brunel's "Shakespeare room," a series of bas-reliefs for Euston Station of the chief cities and towns connected with the North-Western Railway, and a group in high relief of "Britannia Supported by Science and Industry" for the same building'. Gunnis goes on to record, 'Incredible though it may seem, Thomas also worked as an architect and prepared designs for the National Bank of Glasgow; the Royal Dairy at Windsor; the Regent's Park Chapel; Headington House, Oxford; and the Print Room at Windsor Castle'. Thomas exhibited at the Royal Academy between 1842 and 1861, at the British Institution in 1850, and at the 1851 International Exhibition.*

Graves VII, pp. 359–60; Gunnis 1968, pp. 388–90; Thieme-Becker, 33, p. 65; Read 2000.

685: Rachel, the daughter of Laban

signed and dated 1856
Marble
h. 134.5 cm.
257–1885

Signed and dated on the integral base: JOHN THOMAS SC 1856

Given by Sir Henry A. Hunt C.B. in 1885. Transferred on loan to the Bethnal Green Museum in 1928; returned to the Sculpture Department in 1987.

This group was discussed by the *Art Journal* in its review of the Royal Academy exhibition of 1856: '"Rachel, the daughter of Laban", J. Thomas, presents a very elaborate study of drapery; and the accessories of pastoral life assist the spectator to determine the subject' (*Art Journal,* 1 July 1856, p. 222). The subject is taken from Genesis 29, verse 6.

Bibliography
Bequests and Donations 1901, p. 178; Graves VII, p. 359; Gunnis 1968, p. 389; Thieme-Becker, 33, p. 65.

Exhibited
Royal Academy 1856, no. 1250.

Thomas Thornycroft

(b. Cheshire 1815 – d. 1885)

After an ill-suited apprenticeship as a surgeon, Thornycroft was sent to London and apprenticed to the sculptor John Francis (1780–1861). His wife Mary Thornycroft, neé Francis (1814–1895), daughter of the sculptor John Francis, and their son, Sir William Hamo Thornycroft [q.v.], were also sculptors. Thomas Thornycroft produced the bronze group of Boadicea for Westminster Bridge, exhibiting as work in progress the colossal head of Boadicea at the Royal Academy in 1864 (no. 991). He also made the marble group Commerce *for the base of the Albert Memorial in Hyde Park, London; he exhibited the model for this at the Royal Academy in 1868 (no. 1096). He showed works at the Royal Academy between 1836 and 1874. The Thornycroft family archive covering the period 1780 to 1925 is held in the archive of the Centre for the Study of Sculpture, Leeds.*

Graves VII, pp. 383–4; Gunnis 1968, p. 393; Thieme-Becker, 33, p. 92.

686: Equestrian statuette of Queen Victoria
(b.1819; r.1837–1901)

signed and dated 1853
Bronze
h. 55 cm.
A.6–1972

Signed and dated on the base: T.THORNYcroft FECT/LONDON 1853

Originally in the Handley-Read Collection. Purchased from Thomas Stainton, Madeley Penn Road, Beaconsfield, Buckinghamshire in 1972 for £275.

The composition of this statuette (one of several extant versions, see below) is derived from a similar equestrian group executed in marble by Thomas Thornycroft and his wife Mary (1814–1895), which was exhibited at the 1851 International Exhibition (Class XXX, p. 853, pl. 193). The pose of the horse appears however to be taken from an engraving in the *Illustrated London News* of 2 July 1853, commemorating Queen Victoria reviewing the troops at Chobham on 21 June that year (*Illustrated London News*, 2 July 1853, no. 631, XXII, pp. 544–5). The statuettes are therefore adaptations rather than straightforward reductions of the 1851 statue. Thornycroft later used this composition for a colossal bronze equestrian statue of Queen Victoria of 1869 (unveiled on 3 November 1870) to act as a pendant to that of Prince Albert (unveiled on 11 October 1866), erected at Lime Street, St George's Plateau, Liverpool (see Cavanagh 1997, pp. 95–7). The *Art Journal* recorded, 'Mr Thornycroft has just completed a model of a colossal equestrian statue of the Queen, for Liverpool . . . The Queen is represented in the half-military dress she usually wore when visiting the camp at Chobham with the Prince Consort. The features are unmistakably those of the Queen, but very properly the cast is somewhat younger than we now see it . . . The horse is full of impatient action, which tells on the sway of the figure; an effect difficult to express well in sculpture' (*Art Journal*, 1 June 1869, p. 195).

In 1854 Thornycroft exhibited 'Equestrian statue of Her Majesty the Queen; executed in bronze for H.R.H. Prince Albert' at the Royal Academy (Graves VII, p. 384, no. 1417). The *Builder* recorded in 1854, 'We may mention that the equestrian statuette of the Queen, by Mr Thorneycroft [sic], which was submitted to her Majesty and the Prince last week, and elicited warm commendation, is being executed for the Art-Union of London in bronze, and will form most covetable prizes. The execution of the horse is particularly excellent' (*Builder*, 11 February 1854, XII, no. 575, p. 77). The present piece is one of around fifty which were commissioned by the Art Union of London to be distributed as annual prizes between 1854 and 1859. Avery and Marsh recount that 'Hammon, the Queen's favourite horse, came every morning for a canter round the studio . . . the realism of the horse was matched by that of the Queen, who was shown riding side-saddle in a contemporary riding habit, slightly idealized' (Avery and Marsh 1985, p. 329 fig. 5, p. 330 fig. 6 showing Thornycroft with a version of the statuette, p. 331). In 1854, one example was shown at Marlborough House at the request of the Department of Science and Art; another was exhibited at the 1851 Paris Exhibition (no. 1172). An earlier variant of the present piece was sold at Sotheby's London on 9 December 1993, lot 145. A version appeared in the Sotheby's sale, 24 November 1999, lot 78, signed and dated 1853, inscribed Art Union.

BIBLIOGRAPHY

British Sculpture 1850–1914, 1968, p. 32, cat.no. 162; *Handley-Read* 1972, p. 55, cat.no. C61; *Jubilee* 1977, p. 56, cat.no. 88

EXHIBITED

British Sculpture 1850–1914, Fine Art Society, London, 1968, cat.no. 162; *Victorian and Edwardian Decorative Art. The Handley-Read Collection*, Royal Academy, London, 1972, cat.no. C61; *'This Brilliant Year' Queen Victoria's Jubilee 1887*, Royal Academy, London, 19 March to 10 July 1977, cat.no.88.

Sir (William) Hamo Thornycroft

(b. London 1850 – d. Coombe 1925)

The son of the sculptors Thomas [q.v.] and Mary Thornycroft (1814–1895), Hamo initially trained in his father's studio, with whom he collaborated on the Poets' Fountain, Park Lane, London (erected 1875; demolished 1947). He enrolled at the Royal Academy Schools in 1869 and later travelled to Italy to continue his studies. In 1875, whilst at the Royal Academy Schools, he won the Gold Medal for his Warrior and Wounded Youth, *a group which was to mark a turning point in his career, and for which he received widespread critical acclaim. He followed this with* Teucer *in 1881 (now in the Tate Gallery), and later* The Mower, *which reflected a change in the emphasis of his work and a move away from his classically inspired works to more naturalistic pieces in the style of the New Sculpture. As well as ideal works, Thornycroft also executed a number of public monuments in London, including that to General Charles Gordon in Victoria Embankment Gardens. Thornycroft was a founder of the Art Workers' Guild; see entry for cat.no. 401. He exhibited regularly at the Royal Academy from 1872 to 1925, and also taught at the Royal Academy Schools. The Thornycroft family archive covering the period 1780 to 1925 is held in the archive of the Centre for the Study of Sculpture, Leeds.*

How 1893; Spielman 1901, pp. 36–45; Graves VII, pp. 385–7; Manning 1982; Royal Academy VI, pp. 142–3; Thieme-Becker, 33, pp. 91–2; TDA, 30, pp. 761–2 [Manning]; Friedman 1999.

687: Equestrian statuette of Edward I
(b.1239; r.1272–1307)

signed and dated 1884
Plaster with wax detail
h. 72.5 cm.
A.17–2000

Signed twice on the base: once on the ground in front of the horse:

HAMO THORNYCROFT./SC 84 and secondly beneath the inscription: HAMO THORNYCROFT.SC 1884
Inscribed on the base at the front: EDWARD I

There is no information on the provenance of the present piece, which until 2000 was an unregistered object in the Museum.

An old label attached to the object records: FROM/R-C. ART/Principal From/1941
The object may therefore have been presented to the Museum through the Royal College of Art.

This statuette is related to Thornycroft's submission for the proposed Blackfriars Bridge project to display sculpture on four pedestals at the four corners of the bridge. This was originally an open competition organised by the Corporation of London in 1880, with a submission date for designs of 21 March 1881. After much prevarication and committee discussion, the project was eventually confined to equestrian figures depicting English warrior monarchs, and the competition – latterly limited to seven sculptors – was further refined to four in July 1886; models were submitted by Thornycroft, Birch, Armstead and Boehm (Beattie 1983, p. 42). The project did not however come to fruition, and was eventually cancelled later that year (for a full discussion of the competition, see *ibid.*, pp. 41–3; Manning 1982, pp. 97–9).

In an article devoted to Thornycroft in the *Portfolio* of 1888, reference was made to the Blackfriars Bridge competition in connection with a smaller sketch model in wax – Thornycroft's initial competition entry – 'In 1885 the best thing was a small sketch in wax for an Edward I on horseback. The group was one of those intended for Blackfriars Bridge. It would have done credit to the sculptor had it ever been carried out' (Armstrong 1888, p. 114). Spielmann similarly recorded Thornycroft's work on the Edward I figure, '"King Edward I," the model for a statue, was seen the following year [1891]; but I had seen it in progress some years before – in 1884, if my memory serves me well – for the competition for the proposed decoration of Blackfriars Bridge, which undertaking the City of London had projected but from which it incontinently withdrew. In 1894 it was shown again in different form, slightly simplified in surface, broader, and more sculptural in aspect' (Spielmann 1901, p. 40). It is likely that this is one of the one-eighth-size sketch models cited by Beattie, requested by the Committee and Court of Common Council from Thornycroft, George Gammon Adams, C.B. Birch, Thomas Brock, Richard Belt, Hugh Henry Armstead, and Sir Joseph Edgar Boehm (see Beattie 1983, *loc.cit.*).

Elfrida Manning recorded that Thornycroft 'had a special affection for "Longshanks", and in explaining his conception to the Common Council of the City, he wrote that "in order to express the grand, firm and simple character of this most dignified of monarchs, I have purposely avoided any action or momentary movement, either in the horse or the rider" . . . It was a great disappointment to Hamo that he was not allowed to carry out his design. Instead, he used his model to publish "Longshanks" a limited edition of six bronze statuettes 35 inches high and ten half that size, although it is doubtful if they were ever cast to the full number' (Manning 1982, pp. 97, 99; for an example of the bronze statuette of Edward I, 'Longshanks' in the Southampton Art Gallery and Old Bailey London, see *ibid.*, fig. 59 on p. 98; see also Spielmann 1901, illus. on p. 41). In an article of 1893 devoted to Thornycroft, a version is illustrated in his studio (see How 1893, p. 273). A bronze model dated 1894, given by Lady Thornycroft, is in the Birmingham Museum and Art Gallery (see *Birmingham* 1987, p. 92, cat.no. 286, illus. on p. 93). There are differences between the present piece and later *Longshanks* versions.

EXHIBITED

Thornycroft exhibited two versions of the *Edward I* at the Royal Academy. In 1885 he showed 'Edward I; equestrian statuette, wax', and in 1892 'Edward I; design for one of the proposed equestrian statues for Blackfriars Bridge'; the latter may possibly be identified with the present piece, and the wax is probably that commented upon by Armstrong in the *Portfolio* article of 1888 (Graves VII, p. 386, nos. 2133 and 1996 respectively).

George Tinworth

(b. Walworth, London 1843; d. London 1913)

Tinworth was initially apprenticed to his father as a wheelwright, but he enrolled at the Lambeth School of Art in 1861, attending evening classes on modelling and technique, where he studied under John Sparks and Edwin Bale. In 1864 he was admitted to the Royal Academy Schools. He joined the Royal Doulton Potteries, Lambeth in 1867, and remained there until his death in 1913. Spielmann recorded that 'The late Sir Henry Doulton took great interest in the talented lad, who, but for him, might have continued at his father's craft of wheelwright'. Tinworth flourished at the Doulton Potteries, and Spielmann noted, 'apart from the legitimate designs for pottery and the like, dramatic high-relief panels with numerous figures on a small scale have absorbed the energies of Mr Tinworth'. Tinworth exhibited at the Royal Academy between 1866 and 1885; during 1875 he showed a series of small panels depicting religious scenes in terracotta, which were praised by Ruskin, and resulted in his commission for the Crucifixion *reredos at York Minster. Though chiefly known for his religious pieces, Tinworth was also commissioned to produce some public statuary, including the terracotta statue of Henry Fawcett in Vauxhall Park; this statue was the gift of Sir Henry Doulton, further illustrating the close ties between Tinworth and the Doulton Potteries. A cabinet of 1872 designed by Charles Bevan with plaques by George Tinworth is in the Department of Furniture and Woodwork (inv.no. 412–1872). A substantial collection of works of pottery and sculpture by Tinworth is to be found in the Harriman Judd Collection, Los Angeles (Rose 1982). Archival material relating to this sculptor are held at the Sir Henry Doulton Gallery: a manuscript autobiography and correspondence is held at Southwark Local Studies Library.*

Hooe 1880, pp. 23–4; Gosse 1883; Spielmann 1901, pp. 22–4; Tinworth [n.d.]; Graves VII, pp. 397–8; Tinworth 1906; Parkes 1921, p. 95; British Sculpture 1850–1914 1968, pp. 9, 33–4; Read 1982, pp. 311–2; Thieme-Becker, 33, p. 199; Rose 1982, esp. pp.7–61, 153–88 for a chronology of his principal works; Beattie 1983, p. 18. On the Fawcett memorial see Gleichen 1928, pp. 170–1; Blackwood 1989, p. 351.

688: Baptism of Christ

1877
Painted terracotta
h. 23.2 cm. w. (greatest approx.) 34.5 cm.
A.120–1922

Given by Sir William Matthew Trevor Lawrence, Bart., Burford, Dorking in 1922.

This relief, painted black, is the model for part of a font. There are cracks running up the middle area, and another crack through the far right figure; the upper corners are broken away. On acquisition it was recommended that this relief be accepted as an example of 'the religious sculptor George Tinworth', as no other example of his work was represented in the collections. As with much of Tinworth's work, this piece is inspired by medieval sculpture, and is painted black to imitate oak. Rose identifies the present piece as being part of a bowl for a font in salt-glaze stoneware of 1877, which had 16 relief panels (Rose 1982, p. 162).

Bibliography
Rose 1982, p. 162; Thieme-Becker, 33, p. 199.

689: Christ's triumphant entry into Jerusalem

signed and dated 1881
Terracotta
h. 99 cm.
A.4–1935
1881.

Inscribed along the bottom to the left: H DOULTON & CO LAMBETH
Inscribed beneath the figure of Christ on a donkey: I CHR XVI CHA/10
Inscribed beneath the figure of a boy to the right of the relief: NUM XI CHA/29
Signed at the bottom right hand corner: G. TINWORTH

Given by Messrs Doulton & Co Ltd in 1935 and originally assigned to the Bethnal Green Museum. Transferred to the Circulation Department in 1965, and later to the Sculpture Department.

Tinworth's companion relief to the present piece, entitled *Our Lord on His Way to Crucifixion*, was presented to Truro Cathedral by F. Walters Bond in thanks for the safe return of his sons from the South African War. A smaller sketch for the present piece is to be found in the rear wall of the Baptist Church, Wraysbury, Middlesex (Rose 1982, p. 165). Doulton & Co. published a number of catalogues entirely devoted to Tinworth's work, an indicator of the esteem in which he was held, as well as the commercial success of his almost exclusively religious work; see entry for cat.no. 688.

BIBLIOGRAPHY

Gosse 1883 [Tinworth], pp. 74–5, pl. 25; *Tinworth* 1883, pp. 70–2, cat.no. 59; Graves VII, p. 397 (no. 1444); Rose 1982, p. 166.

EXHIBITED

Royal Academy 1881, no. 1444; *Collection of Works in Terra Cotta by George Tinworth*, Conduit Street Galleries, Regent Street, London, 1883.

ALBERT A. TOFT

(b. Birmingham 1862 – d. 1949)

Parkes commented that 'In Albert Toft, England has a type-example of the result of the national system of art-education'. Toft initially studied at the Birmingham School of Art, and later at Hanley and Newcastle-under-Lyme, where he won a National Art Scholarship. Parkes noted that during this period Toft was an apprentice at Wedgwood's, but the award of a scholarship afforded him the opportunity to leave the company to study at South Kensington under the tutelage of Edouard Lanteri [q.v.]. Spielmann commented that 'Mr Toft made his way in the art world with determined perserverance'. In 1889 he executed the nude figure of Lilith, *acquired by the Walker Art Gallery, Liverpool, which increased his reputation. Toft was also commissioned to produce war memorials, including those in Birmingham and Warwickshire. He exhibited at the Royal Academy between 1885 and 1947.*

Spielmann 1901, pp. 118–25; Graves VIII, p.1; Parkes 1921, pp. 122–3; Royal Academy VI, pp. 150–2; Thieme-Becker, 33, p. 248.

690: George Wallis, F.S.A. (1811–1891)

signed and dated 1889
Terracotta
h. 61.5 cm.
30–1892

Signed and dated on the back: Albert Toft/1889

Given by the executors of George Wallis Esq., F.S.A. in 1892 in accordance with the wishes of his children.

According to the obituary notice in the *Art Journal*, George Wallis left the Birmingham School of Design in 1859 to join the staff at the

South Kensington Museum, now Victoria and Albert Museum, becoming Keeper of the Art Collections from 1863 until just before his death in 1891. The writer noted, 'The present complete system of circulation of works of Art to provincial museums now carried on by the Department, owes much to the late keeper of the Art division' (*Art Journal*, December 1891, p. 384).

Original acquisition information records that the Board was pleased to accept this bust as a gift from the family of the late George Wallis, 'in memorial of the valuable services rendered by Mr George Wallis to the Science and Art Department'. In a letter from Wallis's children, the bust was described as 'a most admirable work and a striking likeness of the late Mr Wallis'.

Spielmann commented, 'In his portraiture Mr Toft is dexterous and quick, and his busts are life-like; it is that kind of work which pleases sitters, for, besides resemblance, there are character, refinement, and style' (Spielmann 1901, p. 125).

BIBLIOGRAPHY

Bequests and Donations 1901, p. 259; Spielmann 1901, p. 124.

EXHIBITED

Toft exhibited a terracotta bust of 'George Wallace [sic], Esq FSA' at the Royal Academy in 1887, no. 1810, and in 1890 a bronze bust of 'George Wallis Esq' no. 2001 (Graves VIII, p. 1). Though the present piece is signed and dated 1889, information supplied by the children of the sitter suggests that the present bust was the one exhibited at the Royal Academy in 1887.

ROBERT TOW

(dates unknown; active 1869)

No information has been found on Robert Tow other than his address at 36 Aldenham Street, St Pancras Road, London. He was presumably an amateur sculptor.

691: Grotesque male head

1869
By Robert Tow after Jean Goujon
Copper repoussé
h. 27.2 cm. w. 11.2 cm.
102–1870

Purchased from R. Tow, presumed to be the sculptor, in 1870 for £3 3s.

This grotesque mask, after the original by the French sculptor Jean Goujon (b. about 1510 – d. about 1565), was a prize object from the Society of Arts Art-Workmanship Competition for 1870; see also cat.no. 382. The report on the competition records that Robert Tow was awarded a prize of £7 10s for this object (*Journal for the Society of Arts*, 10 February 1871, XIX, no. 951, p. 230, no. 56).

EXHIBITED

Society of Arts Art-Workmanship Competition of 1869–70.

Peter Turnerelli

(b. Belfast 1774 – d. London 1839)

Turnerelli was the son of an Italian immigrant father and Irish mother. He had originally intended to take up a career in the priesthood, but in 1793 travelled to London and began training as a sculptor, initially under Peter Francis Chenu (b. 1760 – d. after 1822), and later at the Royal Academy Schools. Gunnis recorded, that he was introduced to the Princess of Wales, and was employed to teach her modelling; he was later 'appointed teacher and sculptor to the Queen and the Princesses and consequently was frequently at Windsor. He held the post for three years, and at the end of that time, became Sculptor-in-Ordinary to the Royal Family'. Turnerelli returned to Ireland on a regular basis where, as Gunnis noted, he produced 'his famous bust of Grattan in eleven hours . . . which Canova . . . described as the best modern bust he had seen in England'. He twice declined the offer of a knighthood. He exhibited at the Royal Academy between 1802 and 1838.

Graves VIII, pp. 43–5; Strickland 1913, II, pp. 466–70; Gilmartin 1967; Gunnis 1968, pp. 402–3; Thieme-Becker, 33, pp. 496–7; TDA, 31, p. 477 [Turpin].

692: George III (b.1738; r.1760–1820)

signed; about 1810
Marble
h. 76.2 cm.
A.11–1937

Signed on the base at the side: P. Turnerelli/Fecit

On loan from Dr W.L. Hildburgh F.S.A. from 29 February 1936 (ex-loan no. 4901); acquired as a gift in 1937, given by Hildburgh in honour of the exhibition of *Kings and Queens of England 1500–1900*, held at the Museum during the summer of 1937 to commemorate the Coronation of King George VI and Queen Elizabeth.

Described in the *Review of Principal Acquisitions during the Year 1937*, as 'an excellent example of the work of a sculptor who enjoyed a long and honourable career in the service of early 19th-century royalty and nobility' (*Review* 1937, p. 8). A further version, signed and dated 1812 is in the British Library (I am grateful to Philip Ward-Jackson and Jerry Losty for this information). For a further bust of George III by Turnerelli see cat.no. 693.

Bibliography

Illustrated London News 1937, p. 830 illus.; *Kings and Queens* 1937, illus. p. 36, *Review* 1937, p. 8; Kilmurray 1979, p. 86.

Exhibited

Kings and Queens of England 1500–1900, held at the Victoria and Albert Museum during the summer of 1937, (opened 10 May) in honour of the Coronation of King George VI and Queen Elizabeth.

693: George III (b.1738; r.1760–1820)

signed; 1810
Marble
h. 44 cm.
A.62–1965

Signed on the back beneath the inscription: P. TURNERELLI./Fecit.
Inscribed on the back: G.III.R./JUBILEE BUST.

Bequeathed by Rupert Gunnis, Hungershall Lodge, Tunbridge Wells in 1965.

The bust commemorates the fiftieth anniversary of George III's accession to the throne. Gunnis noted, 'His work for the Royal Family naturally led to the sculptor being given permission to make the Jubilee bust of George III in 1810. The work was an instantaneous success and he received orders for eighty copies in marble from the nobility of England and the Colonies' (Gunnis 1968, p. 402). A further version of 1810 is in the Royal Collection at Windsor Castle; Gunnis recorded replicas in the possession of the Duke of Richmond and Lord Normanton amongst others. Another version dated 1809 is in the National Portrait Gallery (*NPG* 1981, p. 220, no. 3903).

Turnerelli exhibited 'The jubilee bust of His Majesty' at the Royal Academy in 1810, no. 883, presumably the original version now in the Royal Collection (Graves VIII, p. 44, no. 883).

For a further bust of George III by Turnerelli see cat.no. 692.

EXHIBITED

George III. Bicentennial Exhibition, Yorktown Victory Center, Virginia, USA, April 1977 to 31 March 1978.

WAGHORN AND BROWN

The founder William Richard Waghorn established the firm at Nonsuch Pottery, Ewell, Surrey, around 1800. In 1851 the firm was taken over by a Mr Swallow. Jewitt recorded that William Waghorn's produced terracotta tiling, moulded bricks, chimneypots, flowerpots and vases. At some date after 1851 the firm was re-named Waghorn and Brown; it remained at Ewell, producing ornamental works from the local clay, such as the one catalogued below.

Jewitt 1878, pp. 166–7.

694: Vase with egg and dart and vine ornament

about 1800–50
Terracotta
h. 55.5 cm.
A.86–1921

The square base is inscribed on both sides:
Waghorn & Brown/EWELL SURREY

Given by Miss G.M. Butler, Burlingham, Waterden Road, Guildford on behalf of the family of the late T.M. and Mrs Butler of The Firs, London Road, Guildford in 1921, together with cat.no. 715.

Charles V. Walker

(dates unknown; active about 1850 – 1901

I have been unable to find any information relating to Charles V. Walker, presumably a maker of electrotypes.

695: Triumphal entry of Alexander the Great into Babylon

about 1850–1901
By Charles V. Walker after Bertel Thorvaldsen
Electrotype
h. 61 cm. w. 72.5 cm.
5679–1901

Transferred from the Museum of Practical Geology, Jermyn Street, London in 1901, together with cat.nos. 696 and 697. According to Museum records, the Committee met and examined the collections in the Museum of Practical Geology and recommended their transfer in 1901. Included in this suggested transfer were several electrotypes and castings, which had hung on the wall of the Museum.

This is one of three sections of frieze (cat.nos. 695 to 697) which were acquired in 1901, one of which is stamped with Walker's name; cat.no. 696. The original stucco frieze from which these are copied, 32 metres in length, was produced in 1812 by Bertel Thorvaldsen (1768/70–1844) for the Palazzo del Quirinale in Rome. Marble versions exist in the Villa Carlotta at Cadenabbia on Lake Como and in the Christiansborg Palace, Copenhagen (TDA, 30, p. 764 [Jørnaes]). For the version in the Villa Carlotta see *Thorvaldsen* 1990, fig. 8 on p. 121. This section depicts three Babylonian warriors.

696: Triumphal entry of Alexander the Great into Babylon

signed; about 1850–1901
By Charles V. Walker after Bertel Thorvaldsen
Electrotype
h. 60 cm. w. 101.5 cm.
5680–1901

A signature is embossed beneath the incised stamp: Charles V. Walker

Stamped in the bottom left hand corner:
ELECTROTYPED/FOR THE/MUSEUM OF ECONOMIC GEOLOGY

Transferred from the Museum of Practical Geology, Jermyn Street, London in 1901, together with cat.nos. 695 and 697.

This is one of three reliefs which were acquired in 1901 as copies after Thorvaldsen's monumental frieze; see entries for cat.nos. 695 and 697. This section depicts Alexander in a quadriga, driven by Victory.

697: Triumphal entry of Alexander the Great into Babylon

signed; about 1850–1901
By Charles V. Walker after Bertel Thorvaldsen
Electrotype
h. 61.5 w. 91 cm.
5681–1901

A signature is embossed beneath the incised stamp: Charles V. Walker
Stamped in the bottom right hand corner: ELECTROTYPED/FOR THE/MUSEUM OF ECOMONIC GEOLOGY

Transferred from the Museum of Practical Geology, Jermyn Street, London in 1901, together with cat.nos. 695 and 696.

This is one of three reliefs which were acquired in 1901, copies after Thorvaldsen's monumental frieze; see entries for cat.nos. 695 and 696. This section depicts a Babylonian warrior and five children.

Watcombe Terra-cotta Clay Company Ltd

The Watcombe Terra-Cotta Clay Company Ltd was established in 1869 by George Allen at St Mary's Church, Torquay, Devon. It capitalised on the rich deposits of red clay found whilst builders were excavating the foundations for Watcombe House. Initially the company was established as a local consortium of gentlemen, but the business quickly grew. Watcombe specialised in producing quality terracotta ware, including statuary as well as garden ornaments and vases. The company exhibited at the Paris International Exhibition of 1878. The sculptor and potter Robert Wallace Martin [q.v.] worked for Watcombe in 1871. After George Allen's death in 1883, the Watcombe Terra-cotta Clay Company declined, and finally ceased trading under this name in 1901, the year of the gift noted below. In 1903 the company merged with the Royal Aller Vale Pottery to become the Royal Aller Vale and Watcombe Pottery Co, which remained at St Mary's Church, Torquay. This company ceased production on 30 September 1962.

Paris International Exhibition 1878, p. 5; Bergesen 1991, pp. 281–6; Godden 1991, p. 650.

698: Caritas [Charity]

1869–76
Produced by the Watcombe Terra-cotta Clay Co Ltd
Terracotta
h. 56 cm.
3742–1901

Impressed at the back: WATCOMBE/TORQUAY

The socle has number '27' in gold leaf noted on it, and the remnants of a label inscribed: TERRA . . . O . . . TTA/WATC . . .
Stamped on the band beneath the bust: CARITAS

Given by the Watcombe Terracotta Clay Company in 1901.

The present bust is not included in Bergesen's list of known busts produced by Watcombe, and may have been a trial piece. It is based on François Duquesnoy's (c.1594–1643) statue of *St Susanna* in S. Maria di Loreto, Rome; see Hadermann-Misguich 1970, fig. 5 and front cover (I am grateful to Philip Ward-Jackson for this information).

HENRY WEEKES R.A.

(b. Canterbury 1807 – d. London 1877)

Weekes was initially apprenticed in 1822 to the sculptor William Behnes [q.v.], and studied at the Royal Academy Schools from 1823 to 1826. The following year he entered the studio of Sir Francis Chantrey [q.v.], in whose circle he remained until Chantrey's death in 1841, when he took over his studio and completed some of his works. Gunnis commented that Weekes 'is, indeed, chiefly known as a portrait-sculptor and his busts have considerable merit'. He did however also produce commemorative sculpture, and Stocker suggests that the memorial to Percy Bysshe Shelley at Christchurch Priory and that commemorating Samuel and Elizabeth Whitbread in the church of St Mary, Cardington, Bedfordshire, are amongst his greatest works. He exhibited at the Royal Academy between 1828 and 1877, becoming Professor of Sculpture in 1869; he exhibited at the British Institution between 1854 and 1867. Weekes was also involved in the Albert Memorial, executing the marble group depicting Manufactures, *one of the four upper groups symbolising the industrial arts; for the Albert Memorial model, see entry for cat.no. 531. Like his contemporary John Bell [q.v.], Weekes wrote on the state of British sculpture: his review of the fine arts exhibited at the International Exhibition of 1851, entitled* The Prize Treatise of the Fine Arts Section of the Great Exhibition of 1851, *published in 1852, provides an interesting contemporary insight into the sculptors represented. He published his* Lectures on Art, *delivered at the Royal Academy, in 1880.*

Graves VIII, pp. 192–4; Graves 1908, p. 574; Gunnis 1968, pp. 418–20; Thieme-Becker, 35, p. 244; TDA, 33, p. 24 [Stocker]; Getty 1998, p. 117, illus. p. 116.

699: Unknown woman, possibly Mrs George Forbes

signed and dated 1849
Marble
h. (incl. socle) 81 cm.
A.9–1988

Signed and dated on the back: H.WEEKES.SC/1849

Acquired by Mr J.L.N. O'Loughlin around 1968. Given by Mrs Elizabeth O'Loughlin in 1988 in accordance with the wishes of her late husband, Mr J.L.N. O'Loughlin.

In her letter offering this bust to the Museum, Mrs O'Loughlin wrote that the subject of the bust was 'presumed to be Mrs Forbes'. In his justification for acceptance, Anthony Radcliffe remarked, 'The bust, which is big and expansive, and has its original handsome green marble plinth, is a swagger example of English mid-nineteenth century wealthy bourgeois portraiture'. The bust is no longer displayed on its original plinth (inv.no. A.9:A-1988).

BIBLIOGRAPHY
Graves VIII, p. 192, no. 1325; Williamson 1991, p. 876.

EXHIBITED
In 1849 Weekes exhibited a marble bust of Mrs George Forbes at the Royal Academy (no. 1325), possibly the present piece. In its review of the Royal Academy exhibition of 1849, the *Art Journal* commented: 'no. 1325 'Marble Bust of Mrs. George Forbes,' H. WEEKS [sic]. The high and elaborate finish of this bust is instantly declared to the eye. The marble is, in some degree, transparent; which, with the delicacy communicated by minute elaboration, gives an extraordinary softness to the skin textures' (*Art Journal*, 1 June 1849, p. 176).

Henry Weigall

(b. London 1800? – d. 1883)

Forrer recorded that Weigall was initially a gem-engraver and medallist, who later turned to sculpture. Gunnis noted that he produced a number of busts of the Duke of Wellington, showing three busts of the Duke at the Royal Academy in 1849, 1852 and 1853 respectively. He exhibited at the Royal Academy between 1837 and 1854, including proofs of the Flaxman medal produced for the Art Union; he also exhibited at the British Institution between 1850 and 1855.

Graves VIII, p. 199; idem 1908, p. 574; Forrer VI, pp. 422–3; Gunnis 1968, p. 420; Thieme-Becker, 35, p. 276.

700: Arthur Wellesley, 1st Duke of Wellington
(1769–1852)

signed and dated 1851
By Henry Weigall; cast by Elkington & Company
Bronze
h. 77 cm.
777–1864

Inscribed on the truncation: MODELLED FROM SITTINGS TAKEN ON AUG 6 9 11 AND NOV 18 1851/H WEIGALL 27 SOMERSET ST., PUBLISHED OCT 10 1852
Beneath: No 6/Executed by/Elkington Mason & Co

Given by Messrs Elkington & Company in 1864.

Four versions of this bust are cited by Clay in relation to the example held in the Lady Lever Art Gallery. The present piece is not however mentioned (*Lady Lever* 1999, p. 77); it is numbered 6, while the version in the Lady Lever Art Gallery is numbered 7. The busts are casts after the 1851 bust of Wellington exhibited at the Royal Academy in 1852 (no. 1409). Weigall showed a further bronze bust of the late Duke of Wellington at the Royal Academy in 1873 (no. 1398). In 1849 the sculptor had shown another bust of the Duke in marble at the Royal Academy (no. 1306); a similar or the same marble bust was exhibited at the British Institution in 1850 (no. 489).

Bibliography
Inventory 1864, p. 67; *Bequests and Donations* 1901, p. 151.

HENRY WESTMACOTT

(b. 1784 – d. 1861)

Westmacott was a member of the prominent family of eighteenth- and nineteenth-century English sculptors: he was the son of Richard Westmacott the Elder (1747–1808) and father of James Sherwood Westmacott [q.v.]. Henry Westmacott is particularly known for the prodigious quantity of chimneypieces he produced. Gunnis recorded that in 1823 he and his brother George (active 1799–1827), executed the base for the statue of Achilles *at Hyde Park Corner; the figure itself was executed by their brother Sir Richard Westmacott [q.v.]. Henry Westmacott exhibited at the Royal Academy between 1833 and 1835, and at the Royal Scottish Academy between 1831 and 1836.*

Gunnis 1968, pp. 421–2; Royal Scottish Academy 1991, IV, p. 406; Thieme-Becker, 35, p. 453; TDA, 33, p. 100 [Busco].

701: Nicolò Paganini (1782–1840)

signed and dated 1832
Marble
h. (bust) 79.5 cm. h. (pedestal) 110.5 cm.
A.12–1955

Signed and dated on the back: HENRY WESTMACOTT SCULPTOR/ EDINBURGH·1832·

Probably commissioned from the sculptor by Sir Henry Tate, who was a relative of the Booth family (information kindly supplied by Mary K. Macdonald). In the possession of Mr Bromley Booth, then by descent to Mr George E. Booth. Bequeathed to the donor by Mr George E. Booth in 1954. Originally offered by the donor to the Tate Gallery, it was considered a more appropriate acquisition for the Victoria and Albert Museum, a suggestion with which the donor was happy to concur. Given to the Museum by Mrs K. Dawson, 165 Coppice Street, Oldham, together with its original pedestal A.12:A-1955, in 1955.

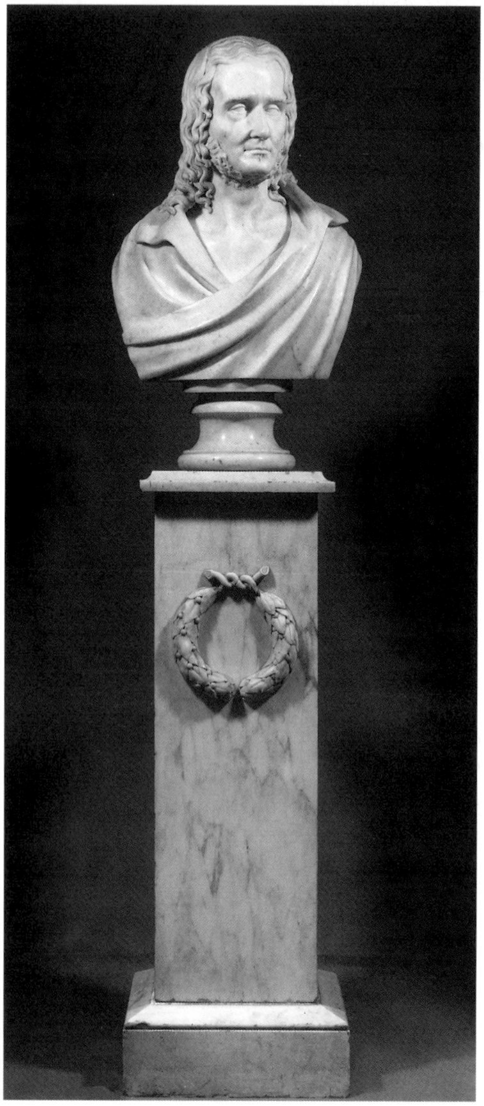

The accompanying illustration shows the bust when displayed on its original pedestal (inv.no. A.12:A-1955).

The bust probably commemorates the only visit made by Paganini, the violin virtuoso, to Britain in 1831–2. Gunnis noted that Westmacott moved to Edinburgh in about 1830 (Gunnis 1968, p. 421).

BIBLIOGRAPHY

Graves VIII, p. 235, no. 1188; Dawson 1935, pp. 457–8, illus. opp. p. 437; Gunnis 1968, p. 421; *Royal Academy* 1968, p. 105, cat.no. 234; *Royal Scottish Academy* 1991, IV, p. 406, no. 335

EXHIBITED

Westmacott exhibited a bust of 'Signor Paganini, . . . from life' at the Royal Scottish Academy, Edinburgh in 1832 (no. 335), presumably the present piece; in 1833 he exhibited at the Royal Academy, London almost certainly the same bust of 'Signor Paganini' (no. 1188); *Royal Academy of Arts Bicentenary Exhibition 1768–1968*, 14 December 1968 to 2 March 1969, cat.no. 234.

James Sherwood Westmacott

(b. London 1823 – d. London 1888 or 1900)

James Sherwood Westmacott, a member of the Westmacott dynasty of eighteenth-and nineteenth-century sculptors, was the son of the sculptor Henry Westmacott [q.v.]. The contemporary commentator William Hooe recorded that Westmacott was 'educated first at Edinburgh, and afterwards at Neuwield on the Rhine, and adopting the profession studied at Dresden, under Professor Rietschel. The ideal and statuettes suitable for private residences have been the class of works mostly produced by his chisel. Among his chief works are the statue of a "Victory" at Dresden, for which he obtained a gold medal, statue of "Peri", and statue of "Alfred the Great". Mr Westmacott was also one of the successful competitors selected by the Royal Commissioners of Fine Arts to execute statues for the House of Lords'. Gunnis noted that Peri at the Gates of Paradise *was exhibited at the Paris Exhibition in 1855, and that it 'became very popular and was illustrated in the Art Journal and other periodicals of the time'. Gunnis also recorded that Westmacott travelled to Rome in 1849, 'and shortly afterwards executed the figure of "Satan Overthrown" for Mr Theophilus Burnard; replicas of this work (in the form of bronze statuettes) were produced in large numbers by Messrs Elkington in 1853'. Westmacott exhibited at the Royal Academy between 1846 and 1885, and at the British Institution between 1852 and 1867. An album of thirty-three of his drawings for sculpture is held in the archive of the Centre for the Study of Sculpture, Leeds.*

Hooe 1880, p. 24; Graves VIII, pp. 235–6; idem 1908, pp. 580–1; Gunnis 1968, p. 422; Thieme-Becker, 35, p. 453.

702: The artist's daughter, possibly Constance Westmacott

about 1872
Marble in wood frame
h. 40 cm.
A.12–1968

By descent from the artist, who was the donor's grandfather, and the sitter's father. Given by Mr H. Barrs-Davies, Grey Roofs, Box, Hand, Gloucestershire, in 1968, together with cat.nos. 113 to 116; see entry for cat.no. 113.

The style of this oval relief is reminiscent of those produced by the Pre-Raphaelite sculptor Alexander Munro (1825–1871), most notably Munro's oval portrait medallion of the *Duchess of Vallombrosa* of 1867, exhibited at the Royal Academy in 1869 (no. 1280); see *Pre-Raphaelite* 1991 [Barnes], p. 130, no. 42.

Bibliography
Graves VIII, p. 236, no. 1581.

Exhibited
In 1872 Westmacott exhibited '"Constance" medallion' at the Royal Academy (no. 1581), possibly the present piece.

SIR RICHARD WESTMACOTT R.A.

(b. London 1775 – d. London 1856)

Westmacott was a member of a family of sculptors: his father was Richard Westmacott the Elder (1747–1808), and his brothers Henry [q.v.] and George Westmacott (active 1799–1827). His son was Richard Westmacott the Younger [q.v.]. Sir Richard Westmacott was renowned for his public and private monuments. Many of his monuments were cast in bronze, including Achilles, *a figure commemorating the Duke of Wellington, at Hyde Park Corner, London (1822). The majority of his commissions were for funerary monuments. He exhibited at the Royal Academy between 1797 and 1839. In 1827 he became Professor of Sculpture at the Royal Academy, and was knighted in 1837. Correspondence relating to this sculptor is held in the Metropolitan Museum of Art, New York.*

Graves VIII, pp. 236–9; Gunnis 1968, pp. 423–8; Penny 1975 [Westmacott]; Busco 1988; Whinney 1988, pp. 384–97; Penny 1991 [Chantrey/Westmacott]; Thieme-Becker, 35, pp. 453–4; Busco 1994; TDA, 33, pp. 99–101 [Busco].

703: Probably Harriet Elizabeth, Lady Beresford
(1790-1825)

about 1825
Possibly by Sir Richard Westmacott
Marble
h. 64 cm.
A.32-1931

Originally in the collection of Thomas Hope (1769–1831); auctioned at the Hope Sale (the Deepdene, Surrey) held by Messrs Fosters on 27 February 1930, lot 130. The annotated copy of the catalogue held in the National Art Library records it was sold to Spink for £3, but also records the name of Balham, perhaps an agent for Spink. It was presumably purchased from Messrs Spink by Dr W.L.Hildburgh F.S.A., who subsequently gave it to the Museum in 1931. The bust was later assigned to the Circulation Department, and was lent to the Victor Batte-Lay Trust and the Minories, Colchester from 1958 to 1972. It was later on loan to 1 Carlton Gardens, London (Foreign and Commonwealth Office) from 1991 to 1993.

Both the identity of the sitter and the sculptor of this bust are uncertain. It was called 'Lady Beresford' in the Hope Sale of 1930, but one of two women with this name and title could be the subject: one is Mrs Louisa Hope, later Lady Beresford (about 1786–1851), the daughter of William Beresford, Archbishop of Tuam; she married Thomas Hope in 1806. Following Hope's death in 1831, she married her cousin, William Carr Beresford, Field Marshall Viscount Beresford in 1832. A painting of Louisa (then the Hon. Mrs Thomas Hope) by G. Dawe shows a fashionable young woman not unlike the present bust (see Law and Law 1925, pl. facing p. 55). However some features – notably the hair and eyes – of a bust of Louisa recently auctioned at Sotheby's, London (14 December 2001, lot 125) by William Behnes [q.v.] dating from 1829 differ in some respects from the present bust. Moreover another bust of Louisa of 1817 by Bertel Thorvaldsen (1768–1844) also seems to show a markedly different physiognomy from the present piece (for the plaster model, see Kai Sass 1963, I, pl. opp. p. 282; see also *idem* III, p. 75, cat.no. 73; both the plaster and the marble are in the Thorvaldsens Museum, Copenhagen; the marble was purchased at the Hope Sale (Humbert & Flint) of 1917, lot 1126).

The more probable subject of the bust is Harriet Elizabeth, Lady Beresford, the daughter of Henry Peirse (d.1824), who married Admiral Sir John Poo Beresford, 1st Baronet (1766–1844) in 1815. Admiral Sir John's half-brother was William Carr Beresford, who was later to marry Louisa (as noted above). Harriet died prematurely in 1825, soon after her father, and they are both commemorated on a joint monument by Sir Richard Westmacott at St Gregory's, Bedale, Yorkshire (see Penny 1975 [Westmacott], fig. 9 on p.124; and Busco 1994, fig. 175 on p.158). Harriet was also portrayed in a painting by Sir Thomas Lawrence, exhibited at the Royal Academy in 1825 (Garlick 1989, p. 151, cat. 96; there catalogued – probably erroneously – as Henrietta, Lady Beresford). The features of the monument and the painting seem closer to the present bust than those seen in images of Louisa, and the bust is therefore here identified as probably Harriet. The blank eyes suggest it is likely to be posthumous, and to date from around the same time as the funerary monument. It may have become part of the Hope collection via the marriage of Louisa to William Carr Beresford, posthumously Harriet's brother-in-law.

The identity of the sculptor is also unclear. A posthumous bust of Lady Beresford (almost certainly Harriet) by Behnes [q.v.] was shown at the Royal Academy in 1826, no. 1045. It is tempting to identify the present piece with this bust, and therefore to ascribe it to Behnes. However stylistically it does not resemble Behnes's works, and seems much closer to the portrayal of Harriet on her monument by Westmacott; it is therefore here attributed to him. Tim Knox and Philip Ward-Jackson have however suggested that stylistically it resembles the works of the Florentine sculptor Lorenzo Bartolini (1777–1850), but no record survives of a commission for a bust of Lady Beresford from this sculptor. We are grateful to Tim Knox, Simon Stock and Philip Ward-Jackson for their comments on this bust.

Bibliography
Review 1931, p. 53.

704: Equestrian statuette of George III
(b. 1738; r. 1760–1820)

about 1831
Anonymous, after Sir Richard Westmacott
Wood
h. 55.5 cm.
A.85–1937

Purchased from Mr Gerald Kerin, 16 Mount Street, London in 1937 for £10.

The right hand of the figure is missing. There are slight traces of paint on the horse.

The colossal equestrian statue to George III, commissioned from Westmacott by George IV, was erected on 24 October 1831 at Snow Hill in Windsor. Busco records that Westmacott appears to have gained this commission following George IV's viewing of the model for the Liverpool monument to George III, which was in the sculptor's studio at the time (Busco 1994, pp. 68–9, and figs. 54 and 55). Prior to its acquisition in 1937 R.P. Bedford [q.v.] wrote, 'I doubt if this wood equestrian figure is a model for Westmacottt's 'Copper' Horse at Windsor. It seems to me to be rather a reduction of it, but it is an interesting contemporary work and I think we would do well to acquire it for the reasonable sum of £10'. According to the *Review of Principal Acquisitions during the Year 1937* the present piece 'cannot be very much later in date [than 1831], but so far it has not been possible to trace the author of it' (*Review* 1937, p. 9). Although it is made of wood, this piece appears to imitate a bronze equestrian statuette.

Bibliography
Review 1937, p. 9.

Richard Westmacott the Younger R.A.

(b. London 1799 – d. London 1872)

Richard Westmacott the younger was one of the Westmacott family of sculptors; his father was Sir Richard Westmacott [q.v.], and his grandfather Richard Westmacott the elder (1747–1808). Gunnis recorded that he joined the Royal Academy Schools in 1818, and spent the period between 1820 and 1826 in Italy. On his return to London, Westmacott trained in his father's studio. Busco records that 'in the 1830s and 1840s, he [Richard Westmacott the younger] appears to have taken over most of his father's practice'. Together with Robert Sievier (1794–1865), he produced two chimney-pieces for Chatsworth House, Derbyshire, which date from around 1840. Gunnis commented, 'His only important work in London . . . is the relief in the pediment of the Royal Exchange, which he executed between 1842 and 1844'. He made his début at the Royal Academy in 1827 and continued to exhibit until 1855, the year in which the bust catalogued below was shown (cat.no. 706). Westmacott also exhibited at the 1851 International Exhibition. He was elected as member of the Royal Academy in 1849, and in 1857 took over the role of Professor of Sculpture from his father.

Graves VIII, pp. 239–40; Gunnis 1968, pp. 428–9; Whinney 1988, p. 397; Thieme-Becker, 35, p. 454; TDA, 33, p. 101 [Busco].

705: Unknown man

signed and dated 1851
Marble
h. 75 cm.
A.14–2000

Signed in monogram: W/R 1851.

There is no information available on the provenance of the present piece, which until 2000 was recorded as an unregistered object in the Museum.

706: Richard Ellison (1788–1860)

signed; about 1855
Marble
h. (incl. socle) 71.5 cm.
236–1881

Signed in monogram on the back: W/R

Inscribed on the front of the socle: R. ELLISON. ESQ.

Given by Mrs Elizabeth Ellison, the widow of the sitter. Received together with the Ellison gift of pictures in 1861, but not formally registered until 1881.

A marble relief at the Royal Academy, which was Westmacott's diploma work, entitled *Go, and sin no more* is signed with the same monogram.

In a published obituary of Ellison (publication unknown; cutting in the Sculpture Department archive), he is described as: 'Possessed of a cultivated taste, an accomplished mind, and more than ordinary attainments, Mr Ellison was a liberal patron of the fine arts. In paintings he was a connoisseur, and possessed one of the finest galleries of water-colour paintings in England. These include many specimens of local subjects by Turner, De Wint, Mackenzie, &c. His library was also very valuable, and the hall at Sudbrooke is replete with rare articles of *vertu* and fine sculpture'.

BIBLIOGRAPHY

Bequests and Donations 1901, p. 152; Graves VIII, p. 240, no. 1544.

EXHIBITED

In 1855 Westmacott exhibited at the Royal Academy 'Bust Richard Ellison Esq, of Sudbrooke Holme, Lincoln', almost certainly the present piece (no. 1544).

JOHN WILLDIGG

(active 1884 – 1886)

I have been unable to locate information on this sculptor other than that which was recorded on acquisition, that he was a National Scholar in the National Art Training Schools, South Kensington, presumably around 1884–6.

707: Jardinière

1884
Terracotta
h. 25 cm.
620–1886

Purchased from the sculptor in 1886 for £3.

A label attached to the inside of the object reads: Gold medal. John Willdigg Hanley. 4.

[Not illustrated].

John Warrington Wood

(b. Warrington 1839 – d. Rome 1886)

Wood began his career as a stonemason, studying in the evenings at the Warrington School of Art. He later travelled to Rome, whence he regularly sent works for exhibition at the Royal Academy between 1868 and 1884. According to Morris, his statue of Eve was to generate much interest amongst Warrington residents, who together subscribed £1,000 to commission Wood to produce a group of St Michael overcoming Satan *for the Warrington Art Gallery. He took Warrington, his native town, as a middle name to distinguish himself from another sculptor called John Wood. He was commissioned to produce an allegorical figure of Liverpool, and statues of Michelangelo and Raphael for the exterior of the Walker Art Gallery; these were installed in 1877. His success in Italy enabled him to purchase the Villa Campana in Rome, the former home of the art collector Pietro Campana. Mary J. Taylor has prepared a dissertation on Wood at Manchester University, part of a Diploma in Art Gallery and Museum Studies, 1984 (information kindly supplied by Edward Morris).*

Wilmot 1891; Graves VIII, p. 338; Grant 1953, p. 272; Thieme-Becker, 36, p. 243; Morris 1995, pp. 6–12.

708: Rt. Hon. Hugh Culling Eardley Childers F.R.S. (1827–1896)

dated 1882
Marble
h. 82 cm.
A.25–2000

Inscribed on reverse: HUGH CULLING EARDLEY CHILDERS/1882

On loan from Miss M. Childers, 6 St George's Place, Hyde Park Corner, London, from 19 March 1896. No contact with the lender had been established since 1918; attempts to locate the family in February 1934 were also unsuccessful. Given to Miss Childers in 1896 on the death of her father, the sitter, who was a politician and statesman (see Stenton and Lees 1978, pp. 65–6). As a redundant loan the present piece was formally accessioned by the Sculpture Department in 2000.

THOMAS WOOLNER R.A.

(b. Hadleigh 1825 – d. London 1892)

Woolner was apprenticed to William Behnes [q.v.], in whose studio he worked for six years, entering the Royal Academy Schools in 1842. Shortly afterwards he met Dante Gabriel Rossetti (1828–1882), and was invited to become a member of the Pre-Raphaelite Brotherhood. Woolner executed a number of portrait medallions of eminent contemporaries, but was unsuccessful in gaining major commissions, and disillusioned emigrated to Australia in 1852, in search of gold. His gold-prospecting hopes were not realised, but he found work there as a sculptor; he returned to London in 1854, following his failure to gain the commission for a statue of William Charles Wentworth in Sydney. In London he executed a number of public statues, including that of Henry Temple, 3rd Viscount Palmerston in Parliament Square, London. His bronze figure of Captain Cook for Hyde Park, Sydney (1879) is considered his masterpiece. Woolner exhibited at the Royal Academy from 1843 until his death, and was elected an Associate of the Royal Academy in 1871 and Member in 1874. In 1877 he was made Professor of Sculpture, a post from which he resigned in 1879, having never lectured. Woolner was also an acclaimed poet. Diaries of the sculptor and related photographs are held in the archive of the Centre for the Study of Sculpture, Leeds. Further papers are held at Oxford University, Bodleian Library, Department of Western Manuscripts.

Graves VIII, pp. 355–7; Gunnis 1968, pp. 443–5; Dolan [n.d]; Pre-Raphaelite 1991 [Read], pp. 21–45, 141–67; Thieme-Becker, 36, p. 251; TDA, 33, pp. 373–5 [Stocker].

709: Captain Francis Fowke, R.E. (1823–1865)

signed and dated 1866
By Minton and Company after Thomas Woolner
Gilded terracotta
h. 57.5 cm.
37–1867

Signed on the left side: T. WOOLNER/1866
Inscribed on the front of the base: CAPTAIN FOWKE
Inscribed on the back: CAPTAIN FOWKE R E/BORN 1823/DIED 1865

Purchased from Messrs Minton and Company in 1867 for £4 1s.

This bust is apparently cast from a plaster model produced by Thomas Woolner, manufactured by Minton and Company. Captain Francis Fowke was the architect and engineer at the Science and Art Department of the South Kensington Museum, now Victoria and Albert Museum. He was responsible for the design of the first permanent buildings on the South Kensington site, and the gallery which housed the Sheepshanks gift of paintings (see Bonython 1982 [Cole], p. 46; Physick 1982, various references).

Physick records that the premature death of Fowke at the age of 42 was one which affected many, including Queen Victoria, who wrote, 'The Queen is truly, deeply grieved at this. It is again one of her beloved, adored Husband's fellow workers in all that was great & good who has been taken away! He is a great, great loss. Pray say so to Mr. Cole' (*ibid.*, p. 107, and n. 33). Physick continues, 'The Board expressed the wish that a commemorative bust of Fowke should be placed in the Museum, and Thomas Woolner was asked to execute this in either marble or terracotta for not more than 100 guineas. On 27 December 1866, Cole, Scott, and Donnelly went to Woolner's studio to see the result, which seemed 'a good likeness'. It was sent to the Paris 1867 Exhibition and is now in the Museum Library' (*ibid.*, p. 108, and notes 35 and 36). A terracotta bust of Fowke was exhibited at the Paris Universelle Exhibition of 1867, no. 14 in part II, the British Section.

Two further versions of the bust were acquired in 1868 from Elkington & Company, (inv.nos. 1154 and 1155–1868); see cat.no. 710; 1154–1868 was de-accessioned in 1933.

BIBLIOGRAPHY
Kilmurray 1981, p. 72; Physick 1982, p. 108.

710: Captain Francis Fowke, R.E. (1823–1865)

signed and dated 1866
By Elkington & Company after Thomas Woolner
Gilt bronze
h. 67 cm.
1155–1868

Signed and dated on the left side: T. WOOLNER SC./1866.
On the right side of the base: ELKINGTON. &. CO/FOUNDERS.
Inscribed on the front of the plinth: CAPTAIN FOWKE

Purchased from Elkington & Company in 1868 for £50.

There is a seam at the side where the two pieces (front and back) of the bust have been joined.

An electro-copper bust of Captain Fowke executed by Elkington's after Woolner, and acquired at the same time as the present piece, was de-accessioned in 1933 (inv.no. 1154–1868).

See entry for cat.no. 709.

Matthew Cotes Wyatt

(b. London 1777 – d. London 1862)

Wyatt was the son of the architect James Wyatt (1746–1813), and father of the sculptor James Wyatt (1808–1893). Three of his other sons also became architects: Matthew Wyatt (1805–1886), George Wyatt (d. 1880), and Henry Wyatt (d. 1899). Matthew Cotes Wyatt was both a painter and sculptor, but from around 1815 he concentrated his attention on sculpture. His first public commission was for the bronze monument to Admiral Lord Nelson (1758–1805), outside the Mansion House in Liverpool; designed by Wyatt in 1813, it was cast in bronze by Sir Richard Westmacott [q.v.]. Several of his public commissions gained a certain amount of notoriety. Gunnis noted that controversy surrounded his statue of George III in Cockspur Street, London; criticised for the inclusion of a pigtail on the figure, there was general dissatisfaction that there had been no competition for the commission, and that it had simply been awarded to Wyatt. Wyatt's equestrian statue of the Duke of Wellington, which was to be erected on top of the arch designed by Decimus Burton (1800–1881) at Hyde Park Corner, similarly gained him widespread critical disclaim. Gunnis recorded that 'Wyatt's last work probably realised the bitterest storm of opposition and was the target of more ridicule than any other statue ever erected in London . . . The result was an equestrian statue nearly 30 ft high, showing the Duke with a huge Roman nose and with his right hand stiffly pointing a baton between his horse's ears'. When the statue was eventually removed from Hyde Park Corner in 1883 as a result of road widening measures, it was taken to Aldershot, Hampshire, and erected at Round Hill near the Royal Garrison Church in 1885 (I am grateful to Ian Maine for this information). Robinson comments that 'Wyatt executed little of his own sculpture. Most of the marble carving and the bronze casting was the work of assistants. He made the designs and supervised the general execution'. Some miscellaneous correspondence is held in the National Art Library.

Graves VIII, p. 375; Gunnis 1968, pp. 446–8; Thieme-Becker, 36, p. 322; TDA, 33, pp. 447–8 [Robinson]; Cavanagh 1997, pp. 51–5.

711: Bashaw, 'The faithful friend of man'

about 1832–4
Marble, plastic, amber, limestone and bronze
h. (dog and cushion) 84 cm.
h. (plinth) 63 cm.
A.4–1960

Commissioned by John William, Lord Dudley and Ward in 1831, for his Park Lane residence; original correspondence relating to the commission between Dudley and Wyatt is held in the Royal Institute of British Architects. Dudley died in 1833 before Wyatt had finished the statue. The executors of his estate queried the £5,000 price, and as the dispute was never resolved, *Bashaw* remained in the possession of Wyatt until his death. Remaining unsold at the sale of the artist's effects, *Bashaw* became the possession of his son, James, who entered it into the sale held at Christie, Manson and Woods, 8 King Street, London, on 7 May 1887, lot 145. In an annotated copy of the catalogue held in the National Art Library it is noted that 'Smith' bid £168 for the piece, though Harris suggests that the sculpture was bought in for 60 guineas, and subsequently became the property of John Corbett of Impney Hall, Droitwich, presumed to have been purchased by him privately. In his possession until sold in the Impney Hall sale held in March 1906. Purchased from the sale by Mr Ernest or Edward Stevens of Prescot House, Stourbridge. Sold at the sale of the effects of Prescot House on 26 November 1957 to Mr W. Malkin of Bygones, 11 Wagon Lane, Sheldon, Birmingham, though the Museum had unsuccessfully put in a bid of £150. Presumably later sold to Snead and Knibbs, Monumental and Ecclesiastical Sculptures. Purchased by the Museum from Messrs Snead and Knibbs, Yardley Road, South Yardley, Birmingham in 1960 for £200. For the history of the ownership of *Bashaw* see Harris 1957.

The plastic foliage, fruit and flowers on the black marble base were added by the Museum's Conservation Department in imitation of the original details, missing on acquisition. Recent conservation on the group carried out in 1999 revealed that some of the original fruits were made of reconstituted amber; the leaves are of gilded plaster. The dog is carved from a white marble which has been inlaid with a black limestone, possibly one of the Ashford Black marbles found in Derbyshire. The dog has been put together in sections; the head is a separate piece. The cushion is of a yellow limestone, possibly Giallo Antico. I am grateful to Alexandra Kosinova and Robin W. Sanderson for this information.

The subject depicted by Wyatt was Lord Dudley's favourite Newfoundland dog, who had already been immortalised by Sir Edwin Henry Landseer (1802–1873) in a painting exhibited at the Royal Academy in 1829 (no. 291); this is now at Elton Hall, Elton, near Peterborough. Harris commented, 'It was intended and was hailed as a serious work of art. Now it evokes amusement and a fragile tenderness for its period flavour'. He went on to record, 'The sculptor was commissioned to produce not only a faithful likeness of Bashaw but also the best piece of sculpture of which he was capable, and was requested to work at unstinted cost' (Harris 1957). The dog, Bashaw, was taken to Wyatt's studio about fifty times to sit for the sculptor.

In his *Prize Treatise of the Fine Arts of the Great Exhibition of 1851*, the sculptor Henry Weekes [q.v.] commented: 'Of Wyatt's "Dog" we shall merely say that it is carefully and truthfully modelled, and elaborately carved; and express our wish that no attempt had been made in it to imitate colour. This was, however, we believe, done by express desire of the nobleman for whom it was intended; if so, the artist is of course not so much to blame' (Weekes 1852, pp. 93–4).

The statue was apparently on display in the Museum by January 1870, exhibited with other loan objects in the newly re-arranged South Court. In connection with some re-arrangement at the South Kensington Museum, an article appeared in the *Art Journal* in January 1870, in which *Bashaw* was singled out: 'The examples of Mosaic-work belonging to the Museum have attained greater prominence by the re-arrangement of the South Court, and the collection is enriched by some interesting pieces on loan. But what claim to its place of honour can be advanced on behalf of the full-sized figure of a Newfoundland dog, in black and white marble – the black varnished to give it its lustre – that stands in the midst of the mosaics? The great placid beast is trampling with calm indifference on a bronze serpent, ingeniously contrived to form a support to the body of the oppressor. A cushion of yellow marble, with ormolu tassels, is under the group; and the whole stands on a black pedestal, decorated on the sides with mosaic work in the style of the beautiful Russian pietra dura. We are glad to learn from the label that this work is only on loan' (*Art Journal*, 1 January 1870, p. 27).

John Ruskin was so moved on seeing *Bashaw* exhibited at the Museum, that he included a lengthy comment on it in a letter dated May 1871, published in *Fors Clavigera*. He wrote: ' I had to go the Kensington Museum; and there I saw the most perfectly and roundly ill-done thing which, as yet, in my whole life I ever saw produced by art. It had a tablet in front of it, bearing this inscription:- "Statue in black and white marble, a Newfoundland Dog standing on a Serpent, which rests on a marble cushion, the pedestal ornamented with pietra dura fruits in relief. – *English. Present Century*. No I". It was so very right for me, the Kensington people having been good enough to number it "I", the thing itself being almost incredible in its one-ness; and, indeed, such a punctual accent over the iota of Miscreation, – so absolutely and exquisitely miscreant, that I am not myself capable of conceiving a Number two, or three, or any rivalship or association with it whatsoever. The extremity of its unvirtue consisted, observe, mainly in the quantity of instruction which was abused in it. It showed that the persons who produced it had seen everything, and practised everything; and misunderstood everything they saw, and misapplied everything they did. They had seen Roman work, and Florentine work, and Byzantine work, and Gothic work; and misunderstanding of everything had passed through them as the mud does through earthworms, and here at last was their worm-cast of a Production' (*Ruskin* 1906, pp. 81–2).

A year later, *Bashaw* was again noted by Ruskin in a lecture entitled *The Power of Modesty in Science and Art*, given on 22 February 1872: 'I should thankfully put upon my chimney-piece the wooden dog cut by the shepherd boy; but I should be willing to forfeit a large sum rather than keep in my room the number I of the Kensington Museum – thus described in its catalogue – "Statue in black and white marble, of a Newfoundland dog standing on a serpent, which rests on a marble cushion; – the pedestal ornamented with Pietra Dura fruits in relief."' (*ibid.*, p. 187).

Bibliography

International Exhibition 1851, p. 854; Weekes 1852, pp. 93–4; *Ruskin* 1906, p. 187; *Ruskin* 1907, pp. 81–2; Harris 1957; Gunnis 1968, p. 447 (there erroneously said to have been auctioned, and bought in, at the Dudley sale in 1887); Penny 1976, p. 303; Bryant 1983 [Bashaw]; TDA, 33, p. 447 [Robinson].

Exhibited

Following the decision of the Executors of Lord Dudley's estate not to honour the commission and pay Wyatt, the statue was exhibited by the sculptor at various venues in an attempt to find a buyer. Initially in the sculptor's studio at Dudley Grove House, London between February and June 1834; at 28 Old Bond Street in July 1834; in Mr Stanley's Great Room at 21 Old Bond Street during January 1835. Exhibited at the International Exhibition 1851, Fine Arts Section, miscellaneous objects displayed in the Main Avenue, as 'The faithful friend of man trampling under foot his most insidious enemy'.

Unattributed Sculpture of the 19th Century

712: Chimneypiece

about 1800
Marble
A.213–1969

Formerly in the study of the house of the donor, Brigadier William Ellis Clark, at 34 Elmstead Lane, Chislehurst. Bequeathed to the Museum by Brigadier Clark in 1969.

[Not illustrated].

713: Bloodhound or basset hound

about 1800
Terracotta
h. 24 cm.
A.10–1954

The present piece and its pendant, cat.no. 714 were said to have formerly been in the Ashburnham collection, presumably at Ashburnham Place, near Battle, Essex. Various sales held by the Trustees of the Ashburnham Settled Estates and the Executors of Lady Catherine Ashburnham were held by Sotheby's during 1953, though it has not been possible to identify the present piece or its pendant in any of these sales. In the possession of the dealer Gerald Kerin prior to 1954. Given by Mr Bill Redford, 15 Davies Street, London in 1954 together with its pendant cat.no. 714.

The tail is broken; there is a crack in the base.

In his recommendation to the Director, H.D. Molesworth [q.v.] wrote, 'I saw these two sketch models of dogs in Kerins some time ago. They came with a block of other things from Ashburnham and the tradition was that they had "been done by an artist who had come down a long time ago and done portraits of all the dogs". They look to me in the 18th or early 19th century tradition and are competently modelled'.

I am grateful to Luisa Pontello of the Kennel Club for her help in identifying the breed of dog.

714: Mastiff

about 1800
Terracotta
h. 21.5 cm.
A.11–1954

Given by Mr Bill Redford, 15 Davies Street, London, in 1954, together with its pendant. See entry for cat.no. 713 for further provenance.

There is a crack in the base.

I am grateful to Luisa Pontello of the Kennel Club for her help in identifying the breed of dog. See also entry for cat.no. 713.

715: Urn

about 1800
Stone
h. 33 cm.
A.85–1921

Given by Miss G.M. Butler, Burlingham, Waterden Road, Guildford on behalf of the family of the late T.M. and Mrs Butler of The Firs, London Road, Guildford in 1921, together with cat.no. 694.

This vase had previously been kept in the garden of The Firs, London Road, Guildford.

716: King John (b.1167; r.1199–1216) handing the Magna Carta to the barons

about 1800–20
Marble in a gilt frame
h. 23 cm. w. 59.5 cm.
1153–1882

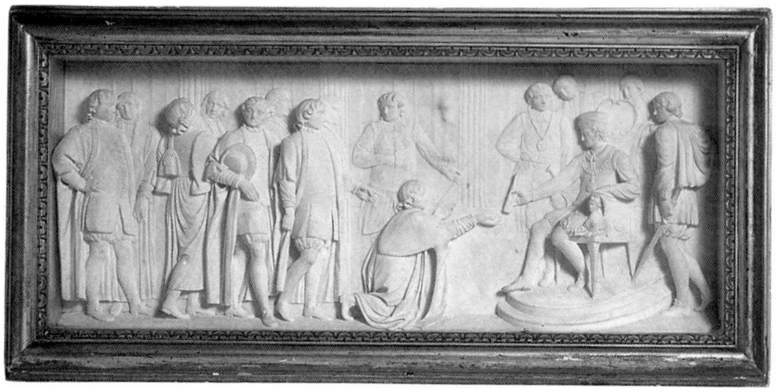

Bequeathed by John Jones as part of the Jones Bequest in 1882.

This marble relief represents the signing of the Magna Carta by King John in June 1215 at Runnymede, Surrey. Its original function is unknown; it may have been an independent piece, or possibly the central relief from a chimneypiece.

Bibliography
Jones 1924, p. 101, cat.no. 395.

717: George III (b.1738; r. 1760–1820)

about 1800–20
Bronze with traces of gilding
h. 71 cm.
A.51–1932

Purchased from W. Hannen Hunn, The Antique Exchange, 171 Fulham Road, Chelsea, London in 1932 for £3.

Eric Maclagan [q.v.] wrote to Buckingham Palace in 1932 prior to the acquisition of the present piece, requesting assistance in identification. A response was sent from the Librarian at Windsor Castle, Owen (later Sir Owen) Morshead, who wrote, ‘Chichester tells me the Queen thinks the three-quarter face photograph bears a distinct resemblance to George III, but that Her Majesty is not so sure about the full face one. Personally I have very little doubt that it does represent him. Among our prints I find one by James Godby after an original drawing by R. Bowyer (drawn 1810; published 1820) . . . I send you a tracing of the relevant portion. I think you will agree that the likeness is considerable. It is an ugly bust – but he was not a beautiful man (in later life)’.

Bibliography
Review 1932, p. 6, pl. 4 facing p. 5.

718: Allegorical scene with animals

about 1800–30
Limestone
h. 22.5 cm. w. 49.5 cm.
A.72–1926

According to the donor, the present piece, together with cat.nos. 719 to 725, originally came from an unidentified house in the City of London, about to be demolished. Between 1878 and 1916 they were placed over fireplaces in 1 Lowther Gardens, Princes Gate, London. Given by Mrs W. Woodbine Parish, 9 Courtfield Road, London in 1926.

On acquisition this group of reliefs (cat.nos. 718 to 725) were thought by Eric Maclagan [q.v.] to be related to the work of John Bacon the Elder (1740–1799), but he considered them to be probably early nineteenth century. The original contexts are unknown.

719: Fisherman

about 1800–30
Limestone
h. 23.5 cm. w. 52 cm.
A.73–1926

Given by Mrs W. Woodbine Parish in 1926.

See entry for cat.no. 718.

720: Two goats

about 1800–30
Limestone
h. 18.5 cm. w. 42. 5 cm.
A.74–1926

Given by Mrs W. Woodbine Parish in 1926.

See entry for cat.no. 718.

721: Ram and a dog

about 1800–30
Limestone
h. 19.5 cm. w. 44 cm.
A.75–1926

Given by Mrs W. Woodbine Parish in 1926.

See entry for cat.no. 718.

721

722: Sheep and a lamb

about 1800–30
Limestone
h. 8.5 cm. w. 46 cm.
A.76–1926

Given by Mrs W. Woodbine Parish in 1926.

See entry for cat.no. 718.

723: Ass and a foal

about 1800–30
Limestone
h. 8 cm. w. 42 cm.

A.77–1926

Given by Mrs W. Woodbine Parish in 1926.

See entry for cat.no. 718.

724: Two boys fishing from a boat

about 1800–30
Limestone
h. 6.8 cm. w. 41 cm.
A.78–1926

Given by Mrs W. Woodbine Parish in 1926.

See entry for cat.no. 718.

725: Two boys and a horse

about 1800–30
Limestone
h. 18 cm. w. 41 cm.
A.79–1926

Given by Mrs W. Woodbine Parish in 1926.

See entry for cat.no. 718.

726: Chimneypiece and grate from 4 Carlton Gardens

about 1817
Marble and ormolu mounts
h. 132 cm.
A.57–1932

From 4 Carlton Gardens, London. Purchased by Mr T. Crowther & Sons, from the contents of the house before its demolition in 1932. Purchased for £100 together with cat.no. 413 from Mr T. Crowther & Sons, 282 North End Road, Fulham, London in 1932, by Mr G. Flint Clarkson, A.R.I.B.A. through the National Art Collections Fund, in memory of Mrs Jane Clarkson. Presented to the Museum in 1932.

The two circular medallions depicting female classical heads in the upper corners of the mantlepiece were reported stolen in 1968.

The Manager of Carron Company, Falkirk wrote to the Museum in 1933, suggesting that the mantlepiece may have been made by Carron's in 1817, or was possibly inspired by works produced by them (departmental records).

The *Review of Principal Acquisitions during the Year 1932* recorded that the present piece was 'decorated with unusually fine ormolu mounts' (*Review* 1932, p. 7). See also the entry for cat.no. 413 for a further chimneypiece from 4 Carlton Gardens.

Bibliography

Review 1932, p. 7, and pl. 5 facing p. 8.

727: Chorus of singers

about 1831
Wood
h. 22.5 cm. w. 22.5 cm.
A.6–1917

Given by Frank Green, Esq, Treasurer's House, York in 1917.

According to the donor this relief was said to have been executed by a York man. It is based on the 1831 engraving of the same subject by George Cruikshank (1792–1878) taken from the etching by William Hogarth (1697–1764) of 1732.

On acquisition, the relief was described as 'certainly not of eighteenth-century work; possibly it may have been executed about the time when the painting was engraved by Cruikshank (1831), a view which is strengthened by the style of the original frame into which the work is fastened' (*Review* 1917, p. 3).

The Hogarth etching shows a rehearsal of the oratorio *Judith* by William Huggins, with music by William Defesch, which was performed on 16 February 1732/3 at Lincolns' Inn Fields (see Burke and Caldwell 1968, no. 140; and Paulson 1965, I, pp. 149–50, cat.no. 127, and III, pl. 133).

BIBLIOGRAPHY
Review 1917, p. 3.

728: Unknown woman

about 1840–50
Plaster
h. 65 cm.
A.6–2000

There is no information available on the provenance of the present piece, which until 2000 was recorded as an unregistered object in the Museum.

729: Unknown woman

about 1840–50
Marble
h. (incl. socle) 70 cm.
A.7–2000

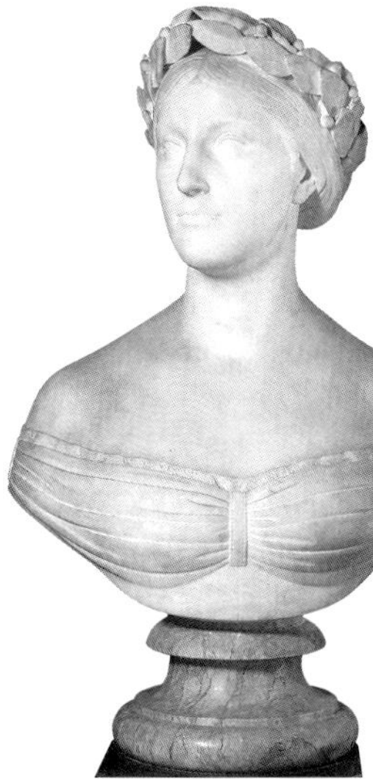

There is no information available on the provenance of the present piece, which until 2000 was recorded as an unregistered object in the Museum.

730: Henry VII (b.1457, r.1485–1509)

about 1850
Anonymous; after the original by Pietro Torrigiano
Bronze
h. 74.5 cm.
7916–1862

In the possession of Mr Henry Catt in 1862. Purchased by the Museum in London in 1862 for £150. Although the vendor is not recorded, it was probably purchased from Mr Henry Catt. On long term loan to Kings College, Cambridge from 1986.

The bust is taken from the effigy to Henry VII in Westminster Abbey, executed by Torrigiano between 1512 and 1519.

At the time of acquisition, this bust was ascribed to Pietro Torrigiano (1472–1528), based on its similarities with the effigy of

Henry VII in Westminster Abbey. It was published by Robinson in the catalogue accompanying the *Special Loan Exhibition* of 1862 as 'apparently a contemporary reproduction by Torregiano [sic] of the bust of the statue from the tomb in Henry VII's chapel at Westminster' (Robinson 1863, p. 28). The bust was also published by Fortnum in his *Descriptive Catalogue of the Bronzes of European Origin in the South Kensington Museum* as Italian, and 'a contemporary reproduction from the tomb in Westminster Abbey' (Fortnum 1876, p. 6). A note attached to the register entry for this bust records a visit to Westminster Abbey in December 1902 by 'W.W.H.', whose exact identity is uncertain. 'W.W.H.' recorded in a memo to Mr Skinner [q.v.] that although the dimensions of the bust were almost identical with the head of the recumbent figure, certain differences were evident. He wrote that the hair on the present bust was fuller than that on the effigy, and that the collar, plain on the present bust, was unlike that in Westminster Abbey, where the surface of the bronze had been inscribed in an attempt to represent fur. He noted, 'this effect could easily be, and probably was, obtained by tooling. The inference is that our bust may not unreasonably be attributed to the hand of Torrigiano'. The dating and attribution of the bust were however subsequently questioned, initially by Maclagan and Longhurst, who suggested the bust was a nineteenth-century reproduction (Maclagan and Longhurst 1932, p. 72). In a letter to Lady Constance Milnes Gaskell dated 10 November 1941, Eric Maclagan [q.v.] noted: 'I was at Windsor last Thursday and noticed a bronze bust of Henry VIIth which I cannot remember to have seen before and which is almost exactly identical with one we have at the Victoria and Albert Museum. I suspect that both of them are 17th century casts from the Effigy in Westminster Abbey'. In a letter of the same date to Owen (later Sir Owen) Morshead, Librarian at the Library, Windsor Castle, Maclagan wrote: 'Very likely you know that we have another version of this bust in the Museum. The actual bust is, I think, identical but ours is on a rectangular base with Gothic decoration. We can trace its history back to the middle of the 19th century; but we have always rather suspected that it was not very old then, and that the base is more in the manner of Pugin than of any of Torrigiano's contemporaries'. The bust is also included in Pope-Hennessy's *Catalogue of Italian Sculpture in the Victoria and Albert Museum* of 1964 in which he noted, 'An exactly similar base occurs beneath a plaster bust of Queen Elizabeth belonging to the Ancient Society of St Stephen's Ringers Bristol (on loan to the Bristol City Art Gallery), of which the upper part depends from the effigy of Maximilian Colt in Westminster Abbey. Both busts appear to date from the first half of the nineteenth century. A number of casts from the heads of the royal effigies at Westminster were made for the exhibitions of 1851 and 1862' (Pope-Hennessy 1964, II, pp. 401–2, cat.no. 418).

BIBLIOGRAPHY

Art Treasures 1857, p. 135, cat.no. 108; Robinson 1863, pp. 4, 28, cat.no. 455; Fortnum 1876, p. 6; Maclagan and Longhurst 1932, pp. 71–2; Pope-Hennessy 1964, II, pp. 401–2, cat.no. 418, and III, fig. 414; Arnoldi 1970, p. 217; Thieme-Becker, 33, p. 306.

EXHIBITED

A bronze bust described as 'Henry VII (Torregiano – ascribed to)', was lent by H. Catt, Esq. to the *Art Treasures of the United Kingdom* exhibition held at Manchester in 1857, cat.no. 108, presumably the present piece; *Special Exhibition of Works of Art of the Medieval, Renaissance, and more recent periods on loan at the South Kensington Museum June 1862,* cat.no. 455; lent by Mr Henry Catt.

731: A laughing child, probably the young Heraclitus

about 1850, after an eighteenth-century original
Marble
h. (incl. socle) 34.5 cm.
A.5–1982

Given by Mr Michael Hall, Connecticut, U.S.A. in 1982.

The model from which the present bust is derived was a popular one in the eighteenth century. The bust of the laughing child has traditionally been associated with Roubiliac's [q.v.] daughter Sophie, but as the bust may often be found paired with a crying child, it has subsequently been suggested that they might represent the young Heraclitus and Democritus, versions of which are known in bronze, marble and terracotta: a Chelsea porcelain version of the laughing child is in the Ashmolean Museum, Oxford (see *Ashmolean* 1992 [III], pp. 17–19, cat.no. 457; see also Baker 1997). A bronze version in a private collection has been dated by Malcolm Baker to about 1750 (Baker 1996 [Production], fig. 8 on p. 151). A pair of terracotta busts depicting a laughing and crying child respectively is in the National Museums of Scotland, Edinburgh, (inv.nos. A.1878.13.16 and A.1878.13.17): Baker has noted that these 'were described on acquisition as by Nollekens, and may be linked to the marble signed by him in the Hermitage'. Baker also records a pair of marble versions in the National Gallery of Victoria, Melbourne (see Baker 1994, p. 851 for the various known versions – I am grateful to Godfrey Evans for drawing this reference to my attention; see also Baker 2000 [Figured in Marble], pp. 91–2, and n. 35 on p. 175). Parian versions were also produced by Minton around 1858, where the types were described as *Mirth* and *Grief* respectively; see Atterbury 1989, pp. 62, figs. 468 (shape 347) and 470 (shape 348) on p. 127. Plaster casts of a 'girl, laughing' and said to be taken from an 'unidentified work of the 19th century', which were offered for sale by the Museum's cast service during the 1930s, appear to be cast from a version of the present piece. A further unidentified girl, described as 'probably French; 18th or 19th century', and given the same reference number, may possibly be identified as a reproduction of the crying child, or Young Democritus (see *Casts* 1939, p. 17, no. 511).

Citing references to busts of laughing and crying children in relation to Roubiliac, Baker has commented, 'Although their authorship is uncertain, there is some circumstantial evidence to suggest that Roubiliac may perhaps have been responsible for the original models. While this remains highly speculative, there can be little doubt that they were particularly well-known in England. It is therefore not surprising that one of them is shown in Mortimer's portrait of Joseph Wilton instructing a student' (Baker 1996 [Production], p. 151 and n. 34).

732: Turkey cock

about 1850
Terracotta
h. 15 cm.
A.21–2000

On loan from the statesman Lord Henry Charles George Gordon Lennox (1821–1886) of 13 Albert Terrace, Regent's Park, London, from 21 February 1866. Lord Lennox died intestate; his widow died in 1903 and no claimant could be found for this object and five ceramic items formerly on loan. Attempts to locate the legal representatives of Lord Henry Lennox, made in June 1918, were unsuccessful. The ceramic objects formally on loan were eventually accessioned by the Department of Ceramics and Glass in 1936 (inv.nos. C.774&A to C.778–1936). As a redundant loan the present piece was formerly accessioned by the Sculpture Department in 2000.

733: Unknown woman

about 1850–60
Marble
h. 43 cm.
A.8–2000

There is no information available on the provenance of the present piece, which until 2000 was recorded as an unregistered object in the Museum.

734: Leda and the swan

signed and dated 1781; but probably about 1850–80
Marble
h. 71.5 cm.
A.46–1935

Signed and dated on the back: Antonio Cannova./fec 1781.

Formerly in the possession of Domenico Brucciani & Co. Transferred from the Department for the Sale of Casts in 1935 and accessioned as a museum object in that year.

There is some damage to the right foot and to the left wing of the swan.

This was one of ten marble sculptures which were included in the assets of the Department for the Supply of Casts, and discovered during stocktaking at the end of March 1934. These had been included with the remaining stock of plaster casts and moulds which were in the possession of the Brucciani cast-selling business, when it was taken over by the Museum agency, the Department for the Sale of Casts, in 1921.

This figure may be Italian or English; when accessioned in 1934 it was tentatively attributed to Canova.

R.P. Bedford [q.v.] wrote in 1934: 'There are a number of works of art in marble in the Brucciani collections whose disposal one should perhaps now consider. None of them seems to have any artistic importance from our point of view with the possible exception of Leda and the Swan signed by Canova and dated 1781 . . . This is a poor work and I doubt if we could in any case exhibit it; we have been unable to find any record of Canova ever having carved such a figure'. Most of these marbles were de-accessioned; a marble bust of Pope Pius IX dating from 1848 by Camillo Pistrucci (1811–1854) is recorded as being lent to the Brompton Oratory, South Kensington in 1934.

Brucciani offered for sale a cast of a slightly smaller statuette of *Leda and the Swan* in his catalogue of around 1870, *Catalogue of Casts for Sale by D. Brucciani, 5 Little Russell Street, Covent Garden, London*: its height was 1ft 6" (46 cm.); it is possible that the present piece is related to these subsequent casts. For Brucciani see also cat.no. 467.

735: Vase

about 1860–85
Blue John fluorspar
h. 17.5 cm.
A.56–1927

Purchased from Cecil Thomas Esq., 7 Gloucester Terrace, Queen's Gate, London in 1927 for £16. Another Blue John vase purchased at the same time from Thomas was stolen in 1974 (inv.no. A.57–1927).

The sculptor Cecil Thomas owned a large collection of Blue John and also wrote on the subject (see Thomas 1921). See also entries for cat.nos. 756 to 760 for examples of Thomas's work bequeathed by the sculptor to the Museum in 1978.

This is one of five items offered for sale by Thomas. He described the present piece, 'Square Tazzae is [sic.] very unusual, as this work was always turned. The two specimens I have are the only examples I have seen or heard of. One corner has been repaired'. Thomas dated this and the other pieces offered for sale from his collection to 1860–1885.

Blue John is the name given to the purple-blue coloured fluorspar which is only to be found in one area, Treak Cliff, near Castleton, Derbyshire. It is a naturally brittle material and not easily worked, though it may be strengthened with the application of resin or hot shellac. For a discussion of the material see Thomas 1921, Clark 1969, and Ollerenshaw [n.d.]).

736: Seated female figure holding her hair

about 1870–90
Plaster on wood base
h. (incl. base) 80.5 cm
A.16–2000

There is no information available on the provenance of the present piece, which until 2000 was recorded as an unregistered object in the Museum.

The number 1789 has been roughly scratched on the back near the base.

737: Left hand of Lord Melbourne, probably William Lamb, 2nd Viscount Melbourne (1779–1848)

about 1845–48
Plaster
l. 26 cm.
1892–128

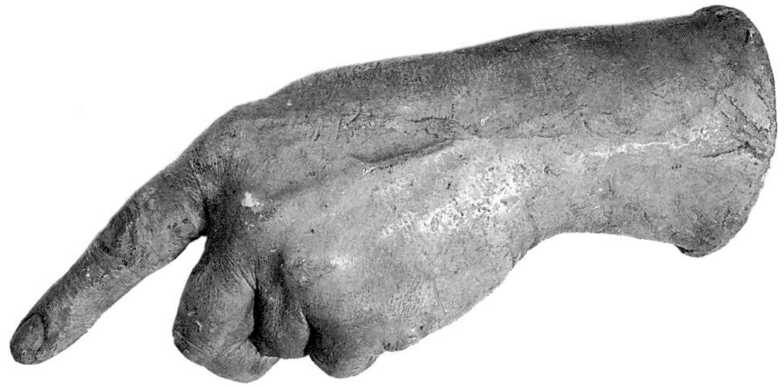

Given by the Executors of the late Sir J.E. Boehm in 1892. Though the present piece and cat.nos. 738 to 740 were acquired with a series of casts of hands through the Executors of the late Sir Joseph Edgar Boehm [q.v.] (see cat.nos. 288, 289, 293, 315, 321 to 336 and 479); the present piece and those listed below have been catalogued as unattributed, since they were executed before 1862 when Boehm settled in London. See entry for cat.no. 288.

BIBLIOGRAPHY
List 1892, p. 17.

738: Right hand of H.R.H. Princess Alice Maud Mary, Princess of Great Britain and Ireland, Duchess of Saxony, later Grand Duchess of Hesse-Darmstadt (1843–1878)

about 1850–5
Plaster
l. 16 cm.
1892–127:1

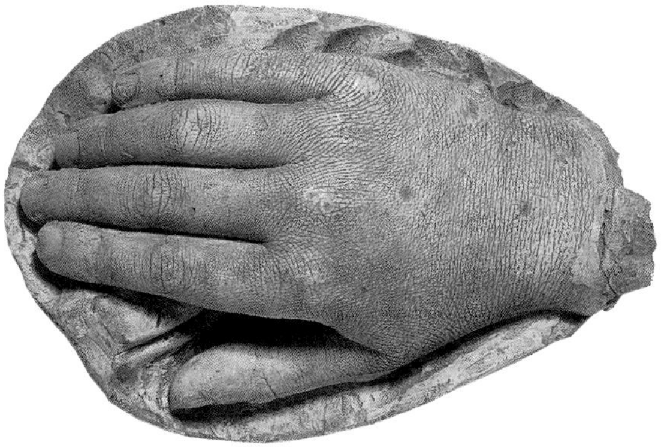

Given by the Executors of the late Sir J.E. Boehm in 1892; see entries for cat.nos. 737 and 288.

The cast was were taken from the subject when a child.

A further virtually identical copy of the cast is possibly taken from the present piece, as it has the inv.no. 1892–127 scratched into the base; see entry for cat.no. 739.

739: Right hand of H.R.H. Princess Alice Maud Mary, Princess of Great Britain and Ireland, Duchess of Saxony, later Grand Duchess of Hesse-Darmstadt (1843–1878)

about 1850–5
Plaster
l. 16 cm.
1892–127:2

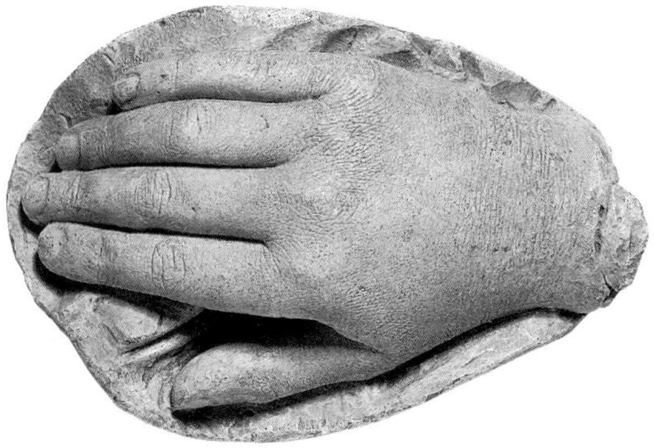

Given by the Executors of the late Sir J.E. Boehm in 1892; see entries for cat.nos. 737 and 288.

This was probably cast from cat.no. 738, as it has the inv.no. 1892–127 scratched into the base.

740: Hands of Count Camillo di Cavour (1809–1861)

about 1858–59
Plaster
l. 24.5 cm.
1892–89

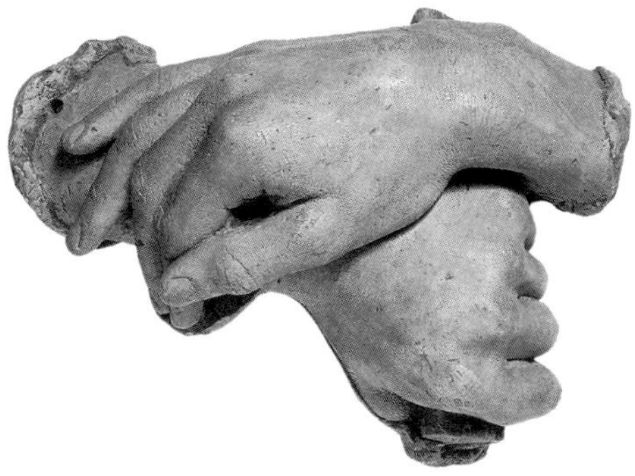

Given by the Executors of the late Sir J.E. Boehm in 1892; see entries for cat.nos. 737 and 288.

BIBLIOGRAPHY
List 1892, p. 13.

THE 20TH CENTURY

The Arts and Crafts Memorial Society

(dates unknown; active 1923)

I have been unable to trace any information on the Arts and Crafts Memorial Society, presumably a group engaged in the promotion of the use of incised lettering, active in 1923.

741: Memorial tablet, HIC JACET

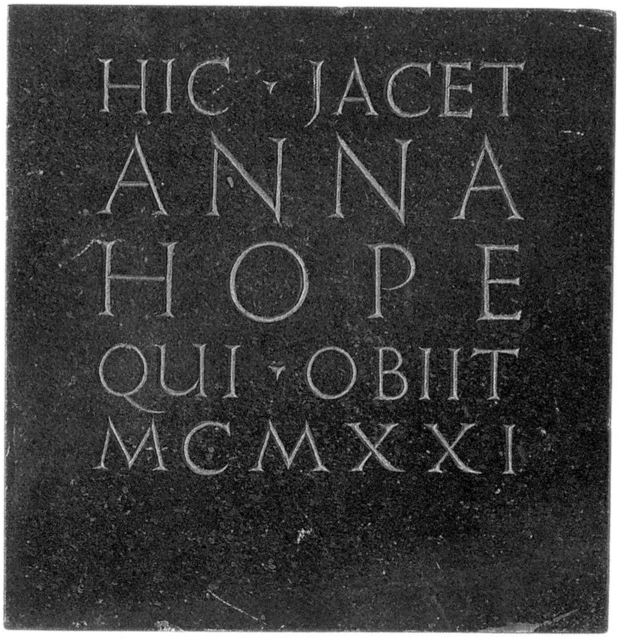

1923
By unrecorded artists at the Arts and Crafts Memorial Society
Slate with incised lettering
h. 15.5 cm. w. 15.5 cm.
A.48–1934

The inscription in Roman lettering reads: HIC JACET/ANNA/HOPE/QUIOBIIT/MCMXXI (Here lies Anna Hope who died in 1921).

Given by the British Institute of Industrial Art to the Victoria and Albert Museum in 1934, together with cat.no. 762. Displayed at the Bethnal Green Museum. Transferred to the Department of Architecture and Sculpture (later Sculpture Department) in 1976.

There are traces of a label on the reverse and two drilled holes.

This tablet was almost certainly acquired by the British Institute of Industrial Art as an example of lettering in stone. On acquisition it was said to date from 1923.

Exhibited
The British Empire Exhibition, Wembley, 1924.

Sir William Reid Dick K.C.V.O., R.A., H.R.S.A.

(b. Glasgow 1879 – d. London 1961)

Reid Dick initially trained at the Glasgow School of Art until 1907. He then attended the City and Guilds School in Kennington. After serving in France and Palestine during the First World War he took up sculpture once more. In 1938 he was appointed Sculptor to George VI, a post he held until 1952. From then until his death he was Queen's Sculptor-in-Ordinary for Scotland. Reid Dick exhibited at the Royal Academy from 1912, and was appointed a member of the Royal Academy in 1928. He also exhibited at the Royal Scottish Academy from 1912 to 1958. He was responsible for a number of war memorials, and for that to George V in Westminster Abbey, erected in 1947. He was knighted in 1935. The Tate Gallery Archive holds material relating to this artist.

Parkes 1921, pp. 137–8; Granville Fell 1945; Tate 1964, pp. 145–6; Who Was Who 1979, p. 946; Sculpture in Britain between the Wars 1986, pp. 52–5; Royal Scottish Academy 1991, I, pp. 412–3; McEwan 1994, p. 169.

742: Pietà from the memorial in St Paul's Cathedral to Field Marshal Horatio Herbert Kitchener, 1st Earl of Khartoum and Broome (1850–1916)

signed and dated 1923
Painted ochre-coloured plaster in wooden frame
h. 60 cm.
A.40–1975

Signed close to Christ's left hand on the base: Reid Dick, ARA 1923.

Formerly in the possession of the sculptor. Given by Lady Reid Dick, the sculptor's widow in 1975, together with cat.no. 743.

This is the model for the Portland stone group surmounting the altar in the Earl Kitchener Memorial Chapel, Chapel of All Souls, St Paul's Cathedral, which was installed in 1925. Granville Fell considered the monument to be 'one of his [Reid Dick's] most important monumental works, commemorative and memorial, more or less associated with its architectural surroundings . . . The *Pietà* in Portland Stone, governed to some extent by traditional conceptions, nevertheless contains some original features; in the head of the Virgin, bowed in reverential attitude over the torn hand of the *Saviour*, in the suggestion of approaching *rigor mortis* in the body of Christ himself and in the well designed lines of the drapery' (Granville Fell 1945, p. vii; for the original group see *ibid.*, pl. 9).

EXHIBITED
Reid Dick exhibited a number of pieces at the Royal Academy connected with the Kitchener memorial yearly from 1922 to 1925, and again in 1942. In 1922 he exhibited 'Earl Kitchener Memorial Chapel – sketch model' (no. 1424), possibly the present piece, although it may be from another part of the memorial, as the present piece is dated 1923. In 1923 he exhibited 'Model for the marble effigy of Earl Kitchener. To be placed in front of the altar in the Memorial Chapel, St Paul's Cathedral' (no. 1503). In 1924 he exhibited 'Pieta (unfinished). Part of the Kitchener Memorial for St Paul's Cathedral (no. 1516); in 1925 'The late Earl Kitchener – recumbent effigy, marble. To be placed in St Paul's Cathedral' (no. 1381). In 1942 he showed what was described as the 'Original sketch-model for Kitchener Chapel, St Paul's Cathedral', no. 829 (see *Royal Academy* II, pp. 162–3).

743: Frieze of dancing putti on the memorial in St Paul's Cathedral to Field Marshal Horatio Herbert Kitchener, 1st Earl of Khartoum and Broome (1850–1916)

about 1923
Painted plaster
h. 54.8 cm.
A.40:A-1975

Formerly in the possession of the sculptor. Given by Lady Reid Dick, the sculptor's widow in 1975, together with cat.no. 742.

This coloured plaster relief showing ten putti dancing with laurel wreaths, cymbals and pipes, is based on Donatello's *Cantoria*, now in the Museo dell' Opera del Duomo, Florence. The present piece was the model for the Portland stone altar frieze in the Earl Kitchener Memorial Chapel, Chapel of All Souls, St Paul's Cathedral, London; see entry for cat.no. 742 for the model of the Pietà from the same memorial.

EXHIBITED
See entry for cat.no. 742.

ROBERT JOHN GIBBINGS

(b. Cork 1889 – d. Oxford 1958)

Gibbings is best known as a book illustrator, wood engraver and writer. Only four sculptures by him are known (including the one catalogued below), probably all produced during the same period (see Empson 1959, illus. pp. 348–50). One of these, entitled The Embrace, *dating from about 1924–33, was acquired by the Reading Museum and Art Gallery in 1989/90, inv.no. 1991–13. A photograph showing* The Embrace *in Gibbings's studio, together with* Tahitian Woman *is illustrated by Empson 1959, p. 348. Papers relating to this sculptor may be found in the Department of Documents at the Imperial War Museum, at Reading University Library and at the University of California Library, Los Angeles, William Andrews Clark Memorial Library.*

Empson 1959; Thirties 1979, p. 290.

744: Tahitian woman

about 1929–31
Hopton Wood stone
h. (incl. base) 74 cm.
A.98–1980

Given to Mrs Hazel Hunkins-Hallinan by the artist around 1940. Purchased from Mrs Hunkins-Hallinan in 1980 for £2000.

On acquisition in 1980 this figure was seen to complement sculptures by Eric Gill [q.v.] already in the collection, as well as the woodcuts, engravings and first edition books by Gibbings, which were held by the Department of Prints and Drawings and the National Art Library respectively. The stone and slate sculptures by Gill were subsequently transferred to the Tate Gallery in 1982.

This figure of a Tahitian woman was almost certainly inspired by a visit made by Gibbings to Tahiti in 1929. The sculpture is not signed or dated, but was probably produced between about 1929 and 1931, when Gibbings was in close contact with Gill, and became interested in sculpture whilst running the Golden Cockerell Press.

BIBLIOGRAPHY
Empson 1959, pls pp. 349–50; *British Art and Design* 1983, pp. 102–3.

(Arthur) Eric (Rowton) Gill

(b. Brighton 1882 – d. Harefield 1940)

Gill is known for his work as a typographic designer and carver of inscriptional lettering, as well as for his sculpture. He initially trained at the Chichester Technical and Art School, and later with the architect William Douglas Caroë (1857–1838), whilst he attended evening classes in masonry at the Westminster Institute. Gill worked as a letter-cutter from 1903, and as a sculptor from 1910. In 1907 he established an artistic community at Ditchling, Sussex. Perhaps his most famous typeface design is Gill Sans, which he designed in 1927. He executed a number of war memorials, and received several church commissions, as well as secular works, including Prospero and Ariel *(1931) for the frontage of BBC Broadcasting House, London, and the* North, South, *and* East Winds *for the London Transport Headquarters (1928). In 1952 a collection of engravings by Gill was given by his widow to the Department of Prints, Drawings and Paintings. Twelve works by Gill (mainly inscriptional lettering) formerly in the Museum were transferred to the Tate in 1983; see appendix I. Two small ivory carvings by Gill remain in the Museum: a* Figure of a Woman *(inv.no. A.39–1928) and a* Madonna and Child *(currently on loan from a private collection). The Tate Gallery Archive holds material relating to this artist.*

Sculpture in Britain between the Wars 1986, pp. 76–83; Peace 1994; Collins 1998; TDA, 12, p. 631 [Stuart-Smith].

745: Memorial tablet, commemorating Museum personnel killed in the First World War (1914–1918)

signed; 1919–20
By Eric Gill with the assistance of Joseph Cribb
Hopton Wood stone
h. 152.5 cm. w. 66 cm.
A.4–1999

The memorial tablet has a lunette-shaped top, containing a laurel wreath in low relief. Below in incised black lettering:/VICTORIA AND ALBERT/MUSEUM

Beneath, in incised red lettering: IN HONOUR OF THOSE/WHO GAVE THEIR LIVES/FOR THEIR COUNTRY/SERVING THE KING/BY LAND AND SEA/IN THE GREAT WAR/MCMXIV – MCMXVIII/

In black lettering below the names of sixteen members of the Museum staff killed in action are listed alphabetically.

J.P. ADAMS/H.F. ARNOTT/E.BIGGS/A. A. BUNTING/L. CALLENDER/A. CLARK/J. FERGUSSON/W. IVES/J.J. LAWES/A. McLEAN/C.G. MILLS/W.F. QUICKENDEN/G.C. SIORDET/T.G. STRATFORD/W.T. TOOMEY/H. WYER/

Beneath is the inscription: Set up by subscription of the whole staff/in memory of their comrades 1920

Commissioned by the Museum from the artist in 1919. The exact cost of this memorial is not recorded. Gill's estimated costing was a nominal sum of between £10 and £20, paid from donations by members of Museum staff. The memorial was to have been acquired using the Museum's purchase grant, and to have been assigned to the Department of Architecture and Sculpture, later the Sculpture Department. As the total sum was raised through subscription, the purchase grant was not used, and the intention of assigning it to Architecture and Sculpture either not carried out or forgotten. The decision to assign the memorial an inventory number was taken in 1999, following the precedents set by other memorials in the Main Entrance of the Museum to staff killed in the Second World War, and to the memory of Dr W.L. Hildburgh F.S.A.; see entries for cat.nos. 755 and 748 respectively.

Gill supplied two corbels for the tablet. Both have a simple insignia symbolising the V&A monogram; the corbel to the left has the initials in smaller lettering, 'J' and 'C' (for Joseph Cribb) incised to each side of the monogram; whilst the other is similarly incised 'E' and 'G 'for Eric Gill. (Herbert) Joseph Cribb (d.1967) was Gill's first apprentice, working with him from June 1906 until 1934. According to Peace, this is one of only three signed examples of Gill's work: it is difficult to attribute lettering solely to Gill after 1906 with the arrival of Cribb in the workshop. This piece is therefore of particular interest as it is signed by both artists.

On the question of a memorial, R.P. Bedford [q.v.] noted in August 1919, 'You will remember that Mr. Maclagan has on several occasions mentioned to you the desirability of having in the collections of sculpture, an example of the lettering of Eric Gill, who is without doubt the foremost of our artists in carved lettering'. Originally a plaque by Gill to the memory of Sir John Charles Robinson [q.v.] was suggested, but Bedford went on to suggest, 'Would it not be possible instead to obtain the services of Eric Gill to carve us a simple tablet in memory of our men, which would be distinguished by its beautiful lettering, and, while being a worthy memorial, would at the same time take its place among the great works in our galleries?' There was seen to be an element of urgency, as it was thought that Gill was intending to enter a religious order, which would have meant that the opportunity of obtaining an example of his work, and of "showing the public the practical interest we take in good memorials" would be missed. The memorial was temporarily displayed in the Main Entrance in April 1920, and later permanently built into the Main Entrance. Gill also produced a First World War memorial for the British Museum, installed in 1921 (see Peace 1994, p. 99).

Gerald Siordet, one of those listed on the memorial, had worked in the Museum as a Temporary Cataloguer prior to 1914 on Margaret Longhurst's *Catalogue of Carvings in Ivory*, and is mentioned by Eric Maclagan [q.v.] in the prefatory note to the catalogue, 'on the outbreak of the War he [George Siordet] enlisted at once as as volunteer and served in the Rifle Brigade, first in France and later in Mesopotamia, where he was killed early in 1917' (Longhurst 1927, p. iv).

Bibliography

Physick 1982, p. 256 fig. 327; Peace 1994, pp. 7, 13–14, 93 cat.no. 365, fig. 36 on p. 95, 177–8; *'One by one'* 1998 [Bilbey], pp. 75–6, no. 72.

Charles Sargeant Jagger M.C., A.R.A., R.B.S.

(b. Kilnhurst 1885 – d. London 1934)

Jagger was a native of Sheffield and began his career as an apprentice silversmith with Mappin and Webb. He later studied under Edouard Lanteri [q.v.] at the Royal College of Art from 1908 to 1911. He visited Italy and North Africa in 1911. He is best known for his monumental war memorials of the 1920s, particularly the Royal Artillery Memorial at Hyde Park Corner, completed during 1921–5. Parkes described Jagger as 'one of the most promising of the younger men'. The Tate Gallery Archive holds material relating to this sculptor.

Parkes 1921, pp. 127–8; Jagger 1933; Jagger 1935; Jagger 1985; Sculpture between the Wars 1986, pp. 94–5; British Sculpture in the Twentieth Century 1981, p. 255; Gingell 1988; TDA, 16, pp. 865–6 [Glaves-Smith].

746: Cathal and the woodfolk

signed; 1914
Bronze in oak frame
relief h. 49.5 cm. w. 77.5 cm.
A.1–1997

Signed in the bottom right hand corner: C. SARGEANT JAGGER. SC.

Included in Sotheby's sale, London, 29 March, 1983, lot 201 (sold for £950); David Roderick Kirch; sold Christie's, London, 2 March, 1995, lot 210 (sold for £2,600). Purchased from Robert Bowman, London in 1997 for £7,130.

This composition is one of Jagger's earliest known works, produced and exhibited at the Royal Academy in 1914, shortly before he enlisted in the Artists' Rifles. It depicts a frieze of revelling nymphs and mythical figures; the central one, Cathal, was a legendary Irish hero. In 1913 Jagger was unsuccessful in his submission of a plaster version of the present piece in the competition for a Scholarship in Sculpture at the British School in Rome, recorded in the *RCA Students Magazine* of May 1913 (see *RCA* 1913, pp. 110–11). A year later in 1914, Jagger's entry into the same competition with a comparable bronze relief entitled a *Bacchanalian Scene* met with success, though he was to renounce the prize in order to enlist in the army (Williamson 1999, p. 788). Two plaster versions of the composition survive; the present locations of these are unknown: one was sold at Christie's, London, 21 May 1992, lot 62 (50.5 x 79 cm.); the other at Sotheby's, London, 16 December 1987, lot 211, described as Bacchanalian scene, (67.5 x 96.5 cm.). A terracotta version purchased from the sculptor by Calouste Gulbenkian is in the Gulbenkian Museum, Lisbon (see *Gulbenkian* 1999, pp. 114–7, inv.no. 576). A bronze version in the possession of Mrs Evelyn Jagger Clarke, the sculptor's widow, was included in the exhibition held at the Fine Art Society in 2001 (see *Fine Art Society* 2001, p. 50, cat. no. 68).

McAllister recorded, 'Bacchanalian subjects have an attraction for Mr. Jagger, as giving plenty of scope for the imaginative faculty with which he is endowed . . . His *Cathal and the Woodfolk* exhib-

ited this year at Burlington House, though classical in treatment, has the unique quality of being very much alive; in fact the whole work is instinct with life and movement to a degree that is particularly noticeable' (McAllister 1914, p. 96).

BIBLIOGRAPHY
McAllister 1914, p. 96; *Royal Academy* 1914, p. 117; *Jagger* 1985, p. 56, fig. 51 on p. 57, 70; *Bowman* 1996, p. 40, illus. on opp. page; *Gulbenkian* 1999, p. 116 (there noted as in the collection of David Roderick Kirch); Williamson 1999, p. 788, fig. XVIII.

EXHIBITED
Royal Academy 146th Summer Exhibition, 4 May to 15 August 1914, cat.no. 2073; *War and Peace Sculpture: Charles Sargeant Jagger*, Imperial War Museum, London, and Mappin Art Gallery, Sheffield, 1 May 1985 to 3 January 1986.

Possibly by Felix Amadeé Joubert

(active 1896 – 1934)

In 1896 Joubert produced a marble monument to Edmund Verney in Stanford, Leicestershire. He was also responsible for some of the internal decoration at Stanford Hall, Leicestershire. He is listed as a sculptor in the Post Office London Directory *for 1896, located in 152 Kings Road, Chelsea, the same address as Amedée Joubert & Son, listed as 'upholsterers and decorators, carton pierre makers and fibrous plaster decorators'. In 1899 Felix Joubert is listed at 2 Jubilee Place, Chelsea, whilst presumably his father's business remained at 152 King's Road. A further member of the Joubert family, Jules Amédee Joubert is also listed as a sculptor, at 4 Jubilee Place, Chelsea. The last entry for Felix Joubert is in 1934, when he was located at 2 & 3 Studios, Jubilee Place, SW3 and 152 King's Road, Chelsea, SW3. (The trade information above was kindly supplied by Norbert Jopek).*

Directory 1896, p. 1156; Directory 1899, p. 1273; Directory 1934, p. 2352; Pevsner 1981 [Northants], pp. 410–11.

747: Geometry and Astrology

about 1896–1934
Possibly by Felix Amadeé Joubert after Giambologna
Bronze
h. 18.5 cm.
A.67–1953

Given by Messrs Kerin and Calmann, 15 Davies Street and Matthiessen, Bond Street, London in 1953.

This bronze was acquired as a known forgery by Joubert (possibly Felix Amadée Joubert), dating from the 19th or early 20th century, after a terracotta by Giambologna or one of his followers, which had been acquired by the Museum in 1937 (inv.no. A.110–1937; Pope-Hennessy 1964, II, pp. 477–8, cat.no. 502, fig. 503; *Giambologna* 1978, p. 230, cat.no. 243). Other bronze variants of this terracotta exist (see *Boymans* 1994, pp. 82–3 cat.no. 18).

Bibliography
Pope-Hennessy 1964, II, p. 477.

David Guy Kindersley

(b. Codicote 1915 – d. 1995)

David Kindersley was a pupil of Eric Gill [q.v.] between 1933 and 1936; he began to work independently in 1937. In 1946 he set up his own workshop at Barton near Cambridge, where he became renowned for his inscriptions; his work has been compared with that of Reynolds Stone [q.v.]. Many examples of Kindersley's work may be found in Cambridge, including inscriptions for King's, and Corpus Christi colleges. Works by Kindersley have also been purchased by the Museum of Modern Art, New York and the Gleeson Library, Williamstown, Massachusetts. An inscribed plaque by Richard Kindersley, David Kindersley's son, is currently on loan to the Museum.

Dreyfus 1957; Kindersley 1967; Kindersley 1976; Kindersley and Cardozo Lopes 1981; Hill 1986; Shaw 1989, esp. pp. 28–30.

748: Memorial tablet to Dr W.L. Hildburgh, F.S.A.
(1876–1955)

1957
Portland stone
h. 30 cm. w. 69 cm.
A.1–1958

The inscription on this plaque in incised lettering reads: TO THE MEMORY OF/WALTER LEO HILDBURGH/1876–1955 GENEROUS/FRIEND OF THE MUSEUM

Commissioned from the artist in 1957 for the sum of £70.

This tablet is set into one of the pillars in the Main Entrance of the Museum, opposite the memorial tablet by Reynolds Stone commemorating Museum staff killed in the Second World War, cat.no. 755.

As well as this tablet commemorating Dr Hildburgh, Kindersley was also commissioned in 1987 to design the inscription found on the exterior wall of the Museum near the Exhibition Road entrance, recording that the damage to the walls of the Museum resulted from bombing during the Second World War. Kindersley felt the inscription would be given greater meaning by its being cut into the surface of one of the sections of bomb-damaged Portland stone (see Shaw 1989, pp. 29–30).

Dr Hildburgh, the American collector and art historian resident in London from 1912 onwards, was a generous benefactor to the Museum, his many gifts culminating in his bequest of 1956 (see TDA, 14, p. 525 [Williamson]).

Maurice Lambert

(b. Paris 1901 – d. London 1964)

Lambert was the son of the painter George Washington Lambert A.R.A. (b.1873). He trained in London from 1919 to 1923 in the studio of Francis Derwent Wood (1871–1926). In 1927 a contemporary commentator, P.G. Konody described Lambert as having 'thrown himself heart and soul into the Modern Movement'. He worked in a wide range of materials, often in combination, including brass, marble, alabaster, lead and aluminium, and executed ideal works as well as portrait busts. Lambert's first major show was in June 1927 at the Claridge Gallery, London. He was Master of Sculpture at the Royal Academy Schools between 1950 and 1958, and was a prolific exhibitor at the Royal Academy from 1938 to 1964. An exhibition of his work was held at the Belgrave Gallery, London in 1988. A marble sculpture by Lambert entitled Man with a bird, *formerly in the Museum's collection, was transferred to the Tate Gallery in 1982; see Appendix I. I am grateful to Vanessa Nicolson for her assistance with some of the biographical details for this sculptor.*

Konody 1927; Lambert 1927; Studio 1932; Royal Academy IV, pp. 214–5; Lambert 1988; Buckman 1998, p. 723.

749: Male and female nudes

signed; about 1930–2
Bronze on a red marble base
h. (group) 9.8 cm.
A.32–2000

Signed in monogram on the base: ML

Initially on loan from Sir Leigh Ashton [q.v.] to the Department of Regional Services (Circulation Department) from 5 January 1953. Transferred from the Circulation Department to the Sculpture Department in 1981. As a redundant loan the present piece was formally accessioned by the Sculpture Department in 2000.

The date of the figure is suggested by its inclusion in a photograph of Lambert's studio taken around 1932 (see *Lambert* 1988; I am grateful to Vanessa Nicolson for this information; see also Nicolson [forthcoming]).

Gilbert Ledward O.B.E., R.A.

(b. London 1888 – d. 1960)

Gilbert Ledward was the second son of the sculptor Richard Arthur Ledward [q.v.]. He studied at the Arts and Crafts School in Langham Place, and at the Chelsea Polytechnic, where he obtained a London County Council scholarship enabling him to attend the Royal College of Art, where he studied under Edouard Lanteri [q.v.]. A contemporary of Charles Sargent Jagger [q.v.], he also studied at the Royal Academy Schools, winning the travelling scholarship in 1913 to become the first Scholar for Sculpture at Rome. He was a committee member of a group named Sculptured Memorials and Headstones, *who promoted the use of British stones for the production of lettered memorials and headstones. He exhibited a plaster copy and relief of the* Mourners *(no. 829) and* Cavalry, *a detail of the memorial to the Rev. Llewellyn P.P. Williams (no. 983), at the War Memorial Exhibition held at the Victoria and Albert Museum in 1919. Ledward produced the Guards' Division Memorial at Horse Guards' Parade, London, perhaps his most prestigious work. Further examples of his work may be found in the permanent collections of the Royal Academy; he also produced some panels for the redecorated interior of Eltham Palace in 1935. During the 1920s he became Professor of Sculpture at the Royal College of Art. Archival material is housed at the Royal Academy, the Courtauld Institute of Art, the Imperial War Museum, Department of Documents, and the Centre for the Study of Sculpture, Leeds. A questionnaire completed by Ledward for Kineton Parkes is held by the Archive of Art and Design AAD/1990/2. A centenary exhibition of his work was held at the Fine Art Society, London in 1988.*

Buckley 1913, pp. 16–17; Sculptured Memorials and Headstones 1934; British Sculpture in the Twentieth Century 1981, p. 256; Skipwith 1988 [Ledward]; Ledward 1988; Turner 1999, pp. 6–7, 25.

750: Richard Redgrave, C.B., R.A. (1804–1888)

signed and dated 1881; this version 1915–16
Marble
h. 64 cm.
A.3–1916

Inscribed on the underside at the side: R·A·LEDWARD/Nov 1881

Given by Gilbert R. Redgrave Esq, Thriftwood, Silverdale, Sydenham, and his sisters in 1916. The sitter was the father of the donors. This bust was presented by Redgrave's children as a memorial to his work at the Victoria and Albert Museum, namely in being 'the first to give the impetus to the formation of an Art Museum', and commemorating his work in securing the Sheepshanks Collection for the Museum.

Richard Redgrave was a close and loyal friend and colleague of Henry Cole [q.v.], and was involved in the embryonic stages of the formation of the South Kensington Museum. He was made Art Superintendent in 1852, Inspector General for Art in 1857, and Director for Art in 1875 (Bonython 1982 [Cole], p. 26).

The bust was executed in marble by Gilbert Ledward during 1915–16 after an original terracotta bust designed and produced by his father, Richard Arthur Ledward in 1881; see entry for cat.no. 485. The terracotta was probably the one exhibited at the Royal Academy in 1882 (no. 1632).

Bibliography
Graves V, p. 15 no. 1632; *Review* 1916, p. 8–9; *Redgrave* 1988, p. 163, no. 162.

Exhibited
Richard Redgrave 1804–1888, Victoria and Albert Museum, and Yale Center for British Art, 16 March 1988 to 7 August 1988, cat.no. 162.

David McGill

(active 1889 – 1927; d. 1947)

David McGill was a sculptor and medallist. He studied at the Royal College of Art and the Royal Academy Schools, where he was awarded the travelling studentship for sculpture. McGill exhibited at the Royal Academy between 1889 and 1924; he also exhibited a number of medals shown at the New York International Medallic Exhibition of 1910. In 1901 Spielmann noted, 'His [McGill's] treatment of the figure is fearless; his style is good, and his future performance should justify its promise'.

Spielmann 1901, pp.147–8; Forrer III, p. 522 and VIII, pp. 1–2; Graves V, p. 139; Royal Academy V, p. 84; McEwan 1994, p. 358.

751: Sir Thomas Armstrong C.B. (1833–1911)

signed and dated 1904
Bronze on a green marble base
h. (incl. base) 65 cm.
A.30–1912

Signed in the front right corner on the plaque at the base of the bust: D M[C] G
Square plaque on integral base is inscribed: Thos: Armstrong C:B/1904

Given by the sculptor in 1912. Previously on loan to the Museum between 1905–6.

Sir Thomas Armstrong [q.v.] was Director of Art in the Department of Science and Art of the South Kensington Museum between 1881 and 1898. On his death a Memorial Committee was set up to organise a suitable commemoration at the Museum. Members included former friends and colleagues such as Sir Edward Poynter and Walter Crane. David McGill, a former South Kensington student, offered to present his bust of Armstrong to the Museum. The bust had already been on loan to the Museum in 1905–6, and the Memorial Committee felt it would be a suitable memorial to Armstong if it were to be taken on permanently. The original loan had been recommended 'as the bust was considered to be an excellent portrait and a fine work of art'. The Armstrong Memorial Committee provided a suitable marble pedestal with the following inscription: THOMAS ARMSTRONG C B. BORN 1833 DIED 1911. DIRECTOR FOR ART 1881–1898. PRESENTED BY FRIENDS IN RECOGNITION OF HIS WORK AS AN ARTIST: IN APPRECIATION OF HIS SERVICES TO EDUCATION IN ART: AND IN REMEMBRANCE OF THE HELP GIVEN BY HIM TO OTHER WORKERS. The bust and pedestal were originally displayed to one side of the Art Library (now National Art Library) doorway. The bust alone is now displayed in the Reading Room of the National Art Library, together with portraits of other former Directors of the Museum; see cat.nos. 753 and 767.

Bibliography
Review 1912, p. 4; *Royal Academy* V, p. 84, no. 1698.

Exhibited
Royal Academy 1905, no. 1698.

Sir Eduardo Paolozzi

(b. Leith, near Edinburgh 1924)

Paolozzi initially studied at the Edinburgh College of Art in 1943, and a year later at St Martin's School of Art, London. Between 1945 and 1947 he studied sculpture at the Slade School of Fine Art, Oxford. He moved to Paris in 1947, where he stayed for two years, and where he met such artists as Georges Braque (1882–1963), Constantin Brancusi (1876–1957) and Alberto Giacometti (1901–1966). Paolozzi taught at the Central School of Art and Design, London from 1949 to 1955. In the early 1950s he became a major influence in what was to become Pop Art. Paolozzi's interest in popular culture is illustrated by his collection of items dating from around 1900 to 1994, which form the Krazy Kat Arkive of Twentieth Century Popular Culture, held at the Archive of Art and Design (AAD/1989/5 also AAD/1994/17). Paolozzi has worked in a number of materials and media, including screenprinting, mosaic and collage.

TDA, 24, pp. 34–5.

752: Dame Elizabeth Esteve-Coll, D.B.E. (b.1938)

signed and dated 1996
By Sir Eduardo Paolozzi; cast at the Arch Bronze Foundry, London
Bronze
h. 71 cm.
A.30–2000

Signed and dated on the front of the integral base: 1996/EduaRdo PAolozzi

Inscribed on a panel on the front of the integral base: DAME ELIZABETH ESTEVE-COLL/DIRECTOR OF THE VICTORIA AND ALBERT MUSEUM/ 1988~1995

Inscribed on a panel on the back of the integral base: TIME PRESENT AND TIME PAST/ARE BOTH PERHAPS PRESENT IN TIME FUTURE/AND TIME FUTURE CONTAINED IN TIME PAST./IF ALL TIME IS ETERNALLY PRESENT/T.S. ELIOT.

[The opening lines of 'Burnt Norton' from Eliot's *Four Quartets*]

Also incised into the base on the left: 'A/C' for artist's copy.

Commissioned from the sculptor by the Museum. This is one of three versions produced by Paolozzi for a total sum of £30,000 plus V.A.T. of £3,520; a total of £33,520. Another version was presented to Elizabeth Esteve-Coll; the third is held in the National Art Library, cat.no. 753.

Elizabeth Esteve-Coll was appointed Keeper and Chief Librarian of the National Art Library from 1985, and was Director from 1988 to 1995. For busts of other former Directors of the Museum, see entries for cat. nos. 751 and 767.

The two reliefs on the pedestal of the figure were inspired by objects in the Museum's collections. The left hand panel is an interpretation of *The Descent from the Cross*, a model in gilt, wax and wood by Jacopo Tatti (Sansovino) (1486–1570) (inv.no. 7595–1861; see Pope-Hennessy 1964, II, pp. 417–9, cat.no. 442; III, figs. 439–40 on pp. 264–5). The right hand panel is inspired by the *Burghley Nef*, a nautilus shell mounted in silver parcel gilt, French, dating from 1482–3 (inv.no. M.60–1959); see Lightbown 1978, cat.no. 19, pp. 28–34.

Also in the Museum's collections are a maquette of the head and torso of the present figure in plaster on a wooden base (h. 28.5 cm; inv.no. A.2–2001), a plaster maquette of the head (h. 8.5 cm.; inv.no. A.3–2001), together with a plaster maquette for the plinth and two for the base (inv.nos. A.6 to 8–2001 respectively). In addition a plaster maquette for the complete figure is in the collection, inv.no. A.5–2001. See also next entry.

753: Dame Elizabeth Esteve-Coll, D.B.E. (b.1938)

signed and dated 1996
By Sir Eduardo Paolozzi; cast at the Arch Bronze Foundry, London
Bronze
h. 68 cm.
A.29–2000

Signed and dated on the front of the integral base: EduaRdo Paolozzi 1996

Inscribed on a panel on the side of the integral base: DAME ELIZABETH ESTEVE-COLL/DIRECTOR OF THE VICTORIA AND ALBERT MUSEUM/ 1988~1995

Inscribed on a panel on the side of the integral base: TIME PRESENT AND TIME PAST/ARE BOTH PERHAPS PRESENT IN TIME FUTURE/AND TIME FUTURE CONTAINED IN TIME PAST./IF ALL TIME IS ETERNALLY PRESENT/T.S. ELIOT.

[The opening lines of 'Burnt Norton' from Eliot's *Four Quartets*]

Commissioned from the sculptor by the Museum. See entry for cat.no. 752.

The arrangement of the base is slightly different to cat.no. 752. The relief inspired by the *Burghley Nef* is at the front, whilst the relief showing *The Descent from the Cross* is at the back.

A plaster maquette for this figure is also in the Museum's collections (inv.no. A.4–2001).

This figure is normally displayed in the National Art Library, where other busts of former Directors of the Museum are also shown; see cat.nos. 751 and 767.

Marcelle Quinton

(b. Berlin)

Marcelle Quinton emigrated to New York from Berlin with her family at the start of the Second World War, and studied at the Art Students League, Bryn Mawr College, Pennsylvania, USA, and later at St Hilda's College, Oxford. Her early works were mainly in alabaster, marble and plaster. A retrospective display entitled Portraits and Figures, *consisting of 23 sculptures in alabaster, bronze and plaster executed between 1967 and 1979, was held at the Ashmolean Museum Oxford, in 1980. Since the early 1980s Marcelle Quinton has specialised in portrait busts of distinguished contemporaries and historical figures, including Harold Macmillan (Members lobby in the House of Commons), Bertrand Russell (Red Lion Square), Margaret Thatcher (Thatcher Centre, Somerville College, Oxford), and Cardinal Newman (Brompton Oratory). She exhibited as a sculptor at the Royal Academy in 1980 and 1984.*

Personal communication; Lloyd-Jones 1978; Marcelle Quinton 1980; Royal Academy 1989, p. 395.

754: The Rt Hon the Lord Carrington K.G., C.H. K.C.M.G., M.C. P.C. (b.1919)

2000
Bronze
h. 45 cm.
A.43–2000

Anonymous gift to the Museum, via the American Friends of the Victoria and Albert Museum in 2000.

Lord Carrington was Chairman of the Board of Trustees at the Victoria and Albert Museum from 1983 to 1988. The bust is currently displayed in the Board Room at the Victoria and Albert Museum.

Reynolds Stone R.D.I., F.R.S.A., C.B.E.

(b. 1909 – d. 1979)

Though chiefly a designer for printed material, including book decoration, Stone was also an engraver, and produced memorial tablets, including the memorial stone to Winston Churchill in Westminster Abbey (1965). In 1930 he began his career as an apprentice in printing at the Cambridge University Press. Practising the art of engraving in his free time, Stone set up on his own as a freelance engraver and designer around 1934. Goodison records that Stone was self-taught in the art of carving lettering in stone, which he took up in 1939, and continues: 'Though embarking upon a new dimension in this departure, the artist and craftsman in Stone were triumphantly successful'. Stone was awarded a C.B.E. in 1953.

Goodison 1979; Who Was Who 1981, p. 762; Stone 1982.

755: Memorial tablet, commemorating Museum personnel killed in the Second World War (1939–1945)

1951–2
Slate with incised gold lettering
h. 46.5 cm. w. 97.5 cm.
A.39–1952

The inscription, in incised lettering, reads: TO THE MEMORY OF THOSE KILLED/IN THE WORLD WAR 1939 – 1945/C.A. CARTER C.J. CHEVERTON W.H. FRENCH/EDNA M. MARR J.E. MELLESS H.G. MOORING/F. MORRIS G.P. MORTON A.E. MUNDAY/J.F.A. ROBERTS P.A. ROUTE E. TICKEL/DOROTHY WILSON A.J.V. WRIGHT

Commissioned by the Museum from the artist in 1951 for £150. The money was provided by the Purchase Grant Fund (£113 6s), and donations from members of staff to the War Memorial Subscription Fund (£36 14s). A memorandum to the then Director records, 'Preliminary enquiries have revealed that his normal fee for such work would be 10/- per letter. We understand that the cost of the stone would be about £50. The total cost therefore would be in the neighbourhood of £150'.

Reynolds Stone was selected in May 1951 by the Committee of the 1939/45 War Memorial Fund to produce this tablet in commemoration of Museum staff lost in the conflict. A precedent had been set by Eric Gill's memorial tablet following the First World War, commissioned in 1919; see cat.no. 745. The Committee were keen for the memorial to be produced by Reynolds Stone, as the Museum would then also obtain an example of the best inscriptive lettering of the period. However, H.D. Molesworth [q.v.], then Keeper of Architecture and Sculpture, expressed his reservations at the suggestion. In a memorandum he noted, 'I of course wholeheartedly support the idea of trying to get a decent memorial rather than a bad one but as "Keeper A&S" I'm in no position to recommend the purchase of modern art at all and secondly I slightly wonder whether anyone would swallow the suggestion that a haphazard group of letters which can neither be photographed or cast or distributed (as in the case of the Gills) was a desirable or reasonable Museum acquisition. Can we however not do something on the grounds that the Museum must have a memorial – must therefore take a lead in ensuring the best memorials and thereby – just as we do presume [to] take care in all our notices & displays justify the expenditure out of one of their housekeeping funds on that account'.

This tablet is displayed in the Main Entrance of the Museum opposite the memorial tablet to Dr W.L. Hildburgh; see cat.no. 748. The memorial by Eric Gill is also displayed in the Main Entrance of the Museum; see cat.no. 745.

CECIL W. THOMAS O.B.E., F.R.B.S.

(b. London 1885 – d. 1976)

In 1901 Cecil Thomas was apprenticed to his father's gem-engraving business in Upper John Street, London. He exhibited at the Royal Academy from 1909 to 1974, initially specialising in gems, medals and seals, but also exhibiting medals and plaquettes. In 1918 he exhibited sculpture at the Royal Academy for the first time, and thereafter became active in this field. Thomas was also a Past Master of the Art Workers Guild. According to Forrer, Thomas was influenced by the work of Onslow Whiting and Richard Garbe. Thomas was awarded an O.B.E. in 1953.

Forrer VI, pp. 69–72; Thieme-Becker, 33, p. 60.

756: Alfred Henry Forster, Lieut. Royal Scots Greys (d.1918)

about 1924
Wood, hardened plasticine and card
h. (incl. candles) 19 cm.
A.50–1978

The maquette is set on a thinly painted wood base, on one side of which is the inscription: IN MEMORY OF ALFRED HENRY FORSTER LIEUTENANT · ROYAL · SCOTS · GREYS ·/WHO DIED MARCH 10 1918 OF/WOUNDS RECEIVED IN ACTION/THIS MONVMENT WAS ERECTED/BY LORD & LADY FORSTER

A coat of arms and insignia are to either side of the inscription. On the other side of the tomb chest is the inscription: ALFRED HENRY FORSTER LIEUT. IN THE/ROYAL SCOTS GREYS DIED MARCH 10 1918/OF WOUNDS RECEIVED IN ACTION/IN MEMORY OF HIS/SACRIFICE BARON/& LADY FORSTER/ERECTED/THIS MONVMENT

To each side are a further coat of arms and insignia.

Bequeathed by the artist in 1978, together with cat.nos. 757 to 760. A collection of gem and seal impressions mostly by Thomas was also bequeathed to the Department of Metalwork. A portrait bust of Howard Marion Crawford by Thomas which formed part of this bequest, inv.no. A.47–1978, was transferred to the Theatre Museum in 1979. Thomas had presented three albums of photographs and illustrations of his works 1901–71, dedicated in memory of his wife Dora Margaret, to the National Art Library in 1972.

This is the working model for Thomas's tomb of Alfred Henry Forster, killed in action during the First World War. Thomas was commissioned by the parents of the deceased, Henry William Lord Forster, Governor General of Australia, and Lady Forster to complete this memorial. The effigy in plasticine shows the young man lying with his right hand over his chest, his left arm by his side. An eagle rests at his feet and a laurel wreath by his head.

According to the albums of Thomas's work (see above), four versions of this tomb were cast in bronze: in Exbury, the New Forest, Hampshire; the Chapel of the Lamp, All Hallows Church, Barking; St John's Church, Southend, Kent, and Newcastle Cathedral, Australia. The tomb in All Hallows Barking was unveiled by Edward Prince of Wales in 1925. The inscriptions were apparently adapted for each version. The inscription on the Exbury Monument records that the monument was erected in memory of Lord and Lady Forster's two sons, John and Alfred, who were both killed during the First World War.

See also cat.no. 760 for another model for a tomb produced by Thomas for All Hallows Barking.

BIBLIOGRAPHY
Thomas Albums, II, pp. 9, 11, 22; *Royal Academy* VI, p. 129; *Royal Society of British Sculptors* 1939, p. 91 illustrates Forster memorial at All Hallows, Barking showing an inscription which differs from that shown on this model.

EXHIBITED
Royal Academy 1924, no. 1363. Included in an exhibition of Thomas's work at the Gieves Art Gallery, 22 Old Bond Street, London, held between 9 and 19 June 1925, were two objects related to the present piece: no. 18, described as: 'Bronze Effigy. The late Lieut. Alfred Forster, Royal Scots Greys, part of a memorial being erected by Lord and Lady Forster', also no. 29: 'Sketch Model. Part of a Memorial being erected by Lord and Lady Forster to their Sons' (*Thomas* 1925, pp. 3, 5).

757: Tomb of the Rt. Rev. Edward Stuart Talbot (1844–1934)

about 1934
Wood, hardened plasticine and card
h. (incl. base) 5.5 cm.
A.52–1978

Inscribed: EDWARD STUART TALBOT/1895 ROCHESTER 1905·1905 SOUTHWARK 1911·1911 WINCHESTER 1923

EDWARD·STUART·TALBOT/1870 KEBLE 1888 1844–1934 1889 LEEDS 1895

Bequeathed by the artist in 1978. See entry for cat.no. 756.

Only the plasticine effigy is illustrated.

This is probably the working model for the tomb of Edward Stuart Talbot, the first Bishop of Southwark, whose tomb in bronze and Hopton-wood stone was erected in the Chancel of Southwark Cathedral. The effigy depicts Talbot in episcopal robes with his hands clasped in prayer; at his feet are two lions, and the Order of the Garter. On one side is the inscription citing the dates and areas in which he had been Bishop; on the other, the period he spent as Warden of Keble College Oxford (1870–88), and Chaplain Ordinary and Vicar and Rural Dean of Leeds (1889–95) is noted. For Talbot, see *Crockfords* 1930, p. 1263.

Three coats of arms are shown on each side, and a coat of arms is also depicted on each end. The first design for the tomb as shown in the *Thomas Albums*, I, p. 13 (see entry for cat.no. 756), shows a canopy surmounted by angels over the tomb. The completed tomb was erected without a canopy (see *Thomas Albums*, II, p. 19).

BIBLIOGRAPHY

Thomas Albums, I, p. 29; II, pp. 12, 13, 19; *Royal Academy* VI, p. 129.

EXHIBITED

In 1938 Thomas exhibited at the Royal Academy 'The Late Bishop Talbot – recumbent effigy' (no. 1545), possibly the present piece.

758: Isabel

about 1950–70
Concrete, painted white, with plaster core
h. 42 cm.
A.49–1978

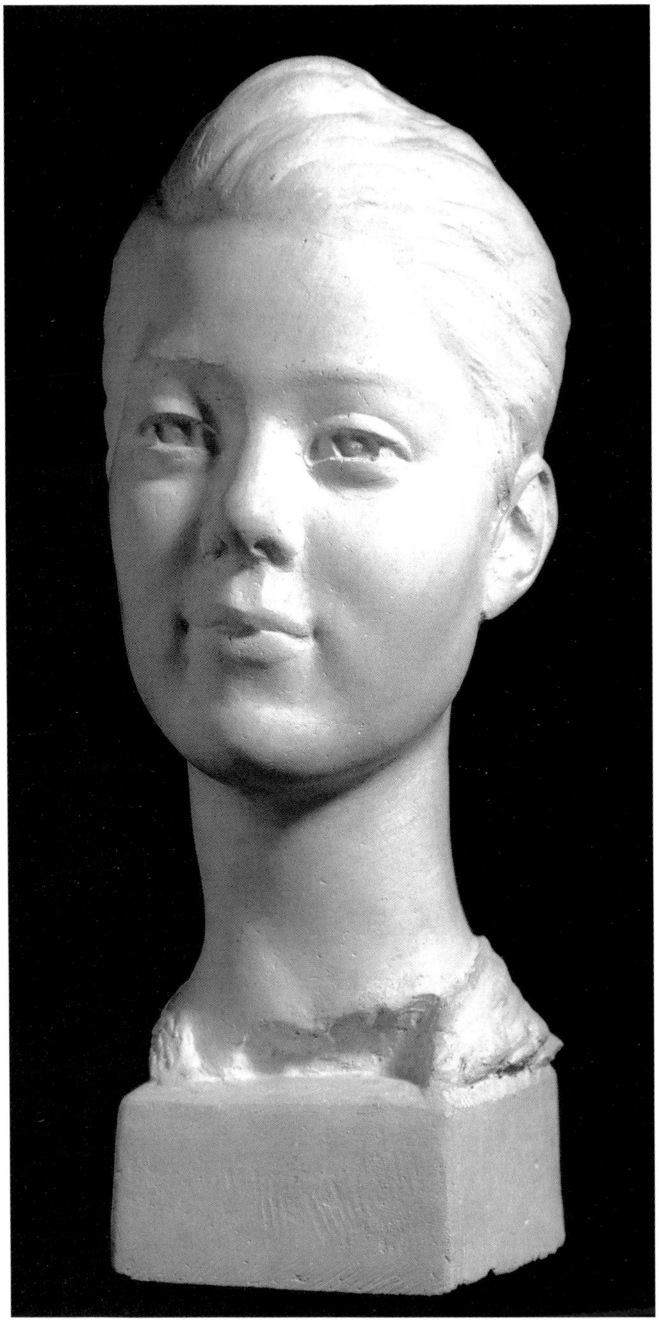

Bequeathed by the artist in 1978. See entry for cat.no. 756.

This bust, possibly a study, is on an integral socle. The identity of the sitter is unknown, the name Isabel being the description in the artist's bequest.

BIBLIOGRAPHY

Thomas Albums, II, p. 31.

759: Leonard Walker (1879–1965)

about 1961
'Snowcrete' (cement and concrete mix)
h. (incl. base) 39 cm.
A.48–1978

Bequeathed by the artist in 1978; see entry for cat.no. 756.

This white bust (with a slightly darker surface wash, peeling in places) is set on a rectangular marble socle, with a label on the side reading: CECIL THOMAS O.B.E./SCULPTOR/108 BROMPTON ROAD/LONDON SW7/TELEPHONE 373 5377

108 Brompton Road (Dora House) is now the home of the Royal Society of British Sculptors; the property, home to Cecil Thomas from 1919 onwards, and named after his wife, Dora, was bequeathed to the R.S.B.S. in 1976.

This is a portrait of Leonard Walker, a designer of stained glass, painter, and Master of the Art Workers' Guild. For an obituary of Walker, see *Journal* 1965, pp. 112–3.

Bibliography
Thomas Albums, II, p. 31; *Royal Academy* VI, p. 130.

Exhibited
Royal Academy 1961, no. 1351.

760: Tomb of the Reverend Philip Thomas Byard Clayton ('Tubby' Clayton) (1885–1972)

about 1972
Wood, hardened plasticine and card
h. (incl. base) 18.5 cm.
A.51–1978

The inscription in gilt lettering on one side reads: PHILIP THOMAS BYARD CLAYTON/CH, MC, DD./1885 1972

The inscription on the other side reads: FOUNDER PADRE OF TALBOT HOUSE·TOC H·/POPERINGHE 1915 ALL HALLOWS 1922

A measuring scale is visible on the unpainted wood base.

Bequeathed by the artist in 1978. See entry for cat.no. 756.

This is the working model for a tomb of the Reverend Philip Thomas Byard Clayton in All Hallows Church, Barking. The recumbent effigy is clothed in vestments, his right hand over his chest, his left arm at his side. A dog sits on a tasselled cushion at his feet. The effigy is supported by four lions at each corner.

The Reverend Clayton was the founding Padre of Toc H (formerly known as Talbot House), a youth movement which sought to encourage racial harmony and philanthropic service. He did much to support East End Clubs and Settlements, and Leprosy Relief, and travelled widely between 1922–66 on behalf of Toc H. Clayton also wrote on religious and social issues (see *Crockfords* 1971, p. 238; Tresham Lever 1971; *Who Was Who* 1981, p. 154). Thomas produced a bronze bust of Clayton for the Tower Hill headquarters of Toc H in 1932 (see *Thomas Albums*, II, p. 32); a plaque commemorating the opening of the Toc H headquarters dedicated by Rev. Clayton on 5 October 1960 (see *ibid.*, p. 8); a carving on the east end of the All Hallows Church in 1962 (see *ibid.*, p. 8); as well as a dedicatory plaque to Rev. Clayton (see *ibid.*, p. 55).

ALFRED TURNER R.A.

(b. London 1874 – d. 1940)

Alfred Turner trained at the South London Technical Art School under W.S Frith (1850–1924) and worked for a time as assistant to Harry Bates (1850–1899). In 1895 he entered the Royal Academy Schools. Spielmann described Turner as a 'highly successful student of the Lambeth and Royal Academy schools, who has also studied abroad, Mr Turner is among the most promising of the youngest generation of sculptors now before the public'. He taught at the Central School of Arts and Crafts, London. Turner was a frequent exhibitor at the Royal Academy between 1905 and 1937, and was elected an Associate of the Royal Academy in 1922, becoming a Royal Academician in 1931; his diploma work, Dreams of Youth, *is in the Royal Academy permanent collection. His daughter, Winifred [q.v.], was a successful sculptor in her own right; see cat.no. 763; a joint exhibition of their work was held at the Ashmolean Museum in 1988 (see Turner 1988). The Tate Gallery Archive holds material relating to this sculptor.*

Spielmann 1901, p. 155; Parkes 1921, pp. 104–5; Grant 1953, p. 249; Royal Academy VI, pp. 170–1; Beattie 1983, p. 252; Turner 1988; Thieme-Becker, 33, p. 491.

761: Mother and child

about 1936
Limestone
h. (incl. base) 103 cm.
A.11–1981

Given together with cat.no. 763 by the artist's daughter Miss Jessica Turner, 44 Munster Road, London in 1981.

This work is based on a smaller group exhibited by Turner at the Royal Academy in 1934, no. 1591.

BIBLIOGRAPHY
Royal Academy VI, p. 170, no. 1507; *Turner* 1988, p. 28, fig.18 on p. 29; Penny 1989, p. 136; *Royal Scottish Academy* 1991, IV, p. 345, no. 47; *Royal Glasgow Institute* IV, p. 242, no. 3.

EXHIBITED
Royal Academy 1936, no. 1507. In 1936 Turner exhibited at the Royal Glasgow Institute of Fine Arts, Glasgow: 'Mother and child – group (bianco del mare) no. 3', priced at £700, possibly the present piece. Similarly in 1938, Turner exhibited at the Royal Scottish Academy, Edinburgh 'Mother and child – bianco del mare', (no. 47), again possibly the same piece.

Laurence Arthur Turner

(b. 1864 – d. 1957)

Turner initially studied at Kennington School of Art. He was an accomplished woodcarver, and was often employed by church architects: he carved William Morris's tomb at Kelmscott, designed by Philip Webb. Turner was a Past Master of the Art Workers Guild, a Fellow of the British Institute of Industrial Art, and a member of a Special Committee of the Institute appointed to report on the 'present position of Monumental Art in Great Britain'. The committee recommended that good examples of monumental art, modern and historic should be displayed in exhibitions organised by the Institute. At the British Empire Exhibition held at Wembley in 1924 Turner exhibited a plaster model of the arms of Queen Elizabeth I for Liberty's new building, and was also involved in the supervision of a room set indicative of the period of 1888. In the 1920s Kineton Parkes sent out questionnaires to sculptors of the period, probably intended as material for a third volume of Sculpture of To-Day. *These questionnaires are held in the Archive of Art and Design, and include one completed by Turner (AAD 12/58–1990).*

British Empire 1924, illus. pp. 143, 147; Gray 1985, p. 357; AAD Turner.

762: In memory of John Stephen Crocket (d.1507?)

1925
Slate, gilded and coloured
h. 52.6 cm. w. 38.2 cm.
A.46–1934

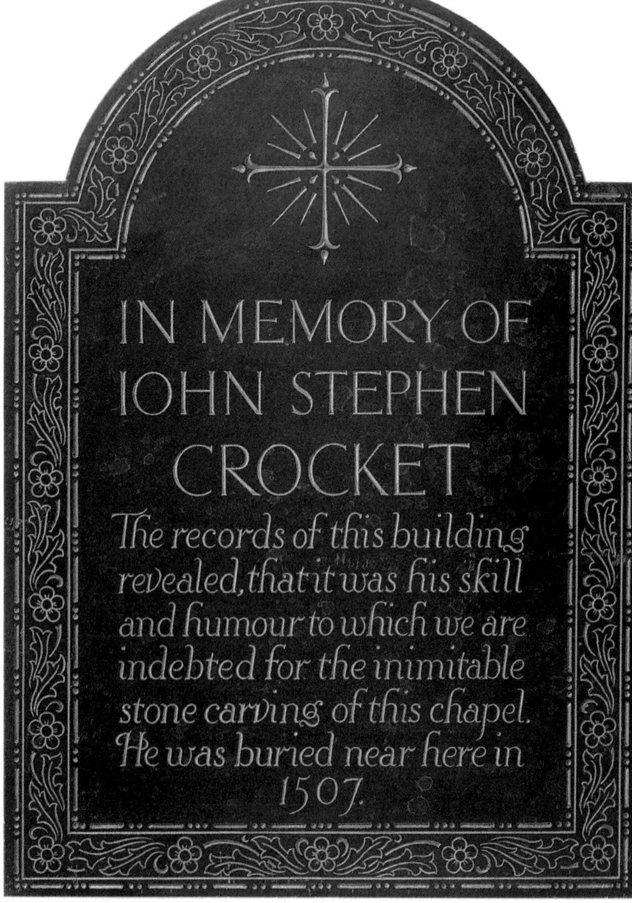

Inscribed: IN MEMORY OF/IOHN STEPHEN/CROCKET/The records of this building/revealed, that it was his skill/and humour to which we are/indebted for the inimitable/stone carving of this chapel./He was buried here in/1507.

Presented to the British Institute of Industrial Art by the artist in 1925. Given by the B.I.I.A. to the Victoria and Albert Museum in 1934 together with cat.no. 741. Transferred from the Department of Architecture and Sculpture (later Sculpture Department) to Bethnal Green Museum in 1936, but returned in 1976.

This slate memorial tablet has an arched top, with incised lettering and a decorative border, gilded and coloured. Other than the details inscribed on this tablet, nothing more is known of John Stephen Crocket. The B.I.I.A. was founded in 1925 with the aim of fostering closer relations between industry and art, and by raising standards in industrial art sought to generate demand for its production. The Institute was finally dissolved in the early 1930s (see Coulson 1979, p. 24 for further information on the B.I.I.A.). In 1934 those objects comprising the Institute's permanent collections were absorbed into the holdings of the V&A.

Exhibited

The Catalogue of the British Institute of Industrial Art Autumn Exhibition illustrating British Industrial Art for the Slender Purse, held in the North Court of the Victoria and Albert Museum, 9 November to 18 December 1929, records a 'Slate Memorial with incised letters in gold with coloured decoration' by Turner (probably the present piece), which was part of the permanent collection of the B.I.I.A. and included in the section on Monumental Art (V).

Winifred Turner

(b. 1903 – d. 1983)

Winifred was the daughter of the sculptor Alfred Turner [q.v.], and the sister of the donor of the sculpture catalogued below, Jessica Turner. Whilst her sister Jessica 'was content to assist her father', Winifred Turner attended the Royal Academy Schools between 1924 and 1929. She was elected Fellow and Associate of the Royal Society of British Sculptors in 1930; she exhibited at the Royal Academy between 1924 and 1962. The Tate Gallery Archive holds material relating to this sculptor.

Royal Academy VI, pp. 172–3; Turner 1988, esp. p. 32; Skipwith 1988 [British sculpture], p. 949.

763: Crouching youth

about 1934
Bronze
h. 101 cm.
A.12–1981

Given together with cat.no. 761 by Miss Jessica Turner, the artist's sister, 44 Munster Road, London in 1981.

This bronze figure has a dark green patination. Penny noted, 'Unlike her father [Alfred Turner], she was primarily a modeller, but much of her [Winifred Turner's] best work was cast in bronze and given a variety of patinas . . . *Youth* . . . has a colour and finish resembling basalt' (*Turner* 1988, p. 36). In a review of the retrospective exhibition of her work, together with that of her father, Skipwith comments, 'On the evidence of the exhibition Winifred Turner at her best was an even better sculptor than her father. *Youth* dominated the show in terms of quality and size. Shown at the R.A. in 1934 it is one of the most important English homages to [Ivan] Meπ troviË [1883–1962]' (Skipwith 1988 [British sculpture], p. 949).

Bibliography
Royal Academy VI, p. 172, no. 1589; *Turner* 1988, cat. no. 16, pp. 36, 47, p. 57 (photograph of the original clay model or a plaster cast after it); Skipwith 1988 [British sculpture], pp. 948–9, illus. 86 (here the plaster model is confused with the present piece); Penny 1989, p. 136; *Society of Women Artists* 1996, IV, p. 161, no. 581.

Exhibited
Probably identical with the bronze statue of *Youth* exhibited by Winifred Turner at the Royal Academy in 1934 (see *Royal Academy* VI, above) no. 1589. Winifred Turner also exhibited a '*Bronze Youth* – bronze' [sic] at the Society of Women Artists in 1939, no. 581, priced at £200; *The Sculpture of Alfred and Winifred Turner*, Ashmolean Museum, Oxford 21 June to 2 October 1988, cat.no. 16.

John Tweed

(b. Glasgow 1869 – d. London 1933)

Tweed initially trained in the studio of Hamo Thornycroft [q.v.] whilst also attending the Royal Academy Schools. The French sculptor Auguste Rodin was to have a major influence on his career; see entry below. In 1902 Tweed was appointed to complete Alfred Stevens's [q.v.] equestrian figure for the memorial to the Duke of Wellington, erected in 1912. He was later commissioned to produce a number of public monuments in London to notable personages, including those at Whitehall to Sir Robert Clive (1912) and Earl Kitchener (1926), and that to Sir George White in Portland Place (1922). Tweed exhibited at the Royal Academy from 1905 to 1932, at the Royal Glasgow Institute of Fine Arts (1888–1922), and at the Royal Scottish Academy (1905–27). A commemorative exhibition of his work was held at the Imperial Gallery of Art, Imperial Institute, London, in 1934.

Spielmann 1901, pp. 152–3; Tweed 1934; Tweed 1936; Royal Academy VI, pp. 174–6; Read 1982, p. 352; Gray 1985, pp. 358–9; Blackwood 1989, pp. 216–7, 276–8, 278–9; Royal Scottish Academy IV, p. 346; Royal Glasgow Institute IV, pp. 243–4; TDA, 31, p. 488 [Stocker].

764: Auguste Rodin (1840–1917)

about 1902
Plaster in wood frame
h. (relief) 39.2 cm; w. (relief) 31.7 cm.
A.29–1924

Bequeathed by Sir Claude Phillips in 1924. A number of works by Rodin were included in the same bequest: a plaster statuette of *Despair*, and a plaster relief of the *Young Mother* by Rodin (inv.nos. A.24 and A.25–1924; see Hawkins 1975, cat.no. 8, pp. 21–2, and cat.no. 6, p. 20 respectively), are both inscribed with a dedication to Phillips, who was a friend of the sculptor. Four dry-points by Rodin from this bequest are in the Department of Prints, Drawings and Paintings (inv.nos. E.2170 to 2173–1924). The present piece was on loan to the Tate Gallery from 1937 to 2000 (inv.no. 6064).

R.P. Bedford [q.v.] noted on the papers relating to the acquisition that the present piece was 'considered the best portrait of the artist'.

The close personal and professional relationship between Tweed and Rodin is discussed in the monograph on Tweed by Lendal Tweed, who noted: '. . . but it was only with the growing friendship with Tweed that his [Rodin's] reputation began to spread considerably on this side of the Channel. It is not too much to say – and Rodin himself freely acknowledged it – that to John Tweed more than to any other man was due the high opinion of the French sculptor that persists in England today . . .' (Tweed 1936, p. 98; for the friendship between Tweed and Rodin, see *ibid.*, pp. 98–110). Rodin's gift to the Museum in 1914 of eighteen examples of his work – presented in admiration of British soldiers fighting alongside his countrymen – was instigated primarily by Tweed (inv.nos. A.33 to A.50–1914; see *Review* 1914, pp. 1–3; *Rodin* 1914; Tweed 1936, pp. 108–9; Hawkins 1975). In 1902 Tweed and his family first visited Rodin at Meudon; the present piece may date from this time.

Bibliography
Rodin 1925, p. 21.

Exhibited
In 1904 Tweed exhibited 'Monsieur A. Rodin' at the Royal Glasgow Institute of Fine Arts (*Royal Glasgow Institute* IV, p. 244, no. 886). A relief of Rodin appeared in the Memorial Exhibition to John Tweed held in 1934 at the Imperial Gallery of Art, Imperial Institute, London (*Tweed* 1934, cat.no. 1). A relief portrait of Rodin by Tweed was lent by Sir Theodore Cook to the Museum for display in the exhibition of works by Rodin held in 1917, on the occasion of the sculptor's death (see *Rodin* 1917). In 1925 the present portrait is recorded as being displayed in the West Hall of the Museum, together with the collection of works by Rodin given by the sculptor.

Leon Underwood

(b. London 1890 – d. London 1975)

In a completed Kineton Parkes questionnaire of about 1926 held at the Archive of Art and Design (AAD 12/59–1990), Underwood listed the details of his career: he studied at the Polytechnic, Regent Street, London 1907; in 1910 he attended the Royal College of Art; in 1913 he travelled to Germany, Poland and elsewhere; he attended the Slade 1919–20. He explained that at this date (1926) he had only recently begun to carve, and that his works were exhibited at the Alpine Club Gallery. Underwood was involved in two publications of 1934: Art for Heaven's Sake, *and* Sermons by Artists, *both published by the Golden Cockerell Press; see cat.no. 765 below. A collection of thirteen wash drawings by the sculptor, given by his son, Garth Underwood, is in the Department of Prints, Drawings and Paintings (inv.nos. E.301 to 313–1982). A further 206 drawings, sketches and paintings were also given to the Museum by Garth Underwood in 1982, and are in the Archive of Art and Design (inv.nos. AAD 4/1 to 4/206–1981). The Tate Gallery Archive holds material relating to this artist: further papers are in the Imperial War Museum, Department of Documents.*

Underwood [Art] 1934; British Sculpture in the Twentieth Century 1981, p. 262; Sculpture between the Wars 1986, p. 142; Thieme-Becker, 33, p. 569; Underwood 1993; Whitworth 2000.

765: Mindslave: The mind in abject subordination to the intellect

1934
Marble
h. (excl. base) 112 cm.
A.1–1981

Given by the artist's son, Garth Underwood, 19 Elm Avenue, Ruislip, Middlesex in 1981.

The block of marble was originally intended for a composition called *Youth*, which in the event the sculptor did not execute (Whitworth 2000, cat.no. 83 on p. 129).

Partly because of the similarities with Michelangelo's *Slaves* in the Louvre, the donor suggested that *Mindslave* attempts to symbolise the struggle to escape from the mental repression prevalent in the totalitarianism of many regimes in Central Europe during the early 1930s. In a Golden Cockerell Press publication of 1934, artists were asked to write a sermon based on a biblical text, which would express their attitude towards life. Underwood contributed one on the Garden of Eden (*Sermons* 1934, p. 70); he wrote: ' Our Garden of Eden would be more readily accessible were we equipped with more of the will of the followers of Gandhi from the dark labyrinths of industrial commercialism that threaten us from the West'. In the light of Underwood's pamphlet of 1934 p.i, *Mindslave* might also be viewed as a representation of the limitations imposed upon the artist by aesthetic dogma: 'If the future is to hold for him further liberation from the bondage of this earth, it can be secured only by his intuition and imagination'.

Bibliography

Underwood 1934 [Leicester], no. 12 on p. 10; *Battersea Park* 1948, cat.no. 40 on p. 12, illus. on p. 39; *Underwood* 1969, cat.no. 114; Neve 1974, p. 152, pl. 108, p. 153; *British Sculpture in the Twentieth Century* 1981, p. 262 (biography) and cat.no. 122; *The Times*, Tuesday 15 September 1981, p. 10 (exhibition review for Whitechapel Art Gallery above); *British Art and Design* 1983, jacket illus.; Whitworth 2000, pp. 19, 34, 51, 53, 55, 90, 93, 129 cat.no. 83, fig. 72 (when displayed at the Beaux Arts Gallery, London in 1953; the figure is just visible in the left hand corner).

EXHIBITED

An exhibition of sculpture, paintings, drawings and engravings by Leon Underwood, The Leicester Galleries, Leicester Square, London, April 1934, no. 12; *Open Air Exhibition of Sculpture at Battersea Park*, May to September 1948, cat.no. 40; *Leon Underwood*, Beaux Arts Gallery, 1 Bruton Place, London, 11 May to 24 June 1953; *Fifth Biennale voor Beeldhouwkunst*, Middelheimpart, Antwerp, May to September 1959, cat.no. 99; *Leon Underwood a retrospective exhibition*, The Minories, Colchester, 1969, cat.no. 114; *British Sculpture in the Twentieth Century*, Whitechapel Art Gallery, London, 11 September to 1 November 1981, part 1, cat. no. 122.

STEPHEN WEBB

(b. 1849 – d. 1933)

Stephen Webb settled in London at the age of sixteen. According to an obituary in the Art News, *within a year of arriving in London Webb was 'carving figures in stone, many of which are still to be seen in the City today'. Amongst his commissions were portraits of Queen Victoria and Gladstone. He later became Professor of Sculpture at the Royal College of Art. In 1893 Webb contributed two essays, 'Woods and other materials' and 'Of Carving' to a publication entitled* Arts and Crafts Essays, *compiled by members of the Arts and Crafts Exhibition Society. A side-table with marquetry designed by Webb is in the Department of Furniture and Woodwork (inv.no. W.32–1954).*

Webb 1893 [Woods]; Webb [Of Carving], 1893; Art News 1933; Thieme-Becker, 35, p. 212.

766: The Arts of Painting and Sculpture

about 1900–3
Plaster in glazed wood frame
h. (incl. frame) 44 cm. h. (relief) 34 cm.
789–1904

Given by Oliver Wheatley Esq., 21 Broomhouse Road, Hurlingham, London in 1904.

The relief depicts a plain shield above two cherubs, between allegories of painting and sculpture respectively: the figure to the left holds a palette and brushes, whilst the other models a statuette of *Victory*.

Lady Désirée Welby (neé Copeland-Griffiths)

(active 1922 – 1952)

Lady Welby, described as a painter and sculptor, exhibited at the Grosvenor Gallery, the Walker Art Gallery, Liverpool, the Royal Academy and the Society of Women Artists.

767: Sir Cecil Harcourt-Smith LL.D., C.V.O.
(1859–1944)

signed; about 1922
Bronze on a marble plinth
h. (incl. plinth) 69 cm.
A.15–1924

Signed on the underside of the truncated left shoulder: D. Welby

Given by the sculptor in 1924.

The sitter was Director & Secretary of the Victoria and Albert Museum between 1909 and 1924. The bust was returned on temporary loan to Lady Welby in 1936 for submission to the Royal Academy Summer exhibition of that year, but was not accepted. The bust is normally displayed in the National Art Library Reading Room, along with busts of other former Directors of the Museum; see also cat.nos. 751 and 753.

Bibliography

Society of Women Artists 1922, p. 27, no. 427; *Review* 1924, p. I; Kilmurray 1981, p. 88; *Society of Women Artists* 1996, IV, p. 228, no. 427.

Exhibited

A bust of Sir Cecil-Harcourt Smith, presumably the present piece,was exhibited at The Society of Women Artists in 1922, no. 427.

Reginald Fairfax Wells

(b. Rio de Janeiro 1877 – d. Worthing 1951)

Wells initially trained at the Camberwell School of Art, and during the late 1890s at the Royal College of Art under the supervision of Edouard Lanteri [q.v.]. He later studied ceramics at the Camberwell School of Arts and Crafts. He became particularly renowned for his small-scale bronzes, most of which were produced between 1900 and 1910. From about 1909 onwards Wells became increasingly interested in ceramics; he established the Coldrum Pottery, Wrotham around 1900; this relocated to Chelsea in 1909. A number of examples of his pottery, mainly acquired in 1919, are in the Ceramics and Glass Department. Three further pieces by him are in the Birmingham Museum and Art Gallery. At the outbreak of the First World War Wells closed the Chelsea pottery, and began designing and manufacturing aircraft. On the failure of his aviation business, he established the London Pottery Company, Chelsea, relaunching the business with the optimistically named 'SOON' ware – 'soon' representing the anticipated timing of his success in the venture.

Studio 1903; Marsh 1925; Beattie 1983, pp. 198–9; Birmingham 1987, pp. 98–9, nos. 303–5 for further examples of his work; Carter 1990, p. 167; Wells 1998.

768: The Sower

signed; about 1900–1900–5
Bronze
h. 29.5 cm.
376–1906

Signed on the base: R.F. WELLS. The numbers 15 and 5 are stamped on one side of the base beneath the signature. There is a label on the underside of the object with the handwritten number '182'.

Purchased from the sculptor in 1906 for £10 10s (10 guineas). Originally held in the Circulation Department, but transferred to the Department of Architecture and Sculpture (later Sculpture Department) in 1956.

The present figure was acquired in 1906 as a characteristic example of Wells's work. An anonymous article on Wells in the *Studio* remarked, 'Some have spoken of Mr Wells as the English Millet of Sculpture, and the phrase seems apposite enough' (*Studio* 1903). Marsh commented that Wells's bronzes have added interest in that 'he has done his own casting throughout, using the cire-perdu process' (Marsh 1925, p. 284). Marsh noted that he first began modelling bronzes in 1900, 'the happiest of these bronzes' included *The Sower*, a version of which was illustrated on p. 285. For a similar example by Wells of a labourer in bronze see *Gibson to Gilbert* 1992 , no. 64, and illus. *Man Leaning on a Staff* c. 1907.

Bibliography
Beattie 1983, p. 252.

Exhibited
Design of the Times: 100 Years of the Royal College of Art, Royal College of Art, London, 7 February to 20 March 1996.

Unattributed Sculpture of the 20th Century

769: The Black Watch

about 1910–20
Stone
25.5 cm sq.
A.19–2000

Latin inscription: NEMO·ME·IMPUNE·LACESSIT (No-one wounds me with impunity), and below: THE BLACK WATCH

There is no information available on the provenance of the present piece, which until 2000 was an unregistered object in the Museum.

Pencil marks are drawn over the relief, and the words 'Not wanted back by W . . . [illegible]' are faintly visible on the surface.

The emblem on the relief is derived from the regimental badge of the Black Watch, the Royal Highland Regiment, which includes the figure of St Andrew. The motto – which refers to the thistle – is taken directly from the regimental badge.

770: Sol Gloria Mundi

about 1924
Anonymous; student of the Leicester College of Art
Marble
h. 19 cm. w. 23 cm.
Circ.637–1924

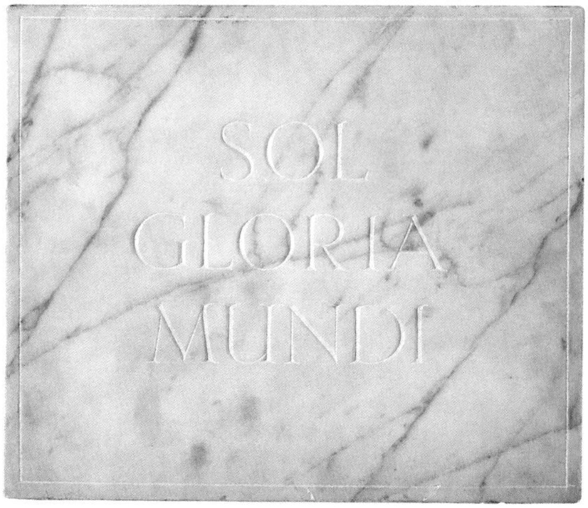

Inscribed on one side: SOL/GLORIA/MUNDI (The sun, the glory of the world)

This tablet has been re-used, on the reverse a previous attempt at inlay, with pencil lines drawn through it, reads: ENGLAND/MY/OWN

Given by the City School of Arts and Crafts, Leicester in 1924. Originally offered as an example of modern inscriptional work to the Circulation Department; it was later transferred from Regional Services (formerly the Circulation Department) to the Sculpture Department in 1978.

The desire for the Museum to have examples of modern inscription for the Circulation Department was noted in a memorandum from the curator H.A. Kennedy to the Director, dated 19 October 1923: 'We are frequently asked for specimens of good incised lettering in stone, and are generally able to meet the request by recourse to casts and photographs. The lettering such as that on the tomb of Henry VII affords an admirable model but it would be useful I think to have a few specimens of good modern lettering as well'.

BIBLIOGRAPHY

AAD Adams George Gammon Adams photograph album and related material (V&A Archive of Art and Design) (reference AAD/1997/12).

AAD Turner Laurence A. Turner, Kineton Parkes questionnaire (V&A Archive of Art and Design) (reference AAD12/58–1990).

Aesthetic Movement **1973** C. Spencer (ed.), *The Aesthetic Movement 1869–1890* (exh. cat.), Camden Arts Centre, London; London, 1973.

Age of Rococo **1958** *The Age of Rococo: Art and Culture of the 18th Century* (exh. cat.), translated by Dr M.D. Senft-Howie and B. Sewell, Council of Europe, Residenzmuseum, Munich, 1958.

Agnew **1981** *Sculpture and Works of Art*, Thomas Agnew & Sons Ltd, London, 29 October – 11 December 1981, London, 1981.

Allen 1981 B. Allen, 'Jonathan Tyers's other Garden', *Journal of Garden History*, I, no. 3, 1981, pp. 215–38.

Allen 1983 B. Allen, 'Joseph Wilton, Francis Hayman and the Chimney-pieces from Northumberland House', *Burlington Magazine*, CXXV, April 1973, pp. 195–202.

L'âme au corps **1993** *L'âme au corps – arts et sciences 1793–1993* (exh. cat.), Grand Palais, Paris; Paris, 1993.

American National Biography **1999** J.A. Garraty and M.C. Carnes (eds.), *American National Biography*, New York and Oxford, 1999.

Antonsson 1942 O. Antonsson, *Sergels Ungdom och Romtid*, Stockholm, 1942.

Architect **1921** Studies of the English Sculptors from Pierce to Chantrey, IV, Caius Gabriel Cibber (1630–1700), *Architect*, CVI, 16 September 1921, pp. 162–5.

Armstong 1881 W. Armstrong, *Alfred Stevens. A biographical study*, London, 1881.

Armstrong 1888 W. Armstrong, 'Mr. Hamo Thornycroft, R.A.', *Portfolio*, XIX, 1888, pp. 111–15.

Arnoldi 1970 F. Negri Arnoldi, 'Scultura Italiano al Victoria and Albert Museum', II, *Commentari*, III, July to September 1970, pp. 201–18.

Art and Design **1987** *Art and Design in Europe and America 1800–1900*, Victoria and Albert Museum, London, 1987.

Art in Rome in the Eighteenth Century **2000** E.P. Bowron and J.H. Rishel (eds.), *Art in Rome in the Eighteenth Century* (exh. cat.), Philadelphia Museum of Art, Philadelphia; The Museum of Fine Arts, Houston; Philadelphia, 2000.

Art Journal **1855** 'Minor Topics of the Month', *Art Journal*, 1 July 1855, p. 217.

Art Journal **1866** *Art Journal*, 1 January 1866, p. 20, illus. opp. p. 20 (engraving by W.W. Stodart).

Art Journal **1873** *Art Journal*, September 1873, p. 268.

Artist's Model **1991** I. Bignamini and M. Postle, *The Artist's Model. Its Role in British Art from Lely to Etty* (exh. cat.), University Art Gallery, Nottingham; The Iveagh Bequest, Kenwood; Nottingham, 1991.

Art News **1933** *The Art News*, New York, XXXI, no. 38, 15 July 1933, p. 6.

Art Treasures **1857** *Catalogue of the Art Treasures of the United Kingdom collected at Manchester in 1857*, London, 1857.

Art Treasures **1932** *Art Treasures Exhibition 1932* (exh. cat.), British Antique Dealers' Association, Christie, Manson & Woods, London, 1932.

Ashmolean **1992** N. Penny, *Catalogue of European Sculpture in the Ashmolean Museum 1540 to the present day*, (3 vols), Oxford, 1992.

Asleson 1999 R. Asleson (ed.), *A Passion for Performance. Sarah Siddons and her Portraitists*, Los Angeles, 1999.

Aslin 1967 E. Aslin, 'The Rise and Progress of the Art Union of London', *Apollo*, LXXXV, January 1967, pp. 12–16.

Athenaeum **1849** *Athenaeum*, 26 May 1849, pp. 549–50.

Athenaeum **1873** *Athenaeum*, 31 May 1873, p. 702.

Atterbury 1989 P. Atterbury (ed.), *The Parian Phenomenon. A Survey of Victorian Parian Porcelain Statuary and Busts*, Shepton Beauchamp, 1989.

Atterbury and Batkin 1990 P. Atterbury and M. Batkin, *The Dictionary of Minton*, Woodbridge, 1990.

Autour du néo-classicisme **1985** *1770–1830. Autour du néo-classicisme* (exh. cat.), Musée communal des Beaux-Arts d'Ixelles, Brussels, 1985.

Avers 1966 H-G. Avers, 'Plastik', *Die Kunst des 19. Jahrhunderts*, Berlin, 1966, no. 11, pp. 153–69.

Avery 1972 C. Avery, 'From David d'Angers to Rodin – Britain's national collection of French nineteenth-century sculpture', *Connoisseur*, CLXXIX, April 1972, pp. 231–9.

Avery 1978 C. Avery, 'Hubert Le Sueur's Portraits of King Charles I in Bronze, at Stourhead, Ickworth and elsewhere', in G. Jackson-Stops (ed.), *National Trust Studies 1979*, London, 1978, pp. 128–47.

Avery 1979 C. Avery, 'Laurent Delvaux's Sculpture in England', *National Trust Studies 1980*, London, 1979, pp. 151–70.

Avery 1983 C. Avery, 'Laurent Delvaux's Sculpture at Woburn Abbey', *Apollo*, CXVIII, October 1983, pp. 312–21.

Avery 1988 C. Avery, 'Hubert Le Sueur, the "Unworthy Praxiteles" of King Charles I' in *Studies in European Sculpture*, II, London, 1988, pp. 145–235 (reprinted from *The Walpole Society*, XLVIII, 1982, pp. 135–209).

Avery and Marsh 1985 C. Avery and M. Marsh, 'The Bronze Statuettes of the Art Union of London. The Rise and Decline of Victorian Taste in Sculpture, *Apollo,* CXXI, May 1985, pp. 328–37.

Avray Tipping 1914 H. Avray Tipping, *Grinling Gibbons and the woodwork of his Age*, London, 1914.

Avray Tipping 1919 (I) H. Avray Tipping, 'Coleshill House. Berkshire. The seat of the Hon. Mrs Pleydell-Bouverie, I', *Country Life*, XLVI, 26 July 1919, pp. 108–116.

Avray Tipping 1919 (II) H. Avray Tipping, 'Coleshill House. Berkshire. The seat of the Hon. Mrs Pleydell-Bouverie, II', *Country Life*, XLVI, 2 August 1919, pp. 138–46.

Avray Tipping 1922 H. Avray Tipping, 'Chesterfield House. Mayfair. A Residence of Viscount Lascelles, K.G.', II, *Country Life*, LI, 4 March 1922, pp. 308–14.

Baarsen 1998 R. Baarsen, 'High rococo in Holland: William IV and Agostino Carlini', *Burlington Magazine*, CXL, March 1998, pp. 172–83.

Baker 1949 C.H. Collins Baker and M.I. Baker, *The Life and Circumstances of James Brydges, First Duke of Chandos, Patron of the Liberal Arts*, Oxford, 1949.

Baker 1982 M. Baker, 'A Glory to the Museum. The Casting of the "Portico de la Gloria"', *Victoria and Albert Museum Album*, I, 1982, pp. 101–8.

Baker 1984 [Robinson] M. Baker, 'Spain and South Kensington. John Charles Robinson and the collecting of Spanish sculpture in the 1860s', *Victoria and Albert Museum Album*, 3, London, 1984, pp. 341–9.

Baker 1984 [Roubiliac] M. Baker, 'Roubiliac and his European background', *Apollo*, CXX, August 1984, pp. 106–113.

Baker 1986 [Cheere] M. Baker, 'Sir Henry Cheere and the Response to the Rococo in English Sculpture', in C. Hind (ed.), *The Rococo in England*. A Symposium, 17–19 May 1984, Victoria and Albert Museum, London, 1986, pp. 143–60.

Baker 1986 [Roubiliac] M. Baker, 'Roubiliac's models and 18th century English sculptors' working practices', *Entwurf und Ausführung in der europäischen Barockplastik* (colloquium papers Bayerischen Nationalmuseums and the Zentralinstituts für Kunstgeschichte, Munich), Munich, 1986, pp. 59–84.

Baker 1990 M. Baker, 'Portrait busts of Architects in Eighteenth Century Britain', in C. Hind (ed.), *The Georgian Group. New Light on English Palladianism* (papers given at the Georgian Group symposium, 1988), London, 1990, pp. 14–30.

Baker 1992 M. Baker, 'Roubiliac's Argyll monument and the interpretation of eighteenth-century sculptors' designs', *Burlington Magazine*, CXXXIV, December 1992, pp. 785–97.

Baker 1993 M. Baker, 'English responses to continental sculpture in the 18th century', *The Grosvenor House Antiques Fair Handbook*, London, 1993, pp. 12–17.

Baker 1994 M. Baker, 'Catalogue of European Sculpture in the Ashmolean Museum, 1540 to the Present Day by N. Penny' (book review), *Burlington Magazine*, CXXXVI, December 1994, pp. 850–1.

Baker 1995 [Garden Sculpture] M. Baker, '"Squabby cupids and clumsy graces": Garden Sculpture and Luxury in Eighteenth-Century England', *Oxford Art Journal*, 18, no. 1, 1995, pp. 3–13.

Baker 1995 [Making of portrait busts] M. Baker, 'The making of portrait busts in the mid-eighteenth century: Roubiliac, Scheemakers and Trinity College, Dublin', *Burlington Magazine*, CXXXVII, December 1995, pp. 821–31.

Baker 1995 [Roubiliac and Cheere] M. Baker, 'Roubiliac and Cheere in the 1730s & 40s: Collaboration and Sub-Contracting in the Eighteenth-Century English Sculptors' Workshops', *Journal of the Church Monuments Society*, X, 1995, pp. 90–108.

Baker 1995 [Wren] M. Baker, 'The Portrait Sculpture', in D. McKitterick (ed.), *The Making of the Wren Library*, Cambridge, 1995, pp. 110–37.

Baker 1996 [Louvre] M. Baker, 'De l'église au musée: les monuments du XVIIIe siècle (fonctions, significations et histoire)' in *Sculptures hors contexte* (actes du colloque international au Musée du Louvre, 29 April 1994), Paris, 1996, pp. 73–92.

Baker 1996 [Production] M. Baker, 'The production and viewing of bronze sculpture in eighteenth-century England', *Antologia di Belle Arti. La Scultura. Studi in onore di Andrew S. Ciechanowiecki,* II, Turin, 1996, pp. 144–53.

Baker 1997 M. Baker, 'Roubiliac and Chelsea in 1745', English Ceramic Circle, *Transactions,* 16, part 2, 1997, pp. 222–5.

Baker 1998 [Materials and processes] M. Baker, 'Limewood, Chiromancy and Narratives of Making, Writing about the materials and processes of sculpture', *Art History*, 21, December 1998, pp. 498–530.

Baker 1998 [Tyers] M. Baker, 'Tyers, Roubiliac and a sculpture's fame: a poem about the commissioning of the Handel statue at Vauxhall', *Sculpture Journal*, II, 1998, pp. 41–5.

Baker 1999 M. Baker, 'Public Fame or Private Remembrance? The Portrait Bust and Modes of Commemoration in Eighteenth-Century England', in W. Reinink and J. Stumpel (eds.), *Memory & Oblivion*, Proceedings of the XXIXth International Congress of the History of Art held in Amsterdam, 1–7 September 1996, Dordrecht, 1999, pp. 527–35.

Baker 2000 [Figured in Marble] M. Baker, *Figured in Marble. The Making and Viewing of Eighteenth-century Sculpture*, London, 2000.

Baker 2000 [Grand Tour] M. Baker, 'La consommation de l'antique: le Grand Tour et les reproductions de sculpture classique', in *D'après l'antique* (exh. cat.), museé du Louvre, Paris, 2000, pp. 69–77.

Baker 2000 [Portrait Bust] M. Baker, 'A Sort of Corporate Company' Approaching the Portrait bust in its setting', *Return to Life. A New Look at the Portrait Bust* (exh. cat.), Henry Moore Institute, Leeds; National Portrait Gallery, London; Scottish National Portrait Gallery, Edinburgh; Leeds, 2000, pp. 20–35.

Baker 2000 [Review] M. Baker, 'Laurent Delvaux. Gand, 1696-Nivelles, 1887 by A. Jacobs' (book review), *Burlington Magazine*, CXLII, December 2000, pp. 781–2.

Baker, Harrison and Laing 2000 M. Baker, C. Harrison and A. Laing, 'Bouchardon's British sitters: sculptural portraiture in Rome and the classicising bust around 1730', *Burlington Magazine*, CXLII, December 2000, pp. 752–62.

Baker forthcoming [Multiple heads] M. Baker, 'Multiple heads: Pope, the portrait bust and patterns of repetition' (forthcoming).

Baker forthcoming [Pitt] M. Baker, 'A case of disputed identity: Henry Cheere's bust of George Pitt' (forthcoming).

Baker forthcoming [Wilton] M. Baker, 'Joseph Wilton's portrait busts of the 10th Earl of Huntingdon and Dr Antonio Cocchi' (forthcoming).

Balderston 1985 G.D. Balderston, 'Roubiliac and Lord Chesterfield', *Apollo*, CXXI, March 1985, p. 189.

Balderston 2001 G.D. Balderston, 'Rysbrack's busts of James Gibbs and Alexander Pope from Henrietta Street', *Georgian Group Journal*, XI, 2001, pp. 1–28.

Baldry 1898 A.L. Baldry, 'The work of F.W. Pomeroy', *Studio*, XV, November 1898, pp. 77–86.

Baldry 1900 A.L. Baldry, 'Our rising artists: Alfred Drury Sculptor', *Magazine of Art*, XXIV, 1900, pp. 211–17.

Baldry 1906 A.L Baldry, 'A notable sculptor: Alfred Drury, A.R.A.', *Studio*, XXXVII, February 1906, pp. 3–18.

Barnes 1999 R. Barnes, *John Bell. The Sculptor's Life and Works*, Kirstead, 1999.

Barrington 1906 R. Barrington, *The Life, Letters and Work of Frederic Leighton*, II, London, 1906.

Bassett and Fogelman 1997 J. Bassett and P. Fogelman, *Looking at European Sculpture. A Guide to Technical Terms*, London, 1997.

Bassi 1943 E. Bassi, *Canova*, Bergamo Milano Roma, 1943.

***Battersea Park* 1948** *Souvenir Catalogue of the Open Air Exhibition of Sculpture at Battersea Park* (exh. cat.), London, 1948.

Bayley 1981 S. Bayley, *The Albert Memorial in its Social and Architectural Context*, London, 1981.

Beard 1936 C.R. Beard, *A catalogue of the collection of Martinware formed by Mr Frederick John Nettlefold, together with a short history of the firm of R.W. Martin and Brothers of Southall*, London, 1936.

Beard 1989 G. Beard, *The Work of Grinling Gibbons*, London, 1989.

Beattie 1983 S. Beattie, *The New Sculpture*, New Haven and London, 1983.

Bell 1938 C.F. Bell (ed.), *Annals of Thomas Banks. Sculptor. Royal Academician*, Cambridge, 1938.

de Bellaigue and Kirkham 1972 G. de Bellaigue and P. Kirkham, 'George IV and the Furnishing of Windsor Castle', *Furniture History*, VIII, 1972, pp. 1–34.

Bellenger 1996 S. Bellenger, 'Henri de Triqueti et l'Angleterre', in A. González-Palacios (ed.), *Antologia di Belle Art. La Scultura. Studi in onore di Andrew S. Ciechanowiecki*, II, Turin, 1996, pp. 183–200.

Bénédite 1903 L. Bénédite, 'Alphonse Legros, Painter and Sculptor', *Studio*, XXIX, no. 123, June 1903, pp. 3–22.

Bennett 1862 G. Bennett, *The History of Bandon*, Cork, 1862.

***Bequests and Donations* 1901** *List of the Bequests and Donations to the South Kensington Museum, now called the Victoria and Albert Museum, completed to 31st December 1900*, London, 1901.

Bergesen 1991 V. Bergesen, *Encyclopaedia of British Art Pottery 1870–1920*, London, 1991.

Betjeman and Piper 1948 J. Betjeman and J. Piper (eds.), *Murray's Buckinghamshire. Architectural Guide*, London, 1948.

Bilbey [forthcoming] D. Bilbey, entry on Margaret Helen Longhurst for *the New Dictionary of National Biography*, Oxford, (forthcoming).

Bindman 1986 D. Bindman, 'The Consolation of Death: Roubiliac's Nightingale Tomb', *Huntington Library Quarterly*, 49, 1986, pp. 25–46.

Bindman 1992 D. Bindman, 'Roubiliac: New Findings', *Sotheby's Review*, January 1992, pp. 2–4.

Bindman 1997 D. Bindman, 'Roubiliac's Statue of Handel and the Keeping of Order in Vauxhall Gardens in the Early Eighteenth Century', *Sculpture Journal*, 1, 1997, pp. 22–31.

Bindman and Baker 1995 D. Bindman and M. Baker, *Roubiliac and the Eighteenth Century Monument. Sculpture as Theatre*, New Haven and London, 1995.

Binney 1983 M. Binney, 'Wentworth Woodhouse Revisited II', *Country Life*, CLXXIII, 24 March 1983, pp. 708–11.

***Birmingham* 1987** E. Silber, *Sculpture in Birmingham Museum and Art Gallery. A Summary Catalogue*, Birmingham, 1987.

Blackburn 1886 H. Blackburn, *Randolph Caldecott. A personal memoir of his early career*, London, 1886.

Blackwood 1989 J. Blackwood, *London's Immortals. The Complete Outdoor Commemorative Statues*, London and Oxford, 1989.

Blomefield 1781 Blomefield, *History of Antiquities of the County of Norfolk containing the hundreds of North Greenhoe, South Greenhoe, Grimshoe, and Guiltcross*, Norwich, 1781.

Boase 1960 T.S.R. Boase, 'John Graham Lough. A transitional sculptor', *Journal of the Warburg and Courtauld Institutes*, XXIII, 1960, pp. 277–90.

Bode 1904 W. Bode, *Königliche Museen zu Berlin. Beschreibung der Bildwerke der Christlichen Epochen. Die Italienischen Bronzen*, II, Berlin, 1904.

Bogler 1855 C. Bogler, *Die Gruppe von San Ildefonso*, Wiesbaden, 1855.

Bolton 1919 A.T. Bolton, *Eighteenth-century Sculpture in Sir John Soane's Museum*, London, 1919.

Bonython 1982 [Album] E. Bonython, 'Sir Henry Cole. First Director of the V&A', *Victoria and Albert Museum Album*, I, London, 1982, pp. 25–30.

Bonython 1982 [Cole] E. Bonython, *King Cole. A picture portrait of Sir Henry Cole, KCB 1808–1882*, London, 1982.

Bonython and Burton 2001 E. Bonython and A. Burton, *The Great Exhibitor: The Life and Work of Henry Cole*, London, 2001.

Boström 2000 A. Boström, 'Giovanni Maria Benzoni, Randolph Rogers and the Collecting of Sculpture in Nineteenth-Century Detroit', *Sculpture Journal*, IV, 2000, pp. 151–9.

Bourne and Brett 1991 J. Bourne and V. Brett, *Lighting in the Domestic Interior. Renaissance to Art Nouveau*, London, 1991.

Bova 1998 A. Bova, 'Murano Glass in the Expositions of the Nineteenth Century', in A. Bora, R. Junck, P. Migliaccio (eds.), *Murrine and Millefiori in Murano Glass from 1832 to 1930*, Venice, 1998, pp. 182–218.

Bowdler 2002 R. Bowdler, 'The Speaker's sepulchre: Chaloner Chute's tomb at The Vyne', *Apollo*, CLV, April 2002, pp. 46–50.

***Bowman* 1996** *Robert Bowman, London. 19th and Early 20th Century Sculpture, Revival of the Romantics, 1996/7*, London, 1996.

***Bowman* 2000** *Robert Bowman, London. 19th and Early 20th Century Sculpture, Power & Passion, 2000/1*, London, 2000.

***Boymans* 1994** E. van Binnebeke, *Bronze Sculpture: Sculpture from 1500–1800 in the Collection of the Boymans van Benningen Museum*, Rotterdam, 1994.

Bradley and Pevsner 1997 S. Bradley and N. Pevsner, *The Buildings of England, London I. The City of London*, London, 1997.

***Brasenose Club* 1888** *Catalogue of a Loan Collection of the Works of Randolph Caldecott, Brasenose Club, Manchester*, March 1888, Manchester, 1888.

Bray 1851 Mrs Bray, *Life of Thomas Stothard, R.A.*, London, 1851.

de Breffny 1986 B. de Breffny, 'Christopher Hewetson', *Irish Arts Review*, 3, no. 3, 1986, pp. 52–75.

Briggs 1934 M.S. Briggs, *Middlesex Old and New*, London, 1934.

Brinckmann 1925 A.E. Brinckmann, *Barock-Bozzetti. Niederländische und Französische Bildhauer*, III, Frankfurt-am-Main, 1925.

***Bristol* 1966** A. Wilson, *Sculpture from the City Art Gallery Bristol*, Bristol, 1966.

***British Art* 1934** *Commemorative Catalogue of the Exhibition of British Art*, Royal Academy of Arts, London; Oxford, 1935.

***British Art and Design* 1983** *British Art and Design 1900–1960*, London, 1983.

***British Artists in Rome* 1974** *British Artists in Rome 1700–1800* (exh.cat.), The Iveagh Bequest, Kenwood; London, 1974.

British Empire 1924 *Illustrated Souvenir of the Palace of Arts, British Empire Exhibition (1924)*, Wembley, London, 1924.

***British Museum* 1999** A. Dawson, *Portrait Sculpture. A Catalogue of the British Museum Collection c. 1675–1975*, London, 1999.

***British Portraits* 1956** *British Portraits. Winter Exhibition*, 1956–57 (exh. cat.), Royal Academy, London, 1956.

***British Sculpture 1850–1914* 1968** *British Sculpture 1850–1914*, The Fine Art Society Ltd (exh. cat.), The Fine Art Society Ltd, London, 1968.

***British Sculpture in the Twentieth Century* 1981** S. Nairne and N. Serota (eds.), *British Sculpture in the Twentieth Century* (exh. cat.), Whitechapel Art Gallery, London, 1981.

Britton and Brayley 1810 J. Britton and E.W. Brayley, *The topographical and historical description of Cumberland*, London, 1810.

Brooks 2000 C. Brooks (ed.), *The Albert Memorial. The Prince Consort National Memorial: its History, Contexts, and Conservation*, New Haven and London, 2000.

Brown 1934 F. P. Brown, *London Sculpture. English Art Series*, III, London, 1934.

Brownlow 1865 J. Brownlow, *The History and Objects of the Foundling Hospital with a memoir of the Founder*, London, 1865.

Brumbaugh 1973 T.B. Brumbaugh, 'John Gibson in Rome: An Unpublished Letter', *Connoisseur*, CLXXXIII, July 1973, pp. 122–6.

Bryant 1983 [Banks] J. Bryant, 'Mourning Achilles': a missing sculpture by Thomas Banks', *Burlington Magazine*, CXXV, December 1983, pp. 742–5.

Bryant 1983 [Bashaw] J. Bryant, *Bashaw*, V&A Masterpiece Sheet, London, 1983.

Bryant 1985 J. Bryant, 'The Church Memorials of Thomas Banks', *Journal of the Church Monuments Society*, I, part I, 1985, pp. 49–64.

Bryant 1991 J. Bryant, 'Thomas Banks's anatomical crucifixion. A tale of death and dissection', *Apollo*, CXXXIII, June 1991, pp. 409–11.

Buckley 1913 H. Buckley, 'A Note on Gilbert Ledward', *The R.C.A. Students' Magazine*, III, no. XVII, November 1913, pp. 16–17.

Buckman 1998 D. Buckman, *Dictionary of Artists in Britain since 1945*, Bristol, 1998.

***Builder* 1852** Architectural Exhibition (review), *The Builder*, CCCLXVIII, X, 17 January 1852, p. 33.

***Builder* 1863 [I]** 'New Materials for the Life of Thomas Banks', *The Builder*, XXI, no. 1039, 3 January 1863, pp. 3–5.

***Builder* 1863 [II]** 'Banks and Northcote', *The Builder*, XXI, no. 1041, 17 January 1863, p. 45.

***Builder* 1867** Obituary for Samuel Cundy, *The Builder*, XXV, no. 1273, 29 June 1867, p. 464.

***Builder* 1871** 'Smithfield Drinking Fountain Competition', *The Builder*, XXIX, no. 1465, 4 March 1871, p. 161.

***Builder* 1882** *The Builder*, XLIII, no. 2074, 4 November 1882, p. 609.

***Builder* 1901** 'The Victoria Memorial', *The Builder*, LXXXI, 3 Aug 1901, pp. 95–6.

***Bulletin* 1968** 'Sculpture Acquisitions', *Victoria and Albert Museum Bulletin*, IV, 1968, pp. 162–4.

Bunt 1931 C.G.E. Bunt, 'A bust of Charles I in chalk-stone', *Apollo*, XIII, February 1931, pp. 106–8.

Burke and Caldwell 1968 J. Burke and C. Caldwell, *Hogarth, The Complete Engravings*, London, 1968.

***Burke's* 1980** *Burke's Peerage and Baronetage*, London, 1980 (first published 1826).

Burlington Fine Arts Club *1912* *Catalogue of a Collection of Pictures, Decorative Furniture, and other Works of Art* (exh. cat.), Burlington Fine Arts Club, London, 1912.

Burton 1999 A. Burton, *Vision & Accident. The Story of the Victoria and Albert Museum*, London, 1999.

Burton and Haskins 1983 A. Burton and S. Haskins, *European Art in the Victoria and Albert Museum*, London, 1983.

Bury 1954 A. Bury, *Shadow of Eros*, London, 1954.

Busco 1988 M.F. Busco, 'The "Achilles" in Hyde Park', *Burlington Magazine*, CXXX, December 1988, pp. 920–4.

Busco 1994 M. Busco, *Sir Richard Westmacott*, Cambridge, 1994.

Caillaux 1935 H. Caillaux, *Aimé Jules Dalou (1838–1902)*, Paris, 1935.

***Caldecott* 1977** *Randolph Caldecott 1846–1886, A Christmas exhibition of the work of the Victorian book illustrator* (exh. cat.), Manchester City Art Gallery, Manchester, 1978.

Calderini 1928 M. Calderini, *Carlo Marochetti Monografia con ritratti, fac-simile e riproduzioni di opere dell'artista*, Turin, 1928.

Cannon-Brookes 1996 P. Cannon-Brookes, 'An alien taste? British collecting of European Baroque and Rococo sculpture', in A. González-Palacios (ed.), *Antologia di Belle Art. La Sculptura. Studi in onore di Andrew S. Ciechanowiecki*, II, Turin, 1996, pp. 201–11.

***Carlton House* 1991** *Carlton House: The Past Glories of George IV's Palace* (exh. cat.), The Queen's Gallery, Buckingham Palace, London, 1991.

***Carlyle* 1954** *Carlyle's house Chelsea: illustrated catalogue chronology and descriptive notes*, London, 1954.

Carter 1990 P. Carter, *A Dictionary of British Studio Pottery*, Aldershot, 1990.

***Casts* 1901** *Catalogue of Casts specially selected for the use of Schools of Art, Art Classes, Technical Schools, and Public Elementary Schools*, London, Chapman and Hall Ltd, April 1901, London, 1901.

***Casts* 1939** *Catalogue of Plaster Casts, Victoria and Albert Museum*, London, January 1939.

Cavanagh 1997 T. Cavanagh, *Public Sculpture of Liverpool*, Liverpool, 1997.

Ceschi 1949 C. Ceschi, *I Monumenti della Liguria e la Guerra 1940–5*, Istituto di Studi Liguri Collezione di Monografie Storico Artistiche, I, Genoa, 1949.

***Chambers* 1996** J. Harris and M. Snodin (eds.), *Sir William Chambers Architect to George III* (exh. cat.), Courtauld Gallery, London; Nationalmuseum, Stockholm; London, 1996.

Chancellor 1911 E. Beresford Chancellor, *The lives of the British Sculptors and those who have worked in England from the earliest days to Sir Francis Chantrey*, London, 1911.

Chancellor 1926 E. Beresford Chancellor, *Lost London. Being a* *description of landmarks which have disappeared pictured by J. Crowther circa 1879–87 and described by E. Beresford Chancellor*, London, 1926.

***Chantrey* 1981** A. Potts, *Sir Francis Chantrey 1781–1841. Sculptor of the Great* (exh.cat.), National Portrait Gallery, London; Mappin Art Gallery, Sheffield; London, 1981.

Charleston and Wills 1956 R.J. Charleston and G. Wills, 'The Bow "Flora" and Michael Rysbrack', *Apollo*, LXIII, April 1956, pp. 125–7.

Charteris 1927 E. Charteris, *John Sargent*, London, 1927.

***Cheere* 1974** *The Man at Hyde Park Corner. Sculpture by John Cheere 1709–1787* (exh. cat.), Temple Newsam, Leeds; Marble Hill House, Twickenham; Leeds, 1974.

Cheetham 1984 F. Cheetham, *English Medieval Alabasters*, Oxford, 1984.

***Chicago Exhibition* 1893** *Royal Commission. Chicago Exhibition (1893). Official Catalogue of the British Section*, London, 1893.

Chute 1888 C.W. Chute, *A History of the Vyne in Hampshire*, Winchester/London, 1888.

Chute 1954 Sir C.L. Chute, ' A Monument by Thomas Carter', *Country Life*, CXV, 27 May 1954, pp. 1733–4.

Clark 1969 D. Clark, 'Blue John', *Forthcoming London Attractions*, June 1969, pp. 22–3.

Clarke 1973 G. Clarke, 'Grecian Taste and Gothic Virtue: Lord Cobham's gardening programme and its iconography', *Apollo*, XCVII, June 1973, pp. 566–71.

***Cleopatra* 2001** S. Walker and P. Higgs (eds.), *Cleopatra of Egypt. From History to Myth* (exh. cat.), British Museum, London, 2001.

Clifford 1985 T. Clifford, 'John Bacon and the Manufacturers', *Apollo*, CXXII, October 1985, pp. 288–304.

Clifford 1990 T. Clifford, 'Vulliamy clocks and British sculpture', *Apollo*, CXXXII, October 1990, pp. 226–37.

Clifford 1992 T. Clifford, 'The plaster shops of the rococo and neo-classical era in Britain', *Journal of the History of Collections*, IV, no. 1, 1992, pp. 39–65.

Clifford Smith 1931 H. Clifford Smith, *Buckingham Palace. Its furniture, decoration and history*, London, 1931.

***Clumber* 1908** 'Clumber. Nottinghamshire. The Seat of the Duke of Newcastle,1', *Country Life*, XXIV, 12 September 1908, pp. 352–9.

Cogo 1996 B. Cogo, *Antonio Corradini Scultore Veneziano 1688–1752*, Este, 1996.

Collins 1998 J. Collins, *Eric Gill. The Sculpture. A Catalogue Raisonné*, London, 1998.

***Colour of Sculpture* 1996** A. Blöhm and P. Curtis (eds.), *The Colour of Sculpture 1840–1910* (exh. cat.), Van Gogh Museum, Amsterdam; Henry Moore Institute, Leeds; Amsterdam, 1996.

Colvin, Ransome and Summerson 1975 H.M. Colvin, D.R. Ransome and J. Summerson, *The History of the King's Works*, III, 1485–1660, (Part 1), London, 1975.

Colvin 1995 H. Colvin, *A Biographical Dictionary of British Architects 1600–1840* (3rd edition), New Haven and London, 1995.

Conforti 1901 L. Conforti, *Das Nazionalmuseum zu Neapel*, Naples, 1901.

Constable 1927 W.G. Constable, *John Flaxman 1755–1826*, London, 1927.

Cooper 1971 J. Cooper, 'John Gibson and his "Tinted Venus"', *Connoisseur*, 178, October 1971, pp. 84–92.

Cooper 1975 J. Cooper, *Nineteenth Century Romantic Bronzes: French, English and American Bronzes 1830–1915*, Newton Abbot, 1975.

Corney 2001 A. Corney, 'Nooks & Crannies', *Keats-Shelley Memorial Association Newsletter*, January 2001, p. 6.

***Cornhill Magazine* 1868** 'Recollections of Gibson the Sculptor', *The Cornhill Magazine*, May 1868, no. 101, pp. 540–6.

***Cornhill Magazine* 1880** 'English Sculpture in 1880', *The Cornhill Magazine*, August 1880, pp. 173–86.

Correia Guedes 1971 N.B. Correia Guedes, *O Palácio dos senhores do Infantado em Queluz*, Lisbon, 1971.

Coulson 1979 A.J. Coulson, *A Bibliography of Design in Britain 1851–1970*, Design Council, London, 1979.

***Country Life* 1928** 'Accessions to the Victoria and Albert Museum, 1926', *Country Life*, LXIII, 17 March 1928, p. xlii.

Coutu 1998 J. Coutu, 'The Rodney Monument in Jamaica and an Empire Coming of Age', *Sculpture Journal*, II, 1998, pp. 46–57.

Coutu 2000 J. Coutu, '"A very grand and seigneurial design" The Duke of Richmond's Academy in Whitehall', *British Art Journal*, I, no. 2, pp. 47–54.

Cox-Johnson 1959 A. Cox-Johnson, 'Gentlemen's Agreement', *Burlington Magazine*, CI, June 1959, pp. 236–42.

Cox-Johnson 1961 A. Cox-Johnson, John Bacon R.A. 1740–1799, *St Marylebone Society Publication*, no. 4, 1961.

Craske 2000 M. Craske, 'Contacts and Contracts: Sir Henry Cheere and the Formation of the New Commercial World of Sculpture in Mid-Eighteenth-Century London', in C. Sicca and A. Yarrington (eds.), *The Lustrous Trade. Material Culture and the History of Sculpture in England and Italy c. 1700-c. 1860* (papers from an international workshop, Opera della Primaziale, Pisa), London and New York, 2000, pp. 94–113.

Cremonicini 1990/1 R. Cremoncini, *Francis Harwood: Scultore Inglese a Firenze nel Settecento*, Phd thesis, University of Siena, Scuola di Specializzazione, Archeologia e Storia dell`Arte, 1990/1.

***Crockfords* 1930** *Crockfords Clerical Directory 1930*, 59th issue, Oxford, 1930.

***Crockfords* 1971** *Crockfords Clerical Directory 1969–70*, 83rd issue, London, 1971.

Croft-Murray 1939–40 E. Croft-Murray, 'An account book of John Flaxman, R.A.', *The Walpole Society*, XXVIII, Oxford, 1939–40, pp. 51–93.

***Cromwell Museum* 1965** *The Cromwell Museum in Huntingdon*, Oxford, 1965.

Cullen 1996 L. Cullen, 'Plaster casts from the studio of George Frampton', *The Medal*, no. 29, 1996, pp. 49–53.

Cundall 1904 H.M. Cundall, 'The Queen Victorial Memorial', *Art Journal*, June 1904, pp. 198–201.

Cundall 1907 F. Cundall, 'Sculpture in Jamaica', *Art Journal*, March 1907, pp. 65–70.

Cunningham 1830 A. Cunningham, *The Lives of the Most Eminent British Painters, Sculptors, and Architects*, III, London, 1830.

Cust 1912 L. Cust, ' A marble bust of Charles I by Hubert le Sueur', *Burlington Magazine*, XX, January 1912, pp, 190, 192–3, 197.

Cust 1914 L. Cust (Sir S. Colvin ed.), *History of the Society of Dilettanti*, London, 1914.

***Dalou* 1978** *Dalou Inédit* (exh. cat.), Galerie Delestre, Paris, 1978.

Darby 1978 E. and M. Darby, 'The National Monument to Victoria', *Country Life*, CLXIV, 16 November 1978, pp. 1647–8, 1650.

Darby 1983 M. Darby, *Victoria and Albert Museum, II, British Art*, London, 1983.

Darke 1991 J. Darke, *The Monument Guide to England and Wales*, London, 1991.

Dart 1723 J. Dart, *Westmonasterium or The History and Antiquities of St Peters Westminster*, I, London, 1723.

Davies 1979 A. Davies, *Dictionary of British Portraiture. The Middle Ages to the Early Georgians – historical figures born before 1700*, I, London, 1979.

Davies 1991 J.P.S. Davies, *Antique Garden Ornament. 300 Years of Creativity: Artists, Manufactures & Materials*, Antique Collectors' Club, Woodbridge, 1991.

Davies 1992 H.E. Davies, *Sir John Charles Robinson (1824–1913): his role as a connoisseur and creator of public and private collections*, Phd thesis, University of Oxford, 1992.

Dawson 1935 F. Dawson, 'Paganini in Leeds January 1832', *Leeds Thoresby Society Miscellanea*, XXXIII, 1935, pp. 447–58.

***DBI* 1994** *Dizionario Biografico degli Italiani*, 44, Rome, 1994.

Dean 1999 P. Dean, *Sir John Soane and the Country Estate*, Aldershot, 1999.

***Death, Passion and Politics* 1995** A. Sumner (ed.), *Death, Passion and Politics. Van Dyck's Portraits of Venetia Stanley and George Digby* (exh. cat.), Dulwich Picture Gallery, London, 1995.

***Della Robbia Pottery* 1980** *An Interim Report Della Robbia Pottery Birkenhead 1894–1906*, Birkenhead, 1980.

Derez, Nelissen, Tytgat, Verbrugge [forthcoming] M. Derez, M. Nelissen, J.P. Tytgat, A Verbrugge (eds.), *Arenberg in der Lage Landen*, Leuven (forthcoming).

Deutsch 1943 O.E. Deutsch, 'Sir William Hamilton's Picture Gallery', *Burlington Magazine*, LXXXII, February 1943, pp. 36–9.

Devigne [n.d.] M. Devigne, 'Achttiend-eewsche Vlaamsche Beeldhouwwerken', pp. 143–7.

***Director* 1807** *The Director. A Literary and Scientific Journal*, London, I, no. 3, Saturday 7 February 1807, footnote on p. 76.

***Directory* 1896** *The Post Office London Directory for 1896*, London, Kelly & Co, London, 1896.

***Directory* 1899** *The Post Office London Commercial and Professional Directory for 1899*, II, London, 1899.

***Directory* 1934** *Post Office London Professional and Commercial Directory for 1934*, London, 1934.

***DNB* 1961** *The Dictionary of National Biography. The Concise Dictionary, 1901–1950*, Part II, Oxford, 1961.

***DNB* 1972** E.T. Williams and H.M. Palmer (eds.), *The Dictionary of National Biography 1951–1960* (first published 1971), Oxford, 1972.

***DNB* 1973** *The Dictionary of National Biography* (first published 1917), Oxford, 1973.

***DNB* 1982** *The Dictionary of National Biography. The Concise Dictionary*, Part II, 1901–1970, Oxford, 1982.

Dobson and Wakeley 1957 J. Dobson and Sir Cecil Wakeley, *Sir George Buckston Browne*, Edinburgh and London, 1957.

Dodsley 1761 R. and J. Dodsley, *London and its Environs Described*, V, London, 1761.

Doin 1911 J. Doin, 'John Flaxman (1755–1826)', *Gazette des Beaux-Arts*, V, 1911, pp. 233–46.

Dolan [n.d.] D. Dolan, 'Thomas Woolner Australia's Pre-Raphaelite', *The Australian Connoisseur and Collector*, 4, pp. 88–91.

Donaldson 1858 T.L. Donaldson, 'Obituary Mr. Thomas Campbell', *Art Journal*, 1 April 1858, pp. 107–8.

Dorment 1985 R. Dorment, *Alfred Gilbert*, New Haven and London, 1985.

Drake 1736 F. Drake *Eboracum: or the History and Antiquities of the City of York. From its original to the present times. Together with the History of the Cathedral Church, and the Lives of the Archbishops of that See*, London, 1736.

Draper 1970 J.D. Draper, 'A Statue of the Composer Grétny by Jean-Baptiste Stouf', *Metropolitan Museum of Art Bulletin*, XXVIII, May 1970, pp. 377–87.

Dreyfous 1903 M. Dreyfous, *Dalou: Sa Vie et son Oeuvre*, Paris, 1903.

Dreyfus 1957 J. Dreyfus, 'David Kindersley's Contribution to Street Lettering', *The Penrose Annual*, 51, 1957, pp. 38–41.

***Dublin* 1853** *Official Catalogue of the Great Industrial Exhibition, (In connection with the Royal Dublin Society)*, Dublin, 1853.

***Dynasties* 1995** *Dynasties: Painting in Tudor and Jacobean England 1530–1630* (exh. cat.), Tate Gallery, London, 1995.

Easter 1995 C. Easter, 'John Weston of Exeter and the Last Judgement', *Journal of the Church Monuments Society*, X, 1995, pp. 84–9.

Eastlake 1870 Lady Eastlake (ed.), *Life of John Gibson, R.A. Sculptor*, London, 1870.

Eatwell 1994 A. Eatwell, 'The Collector's or Fine Arts Club 1857–1874. The first society for collectors of the Decorative Arts', *Decorative Arts Society Journal*, 18, York, 1994, pp. 25–6.

***L'Écorché* 1977** *L'Écorché* (exh. cat.), Museé des Beaux-Arts, Rouen, 1977.

Edwards 1879 M. Edwards, *A Guide to Modelling in Clay and Wax and for terracotta, bronze and silver chasing and embossing, carving in marble and alabaster, moulding and casting in plaster of paris or sculptural art made easy for beginners*, London, 1879.

Edwards 1962 R. Edwards, 'An Inexplicable Miracle', *Apollo*, LXXVII, pp. 464–9.

***Eighteenth Century Portrait Busts* 1959** *Eighteenth Century Portrait Busts* (exh. cat.), The Iveagh Bequest, Kenwood; London, 1959.

Elam 1999 C. Elam, 'Terence Hodgkinson (1913–99)', obituary editorial, *Burlington Magazine*, CXLI, November 1999, p. 655.

Elsen 1974 A.E. Elsen, *Origins of Modern Sculpture. Pioneers and Premises*, London, 1974.

Ely 1900 T. Ely, *Catalogue of Works of Art in the Flaxman Gallery University College, London*, London, 1900.

Empson 1959 P. E. Empson (ed.), *The Wood Engravings of Robert Gibbings*, London, 1959.

***English Chimneypieces* 1928** *A Picture Book of English Chimneypieces*, Victoria and Albert Museum, London, 1928.

***English Medieval Art* 1930** *English Medieval Art* (exh. cat.), Victoria and Albert Museum, London, 1930.

***Eros* 1987** R. Dorment and I. Anscombe, *Eros by Sir Alfred Gilbert* (exh. cat.), The Fine Art Society, London, 1987.

Esdaile 1922 K.A. Esdaile, 'Studies of the English Sculptors from Pierce to Chantrey. IX. Peter Scheemaker (1690–1771?)', *Architect*, CVII, 10 February 1922, pp. 111–14.

Esdaile 1924 [Beckford] K. A. Esdaile, 'Flaxman's design for the Monument to Lord Mayor Beckford at the Guildhall', *Burlington Magazine*, XLV, August 1924, pp. 80–2, 87.

Esdaile 1924 [Trinity College] K.A. Esdaile, *Roubiliac's Work at Trinity College Cambridge*, Cambridge, 1924.

Esdaile 1927 K.A. Esdaile, *English Monumental Sculpture since the Renaissance*, London, 1927.

Esdaile 1928 K.A. Esdaile, *The life and works of Louis François Roubiliac*, Oxford and London, 1928.

Esdaile 1929 [Acquisitions] K.A. Esdaile, 'On decorative sculpture. Some recent Acquisitions of the Victoria and Albert Museum',

Architect and Building News, CXXII, 27 September 1929, pp. 386–7, 390.

Esdaile 1929 [Model] K.A. Esdaile, 'A seventeenth-century model of an English Monument', *Burlington Magazine*, LV, October 1929, pp. 195–7.

Esdaile 1930 K.A. Esdaile, 'The Stantons of Holborn', *The Archaeological Journal*, LXXXV, second series, XXXV, March – December 1928, London, 1930, pp. 149–69.

Esdaile 1935 K.A. Esdaile, 'Notes on three monumental drawings from Sir Edward Dering's Collections in the Library of the Society of Antiquaries', *Archaeologica Cantiana*, XLVII, 1935, pp. 219–34.

Esdaile 1940 [Vyne] K.A. Esdaile, 'A statue by Bacon' (letter), *Burlington Magazine*, LXXVI, January 1940, p. 28 and pl. A.

Esdaile 1940 [William III] K.A. Esdaile, 'A Statuette of William III at South Kensington', *Burlington Magazine*, LXXVI, April 1940, pp. 123–4, pl. on p. 122 (B).

Esdaile 1942 K.A. Esdaile, 'Some Annotations on John Le Neve's "Monumenta Anglica" (1717–19)', *Antiquaries Journal*, XXII, July – October 1942, nos. 3–4, pp. 176–97.

Esdaile 1944 K.A. Esdaile, 'A Group of Terracotta Models by Joseph Nollekens, R.A.', *Burlington Magazine*, LXXXV, September 1944, pp. 220–3.

Esdaile 1946 K.A. Esdaile, *English Church Monuments*, London, 1946.

Esdaile 1947 [Hewetson] K.A. Esdaile, 'Christopher Hewetson and his monument to Dr Baldwin in Trinity College, Dublin', *Journal of Royal Society of Antiquities*, LXXVII, II, December 1947, pp. 134–5.

Esdaile 1947 [Sisters] K.A. Esdaile, 'The Royal Sisters Mary II and Anne in Sculpture', *Burlington Magazine*, LXXXIX, September 1947, pp. 254–7.

Esdaile 1948 [Guelfi] K.A. Esdaile, 'Signor Guelfi, an Italian', *Burlington Magazine*, XC, November 1948, pp. 317–21.

Esdaile 1948 [Taylor] K.A. Esdaile, 'Sir Robert Taylor as sculptor', *Architectural Review*, 103, 1948, pp. 63–6.

Esdaile 1949 K.A. Esdaile, 'The Busts and Statues of Charles I', *Burlington Magazine*, CXI, January 1949, pp. 9–14.

Esdaile MS K.A. Esdaile, *Dictionary of Sculptors English (or working in England, including modellers, artists who designed monuments, and others connected with the art of sculpture)*, compiled by K.A. Esdaile, Manuscript acquired by the National Art Library 1977; ref. MSL/1977/4462; pressmark VI.RC Box 16 files A-J; Box 17 files K-Y.

Estella Marcos 1984 M. Estella Marcos, *La Escultura Barroca de Marfil en España. La Escuelas Europeas y las Coloniales* (2 vols.), Madrid, 1984.

Ettinger 1924 P. Ettinger, 'Portraits of Charles Fox at the Hermitage', *Burlington Magazine*, XLV, August 1924, p. 88.

***Europäische Barockplastik* 1971** *Europäische Barockplastik am Niederrhein. Grupello und seine Zeit* (exh. cat.), Kunstmuseum, Dusseldorf; Dusseldorf, 1971.

***European Sculpture* 2001** R. Butler, S. Glover Lindsay, A. Luchs, D. Lewis, C.J. Mills, J. Weidman, *European Sculpture of the Nineteenth Century. The Collections of the National Gallery of Art*, Washington, New York and London, 2000.

Eustace 1998 K. Eustace, 'The politics of the past. Stowe and the development of the historical portrait bust', *Apollo*, CXLVIII, July 1998, pp. 31–40.

Evans 1982 A. Evans, 'In the old mould', *Interiors*, January 1982, pp. 21–6.

Evelyn 1995 P. Evelyn, 'Hubert Le Sueur's equestrian bronzes at the Victoria and Albert Museum', Shorter Notice, *Burlington Magazine*, CXXXVII, February 1995, pp. 85–92.

Evelyn 2000 P. Evelyn, 'The equestrian bronzes of Hubert Le Sueur', *in Giambologna tra Firenze e l'Europa*, Istituto Universitario Olandese di Storia dell'Arte, Florence, 2000, pp. 141–56.

Evers 1966 H-G. Evers, 'Plastik', in R. Zeitler (ed.), *Die Kunst des 19. Jahrhunderts*, Propyläen Kunstgeschichte, no. 11, Berlin, 1966, pp. 153–69.

***Exposizione Venice* 1897** *Seconda Esposizione Internazionale d'Arte della Città di Venezia*, Catalogo Illustrato, Venice 1897.

Faber 1926 H. Faber, *Caius Gabriel Cibber 1630–1700. His Life and Work*, Oxford, 1926.

***Fake* 1990** M. Jones (ed.), *Fake? The Art of Deception* (exh. cat.), British Museum, London, 1990.

Farquhar 1910 H. Farquhar, *Portraiture of our Stuart Monarchs on their Coins and Medals, II, James II*, London, 1910 (reprinted from the *British Numismatic Journal*, VI, 1910).

***Fine Art Society* 2001** *The Fine Art Society Story. Part 2. 1876–2001* (exh. cat.), London, 2001.

***Fitzwilliam* 1928** *The Fitzwilliam Museum Cambridge. Annual Report for the year ending 31 December 1927*, Cambridge, 1928.

***Fitzwilliam* 1958** *The Fitzwilliam Museum. An illustrated survey*, Château de Boissia, Clairvaux, Jura, 1958.

***Flaxman* 1958** *John Flaxman R.A. Sculptor* (exh. cat.), Hatton Gallery, King's College, University of Durham, Newcastle upon Tyne, Newcastle upon Tyne, 1958.

***Flaxman* 1979** D. Bindman (ed.), *John Flaxman, R.A.* (exh. cat.), Royal Academy, London, 1979.

Fleming and Honour 1968 J. Fleming and H. Honour, 'Francis Harwood. An English Sculptor in XVIII Century Florence', *Festschrift Ulrich Middledorf*, Berlin, 1968, pp. 510–16.

Fletcher 1974 H. Fletcher, 'John Gibson's polychromy and Lord Londonderry's Bacchus', *Connoisseur*, 187, September 1974, pp. 2–5.

Ford 1873 E. Ford, *A History of Enfield in the County of Middlesex including its Royal and Ancient Manors, the Chase, and The Duchy of Lancaster, with notices of its worthies, and its natural history, etc.*, Enfield, 1873.

***Foreign and Commonwealth Office* 1996** *Foreign and Commonwealth Office*, London, 1996 (first published 1991).

Forrer L. Forrer, *Biographical Dictionary of Medallists*, London (8 vols, 1904–30).

Forrest 1988 M. Forrest, *Art Bronzes*, Pennsylvania, 1988.

Forster 1848 H.R. Forster, *The Stowe Catalogue priced and annotated*, London, 1848.

Fortnum 1876 C.D.E. Fortnum, *A Descriptive Catalogue of the Bronzes of European Origin in the South Kensington Museum*, London, 1876.

Foster 1924 W. Foster, *The East India House. Its History and Associations*, London, 1924.

Fothergill 1969 B. Fothergill, *Sir William Hamilton Envoy Extraordinary*, London, 1969.

***French Sculpture* 1979** *French Sculpture* (exh. cat.), Bruton Gallery, Bruton, 1979.

***French Sculpture* 1981** *French Sculpture 1780–1940: Carrier-Belleuse and his circle – origins and influence* (exh. cat.), Bruton Gallery, Bruton, 1981.

Friedman 1973 T.F. Friedman, 'John Cheere's Busts and Statuettes from Kirkleatham Hall', *City of York Art Gallery, Quarterly Preview*, XXV, July 1973, pp. 923–7.

Friedman 1976 T.F. Friedman, 'Sir Thomas Gascoigne and His Friends in Italy', *Leeds Arts Calendar*, 78, 1976, pp. 16–23.

Friedman 1984 T. Friedman, *James Gibbs*, New Haven and London, 1984.

Friedman 1999 T. Friedman, '"Demi-gods in Corduroy": Hamo Thornycroft's Statue of The Mower', *Sculpture Journal*, III, 1999, pp. 74–86.

Fryer 1912 A.C. Fryer, 'Monumental Effigies sculptured by Nicholas Stone', *Archaelogical Journal*, LXIX, no. 275, second series, XIX, no. 3, September 1912, pp. 229–75.

***Fuseli* 1979** N.L. Pressly, *The Fuseli Circle in Rome. Early Romantic Art in the 1770s* (exh. cat.), Yale Center for British Art, New Haven, 1979.

Galvin 1990 C. Galvin, 'The construction of Roubiliac's Shelburne and Argyll models', *Burlington Magazine*, CXXXII, December 1990, pp. 849–50.

Garlick 1989 K. Garlick, *Sir Thomas Lawrence. A complete catalogue of the oil paintings*, Oxford, 1989.

***Garrard* 1961** E. Croft-Murray, *George Garrard 1760–1826. Retrospective Exhibition of the Works of George Garrard, including examples from local country houses* (exh. pamphlet), Cecil Higgins Museum, Bedford, 1961.

Gatty 1900 M. Gatty, *The Book of Sun-dials* (originally compiled by the late Mrs Alfred Gatty, now enlarged and edited by H.K.F. Eden and E. Lloyd), (first published 1872), London, 1900.

***Gentleman's Magazine* 1792** *The Gentleman's Magazine and Historical Chronicle*, compiled by Sylvanus Urban, LXII, London, 1792.

***Georgian Society* 1909** *The Georgian Society. Records of Eighteenth-Century Domestic Architecture and Decoration in Dublin*, I, Dublin, 1909.

***Getty* 1997** P. Fusco, *Summary Catalogue of European Sculpture in The J. Paul Getty Museum*, Los Angeles, 1997.

***Getty* 1998** P. Fusco, P.A. Fogelman, M. Cambareri, *Masterpieces of the J. Paul Getty Museum. European Sculpture*, Los Angeles, 1998.

***Giambologna* 1978** C. Avery and A. Radcliffe (eds.), *Giambologna 1529–1608. Sculptor to the Medici* (exh. cat.), Royal Scottish Museum, Edinburgh; Victoria and Albert Museum, London; Kunsthistorisches Museum, Vienna; Arts Council of Great Britain; London, 1978.

Gibbon 1972 M.J. Gibbon, 'The History of Stowe – XV. Garden ornaments', *The Stoic*, XXV, no. 2, March 1972, pp. 62–8.

***Gibbons* 1998** D. Esterley, *Grinling Gibbons and the Art of Carving* (published to coincide with the exhibition held at the V&A), London, 1998.

***Gibbs* 1972** T. Friedman, *James Gibbs as a Church Designer* (exh. cat.), The Cathedral Church of All Saints at Derby, Derby 1972.

Gibson 1997 K. Gibson, "The Kingdom's Marble Chronicle": The Embellishment of the First and Second Buildings 1600 to 1690', in A. Saunders (ed.), *The Royal Exchange (London Topographical Society Publication 152)*, London, 1997.

***Gibson to Gilbert* 1992** B. Read and P. Skipwith, *Gibson to Gilbert. British Sculpture 1840–1914* (exh. cat.), The Fine Art Society, London, 1992.

***Gilbert* 1936** E. Machell Cox, *Commemorative Catalogue of an exhibition of models and designs by the late Sir Alfred Gilbert R.A.* (exh. cat.), Victoria and Albert Museum, London; Oxford, 1936.

***Gilbert* 1986** R. Dorment, *Alfred Gilbert. Sculptor and Goldsmith* (exh. cat.), Royal Academy of Arts, London, 1986.

Gilbert 1987 C. Gilbert, *The studio diary of Alfred Gilbert for 1899. The identities of the Saints on the Duke of Clarence Memorial*, Newcastle upon Tyne, 1987.

***Gill* 1980** *Strict Delight. The Life and Work of Eric Gill 1882–1940* (exh. cat.), Whitworth Art Gallery, University of Manchester, Manchester, 1980.

Gilmartin 1967 J. Gilmartin, 'Peter Turnerelli Sculptor 1774–1839', *Quarterly Bulletin of the Irish Georgian Society*, X, October – December 1967, pp. 1–17.

Gingell 1988 P.M. Gingell, 'Hands that say it all. Jagger's Louveral Reliefs', *Country Life*, CLXXXII, 21 July 1988, p. 178.

Giometti 1999 C. Giometti, 'Giovanni Battista Guelfi: New Discoveries', *Sculpture Journal*, III, 1999, pp. 26–43.

Girouard 1960 M. Girouard, 'Picton Castle, Pembrokeshire – II', *Country Life*, CXXVII, 14 January 1960, pp. 66–9.

Glaves-Smith 1992 J. Glaves-Smith, 'Frampton's Mysteries', in *Reverie, Myth, Sensuality. Sculpture in Britain 1880–1910* (exh. cat.), Stoke on Trent City Museum and Art Gallery, Bradford, 1992.

Gleichen 1928 Lord E. Gleichen, *London's Open-air Statuary*, London, 1928.

***Glorious Revolution* 1988** *Parliament and the Glorious Revolution 1688–1988* (exh. pamplet), Banqueting House, Whitehall, London, 1988.

Godden 1991 G.A. Godden, *Encyclopaedia of British Pottery and Porcelain Marks*, London, 1991 (first published 1964).

Godwin 1839 G. Godwin, *The Churches of London: A History and Description of the Ecclesiastical Edifices of the Metropolis*, II, London, 1839.

***Going Dutch* 1989** *Going Dutch. Decorative Arts from the Age of William and Mary*, (exh. pamphlet), The Victoria and Albert Museum at the Bank of England, London, 1989.

Gomme 1908 G.L. Gomme, *The Opening of St George the Martyr Churchyard, Southwark, by Mr Stuart Sawley, Chairman of the Parks and Open Spaces Committee of the Council, on Saturday 5 May 1908*, [n.d.].

Goodison 1979 J.W. Goodison, 'Reynolds Stone (1909–1979)' (obituary), *Burlington Magazine*, CXXI, November 1979, p. 728.

Gosse 1883 E.W. Gosse, 'Living Sculptors', *The Century Magazine*, June 1883, pp. 163–85.

Gosse 1883 [Tinworth] E.W. Gosse, *A Critical Essay on the Life and Works of George Tinworth*, London, 1883.

Gosse 1894 E. Gosse, 'The New Sculpture 1879–1894', *Art Journal*, May 1894, pp. 138–42.

***Gott* 1972** T.Friedman and T. Stevens, *Joseph Gott 1786–1860 Sculptor* (exh. cat.), Temple Newsam House, Leeds; Walker Art Gallery, Liverpool; Leeds, 1972.

Graham 1993 C. Graham, 'A noble kind of practice: the Society of Arts Artworkmanship Competitions, 1863–1871', *Burlington Magazine*, CXXXV, June 1993, pp. 411–5.

***Grand Design* 1997** M. Baker and B. Richardson (eds.), *A Grand Design. The Art of the Museum* (exh. cat.), Baltimore Museum of Art, Baltimore; Victoria and Albert Museum, London; New York and London, 1997.

Granville Fell 1945 H. Granville Fell, *Sir William Reid Dick, K.C.V.O., R.A.*, London, 1945.

Grant 1953 C.M.H. Grant, *A Dictionary of British Sculptors from the XIIIth Century to the XXth Century*, London, 1953.

Graphic 1875 'The New Associate of the Royal Academy of Arts', *The Graphic*, XI, January-June 1875, p. 171.

Graves A. Graves, *The Royal Academy of Arts. A Complete*

Dictionary of Contributors and their work from its foundation in 1769 to 1904, (8 vols), East Earsdley, 1905–6.

Graves 1907 A. Graves, *The Society of Artists of Great Britain 1760–1791. The Free Society of Artists 1761–1783*, London, 1907.

Graves 1908 A. Graves, *The British Institution 1806–186. A complete dictionary of contributors and their work from the foundation of the Institution*, London, 1908.

Gray 1985 A. Stuart Gray, *Edwardian Architecture. A Biographical Dictionary*, London, 1985.

Green 1962 D. Green, 'A Lost Grinling Gibbons Masterpiece', *Country Life*, CXXXI, 25 January 1962, pp. 164–6.

Green 1964 D. Green, *Grinling Gibbons*, London, 1964.

Green 1986 C.M. Green, *Finds from the Site of Suffolk Place, Southwark* (project submitted for the Museums Diploma Study Course, Dept of Museum Studies, University of Leicester), October 1986.

Gronau 1909 G. Gronau, *Masterpieces of Sculpture. From Michelangelo to the present day*, II, London and Glasgow, 1909.

Grose 1772 F. Grose, *The Antiquities of England and Wales*, I, 1772.

***Gulbenkian* 1999** M. Rosa Figueiredo, *Calouste Gulbenkian Museum. European Sculpture*, II, Lisbon, 1999.

Gunn and Lindley 1988 S.J. Gunn and P.G. Lindley, 'Charles Brandon's Westhorpe: an Early Tudor Courtyard House in Suffolk', *Archaeological Journal*, CXLV, 1988, pp. 272–89.

Gunnis 1953 R. Gunnis, *Dictionary of British Sculptors 1660–1851*, London, 1953.

Gunnis 1958 R. Gunnis, 'The Carters', *Architectural Review*, CXXIII, 1958, p. 334.

Gunnis 1968 R. Gunnis, *Dictionary of British Sculpture 1660–1851* (revised edition, first published in 1953), London, 1968.

Hadermann-Misguich 1970 L. Hadermann-Misguich, *Les du Quesnoy*, Gembloux: Duculot, 1970.

Halén 1990 W. Halén, *Christopher Dresser*, Oxford, 1990.

Hall 1980 J. Hall, *Dictionary of Subjects and Symbols in Art* (revised edition, first published in 1974), Fakenham, 1980.

Handley Read 1968 L.H-R. Handley-Read, 'Alfred Gilbert: a new assessment, part I: the small sculptures', *Connoisseur*, CLXIX, September 1968, pp. 22–7.

***Handley-Read* 1972** *Victorian and Edwardian Decorative Art; the Handley Read Collection* (exh. cat.), Royal Academy, London, 1972.

Hardy 1989 J. Hardy, 'Important English Furniture', *Christie's International Magazine*, April-May 1989, pp. 102–3.

Hardy 1993 E. Hardy, 'Farmer and Brindley: Craftsman Sculptors 1850–1930', *Victorian Society Annual*, 1993, pp. 4–17.

Harris 1957 J. Harris 'The story of the marble dog', *Country Life*, CXXII, 21 November 1957, p. 1085.

Harris 1971 J. Harris, *A Catalogue of British Drawings for Architecture, Decoration, Sculpture and Landscape Gardening 1550–1900 in American Collections*, New Jersey, 1971.

Hartnoll 1985 P. Hartnoll (ed.), *The Oxford Companion to the Theatre*, Oxford, 1985.

Haskell 1975 F. Haskell, 'Un Monument et ses Mystères. L'art français et l'opinion anglaise dans la première moitiè di XIXe siecle', *Revue de l'Art*, 30, 1975, pp. 61–110.

Haskell 1987 F. Haskell, *Past and Present in Art and Taste. Selected Essays*, New Haven and London, 1987.

Haskell and Penny 1981 F. Haskell and N. Penny, *Taste and the Antique. The Lure of Classical Sculpture 1500–1900*, New Haven and London, 1981.

Haslam 1978 M. Haslam, *The Martin Brothers. Potters*, London, 1978.

Hatton 1903 J. Hatton, 'The Life and Work of Alfred Gilbert RA, MVO, DCL', *The Art Journal*, Easter Art Annual, 1903, pp.1–32.

Hawkins 1975 J. Hawkins, *Rodin Sculptures*, Victoria and Albert Museum, London, 1975.

Haworth-Booth and McCauley 1998 M. Haworth-Booth and A. McCauley, *The Museum and the Photograph. Collecting Photography at the Victoria and Albert Museum 1853–1900* (exh. cat.), Sterling and Francine Clark Art Institute, Williamstown, 1998.

***Hayman* 1987** B. Allen, *Francis Hayman* (exh. cat.), Yale Center for British Art, New Haven, and The Iveagh Bequest, Kenwood, New Haven and London, 1987.

Heugten 1997 S. van Heugten, *Vincent Van Gogh. Drawings: I, The Early Years 1880–1883*, Amsterdam, 1997.

Hepworth-Dixon 1894 M. Hepworth-Dixon, 'Henrietta Montalba:- A Reminiscence', *Art Journal*, July 1894, pp. 215–7.

***Hildburgh* 1957** 'The first pictorial tribute to Walter Leo Hildburgh. A Great American Collector', *Connoisseur Antique Dealers' Fair and Exhibition Number*, June 1957, pp. 18–20.

Hill 1986 R. Hill, 'Both the work and workman show', *Country Life*, CCXXX, 6 November 1986, pp. 1470–1.

Hill 1998 J. Hill, *Irish Public Sculpture. A History*, Dublin, 1998.

Hiscock 1946 W.G. Hiscock, *A Christ Church Miscellany. New Chapters on the Architects, Craftsmen, Statuary, Plate, Bells, Furniture, Clocks, Plays, the Library and other Buildings*, Oxford, 1946.

***Historical Monuments* 1925** *Royal Commission on Historical Monuments (England). An Inventory of the historical monuments in London, West London*, II, 1925.

***Historical Monuments* 1929** *Royal Commission on Historical Monuments (England). An Inventory of the historical monuments in London, The City*, IV, 1929.

***Historical Monuments* 1952** *Royal Commission on Historical Monument (England). An Inventory of the Historical Monument in Dorset, I. West*, London, 1952

Hobhouse 1971 H. Hobhouse, *Lost London. A Century of Demolition and Decay*, London, 1971.

Hodgkinson 1947 T. Hodgkinson, 'A sketch in terracotta by Roubiliac', *Burlington Magazine*, LXXXIX, September 1947, p. 258, illus. on p. 256.

Hodgkinson 1952/4 T. Hodgkinson, 'Christopher Hewetson, an Irish Sculptor in Rome', *The Walpole Society*, XXXIV, Glasgow, 1952/4, pp. 42–54.

Hodgkinson 1965 T. Hodgkinson, 'Handel at Vauxhall', *Victoria and Albert Museum Bulletin*, I, no. 4, October 1965, pp. 1–13.

Hodgkinson 1967 T. Hodgkinson, 'Joseph Wilton and Doctor Cocchi', *Victoria and Albert Museum Bulletin*, III, no. 2, April 1967, pp. 73–80.

Hodgkinson 1969 T. Hodgkinson, 'John Lochée, Portrait Sculptor', *Victoria and Albert Museum Yearbook*, 1969, no. 1, London, 1969, pp. 152–60.

Hodgkinson 1971/2 T. Hodgkinson, 'Monuments from Faxton Church, Northamptonshire in the Victoria and Albert Museum', *Northamptonshire Past & Present*, IV, no. 6, 1971/2, pp. 335–9.

Honour 1959 H. Honour, 'Antonio Canova and the Anglo-Romans. Part II. The first years in Rome', *Connoisseur*, CXLIV, December 1959, pp. 225–31.

Hooe 1880 W. Hooe, *Sculptors of the day: a list of the profession in 1880*, London, 1880.

Hoole [n.d.] *Notes on some works by Alfred Stevens from 1850 to 1857. As shown by the Original Drawings and Models in the possession of Messrs Henry E. Hoole & Co, Ltd, of Green Lane Works*, arranged by H.I. Potter, Sheffield.

Hornblower and Spawforth 1996 S. Hornblower and A. Spawfoth (eds.), *The Oxford Classical Dictionary*, Oxford, 1996.

Houfe 1978 [Chicksands] S. Houfe, 'The Builders of Chicksands Priory II – Since 1753', *Bedfordshire Magazine*, 16, no. 126, Autumn 1978, pp. 228–31.

Houfe 1978 [Dictionary] S. Houfe, *The Dictionary of British Book Illustrators and Cariacturists*, Woodbridge, 1978.

How 1893 H. How, 'Illustrated Interviews XXVI – Mr. Hamo Thornycroft, R.A.', *Strand Magazine*, 6, no. 33, September 1893, pp. 267–79.

Howard 1987 M. Howard, *The Early Tudor Country House. Architecture and Politics 1490–1550*, London, 1987.

Howard 1991 M. Howard, 'Laughton Place: The Tudor house and its terracottas' in J. Farrant, M. Howard, D. Rudling, J. Warren and C. Whittick, 'Laughton Place: A manorial and architectural history, with an account of recent restoration and excavation', *Sussex Archaeological Collections*, 129, 1991, pp. 133–52.

Howarth 1989 D. Howarth, 'Charles I, Sculpture and Sculptors', in A. MacGregor (ed.), *The Late King's Goods. Collections, Possessions and Patronage of Charles I in the Light of the Commonweath Sale Inventories*, London and Oxford, 1989, pp. 73–113.

Hubbard 2001 C. Hubbard, 'Too Big For His Boots – The Relocation of the Wellington Monument model', *V&A Conservation Journal*, no. 39, Autumn 2001, pp. 8–9.

Hughes 1975 J.V. Hughes, *Thomas Mansel Talbot of Margam & Penrice (1747–1813)*, re-printed from *Gower*, XXVI, 1975.

Hughes 1989 E.M. Hughes, *Artists in California 1786–1940*, San Francisco, 1989.

***Huguenots* 1985** *The Quiet Conquest. The Huguenots 1685 to 1985* (exh. cat.), Museum of London; London, 1985.

Hunisak 1977 J.M. Hunisak, *The Sculptor Jules Dalou: Studies in his Style and Imagery*, New York University, Phd thesis, New York and London, 1977.

Hunisak 1978 J.M. Hunisak, 'Jules Dalou: The Private Side', *Bulletin of the Detroit Institute of Arts*, LVI, no. 2, 1978, pp. 132–40.

Hussey 1934 C. Hussey, 'Brocklesby Park – II Lincolnshire. The seat of the Earl of Yarborough', *Country Life*, LXXV, 3 March 1934, pp. 218–24.

Hutchins 1863 J. Hutchins, *The History and Antiquities of the County of Dorset*, (3rd edition corrected, augmented and improved by William Shipp and James Whitworth Hodson), II, London, 1863.

***Ilchester* 1904** *Catalogue of Pictures belonging to the Earl of Ilchester*, London, 1904.

***Illustrated London News* 1846** The National Gallery, *Illustrated London News*, VIII, 21 February 1846, p. 132.

***Illustrated London News* 1857** 'The Milton Vase', *Illustrated London News*, XXX, 31 January 1857, p. 90 and illus.

***Illustrated London News* 1882** *Illustrated London News*, LXXI, 4 November 1882, pp. 465–6.

***Illustrated London News* 1937** *Illustrated London News*, CXC, 8 May 1937, p. 830.

Illustrated Souvenir 1924 *Illustrated Souvenir of the Palace of Arts British Empire Exhibition (1924)*, Wembley, London, 1924.

Inglis-Jones 1950 E. Inglis-Jones, *Peacocks in Paradise. The Story of a House – its Owners and the Elysium they established there, in the mountains of Wales, in the 18th century*, London, 1950.

***Inigo Jones* 1989** J. Harris and G. Higgot, *Inigo Jones: Complete Architectural Drawings* (exh. cat.), Drawing Center, New York; Frick Art Museum, Pittsburg; New York, 1989.

***Inspiration of Egypt* 1983** P. Conner (ed.), *The Inspiration of Egypt. Its Influence on British Artists, Travellers and Designers 1700–1900* (exh. cat.), Brighton Museum; Manchester City Art Gallery, Brighton 1983.

Ingamells 1997 J. Ingamells, *A Dictionary of British and Irish Travellers in Italy 1701–1800 compiled from the Brinsley Ford Archive*, New Haven and London, 1997.

***International Exhibition* 1851** *Great Exhibition of the Works of Industry of All Nations, Official Descriptive and Illustrative Catalogue*, II, London, 1851.

***International Exhibition* 1862** *International Exhibition 1862. Official Catalogue of the Fine Art Department*, London, 1862 (corrected edition).

International Fine Arts Exhibition 1911 *International Fine Arts Exhibition Rome 1911. British Section. Catalogue*, London, 1911.

***Inventory* 1863** *Inventory of the Objects forming the Art Collections of the Museum at South Kensington*, London, 1863.

***Inventory* 1864** *Inventory of the Objects forming the Art Collection of the Museum at South Kensington, Supplement No. 1 for the year 1864*, London, 1864.

***Inventory* 1869** *Inventory of the Plaster Casts of Objecs collected from various sources on the continent and in Great Britain and Ireland and wax impressions of seals in the British Museum produced for the use of schools of art and for general purposes of public instruction, Science and Art Department of the Committee of Council on Education, South Kensington Museum*, London, 1869.

***Irish Art* 1971** *Irish Art in the 19th Century. An exhibition of Irish Victorian Art at Crawford Municipal School of Art* (exh. cat.), Dublin, 1971.

***Irish Portraits* 1969** A. Crookshank and the Knight of Glin, *Irish Portraits 1660–1860* (exh. cat.), National Gallery of Ireland, Dublin; National Portrait Gallery, London; Ulster Museum, Belfast; London, 1969.

***Ironbridge* 1972** *A description and history of Ironbridge Gorge*, Telford, 1972.

Irwin 1966 D. Irwin, *English Neo-Classical Art. Studies in inspiration and taste*, London 1966.

Irwin 1979 D. Irwin, *John Flaxman 1755–1826. Sculptor Illustrator Designer*, London, 1979.

***Italian Art* 1960** *Italian Art and Britain. Winter Exhibition 1960* (exh. cat.), Royal Academy, London, 1960.

Jacobs 1999 A. Jacobs, *Laurent Delvaux 1696–1778*, Paris, 1999.

Jagger 1933 C.S. Jagger, 'Modelling & Sculpture in the Making', *Studio*, 'How to do it Series', London and New York, 1933, pp. 42–51.

***Jagger* 1935** *Charles Sargeant Jagger Memorial Exhibition, War and Peace Sculpture*, Royal Society of Painters in Watercolours, London, 1935.

***Jagger* 1985** A. Compton (ed.), *Charles Sargeant Jagger: War and Peace Sculpture* (exh. cat.), Imperial War Museum, London; Mappin Art Gallery, Sheffield; London, 1985.

Jenkins 1990 I. Jenkins, 'Acquisition and supply of casts of the

Parthenon Sculptures by the British Museum, 1835–1939', *Annual of the British School at Athens*, 1990, no. 85, pp. 89–114.

Jervis 1993 S. Jervis, 'A River God by Caffiéri. An eighteenth-century terracotta on classical theme', *National Art Collections Fund Annual Review*, London, 1993, pp. 81–5.

Jewitt 1878 L. Jewitt, *The Ceramic Art of Great Britain from pre-historic times down to the present day being a history of the ancient and modern pottery and porcelain works of the Kingdom and of their productions of every class*, London, 1878.

Jezzard 1994 A. Jezzard, 'George Frampton: Art-Worker/Medallist', *The Medal*, no. 24, Spring 1994, pp. 53–8.

***Johnson* 1984** *Samuel Johnson 1709–84. A Bicentenary Exhibition* (exh. cat.), Arts Council, London, 1984.

***Jones* 1924** *Catalogue of the Jones Collection, Part II, Ceramics, Ormolu, Goldsmiths' Work, Enamels. Sculpture, Tapestry, Books and Prints, Victoria and Albert Museum*, London, 1924.

***Journal* 1965** *Journal of the British Society of Master Glass Painters*, XIV, 1964–7, no. 2, London, 1965, pp.112–3.

***Jubilee* 1977** *"This brilliant Year" Queen Victoria's Jubilee 1887* (exh. cat.), Royal Academy, London, 1977.

***Jury Reports* 1851** *Exhibition of the Works of Industry of All Nations, 1851. Reports by the Juries on the subjects in the thirty classes into which the exhibition was divided, IV, Reports – Classes XXIX, XXX*, London, 1852.

Kader 1996 A. Kader, 'Four marble busts of artists by Edward Hodges Baily', *Antologia di Belle Arti. La Scultura. Studi in onore di Andrew S. Ciechanowiecki*, II, 1996, pp. 177–82.

Kai Sass 1963 E. Kai Sass, *Thorvaldsens Portrætbuster*, Copenhagen, 1963.

***Katz* 1992** P. Laverack (ed.), *Daniel Katz Ltd 1968–1993. A Catalogue Celebrating Twenty-Five Years of Dealing in European Sculpture and Works of Art*, London, 1992.

***Katz* 1996** J. Auersperg, *Daniel Katz European Sculpture*, New York and London, 1996.

***Katz* 2000** S. Lochhead (ed.), *Daniel Katz European Sculpture*, London and New York, 2000.

***Katz* 2001** K. Zock, *Daniel Katz European Sculpture*, New York and London, 2001.

Keatinge Clay 1918 W. Keatinge Clay, *Prittlewell Priory. An Illustrated History*, Southend-on-Sea, 1918.

Keller-Dorian 1920 G. Keller-Dorian, *Antoine Coysevox (1640–1720). Catalogue raisonné de son oeuvre*, II, Paris, 1920.

Kelly 1973 A. Kelly, 'Decorative stonework in disguise. Plaques and medallions in Coade stone', *Country Life*, CLIV, 29 November 1973, pp. 1797–8, 1800.

Kelly 1980 A. Kelly, 'Coade Stone at National Trust Houses', *National Trust Studies*, 1980, pp. 95–111.

Kelly 1990 A. Kelly, *Mrs Coade's Stone*, Upton-upon-Severn, 1990.

Kemp 1975 M. Kemp (ed.), *Dr William Hunter at the Royal Academy of Arts*, Glasgow; Glasgow, 1975.

Kemp 1983 M. Kemp, 'Glasgow University Bicentenary celebrations of Dr William Hunter (1718–83)' (exh. review), *Burlington Magazine*, CXXV, June 1983, pp. 380–3.

Kenworthy-Browne 1966 J. Kenworthy-Browne, 'Marbles from a Victorian Fantasy' *Country Life*, CXL, September 1966, pp. 708–12.

Kenworthy-Browne 1973 J. Kenworthy-Browne, 'New Sculpture Gallery at the V&A', *Country Life*, CLIII, 8 March 1973, pp. 574–5.

Kenworthy-Browne 1974 J. Kenworthy-Browne, 'The Man at Hyde Park Corner', *Country Life*, CLVI, 1 August 1974, pp. 305–6.

Kenworthy-Browne 1983 J. Kenworthy-Browne, 'Rysbrack, "Hercules", and Pietro da Cortona', *Burlington Magazine*, CXXV, April 1983, pp. 216–9.

Kenworthy-Browne 1985 J. Kenworthy-Browne, 'Rysbrack's Saxon Deities', *Apollo*, CXXII, September 1985, pp. 220–7.

Kenworthy-Browne 1998 J. Kenworthy-Browne, 'Models by Joseph Nollekens, R.A.', *Sculpture Journal*, II, pp. 72–84.

Kerslake 1977 (I) J. Kerslake, *Early Georgian Portraits*, I (text), London, 1977.

Kerslake 1977 (II) J. Kerslake, *Early Georgian Portraits*, II (plates), London, 1977.

Keutner 1969 H. Keutner, *Sculpture: Renaissance to Rococo. A History of Western Sculpture*, London, 1969.

Kilmurray 1979 E. Kilmurray, *Dictionary of British Portraiture, Later Georgians and Early Victorians – historical figures born between 1700 and 1800*, II, London, 1979.

Kilmurray 1981 E. Kilmurray, *Dictionary of British Portraiture, The Victorians – historical figures born between 1800 and 1860*, III, London, 1981.

Kindersley 1967 D. Kindersley, *Mr Eric Gill: further thoughts by an Apprentice*, Cambridge, 1967, republished 1990.

***Kindersley* 1976** *David Kindersley's Workshop* (trade booklet), Cambridge, 1976.

Kindersley and Cardozo Lopes 1981 D. Kindersley and L. Cardozo Lopes, *Letters Slate Cut: Workshop Practice and the Making of Letters*, London, 1981.

***Kings and Queens* 1937** *Kings and Queens of England 1500–1900* (exh. cat.), Victoria and Albert Museum, London, 1937.

Kingsford 1920 C.L. Kingsford, 'Historical Notes on Medieval London Houses', *London Topographical Record*, XII, London, 1920, pp. 1–66.

Kinney 1976 P. Kinney, *The Early Sculpture of Bartolomeo Ammanati*, New York and London, 1976.

Knight Loveday 1957 A. Knight Loveday, 'Statuary from Stowe' (letter), *Country Life*, CXXII, 8 August 1957, p. 267.

Knox 1998 T. Knox, 'Portrait of a Collector: Rupert Gunnis at Hungershall Lodge and his Bequest to the Victoria and Albert Museum', *Sculpture Journal*, II, 1998, pp. 85–96.

Knox 2001 T. Knox, 'Sculpture in Trust. The National Trust as the guardian of outdoor sculpture', *Apollo*, CLIV, September 2001, pp. 26–31.

Konody 1927 P.G. Konody, 'The Art of Maurice Lambert', *Artwork*, 3, no. 11, September-November 1927, pp. 190–3.

Kunst der Historismus 1996 *Der Traum vom Glück. Die Kunst der Historismus in Europa* (exh. cat.), I, Künstlerhaus, Vienna, 1996.

***Lady Lever* 1999** A. Clay, E. Morris, S. Penketh, and T. Stevens, *British Sculpture in the Lady Lever Art Gallery*, Liverpool, 1999.

Laing 1989 A. Laing, 'The Eighteenth-Century English Chimneypiece', *The Fashioning and Functioning of the British Country House*, Studies in the History of Art, 25, National Gallery of Art, Washington, 1989, pp. 241–55.

***Lambert* 1927** *Exhibition of Sculpture by Maurice Lambert at the Claridge Gallery, 52, Brook Street, W1* (exh. leaflet), 13–30 June 1927, London, 1927.

***Lambert* 1988** *Maurice Lambert 1901–1964* (exh. cat.), The Belgrave Gallery, London, 1988.

Lami 1916 S. Lami, *Dictionnaire des Sculpteurs de l'École Française au Dix-Neuvième Siècle*, Paris, 1916.

Landseer **1981** R. Ormond, with contributions by J. Rishel and R. Hamlyn, *Sir Edwin Landseer* (exh. cat.), Philadelphia Museum of Art, Philadelphia; Tate Gallery, London; London, 1981.

Langer, Ufer and Siedentopf 1861 T. Langer, O. Ufer and Siedentopf, *Engravings from original compositions executed in marble at Rome by Iohn Gibson R.A.*, London, 1861.

Lanteri 1902 E. Lanteri, *Modelling. A guide for teachers and students*, I, London 1902.

Lanteri 1904 E. Lanteri, *Modelling. A guide for teachers and students*, II, London 1904.

Lanteri 1911 E. Lanteri, *Modelling. A guide for teachers and students*, III, London 1911.

Lanteri **1920** *Catalogue of the Exhibitions of Sculpture by the late Prof. E. Lanteri, The Leicester Galleries*, Leicester Square, London, 1920.

La Roche 1933 S. von la Roche, *Sophie in London 1786, being the Diary of Sophie von la Roche* (translated from German with an introductory essay by Clare Williams), London, 1933.

Law and Law 1925 H.W. Law and I. Law, *The Book of the Beresford Hopes*, London, 1925.

Ledward **1988** *Gilbert Ledward RA, PRBS, 1888–1960. Drawings for Sculpture. A Centenary Tribute* (exh. cat.), The Fine Art Society, London, 1988.

Leeds **1869** *National Exhibition of Works of Art at Leeds 1868*, Official Catalogue, Leeds, 1869.

Leeds **1996** P. Curtis and T. Friedman (eds.), *Leeds' Sculpture Collections. Illustrated Concise Catalogue*, The Centre for the Study of Sculpture, Leeds, 1996.

Leeuwenberg 1973 J. Leeuwenberg, *Beeldhouwkunst in het Rijksmuseum*, Staatsuitgeverij, ds-Gravenhage, Rijksmuseum, Amsterdam, 1973.

Leighton 1977 M. Leighton, 'Guardians of a heritage', *Illustrated London News*, 265, no. 6946, May 1977, pp. 65–8.

Leighton **1996** *Leighton and his Sculptural Legacy: British Sculpture 1875–1930* (exh. cat.), Matthiesen Gallery, London; Over Wallop, 1996.

Leslie and Taylor 1865 C.R. Leslie and T. Taylor, *Life of Sir Joshua Reynolds*, II, London, 1865.

Lethaby 1906 W.R. Lethaby, *Westminster Abbey & the Kings' Craftsmen. A Study of Medieval Buildings*, London, 1906.

Lewis 1967 L. Lewis, 'Spanish Town and the Rodney Monument' in 'English commemorative sculpture in Jamaica', *Commemorative Art*, February 1967, pp. 365–73.

Liefkes 1994 R. Liefkes, 'Antonio Salviati and the nineteenth-century renaissance of Venetian glass', *Burlington Magazine*, CXXXVI, May 1994, pp. 283–90.

Lightbown 1978 R.W. Lightbown, *French Silver*, London, 1978.

Lindley 1988 P. Lindley, 'The Early Tudor Country House: Architecture and Politics 1490–1550 by M. Howard' (book review), *Oxford Art Journal*, XI, 1988, pp. 64–7.

Lindley 1991 P.G. Lindley, 'Playing check-mate with royal majesty? Wolsey's patronage of Italian Renaissance sculpture', in S.J. Gunn and P.G. Lindley (eds.), *Cardinal Wolsey. Church State and Art*, Cambridge, 1991, pp. 261–85.

Lindley 1995 P. Lindley, *Gothic to Renaissance. Essays on Sculpture in England*, Stamford, 1995.

List **1870** *List of Objects in the Art Division, South Kensington Museum. Lent during the Year 1870, arranged according to dates of loan*, London, 1871.

List **1875** *List of Art Objects in the South Kensington Museum, and in the Branch Museum, Bethnal Green, Lent during the Year 1875*, London, 1876.

List **1876** *List of Art Objects in the South Kensington Museum, and in the Branch Museum, Bethnal Green, Lent during the Year 1876*, London, 1877.

List 1892 *List of Reproductions in Electrotype and Plaster acquired by the South Kensington Museum in the Year 1892*, London, 1893.

List **1908** *List of Reproductions acquired by the Victoria and Albert Museum in the Year 1908.*

Llewellyn 2000 N. Llewellyn, *Funeral Monuments in Post-Reformation England*, Cambridge, 2000.

Lloyd-Jones 1978 H. Lloyd-Jones, *Myths of the Zodiac with sculptures by Marcelle Quinton*, London, 1978.

Loan Exhibition **1932** *A loan exhibition depicting the reign of Charles II* (exh. cat.), 22 and 23 Grosvenor Place, London; London, 1932.

London Exhibition **1871** *Official Catalogue of the Fine Art Department with alphabetical index to artists and contributors, & c*, London, 1871.

London Exhibition **1871 [revised]** *London International Exhibition of 1871. Official Catalogue Fine Arts Department* (3rd revision), London, 1871.

Longhurst 1926 M.H. Longhurst, *English Ivories*, London, 1926.

Longhurst 1927 M. H. Longhurst, *Catalogue of Carvings in Ivory*, I, Victoria and Albert Museum, London, 1927.

Longhurst 1929 M.H. Longhurst, *Catalogue of Carvings in Ivory*, II, Victoria and Albert Museum, London, 1929.

Lord 1988 J. Lord, 'Joseph Nollekens and Lord Yarborough: documents and drawings', *Burlington Magazine*, CXXX, December 1988, pp. 915–9.

Lord 1990 J. Lord, 'J.M. Rysbrack and a group of East Midlands Commissions', *Burlington Magazine*, CXXXII, December 1990, pp. 866–70.

Lord 1992 [Brocklesby] J. Lord, 'The Building of the Mausoleum at Brocklesby, Lincolnshire', *Journal of the Church Monuments Society*, VII, 1992, pp. 85–96.

Lord 1992 [Newton] J. Lord, Sir Isaac Newton, James Thomson, Sir Robert Walpole and Earl Stanhope – a speculative linkage', Newsletter, *Church Monuments Society*, VII, no. 2, Winter 1992, pp. 45–6.

Los Angeles **1987** S. Schaefer and P. Fusco, *European Painting and Sculpture in the Los Angeles County Museum of Art, An Illustrated Summary Catalogue*, Los Angeles, 1987.

Lough and Merson 1987 J. Lough and E. Merson, *John Graham Lough 1798–1876. A Northumbrian Sculptor*, Bury St Edmunds, 1987.

Louvre **1992** *Musée du Louvre. Nouvelles acquisitions du département des Sculptures 1988–1991*, Paris, 1992.

Louvre **1994** J.R. Gaborit, *Le Louvre. La sculpture européenne*, London and Paris, 1994.

Lucas 1861 R.C. Lucas, *The Life of an Artist; being an Autobiography of R.C. Lucas. Sculptor of Chilworth Tower, Hants*, Southampton, 1861 [unpublished manuscript held at Southampton, Collections of Southampton City Cultural Services].

Lucas 1870 R. C. Lucas, *An Essay on Art; especially that of painting, done by R.C. Lucas, sculptor, in the Sky Parlour of his Tower of Winds, Chilworth, Romsey, Hants*, 1870, pp.1–4 (pamphlet, copy held in the National Art Library).

Lucas 1910 P. Lucas, *Heathfield Memorials. Collected from the Parish Records and other unpublished manuscripts*, London, 1910.

MacColl 1903 D.S. MacColl, 'The Wellington Monument of Alfred Stevens. A Description, with Illustrations, of the existing Models and Drawings for the Equestrian Statue', *Architectural Review*, XIII, March 1903, pp. 87–96.

MacGibbon and Ross 1892 D. MacGibbon and T. Ross, *The Castellated and Domestic Architecture of Scotland from the Twelfth to the Eighteenth Century*, V, Edinburgh, 1892.

Maclagan and Longhurst 1932 *Victoria and Albert Museum Department of Architecture and Sculpture. Catalogue of Italian Sculpture*, London, 1932.

***Magazine of Art* 1897** *The Chronicle of Art. Magazine of Art*, XXI, June 1897, p. 106.

***Magazine of Art* 1902** 'The Queen Victoria Memorial', *The Chronicle of Art. Magazine of Art*, XXVI, January 1902, pp. 139–40.

Malcolm 1807 J.P. Malcolm, *Londinium Redivivum or an Ancient History and Modern description of London*, IV, London, 1807.

Mainstone 1976 M Mainstone, *Roubiliac's Handel*, V&A Masterpiece Sheet 4, London, 1976.

Mallet 1962 J.V.G. Mallet, 'Some Portrait Medallions by Roubiliac', *Burlington Magazine*, CIV, April 1962, pp. 153–8.

Manning 1982 E. Manning, *Marble & Bronze. The Art and Life of Hamo Thornycroft*, London, 1982.

Manning and Bray 1814 Rev. O. Manning and W. Bray, *The History and Antiquities of the County of Surrey*, III, London, 1814.

Manwaring Baines 1980 J. Manwaring Baines, *Sussex Pottery*, Brighton, 1980.

***Marble Halls* 1973** J. Physick and M. Darby, *'Marble Halls': Drawings and Models for Victorian Secular Buildings* (exh. cat.), Victoria and Albert Museum, London, 1973.

***Marcelle Quinton* 1980** *Portraits and Figures. Marcelle Quinton* (exh. pamphlet), Ashmolean Museum, Oxford, 1980.

Marsh 1925 E. Marsh, 'R.F. Wells Sculptor and Potter', *Apollo*, I, 1925, pp. 283–9.

Maskell 1905 A. Maskell, *Ivories*, London, 1905.

***Masterpieces* 1951** *Victoria and Albert Museum. Fifty Masterpieces of Sculpture*, London, 1951.

Matthews 1911 T. Matthews, *The Biography of John Gibson, R.A. Sculptor, Rome*, London, 1911.

McAllister 1912 I.G. McAllister, 'Edward Lanteri: Sculptor and Professor', *Studio*, LVII, October 1912, pp. 25–31.

McAllister 1914 I.G. McAllister, 'A Rising British Sculptor: Charles Sargeant Jagger', *Studio*, LXIII, 1914, pp. 84–99.

McAllister 1929 I.G.McAllister, *Alfred Gilbert*, London, 1929.

McCarthy 1973 M. McCarthy, 'James Lovell and his Sculptures at Stowe', *Burlington Magazine*, CXV, April 1973, pp. 221–32.

McCulloch 1994 A. McCulloch (revised and updated by S. McCulloch), *The Encyclopedia of Australian Art*, St Leonards, New South Wales, 1994.

McEvansoneya 2001 P. McEvansoneya, 'Lord Egremont and Flaxman's "St Michael overcoming Satan"', *Burlington Magazine*, CXLIII, June 2001, pp. 351–59.

McEwan 1994 P.J.M. McEwan, *Dictionary of Scottish Art & Architecture, Antique Collectors' Club*, Woodbridge, 1994.

McKay 1917 W.D. McKay, *The Royal Scottish Academy 1826–1916*, Glasgow, 1917.

Medallic Illustrations *Medallic Illustrations of the History of Great Britain and Ireland*, British Museum, London; Oxford (6 vols of plates, 1906–11).

Medwin 1839 T. Medwin, 'Canova', *Corsair*, I, no. 30, 5 October 1839, New York, pp. 169–70.

***Metropole London* 1992** *Metropole London. Macht und Glanz einer Weltstadt 1800–1840* (exh. cat.), Villa Hügel, Essen, 1992.

***Michelangelo* 1992** *The Genius of the Sculptor in Michelangelo's Work* (exh. cat.), Montreal Museum of Fine Arts, Montreal, 1992.

Miller 1900 F. Miller, 'A sculptor-potter, Mr Conrad Dressler', *The Artist*, XXVIII, May to August 1900, pp. 169–76.

Molesworth 1951 H.D.Molesworth, *Sculpture in England: Renaissance to Early XIX Century*, 1951.

de Montaiglon and Guiffrey 1901 M.M.A. de Montaiglon and J. Guiffrey, *Correspondence des Directeurs de l'Académie de France a Rome, XI, 1754–1763*, Paris, 1901.

Moore 1934 W. Moore, *The Story of Australian Art. From the earliest known art of the continent to the art of today*, II, Sydney, 1934.

Moore 1985 S. Moore, 'Hail! Gods of our Fore-fathers, Rysbrack's "Lost" Saxon Deities at Stowe', *Country Life*, CLXXVII, 31 January 1985, pp. 250–1.

Morand 1991 K. Morand, *Claus Sluter. Artist at the Court of Burgundy*, London, 1991.

Mordaunt Crook 1966 J. Mordaunt Crook, 'Sir Robert Peel: Patron of The Arts', *History Today*, XVI, January 1966, pp. 3–11.

Morganstern 1992 A.M. Morganstern, 'Le tombeau de Philippe le Hardi et ses antecédents', *Actes des Journées Internationales Claus Sluter*, Dijon, 1992, pp. 175–91.

Morrell 1944 J.B. Morrell, *The Arts and Crafts in York. York Monuments*, London, 1944.

Morris 1995 E.Morris, *Liverpool Renewed. John Warrington Wood's statue of Liverpool on the Walker Art Gallery and its replacement*, Liverpool, 1995.

Morris 2000 R.K. Morris, 'Architectural Terracotta Decoration in Tudor England', in P. Lindley and T. Frangenberg (eds.), *Secular Sculpture 1300–1550*, Stamford, 2000, pp. 179–210.

***Mosers* 1938** *Mosers of the Borough* (trade pamphlet), London, [n.d.], [1938].

Murdoch 1980 T. Murdoch, 'Roubiliac as an Architect? The bill for the Warkton monuments', *Burlington Magazine*, CXXII, January 1980, pp. 40–6.

Murdoch 1983 T. Murdoch, 'Louis François Roubiliac and his Huguenot Connections', *Proceedings of the Huguenot Society of London*, XXIV, no. I, 1983, pp. 26–45.

Murdoch 1985 T. Murdoch, 'Roubiliac's Monuments to Bishop Hough and the Second Duke and Duchess of Montagu', *Journal of the Church Monuments Society*, I, part I, 1985, pp. 34–48.

Murdoch 2001 T. Murdoch 'Masterpieces from the British Galleries. Lent by the Victoria and Albert Museum to the BADA Antiques and Fine Art Fair', *The British Antique Dealers' Association Yearbook*, 2001/2002, pp. 8–13.

Murdoch 2001 [Supplement] T. Murdoch, 'Masterpieces from the British Galleries. Lent by the Victoria and Albert Museum to the British Antique Dealers' Association Fair at the Duke of York's Headquarters from 21st to 27th March 2001', *BADA, Supplement*, Spring 2001.

Murphy 1999 P. Murphy, 'British Sculpture at the Early Universal Exhibitions: Ireland Sustaining Britain', *Sculpture Journal*, III, 1999, pp. 64–73.

***Musée d'Orsay* 1986** A. Pingeot and L. de Margerie, *Catalogue sommaire illustré des sculptures. Musée d'Orsay*, Paris, 1986.

***Museums Journal* 1926** *The Museums Journal*, XXV, no. 11, May 1926, p. 319.

***Musical Times* 1961** *Musical Times*, no. 1424, October 1961.

NACF **1989** *National Art Collections Fund*, Eighty-sixth Annual Report, London, 1989.

NACF **1990** *Review*, London, 1990.

NACF **1999** *Review*, London, 1999.

NACF **2002** *Review*, London, 2002 (forthcoming).

***National Gallery of Victoria* 1908** *Illustrated Catalogue of the National Gallery of Victoria*, Melbourne, 1908.

***National Gallery of Victoria* 1987** A. Galbally, *The Collections of the National Gallery of Victoria*, Melbourne and Oxford, 1987.

***National Magazine* 1857** J. Saunders and W. Marston (eds.), *The National Magazine*, I, part 5, March 1857, pp. 289, 291.

***National Memorial* 1873** *The National Memorial to His Royal Highness The Prince Consort*, London, 1873.

***National Museum of Wales* 1990** 'Recent acquisitions at the National Museum of Wales', *Burlington Magazine*, CXXXII, October 1990, pp. 752–6.

***Neo-classicism* 1972** *The Age of Neo-classicism* (exh. cat.), Royal Academy and Victoria and Albert Museum, London, 1972.

Neumann 1959 E. Neumann 'Materialien zur Geschichte der Scagliola', *Jahrbuch der Kunsthistorischen Sammlungen in Wien*, 55, XIX, 1959, pp. 75–158.

Neve 1974 C. Neve, *Leon Underwood*, London, 1974.

Nicolson 1972 B. Nicolson, *The Treasures of the Foundling Hospital with a catalogue raisonné by J. Kerslake*, London, 1972.

Nicolson [forthcoming] V. Nicolson, *The Sculpture of Maurice Lambert*, Lund Humphries, London, 2002.

***Nineteenth Century French Sculpture* 1971** *Nineteenth Century French Sculpture. Monuments for the Middle Class* (exh. cat.), J.B. Speed Art Museum, Louisville, Kentucky, 1971.

Noad 1950 A.S. Noad, 'Les Anglais Rococo: the Georgian French', *Art News*, XLIX, no. 3, May 1950, pp. 30–5, and 58–9.

Noble 1908 P. Noble, *Anne Seymour Damer. A woman of art and fashion 1748–1828*, London, 1908.

Noppen 1931 J.G. Noppen, 'A Tomb and Effigy by Hennequin of Liège', *Burlington Magazine*, LIX, September 1931, pp. 114–17.

***Norfolk & the Grand Tour* 1985** A.W. Moore, *Norfolk & the Grand Tour. Eighteenth-century travellers abroad and their souvenirs* (exh. cat.) Norfolk Museums Service, Fakenham, 1985.

***NPG* 1981** K.K. Yung, *National Portrait Gallery, Complete Illustrated Catalogue 1856–1979*, London, 1981.

***NPG* 1985** R. Walker, *National Portrait Gallery. Regency Portraits* (2 vols), London, 1985.

***NSW* 1989** D. Edwards, M. Gowing, *Short Entry Catalogue of paintings, watercolours, sculpture and miniatures. Australian Art Gallery of New South Wales*, Sydney, 1989.

O'Brien 1982 E.S. O'Brien, *Johan Tobias Sergell (1740–1814) and Neoclassicism: Sculpture of Sergell's years abroad, 1767–1779*, I, Phd thesis, University of Iowa, 1982.

O'Connell 1987 S. O'Connell, 'The Nosts: a revision of the family history', *Burlington Magazine*, CXXIX, December 1987, pp. 802–6.

O'Driscoll 1871 W.J. O'Driscoll, *A memoir of Daniel Maclise, R.A.*, London, 1871.

Ollerenshaw [n.d.] A.E. Ollerenshaw, *The history of Blue John Stone. Methods of Mining and Working. Ancient and Modern*, Castleton, [n.d].

Ollett 1963 F.A. Ollett, 'Alfred Stevens (1817–1875)', *Dorset Worthies*, no. 7, 1963, pp. 1–7.

***'One by one'* 1998** L. Cullen, W. Fisher and N. Jopek, *'One by one': European Commemorative Medals of the Great War 1914–1918*, (exh. booklet unpublished; copy held in National Art Library), Victoria and Albert Museum, London, 1998.

***Orient* 1989** *Europa und der Orient 800–1900* (exh. cat.), Martin-Gropius-Bau, Berlin; Munich 1989.

Oswald 1933 A. Oswald, 'West Wycombe Park Bucks. I. The Seat of Sir John Lindsay Dashwood, Bt.', *Country Life*, LXXIII, 6 May 1933, pp. 466–71.

Owsley and Rieder 1974 D. Owsley and W. Rieder, *The Glass Drawing Room from Northumberland House*, London, 1974.

***Painting and Sculpture in England* 1958** *Painting and Sculpture in England 1700–1750* (exh. cat.), Walker Art Gallery, Liverpool, 1958.

***Palace of Arts* 1924** *Catalogue of the Palace of Arts, British Empire Exhibition*, London, 1924.

***Paris Exhibition* 1855** *Paris Universal Exhibition 1855. Catalogue of the Works Exhibited in the British Section of the Exhibition, in French and English*, London, 1855.

***Paris International Exhibition* 1878** *Art Journal. The Illustrated Catalogue of the Paris International Exhibition*, London, 1878.

Parissien, Harris and Colvin 1987 S. Parissien, J. Harris and H. Colvin, 'Narford Hall, Norfolk', *The Georgian Group Report & Journal*, 1987, pp. 49–61.

Parker 1963 J. Parker, 'Designed in the Most Elegant Manner and Wrought in the Best Marbles', *Metropolitan Museum of Art Bulletin*, February 1963, pp. 202–33.

Parkes 1921 K. Parkes, *Sculpture of To-Day*, I, London, 1921.

Parry 1995 G. Parry, *The Trophies of Time. English Antiquarians of the Seventeenth Century*, Oxford and New York, 1995.

Parry-Jones 1981 B. Parry-Jones, 'Peter Hollins at The Warneford Hospital', *Leeds Arts Calendar*, no. 88, 1981, pp. 24–32.

Paulson 1965 R. Paulson, *Hogarth's Graphic Works*, (2 vols), New Haven and London, 1965.

Pavanello 1976 G. Pavanello, *L'opera completa del Canova*, Milan, 1976.

Peace 1994 D. Peace, *Eric Gill. The Inscriptions. A descriptive catalogue*, London, 1994.

***Peasant in French 19th Century Art* 1980** J. Thompson, *The Peasant in French 19th Century Art* (exh. cat.), The Douglas Hyde Gallery, Trinity College, Dublin; Dublin, 1980.

***Peel* 1967** *From Vittoria to Dalou. An Exhibition of European Works of Art*, David Peel, London, 26 April to 19 May 1967, London, 1967.

Penny 1975 [Church Monuments] N.B. Penny, 'English Church Monuments to women who died in childbed between 1780 and 1835', *Journal of the Warburg and Courtauld Institutes*, XXVIII, 1975, pp. 314–32.

Penny 1975 [Westmacott] N.B. Penny, 'The Sculpture of Sir Richard Westmacott', *Apollo*, CII, August 1975, pp. 120–7.

Penny 1976 N. Penny, 'Dead Dogs and Englishmen', *Connoisseur*, CXCII, August 1976, pp. 298–303.

Penny 1977 N. Penny, *Church Monuments in Romantic England*, New Haven and London, 1977.

Penny 1982 N. Penny, 'The Classical Tradition and the Garden Ornament' (book review), F. Souchal, *French Sculptors of the 17th and 18th Centuries. The Reign of Louis XIV* and A. Le Normand, *La Tradition classique et l'esprit romantique*, in *Art History*, 5, no. 2, June 1982, p. 246.

Penny 1989 N. Penny, 'The Turner Sculpture Gift', *NACF Review*, 1989.

Penny 1990 N. Penny, 'Mrs Coade's Stone by A. Kelly' (book review), *Burlington Magazine*, CXXXII, no. 1053, December 1990, pp. 879–80.

Penny 1991 [Chantrey/Westmacott] N. Penny, 'Chantrey, Westmacott and Casts after the antique', *Journal of the History of Collections*, no. 2, 1991, pp. 255–64.

Penny 1991 [Rockingham] N. Penny, 'Lord Rockingham's Sculpture Collection and *The Judgement of Paris* by Nollekens', *The J. Paul Getty Museum Journal*, 19, 1991, pp. 5–34.

Penny 1998 N. Penny, sculpture entries in *The Ford Collection – II*, in L. Herrmann and G. Forrester (eds.), *The Sixtieth Volume of the Walpole Society 1998*, Leeds, 1998.

Petteys 1985 C. Petteys, *Dictionary of Women Artists. An international directory of women artists born before 1900*, Boston, 1985.

Pevsner 1981 [London] N. Pevsner revised by B. Cherry, *The Buildings of England. London, I, The Cities of London and Westminster*, London, 1981 (reprinted 1981 from third edition published 1973).

Pevsner 1981 [Northants] N. Pevsner revised by B. Cherry, *The Buildings of England. Northamptonshire*, Harmondsworth, 1981 (reprinted 1981 from second edition published 1973).

Pevsner 1981 [Suffolk] N. Pevsner revised by E. Radcliffe, *The Buildings of England, Suffolk*, Harmondsworth, 1981 (reprinted 1981 from second edition published 1974).

Phillips 1886 C. Phillips, 'Randolph Caldecott', *Gazette des Beaux-Arts*, XXXIII, 1886, pp. 327–41.

Phillips 1931 P.A.S. Phillips, *John Obrisset Huguenot Carver, Medallist, Horn & Tortoiseshell Worker, & Snuff-Box Maker, With Examples of his Works dated 1705 to 1728*, London, 1931.

Phillips 1964 H. Phillips, *Mid-Georgian London: Topographical and Social Survey of Central and Western London about 1750*, London, 1964.

Physick 1967 J. Physick, 'Some eighteenth century designs for monuments in Westminster Abbey', *Victoria and Albert Museum Bulletin*, III, no. I, January 1967, pp. 26–38.

Physick 1969 J. Physick, *Designs for English Sculpture 1680–1860*, London, 1969.

Physick 1970 [Eastwell] J. Physick, 'Five monuments from Eastwell', *Victoria and Albert Museum Yearbook*, II, 1970, pp. 125–44.

Physick 1970 [Wellington] J. Physick, *The Wellington Monument*, London, 1970.

Physick 1978 J. Physick, *Victoria and Albert Museum Decorative Sculpture*, V&A Masterpiece Sheet, London, 1978.

Physick 1982 J. Physick, *The Victoria and Albert Museum. The history of its building*, London, 1982.

Physick and Ramsay 1986 J. Physick and N. Ramsay, 'Katharine Ada Esdaile 1881–1950', *Journal of the Church Monuments Society*, I, part 2, 1986, pp. 115–36.

***Picture Book* 1927** *Victoria and Albert Museum. A Picture Book of Children in Sculpture*, London, 1927.

Pinkerton 1973 J. Pinkerton, 'Roubiliac's Statue of Lord President Forbes', *Connoisseur*, CLXXXIII, August 1973, pp. 274–9.

***Pioneers* 1973** *Pioneers of Modern Sculpture* (exh. cat.), Hayward Gallery, London, 1973.

Poole 1912 R.L. Poole, *Catalogue of Portraits in the possession of The University Colleges, City and County of Oxford. The Portraits in the University Collections and in the Town and County Halls*, I, Oxford, 1912.

***Pomeroy* 1898** Manuscript letter held in National Art Library from Frederick William Pomeroy to A.L. Baldry, dated 4 August 1898 (NAL pressmark MSL/1972/4950/122).

Pope-Hennessy 1953 J. Pope-Hennessy, 'Some Bronze Statuettes by Francesco Fanelli', *Burlington Magazine*, XCV, May 1953, pp. 157–62.

Pope-Hennessy 1964 J. Pope-Hennessy (assisted by R.W. Lightbown), *Catalogue of Italian Sculpture in the Victoria and Albert Museum*, (3 vols), London, 1964.

Pope-Hennessy 1991 J. Pope-Hennessy, *Learning to Look*, New York, 1991.

Powell 1984 N. Powell, 'Rococo in England', *Apollo*, CXX, August 1984, pp. 98–105.

***Precious* 2001** A. Burton, *Precious. An Illustrated Guide to the Exhibition* (exh. guide), Millenium Galleries, Sheffield, 2001.

***Pre-Raphaelite* 1991** B. Read and J. Barnes, *PreRaphaelite Sculpture. Nature and Imagination in British Sculpture 1848–1914* (exh. cat.), Matthiesen Gallery, London; Birmingham City Art Gallery, Birmingham; London, 1991.

Price Amerson 1975 L. Price Amerson Jr, *The Problem of the Ecorché: A Catalogue Raisonné of Models and Statuettes from the Sixteenth Century and Later Periods*, Phd thesis, Pennsylvania State University, Department of Art History, May 1975.

***Pugin* 1994** P. Atterbury and C. Wainwright (eds.), *Pugin: a Gothic passion* (exh. cat.), Victoria and Albert Museum, London; New Haven and London, 1994.

Puttick 1854 J.F. Puttick, *Roubiliac's statue of Handel, recently purchased by the Sacred Harmonic Society, and now in their office, 6, Exeter Hall*, London, 1854.

Pyke 1973 E.J. Pyke, *A Biographical Dictionary of Wax Modellers*, Oxford, 1973.

***Quick and the Dead* 1997** *The Quick and the dead: artists and anatomy* (exh. cat.), Royal College of Art, London; Mead Gallery, Warwick Arts Centre, Coventry; Leeds City Art Gallery, Leeds; London, 1997.

Rackham 1930 B. Rackham, *Catalogue of English Porcelain, Earthenware, Enamels, and Glass collected by Charles Schreiber Esq. M.P. and The Lady Charlotte Elizabeth Schreiber and presented to the Museum in 1884, II, Earthenware*, London, 1930.

Radcliffe 1964 A. Radcliffe, 'Jules Dalou in England July 1871 to April 1880', *Connoisseur*, CLV, April 1964, pp. 244–5.

Radcliffe 1965 A. Radcliffe, 'Monti's Allegory of the Risorgimento', *Victoria and Albert Museum Bulletin*, I, no. 3, July 1965, pp. 25–38.

Radcliffe and Thornton 1978 A. Radcliffe and P. Thornton, 'John Evelyn's Cabinet', *Connoisseur*, CXCVII, April 1978, pp. 254–62.

***RCA* 1913** 'British School at Rome Scholarship', *The R.C.A. Students' Magazine*, II, no. XIV, May 1913, pp. 110–111.

Read 1894 C.H. Read, *Some Minor Arts*, London, 1894.

Read 1974 B. Read, 'John Henry Foley', *Connoisseur*, CLXXXVI, August 1974, pp. 262–71.

Read 1982 B. Read, *Victorian Sculpture*, New Haven and Yale, 1982.

Read 1996 B. Read, 'Leighton as a sculptor. Releasing sculpture from convention', *Apollo*, CXLIII, February 1996, pp. 65–9.

Read 2000 B. Read, Sculpture and the New Palace of Westminster', in D. Cannandine (*et al.*), I. Ross (ed.), *The Houses of Parliament. History, Art, Architecture*, London, 2000, pp. 253–68, 278.

Réau 1964 L. Réau, *Houdon. Sa vie et son oevre*, Paris, 1964.

Redgrave 1970 S. Redgrave, *A Dictionary of artists of the English Schools*, Bath, 1970 (facsimile from 2nd edition, published 1878).

Redgrave **1988** S.P. Casteras and R. Parkinson, *Richard Redgrave 1804–1888* (exh. cat.), Victoria and Albert Museum, London; Yale Center for British Art, New Haven; London, 1988.

Register Register of Reproductions 1903–8, VII, (unpublished manuscript register in Sculpture Department archive).

Reilly 1995 R. Reilly, *Wedgwood. The New Illustrated Dictionary*, Woodbridge, 1995.

Reilly and Savage 1973 R. Reilly and G. Savage, *Wedgwood. The Portrait Medallions*, London, 1973.

Remnant 1962 G.L. Remnant, 'Jonathan Harmer's terracottas', *Sussex Archaeological Collections*, C, 1962, pp. 142–8.

Remnant 1964 G.L. Remnant, Jonathan Harmer's terracottas (II)', *Sussex Archaeological Collections*, CII, 1964, pp. 52–4.

Rendel 1972 R. Rendel, 'Francis Bird, Sculptor, 1667–1731', *Recusant History*, 11, January 1972, pp. 206–9.

Rendle and Norman 1888 W. Rendle and P. Norman, *The Inns of Old Southwark and their associations*, London, 1888.

Reverie **1992** *Reverie, Myth, Sensuality. Sculpture in Britain 1880–1910* (exh. cat.), Stoke-on-Trent City Museum and Art Gallery, Bradford, 1992.

Review **[1911–1938]** *Victoria and Albert Museum. Review of the Principal Acquisitions during the Year*, London, 1912–1939.

Rhode Island **1991** D. Rosenfeld (ed.), *European Painting and Sculpture, ca. 1770–1937 in the Museum of Art, Rhode Island School of Design*, Providence, 1991.

Robinson [n.d.] J. Robinson, *Descriptive Catalogue of the Lough and Noble Models of Statues, Bas-Reliefs and Busts in Elswick Hall*, Newcastle-upon-Tyne, [n.d.].

Robinson 1856 J.C. Robinson, *Inventory of the Objects forming the collections of the Museum of Ornamental Art*, London, 1856.

Robinson 1860 J.C. Robinson (ed.), *Inventory of the Objects forming the Collections of the Museum of Ornamental Art at South Kensington*, London, 1860.

Robinson 1861 J.C. Robinson, *Inventory of the objects forming the collections of the Museum of Ornamental Art at South Kensington*, London, 1861.

Robinson 1862 J.C. Robinson, *South Kensington Museum. Italian Sculpture of the Middle Ages and Period of the Revival of Art*, London, 1862.

Robinson 1863 J.C. Robinson, *Catalogue of the Special Exhibition of Works of Art of the Medieval, Renaissance, and more recent periods, on loan at the South Kensington Museum June 1862, Section 3. Art Bronzes*, London, 1863.

Rococo **1984** M. Snodin (ed.), *Rococo, Art and Design in Hogarth's England* (exh. cat.), Victoria and Albert Museum, London, 1984.

Rodin **1914** *Catalogue of Sculpture by Auguste Rodin*, Victoria and Albert Museum, Department of Architecture and Sculpture, London, 1914.

Rodin **1917** *Catalogue of Works by Auguste Rodin lent for Exhibition in 1917*, Victoria and Albert Museum, London, 1917.

Rodin **1925** *Catalogue of Sculpture by Auguste Rodin*,Victoria and Albert Museum, Department of Architecture and Sculpture, London, 1925.

Roget 1891 J.L. Roget, *A History of the 'Old Water-colour Society' now the Royal Society of Painters in Water Colours*, I, London, 1891.

Romantic Movement **1959** *The Romantic Movement. Fifth Exhibition to Celebrate the Tenth Anniversary of the Council of Europe* (exh. cat.), Tate Gallery and Arts Council Gallery, London; London, 1959.

Romantics to Rodin **1980** P. Fusco and H.W. Janson (eds.), *The Romantics to Rodin. French Nineteenth-Century Sculpture from North American Collections* (exh. cat.), Los Angeles County Museum of Art; Minneapolis Institute of Arts; The Detroit Institute of Arts; The Indianapolis Museum of Art; Los Angeles and New York, 1980.

Roscoe 1995 I. Roscoe, 'Of Statues, Obelisks, Dyals, and other invegetative Ornaments. Sources and meanings for English garden statues', *Apollo*, CXL, January 1995, pp. 38–42.

Roscoe 1997 I. Roscoe, "'The Statues of the Sovereigns of England': Sculpture for the Second Building, 1695–1831", in A. Saunders (ed.), *The Royal Exchange, London, Topographical Society Publication 152*, 1997, pp. 174–87.

Roscoe 1999 I. Roscoe, 'Peter Scheemakers', *The Walpole Society*, LXI, Leeds, 1999, pp. 163–304.

Rose 1982 P. Rose, *George Tinworth, Chronology of Principal Works, Harrimann-Judd Collection*, I, Los Angeles, 1982.

Royal Academy *Royal Academy Exhibitors 1905–1970. A dictionary of artists and their work in the Summer Exhibitions of the Royal Academy of Arts*, East Ardsley, (6 vols, 1973–82) (normally called Graves; see also under Graves).

Royal Academy **1890** *Royal Academy Winter Exhibition. Drawings and Models by Alfred Stevens* (exh. cat.), Royal Academy, London, pp. 43–53.

Royal Academy **1914** *Royal Academy Summer Exhibition*, 146th (exh. cat.), London, 1914.

Royal Academy **1951** *Winter Exhibition, 1951–52. The First Hundred Years of the Royal Academy 1769–1868* (exh. cat.), London, 1951.

Royal Academy **1968** *Royal Academy of Arts Bicentenary exhibition 1768–1968* (exh. cat.), London, 1968.

Royal College of Physicians **1964** G. Wolstenholme and D. Piper (eds.), *The Royal College of Physicians of London. Portraits*, London, 1964.

Royal College of Physicians **1977** G. Wolstenhome and J. Kerslake, *The Royal College of Physicians of London. Portraits, Catalogue II*, Amsterdam, Holland, New York, 1977.

Royal Glasgow Institute R. Billcliffe, *The Royal Glasgow Institute of Fine Arts 1861–1989. A Dictionary of Exhibitors at the Annual Exhibitions of the Royal Glasgow Institute of Fine Arts*, Glasgow, (3 vols), 1991–92.

Royal Hibernian Academy A.M Stewart, *Royal Hibernian Academy of Arts, Index of Exhibitors 1826–1979*, Dublin, (2 vols), 1985–86.

Royal Institute of Painters in Water Colours **1889** *Royal Institute of Painters in Water Colours. The English Humourists in Art* (exh. cat.), Piccadilly, London, 1889.

Royal Scottish Academy **1991** C. Baile de Laperriere (ed.), *The Royal Scottish Academy Exhibitors 1826–1990. A Dictionary of Artists and their Work in the Annual Exhibitions of The Royal Scottish Academy*, Calne, 1991.

Royal Society of British Sculptors **1939** *R.B.S. Modern British Sculpture*, London, 1939.

Royal Society of British Sculptors **1997** *R.S.B.S. Sculpture '97*, Autumn, London, 1997.

Ruch 1968 J.E. Ruch, 'Regency Coade: a study of the Coade record books, 1813–21', *Architectural History*, 11, 1968, pp. 34–56.

Ruch 1970 J.E. Ruch 'A Hayman Portrait of Jonathan Tyer's family', *Burlington Magazine*, CXII, August 1970, pp. 494–7.

Ruskin **1906** E.T. Cook and A. Wedderburn (eds.), *Lectures on* *landscape, Michelangelo and Tintoret, The Eagles Nest, Ariadne Florentina with notes for Other Oxford Lectures (The Works of John Ruskin)*, XXII, London, 1906.

***Ruskin* 1907** E.T. Cook and A. Wedderburn (eds.), *Fors Clavigera: Letters to the Workmen and Labourers of Great Britain, containing letters 1–36; 1871, 1872, 1873 (The Works of John Ruskin)*, I, London, 1907.

Russell 1925 A.G.B. Russell, 'The Sculpture of Cecil Thomas', *Artwork*, I, no. 4, May-August 1925, pp. 253–7.

Russell 1975 F. Russell, 'Thomas Patch, Sir William Lowther and the Holker Claude', *Apollo*, CII, August 1975, pp. 115–19.

***de Ruyter* 1957** *Michiel de Ruyter 1607–1957* (exh. cat.), Rijksmuseum, Amsterdam and Nieuw Tehuis voor Bejaarden Vlissinger, Amsterdam, 1957.

***Rysbrack* 1932** K.A. Esdaile, *The Art of John Michael Rysbrack in Terracotta* (exh. cat.), Spink & Son Ltd, London, 1932.

***Rysbrack* 1982** K. Eustace, *Michael Rysbrack Sculptor 1694–1770* (exh. cat.), City of Bristol Museum and Art Gallery, Bristol; London, 1982.

Salviati 1862 A. Salviati, *On the gold, silver and coloured enamels employed in the manufacture of mosaics*, London, 1862.

Salviati 1866 A. Salviati, *On Mosaics (generally) and the superior advantages of, adaptability, and general uses, in the past and present age, in architectural and other decorations, of enamel mosaics. With an appendix giving an account of works since executed and a description of the revival of Venetian glass-blowing*, London, 1866.

Sankey 1999 J. Sankey, 'Thomas Brock and the Albert Memorial', *Sculpture Journal*, III, 1999, pp. 87–92.

Sankey 2002 J. Sankey, *Thomas Brock and the Critics: an examination of Brock's place in the New Sculpture movement*, Phd thesis, Leeds University (to be completed 2002).

Saumarez Smith 1989 C. Saumarez Smith, 'Museums, Artefacts, and Meanings', in P. Vergo (ed.), *The New Museology*, London, 1989, pp. 6–21.

***Saur* 1996** *Allgemeines Künstler-Lexikon*, 13, Saur, Munich and Leipzig, 1996.

Scarlett 1980 K. Scarlett, *Australian Sculptors*, Melbourne, 1980.

Schaverien 1998 A. Schaverien, 'Horn, Medals and Straw: A little known link', *The Medal*, no. 32, Spring 1998, pp. 31–8.

***Scheemakers* 1996** I. Roscoe, *Peter Scheemakers 'The Famous Statuary' 1691–1781* (exh. pamphlet), The Centre for the Study of Sculpture, Leeds City Art Gallery, Leeds, 1996.

Schmidt 1957 H. Schmidt, 'Johann Jakob Flatters, ein Krefelder Schüler von Houdon, *Der Niederrhein*, no. 3, 1957, pp. 64–70.

Schmidt 1998 E.D. Schmidt, 'Giovanni Bandini tra marche e Toscana', in *Rivista di Arte Antica e Moderna*, 1998, III, pp. 57–103.

***Schreiber* 1885** *Catalogue of English Porcelain, earthenware, enamels, & c., collected by Charles Schreiber, Esq., M.P., and the Lady Charlotte Elizabeth Schreiber, and presented to the South Kensington Museum in 1884*, London, 1885.

Schroder 1988 T. Schroder, *English Domestic Silver 1500–1900*, New York, 1988.

Scott 1995 Sir G. Gilbert Scott, *Personal and Professional Recollections, (A facsimile of the original edition [1879] with new material and a critical introduction by G. Stamp)*, Stamford, 1995.

***Sculptured Memorials and Headstones* 1934** *Sculptured Memorials and Headstones Carved in British Stones* (trade catalogue), London, 1934.

***Sculpture between the Wars* 1986** B. Read and P. Skipwith, *Sculpture in Britain between the Wars* (exh. cat.), The Fine Art Society, London 1986.

Seeley 1773 B. Seeley, *Stowe: A Description Of the Magnificent House and Gardens Of the Right Honourable Richard Grenville Temple, Earl Temple, Viscount and Baron Cobham* (first published 1759), London, *1773*.

Seeley 1797 J. Seeley, *Stowe. A Description of the House and Gardens of the Most Noble & Puissant Prince, George-Granville-Nugent-Temple Marquis of Buckingham*, Buckingham and London, 1797.

***Sergel* 1990** *Sergel* (exh. cat.), Nationalmuseum, Stockholm; Udderalla, 1990.

***Sermons* 1934** *Sermons by Artists*, Golden Cockerell Press Ltd, London, 1934.

***Shakespeare* 1910** *Shakespeare Memorial and Theatrical Exhibition* (exh. cat.), Whitechapel Art Gallery, London, 1910.

***Shakespeare* 1964** *O Sweet Mr. Shakespeare I'll have his picture. The changing image of Shakespeare's person, 1600–1800* (exh. pamphlet), National Portrait Gallery, London, 1964.

Shaw 1922 H. Shaw, *Stowe House near Buckingham*, 1922.

Shaw 1989 M. Shaw, *David Kindersley: His Work and Workshop*, Cambridge, 1989.

Sherwood and Pevsner 1979 J. Sherwood and N.Pevsner, *The Buildings of England. Oxfordshire*, Harmondsworth, 1979 (reprinted from first edition published 1974).

Sichel 1909 W. Sichel, *Life of Richard Sheridan*, II, London, 1909.

***Siècle de l'élegance* 1959** *Siècle de l'élegance: la Demeure Anglaise au XVIII siécle* (exh. cat.), Museé des Arts Décoratifs, Paris, 1959.

***Singer Sargent* 1989** *John Singer Sargent* (exh. cat.), Tokyo, Yamaguchi, Kumamoto, Otsu, 1989.

Skipwith 1988 [British sculpture] P. Skipwith, 'Some aspects of twentieth century British Sculpture' (exh. review), *Burlington Magazine*, CXXX, December 1988, pp. 948–9.

Skipwith 1988 [Ledward] P. Skipwith, 'Gilbert Ledward R.A. and the Guards' Divison Memorial', *Apollo*, CXXVII, January 1988, pp. 22–6.

Slomann 1932 V. Slomann, 'M.H. Spang En Dansk billedhugger fra det, 18. aarhundrere', *Tilskueren*, March 1932, pp. 177–84.

Smailes 1987 H. Smailes, 'Thomas Campbell and the "camera lucida": the Buccleuch statue of the 1st Duke of Wellington', *Burlington Magazine*, CXXIX, November 1987, pp. 709–14.

Smith 1828 J.T. Smith, *Nollekens and his Times*, II, London, 1828.

Smith 1893 C. Smith, *The Ancient and Present State of the County and City of York. Containing a Natural, Civil, Ecclesiastical, Historical, and Topographical Description Thereof*, I, Cork, 1893.

Smith 1916 A.H. Smith, 'Lord Elgin and his collection', *Journal of Hellenistic Studies*, XXXVI, 1916, pp. 163–372.

Smith 1920 J.T. Smith, *Nollekens and his Times*, (2 vols), edited by W. Whitten, London and New York, 1920 (first published 1828).

Smith 1996 N. Smith, "Great Nassau's Image, 'Royal George's Test", *Georgian Group Journal*, VI, 1996, pp. 12–23.

Snodin 1998 'Sir William Chambers chimneypiece from the Great Dining Room, Gower House', *National Art Collections Fund Review 1997*, London, 1998, p. 103.

Snodin and Styles 2001 M. Snodin and J. Styles, *Design & the Decorative Arts: Britain 1500–1900*, London, 2001.

***SNPG* 1990** *The Concise Catalogue of the Scottish National Portrait Gallery*, compiled by H. Smailes, Edinburgh, 1990.

***Soane* 1999** M. Richardson and M. Stevens (eds.), *John Soane. Architect. Master of Space and Light* (exh. cat.), Royal Academy, London, 1999.

***Society of Antiquaries* 1917** *Proceedings of the Society of Antiquaries of London, 23rd November 1916 to 28 June 1917*, Second Series, XXIX, Oxford, 1917, pp. 214–7.

***Society of Antiquaries* 1977** *National Monuments, Society of Antiquaries of London, Report of the Sepulchral Monuments Committee*, London, 1977.

***Society of Women Artists* 1922** *The Society of Women Artists Sixty-Seventh Exhibition* (exh. cat.), London, 1922.

***Society of Women Artists* 1996** C. Baile de Laperriere (ed.) and J. Soden, *The Society of Women Artists Exhibitors 1855–1996. A dictionary of artists and their works in the annual exhibitions of the Society of Women Artists*, Calne, 1996.

Solkin 1992 D.H. Solkin, *Painting for Money. The Visual Arts and the Public Sphere in Eighteenth-Century England*, New Haven and London, 1992.

Somers Cocks 1976 A. Somers Cocks, 'Intaglios and Cameos in the Jewellery Collection of the V&A', *Burlington Magazine*, CXVIII, June 1976, pp. 366–76.

Southern 1925 R. Southern, 'Alfred Stevens of Blandford. The Perfection of Victorian Art', *The Dorset Year Book*, XXI, 1925, pp. 36–44.

Spencer-Longhurst and Naylor 1998 P. Spencer-Longhurst and A. Naylor, 'Nost's Equestrian George I Restored', *Sculpture Journal*, II, 1998, pp. 31–40.

Spielmann 1901 M.H. Spielmann, *British Sculpture and Sculptors of ToDay*, London, 1901.

Spiers 1919 W.L. Spiers, 'The note-book and account book of Nicholas Stone, Master Mason to James I and Charles I', transcribed and annotated with an introduction by W.L. Spiers, in A.J. Finberg (ed.), *The Seventh Volume of the Walpole Society 1918–19*, Oxford, 1919.

Spink 1976 R. Spink, 'Sculptor of Gods and Madmen. Caius Gabriel Cibber, 1630–1700', *Country Life*, CLIX, 22 January 1976, p. 208.

***Stadhouder-Koning* 1950** *De Stadhouder-Koning en zijn tijd 1650–1950* (exh. cat.), Rijksmuseum, Amsterdam, 1950.

Stainton 1974 L. Stainton, 'A Re-discovered Bas-Relief by Thomas Banks', *Burlington Magazine*, CXVI, June 1974, pp. 327–31.

Staley 1903 E. Staley, 'Edward Lantéri, Artist and Teacher', *Art Journal*, 1903, pp. 241–5.

Stannus 1891 H. Stannus, *Alfred Stevens and his work*, London, 1891.

Staring 1965 A. Staring, 'Een Borstbeeld van de Konig-Stadhouder', *Oud-Holland*, LXXX, no. 1, 1965, pp. 221–7.

Stenton and Lees 1978 M. Stenton and S. Lees, *Who's Who of British Members of Parliament. A Biographical Dictionary of the House of Commons. Based on annual volumes of 'Dod's Parliamentary Companion' and other sources*, 1886–1918, Hassocks, 1978.

***Stevens* 1911** *Catalogue of Loan Collection of Works by Alfred Stevens* (exh. pamphlet), The National Gallery, British Art, London, 1911.

***Stevens* 1912** *Loan Collection of Works by Alfred Stevens* (exh. pamphlet), Mappin Art Gallery, Sheffield, 1912.

***Stevens* 1926** *Victoria and Albert Museum, Picture Book of the Work of Alfred Stevens*, London, 1926.

Stevens 1971 T. Stevens, 'Roman heyday of an English Sculptor', *Apollo*, XCIV, September 1971, pp. 226–31.

***Stevens* 1975** S. Beattie, *Alfred Stevens 1817–75*, London, 1975.

Stevens 1989 [Frampton] T. Stevens, 'George Frampton', in *Patronage & Practice: Sculpture on Merseyside*, P. Curtis (ed.), Liverpool, 1989, pp. 74–85.

Stevens 1989 [Liverpool] T. Stevens, 'Sculptors working in Liverpool in the early Nineteenth Century', in P. Curtis (ed.), *Patronage & Practice: Sculpture on Merseyside*, Liverpool, 1989, pp. 42–9.

Stewart 1978 A. Douglas Stewart, 'New Light on Michael Rysbrack: Augustan England's 'Classical Baroque' Sculptor', *Burlington Magazine*, CXX, April 1978, pp. 214–22.

Stocker 1985 M. Stocker, 'Joseph Edgar Boehm and Thomas Carlyle', *Carlyle Newsletter*, 6, 1985, pp. 11–23.

Stocker 1988 M. Stocker, *Royalist and Realist. The Life and Work of Sir Joseph Edgar Boehm*, New York and London, 1986

***Stone* 1982** *Reynolds Stone 1909–1979*, An Exhibition held in the Library of the Victoria and Albert Museum (exh. cat.), Victoria and Albert Museum, London, 1982.

Strickland 1913 W.G. Strickland, *A Dictionary of Irish Artists*, Dublin and London, 1913.

Stow 1908 J. Stow, *A Survey of London* (reprinted from text of 1603 by C.L. Kingsford), II, Oxford, 1908.

***Studio* 1896** E.B.S., 'A Chat with Mr George Frampton, ARA', *Studio*, VI, January 1896, pp. 205–13.

***Studio* 1899** 'The Work of Christopher Dresser', *Studio*, XV, 1899, pp. 104–14.

***Studio* 1903** 'A Young Sculptor: Mr Reginald F. Wells and his rustic art', *Studio*, XXVIII, no. 119, February 1903, pp. 17–22.

***Studio* 1932** 'New Sculptures by Maurice Lambert', *Studio*, CIII, June 1932, pp. 333–6.

***Style, Truth and the Portrait* 1963** R. G. Saisselin, *Style, Truth and the Portrait* (exh. cat.) The Cleveland Museum of Art, Cleveland, 1963.

Sullivan [forthcoming] G. Sullivan, 'More Revisions to the Nost Family History: Frances Nost, a Monumental Matron' (forthcoming).

***Supplement* [n.d.]** *Illustrated Supplement to the Catalogue of Plaster Casts, Victoria and Albert Museum*, London, undated.

Sutton 1972 D. Sutton (editorial), 'A Born Virtuoso', *Apollo*, XCV, March 1972, pp. 156–61.

Sutton 1973 D. Sutton, 'The faire majestic paradise of Stowe', *Apollo*, XCVII, June 1973, pp. 542–51.

Sutton 1974 D. Sutton (editorial), 'Magick Land', *Apollo*, XCIX, June 1974, pp. 392–407.

Szpila 1997 K. Szpila, 'An eighteenth-century English Artemisia. Sarah Churchill and the Invention of the Blenheim Memorials', in C. Lawrence (ed.), *Women and Art in Early Modern Europe. Patrons, Collectors, and Connoisseurs*, Pennsylvania, 1997.

Tait 1965 H. Tait, 'Cannel carvings and Robert Town of Wigan', *Connoisseur*, CLVIII, February 1965, pp. 92–9.

Tanner 1991 S. Tanner, *'A devoted attention to business: an obituary of Philip Rundell', Silver Society Journal*, Winter 1991, pp. 91–102.

***Tate* 1947** *Tate Gallery Millbank. Catalogue British School*, 25th edition 1936–7, London, 1947.

***Tate* 1953** M. Chamont, *Tate Gallery. British School. A concise catalogue*, London, 1953.

***Tate* 1959** R. Alley, *Tate Gallery. The foreign paintings, drawings and sculpture*, London, 1959.

***Tate* 1963/4** *Tate Gallery Report to the Trustees*, London, 1963/4.

***Tate* 1964** M. Chamont, D. Farr and M. Butlin, *Tate Gallery. The modern British paintings, drawings and sculpture*, I, London, 1964.

TDA J. Turner (ed.), *The Dictionary of Art*, (34 vols), London and New York, 1996.

Thieme-Becker U. Thieme and F. Becker, *Allgemeines Lexikon der Bildenden Kunstler* (37 vols), Leipzig, first published 1907/8 onwards; reprinted 1992.

***Thirties* 1979** J.H. Hawkins and M Hollis (eds.), *Thirties: British Art and Design before the War* (exh. cat.), Hayward Gallery, Arts Council of Great Britain, London, 1979.

Thomas 1921 C. Thomas, '"Blue John" The Collection of the Rt. Hon. the Earl Howe, G.C.V.O.', *Connoisseur*, LXI, November 1921, pp. 147–51.

***Thomas* 1925** *Cecil Thomas. Catalogue of Sculpture Portrait busts, reliefs and statuettes* (exh. cat.), Gieves Art Gallery, London, 1925.

Thomas 1982 T.D.L. Thomas, 'Devotion to natural form. The work of Albert Bruce-Joy (1842–1924)', *Country Life*, CLXXI, pp. 1688–9.

Thomas Albums Three unpublished albums of the work of Cecil Thomas (no text), 1905–1972, held at the National Art Library (inv.nos. L.309 to 11–1972) Pressmark 64.G.57, 64.G.57A and 64.G.57B.

***Thomas Coram Foundation* 1965** *The Thomas Coram Foundation for Children. Catalogue of Pictures, Works of Art and Historical Documents and Relics*, London, 1965.

Thomassin 1694 S. Thomassin, *Recueil des figures, groupes, thermes, fontaines, vases et autres Ornamens tels qui'ls se voyent present dans le Château et Parc de Versailles, grand d'apres les Originaux*, Paris, 1694.

***Thorvaldsen* 1990** E. di Majo, B. Jørnaes, S. Susinno (eds.), *Bertel Thorvaldsen 1770–1844 sculptore danese a Roma* (exh. cat.), Galleria Nazionale d'Arte Moderna, Rome, 1990.

***Three Graces* 1995** H. Honour and A. Weston-Lewis (eds.), *The Three Graces. Antonio Canova* (exh. cat.), National Gallery of Scotland, Edinburgh, 1995.

Throsby 1789 J. Throsby, *Select views of Leicestershire. From Original Drawings: Containing Seats of the Nobility and Gentry, Town Views and Ruins. Accompanied with Descriptive and Historical Relations*, I, Leicester, 1789.

Timbs 1855 J. Timbs, *Curiosities of London exhibiting the most remarkable objects of interest in the Metropolis*, London, 1855.

***Tinworth* [n.d.]** *Catalogue of an exhibition of the works of Mr George Tinworth, held at the premises of Messrs Doulton and Co., Lambeth*, [n.d.] [c.1896/7].

***Tinworth* 1883** *Catalogue of a Collection of Works in Terra Cotta by George Tinworth. The Works of George Tinworth*, introduction by E.W. Gosse (exh. pamphlet), Conduit Street Galleries, Regent Street, London; London, 1883.

***Tinworth* 1906** *Royal Doulton Potteries Sculpture in Terracotta by George Tinworth*, London, 1906.

Tollemache 1949 E.D.H. Tollemache, *The Tollemaches of Helmingham and Ham*, Ipswich, 1949.

Tomalin 1975 G.H.J. Tomalin, *The Book of Henley-on-Thames*, Chesham, 1975.

Tomory 1963 P.A. Tomory, *Sculpture in France, Auckland City Art Gallery*, Auckland, New Zealand, 1963.

***Topographer* 1789** *The Topographer for the year 1789, containing a variety of original articles, illustrative of the local History and Antiquities of England*, I, no. 2, London, May 1789.

Towndrow 1939 K.R. Towndrow, *Alfred Stevens*, London, 1939.

Towndrow 1950 K.R. Towndrow, *The Works of Alfred Stevens in the Tate Gallery*, London, 1950.

Towndrow 1951 K.R. Towndrow, *Alfred Stevens*, Walker Art Gallery monograph, no. 1, Liverpool, 1951.

Toynbee 1928 P. Toynbee, 'Horace Walpole's Journals of Visits to Country Seats, &c', in P. Toynbee (ed.), *The Walpole Society*, XVI, 1927–8, Oxford, 1928, pp. 9–80.

***Treasures* 2000** *Treasures of Catherine the Great* (exh. cat.), Somerset House, London, 2000.

***Treasure Houses* 1985** G. Jackson-Stops (ed.), *Treasure Houses of Britain. Five Hundred Years of Private Patronage and Art Collecting* (exh. cat.), National Gallery of Art, Washington; Washington and New Haven, 1985.

Tresham Lever 1971 *Sir Tresham Lever, Clayton of Toc H*, London, 1971.

Trusted 1992 "'A Man of Talent": Agostino Carlini (c. 1718–1790): Part I', *Burlington Magazine*, CXXXIV, December 1992, pp. 776–84.

Trusted 1993 M. Trusted, "'A Man of Talent": Agostino Carlini (c. 1718–1790): Part II', *Burlington Magazine*, CXXV, March 1993, pp. 190–201.

Trusted 1996 [Dressler] M. Trusted, 'Dressler's terracotta bust of his wife at the V&A', *Apollo*, CXLIII, January 1996, p. 50.

Trusted 1996 [Spanish] M. Trusted, *Spanish Sculpture. A Catalogue of the Post-Medieval Spanish Sculpture in Wood, Terracotta, Alabaster, Marble, Stone, Lead and Jet in the Victoria and Albert Museum*, London, 1996.

Tuff 1858 J. Tuff, *Historical, Topographical and Statistical Notices of Enfield in the County of Middlesex, containing also brief biographical notices of distinguished persons who formerly resided in the parish*, Enfield, 1858.

***Turner* 1988** N. Penny (ed.), *Alfred and Winifred Turner. The Sculpture of Alfred Turner and Winifred Turner* (exh. cat.), Ashmolean Museum, Oxford, 1988.

Turner 1999 M. Turner, *Eltham Palace* (guide book), London, 1999.

***Tweed* 1934** *John Tweed. Memorial Exhibition*, 22 June to 15 July 1934, Imperial Gallery of Art, Imperial Institute, London, 1934.

Tweed 1936 L. Tweed, *John Tweed: Sculptor. A Memoir*, London, 1936.

Underwood 1934 [Art] L. Underwood, *Art for Heaven's Sake*, London, 1934.

***Underwood* 1934 [Leicester]** *Catalogue of an exhibition of sculpture, paintings and engravings by Leon Underwood* (exh. cat.), The Leicester Galleries, Leicester Square, London, 1934.

***Underwood* 1969** *Leon Underwood: a retrospective exhibition* (exh. cat.), The Minories, Colchester, 1969.

***Underwood* 1993** *Pure Plastic Rythym. Leon Underwood 1890–1975. Drawings, watercolours and sculpture, 1922–1939* (exh. cat.), Wolseley Fine Arts, London; Worthing Museum and Art Gallery, Worthing; National Museum of Wales, Cardiff; London, 1993.

Usherwood, Beach and Morris 2000 P. Usherwood, J. Beach and C. Morris, *Public Sculpture of North-East England*, Liverpool, 2000.

***V&A Album* 1988** 'Spotlight on acquisitions', *The V&A Album*, Autumn 1988, p. 8 and front cover.

***V&A Magazine* 1998** *V&A Magazine*, January – April 1998, London, 1998.

***V&A Magazine* 2000 [I]** *V&A Magazine*, May – August 2000, London, 2000.

V&A Magazine 2000 [II] *V&A Magazine*, September – December 2000, London, 2000.
Valadier 1991 *Valadier. Three Generations of Roman Goldsmiths. An Exhibition of Drawings and Works of Art* (exh. cat.), David Carritt Ltd, London, 1991.
Verey 1979 D. Verey, *The Buildings of England. Gloucestershire I. The Cotswolds* (first published 1970), Harmondsworth, 1979.
Verstegan 1634 R. Verstegan, *A Restitution of Decayed Intelligence In antiquities Concerning the most noble, and renowned English Nation. By the study, and travell of R.V.*, London, 1634.
Vertue 1934 *Vertue Note books*, III, *The Walpole Society*, XXII, 1933–4, Oxford, 1934.
Vertue 1938 *Vertue Note books*, V, *The Walpole Society*, XXVI, 1937–8, Oxford, 1938.
Victorian 1978 *Victorian High Renaissance* (exh. cat.), City Art Gallery, Manchester, The Minneapolis Institute of Arts, Minneapolis; The Brooklyn Museum, New York; Minneapolis, 1978.
Victorian Church Art 1971 *Victorian Church Art* (exh. cat.), Victoria and Albert Museum, London, 1971.
Villani 1991 R.R. Villani, 'Il "Busto di Negro" di Francis Harwood del J. Paul Getty Museum di Malibu', *Paragone*, XLII, no. 28, 497, July 1991, pp. 68–74.
Virtue and Vision 1991 F. Pearson (ed.), *Virtue and Vision. Sculpture and Scotland 1540–1990* (exh. cat.), Royal Scottish Academy, Edinburgh, 1991.
Vivian-Neal 1935 A.W. Vivian-Neal, 'Sculptures by Grinling Gibbons and Quellin originally at Whitehall, later in Westminster Abbey, now in the Church of Burnham-on-Sea', *Proceedings of the Somersetshire Archeological and Natural History Society for the Year 1935*, LXXXI, Taunton, 1936, pp. 127–32.
Vlieghe 1987 H. Vlieghe, *Rubens Portraits of identified sitters painted in Antwerp*, II, New York, 1987 (from L. Burchand, XIX, Corpus Rubenianum).

Wake 1988 J. Wake, *Princess Louise. Queen Victoria's Unconventional Daughter*, London, 1988.
Walker 1994 [Dressler] R.P. Walker, 'Conrad Dressler and the Medmenham Pottery', *The Decorative Arts Society Journal*, 18, York 1994, pp. 50–60.
Walker 1994 [Odescalchi] S. Walker, 'The Sculpture gallery of Prince Odescalchi', *Journal of the History of Collections*, 6, no. 2, 1994, pp. 189–219.
Walpole 1927 H. Walpole, *Strawberry Hill Accounts* (originally published 1784), Oxford, 1927.
Ward-Jackson 1992 P. Ward-Jackson,'Birmingham. Pre-Raphaelite sculpture' (exh. review), *Burlington Magazine*, CXXXIV, February 1992, pp. 134–5.
Ward-Jackson 2000 P. Ward-Jackson, 'Carlo Marochetti: Maintaining Distinction in an International Sculpture Market', in C. Sicca and A. Yarrington (eds.), *The Lustrous Trade. Material Culture and the History of Sculpture in England and Italy c. 1700-c. 1860* (papers from an international workshop, Opera della Primaziale, Pisa), London and New York, 2000, pp. 174–90.
Ward-Jackson 2002 P. Ward-Jackson, *Public Sculpture of the City of London*, Liverpool, 2002.
Wardropper 2000 I. Wardropper, 'A Silver Relief of the *Crucifixion of St Peter* by Luigi Valadier', *Sculpture Journal*, IV, 2000, pp. 79–84.
Ware 1796 I. Ware, *A Complete Body of Architecture adorned with plans and elevations from original designs*, London, 1796.
Waring 1863 J.B. Waring, *Masterpieces of Industrial Art and Sculpture at the International Exhibition, 1862*, III, London, 1863.
Wark 1970 R.R. Wark, *Drawings by John Flaxman in the Huntington Collection*, San Marino, 1970.
Waterhouse 1958 E. Waterhouse, *Gainsborough*, London, 1958.
Watson 1963 F.J.B. Watson, 'A Bust of Fiammingo by Rysbrack Rediscovered', *Burlington Magazine*, CV, October 1963, pp. 441–5.
Watson 1986 J.N.P. Watson, 'An affinity with babes and beasts. Randolph Caldecott as animal artist', *Country Life*, CLXXX, July 17 1986, pp. 148–9.
Weaver 1972 L. Weaver, *English Leadwork. Its Art & History*, London, 1972 (first published 1909).
Webb 1893 [Of Carving] S. Webb, 'Of Carving', *Arts & Crafts Essays*, 1893, p. 322.
Webb 1893 [Woods] S. Webb, 'Woods and other materials', *Arts & Crafts Essays*, 1893, p. 345.
Webb 1928 [I] G. Webb, 'Notes on Hubert Le Sueur – I', *Burlington Magazine*, LII, January 1928, pp. 10–16.
Webb 1928 (II) G. Webb, 'Notes on Hubert Le Sueur – II', *Burlington Magazine*, LII, February 1928, pp. 81–8.
Webb 1950 M.I. Webb, 'Sculpture by Rysbrack at Stourhead', *Burlington Magazine*, XCII, November 1950, pp. 307–15.
Webb 1952 M.I. Webb, 'Busts of Sir Isaac Newton', *Country Life*, CXI, 25 January 1952, pp. 216–8.
Webb 1954 M.I. Webb, *Michael Rysbrack Sculptor*, London, 1954.
Webb 1955 M.I. Webb, 'Giovanni Battista Guelfi: an Italian Sculptor working in England', *Burlington Magazine*, XCVII, May 1955, pp. 139–45.
Webb 1958 [I] M.I. Webb, 'Henry Cheere, Sculptor and Businessman and John Cheere' Part I, *Burlington Magazine*, C, July 1958, pp. 232–40.
Webb 1958 [II] M.I. Webb, 'Henry Cheere, Sculptor and Businessman and John Cheere' Part II, *Burlington Magazine*, C, August 1958, pp. 274–9.
Wedgwood 1973 R. Reilly, *Wedgwood Portrait Medallions* (exh. cat.), National Portrait Gallery, London, 1973.
Wedgwood 1995 H. Young (ed.), *The Genius of Wedgwood* (exh. cat.), Victoria and Albert Museum, London, 1995.
Weekes 1852 H. Weekes, *The Prize Treatise of the Fine Arts Section of the Great Exhibition of 1851*, London, 1852.
Weekes 1880 H. Weekes, *Lectures on Art, delivered at the Royal Academy*, London, 1880.
Wells 1998 *Reginald Fairfax Wells Sculptor Potter Designer 1877–1951* (exh. pamplet), Luton Museum and Art Gallery, Luton, 1998.
Westminster Abbey 1995 R. Cocke, *900 Years: The Restoration of Westminster Abbey* (exh. cat.), St Margaret's Church, Westminster and the Masons' Yard, Westminster Abbey, London, 1995.
Wheeler and Hayward 1978 W. Wheeler and C.H. Hayward, *Practical Woodcarving and Gilding*, London, 1978 (first published 1963).
Whiffen 1950 M. Whiffen, *Thomas Archer*, London, 1950.
Whinney 1961 M. Whinney, 'Handel and Roubiliac', *Musical Times*, no. 1416, February 1961, pp. 82–5.
Whinney 1965 M. Whinney, 'Flaxman at Covent Garden', *About the House*, June 1965, pp. 24–9.
Whinney 1971 M. Whinney, *English Sculpture 1720–1830*, London, 1971.
Whinney 1988 M. Whinney, *Sculpture in Britain 1530 to 1830* (revised by J. Physick), London, 1988 (second edition).

Whinney and Gunnis 1967 M. Whinney and R. Gunnis, *The Collection of Models by John Flaxman at University College London*, London, 1967.

Whitaker 1891 C.W. Whitaker, *An illustrated historical, statistical & topographical account of the urban district of Enfield*, London, 1891.

White 1985 A. White, 'Classical Learning and The Early Stuart Renaissance', *Journal of the Church Monuments Society*, I, 1985, pp. 20–33.

White 1999 A. White, 'A Biographical Dictionary of London Tomb Sculptors c. 1560-c. 1660', *The Walpole Society*, LXI, Leeds, 1999, pp. 1–162.

Whitfield 1973 P. Whitfield, 'Bankruptcy and Sale at Stowe: 1848', *Apollo*, XCVII, June 1973, pp. 599–604.

Whitworth 2000 B. Whitworth, *The Sculpture of Leon Underwood*, Much Hadham and Aldershot, 2000.

***Who's Who* 2000** *Who's Who 2000. An annual biographical dictionary*, London, 2000.

***Who Was Who* 1979** *Who Was Who 1961–1970*, VI, London, 1979.

***Who Was Who* 1981** *Who Was Who 1971–1980*, VII, London, 1981.

Wiles [n.d.] R McKeen Wiles, 'The Contemporary Distribution of Johnson's Rambler', *Eighteenth Century Studies*, 2, no. 2, pp. 155–71.

Willame 1914 G. Willame, *Laurent Delvaux 1696–1778*, Brussels and Paris, 1914.

Williamson 1991 P. Williamson, 'Acquisitions of Sculpture at the Victoria and Albert Museum, 1986–1991', *Burlington Magazine*, CXXXIII, December 1991, pp. 876–80.

Williamson 1993 P. Williamson 'John Gordon Beckwith 1918–1991', *Proceedings of the British Academy*, 80, 1991 Lectures and Memoirs, Oxford, 1993, pp. 233–43.

Williamson 1996 P. Williamson (ed.), *European Sculpture at the Victoria and Albert Museum*, London, 1996.

Williamson 1999 P. Williamson, 'Acquisitions of sculpture at the Victoria and Albert Museum, 1992–1999', *Burlington Magazine*, CXLI, December 1999, pp. 783–88.

Wills 1962 G. Wills, 'A Victorian Sculptor: Samuel James Bouverie Haydon (1815–91)', *Apollo*, LXXVI, December 1962, pp. 785–7.

Wilmot 1891 T. Wilmot, 'John Warrington Wood, Sculptor', *Magazine of Art*, XIV, November 1890 to October 1891, pp. 136–140.

Wilson 1896 C.R. Wilson, *List of Inscriptions on tombs or monuments in Bengall Possessing Historical or archaeological interest*, Calcutta, 1896.

Wimsatt 1965 W.K. Wimsatt, *The Portraits of Alexander Pope*, New Haven and London, 1965.

***Wolverhampton* 1913** J. Brownswood, *County Borough of Wolverhampton Art Gallery and Museum, Catalogue of the permanent collection of pictures and other works of art*, Wolverhampton, 1913.

Wood 1912 Sir H.T. Wood, 'The Royal Society of Arts. VIII – The Society and the Fine Arts (1755–1851)', *Journal of the Royal Society of Arts*, LX, 14 June 1912, pp. 732–55.

Wood 1999 J. Wood, 'Raphael Copies and Exemplary Picture Galleries in Mid Eighteenth-Century London', *Zeitschrift für Kunstgeschichte*, 3, 1999, pp. 394–417.

Worsley 1987 G. Worsley, 'Naworth Castle, Cumberland – I. The Seat of the Earl of Carlisle', *Country Life*, CLXXXI, 12 February 1987, pp. 74–9.

***Wren Society* 1930** *The Seventh Volume of the Wren Society 1930. The Royal Palaces of Winchester, Whitehall Kensington, and St James's*, Oxford, 1930.

***Wren Society* 1933** *The Tenth Volume of the Wren Society 1933. The Parochial Churches of Sir Christopher Wren 1666–1718*, II, Oxford, 1933.

***Wren Society* 1940** *The Seventeenth Volume of the Wren Society 1940. Designs and drawings supplementary to volume XII*, 1935, XVII, Oxford, 1940.

Wylde 1981 P. Wylde 'The First Exhibition: The Architectural Association and the Royal Architectural Museum', *The Architectural Association Annual Review*, 1981, pp. 8–14.

***Yale* 1998** *Yale Center for British Art Calendar of Events*, Spring, New Haven, 1998.

Yarrington 1994 A. Yarrington et al., *'The [Chantrey] Ledgers', The Walpole Society, LVI, 1991/1992, An Edition of the Ledger of Sir Francis Chantrey, R.A., at the Royal Academy, 1809–1841*, Leeds, 1994.

Yarrington 1997 A. Yarrington, 'The Female Pygmalion: Anne Seymour Damer, Allan Cunningham and the writing of a woman sculptor's life', *Sculpture Journal*, I, 1997, pp. 32–44.

Yarrington 2000 A. Yarrington, 'Anglo-Italian Attitudes: Chantrey and Canova', in C. Sicca and A. Yarrington (eds.), *The Lustrous Trade. Material Culture and the History of Sculpture in England and Italy c. 1700-c. 1860* (papers from an international workshop, Opera della Primaziale, Pisa), London and New York, 2000, pp. 132–55.

Index of sculptors

INDEX OF SUBJECTS

Index of Provenances and Donors

This index comprises names of previous owners, sale-rooms, and former locations of objects, as well as individuals and institutions who have contributed funds towards acquisitions.

Index of inventory numbers

Appendix I

Transfers of Twentieth-Century British Sculpture from the Victoria and Albert Museum to the Tate Gallery in 1983 (published in *The Tate Gallery. Illustrated Catalogue of Acquisitions 1982–84*, London, 1986), with the exception of the maquettes and later models related to the Waterloo Bridge project by Barbara Hepworth which were transferred in 2001; see below.

Kenneth Armitage (b.1916)
Seated woman with square head, bronze, 1955 (V&A inv.no. Circ.182–1960; Tate inv.no. T03708)

Charles Henry Blaymires (1908–after 1970)
Lettering, 'To be afraid', incised panel, about 1925 (V&A inv.no. Circ.175–1927; Tate inv.no. T03709)

Alan Bridgewater (1903–1962)
Panel in lettering, 'Remember Jane Snowfield 1854–1927', 1927 (V&A inv.no. Circ.636–1927; Tate inv.no. T03710)

Reg Butler (1913–1981)
Crouching woman, wrought iron, 1948 (V&A inv.no. Circ.98–1954; Tate inv.no. T03711)

Lynn Chadwick (b.1914)
Conjunction, wrought iron and composition, 1953 (V&A inv.no. Circ.37–1954; Tate inv.no. T03712)

Geoffrey Clarke (b.1924)
Head, forged iron, 1952 (V&A inv.no. Circ.3–1953; Tate inv.no. T03713)

Robert Clatworthy (b.1928)
Bull, study in cast bronze, 1956 (V&A inv.no. Circ.179–1957; Tate inv.no. T03714)

Hubert Dalwood (1924–1976)
Lucca, cast aluminum sculpture, 1958 (V&A inv.no. Circ.243–1960; Tate inv.no. T03716)

Michael Dillon (b.1941)
Op structure, construction, perspex, 1967 (V&A inv.no. Circ.982–1967; Tate inv.no. T03718)
Op structure, construction, perspex, 1967 (V&A inv.no. Circ.983–1967; Tate inv.no. T03717)

Frank Dobson (1888–1963)
Crouching woman, bronze, 1923 (V&A inv.no. A.32–1971; Tate inv.no. T03721)
Charnaux Venus, model in composition for display figure 'Charnaux Corsets', 1933–4, (V&A inv.no. A.24–1934; Tate inv.no. T03719)
Female kneeling figure, terracotta, 1935 (V&A inv.no. Circ.320–1938; Tate inv.no. T03720)

John Doubleday (b.1947)
Maquette for 'Building blocks', 1964 (V&A inv.no. A.26–1979; Tate inv.no. T03722)

John Ernest (1922–1994)
Triangulated relief 1, relief construction, wood, formica and PVC, 1965 (V&A inv.no. Circ.835–1968; Tate inv.no. T03723)

Frederick Etchells (1886–1973)
Memorial tablet with incised lettering, 'Let us now Praise Famous Men', Hopton Wood stone, 1925 (V&A inv.no. A.47–1934; Tate inv.no. T03724)

Barry Flanagan (b.1941)
Sand muslin 2, 1966, sand and muslin (V&A inv.no. Circ.38&A–1972; Tate inv.no. T03725)

Eric Gill (1882–1940)
Alphabet and numerals, Hopton Wood stone relief, 1909 (V&A inv.no. A.25–1931; Tate inv.no. T03733)
Two alphabets and numerals, Hopton Wood stone relief, 1909 (V&A inv.no. A.26–1931; Tate inv.no. T03734)
Alphabet of capitals, Hopton Wood stone relief, 1909 (V&A inv.no. A.27–1931; Tate inv.no. T03735)
Crucifix, Hopton Wood stone relief, about 1913 (V&A inv.no. A.10–1938; Tate inv.no. T03736)
St Sebastian, Portland stone figure, 1920 (V&A inv.no. A.10–1934; Tate inv.no. T03745)
Plaque with the inscription: 'HOMINES· DIVITES·IN·VIRTUTE/PULCHRITUDINIS STUDIUM·HABENTES/PACIFICANTES·IN·DOMIBUS·SUIS', Portland stone, 1922 (V&A inv.no. Misc.1–1947; Tate inv.no. T03741)
Plaque with the inscription: 'IN TERRA PAX HOMINIBUS/BONAE VOLUNTATIS', slate, 1922 (V&A inv.no. Misc.2–1947; Tate inv.no. T03742)
Plaque with the inscription: 'GLORIA/IN ALTISSIMIS/DEO', slate, 1922 (V&A inv.no. Misc.3–1947; Tate inv.no. T03743)
Sundial with inscription: 'PENSA CHE QUESTO DI/MAI NON RAGGIORNA', slate and metal, 1923–4 (V&A inv.no. Misc.4–1947; Tate inv.no. T03744)
Inscription 'EX DIVINA/PVLCHRITVDINE/ESSE OMNIVM/DERIVATVR', Hopton Wood stone relief, 1926 (V&A inv.no. Circ.959–1926; Tate inv.no. T03738)
Alphabet, Hopton Wood stone relief, 1927 (V&A inv.no. Circ.530–1927; Tate inv.no. T03740)
Alphabet of raised letters, Hopton Wood stone relief, 1927 (V&A inv.no.Circ.531–1927; Tate inv.no. T03739)
Nude figure relief (study in reverse for the North Wind on the East face of the South wing of St James's Park Underground building), stone, 1929 (V&A inv.no A.10–1942; Tate inv.no. T03737)

Dora Gordine (1906–1991)
Guadaloupe head, bronze, about 1925–7 (V&A inv.no Circ.80–1952; Tate inv.no. T03746)

Barbara Hepworth (1903–1975)
Involute II, bronze sculpture one of six casts made, 1956 (V&A inv.no. Circ.249–1960; Tate inv.no. T03749)
Maquette for Waterloo Bridge, limestone, about 1947 (V&A inv.no. Unregistered 347); plus three plaster models made in the 1950s in the Victoria and Albert Museum; transferred in 2001

Anthony Hill (b.1930)
Low relief, perspex, 1955–66 (V&A inv.no. Circ.819–1968; Tate inv.no. T05502)

Relief construction, aluminium and perspex, 1963 (V&A inv.no. Circ.581–1968; Tate inv. no. T03750)

John Hoskin (1921–1990)

Black beetle, iron figure, 1957 (V&A inv.no. Circ.188–1957; Tate inv.no. T03752)

Malcolm Hughes (1920–1997)

Maquette for 'Square relief', card and hardboard, 1968 (V&A inv.no. Circ.76–1969; Tate inv.no. T03753)

Large square relief, plywood, hardboard and PVA, 1968 (V&A inv.no. Circ.77–1969; Tate inv.no. T03754)

Louise Hutchinson (1882–1968)

Three-fold head, terracotta, about 1953 (V&A inv.no. Circ.74–1964; Tate inv.no. T03751)

Sir William Goscombe John (1860–1952)

Pan, bronze statuette, 1901 (V&A inv.no. A.7–1973; Tate inv.no. T03747)

Karin Jonzen (1914–1998)

Head of a youth, terracotta, about 1947–8 (V&A inv.no. Circ.95–1964; Tate inv.no. T03755)

Maurice Lambert (1901–1964)

Man with a bird, marble, 1929 (V&A inv.no. A.35–1930; Tate inv.no. T03756)

F.E. McWilliam (1909–1992)

Mother and daughter, walnut plastic wood group, 1951 (V&A inv.no. Circ.2–1953; Tate inv.no. T03758)

Bernard Meadows (b.1915)

Crab, painted bronze sculpture, 1952 (V&A inv.no. Circ.4–1953; Tate inv.no. T03759)

Henry Moore (1898–1922)

Mask, concrete, 1929 (V&A inv.no. Circ.11–1950; Tate inv.no. T03762)

Reclining figure, lead, 1939 (V&A inv.no. Circ.17–1940; Tate inv.no. T03761)

Three motives against a wall no. 1, 1958, bronze (V&A inv.no. Circ.234–196; Tate inv.no. T03763)

Sir Eduardo Paolozzi (b.1924)

Mr Cruikshank, bronze bust, 1950 (V&A inv.no. Circ.682–1971; Tate inv.no. T03764)

Mr Cruickshank, plaster model for bronze bust, 1950 (V&A inv.no. Circ.683&A–1971; Tate inv.no. T03765)

John Skeaping (1901–1980)

Burmese dancer, alabaster figure, 1928 (V&A inv.no. Circ.79–1964; Tate inv.no. T03768)

Buffalo, lapiz lazuli figure, 1930 (V&A inv.no. A.20–1941; Tate inv.no. T03767)

Joe Tilson (b.1928)

Ziglical column, screenprint on steel, 1966, (V&A inv.no. Circ.984–1967; Tate inv.no. T03772)

William Turnbull (b.1922)

Mask I, bronze, 1953 (V&A inv.no. Circ.194–1964; Tate inv.no. T03773)

Leon Underwood (1890–1975)

Herald of new day, plaster model for a cut brass statuette, 1932–3 (V&A inv.no. A.45–1934; Tate inv.no. T03775)

Gillian Wise (b.1936)

Relief constructed from Unicursal curve no. 2, relief construction, aluminium, cobex and perspex on dural, 1977 (V&A inv.no. Circ.892–1968; Tate inv.no. T03776)

Francis Derwent Wood (1871–1926)

Torso of a girl, plaster, 1903 (V&A inv.no. A.52–1927; Tate inv.no. T03777)

Appendix II

List of the British architectural models compiled from a list supplied by Fiona Leslie. The model for the Albert Memorial is included in the catalogue; see entry for cat.no. 531.

Bristol

Tower of St Mary Redcliffe, plaster (Unregistered 7)

Dublin

St Patrick's Cathedral, spiral staircase for North Transept, wood, 1901, by Sir Thomas Drew (1838–1910) (inv.no. A.169–1929)

London

Albert Hall, seven examples for exterior, four reliefs of window and mouldings, plaster on board, 1868, by Major-General Henry Young Darracott Scott (1822–1883) (inv.nos. A.11 to C–1973)

British Museum Reading Room, plaster, wood and cardboard, about 1853, by Sydney Smirke and Alfred Stevens (inv.no. 349–1890)

Halls of Art and Science, proposed interior (re-named the Albert Hall for its opening in 1871), wood, plaster and paper painted, 1864, by Captain Francis Fowke (1823–1865) (inv. no. A.10–1973)

Marble Arch, plaster, about 1825, by John Nash (1752–1835) (inv.no. A.14–1939)

Royal Exchange, part of building façade, plaster, about 1850, by R. Day (dates unknown), (inv.no. 1069–1873)

St Bartholomew's Hospital, cardboard, (Unregistered 271)

St Paul's Cathedral, cardboard, (6501–1858)

St Paul's Cathedral, cardboard, (Unregistered 820)

Victoria and Albert Museum, Lecture Theatre, semi-dome of the apse, wood, paper and cloth painted, 1869, by Sir Edward Poynter (1836–1919) (inv.no. A.12–1973)

Section of a tower (V&A ?), polychrome wood, nineteenth century (Unregistered 27)

Whitehall government buildings, proposed section of Government office, plaster, wood, cardboard, glass, polychrome, 1869, by Lieutenant-Colonel Andrew Clarke, later Sir Andrew (1824–1902) (inv.no. A.14–1973)

Rome

American Church of St Paul, apse, wood painted, about 1883–4, by Sir Edward Burne-Jones (1833–1898) (inv.no. 365–1895)

St Peter's Basilica, cardboard (6500–1858)

Salisbury

Salisbury Cathedral, plaster (Unregistered 9)

Appendix III

British objects registered in Sculpture Department records following the handing over of Osterley Park House to the National Trust in 1997.

Lawrence Macdonald (1799–1878)

Marble bust, *Lady Sarah Villiers-Child* (b. about 1824?), signed and dated 1845 (inv.no. O.P.H.236–1949)

Marble bust, *Lady Sarah Villiers-Child*, signed and dated 1847 (inv.no. O.P.H.237–1949)

Anonymous

Blue john vase, about 1770 (inv.no. O.P.H.7–1986)

Marble relief, probably *Lady Clementine Villiers* (youngest daughter of Sarah Sophie Villiers), early nineteenth century (inv.no. O.P.H.452–1949)

Appendix IV

British sculpture objects registered in Sculpture Department records following the handing over of Ham House to the National Trust in 1997.

John Cheere (1709–1787)

Bronzed plaster statuette, *John Milton*, about 1750 (inv.no. H.H.559–1948)

Bronzed plaster statuette, *William Shakespeare*, about 1750 (inv.no. H.H.560–1948)

Bronzed plaster statuette, *Edmund Spenser*, about 1750 (inv.no. H.H.561–1948)

Alexander Macdonald (b.1847)

Marble bust, *Sir William John Manners Tollemache, Baron Huntingtower, 9th Earl of Dysart* (1859–1935), signed and dated 1879 (inv.no. H.H.1–1973)

Appendix V

British objects at the Wellington Museum, Apsley House.

George Gammon Adams (1821–1898)

Marble bust, *Arthur Wellesley, 1st Duke of Wellington* (1769–1852), signed and dated 1859 (inv.no. WM.1445–1948)

Sir Francis Chantrey (1781–1841)

Marble bust, *Arthur Wellesley, 1st Duke of Wellington* (1769–1852), signed and dated 1823 (inv.no. WM.1444–1948)

Marble bust, *Robert Stewart, Marquis of Londonderry K.G. (Lord Castlereagh)* (1769–1822) (inv.no. WM.1452–1948)

John Francis (1780–1861) after Joseph Nollekens (1737–1823)

Marble bust, *Arthur Wellesley, 1st Duke of Wellington* (1769–1852), signed and dated 'Francis after Nollekens 1818' (inv.no. WM.1456–1948)

Samuel Joseph (1791–1850)
Marble bust, *Colonel John Gurwood C.B.* (1790–1845), signed and dated 1840 (inv.no. WM.1451–1948)

Joseph Nollekens (1737–1823)
Marble bust, *Arthur Wellesley, 1st Duke of Wellington* (1769–1852), signed and dated 1813 (inv.no. WM.1446–1948)
Marble bust, *Rt. Hon. Spencer Perceval* (1762–1812), signed and dated 1813 (inv.no. WM.1449–1948)
Marble bust, *Rt. Hon. George Canning* (1770–1827), signed and dated 1810 (inv.no. WM.1450–1948)
Marble bust, *Rt. Hon. William Pitt* (1759–1806), signed and dated 1808 (inv.no. WM.1453–1948)

Benedetto Pistrucci (1784–1855)
Marble bust, *Arthur Wellesley, 1st Duke of Wellington* (1769–1852), signed and dated 1832 (inv.no. WM.1448–1948)

Sir John Steell (1804–1891)
Marble bust, *Arthur Wellesley, 1st Duke of Wellington* (1769–1852), signed and dated 1846 (inv.no. WM.1447–1948)

Anonymous
Marble bust, *Sir Frederick Cavendish Ponsonby, K.C.B.* (1783–1837) (inv.no. WM.1457–1948)

APPENDIX VI

Biographical List of Curators and Scholars.

Thomas Armstrong (1832–1911) Painter and designer. Director, Division of Science and Art, South Kensington Museum 1881–98. For a bust of Armstrong, see entry for cat.no. 708 (TDA, 2, pp. 474–5 [Newall]).

Sir [Arthur] Leigh [Bolland] Ashton F.S.A. (1897–1983) Assistant Keeper in the Department of Architecture and Sculpture (later Sculpture Department) between 1922 and 1925, and in the Department of Textiles from 1925 to 1931. Between 1931 and 1937 he was assigned to the Department of Ceramics. In 1937 he became Keeper of Special Collections, and was also Secretary to the Advisory Council from 1935, and Assistant to the Director. His main area of expertise was Oriental art. He was Director and Secretary of the Victoria and Albert Museum between 1945 and 1955, and was responsible for the rearrangement of the Museum's galleries, completed by the end of 1951 (*Who Was Who* 1991, p. 25; Burton 1999, pp. 195–9).

John [Gordon] Beckwith (1918–1991) Joined the V&A in 1948 as Assistant Keeper in the Department of Textiles, where he developed his expertise in Coptic, Byzantine and early medieval objects. In 1955 he transferred to the Department of Architecture and Sculpture, where he was given responsibility for medieval sculpture, and began his study of medieval ivories. Beckwith was responsible for the redisplay of medieval art in Gallery 43 in the mid 1960s. In 1958 he was promoted to Deputy Keeper, and in 1974 became Keeper of the Department of Architecture and Sculpture, and was elected a Fellow of the British Academy. He published widely, most notably on medieval ivories (Williamson 1993).

R. [Richard] P. [Perry] Bedford (1883–1967) Joined the V&A in 1903 as a technical assistant attached to the Department of Woodwork; later he transferred to the Library, and in 1911 was appointed Assistant Keeper in the Department of Architecture and Sculpture. He was Keeper of the Department of Architecture and Sculpture from 1924 to 1938, and Keeper of the Department of Circulation between 1938 and 1946. Bedford was later appointed Curator of Pictures at the Ministry of Works 1947–8. He was also a sculptor in his own right, influenced by Henri Gaudier-Brzeska (1891–1915) (*Bedford* 1961; *Who Was Who* 1979, pp. 78–9).

Sir Henry Cole (1808–1882) The first Director and Secretary of the South Kensington Museum (part of which was later to become the V&A), Cole is also remembered for commissioning the first commercial Christmas card in 1838. He had begun his career earlier that year at the Public Record Office as Assistant Keeper. For his designs and manufactures he used the pseudonym Felix Summerly, and he later established Felix Summerly's Art-Manufactures. Cole played a major role in the organisation of the 1851 International Exhibition, and was later instrumental in the establishment of the Department of Practical Art at Marlborough House, which formed the foundation of the South Kensington Museum, later the V&A, in which he was to play a dominant role until his retirement in 1873. For a bust of Cole by Sir Joseph Edgar Boehm, see entry for cat.no. 286 (Bonython 1982 [Cole]; Bonython 1982 [Album]; TDA, 7, pp. 548–9 [Bonython]; Bonython and Burton forthcoming).

Mrs Katharine Ada Esdaile (1881–1950) Art historian specialising in post-medieval English sculpture. Her publications include *English Monumental Sculpture since the Renaissance* (1927), and *The Life and Works of Louis François Roubiliac* (1928), as well as numerous articles on English sculpture (*DNB* 1959, pp. 239–40; Physick and Ramsay 1986).

Terence Hodgkinson (1913–1999) Joined the V&A in 1946 where he was assigned to the Department of Architecture and Sculpture. He was Assistant to the Director between 1948 and 1962, and was appointed Keeper of the Department of Architecture and Sculpture in 1967, a post he held until 1974. Director of the Wallace Collection from 1974 to 1978 (Elam 1999; *Who's Who* 2000, p. 969).

Margaret Helen Longhurst (1882–1958) Longhurst joined the Museum in 1926. She became the first woman Keeper in the Museum, being appointed Keeper of the Department of Architecture and Sculpture in 1938; she retired in 1942. She published the *Catalogue of Carvings in Ivory* (1927 and 1929) and, together with Eric Maclagan [q.v.], the *Catalogue of*

Italian Sculpture (1932) (TDA, 19, p. 638 [Williamson]; Bilbey [forthcoming]).

Sir Eric Robert Dalrymple Maclagan (1879–1951) Joined the V&A in 1905 as Assistant Keeper in the Department of Textiles, moving to the Department of Architecture and Sculpture in 1909. In 1921 he became Keeper of the Department of Architecture and Sculpture, until his appointment in 1924 as Director, a post he held until 1944. Together with Margaret Longhurst [q.v.] he wrote the *Catalogue of Italian Sculpture* in the Museum, published in 1932 (*DNB* 1971, pp. 672–4; TDA, 20, pp. 26–7).

H. [Hugh] P. [Parker] Mitchell (1871–1926) Joined the South Kensington Museum in 1895 as Junior Assistant in the Art Library. He later transferred to the Art Museum, where he was able to develop his interest in studies of the Middle Ages, becoming a known authority on enamels and English silver. Later he became the Keeper of the Department of Metalwork. His *Catalogue of English Silversmiths' Work* appeared in 1920; he also published many articles on a variety of subjects (*Museums Journal* 1926; Burton 1999, pp. 137–8, 143, 170–1).

H. [Hender] D. [Delves] Molesworth (1907–1978) Joined the V&A as a curator in the Department of Architecture and Sculpture in 1931. In 1936 he was seconded to a post in Jamaica as Curator of the Institute of Jamaica in Kingston, a position he held until 1938. During the Second World War he was attached to the Ministry of Information, and later acted as Press Attaché in Addis Ababa. In 1946 he returned to the Museum as Keeper of the Department of Architecture and Sculpture, a post he held until 1954. From 1954 until his retirement in 1966 he was Keeper of the Woodwork Department (later the Furniture and Woodwork Department). He was Editor of the *Burlington Magazine* from 1978 to 1981 (*Who Was Who* 1981, p. 550; Cannon-Brookes 1996, p. 206).

A. [Adolph] P. [Paul] Oppé (1878–1957) Deputy Director of the Victoria and Albert Museum 1910–13 (TDA, 23, p. 455 [Cast]).

Sir John [Wyndham] Pope-Hennessy (1913–1994) Joined the Museum's Department of Paintings in 1938. After working in Intelligence during the Second World War he returned to the Museum in 1945, where he took up a post in the Department of Architecture and Sculpture, being appointed Keeper in 1955. Director of the Victoria and Albert Museum from 1967 to 1973. Director of the British Museum from 1974 to 1976. He was later appointed as the Consultative Chairman of European Paintings at the Metropolitan Museum of Art, New York (TDA, 25, p. 236; Pope-Hennessy 1991; *British Museum* 1999, pp. 168–9).

Sir [F.] Philip Cunliffe Owen Assistant Director of Administration at the South Kensington Museum; Director of the South Kensington Museum from 1874 to 1893.

Sir Caspar Purdon Clarke Keeper of Art Collections, South Kensington Museum 1891; Assistant Director 1891. Director of the Art Museum (Division of the South Kensington, Victoria and Albert Museum) from 1896 to 1905.

Sir Edward J. [John] Poynter (1836–1919) Painter and designer; he was commissioned to design the Grill Room and Lecture Theatre apse at the Victoria and Albert Museum. In 1871 appointed first Slade Professor at University College, London. Director for Art, Department of Science and Art between 1875 and 1881, and Principal of the National Art Training Schools at South Kensington. In 1894 he was appointed Director of the National Gallery, London, a post he held until 1904 (Physick 1982, pp. 122–4; 139–41; TDA, 25, pp. 406–7 [Inglis]).

Sir John Charles Robinson (1824–1913) Keeper of the Museum of Ornamental Art at Marlborough House (later the South Kensington Museum). Responsible for advising on the acquisition of objects between 1852 and 1867; he acted as Art Referee at the South Kensington Museum between 1863 and 1867. Between 1882 and 1901 he was Surveyor of the Queen's Pictures. His publications include inventories of the collections at the South Kensington Museum, and in 1862 a catalogue of the Museum's collections of *Italian Sculpture of the Middle Ages and Period of the Revival of Art.* For a bust of Robinson by Marochetti, see entry for cat.no. 506 (TDA, 26, pp. 472–3 [Davies]).

A. [Arthur] B. [Banks] Skinner (1861–1911) Assistant Director; Director of the Art Museum (Division of the South Kensington, later Victoria and Albert Museum) 1905–8; Keeper of the Department of Architecture and Sculpture from 1908 until his death in 1911.

Sir Matthew Digby Wyatt (1820–1877) Architect, designer and writer, Wyatt was appointed Special Commissioner and Secretary to the 1851 International Exhibition, and was involved in the reconstruction and interior design of the Courts of Architecture at the Crystal Palace. He acted as Art Referee for the Museum from 1867 (TDA, 33, pp. 449–50 [Robinson]; Burton 1999, pp. 131–2).